CRITICAL SURVEY OF
Poetry
Fourth Edition

American Poets

CRITICAL SURVEY OF

Poetry

Fourth Edition

American Poets

Volume 1
Diane Ackerman—Edward Field

Editor, Fourth Edition
Rosemary M. Canfield Reisman
Charleston Southern University

SALEM PRESS
Pasadena, California
Hackensack, New Jersey

Editor in Chief: Dawn P. Dawson

Editorial Director: Christina J. Moose   *Research Supervisor:* Jeffry Jensen

Development Editor: Tracy Irons-Georges   *Research Assistant:* Keli Trousdale

Project Editor: Rowena Wildin   *Production Editor:* Andrea E. Miller

Manuscript Editor: Desiree Dreeuws   *Page Desion:* James Hutson

Acquisitions Editor: Mark Rehn   *Layout:* Mary Overell

Editorial Assistant: Brett S. Weisberg   *Photo Editor:* Cynthia Breslin Beres

Cover photo: Dorothy Parker (The Granger Collection, New York)

Some of the essays in this work, which have been updated, originally appeared in the following Salem Press publications, *Critical Survey of Poetry, English Language Series* (1983), *Critical Survey of Poetry: Foreign Language Series* (1984), *Critical Survey of Poetry, Supplement* (1987), *Critical Survey of Poetry, English Language Series, Revised Edition*, (1992; preceding volumes edited by Frank N. Magill), *Critical Survey of Poetry, Second Revised Edition* (2003; edited by Philip K. Jason).

∞ The paper used in these volumes conforms to the American National Standard for Permanence of Paper for Printed Library Materials, X39.48-1992 (R1997).

Library of Congress Cataloging-in-Publication Data

Critical survey of poetry. — 4th ed. / editor, Rosemary M. Canfield Reisman.

    v. cm.

Includes bibliographical references and index.

ISBN 978-1-58765-582-1 (set : alk. paper) — ISBN 978-1-58765-583-8 (set : American poets : alk. paper) — ISBN 978-1-58765-584-5 (v. 1 : American poets : alk. paper) — ISBN 978-1-58765-585-2 (v. 2 : American poets : alk. paper) — ISBN 978-1-58765-586-9 (v. 3 : American poets : alk. paper) — ISBN 978-1-58765-587-6 (v. 4 : American poets : alk. paper)

1. Poetry—History and criticism—Dictionaries. 2. Poetry—Bio-bibliography. 3. Poets—Biography—Dictionaries. I. Reisman, Rosemary M. Canfield.

  PN1021.C7 2011

  809.1'003--dc22

2010045095

First Printing

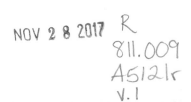
PRINTED IN THE UNITED STATES OF AMERICA

PUBLISHER'S NOTE

American Poets is part of Salem Press's greatly expanded and redesigned *Critical Survey of Poetry* Series. The *Critical Survey of Poetry, Fourth Edition*, presents profiles of major poets, with sections on other literary forms, achievements, biography, general analysis, and analysis of the poet's most important poems or collections. Although the profiled authors may have written in other genres as well, sometimes to great acclaim, the focus of this set is on their most important works of poetry.

The *Critical Survey of Poetry* was originally published in 1983 and 1984 in separate English- and foreign-language series, a supplement in 1987, a revised English-language series in 1992, and a combined revised series in 2003. The *Fourth Edition* includes all poets from the previous edition and adds 145 new ones, covering 843 writers in total. The poets covered in this set represent more than 40 countries and their poetry dates from the eighth century B.C.E. to the present. The set also offers 72 informative overviews; 20 of these essays were added for this edition, including all the literary movement essays. In addition, seven resources are provided, two of them new. More than 500 photographs and portraits of poets have been included.

For the first time, the material in the *Critical Survey of Poetry* has been organized into five subsets by geography and essay type: a 4-volume subset on *American Poets*, a 3-volume subset on *British, Irish, and Commonwealth Poets*, a 3-volume subset on *European Poets*, a 1-volume subset on *World Poets*, and a 2-volume subset of *Topical Essays*. Each poet appears in only one subset. *Topical Essays* is organized under the categories "Poetry Around the World," "Literary Movements," and "Criticism and Theory." A *Cumulative Indexes* volume covering all five subsets is free with purchase of more than one subset.

AMERICAN POETS

The 4-volume *American Poets* contains 398 poet profiles, arranged alphabetically. For this edition, 106 new essays have been added, and 109 have been significantly updated with analysis of recently published books or poems. A significant effort was made to add more women; they include such important figures as Lyn Hejinian, Judith Ortiz Cofer, Laura Riding, and Margaret Walker.

Each volume begins with a list of Contents for that volume, a Complete List of Contents covering the entire subset, and a Pronunciation Key. The poet essays follow in alphabetical order, divided among the four volumes. The fourth volume contains the Resources section, which features three tools for interpreting and understanding poetry: "Explicating Poetry," "Language and Linguistics," and "Glossary of Poetical Terms." The Bibliography, Guide to Online Resources, Time Line, Major Awards, and Chronological List of Poets provide guides for further research and additional information on American poets; comprehensive versions appear in *Topical Essays* and *Cumulative Indexes*. The Guide to Online Resources and Time Line were created for this edition.

American Poets contains a Categorized Index of Poets, in which poets are grouped by culture or group identity, literary movement, historical period, and poetic forms and themes, and a Subject Index. The *Critical Survey of Poetry* Series: Master List of Contents identifies poets profiled in *American Poets* as well as poets profiled in other *Critical Survey of Poetry* subsets. *American Poets* does not contain a geographical index, but all poets in this subset are included in the Geographical Index of Poets and Essays in the *Cumulative Indexes*, which also contains comprehensive versions of the Categorized Index and Subject Index.

UPDATING THE ESSAYS

All parts of the essays in the previous edition were scrutinized for currency and accuracy: The authors' latest works of poetry were added to front-matter listings, other significant publications were added to back-matter listings, new translations were added to listings for foreign-language authors, and deceased authors' listings were rechecked for accuracy and currency. All essays' bibliographies—lists of sources for further consultation—were revised to provide readers with the latest information.

The 109 original poet essays in *American Poets* that required updating by academic experts received similar and even fuller attention: All new publications were added to listings, then each section of text was reviewed to ensure that recently received major awards are noted, that new biographical details are incorporated for still-living authors, and that analysis of works includes recently published books or poems. The updating experts' names were added to essays. Those original articles identified by the editor, Rosemary M. Canfield Reisman, as not needing substantial updating were nevertheless reedited by Salem Press editors and checked for accuracy.

ONLINE ACCESS

Salem Press provides access to its award-winning content both in traditional, printed form and online. Any school or library that purchases *American Poets* is entitled to free, complimentary access to Salem's fully supported online version of the content. Features include a simple intuitive interface, user profile areas for students and patrons, sophisticated search functionality, and complete context, including appendixes. Access is available through a code printed on the inside cover of the first volume, and that access is unlimited and immediate. Our online customer service representatives, at (800) 221-1592, are happy to help with any questions. E-books are also available.

ORGANIZATION OF POET ESSAYS

The poet essays in *American Poets* vary in length, with none shorter than 2,000 words and most significantly longer. Poet essays are arranged alphabetically, under the name by which the poet is best known. The format of the essays is standardized to allow predictable and easy access to the types of information of interest to a variety of users. Each poet essay contains ready-reference top matter, including full birth and (where applicable) death data, any alternate names used by the poet, and a list of Principal Poetry, followed by the main text, which is divided into Other Literary Forms, Achievements, Biography, and Analysis. A list of Other Major Works, a Bibliography, and bylines complete the essay.

- *Principal poetry* lists the titles of the author's major collections of poetry in chronological order, by date of original appearance. If an author has published works in another language and the works have been translated into English, the titles and dates of the first translations are provided.

- *Other literary forms* describes the author's work in other genres and notes whether the author is known primarily as a poet or has achieved equal or greater fame in another genre. If the poet's last name is unlikely to be familiar to most users, phonetic pronunciation is provided in parentheses after his or her name. A Pronunciation Key appears at the beginning of all volumes.

- *Achievements* lists honors, awards, and other tangible recognitions, as well as a summation of the writer's influence and contributions to poetry and literature, where appropriate.

- *Biography* provides a condensed biographical sketch with vital information from birth through (if applicable) death or the author's latest activities.

- *Analysis* presents an overview of the poet's themes, techniques, style, and development, leading into subsections on major poetry collections, poems, or aspects of the person's work as a poet. Although this set focuses on Americans, some of the profiled poets have written works in other languages. As an aid to students, those foreign-language titles that have not yet appeared in translation are followed by a "literal translation" in roman and lowercase letters when these titles are mentioned in the text. If a title has been published in English, the English-language title is used in the text.

- *Other major works* contains the poet's principal works in other genres, listed by genre and by year of publication within each genre. If applicable, the dates and titles of English translations of foreign-language works are listed.

- *Bibliography* lists secondary print sources for further study, annotated to assist users in evaluating focus and usefulness.

- *Byline* notes the original contributor of the essay. If the essay was updated, the name of the most recent updater appears in a separate line and previous updaters appear with the name of the original contributor.

APPENDIXES

The "Resources" section in volume 4 provides tools for further research and points of access to the wealth of information contained in *American Poets*.

- *Explicating Poetry* identifies the basics of versification, from meter to rhyme, in an attempt to demonstrate how sound, rhythm, and image fuse to support meaning.
- *Language and Linguistics* looks at the origins of language and at linguistics as a discipline, as well as how the features of a particular language affect the type of poetry created.
- *Glossary of Poetical Terms* is a lexicon of more than 150 literary terms pertinent to the study of poetry.
- *Bibliography* identifies general reference works and other secondary sources that pertain to American poets.
- *Guide to Online Resources*, new to this edition, provides Web sites pertaining to poetry and American poets.
- *Time Line*, new to this edition, lists major milestones and events in poetry and literature in the United States in the order in which they occurred.
- *Major Awards* lists the recipients of major poetry-specific awards in the United States and general awards where applicable to poets or poetry, from inception of the award to the present day.
- *Chronological List of Poets* lists all 398 poets covered in *American Poets* by year of birth, in chronological order.

INDEXES

The Categorized Index of Poets lists the poets profiled in *American Poets* by culture or group identity (such as Jewish culture, African American culture, and women poets), literary movements (such as Modernism, Beat poets, Confessional poets, New Formalism, and Language poetry), and poetic forms and themes (such as political poets, war poets, ekphrastic poetry, prose poetry, ghazals, and nature poetry). The *Critical Survey of Poetry* Series: Master List of Contents lists not only the poets profiled in *American Poets* but also those in other subsets, allowing users to find any poet covered in the complete series. The Subject Index lists all titles, authors, subgenres, and literary movements or terms that receive substantial discussion in *American Poets*. Listings for profiled poets are in bold face.

ACKNOWLEDGMENTS

Salem Press is grateful for the efforts of the original contributors of these essays and those of the outstanding academicians who took on the task of updating or writing new material for the set. Their names and affiliations are listed in the "Contributors" section that follows. Finally, we are indebted to our editor, Professor Rosemary M. Canfield Reisman of Charleston Southern University, for her development of the table of contents for the *Critical Survey of Poetry, Fourth Edition* and her advice on updating the original articles to make this comprehensive and thorough revised edition an indispensable tool for students, teachers, and general readers alike.

CONTRIBUTORS

Karley K. Adney
University of Wisconsin, Marathon County

John Alspaugh
Richmond, Virginia

Nicole Anae
Charles Sturt University

Andrew J. Angyal
Elon University

Jane Augustine
Stuyvesant Station, New York

Charles Lewis Avinger, Jr.
Washtenaw Community College

Angela Ball
University of Southern Mississippi

Paula C. Barnes
Hampton University

David Barratt
Montreat College

Melissa E. Barth
Appalachian State University

Sharon Bassett
California State University, Los Angeles

Robert Bateman
Concord College

Angela Bates
University of Cincinnati Writing Center

Walton Beacham
Beacham Publishing Corp.

Cynthia S. Becerra
Humphreys College

Kate Begnal
Utah State University

Robert Bensen
Hartwick College

Eleanor von Auw Berry
Milwaukee, Wisconsin

Nicholas Birns
Eugene Lang College, The New School

Patrick Bizzaro
East Carolina University

Franz G. Blaha
University of Nebraska-Lincoln

Lynn Z. Bloom
University of Connecticut

Robert E. Boenig
Texas A&M University

Kevin Boyle
Elon University

Marie J. K. Brenner
Bethel College

Anne Kelsch Breznau
Kellogg Community College

David Bromige
Sonoma State University

Steven Brown
University of Rhode Island, Kingston

Mary Hanford Bruce
Monmouth College

Amy Burnette
Appalachian State University

Alvin G. Burstein
University of Tennessee, Knoxville

Edward Butscher
Briarwood, New York

Susan Butterworth
Salem State College

Ann M. Cameron
Indiana University, Kokomo

David Cappella
Boston University

David A. Carpenter
Eastern Illinois University

Peter Carravetta
Queens College, City University of New York

Henry L. Carrigan, Jr.
Northwestern University

Caroline Carvill
Rose-Hulman Institute of Technology

Leonard R. Casper
Boston College

Mary LeDonne Cassidy
South Carolina State University

Donald Cellini
Adrian College

Allan Chavkin
Southwest Texas State University

Chih-Ping Chen
Alma College

Balance Chow
San Jose State University

Paul Christensen
Texas A&M University

Lindsay Christopher
University of Denver

C. L. Chua
California State University, Fresno

Kevin Clark
*California Polytechnic State
University*

Patricia Clark
Grand Valley State University

Douglas Clouatre
North Platte, Nebraska

David W. Cole
University of Wisconsin Colleges

Caroline Collins
Quincy University

John J. Conlon
*University of South Florida,
St. Petersburg*

Joseph Coulson
Southwest Texas State University

Heidi K. Czerwiec
University of North Dakota

Dolores A. D'Angelo
American University

Robert Darling
Keuka College

Reed Way Dasenbrock
New Mexico State University

Anita Price Davis
Converse College

Delmer Davis
Andrews University

Todd F. Davis
Goshen College

William V. Davis
Baylor University

Frank Day
Clemson University

Mary De Jong
Pennsylvania State University

Bill Delaney
San Diego, California

Lloyd N. Dendinger
University of South Alabama

K. Z. Derounian
University of Arkansas-Little Rock

Mary de Shazer
University of Oregon

Mark DeStephano
Saint Peter's College

Joseph Dewey
University of Pittsburgh-Johnstown

Robert DiYanni
Pace University

Margaret A. Dodson
Boise, Idaho

Georgie L. Donovan
Appalachian State University

David C. Dougherty
Loyola College in Maryland

Theresa E. Dozier
Prince George's Community College

Desiree Dreeuws
Sunland, California

John Drury
University of Cincinnati

Doris Earnshaw
University of California, Davis

Richard A. Eichwald
St. Louis, Missouri

Robert P. Ellis
Worcester State College

Bernard F. Engel
Michigan State University

Thomas L. Erskine
Salisbury University

Jack Ewing
Boise, Idaho

Nettie Farris
University of Louisville

Howard Faulkner
Washburn University

Thomas R. Feller
Nashville, Tennessee

Lydia E. Ferguson
Clemson University

Sandra K. Fischer
*State University of New York
at Albany*

Rebecca Hendrick Flannagan
Francis Marion University

Lydia Forssander-Song
Trinity Western University

Walter B. Freed, Jr.
*State University of New York
at Geneseo*

Lawrence S. Friedman
Indiana University

Jean C. Fulton
Landmark College

Kenneth E. Gadomski
University of Delaware

Ann D. Garbett
Averett University

Elaine Gardiner
Topeka, Kansas

Donna Gerstenberger
University of Washington

Scott Giantvalley
*California State University,
Dominguez Hills*

Kenneth Gibbs
Sturbridge, Massachusetts

Morgan Gibson
Urbana, Illinois

Richard F. Giles
Wilfrid Laurier University

Ronald K. Giles
East Tennessee State University

Vincent F. A. Golphin
The Writing Company

William H. Green
Chattahoochee Valley State College

John L. Grigsby
*Appalachian Research & Defense
    Fund of Kentucky, Inc.*

Daniel L. Guillory
Millikin University

Jeff Gundy
Bluffton College

Kenneth Hada
East Central University

Steven L. Hale
Georgia Perimeter College

Elsie Galbreath Haley
Metropolitan State College of Denver

William T. Hamilton
Metropolitan State College of Denver

Michele Hardy
Prince George's Community College

Maryhelen Cleverly Harmon
University of South Florida

Nelson Hathcock
Saint Xavier University

Robert W. Haynes
Texas A&M University

David M. Heaton
Ohio University

Michael Heller
Stuyvesant Station, New York

Sarah Hilbert
Pasadena, California

KaaVonia Hinton
Old Dominion University

Jeffrey D. Hoeper
Arkansas State University

Hilary Holladay
University of Massachusetts, Lowell

Daryl Holmes
Nicholls State University

Donald D. Hook
Trinity College

Gregory D. Horn
*Southwest Virginia Community
    College*

William Howard
Chicago State University

John F. Hudson
West Concord Union Church

Mary Hurd
East Tennessee State University

Earl G. Ingersoll
SUNY College at Brockport

Tracy Irons-Georges
Glendale, California

Teresa Ishigaki
California State University, Fresno

Maura Ives
Texas A&M University

Helen Jaskoski
California State University, Fullerton

Philip K. Jason
United States Naval Academy

Lesley Jenike
Columbus College of Art and Design

Jeffry Jensen
Pasadena, California

Mark A. Johnson
Central Missouri State University

Sheila Golburgh Johnson
Santa Barbara, California

Judith L. Johnston
Rider College

William Jolliff
George Fox University

Ginger Jones
Lincoln University-Missouri

Leslie Ellen Jones
Pasadena, California

Robert C. Jones
Warrensburg, Missouri

Leela Kapai
Prince George's Community College

James M. Kempf
United States Air Force Academy

Claire Keyes
Salem State College

Karen A. Kildahl
South Dakota State University

Sue L. Kimball
Methodist College

Pam Fox Kuhlken
San Diego State University

Vera M. Kutzinski
Yale University

Rebecca Kuzins
Pasadena, California

Wendy Alison Lamb
South Pasadena, California

L. L. Lee
Western Washington University

Mary Lang
Wharton County Junior College

Susan T. Larson
Clemson University

Patricia Ondek Laurence
*City College, City University of
New York*

William T. Lawlor
*University of Wisconsin-Stevens
Point*

Leon Lewis
Appalachian State University

Rick Lott
Arkansas State University

Michael Loudon
Eastern Illinois University

Bernadette Flynn Low
*Community College of Baltimore
County-Dundalk*

Perry D. Luckett
United States Air Force Academy

Steven R. Luebke
University of Wisconsin-River Falls

Carol J. Luther
Pellissippi State Community College

R. C. Lutz
CII Group

Sara McAulay
California State University, Hayward

Janet McCann
Texas A&M University

Joanne McCarthy
Tacoma Community College

Roxanne McDonald
Wilmot, New Hampshire

Fred R. McFadden
Coppin State College

Ron McFarland
University of Idaho

S. Thomas Mack
University of South Carolina-Aiken

Mary E. Mahony
Wayne County Community College

Joseph Maltby
University of Hawaii at Manoa

Linda K. Martinez
Independent Scholar

Laurence W. Mazzeno
Alvernia College

Julia M. Meyers
Duquesne University

Michael R. Meyers
Pfeiffer University

Jim Wayne Miller
Western Kentucky University

P. Andrew Miller
Northern Kentucky University

Paula M. Miller
Biola University

Mark Minor
Westmar College

Modrea Mitchell-Reichert
Texas State University-San Marcos

Melissa Molloy
*Rhode Island College and University
of Rhode Island*

Christina J. Moose
Pasadena, California

Ronald Moran
Clemson University

Bernard E. Morris
Modesto, California

Claire Clements Morton
Rock Hill, South Carolina

Charmaine Allmon Mosby
Western Kentucky University

C. Lynn Munro
Belton, Missouri

Donna Munro
Bee & Flower Press

Russell Elliott Murphy
University of Arkansas at Little Rock

Cynthia Nichols
North Dakota State University

Edward A. Nickerson
University of Delaware

Holly L. Norton
University of Northwestern Ohio

Michael Paul Novak
Saint Mary College

Arsenio Orteza
WORLD Magazine

Edward F. Palm
Maryville University of St. Louis

Robert J. Paradowski
Rochester Institute of Technology

Jay Paul
Christopher Newport University

David Peck
Laguna Beach, California

Alice Hall Petry
Rhode Island School of Design

Chapel Louise Petty
Stillwater, Oklahoma

Allene Phy-Olsen
Austin Peay State University

Carol Lawson Pippen
Goucher College

Francis Poole
University of Delaware

Laurence M. Porter
Michigan State University

Stanley Poss
California State University, Fresno

Norman Prinsky
Augusta State University

Charles H. Pullen
Queen's University

Thomas Rankin
Concord, California

Honora Rankine-Galloway
University of Southern Denmark

Jed Rasula
University of California, Santa Cruz

John Raymer
Holy Cross College

Rosemary M. Canfield Reisman
Charleston Southern University

Mark Rich
Cashton, Wisconsin

Kelly-Anne Riess
University of Regina

David Rigsbee
Virginia Tech

Dorothy Dodge Robbins
Louisiana Tech University

Danny Robinson
Bloomsburg University

Samuel J. Rogal
Illinois State University

Kathy Rugoff
*University of North Carolina-
Wilmington*

Todd Samuelson
*Cushing Memorial Library &
Archives*

Mark Sanders
College of the Mainland

Alexa L. Sandmann
University of Toledo

Richard Sax
Lake Erie College

Elizabeth D. Schafer
Loachapoka, Alaska

William J. Scheick
University of Texas at Austin

Paul Schlueter
Easton, Pennsylvania

Richard J. Schneider
Wilson, North Carolina

Beverly Schneller
Millersville University

Steven P. Schultz
Loyola University of Chicago

Robert W. Scott
American University

James Scruton
Bethel College

Roy Seeger
University of South Carolina, Aiken

Paul Serralheiro
Dawson College

Emily Carroll Shearer
Middle Tennessee State University

Nancy E. Sherrod
Georgia Southern University

John C. Shields
Illinois State University

Anne Shifrer
Utah State University

R. Baird Shuman
*University of Illinois at Urbana-
Champaign*

Paul Siegrist
Fort Hays State University

Linda Simon
Atlanta, Georgia

Carl Singleton
Fort Hays State University

William Skaff
Baltimore, Maryland

Sherry G. Southard
Oklahoma State University

Virginia Starrett
*California State University,
Fullerton*

Christine Steele
Independent Scholar

Karen F. Stein
University of Rhode Island

Shelby Stephenson
Pembroke State University

Eve Walsh Stoddard
St. Lawrence University

Stefan Stoenescu
Ithaca, New York

Ann Struthers
Coe College

Ryan D. Stryffeler
Ivy Tech Community College

Christopher J. Stuart
*University of Tennessee at
Chattanooga*

Ernest Suarez
The Catholic University of America

James Sullivan
*California State University,
Los Angeles*

Judith K. Taylor
Northern Kentucky University

Betty Taylor-Thompson
Texas Southern University

Jonathan Thorndike
Belmont University

Shelley Thrasher
Lamar State College-Orange

John H. Timmerman
Calvin College

John Clendenin Townsend
Kalamazoo, Michigan

Nance Van Winckel
Lake Forest College

Paul Varner
Oklahoma Christian University

Martha Modena Vertreace-Doody
Kennedy-King College

Edward E. Waldron
Yankton College

Sue Walker
University of South Alabama

Lisa M. Wallace
Sheffield, United Kingdom

Gordon Walters
DePauw University

John Chapman Ward
Kenyon College

Klaus Weissenberger
Rice University

Twyla R. Wells
Lima, Ohio

Craig Werner
University of Wisconsin

Bruce Wiebe
Lakeville, Minnesota

Barbara Wiedemann
Auburn University at Montgomery

Thomas Willard
University of Arizona

Edwin W. Williams
East Tennessee State University

Patricia A. R. Williams
Amherst College

Tyrone Williams
Xavier University

Judith Barton Williamson
Sauk Valley Community College

Rosemary Winslow
The Catholic University of America

Donald E. Winters, Jr.
Minneapolis Community College

Michael Witkoski
University of South Carolina

Chester L. Wolford
Penn State Erie, The Behrend College

Cynthia Wong
Western Illinois University

Philip Woodard
National University

Scott D. Yarbrough
Charleston Southern University

Gay Pitman Zieger
Santa Fe College

CONTENTS

COMPLETE LIST OF CONTENTS

VOLUME 1

VOLUME 2

VOLUME 3

VOLUME 4

RESOURCES

INDEXES

PRONUNCIATION KEY

To help users of the *Critical Survey of Poetry* pronounce unfamiliar names of profiled poets correctly, phonetic spellings using the character symbols listed below appear in parentheses immediately after the first mention of the poet's name in the narrative text. Stressed syllables are indicated in capital letters, and syllables are separated by hyphens.

VOWEL SOUNDS

Symbol	Spelled (Pronounced)
a	answer (AN-suhr), laugh (laf), sample (SAM-puhl), that (that)
ah	father (FAH-thur), hospital (HAHS-pih-tuhl)
aw	awful (AW-fuhl), caught (kawt)
ay	blaze (blayz), fade (fayd), waiter (WAYT-ur), weigh (way)
eh	bed (behd), head (hehd), said (sehd)
ee	believe (bee-LEEV), cedar (SEE-dur), leader (LEED-ur), liter (LEE-tur)
ew	boot (bewt), lose (lewz)
i	buy (bi), height (hit), lie (li), surprise (sur-PRIZ)
ih	bitter (BIH-tur), pill (pihl)
o	cotton (KO-tuhn), hot (hot)
oh	below (bee-LOH), coat (koht), note (noht), wholesome (HOHL-suhm)
oo	good (good), look (look)
ow	couch (kowch), how (how)
oy	boy (boy), coin (koyn)
uh	about (uh-BOWT), butter (BUH-tuhr), enough (ee-NUHF), other (UH-thur)

CONSONANT SOUNDS

Symbol	Spelled (Pronounced)
ch	beach (beech), chimp (chihmp)
g	beg (behg), disguise (dihs-GIZ), get (geht)
j	digit (DIH-juht), edge (ehj), jet (jeht)
k	cat (kat), kitten (KIH-tuhn), hex (hehks)
s	cellar (SEHL-ur), save (sayv), scent (sehnt)
sh	champagne (sham-PAYN), issue (IH-shew), shop (shop)
ur	birth (burth), disturb (dihs-TURB), earth (urth), letter (LEH-tur)
y	useful (YEWS-fuhl), young (yuhng)
z	business (BIHZ-nehs), zest (zehst)
zh	vision (VIH-zhuhn)

CRITICAL SURVEY OF
Poetry
Fourth Edition

American Poets

A

DIANE ACKERMAN

Born: Waukegan, Illinois; October 7, 1948

PRINCIPAL POETRY

The Planets: A Cosmic Pastoral, 1976
Wife of Light, 1978
Lady Faustus, 1983
Reverse Thunder, 1988
Jaguar of Sweet Laughter: New and Selected Poems, 1991
I Praise My Destroyer, 1998
Origami Bridges, 2002
Animal Sense, 2003

OTHER LITERARY FORMS

While Diane Ackerman is known for her poetry, she is better known for her nonfiction work, which includes memoirs and narratives about scientific subjects. Ackerman's early prose work focuses on her personal experiences learning different and unusual occupations. *Twilight of the Tenderfoot* (1980) recounts her time as a cowhand on a cattle ranch, while *On Extended Wings* (1985) focuses on her student pilot experiences. Perhaps her most famous work, *A Natural History of the Senses* (1990), was later adapted into a *NOVA* miniseries for the Public Broadcasting Service (PBS). *The Moon by Whale Light, and Other Adventures Among Bats, Penguins, Crocodilians, and Whales* (1991) contains four essays originally published in *The New Yorker*. Ackerman followed up on these two works with, respectively, *A Natural History of Love* (1994) and *The Rarest of the Rare: Vanishing Animals, Timeless Worlds* (1995). Her essays, which usually focus on science and nature, have been published in *The New York Times*, *Smithsonian*, *Parade*, and *National Geographic*. She edited *The Book of Love* with Jeanne Mackin. *A Slender Thread: Rediscovering Hope and the Heart of a Crisis* (1997)

returned her to writing memoirs, as she recounted her experiences as a crisis hotline counselor. *Deep Play* (1999) suggests ways in which adults can recapture their childhood through play, while *Cultivating Delight: A Natural History of My Garden* (2001) discusses maintenance of her garden. In *The Zookeeper's Wife: A War Story* (2007), Ackerman tells the story of a Polish zoo during World War II. In *Dawn Light: Dancing with Cranes and Other Ways to Start the Day* (2009), Ackerman discusses different facets of nature and dawn throughout the changing of the seasons.

ACHIEVEMENTS

While still in graduate school, Diane Ackerman won the Academy of American Poets College Prize, and in 1985, she won the Peter I. B. Lavan Younger Poets Award from the same organization. She was a panel judge for the New York Foundation for the Arts and the National Endowment for the Arts in 1987 and 1991, respectively. She also received a Guggenheim Fellowship and the John Burroughs Nature Award. Her bestselling book, *A Natural History of the Senses*, inspired a *NOVA* miniseries on PBS called *Mystery of the Senses*, which Ackerman hosted. She was honored as a Literary Lion by the New York Public Library and nominated for a National Book Critics Circle Award for her 1991 book of poetry, *Jaguar of Sweet Laughter*. In 2008, she won the Orion Book Award for *The Zookeeper's Wife*. She also has a molecule, "dianeackerone," named after her.

BIOGRAPHY

Diane Ackerman was born Diane Fink in Waukegan, Illinois, in 1948, to Sam Fink and Marsha Tischler Fink. The family moved to Allentown, Pennsylvania, when Ackerman was eight. Growing up, Ackerman delighted in nature. A tomboy who spent much of her time reading and writing, she often had to hide her interests from her parents, who did not approve of such pursuits. In 1967, Ackerman began attending college at Boston University but, by her sophomore year, had transferred to Pennsylvania State University. It was at Pennsylvania State that she met her husband, Paul West, who was teaching a contemporary literature class and took an interest in her poetry. In 1970, after receiving a bachelor of arts in English, she decided to continue her education at Cornell University, despite wanting to travel. At Cornell, Ackerman earned an M.F.A. (1973), as well as an M.A. (1976) and a Ph.D. (1978), both in English literature. She and her husband settled in Ithaca, New York, in the 1970's.

When working on her dissertation, Ackerman requested a poet, a scientist, and a comparative literature professor to be on her doctoral committee because she felt her studies could not be understood from a single perspective. She believed her work had elements of art, literature, and science in it. Carl Sagan was the scientist assigned to her dissertation committee, and she began working closely with him. In fact, the dedication poem in *Planets* is for Sagan. Also when writing *Planets*, Ackerman spent time doing night watches in a jet propulsion lab and worked with astronomers.

From 1980 to 1983, Ackerman taught English at

Diane Ackerman (©Bob Daemmrich/CORBIS)

Columbia and Cornell universities. She received her pilot's license in Williamsburg, Virginia, in the early 1980's, which served as the inspiration for her memoir *On Extended Wings*. Throughout the 1980's and 1990's, she wrote and published prolifically, drawing on her personal experiences and her love of nature. She also continued to teach writing at various schools, including the College of William and Mary and Ohio University. In 1995, she served as host for PBS's five-episode *NOVA* series *Mystery of the Senses*, based on her book.

ANALYSIS

Influenced by poets such as Pablo Neruda and naturalists such as John Muir, Diane Ackerman frequently combines nature with human emotion or meanings, such as love. As a naturalist, Ackerman believes that humans should view nature as something that they are a part of, rather than something that is outside themselves. Ackerman is a self-proclaimed "sensuist," which she defines as "someone who rejoices in sensory experience," and much of her writing deals with the senses. She believes that people share instincts and feelings with the rest of the natural world and therefore should not attempt to keep themselves separate from nature. Much of her poetry bridges the gap between science, nature, and humanity, and attempts to blend them all into a single entity. Even in her prose, she is lyrical, incorporating bits of unfinished poetry into her prose at times.

PLANETS

As the title suggests, *Planets* focuses on astronomy and the human relation to the universe and Earth. Ackerman strives to express not only how minor humans are in comparison to the universe, but also how closely related poetry and science can be. Ackerman's purpose in *Planets* is to connect poetry with science and space. This work is a series of long poems, one for each planet, and organized as the planets are seen in the sky. Cape Canaveral, asteroids, and the Comet Kohoutek also get poems, and even the dedication and the prologue are given in poem form. In addition to the poetry, Ackerman includes a glossary of scientific terms, as well as a section of notes that link her abstract poetical phrases to the concrete reality of science, literature, and occasionally slang in an attempt to further blend science with the poetic.

Ackerman uses not only words but also visual imagery to convey her meanings in *Planets*. Each of her poems begins with a picture or a diagram of the planet or the topic. Some, like Saturn, have both a picture and diagram. In "Uranus," Ackerman goes even further, by writing the poem (which is actually in the form of a play) lengthwise on the page, so the reader must turn the book on its side to read. As she explains in the endnotes, she uses this tactic because the planet Uranus appears to be sideways when viewed from a telescope, so she forces readers to view her description of Uranus the way they would view the actual planet.

I PRAISE MY DESTROYER

Ackerman's purpose in *I Praise My Destroyer* is to find the good in things that are thought to destroy and to accept those things in life that may be harsh—to find joy in living despite life's negative experiences. The work is divided into sections: "I Praise My Destroyer," "Timed Talk," "By Atoms Moved," "Natural Wonders," "Tender Mercies," "City of Dreams," and "Cantos Vaqueros." Each section's title describes its theme. For example, "Natural Wonders" includes the poem "You Will Think This Is a Dream," which is about the invention of electricity, how a natural wonder (fire) was converted into something helpful to humans. The poem also reflects Ackerman's larger theme of good and evil: "fire was an animal/ whose gold flanks scorched/ and whose galloping/ devoured grasslands as it fled/ No one tamed lions/ no one dreamed of narrowing/ frenzy in its flight." Fire, which was once thought to destroy only, is now harnessed in the form of electricity to create light and warmth, which is beneficial to humanity.

ANIMAL SENSE

Although *Animal Sense* has the same overall theme as that of Ackerman's *A Natural History of the Senses*, this volume of poetry is geared toward children aged eight to twelve. The work is divided into five sections, one for each of the five senses, and the reader is introduced to a different animal in each poem. In each section, Ackerman combines wordplay, lighthearted rhyme, and fantastical imagery with scientific facts about various animals in order to teach, as well as en-

tertain, children. She discusses a variety of animals, including bees, bats, cows, and humpback whales. Frequently, Ackerman gives the animals humanlike emotions while explaining their specific abilities. *Animal Sense* is Ackerman's only book of poetry that is intended for children.

ORIGAMI BRIDGES

In *Origami Bridges*, Ackerman departs from her usual scientific analysis of the world and focuses instead on an inner analysis of the self. This work is the most confessional of any of her longer works, which is likely because of the accidental nature of its conception. Ackerman admits this work was not originally intended to become a book of poetry but was merely the result of a year and a half of psychotherapy, during which she would write poems every day to help her process what she had discovered in her sessions. The poems reflect her feelings during her sessions, explore her relationship with her therapist, and discuss her discoveries about her present and past experiences and desires. As she states in "Omens of Winter," she is using these poems as a continuation of her therapy: "but I do not understand the vernacular/ of fear that jostles me until art occurs,/ or why, knowing you from afar/ spurs hours of working myself into the stars./ Well, I do know, but I fight its common sense:/ I try to stabilize us through eloquence." By writing poetry, Ackerman was able to process and give meaning to the emotions she had discovered in her therapy sessions. Although Ackerman met in person with her therapist once a month, most of their sessions occurred over the phone, so many of the poems in this collection also deal with the nuances of vocal communication in the absence of face-to-face interaction.

OTHER MAJOR WORKS

NONFICTION: *Twilight of the Tenderfoot*, 1980; *On Extended Wings*, 1985 (memoir); *A Natural History of the Senses*, 1990; *The Moon by Whale Light, and Other Adventures Among Bats, Penguins, Crocodilians, and Whales*, 1991; *A Natural History of Love*, 1994; *Monk Seal Hideaway*, 1995; *The Rarest of the Rare: Vanishing Animals, Timeless Worlds*, 1995; *Bats: Shadows in the Night*, 1997; *A Slender Thread: Rediscovering Hope and the Heart of a Crisis*, 1997; *Deep Play*, 1999;

Cultivating Delight: A Natural History of My Garden, 2001; *An Alchemy of Mind: The Marvel and Mystery of the Brain*, 2004; *The Zookeeper's Wife: A War Story*, 2007; *Dawn Light: Dancing with Cranes and Other Ways to Start the Day*, 2009.

EDITED TEXT: *The Book of Love*, 1998 (with Jeanne Mackin; anthology).

BIBLIOGRAPHY

Ackerman, Diane. "Diane Ackerman." http:// diane ackerman.com. The official Web site of Ackerman features a biography and information on her books and appearances.

Christ, Ronald. "The Poet, Words, Truth, and Therapy." Review of *Origami Bridges*. *Santa Fe New Mexican*, March 16, 2003, p. F2. Christ, publisher of Lumen Books, finds Ackerman to be a "tomgirl of poetry and prose," and praises her authentic, multiple voices.

Gossin, Pamela. "Living Poetics, Enacting the Cosmos: The Popularization of Astronomy in Diane Ackerman's *The Planets: A Cosmic Pastoral*." *Women's Studies* 26, no. 6 (October, 1997): 605-639. Contends that Ackerman's poetry, specifically *Planets*, is an important influence on the popularization of space and astronomy. Focuses on Ackerman as a living poet and thus able to actively influence others.

Laszlo, Pierre. "Emotions and Cognitions." *Interdisciplinary Science Reviews* 30, no. 4 (December, 2005): 341-348. Addresses various contemporary scientifically based poems. Discusses how science and poetry can be compatible despite the common conception that they do not have similar goals. Ackerman is used as an example.

Whitcomb, Claire. "Taking Time for the Marvelous." *Victoria* 11, no. 1 (January, 1997): 24-27. Offers a personalized view of Ackerman. Focuses on her personality and everyday life leading up to the publication of *A Natural History of the Senses*.

Angela Bates

LÉONIE ADAMS

Born: Brooklyn, New York; December 9, 1899
Died: New Milford, Connecticut; June 27, 1988

PRINCIPAL POETRY
Those Not Elect, 1925
High Falcon, and Other Poems, 1929
This Measure, 1933
Poems: A Selection, 1954

OTHER LITERARY FORMS

Aside from her poetry, Léonie Adams helped to translate and edit François Villon's lyrics. She also translated some of the poems of Yvan Goll.

ACHIEVEMENTS

Although few talented poets with her longevity have left such a small body of work, Léonie Adams enjoyed quite a distinguished career as poet and teacher. After graduating magna cum laude from Barnard College and publishing her first book of poetry, she was awarded a Guggenheim Fellowship in 1928.

In 1948-1949, she served as consultant in poetry (poet laureate) to the Library of Congress. The National Institute of Arts and Letters gave her its Academy Award in 1949, and in 1951, she was elected a member of the organization. After publishing *Poems* in 1954, she received the Shelley Memorial Award. In conjunction with Louise Bogan, Adams received the Bollingen Prize in poetry the next year. Also in 1955, Adams was appointed as a Fulbright lecturer in France. The National Commission on Arts gave her a sabbatical grant in 1966. Adams received the Brandeis University Poetry Medal in 1969 and the Academy of American Poets Fellowship in 1974.

BIOGRAPHY

Léonie Fuller Adams was born on December 9, 1899, in Brooklyn, New York. Because her grandfather had business interests in Cuba, her father, Charles F. Adams, had been born there. His mother was from Venezuela. Adams's father practiced law in New York.

At the age of eighteen, Léonie Adams enrolled at

Barnard College, where she was soon writing poetry. In 1921, *The New Republic* published her poem "April Mortality," her first published work. After graduating from Barnard, she held various editorial positions while continuing to write poetry. Thanks to assistance from interested friends, she was able to submit a collection of her poems to a publisher who issued it in 1925 under the title *Those Not Elect*, a phrase taken from English writer John Bunyan. Both Allen Tate and Louis Untermeyer reviewed this volume favorably, putting Adams in a position to apply for the then-new Guggenheim Fellowship program. She received the fellowship in 1928.

As a Guggenheim Fellow, Adams traveled to Europe. In Paris, she moved into an apartment that, according to one source, had been lent by Ford Madox Ford to Allen Tate and his wife, Carolyn (later Caroline Gordon). In this small apartment, Adams slept in a closet, the Tates and their daughter taking up the rest of the living space.

In 1929, Adams's second book, *High Falcon, and Other Poems*, appeared. Returning to New York the next year, she took up what was to be a long sequence of teaching appointments, this one at New York University. After two years, she moved to Sarah Lawrence College. She taught at Bennington College and the New Jersey College for Women between 1935 and 1948. In 1947, she began teaching at Columbia University, where she taught for twenty-one years.

In 1933, Adams married William Troy, to whom she remained wed until he died twenty-eight years later. Adams published *This Measure*, a long poem, as a chapbook in the year of her marriage. Although she was to live until 1988, she would publish relatively little new work in the ensuing five and one-half decades. The main exception is *Poems*, which was published in 1954 and includes only twenty-four "new" poems, along with sixty-one poems from her earlier volumes.

In 1948, Adams was selected as consultant in poetry (poet laureate) to the Library of Congress, and in 1951, she became a member of the National Institute of Arts and Letters. She held a sequence of fellowships and distinguished positions as lecturer from the 1950's to the early 1970's. She received the Brandeis University Poetry Medal in 1969.

Retiring at length to the home she and her husband (who had died in 1961) had established in Connecticut, Adams maintained a private life until 1988, when she died in a nursing home in New Milford.

ANALYSIS

Léonie Adams's poetic works are known for their almost obsessive formality. One frequent consequence of writing rhymed and formally metrical verse in English in the twentieth century was obscurity, and Adams's poems are often difficult. This difficulty, along with her lack of the flamboyance or the controversy that characterized many twentieth century poets, resulted in her being referred to in a 1997 review as "the neglected Léonie Adams." Another disadvantage suffered by the reputation of Adams's poetry has been the tendency of critics to compliment her in terms that are ultimately disparaging, as when Allen Tate pronounced, "the fusion of her qualities brings her closer to [Thomas] Carew than to any other poet." This comment, from Tate's 1926 review of *Those*

Léonie Adams (©Oscar White/CORBIS)

Not Elect, set an unfortunate example for future commentators on Adams, some of whom also found it easier to dismiss her with problematic comparisons than to read her difficult poems with an eye to understanding them.

Despite the tendency of critics to explain Léonie Adams by alluding to influences on her or by comparing her to other poets, her work is demonstrably original and often unique in its highly wrought brilliance. Although many of her passages are difficult, she remains one of the finest lyric poets of the twentieth century.

THOSE NOT ELECT

The title poem, which is the first poem in *Those Not Elect*, is a sixteen-line poem in four quatrains of fairly strict form. It begins:

> NEVER, being damned, see Paradise.
> The heart will sweeten at its look;
> Nor hell was known, till Paradise
> Our senses shook.

This and the three succeeding stanzas follow the same pattern. The first line of each of the stanzas lacks a stated subject, unless the subject of each is, as seems likely, the title phrase, "Those Not Elect." In each stanza, the first and third lines end with the same word, while the other lines rhyme. Each stanza begins with the word "never" and ends with a line having fewer than the four stresses of the first three lines. The title is a phrase contained in John Bunyan's tract *Reprobation Asserted: Or, The Doctrine of Eternal Election and Reprobation Promiscuously Handled* (c. 1674), and the phrase refers to those who are reprobate, or damned.

This poem lists pleasures that should be denied to the damned but that evidently are not denied; thus there is a sense of comic futility in the putative assertion of a grim religious doctrine, and the poem's voice becomes an ironic one. It is also highly musical, particularly the third quatrain:

> Never fall dreaming on celestials,
> Lest, bound in a ruinous place,
> You turn to wander with celestials
> Down holy space.

These resonant and mellifluous lines belie their own warning. Surely "to wander with celestials/ Down holy space" does not sound so terrible. As often in Adams's poetry, the reader must consider the music of the language as an essential component of its meaning. Although the poem at first appears to be in accord with a religious doctrine that has seemed to some cruel and unjust, the irony, the playful musicality and ellipticality, and the tone of the poem make it a gentle mockery of such uncompromising attitudes, and the "Never" that begins each stanza is quietly canceled.

Many of the works in this volume share characteristics illustrated by the first poem. Irony, ellipsis, and a strong reliance on musicality of language are, however, accompanied in several poems by imagery and symbolism that seem calculated to work on a subconscious level. Some poems are personal statements that achieve a certain directness. For example, "Quiet" expresses the predicament of the loss of emotional intensity and sensitivity. It begins:

> SINCE I took quiet to my breast
> My heart lies in me, heavier
> Than stone sunk fast in sluggish sand . . .

Desensitized by the loss of emotion, the speaker grieves,

> How could I know I would forget
> To catch breath at a gull's curved wing,
> Strange quiet, when I made thee guest?

The last line of the poem sums up the paradox, "Thou, quiet, hast no gift of rest." Another lyrical and formal piece, this poem achieves the simplicity of song.

Although Adams wrote the poems of *Those Not Elect* in her early twenties, her voice is that of a mature and reflective poet. Deeply concerned with religious themes and concepts as well as with the elusive nature of beauty and the difficulty of art, these poems show a powerful commitment to the exercise of artistic rigor as manifested in controlled poetic form.

HIGH FALCON, AND OTHER POEMS

This volume begins with "Windy Way," a poem of renunciation that is phrased in colloquial speech rhythms, using a rhyme pattern that is notably less strict than that of most of Adams's earlier poems. This poem, in fact, employs quickness of motion as a structural principle, accelerating the departure from remembered love. The narrator declares:

> And somewhere in the running wind
> I cast a thing I had away.
> It was my life, or so I said,
> And I did well, forsaking it,
> To go as quickly as the dead.

Accepting the departure of love and the arrival of an unspecified new guest within her heart, the narrator observes, "The cage is open, he may go./ For since winged love has languished there,/ I'll use no other winged thing so." The effect achieved by altering the brisk, matter-of-fact rhythm of the preceding lines in the concluding two lines is that of hesitation in the word "languishing" and a stumbling or faltering meter in the final line ("winged thing"). This effect undermines the blithe tone of preceding phrases, such as "I did well" and "I did not give a backward look." It suggests instead an intense regret that cannot be entirely concealed by assuming a businesslike manner.

In "Elegy Composed in Late March," Adams represents the beauty that attracts love as "mortal beauty," not something to be represented in inorganic form ("Never hewn in stone") but only in nature. Alluding to Greek myth, she writes:

> To what they loved and destroyed,
> Never had their fill of cherishing and would not save,
> Even the gods fixed no star;
> But more in sign
> The rainbow's meltings and the reed
> And the slight narcissus gave.

The relevant myths are those of Iris (the rainbow), Syrinx (the reed), and the story of Narcissus, and the point seems to be that these are beings who are not constellations in the sphere of the fixed stars but rather part of the realm of the human. In this poem, the phrasing is meditative and not strikingly regular, but the sibilants and liquids furnish a music that, as elsewhere, dimensionalizes and unifies the work. Here also the reader can detect the somewhat suppressed erudition of this poet.

"Song from a Country Fair" represents a paradoxical situation that illustrates the infinite variety of human perspective:

> WHEN tunes jigged nimbler than the blood
> And quick and high the bows would prance
> And every fiddle string would burst
> To catch what's lost beyond the string,
> While half afraid their children stood,
> I saw the old come out to dance.
> The heart is not so light at first,
> But heavy like a bough in spring.

Adams notes the reversal of the convention that the old are more burdened than the young, and her suggestion that they are lightened by the divestiture of their prospects is a merry thought in accord with the music of the lines. These eight lines of regular iambic tetrameter avoid monotony first by requiring some phonological dexterity from the reader ("tunes jigged nimbler," "To catch what's lost") and then by shifting gears but not meter in the final line, where the slow word "heavy" follows a sequence of eighteen tripping monosyllables in the preceding lines, and the line itself expresses both the burden of potentiality and the pressure of the plant sap that loads deciduous trees with leaves in the spring of the year.

"ALAS, KIND ELEMENT"

Adams found the sonnet a congenial literary form. Her love of rhyme, parallelism, ellipsis, and complex but efficient syntax enabled her to write some of the finest sonnets of her day. An example is "Alas, Kind Element," in which she explains that she had entered a period of spiritual dormancy during which she had been immune to pain "like the wintering tree." The octave of the sonnet describes this period, closing with the line, "Thus I lived then, till this air breathed on me," and the sestet begins with a repetition and the statement of a change, "Till this kind air breathed kindness everywhere." The "kind air" brings a new awakening of sensibility, but the speaker knows that it also brings renewed vulnerability. Just as the dormant tree generates new leaves in response to the "kind air" of spring, so it yields to a cycle in which the loss of those leaves is a certainty. As the speaker concludes, "My every leaf leans forth upon the day/ Alas, kind element! which comes to go."

The "wishful leaves" mark the rebirth of hope for

one who has no long-term faith in hope, yet the bittersweet sensations evoked by the "kind element" may not be avoided. Here again one senses Adams's concealed learning, for the word "kind" in Middle English often means "nature."

"THE REMINDER"

Another poem treating the subject of hope is "The Reminder," a description of a wakeful night "With will that churned alone/ And sight pinned bleak as stone/ To what the heart could bring." The contrast between the lonely individual's bleak hope and the majestic spectacle of the cold night sky changes in the third and final stanza as nature alters with the advent of morning and the bustle of daily life resumes, but still, "A lone, a steadfast eye/ Silently looks in." As in "Alas, Kind Element," hope persists, despite its poor prospects.

OTHER MAJOR WORKS

TRANSLATIONS: *Lyrics*, 1933 (with others; of François Villon); *Jean Sans Terre*, 1958 (with others; of Yvan Goll).

BIBLIOGRAPHY

Miller, Brett C. *Flawed Light: American Women Poets and Alcohol*. Urbana: University of Illinois Press, 2009. Miller studies how drinking and alcoholism affected prominent American women poets, and how their struggles were reflected in their poetry. Contains an informative chapter on Adams.

Tate, Allen. "Distinguished Minor Poetry." *The Nation* 122 (March 3, 1926): 237-238. Tate, poet and critic (and later good friend of Adams), traces sources and influences in a discussion of *Those Not Elect*. Tate states that Adams's poetry draws heavily on the work of such British Renaissance poets as John Webster and George Herbert.

Tuthill, Stacy Johnson, ed. *Laurels: Eight Woman Poets*. Catonsville, Md.: SCOP, 1998. This work, which showcases the artistic achievements of the major women poets associated with the Library of Congress in the second half of the twentieth century, includes a chapter on Adams, who held the Chair of Poetry at the library in 1948-1949.

Untermeyer, Louis. "Three Younger Poets." *English Journal* 21 (December, 1932): 796-797. Opposing Yvor Winters's dismissal of Adams as excessively obscure, Untermeyer argues that what seems to be obscure in her poetry is actually originality, and he goes on to argue that her insight actually functions to provide clarity.

Wehr, Wesley. *The Eighth Lively Art: Conversations with Painters, Poets, Musicians, and the Wicked Witch of the West*. Seattle: University of Washington Press, 2000. Vignettes of Adams and others, drawn from the author's journals.

Winters, Yvor. Review of *High Falcon, and Other Poems*. *Hound and Horn* 3 (April-June, 1930): 458-461. Less than enthusiastic about the possibility of there being genuine meaning behind the obscurity of Adams's poetry, Winters grudgingly proposes a suspension of disbelief, which he stipulates "in most cases can be no more than extremely temporary." Unmoved, finally, Winters designates Adams's poems as "momentary luxuries."

Robert W. Haynes

———

AI

Born: Albany, Texas; October 21, 1947
Also known as: Florence Haynes; Pelorhanke Ai Ogawa

PRINCIPAL POETRY

Cruelty, 1973
Killing Floor, 1979
Sin, 1986
Cruelty/Killing Floor, 1987
Fate, 1991
Greed, 1993
Vice: New and Selected Poems, 1999
Dread, 2003

OTHER LITERARY FORMS

Ai (pronounced like the first-person pronoun "I") has written in various genres, including long fiction and short nonfiction for several major publications, though she concentrates on verse forms.

ACHIEVEMENTS

Ai's poetry attracted attention right from the start, with her first publication, *Cruelty*, in 1973, earning as much criticism as praise. *Killing Floor* was named the 1978 Lamont Poetry Selection by the Academy of American Poets. She was awarded the American Book Award from the Before Columbus Foundation (1987) for *Sin* and the coveted National Book Award in Poetry (1999) for *Vice*. She received Guggenheim and Radcliffe fellowships in 1975, a Massachusetts Arts and Humanities Fellowship in 1976, and National Endowment for the Arts (NEA) grants in 1978 and in 1985.

BIOGRAPHY

Ai was born Florence Anthony in Texas in 1947. She did not learn the identity of her biological father until she was well into her twenties. The revelation both shocked and distressed her. Her mother, a married sixteen-year-old, met a Japanese man, Michael Ogawa, at a streetcar stop and, during a brief affair, conceived Florence. When her mother's husband learned of the affair, he began a round of beatings that left family members in a constant state of terror. When Florence realized that her mother's husband was not her father, she changed her name to Ai, which means "love" in Japanese, and embarked on a multicultural identity quest that at times had her feeling she belonged nowhere. She was neither black nor white. She called herself one-half Japanese, one-eighth Choctaw, one-quarter black, and one-sixteenth Irish. When black children at school taunted her as a "nigger-jap," she decided to concentrate on her Japanese heritage. She earned a B.A. in Oriental studies from the University of Arizona in 1969 and an M.F.A. from the University of California, Irvine, in 1971. She married fellow poet Lawrence Kearney in 1975, and they later divorced. During periods of professional unemployment, she found jobs as an antique dealer in New York City, a jewelry designer, and a costume modeler.

She has held teaching positions at many institutions, including the University of Massachusetts and the State University of New York, Binghamton. She was a visiting poet at Wayne State University (1977-1978) and at George Mason University (1986-1987), a writer-in-residence at Arizona State University (1988-1989), an associate professor at the University of Colorado, Boulder in (1996-1997), and the Witte Chair in Creative Writing at Southwest Texas State University (2002-2003). She became a professor at Oklahoma State University in 2004.

ANALYSIS

Ai is a narrative poet who writes short, dramatic monologues, a form that allows her to get into the minds of her characters and speak with their voices. Her narrators are disenfranchised, spiritually bereft outsiders, often the voiceless members of society. She places them in a variety of settings and situations and uses direct, hard-hitting language to convey the essences of people who have no illusions. They do not have pretty lives, but they endure. They are from all races, reflecting America's multiracial, multicultural society. These people assert their wills, understand pain, and want to make an impact. Their messages are gut-wrenching.

In the 1970's, some feminists were so offended by Ai's graphic, violent, and almost pornographic tales about spouse and child abuse, rape, and abortion that they found it hard to appreciate the technical aspects of her early works. They failed to see that she was portraying women as strong survivors. Ai's women suffer from isolation, from being considered chattel by men. They are poverty-stricken. Although Ai purports not to have a political agenda, she does believe that she is recording the United States as it is. She sees Americans as a violent people, in thought and deed.

Ai's poetry reflects the underbelly of the human condition, the thoughts too horrible to express verbally. The urge to kill becomes the need to kill. Passing anger does not pass; rather it leads to unspeakable, depraved actions, showing what monsters ordinary people are capable of becoming. Grim tales fill the newspapers every day, but readers, while stunned, go about their lives thinking that such things happen to other people.

Ai does not celebrate violence, but rather uses it to explore the possibility of achieving a state of grace, a transcendence of the self. She sees the cruelty that is inherent in intimacy. Her characters are both the victims and the victimizers.

CRUELTY

Ai's first collection of poetry, *Cruelty*, created a stir with its vivid details of abominations: mothers and fathers who do unspeakable things to their children, including a mother who feels satisfaction from devising new ways of inflicting pain on her two-year-old; children who enjoy killing; and religious leaders who do not lift up but instead destroy with base instincts that become baser when those who know of the abuses remain silent. Some of the details of physical abuse are too horrifying to give voice to, but Ai's symphonic prose makes the specifics more palatable. It is the eloquence of her poetry, the beautifully expressed concept, the apt word, the melody she creates, the pleasing assonance, the unexpected interior rhyme, the simple language, and uncomplicated form that draw readers to her and allow them to glimpse the dark corners of their psyches.

Ai sees the essentials of life as love and hate, birth and death. Birth is a recurring theme, always matter-of-fact, if not deadly. She does not wonder at the miracle of new life; instead, in "The Country Midwife: A Day," she describes the "scraggly, red child" and the "stink of birth." In another poem, a husband sees his pregnant wife as a "brown walnut waiting to crack open and release her white meat"—no sentimentality here. Sex is always violent and base. In "Prostitute," a woman kills her husband, searches through his pockets, puts on his boots, and holsters his guns, hoping to attract more clients, and then gratifies herself with his dead hand. Other titles attest to the general unpleasantness of Ai's subject matter: "Tired Old Whore" and "A Forty-Three-Year-Old Woman Masturbating." Writer Alice Walker said that this volume was not for those who want nice poetry they can like.

KILLING FLOOR

Killing Floor expands on the themes of violence and sexuality in *Cruelty*; in this volume, Ai creates a wider vision and pushes her poetry toward a more universal view of life and death. She gives snapshot glimpses of the lives of Leon Trotsky, Marilyn Monroe, and Emiliano Zapata. She also creates a German homosexual in Buchenwald, a half-mad Indian bride, a murderous fourteen-year-old boy. "Nothing But Color" is about cannibalistic, homosexual love and suicide.

FATE

Ai alleviates a little of the pain by identifying some of her monologues in *Fate* as "a fiction." She even plays with history, using the facts of important people's lives but altering them in strange ways. Readers can recognize the alterations but still feel the lives and deaths being examined. They can explore the motivating forces behind misdeeds.

In her introduction to *Fate*, Ai says that it is "about eroticism, politics/religion and show business/ as tragicomedy/ performed by women and men/ banished to the bare stage of their obsessions." This nicely stated theme certainly covers her treatment of notables. "Go," dedicated to Edward Kennedy and Mary Jo Kopechne, begins in a familiar way, echoing the opening of Edgar Allan Poe's "The Raven," "Once upon a midnight dreary." In this retelling of the Chappaquiddick incident, she begins with "Once upon a Massachusetts midnight," and gives voice to the dead woman who calls herself unloved and identifies Kennedy as both her lover and her killer. She observes that he carries no traces of her. She thinks of telling her side of the story, of "marching in" to the music of Satchmo (Louis Armstrong), the great trumpeter, who will "blow the walls of this Jericho of lies down." The narrator observes that "Women are always the receivers of what is given without love or permission."

In this collection, readers ride with screen idol James Dean to his death and hear his voice from beyond the grave, saying that he had "devised a way/ of living between/ the rules that other people make." They walk with labor leader Jimmy Hoffa through the parking lot where he was last seen alive. They watch Elvis Presley practice his moves in front of a mirror.

GREED

Greed is about greed in multiple areas: money, power, sex, and love. It deals with consumers gobbling up the images created by advertising executives and wanting more and more. "Riot Act, April 29, 1992" is spoken by a black writer in police custody in South Central Los Angeles, who calls the looting and fires spawned by the acquittal of the police officers in the beating of Rodney King "the day [when] the wealth finally trickled down to the rest of us." In the same poem, he talks about the Reeboks and Nikes that will enable him to fly through the air like basketball players Michael Jordan and Magic Johnson.

In "Self-Defense," Marion Berry, mayor of Washington, D.C., who was arrested and convicted of drug-related charges after the Federal Bureau of Investigation (FBI) filmed him inhaling from a crack cocaine pipe, concludes "that is how you hold the nigger down." He asks, "You think you can chew me up? . . . Reading rights won't make a difference/ if the verdict is already in." Berry claimed that the charges against him were politically motivated and that he had been set up.

Ai enters the worlds of FBI director J. Edgar Hoover, presidential assassin Lee Harvey Oswald, Oswald's assassin Jack Ruby, and a priest-pedophile, all outsiders, out of sync with social and ethical norms. Ai reinvents these people after their deaths and tells more about the American psyche than she does about the real figures.

The poem "Respect" is titled ironically because it details the lack of respect afforded women. A husband/father comes home from work, grumbling about his hard-earned wages going for milk and diapers. He turns on his Aretha Franklin album, counting on her for the understanding he cannot get from other "goddamn women." She represents a life of wine chilled on ice and of chills up the spine. Mainly, she does not talk back.

"Family Portrait" paints an ugly picture of home life, with a wife asking her husband to teach their two girls, ages seven and eleven, how to clean between their legs. He goes through the drill but uses inappropriate language.

VICE

Vice presents a collection of fifty-eight monologues from four earlier books—*Cruelty*, *Killing Floor*, *Sin*, and *Fate*—and seventeen new poems. The older selections resurrect Dean, Hoffa, Hoover, and Lenny Bruce, as well as multiple perpetrators of violence toward women and children. The new poems deal with O. J. Simpson, religious cult leader David Koresh, JonBenét Ramsey, Monica Lewinsky, and the police officer who made dramatic rescues after the 1995 bombing of the Oklahoma City federal building and then killed himself because he felt undeserving of an award. In one poem, a mother matter-of-factly tutors her daughter on how to seduce her father. In another, an aide rapes a comatose patient.

These new poems do not reflect any changes in Ai's subject matter or attitude. In some ways, they display greater anger and greater horror at prevailing social attitudes. However, her technical skills still shine and her ability to seize attention and keep it continue to compel readers and critics. The National Book Award in Poetry gave Ai widespread recognition and acceptance.

OTHER MAJOR WORKS

LONG FICTION: *Black Blood*, 1997.

NONFICTION: "On Being $\frac{1}{2}$ Japanese, $\frac{1}{16}$ Choctaw, $\frac{1}{4}$ Black, and $\frac{1}{16}$ Irish," 1974.

BIBLIOGRAPHY

Cucinella, Catherine. *Contemporary American Women Poets: An A-to-Z Guide*. Westport, Conn.: Greenwood Press, 2002. Contains a biography of Ai with critical analysis of her works.

Huang, Guiyou, and Emmanuel S. Nelson, eds. *Asian-American Poets: A Bio-bibliographical Critical Sourcebook*. Westport, Conn.: Greenwood Press, 2002. Contains a biography of Ai plus bibliographical information.

Ingram, Claudia. "Writing the Crises: The Deployment of Abjection in Ai's Dramatic Monologues." *Literature Interpretation Theory* 8, no. 2 (1997): 173-191. Excellent analyses of the most disturbing elements in Ai's poetry. The notes are particularly telling of the state of society as Ai perceives it.

Jacob, John, and Holly L. Norton. "The Poetry of Ai." In *Masterplots II: African American Literature*, edited by Tyrone Williams. Rev. ed. Pasadena, Calif.: Salem Press, 2009. Provides an in-depth analysis of Ai's poetry, biographical information, and a discussion of the controversy surrounding her early works.

Kilcup, Karen L. "Dialogues of the Self: Toward a Theory of (Re)Reading Ai." *Journal of Gender Studies* 7, no. 1 (1998): 5-20. A discussion of some ways to approach violent literature written by women, including Ai.

Pettis, Joyce Owens. *African American Poets: Lives, Works, and Sources*. Westport, Conn.: Greenwood Press, 2002. Contains an entry on Ai that looks at her life and works.

Seshadri, Vijay. "When Bad Things Happen to Everyone." Review of *Dread. The New York Times Book Review*, May 4, 2003, p. 7. The reviewer notes that Ai's work presents the voices of victims. He finds this collection, which focuses on the September 11, 2001, terrorist attacks on the United States, to be illuminating but less shocking than her early volumes, in part because of the world's raised awareness of violence.

Wilson, Rob. "The Will to Transcendence in Contemporary American Poet, Ai." *Canadian Review of American Studies* 17, no. 4 (Winter, 1986): 437-448. Provides a thorough justification of Ai's use of violence to reach transcendence, a classical device used in literature.

Gay Pitman Zieger

CONRAD AIKEN

Born: Savannah, Georgia; August 5, 1889
Died: Savannah, Georgia; August 17, 1973
Also known as: Samuel Jeake, Jr.

PRINCIPAL POETRY

Earth Triumphant, and Other Tales in Verse, 1914
The Jig of Forslin, 1916
Turns and Movies, and Other Tales in Verse, 1916
Nocturne of Remembered Spring, and Other Poems, 1917
The Charnel Rose, 1918
Senlin: A Biography, and Other Poems, 1918
The House of Dust, 1920
Punch: The Immortal Liar, 1921
Priapus and the Pool, 1922
The Pilgrimage of Festus, 1923
Changing Mind, 1925
Priapus and the Pool, and Other Poems, 1925
Prelude, 1929
Selected Poems, 1929
Gehenna, 1930
John Deth: A Metaphysical Legend, and Other Poems, 1930

The Coming Forth by Day of Osiris Jones, 1931
Preludes for Memnon, 1931
And in the Hanging Gardens, 1933
Landscape West of Eden, 1934
Time in the Rock: Preludes to Definition, 1936
And in the Human Heart, 1940
Brownstone Eclogues, and Other Poems, 1942
The Soldier: A Poem by Conrad Aiken, 1944
The Kid, 1947
The Divine Pilgrim, 1949
Skylight One: Fifteen Poems, 1949
Wake II, 1952
Collected Poems, 1953, 1970
A Letter from Li Po, and Other Poems, 1955
The Fluteplayer, 1956
Sheepfold Hill: Fifteen Poems, 1958
Selected Poems, 1961
The Morning Song of Lord Zero, 1963
A Seizure of Limericks, 1964
Cats and Bats and Things with Wings, 1965
The Clerk's Journal, 1971
A Little Who's Zoo of Mild Animals, 1977

OTHER LITERARY FORMS

Although best known as a poet, Conrad Aiken (AY-kuhn) also published novels, short-story collections, plays, a poetic autobiographical essay, collections of criticism, books for children (including one of limericks), and anthologies of poetry.

ACHIEVEMENTS

From his mature years onward, Conrad Aiken was much honored. In 1930, he received the Shelley Memorial Award and the Pulitzer Prize for *Selected Poems*. He was chosen to edit *A Comprehensive Anthology of American Poetry* for The Modern Library (1929) and published a revision in 1944. In 1941, he was elected a member of the American Academy of Arts and Letters. He was named editor of *Twentieth Century American Poetry* for The Modern Library (1944) and served as consultant in poetry (poet laureate) to the Library of Congress (1950-1952). He continued to receive honors: a Guggenheim Fellowship (1934); the National Book Award in Poetry (1954) for *Collected Poems*, the Bollingen Prize (1956), an Academy of American Poets Fellowship (1957), and the Gold Medal in poetry from the American Academy of Arts and Letters (1958). A special issue of *Wake* magazine (1952), in which there appeared new and reprinted writing by Aiken and others, signaled a step forward in the critical reappraisal of Aiken's contributions.

BIOGRAPHY

Conrad Potter Aiken was the oldest of three sons and one daughter. His father was a surgeon, and the Aikens were well off, but the family was fractured by strife. In "Obiturary in Bitcherel," the last of his *Collected Poems* (1970), and in *Ushant: An Essay* (1952), Aiken records the crescendo of violence that tore his family apart. In "Obituary in Bitcherel," Aiken gives himself a very good beginning, with a distinguished father who was not only a physician and surgeon but also a writer and painter and with a mother, a New England beauty, whose father, William James Potter, a Congregational minister, was a friend of Ralph Waldo Emerson. Two Mayflower passengers and six generations of the Delanos ran in Aiken's veins. His parents reared him to appreciate literature and writing, and he had happy hours of play besides. Then the parents seemed to turn against each other. The atmosphere of the house became strained. Aiken was beaten, barebacked, for reasons unknown. In *Ushant*, he tells of the argument flaring up between his parents early one morning, of his mother's half-smothered cry, of his father's voice counting to three, of the handgun exploding twice, and of the two still bodies lying separately in the dim daylight of the room. Aiken was only eleven years old, and ever after the murder-suicide, he was in search of a literary consciousness that would do his parents credit.

Sent to live with a great-great aunt in New Bedford, Massachusetts, Aiken entered Harvard University in 1907, but in protest at being placed on probation for irregular class attendance, he went on a six-month tour of Europe; he did receive his Harvard degree in 1912. His marriage, the first of three, took place a few days later. After a year of honeymooning in Europe (where he was to return many times), he settled in Cambridge, Massachusetts, devoting full time to writing on a small but independent income.

In 1914, with the publication of *Earth Triumphant,*

Conrad Aiken (Library of Congress)

and Other Tales in Verse, Aiken began a search for poetic monuments to his parents' memory. Although he argued that there was no other possible judge of a poet's excellence than the consciousness of the poet himself, he did reach out to people. There were, for example, his onetime mentor, John Gould Fletcher; his Harvard classmate, T. S. Eliot; and his three children by his first wife. Wherever he took up residence, however, it was the "evolution" of his artistic consciousness, the legacy of his parents, that held first place in his thoughts. Living in England from 1922 to 1925, in Massachusetts, New York City, and again in Georgia, and living as a traveler, Aiken sang with a unique and solitary voice.

His single-minded purpose gained him early recognition. From 1910 to 1911, he published many pieces in the Harvard *Monthly* and the Harvard *Advocate*, of which he served as president. From 1916 to 1922, he was a critic, mainly of contemporary poets, for *The Poetry Journal*, *The New Republic*, and *The Dial*, to which he was one of the contributing editors from 1917 to 1918. He also contributed to *Poetry* and the Chicago *Daily News*, among other periodicals. In the London *Mercury* and the London *Atheneum*, he published "Letters from

America." He also published several volumes of poems during these years, and nearly thirty more thereafter.

There were interesting side excursions from Aiken's main road of poetry and criticism. He spent a year as an English tutor at Harvard (1927-1928) and wrote his play *Fear No More*, based on his short story "Mr. Arcularis." The play was performed in London in 1946, and in Washington, D.C., in 1951. In the 1930's, he conducted a summer school in painting and writing. In spite of his interludes, Aiken spent the last two decades of his life almost exclusively writing and revising his poems.

ANALYSIS

A poet and artist of the second American Renaissance, Conrad Aiken pursued the theme of the poet alone, whose only true friends appear to be the characters of his writings. Technically, his poetry extends from the rhymes and measures of couplet and quatrain and blank and free verse to the more richly concentrated forms of the commemorative ode and "symphony"; the sonnet ("little song") and its sequence, such as "And in the Human Heart"; and the aubade ("morning song"), among a variety of experimental forms.

Aiken's experiments constantly remind readers of the tradition of meter, and especially of rhyme. Even his free verse uses enough rhyme to let one know that Aiken's sense of poetic tradition is important. Aiken is perhaps most admired for his exploration of music within poetic forms as he mixes iambs with polysyllables, ranging from five- to three-stress meters.

Aiken is part of a Romantic humanist tradition that seeks to heal the hurt of human bereavement and the failure of social revolution by substituting the idea of the creator God for the godly creator. The poet-hero shows that it is possible to achieve solitary pleasure in the "resurrected" imagination, and in spite of social failures and inadequacies, there is a type of poetry, a wry music of spiritual revolution, in which lyric narrative and dialogue resist social distress. Aiken creates the enduring mock- or antihero, seen best in Punch in his early writings and in the later figures of the Kid and of Lord Zero.

Aiken's monistic, dreamlike view of life and art is expressed in his protagonists, who range from ironic middle-class types—Forslin and Senlin—to mock- and antihero types—Punch, John Deth, the Kid, and Lord Zero. In Aiken's mythology, death is a regulation, a point of genesis, perhaps because of the traumatic context of the deaths of Aiken's parents. Aiken's ironic rejoinder to death, the binding regulation on life, is the apotheosis of humankind through unity with godhead and nature in an endless cycle of death and rebirth, a pantheistic form of resurrection, as seen, for example, in Aiken's use of the phoenix in *The Morning Song of Lord Zero* and in another late poem, "Thee."

Aiken is a personal Romanticist. In his vaudeville poems, for example, which he wrote off and on well into his seventies, he tells of the sordid lives of the performers whose passions and violence catch the tonal quality of his own terrified childhood recollections. The sad, wry music of Aiken's poetry seems to ask, To what purpose the passion and the violence? Natural death is enough to contend with, without the horror of passion and murder.

Over the stratum of the reality of death, Aiken builds a dreamworld of resurrection in many forms, ranging from the would-be type of Christ, through middle-class "monarchs of all they survey," a Faustian puppet, a master demon and a vampire of the cyclic dance of death, various reincarnations of the American culture hero, to, finally, the apotheosis of humankind in the form of Lord Zero.

THE DIVINE PILGRIM

The Divine Pilgrim is a collection of six "symphonies": *The Charnel Rose, The Jig of Forslin, The House of Dust, Senlin, The Pilgrimage of Festus*, all collected from earlier publications, and *Changing Mind*, which was added in 1925. Aiken spelled out his musical principle in "Counterpoint and Implication" (*Collected Poems*, "Notes"), reprinted as "Aiken, Conrad (1919)," in *A Reviewer's ABC: Collected Criticism Conrad Aiken from 1916 to the Present* (1958). His principle was to build each poem out of its key to emotional masses arranged so that each massing would set an elusively particular musical tone or subtheme to the words, and each masstone, or "sub-key," would dominate a brief movement and its contrapuntal fellows until a "movement," a main section or part, had been stated, developed, and restated to give a general tonality out of the units and subunits of poetic composition.

THE CHARNEL ROSE

The Charnel Rose, in the traditional four-part division of the sonata and symphony, treats carnal love, idealistic or Romantic love, erotically mystical love, and finally, purely mystical love in the crucifixion of Jesus Christ and his resurrection, which for Aiken is the symbol of flesh crucifying itself through its own lusts. At the end of the "symphony," the cycle of humanity is ready to begin again with carnal love. Throughout, the third-person narrator views women, phantoms, and the crucifying crowd as projections of his own frustrated dreams. The entire poem may be considered as having the standard sonata form, with the second main "movement" holding well to the andante tempo while weaving some andante texture into the last two "movements." The whole poem may be viewed as a musical theme with variations, as Aiken's tempos range from allegro quatrains to *allegro manon troppo*.

THE JIG OF FORSLIN

In *The Jig of Forslin*, Forslin is all man, an organic compound of the Latin *forsan* and *fors*, meaning "chanceling" or "weakling." Through all his dreams, ranging from the urge of his body to control his mind to his mind's struggle to control his body, he *is* a man of will, however misdirected. In the aquarium light of his imagination, his adopted personae—the suicidal juggler; the killer of both priest and inebriated sailor, as well as of his children, his wife, and her lover; the alluring lamia; the bodiless voice of Christ; the harlot's lover and the harlot herself—all can, by choice, be resurrected in humankind's dreams. This five-part poem employs both blank verse and free verse, rhymed and rhymeless. The poem is of an earlier, less sophisticated music than *The Charnel Rose* but is placed after it because, apparently, the imagery of *The Jig of Forslin* corresponds more closely to the imagery in *The House of Dust*, which comes next in *The Divine Pilgrim*.

THE HOUSE OF DUST

The House of Dust is another four-part poem that Aiken has compared to a symphonic poem. This poem, however, emphasizes more programmatic detail, and sets forth humankind's innate ability to become divine by becoming divinely conscious of the individual lives of urban residents. The poem points ahead to the Metaphysical period in Aiken's work when, in *Preludes for Memnon* and *Time in the Rock*, the poetic self examines traditional, polarizing concepts of divinity, apparently dispenses with them, and then attempts to set up a new polarity, the self unto itself, in the continuing search for humankind's divine potential.

SENLIN

Senlin is a three-part poem that contains Aiken's most famous composition, the "Morning Song from Senlin" (section two of Part II). Senlin, whose name means "little old man," is an ironic or slightly comical middle-class imperturbable figure, who is potentially explosive and who shines like the sun as he rises from sleep in the morning. "Morning Song from Senlin" is a display of musical prosody, consisting of a variety of adapted ballad stanzas, refrains, and heroic quatrains. An evening ode of Senlin's (section three of Part I), in ternary order, inverts the usual Pindaric or even Cowleyan sequence, and finds its musical echoes in the refrains. Senlin, himself, is both a dreamer and everybody's dream.

THE PILGRIMAGE OF FESTUS

The Pilgrimage of Festus, in five parts and in rhymed free verse, is another step along the road to Lord Zero. Possessed of a Faustian thirst for ultimate knowledge, Festus searches out the world of temporal conquest and then that of spiritual power as he converses to no avail with Buddha, Mephistopheles, Confucius, and Christ. Finally, Festus hears a music that is so lovely that it must be the sign of eternal womanhood, the ultimate symbol of Romantic humanism. Old Man of the Rain, however, Festus's alter ego, soon disillusions him. The music comes from the instruments of a group of butchers on holiday who are still dressed in their spotted aprons. Festus emerges as a wry figure of paternalism in blithe search for truth, to be found only in his private self.

CHANGING MIND

Changing Mind is a poet's poem, in traditional four-part "music." Aiken's stated intention is to enunciate his newfound goal to help humankind "evolve" a higher consciousness pointing toward the divine, but he admits that, as such a helper, he must "die daily" to self. A mixture of farce and brutality, this poem, which moves from free-verse narrative and dialogue to prose and "prayer," advances Aiken from mere hedonism to a kind of creativity that recognizes its source in dust, which is the "true father."

JOHN DETH

John Deth is a rollicking, five-part Hudibrastic literary ballad about John Deth, the master of the death dance, and his two doxies, Millicent Piggistaile and Juliana Goatibed, demons all three. These death demons sleep and dream forever now in the mind of the poet but not until they have led many in the dance to death and have crucified the "god" of beauty itself, Venus Anadyomene. To Aiken, himself never sure of the total meaning of this poem, Deth seems to represent the negative, Piggistaile the positive pole of Aiken's being, while Goatibed stands for the conjoined consciousness of the two poles. Deth is Father Death, capable of using the power of unholy resurrection by word-magic, even as he can do to death by the word of his mouth, always assisted by his magic wand and by the walking dead, who serve as heralds of his deadly work. John Deth is also a grieving antihero, a Comus who, to lust, has added the dimension of death.

"THE ROOM"

"The Room," a marvelous blank verse ode in three stanzas, celebrates memory. An isolated single leaf is able to construct a great tree out of chaos through a reverse creation reflected in the reverse order of the stanzas. The mystic tree of the poem represents a cycle in which both life and death, joined by their intermediary, chaos, deserve praise for perpetuating the cycle. The same theme occurs in *Preludes for Memnon*, composed of sixty-three preludes, in which Aiken attempts to bring order out of chaos and death.

THE MORNING SONG OF LORD ZERO

In expanding and contracting lines of mainly free verse, rhymed and unrhymed, the fourteen poems of *The Morning Song of Lord Zero*, much of the time in dialogue, explore the image of the incarnate word of Romantic humanism, the "I" who has become Lord Zero. Lord Zero, however, is "The Island," death, into which the soul or self takes only a memory of love. The blessed isle of Romantic humanism here presents death as the ultimate identity.

A LITTLE WHO'S ZOO OF MILD ANIMALS

Finally, *A Little Who's Zoo of Mild Animals* mocks its own analysis of an evolved, portmanteau creation and consciousness. In the leaf, there is already the seed, the branch, the trunk, and the root. In the heart of the child is the true beginning of heaven.

OTHER MAJOR WORKS

LONG FICTION: *Blue Voyage*, 1927; *Great Circle*, 1933; *King Coffin*, 1935; *A Heart for the Gods of Mexico*, 1939; *Conversation: Or, Pilgrim's Progress*, 1940; *The Collected Novels of Conrad Aiken*, 1964.

SHORT FICTION: *The Dark City*, 1922; *Bring! Bring!, and Other Stories*, 1925; *Costumes by Eros*, 1928; "Silent Snow, Secret Snow," 1932; *Impulse*, 1933; *Among the Lost People*, 1934; "Round by Round," 1935; *Short Stories*, 1950; *Collected Short Stories*, 1960; *Collected Short Stories of Conrad Aiken*, 1966.

PLAY: *Fear No More*, pr. 1946 (pb. 1957 as *Mr. Arcularis: A Play*).

NONFICTION: *Skepticisms: Notes on Contemporary Poetry*, 1919; *Ushant: An Essay*, 1952; *A Reviewer's ABC: Collected Criticism of Conrad Aiken from 1916 to the Present*, 1958; *Selected Letters of Conrad Aiken*, 1978 (Joseph Killorin, editor).

EDITED TEXTS: *A Comprehensive Anthology of American Poetry*, 1929, 1944; *Twentieth Century American Poetry*, 1944.

BIBLIOGRAPHY

Aiken, Conrad. *Selected Letters of Conrad Aiken*. Edited by Joseph Killorin. New Haven, Conn.: Yale University Press, 1978. Includes a representative sample of 245 letters (from some three thousand) written by Aiken. A cast of correspondents, among them T. S. Eliot and Malcolm Lowry, indexes to Aiken's works and important personages, and a wealth of illustrations, mostly photographs, add considerably to the value of the volume.

Butscher, Edward. *Conrad Aiken: Poet of White Horse Vale*. Athens: University of Georgia Press, 1988. This critical biography emphasizes Aiken's literary work, particularly the poetry. Includes many illustrations, copious notes, and an extensive bibliography that is especially helpful in psychoanalytic theory.

Hamilton, Ian. *Against Oblivion: Some Lives of the Twentieth-Century Poets*. London: Viking, 2002.

Contains an entry on Aiken, examining his life and works.

Hoffman, Frederick J. *Conrad Aiken*. New York: Twayne, 1962. A biography of Aiken that also provides analysis of his works. Contains a chronology, a biographical chapter, and an annotated bibliography.

Lorenz, Clarissa M. *Lorelei Two: My Life with Conrad Aiken*. Athens: University of Georgia Press, 1983. Lorenz, Aiken's second wife, discusses the 1926-1938 years, the period when he wrote his best work. She covers his literary acquaintances, his work habits, and the literary context in which he worked. The book is well indexed and contains several relevant photographs.

Spivey, Ted R. *Time's Stop in Savannah: Conrad Aiken's Inner Journey*. Macon, Ga.: Mercer University Press, 1997. Explores Aiken's thought processes and how they translate to his writings.

Spivey, Ted R., and Arthur Waterman, eds. *Conrad Aiken: A Priest of Consciousness*. New York: AMS Press, 1989. Spivey and Waterman focus on Aiken's poetry. Contains an extensive chronology of Aiken's life and a lengthy description of the Aiken materials in the Huntington Library.

Womack, Kenneth. "Unmasking Another Villain in Conrad Aiken's Autobiographical Dream." *Biography* 19 (Spring, 1996): 137. Examines the role of British poet and novelist Martin Armstrong as a fictionalized character in Aiken's *Ushant*; argues that Aiken's attack on Armstrong is motivated by revenge for Armstrong's marriage to Aiken's first wife.

Fred R. McFadden

Elizabeth Alexander

Born: Harlem, New York; May 30, 1962

PRINCIPAL POETRY

The Venus Hottentot, 1990
Body of Life, 1996
Antebellum Dream Book, 2001
American Sublime, 2005
Miss Crandall's School for Young Ladies and Little Misses of Color, 2007 (with Marilyn Nelson)
Praise Song for the Day: A Poem for Barack Obama's Presidential Inauguration, January 20, 2009, 2009

OTHER LITERARY FORMS

As the chair of African American studies at Yale University, Elizabeth Alexander has published not only poetry but also a number of critical essays on various subjects, almost all of which relate to the African American experience. She has edited *The Essential Gwendolyn Brooks* (2005) and has written a play and two books of essays, *The Black Interior* (2004) and *Power and Possibility* (2007).

ACHIEVEMENTS

Elizabeth Alexander has won a number of awards, including two George Kent Prizes for Poetry (1992, 1997), the Illinois Arts Council Literary Award (1993), the *Kenyon Review* Prize for Literary Excellence (1994), and three Pushcart Prizes (1998, 2000, 2001). *American Sublime* was a finalist for the Pulitzer Prize and was named one of the American Library Association's notable books of the year. Alexander won Connecticut Book Awards in poetry for *American Sublime* and *Miss Crandall's School for Young Ladies and Little Misses of Color* in 2006 and 2008, respectively.

In 2007, Alexander was the inaugural recipient of both the Jackson Poetry Prize from *Poets and Writers* and the Alphonse Fletcher, Sr., Fellowship for her work in improving race relations in the United States. She has also received fellowships from the National Endowment for the Arts and the Guggenheim Foundation. In 2009, she composed *Praise Song for the Day* and delivered it at the inauguration of President Barack Obama. That same year, she received the Stephen E. Henderson Award from the African American Literature and Culture Society.

BIOGRAPHY

Elizabeth Alexander was born in Harlem, New York, but was raised in Washington, D.C., as her father, Clifford Alexander, Jr., served as the chair of the Equal Employment Opportunity Commission during

Elizabeth Alexander (Ficre Ghebreyesus)

the late 1960's and as the first African American secretary of the Army during the administration of President Jimmy Carter. Alexander earned a B.A. from Yale University (1984), an M.A. from Boston University (1987), and a Ph.D. from the University of Pennsylvania (1992).

Alexander began her career as a reporter for the *Washington Post*, but she made the transition to teaching after completing her education. She has taught at a number of prestigious schools, including Northwestern University, the University of Chicago, New York University, and the University of Pennsylvania. In 2000, she joined the faculty at Yale University, where she became the chair of the African American studies department in 2009. In addition to teaching African American studies, Alexander has taught courses in English and gender studies.

Analysis

Elizabeth Alexander's poetry revolves around a celebration of what it means to be both African American and female. In all of her volumes of poetry, Alexander uses riffs on jazz to create a melodious sound when her poems are read aloud. She relies on sensual markers, expressing the senses of touch and sight through words. Rarely venturing out into alternative typographies, Alexander does occasionally use prose poems to form a stream-of-consciousness mentality. Her persona poems are a hallmark of her style, as she attempts to enter in the consciousness of another person and tell his or her story through her poetry.

The Venus Hottentot

The title poem of *The Venus Hottentot* revolves around a historical personage known as the Venus Hottentot, an African woman who was forced to be a sideshow exhibit in the nineteenth century. The poems in this volume reveal a cultural history that ranges from the Venus Hottentot to singer, actor, and activist Paul Robeson to then-imprisoned South African leader Nelson Mandela. "Today's News" celebrates what Alexander sees as a multitude of different types of blackness: "I didn't want to write a poem that said 'blackness/ is,' because we know better than anyone/ that we are not one or ten or ten thousand things."

"The Venus Hottentot" evokes a sense of exploitation and of always being watched by others for unusual behavior. Alexander might be familiar with this feeling, as she grew up in Washington, D.C., as the daughter of a politician, under the watchful eyes of the entire political community. However, the poem also brings forth a sense of physical exploitation, a bodily invasion on the part of another. It is not a theme that continues through this volume but is used later in other books.

The Venus Hottentot also shows the blues and jazz influence of Harlem, as Alexander gives her work a musical quality even as she refers to jazz personages such as Albert Murray, Duke Ellington, and John Coltrane. "John Col" is one of the few poems in which Alexander uses an alternative typography, though only in certain stanzas. She divides syllables and phrases between lines to underline their meaning:

a terrible beau-
ty a terrible
beauty a terrible
beauty a horn

Though divided between lines, the repetition melds itself into the melody of jazz.

BODY OF LIFE

Alexander's second volume, *Body of Life*, also references jazz culture, but the overall theme is memories.
Alexander evokes memories of New York and Chicago, as well of her grandmother. "Butter" is practically mouth-watering as Alexander goes through all the
dishes her mother cooked that contained butter. She
also remembers events such as the Apollo moon landing and, in "Body of Life," explores what it means to
grow up a black woman who is being taught how to be a
diva.

A theme that was mentioned in *The Venus Hottentot*
but not explored in depth until *Body of Life* is that of violation, generally sexual. Alexander brings up incest
and rape in more explicit terms than she used in her previous volume. "In the Small Rooms" describes this in
the most direct way. Alexander asks herself and her
reader "What am I not remembering Why didn't I
tell."

Two poems also deal with acquired immunodeficiency syndrome (AIDS). "Body of Life" tells a story
of wilder years in Alexander's life. One stanza of the
poem, addressed to a friend, ends abruptly with "I'd ask
and you'd tell me, and who died/ and one day you said,
'And I'm living with AIDS.'" "At the Beach" remembers those friends who have died:

> Looking at the photograph is somehow not
> unbearable: My friends, two dead, one low
> on T-cells, his white T-shirt an X-ray
> screen for the virus . . .

Through the entire volume, Alexander relies on memories to guide her poetry.

ANTEBELLUM DREAM BOOK

Alexander celebrates the African American experience in *Antebellum Dream Book*, using dreams rather
than the memories that guided *Body of Life*. A noticeable departure from her other volumes is that instead of
using many persona poems, Alexander includes only

two: "The Toni Morrison Dream," which outlines a
writing experience with Toni Morrison, and "Narrative: Ali," in which Alexander imagines herself as the
narrator of Muhammad Ali's life. Alexander moves
from Ali's birth to his winning and subsequent discarding of the Olympic medal to training to a conversation
with boxer Joe Frazier and to a final statement of who
Ali is.

Many of the poems in *Antebellum Dream Book* deal
with pregnancy, motherhood, and postpartum depression rather than with historical personages. "Gravitas"
and "Baby" explore the dreams that Alexander experienced while pregnant, and "Neonatology" discusses
giving birth and the immediate effects of bringing a
baby home. Three poems discuss postpartum dreams,
which deal with fears about being responsible for another's life. "Neonatology" directly connects the jazz
motion of her other poems with childbearing: "Giving
birth is like jazz, something from silence."

AMERICAN SUBLIME

Although Alexander divided her previous books
into sections, she gives those sections titles for the first
time in *American Sublime*: "American Blue," "Ars Poetica," "*Amistad*," and "American Sublime." Perhaps
the most interesting section is "*Amistad*," which tells
the story of the slave ship *Amistad*. Slaves on board the
vessel revolted but were eventually captured off the
coast of Connecticut in 1839. Abolitionists argued for
the slaves to be set free, as they had been kidnapped,
and in 1841, the U.S. Supreme Court ruled that the Africans on board the vessel were not slaves and could be
returned to Sierra Leone. Alexander arranges her poems almost chronologically, moving through the story
from the beginning with the poem "*Amistad*." "The
Blue Whale" and "Absence" describe life on the ship,
while "Approach" and "Connecticut" describe the arrival of the *Amistad* in New England. Other poems outline life in the United States. Then "Judge Judson" describes the decision that allows the Africans to return
to Sierra Leone.

"The *Amistad* Trail" and "Cinque Redux" are poems that bring the *Amistad* story forward in time.
"Cinque Redux" takes the hero of the *Amistad*, Cinque,
who led the rebellion on board the ship, and expresses
what future generations will make of him and his story:

I will be called bad motherf—ker.
I will be venerated.
I will be misremembered.
I will be Seng-Pieh, Cinqueze, Joseph,
and end up CINQUE.

Alexander depicts the modern-day attitude of a historical figure, and the parallel structure of the first four lines underlines the emphasis of the fifth, the capital letters emphasizing one unique identity.

American Sublime also separates itself from Alexander's previous volumes by using fewer poems based on a persona, although it contains more of these poems than *Antebellum Dream Book* did. This perhaps signals Alexander's becoming comfortable with her own voice and her moving away from the need to speak through another identity. The persona poems are contained in the "*Amistad*" section rather than found throughout the book.

PRAISE SONG FOR THE DAY

Alexander wrote *Praise Song for the Day* for President Barack Obama's inauguration and recited it at the ceremony in Washington, D.C. Although Alexander's other poetry celebrates the African American experience in specific and concete terms, *Praise Song for the Day* celebrates it without being specific, joining the African American with the American experience:

Say it plain: that many have died for this day.
Sing the names of the dead who brought us here,
who laid the train tracks, raised the bridges.

Alexander celebrates the heritage of the United States in this poem, but she departs from her usual focus on the historical and the past to celebrate the future:

In today's sharp sparkle, this winter air,
any thing can be made, any sentence begun.
On the brink, on the brim, on the cusp,

praise song for walking forward in that light.

OTHER MAJOR WORKS

PLAY: *Diva Studies*, pr. 1996.
NONFICTION: *The Black Interior*, 2004; *Power and Possibility*, 2007.
EDITED TEXTS: *Love's Instruments*, 1995 (by Melvin Dixon); *The Essential Gwendolyn Brooks*, 2005.

BIBLIOGRAPHY

Alexander, Elizabeth. "Elizabeth Alexander." http://www .elizabethalexander.net Alexander's official Web site contains information on her life, publications, and teaching philosophies, and reviews of her work. Provides texts of some of Alexander's poetry and some multimedia interviews with the poet.

_____. "The Poetry of Politics: Elizabeth Alexander on Writing the Poem of a Lifetime." Interview by Jeffrey A. Trachtenberg. *Wall Street Journal*, December 20, 2008, p. W4. Alexander talks about writing the poem for President Barack Obama's inauguration, the importance of poetry, and her major influences, including Walt Whitman, Gwendolyn Brooks, and Robert Hayden.

Malamud, Randy. "Walking Forward in a Poet's Light." Review of *Praise Song for the Day*. *The Chronicle of Higher Education* 55, no. 22 (February 6, 2009): B8-B9. Places the poem within the context of the other special presentations at U.S. president Barack Obama's inauguration as well as within the historical context surrounding her reading and the election. Also contains the entire text of the poem.

Pardlo, Gregory. Review of *American Sublime*. *Black Issues Book Review* 8, no. 2 (March/April, 2006): 18. Focuses on each section of the work to explore the messages Alexander's poetry has for African Americans.

Williams, Tyrone. "*The Venus Hottentot*." In *Masterplots II: African American Literature*, edited by Tyrone Williams. Rev. ed. Pasadena, Calif.: Salem Press, 2009. Presents an analysis of Alexander's first book of poetry, looking at themes and meaning and the critical context.

Emily Carroll Shearer

SHERMAN ALEXIE

Born: Spokane Indian Reservation, Wellpinit,
Washington; October 7, 1966

PRINCIPAL POETRY

I Would Steal Horses, 1992
Old Shirts and New Skins, 1993
The Man Who Loves Salmon, 1998
One Stick Song, 2000
Dangerous Astronomy, 2005
Face, 2009

OTHER LITERARY FORMS

In addition to being a significant contemporary
poet, Sherman Alexie has developed an equally prominent status as a writer of fiction through the publication of short-story collections and novels. His first
short-story collection, *The Lone Ranger and Tonto
Fistfight in Heaven* (1993), has become one of the
most-taught Indian literature texts at the college level,
and the short story "This Is What It Means to Say Phoenix, Arizona" was made into the screenplay and film
Smoke Signals (1998). Alexie's novels alone would establish a worthy reputation for any author. In *Reservation Blues* (1995), Alexie fictionally posits that legendary bluesman Robert Johnson did not die in 1938 but
instead hitchhiked his way onto the Spokane Indian
Reservation in 1991, triggering the formation of an all-
Indian blues band, Coyote Springs, in the context of a
compelling narrative. *Indian Killer* (1996), a mystery
story set in Seattle, revolves around the ironically
named John Smith, an Indian adopted as an infant by a
white family. In *Flight* (2007), an orphaned Indian boy
travels back and forth through time, learning and growing through what he experiences. In his acclaimed
young adult novel, *The Absolutely True Diary of a
Part-Time Indian* (2007), Alexie liberally uses elements
of his own childhood—his encephalitic condition, his
Spokane Indian Reservation upbringing, Reardan High
School, and his success in academics and in basketball—to create a heartfelt and memorable work that
employs graphic novel techniques to appeal visually to
a younger reading audience.

ACHIEVEMENTS

Soon after his graduation from Washington State
University, Sherman Alexie won poetry fellowships
from the Washington State Arts Commission (1991)
and from the National Endowment for the Arts (1992).
On the strength of his early poetry and short-story collections, he won the Washington State University Distinguished Alumni Award (1994) and later received the
Regents' Distinguished Alumnus Award from Washington State University (2003). In 1994, he received the
Washington State Book Award. Alexie's stature can be
determined in part by his regional acclaim (Tacoma
Public Library Annual Literary Award, 1998; Western
Literature Association Distinguished Achievement
Award, 2007) and by the national and international notice he has received: *Granta* magazine named him one
of the Twenty Best American Novelists Under the Age
of Forty in 1996, and *The New Yorker* named him one
of the Twenty Writers for the Twenty-first Century in
1999. Among other accolades, Alexie has received the
Lila Wallace-*Reader's Digest* Writers' Award (1994),
the American Book Award from the Before Columbus
Foundation (1996), the PEN/Malamud Award (2001),
a Pushcart Prize for the poem "Avian Nights" (2005),
and the National Book Award in Young People's Literature (2007) and the Boston Globe-Horn Book Award
for Excellence in Children's Literature (2008) for *The
Absolutely True Diary of a Part-Time Indian*. He was
named Most Engaging Author by the Indies Choice
Book Awards in 2009 and received the 2010 PEN/
Faulkner Award for fiction for his short-story collection *War Dances*. He has been granted honorary
degrees from Columbia College, Chicago (1999), and
from Seattle University (2000).

BIOGRAPHY

Sherman Joseph Alexie, Jr., was born on the Spokane Indian Reservation in northwest Washington,
where he spent his childhood. When he was six months
old, he underwent surgery to correct congenital hydro-
cephalus. Although the surgery put him at risk for mental retardation, Alexie suffered no ill effects and became an avid reader in his youth. He attended Reardan
High School, twenty miles south of the reservation
high school, excelling both in the classroom and on the

basketball floor. He earned a scholarship to Gonzaga University and, after two years, transferred to Washington State University, from which he graduated in 1994 with a B.A. in American studies.

At Washington State University, Alexie was influenced by poet and English professor Alex Kuo. Soon after his graduation, he earned multiple poetry fellowships and began to publish collections of his poetry with Hanging Loose Press. Alexie claims that although he struggled with alcoholism throughout his college years, he quit drinking when he received his first acceptance letter from Hanging Loose Press and has been sober since 1990. Alexie began writing and publishing short fiction, then novels, in the mid-1990's.

Alexie has continued to be creative, branching out in multiple genres in addition to fiction and poetry. He has written and directed films and has made many personal appearances before audiences throughout the

Sherman Alexie (Getty Images)

world. In these appearances, he reads his poetry, short stories, and excerpts from his novels and performs stand-up comedy, sometimes accompanied by musician Jim Boyd, whose work appears in both of Alexie's films, *Smoke Signals* and *The Business of Fancydancing* (2002). Alexie won the World Poetry Bout Association competition four years in a row, 1998 through 2001. He has appeared many times on television, including on *The NewsHour with Jim Lehrer*, *Sixty Minutes II*, and *The Colbert Report*. Alexie married Diane Tomhave in 1995, and the couple have two sons, Joseph and David.

ANALYSIS

Sherman Alexie writes both lyric and narrative poetry, usually in free verse, though his poetry sometimes rhymes, and he has rarely but effectively used arcane poetic forms. In "Spokane Tribal Celebration, September 1987," he makes use of the sestina, a form that originated in medieval Provence. Although Alexie invokes Lakota mystic and warrior Crazy Horse as both character and symbol, his poetry is usually set in a very realistic or even surrealistic present, articulating the concerns and struggles of contemporary Indians living in the larger American society through descriptions of powwows, reservation basketball tournaments, the consumption of commodity rather than traditional foods, and the use of old Camaros and pickup trucks instead of horses.

THE BUSINESS OF FANCYDANCING

In the five short stories and forty poems that make up *The Business of Fancydancing: Stories and Poems* (1992), Indian traditions come into conflict with the exigencies of contemporary life on and off the reservation. In the short story "Special Delivery," Junior spends hours watching the automatic door at the trading post open and close, "more fascinated with the useless technology than autistically obsessed." Similarly, reservation storyteller Thomas Builds-the-Fire "spent more than a few moments transfixed by the door, dissonant, like a missed step in a fancydance." Fancydancing, introduced in the title, recurs as one of the controlling metaphors of the collection.

Perhaps the most striking frame of reference is Alexie's invocation of Crazy Horse, a nineteenth century Lakota mystic and warrior, as a symbol of Indian heroism, hope, and failure in "Crazy Horse Dreams," the third and final section of the book. In "Ceremonies," Seymour muses on ". . . Crazy Horse dreams, the kind that don't come true," and Crazy Horse is often transposed into a working-class present that is ironic and sad but often insightful. In "Missing," Crazy Horse gets a job at a 7-11, enjoys the free sodas and cigarettes that the job affords, but ". . . picks up a nicotine habit/ spends breaks lighting up in a cooler, hiding behind the milk and eggs/ because his co-workers told him there's much less smoke that way." In "The Reservation Cab Driver," Crazy Horse is hitchhiking at 3 A.M.; in the prose poem "Basketball," the first-person narrator claims to be "the Reservation point guard with the Crazy Horse jump shot," going home at the end of the story to "hang another shirt in my closet, another Crazy Horse dream without a skeleton or skin."

OLD SHIRTS AND NEW SKINS

Alexie begins *Old Shirts and New Skins* with the equation "Poetry = Anger × Imagination" on the frontispiece and proceeds to document the Indian experience of the 1990's within the context of both traditional and contemporary referents. He continues periodically to reflect on the character and significance of Crazy Horse, especially in apposition to Custer in the parallel poems "Custer Speaks" and "Crazy Horse Speaks." Alexie imagines Crazy Horse saying, as he sits across the fire from Sitting Bull, "We both saw the same thing/ our futures tight and small/ an 8 × 10 dream/ called the reservation./ We had no alternatives/ but to fight again and again/ live our lives on horseback." Alexie exhibits his developing interest in communicating in multiple media in "Powwow Polaroid" and by having poet and artist Elizabeth Woody of the Warm Springs Confederated Tribes contribute twelve illustrations to the volume.

FIRST INDIAN ON THE MOON

In *First Indian on the Moon* (1993), Alexie continues his free-verse ruminations concerning the enduring frustrations and ironies of contemporary American Indian life. In "Reservation Drive-In," he asserts that "we chase the tail of some Crazy Horse dream, chase the theft of our lives." Continuing his interest in figures from American popular culture, in "Vision: From the Drum's Interior," he imagines Bruce Lee as a young Indian boy, envisions Charlie Chaplin as a Spokane In-

dian, and pities Elvis Presley as ". . . a poor white boy . . . trash. He was the dumpster singer who faked guitar and sang black music like it was his." In "My Heroes Have Never Been Cowboys," Alexie suggests that "We've all killed John Wayne more than once" and reflects on "this country of John Wayne and broken treaties," showing Alexie's interest in the well-known motion-picture cowboy whom he would later memorialize in "John Wayne's Teeth," the drum-group song in the film version of *Smoke Signals*. Concerns of racial and individual identity suffuse many poems, as in "Because I Was in New York City Once and Have Since Become an Expert," in which he wonders: "Am I Native American only when I am hated because of it? Does racism determine my entire identity?" The stanza ends without any response to the questions, emblematic of Alexie's penchant to raise compelling, thought-provoking questions that resonate without making a specific reply.

THE SUMMER OF BLACK WIDOWS

In *The Summer of Black Widows*, Alexie uses principally lyric rather than narrative poems to examine the circumstance of being ". . . an Indian/ who knows the difference/ between Monet and Manet" and what significance that might have for him in "Things (for an Indian) to do in New York (City)." Focusing especially on the plight and dilemma of young male American Indians, Alexie sees basketball as a possible outlet for "the twentieth-century warriors who will never kill" in the poem "Defending Walt Whitman." Elegiacally, he feels the need to compose "a poem for people who died in stupid ways" and easily fills twenty-seven stanzas with a litany of human foolishness and stupidity that is tempered with resignation and a poignant sense of pity.

FACE

In *Face*, Alexie's metacognitive and agile poetic perspective creates pages of footnotes and even commentary on his own footnotes as he seeks to convey the complexity of his vision. In "Vilify," he attempts to answer "What is Native American poetry?"—a question that he has most likely fielded many times—by simply responding "funny grief." He shares, in "Tuxedo with Eagle Feathers," that "my literacy/ saved my ass" and suggests that it provided him with the impetus to swear off alcohol, beginning in his early twenties with the publication of his first collection of poetry. In "Unauthorized," he somewhat justifies the number of appearances he makes as a stand-up comedian as he, a resident of Seattle for decades, asserts that "great comedy comes from bad weather" and that "poets and comics share a toolbox."

OTHER MAJOR WORKS

LONG FICTION: *Reservation Blues*, 1995; *Indian Killer*, 1996; *Flight*, 2007.

SHORT FICTION: *The Lone Ranger and Tonto Fistfight in Heaven*, 1993; *The Toughest Indian in the World*, 2000; *Ten Little Indians*, 2003; *War Dances*, 2009.

SCREENPLAYS: *Smoke Signals*, 1998; *The Business of Fancydancing*, 2002.

CHILDREN'S LITERATURE: *The Absolutely True Diary of a Part-Time Indian*, 2007.

MISCELLANEOUS: *The Business of Fancydancing: Stories and Poems*, 1992; *First Indian on the Moon*, 1993; *The Summer of Black Widows*, 1996 (poems and short prose).

BIBLIOGRAPHY

Alexie, Sherman. Interviews. *Conversations with Sherman Alexie.* Edited by Nancy J. Peterson. Jackson: University Press of Mississippi, 2009. This collection of interviews with Alexie provides a great deal of information about his writings, including his poetry.

_____. "shermanalexie.com." http://www.fallsapart .com. The authorized Web site for Alexie features updates on his recent travels, a biography, an academic center, a press center, and links to selected articles and reviews, lists of published books, films, recordings, essays, and awards.

Bruce, Heather E., Anna E. Baldwin, and Christabel Umphrey, eds. *Sherman Alexie in the Classroom: "This Is Not a Silent Movie. Our Voices Will Save Our Lives."* Urbana, Ill.: National Council of Teachers of English, 2008. Seasoned classroom English teachers provide approaches to teach the various works of Alexie in the high school classroom.

Grassian, Daniel. *Understanding Sherman Alexie.* Columbia: University of South Carolina Press, 2005. The first book-length study devoted to Alexie, this work includes discussions of his poetry, short stories, novels, and film, focusing on Alexie's appreciation for popular culture and the manner in which it frames and often distorts the essential meaning and value of Indian cultures.

Herman, Matthew. *Politics and Aesthetics in Contemporary Native American Literature: Across Every Border.* New York: Routledge, 2009. This work on politics and aesthetics in American Indian literature contains a chapter examining Alexie.

James, Meredith K. *Literary and Cinematic Reservation in Selected Works of Native American Author Sherman Alexie.* Lewiston, N.Y.: Edwin Mellen Press, 2005. James examines what has been termed the "reservation of the mind," the attitudes of American Indians raised on the reservation but living elsewhere, by looking at works of Alexie.

Richard Sax

AGHA SHAHID ALI

Born: New Delhi, India; February 4, 1949
Died: Amherst, Massachusetts; December 8, 2001

PRINCIPAL POETRY

Bone-Sculpture, 1972
In Memory of Begum Akhtar, 1979
The Half-Inch Himalayas, 1987
A Walk Through the Yellow Pages, 1987
A Nostalgist's Map of America, 1991
The Belovéd Witness: Selected Poems, 1992
The Country Without a Post Office, 1997
Rooms Are Never Finished, 2002
Call Me Ishmael Tonight: A Book of Ghazals, 2003
The Veiled Suite: The Collected Poems, 2009

OTHER LITERARY FORMS

Agha Shahid Ali (AH-lee) was both a poet and a scholar. In 1986, he published *T. S. Eliot as Editor*, a critical work based on his doctoral dissertation. Ali also was a translator and an editor. With the help of his mother, Sufia Agha Ashraf Ali, he translated the poems of Faiz Ahmed Faiz from Urdu into English, collecting them in *The Rebel's Silhouette: Selected Poems* (1995). In 2000, he edited *Ravishing Disunities: Real Ghazals in English*, with an afterword by Sara Suleri Goodyear.

ACHIEVEMENTS

Agha Shahid Ali won a Pushcart Prize and was a finalist for the National Book Award in 2001. A fellowship from the Ingram Merrill Foundation aided his writing of *A Nostalgist's Map of America* and his work on *The Rebel's Silhouette*. He was also awarded a fellowship from the John Simon Guggenheim Foundation and an Artist's Fellowship for Poetry from the New York Foundation for the Arts, which helped in the writing of *The Country Without a Post Office*. In addition, Ali received fellowships from the Pennsylvania Council on the Arts and the Bread Loaf Writers' Conference. Since 2003, the University of Utah Press and the University of Utah's Department of English have annually awarded the Agha Shahid Ali Prize in Poetry.

These awards are testament to Ali's tremendous contribution to poetry through his successful blending of both Western and Eastern influences in his life and in his writing. His thoughtful responses as a native in the multiracial, multicultural, multireligious, and multilingual environment of India (and Kashmir) and as an immigrant in the United States to racial, cultural, religious, and linguistic differences are reflected throughout his poetry. Furthermore, Ali solidified the North American understanding of the verse form of the ghazal through his translation of Faiz's poetry, his anthology of North American ghazals, and his publication of his own ghazals.

BIOGRAPHY

Agha Shahid Ali was born into a very highly educated, multilingual, and liberal Muslim family. In his introduction to *The Rebel's Silhouette*, he recounts how his paternal grandmother quoted John Milton, William Shakespeare, John Keats, and Thomas Hardy in English; Hafiz and Jalāl al-Dīn Rūmī in Persian; Faiz in Urdu; and Habba Khatun, Mahjoor, and Zinda Kaul in Kashmiri. While he was growing up, his immediate family lived in New Delhi, India; Srinagar, Kashmir;

and Muncie, Indiana, where his parents (Agha Ashraf Ali and Sufia Agha Ashraf Ali) both completed their doctorates in 1964. English, Urdu, and Kashmiri were all spoken in his home. Ali considered English to be his first language (it was the only language in which he wrote) and Urdu to be his mother tongue.

As a child, Ali was educated in Roman Catholic schools, but he attended an American high school while his parents were in graduate school. Ali earned several degrees: a B.A. from the University of Kashmir (1968), an M.A. from the University of Delhi (1970), an M.A. (1981) and a Ph.D. (1984) from Pennsylvania State University, and an M.F.A. from the University of Arizona (1985).

Ali lectured at the University of Delhi from 1970 to 1975 before moving to the United States to teach, study, and write. At Pennsylvania State University, he served as an instructor from 1976 to 1983, and at the University of Arizona, he worked as a graduate assistant from 1983 to 1985. Ali became the communications editor in the marketing department of the JNC Companies from 1985 to 1987 in Tucson, Arizona.

Ali was assistant professor of English and creative writing at Hamilton College from 1987 to 1993. Subsequently, he became an associate professor of English and director of the master of fine arts in creative writing program at the University of Massachusetts in Amherst. Ali also taught in the master of fine arts and doctoral programs at the University of Utah and the master of fine arts program at Warren Wilson College. He attained full professorship at the University of Utah in 1999. He held visiting appointments as professor or writer-in-residence at Princeton University, New York University, and the State University of New York, Binghamton.

Ali visited his parents in the summers in Srinagar, Kashmir, where they remained even after all their children had moved to the United States. However, Ali's mother, accompanied by his father, came to the United States for brain cancer treatment in 1996. She died in 1997. Ali also died of brain cancer four years later.

ANALYSIS

Agha Shahid Ali's elegant, elegiac, expansive, and exilic voice is very clear from the beginning. He mocked it himself very early on in "Introducing" (from *In Memory of Begum Akhtar*): "Death punctuated all my poems./ I tried being clever, white-washed the day,/ exchanged it for the night,/ Bones my masks, Death/ the adolescent password." Apart from the theme of death or loss, which becomes more legitimate and literal toward the end of his career, Ali was also interested in demarcation. He resisted the title "U.S. citizen." He preferred the description "immigrant" or, better still, "exile." He accepted titles such as Kashmiri American, South Asian American, or Asian American. He considered himself conservative in poetic content, form, and technique. He adhered to strict guidelines for the ghazal. In addition, Ali's poetry is rich in allusion to and inclusion of poetic influences from mythology to the works of his contemporary poet friends and larger literary community. His poems are full of dedications to various people in his life. Finally, Ali drew from and portrayed his diverse background and environment. Although conservative in art, he was not conservative in his politics.

Ali's early poems display his most powerful literary influences: British colonization, which gave him the English language, and Eastern poetry (especially ghazals) by Mir Taqi Mir, Mirza Ghalib, and Faiz, sung by Begum Akhtar, whom Ali loved. He writes in the title poem "In Memory of Begum Akhtar," "You've finally polished catastrophe,/ the note you seasoned// with decades of Ghalib,/ Mir, Faiz:// I innovate on a note-less raga." In "dear editor," from his first poetry collection, *Bone-Sculpture*, Ali writes, "they call this my alien language// i am a dealer in words/ that mix cultures/ and leave me rootless." In "The Editor Revisited" (from *In Memory of Begum Akhtar*), he adds, "'A language must measure up to one's native dust.'// Divided between two cultures, I spoke a language/ foreign even to my ears." Later, in his introduction to *The Rebel's Silhouette*, Ali comments on "dear editor," "Rootless? Certainly not. I was merely subscribing to an inherent dominative mode that insisted one should not write in English because it was not an Indian language. . . . But it was mine, ours." Ali had begun to blend and own both his Eastern and Western cultural and linguistic influences.

The Half-Inch Himalayas

Exile is a powerful theme in *The Half-Inch Himalayas*, which opens with an epigraph from Virginia Woolf, ". . . for wherever I seat/ myself, I die in exile." This collection also includes the widely anthologized poems "Postcard from Kashmir," "Snowmen," and "The Dacca Gauzes." In "Homage to Faiz Ahmed Faiz," Ali writes, ". . . Your lines were measured/ so carefully to become in our veins// the blood of prisoners. In the free verse/ of another language I imprisoned// each line—but I touched my own exile." In "A Darkly Defense of Dead White Males" (from *Poet's Work, Poet's Play: Essays on the Practice and the Art*, 2007), Ali states, "A multiple exile, I celebrate myself. *Émigré* and *expatriate* describe me better." He continues, "But as an exile in my own country . . . I use the word for its poetic resonance, for its metaphoric power—I must use the site for the privilege of self-reflection." Strictly speaking, Ali is not an exile because he moved voluntarily. However, as a postcolonial subject, a native of a disputed and unstable territory (Kashmir), and an immigrant, he has experienced enough loss and displacement to be able to lament after and have a desire for "home."

A Nostalgist's Map of America

Loss is a major theme in *A Nostalgist's Map of America*. "Beyond the Ash Rains" contains an epigraph from the Gilgamesh epic (c. 2000 B.C.E.; *Gilgamesh Epic*, 1917): "What have you known of loss/ That makes you different from other men?" Ali's speaker in that poem links loss and exile with this wish of not being ". . . singled/ out for loss in your arms, won't ever again/ be exiled, never again, from your arms." Another poem on loss is "A Rehearsal of Loss." Furthermore, loss is expressed through allusions. The title poem, "A Nostalgist's Map of America," and "In Search of Evanescence" allude to "A Route of Evanescence" by Emily Dickinson, one of Ali's favorite poets. "From Another Desert" alludes to the Arabic love story of Qais (Majnoon) and Laila. The final poem in this collection, "Snow on the Desert," closes with these lines: "a time to think of everything the earth/ and I had lost, of all// that I would lose,/ of all that I was losing."

THE COUNTRY WITHOUT A POST OFFICE

Ali's next three collections—*The Country Without a Post Office*, *Rooms Are Never Finished*, and *Call Me Ishmael Tonight*—display a profound love, sorrow, strength, and hope over the escalating conflict in Kashmir, the illness and death of Ali's mother, and the knowledge of his own imminent passing. Dedications of poems to others increase. In the prologue to *The Country Without a Post Office*, the poignant refrain questions if the blesséd women will brush/rub the ashes together. This image portrays both destruction (ashes of the dead) and construction (making a fire for survival). The prologue is also a lament for Kashmir (the blesséd word). Unsurprisingly, Ali read widely and was widely read. An excerpt from the next poem, "Farewell," is quoted in the epigraph to Salman Rushdie's novel *Shalimar the Clown* (2005), which is dedicated to Rushdie's Kashmiri grandparents.

CALL ME ISHMAEL TONIGHT

Ali began to write more conventional ghazals. In *Call Me Ishmael Tonight*, the ghazal "By Exiles" (which appeared in *Rooms Are Never Finished* as "Ghazal"), Ali returned to the theme of exile. This ghazal contains an epigraph from a poem by Mahmoud Darwish, which also inspires a title of a work by Edward Said. The ghazal begins, "In Jerusalem a dead phone's dialed by exiles./ You learn your strange fate: You were exiled by exiles." The ghazal ends, "Will you, Belovéd Stranger, ever witness Shahid—/ two destinies at last reconciled by exiles?" Ali dedicates "By Exiles" to Said, a fellow exile (a dedication that did not appear in his previous collection).

OTHER MAJOR WORKS

NONFICTION: *T. S. Eliot as Editor*, 1986.

TRANSLATION: *The Rebel's Silhouette: Selected Poems*, 1995 (of Faiz Ahmed Faiz's poetry).

EDITED TEXT: *Ravishing Disunities: Real Ghazals in English*, 2000.

BIBLIOGRAPHY

Ali, Agha Shahid. "Conversation with Agha Shahid Ali." Interview by Christine Benevenuto. *Massachusetts Review* 43, no. 2 (Summer, 2002): 261-268. This interview from the late 1990's examines the poet's life and work.

_____. "A Darkly Defense of Dead White Males." In *Poet's Work, Poet's Play*, edited by Daniel Tobin and Pimone Triplett. Ann Arbor: University of Michigan Press, 2007. Ali writes about the craft of poetry and how being a multiple exile affects his work.

Chiu, Jeannie. "Melancholy and Human Rights in *A Nostalgist's Map of America* and *Midnight's Children*." *Literature Interpretation Theory* 16, no. 1 (January-March, 2005): 25-39. Provides a theoretical framework for discussing nostalgia. Examines Ali's *A Nostalgist's Map of America* and Salman Rushdie's *Midnight's Children* (1981).

Ghosh, Amitav. "The Ghat of the Only World: Agha Shahid Ali in Brooklyn." *Annual of Urdu Studies* 17 (2002): 1-19. An account of Ali's life and work written after Ali's death at his own request.

Hogan, Patrick Colm. *Empire and Poetic Voice*. Albany: State University of New York Press, 2004. Dedicated to Ali and includes an entire chapter on Ali's "From Another Desert" in *A Nostalgist's Map of America*.

Woodland, Malcolm. "Memory's Homeland: Agha Shahid Ali and the Hybrid Ghazal." *English Studies in Canada* 31, nos. 2/3 (June-September, 2005): 249-272. An excellent discussion of Ali's use of the ghazal.

Lydia Forssander-Song

PAULA GUNN ALLEN

Born: Cubero, New Mexico; October 24, 1939
Died: Ft. Bragg, California; May 29, 2008

PRINCIPAL POETRY
The Blind Lion, 1974
Coyote's Daylight Trip, 1978
A Cannon Between My Knees, 1981
Star Child, 1981
Shadow Country, 1982
Wyrds, 1987
Skins and Bones: Poems, 1979-1987, 1988
Life Is a Fatal Disease: Collected Poems, 1962-1995, 1997

OTHER LITERARY FORMS

Paula Gunn Allen's writing helped establish the literature of her American Indian cultural heritage as a legitimate and recognized genre. In addition to her extensive and innovative catalog of poetry, Allen published fiction, nonfiction, biographies, collections of myth and oral tradition, critical essays, pedagogical articles concerning the education of native peoples, and gender and sexuality studies. Allen collected, wrote, and edited personal histories as well as myths and legends of various tribes in her books *The Sacred Hoop: Recovering the Feminine in American Indian Traditions* (1986), *Spider Woman's Granddaughters: Traditional Tales and Contemporary Writing by Native American Women* (1989), and *Grandmothers of the Light: A Medicine Woman's Sourcebook* (1991). Allen's motivation to raise awareness concerning American Indian literature, combined with her innovative academic endeavors, earned her acclaim from critics and readers alike, placing the author at the forefront of the American Indian, feminist, and gay and lesbian literary scenes.

ACHIEVEMENTS

Paula Gunn Allen's literary achievements began in 1978, when the National Endowment for the Arts awarded her a distinguished writing fellowship. She received two postdoctoral fellowships, the first from the University of California in 1981 and the second from the Ford Foundation-National Research Council in 1984. Allen received two awards for her groundbreaking work in 1990: the American Book Award from the Before Columbus Foundation for *Spider Woman's Granddaughters* and the Native American Prize for Literature.

Accolades for Allen's work increased throughout her career, in which she amassed honors such as the Susan Koppelman Award from the Popular Cultural Association and American Culture Association (1991), the Vesta Award for Essay Writing (1991), the Southern California Women for Understanding Award for Literature (1991), an honorary doctorate in humanities from Mills College (1995), the Hubbell Prize for Lifetime Achievement in American Literary Studies (1999), and the Lifetime Achievement Award from the Native Writers' Circle of the Americas (2001). In 2004,

Allen's *Pocahontas: Medicine Woman, Spy, Entrepreneur, Diplomat* (2003) was nominated for a Pulitzer Prize, and in 2007, she received the Lannan Literary Fellowship, designed to honor writers whose impact on English-language literature promotes increased interest and readership in both prose and poetry.

BIOGRAPHY

Paula Gunn Allen was born Paula Marie Francis in 1939 in Cubero, New Mexico, and was raised by her mother and grandmother on the Cubero Land Grant, situated between the Laguna and Acoma Pueblo Reservations. The daughter of a Laguna-Sioux-Scottish mother and a Lebanese American father, Allen cultivated her love and appreciation of the myths and lore of her American Indian ancestors and would perpetuate her desire to be a lifelong student of native culture.

Allen began her higher education at Colorado Women's College, where the work of poet Robert Creeley would have a profound influence on her. She took time off from school to marry and have two children, but the marriage ended in divorce a few years later. She transferred to the University of Oregon, earning a B.A. in English in 1966 and an M.F.A. in creative writing in 1968. At the University of New Mexico, Allen wanted to pursue a doctorate in Native American literature, but the dean informed her that this was not possible as Native American literature was not a canonical genre. Instead, in 1975, Allen received a doctorate in American studies with a concentration on Native American literature.

Following the completion of her doctorate, two divorces, and the birth of three children, Allen began writing from a twentieth century lesbian-feminist perspective. She quickly established herself as a prolific writer and has since been acknowledged as the founder of American Indian literary studies. Seeking to rectify the canonical discrepancies regarding ethnic literature, Allen (after publishing five collections of poetry) turned her focus to the retelling of native myths and to lesbian-feminist literary criticism. In subsequent years, Allen kept working, writing many texts that would become staples in the classroom—providing future generations of students with the types of sources that were unavailable to her during her own education.

ANALYSIS

Paula Gunn Allen's first book of poetry, *The Blind Lion*, contains some of the author's most personal work. The poems in its three sections—"The Blind Lion," "The Amorclast," and "The Separation"—chronicle the dissolution of romantic love, while only subtly referencing her cultural background. The first section records a metamorphosis from the warm comfort of familiarity in "Definition" to colliding and opposing elements in "The Orange on Your Head Is on Fire," in which the man is the "fire/ bird" and the woman is the "cold wind." The lion of the title poem, an animal normally associated with dominance, pride, and courage, is made impotent by its blindness and is transformed into a weeping and pitiable creature. The lion thus becomes a metaphor for the relationship now reduced and defined by isolation. "Cool Life" further elucidates the couple's relationship complications, of which the narrator states: "between us/ we are ice . . ." and "outside of us/ dandelions bloom."

The second section of *The Blind Lion* denotes the irreparable breakage of traditional love and the institution of marriage. The language of the poems becomes increasingly dark and volatile, as the narrator in "The Amorclast" describes, "your fist expresses the rain-/ drops flying around us," culminating with the stark language and imagery of the lover "twisting the handle/ revealing the bone/ of your contempt." Other poems within this section similarly portray the escalating turbulence within the relationship—often represented by aspects of nature such as fog, frost, wind, and shadows. Here, Allen experiments with and reinvents the poetic form in order to fully portray the sporadic and often irrational ways in which people cope with failed relationships.

The third section, "The Separation," portrays the narrator's reclaiming and reinvention of herself, reflected in the increasingly prevalent spiritual and feminist tones of the poems. In "Shadows," the narrator struggles with her sense of identity as "The room comes to me a stranger,/ its familiar things turned/ unfamiliar, as though/ I, a visitor, had just walked in. . . ." Her former life having been forever altered, the narrator cannot recognize where she belongs in her newly realized solitude. "Liebestraume" (German for "dreams

Paula Gunn Allen (©Tama Rothschild)

of love") is perhaps the darkest piece in the collection, wherein "pestilence," "plague," and "rotting velvet" lie under the covers that "half-hid the empty revolver you cocked and used/ to blow open the bone at the back of my skull. . . ." The romantic title belies the poet's emotions as her dreams of love are displaced by dreams of death. However, the narrator ends the poem expressing expectations of hope and rebirth, from which she will arise transformed.

A CANNON BETWEEN MY KNEES

A Cannon Between My Knees, Allen's third collection, builds on the feelings left unresolved at the end of *The Blind Lion*. The fourteen new poems are more noticeably concerned with spirituality, myth, creation, and the roles of women therein. Allen does include two poems dedicated to her father, "Durango Suite" and "Lament of My Father, Lakota," while further exploring the persistence of memory along with the harsh reality of reservation life in "Wool Season: 1973."

Allen's poetry shows a new maturity in this collection. Her feminist voice becomes increasingly impressive, as in "The Beautiful Woman Who Sings," which depicts a hardworking woman of nature who embodies true beauty. In "Poem for Pat," one of Allen's first pieces representing homosexual love and desire, the narrator reminisces, "we found each other again, she said,/ and we were shivering at what we contemplated/ locked together on the sandstone mesas. . . ." In "Suicid/ing(ed) Indian Woman," the poet retells four stories of jilted, misunderstood, and misused women from various native tribes. From their sadness, she creates strength, and as the collection progresses, so too do the references to woman as creator, mother, grandmother, provider, and nurturer.

Accompanying these representations of female empowerment are references to male weaknesses such as addictions to alcohol and gambling, brought on by the emasculation of native men, just two of the results of white colonization of native lands. These references make the phrase "a cannon between my knees" in the final poem of the collection, "Thusness Before the War," especially poignant, as the symbol of military domination and destruction becomes a phallic symbol of feminine virility and authority.

SHADOW COUNTRY

The meaning behind the title of Allen's fifth poetry collection, *Shadow Country*, welcomes reader interpretation, as its pages contain a world that is somehow universal, yet uniquely hers. Neither dark nor light, the title could represent Allen's feelings about her mixed heritage; it could imply the marginalization of native populations or the diminishing of the country's glory; or it could even signify, as in "Que Cante Quetzal," that the country is engulfed in shadow due to its ongoing participation in brutal military conquests worldwide. Allen does not limit herself by any boundaries in her poetic endeavors, as she explores the themes of creation, consumerism, revolution, apocalypse, resurrection, and celebration.

"Los Angeles, 1980" indicts American vanity and the consumerism that results from people's attempts to achieve the public "ideal." This "death culture" dominates the natural world and pollutes the air, then seeks to use the landscape's true beauty to create organic beauty products, natural-fiber clothes, and herbal nutritional supplements. Despite these urges to improve

"naturally," signs reading "Weight and Smoking Control Center" and other such consumer fodder litter the sidewalks. A passerby notices her "average" reflection in the Center's smoky glass, and notes, ". . . death comes in pretty packages too,/ and all around me/ the dying air agreed."

The poems within *Shadow Country*, although certainly concerned with native spirituality, explore the issues of traditional and modern cultures, which are then juxtaposed with political issues. These comparative critiques produce powerful commentary in regard to the conflicting values of white and native societies. Relics and ruins of native cultures, military conquests, and forced removals are present in several poignant poems such as "Another Long Walk," "The Warrior," "Riding the Thunder," and "Off Reservation Blues," in which the dreaming narrator grieves over her imprisonment, which symbolizes the ongoing claustrophobia that resulted from the forced removal of native peoples to reservations, but which gives her poetry meaning: "Open words, openly said/ are not heard."

OTHER MAJOR WORKS

LONG FICTION: *The Woman Who Owned the Shadows*, 1983.

NONFICTION: *Studies in American Indian Literature: Critical Essays and Course Designs*, 1983; *The Sacred Hoop: Recovering the Feminine in American Indian Traditions*, 1986; *Grandmothers of the Light: A Medicine Woman's Sourcebook*, 1991; *As Long as the Rivers Flow: The Stories of Nine Native Americans*, 1996 (with Clark Smith); *Off the Reservation: Reflections on Boundary-Busting, Border-Crossing Loose Canons*, 1998; *Pocahontas: Medicine Woman, Spy, Entrepreneur, Diplomat*, 2003.

EDITED TEXTS: *From the Center—A Folio: Native American Art and Poetry*, 1981; *Spider Woman's Granddaughters: Traditional Tales and Contemporary Writing by Native American Women*, 1989; *Voice of the Turtle: American Indian Literature, 1900-1970*, 1994; *Song of the Turtle: American Indian Literature, 1974-1994*, 1996; *Hozho: Walking in Beauty*, 2001 (with Carolyn Dunn Anderson); *Outfoxing Coyote*, 2002 (with Anderson).

MISCELLANEOUS: *Columbus and Beyond: Views*

from Native Americans, 1992 (with others); *Gossips, Gorgons, and Crones: The Fates of the Earth*, 1993 (foreword by Allen; text by Jane Caputi).

BIBLIOGRAPHY

Allen, Paula Gunn. "A Funny Thing Happened on My Way to Press." *Frontiers: A Journal of Women Studies* 23 (2002): 3-6. This short, autobiographical account of Allen's reactions to the stereotypes of American Indians is a quick yet insightful glimpse into the author's personality, both as an American Indian woman and as a poet.

Forbes, Jack. "Colonialism and Native American Literature: Analysis." *Wicazo Sa Review* 3 (1987): 17-23. Forbes's primary objective in this article is to address questions relating to the term "Native American literature." He examines what constitutes native or ethnic literature, who is "allowed" to write it, and what the literature infers or implies within the social construct of a colonial interpretation.

Jahner, Elaine A. "The Style of the Times in Paula Gunn Allen's Poetry." In *Speak to Me Words: Essays on Contemporary American Indian Poetry*, edited by Dean Rader and Janice Gould. Tucson: University of Arizona Press, 2003. In this article, Jahner writes on Allen's use of formal structures in her poems.

Koehler, Lyle. "Native Women of the Americas: A Bibliography." *Frontiers: A Journal of Women Studies* 6 (1981): 73-101. A comprehensive bibliography of authors and works related to various themes in Native American literature and an invaluable go-to guide for those interested in the genre. The author provides subsections on specific topics such as religion, sexuality, and craftswomen.

Rowley, Kelley E. "Re-inscribing Mythopoetic Vision in Native American Studies." *American Indian Quarterly* 26 (2002): 491-500. Mythopoetic vision refers to the process of making myths and how audiences come to perceive them. Rowley uses Allen's four characteristics of a sacred visionary narrative, "the supernatural characters, the nonordinary events, the transcendent powers, and the pour quoi elements," to further expound on the mythopoetics of Native American texts.

Ruppert, Jim. "Paula Gunn Allen and Joy Harjo: Clos-ing the Distance Between Personal and Mythic Space." *American Indian Quarterly* 7, no. 1 (1983): 27-40. Ruppert discusses the poetry of Allen and Joy Harjo and the ways in which their works address the fusion of mundane and mystic/personal and universal spaces, in order to create harmony between earth, mind, and spirit.

Lydia E. Ferguson

JULIA ALVAREZ

Born: New York, New York; March 27, 1950

PRINCIPAL POETRY

Homecoming: Poems, 1984 (revised and expanded as *Homecoming: New and Collected Poems*, 1996)
The Other Side/El otro lado, 1995
Seven Trees, 1998
Cry Out: Poets Protest the War, 2003 (multiple authors)
The Woman I Kept to Myself, 2004

OTHER LITERARY FORMS

Julia Alvarez (AL-vah-rehz) has published a number of novels, her acclaimed *How the García Girls Lost Their Accents* (1991), *In the Time of the Butterflies* (1994), *¡Yo!* (1997), *In the Name of Salomé* (2000), *The Cafecito Story* (2001), and *Saving the World* (2006); a collection of essays, *Something to Declare* (1998); a nonfiction work, *Once Upon a Quinceañera: Coming of Age in the USA* (2007); and children's books, including *How Tía Lola Came to Stay* (2001) and *A Gift of Gracias* (2005). She has also edited a collection of poetry, *Old Age Ain't for Sissies* (1979).

ACHIEVEMENTS

Julia Alvarez's *How the García Girls Lost Their Accents* received the PEN Oakland/Josephine Miles Book Award (1991) and was selected as a Notable Book by both *The New York Times* (1991) and the American Library Association (1992). The critically acclaimed *In the Time of the Butterflies* was selected as a Notable Book by the American Library Association (1994) and was a finalist for the National Book Critics Circle Award in fiction (1994). *Before We Were Free* (2002) was selected as a Notable Book and Best Book for Young Adults by the American Library Association (2002) and the same year won the Américas Award for Children's and Young Adult Literature and the American Library Association's Pura Belpre Award. Alvarez's literary awards include the La Reina Creative Writing Award for poetry (1982), the Third Woman Press Award (1986), the General Electric Foundation Award for Younger Writers (1986), *American Poetry Review*'s Jessica Nobel-Maxwell Poetry Prize (1995), the Hispanic Heritage Award in Literature (2002), and the Latina Leader Award in Literature (2007). Alvarez has received honorary degrees from several institutions, including the University of Vermont, Burlington (2008), and fellowships from the Bread Loaf Writers' Conference (1986), the National Endowment for the Arts (1987-1988), and the Ingram Merril Foundation (1990).

BIOGRAPHY

Shortly after Julia Altagracia Maria Teresa Alvarez was born in New York City, her family returned home to the Dominican Republic to live among their large, extended family. In 1960, her father took the family back to New York because he was wanted for his involvement in a failed plot to overthrow dictator Rafael Trujillo. Thereafter, Julia Alvarez lived in the United States, making visits to her extended family in the Dominican Republic. She married and became the mother of two children. Along with her husband, she became involved in the political life of the Dominican Republic.

After two years at Connecticut College (1967-1969), Alvarez transferred to Middlebury College, from which she graduated summa cum laude with her bachelor's degree in 1971. She earned a master of fine arts degree from Syracuse University (1975) and attended the Bread Loaf School of English (1979-1980). Alvarez taught in poetry-in-the-schools programs in Kentucky, Delaware, and North Carolina (1977-1979). She has been an instructor of English at Phillips Andover Acad-

emy in Massachusetts (1979-1981), a visiting assistant professor of creative writing at the University of Vermont (1981-1983), the Jenny McKean Moore Visiting Writer at George Washington University (1984-1985), an assistant professor of English at the University of Illinois, Urbana (1985-1988), and an associate professor of English at Middlebury College (1988-1998). In 1998, she became a writer-in-residence at Middlebury College.

ANALYSIS

In her writing, Julia Alvarez has said that she attempts

> to move out into those other selves, other worlds.... By allowing myself to be those mixtures and not having to choose or repress myself or cut myself off from the other, I have become a citizen of the world.

She has stated that she disliked books as a child, except the tales of the Arabian nights, or "one thousand one nights," which she found to be full of both stories and power. She has reflected that she

> just knew words, stories, poems could keep me alive, as they had my first teacher, Scheherazade.... And the best part of the story is that we all have access to that power in the meaning-making, story-telling Scheherazades of the books we read and the books we write.

The power of Alvarez's poetry is in the stories that it tells, stories that transcend one place, one time, and one person's experience.

Alvarez started her career as a poet and still thinks of poetry as her first love. She also believes that being a poet first has had an impact on her fiction, because "writing poetry gives me a kind of intense particularity about words.... [Writing is] a way of being in the world, and the essence of it is paying attention." Attention to the minutiae of everyday life is one identifying characteristic of Alvarez's poetic technique and a vehicle for bringing life and power to the everyday stories she tells in her poems.

HOMECOMING: NEW AND COLLECTED POEMS

Referring to her career as a writer, Alvarez observes that she found herself "turning more and more to writing as the one place where I felt I belonged and could make sense of myself, my life, all that was happening to me." This is certainly true of the poems in *Homecoming: New and Collected Poems*, which capture the ordinary aspects of Alvarez's childhood and her identities as a young girl-woman, daughter, immigrant, and grown woman finding her artistic voice.

The book is organized into six sections: "Homecoming," "Housekeeping," "Heroines," "33," "Redwing Sonnets," and "Last Night at Tía's," followed by an afterword in which Alvarez comments on the changes she made for the revised edition. The 1996 work includes the poems from the 1984 edition of *Homecoming*, some of which were revised to reflect changes the passing years had made in her perspectives. Alvarez also added five sections that explore issues that had become important to her since the book's first publication.

Although *Homecoming*'s central images—the events of a "typical" household day such as cleaning, doing the laundry, cooking, dusting, bed making, and ironing—might be called commonplace or mundane, they are ideal vehicles for exploring powerful, thought-provoking issues. Alvarez accomplishes much more with such simple scenes than merely chronicling the daily chores of a mother and daughter. These small household events allow Alvarez to explore the tensions of family dynamics, the mother-daughter relationship, and the emotional and physical awakening of a young girl to womanhood.

For example, "Storm Windows" not only shows a mother hard at work securing their home but also demonstrates a young girl's need to separate from her mother's protective and domineering grasp:

> I wanted to mount that ladder,
> . . . Then give a kick, unbuckling
> her hands clasped about my ankles,
> and sail up, beyond her reach,
> her house, her yard, her mothering.

The mother-daughter relationship is complex, yet by setting it among the commonplace events of women's daily tasks, Alvarez creates an especially female canvas on which to paint this dynamic and the roles filled by the women in Alvarez's Dominican family. Despite the everyday nature of their "chores," Alvarez reveals

that these women are the artists of the everyday: They bake, select fabric, sew clothing. By definition, such women create things that are designed for use—that will be used up, works of art that will not last: pies, soups, dresses, clean clothes, and sparkling windows.

In "Woman's Work," Alvarez's mother challenges her: "Who says woman's work isn't high art?/ She challenged as she scrubbed the bathroom tiles./ Keep house as if the address were your heart." Ironically, although Alvarez wanted to be different from her mother and wanted to work outside her home, she observes that, as a writer, her work anchors her to her home, the very spot she struggled to escape. She "did not want to be her counterpart!/ I struck out . . . but became my mother's child:/ a woman working at home on her art,/ housekeeping paper as if it were her heart."

The book's remaining sections move away from the family home and sphere of influence. "Heroines" examines the importance of women's friendships ("Woman Friend"), the need for a woman to save herself rather than waiting for Prince Charming ("Against

Julia Alvarez

Cinderella"), and the value of the ordinary life ("Old Heroines").

When asked, "What kind of a woman/ are you?" the poet replies, "I wish I knew, I say, I wish/ I knew and could just put it into words." The sonnets of "33" chart her transition from youth to adult woman, introducing lovers and former lovers, identity crises, successes and failures, political concerns, suicidal times, fears of failure, writer's block, the conflicts associated with being an adult daughter, and the spiritual, emotional, and physical needs of an adult woman. Although they are not always happy or pleasant, these poems make it clear that life's important realities require deep feeling, deep commitment, and a fair amount of pain. "Tell me what is it women want the most?" a man asks her, and this section concludes by powerfully articulating Alvarez's values:

> Sometimes the words are so close I am
> more who I am when I'm down on paper
> than anywhere else . . .
> Those of you lost and yearning to be free,
> who hear these words, take heart from me.
> I once was in as many drafts as you.
> But briefly, essentially, here I am.
> Who touches this poem touches a woman.

The next section, "Redwing Sonnets," describes the emerging writer—stronger, more self-assured and powerful—and demonstrates what the poet has "made" from that small girl first seen making beds with her mother. She has been turned into the inspiration for poetry: "I'm revising/ a poem I've tried for years to make as strong/ as I'm able." This voice is confident, deeply philosophical, and content. It knows what it is meant to do: "affirming that the saying of the world/ is what we're meant to do with chirps or words. . . ."

"Last Night at Tía's," the book's final section, integrates the present with the past: "Remember," says Alvarez, "remember was now the theme/ of all our conversations, the thread holding/ together what was left of our connection." The conclusion of this poem is somewhat bleak: "We had become *the grown-ups* to our young,/ readying ourselves for the big deaths: our own,/ with the future shrieking in the garden,/ and the lighthouse beaming its useless light/ above the dark we

navigate. . . ." Alvarez looks forward into a world from which it is impossible to regain the safety of childhood: ". . . but it was too late./ We had already strayed from that old world/ of the past we had shared with each other."

The Other Side/El otro lado

These poems move from the simple, daily activities of family life, isolated from its Dominican heritage, to a more integrated consideration of how the child became the writer she is today. Like *Homecoming*, *The Other Side/El otro lado* relies heavily on autobiographical material; however, now Alvarez embraces her Dominican heritage, exploring the influence that her childhood and family heritage have had on her as a writer. Moreover, the voice speaking in this volume is more mature, more stable, and more integrated.

The book contains six sections: "Bilingual Sestina," "The Gladys Poems," "Making Up the Past," "The Joe Poems," "The Other Side/El otro lado," and "Estel." While still a central theme, this time the family provides the framework for Alvarez to explore the ways in which her bicultural experience has shaped her development as both a writer and a women. The sections form a closed circle, with the first, "Bilingual Sestina," looking on the ways English, her second language, has constricted her as a writer. Alvarez says that there are experiences, knowledge, and ways of seeing the world that defy translation: "Some things I have to say aren't getting said/ in this snowy, blond, blue-eyed, gum-chewing English . . . *nombres* from that first world I can't translate from Spanish" ("Bilingual Sestina").

The book's remaining sections attempt to integrate these two languages—and the disparate parts of her life that they symbolize: the time before she and her family immigrated from the Dominican Republic; the period during which Alvarez was an "alien" in the United States, learning to "assimilate"; and the experience of returning "home" to the Dominican Republic after having lived as an American for many years. The end result of this quest for self-knowledge, self-acceptance, and a belief in the validity of her poetic voice is the final section, "The Other Side/El otro lado," a sequence purposely given a bilingual title to represent the integration of the old with the new, the Dominican with the American experiences, and the emergence of someone who can no longer go "home" to the Dominican Republic as a Dominican, no more than she can return from there to the United States and forget that she comes from Dominican roots. The poet has stepped through these shaping experiences in both the Dominican Republic and the United States to become a person comfortable in her own skin, comfortable being bicultural, no longer wanting to run back to a time that is inaccessible to her because of her experiences as an outsider, as a minority in the United States. She accepts who she is: an amalgam of all her life.

"The Gladys Poems" depicts life before Alvarez's father became endangered by the political upheavals in the Dominican Republic. As a child, Alvarez lived a life of relative privilege among her extended family, a position of safety with the isolation that money and influence can provide. The poems in this section demonstrate these circumstances through contrasting pictures of the life of Gladys, Alvarez's nanny, and that of the Alvarez family.

In the section "Making Up the Past," "Exile" describes the family's flight to the United States, while "Sound Bites" offers glimpses of assimilation and struggle to assume a bilingual worldview: "There is nothing left to cry for,/ nothing but the story/ of our family's grand adventure/ from one language to another." In "Beginning Again," Alvarez works toward integrating the losses of the past that "can be, not just survived, but made into the matter/ of hope, made into song, not into a hatchet/ to cut off the offending parts, made into poems."

It is not until the section "The Other Side/El otro lado," however, that Alvarez completes her transformation into a new person embodying both her Dominican past and her American present: "I know/ I won't be coming back to live/ in my ex-homeland. A border has closed like a choice/ I can't take back." By reexperiencing her first home now, as an adult, Alvarez discovers that her true identity lies in "a life of choice, a life of words."

The book concludes with "Estel," an enigmatic poem addressed to a mute village child whom Alvarez helped to escape the prison of her disability by enrolling her in a school for the deaf. Like Estel, Alvarez has been "mute," stricken with writer's block, unable to express her dual experiences, "a blank intelligence about to be filled/ with your new life." However, through the school of her experiences she, too, has gained a voice, the proof of which is this book, *The Other Side/El otro lado*.

THE WOMAN I KEPT TO MYSELF

The Woman I Kept to Myself is divided into three sections. The first and last consist of seven poems each, and the midsection contains sixty-one poems. Each section features intensely personal poems written in three ten-line stanzas. The poems relate a wide arc of experiences and reveal Alvarez's life and philosophies. The poet gives the reader a glimpse into both her creative process and her personal life through this vivid collection of autobiographical poems.

The opening section, "Seven Trees," begins with an explanation of the metaphorical family tree, and the succeeding poems either describe a variety of trees that grew in her yard ("Saman" and "Maple, Oak, or Elm") or represent an aspect of her personal life, such as her father's grief over losing his homeland and former life ("Weeping Willow").

From the emphasis on nature in the first section, Alvarez moves to a more explicitly autobiographical description of her childhood and young adulthood in the larger middle section, "The Woman I Kept to Myself." She begins with "Intimations of Mortality from a Collection in Early Childhood" and her experiences as a young Latina in a foreign culture in New York City in the 1950's. She recalls conflicts with other children over her clothes, her accent, and her attitude. Poems such as "Spic," "All American Girl," and "Abbott Academy" detail her painful struggle to adapt to her new environment and to assert herself as a young independent woman. Throughout this difficult process, she is helped and hindered by her relationship with her mother and sisters. Eventually, she moves on to her adult life, and the resulting poems chronicle her highs and lows in dealing with men, jobs, and various personalities in her life such as her landlady. The subjects of her poems range from the description of mundane objects ("Hairband") to consideration of more philosophical concepts, as in "Canons," in which she tries to decide what to put in her limited space on a pack mule, and "Why Don't We Ever See Jesus Laughing?" in which she wonders about various aspects of biblical stories. She writes about her family, her husband, and her grandchildren, as well as famous people such as astronauts and Allen Ginsberg, as she continues to evaluate and examine her life's journey. She relates her physical moves from urban areas to country towns and contemplates the effects on her life. The section concludes with more philosophical poems concerning the art of poetry itself as well as poets she has studied and valued such as Emily Dickinson and Walt Whitman.

The final section of the book, "Keeping Watch," contains poems that reflect on memories of the night watchmen of her childhood ("El Sereno"), stargazing ("Looking Up"), and the redemptive powers of sleep ("What We Ask For"). The last poems in the collection examine the meaning of Alvarez's work in her life and bring the reader full circle to her family. The volume closes with a question concerning the dichotomy of her life in two worlds.

OTHER MAJOR WORKS

LONG FICTION: *How the García Girls Lost Their Accents*, 1991; *In the Time of the Butterflies*, 1994; *¡Yo!*, 1997 (sequel to *How the García Girls Lost Their Accents*); *In the Name of Salomé*, 2000; *The Cafecito Story*, 2001; *Saving the World*, 2006.

NONFICTION: *Something to Declare*, 1998; *Once Upon a Quinceañera: Coming of Age in the USA*, 2007.

CHILDREN'S LITERATURE: *The Secret Footprints*, 2000; *How Tía Lola Came to Stay*, 2001; *Before We Were Free*, 2002; *Finding Miracles*, 2004; *A Gift of Gracias*, 2005; *Return to Sender*, 2009.

EDITED TEXTS: *Old Age Ain't for Sissies*, 1979.

BIBLIOGRAPHY

Alvarez, Julia. "Julia Alvarez." http://www.juliaalvarez .com. The official Web site of Alvarez contains information about appearances as well as a biography and information on her works.

Erickson, Leslie Goss. *Re-visioning of the Heroic Journey in Postmodern Literature: Toni Morrison, Julia Alvarez, Arthur Miller, and "American Beauty."* Lewiston, N.Y.: Edwin Mellen Press, 2006. Contains considerable discussion of Alvarez's *In the Name of Salomé*, which provides perspective on Alvarez.

Garcia-Johnson, Ronie-Richele. "Julía Alvarez." In *Notable Hispanic American Women*, edited by Diane Telgen and Jim Kamp. Detroit: Gale Research, 1993. Provides a basic biography and discussion of Alvarez's works.

Henao, Eda B. *The Colonial Subject's Search for Nation, Culture, and Identity in the Works of Julia Alvarez, Rosario Ferré, and Ana Lydia Vega.* Lewiston, N.Y.: Edwin Mellen Press, 2003. An examination of the search for identity in the works of three Latina writers: Alvarez, Rosario Ferré, and Ana Lydia Vega.

Johnson, Kelli Lyon. *Julia Alvarez: Writing a New Place on the Map*. Albuquerque: University of New Mexico Press, 2005. Provides analysis and literary criticism of Alvarez's writing, with chapters such as "English as a Homeland: Language, Creativity, and Improvisation."

Mujčinović, Fatima. *Postmodern Cross-Culturalism and Politicization in U.S. Latina Literature: From Ana Castillo to Julia Alvarez*. New York: Peter Lang, 2004. Examines Latina literature and analyzes Alvarez's place in that genre.

Ortiz-Marquez, Maribel. "From Third World Politics to First World Practices: Contemporary Latina Writers in the United States." In *Interventions: Feminist Dialogues on Third World Women's Literature and Film*, edited by Ghosh Bishmupriya and Bose Brinda. New York: Garland, 1997. Places *In the Time of the Butterflies* in a political context.

Sirias, Silvio. *Julia Alvarez: A Critical Companion*. Westport, Conn.: Greenwood Press, 2001. This compact volume offers an excellent concise overview of the body of Alvarez's writing.

Melissa E. Barth
Updated by Dolores A. D'Angelo

A. R. AMMONS

Born: Near Whiteville, North Carolina; February 18, 1926

Died: Ithaca, New York; February 25, 2001

PRINCIPAL POETRY

Ommateum, with Doxology, 1955
Expressions of Sea Level, 1963
Corsons Inlet: A Book of Poems, 1965
Tape for the Turn of the Year, 1965
Northfield Poems, 1966
Selected Poems, 1968
Uplands, 1970
Briefings: Poems Small and Easy, 1971
Collected Poems, 1951-1971, 1972
Sphere: The Form of a Motion, 1974
Diversifications, 1975
The Selected Poems, 1951-1977, 1977
The Snow Poems, 1977
Highgate Road, 1978
Six-Piece Suite, 1979
Selected Longer Poems, 1980
A Coast of Trees, 1981
Worldly Hopes, 1982
Lake Effect Country, 1983
The Selected Poems: Expanded Edition, 1986
Sumerian Vistas, 1987
The Really Short Poems of A. R. Ammons, 1990
Garbage, 1993
The North Carolina Poems, 1994
Brink Road, 1996
Glare, 1997
Bosh and Flapdoodle, 2005
A. R. Ammons: Selected Poems, 2006 (David Lehman, editor)

OTHER LITERARY FORMS

Although A. R. Ammons (AM-uhns) is known primarily for his poetry, he also published reviews and essays. Central to an understanding of his work are "A Poem Is a Walk" and his short autobiographical reflection "I Couldn't Wait to Say the Word." Ammons's several published interviews, especially one by Cynthia Haythe, give additional insight into his poetics. *Set in Motion: Essays, Interviews, and Dialogues* (1996) collects his most important writings about poetry.

ACHIEVEMENTS

Throughout a distinguished and prolific career, A. R. Ammons observed and presented the particulars of the world while projecting his longing for a sense of unity. He immersed himself in the flow of things, celebrating the world and the self that sees and probes it.

Ammons's work lies within the Emersonian tradition: He wrote from life without being a slave to any set poetic form. However, more than any other poet since Ralph Waldo Emerson, he developed a transcendentalism rooted in science and in a poetic that includes the self in the work. His epigrams, his short to moderate-length nature lyrics, and his long verse-essays are popular reading among poets.

His many awards include the Bread Loaf Writers' Conference Scholarship (1961), a Guggenheim Fellowship (1966), an American Academy of Arts and Letters Traveling Fellowship (1967), a National Endowment for the Arts grant (1969-1970), the Levinson Prize (1970), a National Book Award (1973) for *Collected Poems, 1951-1971*, an honorary Litt.D. from Wake Forest University (1973), the Bollingen Prize for Poetry for *Sphere* (1975), an Academy Award in Literature from the American Academy and Institute of Arts and Letters (1977), a National Book Critics Circle Award (1981) for *A Coast of Trees*, a John D. and Catherine T. MacArthur Foundation Award (1981), and the North Carolina Award for Literature (1986). In 1990, he was inducted into the American Academy and Institute of Arts and Letters. Ammons won the Lannan Literary Award for Poetry (1992), a second National Book Award (1993) for *Garbage*, the Poetry Society of America's Frost Medal (1994), the Bobbitt National Prize for Poetry (1994), the Ruth Lilly Poetry Prize (1995), and the Wallace Stevens Award (1998). Ammons is recognized as one of the most significant and original voices in twentieth century poetry.

BIOGRAPHY

A. R. Ammons was born Archie Randolph Ammons near Whiteville, North Carolina, in a house bought by his grandfather and situated on the family farm. The main book in the house was the Bible. Ammons's early experiences on the farm, working the land, helped shape his imagination. The self in his poems appears most frequently in relation to the natural world he knew as a child.

He was his parents' fourth child. Three sisters were born before him and two brothers after; one sister lived for only two weeks, and both brothers died, one in infancy and the other at birth. Ammons remembered the deaths of his brothers, saying that they accounted in part for the undercurrent of loss and loneliness in his work.

Upon graduation from high school in 1943, Ammons took a job in the shipyard in Wilmington, North Carolina. In 1944, he joined the U.S. Navy, spending nineteen months in service, including time in the South Pacific, where he began writing poems. Returning home after the war, Ammons attended Wake Forest College (his tuition paid for by the G.I. Bill) and graduated with a B.S. in 1949. That year he married Phyllis Plumbo and took a job as principal of an elementary school in the remote coastal community of Hatteras, North Carolina. From 1950 to 1952, he studied English at the University of California, Berkeley. In 1952, he took a position with his father-in-law's New Jersey medical glassware firm, a job he held for twelve years. He soon began to send poems to literary magazines, and in 1953, *Hudson Review* accepted two of them. His first book of poetry, *Ommateum, with Doxology*, appeared in 1955. Eight years later, *Expressions of Sea Level* appeared. In 1964, he began teaching at Cornell University. Other books of poems followed, and in 1972, most of his poems were published as *Collected Poems, 1951-1971*. *Sphere*, his poem of more than two thousand lines, published in 1974, gained for him the Bollingen Prize in Poetry for 1974-1975. Whitmanesque in its tendency toward democratic feeling, *Sphere* presents Ammons's aesthetic of continual motion and a musical affirmation of interdependence in the energy of all life. Ammons continued to be highly productive in his later years. *The North Carolina Poems* appeared in 1994; *Brink Road* was published in 1996; and his final book during his lifetime, *Glare*, appeared in 1997.

Ammons served for many years as the Goldwin Smith Professor of Poetry at Cornell University. In 1998, the university honored him with a celebration of his monumental achievement. He died from cancer in February of 2001, leaving behind his wife, his son John, and two grandchildren. Throughout his career, Ammons made frequent trips to eastern North Carolina, a place that figures prominently in his poems.

ANALYSIS

In one of A. R. Ammons's early poems, "So I Said I Am Ezra," from *Ommateum, with Doxology*, the speaker is whipped over the landscape, driven, moved by the natural elements. He is at once ordered and disordered, close and far, balanced and unbalanced, and he exclaims, "So I Ezra went out into the night/ like a drift of sand." The line is representative of Ammons's entire body of work, for it announces a search through language in an attempt to mean and to be clear, and failing to succeed completely in such clarity, the line ends by affirming a presence of radiance.

EXPRESSIONS OF SEA LEVEL

Ammons's poems have a tendency, like most contemporary poems, to take their own process, their own making, as a theme. Wanting to express something changeless and eternal, Ammons is constrained by his own intricate mortality. So in the title poem of *Expressions of Sea Level*, he presents the ocean as permanent and impermanent, as form and formlessness. He is interested in what humanity can and cannot know, giving full sway and expression to the ocean's activity: "See the dry casting of the beach worm/ dissolve at the delicate rising touch." The range and flow in Ammons's poetry, his search for balance, moved him to create his philosophical music, using a vocabulary drawn largely from everyday speech. He celebrates the need in every human being to discover a common experience in the least particular thing.

POEMS OF NORTH CAROLINA

Ammons attempts always to render visual details accurately. Some of the most moving poems in this regard are the poems inspired by his background in Columbus County, North Carolina. "Nelly Meyers" praises and celebrates a woman who lived on the farm where Ammons grew up; "Silver" records Ammons's love for and rapport with a mule he used for work. "Hardweed Path Going" tells of his life as a boy, doing chores on the farm, his playtime with a pet bird (a joreet) and a hog named Sparkle. These poems re-create Ammons's past, particularly his boyhood, which he renders in astonishingly realistic details.

CORSONS INLET

Ammons infuses the natural world with his own attuned sensibilities, acknowledging in the title poem of *Corsons Inlet* that "Overall is beyond me." The form of the poem is a walk over the dunes. What lives beyond his perception reassures, although he knows "that there is no finality of vision." Bafflement is a primary feeling in the poem, which may be studied for what it says about the relationship between logic and reason, imposed order and discovered order, art and life, reality and illusion, and being and becoming. "Corsons Inlet" concludes the walk/quest on the note that "tomorrow a new walk is a new walk." Ammons's desire to say something clearly, therefore, is not so much a search for the word as it is an attempt to find original ways to make and shape poetry.

TAPE FOR THE TURN OF THE YEAR

With *Tape for the Turn of the Year*, Ammons writes a long, narrow poem on adding-machine paper. The poet improvises and spontaneously records his thoughts and moods in what resembles a poetic diary. In one place, he praises how writing gets done, suggesting that doing it is almost its own practical reward, as the speaker acknowledges in another poem, "Identity," "it is wonderful how things work."

MAJOR THEMES

By the mid-1960's, Ammons's major themes had emerged, his sensibility oscillating between extremes: formlessness-form, center-periphery, high-low, motion-stasis, order-disorder, and one-many. One of his most constant themes has been the self in the work and in the world. He is concerned not only with the form of natural fact but also with form in the abstract sense, that is, with physical laws that govern the way individual entities act and behave. Ammons reaffirms the resonance of his subject, as in "The Eternal City," in which destruction must "accept into itself piece by piece all the old/ perfect human visions, all the old perfect loves."

Motion within diversity is perhaps Ammons's major theme. In "Saliences," from *Northfield Poems*, he discovers continuity in change. In "Snow Log," from *Uplands*, recognizing that nature's intentions cannot be known, he responds simply as an individual to what he sees in the winter scene: "I take it on myself:/ especially the fallen tree/ the snow picks/ out in the woods to show." In "The City Limits," from *Briefings*, a poem whose urban subject removes the speaker from nature, Ammons celebrates the "gold-skeined wings of flies swarming the dumped/ guts of a natural slaughter or the coil of shit."

COLLECTED POEMS, 1951-1971

Receiving the National Book Award in Poetry in 1973, *Collected Poems, 1951-1971* comprises most of Ammons's first six volumes, except for *Tape for the Turn of the Year* and three long verse-essays—"Extremes and Moderations," "Hibernaculum," and "Essay on Poetics." In "Extremes and Moderations" and "Hibernaculum," Ammons is a seer, lamenting humankind's abuse of Earth and appreciating the immediacy of a world that takes care of itself. "Essay on Poetics" considers the structural advantages and disadvantages of poetry. One reads this essay to appreciate more fully Ammons's views on writing.

SPHERE

In perhaps his major work, the book-length poem *Sphere*, Ammons explores motion and shape in a set form: sentences with no full stops, 155 sections of four tercets each. He relies on colons, perhaps suggesting a democratization and a flow. Shifting freely, sometimes abruptly, within a given stanza, phrase, or word, Ammons says, "I do not smooth into groups." Thus the book explores the nature of its own poetics, the poet searching everywhere for a language of clarity. In one place, he says that he is "sick of good poems." Wanting the smooth and raw together, Ammons reminds the reader that his prejudice against neat, traditional structures in poetry relates to the natural world where "the shapes nearest shapelessness awe us most, suggest the god." He regards a log, "rigid with shape," as "trivial." Ammons, therefore, makes his case for the poem of the open form as opposed to strong, traditional verses.

Ammons demythologizes poetics and language,

while testifying to an Emersonian faith in the universe as flowing freely and spontaneously. At the same time, there is a counter feeling always working. He refers often to clarity and wants his poems to arrive and move forward "by a controlling motion, design, symmetry."

While he is writing the poem, commenting on it, writing himself into it, he shows his instinct for playfulness, for spoofing. This aspect of his work—the clowning humor—adds an inherent drama to his work, as critic Jerald Bullis has written:

> The tone of the poem or, I should say, of the voices of its "parts," ranges and range from that of the high and hard lyric, the crystalline and *as if* final saying, through a talky and often latinate professorial stance, to permutations of low tone: "bad" puns, catalogues that seem to have been lifted from a catalogue, and, in the example below, the high-pressure pitch-man tone of How-To scams: "Now, first of all, the way to write poems is just to start: it's like learning to walk or swim or ride the bicycle, you just go after it."

The poem goes on, praising the ability of humanity to write and to appreciate being alive.

Reverence for creation runs throughout *Sphere*, investing the work with a vision beyond and through the details of the poet's aesthetic. This religious strain has its source in Ammons's absolute reverence for the natural world. A religious vocabulary, then, is no surprise in his work and connects with his childhood, when church services and hymn-sings were dominant parts of his life. As in *Sphere*, he questions what is "true service," saying "it must be a service that is celebration, for we would celebrate even if we do not know what or how, and for He is bountiful if/ slow to protect and recalcitrant to keep." Ammons goes on to say, "What we can celebrate is the condition we are in, or we can renounce the condition/ we are in and celebrate a condition we might be in or ought/ to be in." Ammons fuses and plays on the relationship between creation and imagination, hoping and trying to discover "joy's surviving radiance." In the presence of this radiance—the hues and bends of Ammons's music—exist the crux of his aesthetic, his art and his being: the solitary man never surrendering as he is being imposed on and whipped about, as he writes in one of his earliest po-

ems, "So I Said I am Ezra/ and the wind whipped my throat/ gaming for the sounds of my voice." However, the self is not dwarfed by the world. Ammons understands his moral and aesthetic convictions and will not cease to assert them. Such desire allows the visionary in Ammons constantly to discover new ways to see and understand his life. In this regard, key words crop up often: "salience," "recalcitrant," "suasion," "periphery," "possibility," tentative words that tend to illuminate or seek the proper blend in experience. So *Sphere* ends as it began, clear and free of all encumbrances except the spoken voice: "we're ourselves: we're sailing." The ending is right for the "form of a motion," the sense of wonder and uncertainty going on beyond the finality of the poem. Past, present, and future are one, and the poem and its end recall Walt Whitman's absorption into the dirt in "Song of Myself."

THE SNOW POEMS

In *The Snow Poems*, Ammons continues his experimental attempt to arrange a poetic journal, recounting in lyrical splendor the concerns of daily life, including details about weather, sex, and the poet's attempt to write and to experience a dialogue between the specific and the general. Ammons's work since the mid-1970's marks a return to the more visionary tendencies contained in his earlier terse, fierce lyrics of short or moderate length. "Progress Report" is an epigram from *Worldly Hopes*: "Now I'm/ into things// so small/ when I// say boo/ I disappear." The words flow in natural motion.

LAKE EFFECT COUNTRY

Lake Effect Country continues Ammons's love of form and motion. The whole book represents one body, a place of water, a bed of lively recreation. In "Meeting Place," for example, "The water nearing the ledge leans down with/ grooved speed at the spill then,/ quickly groundless in air." His vision comes from the coming together of the natural elements in the poem, rising and falling, moving and forming the disembodied voices that are the real characters in his poems: "When I call out to them/ as to the flowing bones in my naked self, is my/ address attribution's burden and abuse." "Meeting Place" goes out "to summon/ the deep-lying fathers from myself,/ the spirits, feelings howling, appearing there."

A COAST OF TREES

A major contemporary poem is "Easter Morning," from *A Coast of Trees*. Based on the death in infancy of the poet's younger brother, the poem is filled with reverence for the natural world, Ammons's memory ever enlarging with religious and natural resonances. "I have a life that did not become,/ that turned aside and stopped,/ astonished." The poem carries the contradictory mysteries of the human condition—death, hope, and memory—working together in a concrete and specific aesthetic. Presented in the form of a walk, "Easter Morning" reveals the speaker caught in the motion, as two birds "from the South" fly around, circle, change their ways, and go on. The poem affirms, with the speaker in another poem ("Working with Tools"), "I understand/ and won't give assertion up." Like Ezra going out "into the night/ like a drift of sand," the poet celebrates "a dance sacred as the sap in/ the trees . . . fresh as this particular/ flood of burn breaking across us now/ from the sun." Though the dance is completed in a moment, it can never be destroyed, because it has been re-created as the imagination's grand dance.

SUMERIAN VISTAS

Another major contemporary poem is "The Ridge Farm" from *Sumerian Vistas*. In fifty-one parts, the poem renders the farm itself on a ridge, on the edge of everything and nothing. Ammons's speaker joyfully resigns himself to the "highways" and the dammed-up brooks. The implication is that poetry—like nature—breaks through and flows, exploring the motion and shape of the farm's form. The farm itself is a concrete place wherein Ammons explores the nature of poetics and other realities.

THE REALLY SHORT POEMS OF A. R. AMMONS

In *The Really Short Poems of A. R. Ammons*, the poet continues his necessity to really see the natural world. That seeing becomes the poem; its motion, the story moving through the images. The form and subject move in a terse, fierce way as the poem discovers itself. In "Winter Scene," for example, the natural world changes radiantly when the jay takes over the leafless cherry tree. The landscape transformed, the poet notes what he sees: "then every branch/ quivers and/ breaks out in blue leaves." Motion formerly void of color brightens with vision and sway.

GARBAGE

Many consider *Garbage* to be a capstone of Ammons's maturity. Inspired by a massive landfill along Florida's portion of Interstate 95, this book-length poem continues Ammons's contemplation of and reverence for nature, this time positing the theme of regeneration following decay. It is a theme he applies to the human condition as well as to the sorry condition humanity has brought to nature. According to David Lehman, in his profile of Ammons published in the Summer, 1998, issue of *American Poet*, Ammons was attracted to the garbage mound for several reasons, including its geometry. Writes Lehman,

> The mound struck him as a hierarchical image, like a pyramid or the triangulation of a piece of pie. The pointed top corresponded to unity, the base to diversity. This paradigm of unity and diversity—and the related philosophical question of "the one and the many"—has been a constant feature of Ammons's work from the start.

GLARE

Ammon's penchant for stretching out his thoughts and words is nowhere as evident as in his 1997 volume, *Glare*. Comprising two sections, "Strip" and "Scat Scan," and written in his familiar couplet style, it is a work that is self-deprecating and spontaneous. Ammons speaks of "finding the form of the process," and critics have noted that his apparent ambition in *Glare* was "to make the finished form of the poem indistinguishable from the process of composition." In doing so, it reveals an immediacy of experience and thought, a kind of poetry in real time. In "Strip," he writes, "I have plenty and/ give plenty away, why because here/ at nearly 70 stuff has bunched up/ with who knows how much space to/ spread out into." The themes of "Scat" are harder to discern. Overall, he uses twisted proverbs and recalls Robert Frost's poetry to sum up his life.

OTHER MAJOR WORK

NONFICTION: *Set in Motion: Essays, Interviews, and Dialogues*, 1996.

BIBLIOGRAPHY

Bloom, Harold, ed. *A. R. Ammons*. New York: Chelsea House, 1986. This volume contains eighteen essays on Ammons's work, plus an introductory essay by Bloom. Among the contributors are contemporary poets John Ashbery, Richard Howard, and John Hollander. Perhaps the central theme of all the essays is that Ammons, like Walt Whitman, is a solitary self in the world.

Burak, David, and Rogert Gilbert, eds. *Considering the Radiance: Essays on the Poetry of A. R. Ammons*. New York: W. W. Norton, 2005. A collection of essays on Ammons's poetry, some of which were written by fellow poets.

Elder, John. *Imagining the Earth: Poetry and the Vision of Nature*. Urbana: University of Illinois Press, 1985. Elder writes about poets who remember and re-create Earth. His chapter on Ammons is called "Poetry and the Mind's Terrain." Elder's prose is clear and uncluttered; he presents Ammons from the fresh perspective of contemporary poets. Includes chapter notes and an index.

Hans, James S. *The Value(s) of Literature*. Albany: State University of New York Press, 1990. This book addresses the ethical aspects of literature by discussing three major American poets: Walt Whitman, Wallace Stevens, and A. R. Ammons. The chapter on Ammons is called "Ammons and the One: Many Mechanisms." In a concluding chapter, "The Aesthetic of Worldly Hopes," Hans speculates that one of the reasons poetry is not read widely in the United States is that it is "perceived to have nothing of ethical value inherent in it." What Hans calls "patterns of choice" exist in poems such as "Corsons Inlet" and "Essay on Poetics."

Holder, Alan. *A. R. Ammons*. Boston: Twayne, 1978. This introductory book-length study presents Ammons's life and works through *Sphere*. The text is supplemented by a chronology, notes, a select bibliography (with annotated secondary sources), and an index.

Kirschten, Robert. *Approaching Prayer: Ritual and the Shape of Myth in A. R. Ammons and James Dickey*. Baton Rouge: Louisiana State University Press, 1998. A mythopoetic study of each author that focuses on ceremonial strategies, this analysis examines the nature of Ammons's interest in ancient Sumerian as well as other traditions.

Schneider, Steven P., ed. *Complexities of Motion: New Essays on A. R. Ammons's Long Poems*. Madison, N.J.: Fairleigh Dickinson University Press, 1999. Essays by Helen Vendler, Marjorie Perloff, and other major critics examine the genre of the long poem as individualized by Ammons. Rationale, shape, structure, and strategy are explored, along with recurrent themes.

Sciagaj, Leonard M. *Sustainable Poetry: Four American Ecopoets*. Lexington: University Press of Kentucky, 1999. Along with Ammons, discusses and compares Wendell Berry, Gary Snyder, and W. S. Merwin and their treatment of nature and environmental concerns in their works. Bibliographical references, index.

Spiegelman, Willard. *The Didactic Muse*. Princeton, N.J.: Princeton University Press, 1989. Spiegelman's chapter on Ammons is called "Myths of Concretion, Myths of Abstraction: The Case of A. R. Ammons." Spiegelman ranges over Ammons's work, particularly the longer poems through *Sumerian Vistas*. Spiegelman's concern is the relation between poetry and philosophy. He contends that Ammons's dominant conceit is motion: his attempt to find that place where the conscious and unconscious move, yet stay. The book is important to any student who wishes to see Ammons's work within the larger context of contemporary poetry.

Vendler, Helen, ed. *Voices and Visions: The Poet in America*. New York: Random House, 1987. A companion to *Voices and Visions*, a Public Broadcasting Service television series. Calvin Bedient's essay on Walt Whitman discusses Ammons's *Sphere* within Whitman's energetic thrust out—toward a desire to create a motion within the American attraction for space, for going on, for expanding one's self in a larger world. The book contains pictures of poets, illustrations, notes on chapters, suggestions for further reading, notes on contributors, a list of illustrations, and an index.

Shelby Stephenson; Philip K. Jason
Updated by Sarah Hilbert

MAGGIE ANDERSON

Born: New York, New York; September 23, 1948

PRINCIPAL POETRY

The Great Horned Owl, 1979
Years That Answer, 1980
Cold Comfort, 1986
A Space Filled with Moving, 1992
Windfall, 2000

OTHER LITERARY FORMS

Maggie Anderson has sought to bring attention to the poetry of the Appalachian region that shapes her verse. To that end, she has published a wide range of book reviews and has appeared at countless libraries, schools, and literary conferences. In addition, she edited *Hill Daughter: New and Selected Poems* (1991), by Louise McNeill, designed to introduce longtime (and nearly forgotten) West Virginia poet McNeill to a new audience. A faculty member at Ohio's Kent State University, Anderson coedited *A Gathering of Poets* (1992), which contained poems read at the 1990 ceremonies commemorating the twentieth anniversary of the killing of four young people during a campus rally protesting American involvement in the Vietnam War. Anderson also coedited companion anthologies of works about school, focused primarily on the difficult adolescent years: *Learning by Heart: Contemporary American Poetry About School* (1999) and *After the Bell: Contemporary American Prose About School* (2007).

ACHIEVEMENTS

Maggie Anderson uses the materials of her West Virginia experiences and shapes them into probing, intensely personal lyrical revelations about her perceptions as a mother, a teacher, and, ultimately, a woman. A regional poet whose work has yet to find a national audience, Anderson is vigorously involved with the cultural environment of the Appalachia area. Across more than two decades, she has been awarded numerous fellowships from state committees in West Virginia, Ohio, and Pennsylvania. She has accepted ap-

pointments as writer-in-residence at several universities, most notably the University of Pittsburgh and the University of Oregon. In 2003, Anderson received the prestigious Ohioana Helen and Laura Krout Memorial Poetry Award, given annually to an Ohio poet whose work encourages a wide interest in poetry by attracting readers both in and out of academia, a fitting award for a poet who has championed poetry, in language unadorned with elaborate ornamentation, as the voice of the working class. In 2008, she won the Glenna Luschei *Prairie Schooner* Award for the poem "Black Overcoat."

BIOGRAPHY

It often surprises first-time readers of Margaret Anderson's poetry, with its vivid re-creation of rural Appalachia, that the poet was born and raised in New York City. Her parents were both educators; her father taught English and her mother, political science. To develop their child's artistic appetites, the couple took Anderson to museums and the theater, and lavished her with books. Anderson's mother died when the girl was only eight, but the woman—a dedicated wife and mother who nevertheless managed significant professional success—would give the poet a model for the indomitable woman whose heroic presence would be at the center of much of her poetry. Young Anderson loved language; when she was ten, during an otherwise unremarkable creative writing exercise—she was to describe a tree—Maggie was most impressed by the word "bark" and developed a sophisticated conceit between a tree and a dog.

When Anderson was thirteen, her father moved the family to rural West Virginia (initially Buckhannon in central West Virginia, later Keyser near the Maryland border). Anderson's father's family had lived there for more than a century, and the girl had regularly summered there. Immediately, her creative appetite responded to the sweeping Appalachian landscape. She immersed herself not only in the rugged beauty of Appalachia's natural expanses but also in its culture and its history. After two years (1966-1968) at West Virginia Wesleyan University, a small Methodist university near Buckhannon, Anderson transferred to West Virginia University at Morgantown, from which she received a B.A. in 1970 and an M.A. in 1973. However, Anderson had long been engaged by the people of rural West Virginia—she had listened to the stories her father's family would tell of the hardscrabble life in the mining fields. From 1973 to 1975, Anderson taught in the adult creative writing program at the West Virginia Rehabilitation Center and then worked for two years as a counselor for the blind at the same facility, and she witnessed the impact of the nation's ongoing energy crisis on the livelihood of local residents. Wanting to help, she returned to Morgantown and in 1977 completed a second master's degree in social work. She continued to write, mostly poetry, and served as the poet-in-residence for the public school system of Marshall County from 1977 to 1989.

When Anderson accepted a teaching appointment in the English department at Kent State University in 1989, she had already published three books of poems. As the director and editor of the Kent State's Wick Poetry Center, beginning in 1992, she greatly expanded the scope of the program to publishing chapbooks of promising young poets, presenting poetry programs at high schools and colleges, and expanding scholarship opportunities for writing majors at Kent State. She has continued her work in the classroom and the center and has found success publishing her poetry in a wide variety of university literature journals and through small presses.

ANALYSIS

To read Maggie Anderson's poetry is to appreciate her sense of the poet as illuminator of small things and to understand the unforced grace of moments in extraordinarily ordinary lives. Anderson's poetry—informed by her love of the natural wonder of rural West Virginia and the determined strength of its people—celebrates how the poet's alert and open eye can trigger the epiphany that ultimately becomes the sculpted language of a poem. The language in her poems is carefully worked and elegantly understated, to the point where it seems conversational, an effect that belies the subtle manipulations of phrasing that create Anderson's inviting sound (she has been deeply influenced by music).

COLD COMFORT

With *Cold Comfort*, Anderson's third volume of poetry, she defined herself as a writer confident in both her vision and her craft. Her poetry gives voice to those quiet moments when the natural world or the everyday routine suddenly, unexpectedly, speaks to the heart. These are poems about family dinners, a grandmother doing laundry, a walk in a cemetery, and the cobalt sky that frames the forbidding West Virginia hills. It is the poet, as shaper of lines, who rescues such mundane moments from obscurity. In "The Thing You Must Remember," for example, Anderson creates a sonnet on a child in a school art class creating a clay dog. When the dog does not survive the process of its own creation and is found in shards in the kiln, Anderson, with grace and compassion, sees in the experience a cautionary lesson about the fragility of beauty and the profound frustration of artists who can never quite realize their visions. She upholds, however, the worthiness of the effort. The last image is of the art teacher, coaxing and encouraging, who understands that with art, the effort justifies and sustains.

In the poignant "Heart Fire," Anderson struggles to understand the suicide of a friend's son. Here, memory accommodates such emotional devastation by fashioning a kind of refuge-space where recollection keeps the dead alive and not alone. Drawing on the richly suggestive image of the poet driving across a Pittsburgh bridge and seeing the city lights flicker on, defiant against the descent of the autumn night, Anderson uses the juxtaposition of dark and light, cold and warmth, to offer the fragile comfort of memory in the face of such catastrophic moments as a son's suicide. That elegiac mood dominates the centerpiece effort of *Cold Comfort*, "In Singing Weather." Through a tight cycle of seven poems, Anderson moves with trepidation from late summer to the chilling grip of rural winter. The poems capture the rich colors and the full sensual environment of nature's gradual surrender to winter. Because of Anderson's ear for conversational rhythms, the poems reward recitation, the quiet play of languorous long vowels creating a kind of stay against nature's rush into the dead of winter. The closing image suggests how the poem resists the inevitability of death—as winter commences in earnest, the young poet recollects the dead, hears their lively voices in her imagination, and therein fashions a refuge-space, a bold defiance of death itself.

A SPACE FILLED WITH MOVING

Taking its title from an observation by Gertrude Stein in "The Gradual Making of *The Making of Americans*" (1934) about how vital it is to conceive of space and time as filled with significant movement, Anderson's fourth volume of poetry, *A Space Filled with Moving*, is widely considered her most accomplished. It is divided into three sections. The first, "Where I Live," is a loosely tied collection of meditations on rural life. In each work, the poet taps into a subtle, troubling dimension of loss and collapsing hope, enhanced, as she points out in some of the collection's finest short lyrics, by the wider economic collapse of the Rust Belt itself. In "Ontological," Anderson's most widely anthologized poem, the poet invites the reader not familiar with the country fiddle and deceived by its reputation for barn dances and frenetic rhythms to actually listen to a fiddle player and to be drawn into the lonesomeness and plaintive desolation at the core of bluegrass music.

The second section centers on "Long Story," Anderson's best single work. The poem begins by reminding the reader that people in rural areas, often struggling hard just to get by, have little patience with ornamental language, and therefore, their storytelling favors deadpan delivery uncomplicated by emotional excess. Appropriately, then, the poem begins innocuously enough—the poet, on a walk through town, watches as her docile basset hound suffers the indignities of local children putting scarves and ski caps on its head. As the poet continues her walk, in a devastating quick cut, she tells the harrowing story of how, years ago, after a catastrophic underground explosion, local miners trying to contain a spreading fire had to seal up a mine even though forty men were still alive inside it. By relying on Anderson's crafted deadpan delivery, the poem captures the reality of life in mining country, how every day is vulnerable to the shattering suddenness of death.

In the collection's third section, "A New Life," Anderson offers consolation in poems that celebrate her delight in the everyday—homemade soup, azaleas, wild berries, and pinecones. In the section's most memorable verse, "The Invention of Pittsburgh," the poet's determined effort to eat a more healthful diet by ordering squid in restaurants across the country leads her, during one epiphanic moment while contemplating a plateful of squid in faraway Oregon, to conjure up Pittsburgh with cutting clarity and unaffected homesickness, not as a city on the edge of financial ruin but rather as a vibrant city of street kids on corners with blaring radios on the city's busiest streets under the bright leaves of blossoming sycamores. In the volume's closing poem, a sonnet entitled "The Only Angel," the poet defiantly rejects surrender to pessimism. The angel of death itself speaks and challenges even those most leveled by life's brutalities to resist hungering for the release of death. That heroic defiance is a fitting summary of Anderson's own poetic vision.

OTHER MAJOR WORKS

EDITED TEXTS: *Hill Daughter: New and Selected Poems*, 1991 (text by Louise McNeill); *A Gathering of Poets*, 1992 (with Alex Gildzen and Raymond A. Craig); *Learning by Heart: Contemporary American Poetry About School*, 1999 (with David Hassler); *Working Hard for the Money: America's Working Poor in Stories, Poems, and Photos*, 2002 (with others); *After the Bell: Contemporary American Prose About School*, 2007 (with Hassler); *The Next of Us Is About to Be Born*, 2009.

BIBLIOGRAPHY

Ballard, Sandra L., and Patricia L. Hudson, eds. *Listen Here: Women Writing in Appalachia*. Lexington: University Press of Kentucky, 2004. Anthology that includes four poems by Anderson. Helpful introduction to the major women in a genre dominated by men; the wide-ranging selection gives Anderson's verse a helpful context.

Bryant, Jacqueline, ed. *Gwendolyn Brooks and Working Writers*. Chicago: Third World Press, 2007. Contains an essay by Anderson explaining why she views Brooks as her mentor.

High, Ellesa Clay. "Maggie Anderson: Two Languages." In *Her Words: Diverse Voices in Contemporary Appalachian Women's Poetry*, edited by Felicia Mitchell. Knoxville: University of Tennessee Press, 2002. The most substantive critical look at Anderson. Uses Anderson's urban and rural background to analyze the voice in her poem as both a part of and apart from the West Virginia environment.

Iron Mountain Review (Spring, 2005). This issue of the review, published annually by the English Department of Emory and Henry College in Emory, Virginia, is dedicated to Anderson. Each issue of the review features an Appalachian writer.

Williams, John Alexander. *Appalachia: A History*. Chapel Hill: University of North Carolina Press, 2001. Comprehensive history of the culture of the region that defines Anderson's poetry. Includes an extensive review of the literature of the region.

Joseph Dewey

MAYA ANGELOU
Marguerite Annie Johnson

Born: St. Louis, Missouri; April 4, 1928

PRINCIPAL POETRY

Just Give Me a Cool Drink of Water 'fore I Diiie, 1971

Oh Pray My Wings Are Gonna Fit Me Well, 1975

And Still I Rise, 1978

Shaker, Why Don't You Sing?, 1983

Poems: Maya Angelou, 1986

Now Sheba Sings the Song, 1987 (illustrated by Tom Feelings)

I Shall Not Be Moved, 1990

Life Doesn't Frighten Me, 1993 (juvenile; illustrated by Jean-Michel Basquiat)

On the Pulse of Morning, 1993

The Complete Collected Poems of Maya Angelou, 1994

Phenomenal Woman: Four Poems Celebrating Women, 1994

A Brave and Startling Truth, 1995

Amazing Peace: A Christmas Poem, 2005

Mother: A Cradle to Hold Me, 2006

OTHER LITERARY FORMS

In addition to being a poet, Maya Angelou (AN-juh-lew) is an essayist, playwright, screenwriter, and the author of children's books and other pieces of short fic-

tion. Along with two volumes of her autobiography, her collection of essays *Even the Stars Look Lonesome* (1997) was on *The New York Times* best-seller list for ten consecutive weeks. Her two-act drama *The Least of These* was produced in Los Angeles in 1966. With her screenplay *Georgia, Georgia* she became, in 1972, the first African American woman to have an original screenplay produced. In 1974 she adapted Sophocles' *Aias* (early 440's B.C.E.; *Ajax*, 1729) for the modern stage. Her children's book *My Painted House, My Friendly Chicken, and Me* was published in 1994. Her works have been translated into at least ten languages.

ACHIEVEMENTS

Maya Angelou's work has garnered many prestigious awards. For her writing of the revue *Cabaret for Freedom*, which she and Godfrey Cambridge produced, directed, and performed in 1960 for the purpose of raising money for Martin Luther King, Jr.'s Southern Christian Leadership Conference (SCLC), she was named northern coordinator for the SCLC in 1959. She later worked with civil rights leader Malcolm X. Other honors include a nomination for a National Book Award (1970) for *I Know Why the Caged Bird Sings* (1969), a Pulitzer Prize nomination (1972) for *Just Give Me a Cool Drink of Water 'fore I Diiie*, Antoinette Perry ("Tony") Award nominations (1973 and 1977), a Golden Eagle Award for documentary (1977), a Matrix Award from Women in Communications (1983), the North Carolina Award in Literature (1987), the Langston Hughes Award (1991), the Horatio Alger Award (1992), the Spingarn Medal (1993), a Grammy Award for Best Spoken Word or Non-Traditional Album (1994), the National Medal of Arts (2000), and the prestigious Order of Kilimanjaro Award from the National Association for the Advancement of Colored People (2001). She was named Woman of the Year in Communications and one of the one hundred most influential women by *Ladies' Home Journal* (1976), Distinguished Woman of North Carolina (1992), and Woman of the Year by *Essence* magazine (1992). She also received a Yale University fellowship (1970) and a Rockefeller Foundation scholarship in Italy (1975).

A high school graduate, Angelou has received hon-

Maya Angelou (Getty Images)

orary degrees from Smith College (1975), Mills College (1975), Lawrence University (1976), and Wake Forest University (1977). She was appointed Reynolds Professor of American Studies at Wake Forest University in Winston-Salem, North Carolina, in 1981. She read the poem she had composed in honor of the inauguration of President Bill Clinton at the inaugural ceremonies in January, 1993; only one poet before her, Robert Frost, had been invited to read at an inauguration ceremony. In all, she has received more than thirty honorary degrees.

Although many titles have been assigned to Angelou, one is especially significant to her: the modern female African American Marcel Proust. Angelou is known for addressing the world through the medium of her own life. The first volume of her autobiography made her the first African American woman to appear on nonfiction best-seller lists; four volumes followed the first.

BIOGRAPHY

Born Marguerite Annie Johnson, re-christened Maya, and taking the professional name Angelou (an adaptation of the name of her first husband, Tosh Angelos), Maya Angelou studied music and dance with Martha Graham, Pearl Primus, and Ann Halprin. Her early career was as an actress and singer, to which she quickly added the roles of civil rights worker (as the northern coordinator for the SCLC, 1959-1960), editor (as associate editor for the *Arab Observer*, 1961-1962), educator (beginning with the School of Music and Drama at the University of Ghana's Institute of African Studies, 1963-1966), and finally writer—first as a reporter for the *Ghanaian Times* (1963-1965). During the late 1960's and 1970's, she taught at many colleges and universities in California and Kansas, accepting the post of Reynolds Professor at Wake Forest University in 1981. Since then she has also been a sought-after speaker.

She has told much of her own life's story in her five-volume autobiography. Undoubtedly, Angelou's legacy will be her writings: Although the best-selling *I Know Why the Caged Bird Sings* was censored, her excellent work as an author in all genres has kept her story before the world. Angelou's early years have been burned into the minds of numerous readers. An image from this work centers on three-year-old Marguerite and four-year-old Bailey Johnson aboard a train, alone, traveling from California to their grandmother's home in Stamps, Arkansas, after the breakup of their parents' marriage. The two children wore their names and their destination attached to their clothes. This locomotive quest for family is both a factual part of and an apt metaphor for the life of the world-famous poet. Her first feeling of being truly at home, she has said, came in Africa, after she accompanied her second husband to Egypt and then traveled to Ghana.

A second image from Angelou's childhood involves the seven-year-old's rape by her mother's boyfriend. When no legal punishment followed, the rapist was murdered, possibly by the victim's uncles. Guilt following this incident drove Angelou inward, and she began reading the great works of literature. Reading her way through the Stamps library, she fell in love with William Shakespeare and Paul Laurence Dunbar, among others. The child of a fractured nuclear family came to see herself as a child of the fractured human family.

By age thirteen, Angelou had grown closer to her mother; at sixteen she became a mother herself. To earn a living for herself and her son, Guy, she became a waitress, a singer, and a dancer. These and other occupations were followed by acting, directing, producing, and the hosting of television specials. She loved to dance, but when her knees began to suffer in her early twenties, she devoted her attention to her other love: writing. She began supporting herself through her writing in 1968. Her family came to include "sister friends" and "brother friends," as her troubled brother Bailey became lost in the worlds of substance abuse and prison. She married, but she has refused to attach a number to her marriages, as that might, she says, suggest frivolity, and she insists that she was never frivolous about marriage. To "brother friend" James Baldwin she gives much credit for her becoming an autobiographer. She assisted "brother friends" Martin Luther King, Jr., and Malcolm X in their work and pursued her own work to better the entire human family.

The hope that Angelou found so significant in the 1960's is reflected in the poem she composed for Clinton's presidential inauguration. The dream of King is evident in the words written and delivered by Angelou "on the pulse of [that] morning."

ANALYSIS

Asked in 1983 what she hoped to achieve as a writer, Maya Angelou answered, "to remind us that we are more alike [than un-alike], especially since I've grown up in racial turbulence and unfairness." Two 1990's poems reflect the dichotomy of her declaration: "Human Family" celebrates family likeness, and "Son to Mother" denounces wrongs inflicted by various branches of the human family. Angelou in her poetry dissects and resurrects humankind: She condemns its shamefulness and rejoices in its possibilities and its glories.

STILL RISING

"Some poets sing/ their melodies," writes Angelou in "Artful Pose," published in 1975, "tendering my nights/ sweetly." Angelou, in contrast, chooses to write "of lovers false" "and hateful wrath/ quickly." She adds the word "quickly" to balance and countermand "sweetly." Her style as she speaks to live audiences and to readers, whether her tone is optimistic or pessimistic, reveals a sense of "gusto." In 1982 she offered this bit of self-analysis:

> If you enter a room of hostile strangers with gusto, there are few who can contain, preserve their hostility. . . . [I]t speaks immediately to the gusto in other people.

European American audiences applaud her and purchase her work even as she berates them: "You may write me down in history/ With your bitter, twisted lies," she says in the opening lines of one of her most famous poems, "Still I Rise."

"I'll play possum and close my eyes/ To your greater sins and my lesser lies," she writes in a jump-rope rhythm in "Bump d'Bump." "That way I share my nation's prize," she continues. "Call me a name from an ugly south/ Like liver lips and satchel mouth"; gusto, anger, and a challenge to humankind are integral ingredients of Angelou's poetry.

In "Man Bigot" Angelou writes,

> The man who is a bigot
> is the worst thing God has got
> except his match, his woman,
> who really is Ms. Begot.

Angelou is not unwilling to amuse as she challenges her audience. She did not leave the entertainment field behind when she turned to verse. Other entertaining and uplifting elements of her poetry are sass and the celebration of womanhood. "Men themselves have wondered/ What they see in me," says the speaker of "A Phenomenal Woman." A part of her mystery, she says, is in "the fire in my eyes," "the joy in my feet," and

> The grace of my style.
> I'm a woman
> Phenomenally.
> Phenomenal woman,
> That's me.

SASS AND ANGER

Sass is an element in 1978's "Still I Rise," but anger consistently tempers its speaker's joy. "Does my sassiness upset you?" and "Does my haughtiness offend you?" she asks her European American readers. "Out of the huts of history's shame/ I rise," says her African American speaker. In "Miss Scarlett, Mr. Rhett, and Other Latter-Day Saints," Angelou writes,

> Animated by the human sacrifice
> (Golgotha in black-face)
> Priests glow purely white on the
> bas-relief of a plantation shrine.

In "Slave Coffle" (1983) she speaks as a slave to whom "all the earth is horror," as the speaker realizes "Before the dawning,/ bright as grinning demons" that "life was gone."

Although Angelou has told interviewers that she has mellowed since writing her first volume of poetry, her verse remains harsh to the reader's mind and ear. Shame and ignorance recur as significant themes. Pride, however, is at least as significant.

PRIDE IN ANCESTORS

In 1975, Angelou declared "Song for the Old Ones" her favorite poem. Her celebration of those who kept her race alive remained a favorite theme. Her 1990 volume of poetry, *I Shall Not Be Moved*, has as its title the chorus to the poem "Our Grandmothers." Her sense of pride in these old ones and her sense of kinship with them is evident in the words she gives one of these grandmothers. To those who hurled ribbons of invective into the wind of history,

> She said, But my description cannot
> fit your tongue, for
> I have a certain way of being in this world,
> and I shall not, I shall not be moved.

In "Old Folks Laugh" (1990), she writes that old folks' laughter frees the world. The freedom that the grandmothers offer their children in "Our Grandmothers" is the freedom to be fully human: They tell them, "When you learn, teach. When you get, give."

"I laugh until I start to crying,/ When I think about my folks," says the speaker of "When I Think About Myself." Angelou's poetry shows that the stories of her people continued to fill and to break her heart. The title of the volume containing "Song for the Old Ones," *Oh Pray My Wings Are Gonna Fit Me Well*, seems, as does the title of her 1990 volume, *I Shall Not Be Moved*, to derive from her wish to be worthy of and to emulate the old ones.

That Angelou gives the final position in the 1990 volume to the poem dedicated to other, less great, old ones is significant, as is the idea of that poem: "When great souls die," she says in the final stanza,

> Our senses, restored, never
> to be the same, whisper to us.
> They existed. They existed.
> We can be. Be and be
> better. For they existed.

Unbelievable cruelty has given rise to unbelievable valor. Angelou cannot and will not forget the history of human cruelty as she feels that human beings must learn from their shared history. She continues to show human beings what they must learn that they can be better.

GUILT AND RESPONSIBILITY

Crucial to her overall idea is the shared guilt and responsibility of all history's survivors. In "I Almost Remember" (1975), the speaker recalls smiling and even laughing, but now

> Open night news-eyed I watch
> channels of hunger
> written on children's faces
> bursting bellies balloon
> in the air of my day room.

The speaker's garden, television, and day room suggest the luxuries and the guilt of one of the "haves" as she/he witnesses the suffering of the "have-nots" on the "channels of hunger." Similarly, "Harlem Hopscotch," with a seemingly different tone and a hopscotch rhythm, shows children singing of "good things for the ones that's got." "Everybody for hisself," they continue. The pain of both the television viewer and the children reflects the suffering as well as the scarring of the human psyche.

"Take Time Out" challenges the acceptance of the status quo, challenging the attitude of all human players of life's game:

> Use a minute
> feel some sorrow
> for the folks
> who think tomorrow
> is a place that they
> can call up
> on the phone.

The speaker of this poem asks that kindness be shown for the folk who thought that blindness was an illness that affected eyes alone. "We'd better see," says the speaker,

> what all our
> fearing and our
> jeering and our
> crying and
> our lying
> brought about.

Society is responsible for its children and for its own and its children's attitudes. As she shows in "Faces,"

> the brown caramel days of youth
> Reject the sun-sucked tit of
> childhood mornings.
> Poke a muzzle of war in the trust frozen eyes
> of a favored doll.

This is what humanity has wrought and what it must not accept. Humankind must be rendered both human and kind, the poet seems to say.

NEW DREAMS

Angelou calls repeatedly on the human race to spare itself from suffering. "There's one thing that I cry for I believe enough to die for/ That is every man's responsibility to man," says the speaker of "On Working White Liberals." "Dare us new dreams, Columbus," says the speaker of "A Georgia Song" (1983). In "America" (1975) Angelou speaks of America's promise that "has never been mined": "Her proud declarations/ are leaves in the wind." The United States, says the speaker, "entraps her children/ with legends untrue." This country of such high promise—the promise that all are equally entitled to life, liberty, and the pursuit of happiness—has not yet been discovered. Its citizens are led by their poet laureate to see that it is high time that the discovery be made.

OTHER MAJOR WORKS

SHORT FICTION: "Steady Going Up," 1972; "The Reunion," 1983.

PLAYS: *Cabaret for Freedom*, pr. 1960 (with Godfrey Cambridge; musical); *The Least of These*, pr. 1966; *Encounters*, pr. 1973; *Ajax*, pr. 1974 (adaptation of Sophocles' play); *And Still I Rise*, pr. 1976; *King*, pr. 1990 (musical; lyrics with Alistair Beaton, book by Lonne Elder III; music by Richard Blackford).

SCREENPLAYS: *Georgia, Georgia*, 1972; *All Day Long*, 1974.

TELEPLAYS: *Black, Blues, Black*, 1968 (10 episodes); *The Inheritors*, 1976; *The Legacy*, 1976; *I Know Why the Caged Bird Sings*, 1979 (with Leonora Thuna and Ralph B. Woolsey); *Sister, Sister*, 1982; *Brewster Place*, 1990.

NONFICTION: *I Know Why the Caged Bird Sings*, 1969; *Gather Together in My Name*, 1974; *Singin' and Swingin' and Gettin' Merry Like Christmas*, 1976; *The*

Heart of a Woman, 1981; *All God's Children Need Traveling Shoes*, 1986; *Wouldn't Take Nothing for My Journey Now*, 1993; *Even the Stars Look Lonesome*, 1997; *A Song Flung Up to Heaven*, 2002; *Hallelujah! The Welcome Table: A Lifetime of Memories with Recipes*, 2004.

CHILDREN'S LITERATURE: *Mrs. Flowers: A Moment of Friendship*, 1986 (illustrated by Etienne Delessert); *Soul Looks Back in Wonder*, 1993; *My Painted House, My Friendly Chicken, and Me*, 1994; *Kofi and His Magic*, 1996; *Angelina of Italy*, 2004; *Izak of Lapland*, 2004; *Mikale of Hawaii*, 2004; *Renie Marie of France*, 2004.

MISCELLANEOUS: *Letter to My Daughter*, 2008.

BIBLIOGRAPHY

Angelou, Maya. Interviews. *Conversations with Maya Angelou*. Edited by Jeffrey M. Elliott. Jackson: University Press of Mississippi, 1989. Part of the University Press of Mississippi's ongoing Literary Conversations series, this work is a collection of more than thirty interviews with Angelou, accompanied by a chronology of her life. Provides a multifaceted perspective on the creative issues that have informed Angelou's work as an autobiographer and a poet.

Bloom, Harold, ed. *Maya Angelou*. New York: Bloom's Literary Criticism, 2008. Collection of essays providing criticism of Angelou's works, including her poetry.

Egan, Jill. *Maya Angelou: A Creative and Courageous Voice*. Pleasantville, N.Y.: Gareth Stevens, 2009. A biography of Angelou that sheds light on the thoughts and ideals that are expressed in her actions and her writings.

Gillespie, Marcia Ann, Rosa Johnson Butler, and Richard A. Long. *Maya Angelou: A Glorious Celebration*. Foreword by Oprah Winfrey. New York: Doubleday, 2008. A personal, illustrated biography of Angelou created by long-time friends Gillespie and Long and niece Butler. Contains more than 150 photographs, portraits, and letters.

Hagen, Lynn B. *Heart of a Woman, Mind of a Writer, and Soul of a Poet: A Critical Analysis of the Writings of Maya Angelou*. Lanham, Md.: University Press of America, 1996. This critical volume sur-

veys Angelou's entire opus. Chapters include "Wit and Wisdom/Mirth and Mischief," "Abstracts in Ethics," and "Overview."

Lisandrelli, Elaine Slivinski. *Maya Angelou: More than a Poet*. Springfield, N.J.: Enslow, 1996. Lisandrelli discusses the flamboyance of Angelou, comparing her to the earlier African American author Zora Neale Hurston. Their hard work, optimism, perseverance, and belief in themselves are extolled.

Lupton, Mary Jane. *Maya Angelou: A Critical Companion*. Westport, Conn.: Greenwood Press, 1998. While focusing mainly on the autobiographies, Lupton's study is still useful as a balanced assessment of Angelou's writings. The volume also contains an excellent bibliography, particularly of Angelou's autobiographical works.

Pettit, Jayne. *Maya Angelou: Journey of the Heart*. New York: Lodestar Books, 1996. Includes bibliographical references and an index. Traces Angelou's journey from childhood through her life as entertainer, activist, writer, and university professor.

Williams, Mary E., ed. *Readings on Maya Angelou*. San Diego, Calif.: Greenhaven Press, 1997. This collection of essays by literary scholars and noted faculty offers diverse voices and approaches to Angelou's literary canon.

Judith K. Taylor

JAMES APPLEWHITE

Born: Stantonsburg, North Carolina; August 8, 1935
Also known as: James W. Applewhite

PRINCIPAL POETRY

War Summer: Poems, 1972
Statues of the Grass, 1975
Following Gravity, 1980
Forseeing the Journey, 1983
Ode to the Chinaberry Tree, and Other Poems, 1986
River Writing: An Eno Journal, 1988
Lessons in Soaring, 1989

A History of the River, 1993
Daytime and Starlight, 1997
Quartet for Three Voices, 2002
Selected Poems, 2005
A Diary of Altered Light: Poems, 2006

OTHER LITERARY FORMS

Poetry forms the main body of James Applewhite's work, but *Seas and Inland Journeys: Landscape and Consciousness from Wordsworth to Roethke* (1985) is a critical work in which Applewhite examines the subject that has been so important to his own poetry—the relationship of landscape to the poet's creative perceptions. The work gives particular attention to the Romantic poets William Wordsworth and Samuel Taylor Coleridge as well as to William Butler Yeats and Theodore Roethke. Applewhite also edited two volumes, *Brown Bag* (1971), with Anne Lloyd and Fred Chappell, and *Voices from Earth* (1971).

ACHIEVEMENTS

James Applewhite has been widely recognized as an important lyric poet whose work articulates the scenes and voices of the contemporary South, as his many awards attest. He received a Guggenheim Fellowship in 1976, the Associated Writing Programs' Contemporary Poetry Series Award in 1981, and the North Carolina Literary and Historical Association poetry award in 1981 and 1986. He received a prize in the *International Poetry Review* competition for 1982 and won the North Carolina Poetry Society award in 1990, the American Academy of Arts and Letters's Jean Stein Award in Poetry in 1992, and the North Carolina Award in Literature in 1993. In 2008, he was inducted into the North Carolina Literary Hall of Fame.

BIOGRAPHY

James William Applewhite was born August 8, 1935, in Stantonsburg, North Carolina, a small rural town that, along with his family, has played an important role in the images and voices of his poetry. His grandfather was a farmer; his father owned a gasoline station. Applewhite has frequently recorded the voices of the rural South from the men who worked for his father or who bought gasoline there and in the women

like his mother, voices that shaped his understanding of the world. Growing up in a world at war also shaped the poet's consciousness, as did the constant sense of the American Civil War, a painful event that seemed to the child to have occurred in the recent past.

Applewhite attended Duke University, receiving his bachelor's degree in 1958, a master of arts in 1960, and a doctorate in 1969, eventually making his career at Duke, teaching English until 2008. It was during graduate study, especially during study of the Romantic poets, Applewhite said, that he discovered the power of poetry to address his sense of alienation.

ANALYSIS

James Applewhite's poetry validates the claim that southern literature is often deeply rooted in place. Applewhite's work is steeped in North Carolina, both in Stantonsburg, a small town in the eastern part of the state, and in the area around Duke University and Durham. The sense of history has always been powerful in the South, and his own rootedness in the area has invited Applewhite to examine the relationship between past and present both in personal and historical terms. That relationship often produces a sense of duality that forms an important theme in Applewhite's work.

FOLLOWING GRAVITY

This early volume makes a good introduction to Applewhite's interests and themes. "Tobacco Men," "Drinking Music," "Elegy for a General Store," and "Rooster's Station" all look at the South of the poet's childhood. In the center of the volume, "My Grandmother's Life" uses images of water to link the poet to his grandparents as he seeks out their long-abandoned well. At the end of the volume, in the long poem "The Mary Tapes," a woman tells a tape recorder her life's history in country and town, a history that becomes emblematic of many lives in the "New South."

RIVER WRITING

Applewhite's *River Writing* chronicles a year of hiking and running along the Eno River, a nature preserve in the middle of the increasing urbanization of Durham and Chapel Hill. The poems detail the seasons and sights along the river, its cliffs and boulders, its kingfishers and beavers. The poems also insistently link the writer to his place in the setting, in both the present and past, just as the jonquils he picks in "The Sun's Tone" tie him to the grave of a woman who died in 1914 and yet resemble the jonquils he picks in "House of Seasons" to carry "Home to the living woman I love."

"Sleeping with Stars and Bulbs, Time and Its Signs" is the last poem in the collection. It marks the conclusion of Applewhite's year on the Eno and stands as a fine illustration of the level of lyricism many of the poems achieve. Camping beside the river in winter, the speaker thinks of the jonquil bulbs he dug from an abandoned homestead to plant at his own home. Even now, "each jonquil bulb/ . . . begins to unsheathe its single green claw/ Which will dig a yellow from night." He thinks of the relics of the past he has uncovered along the river, names and dates cut in trees, a "Model-T carcass"—all signs of those who came before him and reminders that others will follow. "All will come/ Round again, will be sounded." Even his own house will some day be a "branch-sketched cinder of rafters." Tonight, in this drowsy meditation, the speaker feels rooted in all he has experienced:

> I expand . . .
> To feel my huge shadow gravity-held,
> On the physical basis of all poetry,
> Nailed to earth's wheel by the stars.

LESSONS IN SOARING

Lessons in Soaring takes its themes from the life of the child who grew up in the rural South during World War II. Physically surrounded by a landscape of burgeoning life, he was also surrounded by adults whose focus was on the killing events abroad, where the technology of death superseded everything else.

Several poems in this collection blend imagery from the war with pictures of rural life, as in the volume's first poem, "The War Against Nature," which pictures the poet as a child watching for enemy aircraft from the observation tower in his father's service station. The adult narrator ponders the implications of the child's eagerness to see planes:

> Bored with a primordial green,
> We wanted experimental designs we'd seen,
>
> The fire it'd have meant had an enemy
> Plane appeared.

As the volunteer watchers gradually return to work on their farms, only the child is left, watching for the foreign shapes:

> Memorizing the chart of possible form:
> Messerschmitt, Wellington, workhorse Douglas.
> Ideas absolute as the blue emptiness.

Somehow the human designs of airplanes have taken on greater power to move the observer than even the absoluteness of the "blue emptiness," a phrase that hints at the emptiness of the human designs and their war against nature.

"The Memory of the Heart" asserts that the whole of the child's experience is written into his physical being. "Deciphering the Known Map" applies that idea to the geography of the family's world. It begins with town names from the family's history, goes on to a family cemetery, and widens its circles to the country music of southern tastes. The very language of this world binds the speaker to it. At a rural general store of the sort still seen throughout the South, the speaker might

> Buy nabs and an orange drink.
> The speech I share
> With the guy behind the counter
> Is as thick as the creek's
> Low water.

The poem concludes at another family graveyard, where the speaker senses his own name on the gravestones. "Among the Old Stones" also deals with a family graveyard (a common interest among southerners); here the setting leads the speaker to a meditation first on the speaker's relationship to the dead and then to the nature of the South and his place in it.

The realities of the modern South are often in tension with the South's romantic vision of itself both now and in its past, a tension that Applewhite articulates in "The Failure of Southern Representation." Here he considers the contradictions between the modern South of shopping centers and interstate highways and the fictional South of romanticized plantation life and the Civil War. The South of slavery and lynchings, the South of music, tobacco, and hurricanes—nothing can create a true picture of a place so riddled with opposites.

"A PLACE AND A VOICE" AND
"A CONVERSATION"

The long poem "A Place and a Voice" is addressed to the poet's mother in her old age, presenting her history in a collage of people, places, and events. The speaker has questions about them. Did her father recover from a buggy accident? Must a Methodist minister always be on the move? The questions suggest the mysteries that inevitably endure in any family's history. Sections 3 and 4 summarize the speaker's childhood in Stantonsburg, where he lived with his parents and brother near his paternal grandfather, enjoying the rich life of an active youth in a small town:

> Starved
> minds never lived in our house.
>
> Was it really the South? Life was
> rich, authentic.

In section 5, Applewhite imagines the tensions his mother endured in her strained relationship with her in-laws; section 6 records his own changing feelings toward his mother in his early maturity. Once she was the best listener to his stories; now he resents her claim on his imagination and simultaneously resents her absence, which leaves him feeling alone even when he is with his wife:

> I hated that you and a place were one,
> so vivid a myth, claustrophobic Eden,
> rich Atlantis in which to drown.

"The Conversation" makes a companion poem to "A Place and a Voice," this time addressed to Applewhite's father, cataloging his legacy as a former wrestler, garage owner, and wartime commander of the home guard. Now the son views his father in his old age; the rebellion of the son's adolescence has mellowed into affection. At the same time, he regrets what is lost: "I worship and regret the other figure,/ The god-king I once wished dead."

DAYTIME AND STARLIGHT

The first poem of *Daytime and Starlight*, "My Grandparents Never Watched *Star Trek*," images the dualities that frequently form Applewhite's themes. Here he pictures the world of his grandparents, the wood-burning stove, the foods they preserved in mason jars, the sausages they made. Since the time he viewed that world as a boy, the world has changed, and he has changed in it. Televised space ships, real and fictional, have carried him away to another planet.

"Botanical Garden: The Coastal Plains" looks at the issue in another way, as the poet tours the coastal plains section of the university's botanical garden. It is a miniature of the land he was born into, but it cannot be the same. Its plants bear the same names, but these are labeled with neat tags. The poet's father is not there. Even the dangers that once attended the water moccasin have been tamed.

The volume contains a number of long-line poems, including several about a trip to Italy, new subject matter for Applewhite. Still, one sees in "Descending in St. Clements" the poet's ongoing interest in the relationship between past and present and in dualities. In this poem, he is underground in an ancient temple of Mithras; above it the Christian basilica of Saint Clement has been built; below it one can hear water rushing. The setting leads the poet to a meditation on the interconnectedness of the pagan god of bull sacrifices depicted at the lowest level and the depictions of Christ, who "shed blood of his own." Also pictured was the watery martyrdom of Saint Clement, including fish and squid. The images and sound of water lead the tourist poet to contemplate the "higher miracle" that extinguished Mithras's flames, leaving that cellar temple as a "time-vein."

"Daytime and Starlight" is the volume's final poem. It pictures small-town North Carolina at dusk, a moment when time is always leaning into the past even while starlight ticks the world forward into its future.

OTHER MAJOR WORKS

NONFICTION: *Seas and Inland Journeys: Landscape and Consciousness from Wordsworth to Roethke*, 1985.

EDITED TEXTS: *Brown Bag*, 1971 (with Anne Lloyd and Fred Chappell); *Voices from Earth*, 1971.

BIBLIOGRAPHY

Applewhite, James. "Illegible Fields and Names in Marble." *Sewanee Review* 103 (1995): 522-537. This thoughtful autobiographical essay discusses the world that created Applewhite's poetic consciousness. The poet re-creates the world of Stantonsburg, where he grew up with his parents and many members of his father's family.

Gwynn, R. S. "What the Center Holds." *Hudson Review* 46, no. 4 (Winter, 1994): 741-750. In this lengthy review article, Gwynn discusses Applewhite's *A History of the River* as part of a general discussion of contemporary American poetry. He notes the poet's deep attachment to North Carolina and says that he can sometimes endow his subjects with "epic grandure," but he faults him for sometimes using imprecise imagery.

Lensing, George S. "Roads from Stantonsburg: The Poetry of James Applewhite." *Southern Review* 31, no. 1 (1995): 139-161. Lensing discusses the relationship between Applewhite's native geography and his writing. He examines the forces of contemporary life which alienate the poet from the natural world and the unpretentious men who are the poet's heroes.

Levine, Philip. "A Conversation with Philip Levine." Interview. *TriQuarterly* 95 (Winter, 1995): 67-83. In this lengthy interview, Levine talks, among other things, about the importance of place for one who wants to write. Although he does not specifically discuss Applewhite, he offers readers an overview of the state of contemporary American poetry.

Publishers Weekly. Review of *A History of the River*. 240, no. 4 (January 24, 1993): 83. In this review, the author describes Applewhite's knowledge of his culture as "impressive" but says that his descriptions are sometimes "excessively nuanced."

Ann D. Garbett

JOHN ASHBERY

Born: Rochester, New York; July 28, 1927

PRINCIPAL POETRY

Turandot, and Other Poems, 1953
Some Trees, 1956
The Tennis Court Oath, 1962
Rivers and Mountains, 1966
Selected Poems, 1967
The Double Dream of Spring, 1970
Three Poems, 1972
Self-Portrait in a Convex Mirror, 1975
Houseboat Days, 1977
As We Know, 1979
Shadow Train, 1981
A Wave, 1984
Selected Poems, 1985
April Galleons, 1987
Flow Chart, 1991
Hotel Lautrémont, 1992
Three Books: Poems, 1993
And the Stars Were Shining, 1994
Can You Hear, Bird: Poems, 1995
The Mooring of Starting Out: The First Five Books of Poetry, 1997
Wakefulness: Poems, 1998
Girls on the Run: A Poem, 1999
Your Name Here, 2000
As Umbrellas Follow Rain, 2002
Chinese Whispers, 2002
Where Shall I Wander, 2005
A Worldly Country: New Poems, 2007
Notes from the Air: Selected Later Poems, 2007
Collected Poems, 1956-1987, 2008
Planisphere: New Poems, 2009

OTHER LITERARY FORMS

Although known mainly as a poet, John Ashbery has produced a number of works in various genres. *A Nest of Ninnies* (1969) is a humorous novel about middle-class American life written by Ashbery in collaboration with James Schuyler. His plays include *The Compromise: Or, Queen of the Carabou* (pr. 1956) and *Three Plays* (1978). He also produced a volume of art criticism, *Reported Sightings: Art Chronicles, 1957-1987* (1989). His Charles Eliot Norton Lectures (given at Harvard University) were collected as *Other Traditions* (2000), an engaging volume of literary criticism about six eccentric poets.

ACHIEVEMENTS

John Ashbery won three major literary awards for *Self-Portrait in a Convex Mirror*: the National Book

Award in Poetry, the Pulitzer Prize, and the National Book Critics Circle Award. Ashbery is a member of the Academy of Arts and Sciences and the American Academy of Arts and Letters (since 1980) and served as chancellor for the Academy of American Poets (1988-1999). He has been honored with two Guggenheim Fellowships, two Fulbright Fellowships, and two National Endowment for the Arts grants. He won the Yale Series of Younger Poets award (1955) for *Some Trees*, Union League Civic and Arts Poetry Prize (1966), an Award in Literature from the American Academy of Arts and Letters (1969), the Shelley Memorial Award (1973), the Levinson Prize (1977), the Jersome J. Shestack Poetry Award (1983), and the Bollingen Prize from Yale University (1985). In 1982, Ashbery was awarded the Fellowship of the Academy of American Poets. In 1985, he was named a winner of both a MacArthur Prize Fellowship and a Lenore Marshall Poetry Prize. He received the Commonwealth Award in Literature (1986), the Ruth Lilly Poetry Prize (1992), the Frost Medal from the Poetry Society of

America (1995), the Gold Medal for Poetry from the American Academy of Arts and Letters (1997), the prestigious Antonio Feltrinelli Prize from the Accademia Nazionale dei Lincei in Rome (1992), the Bingham Poetry Prize (1998), the Wallace Stevens Award (2001), and the Griffin Poetry Prize (2008). In 2002, he was made an officer of the French Legion of Honor by presidential decree.

BIOGRAPHY

Born in Rochester, New York, in 1927, John Lawrence Ashbery grew up in rural Sodus, New York. He attended Deerfield Academy and Harvard University, where he became friends with poet Kenneth Koch. Ashbery received his B.A. from Harvard in 1949 and his M.A. from Columbia University in 1951. After leaving university life, Ashbery worked for various publishers in New York City until he moved to Paris in 1955. He remained in Paris until 1965, writing for the *New York Herald Tribune*, *Art International*, and *Art News*. From 1965 until 1972, Ashbery worked as executive editor for *Art News* in New York, before becoming a distinguished professor of writing at the Brooklyn College campus of the City University of New York. He has also taught at Harvard University. Ashbery became the Charles P. Stevenson, Jr., Professor of Languages and Literature at Bard College in 1990.

ANALYSIS

As a brief review of his biography would suggest, John Ashbery has had a considerable amount of exposure to the world of art and to the language of art criticism. Ashbery spent a full decade of his life in Paris, the art capital of Europe, where he read deeply in French poetry and immersed himself in the day-to-day life of French culture. Readers of Ashbery's poetry, then, should not be surprised to encounter references to art and occasional snatches of the French language as part of the poetic texts. For example, one of his poems is entitled "Le Livre est sur la table." There are other titles in German, Latin, and Russian, and the poetry as a whole bristles with references from every department of highbrow, middlebrow, and lowbrow culture, including cartoons ("Daffy Duck in Hollywood"), silent movies ("The Lonedale Operator"), literature ("Sonnet," "A

John Ashbery (D.C. Public Library)

Long Novel," and "Thirty-seven Haiku"), history ("The Tennis Court Oath"), and linguistics ("The Plural of 'Jack-in-the-Box'").

Because of its unpredictable style and subject matter, Ashbery's poetry has managed to infuriate, befuddle, amuse, delight, and instruct its readers. His work remains some of the most difficult verse produced, for he refuses to provide the reader with a poetic "reality" that is any less complex than the "reality" of the world outside poetry. Ashbery cannot be simplified or paraphrased because his work has no "content" in the ordinary sense. His poetry is "about" the act of knowing, the process of imagining, the curious associational leaps made by the human mind as it experiences any given moment in time. To read Ashbery is to be teased into a whole range of possible meanings without finally settling on a single one. Although this openness might confuse the reader at the outset, the process of reading Ashbery becomes more pleasurable on each encounter. New meanings appear, and Ashbery's voice comes to seem strangely present, as if he were intoning directly into the reader's ear. These poems are filled with little verbal cues and signals aimed directly at the reader; many of the poems depend on a complicated dialogue or interplay between the author and the reader (a technique he exploits masterfully in *Three Poems*). Thus his work is a kind of half-poetry, always requiring an active reader to make it whole. Ashbery achieves his trademark effect of apparent intimacy while simulating the very process of thought itself.

How Ashbery came to create this new kind of poetry is actually a subchapter in the general history of art and culture in the twentieth century. Certainly he benefited mightily from his study of other artists and thinkers. During his formative years in Paris, he absorbed the French language and the famous paintings of the Louvre while immersing himself in all kinds of printed matter: cheap pamphlets and paperback novels bought from the bookstalls, as well as journalistic prose (in French and English) and the rarefied language of art criticism (which he himself was producing).

In addition, it is clear that a strong line of influence connects Ashbery with writers such as Gertrude Stein, who used disjointed syntax and unorthodox grammar as part of her Surrealistic poetry. He owes a clear debt

also to Wallace Stevens, who taught him how to philosophize in poetry and also how to approach subjects obliquely. Stevens, also, was a great lover of French Impressionist painting and Symbolist poetry. From W. H. Auden, who chose Ashbery's *Some Trees* for the Yale Series of Younger Poets, Ashbery learned a conversational naturalness and a lyrical or musical way of phrasing. It might be argued that Ashbery, as a literate artist, was influenced by all the great thinkers of the century, but these poetic debts seem particularly obvious, especially in the early books. He probably learned something from Ludwig Wittgenstein's idea of language as a game, just as he must have responded to Jackson Pollock's expressionist paintings, which use paint in much the same way that Ashbery uses words. Something of the sheer shock value and unpredictability of musicians such as Igor Stravinsky, John Cage, and Anton Webern must have touched him also, since Ashbery is clearly fond of similar effects in his own poems.

These debts to the artistic pioneers of the twentieth century are most obvious in Ashbery's earlier books—that is, those preceding the publication of *Three Poems: Some Trees*, *The Tennis Court Oath*, and *Rivers and Mountains*. All these books are relatively short and compact, typically containing one long or major poem, often positioned near the end of the volume.

Ashbery's characteristic wonder and inventiveness has proven a hallmark of the several volumes published since 1990. During that period, Ashbery wrote and published more and wrote more of the highest quality than at any other time in his career. With Ashbery, there is no limit to the possibilities inherent in human life and to the sheer fun of the mind's response to them. Regular readers of Ashbery will begin to inhabit a world that is larger, more unpredictable, and infinitely more interesting than anything they have known before.

SOME TREES

Typical of Ashbery's early poems are "The Instruction Manual" from *Some Trees* and the title poem from *Rivers and Mountains*, each of which forces the reader to perform another kind of imaginative leaping, one that is different from the mere shock of the surreal. In "The Instruction Manual," the speaker is bored with his job of writing an instruction manual on the uses of a new metal and, instead, falls into a prolonged aesthetic daydream on the city of Guadalajara, Mexico, which he has never visited. He invents this city in magical detail for the rest of the poem. In like manner, the places described on a map and the map itself become utterly indistinguishable in "Rivers and Mountains," as if Ashbery were suggesting that one's most vivid moments are those that have been rescued or resurrected by the fertile powers of the poetic imagination. Ashbery always emphasizes the primacy of the imagination. In his view, the most vivid reality occurs in the poem itself, because that is the precise point where the inner and outer (spiritual and sensory) experiences of life actually intersect.

Two more early poems bear analysis here, because they also illustrate the poetic techniques favored in many of Ashbery's later poems. "Le Livre est sur la table" and "The Picture of Little J. A. in a Prospect of Flowers" (both from *Some Trees*) are magnificent feats of imaginative power, and each operates on the same principle of aesthetic meditation. In each poem, the poet looks at reality through a work of art, or as if it were a work of art (in "The Picture of Little J. A. in a Prospect of Flowers" a photograph is the medium). The effect is largely the same, because the world is always transformed and made into a work of art by the conclusion of the poem. Stevens is probably the model for this kind of poem, exemplified by his "Thirteen Ways of Looking at a Blackbird" and "A Study of Two Pears." Other poets, particularly William Carlos Williams, Marianne Moore, and Elizabeth Bishop, were to involve themselves passionately in the writing of aesthetically oriented poems, and one can look to some of their pioneering work to explain the sureness and control of Ashbery's similar efforts.

In "Le Livre est sur la table," Ashbery offers the reader a number of aesthetic propositions to contemplate, the most important of which is the notion that beauty results from a certain emptiness or from the placement of an object in an unusual or unaccustomed position. In both instances, the viewer is forced to see the object in a new way. Ashbery again underlines the power of the imagination, giving the example of an imaginary woman who comes alive in her stride, her hair, and her breasts as she is imagined. Most important

of all is the artist who creates small artistic catalysts, new and strange relationships that haunt the perceiver with their beauty. Neither the sea nor a simple birdhouse can make for innovative art but placing them together in a fundamental relationship changes them forever:

> The young man places a bird-house
> Against the blue sea. He walks away
> And it remains. Now other
> Men appear, but they live in boxes.

The men in the boxes are the nonartists, who do not realize that the newly created sea is a highlighted thing. All along, the sea has been "writing" a message (with its waves and lines), but only the "young man" (the artist) can read it.

The other "young man," or artist figure, in *Some Trees* is Ashbery himself, described in the snapshot that serves as the aesthetic focal point for the autobiographical poem "The Picture of Little J. A. in a Prospect of Flowers." This little fellow has a head like a mushroom and stands comically before a bed of phlox, but he has the makings of a poet precisely because he appreciates the value of words—especially lost words, those tip-of-the-tongue utterances and slips of the tongue, in which the speaker strains to specify clear meaning. "The Picture of Little J. A. in a Prospect of Flowers" is a typical Ashbery performance, not merely because of its high aesthetic theme but also because of its inclusion of low comedy, irony, and parody. The epigraph—taken from Boris Pasternak's autobiography *Okhrannaya gramota* (1931; *Safe Conduct*, 1945 in *The Collected Prose Works*)—seemingly contradicts the rest of the poem in what is the first of many jokes (Dick and Jane of childhood books become Dick and Genevieve, conversing in complicated Elizabethan sentences). Childhood is full of jokes and embarrassments, like standing in front of the clicking shutter of a camera, but childhood can also be the beginning of the artist's journey: The poem ends by praising the imagination and its ability to rescue this early phase of life through the power of words. "The Picture of Little J. A. in a Prospect of Flowers" is a bittersweet portrait of a self-conscious and precocious young man who was destined to become a great artist.

THE TENNIS COURT OATH

In *The Tennis Court Oath*, the reader encounters the long quasi-epical poem entitled "Europe," a work related in overall form to T. S. Eliot's *The Waste Land* (1922) and to similar efforts by Ezra Pound, Hart Crane, and Williams. In the most general terms, "Europe" here means the accumulated cultural wealth of European history and its ability—or inability—to help the creative artist in the twentieth century. The decay, or "wasteland," of Europe is juxtaposed to or "intercut" (in film terms) with a trivial story of two travelers, Pryor and Collins, whose unheroic status stands in sharp contrast to the old order. As the poem begins, the poet registers all these complex feelings, while focusing on the shocking blueness of the morning sky, here presented surrealistically:

> To employ her
> construction ball
> Morning fed on the
> light blue wood
> of the mouth

The wrecking ball of construction crews is one of the most visible symbols of the typical cityscape, suggesting simultaneously the twin processes of destruction and re-creation. The sudden, destructive impact of the steel ball approximates the elemental power of the morning light as it, too, rearranges and alters the city and all of its facets. The bystander is left openmouthed and speechless, like the sky itself. This analysis does not fully explicate Ashbery's lines, because, like all dream imagery, they resist final explication. One can describe their suggestiveness and allusiveness, but the dream itself remains a mystery, as does this purely perceived moment of an ordinary morning in the city.

THREE POEMS

Some of the poet's greatness is evident on nearly every page of *Three Poems*, the book that many critics cite as Ashbery's masterpiece. The long, meditative work consists of three interlocking prose poems, "The New Spirit," "The System," and "The Recital," and totals 118 densely packed pages of text. Most of that text is written in prose, a highly interactive prose that constantly urges the reader forward, raises questions, voices doubts and suspicions, and generally plunges the reader headlong into a highly meditative process of thinking and reflecting. *Three Poems* is Ashbery at his most difficult and most satisfying, even though there is virtually no story or tidy paraphrase that can be made of the reading experience itself. Nevertheless, a few elusive details do emerge, and one dimly begins to realize that *Three Poems* is an oblique narrative that in general terms charts a deep relationship between two lovers, one that somehow founders, so that the narrator grows more and more self-possessed. The narrator becomes less and less likely to address the familiar "you" who is called upon again and again in the opening pages of the book. By the end, the "you" has virtually disappeared, as if the loss of love might be charted by the absence of the "you" from pages where only the "I" can finally dominate.

The form of *Three Poems* deserves some attention, because the poems are cast in the form of prose, though their imagery, tonal shifts, and complicated rhythms all suggest poetic (not prosaic) form. To complicate matters even further, Ashbery originally published the second section of the work, "The System," in the *Paris Review* in 1971, the year before the whole work appeared in the form of a book. Ashbery specifically allowed "The System" to be published as a prose work, so by titling the whole three-part composition *Three Poems*, he seems to be teasing the reader again on the simplest level and at the same time calling attention to the arbitrariness of literary labels and taxonomy. As if all those complications were not enough, Ashbery carries the joke further by inserting several poems (or at least texts that look like poems) into the longer work. What counts in the end is the sustained act of mediation and empathy with the narrator that these manipulations of typeface and marginal format will induce in the reader.

The reader, facing *Three Poems*, has a Herculean task to perform: absorbing a long, oblique narrative that requires constant reflection, analysis, and thoughtful mediation. The difficulty is an intentional by-product of Ashbery's stated goal on the first page of the book: to leave out as much as possible in order to create a newer and truer form of communication. Any love story the reader could have encountered would have finally become banal; what Ashbery gives, however, cannot grow stale. To read *Three Poems* is to invent on every page the pain and exaltation that make up the essence of a love story. In that way, the "private" person of the book remains mysterious, as all lovers essentially must remain. Thus, one cannot summarize Ashbery's love story, but one can experience it vicariously.

In "The System," the second and most difficult part of the poem, the narrator becomes utterly preoccupied with himself. In "The New Spirit," even small details of urban life were associated with something the beloved had said or done; here, however, the details and the lover have disappeared. Instead, the narrator is trapped in a kind of mental labyrinth, or "system." In one memorable passage, he imagines the members of the human race boarding a train, which is, of course, their whole life. No one has any idea where the train is going or how fast it is moving. The passengers are ignorant of their journey and—the narrator insists—ignorant of their fundamental situation. The very core of their being is ignorance, yet they fail to recognize this crucial fact. Hence, the narrator views them with contempt.

Three Poems concludes on a lighter note, literally on notes of music, which offer a kind of deliverance for the narrator, who has been trapped in the labyrinth of his doleful thoughts. "The Recital" is important because Ashbery often sees music as an analogue to poetry. Indeed, at one point, he had planned to become a musician, and music has remained a rich source of inspiration throughout his career. The power of music and its essential abstractness make a powerful appeal to the narrator, who at this juncture is exhausted by his Hamlet-like speculations. The poem ends, and with it the whole book, with a description of the power of music (and of art)—the power to inspire new beginnings and new possibilities. In a final jest, Ashbery offers the reader an ending that is actually a beginning: "There were new people watching and waiting, conjugating in this way the distance and emptiness, transforming the scarcely noticeable bleakness into something both intimate and noble." With this brilliant virtuoso effect, Ashbery concludes a poem that is at once a continuance of the great Western tradition of meditative writing (one that includes Saint John of the Cross and Sir Thomas Browne)—and a dramatically arresting rendition of how it feels to be alive in the last decades of the twentieth century. The old and the new come together in a synthesis that is as disturbing, fascinating, and elusive as the century that produced it.

Having reached a kind of artistic plateau with *Three Poems*, Ashbery's career took a new direction. In many ways, *Three Poems* occupies the kind of position in his life that *The Waste Land* did for Eliot. Both works explore psychological traumas and deeply sustained anguish; both plumb the depths of despair until a kind of spiritual nadir is reached. After Eliot completed *The Waste Land*, his work took on a new, spiritual dimension, culminating in the complex Christian poem he called *Four Quartets* (1943). Ashbery's work also changed after the publication of *Three Poems*, but he has not embraced Christian or even theistic belief; he has always insisted on a kind of agnostic or even atheistic vision of life, in which art supplants all conventional notions of divinity. Nevertheless, like Eliot, he has passed through the proverbial dark night of the soul, and his work after *Three Poems* is somehow more confident, less self-consciously experimental, and less opaque. The newer poetry is still impossible to paraphrase, but it is much more accessible and more readable (at least on first sight) than the most extravagant of the early poems, and its subject matter generally seems more central to human experience.

SELF-PORTRAIT IN A CONVEX MIRROR

All these tendencies culminate in a book that won the National Book Award, the Pulitzer Prize, and the National Book Critics Circle Award: *Self-Portrait in a Convex Mirror*. Those prizes and the book itself helped put Ashbery on the literary map, so that he could no longer be summarily dismissed as an eccentric aesthete turning out brilliant but inaccessible work. Readers began to look more closely at what Ashbery was saying and to embrace his message (however complex) as never before.

"Self-Portrait in a Convex Mirror," the title poem, is a brilliant piece of autobiographical writing that does not reveal gritty details of Ashbery's personal life so much as his opinions about art and its power to transform the artist. Self-portraits are as old as art itself, but Ashbery as an art critic and former expatriate had encountered some especially powerful examples of the genre. He must have encountered the great self-portraits of Rembrandt van Rijn and Vincent van Gogh, but the particular work that inspired this poem is a famous masterpiece of the High Renaissance, *Self-Portrait in a Convex Mirror* (1524) by Parmigianino (Girolamo Francesco Maria Mazzola), which hangs in the Kunsthistorisches Museum in Vienna. Ashbery tells the reader that he encountered Parmigianino's famous painting in the summer of 1959, during a visit to Vienna. Parmigianino's self-portrait is uniquely circular in overall form and, as the title suggests, resulted from the artist's close inspection of his visage in a convex mirror, an optical device that creates interesting distortions of scale and distance. Parmigianino's hand, for example, is grossly exaggerated and dominates the foreground of the painting, while his head seems undersized and nearly childlike. It is possible that the Italian artist's childlike appearance appealed to Ashbery because it reminded him of the snapshot of little John Ashbery that had inspired his earlier, much shorter autobiographical lyric, "The Picture of Little J. A. in a Prospect of Flowers."

It is in the nature of self-portraits, then, to conceal and reveal simultaneously—hence the appropriateness of the convex mirror, whose powers of transformation and distortion apply equally to Parmigianino and Ashbery. The poet begins the poem by quoting and paying homage to Giorgio Vasari, the first great art critic. (Ashbery too had been an art critic at the time he saw the painting in Venice.) Vasari explains the complicated arrangements that preceded Parmigianino's actual painting: the use of a barber's convex mirror and the necessity of having a carpenter prepare the circular wooden substratum of the painting. These operations are mere preliminaries, however, to the much more important work of the eyes themselves once the painting has been set up. The eyes cannot penetrate the artificial depth created by this strange mirroring device; therefore, everything that results is a kind of speculation—a word that derives from the Latin word for mirror, *speculum*, as Ashbery points out. Thus in the self-portrait one kind of "mirroring" leads to another; what one sees is not precisely what is there. To hold the paradox in the mind is to enter the world of the artist.

The argument that Ashbery then goes on to develop may perhaps be summarized by the adagelike statement that stability (or order) can be maintained in the presence of instability (or chaos). The movements of time, weather, table tennis balls, and tree branches are all potential elements for the synthesizing and harmonizing power of art, no matter if it distorts something in the process. Perhaps the greatest distortion is that of stability; the stable simply cannot be found in nature, as Isaac Newton showed through his laws of thermodynamics. It is only in the mirror of art (a symbol also favored by William Shakespeare) that stability, order, and form may thrive. Since all art is by definition artificial, then, stability also is an artifice.

Nevertheless, artistic stability is all the artist and the race of human beings can rely on to reveal meaning in an otherwise meaningless space. So Parmigianino's Renaissance painting, like all art, is applicable to all future generations, and Ashbery borrows Parmigianino's technique of mirroring until the world seems to spin around him in a merry-go-round of papers, books, windows, trees, photographs, and desks, and "real life" itself becomes a kind of trick painting. Addressing the Italian master, Ashbery admits that the "uniform substance" or order in his life derives from the Italian genius: "My guide in these matters is your self."

He goes on to quote a contemporary art critic, Sydney Freedberg, who finds the idealized beauty and formal feeling of Parmigianino's self-portrait to depend on the very chaos Ashbery had earlier described. For Freedberg this instability is a collection of bizarre, unsettling aspects of reality that somehow the painting enfolds and harmonizes.

Readers might at this point recall similar discussions—though in radically different language—by John Keats, especially in his great meditation on art, "Ode on a Grecian Urn," which asks the reader to accept art precisely because it transforms the chaos and changeability of human life. Ultimately, this process results in a complete fusion of truth (or reality) and beauty (or art), in Keats's formulation. Ashbery is not Keats, but one has to note the similar posture of the two poets, both contemplating the power of art, both commencing with an art object (the Grecian urn and the Italian self-portrait) and concluding on a note of affirmation. For Ashbery, the power of art is not only magnificent but terrifying, like a pistol primed for Russian roulette with only one bullet in the chamber. Art has the potential to "kill" our old perceptions. Some people might consider this power to be only a dream, but for Ashbery the power remains, and art becomes a kind of "waking dream" in the same unhappy world of human beings that Keats evokes in "Ode on a Grecian Urn." Even in the city, which Ashbery imagines as an insect with multifaceted eyes, art somehow survives. He envisions each person as a potential artist holding a symbolic piece of chalk, ready to begin a new self-portrait.

HOUSEBOAT DAYS

Ashbery continues with this more accessible (and essentially more affirmative) kind of poetry in *Houseboat Days*, the title poem of which likens the mind and its vast storehouse of memory to a boardinghouse that is open to everyone, taking in boarders of every possible type and description. This metaphorical way of describing the sensory, intellectual, and imaginative powers of human beings is a valuable clue for understanding another poem in the volume, one of Ashbery's wittiest and most polished performances, "Daffy Duck in Hollywood," a poem that manages to be tender, lyrical, comic, outrageous, and serious without losing its sense of direction.

An obscure opera serves as a kind of grid or structural framework for this rather freewheeling poem. The poem begins with a stupefyingly absurd collection of mental odds and ends, the flotsam and jetsam of a highly cultured and sophisticated mind that also appreciates the artifacts of popular culture: an Italian opera, Rumford's Baking Powder, Speedy Gonzales, Daffy Duck, Elmer Fudd, the Gadsden Purchase, Anaheim (California), pornographic photographs, and the comic-strip character Skeezix. All these apparent irrelevancies are entirely relevant, because they illustrate the random nature of the mind, its identity as a stream of consciousness. However, these items are also a kind of dodge or subterfuge to block out images of a significant other, possibly a lover. Because of the odd way the mind works through the principle of association, however, these same cartoonlike images also remind the narrator of that other person.

As in so many of his other poems, Ashbery is again insisting that the only reality is the one human beings make, and he concludes by wisely noting that no one knows all the dimensions of this mental life or where the parts fit in. The goal, in Ashbery's opinion, is to keep "ambling" on; thus, each person might remain "intrigued" and open to all the extravagant invitations of life. The mind, with its interminable image making, is strangely cut off from life, but when used properly (that is, aesthetically) it can lay hold of the abundant and unanticipated gifts that always surround and endow impoverished human beings.

A WAVE

This optimistic vein is apparent in most of *A Wave* but especially in the title poem, which seems to contrast crests of positive feelings with troughs of despair. The poem is a long discursive work in which Ashbery creates variations on one essential theme: that a fundamental feeling of security (not to be confused with superficial happiness), a deep and abiding sense of the goodness of life, can, in fact, sustain the person through the pain that life inevitably brings. In this poem, human beings do have final control of their destiny because they are supported by something powerfully akin to older notions of grace or faith. Having this power or "balm," as Ashbery terms it, no one is ever really stripped of autonomy: "we cannot be really naked/ Having this explanation."

APRIL GALLEONS

This mood of sustained hope continues in the exquisitely lyrical *April Galleons*, a book that, like *Houseboat Days*, relies on the metaphor of a boat as a vehicle for psychological as well as physical travel. Included is "Ice Storm," a poem that is highly original yet somehow manages to echo Robert Frost (especially "Birches" and "Design"). As Frost did in "Birches," Ashbery describes winter ice in glittering detail. As Frost did in "Design," Ashbery questions the fate of small things that are out of their accustomed places, such as the rose he stumbles on, growing beside a path entirely out of season. However, none of these matters disturbs him fundamentally, because he is beginning to get his "bearings in this gloom and see how [he] could improve on the distraught situation all around me, in the darkness and tarnished earth."

AND THE STARS WERE SHINING

Ashbery's wit and virtuosity are often noted by critics, yet his humanity and intelligence are equally important facets of his work. In *And the Stars Were Shining*, this fact becomes readily apparent when in many of the poems his wisdom of age is blended with a great and tender sadness and bursts of wit and vitality. The title poem harks back to the long poems of another age—Roman numerals mark its sections and its cadences recall a past era—but its direct and relaxed language brings it firmly into the late twentieth century. There are fifty-seven more poems in the volume, displaying Ashbery's characteristic wryness and filled with tragicomic snapshots of our time. The works are also philosophical, as he endeavors to find amusement as well as pain in his autumnal themed poems, including the title poem and "Token Resistance."

YOUR NAME HERE

The title of *Your Name Here* aptly hints at the volume's rambunctious, arbitrary themes and pell-mell performances: Poems include "Frogs and Gospels," "Full Tilt," "Here We Go Looby," "Amnesia Goes to the Ball," and "A Star Belched." While his poetic themes are capricious and whimsical, Ashbery's language is intricate, tightly constructed, rhythmic, and sinuous, with a serious undercurrent of memory, time, loss, angst, and desire. Thus, his tone is at once melancholic and comedic, best demonstrated in "What Is Written."

WHERE SHALL I WANDER

Ashbery is reported to have once said that his ambition was "to produce a poem that the critic cannot even talk about." Most of Ashbery's readers would probably agree that he has satisfied this ambition, although some of the poems in *Where Shall I Wander* are more accessible. For example, "Interesting People of Newfoundland" is quite easy to talk about, with its roll call of characters like Larry, who performed foolishly on street corners, and the Russian who said he was a grand duke—and may have been. Doc Hanks was a good "sawbones" when he was not completely drunk; even half drunk he could perform "decent cranial surgery." Walsh's department store had teas and little cakes and rare sherries from all over. The population was small: "But for all that/ we loved each other and had interesting times." Altogether different in conception, "Novelty Love Trot" is hardly transparent, but it musters some explicable philosophical commentary. The poet's taste in books runs to biographies and cultural studies;

in music, he likes Liszt's Consolations, "though I've never been consoled/ by them." In the poet's view, for most people, religion is about going to Hell: "I'm probably the only American// who thinks he's going to heaven," but first there is "the steep decline/ into a declivity."

The title of the prose piece "From China to Peru" comes from the first two lines of Samuel Johnson's *The Vanity of Human Wishes* (1749), an imitation of Juvenal's tenth satire: "Let observation with extensive view,/ Survey Mankind, from China to Peru." The vanity of the title stands out clearly in Ashbery's version as the speaker finds himself "taunted" for his dark woolen suit when he arrives at some trivial social occasion where the men appear dressed "to go off on a safari." His only recourse is to the bar, where the "unnerving" events around him make him eager for the cocktail hour. The coherence of this satire then dissolves into a typical Ashbery riff on Japan declaring war on Austro-Hungary and his failure to track down a weather report. "The Red Easel" has a rhymed counterpart in "The Bled Weasel," a *jeu d'esprit* that exemplifies the kind of opaque collection of apparently random lines that frustrates so many readers. No weasel appears in the poem but a caterpillar shows up, "Erect on its parasol," while "Glowworms circulated/ under the trees, confirmed [whatever 'confirmed' means] by whimpering Dobermans." This frivolity collapses, appropriately, in a "crazy quilt of expired pageantry."

A WORLDLY COUNTRY

The title poem of *A Worldly Country*, written in long lines worked into couplets, tells of a city that is riotous by day, with "insane clocks" and "the scent of manure in the municipal parterre." Chickens and geese enjoy the leftover bonbons, but even though "all hell broke loose" in the day, all was calm again by evening. The poet's musings lead him to a moral: "And just as waves are anchored to the bottom of the sea/ we must reach the shallows before God cuts us free." In "Autumn Tea Leaves," it is a partial eclipse that violates the normal day, but the poet cannot discern "what is special about this helix." These phenomena raise questions: What blanket will be sufficient for a freezing night? The dancers who celebrated the celestial occasion revealed "faces/ and senses of humor." However, when it all ended, who knows how many cakes were served, "or leaves collected/ in the hollow of a stump"?

In the fifteen four-line stanzas of "Phantoum," the second line of each stanza is repeated as the first line of the next, with other patterns sneaked in as the stanzas proceed. For example, in stanza 5, the second line, "The auks were squawking, the emus shrieking," becomes line 1 of stanza 6. Little Orphan Annie's adoptive father, Daddy Warbucks, makes a guest appearance in stanza 9 ("Daddy Warbucks was sad, but kept his reasons to himself") with no appreciable gain to the plotless but amiable verses.

A line from Auden's poem "At Last the Secret Is Out" provides the title "The Handshake, the Cough, the Kiss," and it is tempting to interpret the secret as Auden's homosexuality. Even though nothing in the poem speaks directly to a sexual theme, stanza 3 encourages speculation: "We risked it anyway,/ out on the ice where it darkens/ and seems to whisper/ from down below. Watch out, it's the Snow Queen. . . ." The poem then evolves into the poet's reminiscences of childhood in the unnamed "port city of his birth," where he was something of a boy wonder, "the local amateur historian." Rambling thoughts about childhood and the city lead to an apparent climax to the poet's relationship with a coworker in the television industry, a man identified only as "him": "look,/ if that's all you can bring to the table, why are we here?" The speaker concludes his critique by lamenting "an academy/ where losers file past, and the present is unredeemed,/ and all fruits are in season." The poems in this volume show no fading of the wit and bright phrasing of the works first published nearly half a century earlier.

OTHER MAJOR WORKS

LONG FICTION: *A Nest of Ninnies*, 1969 (with James Schuyler).

PLAYS: *Everyman*, pr. 1951; *The Heroes*, pr. 1952; *The Compromise: Or, Queen of the Carabou*, pr. 1956; *The Philosopher*, pb. 1964; *Three Plays*, 1978.

NONFICTION: *The Poetic Medium of W. H. Auden*, 1949 (senior thesis); *Reported Sightings: Art Chronicles, 1957-1987*, 1989; *Other Traditions*, 2000; *John Ashbery in Conversation with Mark Ford*, 2003; *Selected Prose*, 2004.

TRANSLATIONS: *Melville*, 1960 (of Jean-Jacques Mayoux); *Murder in Montarte*, 1960 (of Noel Vixon); *The Deadlier Sex*, 1961 (of Genevieve Manceron); *Alberto Giacometti*, 1962 (of Jacques Dupin); *The Landscape Is Behind the Door*, 1994 (of Pierre Martory); *Giacometti: Three Essays*, 2002 (of Dupin); *The Recitation of Forgetting*, 2003 (of Franck André Jamme).

EDITED TEXT: *Best American Poetry, 1988*, 1988.

BIBLIOGRAPHY

Ashbery, John. "John Ashbery in Conversation with Mark Ford." Interview by Mark Ford. In *Seven American Poets in Conversation: John Ashbery, Donald Hall, Anthony Hecht, Donald Justice, Charles Simic, W. D. Snodgrass, Richard Wilbur*, edited by Peter Dale, Philip Hoy, and J. D. McClatchy. London: Between the Lines, 2008. Ashbery talks about his life and works, including his influences.

_____. "A Kind of Musical Spa." Interview by Craig Burnett. *Frieze* 85 (September, 2004). Ashbery identifies and discusses some of his favorite writers—Ronald Firbank, André Breton, and Frank O'Hara. He praises Guy Maddin's films and says he hated writing art criticism.

Bloom, Harold, ed. *John Ashbery: Comprehensive Research and Study Guide*. Philadelphia: Chelsea House, 2004. Overview of Ashbery's published work, discussing his form, complex linguistics, and vision.

Herd, David. *John Ashbery and American Poetry*. New York: Palgrave, 2000. Herd chronicles Ashbery's poetic career, analyzing his continuities, differences, and improvements over time.

Lehman, David. *The Last Avant-Garde: The Making of the New York School of Poets*. New York: Doubleday, 1998. Chronicle of New York School of poets, closely tracing Ashbery's life and analyzing elements contributing to the backdrop of his poetry.

MacArthur, Marit J. *The American Landscape in the Poetry of Frost, Bishop, and Ashbery: The House Abandoned*. New York: Palgrave Macmillan, 2008. Examines the poetry of Ashbery, Robert Frost, and Elizabeth Bishop, noting that all three had the subject of the abandoned house.

Malinowska, Barbara. *Dynamics of Being, Space, and Time in the Poetry of Czesław Miłosz and John Ashbery*. New York: Peter Lang, 2000. Malinowska provides a challenging discussion of poetic visions of reality in the works of Miłosz and Ashbery. She works with Martin Heidegger's philosophy of phenomenology and applies key Heideggerian terms—Dasein, space, time, and culture—to explore the reality created by or alluded to in their writings. Jargon heavy but useful.

Milne, Ira Mark, ed. *Poetry for Students*. Vol. 28. Detroit: Thomson/Gale Group, 2008. Contains an analysis of Ashbery's "Self-Portrait in a Convex Mirror."

Shoptaw, John. *On the Outside Looking Out: John Ashbery's Poetry*. Cambridge, Mass.: Harvard University Press, 1994. Abundant and detailed information about Ashbery's life, publication history, and manuscripts make the book valuable. It offers an intriguing but perhaps overworked and insufficiently proven argument that Ashbery's elusiveness derives from his homosexuality.

Vendler, Helen. "Toying with Words." Review of *Plainsphere*. *The New York Times Book Review*, December 13, 2009, p. 14. Vendler reviews the collection dedicated to Ashbery's partner, David Kermani. She notes his wordplay and praises his lyric poems.

Vincent, John Emil. *John Ashbery and You: His Later Books*. Athens: University of Georgia Press, 2007. Examines *And the Stars Were Shining*, *Your Name Here*, and other later works by Ashbery.

Daniel L. Guillory; Philip K. Jason; Sarah Hilbert
Updated by Frank Day

ROSE AUSLÄNDER

Born: Czernowitz, Bukovina (now Chernivtsi, Ukraine); May 11, 1901
Died: Düsseldorf, Germany; January 3, 1988

PRINCIPAL POETRY
Der Regenbogen, 1939
Blinder Sommer, 1965
36 Gerechte, 1967
Inventar, 1972
Ohne Visum, 1974
Andere Zeichen, 1975
Gesammelte Gedichte, 1976 (expanded 1977)
Noch ist Raum, 1976
Doppelspiel, 1977
Es ist alles anders, 1977
Selected Poems, 1977
Aschensommer, 1978
Es bleibt noch viel zu sagen, 1978
Mutterland, 1978
Ein Stück weiter, 1979
Einverständnis, 1980
Einen Drachen reiten, 1981
Im Atemhaus wohnen, 1981
Mein Atem heisst jetzt, 1981
Schatten im Spiegel, 1981 (in Hebrew)
Mein Venedig versinkt nicht, 1982
Südlich wartet ein wärmeres Land, 1982
So sicher atmet nur Tod, 1983
Gesammelte Werke in sieben Bänden und einen Nachtragsband, 1984-1990 (8 volumes)
Festtage in Manhattan, 1985
Ich zähl die Sterne meiner Worte, 1985
Brief aus Rosen, 1994
Mother Tongue, 1995
Schattenwald, 1995
The Forbidden Tree: Englische Gedichte, 1995

OTHER LITERARY FORMS
The reputation of Rose Ausländer (OWS-lehn-dehr) is based solely on her poetry. Volume 3 of her collected works, containing her writings from 1966 to 1975, includes several short prose pieces; volume 4, containing her writings from the year 1976, comprises, aside from her poetry, only one short autobiographical piece.

ACHIEVEMENTS
In 1957, the highly acclaimed poet Marianne Moore awarded Rose Ausländer the poetry prize of the Wagner College in New York. In 1967, Ausländer received the Meersburger Droste Prize; in 1977, the Ida Dehmel Prize and the Andreas Gryphius Prize; in 1978, the

prize of the Federation of German Industry; and in 1980, the Roswitha Medal of the city of Bad Gandersheim.

BIOGRAPHY

Rose Ausländer was born Rosalie Beatrice Ruth Scherzer on May 11, 1901, to Jewish parents in Czernowitz, the capital of Bukovina. Her mother's name was Etie Binder and her father's, Sigmund Scherzer. Originally her father was supposed to become a rabbi, but later he decided to become a businessman. Until 1918, Bukovina was the easternmost part of the Habsburg Empire. The population of Czernowitz was about 110,000 and consisted of Germans, Romanians, Ukranians, Poles, and a large proportion of Jews. The Jewish population had assumed the role of preserving the German culture and of being an intermediary between it and the Slavic culture. As a child, Ausländer was educated in the German-Austrian school system, but she also learned Hebrew and Yiddish. Through her schooling she became acquainted with the German literary classics, especially those by Johann Wolfgang von Goethe, Friedrich Schiller, and Heinrich Heine. She enjoyed a harmonious childhood, which was filled with love toward her parents and her native country. With the advent of World War I and the Russian occupation of Czernowitz, however, this peaceful existence was abruptly terminated. Ausländer's family fled first to Bucharest and later to Vienna. There they led a life full of suffering and misery. As a result of the Treaty of Versailles, Bukovina became a part of Romania. The family returned to their hometown, where Ausländer finished her secondary education and subsequently attended the University of Czernowitz, majoring in literature and philosophy. At the university, she became especially interested in Plato, Baruch Spinoza, and Constantin Brunner, a follower of Spinoza who lived in Berlin at that time. Later the teachings of Brunner were to become an integral part of her poetry.

Ausländer's studies and her active membership in literary circles exposed her to the poetry of Friedrich Hölderlin, Franz Kafka, Georg Trakl, Rainer Maria Rilke, Else Lasker-Schüler, and Gottfried Benn. Despite their distance from Vienna, the Jewish literary circles in Czernowitz had adopted the Viennese Karl

Kraus as mentor. With the publication of the journal *Die Fackel* (the torch), Kraus had assumed the role of the "high priest of truth," the herald of an ethical humanism and poetry against nationalist chauvinism and the corruption of bureaucracy and politics.

In 1921, as a result of the worsening of the family's already dire financial situation following her father's death, Ausländer decided to emigrate to the United States. She emigrated with her childhood friend Ignaz Ausländer. After failing to establish themselves in Minneapolis-St. Paul, Minnesota, they settled in New York City, where they were married in 1923. Ausländer had a position in a bank, and her husband worked as a mechanic. The marriage was not to last; they separated in 1926 and were finally divorced in 1930. In 1924, Ausländer met Alfred Margul-Sperber, who later became the major sponsor of her poetry after her return to Czernowitz. In 1926, she became a U.S. citizen and in 1927 visited Constantin Brunner in Berlin. She returned to New York in 1928, where she lived with Helios Hecht, a graphologist, a writer, and an editor of several periodicals. She published her first poems in the *Westlicher Herold-Kalender*, a Minneapolis publication, and later published a few poems in the *New Yorker Volkszeitung*. In 1931, she returned to Czernowitz with Hecht and remained there to care for her ailing mother. After her prolonged absence from the United States, her U.S. citizenship was revoked in 1934. Eventually, she and Hecht separated.

Between 1931 and the outbreak of World War II, Ausländer published poems in various periodicals. Margul-Sperber arranged for the publication of her first volume of poetry, *Der Regenbogen* (the rainbow), despite the Romanian government's policy of suppressing non-Romanian literature. In 1941, the Germans occupied Czernowitz, forced the Jews to return to the old ghetto, and periodically deported groups to concentration camps in Transnistria. Ausländer and her mother escaped almost certain death by hiding from the Gestapo in basements where friends supplied them with food and clothes. The experience of persecution and underground existence was to become the motivating force behind Ausländer's later poetry. In secret poetry-reading groups, she met Paul Antschel, who later changed his name to Paul Celan. It was during this time that she came to believe in the existential function of poetry to preserve her own identity in a hostile world.

When the Soviet Union seized Bukovina after World War II, Ausländer, together with her mother and her brother's family, left Czernowitz for Bucharest. With the help of friends in the United States, she was able to obtain an immigration visa but only for herself; her family had to stay behind. In the fall of 1946, she arrived again in New York and found work as a translator and foreign-language secretary for a large shipping company. All her attempts to obtain an immigration visa for her mother proved futile. The news of her mother's death in 1947 caused a psychological breakdown, after which for some time she wrote poetry only in English.

Although Ausländer became naturalized again in 1948, she never felt at home in New York. The American lifestyle remained alien to her. During a visit to Europe in 1957, she again saw Celan, who had emigrated to Paris. He introduced her to contemporary European poetry, which resulted in the rebirth of her poetry in German. The new poems, however, were stripped of all harmonizing prosodic elements.

In 1961, in failing health, Ausländer could not continue her job and was forced to live on her Social Security income. In 1966, she received additional support from the West German government. By that time, she had once again returned to Europe, where she attempted unsuccessfully to settle in Vienna, which was to her the cultural center of the former Habsburg Empire. Finally, she moved to Düsseldorf, West Germany, in 1965. The year 1965 was not only the date of the publication of her second volume of poetry, twenty-six years after her first one, but also the year of her belated reintroduction to a German audience. Although she could not return to her native country, she returned to her mother tongue, the only medium through which she could express her poetic message and establish a dialogue with an audience. In 1970, she moved into Nelly-Sachs-Haus, a Jewish home for the aged, which she made her permanent home. After a long illness and an increasing retreat from the outside world, she died in 1988. She left more than twenty thousand pages of manuscripts and typescripts, as well as numerous notebooks, material that was used to form much of her posthumous collections.

ANALYSIS

Rose Ausländer did not become recognized as a major poet until the late 1960's and early 1970's, when volumes of her poetry appeared in rapid succession. At the same time, various German newspapers and magazines printed some of her poems, and her work appeared in anthologies as well. Because of the outbreak of World War II and her Jewish background, her early writings had never reached a sizable audience beyond her hometown. Not until her visit with Celan in 1957, when she became acquainted with his elliptic Hermetic style and that of his European contemporaries, did she adopt the curt, laconic manner of her mature poetry. In this style, she vividly expressed the horrors of the Nazi persecution and her total desolation and despair, which continued even after the war, in her exile in the United States and later in Germany. Although the trauma of her persecution and exile was not diminished, she was able to transcend the pain of these experiences to reach a level beyond despair, a new affirmation of life and its riches—each object of which becomes the motif for a poem. Perhaps her hard-won message of consolation and redemption explains the increasing recognition of her achievements.

The titles of Ausländer's collections, such as *Blinder Sommer* (blind summer), *Ohne Visum* (without a visa), and *Aschensommer* (ash summer), like the images and motifs in the poems themselves, such as "ash," "smoke," and "dust," clearly reveal that Ausländer's poetry is directly linked to the Holocaust. She deeply identified with the suffering of her people. Even her first volume of poetry in 1939, however, reflected a troubled outlook on life. Here, nature, homeland, and love provide a refuge from a threatening reality, as the danger of national socialism loomed on the horizon. Despite their harmonizing prosodic elements, these early poems are characterized by a beginning awareness of the general crisis during these years. This awareness is put into the cosmogonic perspective of the world's fall from its original godlike state. Poetry became to Ausländer the only means of renewing this divine state. This concept is in direct accordance with Spinoza's philosophical theory of harmonizing microcosm and macrocosm. As acceptable as the harmonizing prosodic elements may be in this idealized conception, however, they are self-contradictory in the poems from the underground, appropriately titled *Ghetto-motifs*. They first became available to a wider audience in volume 1 of *Gesammelte Werke*, containing the poetry from 1927 to 1956. The English poems written from 1948 to 1956 in the United States continue in this style, which Ausländer abandoned when she was confronted with the modern development of poetry during her 1957 visit to Europe.

HOLOCAUST AND PERSECUTION

Aside from the departure from rhyme and classical meters, her change in style can best be seen in the inclusion of the Holocaust into the cosmogonic process and in the reduction of the imagery to key words or constellations. The images of sun, stars, and earth lose all their divine characteristics, and references to the Holocaust are so explicit that they evoke the absolute perversion and denaturalization of the human calling. "Ash-summer," "ash-rain" or "smoke is pouring out of the eyes of the cannibals" are only a few examples. The trauma of persecution is carried into the depiction of Ausländer's experience of exile in the United States. The escape to freedom across the Atlantic resembles the never- ending search of the Flying Dutchman for a final resting place; the Nazi persecution is reenacted in the United States: "Men in Ku Klux Klan hoods, with swastikas and guns as weapons, surround you, the room smokes with danger"; the "ghetto-garb has not been discarded" despite a "fragrant" table full of food. This threat overshadows all personal relationships: "Can it be/ that I will see you again/ in April/ free of ashes?" The exile only reinforces the expulsion from paradise; the house turns into a prison, New York into a jungle, the subway into a funeral procession of war victims, and the summer heat of one hundred degrees evokes the image of the cremations in the concentration camps. Even more significant, the technology and modern civilization in New York are seen as symbols of the absolute denial of God.

YEARNING FOR HER HOMELAND

Against this background of persecution and exile, Ausländer's native country takes on the qualities of a fairy tale—it is a "once-upon-a-time home" representing a "once-upon-a-time existence"—or is mythologized as filled with the presence of God: "the Jordan river emptied into the Pruth" (the Pruth being the main river of Bukovina, the country of beech trees). Although political reality does not allow a physical return to her homeland, Ausländer's "always back to the Pruth" can only be a spiritual return to the full awareness of her cultural, religious, and family roots, to her beginnings; in its "u-topian" fulfillment it would signify the unity of beginning and ending. The poet calls this state "the dwelling," in conscious or subconscious reference to the Kabbalistic *schechina*, which symbolizes the dwelling place of God's bride, or the lowest level of the sefiroth tree. She laments, "Flying on the air swing/ Europe America Europe// I do not dwell/ I only live"; her settling in Germany becomes merely another stage in her continuous exile.

The poet's desire to return to her homeland corresponds to that of the Jewish people to reestablish their homeland in Israel: "Phoenix/ my people/ cremated// risen/ among cypress and/ orange trees." To these "wandering brethren," to "Ahasver, the wandering Jew," she offers the Jewish greeting "Le Cháim": "We/ risen/ from the void/ . . . we are talking/ softly/ with risen/ brethren." Despite that bond, her social and national identity has been lost forever: "born without a visa to this world/ she never looks the other way/ people like us are always/ suspicious." For that reason poetry itself takes over the function of reestablishing a dwelling place that secures Ausländer's spiritual identity.

THE REDEMPTIVE PROCESS

The creative poetic process had to build upon the foundation of annihilation and exile before any redemption and transfiguration could occur. As late as 1979, Ausländer maintained, in a poem: "I do not forget// my family roots/ mother's voice/ the first kiss/ the mountains of Bukovina/ the escape in World War I/ the suffering in Vienna/ the bombs in World War II// the invasion of the Nazis/ the anguish in the basement/ the doctor who saved our lives/ the bitter sweet America// Hölderlin Trakl Celan// my agony to write/ the compulsion to write/ still." In the strictest consistency with her fate, the redemptive process begins, "retracing my steps/ in the urn of memory," and culminates in a paradoxical statement that combines trauma and bliss: "Nothing is lost/ in the urn/ the ash is breathing." The ambiguity of this statement is heightened by the middle line being grammatically linked to both the first and the third lines. This grammatical linking is employed again in these lines: "how beautiful/ ash can blossom/ in the blood." Only by "losing herself in the jungle of words" can Ausländer "find herself again in the miracle of the word," ultimately God's Word, "my word/ born out of despair// out of the desperate hope/ that poetry/ is still possible." Only poetry can grant this renewed existence: "mother tongue is putting me together// mosaic of people" in a space "free of ashes/ among verses." Poetry offers renewed life, the divine breath of life that links past and future in a timeless present: "The past/ has composed me/ I have/ inherited the future// My breath is called/ NOW."

Such stances became more frequent in Ausländer's old age, possibly because the poet, being bedridden, had only poetry left as a means of self-affirmation: "My fatherland is dead/ they have buried it/ in fire// I live/ in my motherland/ the word"—an obvious play on the word "mother tongue," which has taken on the extreme existential function of being the only guarantor of Ausländer's identity. Even then, this process does not entail an escape from reality but rather builds upon "professing to the earth and its dangerous secrets . . . to man I profess myself with all the words that create me." It is a reciprocal act which grants poetic identity by giving meaning to both humankind and life. For that reason, Ausländer can arrive at an otherwise unbelievable statement affirming the poetic process out of the annihilation of humanity: "Magnificent despite all/ dust of flesh// This light-birth/ in an eyelash womb/ Lips/ yes/ much remains/ to be said."

Ausländer has called the specific mode of this poetic process "this dual play/ flower words/ war stammering." It is a play of mediation or reconciliation between language and reality that might result in simplistic affirmation if the never forgotten point of departure were not to forbid such a reduction. On the contrary, this play takes on mystical proportions, striving for the redemption of the world by making it transparent to manifest its divine destiny. This interdependence between language and reality culminates in the image of the crystal, in which microcosm and macrocosm meet, in reverence to Spinoza, who was a lens maker as

well as a philosopher: "My saint/ is called Benedict// He has/ polished/ the universe// Infinite crystal/ out of whose heart/ the light radiates."

Although the later poems, especially those after 1981, reduce the poetic process to such a degree that they can become manneristic, Ausländer's total poetic production clearly shows her to be among the most significant post-World War II poets. She has been able to find meaning in life despite the traumas she has experienced. Her "self-portrait" lists all the conditions that denied her the status of a regular member of society and at the same time testifies to poetry's power to transcend personal tragedy: "Jewish gypsy/ raised/ in the German language/ under the black and yellow flag// Borders pushed me/ to Latins Slavs/ Americans Germanic people// Europe/ in your womb/ I dream/ my next birth."

BIBLIOGRAPHY

Boase-Beier, Jean. "Translating Repetition." *Journal of European Studies* 24, no. 96 (December, 1994): 403. Any literary translation must involve a careful stylistic analysis of the source text, particularly the translation of poetry. Includes an English translation of her poem "Damit kein Licht uns liebe."

Bower, Kathrin M. *Ethics and Remembrance in the Poetry of Nelly Sachs and Rose Ausländer*. Rochester, N.Y.: Camden House, 2000. Critical interpretation of the poetry of Nelly Sachs and Ausländer relating to the Holocaust during World War II. Includes extensive bibliographic references and an index.

_____. "Rose Ausländer." In *Women Writers in German-Speaking Countries: A Bio-Bibliographical Critical Sourcebook*, edited by Elke P. Frederiksen and Elizabeth G. Ametsbichler. Westport, Conn.: Greenwood Press, 1998. Excellent overview of Ausländer's life, the main themes of her poetry, and its critical reception. English translations of German quotations. Includes bibliographies of primary and secondary works and translations.

_____. "Searching for the (M)Other: The Rhetoric of Longing in Post-Holocaust Poems by Nelly Sachs and Rose Ausländer." *Women in German Yearbook* 12 (1996): 125-147. English translations and interpretations of six of Ausländer's poems.

Frederiksen, Elke P., and Elizabeth G. Ametsbichler, eds. *Women Writers in German-Speaking Countries: A Bio-Bibliographical Critical Sourcebook.* Westport, Conn.: Greenwood Press, 1997. Includes a chapter on Ausländer and an introductory essay that examines the history of literature by women in German-speaking countries. Includes an extensive bibliography.

Glenn, Jerry. "Blumenworte/Kriegsgestammel: The Poetry of Rose Ausländer." *Modern Austrian Literature* 12, nos. 3/4 (1979). A brief critical study of selected poems by Ausländer.

Keith-Smith, Brian. "Rose Ausländer." In *Encyclopedia of German Literature*, edited by Matthias Konzett. Vol. 1. Chicago: Fitzroy Dearborn, 2000. Outlines Ausländer's poetic development, from the early influences to the final epigrammatic poems.

Klaus Weissenberger

B

JIMMY SANTIAGO BACA

Born: Santa Fe, New Mexico; January 2, 1952

PRINCIPAL POETRY

Jimmy Santiago Baca, 1978
Immigrants in Our Own Land, 1979
Swords of Darkness, 1981
What's Happening, 1982
Poems Taken from My Yard, 1986
Martín; &, Meditations on the South Valley, 1987
Black Mesa Poems, 1989 (includes *Poems Taken from My Yard*)
Immigrants in Our Own Land, and Selected Earlier Poems, 1990
In the Way of the Sun, 1997
Set This Book on Fire, 1999
Que linda la brisa, 2000 (with Benjamin Alier Sáenz; photographs by James Drake)
Healing Earthquakes: A Love Story in Poems, 2001
C-Train (Dream Boy's Story) and Thirteen Mexicans, 2002
Winter Poems Along the Rio Grande, 2004
Spring Poems Along the Rio Grande, 2007
Rita and Julia, 2008

OTHER LITERARY FORMS

Jimmy Santiago Baca (BAH-kah) has drawn extensively on the difficult circumstances of his early years and on his involvement with the social and political concerns of his cultural community in his poetry. The autobiographical orientation of his writing often results in the placing of prose commentary amid poetry. Similarly, in his memoir *Working in the Dark: Reflections of a Poet of the Barrio* (1992), essays and reflective accounts of his experiences are blended with passages of poetic intensity. *A Place to Stand: The Making of a Poet* (2001) is a recollective re-creation of his youth, adolescence, and years in prison. He also coedited *The*

Heat: Steelworkers Lives and Legends (2001; with Stacy James) and wrote, as well as coproduced, the film *Bound by Honor* (1993; released on video as *Blood in, Blood Out*). The letters that Baca and Denise Levertov exchanged between 1976 and 1987 were issued by the Stanford University Library Department of Special Collections in 1998.

ACHIEVEMENTS

Jimmy Santiago Baca has been recognized for his efforts with a National Endowment for the Arts Literary Fellowship (1986), the Pushcart Prize (1988), the American Book Award from the Before Columbus Foundation (1988), and the International Hispanic Heritage Award (1990). He has also served as the Wallace Stevens Professor at Yale (1989) and held the Regents Berkeley Chair at the University of California (1990), and he was the winner of the International Poetry competition at Taos, New Mexico, in 1996 and 1997. In 2001, he received a Discover Award through Barnes and Noble, as well as an International Hispanic Heritage Award for his memoir *A Place to Stand*. In 2003, he was awarded an honorary doctorate from the University of New Mexico. In 2006, Baca won the Cornelius P. Turner Award for his contributions to education, justice, public service, and social welfare.

BIOGRAPHY

Jimmy Santiago Baca was born José Santiago Baca into the chaos of a fractious family living in an adobe shack on the outskirts of Sante Fe in 1952. His father, Damacio Baca, of Apache and Yaqui lineage, and his mother, Cecilia Padilla, a woman with a Hispanic background, left him with his Indio grandparents when he was two. Baca stayed with them for three years, then was placed in a boy's home and later foster care, before drifting onto the streets of Albuquerque's barrio at thirteen. In and out of detention and correction facilities, he was in prison at seventeen when he "confirmed" or recognized his identity as a Chicano after leafing through a stolen book, *Cuatrocientos cincuenta años del pueblo Chicano = Four Hundred Fifty Years of Chicano History in Pictures* (1976), the only kind of text he could understand, because he was functionally illiterate. Speaking of his father, but alluding to his own situation at that time, he observed, "He was everything that was bad in America. He was brown, spoke Spanish, was from a Native American background, had no education."

In a characteristic act of defiance, he took a guard's schoolbook, glanced at it, and realized that "sounds created music in me and happiness" as he gradually enunciated some lines of a poem by William Wordsworth. Recalling that he was a *vato loco* (crazy dude) serving a five-year term in a federal prison on drug charges, he began a self-directed program of personal education that rapidly led to an explosion of creative energy. Within a short time, he was writing poetry about his present state and his troubled past, composing letters for other inmates, and listening to the stories of older men whose stories "made barrio life come alive." A number of his poems were published in the magazine *New Karui*, and with the assistance of Denise Levertov, a prominent poet and social activist, Baca was able to produce a chapbook, *Jimmy Santiago Baca*, in 1978.

After his release from prison, Baca traveled to North Carolina to live with Virginia Love Long, with whom he had been corresponding, then returned to Albuquerque, where he worked as a janitor at a treatment center for abused teenagers. There, he met Beatrice Narcisco, a therapist who recognized that, in spite of his unsettled nature, "he was great with children," and they were married six months later. During the 1980's, Baca began to build a national reputation as a poet and received a B.A. in English from the University of New Mexico in 1984, but he was unable to completely withdraw from drug addiction. *Martín; &, Meditations on the South Valley*, the first of three books that Baca published with the eminent New Directions press, won the American Book Award, which led to teaching opportunities at Yale and the University of California, Berkeley.

In 1993, Baca cowrote and produced the film *Bound by Honor* and spent much of the 1990's living with his family on the Black Mesa of Albuquerque's South Valley, editing and contributing to various anthologies concerned with issues he cared about, producing films, and reading poetry throughout the Southwest. At the end of the decade, he published two compact books of poetry, the intensely personal *Set This Book on Fire* and

a collaboration with the photographer James Drake and the poet Benjamin Alier Sáenz, *Que linda la brisa*, which included Baca's eight-part searing re-creation of the flow of consciousness of transsexual prostitutes living on the fringes of society. In the twenty-first century, Baca continued to work extensively with at-risk youth in workshops, read his poetry throughout the United States, and declared himself "back in action after a long sabbatical from the publishing world," issuing from Grove/Atlantic a memoir that concentrated on his life inside a maximum security prison, *A Place to Stand*, and a new book of poems, *Healing Earthquakes*, tracing the course of a romantic relationship from beginning to end. In 2005, he created a nonprofit foundation, Cedar Tree, that offers writing workshops and assistance with documentary films. His *Winter Poems Along the Rio Grande* and *Spring Poems Along the Rio Grande* reflect his life and a connection he feels with nature and creativity as he runs along the Rio Grande. More meditative and less intense than his earlier volumes, they were followed by the more intense *Rita and Julia*. In 2009, Baca published his first novel, *A Glass of Water*.

ANALYSIS

Describing himself as a "detribalized Apache"—a man born and raised outside the predominant social patterns of American life—Jimmy Santiago Baca has based his poetry on a commitment to the presentation and preservation of a marginalized, degraded, and often silent segment of American society. Speaking about his utilization of Chicano motifs in his work, he has said that one can "be successful in this society and still offer it all the resources that come from [one's] culture." His faith in the latent redemptive energy inherent in the production of poetry, an act that he regards as responsible for his own survival and that he feels can restore dignity to other people who have struggled with destabilizing psychic states, has enabled him to explore and express conditions of extreme mental and emotional duress. His work, frequently autobiographical in nature, charts a course from near total despair through periods of reversal and dejection toward a life of real accomplishment in literary and social terms.

In conversations about his work, Baca has consistently stressed his belief that poetry is the ultimate act of self-creation, explaining that he has been able to overcome the very grim circumstances of his youth and teenage years through a poetic process of anguished rebirth that he says "gives you a brief view of the intense beauty of life." Because his work deals with the most sordid aspects of existence, the "intense beauty" is not reduced or trivialized by easy emotion or appeals to bogus and shallow sentimentality. Contrary to William Butler Yeats's observation in "The Second Coming" that "the worst/ Are full of passionate intensity," Baca's poetry is an endorsement of the redemptive, inspiring qualities that passion communicated through appropriate language can generate. The "passionate intensity" of Baca's work has lost none of its fiery energy or inventive brilliance.

Martín; &, Meditations on the South Valley

Denise Levertov, who was instrumental in bringing Baca's early work into print, wrote in her eloquent introduction to *Martín; &, Meditations on the South Valley* that the work "draws upon elements in Baca's own history, but does not duplicate them."

The volume consists of two long narrative poems about Baca's semifictionalized figure, who follows a path similar to the author's in a quest for a stable family and a real home. Along the course of this archetypal journey, the narrator passes through a period of personal desolation; a barren, desert landscape; and then on toward a fertile valley, where he establishes a secure place to dwell. The second half of the volume opens with the destruction by fire of the house that represents Martín's initial removal from the poverty of the past, and then proceeds as Martín returns to the barrio, the place of his worst experiences as a young man. Now, seen from a different perspective, the barrio offers a harsh but penetrating vision of beauty that Martín recognizes as one of the sources of the lyric element found in all his work. The poem closes with the reconstruction of the house destroyed by fire and the impulse to write poems to replace the ones lost in the blaze, including the separate poems in the book itself.

Baca called the poem "the rediscovery of who I was" and noted that it marked his reemergence into the world after years lost to drug addiction. He designed

Jimmy Santiago Baca (Lawrence Benton/Courtesy, New Directions)

the poem as an attempt to portray the full scope of a Chicano civilization as opposed to the "official" depiction, "a long poem that could describe what happened here in the last twenty years." Poet Gary Soto described the poem as "a sort of *Ironweed* of the West," with many Spanish words, including abundant street slang, that conveyed the unique flavor of a region essentially invisible prior to the work of Baca and others of his generation.

Immigrants in Our Own Land, and Selected Earlier Poems

In *Immigrants in Our Own Land, and Selected Earlier Poems*, Baca chose a title that expressed his position as an outsider, challenging a dominant culture that had effectively forced his community into a "protective" silence. Most of the poems were written while Baca was in prison, detailing a life in jail often set in sharp contrast with dreams of "the handsome world" outside. The title poem delineates the ways in which inmates establish their own close fraternity of cooperation, and it is characteristic of the ingenuity and methods of endurance to which a beleaguered cohort of society has resorted for survival.

The poems about incarceration are candid and explicit without being brutal, as Baca is not trying to shock a more genteel audience. Their intent is to inform, and the clear-eyed way in which Baca describes his life and the people he met is intriguing without being sensationalistic or falsely romantic. Many of the poems ("In My Land," "So Mexicans Are Taking Jobs from Americans") are specifically political without being polemical, with Baca's stance introducing an element of humor that ameliorates his justified anger. The exuberance of his mocking but ultimately idealistic "The New Warden" is an indication of his unquenchable thirst for a better life and of the guarded optimism that informs his accounts of hard times and hard men.

BLACK MESA POEMS

The Black Mesa near Albuquerque was sacred ground to the Isleta tribal group, Baca's Indio ancestors, and in *Black Mesa Poems*, Baca celebrates the geological features of the land and the generations who lived there. "My book is a homage to the people of the South Valley," Baca observed, "a gift of gratitude for keeping the culture alive." By honoring the Chicano community that he regards as his true spiritual home, Baca traces his evolution from anger on the edge of a violence he feels will always be in his soul to a position where he can accept his obligations as a husband and father.

The endurance and ingenuity of the people he depicts in many poems present examples of maturity and persistence in situations at least equal in difficulty to Baca's own troubled past. In the often anthologized "Green Chile," Baca's tribute to his grandmother, who raised him in his early years, the poet uses the ubiquitous plant, which lends "historical grandeur" to homes and vegetable stands, as a symbol of cultural richness and vividly describes the pleasures involved in the preparation and consumption of a food that permits people to take part in "this old, beautiful ritual" central to Chicano life.

SET THIS BOOK ON FIRE

During the latter part of the 1990's, Baca published his first collection in a decade, *Set This Book on Fire*, and contributed an eight-part sequence to accompany photographs by James Drake (*Que linda la brisa*). *Set This Book on Fire* is divided into three parts, each beginning with a poem—"In '78," "In '88," "In '98"— that sets a tone for the following decade. The initial section is a retrospective consideration of Baca's prison years, centered on the poem "This Dark Side," which Baca acknowledges "has always haunted me." He identifies this psychic demon as something that has been "fiercely adamant in its opposition/ to all the good I create." The manner in which he has been able to resist his "dark side" is discussed in "The Day I Stopped" ("being an alien to myself") and several other poems that conclude the section.

Part 2 is a heartfelt evocation of people who have been close to him and a poignant examination of the contrary impulses to be near his family and to return to a vagabond life. Part 3 is a reflective meditation on what it means to be a poet, with the poems gathered in a narrative that touches on some of his experiences in elite universities and at times when he "took [his] songs to the gutter to sing them to drunks." The disjunction between poetic ambition and the actuality of the poet's life runs through this section like a dark rhythm, summarized in the last poem, "Why and When and How," which concludes with an ongoing query about dreams when "we heard angels/ whisper once in our sleep," which have devolved into moments when words "scatter/ like crumbs on the floor."

QUE LINDA LA BRISA

The eight linked poems in *Que linda la brisa* are efforts by a man who admits that he comes "from a macho side" to "get into" the "skin" of someone who is the polar opposite of himself. The poems attempt to understand the psychology of transvestites from the Mexican interior who are working as entertainers in saloons in Juárez. "Smoking Mirrors" begins in the mind of "A hybrid flower/ Of honey and poison,/ half moon half sun," who is "an constant conflict." Baca's ability to understand something of cross-dressing is a consequence of his own internal divisions, and his capacity to appreciate the position of someone on the margins of society owes something to his own heritage as a person born of a cultural confluence marginalized by mainstream America.

HEALING EARTHQUAKES

In *Healing Earthquakes*, Baca lets loose a flood of confessions, prayers, and odes of love. Using lyricism, Baca explores the human soul, creating a romance from beginning to end. The book introduces the reader to a man and woman before they meet, then describes their meeting and how they fall in love. It follows them through their decision to create a family, the eventual realization of each other's irreconcilable faults, the conflict, and the breakup. It also explores how they get past their bitterness and resentment. Throughout the relationship, readers are shown an array of emotions from loneliness to joy to irritation. Baca also uses the book to explore the beauty and cruelty of the desert, the wisdom of animals, and life on small Chicano farms. The book is heavy with metaphor. "Healing" in the title resonates with the idea of falling in and out of love. The poems in the book are deeply personal and contradictory. "At the airport on the floor with my laptop writing you love poems/ you'll never have a love like mine, Lisana, ever." The book begins in the barrio, with an angry teenager in need of love, and ends in a garage, where the speaker contemplates the Chicano men who change his tires.

C-TRAIN (DREAM BOY'S STORY) AND THIRTEEN MEXICANS

In *C-Train (Dream Boy's Story) and Thirteen Mexicans*, Baca takes a radically different approach to his work. The book is a cross between Allen Ginsberg's "Howl" and Jack Kerouac's *On the Road* (1957). Baca uses a variety of forms, from poetry with short lines to pages and pages of long verse lines with no grammatical punctuation. In this collection, Baca uses intense lyricism to explore the dark underbelly of addiction and shows readers some of what is brutal and unjust in the world. "C-Train" looks at the life of Dream Boy, a young man who finds himself enslaved to cocaine. The work is understanding of how intoxication can be deeply enjoyable, but at the same time laments the fact that people can become powerless to addiction. In "Thirteen Mexicans," Baca writes about the gulf between the American dream and the reality that the Chi-

cano community faces. In elegiac vignettes, Baca shows life in the barrio as beautiful and yet ugly to white society. Baca gives voice to the disenfranchised living in unforgiving landscapes.

WINTER POEMS ALONG THE RIO GRANDE

Winter Poems Along the Rio Grande consists of thirty-nine numbered poems that form a personal meditation on the poet's life. Baca, who often runs alongside the river, uses the rhythm of his footsteps to punctuate descriptions of the plants and animals by the river and his meditations on family, friends, and his life—past, present, and future. Baca sets the theme in the first poem: ". . . I run, I breathe/ shattering my self-centeredness/ against each tree, bush, bird, horse and field I sight," he says, seeking insight from the blue space between boughs "where there is nothing but the sound of silence." After the five-mile run, he stops and prays to the light, the darkness, his ancestors, and the great bear, thanking them and asking for guidance and moral strength.

The poems are positive in nature, despite describing adversity; this optimism is a departure from Baca's earlier, edgier works. In poem 5, he writes ". . . I was thinking/ of my brother, and others who never made it to live the life/ they dreamed." He tries to learn from the Rio Grande, which he likens to "a pair of mother's hands." Like Walt Whitman, Baca uses the natural world to address the universal problems faced by all humans, but he does so while staying grounded in his Chicano and Native American ancestry. In poem 21, he recalls seeing roadrunners in a field as he picks up discarded beer cans from the irrigation ditch and thinks of his brother and parents, killed by alcohol. He notes how children believe in happiness until ". . . the jewels of our eyes shatter/ and sorrow tipped days/ pierce deep into our hearts." He counters this with prayers for a peaceful existence and love for those around him, particularly the mother of his children—"you on the bed, nursing our son,/ your laughter a prayer to the wind." This meditative book uses the river and running to express the spiritual side of Baca.

SPRING POEMS ALONG THE RIO GRANDE

In *Spring Poems Along the Rio Grande*, Baca returns to the landscape and issues explored in *Winter Poems Along the Rio Grande*. In thirty-three titled poems, Baca again describes the land and life along the river, which flows through the poems, creating a natural progression through the seasons. As he runs, he meditates on his hopes and fears, both personal and for the nation. His somewhat more outward orientation is reflected in the opening poem, "The Heart Sharpens Its Machete," which begins "This winter has been a mild one . . ." and contrasts the mildness of the natural world to the horrors of war in the human world: ". . . beyond the bosque/ severe freezing struck the souls of millions." He makes references in some of the poems to his earlier life, but the focus in this volume is on the present and the future. He grounds himself in the present by paying attention to the natural world— blue herons, roadrunners, flowering plum trees, cottonwoods—of the Rio Grande. In "A Green Honesty in Every Leaf," he writes, "The Rio Grande bosque/ doesn't lie—when it's ready to show affection/ it does—there is green honesty in every leaf/ humility in each blade of grass."

OTHER MAJOR WORKS

LONG FICTION: *A Glass of Water*, 2009.

SHORT FICTION: *The Importance of a Piece of Paper*, 2004.

PLAY: *Los tres hijos de Julia*, pr. 1991.

SCREENPLAY: *Bound by Honor*, 1993 (with Floyd Mutrux and Ross Thomas).

NONFICTION: *A Place to Stand: The Making of a Poet*, 2001.

EDITED TEXT: *The Heat: Steelworker Lives and Legends*, 2001 (with Stacy James).

MISCELLANEOUS: *Working in the Dark: Reflections of a Poet of the Barrio*, 1992 (essays, journal entries, and poetry).

BIBLIOGRAPHY

Baca, Jimmy Santiago. "An Interview with Jimmy Santiago Baca." Interview by Frederick Luis Aldama. *MELUS* 30, no. 3 (Fall, 2005): 113-127. Baca talks about *C-Train (Dream Boy's Story)* and *Thir-teen Mexicans* and *The Importance of a Piece of Paper*.

_____. "An Interview with Jimmy Santiago Baca." Interview by Lara Stapleton. *Indiana Review* 28, no. 1 (Summer, 2006) 49-53. Baca discusses his short-story collection, *The Importance of a Piece of Paper*, and *Winter Poems Along the Rio Grande*.

_____. "Jimmy Santiago Baca." http://www.jimmy santiagobaca.com. Official Web site for Baca. Contains a biography and information on Baca's activities. Provides links to other sites with information about the writer.

Coppola, Vincent. "The Moon in Jimmy Baca." *Esquire*, June, 1993, 48-56. A revealing profile that links the poet's life with his work.

Gish, Robert Franklin. *Beyond Bounds: Cross-Cultural Essays on Anglo, American Indian, and Chicano Literature*. Albuquerque: University of New Mexico Press, 1996. Contains an informative essay on Baca's use of the myth of the legendary city of Aztlán and his consideration of the sociology of the border.

Levertov, Denise. Introduction to *Martín; &, Meditations on the South Valley*, by Jimmy Santiago Baca. New York: New Directions, 1987. An extremely incisive discussion by the poet who was instrumental in helping Baca publish his work.

Rector, Liam. "The Documentary of What Is." *Hudson Review* 41 (Summer, 1989): 393-400. One of the best literary analyses of Baca's poetic methods.

St. John, Janet. Review of *Spring Poems Along the Rio Grande*. *Booklist* 103, no. 17 (May 1, 2007): 64. St. John describes the poems as a meditation on season and says that they reveal his sources of poetic inspiration.

Schubnell, Mathias. "The Inner Landscape of the Self in Jimmy Santiago Baca's *Martín; &, Meditations on the South Valley*." *Southwestern American Literature* 21 (1995): 167-173. Focuses on the personal and autobiographical elements.

Leon Lewis
Updated by Kelly-Anne Riess

DAVID BAKER

Born: Bangor, Maine; December 27, 1954

PRINCIPAL POETRY

Laws of the Land, 1981
Summer Sleep, 1984
Haunts, 1985
Sweet Home, Saturday Night, 1991
After the Reunion, 1994
Holding Katherine, 1996 (with Ann Townsend)
The Truth About Small Towns, 1998
Changeable Thunder, 2001
Midwest Eclogue, 2005

OTHER LITERARY FORMS

Aside from his poetry, David Baker has published a book of criticism about poetry for the University of Arkansas Press: *Heresy and the Ideal: On Contemporary Poetry* (2000). More than a decade of critical essays and reviews about the work of modern American poets are included in this collection. Baker edited *Meter in English: A Critical Engagement* (1996), written by and for practicing poets.

The poem "Trees in the Night" was translated into French for the Belgium magazine *Inédit* in 1993. Baker's work has appeared in a variety of anthologies as well as literary magazines such as *The New Yorker*, *The Atlantic*, *American Scholar*, and *Poetry*.

ACHIEVEMENTS

David Baker has been awarded grants and fellowships from the Guggenheim Memorial Foundation, the National Endowment for the Arts, the Poetry Society of America, the Ohio Arts Council, and the Society of Midland Authors. He has been honored with a Pushcart Prize and *Mid-America Review*'s James Wright Prize for Poetry. He was selected the 1991 poet of the year by the Ohio Poetry Association. He won the Ohioana Helen and Laura Krout Memorial Poetry Award in 1998 and the Ohioana Book Award for Poetry in 1999 for *The Truth About Small Towns*. Baker was awarded a student fellowship in 1989 to the famed Bread Loaf Writers' Conference and was named a member of its

faculty in 2001. He has participated in numerous national writers' conferences and judged national poetry contests, including those sponsored by the *Kenyon Review*, where he became poetry editor. Baker has been a member of the National Book Critics Circle and the advisory boards of the literary journal *Pleiades* and Zoo Press, publisher of emerging poets, playwrights, and essayists.

BIOGRAPHY

David Anthony Baker was born in Bangor, Maine, while his father, Donald Baker, was stationed at Dow Air Force Base. When his father accepted a job with the Missouri highway department, Baker moved along with his parents and younger brother Phil to Macon. His father was transferred to the state capital of Missouri, Jefferson City, in 1960. Baker spent his childhood camping and fishing. He went mushroom hunting and learned to identify sea fossils in limestone dynamited by the highway department. An athlete and popular student in high school, Baker cut a record with his fellow students in the jazz band. Baker, a guitarist, took courses in music theory, where he developed his ear for rhythm and harmony.

Gaining experience by playing locally at diners and clubs, Baker, still in high school, performed at the Kansas City Jazz Festival. Immediately following his 1973 graduation, he played banjo for two months in the musical *Hello, Dolly!* at the Cork County Opera House in Ireland and seriously considered a career as a musician.

In 1973, Baker enrolled in Central Missouri State University, where he took a course from English professor Bob Jones, who introduced him to poetry. After deciding to teach English in the high school from which he had graduated, Baker enrolled in every English course the university offered but one. Having taken several advanced placement courses in high school, Baker was able to complete his B.A. and M.A. degrees by 1977. A year earlier, he had published a prose poem, "Stories in the Land," in Northeast Missouri State (now Truman State) University's newly established *Chariton Review*. After receiving his master's degree, Baker accepted a position teaching at Jefferson City High School and married Charlotte Miller in 1978. His early publication encouraged Baker to continue writing, but the demands of high school teaching did not leave him as much time as he needed to do so.

In 1979, Baker accepted a research fellowship at the University of Utah, attracted by its American studies and creative writing programs. At Utah, Baker worked under poet Dave Smith, who often marked Baker's early poetry with different colored inks to show literal, figurative, and potential meanings. During his first two years at Utah, Baker completed a manuscript, *Laws of the Land*, and was urged to submit it to Ahsahta Press. The book, published in 1981, became the core of his dissertation. Baker received his Ph.D. in English in 1983.

Baker refused several tenure-track positions to accept a visiting professorship at Kenyon College, home of the *Kenyon Review*. Besides teaching literature and fiction-writing classes, Baker worked as an assistant editor on the *Kenyon Review*. In 1984, the end of his visiting professorship coincided with the end of his marriage. Baker accepted a tenure-track position at Denison University in Granville, Ohio, where he was granted the Thomas B. Fordam Endowed Chair in Creative Writing in 1996. Baker met his second wife, Ann Townsend, in Ohio. They married in 1987 and had a daughter, Katherine. Together, they wrote *Holding Katherine*, a chapbook about the birth of their daughter.

Analysis

David Baker's poetry reflects the influence of time and space in rural communities and the relationships within them. Baker consistently writes about a future that encroaches on the past, producing images of landscape and stories of long-term personal relationships. His poetry, rooted in the architecture of the human community, tells of the deep histories and the small towns that influence his readers' lives. Baker's poems, written in various forms (he is an expert sonneteer) as well as in free verse, offer an extended and verifiable memory of objects and events, even those not always visible to or recollected by all of his readers.

Empires, and the villages within them, endure when time (permanence, custom) and space (expansion, progress) are held in balance; they decay when either time or space is overemphasized. The United States,

with its bias toward growth and expansion, depends on the work of poets such as Baker, who recall the archeology of specific places and remind their audience of the value of a private history.

Laws of the Land

Baker's earliest collection, *Laws of the Land*, illustrates the emotional attachment to landscape that would later suffuse his work. "Stories in the Land," a prose poem about fossil hunting on Missouri Highway 63, tells readers that "words" found "among the rocks" speak to those who will listen. The land Baker writes of in "History as Place" records the past and is "formed/ by the shape of its dead," by what has lived before.

The carefully metered poems in this collection recall the landscapes of not only Missouri but also Utah and, by incorporating the writing of the eighteenth century spiritual naturalist William Bartram, a lagoon in Florida. The landscapes are connected because Baker shows what the people who live in these landscapes have in common. Bartram, in "Ephemerae," watches the future poet, who watches Bartram "in the sweet/ shade of the past." Baker's family members mentioned in the poem "Antioch Church and Cemetery, 1840-1972," who worked in "the old pit mines," foreshadow the miners mentioned in Utah's "Peabody #7 Strip Mine."

Smith, Baker's former teacher and mentor, writes in the introduction to *Laws of the Land* that Baker wanders the landscape so that his readers may "behold . . . the hope for" and the "idea of home." Indeed, the idea of home, of how long-term relationships influence readers' lives, is like a watermark on the pages of the poems here.

Sweet Home, Saturday Night

Ten years after his first collection, Baker published what writer and *Georgia Review* columnist Judith Kitchen called a "tour de force—as exciting as Eliot's *Waste Land* in its mix of voices, its fractured sensibility, and its visionary sweep." In *Sweet Home, Saturday Night*, the poet analyzes the home he was part of even as he is separating himself from it. Missouri is the home where the poet hears "the oldest voices . . . aching again," saying "This is the living we make. This is our love and pain." Missouri is where the poet fondly recalls attending baseball games in the late 1960's and cheering with his family for the St. Louis Cardinals ("never more perfect than now").

The book's twenty-two-page title poem recalls a Saturday night on "August 15, 1977" at the "Com- On-Inn, Rt. 63, Missouri," where the poet is the lead guitarist in a band playing Lynyrd Skynyrd's "Sweet Home Alabama" as he simultaneously sits at a "solitary corner table" watching the band play. The modernist structure of the poem counterpoints the voices of an observer (the sense of the poet as observer emerges in this poem; later work would expand this theme), a participant, a singer, and a postmodern analyst. This integration of voices and the rhythms in which they overlap underscore the sense of meter Baker learned as a musician. In fact, lyrics from familiar songs accompany Baker's own lyrics throughout this book, and the integration, as Baker writes in "Dixie," a long poem written in septets or seven-line stanzas, "signals the going-on of things."

AFTER THE REUNION

In *After the Reunion*, Baker combines his themes of landscape, home, and the relationships that "connect and so sustain" them. The title poem concerns a family reunion in spring ("The lilac hedge let go its whole bushel of odors") so enjoyable that the poet wants to "keep loving" even though his love is "doomed as a rose." The poems center around Baker's Missouri home and the family that lives and dies there. "What could be sweeter/ than the company of family," the poet writes in "Music in the Smokehouse," a long poem that moves from the poet's past where he was too young to "walk through the doorway" of an uncle's smokehouse where relatives are singing, dancing, and loving each other, to the present, where the poet, an adult, still waits "for someone to let me inside." These are poems about the duration of a home, the architecture of a family, and the poet's struggle to use his private history to love, again.

THE TRUTH ABOUT SMALL TOWNS

Published in 1998, *The Truth About Small Towns*, highlighted by Baker's graceful stanzas and his use of contemporary sonnets, tells of time spent with a grandmother at her cast-iron stove and, in "Home," of the mother who would like him to "come back in." Continuing to explain the pull of land and family, "Dust to

Dust" asks, "Who would guess it takes this long to come home?"

Landscape and one's relationship to it contribute to "Treatise on Touch," a nineteen-stanza poem written in quatrains. The poem details how the poet watches his wife's response to not only being tested in a physician's office for nerve damage but also revisiting the convent school grounds of the Sisters of Divine Providence in Pittsburgh, Pennsylvania, where she becomes "a child/ again watched by . . . watchers." Baker noticeably expands one theme in this collection; he is much more open to showing that he observes, or bears witness to, the past and the present. "Still-Hildreth Sanatorium, 1936" describes a grandmother who worked as a nurse in a "mansion-// turned-sickhouse" in Macon, Missouri, before she lay dying in her daughter's house in Jefferson City. The poem recounts Baker's own suffering of chronic fatigue syndrome, a disease that causes him to die, yet not die, "each night" and imagine his grandmother coming to his room to offer comfort.

As one theme surfaces, another begins to submerge. Though he continues to write about specific places, Baker mentions fewer place-names. The private history that has informed Baker's poetry is beginning to go public.

MIDWEST ECLOGUE

Midwest Eclogue is divided up into five sections. The poems continue Baker's themes of nature, rural life, history, and relationships, including the poet's with his wife and daughter. One poem in the first section notes the paradox of his daughter's hyperactivity being calmed by stimulants. Other poems examine Walt Whitman's journey to Canada and painter Charles Burchfield's journals.

A couple coping with a problem nature has visited on them is at the heart of the title poem of Baker's *Midwest Eclogue*. (An eclogue is a type of poem written in ancient Greece featuring an idyllic rural landscape with shepherds conversing.) Here a couple, newly arrived in an undisclosed locale somewhere in the midwestern countryside, are using rakes to clear a swampy area next to their home so that its tiny water-based ecosystem can once more breathe oxygen. As they struggle, seemingly boorish neighbors, a father named John and his son, not only watch them deal with weeds, muck, and debris, but also offer them unsolicited—and obviously unappreciated—advice. The swamp-raking couple who seem so highly conversant with and attuned to contemporary environmentalist thinking about ecosystems is advised by these uneducated neighbors to give up the meddling with the pond, because John and his son see it a waste of time and effort. John feels that nature not only can but also should care for itself, even though he surely understand that creatures caught in stagnant ponds eventually weaken and die from oxygen deprivation.

Baker seems to set up the reader for a fall, however, by making it seem that this encounter of neighbors amounts to little more than a classic case of rural yahoos versus clever, morally evolved and industrious city people, when actually what is said in "Midwest Eclogue" is far from that simple. For the poem's narrator figure, the male pond-raker, voices frustration with his and his partner's failure to kill pond organisms with the poison copper sulfate pentahydrate, a chemical that causes pond water to shine in an strange, unnerving way. He regrets that all the poison that they used had killed only two carp, carp being a bottom-feeding—and therefore "useless"—fish.

Thus in reference to the natural environment and its care, who are the "yahoos" here? Are they the city slickers with their high degree of formal education or the simple rural folk who live next door to them who advocate a policy of noninterference with nature? In a sense, those who favor natural processes being allowed to take place without human interference—in this case, John and his son—would be more in sync with their landscape than their urbanized newcomer neighbors, whose preoccupation with ecosystem health seems at war with their use of poison to kill organisms they see as detrimental. Moreover, their dredging of the pond to collect weeds and other debris ends up with them piling the shoreline high with dying tadpoles and fish eggs, emblems of a failed attempt to help restore wild habitat. The poem concludes with a reference to smoke drifting from the couple's neighbors' chimney as evening falls; the neighbors are back home, obviously having given up attempts to change the ways of those who will not listen to good advice.

OTHER MAJOR WORKS

NONFICTION: *Heresy and the Ideal: On Contemporary Poetry*, 2000.

EDITED TEXTS: *Meter in English: A Critical Engagement*, 1996; *Radiant Lyre: Essays on Lyric Poetry*, 2007 (with Ann Townsend).

BIBLIOGRAPHY

Collins, Floyd. "Transience and the Lyric Impulse." *Gettysburg Review* 12, no. 4 (Winter, 2000): 702-719. After providing a definition and brief discussion of lyric poetry, Collins reviews the work of three contemporary American poets, including Baker, who, Collins says, captures everyday life in well-crafted lyric poems that reclaim personal history. The basis for his discussion is Baker's *The Truth About Small Towns*.

Dobberstein, Michael. Review of *Laws of the Land*. *Chariton Review* (Spring, 1983). Dobberstein reviews Baker's first book in considerable detail, relating Baker's poetry to the work of William Bartram, calling the poems a tribute to Bartram's spirit. The reviewer finds a solitude and stillness in the poet's voice.

Genoways, Ted. "Our Town." Review of *The Truth About Small Towns*. *Boston Book Review* (May, 1999). The reviewer examines several poems, quoting them at length to illustrate Baker's technical skill. Genoways comments on Baker's graceful and elegant love poems.

Kitchen, Judith. "For the Moment: Essential Disguises." Review of *Sweet Home, Saturday Night. Georgia Review* 46, no. 3 (Fall, 1992): 554-572. Kitchen praises the display of technical skill and postmodern sensibility she finds in *Sweet Home, Saturday Night*. Explaining how all of the poems in the book lead to the title poem, Kitchen remarks that Baker's poetry unifies many aspects of the contemporary self.

Lea, Sydney. "Aging White Men." *Southern Review* 30, no. 4 (Autumn, 1995): 957-973. Lea carefully distinguishes the poems that are in his view the strongest in *After the Reunion*—he calls the title poem "near-perfect"—explaining that Baker has a distinct voice in a consumerist culture and is "on the cusp of major achievement."

Reiter, Thomas. Review of *Haunts. Quarterly West*

(Spring, 1986). Reiter points out that Baker's poetry deals with the personal and the familial, and that this collection is "direct and radiant."

Steinman, Lisa M. "So What Is Poetry Good For?" Review of *Midwest Eclogue*, by David Baker; *Self-Pity*, by Susan Hahn; *Into It*, by Lawrence Joseph; *The Hoopoe's Crown*, by Jacqueline Osherow. *Michigan Quarterly Review* 45, no. 3 (Summer, 2006): 544-661. Extensive review of Baker's work notes his themes of flux and nature.

Ginger Jones
Updated by John Raymer

JOHN BALABAN

Born: Philadelphia, Pennsylvania; December 2, 1943

PRINCIPAL POETRY

After Our War, 1974
Scrisori de peste mare/Letters from Across the Sea, 1979
Blue Mountain, 1982
Words for My Daughter, 1991
Locusts at the Edge of Summer: New and Selected Poems, 1997
Path, Crooked Path, 2006

OTHER LITERARY FORMS

Apart from his volumes of poetry, John Balaban (BAHL-uh-bahn) published a novel, *Coming Down Again* (1985, 1989); a juvenile fable, *The Hawk's Tale* (1988); and several nonfiction books about his Vietnam experience, which include *Vietnam: The Land We Never Knew* (1989) and a memoir, *Remembering Heaven's Face: A Moral Witness in Vietnam* (1991). With coeditor Nguyen Qui Duc, Balaban edited a collection of seventeen short stories, *Vietnam: A Traveler's Literary Companion* (1996). He wrote a screenplay titled *Children of an Evil Hour*, produced in 1969. Balaban has translated Vietnamese poetry into English; some of these translations are in his *Ca Dao Vietnam: A Bilingual Anthology of Vietnamese Folk Poetry* (1974).

ACHIEVEMENTS

John Balaban's deep concern for humanity on the brink of annihilation, which he witnessed during the Vietnam War, is the hallmark of his poetry. Although he explored other areas of human experience, both geographically and historically, as well as his own inner world, the Vietnam factor stayed with him as a sounding board for whatever else came under his scrutiny. In three decades of steady publication, his work accumulated the needful critical mass to secure him an enduring place among the very best poets writing in the United States at the dawn of the twenty-first century.

Among his numerous awards and honors, his first book of poetry published in the United States, *After Our War*, was named the Lamont Poetry Selection by the Academy of American Poets in 1974 and was nominated for the National Book Award in Poetry. His third book, *Words for My Daughter*, was a National Poetry Series selection in 1990; his fourth book of poetry, *Locusts at the Edge of Summer*, was nominated for the National Book Award and won the Poetry Society of America's William Carlos Williams Award.

Balaban was the recipient of literary distinctions or prizes in Romania, the Steaua Prize of the Romanian Writers' Union (1978), and the Prize for Poetry at the Lucian Blaga International Poetry Festival (1999). In Bulgaria, he won the Vaptsarov Medal given by the Union of Bulgarian Writers (1980). In Romania, he held a Fulbright-Hayes Lectureship for 1976-1977 and a Fulbright Distinguished Visiting Lectureship in 1979. After he completed his alternative military service in 1969, he visited Vietnam in 1971 to work on his translation of folk poetry, in 1985 to study the institutions of the unified country, and in 1989 to lecture for a few days at the University of Hanoi.

Between 1994 and 1997, he was president of the American Literary Translators Association. He earned two Pushcart Prizes: for his *Hudson Review* essay "Doing Good" (1978-1979) and for his poem "For the Missing in Action" (1990), originally published in *Ploughshares* and collected in *Words for My Daughter*. Balaban won the National Artist Award of the Phi Kappa Phi Honor Society for 2001-2004 and a John Simon Guggenheim Fellowship in 2003. Balaban has contributed poems, translations, essays and reviews to such periodicals as *American Scholar*, *Asian Art and Culture*, *Hudson Review*, *Modern Poetry in Translation*, *Sewanee Review*, *Southern Review*, *Steaua* (Cluj-Napoca, Romania), *The New Yorker*, and *TriQuarterly*.

BIOGRAPHY

John Balaban was born to Romanian immigrant parents, Phillip Balaban and Alice (Georgies) Balaban, both of peasant stock. The family name Balaban comes from a Polish count who led a force against the Turks in about 1510. Balaban's father, Filip Balaban, was born in Lovrin, a village in the Banat; his mother, Alexandra Georgies, came from a nearby village in southwestern Transylvania. The population was predominantly Romanian in the countryside; however, the people did not enjoy any civic rights and freedoms. After their respective families immigrated to the United States before World War I, Balaban's parents met in 1930 in the United States. They married and had two children, John and his sister, and their assimilation was quick and thorough.

Balaban showed an early bent toward the humanities, became a student at Pennsylvania State University, and majored in English. In 1966, he earned his bachelor's degree with the highest honors. He secured a much-coveted place at Harvard University, where the next year, he received his master's degree. Balaban accepted a position with the International Voluntary Services, a predecessor of the Peace Corps; he fulfilled his alternative service as a conscientious objector during the Vietnam War. As a graduate of Harvard, he received appointment as instructor in literature and descriptive linguistics at the University of Can Tho in South Vietnam (1967-1968).

The next year, Balaban served as field representative for the Committee of Responsibility to Save War-Burned and War-Injured Children, a Boston-based group that offered hospital care to children. It was at this time that he met his future wife, Lana "Lonnie" Flanagan, a teacher. Between 1970 and 1992, he taught English and creative writing at his alma mater, Pennsylvania State University, and taught twice as a Fulbright lecturer in Romanian universities.

In the early 1980's, John's and Lana's only child—a daughter, Tally—was born. A westward trip across the United States, during which he hitchhiked through the desert to escape the "technological sublime," helped him cope with his memories of Vietnam. He recorded what happened during that trip in *Blue Mountain*. *Words for My Daughter* continues his attempt to contain the past, make sense of what happened, and offer wisdom and guidance to his daughter.

From 1992 to 2000, Balaban served as professor of English at the University of Miami. In 2000, he earned appointment as professor of English and poet-in-residence at North Carolina State University in Raleigh.

ANALYSIS

John Balaban's unique experiences as a conscientious objector and eyewitness to the destruction of Vietnam's rural population often figure into his poetry. The uncompromising picture Balban so powerfully paints details the plight of the indiscriminate war casualties among children, women, and elderly peasants. Caught in the crossfire between the belligerent armies, these groups were often victims of "collateral damage."

Balaban's was not a straightforward journalistic account but instead a young humanist's response. To develop a rapport with the centuries-long tradition of Vietnamese folk and written poetry, he went back to Vietnam in 1971 and became fluent in the language of this tradition. The development of his craft came from a sense of urgency and outrage; many of his later experiences yielded poetry from early traumatic events.

"AFTER OUR WAR"

"After Our War," the concluding piece of Balaban's first volume of poetry, is a meditation in the wake of the peace agreement signed between the United States and North Vietnam on January 27, 1973, in Paris. According to that agreement, the United States military would withdraw from the conflict. The poem opens with an apocalyptic vision:

> After our war, the dismembered bits
> —all those pierced eyes, ear slivers, jaw splinters,
> gouged lips, odd tibias, skin flaps, and toes—
> came squinting, wobbling, jabbering back.
> The genitals, of course, were the most bizarre,
> inching along roads like glowworms and slugs.

The tone is bemused, detached, and slightly ironic. The concreteness and specificity of the depiction mark the intensity of the experience. After more details of a like nature, the shocked reader realizes that:

Since all things naturally return to their source,
 these snags and tatters arrived, with immigrant uncertainty,
 in the United States.

The poem concludes with a sequence of questions:

After the war, with such Cheshire cats grinning in
 our trees,
 will the ancient tales still tell us new truths?
 Will the myriad world surrender new metaphor?
 After our war, how will love speak?

In "Gerontion," T. S. Eliot had asked a somewhat similar question: "After such knowledge, what forgiveness?" However, there is a significant difference here: Balaban's knowledge reflects the nightmare of history. Under such circumstances, the poet asks, is it worthwhile to seek after new truths, mediated by new metaphors? Art seems helpless and impotent in the face of twentieth century genocide.

"SITTING ON BLUE MOUNTAIN . . ."

"Sitting on Blue Mountain, Watching the Birds Fly South and Thinking of St. Julien Ravenel Childs," a poem from Balaban's *Blue Mountain*, develops the topic of war and violence in the United States. Sitting, watching, thinking aloud, and addressing the person mentioned in the title is a common stance for Balaban. The poem bears an ominous motto from Harriott Horry Rutledge Ravenel's book on the city of Charleston, South Carolina:

If the new is, or shall be, better,
 purer, braver or higher, it will be well.
 This is the tale of the old and it is done.

While there may be some hope for the future, the past is beyond mending. Forgetful of human history for the moment, the first stanza is about migratory birds heading south toward the Carolinas. After a Whitmanesque catalog, the poet stops and asks himself: "Are these birds worth a whole stanza? Sure,/ they point our noses south; our hearts, to memory."

The entire second stanza is a splendid account of the burgeoning American Civil War, the secession of South Carolina, and the battering of Fort Sumter. The title character of the poem, St. Julien Ravenel Childs, is a southerner steeped in the colonial mentality of the slave-owning class and the grandson of Ravenel, whose book was the source of the motto. Balaban addresses Childs:

In 1922, you soldiered in Santo Domingo.
 With Marines led by a latter General Lee
 you chased bandits through riverine jungles
 and saved the cane crop for a New York bank.

The next stanza casts the same doubt as to the scope and potency of poetry: "We live in a world with a simple sense of use/ that doesn't include poetry and musings." In spite of that declaration, the poet confesses he is a prisoner of his vocation and craft and cannot abandon himself to other pursuits; likewise, his addressee cannot escape his delusions. The poem ends on a resigned note, with an implicit comparison between the Blue Mountain of the poet's sublime idealism and the Atlantis of his interlocutor's incurable "dynastic mind."

"WORDS FOR MY DAUGHTER"

Balaban attempts a solution to the poet's dilemmas in "Words for My Daughter," a frequently anthologized poem. The title recalls William Butler Yeats's "A Prayer for My Daughter"; a comparison of the two poems yields some insight. Balaban seems aware that there is no point in sheltering one's offspring from the harsh reality of living. Yeats, in contrast, directs his prayer toward God and entreats God to protect, insulate, and endow his infant daughter with the graceful arts of gentility. For his daughter, the middle-class Balaban provides an account of his own rough childhood environment to educate her in the difficult art of survival; in this moment, Balaban becomes aware of the healing power he feels as he holds his daughter and of a renewal of hope in his alienated self.

PATH, CROOKED PATH

Path, Crooked Path opens with "Highway 61 Revisited," set in June following the September 11, 2001, terrorist attacks on the United States. The poem reminds readers of the countryside along the legendary road and of Bob Dylan's album *Highway 61 Revisited* (1965). The narrator hopes to find both relief from the summer heat of the city and normality in the farmlands and the songs of crickets and songbirds; the speaker hopes to forget scenes of "the couples holding hands in their slow-motion leaps/ from the skyscraper windows billowing smoke." Reality presents itself, however, when he encounters a soldier who has been mugged and a man who cannot lift his prosthetic legs into a car.

Balaban includes some translations in *Path, Crooked Path*: "Ovid, Tristia V.x: 15-22" (from Ovid), "A Vision" (translated with Elena Christova from the Bulgarian of Kolyo Sevov), "Let Him Be" (translated with Alexandra Veleva from the Bulgarian of Georgi Borrisov), and "Van Gogh" (translated from the Bulgarian with the author, Lyubomir Nikolov). Their inclusion suggests the variety of topics in this collection.

Through his poetry, Balaban chronicles an array of individuals, some famous, some not, and some living, some dead. Balaban offers tribute to his teachers in "The Great Fugue" and to his dog Apples, to Dr. Alice Magheru, and to Vincent van Gogh in the poems named after their subjects. Balaban mentions more than twenty poets, including Georgi Borrisov and Hayden Carruth in the poems bearing their names and Denise Levertov, Theodore Roethke, Sylvia Plath, Cicero, Victor Hugo, and James Wright in "The Lives of the Poets."

Balaban's tolerance of others is apparent throughout the volume but particularly in "Let Him Be," "If Only," and "Leaving." Balaban exhibits respect for other people: a paraplegic in "Eddie," a member of the Sex Change Band in "Poor Boy Slim," and even a feral cat tamed by his daughter in "Big Boy." Balaban's pacifist leanings are evident in "The Lives of the Poets" when he wonders if poetry can "calm the guns" and in "Varna Snow" when he concludes: "Only poetry lasts."

As might be expected for a collection titled *Path, Crooked Path*, Balaban mentions various locales, including Venice Beach (California), Hanoi, and Romania in "Some Dogs of the World"; the Volga River in "Ibn Fadhlan"; Camp Lejeune in "Soldier Home"; the Rio Grande in "Sotol"; the Miami area in "Remembering Miami" and "Dinner in Miami"; and Spain in "Butter People." Not all his scenes are pleasant: an accident victim in "Eddie," Chernobyl and America's cardboard

huts in "Acropolis," losing others in "Goodbyes," and soldiers "smeared on the bushes and grass" in "Soldier Home."

Just as the first poem "Highway 61 Revisited," sets *Path, Crooked Path* on a journey, "Driving Back East with My Dad"—one of the last poems in the collection—ends the trip, mentioning various sites such as Kitty Hawk, North Carolina; the Danube; Philadelphia and Scranton, Pennsylvania; and Kansas. The poet and his father had a difficult trip; at one point, Balaban's father even turns off his hearing aid. Still, Balaban describes their trip—like life itself—as good; they had been ". . . alive together, taking in the road,/ mindful of where we had come, and moving on." Balaban, throughout the entire collection, reminds the reader to value the past, to appreciate the present, and to look forward to the future.

OTHER MAJOR WORKS

LONG FICTION: *Coming Down Again*, 1985, 1989.

SCREENPLAY: *Children of an Evil Hour*, 1969.

NONFICTION: *Vietnam: The Land We Never Knew*, 1989; *Remembering Heaven's Face: A Moral Witness in Vietnam*, 1991.

TRANSLATIONS: *Ca Dao Vietnam: A Bilingual Anthology of Vietnamese Folk Poetry*, 1974; *Vietnam: A Traveler's Literary Companion*, 1996; *Spring Essence: The Poetry of Ho Xuan Huong*, 2000.

CHILDREN'S LITERATURE: *The Hawk's Tale*, 1988.

BIBLIOGRAPHY

Balaban, John. "John Balaban." http://www.john balaban.com. The official Web site of Balaban contains information on his books and poetry as well as links to interviews with him and articles about him.

Beidler, Philip D. *Late Thoughts on an Old War: The Legacy of Vietnam*. Athens: University of Georgia Press, 2004. In his memoir on the Vietnam War, Beidler, an Army calvary platoon leader during the war, describes how his life paralleled that of Balaban in the chapter "Wanting to Be John Balaban."

_____. *Re-writing America: Vietnam Authors in Their Generation*. Athens: University of Georgia Press, 1991. Beidler discusses *After Our War*, which he says shows Balaban's sense of the crucial role of the Vietnam poet in remaking Americans' collective cultural experience of this conflict.

Erhart, W. D. "Soldier-Poets of the Vietnam War." In *America Rediscovered: Critical Essays on Literature and Film of the Vietnam War*, edited by Owen W. Gilman, Jr., and Lorrie Smith. New York: Garland, 1990. The work describes the great effort to absorb the Vietnamese culture made by Balaban, who learned the language and even suffered wounds.

Hillstrom, Laurie Collier. *The Vietnam Experience: A Concise Encyclopedia of American Literature, Songs, and Films*. Westport, Conn.: Greenwood Press, 1998. Contains a chapter on *After Our War*, which discusses the work and Balaban.

Kriesel, Michael. Review of *Path, Crooked Path. Library Journal* 131, no. 3 (February 15, 2006): 119-121. Kriesel notes how Balaban takes readers on a road trip, peopling his poetry with poets and figures ordinary and historical in various locales.

Rignalda, Don. *Fighting and Writing the Vietnam War*. Jackson: University Press of Mississippi, 1994. In the chapter on Vietnam War poetry, Rignalda calls Balaban the "most insistent" of the war poets on "translating the war—on both a figuratively literal and literally figurative level."

Seaman, Donna. Review of *Path, Crooked Path. Booklist*, 102, no. 17 (May 1, 2006): 65. Seaman calls Balaban a "roaming bard" who considers all of humanity and its storms. She notes Balaban's communication of his love of others in his writings although he recognizes their frequent reliance on violence.

Smith, Lorrie. "Resistance and Revision by Vietnam War Veterans." In *Fourteen Landing Zones: Approaches to Vietnam War Literature*, edited by Philip K. Jason. Iowa City: University of Iowa Press, 1991. Smith argues that Balaban implicates the reader in the decision to fight in Vietnam by calling it "our" war in the title of *After Our War*.

Stefan Stoenescu
Updated by Anita Price Davis

MARY JO BANG

Born: Waynesville, Missouri; October 22, 1946

PRINCIPAL POETRY

Apology for Want, 1997
The Downstream Extremity of the Isle of Swans, 2001
Louise in Love, 2001
The Eye Like a Strange Balloon, 2004
Elegy, 2007
The Bride of E., 2009

OTHER LITERARY FORMS

Mary Jo Bang, who came to poetry relatively late in life, has been remarkably prodigious, completing five volumes since the start of the new millennium. Her works of poetry largely define her reputation. Because of her background in teaching and because she regards the explication of poetry as a prime responsibility of practicing poets, she has given numerous interviews in which she discusses the creative process as well as her theories of poetry. Bang has written numerous book reviews and essays, work that inevitably sheds light on her own poetry. Given her extensive theoretical work on the music and rhythms of language, Bang is an adept translator, focusing on the works of Dante.

ACHIEVEMENTS

Although well past middle age, Mary Jo Bang is very much in midcareer. Initially, her poetry reflected her long background in the visual arts (principally photography) and her fascination with the potency and subtleties of language itself. These early works are dense, often experimental in their use of nontraditional rhythms and sonic effects, lyrical in their feel, and abstract in their thematic argument, posing questions about the function of art, the nature of beauty, the logic of time, the implications of mortality, and ultimately, the dynamic relationship between poets and words. The works, often difficult and cerebral, earned lavish praise from academic presses and won prestigious poetry prizes, most notably the Katharine Bakeless Nason Poetry Prize (1996) and the Alice Fay di Castagnola

Award (2001) from the Poetry Society of America. However, in 2004, following the death of her son, a promising artist in his own right, Bang's poetry took a marked turn toward the introspective and the confessional as she examined her private anguish. If her early work was applauded by the academic establishment for its audacity and density, *Elegy* received recognition from a much wider audience of readers (and critics) drawn to the poems' honesty. *Elegy* not only made Bang the subject of numerous national profiles (and much sought after for public readings) but also earned the 2007 National Book Critics Circle Award in poetry.

BIOGRAPHY

Mary Jo Bang was born Mary Jo Ward in the small town of Waynesville, Missouri, but grew up in Ferguson, a northern suburb of St. Louis. Neither her mother, a homemaker, nor her stepfather, a truck driver, had graduated from high school, and Bang grew up with little exposure to literature until she discovered the bookmobile at the age of seven and became a voracious reader. Because of financial restraints and Bang's uncertainty about a course of study—she was sure only that she loved the idea of learning—she attended a number of universities before completing a bachelor of science degree (1971) and a master's degree (1975) in sociology at Northwestern University. Before completing her studies, she was married, had a son, and was divorced. After graduation, enraged over the lingering war in Southeast Asia, Bang moved to Philadelphia to work with a Quaker organization dedicated to social reform. She then found herself drawn to the medical field. She returned to Missouri and received a physician's assistant degree from St. Louis University. In 1978, she married a high school friend who had a son about the same age as hers, and she moved to Evanston, Illinois, where she worked in the medical field for nearly eight years.

Mary Jo Bang (AP/Wide World Photos)

Bang, who now had two children and a hectic professional career, pursued her love of writing by enrolling in a night class in the creative writing program at Northwestern University. During a vacation in France, however, she fell in love with photography. After her husband accepted a job in London, Bang attended the Polytechnic of Central London, graduating in 1989 with a bachelor of fine arts in photography. The couple divorced, and she returned to the United States, certain only that she no longer wanted to pursue medicine. She tried commercial photography in Chicago, but studio work did not satisfy her creative side. She turned to teaching an adult creative writing class at a small college and loved the experience. She was accepted to the writing program at Columbia University. During her time at Columbia, Manhattan's thriving poetry scene convinced her to pursue poetry. After winning a writing contest, Bang published her first book of poetry, *Apology for Want*, one year before she completed her M.F.A. in 1998, at the age of forty-eight. The book received extravagant critical praise, as did her two follow-up volumes, both drawn from her thesis work at Columbia.

In 2000, she returned to St. Louis to join the faculty at Washington University, near where she had grown up. In June, 2004, her thirty-seven-year-old son, Michael Donner Van Hook, an avant-garde artist in New York City with a long history of addictions, died after an overdose of prescription medicine. The experience devastated Bang—and she turned to poetry for solace. *Elegy*, which chronicled the year after her son's death, marked Bang as a major poet. Although she has accepted numerous visiting professorships (most notably at the University of Iowa and Columbia University), Bang has maintained her affiliation with Washington University, serving as the director of its creative writing program from 2005 to 2008, and continuing to teach writing classes. She published *The Bride of E.*, an abecedarian, which, with uncharacteristic wit, uses pop culture icons to investigate Bang's signature themes: time and mortality.

ANALYSIS

Mary Jo Bang's earliest work, poems written during and immediately after her years at Columbia, reflects the eagerness of a student of poetry. Bang is interested in experimenting with form to create the something new that all starting poets seek. Her subject matter seldom reflects her own experience—she strives for an impersonal poetry that focuses on language shaped for sonic effect. The poems construct a suggestive scene rather than telling a story or filling in the details. The reader is set down in an operating room, in a lush park, or on a city sidewalk—but without the reassuring narrative structure of character and situation. The work draws on her two professed influences: the quiet subversive vision of Emily Dickinson and the groundbreaking work of the Beat poets, particularly Lawrence Ferlinghetti, and its endorsement of the delight in radical formal experiments.

Bang's poems are difficult, at times cut with a deliberate ambiguity that leaves the reader suspended just short of clear themes (often the poems play out in a dreamlike ambience); readers are left to savor the lyrical play of language and the rich sense of suggestive imagery. Bang speaks from behind the mask of the poet; indeed the collection *Louise in Love* is a kind of narrative with distinctive characters, notably a woman and her boyfriend. These are poems ultimately about the work of art itself. The poems are often brief, their free structure a complicated weave of accents and pauses, their rhyme achieved through subtle language devices (prominently assonance and consonance), their lines fragmented and elliptical, and their syntax disjointed and abrupt. They are poems of effect.

After the death of her son, when Bang began writing the poem sequence that would become *Elegy*, she maintained her investigation into poetic form, examining how such deep and personal sorrow could shape poems that avoid sentimentality and self-pity and how mourning could not become public theater when transcribed into a poem that assumes a reader, a stranger to her private anguish. That balance between grief and art allowed her to produce her most deeply personal poetry while continuing her work with the formal aspects of poetry, in this case how language—word patterns, line breaks, vocal sounds, and even selected images—can record the recoil from enormous pain.

THE EYE LIKE A STRANGE BALLOON

Bang's fourth collection of poetry, *The Eye Like a Strange Balloon*, most epitomizes her early interest in art itself. Trained in the study of photography, she uses poetry to engage works of modern artists, some well known (Max Ernst, Pablo Picasso, and Willem de Kooning), some more obscure (Cindy Sherman, Sigmar Polke, and David Lynch). In each poem, she uses language, fragmentary and allusive, to detail the selected artwork, to capture its impact—without giving the reader a visual image of the painting. Such poetic endeavor, known as ekphrasis, is, not surprisingly, richly visual, teeming with color and shape, line and shadow. Behind the collection is Bang's own conviction that individual works of art, whether image or text, have the ability to arrest the participatory viewer or reader, to provide a kind of stopped moment that reflects and, in turn, enhances the experience of the artist but provides a similar emotional moment for the audience. Like an Alice in Wonderland figure, the poet in each of the fifty-two poems immerses herself in the selected canvas and speaks from its symbolic landscape. The poems continue the effect begun by the individual painting and participate in the dynamic of art that works only if such constructed pieces engender emotional responses. If there are themes, they are broad—abstract concepts such as beauty, time, and death. The poems are far more about the interplay between the visual arts and the written word, creating a cool feel to the collection and making readers aware they are part of a theoretical excavation into the dynamic of art itself.

ELEGY

Bang readily recalls her first poem, a melodramatic teenaged angst verse written after John Kennedy's assassination in 1963, in which she attempted to use poetry to make sense of a profound loss beyond understanding. Years later, as a mature poet, Bang would begin the difficult process of adjusting to the 2004 death of her son, an avant-garde artist in New York, from a drug overdose, by turning again to poetry. She never considered publishing the poems she wrote after her son's death until her agent urged her to consider organizing the poems into a book. The cycle of sixty-four poems that became *Elegy* roughly chronicles the year of Bang's mourning.

Aware of the long tradition of the elegy form, Bang not only brings to the poems the sharp, precise particulars of her son's death but also informs the event with images and allusions that extend the range beyond the personal. Unlike her earlier work, the poems are relentlessly specific. In countless interviews given in conjunction with the volume's success, Bang has spoken of the elegy as a powerful way that language can maintain a conversation with the deceased, intrude on the anguished distance the bereaved feels, and make immediate a loved one now gone in the most absolute of ways.

The poems resist Bang's signature polish—the language is direct and approachable, with the feeling of being written in an immediacy of distress. The reader is taken to the morgue to identify the body; spends a harrowing night with the poet-mother, who wants only to sleep; and contemplates the cremated remains in an ornate box. Bang speaks in the voice of a wounded poet, an adult who suddenly feels the vulnerability of a child, baffled and hurt. She struggles with responsibility: Should she have been more aggressive in addressing

her son's addictions? In the face of death, the poet longs for the consolation of explanation—knowing, of course, that death defies such tidiness. The poet is left reeling, struggling against the numbness, and working to articulate her grief into something useful, something lasting. Bang's poems avoid the private feel of a mother mourning a son and assume the privilege of art itself, a way for the resilient spirit to handle wounding sorrow.

BIBLIOGRAPHY

Ashley, Renée. Review of *Elegy*. *Literary Review* 51, no. 4 (Summer, 2009): 244-248. A favorable review of Bang's work, which says the poetry "embodies and enacts the numbing impossibility of understanding and the ongoing nature of Bang's suffering."

Bang, Mary Jo. "I. E.: On Emily and Influence." *The Emily Dickinson Journal* 15, no. 2 (2006): 66-70. Revealing analysis that underscores the tremendous influence of Dickinson on Bang. Stresses Bang's signature fragmented line and experimental use of ambiguous imagery.

Hacht, Anne Marie, and David Kelly, eds. *Poetry for Students*. Vol. 23. Detroit: Thomson/Gale, 2006. Contains an analysis of Bang's poem "Allegory."

Heffernan, James A. W. *Museum of Words: The Poetics of Ekphrasis from Homer to Ashbery*. Chicago: University of Chicago Press, 2004. Helpful and accessible, provides context for Bang and her interest in the visual medium. With illustrations.

Jackson, Virginia. *Dickinson's Misery: A Theory of Lyric Reading*. Princeton, N.J.: Princeton University Press, 2005. Helpful explication of Dickinson's lyricism in poetry that, like Bang's, can seem fragmented and harsh.

Ramazani, Jahan. *Poetry of Mourning: The Modern Elegy from Hardy to Heaney*. Chicago: University of Chicago Press, 1994. Important overview of the tradition in which Bang gained national prominence. Investigates the relationship between grief and art, intimacy and publicity, and consolation and self-pity.

Seaman, Donna. Review of *The Bride of E. Booklist* 106, no. 4 (October 15, 2009): 17. The reviewer praises the abecedarian, or book of alphabet poems, by Bang, saying that the poet is "antic and reflective, funny and oracular."

Swensen, Cole, and David St. John, eds. *American Hybrid: A Norton Anthology of New Poetry*. New York: W. W. Norton, 2009. This anthology examines the work of seventy-three poets, including Bang, who combine the traditional and experimental in their poems. Poems from each poet are accompanied by short introductory essays providing background and positioning the poet in the contemporary poetic world.

Joseph Dewey

AMIRI BARAKA
Everett LeRoi Jones

Born: Newark, New Jersey; October 7, 1934
Also known as: LeRoi Jones

PRINCIPAL POETRY

Spring and Soforth, 1960
Preface to a Twenty Volume Suicide Note, 1961
The Dead Lecturer, 1964
Black Art, 1966
A Poem for Black Hearts, 1967
Black Magic: Sabotage, Target Study, Black Art—Collected Poetry, 1961-1967, 1969
In Our Terribleness: Some Elements and Meaning in Black Style, 1970 (with Fundi [Billy Abernathy])
It's Nation Time, 1970
Spirit Reach, 1972
Afrikan Revolution, 1973
Hard Facts, 1975
AM/TRAK, 1979
Selected Poetry of Amiri Baraka/LeRoi Jones, 1979
Reggae or Not!, 1981
Transbluesency: The Selected Poems of Amiri Baraka/LeRoi Jones, 1995
Wise, Why's, Y's, 1995
Funk Lore: New Poems, 1984-1995, 1996
Somebody Blew Up America, and Other Poems, 2003
Un Poco Low Coup, 2004
Mixed Blood: Number One, 2005

OTHER LITERARY FORMS

Amiri Baraka (buh-RAH-kuh) is a protean literary figure, equally well known for his poetry, drama, and essays. In addition, he has written short stories and experimental fiction. Baraka's early plays, notably *Dutchman* (pr., pb. 1964), *The Slave* (pr., pb. 1964), and *The Toilet* (pr., pb. 1964), were produced under his given name, LeRoi Jones, and derive from his period of involvement with the New York City avant-garde. Baraka's critical and political prose has appeared in many collections, and throughout his career, he has been active as an anthologist of African American literature.

ACHIEVEMENTS

Amiri Baraka has been the recipient of many awards and honors. He won the Longview Best Essay of the Year (1961) for his essay "Cuba Libre," the Obie Award for Best American Play of 1964 for *Dutchman*, the American Book Award from the Before Columbus Foundation for *Confirmation: An Anthology of African-American Women* (1984), a PEN-Faulkner Award (1989), the Langston Hughes Award (1989), the Lifetime Achievement Award from the Before Columbus Foundation (1989), Italy's Ferroni Award and Foreign Poet Award (1993), and the Playwright's Award from the Black Drama Festival of Winston-Salem, North Carolina, in 1997. He received fellowships and grants from the John Whitney Foundation, the Guggenheim Foundation, and the National Endowment for the Arts, the Rockefeller Foundation, and the New Jersey State Council for the Arts. He was awarded a doctorate of humane letters from Malcolm X College in Chicago (1972). He also served as poet laureate of New Jersey from July, 2002, until the post was abolished in July, 2003.

BIOGRAPHY

Imamu Amiri Baraka, as he has been known since 1967, was born Everett LeRoi Jones into a black middle-class family in Newark, New Jersey, the son of postal worker-elevator operator Coyette Leroy Jones and social worker Anna Lois Russ Jones. An excellent student whose parents encouraged his intellectual interests, young LeRoi Jones developed lifelong interests in literature and music at an early age. After graduating with honors from a predominately white high school, he was admitted to Rutgers University in 1951. The following year, he briefly attended Columbia University before transferring to Howard University, but he dropped out in 1954 at the age of nineteen. He would later receive M.A. degrees in philosophy from Columbia and in German literature from the New School for Social Research. Jones afterward spent more than two years in the United States Air Force, primarily in Puerto Rico, during which time he began to write. He was promoted to sergeant before receiving an undesirable discharge as a suspected communist.

By 1957, Jones was living a bohemian existence in the creative environment of Greenwich Village and New York's Lower East Side, where he embarked on his literary career while working at a variety of jobs. During the early or "Beat" stage of his career, Jones associated closely with numerous white avant-garde poets, including Robert Creeley, Allen Ginsberg, Robert Duncan, Frank O'Hara, Jack Kerouac, Charles Olson, Gilbert Sorrentino, and Diane di Prima, with whom he founded the American Theatre for Poets in 1961. Such literary figures were important in the development of his voice as a writer, demonstrating by example the many forms that poetry could assume and changing his preconceptions of what poems could or should be.

In 1958, the year he founded Totem Press, Jones married Hettie Cohen, a white woman. They edited their self-published magazine *Yugen* for five years. They had two daughters, Kellie Elisabeth and Lisa Victoria. Jones meanwhile began establishing himself as an important young radical poet, critic, and editor. Among the many magazines to which he contributed was *Down Beat*, the jazz journal where he first expressed the musical interests that had a large impact on his poetry. The political interests that dominated Jones's later work were unmistakably present as early as 1960, when, upon the invitation of Fidel Castro, he toured Cuba with a group of black intellectuals. This event sparked his perception of the United States as a corrupt bourgeois society and seems particularly significant in relation to his later socialist emphasis. Jones's growing political interest conditioned his initial collection of poetry, *Preface to a Twenty Volume Suicide Note*, and to his first produced plays, including the Obie Award-winning *Dutchman*, which anticipated a major transformation in Jones's life.

Following the assassination of Malcolm X in 1965, Jones joined the Black Nationalist movement. He separated from Hettie Cohen, severed ties with his white associates, and moved from the Village to Harlem later that same year. Turning his attention to direct action within the black community, he founded the influential although short-lived Black Arts Repertory Theatre School (BARTS) in Harlem and, following his return to his native city in 1966, the Spirit House in Newark. In 1967, Jones married a black actress and fellow poet, Sylvia Robinson, who became Bibi Amina Baraka. The couple would have five children, one of whom, Shani Isis, was murdered in 2003. In 1967, Jones adopted his new name, Imamu Amiri Baraka, which means "Prince" (Ameer) "the blessed one" (Baraka), along with the honorary title of "Imamu" ("spiritual leader"). In 1966-1967, he lectured at San Francisco State University, just one of several institutions of higher learning where he has taught—including New School University, the University of Buffalo, Columbia, Yale, Rutgers, and George Washington universities—and added to his controversial status by penning a number of poems and articles considered anti-Semitic.

Over the next half-dozen years, as his reputation as a writer and political activist grew, Baraka helped found and mentor the Black Community Development and Defense Organization, the Congress of African Peoples (convened in Atlanta in 1970), and the National Black Political Convention (convened in Gary, Indiana, in 1972). As a leading spokesperson of the Black Arts movement, Baraka provided support for young black poets and playwrights, including Larry Neal, Ed Bullins, Marvin X, and Ron Milner. During the Newark uprising/riot of 1968 after the assassination of Martin Luther King, Jr., Baraka was arrested for unlawful possession of firearms. Although he was convicted and given the maximum sentence after the judge read his poem "Black People!" as an example of incitement to riot, the three-year sentence was reversed on appeal.

Baraka supported Kenneth A. Gibson's campaign to become the first black mayor of Newark in 1970, but he later broke with Gibson over what he perceived as the bourgeois values of the administration. This disillusionment with black politics within the American system, combined with Baraka's attendance at the Sixth Pan-African Conference at Dar es Salaam in 1974, precipitated the subsequent stage of his political evolution. While not entirely abandoning his commitment to confront the special problems of African Americans, Baraka came to interpret these problems within the framework of an overarching Marxist-Leninist-Maoist philosophy and left the Nationalist cause, which he considered racist and fascist, in favor of an anti-imperialist stance. In conjunction with this second transformation, Baraka dropped the title "Imamu" and changed the name of his Newark publishing firm from "Jihad" to "People's War." His attitudes changed again, and he publicly denounced his former biases against women, Jews, and gays, calling for black and white workers of all persuasions to work together in their class struggle for social change.

From 1979 until his retirement in 1999, Baraka taught, lectured, and conducted workshops with the Africana Studies Department at the State University of New York-Stony Brook. In his retirement, he has remained active and has continued to produce work; he has also appeared in more than twenty films, usually as himself. Baraka is noted not only for his writings but also for his influence as an intellectual on young writers and social critics. He was the editor of *Black Nation*, the organ of the League of Revolutionary Struggle, a Marxist organization disbanded in 1990. His influence extends far beyond African American culture and politics to embrace other people of color. Native American writer Maurice Kenney, for example, credited Baraka for teaching ethnic writers how to open doors to important venues for their writing, to "claim and take" their place at the cultural forefront.

ANALYSIS

Amiri Baraka's importance as a poet rests on both the diversity of his work and the singular intensity of his Black Nationalist period. In fact, Baraka's diversity gave his nationalist poetry a symbolic significance with personal, political, and aesthetic dimensions. Perhaps his most substantial achievement is his ability to force

reconsideration of the relationship between the artist, his work, its audience, and the encompassing social context. Reconstructing his own vision of this relationship both at the beginning and at the end of the nationalist period, Baraka has increasingly stressed the necessity for an art that will alter the context and increase the real freedom of both artist and community.

During his Black Nationalist period, Baraka concentrated on exposing the unstated racist premises of Euro-American art while developing an alternative black aesthetic. In part because he had demonstrated mastery of Euro-American poetic modes, Baraka's Black Nationalist philosophy commanded an unusual degree of white attention. Coming from a then-unknown writer, his militant poetry might well have been dismissed as a naïve kind of propaganda. It did, in fact, alienate many earlier admirers, who came to see him as an embodiment of the civil disorders rampant in the

Amiri Baraka (Library of Congress)

mid-1960's. On a more profound level, however, he spurred the more thoughtful of his readers to ponder the complex logic of his transformation and to reassess the political implications of their own aesthetic stances.

Even as Baraka's relationship with the "mainstream" audience underwent this metamorphosis, his call for a militant and, if necessary, violent response to American racism received an affirmative answer from a significant number of younger African American writers. Challenging them to speak directly to and for the African American community, Baraka pursued the implications of his demand and employed his poetry as a direct political force. His subsequent turn to a socialist position, reflecting his growing conviction that simple nationalism unintentionally contributed to capitalist oppression, forced many Black Nationalists to reassess their own positions. Though Baraka again alienated a portion of his audience, he continued to generate serious debate on central issues. Throughout his career, but especially in the 1960's and early 1970's, Baraka has exerted a combined political and aesthetic influence matched by few other figures in American literary history.

Baraka's poetry falls into three distinctive periods, each reflecting an attempt to find a philosophy capable of responding adequately to what he viewed as a corrupt culture. The voice of each period is shaped in accord with a different set of assumptions concerning the nature of the cultural corruption, the proper orientation toward political action, and the poet's relationship with his audience.

During his early period, Baraka built an essentially aesthetic response on premises shared primarily with white poets and intellectuals. Although Baraka always recognized the importance of his racial and economic heritage, the intricate philosophical voice of the early period sounds highly individualistic in comparison with his later work. In his middle, Black Nationalist period, Baraka shifted emphasis to the racial dimension of American culture. The associated voice—much more accessible, though not nearly so simple as it first appears—reflects Baraka's desire to relate primarily to the African American community. Throughout his third and ongoing Marxist-Leninist-Maoist period, Baraka adopted a less emotionally charged voice in accord

with his stance as a scientific analyst of capitalist corruption.

Differing from the voices of the earlier periods—which assumed an equality between Baraka and his audience, whether based on aesthetic awareness or racial experience—this socialist voice frequently takes on the didactic tones of a teacher lecturing an audience unaware of its potential identity as a revolutionary proletariat. The diversity of Baraka's work makes it extremely difficult to find a vocabulary equally relevant to the complex postmodernism of *Preface to a Twenty Volume Suicide Note*, the militant nationalism of *Black Magic*, and the uncompromising economic analysis of *Hard Facts*. Nevertheless, Baraka is not three different people, but one person expressing himself at three different stages of awareness. Anticipations and echoes of all three voices occur during each period. Throughout his career, several constants emerge, most notably a philosophical refusal to conform to the demands of what he views as a corrupt culture and an emphasis on the oral/musical nature of the poetic experience.

Baraka's early work emphasizes the relationship between psychological experience, vocal rhythm, and the poetic line. This aesthetic adapts and develops those of Euro-American poets such as Duncan, Creeley, and Olson, whose essay "Projective Verse" states many of the general premises of the group with which Baraka associated. Olson insists on "the possibilities of breath" as the central element of "Open" verse and develops the idea that "FORM IS NEVER MORE THAN THE EXTENSION OF CONTENT." Given this aesthetic, the poetic voice should embody the precise rhythm and emphasis of the poet's immediate experience and perception.

"DUNCAN SPOKE OF A PROCESS"

The poem "Duncan Spoke of a Process" both explicitly recognizes Baraka's aesthetic affinities (he also inscribed poems to Gary Snyder, Ginsberg, and Michael McClure during this period) and analyzes the experience and premises shaping his voice. The poem typifies Baraka's early work in that it is philosophical, abstract, and nonracial. Although it may obliquely relate to Baraka's experience as a black man, it is equally accessible to a reader whose emotional state derives from different circumstances. In addition, it typifies the early work in its intimation of the deep dissatisfaction with Euro-American culture that led to Baraka's political development.

Assuming an audience familiar with Duncan, Baraka meditates on the emotional and intellectual implications of Duncan's work and revises its aesthetic in accord with his own perceptions. Although he reiterates the word "repeat" three times in the first stanza, he is not simply repeating Duncan's words. The poem most closely resembles Duncan in its syntax, which mirrors the hesitations of a consciousness struggling to embody a natural process in order to find words that repeat experience "as a day repeats/ its color." Frequently "sentences" consist of a string of perceptual units with ambiguous syntactic relationships. Many sentences contain no concrete images ("Before that, what came easiest"); the images that do occur are in relation to poetic consciousness rather than external "reality." Like Duncan's, Baraka's landscape is part psychological and part mythic or archetypal. The image of unidentified people traveling across the "greenest earth" represents his struggle to unite these landscapes, to bring the nurturing archetypal world to life in the persona's mind.

The remainder of the poem, however, emphasizes the persona's inability to achieve this rejuvenating unity. He insists that all abstract ideas and assumptions be validated in relation to memory (of psychological states rather than of external experiences). His memory, however, confronts him with an internal wasteland, "a heap of broken feeling." Starting with this consuming feeling of loss—whether of lover, childhood innocence, affinity with Duncan, or spiritual resiliency remains purposefully ambiguous—the persona's process leads him increasingly toward solipsism. No longer able to distinguish between "love" and "opinion," he feels no sense of the reality of past connections; even the archetypal Eden seems to be an illusion. Existing ". . . where there/ is nothing, save myself. . . . ," he says, "I cannot fill/ myself. . . ." The isolation of the word "myself" in its own line emphasizes the isolation that momentarily overwhelms the persona. Paradoxically, the line expressing the moment of existential terror intimates the pure merging of voice and consciousness associated with the processes of nature in the first stanza.

Perhaps because of this resemblance, the moment generates in the persona a resolve to reestablish contact with the external world. His determination, however, collapses in a way that, at least in retrospect, seems to anticipate Baraka's later political development. His first reaction to the existential terror is a perception of what he "love[s] most." Rather than reassuring him, however, this engenders a cynical determination—perhaps reflecting the continuing sense of loss—that he will "not/ leave what futile lies/ I have." In a context where "love" is a "futile lie," the persona's subsequent decision to "go out to/ what is most beautiful" demands ironic revaluation. The irony increases when the persona derives his conception of the "beautiful" from the platitudinous appeal to nobility of "some noncombatant Greek/ or soft Italian prince," the originators of the Machiavellian slavocracy of Euro-American culture. The persona's concluding questions anticipate the insistence on social and political processes that characterizes Baraka's later works: "And which one/ is truly/ to rule here? And/ what country is this?" Duncan spoke of a process which was essentially mythic, natural, and psychological. While mirroring this process, Baraka's internal processes are clearly carrying him toward the political arena where questions concerning control and possession are central rather than subordinate.

"CROW JANE" AND "LEROY"

Throughout his early work, Baraka tries on a variety of personas, indicating a fascination with masks that provides the center for some of his most interesting early work. The "Crow Jane" sequence, echoing both William Butler Yeats's "Crazy Jane" poems and a blues composition by Mississippi Joe Williams, focuses on the limits of social masking. "Crow Jane," a white woman unconsciously adopting the old Jim Crow racial patterns, attempts to escape her role in "straight" America only to find herself a "wet lady of no image." Even more uncompromising in its dissatisfaction with masks that derive meaning from Euro-American cultural patterns, "An Agony. As Now." develops the image of a persona being burned within a mask of "white hot metal." Tormented by the constrictions of a corrupt, mechanical white role, the persona feels itself "inside someone/ who hates me." Although that someone can easily be seen as a white self, tormenting a black soul, the poem is not developed in explicitly racial terms. It could apply, for example, to a gay person living a "straight" life or a businessperson on the verge of a breakdown. Its implications are clear, however; inexorably, the agony leads to the final line consisting only of the word "screams." Again, the "projective" merging of voice and experience is pure, but the echoes of the scream sound in a voice no longer intended for the ears of the white avant-garde.

Baraka's nationalist voice, collective where the earlier voice was individualistic, aspires to a specifically "black" purity. Even while assuming the role of teacher, Baraka claims authority for his voice only to the extent that it reflects the strength and values of his African American heritage. In "Leroy," he offers up his old voice to the black community, urging it to "pick me apart and take the/ useful parts, the sweet meat of my feelings. And leave/ the bitter . . . rotten white parts/ alone." The alienation associated with Euro-American culture, expressed in the word "alone" as a line by itself, contrasts with the expansive sense of connection felt by the Amiri who rejects the masks of his predecessor "Leroy."

It would be misleading, however, to suggest that Baraka simply rejects all masks imposed by white society in order to reveal his "true" black face. Even while rebelling against the masks associated with his avant-garde personas, Baraka continues to explore the potential of masking in relation to his new orientation. This exploration takes two distinct forms—both designed to bring Baraka closer to the black community. First, he realizes that his own family background distances him from the "black angels" and "strong nigger feeling" described in "Leroy." Even while envisioning Leroy's mother "getting into/ new blues, from the old ones," he sees her "hypnotizing" him as she stares into "the future of the soul." In relation to African American culture, the future of the black bourgeoisie appears increasingly white and alienated. To become "purely black," Baraka must to some extent mask the influence of his class origins. Second, the mask itself is a central image in both African and African American culture. Invoking both the ritual knowledge of Africa and the survival strategy of the black South, the mask has been exploited in African American literature from Charles Waddell Chesnutt and Langston Hughes through Ralph Ellison and William Melvin Kelley. To speak with a black voice, Baraka must, like Br'er Rabbit, present a variety of shifting surfaces, both to defend against and to attack the predatory forces of his environment.

CALL-AND-RESPONSE

These shifting surfaces are extremely elusive, deriving their meaning as much from audience as from speaker. Using musical forms and images as primary points of reference, Baraka explores this relationship between group and individual voices. His music criticism frequently refers to the primacy in African American culture of the call-and-response mode of work songs and spirituals. Playing off this dynamic, many of Baraka's nationalist poems identify his individual voice with that of a group leader calling for an affirmative response from his community. "Three Movements and a Coda," for example, concludes: "These are songs if you have the/ music." Baraka can provide lyrics, but if they are to come alive as songs, the music must be provided by the participation of a responsive community. The conclusion of "Black Art" makes it clear that this music is more than a purely aesthetic response: "Let the world be a Black Poem/ And Let All Black People Speak This Poem/ Silently/ or LOUD." If the world is to be a poem for the black community, a political response must accompany the aesthetic one.

Determining the precise nature of the desired response demands an awareness of the differing implications of Baraka's poetry when interpreted in relation to white and black cultural traditions. Euro-American reactions to Baraka's nationalist voice tend to attribute even its most extreme statements to the poet himself, dismissing the possibility that he is wearing a mask for political purposes. This is particularly significant in relation to the poems in which Baraka appears to suggest random violence against whites. "Three Movements and a Coda" presents the image of looting a drugstore as a guerrilla attack on the "Vampire Nazis." "Black People!" includes the exhortation: "you can't steal nothin' from a white man, he's already stole it he owes/ you anything you want, even his life." The same poem, using profanity as "magic words," pictures looting as a "magic dance in the street."

"A POEM SOME PEOPLE WILL HAVE TO UNDERSTAND"

Frequently, Baraka pictures violence in graphic images of "smashing at jelly-white faces" or "cracking steel knuckles in a jewlady's mouth." Given the unqualified intensity of these images, it hardly seems surprising that many white and less militant black readers dismiss the Baraka of this period as a reverse racist forwarding the very modes of thought he ostensibly rejects. In essence, they take the call that concludes "A Poem Some People Will Have to Understand" on a literal level. When Baraka asks: "Will the machinegunners please step forward," they respond that a military race war can end only in catastrophe for both races.

As the title of the poem suggests, however, the call should not be interpreted simplistically. To be understood, it must be seen in the context of Baraka's view of the historical response of African Americans to racist oppression. Describing a society in which "the wheel, and the wheels, wont let us alone," he points out that blacks have "awaited the coming of a natural/ phenomenon" to effect a release. Only after repeating "But none has come" three times does Baraka summon the "machinegunners." The call sounds Baraka's response to what he sees as the traditional passivity of the African American community. Recognizing that practically all black experience involves direct contact with psychological racism tied to economic exploitation, Baraka treats these shared experiences hyperbolically in order to shake his community into political action. Placed in a social context where violent group rebellion has been the exception, there is much less chance than most white readers believe that his words will be acted on literally. The use of this aesthetic of calculated overstatement demonstrates Baraka's willingness to use the tradition of masking for a new set of political purposes. Where the form of most African American masks has been dictated by their relationship to white psychology, however, Baraka shapes his new masks to elicit response from blacks. Far from oversimplifying his awareness in the nationalist period, Baraka demonstrates his developing sense of the complexity of poetry designed to function in a real social and political context.

The contextual complexity, however, adds a new dimension of seriousness to attacks on Baraka's use of anti-Semitism and racism as rhetorical strategies. Baraka negotiates extremely treacherous territory when and if he expects readers to concentrate on his desire to "Clean out the world for virtue and love" in the same poem ("Black Art") that endorses "poems that kill . . . Setting fire and death to/ whitie's ass." A similar apparent paradox occurs in "Black People!" which says both "Take their lives if need be" and "let's make a world we want black children to grow and learn in." Baraka's aesthetic approach, which vests ultimate authority in the authenticating response, raises the problematic possibility that the audience's real social actions will authenticate the destructive rhetoric rather than the constructive vision.

"IT'S NATION TIME" AND "AFRICA AFRICA AFRICA"

Baraka attempts to diminish this possibility by developing his constructive vision in celebratory nationalist poems such as "It's Nation Time" and "Africa Africa Africa," which introduce a new musical/chant mode to his work. Exhortations such as "Black Art," which, like Baraka's earlier work, manipulate punctuation and syntax to express fully the urgency of an emotional experience, also anticipate the chant poems by introducing oratorical elements reflecting participation in communal ritual. "A Poem for Black Hearts," for example, varies the opening phrase "For Malcolm's eyes" to establish a focal point for audience response. "For Malcolm's words," "For Malcolm's heart," and similar phrases provide a kind of drumbeat for Baraka's meditation on the fallen leader.

In "It's Nation Time" and "Africa Africa Africa," this drumbeat, clearly the constitutive structural element, often sounds explicitly: "Boom/ Boom/ BOOOM/ Boom." Writing primarily in short lines echoing these single drumbeats, Baraka uses reiteration and rhythmical variation to stress his vision of Pan-African unity. The first thirteen lines of "Africa Africa Africa" include no words other than "Africa" and "Africans." Anticipating Baraka's developing interest in reggae music, these poems call for the transformation of the old forms of African American culture into those of a new Pan-African sensibility. "It's Nation Time" phrases this call: "get up rastus for real to be rasta fari." Baraka rejects those "rastus" figures content to wear the passive masks imposed on Africans unaware of their heritage, and celebrates the Rastafarians, a Caribbean sect associated strongly with reggae.

AM/TRAK

The most effective poems of Baraka's socialist period redirect the music of these nationalist chants in an attempt to lead the proletariat, black and white, to a new awareness of the implications of its own experience. *AM/TRAK*, Baraka's celebration of John Coltrane, attempts to chart this new social and aesthetic awareness by relating Baraka's poetic processes to those of the great jazz saxophonist. Beginning with a section that, like the saxophonist's piercing high notes, merges "History Love Scream," Baraka explores the origins of Coltrane's art, which combines individual intensity and the communal response of the bars and churches of Coltrane's Philadelphia. At once purely black and more highly aware than any single voice from the community, Coltrane's voice combines "The vectors from all sources—slavery, renaissance/ bop Charlie Parker/ nigger absolute super-sane screams against reality."

Just as Coltrane's voice incorporates and surpasses that of Charlie "Yardbird" Parker, Baraka's incorporates Coltrane's and places it in a wider socialist perspective. Meditating on the aesthetic "difficulty" of both Coltrane's experimental sounds and his own philosophical works, Baraka considers the threat of losing the communal response: "'Trane you blows too long.'/ Screaming niggers drop out yr solos." Of course, the phrase "drop out" is ambiguous: Even as the audience refuses to make the effort to comprehend the call, the call perfectly expresses the implications of the audience's experience. Such a call, Baraka insists, can never simply fade into silence. Rather, it will receive a response from artists such as Thelonius Monk, the jazz pianist who played "Street gospel intellectual mystic survival codes." Coltrane's audience, according to Baraka, consists largely of fellow artists able to perceive the depths of his involvement with black reality.

By associating his own voice with Coltrane's, Baraka points to the developing distance between himself and his wider audience, a distance reflecting his shift to a socialist stance. The poem's final section, especially,

is much more politically explicit than either the previous sections or Coltrane's music. As he does in numerous poems of the period, including "Dictatorship of the Proletariat" and "Class Struggle in Music," Baraka insists that the capitalist economic system bears full responsibility for the aesthetic and political corruption of American life. Seeing that "the money lord hovers oer us," he concludes, "only socialism brought by revolution/ can win." Meditating on Coltrane's death in relation to the Newark disorders, Baraka responds to his music as an implicit call for the socialist revolution that will "Be reality alive in motion in flame to change." The intensity of the call for change is unmistakable, in both Coltrane's music and Baraka's poetry. Baraka's identification of the change with "socialism brought by revolution," however, seems abstract and unconvincing in contrast, perhaps because of the relative flatness of diction.

As in many of the poems of the socialist period, Baraka's rhetorical strategy seems unclear. *AM/TRAK* contains few indications that the last section should be seen as some type of intricate mask. In fact, American socialist writing lacks a dominant tradition of masking and also tends to reject philosophically anything other than direct confrontation. Still, Baraka certainly retains his knowledge of the African American tradition of masking and has the ability to adjust his voice in accord with shifting social contexts. His extreme didactic stance may be intended as much to spark debate as to enforce agreement. The direct attacks on Don L. Lee (Haki R. Madhubuti) and Nikki Giovanni that occur in Baraka's works, however, suggest that such an interpretation may be overly ingenuous and that Baraka does in fact seek total agreement.

SOCIALIST VOICE

No simple aesthetic analysis suffices to explain either Baraka's new poetic voice or his difficulty in calling forth an affirmative response from either the artistic or the working-class community. Lines such as "This is the dictatorship of the proletariat/ the total domination of society by the working class" can easily be dismissed as lacking either the intellectual complexity or the emotional power of Baraka's earlier work. Such a dismissal, however, risks avoiding the issue of cultural conditioning, which Baraka has come to view as central. Arguing that capitalist control of the media deforms both the proletariat's image of itself as a revolutionary force and its response to a "pure" socialist art, Baraka attempts to shatter the psychological barriers through techniques of reiteration similar to those used in his nationalist poetry. His relationship with the proletariat audience, however, generates a new set of political and aesthetic problems. While the nationalist voice assumed authority only insofar as it was validated by the experience of the African American community, the socialist voice must take on the additional burden of convincing the proletarian audience that its interpretation of its own experience has been "incorrect." If the community does not respond to Baraka's voice as its own, the problem lies with a brainwashed response rather than with a tainted call (the source of the problem in "Leroy"). As a result, Baraka frequently adopts a "lecturer's" voice to provide the "hard facts" that will overcome resistance to political action by proving that capitalism deceives the proletariat into accepting a "dictatorship of the minority."

The lack of response to his poems based on this aesthetic may simply reflect the accuracy of his analysis of the problem. What is certain is that Baraka remains determined to resist corruption in whatever form he perceives it and that he continues to search for a voice like the one described in "Class Struggle in Music (2)," a voice that "even reached you."

SOMEBODY BLEW UP AMERICA, AND OTHER POEMS

The critically acclaimed collection *Somebody Blew Up America, and Other Poems* is dominated by the title poem, Baraka's inflammatory response to the September 11, 2001, terrorist attacks on the United States. The title poem is a sharp thorn among roses of tribute and remembrance, such as "Beginnings: Malcolm," an homage to Malcolm X that raises the issue of Christianity's contribution to the disharmonious state of affairs in the world. The title poem, read publicly beginning on September 19, 2001, and published in November of that year, caused a storm of controversy.

"Somebody Blew Up America" is a polemic that uses a terrorist act of global consequence as a jumping-off point to condemn terrorism in general, and especially the terrorism practiced by whites against minori-

ties, particularly that which occurs in the United States. The poem gathers many threads from Baraka's traditional themes. Racism, corruption, class warfare, government, and imperialism all come under fire in an angry litany of historical outrages—slavery, murder, genocide, market manipulation, Christianity, assassination, capitalism, financial control, and political shenanigans—along with the more recent outrage of passenger-plane attacks against buildings. The poem also brings together elements of Baraka's three creative phases: the intellectual avant-garde, the Black Nationalist, and the radically political.

The structure and tone of the poem owe much to the Beat movement of the 1950's, particularly to Ginsberg's "Howl" (1956). Baraka, in fact, seems to be paying homage to Ginsberg in his repetition of the refrain "Who" and in his reference to an owl in the final stanzas. Stylistically, the poem draws on several traditions: blank verse, spur-of-the-moment rhyme, and repetitious, hip-hop rhythm. Like the Beats, Baraka is not afraid to use a full range of techniques—blunt language, emotionally charged words, racial epithets, Ebonics, slang, and street lingo—to drive home a point. He accuses both the living and the dead (naming such well-known public figures as Trent Lott, David Duke, Rudy Giuliani, Jesse Helms, George W. Bush, Colin Powell, and Condoleezza Rice) of complicity in a five-hundred-year conspiracy to eliminate undesirables, opponents, and the outspoken in an all-consuming effort to dominate the world. Baraka asks tough questions, demanding to know who has historically been the worst mass murderers; who has been the chief aggressors over the ages; who currently controls the oil, the media, and the governments around the globe; and who is responsible for the sad state of the world. The material is based on fact, innuendo, rumor, and wild speculation, making it difficult to distinguish where truth leaves off and fiction begins. The poet's anger is real, and the targets of his vituperation are legion, but he sometimes contradicts himself in his righteous vehemence. After the initial shock of "Somebody Blew Up America" wears off, the thoughtful reader is left with the myriad questions the poem raises, but is provided no answers for how to correct humankind's self-destructive nature or how to change the course of history. Even if reminded of the past, Baraka seems to say, people are condemned to repeat it.

In the poem, Baraka implies that Jews both in the United States and abroad were aware in advance of the September 11 attacks and stayed away from New York City on the day the planes crashed into the Twin Towers. Suggestions like this caused New Jersey's governor to call for Baraka to resign from his post as the state's poet laureate. Baraka, however, refused to do so, and the post was abolished in 2003, ending his appointment.

UN POCO LOW COUP

In contrast to much of Baraka's earlier poetic work, *Un Poco Low Coup* presents brief bursts of inspiration about a range of subjects. The short folio (twenty-three pages) features poems combined with illustrations, photographs, scribbles, and drawings in folk-art style to aid in understanding or to visually expand on a theme. The pieces are experiments in concision, based on the Japanese haiku, the impressionistic seventeen-syllable poem used to express small but significant or profound moments. The title of Baraka's collection (*un poco* means "a little" in Spanish) is an ironic pun on the sound of the word "haiku," in the same vein as such earlier works as *Raise Race Rays Raze: Essays Since 1965* (1971) or *Wise, Why's, Y's* (1995). "Low coup" (LOW-coo) may be presumed to have the opposite intent of the haiku, as filtered through politically motivated, radicalized African American sensibilities, wherein skepticism rules and things are not accepted at face value. The reader is warned in advance that these epigram-like or graffiti-styled efforts, though echoing the brevity of the Japanese verse, do not aim at high art, but low art, since puns are traditionally considered one of the lower forms of humor. Many pieces in *Un Poco Low Coup* do not even attempt to duplicate the precise haiku form, as though the poet, after consciously launching the collection in imitation of a well-established poetic form, found the ancient structure too confining for modern thought.

Reflecting Baraka's lifelong love of music and rhythm, the poems in *Un Poco Low Coup* are like improvisational, jazz-flavored riffs—as though scored for such traditional Japanese instruments as the koto, the shamisen, the hichiriki, or the taiko—touching on fa-

vorite themes. These nuggets of arcane, esoteric wisdom are intended as thought-provoking snacks for the brain, rather than as a filling meal for the soul. Much can be read into them, but the reader has to do most of the work; Baraka's short poems are only a beginning rather than an end, a catalyst to cogitation rather than a completed thought.

It is difficult to argue about the premise of the individual poems. Like the haiku that spawned them, the *Un Poco Low Coup* poems are so brief and so open-ended that interpretation becomes the sole responsibility of readers, all of whom will bring unique personal experiences that contribute to understanding; Baraka proposes, but each person disposes meaning.

In "Ancient Music," for example, Baraka contends that death is humankind's common enemy, and everything else pales by comparison. "In the Funk World," he posits that James Brown deserves more acclaim than Elvis Presley for his contributions to music. The wry "Monday in B-flat" suggests that dialing emergency is more efficacious than prayer in getting results. "Low Coup for Bush 2" recommends imprisonment for George W. Bush. In "Heaven," Baraka implies that the concept of servitude and the idea of slavery was an original tenet of Christianity. Ultimately, the value of the poems of *Un Poco Low Coup* can be summed up in a paraphrase of an older, haiku-like aphorism: "Profundity is in the eye—and ear—of the informed, politically aware beholder."

OTHER MAJOR WORKS

LONG FICTION: *The System of Dante's Hell*, 1965.

SHORT FICTION: *Tales*, 1967; *The Fiction of LeRoi Jones/Amiri Baraka*, 2000; *Tales of the Out and the Gone*, 2007.

PLAYS: *The Baptism*, pr. 1964; *Dutchman*, pr., pb. 1964; *The Slave*, pr., pb. 1964; *The Toilet*, pr., pb. 1964; *Experimental Death Unit #1*, pr. 1965; *Jello*, pr. 1965; *A Black Mass*, pr. 1966; *Arm Yourself, or Harm Yourself*, pr., pb. 1967; *Great Goodness of Life (A Coon Show)*, pr. 1967; *Madheart*, pr. 1967; *Slave Ship: A Historical Pageant*, pr., pb. 1967; *The Death of Malcolm X*, pb. 1969; *Bloodrites*, pr. 1970; *Junkies Are Full of (SHHH . . .)*, pr. 1970; *A Recent Killing*, pr. 1973; *S-1*, pr. 1976; *The Motion of History*, pr. 1977;

The Sidney Poet Heroical, pb. 1979 (originally as *Sidnee Poet Heroical*, pr. 1975); *What Was the Relationship of the Lone Ranger to the Means of Production?*, pr., pb. 1979; *At the Dim'cracker Party Convention*, pr. 1980; *Weimar*, pr. 1981; *Money: A Jazz Opera*, pr. 1982; *Primitive World: An Anti-Nuclear Jazz Musical*, pr. 1984; *The Life and Life of Bumpy Johnson*, pr. 1991; *General Hag's Skeezag*, pb. 1992; *Meeting Lillie*, pr. 1993; *The Election Machine Warehouse*, pr. 1996.

NONFICTION: "*Cuba Libre*," 1961; *The New Nationalism*, 1962; *Blues People: Negro Music in White America*, 1963; *Home: Social Essays*, 1966; *Black Music*, 1968; *A Black Value System*, 1970; *Kawaida Studies: The New Nationalism*, 1971; *Raise Race Rays Raze: Essays Since 1965*, 1971; *Strategy and Tactics of a Pan-African Nationalist Party*, 1971; *Crisis in Boston!*, 1974; *The Creation of the New Ark*, 1975; *Daggers and Javelins: Essays*, 1984; *The Autobiography of LeRoi Jones/Amiri Baraka*, 1984; *The Artist and Social Responsibility*, 1986; *The Music: Reflections on Jazz and Blues*, 1987 (with Amina Baraka); *Conversations with Amiri Baraka*, 1994 (Charlie Reilly, editor); *Jesse Jackson and Black People*, 1994; *Eulogies*, 1996; *Digging: Afro American Be/At American Classical Music*, 1999; *Bushwacked! A Counterfeit President for a Fake Democracy: A Collection of Essays on the 2000 National Elections*, 2001; *National Elections*, 2001; *Jubilee: The Emergence of African-American Culture*, 2003 (with others); *The Essence of Reparations*, 2003; *Home: Social Essays*, 2009.

EDITED TEXTS: *The Moderns: New Fiction in America*, 1963; *Black Fire: An Anthology of Afro-American Writing*, 1968 (with Larry Neal); *African Congress: A Documentary of the First Modern Pan-African Congress*, 1972; *Confirmation: An Anthology of African-American Women*, 1983 (with Amina Baraka).

MISCELLANEOUS: *Selected Plays and Prose*, 1979; *The LeRoi Jones/Amiri Baraka Reader*, 1991; *Insomniacathon: Voices Without Restraint*, 1999 (audiocassette).

BIBLIOGRAPHY

Baraka, Amiri. "Amiri Baraka." http://www.amiri baraka.com. The official Web site for the author contains a brief biography, photographs, descriptions of books, selected poems and essays, recordings of poems, and links to other sites.

_____. Interviews. *Conversations with Amiri Baraka.* Edited by Charlie Reilly. Jackson: University Press of Mississippi, 1994. Offers insights into the black experience through Baraka's experiences during the turbulent later half of the twentieth century, from his ghetto life in the 1940's through the Black Nationalist movement of the 1970's to his intellectual life in the 1990's. Baraka critiques and elucidates his works and underscores his belief in the connection between art and social criticism.

Benston, Kimberly W., ed. *Imamu Amiri Baraka (LeRoi Jones): A Collection of Critical Essays.* Englewood Cliffs, N.J.: Prentice-Hall, 1978. Benston, who also wrote *Baraka: The Renegade and the Mask* (1976), brings together essays that shed light on various aspects of his poetry and drama. Includes a bibliography.

Collins, Lisa Gail, and Margo Natalie Crawford, eds. *New Thoughts on the Black Arts Movement.* Piscataway, N.J.: Rutgers University Press, 2006. This collection of essays discusses the African American renaissance in arts and letters during the 1960's and 1970's and examines the contributions of such influential figures as Baraka.

Epstein, Andrew. *Beautiful Enemies: Friendship and Postwar American Poetry.* New York: Oxford University Press, 2006. This study examines the complex and changeable relationships among and between writers John Ashbery, Frank O'Hara, Baraka and others of various New York intellectual circles, in terms of literary, personal, and philosophical issues.

Finch, Annie Ridley Crane, and Kathrine Lore Varnes, eds. *An Exaltation of Forms: Contemporary Poets Celebrate the Diversity of Their Art.* Ann Arbor: University of Michigan Press, 2002. This collection of essays focusing on contemporary poetic techniques includes a brief piece by Baraka, "The Low Coup as a Contemporary Afro-American Verse Form," explaining his rationale behind the poems in *Un Poco Low Coup*.

Gwynne, James B., ed. *Amiri Baraka: The Kaleidoscopic Torch.* New York: Steppingstones Press,

1985. This collection of poems and essays for and about Baraka includes Richard Oyama's analysis of "The Screamers," titled "A Secret Communal Expression," as well as essays by Clyde Taylor and E. San Juan, Jr.

Smethurst, James Edward. *The Black Arts Movement: Literary Nationalism in the 1960's and 1970's.* Chapel Hill: University of North Carolina Press, 2005. Part of the John Hope Franklin Series in African American History and Culture, this profusely illustrated study focuses on the cultural side of black self-awareness that grew out of the Civil Rights and Black Power movements, including Baraka's contributions to those efforts.

Watts, Jerry Gafio. *Amiri Baraka: The Politics and Art of a Black Intellectual.* New York: New York University Press, 2001. A critical appraisal. Watts argues that Baraka's artistry declined as he became more politically active, though he considers Baraka to be an important poet and lens through which African American political history can be viewed.

Woodard, K. Komozi. *A Nation Within a Nation: Amiri Baraka (LeRoi Jones) and Black Power Politics.* Chapel Hill: University of North Carolina Press, 1999. Revises the common view of Baraka as an extremist, arguing that he became a seasoned political veteran who brought together divergent black factions.

Craig Werner
Updated by Jack Ewing

MARY BARNARD

Born: Vancouver, Washington; December 6, 1909
Died: Vancouver, Washington; August 25, 2001

PRINCIPAL POETRY

"Cool Country" in *Five Young American Poets*, 1940
A Few Poems, 1952
Collected Poems, 1979
Time and the White Tigress, 1986

OTHER LITERARY FORMS

Although Mary Barnard's principal genre was poetry, she also worked with translations from the Greek, most notably in her well-known *Sappho: A New Translation* (1958). The bulk of her fiction, published in widely read periodicals in the 1950's, is as yet uncollected, though *Three Fables* appeared in 1983. Her essays from her research into Sappho, *The Mythmakers* (1966), also inform her poetry collection *Time and the White Tigress.* Perhaps her best-known work, aside from the poetry, is the autobiography *Assault on Mount Helicon: A Literary Memoir* (1984), which features portraits of many of the chief figures in modern American literature but especially of Ezra Pound and William Carlos Williams.

ACHIEVEMENTS

Mary Barnard's work shows the influence of the modernists transposed to a minor key. Although it lacks the cosmopolitan effusiveness of Pound or the cultural skeet-shooting of T. S. Eliot or the secret ambition of Williams, it nevertheless sets forth a legitimate agenda and succeeds in convincing its readers that although it is small as an oeuvre, it is by no means slight. Moreover, the scope belies the small size. If one believes with Samuel Taylor Coleridge that one of the distinguishing characteristics of high art is its ability to pack maximum content into minimum space, then the miniatures of Barnard offer more aesthetic satisfaction than their collective heft would suggest. By invoking the mythical within the ordinary and the everyday within the mythical, she created a resonant parallel device for treating the subjects of her choice: childhood, the meaning of change, the pervasiveness of limits, humanity's relation to nature and to its past, and the fate of women.

Although she wrote essays and fiction as well as translated from the Greek, these endeavors provided—to use one of her favorite images—a spring from which to enlarge and refresh her poetry. In its classical approach to hidden truths about human nature, it bears resemblance to such earlier writers as Léonie Adams and Louise Bogan. Her translations of Sappho show what can be done to breathe life into revered but seldom-read classics, and the autobiographical *Assault on Mount*

Helicon is an important and engaging document of literary history and literary survival from one who wrote from "the far shore" but was nevertheless in the midst of one of the great cultural revolutions of modern times. Her honors and awards include the Levinson Prize from *Poetry* magazine in 1935 and the Western States Book Award for Poetry in 1986 for *Time and the White Tigress*.

BIOGRAPHY

Born of parents who moved west from Indiana, a move inspired in part by the Lewis and Clark Centennial Exposition in Portland, Oregon, in 1905, Mary Barnard was born on December 6, 1909, in Vancouver, Washington. Her father ran a lumber mill, and Barnard was able to grow up happily in congenial surroundings. Her parents encouraged her early interest in poetry, and Barnard—unusual for her time—attended Reed College, where she took creative writing courses and graduated in 1932.

Twice during the 1930's, Barnard took up summer residencies at Yaddo in upstate New York and met a number of writers, including Muriel Rukeyser, Kenneth Fearing, Eleanor Clark, and Delmore Schwartz. It was during this decade that she also began corresponding with Pound and Williams, who further encouraged her. In 1935, she won the Levinson Prize, and her poems were first collected in New Directions' *Five Young American Poets* in 1940. From 1939 to 1943, she worked as curator of the poetry collection at the University of Buffalo, and from 1943 to 1950, she worked as a research assistant to Carl Van Doren and wrote fiction that appeared in such periodicals as *Saturday Review of Literature*, *Kenyon Review*, and *Harper's Bazaar*. *A Few Poems* appeared from Reed College in 1952, and in the mid-1950's she worked on her translations of Sappho. In 1957, simultaneously with the acceptance of her translations, she moved back to the West Coast and settled in Portland, Oregon. Her collection of essays, *The Mythmakers*, appeared in 1966.

The 1979 publication of her *Collected Poems* brought Barnard's poetry to the attention of a new generation of readers. Both this book and her memoir, *Assault on Mount Helicon*, were widely reviewed and warmly received. *Time and the White Tigress* won the 1986 Western States Book Award for Poetry and prompted the jury to cite it as "an impressive achievement from a distinguished writer, and an admirable new American poem." It was her last published poetry collection, and she died in Vancouver in 2001.

ANALYSIS

Mary Barnard's poetic output, while quite slim, nevertheless spans and reflects more than half a century of involvement in the art. Her brief, solicitous early lyrics delineate the natural world of the Pacific Northwest with quiet precision, while her later poems reveal her increasing interest in mythological models. Devoid of gimmick and rhetoric, they are as unassuming and as well made as Shaker furniture. The world described in the earlier poems is a world in transition—mostly gone, a remote place of springs and rivers, of meadows and deer, where railroads provide the transfusions of people and goods necessary for a human population to flourish. The later poems cease to reflect a period aspect and, with increasing awareness and confidence in her powers, rely more heavily on invention than recollection. The dominant elements throughout are water and earth rather than air or fire.

COLLECTED POEMS

Collected Poems opens in childhood, not a childhood toggled to personal memory, but a childhood that any adult might imagine as belonging to a young girl. In "Playroom," there is

> mournfulness of muddy playgrounds,
> raw smell of rubbers and wrapped lunches
> when little girls stand in a circle singing
> of windows and of lovers.

The lives within the playground sing of the life beyond their experience and place, just as the mature poet sings of her "beyond," the past:

> Hearing them, no one could tell
> why they sing sadly, but there is in their voices
> the pathos of all handed-down garments
> hanging loosely on small bodies.

The poem suggests that life itself is a process of outgrowing "garments," that the provisional is the domain of the living. Thus, the girls "sing sadly," not because they understand this condition but because, literally, they embody it.

If the girls have to content themselves with hand-me-downs, a young girl in "The Fitting" must contend with a "trio of hags . . . with cold hands" who roam over her young body and "compress withered lips upon pins" to produce a dress for her. They are the three Fates, who determine the quality and duration of life. As they fit the girl, "The knocking of hammers comes/ from beyond the still window curtain. . . ." Some portion of the future, pertinent to others, is being constructed, but her hands will make nothing: "Her life is confined here, in this depth/ in the well of the mirrors." The poem ends with the soft snipping of scissors and pulled threads—also not to be hers—lying on the carpet. The tiny separations imparted by the scissors suggest many more consequential leave-takings to come.

The understanding of limitations of which the young may only have vague intimations, and their delineation, drawn from images in the natural world, are the subjects of many of Barnard's poems. To define a limit, to put a form to what is already form, is to pay it authentic homage. One of the most elemental limits and the source of centuries of solemn meditation from Homer to Wallace Stevens is the seashore. The sea, as a self-sufficient, obverse universe, confronts people both with their otherness, with respect to their mutually incompatible biologies, and with their own "shores," beyond which begins the vast Not-me, a country about which they are impelled to educate themselves, education being the development of commerce between the two realms. However, their bodies feel a distant affinity to that otherness not easily accessible to language. As the Metaphysical poet Thomas Traherne noted, humanity is "both with moons and tides."

"SHORELINE"

In "Shoreline," one of Barnard's longer poems (and her first published poem), the poet states flatly, "Sand is the beginning and the end/ of our dominion." However, "The way to the dunes is easy," as children, who have not yet transformed the sea and land, water and earth, into concepts, instinctively know: "their bodies glow/ in the cold wash of the beach." When they return from

the beach, "They are unmoved by fears/ that breed in darkening kitchens at sundown/ following storm. . . ." Barnard asserts of the shoreline: "This, then, is the country of our choice." The operative word here is "choice," for one would have thought that limitation was, on the contrary, merely the country of necessity. By choice, however, one stands by the shore "and long[s] for islands"; thus, in some measure, one equally and consciously partakes of one's limitations as well. As one gets older, on the other hand, and one's choices dwindle in the face of increased experience, "We lose the childish avarice of horizons." The poem ends with the refrain, "sand/ is the beginning and the end/ of our dominion," though with a different line break, as if to suggest its shifting against "our dominion." One hears a gentle corrective here both to the infinitude of William Blake's sand and, prophetically, to the sonorous "dominion" of which death shall have none in Dylan Thomas. Barnard's poem seems more thoughtfully located in the actual experiences of people, less in the seductive undertow of language.

Those childhoods, suspended in the ancestral and the domestic, however unique they may seem to the individual and web-spun consciousness of children, carry with them the evidence of their lineages. This evidence, which bespeaks generations of labor needed to produce the child into its time, is present everywhere but especially in those objects that address the body, as in "Beds": "The carved oak headboards of ancestral beds tilt/ like foundered decks from fog at the mouth of the river." The lovely image of care and protection is addressed specifically to the body, whose vulnerability reaches its apex at night. Fear—of being abducted (into the night, into the future, into death)—alternates with remembered or implied assurances of protection:

Lulla, lulla, will there be, will there
always be a place to sleep when smoke gathers in the
    rafters?
. . . .
Lulla, lulla. Flood after flood. When the beds float
downstream, will there be a place to sleep, Matthew, Mark?

Unlike the children's playground, the sanctuary of the bed is permanent, even obligingly providing, although somewhat transformed, humanity's last "resting place." Consequently, the bones' sanctuary posture is the horizontal, and it is through this "angle" that one can see that the eternal nature of the forms links people from biology to biography to history, from their bodies to those of their ancestors and of all humankind:

> The feathers of my grandmothers' beds melted into
>   earlier darkness
> as, bone to earth, I lay down. A trail that leads out, leads
>   back.
> Leads back, anyway, one night or another, bone to earth.

"THE RAPIDS"

Limits, which provide Barnard with so much of her subject matter, are not inert barriers but, because they are "our choice," are rather actively engaged in transformations. In "The Rapids," the poet focuses on the distinction between the boundary as limit and as transformer: "No country is so gracious to us/ as that which kept its contours while we forgot them." The precisely placed "gracious" suggests how accommodating a contour can manage to be to satisfy one's need for orientation and security. At the same time, it is an agency of change: "The water we saw broken upon the rapids/ has dragged silt through marshland/ and mingled with the embittered streams of the sea."

In the last stanza of this three-stanza poem, Barnard telescopes the stationary and the moving into a single image of "ungatherable blossoms floating by the . . . rock." These "have flung light in my face, have made promises/ in unceasing undertone." The promises are guarantees made subliminally that one will be at home in the world, or at least that one can recover his home. "Alienation"—one of the most self-incriminating buzzwords of the twentieth century—and all the philosophical ramifications tangled up with it, are, after all, of human manufacture, and while the mind can surely suffer from alienation, it can also break out of it in an instant. Such an instant constitutes the poetic moment of this and other of Barnard's poems.

"WINTER EVENING"

Being at home in the world means also adjusting to its cyclic nature, which involves death. Usually, human beings do all they can to insulate themselves from its blows, and when the time comes when they can no lon-

ger do that, they remember, if they still can, the traditional loophole, lamentation, channeling their sorrow, paying homage, and letting off the steam of outrage and fear all at once. The ability and courage to confront death (of others and one's own) is inversely proportional to the amount of insulation one has accumulated (in the twentieth century, quite a lot). In "Winter Evening," Barnard examines the mythical place of death, for mythological treatment tends to "naturalize" death and so render it less psychically damaging by treating it as an equal partner in the scheme of things. On the other hand, modern middle-class living has tried, in countless ways and to its detriment, to dust its hands of the unflattering fact of terminal being:

> In the mountains, it is said,
> the deer are dying by hundreds.
> We know nothing of that
> in the suburbs.

Doubtless, suburban life has what passes for myths, too, but these are not "ancestral myth," the myth of origins. Rather, "our century/ clings to the novel./ Coffee and novels." Only the train whistles "howl against death/ . . . like Lear in his heartbreak,/ savage as a new myth." Lear, in his vanity, also upset a primordial set of precedents and suffered madness and death for his trouble. The odd juxtaposition of Lear (though, appropriately, Lear is a winter king) and the suburbanites clearly boosts the latter into a mythical realm of danger, for the forces involved are huge and indifferent to human willfulness. The leveling snow that is the immediate cause of the animals' deaths goes on quietly covering all the houses in the town.

"THE SPRING"

Although Barnard has clearly absorbed the image-based tenets of Pound and Williams, she most clearly follows the homegrown variety of Williams. In the slyly self-referential "The Spring," Barnard follows the course—one is tempted to say "career"—of a spring, "a mere trickle," as it "whispers" out from under a boulder and fills, first, a pond, then travels (somehow keeping its integrity as a separate spring as it does so) over a spillway, fills another pond, and then falls between trees "to find its fate in the river." The poet concludes,

Nameless, it has two little ponds
to its credit, like a poet
with two small collections of verse.

For this I celebrate it.

Executed in Williams-style tercets, the poem concerns the question of poetic identity, as the simile makes clear. It is also a self-celebration, for the spring is a decidedly naturalistic image and so in Barnard's canon gets a de facto seal of approval. From the boulder of obscurity to the river of judgment, the stream has avoided dilution, just as a poet with two small collections will, one hopes, have avoided assimilation. To the untrained eye, however, the spring's continuity, its purposefulness, will be invisible: At the point that it is a pond, it *is* a pond; at the river, the river. Guiding her own stream between the "tall cottonwoods" of Pound and Williams (as one would imagine) becomes a matter of integrity that she does not need to spell out, just as it is an act of homage in form and feeling.

"INHERITANCE"

Barnard's revival ("arrival" might more accurately indicate the tone of her reception) in the late 1970's was to a considerable degree enhanced by her feminist principles. "Inheritance" addresses the theme of the woman's largely forgotten contribution to the settling of America:

Spoon clink fell to axe-chink
falling along the Ohio. These women
made their beds, God bless them,
in the wandering, dreamed, hoped-for
Hesperides, their graves
in permanent places.

The poet admits that, indeed, she was left no tangible inheritance, only pride, and not even pride, but the memory of it, which she identifies as "armor/ . . . against time and men and women." The final placement of women in the list of the enemies of women is a fine idea, and the poem, armored, ends on that note. Barnard obviously believes that one of the chief battles of feminism must be fought on the field of memory, and indeed much of feminist work has been in rectifying the obscured and mystified history of the sex and in transferring future custodianship to women.

"PERSEPHONE"

Barnard's reading of the classics, from which emerged her translations of Sappho, shows up in poems such as "Persephone." Here, the poet disposes of the hierarchical view of the surface as implicitly preferable to the underworld:

I loved like a mole. There were
subterranean flat stone stairways
to columns supporting the earth and its
daffodils. Or shall we say, to the facade
of the hiding place of earth's treasure?

Nostalgia has no place in the erection of hell: "Homesickness here/ is for the raw working and scars of the surface. . . ." Persephone will make do with what is at hand and will not be enticed into living by "hunger—to which/ . . . surrender is death." She will return to the surface, but not by giving in to her hunger for it. Rather, she will have her pride, and presumably the memory of it, to strengthen her for her return:

How many times it is said to the living,
Conquer hunger! If you
want to go back, up, up where the sun falls
warm on flowering rock and make garlands again.

Barnard puts an effective feminist spin on Persephone's self-denial: Neither the hunger for the world nor the conquering of it is tinged with the desire to return to men (they are conspicuously absent from the poem); rather, Persephone's desire is "to make garlands again."

"ONDINE"

The image of another "buried" woman appears in "Ondine." Here, the speaker has invited the mermaid into her house to eat, but instead of eating, she sits weeping and blames the speaker for stealing driftwood to burn, a charge the speaker denies. At this, the mermaid stands up and wrings her hair "so that the water made a sudden splash/ on the round rug by the door" and leaves to return to the sea. The speaker throws the knot of wood where the mermaid had sat into the fire ("I beat it out with a poker/ in the soft ash"). At length, she comes to regret her fit of anger:

Now I am frightened on the shore at night,
and all the phosphorescent swells that rise
come towards me with the threat of her dark eyes
with a cold firelight in them . . .

Her sense of self-reproach at her inability to establish any but the most cursory of relationships with the strange creature gives way to anxiety and guilt. The poem ends with an apocalyptic image that hints at the psychological forces involved in her failure:

Should she return and bring her sisters with her,
the withdrawing tide
would leave a long pool in my bed.
There would be nothing more of me this side

the melting foamline of the latest wave.

"FABLE FROM THE CAYOOSH COUNTRY"

It is in her mythological voice that Barnard most comfortably addresses the larger themes. In one of these, "Fable from the Cayoosh Country," the subject is the power and influence of language. The poet and an unnamed companion lie beside a lake in a pastoral setting. Aware of the nature surrounding them, their thought "pushed forward into the margins of silence/ . . . the boundaries of an inarticulate world." Falling asleep, she dreams of being a missionary of language to the beasts:

I preached the blessing of the noun and verb,
but all was lost in the furred ear of the bear,
in the expressive ear of the young doe.
What the doe said with her ear, I understood.
What I said, she obviously did not.

Exasperated, she hurls her grammar books into a pool that immediately begins to address her. It relates the story of a time when all nature could speak with the eloquence that human beings have, but found it was a curse, not a blessing:

. . . The blade of this tool, useless for digging, chopping,
shearing, they used against each other with such zeal
they all but accomplished their own extermination.

The creatures of nature therefore "abandoned speech" yet "retained cries expressive of emotion,/ as rage,/ or love." The pool adds, "They have never seen any cause to repent their decision." The speaker then dreams that the lake has risen over them and confesses, "My consternation was that of a poet, whose love/ if not his living was gravely endangered." She wakes and, finding the lake in place as before, wonders whether it is not a pity that it had not, in fact, flooded over them. As a visionary poem, "Fable from the Cayoosh Country" locates in language not the tool that binds human beings together in a mutually satisfying quest for articulation, but a tempting means to allow oneself to become separate from nature and from one's self. Unfortunately, language cannot police its abuses. In fact, it is not usually aware of them until the harm has been done. Obviously, the poem is a retelling of the Fall, and the striving after language (not in the sense of naming but in the proud rise to eloquence) becomes an activity inappropriate to either Paradise or redemption, the beasts having already fallen and redeemed their natures through a return to the inarticulate. The triumph and burden of language being the human lot, however, the wish to do as the beasts do becomes moot, as language is, for humankind, an irreversible phenomenon.

"LETHE"

Another fine poem that speculates on erasure (and mentioned approvingly by Pound) considers the return to the tabula rasa of the soul recycled and made ready for reincarnation by the waters of Lethe. The soul in "Lethe" pauses over the waters and ponders the enormous human loss necessary to prepare the soul for return to Earth:

Will a few drops on the tongue
like a whirling flood submerge cities,
like a sea, grind pillars to sand?
Will it wash the color from the lips and the eyes
beloved? It were a thousand pities
thus to dissolve
the delicate sculpture of a lifted hand. . . .

The cost of such forgetting is, for a poet, unbearable, even as it is inevitable. Oblivion is the exact enemy of art, just as Satan is the enemy of virtue, and the poet, "hesitant, unwilling to drink," is ennobled by her resistance.

TIME AND THE WHITE TIGRESS

Time and the White Tigress is a series of verse essays (Barnard refers to it as a single long poem) about the celestial and natural cycles and their impact on humanity's understanding of its place in the cosmos. Harking back to her classical studies and the archaeological arcana of *The Mythmakers*, the poems present, complete with contextual notes, a rationale for the capture and implementation of time as a series of demarcations suitable to the use of custom, since there is "no society without customs. . . ." Hence, the possession of knowledge about time is power inasmuch as it gives its possessor(s) knowledge of the cycles through which one conducts one's life:

> A rhythm established by moon after moon,
> tide after tide, and year after year
> has formed the framework for all our cultures,
> a pattern of custom that echoes the pattern
> woven by time in the heavens.

Principally, it is to the ancient astronomers, whose priestly function it was to observe and mime the activities of the sky, that beginnings of mythology can be traced: the Twins (dark and light), the signs of the Zodiac, the gods and goddesses of the ancient religions. Far from pushing mythology deeper into the mists, however, Barnard shows that the sky watchers were pragmatic sages who interpreted the heavens in ingenious and economic ways and set the stage for the growth of civilization, from the role of priests and kings to the use and democratization of time to the techniques of mythologizing as a form of advancing out of the darkness. Miming her own subjects, she writes,

> We are following here the spoor
> of a White Tigress who prowled
> Time's hinterlands . . .
>
> . . . .
>
> Her teats, dripping a moon-milk,
> suckled the Twins. The savor,
> still on our tongues, is fading.
>
> Here, a pug-mark in the path.
> There, bent grass where she crouched.
> From this I construct a tigress?
>
> A mythical one?
> Perhaps. Why
> should we cease to make myths?

One of Barnard's achievements was a conscious invention and perpetuation of myths, which are the "necessary fictions" by which human beings try to invoke principles of memory and harmony in their otherwise partial and painful existence through time's indifferent hallways.

OTHER MAJOR WORKS

SHORT FICTION: *Three Fables*, 1983.

NONFICTION: *The Mythmakers*, 1966; *Assault on Mount Helicon: A Literary Memoir*, 1984; *Nantucket Genesis: The Tale of My Tribe*, 1988; *The Diary of an Optimist*, 1995.

TRANSLATION: *Sappho: A New Translation*, 1958.

BIBLIOGRAPHY

Barnard, Mary. "Dialogue with Mary Barnard." Interview by Anita Helle. *Northwest Review* 20, no. 2/3 (1982): 188-198. Few biographical sources on Barnard exist, therefore this interview is very important. Barnard explains that she uses myth to reveal lost history, especially the history of women in Western society. Interesting for all students.

Fantazzi, Charles E. Review of *The Myth of Apollo and Daphne from Ovid to Quevedo*. *Choice* 25 (September, 1987): 112. Fantazzi comments on Barnard's highly learned book of comparative literature, which traces the story of Apollo and Daphne from Ovid to the Spanish Golden Age. Barnard's facility with myth is apparent here, as it is in her poetry. Gives an idea of the breadth of Barnard's accomplishment as a writer.

McDowell, Robert. "New Schools and Late Discoveries." *Hudson Review* 34 (Winter, 1987). Discusses the unusual fusion of poetry and explicative essay in Barnard's *Time and the White Tigress*.

Swift, John. "Separations." *Northwest Review* 18, no. 3 (1980): 114-119. Swift explains Barnard's attempt to separate the idea of boundaries as limits and the notion of limits as powers that enable transformation. This is related to Barnard's connection with the land of the Pacific Northwest.

Van Cleve, Jane. "A Personal View of Mary Barnard." *Northwest Review* 18, no. 3 (1980): 105-113. Barnard's work did not find a large audience until the late 1970's, when feminist writing came into vogue. Van Cleve discusses how Barnard's poetry affects Van Cleve as a woman.

Whitman, Ruth. Review of *Time and the White Tigress*. *Choice* 24 (December, 1986): 620. Whitman calls Barnard's book of poetry "extraordinary." She describes how it weaves comparative mythology with comparative science in a beautiful, simple way. Provides students with a helpful overview and understanding of Barnard's book. Informative for all students.

David Rigsbee

PAUL BEATTY

Born: Los Angeles, California; 1962

PRINCIPAL POETRY

Big Bank Take Little Bank, 1991
Joker, Joker, Deuce, 1994
Slam! Poetry: Heftige Dichtung aus Amerika, 1994

OTHER LITERARY FORMS

After publishing three books of poetry, Paul Beatty (BAY-tee) turned to fiction, becoming widely known as a novelist. His novels, *The White Boy Shuffle* (1996), *Tuff* (2000), and *Slumberland* (2008), are comedic satires that address the complexities of African American and mainstream American culture at the turn of the millennium. Like his poetry, Beatty's novels are praised for their urban lyricism, quick wit, and wide-reaching social commentary. Beatty has also published an eclectic and controversial collection of African American humor entitled *Hokum: An Anthology of African American Humor* (2006).

ACHIEVEMENTS

Before trying his hand at fiction, Paul Beatty was known as a preeminent hip-hop poet and performance artist. He was crowned the Grand Slam Champion of the New York City-based Nuyorican Poets Café in 1991 for his work as a performance poet. That same year, the *Village Voice* named *Big Bank Take Little Bank* one of the best books of the year, and soon after *Newsweek* declared him "the premier bard of hiphop." Beatty's poetry is widely acclaimed for its sharp, postmodern edge and blend of high and low cultural references, a mix that is indebted to rap music but explodes beyond its urban borders. After carrying this hip-hop aesthetic from poetry into fiction, Beatty has secured a reputation for writing dazzling novels known for their percussive language, unflinching humor, and broad cultural references. Upon publication of his first novel, *The White Boy Shuffle*, *The New York Times* declared Beatty a new fiction writer to watch. In 2009, he received a grant from the Creative Capital Foundation. Beatty is considered a premier African American poet, novelist, satirist, and cultural commentator.

BIOGRAPHY

Paul Beatty was born in Los Angeles in 1962 and moved to West Los Angeles with his mother and two sisters when he was eight years old. In his introduction to *Hokum*, Beatty admits that by this time he had already been combing through his mother's library, reading impressive amounts of literature from E. L. Doctorow to *Mad* magazine. Beatty, reared on cartoons and comics, was first exposed to African American literature between middle and high school, when he was given a copy of Maya Angelou's novel *I Know Why the Caged Bird Sings* (1969). He claims that after reading three pages, he discarded the work, upset by what he believed to be its maudlin content, and consequently, he did not read African American literature again until ten years later.

After high school, Beatty moved to Boston, where he earned an M.A. in psychology at Boston University. During his time as a graduate student and teaching assistant, he began to write poetry. He then moved to New York City, where he earned an M.F.A. in creative writing from Brooklyn College. Although Beatty studied with the consummate Beat poet Allen Ginsberg, his fellow graduate students and some professors often failed to understand the urban sensibilities in his work, and for a time, Beatty struggled to find his poetic voice.

Soon after he graduated, Beatty began teaching in East Harlem and performing slam poetry at the newly reopened Nuyorican Poets Café. After Beatty won the first Nuyorican Grand Slam, the Café press published Beatty's first book of poetry, *Big Bank Take Little Bank*, which was received as a rhythmic and smart collection of urban poems. Penguin published Beatty's second book of poetry, *Joker, Joker, Deuce*, as a Penguin Poets selection, establishing his reputation as a poet. Critics hailed the poems as lyrical, humorous poems that demand oral performance. Beatty was, however, uneasy with what he termed the insincerity and complacency of contemporary and performance poets and admitted in a *BOMB Magazine* interview that after a time, "poetry got boring." After his short story "'What Set You from, Fool?'" appeared in Eric Liu's *Next: Young American Writers on the New Generation* (1994), Beatty crossed over to literature with his first novel, *The White Boy Shuffle*.

The receipt of a grant in 1996 allowed Beatty to move to Berlin, where he started writing his second novel, *Tuff*. After returning to the United States, he published several short stories, including "A Spoonful of Borscht" (2000), which appeared in the literary journal *Transition*. Beatty also published essays and another novel, *Slumberland*. His novels have been translated and are studied in academic publications.

ANALYSIS

Reviewers and critics often call Paul Beatty a hip-hop poet, a categorization that Beatty himself finds easy and superficial. He admits to being influenced by hip-hop, but resists wholly defining his poetry in those terms. Like hip-hop itself, Beatty's poetry lives on the page as a model of innovation and change, yet resists being formulaically labeled as part of the African American oral tradition. For Beatty, the vernacular tradition, from the oral poems of the Greeks to the rhymes of hip-hop artists, is founded on multiplicity of meaning. He believes these forms should be looked to as a way to balance and blend seemingly incompatible things, such as playwright William Shakespeare's timeless wit with rap artist Biggie Smalls's keen grandiloquence. Recognizing this, critics also attempt to situate Beatty's work as postmodern due to its ironic blending of multiple narratives across time and culture. Indeed, his influences range from blues and jazz music to cartoons, Jap-

anese literature and film, the Enlightenment philosopher Voltaire, and comedian Richard Pryor.

For Beatty, who wrote two books of poetry while performing spoken word, recording language is a difficult, meandering process that cannot be bound by audience needs and expectations. While performing his poetry, Beatty found that his audiences, often solely white or multiracial, missed many of the cultural references readily understood by black culture. Rather than adjusting his style, Beatty decided to allow readers to have their own struggles when accessing his work and eventually found that audiences who gained exposure to hip-hop or urban language would come to appreciate and understand his work. Limiting his poetic voice was never an option, and by forging ahead, Beatty found much fun and absurdity in observing audience responses to his far-reaching and irreverent work.

On the page, Beatty's poems take on an intentionally rollicking form and rely on the placement of words on the page and the use of white space to control the movement of language. Read aloud, the rhythms of rap and hip-hop are evident as the poems speed to their often elusive conclusions. Beatty's imagery and dramatic situations freely borrow from both "the 'hood" and "the academy" as well as from everywhere in between. In doing so, the poems attempt to reconcile the false notion that low and high culture are mutually exclusive. The resulting collections showcase how critical comparisons of seemingly incompatible cultural forms can often yield rich readings. Forging these connections against a backdrop of concern and sometimes anger, Beatty's poems remain quick and light, strikingly satirical and funny. Beatty's work is often anthologized and discussed in book reviews, journal articles, and in interviews with the author.

BIG BANK TAKE LITTLE BANK

Beatty's first book of poems, *Big Bank Take Little Bank* was well-received, despite the fact that the language and style were unfamiliar to many readers. The title phrase, "big bank take little bank," is an expression that refers to the circumstance under which the person with the most possessions will eventually acquire all others' property. With its urban, insider orientation, the title forecasts the poetry's linguistic mix of street culture and pop references. One *Library Journal* reviewer cited the text as a "pop-modern" deluge that records how the poet experienced the 1980's. Beatty's poems are not only funny, but also explosive, taking on dynamic forms that scatter words and lines across the page. The effect mimics hip-hop rhythms and shows a poet attempting to find his voice through experimentation and play.

The most anthologized poem in the collection, "Aa Bb Cc . . . Xx Yy and Zzing," is an epigram that questions an elementary teacher's assumption that the tenets of equality and opportunity found in the Declaration of Independence can be an inspiration to all young students, regardless of race and class. True to the form, the poem is short, witty, and unapologetically cross-referential, as it smugly compares the speaker's chances of becoming the president to the famous panda bear Ling Ling's cubs' chances of surviving. As it jaunts through inner-city America and explores the lines between black authenticity and appropriation, the collection is concerned about the social and political state of young African Americans, but it is not overtly political. Instead, it trades somber messages for wily observation and intense humor.

JOKER, JOKER, DEUCE

Beatty's second collection, *Joker, Joker, Deuce*, gains velocity and hurtles through what seems to be the poet's mounting anger at and frustration with racial politics and poetic chicanery. Rather than rant, however, Beatty again relies on satire, humor, and volatile rhythms to critique and caricature American culture. In "That's Not in My Job Description," Beatty turns the tables on traditional racial discourse by posing as an ethnographer embedded in a corporate environment to study the habits of "whitey." The white boys invite him out for an awkward, obligatory drink, and although they presume to know something about being black in the United States, the speaker, unlike Beatty, resentfully holds his tongue. Beatty also explores the differences between white and black humor in "Why That Abbott and Costello Vaudeville Mess Never Worked with Black People." This poem, masquerading as a haiku, simply reads: "who's on first?/ i don't know, your mama."

No one, including African Americans, is untouched by Beatty's critical ire. He deconstructs what it means to act black in a society that increasingly commodifies black culture, and he struggles to meaningfully challenge racial injustice. He parodies the use of famous black figures to sell items such as tennis shoes by imagining the civil rights leader Martin Luther King, Jr., sporting Nike shoes throughout his many civic demonstrations. In "Verbal Mugging," a title that critics have used to describe the tone of the collection, Beatty confronts performance poetry itself by drawing attention to insincerity on the part of the poet and the audience: "you don't have to think// cause i illustrate my words/ with some cheesy rip off diana ross four tops hand gestures." Throughout its shouts and slams, *Joker, Joker, Deuce*, like all Beatty's poetry, remains mirthful and slick, adroitly dodging any phraseology that would nail down his racial or social allegiances.

OTHER MAJOR WORKS

LONG FICTION: *The White Boy Shuffle*, 1996; *Tuff*, 2000; *Slumberland*, 2008.

EDITED TEXTS: *Hokum: An Anthology of African American Humor*, 2006.

BIBLIOGRAPHY

Ashe, Bertram. "Paul Beatty's *White Boy Shuffle* Blues: Jazz Poetry, John Coltrane, and the Post-Soul Aesthetic." In *Thriving on a Rift: Jazz and Blues Influences in African American Literature and Film*, edited by Graham Lock and David Murray. New York: Oxford University Press, 2009. This chapter examining *The White Boy Shuffle* deals with jazz poetry and Beatty's style.

Grassian, Daniel. *Writing the Future of Black America: Literature of the Hip-hop Generation*. Columbia: University of South Carolina Press, 2009. Contains a chapter on Paul Beatty.

Rankin, Thomas. "*Joker, Joker, Deuce*." In *Masterplots II: African American Literature*, edited by Tyrone Williams. Rev. ed. Pasadena, Calif.: Salem Press, 2009. Provides an in-depth analysis of this work.

Selinger, Eric Murphy. "Trash, Art, and Performance Poetry." Review of *Joker, Joker, Deuce*. *Parnassus: Poetry in Review* 23, nos. 1/2 (1998): 356-382. Reviews *Joker, Joker, Deuce* in the context of Beatty's production as a performance poet. One of the few full-length analyses of Beatty's poetry, this article provides insight into the work's motivations and impact.

Svboda, Terese. "Try Bondage." Review of *Joker, Joker, Deuce*. *Kenyon Review* 17, no. 2 (1995): 154-160. Reviews Beatty's book *Joker, Joker, Deuce* along with collections by Lois-Ann Yamanaka, Sapphire, and Marilyn Chin. Shows how Beatty deconstructs African American myths through his edgy, explosive rhymes while it praises the collection's veracity, sharp wit, and moral stance.

Thomas, Lorenzo. "'Stuck in the Promised Land': African American Poets at the Edge of the Twenty-first Century." In *Black Liberation in the Americas*, edited by Fritz Gysin and Christopher Mulvey. Munster, Germany: Lit Verlag, 2001. Discusses the work of five young African American poets writing in the 1990's and closely reads selections from Beatty's *Joker, Joker, Deuce*. Attempts to situate their poetry as simultaneously responding to and breaking away from earlier African American literary traditions in the face of an increasingly commodified and postmodern cultural landscape.

Lindsay Christopher

ROBIN BECKER

Born: Philadelphia, Pennsylvania; March 7, 1951

PRINCIPAL POETRY

Personal Effects, 1976 (with Helena Minton and Marilyn Zuckerman)
Backtalk, 1982
Giacometti's Dog, 1990
All-American Girl, 1996
The Horse Fair, 2000
Domain of Perfect Affection, 2006

OTHER LITERARY FORMS

As a poetry editor for the *Women's Review of Books*, Robin Becker has published numerous articles reviewing scholarly works on Elizabeth Bishop. Two such articles, reviewing Bonnie Costello's *Elizabeth Bishop: Questions of Mastery* (1991) and Lorrie Goldensohn's *Elizabeth Bishop: The Biography of a Poetry* (1992), appeared in the *Women's Review of Books* (July, 1992). Becker has published other book reviews in *Belles Lettres*, *Boston Globe*, *Boston Review*, and *Prairie Schooner*.

ACHIEVEMENTS

Robin Becker has been honored many times for her work and has achieved a reputation as one of America's premier lesbian poets. She has received several fellowships: a Massachusetts Artist Foundation Fellowship in Poetry (1985), a fellowship in poetry from the National Endowment for the Arts (1990), and a fellowship from the Bunting Institute of Radcliffe College (1995-1996). She received Lambda Literary Awards for *All-American Girl* and *The Horse Fair*. Her other literary honors include the Virginia Faulkner Prize for Excellence in Writing from *Prairie Schooner* (1997), a position as visiting scholar at the Center for Lesbian and Gay Studies (CLAGS) at the City University of New York (1998), and an invitation to serve as the William Steeple Davis Artist-in-Residence (2000-2001).

BIOGRAPHY

Robin Becker was born March 7, 1951, in Philadelphia, Pennsylvania, to realtors Benjamin Becker and Ann Weiner Becker. She entered Boston University in 1969, earning her B.A. in 1973 and her M.A. in 1976. Her teaching career has been long and varied: She taught at the Massachusetts Institute of Technology, first as a lecturer in creative writing and humanistic studies (1977-1983) and then as an assistant professor of exposition and rhetoric (1983-1987); she was a writer-in-residence for the Wyoming Council on the Arts, in Sheridan, and the Writers' Place, in Madison, Wisconsin (both in 1991). She was a visiting professor of writing at Kent State University (1992) and Pennsylvania State University (1993-1994); an *American Poetry Review* scholar-in-residence at Central High School, in Philadelphia (1994); and professor of English and women's studies at Pennsylvania State University (beginning in 1994). Besides her teaching, Becker has been active in other areas: She was co-coordinator of a reading series at New Words Bookstore (1981-1983), served as poetry editor for *Women's Review of Books* and as a member of the board of directors of Associated Writing Programs (1992-1995), and was a CLAGS visiting scholar during the 1998-1999 academic year.

ANALYSIS

Throughout Robin Becker's poetry, there exists a sense of alienation and otherness. As a woman, as a Jew, and as a lesbian, Becker has faced the difficulties of living in the male-, Christian-, and heterosexual-centered United States with humor, intelligence, and tenacity. Her writing is specifically intended to honor and explore "issues dealing with sexual identity, relationships, and Jewish identity."

PERSONAL EFFECTS

Becker's first collection of poems, *Personal Effects*, gives the reader a glimpse of the poet's lifetime journey of self-discovery. Just as in later books, the poet writes verse celebrating her grandmother, examining her emergent sexuality, relating her childhood experiences, and discovering the breadth and scope of the wider world. Despite being fully aware of the differences between the dominant culture and her own sensibilities, Becker stands unafraid. She accepts her Jewishness, her sexuality, and her femininity in strong yet graceful lines.

BACKTALK

Backtalk explores the often complex relationship among family members, friends, lovers, and pets. It describes the balances created between people and their loved ones, between people and the places they travel, and between people and their memories. These poems sort out the complexities of existence: "I remember the globe that was a pencil sharpener," says the speaker in "A Long Distance":

> I remember standing in the lunchroom
> & trying to figure out
> how I could be standing in the lunchroom
> & standing on the earth which was the globe.

The pencil sharpener—a small, concrete, graspable object—is connected to the larger idea of the world beneath her feet—an idea hard to fathom but easy to experience. This difficulty of conception, yet ease of experience, not only describes standing on earth but also describes the emotions of love and worship. As de-

scribed by one critic in the *Valley Advocate*, Becker's poems tell truths of the gut and the groin. They are one half of a dialogue; communication from one individual to another rather than the meditation of a solitary individual; literally, the poems are "talking back."

GIACOMETTI'S DOG

Each poem in Becker's third book of verse, *Giacometti's Dog*, is a tribute to the impact of her visual imagery. Many of the poems, particularly "Grief," which recounts the suicide of Becker's sister, and "Good Dog," which refers to the accidental death of her beloved pet, are paeans to the sorrows of her life. The feelings expressed are raw and unrestrained, but Becker uses the very details of her works as a purgative. These poems, widely ranging in their emotional content, give voice to loss, guilt, and erotic yearning and describe the consolation that love, creativity, and friendship can provide. Becker seems to gain in wisdom as she travels, and her desire to understand the cultures of Europe and the American Southwest give the poems a depth rarely found in "travel poems."

In "The Children's Concert," Becker and her younger sister have been taken, once a month, to listen to music played at a children's concert series. She recalls, guiltily, how she lied about her mother's intentions to her younger, more innocent sibling, and convinced her that their mother was, in fact, abandoning them. This lie turns what had been a pleasurable activity into a source of almost paralyzing anxiety for the younger girl, and Becker's recollections carry an unmistakable sense of guilt when she realizes how cruelly she was tormenting her sister. The cultural value of the concerts is lost in the face of the younger girl's panic, but it is not until Becker's sister's suicide years later that Becker regrets her actions.

"Grief," too, expresses Becker's unswerving self-condemnation as openly as "the kindness of the rabbi I remember now." The poem moves from a Philadelphia cemetery to Florence and Venice, Italy, comparing Becker's sister's life to "a place I visited by boat." Becker finds that only in the distance of poetry can she gain some kind of peace and contentment.

ALL-AMERICAN GIRL

Becker's fourth book of verse, *All-American Girl*, has the greatest scope of geographical distance of her early works. Many places—the site of a Quaker meeting in Philadelphia; a drugstore in Buffalo, Wyoming; pueblos in the American Southwest—are only a few of the vast distances traveled in the scope of this small volume, which also explores the vastness of inner space. Becker drives from Taos to Sante Fe, New Mexico; goes contra dancing in New Hampshire; and dresses up as Peter Pan and "flies" onstage. Her movements are quick, sure, and far-reaching. The only constant is her voice, daring the reader to follow her farther into her vision and pain. Every poem describes a revolution, a breakup, or a sorrow. Love ends, families dissolve, and childhood innocence is ended.

All-American Girl, like *Giacometti's Dog*, describes loss and acceptance of loss. Becker seems to struggle for order and strives to make sense out of the chaos of her life. "The Star Show," with its chaotic universe, is no more out-of-control than Becker; its planetarium commentator, who "[throws] stars across the sky, [flings] meteors/ carelessly . . ./ . . . punctur[ing] the darkness with white bullets," is no more destructive than the forces that make Becker's life difficult. Becker truly is an all-American girl: She loves her dog and horses, enjoys the vigorous exercise of skiing, hiking, and skinny-dipping at midnight. She finds pleasure in her femininity, although she wishes that she could enjoy the benefits of being male:

> . . . the boy across the street
> who hung upside down from a tree and didn't care
> that his shirt fluttered over his bare chest.

However, all of these things pale beside the death of her sister and the dissolution of her grieving family.

Becker's fourth book follows the pattern set by her third, *Giacometti's Dog*, in that she revisits her Philadelphia childhood, her Jewish family, her constant travel, and her blossoming sexuality. Both volumes tend toward the humorous and rely on strong narrative structure for the progression of their themes, but *All-American Girl* is a more contemplative and thorough examination of the development of Becker's lesbian poetic persona. It is also more erotic and, though often droll, reflects more deeply on the pain of embracing an "alternative lifestyle." "Philadelphia, 1955," for example, shows the young Becker as she

> . . . in a nightgown
> closes the door and walks barefoot
> on the black grass. Stars have grouped
> like families into their fixed relations.
> She welcomes the great indifference
> of the street. . . .

That "indifference" demonstrates the distance she feels between the silently sleeping families and her burgeoning desires: "Everything that is her own is suddenly here revealed, separate as her body."

"A History of Sexual Preference" further demonstrates this new, proud sexuality in a way that the poems in *Giacometti's Dog* failed to do. Becker, in her quest for equal rights for women, casts herself as "seventeen and tired of fighting for freedom/ and the rights of men." She is preparing her own declaration of independence and is "already dreaming of Boston—/ city of women." It is here that Becker and her girlfriend have their first sexual encounter, "in a hotel room on Rittenhouse Square":

> And I am happy as the young
> Tom Jefferson, unbuttoning my collar, imagining his
>   power,
> considering my healthy body, how I might use it in the
>   service
> of the country of my pleasure.

Thus, Becker's restlessness and her constant movement help her deal with her internal discomfiture; she is converting her inner pain into movement. Though love fails and families suffer, she knows that greater wisdom awaits those who seek it. In "Shopping," she says that "If things don't work out/ I'll buy the belt/ with the fashionable silver buckle," acknowledging the frivolous ways in which women use clothing to control their internal suffering: "I'll do what my mother did/ after she buried my sister:/ outfitted herself in an elegant suit/ for the rest of her life." Clothing masks sadness because it can make the most distraught woman more attractive and, thus, attract the comforting words of even strangers. On the other hand, comments Becker in "Santo Domingo Feast Day," "there are no remedies for great sorrow . . . only dancing and chanting, listening and waiting."

THE HORSE FAIR

In *The Horse Fair*, Becker questions the nature of citizenship; she examines the ways in which human beings, both male and female, market their bodies, their ideas, and their belongings. She observes and criticizes the myriad ways in which the most restricted members of a society must create false personae simply for survival in a society that demands uniformity and conventionality. Unlike the solid uniformity of her earlier collections of poetry, *The Horse Fair* celebrates multiple viewpoints and multiple voices. Rosa Bonheur, the nineteenth century French painter who created the painting that inspired the book's title, is described as a woman caught up by the pain of her culture. In another poem, Becker becomes Charlotte Salomon, child of German Jews, killed by the Nazis at the age of twenty-six. In this portrait, Becker establishes a parallel structure that compares sections of the Rosh Hashanah and Yom Kippur services with stanzas that mourn her sister's death and stanzas that celebrate nontraditional families. Organized around long meditations, other poems show Becker's dexterity with formal verse (she uses the sestina and sonnet forms with ease) and free verse.

The Horse Fair serves as the instrument with which Becker explores anti-Semitism, cross-dressing, and homosexuality—the sexual orientation of both Becker and Bonheur. The volume presents the reader with the marketplace, the communal spaces where purchases of self and lifestyle are made. The best part of Becker's poems is how much the world is with her in these lyrics; characters, histories, animals, places, and things crowd onto the pages, inscribing them with living, breathing voices.

DOMAIN OF PERFECT AFFECTION

Domain of Perfect Affection addresses a familiar series of concerns: family, nature, and the reassessment of youthful experiences. The poet's maturity and confidence allow her to examine past obsessions with a more relaxed, leisurely air that speaks of increasing wisdom and gravity. For example, in the opening section, Becker creates a found poem from the lines of Meriwether Lewis and William Clark, "Manifest Destinies," that contrasts the expansion of the West with the tight spaces she personally experienced in her youth

and her own, wistful desire to take on the greater perceived freedoms of masculinity. Similarly, in "A Pasture of My Palm," Becker recalls a childhood incident in which she stole a trinket—a glass horse—from a neighborhood store's display case and was forced to return it the next morning with her angry mother by her side. She had seen the palomino horse as a symbol for her own, tightly controlled soul and wished to free it (and, symbolically, herself) from its confines, but her mother's fury turned a moment of bad judgment into an indictment of her daughter's character. Becker's flood of tears is a painful reminder of a childhood shaming that the adult Becker is able to put into perspective only when she compares it with the greater trauma of the repression of her "corralled" sexuality and self-awareness. *Domain of Perfect Affection* also has an inner tension that relies on Becker's dualistic view of life—she both needs and rejects greater society's expectations for her.

Another found poem, the "Qualities Boys Like Best in Girls," demonstrates Becker's intense awareness of the irony of living as a lesbian in an inherently masculine society. Although she intuitively understands the attractiveness of traditional feminine beauty, she does not associate such traditions with herself and must, paradoxically, both accept the validity of a "masculine" desire that she herself feels and reject such desire's deprecating boundaries. Coping with disappointment has always played a role, at times greater and at times lesser, in Becker's works, and the tight control of self has always been observable in the restrictions she places on the structure and themes of her poems. By stealing the glass palomino horse, Becker is trying to rescue a kind of anima from the "corral" of the glass display case. Her actions invite extreme punishment and shame for allowing the trinket its "liberty."

BIBLIOGRAPHY

Becker, Robin. "Robin Becker." Interview by Rosemarie C. Sultan. In *Truthtellers of the Times: Interviews with Contemporary Women Poets*, edited by Janet Palmer Mullaney. Introduction by Toi Derricotte. Ann Arbor: University of Michigan Press, 1998. Becker discusses her life and writings and her perspective as a Jewish lesbian.

Ciuraru, Carmela. Review of *The Horse Fair. The New*

York Times Book Review, September 24, 2000, p. 22. Ciuraru describes Becker as "honest" in describing her Judaism, complicated relationships, and unconventional sexuality, and she sees her as a poet who fearlessly confronts events and emotions. Ciuraru defines Becker's poems as paeans to animals, lovers, and family members, who have taught her the more important lessons in life.

Frank, Allen. "*Giacometti's Dog*." Review of *Giacometti's Dog. Poet Lore* 85, no. 4 (Winter, 1990/1991): 49. Frank celebrates the tenacity of Becker's vision in this book review. He establishes the fluidity of her verse while recognizing the sometimes brutal impact of the described scenarios.

Grosholz, Emily. "Flint and Iron." *Hudson Review* 53, no. 3 (Autumn, 2000): 495-505. Grosholtz compares Becker's poetry with the "fire" created from the clashing of divergent parts of Becker's life—the "flint" and "iron." She describes the revolutionary spirit that fuels Becker's poetry while still acknowledging the delicacy of her work.

Schwartz, Patricia Roth. "Profound Pitt Poets." *Lambda Book Report* 9, no. 2 (September, 2000): 21. Characterizing Becker as a thoroughly erudite and often witty lesbian, Schwartz honors Becker for her five books of poetry and her National Endowment for the Arts Fellowship. Schwartz confirms that Becker has chosen to be not simply a lesbian poet; instead, Becker has achieved a larger artistic acceptance without compromising her lesbian identity. She comments on knowing Becker personally and seeing her work mature from *Backtalk*, where the focus is her relationships, her sister's suicide, her family, and her own often-troubled past, through *Giacometti's Dog* and *All-American Girl*, where the focus is more complex.

Shomer, Enid. "Hungry for the World." *Women's Review of Books* 18, no. 1 (October, 2000): 16. Shomer argues that Becker's poems reflect the poet's sexual and social identities in startlingly apt metaphors. Describes the poet's careful handling of the widely varying scenery in *The Horse Fair*: Meeting and melding in "surprising satisfying juxtapositions" are the Philadelphia of Becker's girlhood, her ancestral links to the shtetls of Eastern Europe, the mesas of New Mexico (one of her favorite landscapes), and the towns and people of Italy. Describes Becker's poetic technique as combining irony and directness.

Slate, Ron. "On Robin Becker's *Domain of Perfect Affection*." Review of *Domain of Perfect Affection. Prairie Schooner* (Fall, 2007): 149-153. In *Prairie Schooner*, Slate is taken with Becker's increasing maturity as a poet. He finds her narrative voice to be stronger and more self-assured with the passage of time and states that she has gained greater wisdom and understanding of herself and her place in an increasingly accepting society.

Yannone, Sandra. Review of *All-American Girl. Prairie Schooner* 72, no. 4 (Winter, 1998): 195-198. Yannone describes Becker's work as roving the terrain of loss and grief: the streets of Becker's childhood in Philadelphia, where she courts other women; the arid deserts of the Southwest, where she examines her childless, often partnerless life; and the romantic tapestry of Italy, where she struggles as an outsider to make a life with other women.

Julia M. Meyers
Updated by Meyers

BEN BELITT

Born: New York, New York; May 2, 1911
Died: Bennington, Vermont; August 17, 2003

PRINCIPAL POETRY

The Five-Fold Mesh, 1938
Wilderness Stair, 1955
The Enemy Joy: New and Selected Poems, 1964
Nowhere but Light: Poems, 1964-1969, 1970
The Double Witness: Poems, 1970-1976, 1977
Possessions: New and Selected Poems, 1985
This Scribe, My Hand: The Complete Poems of Ben Belitt, 1998

OTHER LITERARY FORMS

Ben Belitt (buh-LIHT), a major translator of verse into English, translated works by Arthur Rimbaud,

Jorge Luis Borges, Federico García Lorca, Rafael Alberti, and, preeminently, Pablo Neruda. He also wrote about both the problems of translation and poetics in general.

ACHIEVEMENTS

Ben Belitt's poetry is, by common assent, difficult, owing to its casual erudition, allusiveness, exacting vocabulary, and compact figuration. He so assiduously avoided being a public poet that his reserve seems an explanation of why his work is not more anthologized. Nevertheless, his poetry has not escaped recognition: Belitt received the Shelley Memorial Award (1937), the Oscar Blumenthal Award (1957), the Union League Civic and Arts Poetry Prize (1960), the National Institute of Arts and Letters Award (1965), and the Russell Loines Award (1981). He was twice a candidate for the National Book Award (in poetry and in translation), and he was a recipient of fellowships and grants from the Guggenheim Foundation and the National Endowment for the Arts.

BIOGRAPHY

Ben Belitt was born in New York City in 1911, the son of a teacher, Lewis Belitt, and Ida Lewitt Belitt. He earned his bachelor's, master's, and doctoral degrees at the University of Virginia and served in the U.S. Army during World War II.

Belitt joined the faculty of Bennington College (Vermont) in 1938; he remained on Bennington's faculty and continued to teach on an occasional basis and to live in Bennington until his death in 2003. He preferred a provincial to an urban setting for what he called his "obsessional" writing habits. His poems and translations, however, reveal the least provincial of men. In 1936 and 1937, while still working on a doctoral degree (which he never finished) at the University of Virginia, he served as an assistant literary editor of *The Nation*, and late in World War II, he served with the U.S. Army Department of Historical Films.

Belitt was orphaned early in life after the death of his father and subsequent abandonment by his mother. He and his sisters returned to their mother after her remarriage, but Belitt felt permanently isolated where family was concerned. He was not a confessional sort

of poet, but this experience and its consequences are presented in his poem "Orphaning" and elsewhere.

ANALYSIS

From the outset, Ben Belitt's poetry was aurally remarkable. Though his first volume was excessively alliterative and was spoken in a too-mannered voice, it revealed a poet whose first priority was control of traditional forms, in terms of meter and stanza. He managed this with a fluent prosody driven equally by the line and the sentence. After that first volume, Belitt wrote a freer verse in accommodating his times and the dictates of his own sensibility. His genius for linking the sounds of words abided, however, and he would rather have risked verbal excess than spoken flatly.

Belitt's imagination is demanding. Images and the terms of his similes and metaphors are brought together rapidly in his work. The reader may feel that some unimaginable step by which the poet mediated the associations has been left out. Moreover, Belitt requires intellectual rigor from his reader. Often, he brings an immediately realized object or event into relation with historical figures and their ideas. His practice assumes that these unions are self-evident.

PLACE

Perhaps more than anything else, Belitt's poems strive to realize and throw light on the nature of place and his response to place, which originates in alienation and need, moves on to solace and immersion and thence to a mature acceptance of rootlessness. (The reader who interprets this as the displacement of childhood anxieties overlooks the philosophical richness of Belitt's mind.) This enterprise is only roughly chronological in his work, as Belitt works by perpetually reconnoitering the old ground of his thought. As he goes, place is always complex, sometimes consoling, sometimes inscrutable, sometimes antagonistic; it can be all these at once.

The reader sees then that place, though sharply focused and delineated by Belitt, is rendered in an essentially impressionistic manner and stands more for the poet's metaphysical and aesthetic probings than for its own pictorial value. Thus his common practice of envisioning place through contrasting entities such as stone and tree, gem and flower, desert and water, is deeply related to his existential struggle to achieve, without self-delusion or the consolations of defunct mythologies, a stable and abiding worldview. It is not surprising that such a poet would eventually write a book titled *Nowhere but Light*, having touched with clarity the innumerable dark places of his outer and inner landscapes.

THE FIVE-FOLD MESH

In a prefatory note to *The Five-Fold Mesh*, Belitt speaks of two of its sequences, "Many Cradles" and "In Time of Armament," as dealing, respectively, with a "problem in orientation" and an "expanding record of change." The whole collection he sees as moving from "simple responses to the natural world" to "usable relationships between the personal and the contemporary world." This is the case. The poet is lost in the face of absolute flux. His "contemporary world" is not rife with technological paraphernalia; it is the psychological state of incertitude in the province of metaphysics and value. Thus he says in "The Unregenerate": "Cherish this disbelief/ For final truth, although the end be grief." The "heart," he argues, should confront and "accept this thing" (disbelief); the mind has been long aware of it. This collection then is largely about the heart and mind's taking up the "problem in orientation" to utter mutability.

Many of the poems, to test the poet's integrity, confront suffering and death. In these provinces, mutability is most vexing and makes disbelief small consolation. "John Keats, Surgeon" is preeminent in this category. It goes beneath the ceaselessly kindling fever of that poet's tubercular dying to discover first his broken heart and then his great integrity. He sees every impulse of Keats as rejecting the balm of easy, traditional consolation (the "kindly unguent") and, equally, any kind of nepenthe. Better to treasure the merciless truth, a poet's duty, and be left with the "ruined heartbeat ailing still." This is the archetypal spirit of the poet, who must be surgeon to himself. If darkness and this tragic unconsolability mark much of the collection, however, it is noteworthy that Belitt closes with the more hopeful touches of "Battery Park: High Noon." Here the controlled and behatted individual of workaday lower Manhattan is pulled irresistibly toward the allurements of nature's ancient condition by a concert of spring's forces.

WILDERNESS STAIR

Wilderness Stair continues in a dark vein, its concluding sequence of war poems contributing largely to that effect. There is, however, much balance of joy and despondency here, an "equilibrium" in Belitt's lexicon.

Four sequences make up the volume. The first, "Departures," dominates by length. Its main body is a tour of places, each a blend of antithetical features that usually astound by their grace on one hand and their starkness on the other. A maple in a Vermont quarry constitutes the wholeness of fragile fruitfulness and hard duration. A dead bull in a Mexican bull ring testifies to the commingling of dark and light: the "hilt . . . in a column of gristle" but also "Dionysus drowsing in a meadow." The second section, "The Habit of Angels," suggests transcendence and entails a struggle with the inner conflict created by the world's wildness. Belitt is moved by the call of moral rectitude, sent to one sensually engaged on the "wilderness stair." (Stairwells and ladders, venues of psychological and spiritual ascent and descent, make up much of Belitt's terrain.) However, his testament is, finally, an affirmation of the worldly stance, there being a "void at the sheer of the stair" and a fading godhead at the "place of the rock and the ladder."

The third section, "Karamazov," gets at the wish to murder the father. It is a tribute to Fyodor Dostoevski, like Keats esteemed by Belitt, and an exploration of the oedipal urge. Certainly, the section has biographical overtones but is very distanced in accepting a mother's peaceful counsel, which leads to the poet's generic blessing of the father.

Four grim war poems make up "In Agamemnon's Color." A paratrooper's "Descent in a Parachute" renders his fall a traumatic birth. Fumbling the cord ("on his broken navel"), what he had expected to be easeful becomes only a terrifying "question" in "his brute and downward waste." "The Spool" is a cinematic account of a day at war. The most rhetorically straightforward poem in Belitt's whole corpus, it is a narrative of filmed action, beginning with the routine of the morning march and ending with the field surgeon's rubber-gloved hands poised above a "nerveless and saline wound." The surgeon's "mouth rejects contemplation" as Belitt mines a dark vein.

THE ENEMY JOY

Belitt's title for his third collection, *The Enemy Joy*, comes from a poem published in *The Five-Fold Mesh* that is reprinted there, though not among the new poems. It is significantly positioned, however, as the book's final piece. The paradoxical title refers to Belitt's sense that joy is always accompanied by its antagonist. In the poem, which is basic to understanding the continued balancing of the contrarieties of place in the new work, a bird "in jackal country" sings "for pure delight." The bird suggests Thomas Hardy's darkling thrush, but Hardy's bird seemed to announce some hope of which Hardy remained unaware. Belitt's bird sings "the enemy joy as it were grief"; its utterance is powerful, manifold, and paradoxically evident to Belitt. Simply put, this bird is the spirit of Keats, of the "Ode on Melancholy."

Thus, a quite productive orientation to the new poems may be to approach them in terms of aesthetics or of art understood as worldview, though life per se is nowhere shunned by Belitt. "Battle-Piece," a poem in five parts, is not simply an extension of the interest in war that was the finale to *Wilderness Stair*. It is an envisioning of Paolo Uccello's painting *Battaglia di San Romano* (1456-1460). Belitt regards the "champion" of the field as awaiting some interpretation of the deadly event. The poet concludes simply with "Nothing responded." This is not just colloquial; this is the veritable "nada" of a nihilistic insight. It is the artistic representation, ostensibly by Uccello but really by Belitt, of that "nerveless wound" speaking in the face of the surgeon's stilled mouth. In the penultimate line of this brilliant sequence, Belitt uses the word "placeless" with a cunning ambiguity. In one of its principal designations, it states the irreducible position of the artist. He is the poem's "Begetter," whose vision goes beyond the "landscape." He is the one to "fight that battle after the battle,/ Inward and naked." A commensurate realization caps "Memorial Hospital: Outpatient," dedicated to a physician. It is conveyed by the utterance "There is nowhere but light."

NOWHERE BUT LIGHT

That line, of course, prefigures the title of Belitt's fourth volume. It derives, as mentioned, from his steady effort to illuminate the darkness of the world and of his experience. *Nowhere but Light* also points, however, to the acceptance of a placeless condition, to some vanquishing of an old desire. The zone of his concern shifts here to being itself. Indeed, the first line of the first poem is merely "To be." Nevertheless, place, especially contrastive place, though differently regarded, remains important.

Thus, the sequence titled "Antipodal Man" comes to a head in "Siesta: Mexico/Vermont." (The term "antipodal man" appears here.) Like many of Belitt's poems, this one suggests the Hartford/Florida and Nova Scotia/Brazil frames of reference of Wallace Stevens and Elizabeth Bishop. All have required antitheses of climate and topography for their work; yet here it is the light of a dual setting, glimpsed in siesta, that dominates and grants the "antipodal man" his bearing. He enters simultaneously "the tropic/ and the polar fires." There is a mystic, albeit humanistic, dimension to this; the poem is about the rarefied human experience in which the poet enters fire and circles "the precision/ of a moment." Specific place yields to archetypal place, which yields to light, which yields to an enlightened moment.

The volume's first poem, one of Belitt's finest, "The Orange Tree," sets the stage for such experience. Belitt meditates on the idea that if one can "live in the spirit," perhaps it is a state analogous to "the orange's scent/ in the orange tree." It is the marriage of the palpable tree and the ephemeral scent that excites the poet's imagination. In tying that union to conceivable spirituality, he arrives at a synesthetic figure in which the tree's branch, then twig, then leafage lead irrepressibly to the "sunburst of white in the leaves," which he calls "the odor's epiphany." Scent inhabits color. This natural epiphany dictates a paring of excess to Belitt, a search for the "minimal." The epiphany and its lesson stand as emblems of the questing and goal particular to this collection that, with *The Enemy Joy*, considerably broadens Belitt's use of his materials and his idea of his art.

THE DOUBLE WITNESS

Belitt continues to explore his isolation in *The Double Witness*, though he employs "we" more than before. The title comes from the opening poem, "Xerox," wherein an "original" man lies down on a copy machine's glass to double all that was "lonely, essential, unique." In witty prayerfulness, he calls from the machine's inky pit, "Forgive our duplicity." Belitt uses the volume to track the individual into the species, locating a range of doubles. The poems are worlds of mirroring.

The volume's key piece is the sequence "This Scribe My Hand," about Belitt's relation to Keats, which is represented by the contact of their pens' nibs as Keats writes on the underside of Belitt's page. Its exquisite realization of psychological pain does not check its despair and nihilistic feeling. These become the dominant tones of the volume's final section, where "chaos" rules and the mundane lament that "nothing will happen today" is a refrain. Belitt's despair is attributable to his continuing appraisal of his art, which—especially in "This Scribe My Hand"—grows utterly pessimistic in this volume. He feels his own work as posthumous and envisions Keats writing his own solitude "in water" on his side of the page. He sees that "something murderous flows/ from that page," a silence that stills their language and is the fate of which they are the double witness. He calls the silence "mortal."

These are the poems of a poet's most extreme crisis, come inexorably to haunt his sixties. They give us suicides, exiles, and deep anxiety about the poet's own enterprise. Belitt's skill in connecting detail within and between them, his management of paradox and the forthrightness of his self-questioning, all preserve integrity in a volume menaced by disintegration. Belitt has always considered poetry his talisman. That these poems so thoroughly doubt themselves philosophically yet remain so exquisitely executed suggests that for Belitt the true poem of the chaotic, even one written against itself, retains its talismanic power.

POSSESSIONS

There are only twelve new poems in *Possessions*. They are not easily characterized, as each picks up on some dominant strain long at work. "Graffiti" is a "vandal's dream" in which Belitt writes himself large and pervasively, in his "double initials," on a subway's every surface. It is, first, an absurd fantasy of a literary status denied and, second, a dealing with the commensurate sense that his work has only posthumous prospects. "Walker" is an old woman's revery of dancing as she stands, bound to her home and stalled, before her doorframe, which holds the image of Candlewood Mountain at an impossible distance. Belitt does not let her drift into a nostalgic past; rather, he makes up the fantastic satisfaction of her longing from her present condition. "Walker" belongs to a group that takes the difficult lives of elderly women as its subject. It originates with the excellent "Charwoman" (*The Five-Fold Mesh*) and comes to full development both here and in "A Suicide: Paran Creek" (*The Double Witness*).

The poem titled "Possessions" glimpses King Tutankhamen's realization that grave robbers have done him out of the wherewithal of his immortality. Belitt takes the point to heart, seeing his own desire through the boy king's. Each of the volume's poems ties in with "Possessions" in some way. The quite dissimilar "Sumac" ends with a remark about how the "marauders move in," and the subterranean setting of "Graffiti" is characterized as "the tomb-robber's darkness."

"On Paran Creek" and "Voyage of the *Beagle*" get finely at Henry David Thoreau's and Charles Darwin's probing to discover precisely why certain particulars and not others constitute the world. The poems relate to "Possessions" and its spiritual search to locate and possess what can bestow some abiding meaning on human existence. Belitt knows that nothing can be so possessed except in illusion, and that everyone is robbed even of that, one way or another. Though *Possessions* is a small volume, it is not skimpy. It is a plenitude from the lively mind of a poet in his seventies.

OTHER MAJOR WORKS

NONFICTION: *Four Poems by Rimbaud: The Problem of Translation*, 1947; *Adam's Dream: A Preface to Translation*, 1978; *The Forgèd Feature: Toward a Poetics of Uncertainty—New and Selected Essays*, 1995.

TRANSLATIONS: *Poet in New York*, 1955 (of Federico García Lorca); *Selected Poems of Pablo Neruda*, 1961; *Juan de Mairena*, 1963 (of Antonio Machado); *Selected Poems of Rafael Alberti*, 1965; *Poems from the Canto General*, 1968 (with Alastair Reid; of Pablo Neruda); *A New Decade: Poems, 1958-1967*, 1969 (of Neruda); *A la pintura*, 1972 (of Rafael Alberti); *Jorge Luis Borges: Selected Poems*, 1972; *New Poems, 1968-*

1970, 1972 (of Neruda); *Splendor and Death of Joaquin Murieta*, 1972 (of Neruda); *Five Decades: Poems, 1925-1970*, 1974 (of Neruda); *Sky-stones*, 1981 (of Neruda); *The New York Poems: Poet in New York/ Earth and Moon*, 1982 (of García Lorca); *Late and Posthumous Poems, 1968-1974*, 1988 (of Neruda).

BIBLIOGRAPHY

Boyers, Robert. "Ben Belitt." *Salmagundi* 141/142 (Winter, 2004): 56. The editor of this magazine describes his personal impressions of Belitt and his poetry in this obituary.

Goldensohn, Lorrie. "Witnessing Belitt." *Salmagundi* 44 (1979): 182-196. Analyzes Belitt's habit of "cannibalizing" prior books so as to enrich his current approach to a theme, a habit that goes beyond the borrowing of a line or image; it entails whole poems, which when newly placed revisit, enlarge, and reshape a concern. Also offers insight into Belitt's "gloominess" and spirituality.

Landis, Joan Hutton. "A Wild 'Severity': Toward a Reading of Ben Belitt." In *Contemporary Poetry in America*, edited by Robert Boyers. New York: Schocken, 1974. Excellent overview of Belitt's work (excepting the new poems in *Possessions*) links the poet's dominant attitude to Keats's "melancholy." Treats also the recurrent balancing of opposites in the poems, whether the rock and flower of the world or the joy and despair of humanity.

Nemerov, Howard. "The Fascination of What's Difficult." In *Reflexions on Poetry and Poetics*. New Brunswick, N.J.: Rutgers University Press, 1972. Nemerov argues the efficacy of Belitt's difficult-to-grasp verbal associations and demanding vocabulary. He sees Belitt's typical manner as a blending of "great elaboration" and "great intensity" (conciseness) and contends that one must read "around" rather than "through" his lyrics and see them in combination.

Salmagundi 87 (1990): 3-231. An indispensable issue devoted to readings of Belitt's poems. Mary Kinzie's "A Servant's Cenotaph" is broadest in scope, taking up the whole of *The Double Witness* and noting that there as elsewhere Belitt's "vision of human experience is fateful and symbolic." Hugh Kenner's "Med-itations on 'Possessions'" deals with Belitt's predilections for lists and the "rite" of naming. He sees these characteristics as the poet's means for manifesting both the intense particularity of things and the dilemma of valuing what one is attached to but cannot possess. Terence Diggory's "On Ben Belitt's 'The Bathers: A Triptych'" discusses the poet's work as frequently conscious of itself as art. It characterizes Belitt's particularly rich way of revealing the division between the work and the object it contemplates.

David M. Heaton

MARVIN BELL

Born: New York, New York; August 3, 1937

PRINCIPAL POETRY

Things We Dreamt We Died For, 1966
A Probable Volume of Dreams, 1969
Escape into You, 1971
Residue of Song, 1974
Stars Which See, Stars Which Do Not See, 1977
These Green-Going-to-Yellow, 1981
Drawn by Stones, by Earth, by Things That Have Been in the Fire, 1984
New and Selected Poems, 1987
Iris of Creation, 1990
The Book of the Dead Man, 1994
A Marvin Bell Reader: Selected Poetry and Poems, 1994
Ardor: The Book of the Dead Man, Volume 2, 1997
Rampant, 2004
Mars Being Red, 2007
Seven Poets, Four Days, One Book, 2009 (with others)

OTHER LITERARY FORMS

Although Marvin Bell published mainly poetry, he wrote essays about poetry in *Old Snow Just Melting: Essays and Interviews* (1983). Bell also collaborated with poet William Stafford on two books, *Segues: A Correspondence in Poetry* (1983) and *Annie-Over* (1988). He also made a sound recording of *The Self and the Mulberry Tree* (1977) for the Watershed Foundation. His poetry has appeared in many anthologies, and in 1998, he published some of his collected poems in *Wednesday: Selected Poems, 1966-1997* in Ireland.

Bell has extensive editing experience, first with *Statements* (1959-1964), which he founded, and later as poetry editor for the *North American Review* (1964-1969) and the *Iowa Review* (1969-1971). Partly because of his long association with the *Iowa Review* and the University of Iowa, he was twice interviewed at length by the editors of the *Iowa Review*: in the winter edition of 1981 and in the fall issue of 2000.

ACHIEVEMENTS

Marvin Bell has steadily acquired critical acclaim. He won the James Laughlin Award from the Academy of American Poets for *A Probable Volume of Dreams* and the Bess Hokin Award from *Poetry* magazine, both in 1969; the Emily Clark Balch Prize from the *Virginia*

Marvin Bell (©Erik Borg)

Quarterly Review in 1970; and the prestigious Literature Award from the American Academy of Arts and Letters in 1994. He was also the recipient of a Guggenheim Fellowship (1976) and National Endowment for the Arts Fellowships (1978 and 1984). He has twice held Senior Fulbright Scholarships (Yugoslavia, 1983; Australia, 1986) and has served as visiting professor at several universities. In 1986, his alma mater, Alfred University, awarded him the Lh.D., and in 2000, he was named the first poet laureate in Iowa; he served two terms.

BIOGRAPHY

Marvin Hartley Bell was born in New York City but spent his childhood in Center Moriches, a small Long Island town sixty miles from Manhattan. His parents, Saul Bell and Belle Bell, were the children of Russian Jews who had emigrated to escape persecution. In his boyhood, Bell played on soccer, baseball, and basketball teams, became a ham radio operator, and played the trumpet in a jazz group. His early writing experience consisted of writing a column about school events for the local weekly newspaper.

After high school, Bell attended Alfred University in upstate New York. There he continued with his trumpet playing in the university orchestra; worked for the yearbook and *Fiat Lux*, the weekly newspaper, which he edited his senior year; and became interested in ceramics and photography. Bell was initially more attracted to journalism than to literature, and when he found appropriate political causes (discriminatory clauses in sororities and fraternities, for example), he wrote and mimeographed an underground newsletter. After graduation from Alfred, Bell enrolled in the graduate journalism school at Syracuse University, where he met Al Sampson, who became a lifelong friend, and Mary (Mickey) Mammosser, who became his first wife. The couple then moved to Rochester, where they founded *Statements*, a journal that enabled them to include both literature and photography.

At the urging of Sampson, who was now studying literature at the University of Chicago, the Bells moved to Chicago in 1958. Bell enrolled in the M.A. program in English at the University of Chicago, continued to publish *Statements* (five issues ultimately appeared), wrote poems, and did still photography. His marriage to Mickey ended after the birth of their son Nathan, who stayed with Bell. He later married Dorothy Murphy, with whom he had another son, Jason, in 1966. Bell comments, "My story since 1960 is forever woven together with the stories of Dorothy, Nathan, and Jason." The three often appear in Bell's poems.

While in Chicago, Bell took a writing seminar with John Logan, who had encouraged Bell to contribute an article and a photograph to *Choice*, which Logan had just founded. When Logan recommended the Writers' Workshop in Iowa, Bell applied for the doctoral program at the University of Iowa and was accepted. Studying with Donald Justice and Paul Engel, Bell writes, "In the midst of a swirl of literary fellowship, I still felt that I was following my own road." Bell, however, left Iowa to go on active duty with the U.S. Army (he had been in the Reserve Officers' Training Corps program at Alfred) in 1965. After his military tour of duty, Bell returned to Iowa City, where he taught with Justice and George Starbuck in the Writers' Workshop. After 1966, when his first volume of poems appeared, Bell published a poetry volume about every three years, while also serving as poetry editor for the *North American Review* (1964-1969) and the *Iowa Review* (1969-1971). He continued to teach at Iowa until 2005, but he also taught abroad and at other universities in the United States. After 1985, he divided his time between Iowa and Port Townsend, Washington, where he bought a house. In the 1990's, a series of fellowships took him to several universities and colleges, including the University of Redlands (1991-1993), St. Mary's College of California (1994-1995), Nebraska-Wesleyan University (1996-1997), and Pacific University (1996-1997) in Oregon, where he also taught in the M.F.A. graduate program. He frequently acts as judge for various writing competitions. He was named the first poet laureate of Iowa in 2000 and served two terms.

ANALYSIS

The dominant themes and motivations of Marvin Bell's poetry perhaps can be best understood by hearing him speak of his own work. Discussing his personal aesthetic, he told Wayne Dodd and Stanley Plumly in an *Ohio Review* interview,

I would like to write poetry which finds salvation in the physical world and the here and now and which defines the soul, if you will, in terms of emotional depth, and that emotional depth in terms of the physical world and the world of human relationships.

Indeed, Bell is a poet of the family and the relationships within. He writes of his father, his wives, his sons, and himself in a dynamic interaction of love and loss, accomplishment, and fear of alienation. These are subjects that demand maturity and constant evaluation. Bell's oeuvre highlights his ability to understand the durability of the human heart. As a son of a Jew who immigrated from Ukraine, Bell writes of distance and reconciliation between people, often touching on his complex relationship to his heritage.

While concern with the self and its relationships provides a focal point in Bell's early poetry, many of his poems have crystallized around a reflection on the self in relation to nature, evident in collections such as *Stars Which See, Stars Which Do Not See*. Growing up among farmers, Bell has always felt nature to be an integral part of his life. The rural life that so fascinated other writers during the 1960's back-to-nature movement was not Bell's inspiration. Rather, nature forms a critical backdrop for events and relationships in his life, and in that sense, he says, "I *am* interested in allowing nature to have the place in my poems that it always had in my life."

Bell further notes that

contemporary American poetry has been tiresome in its discovery of the individual self, over and over and over, and its discovery of emotions that, indeed, we all have: loneliness, fear, despair, ennui. . . . I think it can get tiresome when the discovery of such emotions is more or less all the content there is to a poem. I think, as I may not always have thought, that the only way out of the self is to concentrate on others and on things outside the self.

Thus, Bell has evolved his ability to perceive and praise small wonders in a quiet and reserved fashion and, as one critic noted, "has found within his *own* voice that American voice, and with it the ability to write convincingly about the smallest details of a personal history."

A Probable Volume of Dreams

"An Afterword to My Father," which ironically begins *A Probable Volume of Dreams*, is a fairly typical early Bell poem. The "probable" part of the book's title and the placement of an "afterword" at the beginning of a poem reflect Bell's characteristic ambiguity and uncertainty.

> Not so much "enough,"
> there is more to be done,
> yes, and to be done with.
>
> You were the sun and moon.
> Now darkness loves me;
> the lights come on.

Here Bell uses cliches, an allusion ("done") to Donne, and metaphors (father as sun and moon). What remains to be "done" must also be "done with," moved beyond. The father, a recurrent image in Bell's poems, was the poet's source of light; the darkness that follows the father's death now provides light, but what is illumined is not stated, nor is it necessarily positive.

Escape into You

Escape into You chronicles the breaking up of a marriage and a poet's gradual coming to terms not only with a wife and sons but also with himself. As Arthur Oberg puts it, the poems describe "a poetic self that is still learning to bury the dead and to walk among the living." "Homage to the Runner," also the title of a column Bell wrote, is about running, one of Bell's athletic outlets, but also about poetry and how poetry affects others. Running and poetry both involve "pain," and "the love of form is a black occasion/ through which some light must show/ in a hundred years of commitment." While there is "some light," the occasion is "black." The runner and poet "ache" to end the race and poem, which begin in darkness, but there "is no finish; you can stop [running or writing] for no one," not even family, as much as you care for them.

Residue of Song

Residue of Song contains thirteen poems to Bell's father and concerns loneliness. "Residue of Song" begins by stating that "you were writing a long poem, yes,/ about marriage, called 'On Loneliness.'" Like the "probable" in his *A Probable Volume of Dreams*, the "residue" also undercuts its subject matter. In fact, in "Residue of Dreams" "you" decide not to write the poem. In Bell's poem it is the speaker who is the lonely one as he describes a woman's egotism and violence and his callous responses to her; but, as is usually the case with Bell, the poem ends in bittersweet acceptance of the "residue" in a relationship:

> Your cries,
> for ecstatic madness, are not sadder than some things.
> From the residue of song, I have barely said my love
>> again,
> as if for the last time, believing that you will leave me.

The use of "barely" and "as if" is part of Bell's tendency to qualify, to undercut, and to leave meaning implied but not defined.

Stars Which See, Stars Which Do Not See

Stars Which See, Stars Which Do Not See contains poems about Dorothy, Bell's wife, but also includes several poems about poetry. In his "To a Solitary Reader," an allusion to William Wordsworth's poem about the solitary reaper, Bell discusses the development of his poetry: "If once he slept with Donne/ (happily) now he sleeps/ with Williams/ the old Williams." Bell thereby indicates his movement from John Donne's metaphysical style to William Carlos Williams's stress on a poem being, rather than meaning. The remainder of the poem distinguishes between "memory," which is what we "are" in the sense that "they/ think they know us," and what our "being" is, that which is inexplicable, without meaning. The poem concludes, "Time's determinant./ Once I knew you." Bell leaves behind certainty and memory and instead embraces the idea that nothing can be "known."

These Green-Going-to-Yellow

In the title poem of *These Green-Going-to Yellow* the poet states, "I'm raising the emotional ante" by attempting to align himself with nature, particularly the leaves of a gingko tree someone planted in New York City. The poem concerns people's perspectives on life and asks if they really see beauty. Of course, the answer is "no." People look down "not to look up" and "look at the middles of things." Comfortable with mediocrity, like the seasons, people go from green to yellow, age like autumn, and lose their creative powers. Bell declares that people's perspective would be different "if we truly thought that we were gods." This line denies people even an erroneous presumption about their place in the universe, but in his acceptance of the situation Bell somehow remains "green." He has said, "I started out green and I intended to remain so."

THE BOOK OF THE DEAD MAN AND ARDOR

In the Dead Man poems in *The Book of the Dead Man* and *Ardor*, Bell moves in a new direction, adopting a persona or mask that he often denies but on at least one occasion accepts: "He was my particular and my universal./ I leave it to the future to say why." The Dead Man has enabled Bell to erase distinctions such as the one between life and death. In "About the Dead Man" the poet writes, "He [the Dead Man] thinks himself alive because he has no future." Statements like this, especially when they are preceded by and followed by other seemingly unrelated statements, would appear to be incredibly complicated, but Bell asserts that they are complex, rather than complicated. Complexity, for him, is "the fabric of life and the character of emotion." In his poetry things "connect," even if the connections are not always apparent to the reader.

The "Baby Hamlet" poem in this section embodies Bell's ideas about complexity, which requires "a fusion of many elements, some of them seemingly disparate, even contradictory." Hamlet's indecision is fused with the world's indecision, its "hopeless pacifism" and the "Platonic ideal carried to its logical inconclusion." According to Bell, "It doesn't seem a stretch to me to parallel Hamlet's indecision with the world's reluctance to act early and decisively against the Nazis." After all, "events occur while waiting for the news./ Or stuck in moral neutral."

OTHER MAJOR WORKS

NONFICTION: *Old Snow Just Melting: Essays and Interviews*, 1983.

MISCELLANEOUS: *Segues: A Correspondence in Poetry*, 1983 (with William Stafford); *Annie-Over*, 1988 (with Stafford).

BIBLIOGRAPHY

Bell, Marvin. "An Interview with Marvin Bell." Interview by David Hamilton. *Iowa Review* 30 (Fall, 2000): 3-22. Because Bell was the first poetry editor for the *Iowa Review*, which interviewed him in 1981, this review provides an excellent overview of Bell's writing career. Hamilton discusses the development of the Dead Man poems, beginning with *Iris of Creation* with later appearances in *A Marvin Bell Reader* (1994). These lead to *The Book of the Dead Man* and *Ardor*. The Resurrected Dead Man first appeared in *Wednesday* (1997), published in Ireland. Hamilton describes the Dead Man as "an archetypal figure with sacramental dimensions." Bell distinguishes between the two figures by stating that a Dead Man poem is a field, but a Resurrected Dead Man poem is a path: "I go first. If you want to follow me, you have to stay on the path."

_____. "My Twenties in Chicago: A Memoir." *TriQuarterly* 60 (Spring/Summer, 1984): 118-126. Bell's vivid account of the years 1958 to 1961, which he spent in the artistic neighborhood of Hyde Park in Chicago. Bell describes the "activist" nature of the neighborhood, his growing involvement with photography, his master's writing classes at the University of Chicago, and his many colleagues, friends, and teachers. John Logan, poet and professor, is discussed at length. Of special interest is his discussion of the Chicago artistic and literary scene, including the work of several prominent Beat poets such as Jack Kerouac, Allen Ginsberg, and Gregory Corso.

Harp, Jerry. "Inexactly Dead: On Marvin Bell's *Mars Being Red*." *Pleiades* 28, no. 2 (2008): 177-183. A thorough review of Bell's 2007 poetry collection *Mars Being Red*. Examines how many of the poems in this book are "extended meditation[s] on multiple senses of time, as well as on the times."

Jackson, Richard. "Containing the Other: Marvin Bell's Recent Poetry." *North American Poetry Review* 280 (January/February, 1995): 45-48. Jackson focuses on *The Book of the Dead Man*, which he finds rich in complexity. For Jackson, Bell extends his emphasis on inclusiveness and counterpointing in the Dead Man poems. The book begins with poems about feeling and sensing, moves to dreams and the psychic life, and concludes "with two poems about our relation to the cosmos." Jackson finds in Bell's poetry the joy of life.

Kitchen, Judith. "'I Gotta Use Words. . . .'" *Georgia Review* 51 (Winter, 1997): 756. Kitchen believes that in the Dead Man poems, Bell has found "a liberating spirit, someone who could serve his poetic innovation." She finds *Ardor*, not surprisingly, more passionate than *The Book of the Dead Man* and sees Bell moving from a forward look at death to a backward look at life. As a result, she claims, the poems in the later book to be a cohesive whole, to be able to create a contextual world and then provide a "take" on that world. For her, Bell is sending poetry into new and original territory.

Thomas L. Erskine
Updated by Sarah Hilbert

STEPHEN VINCENT BENÉT

Born: Bethlehem, Pennsylvania; July 22, 1898
Died: New York, New York; March 13, 1943

PRINCIPAL POETRY
Five Men and Pompey, 1915
Young Adventure, 1918
Heavens and Earth, 1920
King David, 1923
Tiger Joy, 1925
John Brown's Body, 1928
Ballads and Poems, 1915-1930, 1931
A Book of Americans, 1933 (with Rosemary Carr Benét)
Burning City, 1936
The Ballad of the Duke's Mercy, 1939
Western Star, 1943

OTHER LITERARY FORMS
Stephen Vincent Benét (beh-NAY) made his major contribution to literature as a poet and primarily as the author of the book-length poem *John Brown's Body*. Benét was a prolific writer in several genres, however, and his canon includes short stories, novels, radio scripts, and nonfiction.

Benét's short stories are collected in *Thirteen O'Clock* (1937) and *Tales Before Midnight* (1939). The first collection contains the well-known "The Devil and Daniel Webster," which he adapted as a play, opera, and film script. He wrote several novels: *The Beginning of Wisdom* (1921), *Young People's Pride* (1922), *Jean Huguenot* (1923), *Spanish Bayonet* (1926), and *James Shore's Daughter* (1934). Benét chose to support himself and his family as a writer and, as a result, his short stories and novels often were hack work churned out for whoever would pay him the most money.

Benét also composed radio scripts, collected in *We Stand United, and Other Radio Scripts* (1945), plays, and a short history. These writings were propagandistic, wartime efforts that he felt he had to do no matter what the effect on his literary reputation.

The best collections of Benét's works are the two-volume hardback edition, *Selected Works of Stephen Vincent Benét* (1942; Basil Davenport, editor), and the paperback edition, *Stephen Vincent Benét: Selected Poetry and Prose*, also edited by Davenport (1942).

ACHIEVEMENTS
Stephen Vincent Benét's achievements began early in his life. In 1915, when he was only seventeen years old, he made his first professional sale of a poem—to *The New Republic*—and published his first book of poems (*Five Men and Pompey*). He published his second book of poems (*Young Adventure*) in 1918 just before he was twenty years old. Between 1916 and 1918, while at Yale, he was first on the editorial board of the *Yale Literary Magazine* and then became chairman. He received a traveling fellowship from Yale in 1920 that enabled him to go to Paris, where he completed his first novel, *The Beginning of Wisdom*.

Benét received many literary and academic awards throughout his life, and he was popular with the public. His collection of poems *King David* received *The Nation*'s poetry prize in 1923, when he was twenty-five years old. A Guggenheim Fellowship allowed him to return to Paris, where he worked on *John Brown's Body*. In 1929, a year after the publication of *John Brown's Body*, when he was thirty-one years old, he received the prestigious Pulitzer Prize in poetry and became famous overnight.

Benét accepted the editorship of the Yale Series

of Younger Poets competition in 1933, and in 1935, he began regular reviewing for the New York *Herald Tribune* and the *Saturday Review of Literature.* He was elected to the National Institute of Arts and Letters in 1929 and to the American Academy of Arts and Letters in 1938, and he received the Theodore Roosevelt Medal for literary accomplishment in 1933. Benét won the O. Henry Memorial Prize for the best American short story of the year several times; among his winning stories were "The Devil and Daniel Webster" and "Freedom's a Hard-Bought Thing." Finally, he received posthumously the Gold Medal for Literature from the National Institute of Arts and Letters and the Pulitzer Prize a second time for the unfinished epic poem *Western Star.*

BIOGRAPHY

Stephen Vincent Benét was born July 22, 1898, in Bethlehem, Pennsylvania. His parents were Frances Neill Rose Benét and James Walker Benét, captain of ordnance, U.S. Army, a man with poetic and literary tastes. Stephen was their third child and second son; his sister and brother were Laura Benét and William Rose Benét, who were both active in the literary world. Well-read from his youth and thoroughly educated, Benét began writing early in his life.

During Benét's childhood, his family moved throughout the United States because of his father's position in the Army. Benét and his family were at the Vatervliet, New York, Arsenal from 1899 until 1904; the Rock Island, Illinois, Arsenal during 1904; the Benicia, California, Arsenal from 1905 until 1911; and the Augusta, Georgia, Arsenal from 1911 until he graduated from a coeducational academy and entered Yale College in 1915. There he was with such undergraduates as Archibald MacLeish, Thornton Wilder, Philip Barry, and John Farrar. He left Yale after completing his junior year in 1918 to enlist in the Army, but was honorably discharged because of his bad eyesight. After working briefly for the State Department in Washington, D.C., he reentered Yale. Benét received his B.A. degree in 1919 and his M.A. degree in 1920. At that time, he was given a traveling fellowship by Yale and went to Paris, where he completed his first novel.

Unlike other expatriates in Paris, Benét was not dis-

Stephen Vincent Benét (Library of Congress)

illusioned or dissatisfied with America; he went to Paris because he could live there cheaply. He was very patriotic and loved his country deeply. While in Paris, he met Rosemary Carr; about a year later, in 1921, they were married in her hometown of Chicago. Their marriage was a happy one, producing three children: Stephanie Jane, born in 1924; Thomas Carr, born in 1925; and Rachel, born in 1931.

Benét earned his living by writing. To support his family, he was often forced to devote less time than he would have liked to his serious writing—rather than concentrating on his poetry, he sometimes had to spend time and energy writing short stories and novels that would bring in money. Although *John Brown's Body* generated substantial sales, he lost most of his capital in the crash of 1929 and never again enjoyed financial security.

When World War II broke out, fiercely loyal to

democracy, Benét felt compelled to contribute to the war effort as much as he could. As a result, in the early 1940's, he devoted much of his time and energy to writing propagandistic radio scripts and other needed pieces.

During Benét's most creative years, he was handicapped by poor health; from 1930 until his death in 1943, he suffered from arthritis of the spine and other illnesses. He was hospitalized for several weeks in 1939 for a nervous breakdown caused by overwork. On March 13, 1943, when he was forty-four years old, he died in his wife's arms following a heart attack.

ANALYSIS

In the nineteenth century, Walt Whitman called for a national poet for the United States and sought to be that poet. While he envisioned himself as the poet working in his shirt sleeves among the people and read by the population at large, he was never really a poet of the people, absorbed by the people. Ironically, Stephen Vincent Benét became the poet that Whitman wanted to be. Although Benét's approach as a poet was a literary, academic one, his poetry was widely read and popular with the public.

Using American legends, tales, songs, and history, Benét was most effective writing in epic and narrative forms, especially the folk ballad. Benét's primary weakness is related to his strength. He lacks originality; he takes not only his subjects but also his techniques from other sources. In his first published poems, a series of dramatic monologues called *Five Men and Pompey*, the influence of Robert Browning and Edwin Arlington Robinson is evident. As Donald Heiney indicates in *Recent American Literature* (1958), Benét never developed a single stylistic quality that was his own.

Benét's poetry, particularly *John Brown's Body*, is nevertheless worth reading for its presentation of American folklore and history. As he himself indicated in a foreword to *John Brown's Body*, poetry, unlike prose, tells its story through rhyme and meter. By using such a method to tell stories and convey ideas, the poet can cause the reader to feel more deeply and to see more clearly; thus, the poet's work will remain in the reader's memory.

TIGER JOY

Benét's strengths are evident in the volume preceding *John Brown's Body*, *Tiger Joy*. The best poems in this collection include an octave of sonnets, "The Golden Corpse," and two very good ballads "The Mountain Whippoorwill: Or, How Hill-Billy Jim Won the Great Fiddlers' Prize" (subtitled "A Georgia Romance"), and "The Ballad of William Sycamore."

In "The Mountain Whippoorwill," Benét uses the dialect of the inhabitants of the Georgia hills. The rhythm of the poem suggests the music that is produced as Big Tom Sargent, Little Jimmy Weezer, Old Dan Wheeling, and Hill-Billy Jim attempt to win the first prize at the Georgia Fiddlers' Show. The mountain whippoorwill serves as a unifying element; initially, the whippoorwill is supposedly the mother of Hill-Billy Jim, the narrator, but then becomes symbolic of him as fiddler and of his genius.

"THE BALLAD OF WILLIAM SYCAMORE"

"The Ballad of William Sycamore," one of Benét's frequently anthologized poems, is the autobiography of William Sycamore, an archetype of the pioneer. The son of a Kentucky mountaineer, Sycamore was born outdoors near a stream and a tall green fir. Following a childhood during which he learned his woodsman's skills from his father, he and his wife were part of the westward movement; he lost his eldest son at the Alamo and his youngest at Custer's last stand, and died with his boots on. At the end of the poem, he tells the builders of towns to go play with the towns where they had hoped to fence him in. He has escaped them and their towns, and now sleeps with the buffalo. According to Heiney, the poem differs from the traditional ballad primarily in that it is written in the first person and covers Sycamore's life from his birth to his death.

JOHN BROWN'S BODY

John Brown's Body, a book-length narrative poem, became immediately popular with the American public when it was published in 1928; it was the poem that established Benét's position in American literature. Although many critics have complained that a major weakness of the poem is a lack of unity, Parry Stroud points out, in *Stephen Vincent Benét* (1962), several ways in which the epic is unified—through the characters, through the symbolism, and through the consistent and purposeful use of several meters.

First, John Brown himself and the imaginary characters representing the major regional areas of America serve to unify the poem. Jack Ellyat, a Connecticut boy who enlists in the Union army, is the counterpart of Clay Wingate, a Southerner from Wingate Hall, Georgia. Ellyat eventually marries Melora Vilas, who, with her father, stands for the border states and the West. At the end of the war Wingate also marries the woman he loves, the Southern belle Sally Dupre. There are several other minor fictional characters typifying various regions and classes in America: Lucy Weatherby, a Southern coquette; Spade, a slave who runs away; Cudjo, a slave who remains loyal to the Wingates; Jake Diefer, a stolid Pennsylvania farmer for whom Spade works after the war; Luke Breckinridge, an illiterate Tennessee mountaineer who fights for the South; and Shippey, a spy for the North. The war resolves the fates of most of these fictional characters.

Parry Stroud disagrees with the many critics who believe that Benét's style disrupts the unity of the poem. Benét uses three basic meters: traditional blank verse, heroic couplets, and what Benét called his "long rough line." This versatile long line approximates the rhythm of everyday speech more than traditional meters do. Benét also uses rhythmic prose and lyrics. In the foreword that he wrote for the poem in 1941, he states that he intentionally used a variety of meters. For example, he used a light, swift meter for the episodes concerning Clay Wingate, the Southerner, to suggest dancing, riding, and other aspects of Southern culture.

In the foreword, Benét indicates that the poem deals with events associated with the American Civil War, beginning just before John Brown's raid on Harpers Ferry and ending just after the close of the war and the assassination of U.S. president Abraham Lincoln. Although he did not intend to write a formal history of the Civil War, he did want the poem to show how the events presented affected different Americans; he was concerned with the Americans of the North and South as well as those of the East and West.

By describing the American landscape and people, Benét gives American historical events a reality greater than mere names and dates can confer. He believed that the people living during the Civil War encountered problems similar to those of his time and that the decisions they made then had a great effect upon future generations of Americans.

Growing out of Benét's fondness for his country, *John Brown's Body* will have a permanent place in American literature because it is an epic having uniquely American themes and qualities. Benét researched the historical details of the war extensively, but he also understood the human complexities involved. Exhibiting a high level of narrative skill, he presented five of the most crucial years in American history, poetically interpreting part of the great heritage of the United States.

WESTERN STAR

Western Star, a fragmentary work, which was to have been another epic like *John Brown's Body*, was published after Benét's death in 1943. He had begun writing *Western Star* before World War II, but upon the entry of the United States into the war, he put the manuscript aside, planning to resume work on it when peace was achieved. *Western Star* was to have been Benét's interpretation of the settlement of the United States and of the westward movement of frontier life. He intended to present frontier life in a way similar to that he had used to present the Civil War in *John Brown's Body*—by using actual events and both actual and imaginary persons for his characters. Unfortunately, his early death prevented his completing this work.

OTHER MAJOR WORKS

LONG FICTION: *The Beginning of Wisdom*, 1921; *Young People's Pride*, 1922; *Jean Huguenot*, 1923; *Spanish Bayonet*, 1926; *James Shore's Daughter*, 1934.

SHORT FICTION: *Thirteen O'Clock*, 1937; *Tales Before Midnight*, 1939; *Twenty-five Short Stories*, 1943.

PLAYS: *Nerves*, pr. 1924 (with John Chipman Farrar); *That Awful Mrs. Eaton*, pr. 1924 (with Farrar); *The Headless Horseman*, pr., pb. 1937; *The Devil and Daniel Webster*, pr. 1938.

RADIO PLAY: *We Stand United, and Other Radio Scripts*, 1945.

NONFICTION: *America*, 1944; *Stephen Vincent Benét on Writing: A Great Writer's Letters of Advice to a Young Beginner*, 1946; *Selected Letters of Stephen Vincent Benét*, 1960.

MISCELLANEOUS: *Selected Works of Stephen Vincent Benét*, 1942 (Basil Davenport, editor); *Stephen Vincent Benét: Selected Poetry and Prose*, 1942 (Davenport, editor); *The Last Circle: Stories and Poems*, 1946.

BIBLIOGRAPHY

Benét, Laura. *When William Rose, Stephen Vincent, and I Were Young*. New York: Dodd, Mead, 1976. A memoir of the childhoods of Laura, William Rose, and Stephen Vincent Benét. Includes black-and-white photographs.

Benét, Stephen Vincent. *Selected Letters of Stephen Vincent Benét*. Edited by Charles A. Fenton. New Haven, Conn.: Yale University Press, 1960. A broad selection of letters reflecting Benét's moods and perceptions about places in the United States and Europe, the people and the literary and social scenes, especially during the 1920's, 1930's, and the few years that he lived in the 1940's.

Benét, William Rose. *Stephen Vincent Benét*. 1943. Reprint. Folcroft, Pa.: Folcroft Library Editions, 1976. A look at the poet's life from his brother. Includes a bibliography.

Davenport, Basil. Introduction to *Stephen Vincent Benét: Selected Poetry and Prose*. New York: Rinehart, 1960. This essay is a good overview of Benét's life and literature for those unfamiliar with his writing. Davenport stresses how unusual Benét's Americanism seemed during a time when Paris overflowed with expatriates cynical of American idealism. The poet is seen as essentially a romantic, able to show extraordinary feeling for his subjects.

Fenton, Charles A. *Stephen Vincent Benét: The Life and Times of an American Man of Letters*. 1958. Reprint. Westport, Conn.: Greenwood Press, 1978. A definitive biography that not only presents the well-documented life of Benét but also comments on the works. Fenton had the cooperation of Rosemary Carr (Benét's wife) and access to Benét's diaries.

Izzo, David Garrett, and Lincoln Konkle, eds. *Stephen Vincent Benét: Essays on His Life and Work*. Jefferson, N.C.: McFarland, 2003. Eleven essays (four on Benét's life) are collected here by the editors in an effort to rekindle interest in the Pulitzer Prize-winning author and poet. Izzo and Konkle set his works alongside those of his modernist contemporaries and review his achievements in this context.

Roache, Joel. "Stephen Vincent Benét." In *American Short-Story Writers, 1910-1945, Second Series*, edited by Bobby Ellen Kimbel. Vol. 102 in *Dictionary of Literary Biography*. Detroit: Gale Research, 1991. Delineates the writings of Benét and provides a short biography. A straightforward and readable article, succinctly written.

Snow, Richard F. "Benet's Birthday." *American Heritage* 49 (October, 1998): 6-7. A biographical sketch that comments on Benét's winning of the Pulitzer Prize and his attempts to forge a clear American language that was large enough for poetry but also idiomatic and spare.

Stroud, Parry. *Stephen Vincent Benét*. New York: Twayne, 1962. A critique that focuses on Benét's liberalism, reflected in his writings. Stroud places the writer in a historical and cultural frame in an interpretation of Benét's themes. The analysis is clear in its literary perspective and its biographical framework.

Sherry G. Southard

WILLIAM ROSE BENÉT

Born: Brooklyn, New York; February 2, 1886
Died: New York, New York; May 4, 1950

PRINCIPAL POETRY
Merchants from Cathay, 1913
The Falconer of God, and Other Poems, 1914
The Great White Wall, 1916
The Burglar of the Zodiac, and Other Poems, 1918
Perpetual Light: A Memorial, 1919
Moons of Grandeur, 1920
Poems for Youth: An American Anthology, 1925
Man Possessed: Being the Selected Poems of William Rose Benét, 1927

Rip Tide, 1932

Starry Harness, 1933

Golden Fleece: A Collection of Poems and Ballads Old and New, 1935

Harlem, and Other Poems, 1935

With Wings as Eagles: Poems and Ballads of the Air, 1940

The Dust Which Is God, 1941

Day of Deliverance: A Book of Poems in Wartime, 1944

The Stairway of Surprise, 1947

Poetry Package, 1949 (with Christopher Morley)

The Spirit of the Scene, 1951

OTHER LITERARY FORMS

Though William Rose Benét (beh-NAY) dabbled in other literary forms—fiction for adults and children, drama, and essays and other nonfiction—he is mostly remembered for his poetry and his efforts to promote poetry as an associate editor at the *Saturday Review of Literature* (after 1952, known simply as the *Saturday Review*) and the editor of several anthologies of verse.

ACHIEVEMENTS

William Rose Benét's long tenure as an editor at the *Saturday Review of Literature* over the first half of the magazine's sixty-year existence helped make the publication one of the more influential periodicals in providing literary commentary and book reviews. While extolling the virtues of prominent nineteenth century writers, the magazine also helped introduce such twentieth century authors as Edith Wharton, Ernest Hemingway, Sinclair Lewis, William Faulkner, Robert Benchley, and Ring Lardner.

Benét also earned a reputation as a competent—if not always inspired—craftsman of traditional rhyming poetry. Benét's longevity as a poet and his technical abilities in composing verse were eventually recognized toward the end of his life. He received the Pulitzer Prize in poetry in 1942 for *The Dust Which Is God*, giving the Benét family a pair of Pulitzer winners: his brother Stephen Vincent Benét won the award twice for his epics *John Brown's Body* (1928) and *Western Star* (1943). He served as chancellor for the Academy of American Poets from 1946 to 1950.

BIOGRAPHY

William Rose Benét was born into a family of logophiles whose ancestors had come from Minorca to America, settling in Florida during the eighteenth century. His grandfather was General Stephen Vincent Benét (1825-1895), a West Point graduate, writer of military treatises, and Civil War veteran who became chief of U.S. Army Ordnance. William's father, Colonel James Walker Benét, was likewise a career Army officer, also in ordnance; his mother was Frances Neill Rose Benét. William was the middle of three children. William, his younger brother Stephen Vincent, and his elder sister Laura would all earn reputations as writers and editors, influenced and inspired by their father's love of quality literature, particularly poetry; the brothers would both receive Pulitzer Prizes for their verse. The Benét family moved several times as the children were growing, following Colonel Benét to postings at government arsenals in Pennsylvania, Georgia, New York, and California.

William Rose Benét originally intended to follow his father into the military, and toward that end, he attended Albany Academy in New York, where he began to write. At the age of fifteen, he won a silver medal for "The Harvest," a poem published in *St. Nicholas Magazine for Boys and Girls*. Eschewing a military career for the literary life, Benét attended Yale University, where he became editor of the *Yale Record*, the institution's longtime humor magazine. Following graduation in 1907, Benét found employment at a number of publications, including *Literary Review*, *New York Evening Post*, and *Century Magazine* (where he was office boy from 1911 to 1914, and assistant editor from 1914 to 1918). While working at *Century Magazine*, Benét published his first collection of verse, *Merchants from Cathay*. Many of the poems in this collection had already appeared in such popular periodicals as *American Magazine*, *Poet Lore*, *Harper's Weekly*, *Bookman*, *Poetry Review*, *Lippincott's Magazine*, *North American Review*, and *Poetry*.

Merchants from Cathay was just the opening salvo in a productive writing career spanning more than three decades that incorporated numerous volumes of poetry; a novel in verse; a play; several nonfiction works, including a memoir about growing up with his famous younger brother; children's stories; and a variety of edited texts, notably *The Oxford Anthology of American Literature* (1938; with Norman Holmes Pearson) and *The Reader's Encyclopedia: An Encyclopedia of World Literature and the Arts* (1948). Benét married for the first time in 1912, to Teresa Frances Thompson, and fathered three children—James Walker, Frances Rosemary, and Kathleen Anne—before Teresa died in 1919 during the influenza pandemic.

After the United States entered World War I in 1917, Benét volunteered for military service and was briefly enlisted in flight school, where his weak eyesight resulted in an honorable discharge. He subsequently wrote advertising copy in New York City before joining the staff of *Nation's Business* in Washington, D.C. In 1924, Benét cofounded (with Amy Loveman, Henry Seidel Canby, and others) *Saturday Review of Literature*, where he worked as an editor and wrote a column, "The Phoenix Nest," for the remainder of his life; the magazine would continue without him until 1986, when it folded.

William Rose Benét (The Granger Collection, New York)

Benét was married for a second time, in 1923, to poet-novelist Elinor Wylie, who died in 1928, although they lived apart by mutual consent. A third marriage, in 1932 to Lora Baxter, ended in divorce five years later. His fourth marriage, to Marjorie Flack in 1941, lasted until his death in 1950 from a heart attack.

ANALYSIS

A classically educated man who straddled the nineteenth and twentieth centuries, William Rose Benét, judged by his poetry, seems to belong more to the leisurely Victorian era into which he was born than to the hectic modern period in which he flourished. Benét's adherence to medieval French poetic forms (particularly in his earlier work), his choice of subject matter, and his florid writing style all reinforce this impression. Benét's verses are typically composed according to the rules of their type—rondeau, cinquain, lai, chanson, triolet, iambe, sestina, villanelle, sonnet, or ode—each of which demands a particular syllabic rhythm and fixed rhyme scheme. Many of his poems would not be out of place in the Romantic tradition; they are replete with symbolism and full of controlled emotion. Some deal colorfully and imaginatively with exotic, faraway places, and long-ago times. Others are impassioned paeans to aspects of nature, explorations of self, musings on spirituality, love poems, or combinations of various ideas.

Benét's verse contains more exclamation points than is considered seemly by twenty-first century writers. He occasionally resorts to such outmoded devices as feminine rhyme (using two rhyming syllables instead of a single syllable at the end of a line, as in "gave me/save me"). He inserts obsolete expressions (for example, "Thee, "doth," and "Lackaday") to add the flavor of yesteryear to a piece. He employs old-fashioned expressions such as "o'er" for "over" or "'neath" for "beneath," and applies antique pronunciations (such as REACH-ed) to improve scansion. The poems often rely on arcane allusions from history and mythology that require annotations or research to gain fuller understanding, or dwell on larger-than-life figures and monumental events.

However, despite such potential drawbacks, Benét can still be appreciated as a master craftsperson of great technical skill and is a worthy model for traditionalists. His interests are far ranging and creatively presented. As he matured as a poet, Benét dealt with more modern topics, but with few exceptions, he approached them through well-wrought rhyme that became increasingly more free-form and less dependent on past conventions, and as a consequence, he produced work unique in style, tone, and substance. Benét's rhymes are for the most part true, with great attention paid to varying the choice of words to end lines (as in "beau," "flow," "so," and "dough") to keep the reader's visual interest high. Though generally adhering to established rhyme schemes, Benét was canny enough to avoid reader monotony and to impart a feeling of spontaneity and freshness by incorporating stanzas in different rhythmic or rhyming patterns (as in trimeter versus pentameter or hexameter), by adding or subtracting syllables from his usual iambic verse, by using enjambment or internal rhyme, or by repeating key concepts or phrases.

MERCHANTS FROM CATHAY

The seventy-eight poems in the author's first collection, *Merchants from Cathay*, provide an excellent introduction to Benét's versatility of style within the confines of conventional form and to the multiplicity of subjects he addressed in verse. Published when the author was in his mid-twenties and encompassing work completed while he was in his teens, *Merchants from Cathay* demonstrates a remarkable familiarity and facility with classical verse forms and sophistication beyond Benét's years in the ability to bend those forms to his specific purpose. The poems—here in brisk quatrains, there in longer, more convoluted stanzas—move glibly among a variety of lengths, rhyme patterns, rhythms, and conceits. A sober consideration of a small, everyday thing of quiet beauty will follow the unabashed flamboyance of a historical re-creation or a mythological fantasy. An impassioned love poem will precede a profound contemplation of an individual's place in the universe. There is something for every taste, every mood, and every occasion. Though there may not be a plethora of timeless quotable lines to be gleaned from Benét's works, individually and collectively, his poems are thoughtfully conceived and expertly constructed to produce a desired effect.

All the Romanticist's primary preoccupations are well represented here. There are thoughtful examinations of the natural world as it relates to humans (such as "The Awakening of the Trees," "The Bird Fancier," "The Boast of the Tides"). There are vignettes capturing bygone times ("The Brawl," "The Parlous Thing") and distant places ("The Merchants from Cathay"). There are contemplations of fate and spirituality ("The Anvil of Souls," "The Young Brother," "Lightning"). There are exuberant studies of historical figures ("The Drowned Hidalgo Dreams," "The Marvelous Munchausen") and mythological figures ("Song of the Satyrs to Ariadne," "The Lost Gods Abiding"). There are poems of love ("The Heart's Colloquy," "The Second Covenant"), as well as sentimental pieces, reminiscences, and children's fantasy verses.

THE DUST WHICH IS GOD

The Dust Which Is God is Benét's thinly disguised semi-autobiographical novel in verse-narrative form. Although the quality of the poetry is uneven—it is difficult to sustain white-hot enthusiasm for a project over hundreds of pages that consume thousands of hours of thought and work—there are many well-turned passages of emotional depth throughout the work. *The Dust Which Is God* contains many allusions to early twentieth century American literary history, with glimpses of people from Benét's social circle—Christopher Morley (called "Darlington Tracy"); his late wife, Wylie (called "Sylvia"); his brother, Stephen Vincent (called "Peter"); Dorothy Parker; George Gershwin; Benchley; and others—in the process of putting forth the case that poetry is valuable in appreciating the finer aspects of the human experience and understanding the dynamics that apply to relationships, emotions, and beliefs. This work, for which Wallace Stevens praised the author as a "virtuoso and a voluptuary of language," received the Pulitzer Prize.

THE STAIRWAY OF SURPRISE

The Stairway of Surprise, the last solo effort published during Benét's lifetime, demonstrates that though his poetic skills had grown, his major areas of concentration had not changed. The book is divided into nine parts; each section contains poems loosely grouped around a particular subject. The title of the first part, "Center Is Everywhere," is based on a line from a lost treatise by Empedocles concerning the nature of God, and most of the twenty-one rhyming poems (including "Supreme Being," "The Incarnate," and "Deus") at least touch on some aspect of spirituality. The poems in "The Noblest Frailty" deal with love, those in "Gallery" portray individuals from history and mythology, and those in "High Fantastical" are what-if speculations. Interestingly, *The Stairway of Surprise* contains two of Benét's rare unrhymed, blank-verse efforts: the mythology-steeped "Brigand of Eleusis" and the seafaring epic "The Fire in the Crystal," which exceeds twelve hundred lines.

OTHER MAJOR WORKS

LONG FICTION: *The First Person Singular*, 1922.

PLAY: *Day's End: A Fantasia in One Act*, pr., pb. 1939.

NONFICTION: *Saturday Papers: Essays on Literature from "The Literary Review,"* 1921 (with Henry Seidel Canby and Amy Loveman); *Wild Goslings: A Selection of Fugitive Pieces*, 1927; *Stephen Vincent Benét: My Brother Steve and For the Record*, 1943 (with John Chipman Farrar).

CHILDREN'S LITERATURE: *The Flying King of Kurio: A Story for Children*, 1926; *Adolphus: Or, The Adopted Dolphin and the Pirate's Daughter*, 1941 (with Marjorie Flack); *Timothy's Angels*, 1947 (with Constantin Alajal).

EDITED TEXTS: *Twentieth Century Poetry*, 1929 (with John Drinkwater and Canby); *The Collected Poems of Elinor Wylie*, 1932; *Fifty Poets: An American Auto-Anthology*, 1933; *The Pocket University Guide to Daily Reading*, 1934 (with Canby and Christopher Morley); *The Prose and Poetry of Elinor Wylie*, 1934; *Mother Goose*, 1936 (with Roger Duvoisin); *Great Poems of the English Language*, 1937 (with Wallace Alvin Briggs); *The Oxford Anthology of American Literature*, 1938 (with Norman Holmes Pearson); *Poems for Modern Youth*, 1938 (with Adolph Gillis); *An Anthology of Famous English and American Poetry*, 1945 (with Conrad Aiken); *The Poetry of Freedom*, 1945 (with Norman Cousins); *The Oxford Anthology of American Literature, Volume 2*, 1946 (with Pearson); *The Reader's Encyclopedia: An Encyclopedia of World Literature and the Arts*, 1948.

MISCELLANEOUS: *A Baker's Dozen of Emblems: Collected from Various Numbers of the "Saturday Review of Literature" Issued in 1927 and 1928*, 1935.

BIBLIOGRAPHY

Brennan, Elizabeth A., and Elizabeth C. Clarage. *Who's Who of Pulitzer Prize Winners*. Phoenix, Ariz.: Oryx Press, 1999. This useful reference work—constantly updated on the Pulitzer Web site (http://www.pulitzer.org)—includes information on winners in each category, names of other finalists, and names of jurors. Links to the text of the prizewinning entries are included on the Web site.

Gregory, Horace, and Marya Zaturenska. *A History of American Poetry, 1900-1940*. 1946. Reprint. New York: Gordian Press, 1969. This classic work contains a chapter on the influence of Benét that shows his importance in the first half of the twentieth century.

Hively, Evelyn Helmick. *A Private Madness: The Genius of Elinor Wylie*. Kent, Ohio: Kent State University Press, 2003. A study of the author and her work, with an emphasis on her troubled personal life—which included a marriage of five years' duration to Benét—that shaped her fiction and poetry.

Mitchell, Ruth Comfort. *Narratives in Verse*. 1923. Reprint. Whitefish, Mont.: Kessinger, 2005. This is a reprint of a volume brought out under a pseudonym by magazine writer Mrs. Sanborn Young, which includes a contribution on the subject of narratives in verse from Benét.

Jack Ewing

CHARLES BERNSTEIN

Born: New York, New York; April 4, 1950

PRINCIPAL POETRY
Asylums, 1975
Parsing, 1976
Shade, 1978
Poetic Justice, 1979
Controlling Interests, 1980

Legend, 1980 (with Bruce Andrews, Steve
   McCaffery, Ron Silliman and Ray DiPalma)
Stigma, 1981
Islets/Irritations, 1983
The Sophist, 1987
The Nude Formalism, 1989
Rough Trades, 1991
Dark City, 1994
Republics of Reality: 1975-1995, 2000
With Strings, 2001
Shadowtime, 2005
Warrant, 2005
Girly Man, 2006
All the Whiskey in Heaven: Selected Poems, 2010

OTHER LITERARY FORMS

Charles Bernstein has written collections of essays, including *Artifice of Absorption* (1987), *Content's Dream: Essays, 1975-1984* (1986), and *A Poetics* (1992). In *Content's Dream*, Bernstein examines the difference and connection between poetry and prose and also argues against the current critical establishment and its institutionalized encouragement of homogenized mainstream poetry. *A Poetics* looks at poetics, philosophy, and the social aspects of text. Bernstein also published *A Conversation with David Antin* (2002) and *My Way: Speeches and Poems* (1999). Bernstein has written the libretti for operas, and he translated *Red, Green, and Black* (1990) by Olivier Cadiot and *The Maternal Drape* (1984) by Claude Royet-Journoud. Bernstein's poetry has appeared in several editions of *The Best American Poetry* series. His work has also regularly appeared in *Harper's Magazine*, *Poetry* magazine, and *Critical Inquiry*.

ACHIEVEMENTS

Charles Bernstein is a foundational member of the Language poets and has been honored for his poetry and his teaching. He received the Roy Harvey Pearce/Archive for New Poetry Prize by the University of California in 1999 for his lifetime contributions to poetry and literary scholarship, and he was made a fellow of the American Academy of Arts and Sciences in 2006. From 1990 to 2003, Bernstein was the David Gray Professor of Poetry and Letters at the State Uni-

versity of New York at Buffalo and director of the poetics program, which he cofounded with Robert Creeley. He was appointed a State University of New York Distinguished Professor in 2002. He received the Dean's Award for Innovation in Teaching from the University of Pennsylvania in 2005. He was the recipient of a number of prestigious fellowships, which include the William Lyon Mackenzie King Fellowship at Simon Fraser University (1973), the National Endowment for the Arts Creative Writing Fellowship (1980), the John Simon Guggenheim Memorial Fellowship (1985), the University of Auckland Foundation Fellowship (1986), and New York Foundation for the Arts Poetry Fellowships in 1995 and 1990.

BIOGRAPHY

Charles Bernstein was born in New York City to Jewish parents and grew up near Central Park. His father worked in the garment industry. Bernstein attended the Bronx High School of Science, where he edited the school newspaper. He entered Harvard in 1968, the same year he met his future wife, Susan Bee. During his university years, Bernstein protested against the Vietnam War and worked on the freshman literary magazine. He also published *Writing*, a photocopied magazine. Bernstein wrote his senior thesis on two writers who influenced his later poetry, Gertrude Stein and Ludwig Wittgenstein. In 1973, Bernstein received the William Lyon Mackenzie King Fellowship at Simon Fraser University in British Columbia, Canada. From there, Bernstein moved to Santa Barbara, California, where he worked part-time at a community free clinic. Bernstein spent about twenty years working as a medical and healthcare editor and writer; this experience has partially informed his poetry. Bernstein also served as the associate director of the Comprehensive Employment and Training Act (CETA) Artists Project.

In 1975, Bernstein and Bee moved back to New York; they married two years later and had two children, Emma and Felix. Bernstein became very active in the New York poetry scene. Bernstein and his wife founded Asylum's Press, which published his first two books, *Asylums* and *Parsing*. In 1978, he and Ted Greenwald established the Ear Inn series, which went on to be a significant venue for emerging writers. That same year, Bernstein and Bruce Andrews created $L=A=N=G=U=A=G=E$ magazine. Although its production value was quite low—the books were photocopied and stapled together without covers—the magazine was an important publication. In 1984, three years after the magazine had ceased publication, Bernstein and Andrews selected pieces from the thirteen issues and published them as *The L=A=N=G=U=A=G=E Book*.

Bernstein was awarded a University of Auckland fellowship in 1986, which helped him develop his international reputation. In 1999, Bernstein played Dr. Simon in a number of television commercials with Jon Lovitz for the Yellow Pages. The following year, he appeared in the film *Finding Forrester* (2000), which starred Sean Connery. Bernstein has been writer-in-residence or visiting faculty at Columbia, Princeton, Brown, and Temple universities; Bard College; the New School for Social Research; Queens College; and the University of California, San Diego.

At the State University of New York at Buffalo, Bernstein served as David Gray Professor of Poetry

Charles Bernstein (©Christopher Felver/CORBIS)

and Letters and as director of the poetics program from 1990 to 2003. He cofounded the Electronic Poetry Center with Loss Glazier. In 2003, Bernstein became the Donald T. Regan Professor of English and Comparative Literature at the University of Pennsylvania, where, with Al Filreis, he was confounder and coeditor of PENNsound, an archive of recorded poetry.

ANALYSIS

Charles Bernstein is a leading postmodern poet who was one of the first creators of Language poetry, which came out of New York City in the late 1970's and early 1980's. Language poetry calls attention to language itself, rather than to a persona. It follows the ideas of objectivism and Ezra Pound's experimental poetics. Bernstein's iconoclastic and radically inventive verse challenges traditional ideas about poetry. His poetry does not assume a syntax, subject matter, or structure. It pays attention to language and how it makes meaning. Bernstein has worked against the idea of using a consistent narrating voice in poetry, which was a popular convention in the 1970's. Bernstein has aimed to put the art back in poetry by allowing one phrase to collide with the next. His poems use widely variant forms of language and make a rhythm from the types of language used. As a writer, Bernstein has examined the ways that meanings and values are exposed through the written word, which is meant to unlock poetic activity, not close it. The common thread throughout Bernstein's work is the wide-ranging referential power of words, which can be denotative, connotative, and associational. Words can partake in social and political activity as well as be used for aesthetics. Bernstein's work is driven by social passions. His poetry graphically explores contemporary half-truths, speech forms, and modes of expression. Bernstein's language-oriented work can be minimalist in style. He has also written a number of prose poems and collage pieces.

POETIC JUSTICE

Poetic Justice includes one of Bernstein's most-cited poems, "Lift Off," which is made from fragments of words and what seem to be randomly positioned punctuation marks and spaces. The sense-defying poem is the transcription of the correction tape from a self-correcting typewriter. *Poetic Justice* includes prose poems such as "Lo Disfruto": "One a problem with a fragment sitting. Wave I stare as well at that only as if this all and not form letting it but is it." The book also includes poems such as "eLecTrIc" and "AZOOT D'PUUND," a poem in which Bernstein experiments with dislocated typography in the spirit of Jackson MacLow's change permutations: "iz wurry ray aZoOt de pound in reducey ap crrRisLe/ ehk nugkinj sJuxYY senshl. Ig si heh hahpae uvd r/ fahbeh at si gidrid. ImpOg qwbk tuUg. jr'ghtpihqw." This passage is intended to make readers wonder what they are supposed to see in the text when they cannot be drawn in by actual words.

THE SOPHIST

The Sophist includes "Dysraphism," which has come to be considered one of Bernstein's major works. The poem's title reflects Bernstein's medical experience ("raph" means "seam"); the "mis-seaming" of "dysraphism" is clear in the sound-based juxtaposition of its words. For example, "blinded by avenue and filled with adjacency" demonstrates exactly how this "seaming" works. "Dysraphism" exploits rhetorical figures such as the pun, anaphora, epiphora, metathesis, epigram, anagram, and neologism to create a seamless web of reconstituted words. The poem is a disturbance of stress, pitch, and rhythm of speech. The sound of "Dysraphism" could almost be called a rhapsody.

The Sophist combines traits from Bernstein's earlier works, which include an intense assemblage of sounds and a dense mix of voices. By this combination, Bernstein has created a model for a rhetorical poetry that questions truth in the name of reason. Other poems in the book include "Fear and Trespass," a dense prose piece; "The Years of Swatches," a long, single stanza composed of very short lines; "Hitch World," a three-page poem with stanzas; and "Like DeCLAraTionS in a HymIE CEMetArY," which begins "WheTHer orientated or RETurned to/ STAndiNg posture/ ACCUMU-LAteD/ *advicement and bASicALly*." From this list, one can see how *The Sophist* can stagger from text to text.

WITH STRINGS

With Strings compiles sixty-nine poems in various forms and styles that mostly date from the 1990's. *With Strings* incorporates fractured nursery rhymes, distressed mottoes, runcible riddles, and inscrutable sayings. The book ventures into the comic, the political,

the whimsical, and the elegiac. At times, the work twists toward vaudevillian satire: "the toilet seat is down now/ it's there I plan to sit/ until I find that doggy bag/ I lost while just a kid." One of the forms used by Bernstein is the inverted ballad, as in "Besotted Desquamation." Every line of this poem contains four words that begin with the same letter and are engaged with the quotidian. The musical element of the poems is suggested in the title of the book, *With Strings*. Bernstein samples everyday life and at times uses wild iambic beats. The poems collectively ask: What is art? Why is it? How is it? By asking these questions, one discovers a presence of artlessness.

GIRLY MAN

After the terrorist attacks of September 11, 2001, some members of the literary world declared postmodernism and irony dead. Bernstein used *Girly Man* to show that this was not true. The poems in this book are elegiac, satiric, and defiant, coming close to song. The work responds to the historical moments that occurred while it was written. *Girly Man* includes poems written on the evening of September 11 and verse written in response to the subsequent war in Iraq.

In this volume, Bernstein mixes self-deprecating humor with philosophical and political thinking. The poems deal with moments of crisis and comedy and confront what is illogical about political consciousness. The book battles clichéd questions such as What are we fighting for? The book also examines the music created by Tin Pan Alley, a group of New York City songwriters working in the late nineteenth and early twentieth centuries. This is reflected in the title poem, "Girly Man": "So be a girly man/ & sing this gurly song/ Sissies & proud/ That we would never lie our way to war." Tin Pan Alley is not the only source of inspiration in *Girly Man*. Poems are also based on paintings and highway signs.

ALL THE WHISKEY IN HEAVEN

All the Whiskey in Heaven is a collection of Bernstein's work during a thirty-year period. It looks at how language can both limit and liberate thought. Despite this overarching theme, each poem is quite distinct. Using sound play, Bernstein alternates between the comic and the darkly tragic, demonstrating lyric excess and great emotional range. *All the Whiskey in Heaven* is radical, socially engaged, and philosophical, using satire, irony, and wit. Bernstein's intention is to get the reader to think in unaccustomed ways. The poems address public, private, and poetic matters. The title poem, "All the Whiskey in Heaven," was first published in *The Nation* in 2008. It is a list poem, in which almost every line begins with "Not for" and demonstrates how the speaker will not give up his love for anything in the world. "Not for an empire of my own . . ./ I'll never stop loving you/ Not till my heart beats its last/ And even then in my words and my songs/ I will love you all over again."

OTHER MAJOR WORKS

PLAYS: *Blind Witness News*, pr. 1990 (libretto; with Ben Yarmolinsky); *The Lenny Paschen Show*, pr. 1992 (libretto; with Yarmolinksy; also known as *Abacus*); *The Subject: A Psychiatric Opera*, pr. 1992 (libretto; with Yarmolinsky); *Shadowtime*, pr. 2004 (with Brian Ferneyhough).

NONFICTION: *Content's Dream: Essays, 1975-1984*, 1986; *Artifice of Absorption*, 1987; *A Poetics*, 1992; *A Conversation with David Antin*, 2002.

TRANSLATIONS: *The Maternal Drape*, 1984 (of Claude Royet-Journoud); *Red, Green, and Black*, 1990 (of Olivier Cadiot).

EDITED TEXTS: *The L=A=N=G=U=A=G=E Book*, 1984 (with Bruce Andrews); *The Politics of Poetic Form: Poetry and Public Policy*, 1990; *Thirteen North American Poets*, 1993 (with Susan Howe); *Close Listening: Poetry and the Performed Word*, 1998; *Poetry Plastique*, 2001 (with Jay Sanders); *Louis Zukofsky: Selected Poems*, 2006.

MISCELLANEOUS: *My Way: Speeches and Poems*, 1999.

BIBLIOGRAPHY

Bernstein, Charles. "A Conversation with Charles Bernstein." Interview by David Caplan. *Antioch Review* 62, no. 1 (Winter, 2004): 131-141. Bernstein and Caplan talk about what makes poetry innovative and about Bernstein's interest in exploring the vernacular. There is also discussion of Bernstein's thoughts on metric poetry and free verse, as well as his ideas for teaching poetry in the classroom.

_____. "An Interview with Charles Bernstein." Interview by Allison M. Cummings and Rocco Marinaccio. *Contemporary Literature* 41, no. 1 (Spring, 2000): 1-21. Bernstein speaks about both his commitment to poetic language as a vehicle for "truths" rather than Truth and his intention to liberate language from the depleted mines of mainstream poetic conventions.

Golding, Alan. "Charles Bernstein and Professional Avant-Gardism." *Talisman* (Winter, 2009): 29-42. Looks at Bernstein's career as an avant-garde poet.

Hennessey, Michael S. "From Text to Tongue to Tape: Notes on Charles Bernstein's '1-100.'" *English Studies in Canada* 33, no. 4 (December, 2007): 67-72. The essay on an early recording of Bernstein's, "1-100," talks about how Bernstein underscores the semantic tension between the performance of the words and the words themselves, downplaying the latter for the sake of the former.

McGuirk, Kevin. "*Rough Trades*: Charles Bernstein and the Currency of Poetry." *Canadian Review of American Studies* 27, no. 3 (1997): 205-214. Discussion of *Rough Trades* examines whether Bernstein's poetry is marked by trade and talks about how Bernstein's name typically functions as a metonym for Language poetry.

Mack, Anne, Georg Mannejc, and J. J. Rome. "Private Enigmas and Critical Functions with Particular Reference to the Writing of Charles Bernstein." *New Literary History* 2 (Spring, 1991) 441-464. Explores Bernstein's arbitrary construction of poetry, which can combine various allusions, for example, in one poem, or seemingly disconnected segments that reference Lord Byron and nursery doggerel.

Nathanson, Tenney. "Collage and Pulverization in Contemporary American Poetry: Charles Bernstein's *Controlling Interests*." *Contemporary Literature* 33, no. 2 (Summer, 1992): 302-318. Looks at Bernstein's use of disenchantment with unimpeded narrative, focusing on *Controlling Interests*.

Quinn, Paul. "Bernstein's Republics: The Horizon of Language." *PN Review* 27, no. 2 (2000): 32-35. Discusses how Bernstein's poetic thinking can serve as a model of an autonomous, creative society.

Kelly-Anne Riess

DANIEL BERRIGAN

Born: Virginia, Minnesota; May 9, 1921

PRINCIPAL POETRY

Time Without Number, 1957
Encounters, 1960
The World for Wedding Ring, 1962
No One Walks Waters, 1966
Crime Poems, Trial Poems, 1968 (also known as
    *Poems by Daniel Berrigan: Crime Poems, Trial
    Poems*)
*Love, Love at the End: Parables, Prayers, and
    Meditations*, 1968
*Night Flight to Hanoi: War Diary with Eleven
    Poems*, 1968
False Gods, Real Men: New Poems, 1969
Trial Poems, 1970 (with Tom Lewis)
Prison Poems, 1973
Selected and New Poems, 1973
May All Creatures Live, 1984
Block Island, 1986
Jubilee!, 1991
Homage to Gerard Manley Hopkins, 1993
And the Risen Bread: Selected Poems, 1957-1997,
    1998
Tulips in the Prison Yard, 1999

OTHER LITERARY FORMS

Though he first gained recognition as a poet, Daniel Berrigan (BEHR-ih-gan) also became well known for his writings on religion, peace, and politics. As part of his mission as a Jesuit priest, he has published many books on religion and spirituality, from *The Bride: Essays in the Church* (1959) through such books as *Jesus Christ* (1973) and *The Words Our Savior Gave Us* (1978) to such later works as *Job: And Death No Dominion* (2000) and *Wisdom: The Feminine Face of God* (2002). To explain his civil disobedience, he has written a play, *The Trial of the Catonsville Nine* (pr., pb. 1970), which was produced off and on Broadway and all over the world (most notably by prisoners released after the defeat of the junta in Greece). To communicate his pacifistic message, he has used a variety of other genres, including parables (*A Book of Parables*, 1977), diaries (*Lights on in the House of the Dead: A Prison Diary*, 1974), and journals (*Steadfastness of the Saints: A Journal of Peace and War in Central and North America*, 1985). He has also published *To Dwell in Peace: An Autobiography* (1987), which is also a poetic meditation on his times.

ACHIEVEMENTS

Daniel Berrigan's first book of poetry, *Time Without Number*, was nominated for a National Book Award and was named the Lamont Poetry Selection by the Academy of American Poets in 1957. Two other National Book Award nominations followed, for *No One Walks Waters* in 1967 and *No Bars to Manhood* in 1970. *The Trial of the Catonsville Nine* received several awards in 1971, including an Obie Award for Distinguished Production and two Los Angeles Drama Critics Awards. In 1974, the War Resisters League presented him with its award, which had previously been given to such people as Dorothy Day and Norman Thomas. In 1988, Berrigan received the Thomas Merton Award in recognition of his struggle for justice. The next year, he was honored with the Pax Christi USA Pope Paul VI Teacher of Peace Award. In 1993, he received the Pacem in Terris Peace and Freedom Award; previous winners included such distinguished recipients as President John F. Kennedy, Martin Luther King, Jr., and Mother Teresa. In 2000, Berrigan and his brother Philip were honored with the Vasyl Stus Award from PEN of New England. Berrigan was granted an honorary degree from the College of Wooster in 2008. When one of his publishers asked Berrigan to list his awards and honors, he impishly included his indictment and "4 felonies."

BIOGRAPHY

Daniel Berrigan was born the fifth of six sons to Thomas Berrigan and Frieda Fromhart Berrigan, who were married in northern Minnesota by a priest who had served Native Americans. Berrigan described his Irish father as an "extraordinary conglomerate of passion and illusion," whereas his German-born mother was practical and deeply devout. When Daniel was five, the family moved to a farm near Syracuse, New

York, where he was educated at St. John the Baptist, a schooling that he felt was a "mitigated catastrophe," since most of the nuns, "ignorant and unhappy," made sure that these traits flourished in their charges. His father, a poet manqué, familiarized his son with such Romantics as Lord Byron, but his son preferred the poets of his own time. In high school, a nun who manifested a humanitarianism and holiness that he found attractive saw him as a potential priest, as did a friend and classmate. After graduation, he decided to enter the Society of Jesus because of this religious order's "revolutionary history."

His life as a Jesuit began on August 14, 1939, when he entered the novitiate at St.-Andrew-on-Hudson near Poughkeepsie, New York. After two years of ascetical and spiritual training, he took his perpetual vows of poverty, chastity, and obedience. This was followed by two years of literary studies in the Latin and Greek classics. During this time, he published his first poem,

Daniel Berrigan (AP/Wide World Photos)

which he later described as a postadolescent "Marian effusion," in the Jesuit magazine *America*. The next phase of his Jesuit training occurred at Woodstock in the Maryland countryside, where he studied Scholastic philosophy. He experienced World War II vicariously through his brothers, who fought in Africa and Europe, and he learned of the atomic bombing of Hiroshima while he was a patient in a Baltimore hospital. The horrors of this war helped to solidify his growing pacifist outlook.

From 1946 to 1949, he taught at St. Peter's Preparatory School in Jersey City, New Jersey. He also met Dorothy Day, the founder of the *Catholic Worker*, who encouraged him to minister to the poor. After returning to Woodstock to pursue his theological studies, he was ordained a priest on June 19, 1952, and was soon sent to France. The time Berrigan spent in France, where he met men who had been engaged in the Resistance and others who participated in the worker-priest movement, was particularly important in shaping his formation as a social and political activist. He returned to New York in 1954, and during the next decade, while he first taught at a Jesuit school in Brooklyn and then a Jesuit college in Syracuse, he devoted more and more time to his avocations of poetry and political activism. Through letters and meetings, he became friends with the Trappist monk Thomas Merton, who was an accomplished poet and spiritual writer. Merton tried to mitigate Berrigan's increasing radicalism, particularly after Roger LaPorte, a member of the Catholic Worker movement, burned himself to death in the United Nations Plaza to protest the Vietnam War. Berrigan participated in services honoring the "sacrifice" of this young man, which he compared to the crucifixion of Christ. Berrigan's activities disturbed Church and Jesuit authorities, and he was sent to Mexico and South America.

Upon his return to the United States, Berrigan, increasingly distraught over the war in Vietnam, became even more politically active. Early in 1968, he traveled with historian Howard Zinn to Hanoi, where they negotiated the release of several captured American pilots. Later that year, Berrigan, his brother Philip, and seven other Catholics forced their way into a federal office in Catonsville, Maryland, removed draft files, and burned them with homemade napalm. They were taken into custody, indicted, convicted, and sentenced. During the summer of 1970, Daniel Berrigan avoided imprisonment by going underground, embarrassing the Federal Bureau of Investigation (FBI) by his writings and public appearances, including an interview in Lee Lockwood's documentary *The Holy Outlaw*. He was captured on August 11, 1970, and sent to the federal prison in Danbury, Connecticut, to begin serving his three-year term. While a prisoner, he wrote poetry and prose, ministered to his fellow inmates, and even met with the musician Leonard Bernstein, who was seeking advice on a Mass he was composing. FBI chief J. Edgar Hoover, through Attorney General John Mitchell, brought indictments against Philip Berrigan and others for an alleged plot to kidnap National Security Adviser Henry Kissinger and destroy heating tunnels in Washington, D.C. The case was thrown out of court in 1972.

Daniel Berrigan was released from prison in February, 1972. By the mid-1970's, he was living in a Jesuit community in upper Manhattan, where he continued to write, mostly religious and pacifist books, and to be politically active. For example, in 1980, Berrigan, his brother Philip, and others broke into a General Electric plant making nuclear missiles in King of Prussia, Pennsylvania; they then hammered and poured blood on unarmed Mark 12A nose cones. This led to more time in law courts, but this did not prevent Daniel Berrigan from participating in other acts of civil disobedience. He spoke out on a variety of issues, including the Israeli invasion of Lebanon and treatment of Palestinians, covert U.S. military activities in Central America, the Gulf War, and the American invasions of Iraq and Afghanistan. During the 1980's and 1990's, he devoted much of his time to patients dying of acquired immunodeficiency syndrome (AIDS) and other diseases. In the first decade of the twenty-first century, he brought his message of peace to many places in the United States and abroad. He has stated that he finds it impossible to retire from his efforts to bring about a peaceful world and hopes that God grants him his wish to "die with his boots on."

ANALYSIS

Daniel Berrigan's poetry reflects his complex evolution as a human being, a Roman Catholic, a Jesuit priest, a peace activist, and a humanitarian. His poems,

created over more than seven decades, exhibit wideranging subjects, tone, and techniques. Because of his notoriety as an activist, he has been called "the most overlooked poet of our time." His poetry is rooted in his religious vocation, and the American writer Kurt Vonnegut once called him "Jesus as a poet." Some critics have found echoes of fellow Jesuit poet Gerard Manley Hopkins, particularly in Berrigan's early poems, but his poetry does not manifest the same fascination with rhythm, neologistic language, and form as that of Hopkins, and though Berrigan's oeuvre is much more extensive than that of his Jesuit counterpart, it has not yet achieved the stature and influence of Hopkins's more modest output. In his later works, Berrigan refused to separate religion, politics, and poetry, and some critics have praised this mature work as the product of a passionate sensibility refined by his sufferings in and out of prison. However, other critics think that Berrigan's intertwining of politics and poetry has led to didactic productions that purvey ideas, not imaginative experiences. For them, these later poems lack the mastery of metaphor and emotional insights that characterized his early creations. Berrigan himself feels that his primary responsibility is not to the critics but to the community of peacemakers.

TIME WITHOUT NUMBER

Berrigan's first book, *Time Without Number*, whose poems were written during his years of Jesuit training and his early work as a priest, reverberates with his reactions to life in the Catholic Church during the years before the revolutionary changes brought about by the Second Vatican Council. He found that his soul was "moving in a contrary wind" to conservative Catholicism, and his poems were largely the product of his lonely meditations and social activism. Influenced by Day, he identified with those priests and laypersons who were fighting against poverty, militarism, and racism. In the course of these experiences, Berrigan met a young editor who had heard of his poems, which Berrigan was reluctant to publish. He made an agreement with this editor that, if a "scrupulous and demanding reader" found his poems commendable, then he would agree to publication. The discerning reader was the great American poet Marianne Moore, who became a passionate advocate for Berrigan's poetry.

In Berrigan's estimation, his first book was a "mini-triumph," but other readers were more effusive in their praise. Highly honored, this book served as a provocative prelude to all the poems that were to follow. Some of these early poems derive from Berrigan's experiences of the natural world. For example, "Its Perfect Heart" begins with the poet's observation of a gray-blue heron in a November dawn. The Hebrews considered these long-necked, long-legged birds to be unclean, but the poet admires the "invisible fire" that enlivens the bird's heart and drives it north to breed. While humans huddle by their firesides, the heron labors day and night, following the promptings of "its perfect heart."

Other poems in this collection have a biographical source, such as "You Vested Us This Morning," dedicated to his "soldier-brothers" serving in World War II. He dedicates "The Innocent Throne" to his brother Philip; it contains references to their childhood and to Daniel's physical and emotional breach with his mother when he entered the Society of Jesus. According to Jesus Christ, his close followers have to leave father and mother and dedicate themselves totally to his service, a teaching that Jesus himself realized was difficult and that the poet feels is brutal, even tragic, as he "snatches his heart away" from his mother, leaving her with a stranger who ". . . suddenly/ stands at her door." The religious poems in this first collection prompted some readers to find influences on Berrigan from such seventeenth century Metaphysical poets as John Donne and George Herbert. Although most critics commended the efforts of this poetic novice, some reviewers objected to the preachy tone of some of the poems, while others found that the twisted syntax and cryptic language often muddied the poet's messages. Still other reviewers observed that the meters and rhythms of certain poems were often at odds with their themes. Despite these criticisms, judges from the Academy of American Poets and the National Book Award found the young poet's collection extraordinarily promising.

False Gods, Real Men

By 1969, when this seventh book of Berrigan's poetry was published, he had become more famous for his public protests than his poetry. He had participated in civil rights marches with Martin Luther King, Jr., and in protests against the Vietnam War with priests, ministers, nuns, and rabbis. Politics certainly entered his poetry, but politics in the way that the British writer George Orwell understood it: the desire to change people's minds and hearts about the type of society to which they should aspire. Berrigan's politicized poems attracted some readers while alienating others. The book's title, *False Gods, Real Men*, comes from its first poem, which is actually a compendium of nine poems, the first long, the rest short. The first centers on Berrigan's family, which has been transformed from "Acceptable Ethnic" to "Ideal American" by four sons who fought in World War II and has become an "Ideal Catholic" family by the good works of those family members who became priests and a nun. However, two son-priests, Daniel and Philip, now find themselves "in and out of jail," and the poem ends with a quotation from their indictment for destroying draft records at Catonsville. Other poems (4, 7, and 8) end with quotations from the Associated Press, *The New York Times*, and *Time* magazine, respectively, dealing with the Berrigan brothers' destruction of draft records, and reactions to it. The ninth poem, dedicated to Philip Berrigan, is infused with brotherly love as Daniel Berrigan seeks to discover clues to their fate in the physical laws of the universe and in the biological laws governing their "mother's body." What unifies these poems is the poet's search for ways to become a complete human being.

Other poems also develop this theme of how to become a genuine person in a secular world that often interferes with the laws that the Creator God instilled into human hearts and that the man-God Jesus Christ taught was the chief task of every person. In striving to become such a genuine person, the poet traveled to Hanoi, the subject of some of the poems. Other poems derive from his visits to Europe, and still others from his experiences in New York City, for example, his visit to Central Park Zoo, where a seal reminds him of God the Father.

Some critics, particularly those who shared his political views, found the poet's cries of despair, appeals to conscience, and pleas for nonviolent protest relevant and heartrending, but others thought that Berrigan's emphasis on human failures and suffering was entirely too bleak in the light of the essential optimism of the Christian message. For them, he dwelled too much on Good Friday and not enough on Easter Sunday. Consequently, his poems tended to mourn more than they exalt. One critic found only five of the seventy-seven poems successful, a pessimistic assessment clearly not shared by others.

PRISON POEMS

Berrigan wrote the poems in *Prison Poems*, which some critics consider his best work, while he was serving his sentence in Danbury Federal Correctional Institution. Many of the poems represent the emotional struggles of a priest who is dedicated to enhancing human life but who has to endure the enforced discipline in what the once-imprisoned Russian writer Fyodor Dostoevski called "the house of the dead." In the book's foreword, Philip Berrigan explains that his brother was motivated to write these poems by his vision of nonviolent resistance to evil and faithfulness to the Christian goal of a community of love. He believes that "these poems, born of the grief and glory of prison life, are doorways to a great spirit."

"My Father" is the longest poem in the collection, and one reviewer praised it as "one of the most beautiful extended lyrics in contemporary poetry." It is in twelve numbered sections, and the first deals with Berrigan's father's death, surrounded by "the symbols of mortician culture." The second section begins with his brother Philip entering a Harrisburg, Pennsylvania, prison in chains, while the poet sits in a prison ward nursing an ulcer. In the third section, the poet wonders if he ever loved his father or whether his father ever loved him. Toward the end of this section, he imagines his father's "ironic ghost," whom he thanks for bequeathing to him what his enemies call madness and his friends, arrogance. The next several sections deal with the poet's reactions to contemporary events, such as the president's defending, during Holy Week, the "national honor" in what Berrigan views as a hellish war. The poet also turns his attention to Catonsville Court, where ideologies broke "like rot under the judge's hammer." (The judge in the case did state that the American legal system does not recognize religious or moral convictions as justifications for breaking the law.) In other

sections, the poet attempts to make emotional sense, from his prison perspective, of his education at St. John the Baptist and his relationships with aunts and uncles, priests and nuns, while returning, again and again, to his father, whom he calls the "old pirate" and "old mocker." His father was actually dying while he and his brother Philip were being convicted and sentenced. The poem's final section returns to his father's death in 1969. The family gathered his worldly possessions "in 2 brown sacks," an "immigrant pauper's bundle." Although the poet reacts with a mixture of hatred and love to his father, the poem ends hopefully on Easter morning, with Christ's promise that, on the day of judgment, ". . . graves shall open/ the dead arise. . . ." The poem concludes with "Alleluia."

Other poems in this collection deal more directly with the poet's experiences in prison, such as "We Used to Meet for Classes, Sometimes It Was Ecstasy, Sometimes Blah," while others deal with nature. For example, "A Hermit Thrush in Autumn, Over the Wall" describes a hermit thrush that freely flits "ragged as a bat from tree to tree," while the thrush's song filters through the poet's barred window. In another, entitled "The Day the Humming Birds Returned, and Why," the poet asks the birds to bear witness to the caged prisoners who have been convicted of breaking and entering, safecracking, and burning draft records ("yours truly"). A skunk that bumbles into the prison becomes another subject for the poet's reflections. In "Skunk," the poet whimsically opines that the prisoners did not ". . . want additional/ prisoners, even dumb ones." What the inmates really want are atavistic skunks that will raise a stink against the proponents of law and order.

Some readers praised *Prison Poems* as worthy of being categorized with such classic prison literature as Dietrich Bonhoeffer's *Widerstand und Ergebung: Briefe und Aufzeichnungen aus der Haft* (1951, 1964, 1970; *Letters and Papers from Prison*, 1953, 1967, 1971) and Nelson Mandela's *Long Walk to Freedom* (1994). A *New Republic* critic thought that the book contained "the best poems of Berrigan's career." A *National Review* critic, whose political views were clearly antagonistic to Berrigan's, stated bluntly that Berrigan is "not a poet" and that his imagery and language are as "humdrum as check stubs." As might be expected, those readers who saw the activities of the Berrigan brothers as immoral and criminal interpreted some of the poems as improperly justifying, even glorifying, illegal entry and destruction of government property. *Prison Poems* did not mark the end of Berrigan's "apology for his life," for he continued to defend his actions in poems that became part of later collections.

OTHER MAJOR WORKS

SHORT FICTION: *A Book of Parables*, 1977.

PLAY: *The Trial of the Catonsville Nine*, pr., pb. 1970.

SCREENPLAY: *The Trial of the Catonsville Nine*, 1972 (adapted from the stage play; with Saul Levitt).

NONFICTION: *The Bride: Essays in the Church*, 1959; *The Bow in the Clouds: Man's Covenant with God*, 1961; *They Call Us Dead Men: Reflections on Life and Conscience*, 1966; *Consequences: Truth and . . .* , 1967; *Go from Here: A Prison Diary*, 1968; *No Bars to Manhood*, 1970; *The Dark Night of Resistance*, 1971; *The Geography of Faith*, 1971 (with Robert Coles; also known as *The Geography of Faith: Conversations Between Daniel Berrigan, When Underground, and Robert Coles*); *Absurd Convictions, Modest Hopes: Conversations After Prison with Lee Lockwood*, 1972; *America Is Hard to Find*, 1972; *Jesus Christ*, 1973; *Lights on in the House of the Dead: A Prison Diary*, 1974; *The Raft Is Not the Shore*, 1975 (with Thich Nhat Hanh; also known as *The Raft Is Not the Shore: Conversations Towards a Buddhist/Christian Awareness*); *Beside the Sea of Glass: The Song of the Lamb*, 1978; *Uncommon Prayer: A Book of Psalms*, 1978 (illustrated by Robert McGovern); *The Words Our Savior Gave Us*, 1978; *The Discipline of the Mountain: Dante's Purgatorio in a Nuclear World*, 1979; *We Die Before We Live: Talking with the Very Ill*, 1980; *Ten Commandments for the Long Haul*, 1981; *Portraits— Of Those I Love*, 1982; *The Nightmare of God*, 1983; *Steadfastness of the Saints: A Journal of Peace and War in Central and North America*, 1985; *The Mission: A Film Journal*, 1986; *To Dwell in Peace: An Autobiography*, 1987; *The Hole in the Ground: A Parable for Peacemakers*, 1987; *Stations: The Way of the Cross*, 1989 (with Margaret Parker); *Isaiah: Spirit of Courage, Gift of Tears*, 1996; *Ezekiel: Vision in the Dust*, 1997; *Daniel: Under the Siege of the Divine*, 1998; *Jer-*

emiah: The World, the World of God, 1998; *Job: And Death No Dominion*, 2000; *Lamentations: From New York to Kabul and Beyond*, 2002; *Wisdom: The Feminine Face of God*, 2002; *Testimony: The Word Made Fresh*, 2004; *Genesis: Fair Beginnings, Then Foul*, 2006; *The Kings and Their Gods: The Pathology of Power*, 2008.

BIBLIOGRAPHY

Aguilar, Mario I. *Contemplating God, Changing the World*. New York: Seabury Books, 2008. Aguilar looks at Berrigan and other political and social reformers such as Thomas Merton, Ernesto Cardenal, and Desmond Tutu.

Cargas, Harry J. *Daniel Berrigan and Contemporary Protest Poetry*. New Haven, Conn.: College and University Press, 1972. In this controversial brief book, the author so identifies with Berrigan's activism and his poetry that he interprets the burning of draft records as "his finest poem." He situates Berrigan's protest poetry in the context of the work of Robert Lowell, Allen Ginsberg, and Amiri Baraka. Notes and references, as well as an index.

Casey, William Van Etten, and Philip Nobile, eds. *The Berrigans*. New York: Praeger, 1971. This book originated in a special issue of the *Holy Cross Quarterly*, which needed to print more than sixty thousand copies because of the surprising demand. Such notable figures as Noam Chomsky, Robert McAfee Brown, and Gordon C. Zahn reflect on the meaning and morality of the Berrigans' civil disobedience. However, Father Andrew M. Greeley's article, in which he argues that the Berrigans' activities prolonged the Vietnam War, does not appear because Greeley did not grant reprint rights.

Deedy, John. *Apologies, Good Friends . . . : An Interim Biography of Daniel Berrigan*. Chicago: Fides/ Claretian, 1981. This short account provides a well-written introduction to the first two-thirds of Berrigan's life, with an emphasis on his peace activities.

Gray, Francine du Plessix. *Divine Disobedience: Profiles in Catholic Radicalism*. New York: Knopf, 1970. The bulk of this book first appeared in *The New Yorker*, and it is now widely available as a Vintage paperback. The author devotes well over half of her account to the Berrigans. While her principal concern is their political activism, she does show how Daniel Berrigan's poetry served his efforts against war and for peace. Index.

Polner, Murray, and Jim O'Grady. *Disarmed and Dangerous: The Radical Lives and Times of Daniel and Philip Berrigan*. New York: BasicBooks, 1997. The authors trace the paths of the Berrigans as they become activist priests and analyze their legacy.

True, Michael, ed. *Daniel Berrigan: Poetry, Drama, Prose*. Maryknoll, N.Y.: Orbis Books, 1988. This anthology contains selections from all the genres in which Berrigan has written, from poetry and parables to essays and autobiographical pieces. The book contains a helpful introduction and chronology (1921 to 1987), as well as a section on Berrigan's books, films, and recordings.

Robert J. Paradowski

TED BERRIGAN

Born: Providence, Rhode Island; November 15, 1934
Died: New York, New York; July 4, 1983

PRINCIPAL POETRY

The Sonnets, 1964, 2000
Living with Chris, 1965 (with Joe Brainard)
Bean Spasms, 1967 (with Ron Padgett)
Many Happy Returns to Dick Gallup, 1967
Doubletalk, 1969 (with Anselm Hollo)
In the Early Morning Rain, 1970
Memorial Day, 1971 (with Anne Waldman)
Train Ride, 1971
Back in Boston Again, 1972 (with Padgett and Tom Clark)
The Drunken Boat, 1974
A Feeling for Leaving, 1975
Red Wagon, 1976
Nothing for You, 1977
So Going Around Cities: New and Selected Poems, 1958-1979, 1980

In a Blue River, 1981
A Certain Slant of Sunlight, 1988 (Alice Notley, editor)
Selected Poems, 1994
Great Stories of the Chair, 1998
The Collected Poems of Ted Berrigan, 2005 (edited by Notley, with Anselm Berrigan and Edmund Berrigan)

OTHER LITERARY FORMS

Ted Berrigan (BEHR-ih-gan) is primarily known as a poet. However, he has edited collections of poetry as well as works about poetry, including a book by underground artist and poet Tom Veitch, *Literary Days: Selected Writings* (1964), which he edited with Ron Padgett. He founded and was the primary editor for the poetry press C Press in New York for several years, publishing collections by such poets as Kenward Elmslie, Dick Gallup, Joe Ceravolo, Michael Brownstein, and his frequent collaborator Padgett. He also served as the organizer of and an instructor for the very successful St. Mark's Poetry Project in New York City.

ACHIEVEMENTS

Ted Berrigan's most famous collection, *The Sonnets*, won the Poetry Foundation Award and placed Berrigan on the literary map of American poetry. In 1967, he won a Poetry Foundation Grant and a National Anthology of Literature Award for an interview with John Cage. He supported and influenced a number of rising stars of poetry through his work with the C Press and through his work with the St. Mark's Poetry Project. Like such contemporaries as poets Padgett and Frank O'Hara, Berrigan believed in wedding the everyday to the ephemeral, and as an artist, editor, and teacher, he significantly influenced a generation of poets to come. He was awarded a Community Arts Project (CAPS) grant in 1977 for his collection *Nothing for You*. In 1979, he received a National Endowment for the Arts grant.

BIOGRAPHY

Born in Providence, Rhode Island, in 1934, Edmund Joseph Michael Berrigan, Jr., briefly attended Providence College before joining the U.S. Army and serving during the Korean War. Although he never engaged in combat, Berrigan spent three years in the U.S. Army. He subsequently attended the University of Tulsa in Oklahoma, earning a B.A. in 1959 and an M.A. in 1962. In Tulsa, he met young poets and future collaborators Padgett and Joe Brainard, who would be among Berrigan's closest friends for the rest of his life.

In 1960, Berrigan moved to New York to make the connections needed for success in the poetry world. There he met Sandra Alper, also a poet. They married, eventually having two children, David and Kate. The New York City poetry scene in the early 1960's was particularly vital, featuring not only the established poets O'Hara and Kenneth Koch but also younger poets such as Berrigan and his friend Padgett; in all they were part of the New York School of poetry. Although Berrigan may not have been as influential as his friend O'Hara, he was nevertheless essential to the group.

In 1964, Berrigan published *The Sonnets*, which established his reputation and his career. That same year, he began *C* magazine and then C Press, where he published the works of many of his friends as well as those of new poets who shared his sensibilities. In 1966, he helped organize the Poetry Project at St. Mark's Church-in-the-Bowery, where he would teach workshops and support the project for years to come.

Berrigan was a visiting lecturer in the prestigious University of Iowa writing program from 1968 to 1969; he also taught for short periods at a number of colleges, including the University of Michigan, Yale University, Buffalo University, Northeastern Illinois University, and the University of Essex. Berrigan became known as a particularly gifted and insightful teacher and was often sought out for advice. While at Michigan in 1971, he divorced his first wife and married his student, the poet Alice Notley, with whom he would have two sons, Anselm (named for Berrigan's friend, poet Anselm Hollo) and Edmund. Although Berrigan remained prolific throughout his career, his reputation was largely founded on his work during the 1960's and early 1970's. He died of hepatitis in 1983 at the age of forty-eight. His health had been compromised by recurring episodes of methamphetamine abuse.

ANALYSIS

Ted Berrigan was an integral part of the New York School of poetry and the general movement toward expressionism in American poetry. Loosely put, works of literary expressionism focus more on the personal than the abstract and more on the day to day than the political. From an aesthetic point of view, expressionist works tend to follow the free-associative quality of everyday speech rather than the more rigid and uniform rules of more traditional forms. In the 1950's and early 1960's, literary expressionism manifested itself in three primary forms in American literature: the works of the confessional poets (including Robert Lowell, Elizabeth Bishop, and Sylvia Plath), which focused on the personal experience; the literature of the Beat writers (including novelist Jack Kerouac and poet Allen Ginsberg), which emphasized energetic and "spontaneous" creativity in writing; and the works of the New York School, which combined approaches from each of the former schools while generating its own voice. The first poet associated with the New York School was O'Hara, whose literary reputation quickly rose before his untimely death at the age of forty. While showing the influence of O'Hara and other New York School poets in his appreciation of the everyday reality of life, Berrigan also brought to the movement a lyrical sensibility and a wry sense of humor.

In his poetry, Berrigan demonstrated his conversance with a diversity of poetic forms and styles. He composed in free verse with long lines, short lines, and spaced lines; he wrote sonnets and prose poetry. The scattered spacing of his famous early poem "Tambourine Life" (anthologized in *The Young American Poets*, 1968), for example, contributes to the expressionistic, "take life by the horns" attitude of the poem. Additionally, his tendency to be more lyrical and imagistic than other members of the New York School is on display in poems such as "Sonnet LXXIV" (from *The Sonnets*), in which he writes that ". . . The only travelled sea/ that I still dream of/ is a cold black pond, where once/ on a fragrant evening fraught with sadness/ I launched a boat frail as a butterfly."

Despite his departure from the familiar, however, Berrigan is often at his most successful and his most touching when he sticks to the common truths, as shown in his poem "Words for Love" (from *Many Happy Returns to Dick Gallup*), where the speaker states, ". . . If/ I sometimes grow weary, and seem still,/ nevertheless// my heart still loves, will break." More than any spontaneous or expressionist style, however, the content that informed Berrigan's poetry throughout his entire career largely consisted of the personal and everyday. Such a focus is, in a way, a democratization of poetry: One does not have to have read important philosophy, consider world religions, or participate in armed conflicts to write poems. Berrigan seems to address his focus in poetry in "Around the Fire" (from *So Going Around Cities*), where the speaker claims, ". . . I'm interested in/ anything. Like I could walk out the door right now and go some-/ where else. I don't have any center in that sense. . . ." However, he goes on to say, "My heart and my head feel exactly the same."

Humor is an essential part of Berrigan's oeuvre as well, as shown in "Hearts" (from *Nothing for You*), with its wry sendup of conflicting poetic traditions:

> At last I'm a real poet I've written a
> ballade a sonnet a poem in spontaneous
> prose and even a personal poem 　　　I can use
> punctuation or not and it doesn't even
> matter . . .

Many of Berrigan's greatest strengths are brought together in his elegies, from the everyday listing of the dead in "People Who Died" (from *In the Early Morning Rain*), including his grandfather, father, O'Hara, folksinger Woody Guthrie, Kerouac, and Beat icon Neal Cassady, to the masterful elegy "Frank O'Hara" (from *Red Wagon*), which unites his sense of humor, his lyrical sensibilities, and his personal loss:

> 　　　　　You are dead. And you'll never
> write again about the country, that's true.
> But the people in the sky really love
> to have dinner & take a walk with you.

THE SONNETS

Berrigan's first book published other than through private means, *The Sonnets*, was the one that would cement his career and stay with him for the rest of his life. The poems making up this 1964 collection are each fourteen lines long but eschew other requirements of the form, such as iambic pentameter, formalized rhyme schemes, and a turn (or *volta*), where the theme changes or develops in the latter part of the poem. Furthermore, Berrigan forgoes the traditional focus of sonnets—courtly love—and tackles a variety of subjects. "Sonnet XV" is about Marilyn Monroe's death; others are about writing, friendship, and sex. The humor and expressionism that became Berrigan hallmarks are made manifest in "Sonnet LII," in which the narrator states, "It is a human universe: & I/ is a correspondent. . . ." The personal and emotional appeal of his later poetry is on full display in the sonnets as well, as shown when Berrigan's narrator calls out in "Sonnet XVII," "Dear, be the tree your sleep awaits/ Sensual, solid, still, swaying alone in the wind." Furthermore, although *The Sonnets* are not solely concerned with love, many of them do deal with romantic love, albeit in Berrigan's idiosyncratic way.

PERSONAL POEMS

Berrigan titled a number of his poems "Personal Poems" in the earlier years of his career; many later poems also very clearly detail facts of the narrator's personal life and world. The influence of Berrigan's friend O'Hara seems more prevalent in such poems. "Personal Poem #9" (from *Many Happy Returns to Dick Gallup*), for example, begins, "It's 8:54 a.m. in Brooklyn it's the 26th of July/ and it's probably 8:54 in Manhattan but I'm/ in Brooklyn 　　I'm eating English muffins and drinking/ Pepsi . . . ," very much echoing O'Hara's famous "The Day Lady Died," which starts "It is 12:20 in New York a Friday." As his poetry grew and matured, Berrigan avoided the trap of self-indulgence that makes such poetry problematic; instead, the personal nature of his poems makes the poet more accessible and human to the reader. This transformation is manifested in "Ann Arbor Song" (from *In the Early Morning Rain*), a 1969 poem in which a complaint about having to attend a reading becomes an elegy for Kerouac and a contemplation of the nature of loss. "I won't be at this boring poetry reading/ again!" begins the speaker, who then goes on to say, "Anne won't call me here again,/ To tell me that Jack is dead." Despite the speaker's sense of loss—not only of his friend but also of his life at that time in itself—he will not "cry for Jack here again."

OTHER MAJOR WORKS

NONFICTION: *On the Level Everyday: Selected Talks on Poetry and the Art of Living*, 1997 (Joel Lewis, editor).

PLAYS: *Seventeen: Plays*, 1964 (with Ron Padgett).

EDITED TEXTS: *Literary Days: Selected Writings*, 1964 (with Padgett); *Fits of Dawn*, 1965 (with Joseph Ceravolo).

BIBLIOGRAPHY

Berrigan, Ted. *On the Level Everyday: Selected Talks on Poetry and the Art of Living*. Edited by Joel Lewis. Jersey City, N.J.: Talisman House, 1997. A collection of speeches, notes, and commentaries by Berrigan on the craft of poetry and the writing process.

Lopez, Tony. "'Powder on a Little Table': Ted Berrigan's Sonnets and 1960's Poems." *Journal of American Studies* 36, no. 2 (August, 2002): 281-292. A thorough discussion of Berrigan's *The Sonnets* that investigates his technical use of the form as well as his development away from simply writing "personal" poetry.

Padgett, Ron. *Ted: A Personal Memoir of Ted Berrigan*. Great Barrington, Mass.: The Figures Press, 1993. Padgett was a friend and a frequent collaborator with Berrigan; this memoir is particularly insightful into Berrigan's creative process as well as his generosity to fellow poets.

Rifkin, Libbie. "'Worrying About Making It': Ted Berrigan's Social Poetics." *Contemporary Literature* 38, no. 4 (Winter, 1997): 640-671. A long article that examines Berrigan in terms of his influence on other poets, considering his work with *C* magazine and his development of social support groups of poets.

Waldeman, Anne, ed. *Nice to See You: An Homage to Ted Berrigan*. Minneapolis: Coffee House Press, 1991. A book-length collection of letters, memoirs, and journal entries about Berrigan's life and work by such poets and literary lights as Ron Padgett, Clark Coolidge, Tom Clark, and Robert Creeley, among many others. The collection also contains many of Berrigan's personal letters and commentaries on writing.

Scott D. Yarbrough

WENDELL BERRY

Born: Henry County, Kentucky; August 5, 1934

PRINCIPAL POETRY

November Twenty-six, Nineteen Hundred Sixty-three, 1963
The Broken Ground, 1964
Openings, 1968
Findings, 1969
Farming: A Hand Book, 1970
The Country of Marriage, 1973
An Eastward Look, 1974
Horses, 1975
Sayings and Doings, 1975
To What Listens, 1975
The Kentucky River: Two Poems, 1976
There Is Singing Around Me, 1976
Three Memorial Poems, 1976
Clearing, 1977
The Gift of Gravity, 1979
A Part, 1980
The Wheel, 1982
Collected Poems, 1957-1982, 1985
Sabbaths, 1987
Traveling at Home, 1989
Sabbaths, 1987-1990, 1992
Entries, 1994
The Farm, 1995
The Selected Poems of Wendell Berry, 1998
A Timbered Choir: The Sabbath Poems, 1979-1997, 1998
Given: New Poems, 2005
The Mad Farmer Poems, 2008
Leavings, 2010

OTHER LITERARY FORMS

In addition to poetry, Wendell Berry has written nonfiction, fiction, essays, and a biography of Harland Hubbard. He has also been the subject of numerous published interviews.

ACHIEVEMENTS

Wendell Berry first achieved regional and then national prominence as a poet, essayist, and novelist who writes about the small farmers of his fictional Port William community in northern Kentucky. As a poet, Berry has published widely since 1957, in small magazines, poetry volumes, private printings, and collections of his verse in 1985 and 1998. He won the Bess Hokin Prize from *Poetry* magazine (1967), an Academy Award in Literature from the American Academy of Arts and Letters (1971), the Jean Stein Award in Nonfiction (1987), the Aiken Taylor Award in Modern American Poetry (1994), the T. S. Eliot Award for Creative Writing from the Ingersoll Foundation (1999), the Thomas Merton Award (1999), and the Poets' Prize (2000). His major topics are the land, the family, and the community, especially the way that each has been affected by greed and indifference. Berry is a deeply traditional poet in theme and form, celebrating a timeless agrarian cycle of planting and harvest. He affirms a strong sense of place and ancestral inheritance, stemming from local family ties stretching back almost two centuries. His values are a curious blend of conservative and radical, combining a strong commitment to marriage and family with a pacifist stance and criticism of corporate exploitation of rural Appalachia. His voice is that of the farmer-poet, husband, father, and lover. For many readers and critics, he has reached the stature of a major contemporary philosopher.

BIOGRAPHY

Born in Henry County, Kentucky, on August 5, 1934, Wendell Erdman Berry grew up in a family of strong-willed, independent-minded readers and thinkers. His father, John M. Berry, was an attorney and a leader of the Burley Tobacco Growers Association. After attending the University of Kentucky for his bachelor's and master's degrees, Berry was married and taught for a year at Georgetown College in Kentucky. He then accepted a Wallace Stegner Fellowship in creative writing (1958-1959) at Stanford University. A Guggenheim Foundation award allowed him to travel to Europe in 1962 before he returned to teach English at New York University from 1962 to 1964. Berry wrote a moving elegy for President John F. Kennedy that won critical praise, and his first major poetry volume, *The Broken Ground*, appeared in 1964.

Berry and his family returned to Kentucky in 1964, when he was appointed to the English Department at the University of Kentucky in Lexington. He purchased Lane's Landing Farm in Port Royal in 1965 and moved back to his native county, where he has continued to farm and write. Berry has also served as a contributing editor to Rodale Press. He and his wife, Tanya (Amyx) Berry, raised two children, Mary and Pryor Clifford, on that farm.

ANALYSIS

Wendell Berry is a poet of deep conviction. Like Henry David Thoreau, he has felt a need to reestablish himself from the ground up by articulating the ecological, economic, and religious principles by which he would live, and by trying to live and write in accordance with those principles. He has striven to achieve a rigorous moral and aesthetic simplicity in his work by reworking the same basic themes and insights: the proper place of human life in the larger natural cycle of life, death, and renewal; the dignity of work, labor, and vocation; the central importance of marriage and fam-

Wendell Berry (©Dan Carraco/Courtesy, North Point Press)

ily commitments; the articulation of the human and natural history of his native region; and precise, lyrical descriptions of the native flora and fauna of his region, especially of the birds, trees, and wildflowers. Expanding on these basic themes, he has included elegies to family members and friends, topical and occasional poems (especially antiwar poems expressing his strong pacifist convictions), didactic poems expressing his environmental beliefs, and a surprising number of religious poems expressing a deeply felt but nondenominational faith.

One finds in Berry's verse a continual effort to unify life, work, and art within a coherent philosophy or vision. Put simply, that vision includes a regional sensibility, a farming avocation, a poetic voice of the farmer-husband-lover-environmentalist, and a strong commitment to a localized environmental ethic. His most notable persona is the "Mad Farmer," though it is not clear why he is "mad"—does Berry mean passionate, exuberant, or merely eccentric? From childhood, Berry always hoped to become a farmer, and his verse celebrates the life of the land. His vision, however, is that of simplicity: of the land, of the community, and even of his art. In his literary works, Berry expresses nostalgia for the kind of small-scale, labor-intensive farming that was practiced in his region before World War II. His style of unmechanized organic farming is practiced today mainly by the Amish and the Mennonites. Berry has admitted that farming his hilly, eroded land has not been profitable, and while it may be ethically admirable to restore damaged land to production, it is generally not economically feasible without another source of income.

One senses in Berry's poetry a keen awareness of living in a fallen world, to be redeemed, if at all, through hard work, disciplined self-knowledge, and a gradual healing of the land. However, though he is a lyric poet, too often his lyrics do not sing: His muse is Delphic rather than Orphic, prophetic instead of lyrical. His verse is carefully worked and thoughtful but burdened at times by didacticism. The Berry persona is sometimes detached and impersonal, preoccupied with its own sensibility or with an environmental theme. His lyrics are often descriptive meditations in which little happens aside from the registration of impressions on

the poet's sensibility. Still, the simplicity of his verse is often lightened by a sense of humor, a sense of proportion, and awareness of others. However, sometimes his lyrics seem sanctimonious or self-righteous. His verse echoes the rhetorical question of Robert Frost's "The Oven Bird"—"What to make of a diminished thing?"—and the answer is hard-won redemption.

Berry first published many of his poems in literary journals or small magazines or specialty presses, so that original editions of his works are often hard to find. His individual poetry volumes were published first with Harcourt Brace (*The Broken Ground*, *Openings*, *Farming*, *The Country of Marriage*, and *Clearing*) and later with North Point Press (*A Part*, *The Wheel*, *Collected Poems, 1957-1982*, and *Sabbaths*). The pieces in *Collected Poems, 1957-1982* are selected from each volume, but the collection is not entirely inclusive. He did add some important poems, such as the contents of the volume *Findings*, which was originally published by a small specialty press and is out of print.

Berry's poetry marks him as one of the most important modern American nature poets. His sense of the sacredness and interdependence of all life places him within the tradition of Ralph Waldo Emerson, Walt Whitman, and Henry David Thoreau. He is also one of the foremost American regional writers, insisting that his poetry be firmly rooted in a sense of place. His poetry reflects the same deep concern for the natural environment and for sound conservation and farming practices that is evident in his essays and fiction. His emphasis on marriage, family, and community allows him to affirm these necessary human bonds. His poems reflect his loyalty to his native region, his love of farming, his view of marriage as a sacrament, and his deep awareness of the beauty and wonder of the natural world.

ELEGIAC POETRY

Though Berry had been publishing poems in literary magazines and journals since the mid-1950's, his first critical recognition came in 1964, with the appearance of *The Broken Ground*, his first poetry volume, and *November Twenty-six, Nineteen Hundred Sixty-three*, his elegy for John F. Kennedy, which first appeared in the December 21, 1963, issue of the *Nation*. Berry's elegy, which was accompanied by woodcuts by Ben Shahn, has been called the most successful commemoration of Kennedy's death. Though written in free-verse form, Berry's elegy makes use of a traditional stanzaic organization and refrain and incorporates the traditional elegiac cycle of grief, mourning, the funeral procession, the interment, and the apotheosis of the subject's memory. Berry's interest in the elegy was also apparent in "Elegy," the opening poem in *The Broken Ground*. Other elegiac works include "Three Elegiac Poems" (*Findings*), "In Memory: Stuart Engol" (*Openings*), and "Requiem" and "Elegy" (*The Wheel*). Death is always present in Berry's work, but it is presented naturalistically, without a compensating carpe diem theme or renewal, except in the natural cycle of life.

THE BROKEN GROUND

The Broken Ground is a collection of thirty-one free-verse lyrics with a distinctly regional flavor, twenty of which were later included in his *Collected Poems, 1857-1982*. Many of these poems first appeared in *Stylus*, *Poetry*, *The Nation*, and *The Prairie Schooner*. This early collection introduces the Berry voice and some of his major themes: the cycle of life and death, a sensitivity to place, pastoral subject matter, and recurring images of water, the Kentucky River, and the hilly, pastoral landscape of north-central Kentucky. His language is terse, intense, and compressed, his style imagistic and at times almost epigrammatic. The stylistic influence of William Carlos Williams and the Orientalism of Kenneth Rexroth seem apparent in these early poems. Berry's sharp, sculpted images also recall those of his friend and fellow poet Gary Snyder. Some of the poems seem curiously detached and impersonal. They are animated by no great myths, legends, or events, aside from the figures of Daniel Boone and other early settlers. Instead, the poems are intensely private, detached, and descriptive. Although many of them are set in his native Kentucky, the Berry persona seems curiously detached from members of his local community beyond his family. One does not find the social engagement Williams shows in his Patterson poems, a warmth that came from his lifelong involvement as a local pediatrician. Instead, the Berry persona seems solitary and austere: too much the detached observer, quiet and understated, though perhaps not intending to project a

sense of social isolation. The parallels with Williams are instructive: While Williams was a practicing local physician whose poetry often reflects his sympathetic understanding of his patients and their families, Berry presents himself as a working farmer whose poetry reflects his love of his work. What redeems Berry's poems is his love of farming and the rhythms of physical labor: its purposefulness, its physicality, and its tangible rewards, including a sense of psychological and natural harmony.

LOST PARADISE AS THEME

Berry's poems contain a mythic vision of a lost, primeval paradise, a fall from grace, and a guarded hope in work, discipline, and renewal. "Paradise might have appeared here," he announces in "The Aristocracy," but instead he finds a wealthy old dowager airing her cat. Like Robert Frost's pastoral world of a diminished New England landscape, Berry's Kentucky River Valley has suffered from neglect and abuse. The moments of grace are few—bird songs, the return of spring, the cycle of the seasons, glimpses of the natural order—and death is always present. Like Frost, Berry has chosen to make a "strategic retreat" to a pastoral world in which the poet-farmer can take stock of his resources, but his sensibility differs from Frost's. For Frost, the sense of diminishment came from the abandonment of farms in rural New England after the Civil War, while for Berry the sense of loss comes from environmental despoliation of the Cumberland plateau, first by careless farming practices and later by timber interests and the big coal companies. The villain in Berry's loss of paradise is the machine in the garden—modern technology—for which Berry never has a kind word.

Berry's version of the Paradise Lost myth centers on the massive environmental destruction by modern technology visited on the Cumberland region by absentee corporate owners. He has been radicalized by Kentucky's legacy of corrupt government and indifference to environmental concerns, which has left the region virtually a Third World economy, based on cheap, large-scale mineral extraction with little regard for the human or environmental consequences of pit or surface mining. The practice of strip-mining has been particularly devastating to the land and water resources, given the use of bulldozers and other machinery never contemplated when the rights to access the coal were sold a century or more ago. Living downstream from the despoiled hills and polluted creeks of Appalachia, Berry has seen at first hand the flooding and water pollution that have occurred on the Kentucky River.

THE KENTUCKY RIVER AND FINDINGS

As Berry recounts in *The Kentucky River*, the first white settlers who entered the Kentucky territory were unable to respond to the richness and abundance of natural resources except by exploitation. Hence, in "July, 1773," the first of the "Three Kentucky River Poems," young Sam Adams fires heedlessly into a herd of peacefully grazing buffalo at a salt lick, a clear parallel to the extensive hunting and killing done by early Kentucky settlers such as Daniel Boone, which soon changed the face of hunting in the area.

Not only did the publication of Berry's *Collected Poems, 1957-1982* permit the republishing of nearly two hundred poems from his previous eight volumes, many of which were by then out of print, but it also allowed him to select which poems he could retain and which he would drop from those early volumes. Among Berry's best early work was the sequence of three long poems from *Findings*. "The Design of a House" is about beginnings and intentions, the conscious fabrication of a dwelling and a marriage relationship that had previously existed merely as a vague dream or desire, and a wish to reestablish roots in one's native place. It becomes a nuptial poem, the speaker's dedication of his love to his wife, Tanya, and his daughter, Mary, and the continuation of their life together. The design of their house comes to signify the design of their family relationship.

The second poem in *Findings*, "The Handing Down," continues this theme of family and place, this time in terms of an old man's memories and reflections and his sense of satisfaction with the life he has led, as expressed through conversations with his grandson. The speaker in this poem recalls Jack Beecham, the protagonist of Berry's novel *The Memory of Old Jack* (1974). Both the poem and the novel have to do with an old man's preparations for death, his gradual letting go of life through the memories that run through his mind. The third part of *Findings*, "Three Elegiac Poems," commemorates the death of the old man, which the speaker hopes will occur quietly at home, away from the sterile coldness and isolation of hospital wards and the indifference of physicians.

CELEBRATION OF NATURE AND LAND

Openings, *Farming*, *The Country of Marriage*, and *Clearing* celebrate Berry's return to Kentucky and the satisfaction he found in taking up farming. After living in California, Europe, and New York City, he came to appreciate the possibilities of writing about his native region. Berry was particularly impressed with the hill farms of Tuscany, around Florence, which showed him that such "marginal land" might remain productive for many centuries with the proper care and attention. The quality of these farms led him to rethink the possibilities of hill farming in his native Kentucky. As he indicates in the autobiographical title essay in *The Long-Legged House* (1969), he kept feeling himself drawn back home, particularly to the small cabin built on the Kentucky River by his uncle Curran Matthews. After it was flooded, Berry moved this house farther up the riverbank and rebuilt it to create his writer's study.

Berry's poems in these middle volumes show a new depth of craft and responsiveness to nature. They celebrate the values of land and nature, family and community, marital love and devotion. They are quietly attentive to the cycle of seasons, of the organic cycles of growth and decay, of the subtle beauty of the native flora and fauna. As philosopher, visionary, and political activist, his "Mad Farmer" persona speaks out against war, wastefulness, and environmental destruction. He dreams of a new, gentler orientation to the land that will encourage people to cherish and preserve their natural heritage. He finds deep spiritual sustenance as he reflects on the beauty and fitness of the natural order and the richness of the present moment.

Berry's poems are broadly pastoral in orientation, but they reflect the Kentucky frontier tradition of pioneer homesteading and yeoman farming rather than artificial literary tradition. Some pastoral themes evident in his work include an idealization of the simple life, an implied city-country contrast, a yearning for a past "golden age" of rural life, a celebration of the seasonal tasks of farming life, a strong affirmation of small-scale, organic farming, and an identification of the poet with his native region.

OPENINGS

In *Openings*, "The Thought of Something Else" announces the speaker's desire to leave the city for country life, but first he must make peace with the legacy of the past, which he does in "My Great-Grandfather's Slaves." The next three poems are autumnal in tone, establishing the speaker within a seasonal cycle. In "The Snake," he comes upon a small reptile preparing for winter hibernation. The "living cold" of the snake, replete with its engorged meal, parallels the contented winter solitude of the speaker in the next poem, "The Cold." The starkly descriptive "Winter Rain" leads to "March Snow" and "April Woods: Morning," which resemble haiku in their delicate imagery. In "The Porch over the River," the speaker establishes himself in his riverside writer's cabin, like the classical Chinese poet Du Fu. In "The Dream," he imagines the surrounding countryside restored to its pristine beauty, unspoiled by greed or acquisitiveness. The tree celebrated in "The Sycamore," a venerable specimen whose gnarled trunk is scarred by lightning, becomes a symbol of natural resiliency. Like the tree, the poet wishes that he might be shaped and nurtured by his native place. "Grace" and "A Discipline" reflect the strength the speaker draws from nature, allowing him to withstand the destructiveness of his culture, in which people are at war with the environment, one another, and themselves.

FARMING AND THE COUNTRY OF MARRIAGE

Farming and *The Country of Marriage* are less solitary in mood. They introduce the colorful persona of the "Mad Farmer," an exuberant, Bunyanesque figure who flaunts social convention in "The Mad Farmer's Revolution" and "The Contrariness of the Mad Farmer," dances in the streets in "The Mad Farmer in the City," and—through his prayers, sayings, satisfactions, and manifestos—offers a wry and humorous commentary on Berry's own views as expressed in his books and essays. "The Birth," a dramatic dialogue, constitutes an interesting departure from Berry's customary lyrical verse. A group of farmers, up late with lambing on a cold winter night, unexpectedly come upon a couple and child who have taken sanctuary in their barn for their own nativity. Berry's poem captures the cadences and flavor of ordinary country talk, in which more is implied than said.

Berry's poems are noted for quiet attentiveness to surroundings, almost as if the speaker tried to make himself part of his habitat. His farmer persona is a keen naturalist, carefully observing the seasonal behavior of the birds and animals. His speaker is especially attuned to bird songs, and the variety of birds mentioned in his poems is notable—kingfishers, song sparrows, phoebes, herons, wild geese, finches, wrens, chickadees, cardinals, titmice, and warblers. Implicit in his poems is a sense of grace and renewal, a deep satisfaction and contentment.

Berry's relationship with his wife and children has been central to his task of renewal as a pastoral poet. An accomplished love poet, Berry has written many poems to his wife, Tanya, on the anniversaries of their marriage or to express his gratitude for their common life. For his children, too, Berry has written poems on their births, comings of age, and marriages, and on the births of grandchildren. In "The Gathering," the speaker recalls that he now holds his son in his arms the way his father held him. In "The Country of Marriage," farming and marriage serve as complementary and inseparable extensions of each other. Husbandry and marriage are recurring tropes in Berry's poetry, illustrated in clearing fields, sowing crops, planting a garden, tending livestock, mowing hay, and taking in the harvest. He celebrates farming as a labor of love, a work of regeneration and fecundity that is at once vital and procreative.

CLEARING

The poems in *Clearing* articulate Berry's sense of region and place. "Where" is a long pastoral meditation on the history and ownership of the fifty-acre farm, Lane's Landing, which the Berrys purchased between 1965 and 1968. The history of the farm provides a case study in attitudes toward stewardship and land use, from the earliest settlers to the developer from whom Berry bought the farm. The transition from wilderness to settlement to worn-out land rehearses an ecological myth of the fall from primeval abundance to reckless waste and decay. Berry presents the history of his farm as a parable of the American frontier and an indictment of the reckless habits that quickly exhausted the land's natural richness and abundance. "Where" is both a personal credo and a contemporary ecological statement of what needs to be done, both in terms of land management and in changing cultural attitudes toward the land.

A PART

Berry's next two poetry volumes, *A Part* and *The Wheel*, reflect in their titles his deepening ecological awareness. *A Part* includes short pastoral lyrics; some religious verse; translations of two poems by the sixteenth century French poet Pierre de Ronsard; "Three Kentucky River Poems," a narrative triptych based in part on historical accounts of the McAfee brothers' 1773 expedition into Kentucky; and "Horses," a verse tribute to the skills of working draft horses, in which Berry excoriates tractors and internal combustion engines for destroying the quiet pleasures of farming.

THE WHEEL

The Wheel takes its title image from the mandala, or "wheel of life," of which Sir Albert Howard speaks in his classic study *An Agricultural Testament* (1943), which influenced Berry's thinking about organic farming. This collection is a book of elegies of remembrance and praise, celebrating the continuities of birth, growth, maturity, death, and decay. An increasing self-assurance is evident in Berry's voice, a relaxed, self-confident voice free of anxiety. His verse forms also become more formal, with an increased use of rhyme and regular stanzaic form, though he still seems to prefer a short line.

"Elegy," one of Berry's finest poems, appears in this collection. A pastoral elegy, it is one of a series of three poems dedicated to Owen Flood, whom Berry honors as a teacher and friend. The first poem, "Requiem," announces his passing, though his spirit remains in the fields he had tended. "Elegy" pays tribute to the quality of Flood's life in eight sections, invoking the spirits of the dead to reaffirm the traditional values that Flood embodied: duty, loyalty, perseverance, honesty, hard work, endurance, and self-reliance. It reaffirms the continuity of the generations within a permanent, stable agricultural order. There is a sense of recycling human life, as nature recycles organic materials back into the soil to create fertile organic humus. The poem also celebrates human permanences: marriage, work, friendship, love, fidelity, and death. The dominant image is of life as a dance within the circle of life, implying closure, completeness, and inclusion. "Elegy" affirms farm labor as an honorable calling, true to the biblical injunction to live by the sweat of one's

brow. The opening line of the poem reaffirms an implicit purpose in all Berry's work: "To be at home on its native ground." The poem honors the elders of the community who were the speaker's teachers, including Flood, and concludes with the affirmation that "the best teachers teach more/ than they know. By their deaths/ they teach most."

Another important poem in this collection, "The Gift of Gravity," reaffirms the life-sustaining cycles of sunlight, photosynthesis, growth, decay, and death. The poem announces its major theme, "gravity is grace," with the dominant image of the river of life and the return of all life to its source. There is an almost mystical unity conveyed in the opening lines: "All that passes descends,/ and ascends again unseen/ into the light." Two other poems, "The Wheel" and "The Dance," affirm the interlocking unities that knit the community together in festive celebrations of song and dance.

Dissatisfied with Harcourt Brace, Berry changed publishers in the early 1980's, moving to North Point Press, a small publisher in Berkeley, California. One immediate result was the issuing of his *Recollected Essays, 1965-1980* (1981) and *Collected Poems, 1927-1982*, which includes the better part of his first eight volumes of poetry.

SABBATHS

Sabbaths marks something of a departure in tone and style from Berry's earlier work. It is at once more formal, more structured, and more overtly religious in its sensibility. The forty-six poems in this collection were written over a six-year period, from 1979 to 1985. The poems are untitled, arranged by year, and identified only by their first line. There are quiet, restrained, almost metaphysical meditations that incorporate a number of lines from Scripture. Here Berry makes use of traditional rhyme and meter. These poems show a deep, nonsectarian religious sensibility, akin to the personal faith of the New England Transcendentalist poets, especially Emily Dickinson. Like Dickinson, Berry applies Christian tropes to nature to imply a natural religion. The many allusions to Eden, Paradise, worship, hymns, song, grace, gift, the Maker, heaven, resurrection, darkness, and light invoke a kind of prophetic vision of a new Earth, healed and reborn—a paradise regained. Berry again describes the primal fertility and richness of the Kentucky landscape before it was ruined by the rapacious settlers. His poems combine a moral awareness of a deep wrong done to Earth by human greed and ignorance with an ecological awareness of the need for a change that can come only from within individuals and local communities.

The overall theme of *Sabbaths* is the need for rest and renewal—both within human hearts and in the natural world. People need to take time away from their heedless ravaging of the environment to try to understand and appreciate Earth's beauty and strength. Berry calls for the cultivation of a different kind of sensibility—less inclined to impose human will on nature and more inclined to appreciate the natural world on its own terms, as a kind of heaven on Earth. Berry weaves many scriptural allusions into his poems, quoting from the Psalms, the Old Testament prophets, and the New Testament. The poems manage to convey a deep meditative sensibility without making any formal religious affirmations except by implication. The speaker comes across as a deeply thoughtful but independent spirit, reverent but unchurched. One finds in *Sabbaths* a new blend of spiritual and ecological awareness, a sense of life and of the land, as worthy of the deepest veneration. This meditative cycle of poems is extended in *A Timbered Choir*.

GIVEN

These poems were written between 1994 and 2004, late in Berry's career. The first three sections of the volume are most notable for "Some Further Words," which sets out in considerable detail Berry's most important beliefs, including that the world of nature outranks the domestic world of humans, that the rich are mostly thieves, that most intellectuals are (figuratively) prostitutes, that stockpiling weapons for war is not something that enourages peace, that health is not equivalent to medication, that science used by corporations is "knowledge reduced to merchandise," which is a "whoredom of the mind" and not progress, that machines should be gone, and that capitalism is fantasy (and the stock market fall should evoke "long live gravity!"). Rather, the poem endorses "old intelligence of the heart," as in love and respect for one another and everything else.

Part 4, "Sabbaths 1998-2004," fills two-thirds of the volume, and like *Sabbaths*, his 1987 collection, these new Sabbath poems are formal in structure and often overtly religious. For example, the fifth poem in "Sabbaths 1999" is a sonnet, celebrating both human, earthly love and the realization that such love is also eternal, religious love, which humans learn on reaching heaven. The natural world, of course, is a major element in Berry's religious vision, as in poem 5 of "Sabbaths 2000," in which the poet visits a favorite nature scene as "one of the thresholds/ between Earth and Heaven," where he can detach from himself and be free. Even in these religious poems, however, Berry continues to satirize the excesses of American capitalism, as in poem 4 in "Sabbaths 2001," with the "country smeared" because of human stupidity, with freedom unappreciated and unexercised, with the "idiot luxury" replacing true religious faith, and with beauty, closely associated with religious faith and love, sold in the marketplace. Also, in poems 6 and 9 of "Sabbaths 2002," modern technology in the form of boats on the river is again satirized, with the river "bedeviled" (word choice deliberate for its Satanic overtones) by the engines, which fill "the air with torment." Even more powerfully satiric are the post-September 11, 2001, Sabbath poems, including poem 3 from "Sabbath 2003," with its depiction of the "Lords of War," driven by greed and wrath, destroying any place based on "their willingness to destroy every place." The poet urges the alternative of "saying yes/ to the air, to the earth, to the trees" and to all living therein. Also, poem 7 of "Sabbaths 2003" satirizes the sworn defenders of freedom who are snuffing out freedom's candle while chanting praise for freedom. This poem also satirizes artists for creating art for art's sake while keeping their university jobs and literary awards and argues for no art if it "cannot speak freely in defiance/ of wealth self-elected to righteousness." With their important ideas conveyed by sophisticated literary techniques such as oxymorons ("silenced into song, blinded into light"), literary allusions (estranged hearts like Hemingway's "islands parted in the sea"), and metaphors (aged poet as gray heron, withdrawing in peace), Berry's Sabbath poems from 1998 through 2004 rank with the very best poetry.

OTHER MAJOR WORKS

LONG FICTION: *Nathan Coulter*, 1960, 1985; *A Place on Earth*, 1967, 1983; *The Memory of Old Jack*, 1974; *Remembering*, 1988; *A World Lost*, 1996; *Jayber Crow*, 2000; *Hannah Coulter*, 2004; *Andy Catlett: Early Travels*, 2006.

SHORT FICTION: *The Wild Birds*, 1986; *Fidelity*, 1992; *Watch with Me*, 1994; *Three Short Novels*, 2002; *That Distant Land: The Collected Stories*, 2004.

NONFICTION: *The Long-Legged House*, 1969; *The Hidden Wound*, 1970; *The Unforeseen Wilderness*, 1971; *A Continuous Harmony*, 1972; *The Unsettling of America: Culture and Agriculture*, 1977; *The Gift of Good Land*, 1981; *Recollected Essays, 1965-1980*, 1981; *Standing by Words*, 1983; *Home Economics*, 1987; *Harland Hubbard: Life and Work*, 1990; *What Are People For?*, 1990; *The Discovery of Kentucky*, 1991; *Standing on Earth*, 1991; *Sex, Economy, Freedom, and Community*, 1993; *Another Turn of the Crank*, 1995; *Life Is a Miracle: An Essay Against Modern Superstition*, 2000; *The Art of the Commonplace: The Agrarian Essays of Wendell Berry*, 2002 (Norman Wirzba, editor); *In the Presence of Fear: Three Essays for a Changed World*, 2002; *Citizenship Papers: Essays*, 2003; *Standing by Words: Essays*, 2005; *The Way of Ignorance, and Other Essays*, 2005; *Bringing It to the Table: On Farming and Food*, 2009; *Imagination in Place: Essays*, 2010; *Conversations with Wendell Berry*, 2007 (Morris Allen Grubbs, editor).

CHILDREN'S LITERATURE: *Whitefoot: A Story from the Center of the World*, 2009.

EDITED TEXT: *Blessed Are the Peacemakers: Christ's Teachings of Love, Compassion, and Forgiveness*, 2005.

BIBLIOGRAPHY

Angyal, Andrew J. *Wendell Berry*. New York: Twayne, 1995. A standard critical biography in the Twayne United States Authors series.

Berry, Wendell. Interviews. *Conversations with Wendell Berry*. Edited by Morris Allen Grubbs. Jackson: University Press of Mississippi, 2007. A collection of interviews in which Berry covers most aspects of his work and life.

Basney, Lionel. "Having Your Meaning at Hand: Work in Snyder and Berry." In *Word, Self, Poem: Essays on Contemporary Poetry from the Jubilation of Poets*, edited by Leonard M. Trawick. Kent, Ohio: Kent State University Press, 1990. Discusses Berry's early volumes as articulating a work ethic that is rooted in a person's interaction with a particular place, with a sense of community, and with an uneasy Christian sacramental vision.

Bonzo, J. Matthew, and Michael R. Stevens. *Wendell Berry and the Cultivation of Life*. Grand Rapids, Mich.: Brazos Press, 2008. An in-depth study that attempts to capture Berry's religious vision, arguing that the writer is the one person to whom contemporary Christians need to listen.

Cornell, Daniel. "*The Country of Marriage:* Wendell Berry's Personal Political Vision." *Southern Literary Journal* 16 (Fall, 1983): 59-70. Through a close reading of the poems in *The Country of Marriage*, Cornell offers a thoughtful examination of the thematic implications of Berry's pastoral metaphors. Cornell locates Berry within an agrarian populist tradition that defies conventional conservative or liberal labels.

Freeman, Russell G. *Wendell Berry: A Bibliography*. Lexington: University of Kentucky Libraries, 1992. This is the place to begin straightening out the history of Berry's nonstop, multigenre publishing career.

Goodrich, Janet. *The Unforeseen Self in the Works of Wendell Berry*. Columbia: University of Missouri Press, 2001. Goodrich argues that whether Berry is writing poetry, fiction, or prose, he is reimagining his own life and thus belongs to the tradition of autobiography. A fresh approach to Berry's literature.

Hicks, Jack. "Wendell Berry's Husband to the World: *A Place on Earth.*" *American Literature* 51 (May, 1979): 238-254. Perhaps the best critical overview of Berry's earlier work. Examines the farmer-countryman vision in Berry's fiction. Hicks traces thematic connections between Berry's essays, poetry, and fiction.

Peters, Jason, ed. *Wendell Berry: Life and Work*. Lexington: University Press of Kentucky, 2007. This collection of essays focuses on Berry's values of agrarianism, family, and community.

Shuman, Joel James, and L. Roger Owens, eds. *Wendell Berry and Religion: Heaven's Earthly Life. Lexington: University Press of Kentucky, 2009. A collection of essays examining Berry's religious point of view. The work is divided into four sections: "Good Work," "Holy Living," "Imagination," and "Moving Forward."

Andrew J. Angyal; Philip K. Jason
Updated by John L. Grigsby

JOHN BERRYMAN

Born: McAlester, Oklahoma; October 25, 1914
Died: Minneapolis, Minnesota; January 7, 1972

PRINCIPAL POETRY

Five Young American Poets, 1940 (with others)
Poems, 1942
The Dispossessed, 1948
Homage to Mistress Bradstreet, 1956
His Thought Made Pockets and the Plane Buckt,
    1958
Seventy-seven Dream Songs, 1964
Berryman's Sonnets, 1967
Short Poems, 1967
His Toy, His Dream, His Rest, 1968
The Dream Songs, 1969
Love and Fame, 1970, 1972
Delusions, Etc. of John Berryman, 1972
Henry's Fate, and Other Poems, 1977
Collected Poems, 1937-1971, 1989
Selected Poems, 2004

OTHER LITERARY FORMS

In addition to his poetry, John Berryman produced a considerable number of reviews and critical pieces. A posthumous collection, *The Freedom of the Poet* (1976), gathers a representative sample of his criticism, published and unpublished. Berryman did not produce much prose fiction, preferring to use verse as a narrative vehicle. He did, however, write several short stories, and an unfinished novel, *Recovery* (1973), was published as he left it at his death. Other critical writing

includes *Stephen Crane* (1950), a critical biography with a psychological slant, and *The Arts of Reading* (1960), a collection of essays coauthored with Ralph Ross and Allen Tate. Berryman also edited a 1960 edition of Thomas Nashe's *The Unfortunate Traveller: Or, The Life of Jack Wilton*. Berryman may be heard reading his poems on several recordings produced by the Library of Congress.

ACHIEVEMENTS

In *Beyond All This Fiddle* (1968), A. Alvarez remarks that

> John Berryman is one of those poets whom you either love or loathe. Yet even the loathers have grudgingly to admit that the man is extraordinary . . . with a queer, distinct voice of his own.

No doubt, there are "loathers" who would apply "extraordinary" in no laudable sense, and who would use far cruder adjectives than "queer" and "distinct" in describing Berryman's voice. Still, decades after his death, Berryman's place in modern poetry seems as secure as that of any of his contemporaries, living or dead—Robert Lowell, Delmore Schwartz, Richard Wilbur, Adrienne Rich, or W. D. Snodgrass. Though he died a most unsatisfied man, his poetic career certainly brought him his share of recognition and praise: the Levinson (1950) and Guarantors Prizes from *Poetry* and the Shelley Memorial Award (1949), an Award in Literature from the American Academy of Arts and Letters (1950), the University of Chicago's Harriet Monroe Poetry Prize (1957), the Brandeis Creative Arts Award (1960), the American Academy of Arts and Letters' Russell Loines Award (1964), the Pulitzer Prize in poetry (1965) for *Seventy-seven Dream Songs*, and both the National Book Award and the Bollingen Prize for Poetry, shared with Karl Shapiro, (1969) for *His Toy, His Dream, His Rest*. He became a member of the American Academy of Arts and Letters in 1965 and served as chancellor for the Academy of American Poets from 1968 to 1972. In addition, he won grants and fellowships from such organizations as the Guggenheim Foundation (1952, 1966), the Rockefeller Foundation (1944), the National Institute of Arts and Letters (1950), and the Academy of American Poets

(1966). He was much in demand for public readings, even though, especially toward the end of his career, his alcoholism and unpredictable personality made some of these appearances traumatic for both poet and audience.

In his poetry, Berryman moved from an ordered, restrained style, imitative of William Butler Yeats and W. H. Auden to a passionate, energetic, deeply personal mode of expression, held in check—though just barely in places—by skilled attention to rhythm and sound. So decisive was this movement that comparing such early poems as "Winter Landscape" with a random sample from his later work, *The Dream Songs*, is almost like comparing two different poets. It is easy enough to look back at Berryman's early work and find it too poised, too urbane and academic. A number of critics, however, have objected to much of his later work, finding in it too little restraint and much too large a dose of the poet's raw experience. He is placed by some, with Anne Sexton and Lowell, in the "confessional school." The label does not quite apply, for

John Berryman (©Tom Berthiaume/ Courtesy, Farrar, Straus and Giroux)

Berryman's work at its best—and, unfortunately, he did frequently allow it to be published at its worst—remained for him a means of using personal experience to get at human experience. He retained too much formal control to be considered a Beat poet and was too inventive in his use of language to be classed with the vernacular mode of William Carlos Williams. Whatever else may be said about him, Berryman is one of the most individual voices in twentieth century American poetry.

In spite of his successes, however, it is difficult not to wonder whether Berryman has been overpraised. His *Homage to Mistress Bradstreet*, for example, was extolled by Robert Fitzgerald (*American Review*, Autumn, 1960) as "the poem of his generation," while Edmund Wilson, solicited for a back-cover blurb for a 1968 paperback edition of the poem, responded with, "the most distinguished long poem by an American since [T. S. Eliot's] *The Waste Land*." There must certainly be a middle stance, somewhere between overpraise and Stanton Coblentz's view that "*Seventy-seven Dream Songs* has all the imaginative fervor of a cash register." Such a moderate perspective would see Berryman as a major poet of his generation, and view *Seventy-seven Dream Songs* as one of the major poetic events of the 1960's. His *Collected Poems, 1937-1971*, was published in 1989.

BIOGRAPHY

John Berryman was born John Allyn Smith, in McAlester, Oklahoma, the eldest son of a banker and a schoolteacher. His early childhood, spent in various small Oklahoma towns, was normal enough until his father's work took the family to live in Tampa, Florida. Marital problems developed and the boy's father became increasingly troubled and unstable, until in June, 1926, he shot himself in the chest at the family's vacation home across Tampa Bay. Young John heard the shot just outside his window—one sharp report that would echo through his consciousness for the rest of his life. When the boy's mother moved to New York and remarried, his name was changed to John Allyn McAlpin Berryman. Berryman wrote many letters to his mother as an adult, which were published as *We Dream of Honour: John Berryman's Letters to His Mother* in 1988.

Berryman attended a Connecticut prep school, South Kent; though he showed great intellectual promise, he was only intermittently moved to apply it. He graduated in 1933 and went on to Columbia University in New York. There he felt much more at home academically and socially, and there he began a lifelong friendship with Mark Van Doren, who, by Berryman's account, was the first person to inspire and encourage him to be a poet. Not long after this association began, Berryman published his first poem, an elegy on Edwin Arlington Robinson, in the *Nation*. In 1936, he received his bachelor's degree from Columbia, Phi Beta Kappa, and won the University's Kellett Fellowship, which he used to pursue further studies at Clare College, Cambridge University. Academically, his Cambridge experience was extremely rewarding. In 1937, he served as Oldham Shakespeare Scholar, and he received a bachelor of arts degree in 1938. His social contacts were rewarding, to say the least, including as they did William Butler Yeats, W. H. Auden, and Dylan Thomas.

Back in New York, Berryman was a friend of another young poet, Delmore Schwartz, and became poetry editor of the *Nation*. His teaching career began in 1939 at Wayne State University in Detroit. After a year there, Berryman took a position at Harvard, where he remained until 1943. During this time, his first published collection of poems appeared in *Five Young American Poets* (1940). His work was well received, as were the poems of another promising young talent, Randall Jarrell. In 1942, Berryman published a self-contained selection, *Poems*. On October 24 of the same year, he married Eileen Patricia Mulligan. From 1943 to 1951, Berryman lectured in creative writing at Princeton, taking time out frequently, with the help of grants and fellowships, to write poetry and criticism, as well as a few short stories. In 1948, he published a new book of poems, *The Dispossessed*, which was received more politely than enthusiastically. His most significant work while at Princeton was his critical study, *Stephen Crane*. His psychoanalytic approach was not popular with most reviewers, but the book, on the whole, attracted a good deal of praise.

In 1951, Berryman accepted a one-year position as Elliston Lecturer in Poetry at the University of Cin-

cinnati and spent the next academic year in Europe with the help of a Guggenheim Fellowship. While in Europe, he completed the poem that, on its publication in 1956, would bring him his first great critical success as a poet—*Homage to Mistress Bradstreet*. The price of this success, however, was high. Berryman later cited his preoccupation with the poem, coupled with an increasing dependence on alcohol, as the cause of his separation in 1953 from his first wife. Certainly, the marriage had not been helped by an intense, guilt-ridden love affair in which Berryman had indulged during the summer of 1947, an affair portrayed in painful detail in the sequence *Berryman's Sonnets*. In the meantime, however, Berryman's academic and literary careers proceeded without serious hindrance. In the fall of 1954, having spent the preceding spring and summer semesters, respectively, at the University of Iowa and at Harvard, he began his long tenure as a professor of humanities at the University of Minnesota in Minneapolis, where he became a popular, if eccentric, academic figure. In 1969, he received the university's most prestigious faculty award, a Regents' Professorship, and he remained on the faculty there until his death.

In 1956, Berryman divorced Eileen and married Ann Levine, who gave birth to a son in 1957. The marriage lasted only until 1959. When he again remarried, in 1961, it was to Kathleen Donahue, twenty-five years his junior. In the same year, he lectured at Indiana University, then moved on, in 1962, to a visiting professorship at Boon University. During that year, Kathleen gave birth to a daughter, Martha. In 1965, Berryman won the Pulitzer Prize for *Seventy-seven Dream Songs*; his place as a major contemporary poet seemed secure. He had begun work on these "songs" around 1955, and continued to work in this form for nearly twenty years, publishing in 1968 *His Toy, His Dream, His Rest*, a collection of 308 more poems that won the National Book Award in 1969. The two volumes were combined in *The Dream Songs* (1969).

The 1960's was a time of triumph for Berryman. The decade saw, along with *The Dream Songs*, the long-delayed publication of *Berryman's Sonnets*, and of *Short Poems*, a compilation of the earlier collections, *The Dispossessed* and *His Thought Made Pockets and the Plane Buckt*, with the addition of "Formal Elegy," a poem on the death of John F. Kennedy. However, the kind of success that most poets only dream of left Berryman dissatisfied and unfulfilled. His drinking problem became more serious than ever, interfering not only with his family life but also with his professional responsibilities, disrupting classes and public readings, much to the dismay of students, admirers, and colleagues.

Berryman's next book of poems, *Love and Fame*, did not fare well with the critics, and the poet took their disapproval hard. He had been, by this time, in and out of alcohol treatment programs, and although he had found some consolation in a renewal of his Roman Catholic faith, he could not overcome his addiction to alcohol; drinking had for too long been, in Joel Conarroe's words, "both stabilizer and destroyer, midwife and coroner, focuser and depressant." He spent many weeks of 1971 in the alcohol treatment facility at St. Mary's Hospital in Minneapolis, the hospital that provided the setting for *Recovery*. He remained, however, busy. He prepared a new book of poems for publication, and his plans for work included a translation of Sophocles and a book or two on Shakespeare. Unfortunately, the prospect of hard work, the comfort of family and friends, his affection for his daughters, Martha and Sarah—these were not enough.

On January 7, 1972, readers of the *St. Paul Dispatch* were greeted with the front page headline: "Poet Berryman Leaps to Death." That afternoon, Berryman had thrown himself some one hundred feet from the railing of a bridge in Minneapolis; his body was recovered from among the rocks on the frozen west bank of the Mississippi. In a circumstance worthy of the most bitterly ironic of his poems, the only identification he carried was a blank check. After a Requiem Mass, he was buried in Resurrection Cemetery in St. Paul.

ANALYSIS

In his essay "Tradition and the Individual Talent," T. S. Eliot asserts that

> the more perfect the artist, the more completely separate in him will be the man who suffers and the mind which creates; the more perfectly will the mind digest and transmute the passions which are its material.

Poetry, to Eliot, is "not a turning loose of emotion, but an escape from emotion; it is not the expression of personality, but an escape from personality." Regardless of what Eliot's critical stock is worth these days, there is an essential truth in what he says. Of course, poetry has brought to its readers the sweetest joys and the bitterest sorrows that human flesh is heir to, from "sweet silent thought" to "barbaric yawp." To the extent, however, that poets present their passions to the reader undigested, untransmuted, they damage the quality of their work as poetry. The more loudly personality speaks in a poem, the more art is forced to falter, to stutter. The poem—and the poet, and the reader—suffers.

To the extent to which "the man who suffers" and "the mind which creates" are not kept separate, to that extent will that poet's art be imperfect. A case in point is Berryman. There is much in his work that is brilliant; since his death, his stature has grown. There is no denying that he suffered much in his life, and risked much, dared much, in his poetry. What he was never really able to do was to find the voice and mode that would allow him, not to banish personality from his poems but to keep personality from getting in the way, from obstructing the proper work of the poem.

BERRYMAN'S SONNETS

Berryman's Sonnets, though unpublished until 1967, was written mostly some twenty years earlier. These poems are the poet's first sustained use of what may be called his "mature style," much of his previous work being rather derivative. The 115 sonnets form a sequence that recounts the guilty particulars of an adulterous love affair between a hard-drinking academic named Berryman and a harder-drinking woman named Lise, with the respectively wronged wife and husband in supporting roles. The affair, as the sonnets record it, is a curious mixture of sex, Scotch, and Bach (Lise's favorite, her lover preferring Mozart), punctuated by allusions right out of a graduate seminar, from the Old Testament to E. E. Cummings.

In form, the sonnets are Petrarchan, with here and there an additional fifteenth line. In his adherence, more or less, to the stanzaic and metric demands of the sonnet, Berryman pays a sort of homage to earlier practitioners of the form. At the same time, he is attempting to forge a mode of expression that is anything but Petrarchan, in spite of the fact that, as Hayden Carruth pointed out in a review in *Poetry* (May, 1968), the poems "touch every outworn convention of the sonnet sequence—love, lust, jealousy, separation, time, death, the immortality of art, etc." Carruth points out in the same review that "the stylistic root of *The Dream Songs*" is present in the sonnets, with those attributes that came to be trademarks of Berryman's style— "archaic spelling, fantastically complex diction, tortuous syntax, formalism, a witty and ironic attitude toward prosody generally." A concentrated if somewhat mild example of how Berryman combines any number of these traits within a few lines is the octet of "Sonnet 49":

> One note, a daisy, and a photograph,
> To slake this siege of weeks without you, all.
> Your dawn-eyed envoy, welcome as Seconal,
> To call you faithful . . . now this cenotaph,
> A shabby mummy flower. Note I keep safe,
> Nothing, on a ration slip a social scrawl—
> Not that it didn't forth some pages call
> Of my analysis, one grim paragraph.

There are enjoyable juxtapositions here. Outdated words such as "slake" and "cenotaph," the oversweetness of "dawn-eyed envoy," ranged about the all-too-contemporary simile, "welcome as Seconal," are no accident. There is an irreverent literary mind at work here, orchestrating intentionally a little out of tune. It is harder to appreciate or justify a phrase such as "not that it didn't forth some pages call/ Of my analysis." Such syntax is a high price to pay for a rhyme, and much more extreme examples could be cited.

On the whole, the sequence is successful, but the seeds of Berryman's eventual undoing are here. The confessional nature of the poems (Berryman did experience just such an affair in 1947, and required a good deal of psychoanalysis afterward) makes it plain enough why their publication was delayed so long, but it also leads the reader to wonder whether they should have been published at all. In his attempts to work within a fairly strict form, he shows a tendency to force rhyme and overburden meter. His literary name-dropping ("O if my syncrisis/ Teases you, briefer than

Propertius' in/ This paraphrase by Pound—to whom I owe three letters"), private allusions, and inside jokes present a dangerous intrusion of the idiosyncratic, the personal. With more shaping, more revision, more distance generally, the sequence could have been much more artistically successful than it is. Perhaps part of Berryman's intention was to get the thing on paper "as it was," to share his raw feelings with the reader. The best of the sonnets, by their wit and craft, speak against such a supposition. They contain, as a group, too much undigested Berryman to be placed, as some have placed them, beside the sonnets of William Shakespeare. Lise is all too actual, "barefoot . . . on the bare floor riveted to Bach," no Dark Lady. Further, while Shakespeare's sonnets have much to say about love, loss, youth, age, success, and failure, they tell the reader little if anything about William Shakespeare, while Berryman's sonnets reveal more than one may care to know about Berryman.

HOMAGE TO MISTRESS BRADSTREET

Not long after the strenuous summer of the sonnets, Berryman began a poem on the seventeenth century American Puritan poet, Anne Bradstreet. Part of the initial task was to find the right stanza for the job; an eight-line stanza suggested itself, the pattern of feet running 5-5-3-4-5-5-3-6, with a rhyme scheme of *abcbddba*. Neither meter nor rhyme is adhered to inflexibly in the resulting poem, *Homage to Mistress Bradstreet*, but for the most part Berryman succeeded in his choice of a stanza "both flexible and grave, intense and quiet, able to deal with matter both high and low." He achieves beautiful effects in the fifty-seven stanzas of this poem. The birth of Bradstreet's first child after several years of barrenness is portrayed in images wonderfully right: "I press with horrible joy down/ my back cracks like a wrist." The words sweep forward, charged with the urgency of this experience, "and it passes the wretched trap whelming and I am me/ drencht & powerful, I did it with my body!/ One proud tug greens Heaven. . . ." In fact, some of the most touching moments in the poem focus on Bradstreet and her children, whether the occasion be death, as in stanza 41, "Moonrise, and frightening hoots. 'Mother,/ how *long* will I be dead?'" or nothing more than a loose tooth, as in stanza 42: "When by me in the dusk my child sits down/ I am myself. Simon, if it's that loose,/ let me wiggle it out./ You'll get a bigger one there, & bite." Moving outdoors, away from the hearth, there are lovely scenes of natural description: "Outside the New World winters in grand dark/ white air lashing high thro' the virgin stands/ foxes down foxholes sigh. . . ."

Berryman, however, has his problems with the poem. As in the sonnets, he sometimes tangles his syntax unnecessarily: "So were ill/ many as one day we could have no sermons." To write "so were ill many" instead of "so many were ill," without even the excuse of a stubbornly kept rhyme scheme, seems at best eccentric, at worst, sloppy. As in the sonnets, also, there is an unfinished quality about the poem. Tangled phrasing, the inconsistent use of a rather carefully established rhyme scheme—these in spite of the fact that Berryman spent years on the poem, even blamed the demise of his first marriage partly on the intense effort that the work required. One may wonder, in spite of his long labors, whether he relinquished it to the public a bit unfinished.

The major flaw in *Homage to Mistress Bradstreet*, however, has not so much to do with details of diction or prosody. Bradsteet was, by historical accounts, a happily married, deeply religious woman, devoted to her husband and children, who happened to write poetry. Berryman needed for his poem a passionately suffering artist, plagued by religious doubt, resentful of her husband and family, and thwarted in her dream of artistic commitment, so he altered the historical Bradstreet to suit his purposes. This reshaping of history is necessary for the centerpiece of the poem—a seduction scene between a modern poet and a woman three hundred years buried. In an understandably surrealistic dialogue, the poet speaks his love for the poor, tormented Bradstreet in a rather far-fetched variation of the designing rake's "Let me take you away from all this." Bradstreet (Berryman's, that is) is tempted to religious doubt, to extramarital dalliance (she does ask the poet for a kiss), to despair over her misunderstood lot. Her domestic commitments, however, overrule her temptations, and the poem ends with the modern poet standing before Bradstreet's grave and uttering words that are supposed to be touching and solemn, but which somehow fail to convince:

> I must pretend to leave you . . . O all your ages at the
>   mercy of my loves
> together lie at once, forever or
> so long as I happen.
> In the rain of pain & departure, still
> Love has no body and presides the sun . . . Hover, utter,
>   still
> a sourcing whom my lost candle like the firefly loves.

The rhyming of "still" with itself is a nice touch, and "the rain of pain & departure" rings true, but the passage has a disturbing, self-conscious quality that is not at all helped by a reference, in one of the closing stanzas, to contemporary (post-World War II) anxieties—"races murder, foxholes hold men,/ reactor piles wage slow upon the wet brain rime."

The foregoing summary oversimplifies and leaves much unsaid. In all fairness, there are many brilliant moments in Berryman's poem, but, as a whole, *Homage to Mistress Bradstreet* is somewhat less than brilliant. John Frederick Nims, reviewing the poem in *Prairie Schooner*, termed it a "gallant failure," finding it "magnificent and absurd, mature and adolescent, grave and hysterical, meticulous and slovenly." In the end, his major complaint is that the poem,

> purportedly concerned with Anne Bradstreet . . . is really about "the poet" himself, his romantic and exacerbated personality, his sense of loneliness, his need for a mistress, confidante, confessor. One might think there would be more satisfactory candidates for the triple role among the living.

Nims's position is persuasively put and strikes at the heart of what is wrong with *Homage to Mistress Bradstreet*. Rather than conveying any true homage to this first American poet, Berryman lets his own personality, his own needs and concerns, dominate the stage, to the extent that the Bradstreet of his poem becomes just a version of himself. Far from "escaping personality," to recall Eliot's term, Berryman forces Bradstreet into the mold of his own personality.

THE DREAM SONGS

From "Berryman" of the sonnets, to "the poet" of *Homage to Mistress Bradstreet*, Berryman moved on to "Henry," the narrator and protagonist of *The Dream Songs*, the sequence of 385 poems that is considered to be his major work. Berryman apparently began with the notion of writing another long poem, about as long as Hart Crane's *The Bridge* (1930). What resulted, however, was something closer to Ezra Pound's *Cantos* (1925-1972). At the center of the poems is a character known variously as Henry House, Henry Cat, Pussycat, and Mr. Bones. Within flexibly formal songs of three sestets apiece, Berryman reveals Henry's trials and sufferings, which in many cases are the reader's as well. Too often, however, the songs are about Berryman.

There is real feeling in *The Dream Songs*. Too much suffering, however, spread not at all thinly over seven thousand lines and interspersed with proportionately more of the same sort of name-dropping and private allusion encountered in the sonnets, becomes oppressive and even boring. There are wonderful moments, notably in the elegies for dead friends—Jarrell, Schwartz, Sylvia Plath. The obsession with suicide that laces many of the poems is lent a special poignance when considered in the light of the suicides of Berryman's father's and Berryman himself. Not surprisingly, Henry's father took his life when he was young. Still, readers must be very interested in Berryman as a person to wade through these 385 poems, for Berryman is once again the center of attention, the "star" of his own epic, despite his coy disclaimer that Henry is "not the poet, not me."

In his continuing inability to distance himself sufficiently from his poetry, Berryman places the reader in an awkward position. In *The Personal Heresy: A Controversy* (1939), C. S. Lewis describes the necessity of keeping one's response to a poem separate from one's response to the personality of the poet, a task that Berryman makes unfairly difficult. When readers mix the two, says Lewis, they offend both poet and poem. "Is there, in social life," he asks, "a grosser incivility than that of thinking about the man who addresses us instead of thinking about what he says?" No, says Lewis, "We must go to books for that which books can give us—to be interested, delighted, or amused, to be made merry or to be made wise." As for personalities, living or dead, the response should be some "species of love," be it "veneration, pity," or something in between.

Berryman's personality is hard to love, easier to pity, but what is truly to be pitied is the fact that, had his skills as a poet been a match for his troubled personality, he would without question have been one of the greatest poets of his time.

OTHER MAJOR WORKS

LONG FICTION: *Recovery*, 1973.

NONFICTION: *Stephen Crane*, 1950; *The Arts of Reading*, 1960 (with Ralph Ross and Allen Tate); *The Freedom of the Poet*, 1976; *We Dream of Honour: John Berryman's Letters to His Mother*, 1988.

EDITED TEXT: *The Unfortunate Traveller: Or, The Life of Jack Wilton*, 1960.

BIBLIOGRAPHY

Bloom, Harold, ed. *John Berryman*. New York: Chelsea House, 1989. Collects twelve critical essays on Berryman's poetry, representing a variety of approaches. Contains a good index, a chronology, and a bibliography.

Haffenden, John. *John Berryman: A Critical Commentary*. New York: New York University Press, 1980. This rather dense study examines Berryman's major poetry, showing the connections between Berryman's personal and poetic challenges. Although students may find this work difficult, they will be enlightened by the extensive reproductions of Berryman's drafts, notes, and diary entries. Includes a composition chronology and an index.

_____. *The Life of John Berryman*. Boston: Routledge & Kegan Paul, 1982. This long and sometimes difficult volume draws heavily on Berryman's unpublished diaries, letters, and notes to tell the story of the poet's life from his father's suicide to his own. The contrast between Berryman's artistic successes and personal failures is at the center of this unblinking biography.

_____, ed. *Berryman's Shakespeare: Essays, Letters, and Other Writings by John Berryman*. New York: Farrar, Straus and Giroux, 1999. In this collection of Berryman's best short writings on Shakespeare, he explores the complex power of England's greatest dramatist and how knowledge of his work might be enlarged. An intimate, intricate view of Shakespeare's work.

Halliday, E. M. *John Berryman and the Thirties: A Memoir*. Amherst: University of Massachusetts Press, 1987. A close friend of Berryman, Halliday presents his recollections of his friendship with Berryman from 1933 to 1943. An account of college life in the 1930's, glimpses of other writers, and excerpts from Berryman's letters to Halliday make this a touching and fascinating memoir.

Hamilton, Ian. *Against Oblivion: Some Lives of the Twentieth-Century Poets*. London: Viking, 2002. Contains an entry on Berryman, examining his life and works.

Kirsch, Adam. *The Wounded Surgeon: Confession and Transformation in Six American Poets—Robert Lowell, Elizabeth Bishop, John Berryman, Randall Jarrell, Delmore Schwartz, and Sylvia Plath*. New York: W. W. Norton, 2005. This discussion of how these six poets treat confession and transformation in their works contains a chapter on Berryman.

Linebarger, J. M. *John Berryman*. New York: Twayne, 1974. After a brief biographical chapter, Linebarger examines Berryman's poetry, dividing it into four periods. The volume includes a chronology, an annotated bibliography, and an index, but contains few quotations from the poetry.

Mariani, Paul. *Dream Song: The Life of John Berryman*. New York: William Morrow, 1990. This highly readable biography conveys at every point Mariani's admiration for Berryman. As he traces Berryman's brilliant and tragic life, Mariani does not flinch from what was unattractive about the poet. Instead, he describes with respect Berryman's struggles to overcome his weaknesses. Includes extensive quotations from letters, essays, and poems, and numerous photographs.

Thomas, Harry. *Berryman's Understanding: Reflections on the Poetry of John Berryman*. Boston: Northeastern University Press, 1988. A collection of critical essays, reviews, interviews, and memoirs. Covers the canonical criticism of Berryman's work and the uses of that criticism to document the ongoing work of intelligent, imaginative reading.

Richard A. Eichwald

FRANK BIDART

Born: Bakersfield, California; May 27, 1939

PRINCIPAL POETRY

Golden State, 1973
The Book of the Body, 1977
The Sacrifice, 1983
In the Western Night: Collected Poems, 1965-1990, 1990
Desire, 1997
Music Like Dirt, 2002
Star Dust, 2005
Watching the Spring Festival, 2008

OTHER LITERARY FORMS

Frank Bidart (BIH-durt) is known primarily for his poetry. He also coedited the monumental *Collected Poems of Robert Lowell* (2002).

ACHIEVEMENTS

Deeply engaged in the moral issues of both personal and cultural guilt, Frank Bidart's poetry has won praise for the intensity with which it documents the struggle between the limits imposed by the body and the ideals envisioned by the mind. In 1981, Bidart won the *Paris Review*'s first Bernard F. Conners Prize for Poetry for his long poem "The War of Vaslav Nijinsky." This extended dramatic monologue highlights Bidart's unique talents: an unsettling insight into the psychology of guilt and anger, a singular style of narrative poetry based on abstract speech with little reliance on traditional poetic devices, and a thematic focus on the suffering occasioned by humankind's ambiguous intermixture of body and spirit. In 1998, *Desire* won the Bobbitt National Prize given by the Library of Congress, the Bingham Poetry Prize from the *Boston Book Review*, and the Theodore Roethke Memorial Poetry Prize from Saginaw Valley State University, and was a finalist for the Pulitzer Prize. Bidart received the Lila Wallace-*Reader's Digest* Writers' Award (1991), the Morton Dauwen Zabel Award (1995), the Shelley Memorial Award of the Poetry Society of America (1997), the O. B. Hardison, Jr., Poetry Prize (1997), the Lannan

Literary Award for Poetry (1998), the Wallace Stevens Award of the Academy of American Poets (2000), the Levinson Prize from *Poetry* magazine (2005), and the Bollingen Prize for poetry (2007). His *Watching the Spring Festival* was a finalist for the Pulitzer Prize in poetry and won the Los Angeles Times Book Prize for poetry (2008). Bidart served as a chancellor of the Academy of American Poets (2003-2009) and was elected a member of the American Academy of Arts and Letters in 2006.

BIOGRAPHY

Frank Leon Bidart, Jr., was born in 1939 in Bakersfield, California, where he grew up, in his words, "obsessed with his parents." After he was graduated from the University of California, Riverside, he attended graduate school at Harvard University. He formed a close relationship with poet Robert Lowell while residing in Cambridge, Massachusetts, and soon after began to write poetry with a style and content distinctive from those of his illustrious mentor. In 1972, Bidart accepted a position at Wellesley College, later becoming Andrew W. Mellon Professor of English.

ANALYSIS

Frank Bidart's poetry is decidedly original in style and content. Thematically, his work resembles confessional poetry, since it is obsessed with the family drama along with the attendant guilt and longing for forgiveness. Like Lowell's groundbreaking *Life Studies* (1959), Bidart's poetry abounds with autobiographical revelations of sexual perversion and neurotic family dynamics; like Lowell, Bidart develops personae that dramatically present these topics with an excruciating anguish that often borders on insanity. Unlike Lowell, however, Bidart presents the guilt and suffering of the mind embedded in the raging emotions and chaotic desires of the body with singular directness.

Whereas Lowell's poetic style has a rhetorical eloquence fashioned from the New Critical techniques of irony, fragmentation, and detailed imagery, Bidart's develops directly from an impassioned narrative voice that is abstract rather than particular, flatly prosaic rather than rhythmically colloquial. In Bidart's poetry, the line breaks and the idiosyncratic punctuation func-

tion to reproduce the "pauses, emphases, urgencies and languors in the voice." Often the syntax is complex; sometimes sentences stretch over a page or more and are rife with qualifications and contradictions, all signs of an active mind that, though speaking with the eloquence of polite, educated conversation, is in the grip of strong emotion. Bidart's dependence on an articulate, abstract style risks prosaic blandness, but the reward is a remarkably faithful fastening of his distinctive voice to the page.

GOLDEN STATE

Bidart's first collection, *Golden State*, begins with the poem "Herbert White," a dramatic monologue prefiguring the thematic focus on insanity and morality in his prizewinning poem "The War of Vaslav Nijinsky," published ten years later in *The Sacrifice*. At first the eponymous narrator of "Herbert White" views his murder and rape of a young child as morally justifiable because the act comes from a unity of body and desire:

Frank Bidart (Getty Images)

"When I hit her on the head, it was good." From this point of view, however, life is "without sharpness, richness or line." Only when White splits his awareness from his physical desires does suffering, and hence morality, commence:

> —Hell came when I saw
> > MYSELF . . .
> > > and couldn't stand
> what I see. . . .

Coordinate with White's separation from and feeling of revulsion for the body and natural processes is the advent of Bidart's characteristic stylistic devices. Before the foregoing lines occur, the verse in "Herbert White" is irregular, but when the narrator's split consciousness focuses on the agony of parental rejection, the gnawing guilt of his familial relationships, his sexual perversity, and the suffering occasioned by his body's unbridled instincts, the line breaks become directly reflective of emotional urgency and certain words, such as "MYSELF," are capitalized in order to reproduce the sonic dynamics of impassioned speech. Significantly, the suffering and the guilt cannot be ameliorated by appeal to a higher plane of understanding such as that normally supplied by religion. Devoid of absolutes, the narrator's voice exists only in the domain of his suffering, a voice universalized by the sound, grammar, and vocabulary of the relentless anguish of self-awareness.

The autobiographical poem "Golden State" reveals one of the sources of the emotional distress pervading Bidart's poetry: his father, a millionaire farmer described in the poem as "the unhappiest man/ I have ever known well." The father's unhappiness results not only from his pathetic desire to be a film star, cowboy, or empire builder but also from a "radical disaffection/ from the very possibilities/ of human life." Disconnected from himself and from his family, the father demonstrates to the poet that the search for connections is both initiated and frustrated by the family:

> > > The exacerbation
> of this seeming *necessity*
> for connection—;
> > > you and mother taught me
> there's little that's redemptive or useful
> in natural affections. . . .

Bidart is subject to the compelling human need to make something—some meaning, some pattern—out of these natural affections, but he finds little assistance from the conventional means toward establishing a relationship between his life and a larger realm of understanding. In section 4 of "Golden State," Bidart considers and rejects the efficacy of what his education has given him as an aid to understanding the mysterious hold his father wields on his innermost being: "the lies/ of mere, neat poetry"; his readings of Carl Jung that "never get to the bottom/ of what is, or was"; and the very "patterns and paradigms" of his Harvard studies that are rendered effete by his father's sarcasm, "How are all these bastards at Harvard?" Mere objective insight is rejected in section 5, and section 7 demonstrates the inadequacy of psychiatry to effect a reconciliation between the son and his memories of his dead father. Prayer is discovered to be ineffective in section 8. Only by entering into the words of his poem "to become not merely/ a speaker, the 'eye,' but a character" can Bidart represent the actual shape of his inner life. It is precisely in order to represent his inner life that Bidart has developed poetic techniques that eschew the artificiality of traditional prosody, with its dependence on meter, metaphor, image, and irony. Bidart's poetry demands directness, a physical entering of the self into the poem, an embodiment, that reifies the relentless agony and violence of human experience.

THE BOOK OF THE BODY

The Book of the Body, Bidart's next collection of poetry, presents the poet's sheer disgust at having to enter aesthetically into "the stump-filled material world// things; bodies;/ CRAP." These lines are from the first poem of the book, titled "The Arc," which sets the collection's pervasive tone of physical laceration (the poem's narrator has lost his arm as a result of a senseless accident) and bodily anxiety ("I'm/ embarrassed to take my shirt off"). An arc could geometrically be part of the unity of a circle, but in this poem, an arc is seen as irremediably cut off from wholeness, as is the arm of the amputee-narrator; it is an unredeemed segment of time, like a person's life bounded by its birth date and death date between parentheses. Unable to transcend the suffering of his limited physical existence, the narrator can achieve only the equivocal resolution of contemplating "how Paris is still the city of Louis XVI and/ Robespierre, how blood, amputation, and rubble// give her dimension, resonance, and grace."

Having explored his obsession with his father in "Golden State," Bidart now turns to his mother in the poem "Elegy." References to laceration abound: the chewing done by his mother's pet dog Belafont, his mother's reply of "gelding" to the narrator's ambition to become a priest, a love affair that leads to abortion, the envisioning of death and memory as "a razor-blade without a handle." Especially interesting is the interconnection made between being cut off from a satisfying relationship with his mother as well as himself and discussions of impotent mouths and mutilated breasts. When dreaming of the dog Belafont, the narrator recalls how the dog attempted to kiss him, but "carefully avoiding the mouth, as/ taught." In the section grotesquely entitled "Pruning," his mother exclaims, "I'd rather die than let them/ take off a breast." Mouths that cannot make contact, breasts that are threatened with excision indicate a lack of connection with the physical world as matter, "mother."

A morbid rejection of matter and of eating, an act that implicates the self in matter, forms a large portion of the theme of Bidart's great dramatic monologue from *The Book of the Body*, "Ellen West." Assuming the mask of the anorexic Ellen West, Bidart dramatizes how acquiring a body that is the image of the soul necessitates destroying that very body. To West, food is inextricably entangled with sex, death, and the material world:

> Even as a child,
> I saw that the "natural" process of aging
> is for one's middle to thicken—
> one's skin to blotch;
>
> as happened to my mother.
> And her mother.
>   *I loathed "Nature."*

Only by opposing the body—as, in the poem, did Maria Callas, the great opera singer, when she drastically trimmed her once-ample body by sixty pounds, illustrating how her soul "loved eating the flesh from her bones"—can an ideal approaching great art be realized.

Such an art records the unending struggle of the spirit to embody and manifest itself in a medium that it finds repulsive. Finally, each attempt to reconcile the body and the spirit heightens a hunger that neither food nor ink, the food of art, can satisfy. At the end of the poem, West poisons her body to achieve the ideal self that the world has sought to poison through food.

THE SACRIFICE

Although Ellen West sacrifices her body for an ideal in "Ellen West," that ideal cannot be directly embodied in art, for art as physical representation partakes of the body, not the soul. What can be recorded is the struggle itself, the sacrifice—and that is the central theme of Bidart's *The Sacrifice*.

One of the major poems in *The Sacrifice*, "Confessional," extends the thematic conflict of an earlier poem centered on Bidart's mother, "Elegy." In "Confessional," the body, the material world, presents a terrain on which it is impossible for mother and son to find harmony, for in the physical world dwell anger and unredeemable guilt occasioned by Bidart's memory of his childhood predatory wish to supplant both his father and his stepfather in his mother's affections, a situation exacerbated by the mother's excessive emotional dependence on him when he was a child. In an extreme contrast to the condition between the poet and his mother, sections from *Confessiones* (397-401; *Confessions*, 1620) that depict the relationship between Saint Augustine and his mother, Monica, constitute a major portion of the poem. Like Bidart in his childhood, Augustine supplanted his own father to the extent that Monica wished to be buried next to him, not her husband. The unbridgeable gap between Saint Augustine and his mother, on one hand, and Bidart and his mother, on the other, results from Saint Augustine and Monica's ability within the framework of the Christian mythos to transcend the "tumult of the flesh" and ascend to "the WISDOM that is our SOURCE and GROUND." Entangled in the confusions and desires of the body, Bidart's poetry cannot appeal to a higher level of meaning, however strongly craved: "*Man needs a metaphysics;/ he cannot have one.*" As in the poem "Genesis," a reworking of the first two books of the Bible into Bidart's poetic voice, not only did God rest after the days of creation, but God also "ceased." In the absence of an absolute, no anagogic, no symbolic function of language can mend the chasm between the mutually exclusive pairs: Saint Augustine and his mother with their harmonious heavenly vision, Bidart and his mother with their unappeasable anger, and remorse.

Also contained in *The Sacrifice* is the remarkable long poem "The War of Vaslav Nijinsky," a dramatic monologue in the persona of Vaslav Nijinsky (1890-1950), a famous dancer who had a formidable talent to turn his body into symbol. Nijinsky is presented as a figure that would—as Friedrich Nietzsche did in his unconditional acceptance of eternal return and thus the cycles of physical existence—say yes to life, were it not for his realization that he is not Nietzsche but the "bride of Christ." The dowry of the bride of Christ is an unrelenting guilt that leads to the rejection of life. There is no relief from this guilt, for "God was silent.// Everything was SILENT." Love, religion, philosophy, art, and mythology cannot assuage Nijinsky's insight that "All life exists// at the expense of other life" and that war is a given of life. Only sacrifice serves to atone for the guilt and suffering of the world, and Nijinsky, therefore, according to Bidart, danced "the Nineteenth Century's/ guilt," World War I, on January 19, 1919, in order to redeem, or perhaps destroy, the earth. Like Ellen West, Nijinsky can overcome the body and, by extension, earthly existence only through annihilation of the body. At the end of the poem, Nijinsky feels a "need to be as low down as possible" in his bed at an asylum in Zurich, Switzerland. He has sacrificed his body to his art.

IN THE WESTERN NIGHT

In the Western Night, Bidart's first three books plus two previously unpublished collections, confronts the reader with an odd ordering of these works: A new collection, *In the Western Night*, precedes the three previously published books, which are in reverse chronological order, and another new collection, *The First Hour of the Night*, ends the entire poetry collection. A possible reason for this arrangement is that *In the Western Night* underscores a theme that has been muted in the previous works, a theme that revalues those works and resolves itself in the final collection, *The First Hour of the Night*. In his 1990 review of *In the Western Night*, Denis Donoghue noted that "several of Bidart's most urgent poems are, in some sense that is hard to describe,

mystical." Odd as it may sound, Bidart's earthbound poetry possibly conceals a strong mystical impulse that intuits meaning beneath or beyond physical appearance. Such a mystical theme is strongly suggested in the first poem of the volume, "To the Dead":

once we'd been battered by the gorilla

we searched the walls, the intricately carved
impenetrable paneling

for a button, lever, latch

that unlocks a secret door that
reveals at last the secret chambers,

CORRIDORS within WALLS

(the disenthralling, necessary, dreamed structure
beneath the structure we see)

After the poem's "we" have been battered by the gorilla-like physical life, a secret chamber hidden behind the veil of material appearance is revealed. This innermost structure is "disenthralling," liberating from the prison of the body and the material world.

The working out of the mystical implications of "To the Dead" occurs, as it should, in the last poem in *In the Western Night*, "The First Hour of the Night." Perhaps Bidart's most ambitious poem, it balances the Western philosophical tradition against the poet's personal feelings of guilt, putting in equilibrium both "*wound and balm*." The occasion of the poem is the return of the poet to the house of a dead friend, at the invitation of the friend's son. The son and the poet discover that they share a sense of unresolved guilt: the son over the death of his father, the poet over the death of a pony that had been his close companion when he was young. Late that night, the poet retires to the guest bedroom and dreams two dreams. In one dream, he enters into an etching of *The School of Athens* by the Renaissance painter Raphael, which presents the ancient philosophers unified around the opposing but balanced gestures of Aristotle, representing matter, and Plato, representing spirit. Before entering into this painting in a dream state, the poet describes the panorama from an intellectual, objective point of view that sees a Janus-like unity in the divided philosophical positions of the ancient philosophers. Once embodied in the dream, however, the poet is weighed down by humiliation and guilt and strives unsuccessfully to regain a sense of unity. Philosophers who lived and wrote after the execution of Raphael's painting join the original group, bringing a cacophony of opinions that result in irreparable chaos. Finally, the poet awakes from this dream into "the desolation of/ HISTORY's/ leprosy,—LEPROSY of SPIRIT."

The first dream ends in Bidart's customary vision of spirit hopelessly mired in a diseased, repulsive physical state. In the second dream, the poet discovers that he has been carrying the entrails of his pet pony on his back ever since the animal died (when the poet was nine). Entrails not only suggest eating and the processes of the body but also haruspication, the divination of spirit. For the first time in Bidart's poetry, the mouth, the agent of eating and sexuality, joins with the breast, no longer seen as repulsive as it was in "Elegy" from *The Book of the Body*:

> hungry, SUCKING mouths stretched toward
> swollen, distended udders that I saw must be
>
> painful *unless* sucked —;
>
> . . . RECIPROCITY,—
>   I thought,—
>   *not the chick*
>   *within*
> *the egg, who by eating its way*
> *out, must DESTROY the egg to become itself . . .*

Destroying in order to become, the way of sacrifice, is abandoned in favor of reciprocity, the interpenetration of matter and spirit. Thus "The First Hour of the Night" ends with a tentative glimmer of transformation possible in the physical world.

Although his later work intimates a conditional transcendence, the bulk of Bidart's poetry to this point envisions the self trapped in history, sunk in the body, devoid of wholeness. Like an animal in a snare, the frustrated spirit experiences only torment, rage, grief, and guilt. The language of his poetry seldom soars, but remains earthbound, flat, prosaic, and lexically abstract.

DESIRE

Many of the same features characterize Bidart's next book, *Desire*, published to much acclaim after a period of silence. There is, in this prizewinning collection, less flatness and more lyricism, though it is indeed a dark lyricism. These poems draw heavily on the history of the Roman Empire and on Greek and Roman mythology, arguing in various ways that one is what one desires. Is desire, or will, only an illusion, or is it a dependable, controlled spring for action? Is it destiny? Bidart wrestles profoundly with such questions, enlarging the spiritual questing evident in his earlier work. More than half of *Desire* is taken up by a contemporary masterpiece, "The Second Hour of the Night," which may be Bidart's most significant achievement and one of the great meditative-dramatic poems of the late twentieth century. It recounts the story of Myrrah, the mother of Adonis, whose desire led her to sleep with her father, after which she found both life and death unbearable. The gods transform her into a tree: "She must/ submit, lose her body to an alien/ body not chosen, as the source of ecstasy is/ not chosen." Bidart's poetry documents the contemporary moral and psychological state of humankind, often through the vehicle of classical allusion, with such excruciating intensity that it resonates in the depths of every reader.

MUSIC LIKE DIRT

Music Like Dirt gets its title from a phrase in Desmond Dekker's song "Intensified" and is the only chapbook ever to be nominated for a Pulitzer Prize. Bidart explains that he wanted to create a sequence dramatizing "the human need to make." The theme of making appears prominently in "Young Marx," in which Marx muses on how though it is human nature to labor, people cannot find themselves in their labor and are thus estranged from themselves. Something of Bidart's own ideology emerges in the last line when he remarks that "too many sins were committed in his name." The theme of making continues in "Advice to the Players," which identifies Bidart's parents as frustrated makers and asserts that without clarity "the need to make is a curse." In "Two Tramps in Mud Time," Robert Frost had insisted that one's vocation and one's avocation should be one, a theme that Bidart repeats in "Advice to the Players." In "Lament for the Makers,"

Bidart claims that many creatures have it in their nature to make but only humanity *"must seek/ within itself what to make"* and he begs the masters to teach him their art.

STAR DUST

Star Dust returns to the theme of making and of how it is paired in human nature with the impulse to destroy. "Curse," the first poem, treats making a curse on those responsible for the September 11, 2001, terrorist attacks on the United States: "May what you have made descend upon you./ May the listening ears of your victims their eyes their/ breath/ enter you, and eat like acid/ the bubble of rectitude that allowed you breath." "Curse" is a powerful poem, one of Bidart's best. "Romain Clerou" remembers—after twenty-eight years—the way Dr. Clerou faces the last dying minutes of Martha, a longtime friend. Bidart's observation is chilling when he says, "he watched Martha face the void." The long poem "The Third Hour of the Night" takes up forty-four of *Star Dust*'s eighty pages with part 2 claiming thirty-four pages in an account of Benvenuto Cellini's ragged life. The sixteenth century Cellini was both an artistic genius and a multiple murderer, making him an apt subject for Bidart's thesis that humans are impelled both to create and to destroy. Cellini expresses his helplessness in the lines "As the knife descended (forgive me, O God of/ Nature, but *thus* you have arranged it)." It is a fine poem with not only a narrative of Cellini's struggles but also a sympathetic picture of his father, a vivid evocation of his artistic rival Bandinelli, and the story of his struggle with his bronze statue of Perseus.

WATCHING THE SPRING FESTIVAL

In *Watching the Spring Festival*, the poem "Tu Fu Watches the Spring Festival Across Serpentine Lake" is a story of court intrigue and violence. The Mistress of the Cloud-Pepper Apartments arranges her cousin's appointment as first minister, but in three years, he will be executed and she carried on a palanquin to a Buddhist chapel and strangled. Thus, uneasy lies the head that wears a first minister's hat—and that of his patroness. Bidart returns to a familiar theme in "The Old Man at the Wheel," an elegy for one who survived *"By submission, then making."* The last two lines are splendid: "Now you must drive west, which in November/ means

driving directly into the sun." "Little *O*" confronts the problems of making by observing that "disgust with the banality of naturalistic representation" is "necessary" and that art grows from a dialectic of refusals. French critics were wrong to judge Shakespeare a "barbarian" lacking in decorum: He was "remaking art." One of the longer poems in this volume, "Seduction," traces an ongoing teasing sexual rite that prompts the question of what impels people to "interpenetrate flesh." "If See No End in Is" is exceptional in this collection for its eight tightly constructed six-line stanzas on the bleak theme of "What none knows is when, not if." The inability to change lacerates the heart with guilt, and to fail the love of a mother leads to the central stanza in this powerfully moving poem:

> *Familiar spirit, within whose care I grew, within*
> *whose disappointment I twist, may we at last see*
> *by what necessity the double bind is in the end*
> *the figure for human life, why what we love is*
> *precluded always by something else we love, as if*
> *each no we speak is yes, each yes no.*

OTHER MAJOR WORK

EDITED TEXT: *Collected Poems of Robert Lowell*, 2002 (with David Gewanter).

BIBLIOGRAPHY

Bergman, Susan. "Frank Bidart's Personae: The Anterior 'I.'" *Pequod* 43 (2000): 100-111. Bidart's dramatic or persona poems are based on the stance that "self precedes and centers expression." Bergman underscores what is unique in Bidart's version of the vogue for persona poems, providing excellent close readings of many key passages.

Bidart, Frank. "Frank Bidart." Interview by Christopher Hennessy. In *Outside the Lines: Talking with Contemporary Gay Poets*, edited by Hennessy. Ann Arbor: University of Michigan Press, 2005. Bidart discusses his poetics of embodiment and what it is like to be an outsider.

_____. "In Conversation with Frank Bidart." Interview by H. L. Hix. *Madison Literary Review* 53, no. 1 (Fall, 2009): 191-200. Discusses "Ellen West," "Herbert White," and *Watching the Spring Festival*, as well as structure in poetry.

Birkerts, Sven. "Frank Bidart's Ambivalent Appetite." Review of *Watching the Spring Festival. Boston Phoenix*, June 17, 2008. Identifies the essence of Bidart's vision as "the clarification and underscoring of ambivalence." This is the focus of the short poems in *Watching the Spring Festival* just as in the earlier long poems.

Crenshaw, Brad. "The Sin of the Body: Frank Bidart's Human Bondage." *Chicago Review* 33 (Spring, 1983): 57-70. This article contains an insightful discussion of "Ellen West" and clarifies Bidart's construction of an art that presents the ethical paradox of carnality. Crenshaw discusses how Bidart has contracted human ethics within bodily limits, so that customary morality with its exaltation of the spirit becomes severely modified.

"Frank Bidart." In *Contemporary Poets*, edited by Thomas Riggs. 7th ed. New York: St. James Press, 2001. An in-depth profile of the poet's work.

Hammer, Langdon. "Frank Bidart and the Tone of Contemporary Poetry." *Southwest Review* 87, no. 1 (Winter, 2002): 75. Argues that Bidart's work is important and representative because it struggles against the flatness of voice found in much contemporary poetry.

Kelly, David, ed. *Poetry for Students*. Vol. 26. Detroit: Thomson/Gale, 2007. Contains an analysis of Bidart's "Curse."

Rector, Liam, and Tree Swenson, eds. *On Frank Bidart: Fastening the Voice to the Page*. Lansing: University of Michigan Press, 2007. Gathers thirty-six appreciations by such prominent poets as Elizabeth Bishop, Donald Hall, and Seamus Heaney.

Robbins, Michael. Review of *Watching the Spring Festival. Poetry* 193, no. 3 (December, 2008): 269-273. Notes that the poems are shorter than many of Bidart's poems and calls his poetry a "distinctive and bizarre art, less confessionalist than shock therapist." Praises "The Third Hour of the Night."

Warren, Rosanna. *Fables of the Self: Studies in Lyric Poetry*. New York: W. W. Norton, 2008. Includes an essay on "Contradictory Classicists: Frank Bidart and Louise Glück."

Kenneth Gibbs; Philip K. Jason
Updated by Frank Day

ELIZABETH BISHOP

Born: Worcester, Massachusetts; February 8, 1911
Died: Boston, Massachusetts; October 6, 1979

PRINCIPAL POETRY

North and South, 1946
Poems: North and South—A Cold Spring, 1955
Questions of Travel, 1965
Selected Poems, 1967
The Ballad of the Burglar of Babylon, 1968
The Complete Poems, 1969
Geography III, 1976
The Complete Poems, 1927-1979, 1983

OTHER LITERARY FORMS

In addition to her poetry, Elizabeth Bishop wrote short stories and other prose pieces. She is also known for her translations of Portuguese and Latin American writers. *The Collected Prose*, edited and introduced by Robert Giroux, was published in 1984. It includes "In the Village," an autobiographical revelation of Bishop's youthful vision of, and later adult perspective on, her mother's brief return home from a mental hospital. Like her poetry, Bishop's prose is marked by precise observation and a somewhat withdrawn narrator, although the prose works reveal much more about Bishop's life than the poetry does. Editor Giroux has suggested that this was one reason many of the pieces were unpublished during her lifetime. *The Collected Prose* also includes Bishop's observations of other cultures and provides clues as to why she chose to live in Brazil for so many years.

ACHIEVEMENTS

Elizabeth Bishop was often honored for her poetry. She served as consultant in poetry (poet laureate) to the Library of Congress in 1949-1950. Among many awards and prizes, she received an Award in Literature from the American Academy of Arts and Letters (1951), the Shelley Memorial Award (1953), the Pulitzer Prize in poetry (1956), the Academy of American Poets Fellowship (1969), the National Book Award in Poetry (1970), and the National Book Critics Circle

Elizabeth Bishop (J. L. Castel)

Award in poetry (1976) for *Geography III*. She became a member of the American Academy of Arts and Letters in 1954 and served as chancellor for the Academy of American Poets from 1966 to 1979. However, as John Ashbery said, in seconding her presentation as the winner of the *Books Abroad*/Neustadt International Prize for Literature in 1976, she is a "writer's writer." Despite her continuing presence for more than thirty years as a major American poet, Bishop never achieved great popular success. Perhaps the delicacy of much of her writing, her restrained style, and her ambiguous questioning and testing of experience made her more difficult and less approachable than poets with showier technique or more explicit philosophies.

Bishop's place in American poetry, in the company of such poets as Marianne Moore, Wallace Stevens, and Richard Wilbur, is among the celebrators and commemorators of the things of this world, in her steady conviction that by bringing the light of poetic intelligence, the mind's eye, on those things, she would enrich her readers' understanding of them and of themselves.

BIOGRAPHY

Elizabeth Bishop is a poet of geography, as the titles of her books testify, and her life itself was mapped out by travels and visits as surely as is her poetry. Eight months after Bishop's birth in Massachusetts, her father died. Four years later, her mother suffered a nervous breakdown and was hospitalized, first outside Boston, and later in her native Canada.

Elizabeth was taken to Nova Scotia, where she spent much of her youth with her grandmother; later, she lived for a time with an aunt in Massachusetts. Although her mother did not die until 1934, Bishop did not see her again after a brief visit home from the hospital in 1916—the subject of "In the Village."

For the rest of her life, Bishop traveled: in Canada, in Europe, and in North and South America. She formed friendships with many writers: Robert Lowell, Octavio Paz, and especially Marianne Moore, who read drafts of many of her poems and offered suggestions. In 1951, Bishop began a trip around South America, but during a stop in Brazil she suffered an allergic reaction to some food she had eaten and became ill. She remained in Brazil for almost twenty years. During the last decade of her life, she continued to travel and to spend time in Latin America, but she settled in the United States, teaching frequently at Harvard, until her death in 1979.

ANALYSIS

In her early poem "The Map," Elizabeth Bishop writes that "More delicate than the historians' are the map-makers' colors." Her best poetry, although only indirectly autobiographical, is built from those map-makers' colors. Nova Scotian and New England seascapes and Brazilian and Parisian landscapes become the geography of her poetry. At the same time, her own lack of permanent roots and her sense of herself as an observer suggest the lack of social relationships one feels in Bishop's poetry, for it is a poetry of observation, not of interaction, of people as outcasts, exiles, and onlookers, not as social beings. The relationships that count are with the land and sea, with primal elements, with the geography of Bishop's world.

For critics, and certainly for other poets—those as different as Moore and Lowell, or Randall Jarrell and John Ashbery—Elizabeth Bishop is a voice of influence and authority. Writing with great assurance and sophistication from the beginning of her career, she achieved in her earliest poetry a quiet, though often playful, tone, a probing examination of reality, an exactness of language, and a lucidity of vision that mark all her best poetry. Her later poetry is slightly more relaxed than her earlier, the formal patterns often less rigorous; but her concern and her careful eye never waver. Because of the severity of her self-criticism, her collected poems, although relatively few in number, are of a remarkably even quality.

History, writes Bishop in "Objects and Apparitions," is the opposite of art, for history creates ruins, while the artist, out of ruins, out of "minimal, incoherent fragments," simply creates. Bishop's poetry is a collection of objects and apparitions, of scenes viewed and imagined, made for the moment into a coherent whole. The imaginary iceberg in the poem of that name is a part of a scene "a sailor'd give his eyes for," and Bishop asks that surrender of her readers. Her poetry, like the iceberg, behooves the soul to see. Inner and outer realities are in her poetry made visible, made one.

"SANDPIPER"

In Bishop's poem "Sandpiper," the bird of the title runs along the shore, ignoring the sea that roars on his left and the beach that "hisses" on his right, disregarding the interrupting sheets of water that wash across his toes, sucking the sand back to sea. His attention is focused. He is watching the sand between his toes; "a student of [William] Blake," he attempts to see the world in each of those grains. The poet is ironic about the bird's obsessions: He is "finical"; in looking at these details he ignores the great sweeps of sea and land on either side of him. For every point in time when the world is clear, there is another when it is a mist. The poet seems to chide the bird in his darting search for "something, something, something," but then in the last two lines of the poem the irony subsides; as Bishop carefully enumerates the varied and beautiful colors of the grains of sand, she joins the bird in his attentiveness. The reward, the something one can hope to find, lies simply in the rich and multivalent beauty of what one

sees. It is not the reward of certainty or conviction, but of discovery that comes through focused attention.

The irony in the poem is self-mocking, for the bird is a metaphor for Bishop, its vision like her own, its situation that of many of her poetic personas. "Sandpiper" may call to mind such Robert Frost poems as "Neither out Far nor in Deep" or "For Once, Then, Something," with their perplexity about inward and outward vision and people's attempt to fix their sight on something, to create surety out of their surroundings. It may also suggest such other Bishop poems as "Cape Breton," where the birds turn their backs to the mainland, sometimes falling off the cliffs onto rocks below. Bishop does share with Frost his absorption by nature and its ambiguities, the ironic tone, and the tight poetic form that masks the "controlled panic" that the sandpiper-poet feels. Frost, however, is in a darker line of American writers: His emphasis is on the transitoriness of the vision, the shallowness of the sea into which one gazes, the ease with which even the most fleeting vision is erased. For Frost's poet-bird, "The Oven Bird," the nature he observes in midsummer is already 90 percent diminished. Bishop, rather, prefers the triumph of one's seeing at all. In her well-known poem "The Fish," when the persona finally looks into the eyes of the fish she has caught—eyes, the poet notes, larger but "shallower" than her own—the fish's eyes return the stare. The persona, herself now caught, rapt, stares and stares until "victory fill[s] up" the boat, and all the world becomes "rainbow, rainbow, rainbow." Like the rainbow of colors that the sandpiper discovers, the poet here discovers beauty; the victory is the triumph of vision.

Like the sandpiper, then, Bishop is an obsessive observer. As a poet, her greatest strength is her pictorial accuracy. Whether her subject is as familiar as a fish, a rooster, or a filling station, or as strange as a Brazilian interior or a moose in the headlights of a bus, she enables the reader to see. The world for the sandpiper is sometimes "minute and vast and clear," and because Bishop observes the details so lucidly, her vision becomes truly vast. She is, like Frost, a lover of synecdoche; for her, the particulars entail the whole. Nature is the matter of Bishop's art; to make her readers see, to enable them to read the world around them, is her purpose. In "Seascape," what the poet finds in nature, its potential richness, is already like "a cartoon by Raphael for a tapestry for a Pope." All that Bishop must accomplish, then, as she writes in "The Fish," is simply "the tipping/ of an object toward the light."

"OBJECTS AND APPARITIONS"

Although the world for the sandpiper is sometimes clear, it is also sometimes a mist, and Bishop describes a more clouded vision as well. She translated a poem by Paz, "Objects and Apparitions," that might indicate the fuller matter of her own work; the objects are those details, the grains of sand that reveal the world once they are tipped toward the light. The apparitions occur when one sees the world through the mist and when one turns vision inward, as in the world of dreams. Here, too, the goal is bringing clarity to the vision—and the vision to clarity. As Bishop writes in "The Weed," about drops of dew that fall from a weed onto a dreamer's face, "each drop contained a light,/ a small, illuminated scene."

Objects and apparitions, mist and vision, land and sea, history and geography, travel and home, ascent and fall, dawn and night—these oppositions supply the tension in Bishop's poetry. The tensions are never resolved by giving way; in Bishop's world, one is a reflection of the other, and "reflection" becomes a frequent pun: that of a mirror and that of thought. Similarly, inspection, introspection, and insight suggest her doubled vision. In "Paris, 7 A.M.," looking down into the courtyard of a Paris house, the poet writes, "It is like introspection/ to stare inside," and there is again the double meaning of looking inside the court and inside oneself.

"THE MAN-MOTH"

No verbs are more prevalent or important in Bishop's poetry than those of sight: Look, watch, see, stare, she admonishes the reader. From "The Imaginary Iceberg," near the beginning of her first book, which compares an iceberg to the soul, both "self-made from elements least visible," and which insists that icebergs "behoove" the soul "to see them so," to "Objects and Apparitions" near the end of her last book, in which the poet suggests that in Joseph Cornell's art "my words became visible," one must first of all see; and the end of all art, plastic and verbal, is to make that which is invisible—too familiar to be noticed, too small to be important, too strange to be comprehended—visible.

In "The Man-Moth," the normal human being of the first stanza cannot even see the moon, but after the man-moth comes above ground and climbs a skyscraper, trying to climb out through the moon, which he thinks is a hole in the sky, he falls back and returns to life belowground, riding the subway backward through his memories and dreams. The poet addresses the readers, cautioning them to examine the man-moth's eye, from which a tear falls. If the "you" is not paying attention, the man-moth will swallow his tear and his most valuable possession will be lost, but "if you watch," he will give it up, cool and pure, and the fruit of his vision will be shared.

QUESTIONS OF TRAVEL

To see the world afresh, even as briefly as does the man-moth, to gain that bitter tear of knowledge, one must, according to Bishop, change perspectives. In *Questions of Travel*, people hurry to the Southern Hemisphere "to see the sun the other way around." In "Love Lies Sleeping," the head of one sleeper has fallen over the edge of the bed, so that to his eyes the world is "inverted and distorted." Then the poet reconsiders: "distorted and revealed," for the hope is that now the sleeper sees, although a last line suggests that such sight is no certainty. When one lies down, Bishop writes in "Sleeping Standing Up," the world turns ninety degrees and the new perspective brings "recumbent" thoughts to mind and vision. The equally ambiguous title, however, implies either that thoughts are already available when one is upright or, less positively, that one may remain inattentive while erect.

The world is also inverted in "Insomnia," where the moon stares at itself in a mirror. In Bishop's lovely, playful poem "The Gentleman of Shalott," the title character thinks himself only half, his other symmetrical half a reflection, an imagined mirror down his center. His state is precarious, for if the mirror should slip, the symmetry would be destroyed, and yet he finds the uncertainty "exhilarating" and thrives on the sense of "re-adjustment."

"OVER 2000 ILLUSTRATIONS AND A COMPLETE CONCORDANCE"

The changing of perspectives that permits sight is the theme of Bishop's "Over 2000 Illustrations and a Complete Concordance." The poet is looking at the illustrations in a gazetteer, comparing the engraved and serious pictures in the book with her remembered travels. In the first section of the poem, the poet lists the illustrations, the familiar, even tired Seven Wonders of the World, moving away from the objects pictured to details of the renderings, until finally the "eye drops" away from the real illustrations, which spread out and dissolve into a series of reflections on past travels. These too begin with the familiar: with Canada and the sound of goats, through Rome, to Mexico, to Marrakech. Then, finally, she goes to a holy grave, which, rather than reassuring the viewer, frightens her, as an amused Arab looks on. Abruptly, the poet is back in the world of books, but this time her vision is on the Bible, where everything is "connected by 'and' and 'and.'" She opens the book, feeling the gilt of the edges flake off on her fingertips, and then asks, "Why couldn't we have seen/ this old Nativity while we were at it?" The colloquial last words comprise a casual pun, implying physical presence or accidental benefit. The next four lines describe the nativity scene, but while the details are familiar enough, Bishop's language defamiliarizes them.

The poet ends with the statement that had she been there she would have "looked and looked our infant sight away"—another pun rich with possibilities. Is it that she would have looked repeatedly, so that the scene would have yielded meaning and she could have left satisfied? Do the lines mean to look away, as if the fire that breaks in the vision is too strong for human sight? The gazetteer into which the poet first looked, that record of human travels, has given way to scripture; physical pictures have given way to reflected visions and reflections, which, like the imaginary iceberg, behoove the soul to see.

"THE RIVERMAN"

Bishop participates in the traditional New England notion that nature is a gazetteer, a geography, a book to be read. In her poem "The Riverman," the speaker gets up in the night—night and dawn, two times of uncertain light, are favorite times in Bishop's poetic world—called by a river spirit, though at first the dolphin-spirit is only "glimpsed." The speaker follows and wades into the river, where a door opens. Smoke rises like mist, and another spirit speaks in a language the narrator does not know but understands "like a dog/

although I can't speak it yet." Every night he goes back to the river, to study its language. He needs a "virgin mirror," a fresh way of seeing, but all he finds are spoiled. "Look," he says significantly, "it stands to reason" that everything one needs can be obtained from the river, which draws from the land "the remedy." The image of rivers and seas drawing, sucking the land persists in Bishop's poetry. The unknown that her poems scrutinize draws the known into it. The river sucks the earth "like a child," and the riverman, like the poet, must study the earth and the river to read them and find the remedy of sight.

PICTORIAL POETRY

Not only do the spirits of nature speak, but so too for Bishop does art itself. Her poetry is pictorial not only in the sense of giving vivid descriptions of natural phenomena but also in its use of artificial objects to reflect on the self-referential aspect of art. Nature is like art, the seascape a "cartoon," but the arts are like one another as well. Bishop is firmly in the *ut pictura poesis* tradition—as is a painting, so a poem—and in the narrower tradition of ekphrasis: Art, like nature, speaks.

In "Large Bad Picture," the picture is an uncle's painting, and after five stanzas describing the artist's attempt to be important by drawing everything oversized—miles of cliffs hundreds of feet high, hundreds of birds—the painting, at least in the narrator's mind, becomes audible, and she can hear the birds crying.

In the much later "Poem," Bishop looks at another but much smaller painting by the same uncle (a sketch for a larger one? she asks), and this time the painting speaks to her memory. Examining the brushstrokes in a detached and slightly contemptuous manner, she suddenly exclaims, "Heavens, I recognize the place, I know it!" The voice of her mother enters, and then she concludes, "Our visions coincided"; life and memory have merged in this painting as in this poem: "how touching in detail/ —the little that we get for free."

"THE MONUMENT"

Most explicitly in "The Monument," Bishop addresses someone, asking her auditor to "see the monument." The listener is confused: the assemblage of boxes, turned catty-corner one on the other, the thin poles hanging out at the top, the wooden background of sea made from board and sky made from other boards:

"Why do they make no sound? . . . What is that?" The narrator responds with "It is the monument," but the other is not convinced that it is truly art. The voice of the poet again answers, insisting that the monument be seen as "artifact of wood" which "holds together better than sea or cloud or sand could." Acknowledging the limitations, the crudeness of it, the questions it cannot answer, she continues that it shelters "what is within"—presenting the familiar ambiguity: within the monument or within the viewer? Sculpture or poem, monument or painting, says the poet, all are of wood; that is, all are artifacts made from nature, artifacts that hold together. She concludes, "Watch it closely."

Thus, for Bishop, shifting perspectives to watch the natural landscape (what she quotes Sir Kenneth Clark as calling "tapestried landscape") and the internal landscape of dream and recollection are both the matter and the manner of art, of all arts, which hold the world together while one's attention is focused. The struggle is to see; the victory is in so seeing.

POEMS OF QUESTIONING

Bishop's poetry is not unequivocally optimistic or affirmative, however. There are finally more ambiguities than certainties, and—like her double-edged puns—questions, rhetorical and conversational, are at the heart of these poems. Bishop's ambiguity is not that of unresolved layers of meaning in the poetry, but in the unresolvable nature of the world she tests. "Which is which?" she asks about memory and life in "Poem." "What has he done?" the poet asks of a chastised dog in the last poem of *Geography III*. "Can countries pick their colors?" she asks in "The Map." *Questions of Travel* begins with a poem questioning whether this new country, Brazil, will yield "complete comprehension"; it is followed by another poem that asks whether the poet should not have stayed at home: "Must we dream our dreams/ and have them, too?" Bishop poses more questions than she answers. Indeed, at the end of "Faustina," Faustina is poised above the dying woman she has cared for, facing the final questions of the meaning that death gives to life: Freedom or nightmare?, it begins, but the question becomes "proliferative," and the poet says that "There is no way of telling./ The eyes say only either."

Knowledge, like the sea, like tears, is salty and bitter, and even answering the questions, achieving a mea-sure of knowledge, is no guarantee of permanence. Language, like music, drifts out of hearing. In "View of the Capitol from the Library of Congress," even the music of a brass band "doesn't quite come through." The morning breaks in "Anaphora" with so much music that it seems meant for an "ineffable creature." When he appears, however, he is merely human, a tired victim of his humanity, even at dawn. However, even though knowledge for Bishop is bitter, is fleeting, though the world is often inscrutable or inexplicable, hers is finally a poetry of hope. Even "Anaphora" moves from morning to night, though from fatigue to a punning "endless assent."

POETIC FORM

Bishop's poetry is often controlled by elaborate formal patterns of sight and sound. She makes masterful use of such forms as the sestina and villanelle, avoiding the appearance of mere exercise by the naturalness and wit of the repetitions and the depth of the scene. In "The Burglar of Babylon," she adopts the ballad form to tell the story of a victim of poverty who is destroyed by his society and of those "observers" who watch through binoculars without ever seeing the drama that is unfolding. Her favorite sound devices are alliteration and consonance. In "The Map," for example, the first four lines include "shadowed," "shadows," "shallows," "showing"; "edges" rhymes with "ledges," "water" alliterates with "weeds." The repetition of sounds suggests the patterning that the poet finds in the map, and the slipperiness of sounds in "shadows"/"shallows" indicates the ease with which one vision of reality gives place to another. The fifth line begins with another question: "Does the land lean down to lift the sea?," the repeated sound changing to a glide. "Along the fine tan sandy shelf/ is the land tugging at the sea from under?" repeats the patterning of questions and the *sh* and *l* alliteration, but the internal rhyme of "tan" and "sandy," so close that it momentarily disrupts the rhythm and the plosive alliteration of "tan" and "tugging," implies more strain.

Being at the same time a pictorialist, Bishop depends heavily on images. Again in "The Map," Norway is a hare that "runs south in agitation." The peninsulas "take the water between thumb and finger/ like women feeling for the smoothness of yard-goods." The reader is brought up short by the aptness of these images, the familiar invigorated. On the map, Labrador is yellow, "where the moony Eskimo/ has oiled it." In the late poem "In the Waiting Room," a young Elizabeth sits in a dentist's waiting room, reading through a *National Geographic*, looking at pictures of the scenes from around the world. The experience causes the young girl to ask who she is, what is her identity and her similarity, not only with those strange people in the magazine but also with the strangers there in the room with her, and with her Aunt Consuela, whose scream she hears from the inner room. Bishop's poetry is like the pictures in that magazine; its images offer another geography, so that readers question again their own identity.

USE OF CONCEIT

This sense of seeing oneself in others, of doubled vision and reflected identities, leads to another of Bishop's favorite devices, the conceit. In "Wading at Wellfleet," the waves of the sea, glittering and knifelike, are like the wheels of Assyrian chariots with their sharp knives affixed, attacking warriors and waders alike. In "The Imaginary Iceberg," the iceberg is first an actor, then a jewel, and finally the soul, the shifting of elaborated conceits duplicating the ambiguous nature of the iceberg. The roads that lead to the city in "From the Country to the City" are stripes on a harlequin's tights, and the poem a conceit with the city the clown's head and heart, its neon lights beckoning the traveler. Dreams are armored tanks in "Sleeping Standing Up," letting one do "many a dangerous thing," protected. In the late prose piece "12 O'Clock News," each item on a desk becomes something else: the gooseneck lamp, a moon; the typewriter eraser, a unicyclist with bristly hair; the ashtray, a graveyard full of twisted bodies of soldiers.

Formal control, a gently ironic but appreciative tone, a keen eye—these are hallmarks of Bishop's poetry. They reveal as well her limitation as a poet: a deficiency of passion. The poetry is so carefully controlled, the patterns so tight, the reality tested so shifting, and the testing so detached, that intensity of feeling is minimized. Bishop, in "Objects and Apparitions," quotes the painter Edgar Degas: "'One has to commit a painting . . . the way one commits a crime.'" As Richard Wilbur, the writer whom she most resembles in her work, has pointed out, Degas loved grace and energy, strain coupled with beauty. Strain is absent in Bishop's work.

CHARACTER SKETCHES

Although there are wonderful character sketches among her poems, the poetry seems curiously underpopulated. "Manuelzinho" is a beautiful portrait of a character whose account books have turned to dream books, an infuriating sort whose numbers, the decimals omitted, run slantwise across the page. "Crusoe in England" describes a man suddenly removed from the place that made him reexamine his existence. These are people, but observers and outsiders, themselves observed. The Unbeliever sleeps alone at the top of a mast, his only companions a cloud and a gull. The Burglar of Babylon flees a society that kills him. Cootchie is dead, as is Arthur in "First Death in Nova Scotia," and Faustina tends the dying. Crusoe is without his Friday, and in "Sestina," although a grandmother jokes with a child, it is silence that one hears, absence that is present. There is little love in Bishop's poetry. It is true that at the end of "Manuelzinho," the narrator confesses that she loves her maddening tenant "all I can,/ I think. Or do I?" It is true that at the end of "Filling Station," the grubby, but "comfy" design of the family-owned station suggests that "Somebody loves us all," but this love is detached and observed, not felt. Even in "Four Poems," the most acutely personal of Bishop's poems and the only ones about romantic love, the subject is lost love, the conversation internal. "Love should be put into action!" screams a hermit at the end of "Chemin de Fer," but his only answer is an echo.

OTHER MAJOR WORKS

SHORT FICTION: "In the Village," in *Questions of Travel*, 1965.

NONFICTION: *The Diary of "Helena Morley,"* 1957 (translation of Alice Brant's *Minha Vida de Menina*); *Brazil*, 1962 (with the editors of *Life*); *One Art: Letters*, 1994; *Words in Air: The Complete Correspondence Between Elizabeth Bishop and Robert Lowell*, 2008 (with Robert Lowell).

EDITED TEXT: *An Anthology of Twentieth Century Brazilian Poetry*, 1972 (with Emanuel Brasil).

MISCELLANEOUS: *The Collected Prose*, 1984 (fiction and nonfiction); *Edgar Allan Poe and the Juke-Box: Uncollected Poems, Drafts, and Fragments*, 2006 (Alice Quinn, editor); *Poems, Prose, and Letters*, 2008.

Bibliography

Bishop, Elizabeth. Interviews. *Conversations with Elizabeth Bishop*. Edited by George Monteiro. Jackson: University Press of Mississippi, 1996. These interviews with Bishop reveal the unusual artistic spheres in which she moved. Monteiro's lucid introduction respects the complexities of both Bishop and her repressive historical moment.

Bloom, Harold. *Elizabeth Bishop: Modern Critical Views*. New York: Chelsea House, 1985. Bloom has gathered fifteen previously published articles on separate poems and on Bishop's poetry as a whole, as well as a new article, "At Home with Loss" by Joanne Feit Diehl, on Bishop's relationship to the American Transcendentalists. "The Armadillo," "Roosters," and "In the Waiting Room" are some of the poems treated separately. A chronology and a bibliography complete this useful collection of criticism from the 1970's and early 1980's.

Costello, Bonnie. *Elizabeth Bishop: Questions of Mastery*. Cambridge, Mass.: Harvard University Press, 1991. Provides a comprehensive view of Bishop's visual strategies and poetics, grouping poems along thematic lines in each chapter. She examines the poet's relationship to spirituality, memory, and the natural world by exploring her metrical and rhetorical devices.

Goldensohn, Lorrie. *Elizabeth Bishop: The Biography of a Poetry*. New York: Columbia University Press, 1992. Analyzing Bishop's life through the lens of her verse, Goldensohn probes the lesbianism and alcoholism that Bishop wished to conceal in her life and examines the role that Brazil played in shaping Bishop's works.

Harrison, Victoria. *Elizabeth Bishop's Poetics of Intimacy*. New York: Cambridge University Press, 1993. Harrison's application of critical theory to Bishop's work reveals new facets of Bishop's art. She examines Bishop's language, poetics, and prosody via postmodern theory, feminist theory, and cultural anthropology. Takes advantage of the ample manuscript materials available.

Miller, Brett C. *Elizabeth Bishop: Life and the Memory of It*. Berkeley: University of California Press, 1993. The first critical biography of Bishop, this resource combines the subject's life and writings. Numerous notebook entries and letters are uncovered as sources for later poems, and Bishop's alcoholism is discussed.

_____. *Flawed Light: American Women Poets and Alcohol*. Urbana: University of Illinois Press, 2009. Miller studies how drinking and alcoholism affected certain prominent American women poets, and how their struggles were reflected in their poetry.

Parker, Robert Dale. *The Unbeliever: The Poetry of Elizabeth Bishop*. Urbana: University of Illinois Press, 1988. Parker has the advantage of a longer view of Bishop's writings and criticism. His wide grasp of her life and work leads him to shape her development into three stages: poems of wish and expectation, resignation into poems of place, and finally, as is natural with maturity, poems of retrospection. He focuses on the major poems in each area, with a last chapter on the later poems, some of which, such as "The Moose," had been in her mind for twenty years. Includes particularly fine notes and an index.

Schwartz, Lloyd, and Sybil P. Estess. *Elizabeth Bishop and Her Art*. Ann Arbor: University of Michigan Press, 1983. This indispensable source gathers critical articles from many admirers, as well as interviews, introductions at poetry readings, explications of specific poems, and a bibliography (1933-1981). Some of Bishop's journal passages demonstrate why she is a preeminent American poet—her realism, common sense, lack of self-pity over losses—as James Merrill calls her, "our greatest national treasure."

Travisano, Thomas. *Elizabeth Bishop: Her Artistic Development*. Charlottesville: University Press of Virginia, 1988. This comprehensive study of Bishop's career traces the evolution of her prose and poetry through three phases. The first, "Prison," uses enclosure as its metaphor; the second, "Travel," breaks through into engagement with people and places; and the third, "History," reconciles her life of loss and displacement to a calm, mature mood of courage and humor. Complemented by a chronology, a bibliography, and an index.

Howard Faulkner

JOHN PEALE BISHOP

Born: Charles Town, West Virginia; May 21, 1892
Died: Hyannis, Massachusetts; April 4, 1944

PRINCIPAL POETRY
Green Fruit, 1917
The Undertaker's Garland, 1922 (with Edmund
    Wilson; includes poetry and stories)
Now with His Love, 1933
Minute Particulars, 1935
Selected Poems, 1941
The Collected Poems of John Peale Bishop, 1948

OTHER LITERARY FORMS

The literary reputation that John Peale Bishop retains is connected almost solely to his work as a poet, but he also was involved in journalism as an editor for *Vanity Fair* (1922), and he wrote for that magazine in the 1920's. He produced a volume of short stories, *Many Thousands Gone*, in 1931 and a novel, *Act of Darkness*, in 1935.

ACHIEVEMENTS

John Peale Bishop was a member of the literary establishment of New York in the early 1920's but spent most of the decade living in Europe. He never won a major prize for his work, but in 1931, his short story "Many Thousands Gone" won the *Scribner's Magazine* annual short-story prize. He was respected as a critic, and in 1940, he worked as the poetry reviewer for the periodical *The Nation*.

In 1943, Bishop was honored by the appointment as resident fellow at the Library of Congress in Washington, D.C., but ill health forced him to resign; he died soon after.

BIOGRAPHY

John Peale Bishop was born in Charles Town, West Virginia, to a family of substantial wealth. He began writing poetry in his late teen years; *Harper's Weekly* published a poem by him in 1912, a year before he entered Princeton University. He came to university somewhat later than most because of serious illness in his late youth. At Princeton, he was part of the literary coterie that included F. Scott Fitzgerald. After graduation in 1917, he earned a commission in the U.S. Army and served until the end of World War I.

In 1920, he became a prominent member of the New York City literary circle, working as an editor at *Vanity Fair* as well as writing poems, reviews, and comic pieces. He married Margaret Hutchins in 1922, and they went off to tour Europe. In 1924, they returned to New York, and Bishop worked in the office of Paramount Pictures. He also contributed occasional work to New York magazines. Dissatisfied with intellectual life in the United States, he returned to Europe, living in a chateau in rural France, but he continued to write for American publications. While there he published a book of short stories and a book of poems, *Now with His Love*.

Bishop returned to the United States in 1933, living for a short time in Connecticut, then in New Orleans. In 1935, he settled on Cape Cod, where he wrote some of his best poems. The December, 1940, death of F. Scott Fitzgerald was remembered in "The Hours," and a series of somber, sonorous poems followed. Constantly troubled by serious illness, Bishop worked when he was able, in New York in the Office of the Coordinator of Inter-American Affairs and in editorial work. In 1942, his health forced him to return to Cape Cod. In 1943, he tried to work at the Library of Congress with the poet Archibald MacLeish but suffered a heart attack soon after his arrival. He returned to the Cape, where he continued to write poetry. He died in Hyannis Hospital on April 4, 1944.

ANALYSIS

The reputation of poets is often fragile, dependent on changes in taste for certain themes, tonalities, and technical enthusiasms. This is particularly true of John Peale Bishop (who was ruefully aware of it), for he was rarely chosen for poetry anthologies and of little interest to the critics.

His major limitations were his lack of a singular voice or an individual style. His early poetry was influenced by several nineteenth century poets, including John Keats, Percy Bysshe Shelley, and Algernon Charles Swinburne, and his later work revealed an enthusiasm for the twentieth century poets William Butler Yeats, T. S. Eliot, and Ezra Pound. His poems are often clever but lack originality (a touchstone for artistic praise) and that indefinable artistic sense of power that marks the great poet. His later poetry, however, often manages interesting ideas and possesses a laconic tone that is attractive.

"SPEAKING OF POETRY"

The first poem in his 1933 collection *Now with His Love* uses a central problem of William Shakespeare's *Othello, the Moor of Venice* (pr. 1604, pb. 1622; revised 1623) as a metaphor for the relation of poetry to ordinary life. How can Desdemona, so civilized and cultivated, so delicate and fastidious, be attracted to the rough animality of Othello? Unlike most twentieth century lyric poets, Bishop does not quite answer the question, although the poem is reminiscent of the problem poems of Yeats and W. H. Auden in which some final solution is reached.

Desdemona represents, for Bishop, the intellect, the world of European culture, restraint, and the feminine, while Othello represents the emotions, the dark uncivilized African, the masculine. "For though Othello had his blood from kings/ his ancestry was barbarous, his ways African,/ his speech uncouth." Bishop explores the nature of their coming together in a way that suggests that such is how art is made, in a coming together of the traditions and disciplines of the form wedded to the unconscious, the wayward, dark aspects of the poetic imagination.

It is a tonally tough poem, cool in its comparison of the act of artistic creation with the sexual attraction of Desdemona "small and fair,/ delicate as a grasshopper" and Othello, "his weight resilient as a Barbary stallion's." All the trappings of "poetic" language that mar so many of Bishop's early poems are left behind here for an informal, angular verse, with intimate conversational simplicity. The question of how culture is related to ordinary life was common with Bishop and shows up most successfully in his later work in *Minute Particulars* in "The Freize" and "Your Chase Had a Beast in View," in which the artist is praised for the ability to bring order and meaning out of humanity's base existence.

NOW WITH HIS LOVE

Bishop had a wide range of subject matter, and in *Now with His Love*, he faces the horror of his service in World War I, juxtaposing the innocence of daily life behind the battle lines with the existential facts of daily slaughter. His gift for the description of the indifferently beautiful world of nature makes the facts of life even more intensely sad. The dead are buried close to their billets in "In the Dordogne":

> the young men rotted
> under the shadow of the tower
> in a land of small clear silent streams
> where the coming on of evening is
> the letting down of blue and azure veils
> over the clear and silent streams
> delicately bordered by poplars.

The senselessness of the fighting is conveyed not by heroic posturing or heightened emotion but rather by a distasteful rigor and a recognition of the sad foolishness of the idealizations of the young men. Relentless in tone and intelligent candor, bone thin in its refusal to glorify, it is war poetry of considerable power.

"Young Men Dead" is a powerful evocation of three boys slain in France, one who might have become a formidable man in time, one a great lover "who had so many dears/ Enjoyed to the core," and "Newlin who hadn't one/ To answer his shy desire." However different they may be, they are "blanketed in the mould." The emotional tightness of the poem, the terse bleakness of the memory is brought to a deadening conclusion in the muted admission that "I who have most reason/ Remember them only when the sun/ is at his dullest season."

"FIAMETTA" AND "METAMORPHOSES OF M"

These two poems are also from *Now with His Love*. Bishop wrote love lyrics from early in his career, but it was only in his later years that he was consistently able to find an economical, intensely direct way to deal with the subject. He did, however, show signs of power early on, as in "Fiametta," written in the early 1920's. The poem is metrically very strict for the first two six-line stanzas; the final stanza is somewhat looser and provides a pleasing contrast. It is a poem that displays how technically skilled Bishop was at an early age. It is a simple song of outright adoration of female beauty, full of color and sensitive evocations of sexual excitement: "In a gown the color of flowers;/ Her small breasts shine through the silken stuff/ Like raindrops after showers." The poem is not without a glint of wit: "Whatever her flaws, my lady/ Has no fault in her young body."

In 1933, this sexual adoration appears again, with even greater success, in "Metamorphoses of M." This poem is strongly reminiscent of Yeats but remains a successful evocation of adoration of the female. In this love poem written on the morning after a night of sexual pleasure, the lover contemplates the beauty fit for Venetian craftsmen to adorn. "I could have sworn Venetian artisans/ Had all night been awake, painting in gold,/ To set your beauty on appropriate heels."

Bishop, deeply lettered in literature and history, often subtly infuses his poetry with cultural references, and William Shakespeare's Cleopatra is hinted at in "Your beauty is not used" as the lover marvels at the unspoiled perfection of the loved one. There is also a touch of the Metaphysical poets in his logic-chopping consideration of the woman, sexually active, yet so beautiful that a kind of virginity surrounds her. "Though you have lain/ A thousand nights upon my bed, you rise/ Always so splendidly renewed that I have thought" that "even the unicorn" would be "so marvelled by virginity/ That he would come, trotting and mild,/ To lay his head upon your fragrant lap/ And be surprised."

"A SUBJECT OF SEA CHANGE"

The longer poems, gathered in *The Collected Poems of John Peale Bishop* under "Uncollected Poems, 1937-1945," are examples of his ability to sometimes, but not always, organize his work with a happy conjunction of technical and aesthetic success. Sea Change was the name of the house he had built on Cape Cod, the name coming from Shakespeare's *The Tempest* (pr. 1611, pb. 1623) in a passage describing the act of drowning, an act in which all is changed forever. In the poem "A Subject of Sea Change," the speaker reflects on life, public and private, as he looks out to the shore and the rolling sea. Bishop had considerable sensitivity in the description of nature, and the beginning section places the house within the beach landscape. "I have built my house amid sea-bitten green,/ Among the pitch pines of a dispersed wood." The time is ominous, that of World War II: "I hear the great bombs drop." Humanity's limited hold on time, and its failures, are put

into the context of the long run, of the ability to accept failure and responsibility, but to maintain a sense of life having meaning.

> Time is man's tragic responsibility
> And on his back he bears
> Both the prolific and destroying years.
> . . . he must surround each act
> With scruples that will hold intact
> Not merely his own, but human, dignity.

"THE HOURS"

Something of similar thoughtfulness and tender passion can be seen in "The Hours," the elegy written on the death of F. Scott Fitzgerald. The Cape Cod landscape is used with relentless force in pastoral sympathy. "The sky is overcast,/ And shuddering cold as snow the shoreward blast./ And in the marsh, like a sea astray, now/ Waters brim." John Milton's "Lycidas" (1638) may be the inspiration behind the poem, but Milton had never met the young man who was the subject of that poem, nor had the boy done anything significant with his life. By contrast, Bishop was an intimate of Fitzgerald, and Fitzgerald was one of the finest American novelists of his time. The poem has an intimacy that Milton's poem lacks: "None had such promise then, and none/ Your scapegrace wit or your disarming grace." The poem concludes in acceptance of eternal loss. "I cannot pluck you bays,/ Though here the bay grows wild. For fugitive/ As surpassed fame the leaves this sea-wind frays/ Why should I promise what I cannot give?"

OTHER MAJOR WORKS

LONG FICTION: *Act of Darkness*, 1935.

SHORT FICTION: *Many Thousands Gone*, 1931.

NONFICTION: *The Collected Essays of John Peale Bishop*, 1948; *The Republic of Letters in America: The Correspondence of John Peale Bishop and Allen Tate*, 1981.

EDITED TEXT: *American Harvest*, 1942 (with Allen Tate).

BIBLIOGRAPHY

Arrowsmith, William. "An Artist's Estate." *Hudson Review* 2 (1949): 118-127. A short account of the

Bishop poetry and its relation to early twentieth century literary movements.

Bier, Jesse. *A Critical Biography of John Peale Bishop.* Ann Arbor, Mich.: University Microfilms, 1957. This thesis for Princeton University is one of the rare biographical works on Bishop.

Bratcher, James T. "'Chickimee Craney Crow': A Game as Explanation of an Obscure Poem by John Peale Bishop." *Notes and Queries* 55, no. 4 (December, 2008): 481-484. The author uses chickimee craney crow, a game played in the South in the nineteenth and early twentieth centuries, to explain the poem "A Charm."

Frank, Joseph. "The Achievement of John Peale Bishop." *Minnesota Review* 2 (1962): 325-344. Bishop often used mythological themes in his poetry; Frank spends considerable time on that aspect of the work but also examines the later poetry with considerable sensitivity.

Hyman, Stanly Edgar. "Notes on the Organic Unity of John Peale Bishop." *Accent* 4 (1949): 102-113. A comment on the complexity of some of the poetry.

Spindler, Elizabeth Carroll. *John Peale Bishop: A Biography.* Morgantown: West Virginia University Press, 1980. Includes bibliographical references, index.

Tate, Allen. "A Note on Bishop's Poetry." *Southern Review* 1 (1935): 357-364. Tate, a good poet and distinguished critic, was Bishop's closet literary confidant and a personal friend; his judgment of the Bishop work is probably the best available.

Tate, Allen, and John Peale Bishop. *The Republic of Letters in America: The Correspondence of John Peale Bishop and Allen Tate.* Lexington: University Press of Kentucky, 1981. The sparsity of criticism of Bishop's work can, in part, be alleviated by his long personal and critical correspondence with fellow poet Allen Tate. They discuss the problem of making art in the United States.

White, Robert Lee. *John Peale Bishop.* 1966. Reprint. Detroit: Gale Group, 1983. A widely accessible, full-length study of the poet. It is sensible and thorough, dealing with his life and his full range of literary endeavors. A good source for student study.

Charles H. Pullen

PAUL BLACKBURN

Born: St. Albans, Vermont; November 24, 1926
Died: Cortland, New York; September 13, 1971

PRINCIPAL POETRY

The Dissolving Fabric, 1955
Brooklyn-Manhattan Transit: A Bouquet for Flatbush, 1960
The Nets, 1961
Sing-Song, 1966
Sixteen Sloppy Haiku and a Lyric for Robert Reardon, 1966
The Cities, 1967
The Reardon Poems, 1967
In. On. Or About the Premises: Being a Small Book of Poems, 1968
Two New Poems, 1969
The Assassination of President McKinley, 1970
Gin: Four Journal Pieces, 1970
Three Dreams and an Old Poem, 1970
The Journals: Blue Mounds Entries, 1971
Early Selected Y Mas: Poems, 1949-1966, 1972
Halfway Down the Coast: Poems and Snapshots, 1975
The Journals, 1975 (Robert Kelly, editor)
By Ear, 1978
Against the Silences, 1980
The Selection of Heaven, 1980
The Collected Poems of Paul Blackburn, 1985

OTHER LITERARY FORMS

Paul Blackburn was an ambitious translator, not only of such modern Spanish-language writers as Federico García Lorca, Julio Cortázar, and Octavio Paz but also of the medieval troubadours, who had some influence on his own verse. Although his work in the Provençal poets was primarily finished by the late 1950's, Blackburn continued to revise his translations for the rest of his life. The substantial manuscript was eventually edited by his friend, the scholar of medieval literature George Economou, and published posthumously as *Proensa: An Anthology of Troubadour Poetry* (1978).

ACHIEVEMENTS

Appreciated as a translator, Paul Blackburn limited his reputation as a poet during his lifetime by publishing only a small portion of his poetry and then in very limited editions. His position in literary history can be appreciated through the inevitable comparison with Frank O'Hara. Both poets were born and graduated from college in the same years; both were celebrators of the city, primarily New York, in verse that revealed their awareness of centuries of literary history at the same time that they were pursuing some of the more radical modernist innovations in poetic structure and idiom; and both bodies of work reveal warm, generous, witty sensibilities; unfortunately, both poets also died young. Blackburn and O'Hara were, in fact, simultaneously experimenting with the open-form poem, the poem that strives to convey the immediacy of life by presenting the poet's situation, observations, and responses as directly and precisely as possible, according to the chronology of the events themselves as they happened, thus giving the illusion of both inclusiveness and inconclusiveness. The mediating consciousness that shapes and judges experience, that yields a crafted, discursive, linearly logical development of images progressing to a closure that both evolves from and unifies them, is seemingly denied. O'Hara's affinities, however, are with the French: the post-Symbolists Pierre Reverdy and Guillaume Apollinaire, and the Surrealists. Consequently, his "lunch poems" retain a sense of a consciousness willing and directing, a gesture akin to that of the analogical subconscious managing the flow of his "automatic" texts. Blackburn, however, places the reader almost completely in reality, in the experience itself, perhaps because he is working within the more objectivist American tradition.

Blackburn readily acknowledged that Ezra Pound had the most influence on his work, along with William Carlos Williams, whom he first encountered through the poetry of Robert Creeley. Charles Olson's essay "Projective Verse" (1950) provided added incentive, as did the poetry of Louis Zukofsky. Blackburn worked in the modernist poetic technique pioneered by Pound and Williams, and E. E. Cummings and T. S. Eliot as well, and defined in 1945 by Joseph Frank in a seminal essay as "spatial form." This technique complements a nondiscursive content by replacing the linear conventions of typographically recorded language, appropriate to discursive content, with a two-dimensional, spatially oriented presentation. The unconventional spacing of words or phrases can establish rhythm by indicating length of pause between verbal elements, and calculated rather than conventional line endings can provide emphasis whenever strategically desirable. Blackburn consistently avails himself of both of these features of spatial form, as did his predecessors.

Blackburn's unique contribution to modernist poetics, however, is to use juxtaposition, the primary aspect of spatial form that yields thematic meaning, in the spontaneous, open-form poem of immediate experience to convey definite, if subtle, complex meanings within verse that appears simply to be recording random observations of the ongoing flow of life. The placing of material in different areas on the page according to subject not only isolates particular experiences, preserving their phenomenal integrity, but also facilitates a more profound kind of relationship between them. When Blackburn is at his best, he is shrewdly choosing for a given poem inherently related experiences that

Paul Blackburn (©Thomas Victor)

comment on one another, yet describing them with complete fidelity to their objective reality and presenting them nonchalantly, extemporaneously, as if they are insignificant coincidences. In this way, Blackburn creates in his poems a living world of joyous activity and sensuous appearance that is nevertheless intrinsically meaningful.

Blackburn was aware, however, that a poem is not merely a written, visual product, but also a spoken, aural event. What made Blackburn the complete poet, the virtuoso, was the other great influence on his poetic career besides Pound: the troubadours. Music in poetry was for Blackburn at once formal, the orchestration of material for thematic and emotional impact, and aural, the rhythm and sound of the language itself. To be sure, Blackburn, like his contemporaries, sought American speech rhythms and conversational diction, an aesthetic inaugurated by Walt Whitman. Blackburn had a fine ear for colloquialisms and slang, but that ear was also trained by Provençal. Consequently, the play of assonance, consonance, internal rhyme, off-rhyme, and rhythmic nuance inspired by troubadour lyric can be found at times alternating, or even blending, with modern idiom, for atmosphere, emphasis, or wit. Blackburn's range of diction, in fact, enables him to enliven his poetry with irony and humor, formal diction and slang clashing unexpectedly. Despite the minimalist tendencies of many of his contemporaries to strip poetry of all rhetorical beauty, Blackburn found ways to preserve the varied aural richness of language.

The troubadours may also be responsible, along with Blackburn's avowed Mediterranean sensibility, for the one quality of his poetry that is very rare in English verse: the comfortable ease, the relaxed poise, with which he treats the erotic. Cummings was, of course, always aware of the shock that he was creating with his references to sexual love. John Donne and even Robert Herrick are self-conscious by comparison. One would have to go back to Geoffrey Chaucer for a similar natural acceptance of sensuality. Certainly Blackburn's stature as an American poet is enhanced, not diminished, by such a foreign influence as Provençal poetry. A melting-pot culture remains vital by renewing component cultures latent in its native tradition, a program that Pound, as well as Eliot, followed.

As Blackburn deliberately takes his place in the tradition of poetry from the Middle Ages on through his work with the troubadours, so he openly acknowledges a similar tradition of modern poetry by occasionally parodying or quoting poets of the immediate past, including Pound, Williams, Eliot, Robert Frost, Walt Whitman, William Butler Yeats, and Gerard Manley Hopkins.

This inclusive view of the modern poetic tradition is indicative of the richness of Blackburn's own poetry: its technical innovations with spatial form, sound and rhythm, and diction; its thematic and emotional range; and its ability to perceive, in the immediate and the personal, the general and the universal. Blackburn's verse is always grounded in private experience, yet it expresses the common concerns of humanity. He is able to structure the immediate without violating it, whereas others of his generation were only able, or simply content, to record. Thus, poetry for him is never therapy through confession, or a notebook of fragments from his reading, or a self-absorbed diary. When one speaks of significant postwar poets, one cannot with any justice mention any one of his contemporaries, no matter how well-respected at the present time, without mentioning Blackburn's name in the same breath.

BIOGRAPHY

Paul Blackburn was the son of the poet Frances Frost. Having been reared in Vermont, New Hampshire, South Carolina, and New York City, he attended New York University and the University of Wisconsin, where he received a B.A. degree in 1950. While at Wisconsin, Blackburn began corresponding with Ezra Pound, whose poetry he admired, and then occasionally visited Pound in St. Elizabeths Hospital, Washington, D.C. At Pound's suggestion, Blackburn began writing to Robert Creeley, who eventually published his poems in the *Black Mountain Review* and put him in touch with Cid Corman, who, in turn, published Blackburn's poems in *Origin* (a quarterly for the creative) and introduced him to Charles Olson, though Blackburn was never to study or teach at Black Mountain College. Pound also encouraged Blackburn's interest in the troubadours, which began when Blackburn encountered Pound's own quotations and imitations of

Provençal verse in *Personae* (1909) and the *Cantos* (1925-1972). In 1953, Blackburn published a small volume of translations through Creeley's Divers Press, the early *Proensa*, that earned him a Fulbright scholarship in 1954 to do research in Provençal poetry at the University of Toulouse in southern France, and he returned as *lecteur américain* the following year. He remained in Europe, principally in Málaga, Spain, and Bañalbufar, Mallorca, with Winifred McCarthy, whom he married in 1954, until 1957, when they returned to New York.

For the next ten years in New York City, in addition to writing and translating, Blackburn worked to establish a sense of community among the poets centered on St. Mark's Church in the Bowery. As well as offering help and encouragement, he organized and tape-recorded weekly poetry readings at the church. His efforts eventually led to the funded Poetry Project at St. Mark's in 1967. He also conducted a "Poet's Hour" on radio station WBAI. In 1963, he was divorced from his first wife and married Sara Golden; that marriage also ended in divorce in 1967, around the time that he was poet-in-residence at the Aspen Writers' Workshop in Colorado. That year also saw the appearance of his most widely circulated collection of poems, *The Cities*, published by Grove Press. Toward the end of 1967, he returned to Europe on a Guggenheim Fellowship, where he met Joan Miller, whom he married in 1968, and with whom he had a son. In September, 1970, he assumed a teaching position at the state college in Cortland, New York, where he died of cancer the following year.

ANALYSIS

Because Paul Blackburn is a poet of immediate observation and spontaneous response, his poetry thrives on particular places. His work, however, is not rooted in a specific geographical location that is transformed into a frame of mind, as is Frost's New England, or that is elevated to a latter-day myth, as is Williams's Paterson. Blackburn's places are the environments in which he happens to be: a town plaza, a boat at sea, a wooded hill, a city street, a subway car, a tavern, a luncheonette, a kitchen, a bedroom. He would often generate a poem by immersing himself in his surroundings until man and place were one, the identification stirring in him a particular thought or emotion, a combination of his mood and the suggestion of that particular rush of outside activity. Although his thematic preoccupations and technical goals remain fairly uniform throughout the course of his work, he did tend to prefer certain themes and to express certain emotions through certain techniques when he was living in European cities, and others when he was living in New York. Perhaps because he could see sheep grazing in the town square in Málaga or burros passing through Bañalbufar, when Blackburn was living in Europe he often considered the relationship between humans and nature through such concepts as freedom, mutability, eternity, and religiosity; love is portrayed as sentiment. Perhaps because his mind was on the troubadours, living with his hands on their manuscripts near Provence, Blackburn's European poetry tends to be meditative and pensive, the soundplay more melodious, the language more metaphorical. When he was living in New York, in the densely populated modern city, where concrete substituted for grass, Blackburn focused on interpersonal relations, including friendship, complicity, estrangement, and anonymity; love becomes erotic energy. In a city whose traffic rushes and whose subway rumbles and roars, Blackburn's poetry becomes more immediate and involved, conversational and wtty; sound is orchestrated for dissonance; metaphor, if resorted to at all, is unexpected, shocking; but the occasional use of symbol is retained.

EARLY SELECTED Y MAS

Blackburn is best read, then, chronologically, according to the place where he was living and writing. The dates given for the poems gathered in *Early Selected y Mas*, which includes the small, early books of limited circulation, makes such a reading possible for most of the first half of his work. In the poetry written or set in Europe between 1954 and 1958, Blackburn explores the existence of humans as creatures both fundamentally part of nature, with physicality and sensuousness, and separate through consciousness, will, and ephemerality.

In "A Permanence," Blackburn uses the seven-star constellation the bear to present nature as an eternal force separate from humanity: The bear "is there/ even in the day, when we do not see him." Nevertheless, humans cannot help responding to nature's perpetually changing life, being natural themselves. The lovers in "The Hour," for example, are "hungering" not only for food but also for the first sign of spring after a long winter: They sit "listening to the warm gnawing in their stomach/ the warm wind/ through the blossoms blowing." These lines exemplify the rich grammatical ambiguity made possible by spatial form: The appetites for food and for seasonal renewal are associated not only by repetition of the adjective "warm" but also by the possibility that "wind" as well as "gnawing" can be the object of the preposition "to," modifying "listening."

Separation from and unity with nature are confronted simultaneously in "Light." Initially, humanity and sea are only linguistically related through a simile; day moves inevitably into night, but an effort of the will is required for human action: "My thought drifts like the sea/ No grip between it and my act." By the end of the poem, however, the dark, drifting sea complements and then merges with the poet's gloomy mood. The assertion is metaphoric, but the poet's mind and his perceptual experience have indeed become one: "The sea flashes up in the night/ to touch and darken my sea."

"MESTROVIĆ AND THE TREES"

From this contemplation of the relationship between humans and nature, a religious sense develops, as expressed in "Mestrović and the Trees." For Blackburn, a feeling for the divine is unavoidable: "You never get passed the wood" where "The beginnings of things are shown." Religion for him is a matter of origins, and this poem is Blackburn's own version of the cosmological argument. From humanity's own existence, which cannot be denied—"Yes we are"—he moves back to origins—"Our mother and father," and by implication, Adam and Eve—to their origin, in nature, through God: "So these trees stand there, our/ image, the god's image." The trees "stand there/ naked" just as humans enter the world, their unity with nature now binding them also to the divine. By using the lower case for God and preceding his name with the definite article, Blackburn indicates that his religion is natural rather than orthodox. Although Blackburn is certain of the existence of the divine, its nature remains an enigma.

"HOW TO GET THROUGH REALITY"

This mystery, essential to Blackburn's religious experience, is in itself sacred for him and not to be violated by forms and formulas that he considers to be ultimately human fabrications, at best mere approximations of the divine. In "How to Get Through Reality," Blackburn insists on the separation, epistemological despite a metaphysical complicity, between the temporal and the divine, that is, "Those who work with us . . . who create us from our stone." An impenetrable glass wall separates the two realms, and he celebrates the divine only in the most general of ways, aesthetically: "Our beauty under glass is your reality, unreachable/ sliding our gift to you." The insistence on the unintelligibility of the divine is portrayed grammatically with a sentence that ends incompletely just at the point God is to be named: "Beauty is the daily renewal in the eyes of." Feeling, the basis of his perception of beauty, provides his only sense of the divine: "One could kick the glass out, no?/ No./ Pass through." Breaking the glass, transcending the temporal, for direct communication with and precise knowledge of the supernatural is impossible; only intimations, illuminations, can pass through the transparency of the glass. A similar warning is sounded in "Suspension," where the poet's vision of the moon is obscured by tree branches: "—Shall I climb up and get it down?/ —No. Leave it alone."

"RITUAL I"

As a consequence, Blackburn's attitude toward orthodox religious forms—language, ceremony, observance—is ambivalent. "Ritual I" presents a religious "Procession," as it moves "with candles" from the church through the various streets of the Spanish town to the chant of "Ave Maria." Because the "fiesta" does not "celebrate," but rather "reenacts" the "event," *time emerges.* Blackburn is observing that the religious ritual is "a timeless gesture" because its origin cannot be traced or dated, because it has been perpetuated throughout the course of history, and because it creates anew the event each time it is performed. Through this persistence of religion, this infinite renewal, this timelessness, human time is made possible: The participants too are renewed along with the ritual. Blackburn continues, however, to enlarge the concept of ritual to encompass secular as well as religious life. Midway through the poem a "lady tourist/ . . . joined the procession"; she appeared an "anomaly": "Instead of a rosary, carried/ a white pocketbook." After this secular irregularity in the religious ceremony, Blackburn immediately introduces what appear to be irregularities of subject in a poem describing a sacred ritual: He tells the reader that he rises everyday "in the dawn light"; he eats "Meat every Thursday/ when the calf/ is killed"; he gets "Mail from the bus at 4:30/ fresh milk at 5." What Blackburn is implying through these juxtapositions is that our everyday lives are composed of rituals that renew life on a daily basis, that make life itself possible. The "german anthropologist," then, "her poor self at the end of the line," is really not at a terminal point; for life, like this yearly ritual, is a perpetual process of renewal, a series of rebirths: "End of a timeless act of the peoples of the earth," hardly an end at all.

"RITUAL IV"

In poetry written after Blackburn's return to New York in 1957, the religious and the secular merge for him to the point where his rituals consist entirely of various activities repeated on a daily basis. Religion becomes the celebration of life, since the divine is immanent in the world itself. In "Ritual IV," for example, Blackburn juxtaposes a description of plants growing in his kitchen with a reenactment of a Saturday morning breakfast with his wife, in order to express the unity of all living things. "You sit here smiling at/ me and the young plants," as the "beams" of sunlight reveal the "dust" that "float[s]" from the plants to them. The poet concludes: "Everything/ grows,/ and rests."

"LINES, TREES, AND WORDS"

Having united the sacred and profane to such a degree, Blackburn occasionally grows impatient with orthodox ceremony. In "Lines, Trees, and Words," walking through a park and overhearing children singing a hymn off-key, a friend observes how they are mutilating "it." Blackburn, however, willfully misunderstands the referent of the pronoun to be the divine and replies, "Don't we all." Any verbal attempt to embody the spiritual will result in such travesty: "Give the child words, give him/ words, he will use them." Characteristically, the poem ends with the preferred indefinite, natural, religious note: "How the trees hang down from the sky."

At times, Blackburn will even imply that the more Puritanical strain in orthodox religion might very well obstruct his and others' more spontaneous celebration of the divine through joyous living, as in "Ash Wednesday, 1965."

"THE PURSE SEINE"

Most of the poetry that Blackburn wrote between 1958 and 1967 had New York City for its setting and focused intimately on human psychology: the ways in which people relate to one another, how they react to the world in which they find themselves, and how they regard their own personalities and bodies. In Blackburn's love poems of this period, two symbols, fishing nets and the sea, continually recur, helping him to express his vision of love as unavoidable and overwhelming, as the persistent tide of the sea, and therefore frightening, threatening, as the confining fishing net, at first unnoticed. Love for Blackburn is a force that one can resist only for so long; then one gives in wholeheartedly, though with trepidation. "The Purse Seine" accumulates a number of aquatic images that express this ambivalence: what "gulls" "do that looks so beautiful, is/ hunt"; at once they are "crying freedom, crying carrion"; the eye of the gull, merging with that of his lover, "frightens," for both are the "beautiful killer"; "the net/ is tight," and then "The purse closes" and "we drown/ in sight of/ I love you and you love me." In "Park Poem," the poet reels from "the first shock of leaves their alliance with love"—the complicity of nature in romance. "How to Get up off It" is a contemporaneous poem that juxtaposes several random events ultimately related to the persistence of love in nature, and thus in human beings. The poet begins the poem by recalling a mountain climber's words: "Am I ready for this mountain?" As "they go up," so does the poet climb love's mountain, sitting with his second wife in front of the Public Library, next to a girl writing a letter to her boyfriend; they are passed by a couple holding hands who wave to them and then witness a mating dance: "The pigeons never seem to tire/ of the game," and neither do people, as the events recorded in the poem demonstrate.

"CALL IT THE NET" AND "THE NET OF MOON"

Depending on his mood, Blackburn can portray love as simply the drive of blind passion that results in a loss of freedom through its satisfaction. In such poems as "Call It the Net," love is a "silken trap . . . the net of lust." In "The Sea and the Shadow," that "damned sea" of sexuality will drive him back to his lover despite his anger at her; the waves become the rhythm of the sexual act: "I will come into your belly and make it a sea rolling against me." At other times, however, sexual love will be a joyous occasion, as in "lower case poem": "of that spring tide i sing/ clutched to one another." At such times, as Blackburn explains in "The Net of Moon," the lovers have achieved a union of the physical and the spiritual, "a just balance be-/ tween the emotion and the motion of the wave on the bay," lust being transformed into love. What Blackburn finds most striking, in the end, is the inevitable nature of both sexuality and love. On seeing a pretty girl on the street in "The Tides," the poet exclaims: "Terrible indeed is the house of heaven in the mind." After recalling the act of love, "its flood/ its ebb," the poet can only conclude: "What the man must do/ what the woman must do."

EROTIC POEMS

Blackburn accepts, as a natural dimension of human relations, this constant attraction between men and women, which exists as much on the physical as on the emotional level. Rather than trying to resist or repress the erotic impulse, Blackburn celebrates it in a series of erotic poems unique in the language. Never vulgar, tawdry, or exhibitionistic, they involve a drama of emotion as well as of desire, for Blackburn portrays the woman as well as the man being caught in the erotic moment and enjoying it with equal relish. This mutual, if often covert, complicity results in a sense of the erotic as all-pervasive and joyous rather than predatory or compromising. These poems are usually contemporaneous with the events and feelings they describe and involve witty shifts of tone through incongruous diction, ranging from colloquial ("all very chummy") to tabloid cliché ("the hotbed of assignation") to scientific jargon ("hypotenuse," "trajectory").

Two of his best erotic poems appear in *Brooklyn-Manhattan Transit,* for the subway is one of the more likely places to afford the modern troubadour an opportunity to admire the feminine. In "The Once-Over," a pretty blond woman is being appreciated by the poet and the other riders of the car. According to the poet,

however, she is deliberately inviting their admiration: She is "standing/ tho there are seats"; "Only a stolid young man . . . does not know he is being assaulted"; "She has us and we her." In "Clickety-Clack," Blackburn is reading out loud a blatantly erotic passage from one of Lawrence Ferlinghetti's poems on the subway car, much to the amusement (and arousal) of a young lady, despite her frown, as the negative prefix split by the line ending from the rest of its root word indicates: She "began to stare dis-/ approvingly and wiggle." "The Slogan" records the provocative stroll of a "wellknit blonde in a blue knit dress" past a group of utility workers, Blackburn describing her walk with terms borrowed from physics. "Hands" portrays a girl entering her room and going to open a window with her boyfriend in pursuit, "bringing/ one thing up, & another down." Even in "The Assassination of President McKinley," the opportunistic proprietor of the drapery shop is not the only one who enjoys "the last rite/ for the assassinated Mr. McKinley."

AGAINST THE SILENCES

Blackburn's one long cycle of poems on love, published posthumously as *Against the Silences,* was written between 1963 and 1967, and deals with the dissolution of his second marriage. The cycle moves from uneasy marital contentment ("knowing we love one another/ sometime," from "The Second Message"), to the beginning of estrangement ("the thought dissolves & only/ fact remains," from "Slippers, Anyone?"), to argument resulting from a misunderstanding of the husband's deepest personal allegiances ("The Value"), to the wife's infidelity ("What Is It, Love?"), and finally to divorce ("Scenario for a Walk-On," in which the poet depicts the separation as the ending of a film). The sequence recalls George Meredith's *Modern Love* (1862), a series of fifty sixteen-line sonnets portraying the psychological dilemmas of an unhappy married couple through dramatic monologue or silent rumination, written the year after Meredith's divorce from his first wife. Because Blackburn's poems focus specifically on the intimate details of his own marriage, automatically recorded in the contemporaneous open-form poem of immediate experience, his cycle has somewhat greater emotional range and depth than Meredith's, which is a more conscious attempt to generalize from personal experience about the condition of romantic love in the modern world, as the title suggests.

In *Against the Silences*, the complexity of the beleaguered husband's feelings is captured in poems that often portray several conflicting emotions at once: confusion, frustration, pain, humiliation, anger, disgust, fear, loneliness. The subtle role that sexual passion assumes in the relationship is also treated. In the early "So Deep We Never Got," the poet wishes his wife to make love to him as a reassurance of her affection: Resorting to a favorite symbol, he needs to be with her "chest-deep in the surf/ and those waves coming and coming." In "Monday, Monday," however, the husband uses an offer of sex in an attempt to keep his wife from meeting her lover, but the response remains the same throughout the poem: "away,/ her body pushed me away." In this sequence, Blackburn's idea of love as a net to which one deliberately surrenders oneself attains its most explicit statement. Although staying with his wife was always an "act of will" ("The Second Message"), "reasons of choice" are "so obscure" that the process of choice can never ensure happiness; he can only "choose and fear and live it thru" ("Accident"). The result is equally ironic: The possessor of another in love becomes "possessed" by that very love ("The Price").

ELEGIES

If Blackburn adds a new genre to English-language verse, or revives one long defunct, through his erotic poems he contributes to an ongoing tradition with his elegies, which he composed throughout his career. In "The Mint Quality" (1961), the poet attempts to "Sing/ straight as I can" about the death of a vivacious young woman by first giving the details of her automobile accident in France and then presenting her monologue to her friends from the other side of death. The poem becomes ironic when Christiane assures them that *"next time"* she will *"wait til the middle of life/ know what you know/ just to understand."* The poem began with the poet, at middle age, professing his complete incomprehension of the cycle of life and death: "two friends'/ wives/ are near their term and large./ . . . One/ girl is dead. No choice."

THE REARDON POEMS

The Reardon Poems is a sequence of seven poems written in memory of Blackburn's friend Robert Reardon: "Bluegrass" presents the unsuccessful operation to save his life; "The Writer" tells of Reardon's vocation, novelist; "The Husband" treats his relationship with his wife and presents her disorientation and loneliness; "Sixteen Sloppy Haiku" are brief glimpses or thoughts of Reardon's last days of life; "The List" consists of Reardon's last rites, as specified by him before his death; and "St. Mark's-in-the-Bouwerie" is an elegy proper on death, its inexplicability amidst life ("When there's nothing anyone can do,/ reality/ comes on fast or slow"). "Seventeen Nights Later at McSorley's" is the epilogue, employing recorded conversation with great thematic effect; Blackburn is speaking to Reardon's former roommate in the hospital:

> You won't see him again, sez I
> "No?"
> No. You're well again? Mazeltov.
> "No?"
> No.

Perhaps Blackburn's finest elegy is "December Journal: 1968," on the death of his third wife's father, in which practically all his formal poetic resources come into play. The poem begins with the telephone call informing them of the death and moves through grief and tears to the wake and funeral in a passage in which breakfast and the Eucharist are superimposed; to a meditation on the mystery of life and death, creation and destruction, inspired by an open journal on alchemy lying before the poet; and finally to lovemaking and a renewal of domestic patterns ("'You have to get up and move the car.'/ I existed again, I/ was married to my wife!"). Inspired by his alchemical reading, the poet realizes that life mysteriously renews itself within materials that compose rock; that is, life dwells in and is sustained by essentially inanimate matter, a theme first heard in "How to Get Through Reality." This miracle, and the miracle of the living child in his wife's womb, has by the end of the poem put him at ease.

OTHER MAJOR WORKS

NONFICTION: "Das Kennerbuch," 1953; "Writing for the Ear," 1960; "The American Duende," 1962; "The Grinding Down," 1963.

TRANSLATIONS: *Proensa*, 1953; *Poem of the Cid,*

1966; *End of the Game, and Other Stories*, 1967 (of Julio Cortázar); *Hunk of Skin*, 1968 (of Pablo Picasso); *Cronopios and Famas*, 1969 (of Cortázar); *Peire Vidal*, 1972; *The Treasure of the Muleteer, and Other Spanish Tales*, 1974 (of Antonio Jimenez-Landi); *Guillem De Poitu: His Eleven Extant Poems*, 1976; *Proensa: An Anthology of Troubadour Poetry*, 1978; *Lorca/Blackburn: Poems of Federico García Lorca Chosen and Translated by Paul Blackburn*, 1979.

BIBLIOGRAPHY

Malkoff, Karl. *Crowell's Handbook of Contemporary American Poetry*. New York: Thomas Y. Crowell, 1973. The entry on Blackburn lists him not only as a Black Mountain poet but also as a Projectivist, although like most Projectivists, his poetry is individualistic. Mentions his long sojourns abroad and discusses two of his works, *The Cities* and *The Nets*. Other than some insightful comments about Projectivist poetry—for example, that there is no real distinction between the inner and outer world—there is little noteworthy criticism here.

Marowski, Daniel G., and Roger Matuz, eds. *Contemporary Literary Criticism*. Vol. 43. Detroit: Gale Research, 1987. Lists Blackburn as a noted translator, scholar, and poet, whose poetry combines structural experimentation with colloquial forms. This combination creates a "visual, aural, and psychological reading experience." Gathers together some fine reviews of Blackburn's work, in particular critical commentary of his most widely acclaimed work, *The Journals*. Also notes that since the posthumous publication of *The Collected Poems of Paul Blackburn*, his verse has attracted a wider audience and has undergone critical reevaluation.

Rosenthal, M. L. Review of *The Cities*. *Poetry* 114 (May, 1969): 129-130. Comments on Blackburn's love of American lingo and his emphasis on the quality of movement, both of which lend his poems qualities of "humor and sensuality." Appreciates Blackburn's focus on the process of the poet's involvement in the poem as a "disciplining subject of the poem, as well as its range in action."

Stephens, Michael. "Common Speech and Complex Forms." *The Nation* 223 (September 4, 1976): 189-190. Reviews *The Cities*, *The Journals*, and *Halfway down the Coast*, which he considers a suitable introduction to Blackburn. Notes that the possibility of death that Blackburn explores in *Halfway* becomes the reality of dying in *The Journals*. Commends Blackburn for his ability to appreciate "overheard cadences in common speech," which he says is indicative of Blackburn's love of people.

William Skaff

ROBERT BLY

Born: Madison, Minnesota; December 23, 1926

PRINCIPAL POETRY

The Lion's Tail and Eyes: Poems Written out of Laziness and Silence, 1962 (with James Wright and William Duffy)
Silence in the Snowy Fields, 1962
The Light Around the Body, 1967
The Teeth Mother Naked at Last, 1970
Jumping out of Bed, 1973
Sleepers Joining Hands, 1973
Old Man Rubbing His Eyes, 1974
Point Reyes Poems, 1974
The Morning Glory, 1975
This Body Is Made of Camphor and Gopherwood, 1977
This Tree Will Be Here for a Thousand Years, 1979
The Man in the Black Coat Turns, 1981
Out of the Rolling Ocean, and Other Love Poems, 1984
Loving a Woman in Two Worlds, 1985
Selected Poems, 1986
The Apple Found in the Plowing, 1989
What Have I Ever Lost by Dying: Collected Prose Poems, 1992
Meditations on the Insatiable Soul, 1994
Morning Poems, 1997
Eating the Honey of Words: New and Selected Poems, 1999
The Night Abraham Called to the Stars, 2001

My Sentence Was a Thousand Years of Joy, 2005
The Urge to Travel Long Distances, 2005
Reaching out to the World: New and Selected Prose Poems, 2009

OTHER LITERARY FORMS

Robert Bly has been a prolific critic, translator, and anthologist. His work in these areas complements his poetic accomplishments and was a significant influence on the internationalization of the literary community in the last third of the twentieth century. His most important works include translations of the poems of Georg Trakl, Juan Ramón Jiménez, Pablo Neruda, Tomas Tranströmer, Federico García Lorca, Jalāl al-Dīn Rūmī, Kabir, and Antonio Machado. He has also called attention to the work of other poets through anthologies: *News of the Universe: Poems of Twofold Consciousness* (1980), *The Winged Life: The Poetic Voice of Henry David Thoreau* (1986), *The Rag and Bone Shop of the Heart: Poems for Men* (1993), and *The Soul Is Here for Its Own Joy: Sacred Poems from Many Cultures* (1995).

Bly's writings about the practice of poetry have been published as *Leaping Poetry: An Idea with Poems and Translations* (1975) and *American Poetry: Wildness and Domesticity* (1990). His social criticism has ranged from *A Poetry Reading Against the Vietnam War* (1966; with David Ray) to *Iron John: A Book About Men* (1990), the best seller that became a primer for the men's movement of the 1990's. It was followed by similarly controversial studies, including *The Spirit Boy and the Insatiable Soul* (1994) and *The Sibling Society* (1996).

ACHIEVEMENTS

Robert Bly is the central poet of his generation. His wide-ranging achievements in poetry, criticism, and translation, as well as his work as editor and itinerant apologist for poetry and various social causes, have made him one of the most conspicuous, ubiquitous, and controversial poets in the United States since the mid-1960's. His significance and influence extend well beyond his own work.

Bly's various accomplishments have been rewarded by a Fulbright Fellowship for translation (1956-1957),

the Amy Lowell Traveling Fellowship (1964), two Guggenheim Fellowships (1965 and 1972), a Rockefeller Foundation grant (1967), and a National Institute of Arts and Letters Award (1966). In 1968, *The Light Around the Body*, his most controversial collection of poetry, won the National Book Award. Bly received the McKnight Distinguished Artist Award (2000) and the Minnesota Book Award (2002) for *The Night Abraham Called to the Stars*. In 2008, his poem "War and Childhood," won the Theodore Roethke Prize from *Poetry Northwest*.

BIOGRAPHY

Born in the small farming community of Madison, Minnesota, Robert Elwood Bly grew up, as he said, a "Lutheran Boy-god." He attended a one-room school in his early years. Upon graduation from high school, he enlisted in the U.S. Navy, where he first became interested in poetry. After the war, Bly enrolled at St. Olaf's College in Northfield, Minnesota, but after only one year there, he transferred to Harvard University. At Harvard, he read "the dominant books" of contemporary American poetry, associated with other young writers (among them John Ashbery, Frank O'Hara, Kenneth Koch, Adrienne Rich, and Donald Hall), worked on *The Harvard Advocate* (which he edited in his senior year), delivered the class poem, and graduated magna cum laude in 1950.

Having decided to be a poet and seeking solitude, Bly moved back to Minnesota; then, in 1951, still "longing for 'the depths,'" he moved to New York City, where he lived alone for several years, reading widely and writing his early poems. In 1953, he moved to Cambridge, Massachusetts, and in 1954 to Iowa City, where he enrolled in the creative writing program at the University of Iowa. His M.A. thesis consisted of a short collection of poems titled "Steps Toward Poverty and Death" (1956). Bly was married to Carolyn McLean in 1955, and in 1956, they moved to Oslo, Norway, via a Fulbright grant. In Norway, Bly sought out his family roots, read widely, and translated contemporary Norwegian poetry.

In 1957, back in Minnesota, living on the family farm, Bly continued his work as a translator. In 1958, he founded a magazine, *The Fifties* (which would become *The Sixties*, *The Seventies*, and *The Eighties*), in which he published his translations and early literary criticism. He did not publish his first book of poetry, "Poems for the Ascension of J. P. Morgan," but in 1962, he published two books: *The Lion's Tail and Eyes* (written with his friends James Wright and William Duffy), and *Silence in the Snowy Fields*, his first independent book of poetry.

By the mid-1960's, Bly was actively engaged in the anti-Vietnam War movement. He and David Ray formed a group called American Writers Against the Vietnam War, and they published an anthology titled *A Poetry Reading Against the Vietnam War* (1966). Bly attended draft card turn-ins, and he demonstrated at the Pentagon in 1967. When his second book of poems, *The Light Around the Body*—filled with his outspoken poems against the war—won the National Book Award in 1968, Bly donated the prize money to the draft resistance.

During the 1970's, Bly's interests and activities diversified considerably. He studied Sigmund Freud,

Robert Bly (©Jerry Bauer/Courtesy, HarperCollins)

Carl Jung, Eastern meditation, myths and fairy tales, philosophy, and psychology. He organized conferences on "Great Mother and New Father" culture and consciousness. Bly's poetry, social commentary, and literary criticism during this period reflected his wide-ranging interests. By this point in his career, he said, he believed that he had "gotten about half-way to the great poem."

In 1979, Bly and his wife of more than twenty-five years were divorced. In 1980, he was married to Ruth Ray; they moved to Moose Lake, Minnesota, and lived there for ten years before moving to Minneapolis in 1990.

During the 1980's and 1990's, Bly continued to work at a rapid pace, writing and publishing widely in several genres, translating, giving readings throughout the United States and overseas, and holding meetings and seminars for groups of women and men. His books during and since the 1980's document, as well as anything, the life and activities of this exceedingly visible and yet, ultimately, extremely private individual.

ANALYSIS

Since Robert Bly has habitually brought his wide-ranging interests in literary history, myth, fairy tales, philosophy, psychology, politics, social concerns, and poetry past and present into his own work, his poetry reflects these interests and is enriched by them. Furthermore, because he has been prolific and unsystematic, even at times seemingly self-contradictory, he is extremely difficult to categorize and analyze. Nevertheless, it is possible—indeed necessary—to consider Bly's poetry in terms of the series of various phases it has gone through. These phases, although they are also reflected in Bly's other writings and involvements, are most evident in his poetry.

SILENCE IN THE SNOWY FIELDS

Bly's first published book of poetry, *Silence in the Snowy Fields*, remains one of the best examples of his deepest obsession: the notion that a personal, private, almost mystical aura adheres to and inheres with the simplest things in the universe—old boards, for example, or a snowflake fallen into a horse's mane. These things, observed in the silence of contemplation and set down honestly and simply in poems, may, Bly believes, inform human beings anew of some sense of complicity, even communion, they have always had with the world, but have forgotten. Bly's focus has caused his work to be labeled Deep Image poetry. In a 1981 essay, "Recognizing Image as a Form of Intelligence," he explained the term's application to his work: "When a poet creates a true image, he is gaining knowledge; he is bringing up into consciousness a connection that has been largely forgotten." In this sense, these early poems provide the reader with the re-created experience of Bly's own epiphanic moments in the silences of "snowy fields," and they become his means of sharing such silences with his readers.

The epigraph to *Silence in the Snowy Fields*, "We are all asleep in the outward man," from the seventeenth century German mystic Jacob Boehme, points up both the structural and the thematic principles on which Bly builds his book. The three sections of the book suggest a literal and a mental journey. The second, central section, "Awakening," contains twenty-three of the forty-four poems in the book and serves as a structural and thematic transition from "Eleven Poems of Solitude," the first section, to the final section, "Silence on the Roads," which sends both book and reader, via the central "awakening," outward into the world. The solitude and contemplative silence of this first book, then, prepare both poet and reader for the larger world of Bly's work.

THE LIGHT AROUND THE BODY

The way the world impinges on private life is immediately evident in Bly's next book, *The Light Around the Body*. This is his most famous (or for some, most infamous) book. Like *Silence in the Snowy Fields*, *The Light Around the Body* shows the strong influence of Boehme (four of the five sections of the book have epigraphs from Boehme), especially in terms of the dichotomy of the inward and the outward person, the "two languages," one might argue, of Bly's first two books. If *Silence in the Snowy Fields* deals primarily with the inward being, clearly the focus of *The Light Around the Body* is on the outward being—here seen specifically in a world at war.

The Light Around the Body was published in the midst of the American obsession with the Vietnam War, and most of the poems in it are concerned with that war, directly or indirectly. The third section of the

book (following sections titled "The Two Worlds" and "The Various Arts of Poverty and Cruelty") is specifically titled "The Vietnam War." This is the most definitive, the most outspoken and condemnatory group of poems—by Bly or anyone else—on the war in Vietnam. Bly reserves his harshest criticism for American involvement in the war. He does not mince words, and he names names: "Men like [Dean] Rusk are not men:/ They are bombs waiting to be loaded in a darkened hangar" ("Asian Peace Offers Rejected Without Publication").

Perhaps the most famous poem Bly has written is also his most definitive criticism of the Vietnam War. In "Counting Small-Boned Bodies," the speaker of the poem has been charged with keeping the grisly count of war casualties to be reported on the evening news. Shocked by the mounting death tolls, he finds himself trying to imagine ways to minimize these terrifying statistics. The refrain that runs through the poem is, "If we could only make the bodies smaller." The implication is that if the bodies could be made smaller, then people might, through some insane logic, be able to argue the war away. Bly's poems in *The Light Around the Body* ensure that the war will never be forgotten or forgiven.

The last two sections of *The Light Around the Body* ("In Praise of Grief" and "A Body Not Yet Born") move back "inward" from the "outward" world of the war, just as the first two sections of the book had moved "outward" from the "inward" world of *Silence in the Snowy Fields*. Since the war, however, this new inward world can never again ignore or fail to acknowledge the outward world. Therefore, Bly writes "in praise of grief" as a way of getting through, psychologically speaking, both outward and inward conflicts.

The first three poems of the fourth section of the book define a progression back toward a place of rest, calm, peace. In the third poem, the body is described as "awakening" again and finding "nourishment" in the death scenes it has witnessed. Such a psychic regeneration, which parallels the inevitable regeneration of nature after a battle, is what is needed to repair the damage the war has done if people are to be restored to full human nature. Thus, in the final section of the book, although the new body is not yet fully born, it is moving toward birth, or rebirth.

Although *The Light Around the Body* will no doubt be most often remembered for its overt antiwar poems, from the point of view of Bly's developing poetic philosophy, it is best seen as a description of the transition from the outer world back into the inner world.

SLEEPERS JOINING HANDS

The psychological movement first suggested and then begun in *The Light Around the Body* is followed further inward by Bly's next important book, *Sleepers Joining Hands*. This book contains three distinctly different sections. The first section consists of a series of short lyric poems. Beginning with "Six Winter Privacy Poems," it comes to a climax with a long poem, "The Teeth Mother Naked at Last," Bly's final, psychological response to the war in Vietnam.

The second section of *Sleepers Joining Hands* consists of an essay in which Bly documents many of the philosophical ideas and psychological themes with which he has long been obsessed and which he has addressed (and will continue to address) both in his poetry and in his criticism. Bly here summarizes his thinking in terms of Jungian psychology, father and mother consciousness, the theory of the three brains, and other ideas that he groups together as "mad generalizations." This essay, although it is far from systematic, remains an important summary of the sources of many of Bly's most important poems and ideas.

Thus, although *Sleepers Joining Hands* does not contain Bly's most important poetry, it does deal with most of the elements of the literary theory behind that poetry, and it is an extremely important book. In the central essay, Bly describes in detail the way in which "mother consciousness" has come to replace "father consciousness" during the last several centuries. Four "force fields" make up the Great Mother (or Magna Mater), which, according to Bly, is now "moving again in the psyche." The Teeth Mother, one of these force fields, attempts to destroy psychic life. She has been most evident in the Vietnam War and has caused the "inward" harm that that war has brought to the world. "The Teeth Mother Naked at Last," the climactic poem in the first section of *Sleepers Joining Hands*, like the earlier antiwar poems in *The Light Around the Body*, describes the conditions of psychic reality in terms of the presence of the Teeth Mother. It argues that once

the Teeth Mother is acknowledged (made "naked at last"), she can be dealt with and responded to, and then the outward physical world can be effectively reconnected with the inward psychic or spiritual world.

"Sleepers Joining Hands," the long title poem that constitutes the collection's third section, is an elaborate and challenging poem, a kind of dream journal or a journey, with overt Jungian trappings. Thematically, it shifts back and forth between dreamed and awakened states. These thematic shifts are evidenced in the structure of the poem. The poem as a whole is a kind of religious quest based in large part on the Prodigal Son story—one of the great paradigms of the journey motif in Western culture. At the end of the poem, bringing to climax so many of his themes, Bly provides "An Extra Joyful Chorus for Those/ Who Have Read This Far" in which "all the sleepers in the world join hands."

THE MORNING GLORY

The next several books in Bly's canon consist of prose poems. Bly believes that when a culture begins to lose sight of specific goals, it moves dangerously close to abstraction, and that such abstraction is reflected in the poetry of the time. Prose poetry, then, often appears as a way of avoiding too much abstraction. Whether this theory holds up historically or not, it certainly can be made to apply in Bly's case, even if only after the fact—the theory having been invented to explain the practice. Certainly, there is ample reason to think that Bly believed that his own work, influenced by the events the world was witnessing, was moving dangerously toward "abstraction," perhaps most conspicuously so in *Sleepers Joining Hands*. For whatever reason, then, Bly turned, in the middle of his career, to the genre of the prose poem. His prose poems of this period are extremely strong work, arguably some of his strongest poetry.

The two most important collections of prose poems are *The Morning Glory* (which includes as its central section the ten-poem sequence "Point Reyes Poems," published separately the year before, and one of the most powerful sequences of poems Bly has written) and *This Body Is Made of Camphor and Gopherwood*. All these prose poems move "deeply into the visible," as the old occult saying Bly quotes as epigraph to *The Morning Glory* demands, and they are poems written "in a low voice to someone he is sure is listening," as Bly suggested they should be in his essay "What the Prose Poem Carries with It" (1977).

The Morning Glory, like *Silence in the Snowy Fields*, contains forty-four poems. It suggests of a new beginning in Bly's career. These poems follow a rather typical pattern. They begin in offhanded ways, frequently with the speaker alone outdoors, prepared, through his openness to all possibilities, for whatever he may find there. The poems, then, are journeys; they move from the known to the unknown. Even so, what can be learned from them is often difficult to analyze, especially since Bly frequently only suggests what it is or might be. Indeed, often it seems to be something that the body comes to know and only later—if at all—the mind comprehends. In this sense these are poems of preparation, and they frequently imply apocalyptic possibilities.

The Morning Glory ends with several poems that describe transformations. One of the most important of these, "Christmas Eve Service at Midnight at St. Michael's," involves the personal life of the poet, who, six months after his only brother has been killed in an automobile accident, attends a Christmas Eve service with his parents. He and his parents take Communion together and hear the Christian message. Coming so soon after his brother's death, however, the message is "confusing," since the poet knows that "we take our bodies with us when we go." The poem ends in a reverie of transfiguration in which a man (both brother and Christ), with a chest wound, flies out and off over the water like a large bird.

THIS BODY IS MADE OF CAMPHOR AND GOPHERWOOD

The basic "religious" theme begun in *The Morning Glory* is continued in *This Body Is Made of Camphor and Gopherwood*. Here Bly writes overtly religious meditations, thus picking up again the aura of the sacred that has been important in his work since the beginning. Indeed, this book immediately reminds the reader of *Silence in the Snowy Fields*, both thematically and in terms of Bly's basic source material.

There are twenty poems in *This Body Is Made of Camphor and Gopherwood*; they are divided into two thematic units. The first ten poems describe, often

through dreams, visions, or dream-visions, "what is missing." Not surprisingly, given this theme, Bly frequently uses the metaphor of sleep and awakening. Indeed, the first poem in the book begins, "When I wake." This awakening is both a literal and an imaginative or metaphoric awakening, and it signals at the outset the book's chief concern.

The second section of the book is filled with intensely heightened, almost ecstatic, visionary poems. The crucial transitional poems in *This Body Is Made of Camphor and Gopherwood*—which is itself a crucial transition in Bly's canon—are "Walking to the Next Farm" and "The Origin of the Praise of God." "Walking to the Next Farm" describes the culmination of the transition "this body" has been going through as the poet, his eyes wild, feels "as if a new body were rising" within him. This new body and the energy it contains are further described and defined in the other central poem, "The Origin of the Praise of God." It begins with exactly the same words that begin several other poems in this book: "My friend, this body." This poem, in the words of Ralph J. Mills, Jr., "a visionary hymn to the body, . . . dramatizes [the] experience of the inner deity" and thus is the paradigm of the entire prose-poem sequence. By the end of the book, this visionary, mystical, yet still fully physical body is finally fully formed and is "ready to sing" both the poems already heard and the poems ahead.

THIS TREE WILL BE HERE FOR A THOUSAND YEARS

This Tree Will Be Here for a Thousand Years is a second collection of "snowy fields" poems. Bly said that it should be understood as a companion volume to *Silence in the Snowy Fields*. In this sense, then, *This Tree Will Be Here for a Thousand Years* is a specific, overt attempt on Bly's part to return to his beginnings. Just as it is a return, however, it is also a new beginning in the middle of his career. Bly is clearly a poet obsessed with a need for constant renewal, and in many ways each of his books, although taking a different direction, also retraces each earlier journey from a different vantage point.

Perhaps it is not surprising that, although *This Tree Will Be Here for a Thousand Years* is a new beginning for Bly, it is also a darker beginning, a darker journey than the journey he took in *Silence in the Snowy Fields*. Here the journey envisions its end. This, then, is the book of a man facing his mortality, his death, and walking confidently toward it. As Bly puts it in one of these poems, "there are eternities near." At the same time, there is the inevitable paradox that poems outlive the poet who has written them—and, thus, even poems that speak of death outlive the death of their speaker.

THE MAN IN THE BLACK COAT TURNS

Two later books may be seen as companions to each other: *The Man in the Black Coat Turns* and *Loving a Woman in Two Worlds*. Like *This Tree Will Be Here for a Thousand Years*, these books circle back to Bly's beginnings at the same time that they set out on new journeys. Furthermore, these books are among the most personal and private he has published, and thus they are particularly immediate and revealing.

The Man in the Black Coat Turns is divided into three sections, the central section, as in *The Morning Glory* and *This Body Is Made of Camphor and Gopherwood*, being made up of prose poems. The prose poems here, however, are different from their predecessors in being much more clearly related to Bly's personal experiences; as he says in the first of them, "Many times in poems I have escaped—from myself. . . . Now more and more I long for what I cannot escape from" ("Eleven O'Clock at Night").

More than anything else, the poems in *The Man in the Black Coat Turns* are poems about men. The dominant theme of the book is the father-son relationship. This theme and its association with the book's title is immediately, and doubly, announced at the outset of the book, in the first two poems, "Snowbanks North of the House" and "For My Son, Noah, Ten Years Old," as Bly works the lines of relationship through the generations of his own family: from his father to himself as son, then, as father, through himself to his own son, Noah. The third poem, "The Prodigal Son," places the personal family references into a larger context by relating them to the father and son in the New Testament parable. In the final poem in this first section of the book, "Mourning Pablo Neruda," Bly extends the father-son relationship again—this time to include one of his own important poetic "father figures," Pablo Neruda, a poet he has often translated.

The final section of *The Man in the Black Coat Turns* draws all these themes together in "The Grief of Men." This poem is clearly the climactic thesis piece for the whole book. There are, however, a number of important poems grouped together in this last section: "Words Rising," "A Meditation on Philosophy," "My Father's Wedding," "Fifty Males Sitting Together," "Crazy Carlson's Meadow," and "Kneeling Down to Look into a Culvert." In the last of these poems, via the account of a symbolic, ritualized sacrificial death, the poet completes his preparations for another new life.

LOVING A WOMAN IN TWO WORLDS

The poems of *Loving a Woman in Two Worlds* are, for the most part, short—almost half of them contain fewer than eight lines, and eleven of them are only four lines long. Technically speaking, however, this book contains poems in most of the forms and with most of the themes Bly has worked in and with throughout his career. In this sense, the collection is rather a tour de force. Many of these poems of *Loving a Woman in Two Worlds* are love poems, and some of them are quite explicitly sexual. The book can be read in terms of the stages of a love relationship. These are poems that focus on the female, on the male and female together, and on the way the man and the woman together share "a third body" beyond themselves, a body they have made "a promise to love."

This book thus charts another version of the "body not yet born" journey with which Bly began his poetry. In the final poem in *Loving a Woman in Two Worlds*, Bly, speaking not only to one individual, but also to all of his readers, writes, "I love you with what in me is unfinished.// . . . with what . . . is still/ changing."

SELECTED POEMS

In *Selected Poems*, in addition to poems from all of Bly's previous major collections (some of the poems have been revised, in some cases extensively), he has included some early, previously uncollected poems. A brief essay introduces each of the sectional groupings of this book. *Selected Poems*, then, is a compact, convenient collection, and it succinctly represents Bly in the many individual phases of his work.

MORNING POEMS

Bly's later collections continue to develop, without any loss of power, his distinctive vision and manner.

Morning Poems is something of a departure, revealing a rich vein of humor and growing out of the discipline of writing a poem a day. These poems capture the speaker's amazement at newness, the splendor of re-awakening, but they also do their share of mourning. In an unexpected and powerful sequence, Bly presents an imagined interchange with Wallace Stevens, a somewhat surprising father figure for Bly.

THE NIGHT ABRAHAM CALLED TO THE STARS

In *The Night Abraham Called to the Stars*, Bly employs the leaps of the ghazal, a poetic form developed in Persia and Arabia in the seventh century in which each stanza exists as an independent poem. At once seemingly and simultaneously opened to everything and closed upon themselves, these poems, with their leaping shifts of focus, underscore the great range of Bly's curiosity, his reasonable argument against reason, his quest for a mystical simplicity and unity that does not deny the power of the particular. Biblical allusions permeate this collection, as do historical references and legends. As ever, Bly oscillates between the generic and the generative.

MY SENTENCE WAS A THOUSAND YEARS OF JOY

My Sentence Was a Thousand Years of Joy continues Bly's exploration of the ghazal. The ghazal consists of a series of seemingly discontinuous tercets that thematically turn the real into the surreal and often conflate the inward world of consciousness with elements of the outward world by forcing them to collide or collapse into one another. The poem concludes with a moment of insight or illumination. Since, traditionally, the poet's name is mentioned at the end of a ghazal (usually in the penultimate line), the illumination that the poem elicits provides a eureka moment for the poet and for the reader simultaneously. As such, the ghazal, with its series of statements and questions—which often enough seem to be a series of non sequiturs—is an almost inevitable form for Bly. Indeed, it would seem to be the natural outgrowth of the kind of "leaping" poetry that has been his most conspicuous trademark since the beginning of his career.

My Sentence Was a Thousand Years of Joy consists of forty-eight ghazals, each made up of six tercets. Keeping to the tradition of the ghazal, Bly includes his own name (typically at the outset of the final tercet) in one third of these poems. In addition to satisfying the demands of the ghazal, several of the poems also make use of conspicuous patterns of repetition. For instance, each tercet of "The Blind Tobit" ends with the phrase "so many times," while in "Growing Wings," nine of the lines (exactly one half of the poem) begin with the phrase "It's all right."

Bly weaves references to numerous literary and historical figures through these poems. There are explicit references to Plato, Paul Cézanne, Neruda, Anna Akhmatova, Freud, Thoreau, Frederick Douglass, Rembrandt, Johannes Brahms, Søren Kierkegaard, Franz Kafka, Herman Melville, Johann Sebastian Bach and Robinson Jeffers, as well as many others. It is as if Bly wishes to include the whole of the world in this book and to stress the universality of these otherwise seemingly personal and private poems.

Ultimately, however, the vivid metaphors and all the allusions serve to support Bly's overarching theme of the transience of life and the need for joy even in the midst of the pain and pitfalls of existence. This theme is perhaps made most obvious in two poems ("Brahms" and "Stealing Sugar from the Castle"), both of which directly allude to a well-known passage in Saint Bede the Venerable's *Ecclesiastical History of the English People* (731). In it, Bede compares human life to the flight of a sparrow through a hall during a wintery day. The bird flies in at one door and out another, experiencing only momentary comfort and safety from the winter's storm before it vanishes into the unknown from whence it came. In these short lyrics, Bly extends the "brief moment" of the ghazal to create a "sentence" that becomes the "thousand years of joy" alluded to both in his title and in the final line of the book.

OTHER MAJOR WORKS

NONFICTION: *Leaping Poetry: An Idea with Poems and Translations*, 1975; *Talking All Morning*, 1980; *American Poetry: Wildness and Domesticity*, 1990; *Iron John: A Book About Men*, 1990; *The Spirit Boy and the Insatiable Soul*, 1994; *The Sibling Society*, 1996; *The Maiden King: The Reunion of Masculine and Feminine*, 1998 (with Marion Woodman).

TRANSLATIONS: *Twenty Poems of Georg Trakl*,

1961 (with James Wright); *Forty Poems*, 1967 (of Juan Ramón Jiménez); *Hunger*, 1967 (of Knut Hamsun's novel); *I Do Best Alone at Night*, 1968 (of Gunnar Ekelöf); *Twenty Poems of Pablo Neruda*, 1968 (with Wright); *Neruda and Vallejo: Selected Poems*, 1971; *Ten Sonnets to Orpheus*, 1972 (of Rainer Maria Rilke); *Lorca and Jiménez: Selected Poems*, 1973; *Friends, You Drank Some Darkness: Three Swedish Poets, Harry Martinson, Gunnar Ekelöf, and Tomas Tranströmer*, 1975; *The Kabir Book: Forty-four of the Ecstatic Poems of Kabir*, 1977; *Twenty Poems*, 1977 (of Rolf Jacobsen); *Truth Barriers*, 1980 (of Tomas Tranströmer); *Selected Poems of Rainer Maria Rilke*, 1981; *Times Alone: Selected Poems of Antonio Machado*, 1983; *The Half-Finished Heaven: The Best Poems of Tomas Tranströmer*, 2001; *The Roads Have Come to an End Now: Selected and Last Poems of Rolf Jacobsen*, 2001 (with Roger Greenwald and Robert Hedin); *Horace: The Odes*, 2002 (with others; J. D. McClatchy, editor); *The Winged Energy of Delight: Selected Translations*, 2004; *The Angels Knocking on the Tavern Door: Thirty Poems of Hafez*, 2008 (with Leonard Lewisohn); *The Dream We Carry: Selected and Last Poems of Olav H. Hauge*, 2008 (with Robert Hedin).

EDITED TEXTS: *A Poetry Reading Against the Vietnam War*, 1966 (with David Ray); *News of the Universe: Poems of Twofold Consciousness*, 1980; *The Winged Life: The Poetic Voice of Henry David Thoreau*, 1986; *The Rag and Bone Shop of the Heart: Poems for Men*, 1993; *The Soul Is Here for Its Own Joy: Sacred Poems from Many Cultures*, 1995.

BIBLIOGRAPHY

Davis, William V. *Critical Essays on Robert Bly*. New York: G. K. Hall, 1992. An excellent selection of essays, reviews, and overviews of Bly's work, together with a detailed critical introduction documenting his career to the early 1990's.

_____. *Robert Bly: The Poet and His Critics*. Columbia, S.C.: Camden House, 1994. This chronological study traces the twists and turns of Bly's reputation, accounting for both the aesthetic and nonaesthetic components of critical judgments.

_____. *Understanding Robert Bly*. Columbia: University of South Carolina Press, 1988. A book-length study of Bly's poetic career, geared to an understanding of the chronological development and ongoing significance of Bly's life and work through a detailed analysis of individual poems and an in-depth consideration of each of the major books. Includes a primary and secondary bibliography and an index.

Harris, Victoria Frenkel. *The Incorporative Consciousness of Robert Bly*. Carbondale: Southern Illinois University Press, 1992. This in-depth study examines Bly's poetry in terms of his idea of universalizing poetic processes. Contains an exhaustive bibliography of work by and about Bly.

Hertzel, Laurie. "The Poet Comes Home: Reckless Youth. War protester. Translator. Men's-Movement Guru. Through It All, Robert Bly's Enduring Passion Has Been for His Poetry." *Star Tribune*, September 27, 2009, p. E1. This profile of Bly looks at his life and his love for poetry, which he says should have a quality of "wildness." Discusses his Madison home and the men's conferences that his book spawned.

Jones, Richard, and Kate Daniels, eds. *Of Solitude and Silence: Writings on Robert Bly*. Boston: Beacon Press, 1981. A miscellany of materials on Bly, including essays, memoirs, poems, notes, and documents, as well as new poems and translations by Bly. Includes an extensive primary and secondary bibliography.

Nelson, Howard. *Robert Bly: An Introduction to the Poetry*. New York: Columbia University Press, 1984. A detailed critical introduction to and analysis of Bly's career through *The Man in the Black Coat Turns*, stressing the ways in which his various theories illuminate his poems. Includes a chronology of his life, a primary and secondary bibliography, and an index.

Peseroff, Joyce, ed. *Robert Bly: When Sleepers Awake*. Ann Arbor: University of Michigan Press, 1984. A substantial collection of reviews and essays (including several previously unpublished) on Bly and his work through *The Man in the Black Coat Turns*. Includes an extensive primary and secondary bibliography but no index.

Quetchenbach, Bernard W. *Back from the Far Field: American Nature Poetry in the Late Twentieth Century*. Charlottesville: University of Virginia Press, 2000. In a lengthy chapter on Bly, the author explores Bly's concept of a true humanity, including his insistence that consciousness be linked to the environment or disaster will follow.

Sugg, Richard P. *Robert Bly*. Boston: Twayne, 1986. An introductory critical overview of Bly's work and career stressing a Jungian interpretation, through *The Man in the Black Coat Turns*. Includes a selected bibliography of primary and secondary sources and an index.

William V. Davis; Philip K. Jason
Updated by Davis

LOUISE BOGAN

Born: Livermore Falls, Maine; August 11, 1897
Died: New York, New York; February 4, 1970

PRINCIPAL POETRY

Body of This Death, 1923
Dark Summer, 1929
The Sleeping Fury, 1937
Poems and New Poems, 1941
Collected Poems, 1923-1953, 1954
The Blue Estuaries: Poems, 1923-1968, 1968, 1977

OTHER LITERARY FORMS

There are two collections of the criticism of Louise Bogan (boh-GAN), most of which consists of articles and reviews from her many years with *The New Yorker*: The posthumously published *A Poet's Alphabet: Reflections on the Literary Art and Vocation* (1970), edited by Robert Phelps and Ruth Limmer, contains all the pieces from *Selected Criticism: Prose, Poetry* (1955) plus other writings previously uncollected. Bogan's brief history of modern American poetry, *Achievement in American Poetry*, appeared in 1951. Her translations include *The Glass Bees* by Ernst Jünger (1960, with Elizabeth Mayer), and three works of Johann Wolfgang von Goethe: *Elective Affinities* (1963), *Novella* (1971), and *The Sorrows of Young Werther* (1971); she also edited a translation of *The Journal of Jules Renard* (1964). Ruth Limmer, Bogan's friend

and literary executor, brought out two posthumous collections of personal writings: *What the Woman Lived: Selected Letters of Louise Bogan 1920-1970* (1973) and *Journey Around My Room: The Autobiography of Louise Bogan* (1980), a chronological selection from diaries, letters, and other published and unpublished papers.

ACHIEVEMENTS

Louise Bogan devoted her life to poetry in writing, criticism, reviews, lectures, and consulting, and she was recognized with "all the honors that are an honor" for a poet in the United States. She received three Guggenheim Fellowships (1922, 1933, and 1937), the John Reed Memorial Prize from *Poetry* magazine (1930), the Levinson Prize from *Poetry* magazine (1937), the Harriet Monroe Award from the University of Chicago (1948), a National Institute of Arts and Letters Award (1951), the Bollingen Prize (1955), the Academy of American Poets Fellowship (1959), and the Senior Creative Arts Award from Brandeis University (1962). She served as the consultant in poetry (poet laureate) to the Library of Congress in 1945-1946. Western College for Women and Colby College bestowed honorary degrees. She was elected a fellow in American Letters of the Library of Congress and a member of the American Academy of Arts and Letters in 1952. She served as chancellor for the Academy of American Poets from 1961 to 1970.

These honors came in recognition of a substantial body of prose as well as poetry. From 1931 until 1968, Bogan regularly reviewed poetry for *The New Yorker*, contributing notes and reviews on twenty to forty books of poetry every year. Her published criticism helped shape the taste of generations of readers. Less well known but also influential was Bogan's second career as teacher, lecturer, and poet-in-residence. In 1944, she delivered the Hopwood Lecture at the University of Michigan, and for the next twenty-five years she lectured and taught at universities from Connecticut to Arizona and Washington State to Arkansas.

Bogan never cultivated popularity, and, despite the many academic and official honors, popular acclaim for her work has been scant. She received neither the Pulitzer Prize nor the National Book Award. More puzzling has been the neglect by the academic establishment; few scholars have undertaken the thorough examination of her work that has been accorded such contemporaries as Theodore Roethke and Marianne Moore. In the late 1970's, however, stimulated by feminist criticism and an awakening interest in women authors, literary scholars began more extensive studies of Bogan's works.

BIOGRAPHY

About the details of her life, Louise Marie Bogan maintained a deliberate and consistent reticence. However, she also claimed that she had written a searching account of her life; it was all in her poetry, she said, with only the vulgar particulars omitted. The information available about her life substantiates her claim.

The earliest theme to emerge in Bogan's life is the struggle for order amidst chaos and violence. She was born in Livermore Falls, Maine, on August 11, 1897, the second child and only daughter of Mary Helen Shields and Daniel J. Bogan. During the next twelve years, the family lived variously in Milton and Man-

Louise Bogan (©Bettmann/CORBIS)

chester, New Hampshire, and in Ballardvale, Massachusetts, before settling, in 1910, in Boston. Life was characterized by extremes of physical and psychological violence between the parents, and between mother and children. Although Bogan's father is almost totally absent from her recollections, her mother, a woman of elegance, taste, and ferocious temper, imposed an unpredictable and almost overwhelming presence on the young girl's life. There are startling gaps in memory: an unexplained year in a convent boarding school, two days of blindness at the age of eight. The convent year, the boardinghouse in Ballardvale, and an art teacher in Boston, however, represented relief from the constant struggle for sanity and order in the chaotic Bogan household. As a child, Louise relished the soothing atmosphere of order, cleanliness, and competence found in the boardinghouse, and later the enchantment of Miss Cooper's studio with its precious trinkets and carefully ordered tools. During her teens, Bogan's five years at Boston's Girls' Latin School enlarged her experience of both discipline and disorder; it was here that she received the thorough classical education she treasured so, and here that she encountered firsthand the vigorous New England Protestant bigotry against the Irish. To her classmates, Bogan was a "Mick," and she kept this consciousness of class distinctions throughout her life. The revelation must have amazed the girl steeped in a rich and intricate Catholicism. During this period of childhood and youth, which ended with marriage after one year at Boston University, she began to write.

In 1916, against the strong objections of her mother, Bogan forfeited her scholarship to Radcliffe and married Curt Alexander, a private in the U.S. Army. Her overriding motive was escape from a constricting life, but that illusion was very short-lived. Exactly one year after joining her husband in Panama, where she gave birth to a daughter, Maidie, Bogan returned with the child to Boston. Later, she and Alexander attempted to revive the marriage, living first near Portland, Maine, and later in Hoboken, New Jersey; all they had in common, Bogan recalled, was sex. She began to publish more, establishing a literary life as part of the Greenwich Village artistic milieu, and eventually the two separated. In 1918, Bogan's brother Charles was killed in France, and two years later Curt Alexander died. In 1923, her first collection, *Body of This Death*, came out.

The next twelve years of her life reflected a pattern of increasing professional skill and discipline together with a persistently troubled personal life. From 1925 to 1937, she was married to Raymond Holden. The relationship was stormy, not least because of Holden's infidelities, and marked by a series of moves—to Santa Fe, to Hillsdale, to various addresses in New York City. Material losses took a toll: In 1929, the couple's house burned, destroying books, pictures, and manuscripts, and in 1935, while she was separated from Holden, Bogan was evicted from her apartment. In 1937, her mother died. During this period of her life, Bogan was hospitalized twice for depression and nervous collapse. She later speculated on the relationship between childhood experience and memory and the many upheavals of her young adult life, locating the beginning of her depression in a visit to the earliest neighborhood the Bogans had lived in after coming to Boston. She continued writing; in 1937, *The Sleeping Fury* appeared.

The period 1937 to 1965 marked a time of maturity, productivity, and fulfillment. In 1937, Bogan moved to the New York apartment that would be her home thenceforth. Three volumes of poetry, as well as two critical works, an anthology, and translations were published. Awards and honors came almost yearly, along with invitations to lecture, read, and consult.

Turmoil and controversy reappeared in her life in 1965, when another depression resulted in hospitalization. The 1960's also saw Bogan's first public political activity, when she took part in the protests against the war in Vietnam. She continued lecturing, reading, and reviewing until, at the age of seventy-two, she resigned from her position as poetry reviewer for *The New Yorker*. Her last collection of poems, *The Blue Estuaries*, appeared in 1968, and she completed the compilation of her reviews that was published as *A Poet's Alphabet*. On February 4, 1970, Bogan died alone in her New York apartment.

ANALYSIS

Louise Bogan's well-known reticence about the details of her personal life extended to her poetry. She said that she had written down her experience in detail, omitting only the rough and vulgar facts. This dichotomy of fact and experience lies at the heart of her poems: They are about experience, not about facts. Four basic thematic concerns emerge in Bogan's work. Many poems center on women or womanhood. This was a theme to which Bogan returned often in her criticism, and her history of modern American poetry is one of the few to acknowledge the contributions of women. A second theme emerges in the many poems that explore the universal human condition of fleshly existence and the disasters and delights of love. Another preoccupation is art, the process of making art, and the artist and his commitment. Finally, the struggle of the mind and spirit for sanity and consolation in the face of insanity, chaos, and meaninglessness inspired the greatest of her poems.

WOMEN AS THEME

"Women" may be Bogan's most frequently anthologized poem, and it has certainly troubled feminist critics more than any other. The poem is cast as a diatribe by a male speaker who generalizes about women as "they." This catalog of faults outlines the stereotype of "woman" that Bogan herself referred to impatiently in several of her essays. The speaker's harsh tone modulates toward pity for women's habit of using their own benevolence against themselves, but he does not speculate on the causes of the many flaws in women. Neither did Bogan, as evidence by her letters and criticism: She inherited, without question, the Victorian and Romantic view that applied the dichotomies of emotion and intellect to woman and man, respectively, and then raised those parallel associations to the status of natural law.

In her poems, however, Bogan's perception of stereotypes of gender reflects a more complex vision. "The Romantic," for example, mocks the sentimental ideal of the passionless woman. The romantic had sought to impose his vision of femininity on the young woman and lost both woman and ideal. In both "Women" and "The Romantic" the poet distances herself from the subject. In the first, a presumptively male voice discourses, not about any real woman but about the idea of women, while in the second, a voice of unspecified gender addresses a man about a woman who has vanished.

Other poems confront more directly the particular heartaches, upheavals, and joys of being a woman, but in these, too, the approach is ordered and the thought kept coherent by various techniques of distancing. In each of the three poems, "The Changed Woman," "Chanson un peu naïve," and "For a Marriage," an anonymous speaker talks about a woman who also remains unspecified and anonymous. "Chanson un peu naïve" expresses an ironic, despairing pity at the destructive results of frequent childbearing and an apparent self-deception that permits its continuance. In "For a Marriage," a dispassionate onlooker reflects on intimacy as a sharing of pain, in this instance the woman's revelation of her pain to be shared by her husband. "The Changed Woman" is more obscure, referring perhaps to a miscarriage or abortion; the quality of the experience, the dream denied and driven, supersedes factual references. Another treatment of the theme is "The Crossed Apple": Here an older person, man or woman, directly addresses a young girl and offers the gift of an apple. The poem invokes the creation myth in Genesis, as the voice suggests that eating the fruit means knowledge as well as sustenance: She will taste more than fruit, blossom, sun, or air.

Such distancing brings order to the chaotic, impulsive, often outrageous realities of women's lives, placing those realities within the bounds of an art that can illuminate and make them meaningful. Those poems in which Bogan uses a woman's voice to articulate a woman's point of view also find means to distance and thus order her subject. "Men Loved Wholly Beyond Wisdom" generalizes about men and women according to familiar stereotypes. For the first five lines, women love and therefore demand love excessively, and in the remaining eight lines, the speaker resorts to harsh suppression of her emotions as the solution to the dilemma presented by her feelings and her perceptions of them. "Girl's Song" implies the same problem: The speaker addresses the man who has abandoned her in favor of another woman who, it is implied, will likewise love him in a sacrificial, even destructive way. Although this poem expresses resignation rather than the fierce despair of "Men Loved Wholly Beyond Wisdom," the view of women's nature and circumstances is the same: Women love excessively, to their sorrow and destruction.

WOMEN IN LATER POETRY

Both of the foregoing poems come from Bogan's early work, and they, like many of the early poems, express the tension between matter and form, instinct and reason, in terms of the relationships between women and men. In three poems published much later in her life, she spoke less generally and more directly in the persona of a particular woman with a specific history.

In "The Sorcerer's Daughter" and "Little Lobelia's Song," women speak of their own experience, and both poems spring from recognition of that most fundamental of connections, the relationship between parent and child. The sorcerer's daughter, who can read signs and auguries, finds herself bound to an unfortunate fate. The poem echoes the prophetic pessimism of "Cassandra" without the formal restraint and emotional tension of the earlier poem. "The Sorcerer's Daughter" is no tragedy; from her father the speaker inherits, chiefly, bad luck. In "Little Lobelia's Song" the piteous, helpless, inarticulate voice is an infant addressing its mother. Reflections on Bogan's tumultuous relationship with her own mother are inevitable, although the poem contains no details. The speaker's expression of identity with its mother, and the agony of separation, invite Freudian interpretation. Bogan's own acquaintance with modern psychology emerged from experience as well as theory, and the poem, published not long after her last stay in a mental hospital, is one of a group of three including "Psychiatrist's Song." Seldom did Bogan permit expression of such unalloyed pathos, yet the poem achieves power precisely through its rigid form and the distancing created by the artificial persona; the poet even succeeds with that commonest of clichés, flower as metaphor for child.

"Masked Woman's Song," the third poem of this trilogy, speaks most specifically yet most enigmatically about Bogan's own experience. Although the other poems use personas as disguise, the masked woman acknowledges her disguise and thus disarms skepticism. The singer seems to disown her previous sense of the value of artistic and moral order. The poem contains more physical description than most: The man is tall, has a worn face and roped arms. These are matters of fact, not experience, and the poem remains virtually impenetrable. The poet has moved beyond the classical values and virtues to a realm so resistant to description that it defies metaphor, where the familiar images of male and female no longer serve.

LOVE AS THEME

As is already evident, Bogan made love in its many varieties a major theme in her poetry. She framed her exposition generally in the Renaissance terms of flesh and spirit, passion and reason. The classical understanding of passion, derived from *passio* (suffering, submission) and related to "passive," regarded the lusts of the flesh not as mere sentiment or feeling but as the fundamental, chaotic, instinctual life of man that provides all force for ongoing life and regeneration, but that also constantly moves to overwhelm and subsume the cognitive being. Thus, the great human enterprise is to balance and harmonize both the instinctual and the mental, the flesh and the spirit.

Bogan's poems express disdain for excess in either direction. In "Several Voices out of a Cloud" the drunks, drug-takers, and perverts receive the laurel, for they have—whatever their flaws—been committed, they have used their creative energy. The pallid, the lifeless, punks, trimmers, and nice people—all those who denied life in favor of empty form—forgo eternity. The conception, the thesis, and even the terminology are Dantean.

Two poems about men suggest the peculiar dangers of trying to avoid confrontation with passion. In "The Frightened Man" the speaker explains that he feared the rich mouth and so kissed the thin; even this contact proved too much as she waxed while he weakened. His shattered image of the docile woman implies a self-destructive loathing of the real and the fleshly. "Man Alone" explores the subtle complexities of this solipsistic position. The man of the title seems to exist in a hall of mirrors; unable to confront and acknowledge the common humanity and individual otherness of his fellow human beings, he persists in a state of autistic rage. Literally and figuratively, he cannot face another person. The man does not suffer an excess but rather a perversion; passion misplaced has devolved into self-absorbed rage and infatuate isolation.

Most of Bogan's poetic statements on the subject of passionate love decry its excesses. She acknowledged and even emphasized the urgency of fleshly desire, but rarely celebrated it for itself. In her poems, giving oneself to overwhelming passion means capitulation, not liberation. Variations on this theme are played in "Women," in "Men Loved Wholly Beyond Wisdom," in "Chanson un peu naïve," and in "Girl's Song." Bogan's clearest critique of excessive love is in "Rhyme," with its echoes of William Shakespeare's sonnet, "The expense of spirit in a waste of shame." In Bogan's poem, a lover recollects a former love, addressing the absent one in a tone of wry nostalgia. The speaker articulates the Renaissance perception of excessive love as a form of idolatry, yet also acknowledges the nourishing function that passion can have, for the loved one had been heart's feast to the lover.

"Second Song" and "At a Party" describe the destructiveness of undisciplined love. In "Second Song," the speaker bids farewell to passion, which has garnered mere trinkets and a poisoned spiritual food. The speaker has undergone passion, has suffered it in the classical sense, as a pensioner, and so chooses to become detached from it. Like the speakers in "Rhyme" and "Second Song," the voice in "At a Party" has no specified gender; nor does this persona speak from behind mask or disguise, as do the speakers in many poems about women. When she spoke most directly, Bogan framed her persona as androgynous. This is a Renaissance ideal; one image for the integration of opposing dualities was the figure of the androgyne. "At a Party," however, treats the more cosmic theme of the corruption of nature that can follow from worship of the flesh. The speaker observes a dizzy, drunken revelry that ignorantly mocks the ordered progress of the stars, and then orders flesh to assert primacy over spirit and proclaim the tyranny of the material and the final corruption of value and beauty. Against this projected debacle, the speaker then invokes malice and enmity, which may bring salvation. The philosophy and the images recall John Donne and Dante: Disorder and perversion affront the natural order of the universe and require stern correctives.

ART AS THEME

Although Bogan's poems on the subject of love consistently treat the hazards and disasters of passion, models of harmonious, productive love exist mainly in the ideal implied by negative examples. The integration of duality, a fruitful union of passion and intellect, is imaged not in the lover, but in the artist.

Bogan expressed more than once her faith in art as a means to sanity and salvation in her troubled personal world, and two of her poems on art specifically explore the great power she attributed to it. "M., Singing" celebrates the capacity of art to articulate the unspeakable. The speaker finds that the melancholy words and subtle music of M.'s song cause the soul's hidden demons to step forth into the light of day. This is healing music, for these corrupt creatures abandon their unseen work of destruction and become subject to rational examination in human space; evil can be neutralized. "Song for a Slight Voice" returns to the theme of possessive love. The discipline of art, the speaker implies, has overcome the exigencies of passion, and the lover's stubborn heart will become an instrument for music, will hear the dance. Art can triumph over witless passion.

In two poems that explore the traditional theme of nature versus art, however, Bogan does not offer a clear-cut statement of superiority for either side. "To an Artist, To Take Heart" is an epigram in which the speaker contrasts the violent ends of William Shakespeare's characters Hamlet, Othello, and Coriolanus with the peaceful death of the author who outlived them all. Neither nature nor art wins supremacy, but each finds its fulfillment. The speaker's wry view of the artist as parent to his creations is adumbrated in the title: The work of art does not kill the artist, for the author lives even though his characters die. Verb tenses, however, signify the reverse: "Shakespeare died" in the past, once and for all, whereas "Hamlet, Othello, Coriolanus fall" in the present, as the creation lives after the creator dies.

"Animal, Vegetable, Mineral" is an uncharacteristically long poem of sixty-five lines in rhymed five-line stanzas. It is a meditation on the subject of cross-pollination, which is a work of nature; but it takes as its starting point art objects twice removed from the natural world: a publication of color plates depicting glass models of flowers. Both language and subject matter point to the pervasive theme of cross-pollination, or integration, of nature and art, instinct and mind. Blossoms are gothic or baroque, bees are Empire. The precise workings of instinct and of natural functions stim-

ulate thought in the human mind, here represented by Charles Darwin, and provide occasion for almost incomprehensible devotion to craft in the work of the Blaschkas, the Czech family of glassblowers who worked for fifty years to produce the botanical models. The speaker remains awed by cross-pollination of science, art, and nature: It is the process itself that is valuable, unfathomable, a loud mystery.

Like "Animal, Vegetable, Mineral," "Roman Fountain" and "Italian Morning"—two poems set in Italy—take visual art as their theme. The first emphasizes the process of making art, while the latter focuses on the work of art. Each, too, expresses a quintessential Renaissance theme, the triumph of art over time. In "Roman Fountain," the speaker is a poet sustained and reinvigorated on seeing water rising and falling in an ornate fountain. The gushing, noisy, ceaselessly moving water fructifies and enlivens the poet's imagination, but it does so because it has been shaped and directed by the carefully wrought fountain created by hands long dead. This perfect union of nature and art elates and inspires the poet. In "Italian Morning," the work of art confronts the speaker with human mortality. Two people awaken in an ornately decorated room, and the calm, silent presence of the painted fruit and flowers conveys a sense of timelessness. In contrast, the speaker's perception of time—placing the hour, naming the year—indicates a paradoxical poverty in human life: Time evaporates in the act of being possessed.

These poems suggest a mystical dimension to art that is made even more explicit in two others, "The Alchemist" and "Musician." In the former, the alchemist speaker represents the artist who has taken his own self as the base material for transmutation. The alchemist renounces material life and its rewards in search of a wholly spiritual existence and pleasure. Mere breathing will become the vehicle for ecstasy. The connection between breath and transcendent contemplation occurs in mystical traditions of both East and West; in the case of Bogan's alchemist, the long search culminates in a vision of reality stripped of illusion, of pure substance without the accident of meaning.

"Musician" portrays process and performance in terms similar to some types of Zen Buddhist aesthetics. Musician and instrument join to produce harmony so effortless and perfect that it seems the instrument has a life of its own. The agent is subsumed in perfect art. Like the figure of the androgyne, the image of the musician with instrument represented to the Renaissance mind the perfect dynamic balance of material and spiritual, matter and form. This ideal of vital integration of opposites pervades Bogan's poems about art, most clearly in the many poems centering on the image of the musician.

PSYCHOLOGY AS THEME

Bogan's preoccupation with the achievement of balance, harmony, and fruitfulness through reconciliation of opposites receives its finest expression in the poems that present most explicitly the struggle of the human mind to avert chaos and integrate impulse. Two poems that take a merely clinical look at the issue, "Evening in the Sanitarium" and "Psychiatrist's Song," recall her own experiences with the institutional view of mental illness. These poems are closer to the factual end of the fact-experience continuum, as is "Animal, Vegetable, Mineral," and all three are also very discursive and formally loose by comparison with her other works. For Bogan, it was formal rigor that produced the tension needed to convey intensity of thought and feeling.

Four poems deserve special notice as preeminent expressions of this struggle of the spirit. "Exhortation," "Simple Autumnal," "Kept," and "Henceforth, from the Mind" focus in turn on hate, grief, renunciation, and sublimation as healing powers.

"Exhortation" further elaborates the ideas expressed in "At a Party": The person who is conscious and moral and therefore alive lives in a world of the walking dead—the callous and the ignorant who are impervious to insight or ethics. In material terms, the latter always wins; success and failure rather than good or evil are the terms on which they operate. The speaker in the poem counsels detachment as the only remedy for the thinking, feeling person. The listener is advised to renounce both joy and rage, to leave behind the comforts of love and grief, and to cultivate indifference. This is a harsh doctrine, uncongenial to a vision of humanity as naturally good or perfectible. It has been called stoic; certainly, it accords with the Catholic philosophy of Bogan's early education, which emphasized the Fall of Man and a resultant debility of spirit. At the heart of the poem lies a crucial distinction, however: The living

dead, preoccupied with trivia and sated with insolence, exist in a state of moribund sterility, passionless and bleak. The speaker's renunciation of passion and rage, grief and joy, does not deny these elements of human life, but rather requires a full realization (in its root meaning) of them. Discipline and detachment, superficially similar to indifference, sustain life in the face of mere repression and ignorance. "Simple Autumnal," one of Bogan's few sonnets, makes a contrasting assertion: Grief denied repudiates both life and death. The speaker compares delayed autumn with delayed grief; time is frozen and so is life. The maturing process seems to come to a standstill in nature as it mirrors the person who refuses grief, so that nature takes on the static character of art and is therefore unnatural. Sorrow could heal, fulfilling life's intent, but feelings remain unreachable. The poem expresses the experience of living death referred to in "Exhortation," but with one difference: In "Simple Autumnal" the speaker comprehends the situation of lifelessness fully, and suffers intensely thereby. The sense of the poem recalls many of Emily Dickinson's works, in particular those such as "Pain Has an Element of Blank" which explore the experience of unreleased pain.

Reminiscent of Dickinson also is the emphasis on renunciation in "Kept." Again, the speaker takes up the theme of movement versus stasis, life against lifelessness. Those who would cling to the past as represented by its artifacts, dolls, and toys, will never be free of it. Nostalgia can trap one in everlasting childishness, for the past must be destroyed to be the past. Growth and maturity can occur only in the passage of time. Without the process of growth, a reverse process takes place: The person existing in an artificial world diminishes and indeed begins to metamorphosize until only an object remains. As in the two preceding poems, sanity is a function of conscious, heartfelt, and disciplined submission to the natural processes of life and death, growth and decay.

In "Henceforth, from the Mind," Bogan reaches beyond the pain of discipline and renunciation to affirm the final achievement of sublimation. The speaker does not advocate substitution or repression, as the notion of sublimation is often wrongly understood. It is real joy that will spring from the mind, from the tongue—the selfsame exaltation that the younger person ascribes to passion. The form of the poem harmonizes with this theme. The forward motion of the first two stanzas takes momentum from the "henceforth" that begins each and from the emphatic reversal of verb and subject in the two main clauses; the repetition of the rhyming couplets ending each stanza counterbalances this same forward motion. The last two stanzas mirror in their form the perfect transmutation of the material and spiritual that the poem asserts. In a single twelve-line sentence as convoluted as the image of the shell in the first line, syntactical momentum builds until the verb and—finally—the subject appear at the end of the sentence, which is also the end of the poem. This reversal of the usual sentence structure is itself a form of echoing: The sea and earth that will henceforth be known from their echoes within memory and imagination sound back to the resonating shell in a grammatical spiral that imitates the convolvulus's physical shape. The shell encloses the ocean, echoing a knowledge of that sea from which it is itself sundered. Sound and motion prevail in the rocking, cradling rhythms of bell and wave, the music of transcendent illumination, echoing through the depths within depths of perfect harmony.

OTHER MAJOR WORKS

NONFICTION: *Achievement in American Poetry*, 1951; *Selected Criticism: Prose, Poetry*, 1955; *A Poet's Alphabet: Reflections on the Literary Art and Vocation*, 1970; *What the Woman Lived: Selected Letters of Louise Bogan, 1920-1970*, 1973; *Journey Around My Room: The Autobiography of Louise Bogan*, 1980.

TRANSLATIONS: *The Glass Bees*, 1960 (with Elizabeth Mayer; of Ernest Jünger); *Elective Affinities*, 1963 (with Mayer; of Johann Wolfgang von Goethe); *Journal*, 1964 (with Elizabeth Roget; of Jules Renard); *Novella*, 1971 (of Goethe); *The Sorrows of Young Werther*, 1971 (of Goethe).

EDITED TEXT: *The Golden Journey: Poems for Young People*, 1965 (with William Jay Smith).

BIBLIOGRAPHY

Bowles, Gloria. *Louise Bogan's Aesthetic of Limitation*. Bloomington: Indiana University Press, 1987. Bowles uses a feminist perspective to examine Bogan and her work and asserts that the poet's "limitation" results from her notion of what she could and could not do within the male literary tradition. The author identifies Bogan as a modernist and explores a variety of influences, including William Butler Yeats and the Symbolists, on Bogan's poetry.

Collins, Martha, ed. *Critical Essays on Louise Bogan*. Boston: G. K. Hall, 1984. The first collection of scholarly essays on Bogan ever published. Topics discussed are varied and range from the tendencies to misunderstand Bogan's work to feminist responses to her poetry. Collins has written an extensive and enlightening introduction.

Dodd, Elizabeth Caroline. *The Veiled Mirror and the Woman Poet: H. D., Louise Bogan, Elizabeth Bishop, and Louise Glück*. Columbia: University of Missouri Press, 1992. Dodd identifies a strain in women's poetry she calls "personal classicism": poetry grounded in the writer's private experience yet characterized by formal and tonal restraint. Includes a bibliography and an index.

Frank, Elizabeth. *Louise Bogan: A Portrait*. New York: Alfred A. Knopf, 1985. Although this book is intended for the general reader, it will also satisfy and inform Bogan scholars. Deftly examines the relationship between Bogan's life and work, using a variety of sources, including letters, diaries, recollections of people who knew her, and unpublished and uncollected works. The author is eminently qualified for this ambitious work, as she has studied Bogan for many years.

Knox, Claire E. *Louise Bogan: A Reference Source*. London: Scarecrow Press, 1990. Knox draws on files of *The New Yorker* (where Bogan was poetry editor from 1931 to 1969), the Berg Collection at the New York Public Library, collected materials at Harvard and Amherst Universities, and the Library of Congress (where Bogan was consultant in poetry) to compile this exhaustive, annotated bibliography.

Llanas, Sheila Griffin. *Modern American Poetry, "Echoes and Shadows."* Berkeley Heights, N.J.: Enslow, 2009. An exploration of modern American poetry that contains a biography and critical analysis of Bogan.

Miller, Brett C. *Flawed Light: American Women Poets*

and Alcohol. Urbana: University of Illinois Press, 2009. Miller studies how drinking and alcoholism affected certain prominent American women poets, and how their struggles were reflected in their poetry. Contains an informative chapter on Bogan.

Ridgeway, Jaqueline. *Louise Bogan.* Boston: Twayne, 1984. This ambitious book explores childhood experiences that influenced Bogan's poetry, the symbols that express her poetic statements, and her use of the formal lyric style long after it had fallen out of favor with her contemporaries. Also examines a rarely discussed topic: Bogan's influence on other poets.

Simmons, Thomas. *Erotic Reckonings: Mastery and Apprenticeship in the Work of Poets and Lovers.* Urbana: University of Illinois Press, 1994. Examines the mentor-apprenticeship relationships between three pairs of twentieth century poets: Ezra Pound and H. D., Yvor Winters and Janet Lewis, and Bogan and Theodore Roethke. Explores the force of biographical and literary events on the mentor, then traces the mentor's impact on the apprentice.

Helen Jaskoski

ARNA BONTEMPS

Born: Alexandria, Louisiana; October 13, 1902
Died: Nashville, Tennessee; June 4, 1973

PRINCIPAL POETRY
"Hope," 1924
Personals, 1963

OTHER LITERARY FORMS

Arna Bontemps (bon-TAHM) contributed to many genres of literature. He decided to concentrate on writing poetry after moving to Harlem in 1924 and because he felt that the mind-set of the early artists, writers, and musicians who lived there was particularly attuned to the rhythm and sound of poetry. In the 1930's, he turned to the novel as a vehicle for attempting to right the wrongs of an educational system that minimized black contributions to society, often devoting only two paragraphs to blacks—one dealing with Africa and the other with slavery in the Americas. His best-known novel, *Black Thunder* (1936), told the story of Gabriel Prosser, a slave who orchestrated an unsuccessful revolt in 1800. Hoping to gain a readership whose minds were less skeptical and more malleable than adults, he collaborated on several children's books with Langston Hughes and Jack Conroy and wrote several of his own, including *You Can't Pet a Possum* (1934). He later began to concentrate on history and biography for children with such books as *The Story of George Washington Carver* (1954) and *Frederick Douglass: Slave, Fighter, Freeman* (1959). He wanted young blacks to understand their racial past and gain a sense of pride in what blacks had achieved despite the obstacles they faced. Bontemps, indeed a prolific writer, was writing his autobiography when he died in 1973.

ACHIEVEMENTS

Arna Bontemps was showered with awards and recognition for his literary works. He won the Alexander Pushkin Award for Poetry from *Opportunity: A Journal of Negro Life* for "Golgotha Is a Mountain" in 1926 and for "The Return" in 1927. Also in 1927, he was awarded First Prize in Poetry for "Nocturne at Bethesda" by *The Crisis*, published by the National Association for the Advancement of Colored People (NAACP). He went on to win *Opportunity*'s short-story prize in 1932 for "A Summer Tragedy," a powerful tale that is included in many anthologies. He was granted two Julius Rosenwald Fellowships for travel, study, and writing, the first in 1938-1939 and the other in 1942-1943, and two Guggenheim Fellowships in 1949 and 1954. He received the Jane Addams Children's Book Award in 1956 for *The Story of the Negro*.

BIOGRAPHY

Arna Wendell Bontemps was born in Alexandria, Louisiana, in 1902, to a Roman Catholic brick mason and accomplished trombonist, Paul Bismark Bontemps, and a Methodist schoolteacher, Marie Carolina Pembrooke. His father, who left the Roman Catholic Church to become a lay minister with the Seventh-day Adventists, was a somewhat distant, practical man who hoped his son would join the family trade in build-

Arna Bontemps (Library of Congress)

ing construction and masonry. From the start, however, Bontemps's mother instilled in him a love of reading and encouraged him to give his imagination free rein. Her free-spirited creativity had a great influence on him.

Bontemps had just turned three when the family moved to the Watts area of California because his father had grown tired of the indignities suffered by blacks in the South. Bontemps's father had been walking down the sidewalk when a pair of drunken white men grew close; when they hurled an epithet, his father, following convention, had stepped down into the street to avoid a confrontation. The three-year-old Bontemps was too young to understand the full implications of the incident, and when at age twelve, after his mother's death, he was sent to San Fernando Academy, a mostly white boarding school, he misunderstood his father's admonition that he not "act all colored" at the school. He saw this warning not as the safety measure it was designed to be, but as an attempt to make him forget his past, to negate everything in him that was black. His father was trying both to protect him and to get him away from the influence of his uncle Buddy, who drank heavily, loved tall tales told in dialect, and believed in ghosts. The young Bontemps, however, admired and enjoyed Uncle Buddy's energy and good humor, as well as the company of his friends. Physical separation did not remove his uncle from his mind; Bontemps even based the main character of his first novel, *God Sends Sunday* (1931), on him.

The idea that he was being miseducated, that he was expected to assimilate into white society and to be no different, stayed with Bontemps for many years and perhaps created in him a desire to change things, to learn about his heritage, and to alter misconceptions about black people. Because he believed that fiction was often more successful than scholarly writings in conveying history, he decided to become a writer. After receiving a bachelor of arts degree from Pacific Union College in Angwin, California, in 1923, he moved to Harlem to be among like-minded people with interests in literature, art, and music, and to teach at Harlem Academy, the largest Seventh-day Adventist school in the nation. He published his first poem, "Hope," in 1924 in *The Crisis*. He married Alberta Johnson in 1926; the couple would have six children.

In 1931, Bontemps accepted a teaching position at Oakwood Junior College, in Huntsville, Alabama. He loved the softness of the South, the greenery, the agriculture, and the slower life. Unfortunately, he was in Alabama during a turbulent time when nine young men (known as the Scottsboro boys) were wrongfully accused and ultimately convicted of raping two white girls. The trial in nearby Decatur, Georgia, attracted the attention of the nation, and many friends from his Harlem days—Hughes and Countée Cullen among them—stopped to visit Bontemps and his family on their way to hold protests at the courthouse where the trial was held. The school administration became concerned because of the influx of black activists as well as Bontemps's mail orders for black history books. He was told that if he wanted to keep his position, he would have to burn some of his more radical works, such as books by W. E. B. Du Bois and Frederick Douglass. The administrators wanted some public display of his break from radical politics. Appalled, Bontemps quietly resigned at the end of the spring semester, 1934.

About a year later, he accepted a position at the Shiloh Academy in Chicago. In 1938, he became an editorial supervisor for the Federal Writers' Project of the Illinois Works Progress Administration, where he met writers such as Conroy, Nelson Algren, Richard Wright, Margaret Walker, and Saul Bellow. His third novel, *Drums at Dusk*, was published in 1939, and he continued to write children's books, as he would into the 1970's. He received a master's degree in library science from the University of Chicago in 1943 and was appointed a librarian at Fisk University in Atlanta, where he would remain until his retirement in 1965. At Fisk, he found just the kind of life for which he had hoped. He became instrumental in building up the library's African American archives, bringing in Hughes's papers and developing a serious focus on black writers, artists, and musicians. With Hughes and later on his own, Bontemps edited several collections of poetry and other works by African Americans. His only collection of poetry, *Personals*, containing twenty-three poems from the 1920's, was published in 1963. In his later years, he served as curator of the James Weldon Johnson Collection at Yale University, visiting scholar at the University of Illinois, and poet-in-residence at Fisk University.

ANALYSIS

Several themes dominate Arna Bontemps's poetry: protest against social inequity, the decline in religious belief, and the search for identity through examination of the past. His social protest was more suggested than directly stated, however. He always wrote in a brooding, sad way, never showing joy or laughter. His dismay at what he considered the loss of right behavior, ethics, responsibility, and faith is pronounced in some of his poetry. However, his greatest interest was in exploring roots, most often African, summoning up the past by returning to it and seeing what could be learned. The return could be to a memory or be an actual relocation to a place or to a loved one. The Africa of his poetry is a bit idealized, with verdant grasses and scarlet birds in lush palms and tom-toms beating out hypnotic rhythms and never sounding warnings of impending danger.

"GOLGOTHA IS A MOUNTAIN"

Often, further study is necessary for a complete understanding of Bontemps's poetry, in which biblical references abound. For example, the poem "Golgotha Is a Mountain" refers to Golgotha, a hill near Jerusalem believed to be the site of the crucifixion of Jesus Christ. The name of the hill comes from an Aramaic word that means "place of the skull." Golgotha is a place of death, as evidenced through Bontemps's oblique reference to those who ". . . hanged two thieves there,/ And another man," causing a flood of tears then and now, enough to make a river. Romans and Jews in biblical times carried out executions on the outskirts of cities, preferably on elevated spots so that the executions would serve as warnings to passersby. In this poem, Bontemps may be linking the suffering of Jesus with that of blacks. The excavation at the mountain could serve as a reminder that the Africans who dig precious stones out of mountains get no recompense. The mountains are theirs, but the wealth eludes them.

"THE RETURN"

"The Return" describes the poet's attempt to summon up the past and understand it, one of Bontemps's major themes. The poet states, "The throb of rain is the throb of muffled drums;/ darkness brings the jungle to our room// . . . This is a night of love/ retained from those lost nights our fathers slept/ in huts; this is a night that cannot die." He hopes that calling up the sounds and smells of Africa will give life to racial memory, saying, "Oh let us go back and search the tangled dream." He knows that such trips are only temporary, soon interrupted by reality, with street noise, weather, and birds.

"NOCTURNE AT BETHESDA"

The Bethesda of the poem "Nocturne at Bethesda" is the biblical site of miracles, where the afflicted gather and wait for angels to stir up the waters of a pond. Those who enter the pool before the water settles are released from pain. According to the biblical account, a man, hobbled for thirty-eight years, was too crippled to reach the pool in time, so Jesus healed him. In modern times, a person might wait at that ancient pool for some kind of revelation or cleansing, but it will not come. Bontemps reflects on the twentieth century's demise of faith and concludes that the forces that once sustained people no longer have the power to heal or transform. He laments that the healing waters are no longer there to help blacks, noting, ". . . This ancient pool that Healed/ A host of bearded Jews does not awake// . . . No Saviour comes/ with healing in his hands. . . ." There is no solace for blacks at this site, causing him to ask ". . . why/ Do our black faces search empty sky?" He looks for an answer and mourns the loss of spiritual values where God was once immanent: "I may pass through centuries of death/ with quiet eyes, but I'll remember still/ a jungle tree with burning scarlet birds.// I shall be seeking ornaments of ivory,/ I shall be dying for a jungle fruit."

"A BLACK MAN TALKS OF REAPING"

The last poem in *Personals*, "A Black Man Talks of Reaping," is probably the most anthologized. In this poem, a man who has prepared his land well, planting his seeds deeply enough to save them from the wind and birds, takes pride in rows that could, in his mind, run from "Canada to Mexico." However, the times are bad and the crops have not done well. The man, like many blacks after the Emancipation, is either a tenant farmer or a sharecropper, and finds that he has nothing to pass down to his children. He says his children "glean" or take from "fields" they have not sown and "feed on bitter fruit." Bontemps feels it is unnatural and disastrous for humans not to be able to reap what they sow, but he credits blacks for their endurance and for believing that a better day will come. In "Day-Breakers," he wrote lines conveying this mind-set: "Yet would we die as some have done./ Beating a way for the rising sun."

OTHER MAJOR WORKS

LONG FICTION: *God Sends Sunday*, 1931; *Black Thunder*, 1936; *Drums at Dusk*, 1939.

SHORT FICTION: *The Old South*, 1973.

PLAY: *St. Louis Woman*, pr. 1946 (with Countée Cullen).

NONFICTION: *Father of the Blues*, 1941 (with W. C. Handy; biography); *They Seek a City*, 1945 (with Jack Conroy; revised as *Anyplace but Here*, 1966); *One Hundred Years of Negro Freedom*, 1961; *Free at Last: The Life of Frederick Douglass*, 1971; *Arna Bontemps—Langston Hughes Letters: 1925-1967*, 1980.

CHILDREN'S LITERATURE: *Popo and Fifina: Children of Haiti*, 1932 (with Langston Hughes); *You Can't*

Pet a Possum, 1934; *Sad-Faced Boy*, 1937; *The Fast Sooner Hound*, 1942 (with Conroy); *We Have Tomorrow*, 1945; *Slappy Hooper: The Wonderful Sign Painter*, 1946 (with Conroy); *Story of the Negro*, 1948; *Chariot in the Sky: A Story of the Jubilee Singers*, 1951; *Sam Patch*, 1951 (with Conroy); *The Story of George Washington Carver*, 1954; *Lonesome Boy*, 1955; *Frederick Douglass: Slave, Fighter, Freeman*, 1959; *Famous Negro Athletes*, 1964; *Mr. Kelso's Lion*, 1970; *Young Booker: Booker T. Washington's Early Days*, 1972; *The Pasteboard Bandit*, 1997 (with Hughes); *Bubber Goes to Heaven*, 1998.

EDITED TEXTS: *The Poetry of the Negro*, 1949, 1971 (with Hughes); *The Book of Negro Folklore*, 1958 (with Hughes); *American Negro Poetry*, 1963; *Great Slave Narratives*, 1969; *Hold Fast to Dreams*, 1969; *The Harlem Renaissance Remembered*, 1972.

BIBLIOGRAPHY

Bloom, Harold, ed. *Black American Poets and Dramatists of the Harlem Renaissance*. New York: Chelsea House, 1995. Contains an essay on Bontemps that places him within the greater context of the Harlem Renaissance.

Bontemps, Arna. *Personals*. 1963. Reprint. Alexandria, Va.: Chadwyck-Healey, 1998. Bontemps's preface to his poetry collection details his great excitement at reaching Harlem in 1924, describing the city as a "foretaste of paradise."

_____, ed. *American Negro Poetry: An Anthology*. Rev. ed. New York: Hill and Wang, 1996. In his eloquent introduction, Bontemps discusses the importance of poetic expression in African American culture.

Drew, Bernard A., ed. *One Hundred Most Popular African American Authors: Biographical Sketches and Bibliographies*. Westport, Conn.: Libraries Unlimited, 2007. Contains an entry on Bontemps that describes his life and lists his works.

Gates, Henry Louis, Jr., and Evelyn Brooks Higginbotham, eds. *Harlem Renaissance Lives: From the African American National Biography*. New York: Oxford University Press, 2009. Gates, one of the leading scholars in African American studies, helped edit this work, which contains an informative introduction as well as a section with a comprehensive discussion of the life and works of Bontemps. Especially good for its biographical time line.

Jones, Kirkland C. *Renaissance Man from Louisiana: A Biography of Arna Wendell Bontemps.* Westport, Conn.: Greenwood Press, 1992. This biography of Bontemps stresses his many talents in various areas.

Pettis, Joyce Owens. *African American Poets: Lives, Works, and Sources.* Westport, Conn.: Greenwood Press, 2002. Contains an entry on Bontemps that looks at his life and poetic works.

Gay Pitman Zieger

PHILIP BOOTH

Born: Hanover, New Hampshire; October 8, 1925
Died: Hanover, New Hampshire; July 2, 2007

PRINCIPAL POETRY

Letter from a Distant Land, 1957
The Islanders, 1961
Weathers and Edges, 1966
Margins: A Sequence of New and Selected Poems, 1970
Available Light, 1976
Before Sleep, 1980
Relations: Selected Poems, 1950-1985, 1986
Selves: New Poems, 1990
Pairs: New Poems, 1994
Lifelines: Selected Poems, 1950-1999, 1999
Crossing, 2001 (juvenile)

OTHER LITERARY FORMS

Philip Booth's poetry forms the basis of his literary reputation. He gave readings of his works on both radio and television, and he edited several volumes of poetry. His essay collection, *Trying to Say It: Outlooks and Insights on How Poems Happen*, appeared in 1996.

ACHIEVEMENTS

The finely crafted poetry of Philip Booth has a strong, clear connection with his ancestral home of Castine, Maine, a colonial coastal village of fewer than seven hundred year-round residents. Through his poetry, Booth carefully captured this place; he was at home with its blustery winters, its tides and charts, its starkness, its dry humor, its sparse, homely conversation, and its flora, fauna, and animals. However, like Emily Dickinson, through an intimate closeness with one place, the poet spoke of a common humanity and universal themes.

Booth's poems move from engaging openings to clear, satisfying conclusions and are meticulously placed in each volume, moving toward a final resolution of their themes. Booth husbanded his language, but his poems hold a richness of meaning and look with curiosity and wonder at the miracle of human life. The poet, whose works have been translated into French, Portuguese, Finnish, Dutch, and Italian, and have been lauded by fellow poet Maxine Kumin as having a "wonderfully consistent tone," is recognized as one of the best of late twentieth century writers.

Booth's first collection of poems, *Letter from a Distant Land*, was named the 1956 Lamont Poetry Selection by the Academy of American Poets. Additional honors include the Bess Hokin Prize from *Poetry* magazine (1955), Guggenheim and Rockefeller Fellowships, grants from the National Institute of Arts and Letters (1967) and from the National Endowment for the Arts, and awards from *Poetry*, *Saturday Review*, *Virginia Quarterly Review*, and *Poetry Northwest*. In 1983, Booth received an Academy of American Poets Fellowship. His 1986 collection *Relations* earned for him the Maurice English Poetry Award. In 2001, Booth was awarded the Poets' Prize by the Academy of American Poets.

BIOGRAPHY

As his poetry suggests, Philip Edmund Booth was a New Englander, a man of Down East sensibilities and humor. Born in 1925 in Hanover, New Hampshire, to a Dartmouth English professor, and having grown up both in New Hampshire and in Maine, he settled in the white-clapboard, black-shuttered, 130-year-old house in Castine, Maine, which belonged to his family for five generations. Thomas Jefferson had appointed Booth's maternal great-great-grandfather to serve as customs collector in Castine two hundred years before, and the Greek Revival house on Main Street where the poet would reside belonged to his mother's family for nearly a century.

Booth received his undergraduate degree at Dartmouth College in New Hampshire; there, as a freshman in a noncredit seminar during the summer of 1943, he met Robert Frost, who acted as an occasional grandfather for Booth's three daughters during the early years of his marriage (in 1946, to Margaret Tillman). Booth graduated from Dartmouth in 1947, taught at Bowdoin College in Maine in 1949, and then stopped teaching for a while. He hoped to be a novelist and, to pay the bills for the next four years, worked in both Vermont and New Hampshire at jobs that included a stint in Dartmouth's admissions office, work as a traveling ski-book salesperson, and some time in a carpentry shop. After deciding that he was not a good storyteller but rather a good wordsmith, Booth turned his attention to writing poetry. He earned his master's degree at Syracuse University, and for the next twenty-five years, he served as senior poet in the creative writing program there. During these years he edited several volumes of *Syracuse Poems*.

Booth published poetry in many leading literary magazines and journals, including *Harper's*, *Kenyon Review*, *The New Yorker*, and *Saturday Review*. He developed Alzheimer's disease and died in Hanover on July 2, 2007.

ANALYSIS

Philip Booth's list of accomplishments is impressive, and his reputation is international, but he was, most of all, a humanist speaking to an individual audience, one person at a time. Although he is widely identified as a regional poet who wrote of life in a harsh, cold northern climate, Booth's subjects cover the whole range of human experience. The powerful forces of nature and how humans relate to them play prominently in his work, but his poems also speak of other human concerns: love, sex, marriage, children, aging, poverty, death, and the mysteries of existence. In his earliest collection, *Letter from a Distant Land*, his poetic patterns are fairly traditional; however, later poems exhibit less attention to traditional form and sometimes an aban-

donment of rhyme and stanza. In all Booth's works, the struggle of form and matter are present; his themes are of human loneliness and vulnerability set against the impersonal forces of nature. This struggle is never fully reconciled, but the poet examines the need for the coexistence of humankind and the natural world.

LETTER FROM A DISTANT LAND

In the sonnet "Good Friday, 1954," which appears in *Letter from a Distant Land*, the number of lines and the rhyme scheme follow the traditional pattern, but the poet uses slant rhyme, with "lodged" and "judged" ending the sixth and eighth lines. The poem's final line reveals Booth's closeness to the New England school headed by Robert Frost and its belief in the moral function of poetry: "To spike a rumor sacrifice a man." "The Wilding," another early poem, issues a springtime call to love; Booth plays on the sexual suggestiveness of jack-in-the-pulpits and maidenhair fern. E. E. Cummings's playfulness is echoed in "a sweet fern questionmark/ whorls green as green is today,/ and ferns ask no answer a swallow/ can't fly." The youthful joy and exuberance of this poem fill the reader with hope and expectation. Another early poem, "First Lesson," instructs a daughter about trusting the father who is cradling her head in the "cup" of his hand as he gently urges her to learn to swim. Just as the swimmer learns to trust the sea, a person can learn to survive by remembering experiences that, like the sea, "will hold you." "Chart 1203" captures the essence of sailing's allure and challenge in saying of the sailor, "He knows the chart is not the sea." The Atlantic coast is threatening, Booth says, only for the sailor who is not familiar with its eccentricities and relies on charts and maps alone to guide him. The sailor must have "local knowledge of shoal/ or ledge." The poem celebrates the thrill of meeting a challenge and surviving through a combination of good luck and skill.

The volume's title poem, "Letter from a Distant Land," combines slant rhyme and true rhyme. The poem, a lengthy meditation about the area around Henry David Thoreau's Walden Pond and the changes it has undergone since the nineteenth century, is written in terza rima, with long sentences and a doubly alternating rhyme scheme. The rhyme and meter are, nevertheless, so subtle, with approximate combinations such as "desk" and "risk," that the reader hardly notices them. In this way the poem does have the flavor of a letter written from a distant land to a friend, with themes of the connectedness of writer and reader, the natural world and human values.

WEATHERS AND EDGES

In *Weathers and Edges*, New England voices speak with terse language and dry humor. The arrangement of the poems moves from works such as "Heart of Darkness," which deals with large human concerns, to personal poems of private experience such as "Cleaning Out the Garage," and then outward again to a series of sea poems set on the Maine coast. The reader of "Heart of Darkness" is struck by the short lines arranged as a column on the page: The poem itself is presented as "some sort of base/ to start out from." The stanza arrangement in "Cleaning Out the Garage" is less lean. Filling out the page, its four stanzas move from nine to ten to eleven and finally to twelve lines, ironically accumulating lines as the garage is cleaned out and its contents diminished, and ending with an almost Frostian moral: The speaker has learned, after discarding all the "useless stuff" stored since his boyhood, "how to let go what won't do." "Report from the Scene," an immediate description of the effects of severe local thunderstorms on boats moored in a Maine harbor, is arranged in eleven two-line stanzas; in it, the forces of nature seem nearly overwhelming, but two people "with reflex love" reach for each other and face the storm. The individuals watching the violent storm are an image of human vulnerability in the face of natural forces, but as the two reach out toward each other, they and the storm are able to coexist.

AVAILABLE LIGHT

Several works in *Available Light* try to come to terms with harsh winters, the freeze of a late spring, the poet's Puritan need to take inventory constantly, and the nearly mystical experience of a dream. "Entry," a terse, honed poem that is skinny on the page, describes bitter cold weather that has lasted for four days, drifted snow coming in large flakes, and a "small sun." The poet's words "quicken," or give life to, the silence and allow an entry for him, suggesting Booth's fascination with the life-giving power of words. "Adding It Up" uses what light is available as the speaker's mind be-

gins to open up before dawn, while he lies in bed tallying his life and its concerns. As his mind opens and he meticulously counts, his body prepares for the first humorously ordinary job of the day: "cleaning up after/ an old-maid Basset in heat." With humor the speaker looks at himself and inventories his Puritan characteristics: being sorry, worrying, counting.

Set against such straightforwardness, "Dreamscape" has a visionary quality in its carefully shaped free verse. In contrast to "Supposition with Qualification," in which the speaker struggles with wanting to give himself up to experience, the speaker in "Dreamscape" lets the dream experience take control of the poem. The opening stanza describes the familiar road to town as the speaker has "always" known it: the steep hill, the filled-in old British canal, the spruce trees, the five houses. The certainty of "always," however, is denied by the vision of the road in the dream. In the second stanza, beginning with the word "but," the poet presents the road in his dream, with the left side now cleared into pasture in which "miniature bison" are kneeling. Avoiding the questioning of experience found in some

Philip Booth (©Rollie McKenna)

of Booth's earlier works, he neither can nor wants to explain this dreamscape. The organic process of the poem takes on a life of its own, offering a sharing of the dream's experience and suggesting the chance that this dream experience opens up a wholly new perspective.

"How to See Deer" comments directly on the subtler theme of an earlier poem, "Shag." "Shag" first describes the poet's observations of seven cormorants (shags), follows with ruminations about what ornithologists say regarding their strange flights, and concludes as the poet continues to observe and to row "as if/ on vacation from knowledge." Here Booth has tried to let the experience speak for itself, and to avoid explaining it or generalizing from it. "How to See Deer" makes a similar point, but much more overtly, in contrast to Booth's usual practice: by advising, if one purposely sets out to see deer—or, by extension, to experience anything—that the deer will not be seen. Serendipity is a factor; however, taking "your good time," trusting "your quick nature," learning to listen and to observe, to "see/ what you see," will permit one to experience joy. Perceptions and experiences cannot be forced; if, however, one is alert and receptive, one is able to participate in life.

BEFORE SLEEP

Like Booth's earlier works, *Before Sleep* is divided into parts, but they are concurrent rather than consecutive, with tightly woven interaction. These pieces are separated into poems and "Night Notes": The forty-three poems appear on numbered pages indicated in the table of contents; the eighteen "Night Notes," offering commentaries on the poems to which they are juxtaposed, appear between listed poem titles and are not given page numbers. The collection's title, reminiscent of the famous Frost poem "Stopping by Woods on a Snowy Evening," brings to mind the long sleep of death. The poems themselves, however, offer meditations on how to live life. There are no formal stanzaic patterns here; rhyme and even approximate rhyme are absent. Figurative language is also sparse; Booth uses mostly simple words and gives particular attention to the word "nothing," which exists by itself, contradicting the view—held by Booth in his early years—that nothing exists in isolation.

The opening poem, "Not to Tell Lies," describes a man who wishes to strip life down to the barest essentials. Initially, the lines are short, but they quickly become longer, only to shorten again to the single word "lies." This arrangement is striking, for it suggests a wedge used to force the truth into a limited space, without anything extraneous. The poet is coming to terms with his age, having reached his sixth decade and returned to live year-round in the ancestral Maine home. Items in his upstairs room, "which corners late sun," include a schooner model, the portrait of a daughter, a rock brought from Amchitka by the speaker's doctor, an ancestor's photograph, and books by Henry David Thoreau and Herman Melville—men who also made outward and inward journeys. As in earlier poems, Booth uses sea metaphors—for example, his bed has been:

> moored . . .
> perpendicular to the North wall,
> whenever he rests his head is compassed barely west
> of Polaris

All the poem's other words catalog what he has gathered and sorted through "in order not/ to tell/ lies." Following this poem, and integral to its meaning, is a "night note" introducing the idea of "nothing." The room just described is nothing, Booth says, when separated from the life he lives within it; the person, the poet, is more "vital" than the room, and his "virtue" is "not/ in my own life to live/ as if nothing/ were more important."

As the collection progresses, one senses the nothingness of death but also the meaning and sometimes the meaninglessness of life. "The House in the Trees," the collection's final entry, pictures a continuous moving toward life, affirming the possibility of continuing to build for the future, although, like the house "in the process/ of being built," the poet's life and art may not reach complete fulfillment before his death. In this process, in the sense of "constantly being arrived at," life and art are affirmed.

RELATIONS

The title poem of *Relations* is a poem of affirmation; the speaker does not deny life's uncertainties, but wonders at the miracle of each moment, amazed at the movement of the spheres,

> . . . by how
>   to each other
> we're held, we keep
>
> from spinning out
>   by how to each other
> we hold.

The staggered placement of the poem's lines suggests how each line relates to those that follow and precede it. "From broken dreams," says the poem, "we wake to every day's/ brave history." That all persons do this, that history involves experience, and perhaps as well that opening oneself to each day's experience is "brave" indicate the commonality of persons, their dependence on one another. As the poem progresses, the speaker becomes more personal, naming his village's zip code, 04421, and a specific woman. Janet, the town's postmaster, is "spun into light" by the planets' movements, as all people are. Moving from the specific person in Castine to the inclusive "we" once more, Booth combines thanksgivings for his peninsular village and, by extension, for life.

Relations includes selections from all Booth's previous collections, as well as thirty-one new poems. The later works use terse Down East language, slanted syllables, and simple Anglo-Saxon diction, omitting rhyme and meter. The fragmentation of short lines and stanzas gives these poems a conversational quality. Woven into these works is the theme of human isolation but also of love and connectedness with the world, for the poet often looks to nature for answers and for the reassurance of order. The title poem, "Relations," explores relationships not only of people to one another over space and time but also among lines in a poem, of words to other words, and of the limits the poet imposes on them. These poems do not offer certainties for the reader, but rather uncertainties, as the poet struggles to find his way through questions such as "Where did I come from?" and "Where am I going?" Booth speaks of this searching as a "coming to terms" with experience, and of human relationships as giving meaning to life.

Originally published in *Margins*, "Supposition with Qualification" questions the eternal mystery of being. The speaker discusses a man who "if he could say it" certainly meant to do so, but who is never clear about what "it" means. Instead, the man intended to say "how it felt when he let himself/ feel." It is, however, difficult for him to let himself feel anything without allowing his mind to get in the way. The poem includes several question words: "what," "how," "when." Even with the need to know suggested by these words, the man does not want to intellectualize but to feel, to "give himself up," although the qualification itself, "if he could say it," suggests his inability to do so, as well as the human need to question and articulate experience.

"The Man on the Wharf," which is arranged in direct two-line stanzas, describes a man, drunk with Jim Beam whiskey, who has lost his woman. He watches another man shuck clams; although he does not know why he watches, one senses in him a questioning about his life and his loss: He "swallows no answer/ but questions in bourbon this seeming harbor." "Seeming harbor" questions what is real and what is imagined, while the man turns to perhaps the most fundamental source for answers in the poem's concluding lines: "The sea is all he can ask."

"The Stranding" journeys inward, as the first-person speaker puts his eyes to the eyes of his own skull to look through both pairs of eyes into his own head, only to find a "stranding," a sense of being left alone in a helpless position, of being separated from his essential self. The speaker, though, can hardly see himself, and, when he considers calling to his inner self by name, he realizes that the inner self whom he can barely see is listening to porpoises, not to the self on the outside calling to him. Perhaps in answer to the universal question "Who am I?" the speaker finds isolation. In simple, carefully sharpened language arranged in stanzas of three short lines each, the poem successfully creates the effect of the speaker explaining to an individual listener what happened as he searched for himself.

Reminding one of David Wagoner's "Return to the Swamp," "The Question Poem" also deals with eternals. What does the wind mean? What "sudden discipline" determines the course of birds' migrations? Do the seabirds fish for answers, too? No answers are offered, but like any human being, the speaker finds it impossible to imagine a world in which he himself is absent. He does seem to find some hint of a response to his questions in the mysteries of the sea and its creatures as they move in their carefully ordered, delicately balanced relationships to one another.

SELVES

Booth alludes to the theme of *Selves* in *Vermont Academy Life* (Fall/Winter, 1979/1980): "I read because . . . my many selves . . . need to experience other lives." In *Selves*, once again, he presents beautifully moving, tightly made, sometimes humorous poems that employ a minimum of figurative language. The volume's prologue, from Wallace Stevens's *Esthétique du Mal* (1945), introduces the theme of the many selves within each human being. Participation in these poems allows the reader to become part of the creative process and, in turn, to begin to discover his or her own many selves. The poems combine philosophical speculation about universal mysteries with ordinary, mundane topics such as losing a glove, splitting wood with a wedge and an ax, and spreading manure. While commenting on each person's inability to feel another's feelings completely, and while expressing concern for the future given past and present ecological disasters, these poems give thanks for life, music, sex, food, and relationships, for awareness, consciousness, and wonder. Traditional rhyming and restrictive forms are eschewed in favor of the comfortable patterns of common speech, so that these works are very accessible.

The epigraph poem "Reaching In," with parallels from physics and probability theory, expresses deep concern with and respect for how each reader experiences the poem. Booth asks his readers to "weigh each word before you believe me"; there is an implied reward for the reader who follows this directive. The first "reaching" in the poem is that of the physicist who reaches in to measure momentum. The second use of the word is literal: The poet reaches through the dark at night on his way to the bathroom, and like the physicist's changing of the photon's position, the poet's "feet displace the shape of the dark." The third "reaching" is internal but also cosmic: "Reaching in, I trembled the landscape." The unusual transitive use of "trembled" continues the opening image. The word "you" in stanza 3 begins in reference to a particular person but subsequently moves to the individual reader and beyond. This poem suggests how to experience the poems that follow.

Some of the poems in part 1 are eloquent pictures of rural poverty. With simple, direct language "Poor" describes the impossibility of planning ahead when one has very little. Moose Coombs has never been able to afford the time to seek out seasoned wood for heating the kitchen stove. Instead he has brought home green wood, which burns too intensely and coats the chimney with creosote; the result is a sudden fire that destroys his wife and his house. There are no metaphors here, but the ordinary language brings the event home and shows its pointless tragedy.

In "Civilities," with humor, fondness, and appreciation, the poet turns to his grandmother's knowledge of "right words, and which/ to use when." Without ever using the four-letter word for excrement, Booth makes it humorously present. His portraits of Mr. Bowden delivering and of Mrs. Hooke paying for "spring dressing" are painted with tender humor and fond respect, as the poet, years later, prepares the same perennial garden they tended with "lovely dark clouds of cowdung."

Further poems in this volume speak of the isolation of aging, of survival, and of the hopefulness of life. "Fallback" poignantly describes an elderly couple imprisoned in a home for the aged. Concrete, direct language brings home the predicament of the old couple, who have been together for sixty-two years. They are now perfunctorily tended by a young nurse who "looks like a grebe" and who cannot and probably does not care to know the elderly woman's tender memories of love and caring: how her husband in years past spread out his jacket for picnics and how they "made love/ in the sweetfern high on an island." The husband's mind is now gone, and the wife's body is impossibly frail, but the memories are sturdy and real.

"Provisions," in reaction to a book on survival tactics left on an airplane, speaks against the directions it offers about what to take when one is dealing with a nuclear disaster and agrees only with the advice "Leave objects behind" (especially, Booth says, the survival book itself). His advice, instead, is to take poems, Thoreau, the memory of a tune by Bach, and sustaining memories. As the old woman in "Fallback" finds, it is the experiences of life that will sustain one.

The final piece in the collection, "Presence," is a

poem of wonder. In simple, two-line stanzas, the poet speaks of the singular mystery "that we are here, here at all." The very title suggests an almost worshipful attitude toward life, that there is a being, a presence, a hint of a supernatural influence felt nearby. "Presence" offers the opportunity for joy in life, brief as it is, and an affirmation of being.

LIFELINES

In *Lifelines*, the new poems comprise a final section. In this grouping, Booth enjoys more than even the formal play that is his hallmark, though with a continuing loosening of exterior borders. Understandably, many of these poems (as do several in *Pairs*) flirt with the impingement of aging. Memories have further to travel. Losses pile up. However, Booth's clipped, dignified style—and his occasional humor—hold despair in check. A long poem, "Reach Road: In Medias Res," follows an old mailman over the rural route he has traversed for decades, defined by the familiar blend of nature and neighborhood. His larger route, his lifepath, takes the mailman and the reader in and out of the books that define another kind of journey, the life of intellect and art that is Booth's own. At once narrative and meditative, "Reach Road" is a late marvel in a career of many marvels. It is a brilliant, if premature, review of Booth's territory—a summation.

Although all Booth's poetry explores the struggle and isolation of human existence, his ultimate response to both is positive. He embraces the old but important observation of John Donne that we are all, with our fears, affirmations, sorrow, and happiness, joined in the large human family. We are part of one another, and we share in the sorrows, mysteries, and joys of life. Booth's poems, with their universal themes and simple language, enlarge and expand that life.

OTHER MAJOR WORK

NONFICTION: *Trying to Say It: Outlooks and Insights on How Poems Happen*, 1996.

BIBLIOGRAPHY

Booth, Philip. Interview by Rachel Berghash. *American Poetry Review* 18 (May/June, 1989): 37-39. The poet discusses his sense of place and roots in Castine, offering some biographical information. He also talks about his views on survival, his philosophy of poetry, and his collection *Relations*.

_____. Interview by Stephen Dunn. *New England Review and Bread Loaf Quarterly* 9 (Winter, 1986): 134-158. Dunn is one of the four former students to whom Booth dedicated *Selves* and from whom the poet says he is still learning. This interview offers good insight into the poems of Booth's seventh volume, *Relations*.

Marquard, Bryan. "Philip Booth: Poetry and Maine Were the Core of His Life, at Eighty-One." *Boston Globe*, July 12, 2007, p. D7. This obituary of Booth examines his life and work, with an emphasis on his connection to Maine.

Phillips, Robert. "Utterly Unlike." *Hudson Review* 52, no. 4 (Winter, 1999): 689-697. Phillips contrasts Booth's style and thematic focus in *Lifelines* with two other works in this celebration of poetic diversity.

Rotella, Guy L. *Three Contemporary Poets of New England: William Meredith, Philip Booth, and Peter Davison*. Boston: Twayne, 1983. Rotella places Booth in a New England regional context, providing biographical information and analysis of the poetry.

Taylor, John. Review of *Lifelines*. *Poetry* 177, no. 1 (January, 2001): 272-273. Taylor notes that Booth's realism is often overcast with a dreaminess that invites introspection and meditation.

Tillinghast, Richard. "Stars and Departures, Hummingbirds and Statues." *Poetry* 166, no. 5 (August, 1995): 295-297. Tillinghast appreciates Booth's Yankee sensibility, close observation, and the way in which he avoids forcing his material into themes.

Linda K. Martinez
Updated by Philip K. Jason

DAVID BOTTOMS

Born: Canton, Georgia; September 11, 1949

PRINCIPAL POETRY

Jamming with the Band at the VFW, 1978
    (chapbook)
Shooting Rats at the Bibb County Dump, 1980
In a U-Haul North of Damascus, 1983
Under the Vulture-Tree, 1987
Armored Hearts: Selected and New Poems, 1995
Vagrant Grace, 1999
Waltzing Through the Endtime, 2004

OTHER LITERARY FORMS

Although David Bottoms has primarily made his reputation as a poet, he has published a number of other interesting and important works. As an editor, he collaborated with poet Dave Smith on the influential anthology *The Morrow Anthology of Younger American Poets* (1985). He also published the novels *Any Cold Jordan* (1987) and *Easter Weekend* (1990). Both novels earned generally favorable notices, but his poetry has typically received more attention. In 2001, he collaborated with photographer Diane Kirkland to produce *Oglethorpe's Dream: A Picture of Georgia*, a collection of photographs of the Georgia landscape with commentary by Bottoms.

ACHIEVEMENTS

David Bottoms's first full collection of poetry, *Shooting Rats at the Bibb County Dump*, was selected from a field of more than thirteen hundred submissions by famous novelist and poet Robert Penn Warren to receive the Walt Whitman Award from the Academy of American Poets in 1979. His next two collections of poetry, *In a U-Haul North of Damascus* and *Under the Vulture-Tree*, won Georgia Author of the Year Awards from the Council of Authors and Journalists (later the Georgia Writers Association) in 1983 and in 1988, respectively; Bottoms also won the Georgia Author of the Year Award for *Vagrant Grace* in 1999. His other awards include the Levinson Prize (1985) and the Frederick Bock Prize (2002) from *Poetry* magazine,

an Academy Award in Literature from the American Academy and Institute of Arts and Letters (1988), the Ingram Merrill Award (1988), and the James Boatwright III Prize for Poetry (2007). He was granted fellowships by the National Endowment for the Arts (1988) and the Guggenheim Foundation (1999). In 2000, he became the poet laureate for the state of Georgia, and in 2009, he was inducted into the Georgia Writers Hall of Fame.

BIOGRAPHY

Although David Bottoms's themes are seen as broadly construed and he has in some ways escaped the label of being a southern writer, his works are nevertheless intimately tied to the Georgia landscape where he has lived for most of his life. Bottoms was born in Canton, a small town in northern Georgia, where he graduated from Cherokee High School in 1967. He earned a B.A. in English in 1971 from Mercer University in Macon, Georgia, and an M.A. from West Georgia College in 1973. He married Margaret Bensel, an elementary school teacher, in 1972. From 1974 to 1978, he taught high school English, participating in the Georgia Poets in the Schools program sponsored by the Georgia Poetry Society. After receiving the Walt Whitman Award in 1979, he accepted a graduate fellowship at Florida State University in Tallahassee, where he earned a doctorate in creative writing and American poetry in 1982. Tallahassee would serve as the setting for his novel *Any Cold Jordan*, just as Macon would be the setting for *Easter Weekend*. In 1982, Bottoms became a professor of creative writing at Georgia State University, where he later would hold the Amos Distinguished Chair in English Letters. Other than a brief hiatus as the Richard Hugo Poet-in-Residence at the University of Montana, Bottoms has remained at Georgia State University. He and his wife divorced in 1987, and he married attorney Kelly Jean Beard (whom he met in Montana) in 1989. Their daughter Rachel was born in 1991.

ANALYSIS

It is fitting that David Bottoms was, in effect, discovered by Pulitzer Prize-winning poet and novelist Warren. The works of Bottoms and those of Warren reveal that although both writers were deeply affected by the cultural milieu of the South in their youths, their southern upbringing does not completely define and restrain their writing. Essentially, Bottoms's poetry not only manages to extract all the available benefits from his childhood but also progresses beyond the poet's experiences growing up in small-town Georgia. As much as he focuses on the rural South in early poems such as "Shooting Rats at the Bibb County Dump" and later poems such as "Homage to Buck Cline" (from *Waltzing Through the Endtime*), he is also concerned with father-son and father-daughter relationships (as in "The Desk" from *Under the Vulture-Tree* and "My Daughter at the Gymnastics Party" from *Vagrant Grace*) and with the disappearance of the natural world as the industrial world encroaches, as in "A Walk to Carter's Lake" (from *Vagrant Grace*). Bottoms has also written a number of poems in tribute to musicianship and musicians, including homages to such varied artists as bluegrass musician Lester Flatt, banjo player Little Roy Lewis, and the Allman Brothers, the 1970's rock group.

Bottoms is interested in how the world has changed since his youth, but at the same time, he does not fall prey to romanticizing or waxing nostalgic about the past. He is, however, curious about questions of fate and destiny. For example, Bottoms's father served aboard the U.S.S. *Atlanta* during World War II and floated for hours in the sea after being badly wounded at the Battle of Guadalcanal in November, 1942. Bottoms returns to this image again and again in his poems, partly, perhaps, in tribute to his father's courage and partly because of morbid curiosity: If the poet's father had died in 1942, then Bottoms never would have been born. In "Country Store and Moment of Grace" (from *Vagrant Grace*), he imagines his grandmother having received the news, picturing his ". . . grandmother collapsing one morning/ by the mailbox." The poet thinks of how for "Fifteen months she thought him dead," until a woman in her ". . . church dreamed him wounded/ but faceup,/ alive in burning water. . . ."

SHOOTING RATS AT THE BIBB COUNTY DUMP AND IN A U-HAUL NORTH OF DAMASCUS

Bottoms's first two collections of poetry fit most obviously into the tradition of southern poetry. They focus on the endemic problems of the twentieth century South: the loss of identity, racism, the disappearance of the rural world into suburbia, and the frustrations that come about from living lives of limited potential and opportunity. In "Shooting Rats at the Bibb County Dump," the narrator states, "It's the light they believe kills./ We drink and load again, let them crawl/ for all they're worth into the darkness we're headed for." It is the light of hope that is most damning and frustrating to the small-town men leading shackled lives. In the prayer that forms the titular poem of *In a U-Haul North of Damascus*, the narrator asks, "Jesus, could the irony be/ that suffering forms a stronger bond than love?"

UNDER THE VULTURE-TREE

Shooting Rats at the Bibb County Dump was an extraordinarily auspicious beginning for Bottoms's career, but *Under the Vulture-Tree* could be said to be the book that cemented his place in the forefront of his generation of poets. The book not only earned awards and honors but also tied together many of Bottoms's primary interests and themes. The title poem describes the narrator drifting down a river in a boat and passing under a tree laden with vultures. Looking up into the tree as the boat passes beneath, the narrator says, "The black leaves shined, the pink fruit blossomed/ red, ugly as a human heart." To his surprise, though, passing closely, he sees that the faces, and presumably the dreams, of the vultures with their "raw fleshy jowls" are "wrinkled and generous, like the very old/ who have grown to empathize with everything." Life is ugly, perhaps, and people are always under the shadow of the vulture; yet life is beautiful as well. This theme is reflected in "The Anniversary," a poem about the poet's veteran father's ritual handling of a Japanese knife on the anniversary of his wounding in World War II, acknowledging how close he was to being dead and gone. Bottoms's fascination with his father's example and life is developed even further in the book's ultimate poem, "The Desk," which tells how the poet, as a young man, broke into the school where his father had once carved his name into a desk in order to steal the desktop. Years later, his gaze falls onto the desk and the narrator wonders ". . . what it means/ to own my father's name."

VAGRANT GRACE AND WALTZING THROUGH THE ENDTIME

Bottoms's later books, such as *Vagrant Grace* and *Waltzing Through the Endtime*, continue to follow the thematic road maps of his earlier works, examining the importance of family, particularly from the standpoint of being a son to his father and a father to his daughter; the gravitational pull of the past in the South; the importance of the soul-soothing yet vanishing natural world in the human world; and humankind's fragile mortality. In "Bronchitis" (from *Vagrant Grace*), the narrator, who is reading about the Battle of Kennesaw Mountain in the American Civil War, is not so much struck by the battlefield tactics but by the death of a small girl killed by a Union shell: "I think of her sporadically, shell crater and spaniel,/ powder stench, geyser of dust settling/ as her mother staggers/ onto the porch—." This concern for the child is mirrored in "My Daughter at the Gymnastics Party," when the narrator watches his daughter Rachel, "the smallest child in class," climb the rope to the ceiling, ". . . ponytail swinging, fifteen, twenty,/ twenty-five feet, the pink tendrils of her leotard/ climbing without effort/ until she'd cleared the lower rafters." She does all this without consideration of all the children who have died, such as a skater on a frozen lake or a boy killed by falling off a horse; the narrator, her father, can think of little else.

Bottoms's poems often point out the danger of nostalgia; even as he considers the past of his grandfather's general store in the long poem "Country Store and Moment of Grace," he asks, "What's left in these last moments but memory?/ And what is memory/ but the mirror image of hope?" His feelings here are mirrored in his poem, "Homage to Buck Cline," about a run-in with a notorious small-town police officer when he was still a teenager. As the narrator considers how the world has changed and how his memory plays tricks, arranging itself into squared and focused stories for his readers' consideration, he also thinks of how the things that once haunted people as children slowly pare away until they are left with the bones of life, the most essential things of all:

Maybe in the long haul,
as a friend says, most everything blows off steadily to
   the shoulder
of the road and wallows like litter
               in the dark we leave behind, things
that have disheartened, haunted, obsessed, delighted,
until finally there's nothing to distract us
from that last curve opening
                onto the homestretch . . .

OTHER MAJOR WORKS

LONG FICTION: *Any Cold Jordan*, 1987; *Easter Weekend*, 1990.

EDITED TEXT: *The Morrow Anthology of Younger American Poets*, 1985 (with Dave Smith).

MISCELLANEOUS: *Oglethorpe's Dream: A Picture of Georgia*, 2001 (with photographer Diane Kirkland).

BIBLIOGRAPHY

Hill, Jane. "'To Own My Father's Name': Not Hiding the Masculine in the Poems of David Bottoms." *Studies in the Literary Imagination* 35, no. 1 (2002): 25-59. A thorough consideration of the masculine codes, as well as the relationships between father and son, in Bottoms's poetry.

Hill, Robert W. "Warbling with TV in the Background: David Bottoms in the Suburbs." *Southern Quarterly* 37, nos. 3/4 (1999): 80-84. A discussion that points out Bottoms's departure from southern clichés and stereotypes.

Murray, G. E. "The Collective Unconscious." *Southern Review* 37, no. 2 (Spring, 2001): 404-421. A review/analysis of the works of a number of southern poets that demonstrates how certain themes about manhood, fathers, overcoming the past, and racism appear repeatedly. The analysis provides thorough readings of poems from Bottoms's first and third books.

Russ, Don. "'Up Toward the Light': Resurrection, Transfiguration, Metamorphosis, and Evolution in David Bottoms's *Armored Hearts*." *Southern Quarterly* 37, nos. 3/4 (1999): 66-72. Although this article is primarily a consideration of Bottoms's collection *Armored Hearts*, its discussion of nature imagery in his work applies to many of his poems, early and late.

Suarez, Ernest. "A Deceptive Simplicity: The Poetry of David Bottoms." *Southern Quarterly* 37, nos. 3/4 (1999): 73-79. Suarez provides a useful analysis of Bottoms's technique, demonstrating his use of figurative detail and distracting narratives.

Scott D. Yarbrough

EDGAR BOWERS

Born: Rome, Georgia; March 2, 1924
Died: San Francisco, California; February 4, 2000

PRINCIPAL POETRY
The Form of Loss, 1956
The Astronomers, 1965
Living Together, 1973
For Louis Pasteur, 1989
Collected Poems, 1997

OTHER LITERARY FORMS
Edgar Bowers is known primarily for his poetry.

ACHIEVEMENTS
Edgar Bowers's poetry was championed by Yvor Winters, who offered the first critiques of Bowers's poetry in his critical book *Forms of Discovery* (1967). Winters's analysis was based on Bowers's first two books, *The Form of Loss* and *The Astronomers*. Winters was drawn to Bowers's imagery, his word choice, and his capable use of meter. He noted that Bowers's "vision" was shaped by many factors, including the war, his reading, and his intellectual interests. In his *Lives of the Poets* (1998), Michael Schmidt includes Bowers as one of the representative poets of the modern era and notes the influence on Winters on Bowers's style, describing the "harsh discipline" of Winters's teaching of poetry writing as having produced rigorously formal poetry linked to stoicism.

Bowers received many awards and honors in his career. In 1950, he was awarded a Fulbright Fellowship for study in England. In 1955, he won the Swallow Press Prize for Poetry. He received two Guggenheim Fellowships, in 1958 and 1969. In 1973, he received the Silver Medal in poetry from the Commonwealth Club of California for *Living Together*. In 1989, Bowers won both the Bolligen Prize and the Harriet Monroe Prize for excellence in poetry.

BIOGRAPHY
Edgar Bowers was born in Rome, Georgia, to William Edgar Bowers and Grace Anderson Bowers. His father, who was from South Carolina, graduated from Clemson University, served in World War I, briefly taught at Virginia Polytechnic University, and ended his career as a nurseryman in Stone Mountain, Georgia. His mother was a graduate of Agnes Scott College and a native of Iowa. She was a schoolteacher and an accomplished painter. Bowers had one sister, Eleanor, who predeceased him.

Between 1943 and 1946, Bowers, who was a French and German major at the University of North Carolina, served in the U.S. Army with the 101st Airborne's unit in counterintelligence. His role included service in Germany, where he acted as a translator and where he saw many scenes of devastation and despair. These would figure later in the sensibility of his poetry. After his tour ended, Bowers returned to finish his education on the G.I. Bill. He earned his B.A. in 1947 and enrolled in the Stanford M.A. program, where he would study with poet-critic Yvor Winters. He earned his degree in 1949 and followed that with a Ph.D. from Stanford in 1953. Bowers went on to teach at Duke University and Harpur College. In 1958, he joined the English faculty at the University of California, Santa Barbara, from which he would retire in 1991. He then moved to San Francisco, where he died of lymphatic cancer on February 4, 2000.

ANALYSIS
Edgar Bowers's poetry has been praised for its technical skill, its smooth integration of philosophical ideas, and its intellectual rigor. He was described by Dick Davis, a fellow poet and professor of Persian at Ohio State University, as "a cerebral poet," while the *Oxford Companion to Poetry* states Bowers's poetry shows "great intellectual sophistication" as he writes "with unmannered dexterity."

Bowers's greatest achievement was in his use of blank verse for poetry on contemporary themes and issues. Bowers kept aspects of the Elizabethan style, such as that of Ben Jonson, alive in his poetry. He wrote on a range of subjects, effectively blending elements of past literary traditions with contemporary concerns. He could be characterized as a poet of World War II in the sense that the war remained central to his writing. As late as the "New Poems" in the *Collected Poems* published in 1997, Bowers dealt with the way the war had changed his perceptions of life. Technically, he is a postwar poet, having published his first book of verse, written after the war, in 1956. Bowers never attempted to reconcile the war's experiences with his situation, nor did he moralize about the wrongs of war. His use of the war was as setting and a platform for deeper reflection on human nature and the way circumstances affect the course of life.

For someone who was counted in the company of

Edgar Bowers (©Miriam Berkley)

such notable poets as Howard Nemerov and Louis Simpson, Bowers received little critical attention after the publication of Yvor Winters's 1967 book that discussed him. Bowers's verse is the work of a serious observer of himself and human nature. The poetry is marked by its keen attention to details in both physical and abstract nature. The poems have great range and often accumulate information from various sources, which enables the poems to appeal to a variety of readers.

THE FORM OF LOSS

Published in 1956, *The Form of Loss* has twenty-six poems composed between 1947 and 1955. "To the Reader," which opens the collection, and "To this Book" were the last poems written in 1955. The primary images in the book are derived from nature. Bowers uses the image of snow, for example, to show mutability.

The Form of Loss demonstrates Bowers's use of rhetorical figures, stanza forms, rhymes, and meters in an unobtrusive manner in these poems based on his travels, his Army experiences, and his personal life. In the poem "Dark Earth and Summer," Bowers uses an alternating rhyme in the quatrains to counterpoint the words in the unrhymed lines to great effect. "To W. A. Mozart" is based on the time Bowers found himself in a German castle, where he was able to play a tune on Mozart's own clavier.

Other poems in the collection are topical, bringing together Bowers's interests in the lives of his friends, historical subjects, and the arts. "The Prince," a poem praised by Winters, combines the themes that dominate the book—time, loss, perception, and perspective—with a formal elegance and expertise. The poem is a dramatic monologue spoken by a father whose son has been executed as a spy in wartime. The title of the collection comes from "The Prince" as he says, "My son, who was the heir/ To every hope and trust grew out of caring,/ Into the form of loss as I had done,/ And then betrayed me who betrayed him first."

THE ASTRONOMERS

Bowers's 1965 collection of fifteen poems, *The Astronomers*, was dedicated to his mother and his aunts, who were formative influences in his education. The majority of these poems were written in Santa Barbara, after Bowers assumed his faculty position. Blank verse dominates the collection, as rhyme recedes and the poems become more conversational and evenly paced.

Death and the passage of time continue as important themes in this book. Two poems that stand out in this book are the sonnet "The Mirror," in which the poet-speaker addresses his father and their similarities in personality, and "Autumn Shade," a poem of ten numbered sections. The poem describes the sensations of coming home, the loss of innocence associated with aging, lost childhood, and the passage of time as the personality of the speaker has been changed by time, death, and experiences. The poem is rich in natural imagery, philosophical concepts, and lived experience.

LIVING TOGETHER

Bowers's third book, *Living Together*, is concentrated on the theme of love lost. Not based on any one experience, the poems are an assimilation of all people's experiences of sadness when relationships fail. The poems were composed between 1964 and 1971 in Santa Barbara.

"Living Together" in eight lines provides the themes of memory, love, loss, and loyalty. The poem "Wandering" charts the breakup of a relationship and ends with the speaker both literally sick in bed with the flu and emotionally heartsick. This is one instance of Bowers's use of comic or situational irony. "Insomnia" is a fine ten-line poem about the speaker's insomnia and his hope to wake up one morning with "the need to have no need." This collection shows Bowers's mastery of the shorter lyric, rich with formal elegance and vivid language.

FOR LOUIS PASTEUR

Of all his books, Bowers declared *For Louis Pasteur* his favorite for its technical skill, its variety in the use of blank verse for many diverse themes, and its alliance with his own interests. This is the book that best represents Bowers. The cover of the book is a painting by Bowers's mother, "The Big Oak."

The collection is divided into three numbered sections. Part 1 contains the title poem and two sequences of short poems—"Thirteen Views of Santa Barbara" (with its allusion to Wallace Stevens's "Thirteen Ways of Looking at a Blackbird")—and "Witnesses," in which Old Testament people—Adam, Eve, Cain, Noah, and Jacob— have a say about creation. "Thirteen Views"

begins with the highly visual poem "Hang Gliding," which uses language of flight and falling to connect the picture of the hang glider "leaping out from the fartherest ridge" with the soldier's memory of being a parachutist. Falling would have killed both these men, who hang precariously on the wind.

The second section of the book is composed of seven poems. These include a description of Dick Davis reading his poetry, with an emphasis on how he sounds when he reads and how the reading stops time and the noises of the environment in Los Angeles. "Mary" is a long narrative about Bowers's aunt, and "Elegy: Walking the Line" begins, "Every month or so, Sundays, we walked the line." It largely describes in rich visual language walking through the nursery on Stone Mountain and remembering all that happened there as well as the family that called it home.

The third section of the book has five poems on subjects that merge philosophical concepts with historical moments. The central poem of this section is "Chaco Canyon," which is at once topographical, experiential, and philosophical as the canyon is likened to Plato's cave from which knowledge of the world came.

The themes of this book advance those of the previous books with a new emphasis on ordering experiences and memories to make life less chaotic. The opening lines of "For Louis Pasteur" set the tone for the rest of the book as the speaker ponders: "How shall a generation know its story/ Of it will know no other?" This is elaborated on in stanza 2, "How shall my generation tell its story?" These are the seminal questions of Bowers's oeuvre and express what he is trying to accomplish in his poetry. As a poet who served in World War II, Bowers seeks to answer questions raised by subsequent generations about the meaning of war and such experience in everyday life.

The elegant poem "In Defense of Poetry," which ends the collection, begins, "Childhood taught us illusion," and it proceeds from there to address the theme of forms of deception, which Winters had first noticed in Bowers's verse. Here films, books, and education emphasizing self-esteem are the culprits in the false sense of security and accomplishment people have. In the final lines, the poet looking around at these people of the suburbs sees in his mind's eye Polish families on the trains to their deaths. Without saying anything more than just what the memory flash is, the poem effectively makes its point about the fragility of human life and civilization.

COLLECTED POEMS

Bowers's final book, *Collected Poems*, is a compilation of the previous books in total, but they are presented in reverse chronological order. The effect of this structure is to allow the reader to hear the different voices in Bowers's poetry and to chart its evolution from the present to the past. When the reader comes to *The Form of Loss*, it is clear how Bowers moved beyond his early rigorous use of form to create a more subtly crafted poem in which rhyme, meter, and rhetorical devices become a necessary extension of expressing the ideas of the poems. Taken together, one sees continuity in Bowers's interests and the development of traditional themes over time. From last to first book, the impression of Bowers's poetry is that it is a consistent exploration of universal ideas couched in a range of experiences.

The book opens with twenty-five new poems under eleven titles. There is one lyric sequence called "Mazes," which is composed of fourteen poems on time, space, nature, and ideas. "New Poems" opens with a long lyric in memory of John Finlay, a poet who died of acquired immunodeficiency syndrome (AIDS). The second poem, "Clear-seeing," about a clairvoyant in Germany during the war, complements the two poles of Bowers's poetic experiences: now and then. Other poems address preparing for death and remembrances. The poem "The Poet Orders His Tomb," with its allusion to Robert Browning's "The Archbishop Orders His Tomb," opens with an appeal to art historian Erwin Panofsky to design a tomb rich with animal imagery and symbols. As the poem speeds along in rhymed quatrains, stanza 8 provides a glimpse at Bowers's definition of his role as a poet: "I who have sought time's memory afoot,/ Grateful for every root/ Of trees that fill the garden with their fruit,/ Their fragrance and their shade?"

As these stanzas suggest, Bowers's poetry is not easily reducible to a core set of stylistic preferences or themes. He showed great skill with the short lyric, stan-

zas, and the long narrative. Significantly, he extended the possibilities for blank verse as a tool for poets wanting to write meaningful poetry in a formal mode. His themes were varied, but they seem to center on such concepts as loyalty, love, honor, courage, and beauty.

BIBLIOGRAPHY

Akard, Jeffery, and Joshua Odell. *A Bibliography of the Published Works of Edgar Bowers*. Barth Bibliographies 3. Santa Barbara, Calif.: J. Akard, 1988. Provides technical descriptions of the books published before 1988 and includes listings of the periodicals in which many of the poems were first published. Bowers provided a chronology for the poems as well.

Davis, Dick. "The Mystery of Consciousness: A Tribute to the Poet Edgar Bowers." *Poets and Writers*, July/August, 2000, 14-19. A tribute to Bowers and analysis of some of his poetry by his friend Dick Davis.

Fraser, Russell. "Edgar Bowers: His Little Book and All the Rest." *Yale Review* 96, no. 1 (January, 2008): 24. Fraser reflects on his friendship with Bowers and Bowers's poetry.

Schmidt, Michael. *Lives of the Poets*. London: Weidenfeld & Nicolson, 1998. Places Bowers in the context of a discussion of Yvor Winters's poetry and notes the influence of Winters on Bowers's use of language and uses of poetic form.

Wilmer, Clive. "Obituary: Edgar Bowers, American Poet Exploring the Mysteries of Life with an Aesthetic and Sensitive Intellect." *The Guardian*, February 15, 2000, p. 22. Obituary details Bowers's life and describes his poetry as having an "extreme aesthetic refinement and an intense feeling for the mystery of things."

Winters, Yvor. *Forms of Discovery*. Denver, Colo.: Alan Swallow Press, 1967. Winters studies Bowers's first two books and analyzes their strengths and weaknesses. Winters also edited two collections of poetry in which he included Bowers's verse: *Poets of the Pacific* (1949; second series) and *Quest for Reality* (with Kenneth Fields, 1969).

Beverly Schneller

ANNE BRADSTREET

Born: Northampton, Northamptonshire, England; 1612(?)

Died: Andover, Massachusetts Bay Colony (now in Massachusetts); September 16, 1672

PRINCIPAL POETRY

The Tenth Muse Lately Sprung Up in America: Or, Several Poems Compiled with Great Variety of Wit and Learning, Full of Delight, 1650 (revised and enlarged 1678 as *Several Poems Compiled with Great Variety of Wit and Learning, Full of Delight*)

OTHER LITERARY FORMS

Anne Bradstreet's published collection of 1650 and its revised edition of 1678 consist entirely of poetry, and her reputation rests on her poems. She left in manuscript the prose "Meditations Divine and Morall" (short, pithy proverbs) and a brief autobiography written especially for her children.

ACHIEVEMENTS

Anne Bradstreet and Edward Taylor are the two foremost Colonial American poets. They form a classic study in contrasts: She was emotional, he cerebral; she secular, he spiritual; she feminine, he masculine; she stylistically straightforward, he complex; she generically varied, he generically limited; she well known by her contemporaries, he little known until the twentieth century. These are only generalizations; however, they suggest a special problem that Bradstreet criticism has overcome: the inability to divorce her work from biographical, historical, and personal elements.

One of Bradstreet's distinctive poetic strengths is her generic variety. She wrote epics ("The Four Monarchies" and the "Quaternions"), dialogues ("A Dialogue Between Old England and New," among others), love lyrics, public elegies (on Sir Philip Sidney, Guillaume de Salluste Du Bartas, and her parents, for example), private elegies (on her grandchildren and daughter-in-law), a long meditative poem ("Contemplations"), and

religious verse. Few other Puritan poets successfully tackled so many genres.

Although Bradstreet's contemporaries admired her early imitative poetry ("The Four Monarchies," the "Quaternions," and the elegies on Sidney, Du Bartas, and Queen Elizabeth I), her later personal poetry is what endures (and endears). Poems included in *Tenth Muse Lately Sprung Up in America* fall within an essentially Renaissance tradition, while those in *Several Poems Compiled with Great Variety of Wit and Learning, Full of Delight* initiate a distinctive tradition of American literature. Bradstreet's love poems to her husband are admired for their wit, intricate construction, emotional force, and frank admission of the physical side of marriage: As she says in "To my Dear and Loving Husband," "If ever two were one, then surely we./ If ever man were lov'd by wife, then thee." Bradstreet's personal elegies on her grandchildren skillfully dramatize the Puritans' unremitting battle between worldliness (grieving for the dead) and unworldliness (rejoicing in their salvation). However,

Anne Bradstreet (The Granger Collection, New York)

her masterpiece is probably her long meditative poem "Contemplations," praised for its maturity, complexity, and lyricism. Her love poems, personal elegies, and "Contemplations" reveal the human side of Puritanism from a woman's vantage point.

BIOGRAPHY

Through her poetic voices, Anne Bradstreet assumes a clear (but complex) presence, yet factual data about her are surprisingly scant. Joseph McElrath, editor of *The Complete Works of Anne Bradstreet* (1981), shows that even her birth date is uncertain. She was born Anne Dudley, one of Thomas Dudley and Dorothy Yorke's six children, probably in 1612 in Northampton, England, but she may have been born as late as 1613.

In 1619, the family moved to Sempringham, where Thomas Dudley became steward to the earl of Lincoln. Both he and his employer allowed the prospective poet an unusually good education for a woman. Scholars even speculate that she had access to the earl's library. There she may have read staples of humanism: William Shakespeare, Sir Philip Sidney, Sir Walter Raleigh, Du Bartas, and Miguel de Cervantes. In 1621, Simon Bradstreet joined the earl's household to assist Dudley; but in 1624, the Dudleys moved to Boston, England, and Simon Bradstreet left to work for the countess of Warwick.

When the poet was about sixteen, as she records in her autobiographical prose, "the Lord layd his hand sore upon me & smott mee with the small pox." After her recovery in 1628, she and Simon Bradstreet married, and two years later, the Dudley and Bradstreet families left for America aboard the *Arbella*.

For Anne Bradstreet, the transition was not entirely smooth, and her prose autobiography speaks of "a new World and new manners at which my heart rose. But after I was convinced it was the way of God, I submitted to it & joined to the chh., at Boston." After brief spells in Salem, Boston, Cambridge, and Ipswich, the Bradstreets moved to North Andover, Massachusetts Bay Colony, where Anne Bradstreet reared eight children, wrote, and shared her husband's life as he rose from judge to governor of the colony. Although the poet was susceptible to many illnesses and was childless for several years, her supremely happy marriage compensated for, and helped her to overcome, these "trials."

As the governor's wife, Bradstreet enjoyed a socioeconomic status conducive to writing. In the mid-1640's, Bradstreet had completed the poems that appeared in her first collection. Bradstreet herself did not supervise their printing; John Woodbridge, her brother-in-law, probably carried the manuscript to London, where it was published in 1650. Bradstreet expresses mixed feelings about its publication, largely because of the printing errors. The poem "The Author to Her Book" mildly chides "friends, less wise than true" who exposed the work "to publick view." Poems in the collection are mainly public in tone and content, while those in her second collection (published posthumously in 1678) are mainly private and personal.

Bradstreet was a known, respected, and loved poet in both the Old and New Worlds. Her death in 1672 called forth elegies and eulogies. These lines from the preface to *The Tenth Muse Lately Sprung Up in America*, probably written by Woodbridge, best convey Bradstreet's qualities: "It is the Work of a Woman, honoured, and esteemed where she lives, for her gracious demeanour, her eminent parts, her pious conversation, her courteous disposition, [and] her exact diligence in her place."

ANALYSIS

Anne Bradstreet wrote poetry from the 1640's to her death in 1672. Naturally, her work developed and deepened over this thirty-year period. The critic Kenneth Requa's distinction between her public and private poetic voices (in "Anne Bradstreet's Poetic Voices," *Early American Literature*, XII, 1977) is a useful way to assess her poetic development. Her public voice, which dominates the early poetry, is eulogistic, imitative, self-conscious, and less controlled in metaphor and structure. Most of the poems in *The Tenth Muse Lately Sprung Up in America* illustrate these traits. Her private voice—more evident in *Several Poems Compiled with Great Variety of Wit and Learning, Full of Delight*—is often elegiac, original, self-confident, and better controlled in metaphor and structure. Any attempt to divide Bradstreet's work into phases has its dangers. Here, however, it is convenient to consider representative elegies from three roughly chronological stages: "poetic" involvement, conventional involvement, and personal involvement.

FIRST PHASE

Almost all the verse in her first collection conveys Bradstreet's public, poetic involvement. Specifically, in secular poems such as the "Quaternions," "The Four Monarchies," and the elegies on famous Elizabethans, Bradstreet as professional poet or bard dominates and controls. "In Honour of Du Bartas" (1641) contains the typical Renaissance characteristics of public content, imitative style, classical allusions, and secular eulogy. The poem's content could hardly be more public, since it dutifully details the accomplishments of Bradstreet's mentor Du Bartas—his learning, valor, wit, and literary skill. Although Bradstreet contrasts her meager poetic powers with Du Bartas's unlimited powers, her involvement is not personal; rather, it eventually points to a favorite moral for Renaissance poets. No matter how bad the writer, the dead person (in this case a poet, too) will "live" in the poem's lines. The "Quaternions"—a quartet of long poems on the four elements, the four humors, the four ages of man, and the four seasons—and the interminable rhymed history "The Four Monarchies" are similarly public in content.

An extension of public content and bardic involvement is imitative style. For example, "In Honour of Du Bartas" contains conventional images like the simile comparing Bradstreet's muse to a child, the hyperbole declaring that Du Bartas's fame will last "while starres do stand," and the oxymoron in "senslesse Sences." Although Bradstreet's early imitative style is skillful, it hinders her from expressing the unique voice of her later work. Furthermore, tradition compels her to scatter her public poems with classical allusions. In the three elegies on Du Bartas, Sidney, and Queen Elizabeth I, these allusions are a conventional part of the Renaissance pastoral elegy, and in the "Quaternions" they imitate the medieval/Renaissance debates.

Finally, these lengthy early poems may contain secular eulogy, also a characteristic of the pastoral elegy, and hyperbole, common in the debate form. The opening lines of "In Honour of Du Bartas," for example, state that Du Bartas is "matchlesse knowne" among contemporary poets. In such a richly literary age, Bradstreet obviously uses hyperbole and eulogy to emphasize Du Bartas's greatness for her.

SECOND PHASE

The second phase—conventional involvement—includes religious poems within a public or orthodox context. In many ways this is a transitional voice, for some poems recall the imitativeness and bardic self-consciousness of the first phase, while others anticipate the domestic content and individual voice of the third phase. A few poems (such as "David's Lamentations for Saul" and "Of the vanity of all worldly creatures") are from *The Tenth Muse Lately Sprung Up in America*; more are from her second collection (the elegies on Thomas and Dorothy Dudley and "The Flesh and the Spirit," for example). In this poetry, Bradstreet moves closer to mainstream Puritan verse. The elegies on her parents are conventionally formal and fit the pattern of the New England funeral elegy, whose hallmark was public praise of the dead one's life and virtues to overcome personal grief. "The Flesh and the Spirit," "As weary pilgrim now at rest," and "Of the vanity of all worldly creatures" treat the theme of worldliness versus unworldliness generally and impersonally to reach orthodox conclusions.

Bradstreet's elegy on her father, "To the memory of my dear and ever honoured Father Thomas Dudley," begins with an apparently personal touch: Bradstreet's claim to write from filial duty, not custom. Even so, as she reminds her readers, this filial duty allows her to praise her father's virtues fully and publicly, not partially and privately. In later elegies, Bradstreet does not explain so defensively why she follows certain conventions; indeed, she frequently modifies or ignores them. In this early elegy, however, these conventions constrain Bradstreet's own voice so that she writes forced lines such as these: "In manners pleasant and severe/ The Good him lov'd, the bad did fear,/ And when his time with years was spent/ If some rejoyc'd, more did lament." Lacking are the emotional force, personal involvement, and dramatic struggle between flesh and spirit found in the later poems.

Another characteristic apparent in the second phase is Bradstreet's use of fairly standard poetic structure. "The Flesh and the Spirit," for example, is in dialogue/ debate form, while "As weary pilgrim, now at rest" and "Of the vanity of all worldly creatures"—both meditations—examine the battle between body and soul to attain the eternal peace that only Christ's love will bring. "David's Lamentations for Saul" is a versified retelling of the scriptural story. Bradstreet's epitaphs on her mother and father, as already stated, follow the form of the Puritan elegy.

Standard, often biblical, imagery is another distinct aspect of the second phase. While this imagery is to some extent present in the earlier and later phases, it is particularly evident in the middle stage. In the first stage, Bradstreet's images are traditionally Renaissance, and in the third stage, they are biblical but infused with emotive and personal force. The elegy on Thomas Dudley illustrates the traditionally biblical images found in phase two: Dudley has a "Mansion" prepared above; and, like a ripe shock of wheat, he is mown by the sickle Death and is then stored safely. The other orthodox poems also use biblical images almost exclusively.

Appropriately, in these poems, Bradstreet generally excludes the personal voice. Only "As weary pilgrim, now at rest," the theme of which is the heaven-bound soul housed within the "Corrupt Carcasse," succeeds in combining the general and individual situations. Universality and individuality form the special strength of Bradstreet's masterpiece, "Contemplations." This thirty-three-verse meditative poem fits best into the second stage because of its spiritual content. Given the poem's importance, however, it must be discussed separately. Bradstreet skillfully evokes a dramatic scene—she walks at dusk in the countryside—then uses it to explore the relationships among man, God, and nature.

In stanzas one to seven, the poet acknowledges nature's potency and majesty by looking first at an oak tree and then at the sun. If they are glorious, she muses, how much more glorious must their creator be? Stanzas eight to twenty recall man's creation and fall, extending from Adam and Eve to Cain and Abel and finally to Bradstreet's own day. The answer to man's misery, however, is not nature worship. Instead, man must acknowledge that God made him alone for immortality. In stanzas twenty-one to twenty-eight, the poet considers the amoral delight of nature—the elm, the river, the fish, and the nightingale—incapable of the tortures of free will. Stanzas twenty-nine to thirty-three show that beyond the natural cycle, only man ("This lump of wretchedness, of sin and sorrow," as the poet states) can be resurrected within the divine cycle.

"Contemplations" contains some of Bradstreet's most original and inspired poetry within the three-part structure of the seventeenth century meditation. These parts correspond to the mental faculties of memory, understanding, and will. In the first part, the person creates or recalls a scene; in the second part, he analyzes its spiritual significance; and last, he responds emotionally and intellectually by prayer and devotion. Clearly, these are the three basic structural elements of "Contemplations." Although Bradstreet ultimately returns to orthodoxy, this poem is no mere religious exercise; it is "the most finished and musical of her religious poems."

THIRD PHASE

The third phase of Bradstreet's poetry includes love lyrics, elegies on grandchildren and a daughter-in-law, and other works inspired by private matters (the burning of Bradstreet's house, the publication of her first collection, the poet's eight children). However, unlike the poems of the previous stage, which are overwhelmingly spiritual, the poems of the third phase are primarily secular. If they deal with religious matters—as the elegies do, for example—it is within a personal context. One critic calls Bradstreet "the worldly Puritan," and these late poems show the material face of Puritanism. Bradstreet's personal involvement affects structure, tone, rhythm, and metaphor. "In memory of my dear grand-child Elizabeth Bradstreet" illustrates many of these changes.

Because she was more comfortable writing of private matters in a private voice, Bradstreet's poetic structure arises naturally from content and context. The elegy on Elizabeth, for instance, divides into two seven-line stanzas (it is a variation of the sonnet form). In stanza 1, the poet says farewell to her grandchild and questions why she should be sad since little Elizabeth is in Heaven. In stanza 2, Bradstreet explains that nature's products perish only when they are ripe; therefore, if a newly blown "bud" perishes, it must be God's doing. The structure aptly complements the poet's grief, disbelief, and final resignation. Both stanzas effortlessly follow the rhyme scheme *ababccc*. Bradstreet's love poems are also constructed in an intricate but uncontrived way. Both poems titled "Another [Letter to Her Husband]" show careful attention to structure. The first poem of this title personifies the sun and follows the sun's daily course; the second ties together three images and puns suggesting marital harmony (*dear/deer, heart/hart,* and *hind/hind*).

A marked difference in the poetry of the third phase is its tone. Instead of sounding self-conscious, bookish, derivative, overambitious, or staunchly orthodox, Bradstreet's later poetry is poised, personal, original, modest, and unwilling to accept orthodoxy without question. Another tonal change is subtlety, which the elegy on Elizabeth illustrates well. Throughout the poem Bradstreet hovers between the worldly response of grief and the unworldly one of acceptance. This uneasy balance, finally resolved when Bradstreet accepts God's will, makes the elegy especially poignant. The poet's other late elegies on her grandchildren Anne and Simon and her daughter-in-law Mercy are also poignant. The secular love poetry that Bradstreet wrote to her husband—often while he was away on business—conveys playfulness, longing, and, above all, boundless love. The tone of Bradstreet's late poetry tends to be more varied and complex than the tone of her early poetry, the only notable exception being "Contemplations," placed in phase two.

Bradstreet's rhythm reflects her increased poetic self-confidence. Gone are the strained lines and rhythms characteristic of the "Quaternions" and "The Four Monarchies"; instead, the opening lines of Bradstreet's elegy on Elizabeth show how private subject matter lends itself to natural, personal expression: "Farewel dear babe, my hearts too much content,/ Farewel sweet babe, the pleasure of mine eye,/ Farewel fair flower that for a space was lent,/ Then ta'en away unto Eternity." The delicate antithesis in lines one to three and the repetition of "Farewel" add emotional force to the content and emphasize Bradstreet's difficulty in accepting Elizabeth's death. The other late elegies are rhythmically varied and use antithesis to underscore life's ever-present duality: flesh/spirit, worldliness/unworldliness. For example, within the elegy on three-year-old Anne, Bradstreet conveys her problem in coming to terms with yet another grandchild's death when she uses this forced, monosyllabic rhythm, "More fool then I to look on that was lent./ As if mine own, when thus impermanent." The love poetry is also written with special attention to rhythmic variety.

The poet's metaphoric language in the later works is free of bookishness and imitativeness. She does not resort to classical allusions or literary images but chooses familiar, often domestic or biblical, metaphors. In the elegy on Elizabeth, the entire second stanza comprises a series of images drawn from nature. Bradstreet heightens her grandchild's death by saying how unnatural it is compared with the natural cycle of trees, fruit, corn, and grass. The love poetry draws on nature images too—the sun, fish, deer, and rivers, for instance. In her late personal poetry, Bradstreet also feels comfortable using some extended images. "The Author to Her Book," for example, extends the metaphor of Bradstreet's relationship as author/mother to her book/child, while "In reference to her Children, 23 June 1659" humorously compares Bradstreet and her children to a mother hen and her chicks. These images are original in the sense that they arise in an unaffected, apparently spontaneous, way. They are not original in the sense of being innovative.

The elegies on Du Bartas, Thomas Dudley, and Elizabeth Bradstreet are representative of stages in Bradstreet's poetic career. Her poetry has always been known, but now, more than ever, critics agree on her importance as one of the two foremost Colonial poets. Until recently, scholarship focused on biographical and historical concerns. Modern criticism, however, concentrates on structure, style, theme, and text. This move toward aesthetic analysis has deepened scholarly appreciation of Bradstreet's talent. In addition, the rise of women's studies ensures her place as a significant female voice in American poetry. She has stood the test of time as "a writer of unquestionably major stature."

OTHER MAJOR WORK

MISCELLANEOUS: *The Complete Works of Anne Bradstreet*, 1981 (Joseph R. McElrath and Allan P. Robb, editors).

BIBLIOGRAPHY

Boschman, Robert. *In the Way of Nature: Ecology and Westward Expansion in the Poetry of Anne Bradstreet, Elizabeth Bishop, and Amy Clampitt.* Jefferson, N.C.: McFarland, 2009. Boschman analyzes the poetry of Bradstreet, Elizabeth Bishop, and Amy Clampitt, paying attention to travel, geography, and attitudes toward the New World.

Cowell, Pattie, and Ann Stanford, eds. *Critical Essays on Anne Bradstreet*. Boston: G. K. Hall, 1983. An excellent collection of essays by a variety of Bradstreet scholars. Part 1 includes criticism from the colonial period to the twentieth century. The essays cover issues as diverse as Bradstreet's role in the American female literary tradition, the role of religion in the poet's life and work, and her inventive use of language.

Dolle, Raymond F. *Anne Bradstreet: A Reference Guide*. Boston: G. K. Hall, 1990. An exhaustive summary of all commentaries on Bradstreet written between 1650 and 1989.

Gordon, Charlotte. *Mistress Bradstreet: The Untold Life of America's First Poet*. New York: Little, Brown, 2005. A biography of the poet with special emphasis on the context of her time and place, seventeenth century colonial Massachusetts.

Hammond, Jeffrey. *Sinful Self, Saintly Self*. Athens: University of Georgia Press, 1993. Grounded in solid scholarship, this study compares works by Bradstreet, Michael Wigglesworth, and Edward Taylor. Hammond finds unexpected resemblances in the ways in which these three Puritan poets responded to their projected audiences. Clearly written and carefully documented.

Martin, Wendy. *An American Triptych: Anne Bradstreet, Emily Dickinson, Adrienne Rich*. Chapel Hill: University of North Carolina Press, 1984. Examines how the American experience has been transformed in the works of three American poets. The section on Bradstreet focuses on the relationship between the poet's commitment to the religious values of her culture and her desire to create an alternative vision in her art.

Rosenmeier, Rosamond. *Anne Bradstreet Revisited*. Boston: Twayne, 1991. Intended to supersede Josephine K. Piercy's study for the same publisher, this work's format is unusual in a Twayne book. Its approach is suggested by the titles of the three main chapters: "Daughter-Child: Actualities and Poetic Personas," "Sister-Wife: Conflict and Redefini-

tions," and "Mother Artist: A Typology of the Creative."

Scheick, William J. *Authority and Female Authorship in Colonial America*. Lexington: University Press of Kentucky, 1998. Scheick searches for aesthetic and thematic dissonance in texts such as Mary English's acrostic poem or Elizabeth Ashbridge's autobiography. The choice of authors spans a provocatively wide sample of women's writing, including Bradstreet's.

Stanford, Ann. *Anne Bradstreet: The Worldly Puritan*. New York: Burt Franklin, 1974. Written as an introduction to the works of Bradstreet. Discusses the body of the author's poetry in the light of the prevailing literary forms and examines how Bradstreet fashioned these forms into a personal voice for argument between the world she knew and the greater world she envisioned. Contains extensive notes, a bibliography, and appendixes.

White, Elizabeth Wade. *Anne Bradstreet: The Tenth Muse*. New York: Oxford University Press, 1971. Although Bradstreet's writing became the object of increasing interest and discussion in the twentieth century, White maintains that her life and historical background have been neglected. Calls Bradstreet the first resident poet of English-speaking North America and the first significant British poet. Contains numerous illustrations, an appendix, and a bibliography.

K. Z. Derounian

EDWARD KAMAU BRATHWAITE

Born: Bridgetown, Barbados; May 11, 1930
Also known as: Kamau Brathwaite

PRINCIPAL POETRY
Rights of Passage, 1967
Masks, 1968
Islands, 1969
The Arrivants: A New World Trilogy, 1973
    (includes *Rights of Passage*, *Masks*, and *Islands*)
Days and Nights, 1975

Other Exiles, 1975

Black + Blues, 1976

Mother Poem, 1977

Word Making Man: Poem for Nicolás Guillén in Xaymaca, 1979 (bilingual edition, with Spanish version by J. R. Pereira)

Sun Poem, 1982

Third World Poems, 1983

Jah Music, 1986

X/Self, 1987

Sappho Sakyi's Meditations, 1989

Shar, 1990

Middle Passages, 1992

Trench Town Rock, 1994

DreamStories, 1994

Words Need Love Too, 2000

Ancestors: A Reinvention of "Mother Poem," "Sun Poem," and "X/Self," 2001

Born to Slow Horses, 2005

DS (2): dreamstories, 2007

Elegguas, 2010

OTHER LITERARY FORMS

Edward Kamau Brathwaite (BRATH-wayt) has published scores of books, articles, and reviews as a historian and literary critic. Among his historical studies are *The Development of Creole Society in Jamaica, 1770-1820* (1971), which was his dissertation in college in the 1960's; *Contradictory Omens: Cultural Diversity and Integration in the Caribbean* (1974); *Caribbean Man in Space and Time* (1974); and *History of the Voice: The Development of Nation Language in Anglophone Caribbean Poetry* (1984). His historical studies have delineated the historical pressures that have shaped modern-day Caribbean life. He is particularly interested in the transmission of African culture to the New World, the "'little' tradition of the ex-slave," and its promise to serve as a "basis for creative reconstruction" in postemancipation, postcolonial Creole society. His literary criticism has sought out the presence of African traditions in Caribbean literature and has helped to develop a vigorous, indigenous school of West Indian criticism. Brathwaite's work as poet, critic, and historian has made available to a wide audience the rich cultural heritage of Caribbean people.

ACHIEVEMENTS

Edward Kamau Brathwaite is one of the most popular and critically acclaimed writers to emerge in the West Indies during the remarkable period in the region's history and literature following World War II. He epitomizes the intensified ethnic and national awareness of his generation of writers—which includes Derek Walcott, Wilson Harris, Michael Anthony, Martin Carter, Samuel Selvon, John Hearne, and Austin Clarke, to name several of the more prominent—whose writing seeks to correct the destructive effects of colonialism on West Indian sensibility.

For his efforts, Brathwaite has earned a number of honors. He received an Arts Council of Great Britain bursary and a Camden Arts Festival prize (both in 1967), the Cholmondeley Award (1970) for *Islands*, a Guggenheim Fellowship (1972), a City of Nairobi Fellowship (1972), the Bussa Award (1973), a Casa de las Americas Prize for Poetry (1976), a Fulbright Fellowship (1982), an Institute of Jamaica Musgrave Medal (1983), the Neustadt International Prize for Literature (1994) and the Griffin Poetry Prize (2006) for *Born to Slow Horses*. He has served on the board of directors of UNESCO's History of Mankind project since 1979 and as cultural advisor to the government of Barbados from 1975 to 1979 and again beginning in 1990. Over the years, Brathwaite has taught at a number of universities, including the University of the West Indies, University of Nairobi, Harvard University, Yale University, and New York University, where he became professor of comparative literature.

BIOGRAPHY

Lawson Edward Kamau Brathwaite was born Lawson Edward Brathwaite in Bridgetown, Barbados, on May 11, 1930, the son of Hilton Brathwaite and Beryl Gill Brathwaite. He enrolled at Harrison College in Barbados, then in 1949, he won the Barbados Scholarship, enabling him to read history at Pembroke College, Cambridge University, in 1950. He received an honors degree in 1953 and the certificate of education in 1955.

His earliest published poems appeared in the literary journal *Bim*, beginning in 1950. The poems of that decade, some of which are collected in *Other Exiles* and, in revised form, in *The Arrivants*, portray an estranged world fallen from grace, a world that can be re-deemed through poetic vision—a creative faith that sustains the more complex fashionings of his later work. Brathwaite shared with other West Indian writers of his generation a strong sense of the impossibility of a creative life in the Caribbean and the equal impossibility of maintaining identity in exile in England or North America. He understood this crisis of the present as a product of his island's cultural heritage being fragmented among its sources: European, African, Amerindian, and Asian.

His reading of history at Cambridge heightened both his sense of the European culture that had been the dominant official culture of the West Indies and his need to understand the African culture that had come with the slaves on the Middle Passage. His search led him to Africa, where he served as an education officer in Kwame Nkrumah's Ghana from 1955 to 1962. His career in Ghana (and in Togoland in 1956-1957 as United Nations Plebiscite Officer) provided the historical and local images that became *Masks*, the pivotal book of *The Arrivants*. In Ghana, he established a children's theater and wrote several plays for children (*Four Plays for Primary Schools*, pr. 1961, and *Odale's Choice*, pr. 1962). He married Doris Monica Wellcome in 1960, and he has a son, Michael Kwesi Brathwaite.

Brathwaite returned to the West Indies after an exile of twelve years to assume a post as resident tutor at the University of the West Indies in St. Lucia (1962-1963) and to produce programs for the Windward Islands Broadcasting Service. His return to the Caribbean supplied the "center" that his poetry had lacked:

> I had, at that moment of return, completed the triangular trade of my historical origins. West Africa had given me a sense of place, of belonging; and that place . . . was the West Indies. My absence and travels, at the same time, had given me a sense of movement and restlessness—rootlessness. It was, I recognized, particularly the condition of the Negro of the West Indies and the New World.

The exploration of that sense of belonging and rootlessness in personal and historic terms is the motive for Brathwaite's subsequent work in poetry, history, and literary criticism. He began in 1963 as lecturer in history at the University of the West Indies at Kingston,

Jamaica; he became a professor of social and cultural history there. He earned his Ph.D. at the University of Sussex in England (1965-1968). His dissertation became *The Development of Creole Society in Jamaica, 1770-1820*, a study of the assimilation of cultures by various groups within the colonial hierarchy. In 1971, in Kingston, he launched *Savacou*, the journal for the Caribbean Artists Movement (CAM), which he cofounded in 1966 in London.

His poetry continues to explore the cultural heritage of the West Indies in historical and personal terms. During the 1980's, Brathwaite continued to produce important literary criticism and poetry collections. The death of Brathwaite's wife, Doris, in 1986 marked a critical juncture in his career. The shock came in the midst of a publishing a retrospective collection of poems (*Jah Music*) and Doris's own labor of love, the bibliography *EKB: His Published Prose and Poetry, 1948-1986*. Another blow came in 1988, when Hurricane Gilbert virtually destroyed Brathwaite's house and buried most of his library in mud, entombing an unequaled collection of Caribbean writing as well as Brathwaite's own papers. Even more harrowing was a 1990 break-in and physical attack against Brathwaite in his Marley Manor apartment in Kingston. These events helped in his decision to leave Jamaica in 1991, when he began his tenure at New York University, teaching comparative literature. From 1997 to 2000, he resided in Barbados; during this period, he married Beverley Reid, a steady source of his inspiration.

ANALYSIS

Edward Kamau Brathwaite's aim, as he has described it, is to "transcend and heal" the fragmented culture of his dispossessed people through his poetry, reexamining the whole history of the black diaspora in a search for cultural wholeness in contemporary Caribbean life. Brathwaite offers his poetry as a corrective to the twin problems of the West Indian: dispossession of history and of language. The West Indian writer labors in a culture whose history has been distorted by prejudice and malice, the modern version of which is the commonplace notion, after James Anthony Froude and V. S. Naipaul, that nothing was created or achieved in the West Indies. The Afro-Caribbean's history is the record of being uprooted, displaced, enslaved, dominated, and finally abandoned. Brathwaite's reclamation of racial pride centers on rectifying the significance of the Middle Passage not as the destroyer but as the transmitter of culture.

The second problem that the writer confronts, that of language, is an aspect of cultural dispossession. The diversity of Creole languages, hybrids of many African and European tongues, reinforces the insularity of the individual and devalues the expressively rich languages that the people use in their nonofficial, personal, most intimate lives. Brathwaite's poems in Bajun dialect extend the folk traditions of Claude McKay and Louise Bennett and ground his work in the lives of the people for and about whom he writes.

The problem of language, however, is not a matter of choosing the Creole over the metropolitan language. It is a deeply political and spiritual problem, since, as Brathwaite writes, it was with language that the slave was "most successfully imprisoned by the master, and through his (mis)use of it that he most effectively rebelled." With nearly all other means of attaining personal liberty denied, the slave's last, irrevocable instrument of resistance and rebellion was language. For Brathwaite, a West Indian writer, Caliban in William Shakespeare's *The Tempest* (pr. 1611), written at the beginning of England's experiment in empire, is the archetype of the slave who turns his borrowed language against his master. To turn his instrument of rebellion into one of creation is Brathwaite's task.

"CALIBAN"

Accordingly, in his poem "Caliban" (from *The Arrivants*), Brathwaite's persona begins by celebrating the morning of December 2, 1956, the start of the Cuban Revolution, which remains a symbol of self-determination in the region. In the second section of the poem, Brathwaite adapts Shakespeare's "'Ban Ban Caliban,'/ Has a new master" curse-chant to the hold of a slave ship, articulating a spirit of resistance that turns in the final section to an assertion of endurance. At the end of the poem, the slaves' nightly limbo on deck becomes the religious ceremony—the seed of African culture carried to the New World—of the assembled tribes, who are able to raise their ancestral gods and be for the moment a whole people.

NATION LANGUAGE

What he achieves in "Caliban," Brathwaite achieves in his poetry at large: He uses his languages, both Creole and metropolitan English, to define the selfhood of the group in positive terms, contrary to the negations of the colonizers. "Within the folk tradition," Brathwaite writes, "language was (and is) a creative act in itself; the word was held to contain a secret power." His term "nation language" (defined in *History of the Voice*) for the language of the people brought to the Caribbean, as opposed to the official language of the colonial power, has profoundly influenced the theory and criticism of African American literature. Brathwaite continues in *Mother Poem* and *Sun Poem* to explore the resources of both his native Bajun dialect and contemporary standard English. In his poetry, the power of the word is to conjure, to evoke, to punish, to celebrate, to mourn, and to love. He uses language boldly as one who seeks its deepest power: to reveal and heal the wounds of history.

Brathwaite's early poetry in *Bim*, collected later in *Other Exiles*, with its themes of anxiety and alienation, changed under the search for racial and cultural identity while in exile. Brathwaite became surer of his European heritage while he was a student in England and recovered the remnants of his African heritage while working in Ghana. Those two great cultures, in conflict in the New World for the last four centuries, are the forces that shape Brathwaite's personal and racial history and the poetics through which he renders his quest for wholeness.

He is equally indebted to the Euro-American literary tradition through the work of T. S. Eliot and to the Afro-West Indian tradition through the work of Aimé Césaire. Brathwaite draws upon Eliot's musical form in *Four Quartets* (1943) for his own use of musical forms developed in stages of the black diaspora—work song, shanto, shango hymn, spiritual, blues, jazz, calypso, ska, and reggae—for his poetic rendering of historic and lyric moments. He also draws his aesthetic for rendering modern industrial and mercantile society in the United States and the Caribbean from Eliot's *The Waste Land* (1922). From Césaire's *Cahier d'un retour au pays natal* (1968; *Notebook of the Return to My Native Land*, 1995), Brathwaite derives the epic and dialectical structure of his trilogy as well as the surrealistic heightening of language that propels the movement from the reality of the Caribbean as wasteland to the vision of the Caribbean as promised land.

THE ARRIVANTS

That change in visions of the Caribbean can be discerned in the three books of *The Arrivants* through the poet's reconstruction of racial history and his tracing of his personal history. *Rights of Passage*, the first book of the trilogy, contains the restless isolation of Brathwaite's early life in Barbados that sends him into exile in England and Africa, as well as a recollection of the first phase of the black diaspora, the advent of the slave trade and the Middle Passage. The original dispersal of tribes from Ethiopia to West Africa, as well as his own search for his African origins, is the subject of *Masks*. In *Islands*, racial and personal history merge in the exile's return to the West Indies. The fruits of that return would become manifest in his second trilogy, *Ancestors*.

Readers of *The Arrivants* who focus on its historical dimension figure Brathwaite as the epic poet of the black diaspora, while those who focus on the autobiography make him the hero of the poem. Taking both approaches as valid, with the binocular vision that the poem requires, one can see that the central figure of the rootless, alienated West Indian in exile and in search of home is the only possible kind of hero for a West Indian epic. That questing poet's voice is, however, often transformed into the voice of a precolonial African being fired on by a white slaver; the Rastafarian Brother Man; Uncle Tom; a *houngan* invoking Legba; or some other historic or mythic figure. Brathwaite's use of personas, or masks, derives equally from the traditions of Greek drama (dramatic monologue) and African religious practice (chant or invocation). One communal soul speaks in a multiplicity of guises, and the poet thereby re-creates not only his own quest as victim and hero but also the larger racial consciousness in which he participates. The poet's many masks enable him to reconstruct his own life and the brutal history that created "new soil, new souls, new ancestors" out of the ashes of the past.

Combining racial history and personal quest in *The Arrivants*, Brathwaite has fashioned a contemporary West Indian myth. It is not the myth of history petrified into "progress" but that of a people's endurance through cycles of brutal oppression. Across centuries, across the ocean, and across the three books of this poem, images, characters, and events overlie one another to defy the myth of progress, leading in the poem only to heaven swaying in the reinforced girders of New York, and to the God of capitalism floating in a soundless, airtight glass bubble of an office, a prisoner of his own creation. For the "gods" who tread the earth below, myth is cyclical, and it attaches them to the earth through the "souls" of their feet in repetitions of exodus and arrival.

The trilogy begins with one tribe's ancient crossing of the Sahara desert, their wagons and camels left where they had fallen, and their arrival at a place where "cool/ dew falls/ in the evening." They build villages, but the cattle towns breed flies and flies breed plague, and another journey begins, for across the "dried out gut" of the riverbed, a mirage shimmers where

> trees are
> cool, there
> leaves are
> green, there
> burns the dream
> of a fountain,
> garden of odours,
> soft alleyways.

This is the repeated pattern of their history: exodus across desert, savanna, ocean; in caravan, ship, or jet plane; visitations of plague, pestilence, famine, slavery, poverty, ignorance, volcanoes, flood. The promised land is always elsewhere, across the parched riverbed ("Prelude") or in the bountiful fields of England, not in Barbados ("The Cracked Mother").

The connections between history and biography and the difficult process of destroying the colonial heritage in favor of a more creative mode of life are evident in the six poems that constitute the "Limbo" section of *Islands*. In "The Cracked Mother," the first poem of "Limbo," the dissociation of the West Indian's sensibility—regarding attitudes toward self, race, and country—threatens to paralyze the poet's dialectical movement toward a sustaining vision. The poet's rejection of his native land in favor of England is an acceptance of the colonial's position of inferiority. That attitude is instilled in young West Indians, such historians as Walter Rodney, Frantz Fanon, and Brathwaite have argued, by the system of colonial education that taught an alien and alienating value system. The debilitating effects of such an education are the subject of "The Cracked Mother." The three nuns who take the child from his mother to school appear as "black specks . . ./ Santa Marias with black silk sails." The metaphor equates the nuns' coming with that of Columbus and anticipates the violence that followed, especially in the image of the nuns' habits as the sails of death ships. With her child gone, the mother speaks in the second part of the poem as a broken ("cracked") woman reduced to muttering children's word games that serve as the vehicle for her pain:

> See?
> She saw
> the sea . . .
> I saw
> you take
> my children . . .
> You gave your
> beads, you
> took
> my children . . .
> Christ on the Cross
> your cruel laws teach
> only to divide us
> and we are lost.

History provides the useful equation of nuns' habits with sails and the nuns' rosary with the beads that Columbus gave to the inhabitants of his "discovered" lands, but it is Brathwaite's own biography that turns metaphor into revelation in the last two parts of the poem, showing how ruinous the colonial mentality is, even to the point of rejecting the earth under one's feet (another "cracked mother") because it is not England.

Brathwaite's corrective begins in "Shepherd," the second poem of the "Limbo" section. Having recalled the damage of his early education and having felt again some of the old abhorrence of the colonial for himself, the poet returns to the African drumbeats of *Masks* to chant a service of possession or reconnection with the

gods of his ancestors. The poet then addresses his peers in proverbs, as would an elder to his tribe:

> But you do not understand.
> For there is an absence of truth
> like a good tooth drawn from the tight skull
> like the wave's tune gone from the ship's hull
> there is sand
> but no desert where water can learn of its loveliness.

The people have gifts for the gods but do not give them, yet the gods are everywhere and waiting. Moving in *Islands* toward the regeneration promised in *Masks*, Brathwaite continues with "Caliban" to explore the potential for liberty inherent in the Cuban Revolution, then moves at the moment of triumph back into the slave ship and the limbo that contained the seeds of African religion and identity.

The "Limbo" section ends with the beautiful poem "Islands," which proposes the alternatives that are always present in every moment of Caribbean history: "So looking through a map/ of the islands, you see/ . . . the sun's/ slums: if you hate/ us. Jewels,/ if there is delight/ in your eyes." The same dichotomy of vision has surrounded every event and personage in the poem, all folded in upon the crucial event of the Middle Passage: Did it destroy a people or create one? Brathwaite's account of the voyage in "New World A-Comin" promises "new worlds, new waters, new/ harbours" on the one hand, and on the other, "the flesh and the flies, the whips and the fixed/ fear of pain in this chained and welcoming port."

The gods have crossed with the slaves to new soil, and the poet has returned to the origin of his race to discover his communal selfhood in African rite, which requires participation by all to welcome the god who will visit one of them. *The Arrivants* is a long historical and autobiographical poem, and it is also a rite of passage for the poet-priest who invites the god to ride him. Brathwaite's incantatory poems in *Masks* are his learning of the priest's ways, which restores his spirit in *Islands*. The refrain "*Attibon Legba/ Ouvri bayi pou'moï*" (Negus) is the Voodoo *houngon*'s prayer to the gatekeeper god Legba to open the door to the other gods. The prayer is answered in the final poem "*Jou'vert*" ("I Open"), where Legba promises

hearts
no longer bound
to black and bitter
ashes in the ground
now waking
making
making with their
rhythms some-
thing torn
and new.

ANCESTORS

The use of the trilogy as a structuring framework in *The Arrivants* has allowed Brathwaite to organize separately published volumes of poetry into a complex but unified and dynamic narrative of national proportions. This is a strategy with profound implications for postcolonial literature because it helps to address the fundamental problem of fragmentation—a significant challenge confronting marginalized writers of the periphery (as opposed to cosmopolitan writers of the center). A sense of postcolonial identity capable of engendering a common national culture is made possible by this ingenious application, first used in Brathwaite's *The Arrivants* and once again employed in *Ancestors*, the long-awaited Bajan trilogy based on three previously published volumes: *Mother Poem*, *Sun Poem*, and *X/Self*.

MOTHER POEM

In *Mother Poem*, the first book of Brathwaite's second trilogy, the central figure is not the restless poet but the mother he has left and to whom he has returned, the source of his life. The types of motherhood established in "The Cracked Mother" (from *The Arrivants*) are reiterated here as the poet's human mother and his motherland, Barbados. Both "mothers" are established in the first poem, "Alpha." Barbados is the mother-island of porous limestone (thus absorbing all influence of weather and history), cut by ancient watercourses that have dried up in sterility. Her dead streams can be revived only by the transfigured human mother who "rains upon the island with her loud voices/ with her grey hairs/ with her green love." The transfiguration that occurs in the last lines of the book must wait, however, for the woman to endure the dream-killing, soul-killing life of the island that is dominated by "the man

who possesses us all," the merchant, the modern agent of bondage ("name-tracks").

The mother is the merchant's victim, no matter whether she "sits and calls on jesus name" waiting for her husband to come home from work with lungs covered with jute from the sugar sacks, or whether she goes out after his death to sell calico cloth, half-soled shoes, and biscuits, or persuades her daughter to sell herself to the man who is waiting: "It int hard, leh me tell you/ jess sad/ so come darlin chile/ leh me tell he you ready you steady you go" ("Woo/Dove").

She gets no help from her men, who are crippled, destroyed, frightened, or sick from their lives of bondage to the merchant. One man goes to Montreal to work for nine years and sends back nothing ("Woo/Dove") and another goes to work for life in the local plantation, brings nothing home, and loses three fingers in the cane-grinder ("Milkweed"). Nor does she receive comfort from her children, "wearing dark glasses/ hearing aids/ leaning on wine" ("Tear or pear shape"), who were educated by Chalkstick the teacher, a satirical composite of the colonial educator whose job is to see that his pupils "don't clap their hands, shake their heads, tap their feet" or "push bones through each others' congolese nostrils" ("Lix"). Nor does her help come from her sisters ("Dais" and "Nights") or her Christianity ("Sam Lord").

Rather, the restoration of her powers as life-giver begins in the guttural, elemental, incantatory uttering of "Nametracks," where, as a slave-mother beaten by her owner, she reminds herself and her huddled children in dark monosyllables like the word game of "The Cracked Mother" that they will endure while "e di go/ e go di/ e go dead," that despite all his power, he "nevver maim what me." Her eyes rise from the plot of land she has bought with her meager earnings, the land that has sustained her and her children, to the whole island and a vision of revolutionary solidarity with her people: "de merchants got de money/ but de people got de men" ("Peace Fire"). With full realization that her child will be born to the life of "broken islands/ broken homes" ("Mid/Life"), in "Driftwood," the human mother still chooses to suffer the "pour of her flesh into their mould of bone." The poem ends with the mother re-created in clay by the potter who can work again, in stone by the sculptor whose skill has returned, and in her words gathered by the poet as rain gathering in the dry pools flows once more past the ruins of the slave and colonial world, refreshing and renewing the ancient life of the island.

SUN POEM

Brathwaite's *Sun Poem* moves from *Mother Poem*'s focus on the female characters (and character) of the island to the male principle of the tropical sun and of the various sons of Barbados. The pun of sun/son is derived from a number of historical and mythological associations, including that of Christianity (Brathwaite renames himself Adam as the boy-hero of the poem, and spells the pronoun "his" as "ihs" or Iesu Hominum Salvator) and various African traditions. The sun, for instance, contains "megalleons of light," the invented word associating it with the Egyptian god Ra's sun-ship, the galleons of European explorers, and the enormous nuclear energy that eclipses or perhaps anticipates the holocaust that Western humans have in their power. The complexity of the sun/son as controlling metaphor, as it evokes various ethnic and historical images, extends through time and geographic space the significance of the narrative, even as it complements and completes the female principle of *Mother Poem*.

The mythologies evoked in the poem contribute to the meaning of the life of the son Adam, as he begins to understand the West Indian man's sunlike course of ascent, dominance, and descent, played out through the rituals of boyhood games and identity seeking, adolescence, adult sexual experience, marriage and paternity, and finally death. In an early encounter, Adam wrestles the bully Batto underwater in a life-or-death rite of passage that initiates him into the comradeship of his peers, but which, Brathwaite suggests, fails (as do the other games that "had little meaning") to prepare him for the struggles of adult manhood ("Son"). The types of fathers portrayed ("Clips") fall into roles available from Christian, bourgeois, and Rastafarian cultures that are equally dead-ended. These fathers are unable to pass on to their sons any mode of fulfilling identity or action, even as in his soliloquy, the father laments his own diminishment, his being displaced as the head of his family by his own son.

The central incidents of Adam's life introduce him to the cares and costs of adulthood. On his Sunday school trip to the Atlantic coast, he enters the adult world, in part by hearing the story of Bussa's slave rebellion, a story of the painful price one pays for asserting his personhood ("Noom"). He conducts his courtship of Esse ("Return of the Sun") with a blithe but growing awareness of the consequences of one's sexual life in determining social and political roles ("Fleches"). The death of Adam's grandfather ("Indigone"), the final event in the poem, reveals to him the cyclical nature of manhood in which he begins to locate himself: "and i looked up to see my father's eye: wheeling/ towards his father/ now as i his sun moved upward to his eye." The cultural determinants of dispossession and lack of identity that so condition the natural progress and decline of masculine life are transcended in the poem's ultimate vision of a world capable of beginning anew. The final section ("Son") returns to the cosmic, creative domain of the poem's invocation ("Red Rising"), but with a clarified focus on creation and growth as the first principles of the natural and hence human world. The image of emerging coral returns the reader to the genesis of the island at the beginning of *Mother Poem* ("Rock Seed"), completing the cycle of the poems with the "coming up coming up coming up" of his "thrilldren" to people a world renewed.

X/SELF

X/Self, the third volume of *Ancestors*, is conceived as an exploration of the question of the self engendered by the figures of the mother and the son. When published as a separate volume in 1987, *X/Self* contained eighteen pages of notes citing references and allusions that constitute a montage of heterogeneous texts, partly as an aid to readers and partly as a parody of Eliot's pseudo-academic annotations for *The Waste Land*—a poem that *X/Self* appears to echo. The *X/Self* poems appear to be organized around the perspective (or consciousness) of the son, who is addressing his "Dear mumma" by writing a letter from the United States ("X/ Self xth letter from the thirteenth provinces") using a computer, obviously fascinated by its jinn-like capabilities. Speaking with a voice like that of the all-knowing and all-experiencing Tiresias in *The Waste Land*, the narrator of the *X/Self* poems observes and critiques from a transhistorical and cross-cultural perspective the rise and fall of civilizations, during which the masses of the world often are subjected to war, slavery, domination, and oppression. Using the lines "Rome burns/ & our slavery begins" as the leitmotif and making allusions to the Trojan War, Augustus Caesar, Hannibal, Charlemagne, Christopher Columbus, Prospero, and Richard Nixon as frames of reference, Brathwaite constructs the figure of the Caliban-like X/Self to characterize the Bajan as a complex identity emerging from the history of slavery, colonial conquest, and imperialism. This complex X/Self identity is unknown or unknowable due to the destructive erasures caused by slavery; it is also a hybrid identity, a Creolized self, produced by mixing or cross-breeding different sets of cultures (master and slave; the colonial and the colonized; the West and the Third World). An "ex-self" that calls into question preconceptions about identity, the "X/Self" is a crossed-out self that is being deconstructed even as it is being shaped.

With *X/Self* and *Ancestors*, Brathwaite developed a signature style of page layout in which his poems use a variety of fonts produced by the computer and the dot-matrix printer. Known as the Sycorax style "video text," this experimental form allows Brathwaite to create a postcolonial means by which, metaphorically, the Caliban-poet might be able to manipulate the colonial language imposed on him to pay tribute to his mother, Sycorax. This video text continues to be used in virtually all of Brathwaite's creative writing.

MIDDLE PASSAGES

A collection of fourteen poems (mainly culled from previously published volumes), *Middle Passages* employs a running theme regarding the effects of slavery on Caribbean culture and on the world. The title alludes to the Atlantic slave trade as the crucial experience in the existential struggles of the people of the African diaspora past and present, but it also reenvisions the Middle Passage in the context of postcolonial resistance and reconstruction. The title also seems to evoke the grief caused by his first wife's death in 1986, an event he referred to as "middle passages" in *The Zea Mexican Diary* (1993). Thus the title also suggests a spiritual passage that death entails for both the dead and the living. The idea of journeys, especially those to African roots, is a recurring theme in this volume, which is ded-

icated to the memory and honor of jazz musicians (Duke Ellington in "Duke"), poets (Nicolás Guillén in "Word Making Man"), scholars (Walter Rodney in "How Europe Underdeveloped Africa"), and African leaders fighting for freedom (Nelson Mandela in "Soweto").

To delineate the Middle Passage as he reenvisions it, Brathwaite uses the figure of Columbus as the harbinger of destruction on his arrival in Hispaniola. "Columbe" suggests the beauty that Columbus and his entourage must have discovered on their arrival in the Caribbean: "Yello pouis/ blazed like pollen and thin waterfalls suspended in the green." Told from the perspective of an island inhabitant watching the arrival, it also asks whether Columbus understood the violence to which his discovery would lead: "But did his vision/ fashion as he watched the shore/ the slaughter that his soldiers/ furthered here?"

The history of violence against Africans and other people of color indeed plays a dominant role here, as it does in so many of Brathwaite's literary works. However, the violence that arises in the context of anticolonial and Third World struggles appears to strike a resounding note in *Middle Passages*. "The Visibility Trigger," which surveys the history of Europeans using guns to kill and subdue Third World peoples, pays tribute to leaders such as Ghana's Nkrumah. Another poem exemplifying this theme of struggle, "Stone," is dedicated to Mickey Smith, a poet and political activist who was "stoned to death on Stony Hill, Kingston" in 1983.

Music and musicians are a strong presence in the collection. "Duke Playing the Piano at Seventy" pictures Duke Ellington's wrinkled hands as alligator skins gliding along a keyboard. Brathwaite uses a number of devices to evoke a sense of music on the printed page. Several poems call on the rhythm and cadence of different instruments to heighten the theme at hand: "Flutes" lyrically describes the sounds of bamboo flutes, while "Soweto," written about the Soweto uprising (June, 1976), draws on the rhythm of drums.

DS (2)

Brathwaite's creative work becomes intensely traumatic and foreboding during his "Time of Salt" (roughly, 1986 to 1990) as a result of the death of his wife (and personal bibliographer), Doris, in 1986 (commemorated in *The Zea Mexican Diary*); the destruction of his house, library, and archive in Kingston by Hurricane Gilbert in 1988 (in *Shar*); and the devastating robbery and assault in 1990 (in *Trench Town Rock*). Surviving these deadly catastrophes, Brathwaite is inspired to strengthen the connection between the personal, spiritual experience of the traumatized individual and the catastrophe-ridden social history and political reality of the African diaspora. The result of this deepened connection is his ongoing series of "dreamstories," which are written partly in prose and partly in verse, and printed in the style of the "video text" of Sycorax. Both fictional and autobiographical, these dream stories are like fables and parables designed to chronicle or dramatize the physical and spiritual struggles of the traumatized individual, who must also come to grips with the trials and tribulations of the people of African descent in a hostile world.

Most of the entries in *DreamStories* reappear in the larger collection *DS (2)*. "Dream Chad," which appears only in *DreamStories*, possesses great significance because of the emergence of a woman named Dream Chad, the poet's new muse, who in turn could also be a personification of the life force of Lake Chad. In this dream story, Brathwaite learns to use the Macintosh computer—an act that symbolizes how he copes, with help from Chad, with the fear of the destruction of his memories and archives. In a dreamy, surreal state, the narrator is later visited by the spirit of his deceased wife, who clamors for his attention and warns him—as if in retaliation for his lapse—of impending calamities. A tremendous anguish arises in "4th Traveller" (written "for Dream Chad"; found also in *DS (2)* with revisions), a dream story in which the narrator, along with his father, mother, and the unidentified "4th traveller," makes a journey to the dark village of the dead and is met with great hostility. The dream sequence is infused with suggestions of fear, guilt, hypocrisy, remorse, and various negative emotions indicative of the narrator's self-flagellating state of mind. At the end of the sequence, there are hints that the "4th Traveler" dies, "perishing alone out there on the night of the hillside . . . not of his dreams but our noiseless galloping nightmare." Suggestive of Dante's descent into the City of Dis (Inferno), "4th Traveler" serves as an allegory of the journey into the dark night of the soul, an undertaking that does offer prospects of cathartic expiation and renewal.

BORN TO SLOW HORSES

In the "post-salt" years, Brathwaite continues to be inspired by Chad and dedicates a volume of love poetry, titled *Words Need Love Too*, to her in gratitude for her "three DreamChad years of love and understanding." The major work to appear in this new phase of Brathwaite's poetic output, however, is *Born to Slow Horses*, the winner of the prestigious Griffin Poetry Prize. In awarding the prize, the judges cite the book as "an epic of one man (containing multitudes) in the African diaspora" and recognize it for containing "what may well be the first enduring poem on the disaster of 9/11" by turning Manhattan into "another island in the poet's personal archipelago." Asked about the title of the volume, Brathwaite explains that lazy horses sometimes pass onto the "basseterre" (cow pasture) he owns in Barbados and that "slow horses are what we call the waves that come over the reefs." More specifically, the title comes from the poem "Kumina," written on the occasion of Dream Chad's loss of her twenty-nine-year-old son, Mark, to a horrific act of violence in Kingston. In the poem, the heartbroken mother vows that there will be no rest until she finds her son again and brings justice back with her, because she was "[never] born to blue nor no slow horses." The poet characterizes the poem, in the epigraph, as his attempt to "speech my heart yr heart from breaking"; using the twenty-one-day Kumina ceremony associated with funerals (from the wake to the burial) as a framework for the poem, he re-creates the tremendous pain of the mother. In the reenactment of the communal ritual, the poem brings about a catharsis for its audience as well when they assimilate the experience of grief (and transform the emotion into their own) through participation, identification, and empathy.

The transference and distribution, of intense emotions by means of ritualistic evocation and identification is the same kind of process occurring in the poetic sequence commemorating the September 11, 2001, terrorist attacks. The poetic sequence is supposed to be the sixth in the volume and should be designated with the Roman numeral "VI," but Brathwaite deliberately uses

"9/11" instead, so that the sequence is designated as "9/11   Hawk," thus drawing special attention to the significance of the historic event. The first few lines of the sequence, serving as an alternative title, indicate that the poem is conceived as a memorial inspired by American jazz tenor saxophonist Coleman Hawkins (1904-1969): "Hawk's Last Body_Soul/ Ronnie Scott's in London/ 11 Sept 1967_Counting." The poem begins with the music of "Hawk" playing at the moment the Twin Towers were falling and shifts back in time to a different September 11, in London in 1967—a "golden" time celebrated in wonderful jazz as the narrator remembers it, when "Rollins Bridge is fallin down"—alluding to the collapse of the British Empire as many of its colonies became decolonized (Barbados gained independence in 1966). The meditative dramatization of the September 11 terrorist attacks is then carried out, as the poem continues, in the contexts of a large array of social upheavals and historical events characterized by systematic, organized violence: colonial exploitation in the Belgian Congo, the use of atomic bombs on Hiroshima and Nagasaki, the killing fields in Cambodia under Pol Pot, ethnic cleansing in Rwanda, the suppression of civil rights in American cities such as Birmingham, Alabama, and the invasion of Afghanistan and Iraq. The poetic critique reaches far and wide on the political front, but it is also deeply soul searching on a personal and spiritual level. The two events—the collapse of an empire and the destruction of the World Trade Center's Twin Towers—are tied together because the narrator links Hawkins's 1967 performance with the recorded version, playing in the present, of "Body and Soul," a masterpiece that carries much symbolic significance: "these words of love to sovereign wars of lust/ to lose/ u/even in the burn-/ing towers of this saxophone/ o let me love you love you love you love you/ vivid + green + golden/ ./ body/ body & soul." As a memorial to a tragedy that has yet to be connected to many other no-less tragic disasters and catastrophes, "9/11   Hawk" strikes a profound note with its communal message of love, "o let me love you . . . body & soul."

Although Brathwaite continues to use his Sycorax video-text style, with *Born to Slow Horses*, he begins to explore other ways to expand the potential of his poetry. The postscript to "9/11   Hawk" includes instructions on how to stage a performance of the "Audioglyph" version of the poem with murals, music, and sound effects. The cover of the book contains an intriguing photograph Brathwaite took of a spider, which somehow turned into "Namsetoura," a woman (or woman-spirit) and became a new subject in some of his later writings. Explicitly, in the epilogue to *Born to Slow Horses*, Brathwaite draws attention to the "transboundary" development of his writing and alludes to "tidalectics" and "tripartite exploration" in his ongoing aesthetic experimentations. These gestures portend new ideas being marshaled by the poet for another outpouring of poetic energy.

OTHER MAJOR WORKS

PLAYS: *Four Plays for Primary Schools*, pr. 1961; *Odale's Choice*, pr. 1962.

NONFICTION: *Folk Culture of the Slaves in Jamaica*, 1970; *The Development of Creole Society in Jamaica, 1770-1820*, 1971; *Caribbean Man in Space and Time*, 1974; *Contradictory Omens: Cultural Diversity and Integration in the Caribbean*, 1974; *Our Ancestral Heritage: A Bibliography of the Roots of Culture in the English-Speaking Caribbean*, 1976; *Wars of Respect: Nanny, Sam Sharpe, and the Struggle for People's Liberation*, 1977; *Barbados Poetry, 1661-1979: A Checklist*, 1979; *Jamaica Poetry: A Checklist*, 1979; *The Colonial Encounter: Language*, 1984; *History of the Voice: The Development of Nation Language in Anglophone Caribbean Poetry*, 1984; *Roots: Essays in Caribbean Literature*, 1993; *The Zea Mexican Diary*, 1993; *LX, the Love Axe/l*, 2002.

EDITED TEXTS: *New Poets from Jamaica: An Anthology*, 1979.

BIBLIOGRAPHY

Bobb, June. *Beating a Restless Drum: The Poetics of Kamau Brathwaite and Derek Walcott*. New York: Africa World Press, 1997. Exploring the commonalities and differences between Braithwaite and Walcott, this study focuses on their engagements with the history, culture, and mythology of the Afro-Caribbean experience and their contributions to the development of modern Caribbean poetics.

Brown, Stuart. *The Art of Kamau Brathwaite*. Bridgend, Mid Glamorgan, Wales: Seren, 1995. This collection of critical essays presents some of the most informed and cogent ways to approach Brathwaite's varied body of work. By looking at most of his work, it allows the reader to discover Brathwaite the critic, the historian, the poet, and the essayist.

Naylor, Paul. "Kamau Brathwaite: Tidalectic Rhythms." *Poetic Investigations: Singing the Holes in History*. Evanston, Ill.: Northwestern University Press, 1999. The author argues that Brathwaite's work can be understood as a "creolization" of Caribbean, African, and Euro-American culture.

Pollard, Charles W. *New World Modernisms: T. S. Eliot, Derek Walcott, and Kamau Brathwaite*. Charlottesville: University of Virginia Press, 2004. Pollard argues that the cosmopolitanism of postcolonial writers like Walcott and Brathwaite has been influenced and informed by Eliot's modernist principles including tradition, poetry's relation to speech, and the social function of poetry.

Reiss, Timothy J., ed. *For the Geography of a Soul: Emerging Perspectives on Kamau Brathwaite*. Trenton, N.J.: Africa World Press, 2002. A large collection of essays on Brathwaite's writings and his significance in poetry and literature, historical and sociological research, and cultural and literary criticism; includes three memoirs by fellow Caribbean figures close to him.

Rohlehr, Gordon. "Dream Journeys." Introduction to *DreamStories*, by Edward Kamau Brathwaite. Essex, England: Longman, 1994. University of West Indies scholar Rohlehr combines critical and textual analysis with biographical and personal information provided by Brathwaite, clarifying the contexts and the substance of the dense, obscure dream stories.

Ten Kortenaar, Neil. "Where the Atlantic Meets the Caribbean: Kamau Brathwaite's *The Arrivants* and T. S. Eliot's *The Waste Land*." *Research in African Literatures* 27, no. 4 (Winter, 1996): 15-27. Brathwaite has acknowledged Eliot as a poetic precursor. Parallels between Brathwaite's trilogy *The Arrivants* and Eliot's *The Waste Land* are examined.

Torres-Saillant, Silvio. *Caribbean Poetic: Towards an Aesthetic of West Indian Literature*. New York: Cambridge University Press, 1997. The author advocates a new system of canon formation and argues that Caribbean discourse in European languages is a discrete entity. Offers scholarly, in-depth studies of Brathwaite, René Depestre, and Pedro Mir.

Williams, Emily Allen. "Historical Empowerment in Edward Kamau Brathwaite's *The Arrivants*." In *Poetic Negotiations of Identity in the Works of Brathwaite, Harris, Senior, and Dabydeen: Tropical Paradise Lost and Regained*. Lewiston, Pa.: Edwin Mellen Press, 1999. Williams explores the question of identity in Brathwaite's *The Arrivants*.

_____, ed. *The Critical Response to Kamau Brathwaite*. Westport, Conn.: Praeger, 2004. An extensive collection of essays focusing on the poetry of Brathwaite arranged by decade since the 1960's; it includes an interview conducted in 2002 as well as a chronology and introduction by the editor.

Robert Bensen; Sarah Hilbert
Updated by Balance Chow

RICHARD BRAUTIGAN

Born: Tacoma, Washington; January 30, 1935
Died: Bolinas, California; September, 1984

PRINCIPAL POETRY

The Return of the Rivers, 1957
The Galilee Hitch-Hiker, 1958
Lay the Marble Tea: Twenty-four Poems, 1959
The Octopus Frontier, 1960
All Watched over by Machines of Loving Grace, 1967
The Pill Versus the Springhill Mine Disaster, 1968
Please Plant This Book, 1968
Rommel Drives on Deep into Egypt, 1970
Loading Mercury with a Pitchfork, 1976
June 30th, June 30th, 1978

OTHER LITERARY FORMS

Richard Brautigan is best known for capturing the spirit of the 1960's counterculture. His earliest novels—*A Confederate General from Big Sur* (1964), *Trout Fishing in America* (1967), and *In Watermelon Sugar* (1967)—were extremely popular, especially among younger readers; *Trout Fishing in America* sold millions of copies worldwide. His later works (such as *The Abortion: An Historical Romance*, 1971, and *The Hawkline Monster: A Gothic Western*, 1974) continued the 1960's zeitgeist into the 1970's but were considerably less popular. Brautigan also published a collection of his short stories, *Revenge of the Lawn: Stories, 1962-1970* (1971).

ACHIEVEMENTS

Richard Brautigan can best be understood as providing the bridge from the writers of the Beat movement of the 1950's (Allen Ginsberg and Jack Kerouac) to those of the literary counterculture of the 1960's and early 1970's (Ken Kesey and Tom Robbins). Brautigan exploded onto the literary scene in the middle of the 1960's and became—like Hermann Hesse and J. R. R. Tolkien—a cult writer for younger readers. He was a poet-in-residence at the California Institute of Technol-

Richard Brautigan (Library of Congress)

ogy in 1967 and won a National Endowment for the Arts grant in 1968. It is hard to think of another writer whose rise was so meteoric, but Brautigan started out reading his own poetry on the streets of San Francisco and just a few years later was invited to read at Harvard University. His reputation has not lasted (in comparison to that of his contemporary, the California poet Gary Snyder), but for some years, he helped shape the dreams and attitudes of the younger generation.

BIOGRAPHY

Richard Gary Brautigan was born in Tacoma, Washington, and lived his early life in the Pacific Northwest. His father abandoned the family a few months after he was born, and Brautigan's childhood contained both poverty and abuse at the hands of a stepfather. He graduated from high school in Eugene, Oregon, but in a year had gravitated to the literary scene in San Francisco. He was a street poet in his first literary role, performing at coffeehouses and poetry clubs. Local presses published several collections of his poems in the late 1950's, but Brautigan was definitely viewed as a regional poet. He first won fame through his novels, especially after *Trout Fishing in America* and *A Confederate General in Big Sur* were reissued by the New York publisher Delacorte at the suggestion of the writer Kurt Vonnegut. Brautigan continued to publish both novels and poetry into the 1970's, but his popularity and his powers waned at the end of the 1960's.

Brautigan was twice married and had a daughter with his first wife, but he suffered from alcoholism, among other troubles, and he ended his life with a handgun in the fall of 1984. The exact date is unknown because his body was not discovered until some weeks after his death. He taught at Montana State University in 1982 and traveled extensively in Japan, but he lived mostly in the San Francisco area and died in his last home in Bolinas, just up the coast from the city.

ANALYSIS

Richard Brautigan's poems are usually brief, often humorous, sometimes childlike in their innocence, and decidedly antipoetic. Much of his poetry sounds like prose, in the same way that the prose of his novels is often poetic. "January 17" (from *Rommel Drives on Deep into Egypt*) reads simply, "Drinking wine this afternoon/ I realize the days are getting/ longer." His best poems resemble brief haiku, and some have a Zen Buddhist quality to them. The short verse "Haiku Ambulance" (from his popular collection *The Pill Versus the Springhill Mine Disaster*) reads, in its entirety, "A piece of green pepper/ fell/ off the wooden salad bowl:/ so what?" His imagination is sometimes startling, and his images and metaphors often surprise the reader, although they rarely leave an aftertaste.

Many of his poems are nonsense verse; for example "The Amelia Earhart Pancake" (from *Loading Mercury with a Pitchfork*) tells readers that he is giving up trying to find a poem to fit this title, and in several cases, he prints titles with no poems beneath them, as in "A 48-Year-Old Burglar from San Diego" and "1891-1944" (both from *Rommel Drives on Deep into Egypt*). A good number of his poems are about love, love found and love lost (some in his first collection are dedicated "For Marcia" or simply "For M"), and some have explicit sexual images and language at their center.

His poetic voice is simple and direct, capturing the rhythms of the spoken word and providing easy access to his thoughts. A few of his poems are longer than a page, but most of his poems are only a few lines long. However, "The Galilee Hitch-Hiker" section of *The Pill Versus the Springhill Mine Disaster* contains nine linked poems, all but the last featuring the nineteenth century French poet Charles Baudelaire in twentieth century America; the "Group Portrait Without the Lions" section of *Loading Mercury with a Pitchfork* has fourteen short poems (part 9, "Betty Makes Wonderful Waffles," reads simply, "Everybody agrees to/ that"); and the "Good Luck, Captain Martin" section of the same collection has seven poems. The last poem in the series, "Put the Coffee On, Bubbles, I'm Coming Home," consists of two lines, "Everybody's coming home/ except Captain Martin."

Brautigan's rise was sudden. He was known as a West Coast poet for about a decade, until the publication of his first major collection, *The Pill Versus the Springhill Mine Disaster*, in 1968, and for the next ten years—through his final three collections, *Rommel Drives on Deep into Egypt*, *Loading Mercury with a Pitchfork*, and *June 30th, June 30th*—he was a popular poet who was closely associated with the San Francisco cultural scene of rock bands, flower children, and drugs. Many of the poems in the first and second collections published during the peak of Brautigan's popularity first appeared in *Harper's*, *Mademoiselle*, *Poetry*, and *Rolling Stone* magazines. His later poetry collections, however, showed a falling off of poetic inspiration and imagination: More of the poems were flat or nonsense prose, with fewer startling images and metaphors than in his earlier collections.

THE PILL VERSUS THE SPRINGHILL MINE DISASTER

Although Brautigan had been publishing in small presses and reading his own poetry in the late 1950's and early 1960's, his 1968 collection, *The Pill Versus the Springhill Mine Disaster*, was the first to gain wide popularity with young American readers. The ideas and images expressed in this work seemed to capture the magical, antiauthoritarian spirit of the late 1960's. Brautigan's novels, along with those of writers such as Peter S. Beagle (*The Last Unicorn*, 1968) and Kurt Vonnegut (*Slaughterhouse-Five: Or, The Children's Crusade, a Duty-Dance with Death*, 1969), were also vehicles of the counterculture.

The title poem of Brautigan's first major collection conveys its tone:

> When you take your pill
> it's like a mine disaster.
> I think of all the people
> lost inside of you.

The metaphor jolts readers with its juxtaposition of images, and the poem becomes a kind of ironic haiku on the birth control pill. It was the poetic language, particularly the images and metaphors, of this collection that struck readers most forcefully. Death was ". . . a beautiful car parked only/ to be stolen . . . ," a dish of ice cream looked "like Kafka's hat." The last three lines of "Your Departure Versus the Hindenburg" read, "When you leave the house, the/ shadow of the Hindenburg enters/ to take your place." Even in this collection, there were poems that fit the definition of poetry only by virtue of their linear spacing: "Widow's Lament" reads, "It's not quite cold enough/ to go borrow some firewood/ from the neighbors." Brautigan was drawing on William Carlos Williams and the Imagists, but often without a strong enough central image, and creating haiku without a sharp enough picture.

ROMMEL DRIVES ON DEEP INTO EGYPT

Brautigan's second major poetry collection, *Rommel Drives on Deep into Egypt*, had many of the same qualities—the cryptic humor, the naïve tone, and the nonsense lyrics—but there seemed to be fewer fresh metaphors, and more poems seemed to be self-referential. "Critical Can Opener," for example, reads, "There is something wrong/ with this poem. Can you/ find it?" "Third Eye/ For Gary Snyder" reads simply, "There is a motorcycle/ in New Mexico," and "April 7, 1969" consists of the simple four-line lament: "I feel so bad today/ that I want to write a poem./ I don't care: any poem, this/ poem." Still, there were enough poems in which the images surprised and puzzled readers to maintain Brautigan's reputation, such as the two-line "Cellular Coyote": "He's howling in the pines/ at the edge of your fingerprints."

LOADING MERCURY WITH A PITCHFORK

Brautigan's third popular collection, *Loading Mercury with a Pitchfork*, continued the hip Brautigan poetic style, with images such as those in the title poem; jokes such as that in the one-line poem "Nine Crows: Two Out of Sequence," which reads, "1,2,3,4,5,7,6,8,9"; and the haiku-like brevity and irony of "Curiously Young Like a Freshly-Dug Grave":

> Curiously young like a freshly-dug grave
> the day parades in circles like a top
> with rain falling in its shadow.

Similarly, "Impasse" reads, "I talked a good hello/ but she talked an even/ better good-bye." He writes "the moon shines like a dead garage" in one poem and snowflakes in New York City appear ". . . like millions/ of transparent washing machines swirling/ through the dirty air of this city, washing/ it" in another. More poems, however, devolve into prose in this collection: "Ginger" reads simply, "She's glad/ that Bill/ likes her," and "Two Guys Get out of a Car," consists of three simple lines:

> Two guys get out of a car.
> They stand beside it. They
> don't know what else to do.

Other poems contain antipoetic gestures. In "Death Like a Needle," Brautigan writes, ". . . [I can't make/ the next two words out. I first/ wrote this poem in long-hand]. . . ." Brautigan seems less imaginative and figurative in this collection and more inclined to write poems just to poke fun at the poetic process. As the spirit of the 1960's dissipated, so too did Brautigan's imaginative powers and popularity.

OTHER MAJOR WORKS

LONG FICTION: *A Confederate General from Big Sur*, 1964; *Trout Fishing in America*, 1967; *In Watermelon Sugar*, 1967; *The Abortion: An Historical Romance*, 1971; *The Hawkline Monster: A Gothic Western*, 1974; *Willard and His Bowling Trophies: A Perverse Mystery*, 1975; *Sombrero Fallout: A Japanese Novel*, 1976; *Dreaming of Babylon: A Private Eye Novel, 1942*, 1977; *The Tokyo-Montana Express*, 1980; *So the Wind Won't Blow It Away*, 1982; *An Unfortunate Woman*, 2000 (wr. 1982; first published in French as *Cahier d'un Retour de Troie*, 1994).

SHORT FICTION: *Revenge of the Lawn: Stories, 1962-1970*, 1971.

MISCELLANEOUS: *The Edna Webster Collection of Undiscovered Writings*, 1995.

BIBLIOGRAPHY

Abbott, Keith. *Downstream from "Trout Fishing in America."* Santa Barbara, Calif.: Capra Press, 1989. Abbott describes his friendship with Brautigan, from their meeting in 1966 through their parting in 1982 in San Francisco.

Barber, John F., ed. *Richard Brautigan: Essays on the Writings and Life*. Jefferson, N.C.: McFarland, 2007. The volume contains thirty-two memoirs and articles, many of them brief, including tributes by Michael McClure and Robert Creeley. A longer, more analytical piece is Steven Moore's "Paper Flowers: Richard Brautigan's Poetry," originally intended as the introduction to a volume of Brautigan's collected poetry that was never published.

Boyer, Jay. *Richard Brautigan*. Western Writers Series 79. Boise, Idaho: Boise State University Press, 1987. This early appraisal captures the Brautigan mystique in the 1960's, especially as readers discovered it in the novels.

Brautigan, Ianthe. *You Can't Catch Death: A Daughter's Memoir*. New York: St. Martin's Press, 2000. Brautigan's daughter, not satisfied with the portrayal of her father in his obituaries, writes of her childhood spent bouncing between the homes of her two bohemian parents.

Cutler, Edward. "Richard Brautigan." In *Twentieth Century American Western Writers, First Series*. Vol. 206 in *Dictionary of Literary Biography*. Detroit: Gale, 1999. Cutler approaches Brautigan both as a unique voice in Western literature and as an early postmodernist laying bare the relationships of language and representation.

Foster, Edward Halsey. *Richard Brautigan*. Boston: Twayne, 1983. Part of Twayne's United States Authors series. Foster includes an incisive analysis of the poetry as well as long discussions of the novels.

McDermott, James Dishon. *Austere Style in Twentieth-Century Literature: Literary Minimalism*. Lewiston: Edwin Mellen Press, 2006. This discussion of minimalism looks at Brautigan as well as Ludwig Wittgenstein, Raymond Carver, and David Mamet.

David Peck

WILLIAM BRONK

Born: Fort Edward, New York; February 17, 1918
Died: Hudson Falls, New York; February 22, 1999

PRINCIPAL POETRY

Light and Dark, 1956
The World, the Worldless, 1964
The Empty Hands, 1969
That Tantalus, 1971
To Praise the Music, 1972
Utterances: The Loss of Grass, Trees, Water; The Unbecoming of Wanted and Wanter, 1972
Looking at It, 1973
Silence and Metaphor, 1975
The Stance, 1975
Finding Losses, 1976
The Meantime, 1976
My Father Photographed with Friends, and Other Pictures, 1976
Twelve Losses Found, 1976
That Beauty Still, 1978
Life Supports: New and Collected Poems, 1981
Light in a Dark Sky, 1982
Careless Love and Its Apostrophes, 1985
Manifest and Furthermore, 1987
Death Is the Place, 1989
Living Instead, 1991
Some Words, 1992
The Mild Day, 1993
Our Selves, 1994
Selected Poems, 1995
The Cage of Age, 1996
All of What We Loved, 1998
Metaphor of Trees and Last Poems, 1999

OTHER LITERARY FORMS

Although William Bronk was one of the most prolific American poets of the post-World War II era, he also published a substantial body of nonfiction essays that explored the themes that shaped his poetic vision. When still involved with the academic world in the late 1940's, Bronk authored a collection of groundbreaking essays on nineteenth century American writers, most prominently Herman Melville and Henry David Thoreau, that he would not publish until 1980 as *The Brother in Elysium: Ideas of Friendship and Society in the United States*. Late in his life, Bronk collected three decades of prose writings in *Vectors and Smoothable Curves: Collected Essays* (1983). The collection included selections from *The Brother in Elysium* and two earlier limited editions, *The New World* (1974) and *A Partial Glossary: Two Essays* (1974). The essays treat a wide range of topics, including Bronk's investigations into Mayan and Incan civilizations, his meditations on the relationship between time and space, and his theories on the nature of desire.

ACHIEVEMENTS

Because of the density and the intellectual passion of his poetry, William Bronk for decades maintained a secure, if quiet, reputation as a poet's poet. Two generations of fellow poets admired and respected Bronk, finding the same satisfying illuminations in Bronk's investigations into the nature of time, the elusiveness of truth, the implications of desire, the difficult work of defining reality, and the role of art and language within the process of acquiring knowledge as they had in the works of landmark philosophical poets of an earlier generation, most prominently T. S. Eliot and Wallace Stevens. Bronk's poems are seldom more than twenty lines long, but despite their haiku-like concision, they manage to raise profound epistemological questions about the universe. Bronk, a successful business owner who seldom traveled far from his upstate New York home, wrote verse not to secure academic appointments, to enhance his own celebrity, or to gain financial remuneration, but rather to make his own complicated interrogations into the nature of reality. Bronk's poetry maintained its narrow, if appreciative, readership until his collected poems, *Life Supports*, was awarded the National Book Award in 1982. Over the next decade, Bronk's writings became the subject of much discussion in academic circles. He received the Lannan Literary Award for Poetry in 1991. At the time of his death, he was widely recognized as a major figure in late twentieth century American verse.

BIOGRAPHY

Not surprisingly, given William Bronk's esoteric investigations into big cosmic questions, the facts of his own biography seldom affected his verse. He was born the youngest of four children and lived most of his life in upstate New York. A remarkably astute student who began writing poetry in high school, he was accepted for study at Dartmouth when he was only sixteen. There he studied most memorably under Robert Frost, whose meditations on the widest implications of human existence in a universe far emptier than any conceived by the imagination impressed the young Bronk. After a single semester at Harvard, Bronk left to complete a most unconventional study on nineteenth century American writers, including Thoreau and Mel-

ville, that he would not publish until nearly three decades later.

After serving in World War II, Bronk briefly tried teaching at Union College in Schenectady but found the academic environment stifling to his creativity; teaching, which he loved, required too much energy and any long-term career in academics would ultimately require that Bronk return to school for postgraduate work. In 1946, Bronk abandoned academia entirely and returned to Washington County, to Hudson Falls. Within a year, he agreed to take over executive operations for the family business, the William M. Bronk Coal and Lumber Company, which had been run by his uncle after the unexpected death of Bronk's father five years earlier. Initially, Bronk assumed the position temporarily, but he never left, successfully managing the company for thirty years, until he retired in 1978.

Beginning in 1956, Bronk published slender collections of poetry with small (if prestigious) presses. Financially secure, Bronk was free to write whatever he chose, and he composed poetry that grappled with abstract questions about the nature of time, space, memory, and perception. Although he was remarkably prolific, his work never sold widely. However, across more than four decades, his poetry generated genuine enthusiasm among academics and critics who found in Bronk's invigorating intellectualism a welcome respite from the exorcism of private demons that dominated the poems of postwar confessional poets. Despite growing interest in his work, Bronk maintained a decidedly solitary existence—he refused to pursue celebrity, refused academic appointments, and never gave public readings. Indeed, he seldom left his spacious Victorian home in Hudson Falls, never even obtaining a driver's license. He was hardly a recluse, however, welcoming fellow poets, students of literature, academics, and admirers with warmth and hospitality. Bronk never directly treated his homosexuality in his verse—indeed, it was something of a surprise to many of his readers when his poetry was included in Timothy Liu's *Word of Mouth: An Anthology of Gay American Poetry* published in 2000, just after Bronk's death.

After publishing more than twenty volumes of poetry, Bronk earned a kind of celebrity when *Life Supports* was awarded the National Book Award in Poetry in 1982 and again in 1991 when he received the Lannan Literary Award for Poetry. Then in his seventies, Bronk became the subject of scholarly investigations that sought to rescue him from obscurity by positioning him within a tradition of American philosophical poetry that included Frost, Eliot, Stevens, Hart Crane, and Ralph Waldo Emerson. He continued to publish until his death, at the age of eighty-one, in 1999.

ANALYSIS

The poetry of William Bronk is strikingly (and deliberately) out of step with most postwar American poetry. He does not draw from his own emotional life or presume the intimacy of confessional poetry, and his verse does not employ striking and original ornamental language that foregrounds the poet's cleverness and craft. His are not the kind of poems that easily invite readers; they lack the emotional drama of most poetry and draw their boldness from testing premises, raising questions, and extracting from phenomena significant uncertainties over their very existence. Therefore, the poems can seem forbidding, even intimidating. Bronk is compelled by a restless intelligence, a curiosity about the very nature of the material world and the relationship between the mind and that world, how people go about determining what they call reality and what they call truth. His poetic voice is thus disembodied, stately (he is most comfortable with the gravitas of iambic pentameter), austere, and cool to the point of cerebral. Bronk's verse lines are clean and chiseled, economic and careful, and, with jarring directness, pose provocative, complex metaphysical questions without demanding or even expecting answers.

Appreciation of his verse was never universal. Critics found his verse too abstract in its argument and too consistent in its sensibility and in the questions it raised over the many decades in which he wrote it. Because Bronk seldom engaged a world wider than that of his own business and his own home, critics argue, his poetry largely reflected the unsettling isolation of the human mind distracted only by the relentless questioning into its own functions. However, Bronk's verse came to influence a wide range of younger poets who found in such metaphysical verse a liberating sense of art tangling with big questions, trying to define its own reach against the threat of surrendering to the obvious absurdity of postmodern existence.

THE WORLD, THE WORLDLESS

The World, the Worldless, Bronk's second published volume, embodies the bracing cerebral energy of his early work. Although it generated lavish critical praise, sales were disappointing, as readers were puzzled by the gnomic quality of the poems. As the title indicates, by juxtaposing the material universe against its absence, Bronk introduces one of the volume's dominant themes: the nature of perception and the sheer power of the mind to create—and uncreate—worlds. As he argues in "Blue Spruces in Pairs, a Bird Bath Between," the mind apprehends a variety of worlds simultaneously; thus the world itself is not fixed until created into form by perception itself. The poems are thus drawn to images of light and illumination—morning light, winter light, starlight, and candlelight—suggestive of Bronk's own grasping, groping, and questioning, and his struggle to understand the process of defining the material world, how intently the mind pursues order in a universe that seems in its every expression to be chaotic and disordered.

That subtle celebration of the mind ultimately centers on what is apparently a collection of discrete, beautifully chiseled meditations. Any item in the material world—ice in February, a backyard shrub, his newly painted house, the Incan ruins at Machu Picchu, a clump of skunk cabbage—subtly morphs into an occasion for Bronk as poet to interrogate the nature of a range of abstractions, including desire, permanence, and the threat of nothingness; ultimately, Bronk does not endorse any single perception (hence the volume's lack of traditional themes) but rather the radical energy of the engaged mind itself. It is, as he argues in "Aspects of the World like Coral Reefs," the work of the mind to describe the world by aspects that, while not real themselves, have sturdiness and apparent reliability like a coral reef thrown up against and amid a raging sea. For Bronk, the poem is itself at once intricate and simple, fragile and resilient, vulnerable and durable. The world is all people have to explore; their perceptions are the only reality they can accept, but the more people explore the world, the more it eludes definition. People are thus left with the need to understand the most complex questions of existence itself, certain only that answers cannot stand without irony.

DEATH IS THE PLACE

Death Is the Place, published about a decade before Bronk's death, reflects an evolution in his poetic form. In this volume, Bronk's poetry has assumed a stark, zenlike simplicity; few of the poems are more than a handful of lines. The threat here is nothingness, the extinction of the restless perception, and a universe uncontained by the mind (each poem, on its own page, stands as a few lines of type surrounded by an intimidating blank area). Approaching the reality of his own finitude (the poems draw on images of sleep and descending nightfall), Bronk distilled his poetic line into stark concision; his lines are fragmented and elliptical, and his thoughts are often obscure and abstract. However, despite a title that appears to promise elegiac musings, Bronk's voice is resilient, his mind engaged and still won by the beauty of a material world that refuses to concede the obvious tragedy of its own brevity.

Poems, Bronk argues, are ultimately acts of love that depend on responding to a world that is imperfect and temporary. There is a clean, hard music to the poems in this volume. They reward recitation; the cool exactness and the colloquial feel are revealed when they are heard in a slow, subtle cadence. Past seventy and at an age when cynicism and even pessimism would be understandable, Bronk offers a subtle kind of resilient optimism. If flesh is impermanent, the apprehension of beauty is not—that perception process, that energy, is immortal. Only because people are mortal, he argues in "Vicarious," can they know how beautiful the brief world of their perception is. How thin life would be, he says in "Elder Brother," the collection's penultimate offering, without death's company. Against the oppressive pull of night, the collection offers poems of awakening and arising, poems of early morning, that reassure the vitality of perception and the vigor of the mind.

OTHER MAJOR WORKS

NONFICTION: *The New World*, 1974; *A Partial Glossary: Two Essays*, 1974; *The Brother in Elysium: Ideas of Friendship and Society in the United States*, 1980; *Vectors and Smoothable Curves: Collected Essays*, 1983.

BIBLIOGRAPHY

Clippinger, David W. *The Mind's Landscape: William Bronk and Twentieth-Century American Poetry*. Newark: University of Delaware Press, 2006. Draws on Bronk's considerable work in American literary scholarship to structure a broad reading of Bronk's era. Useful because it places Bronk within the context of his contemporaries.

Foster, Edward, and Joseph Donahue, eds. *The World in Time and Space: Towards a History of Innovative Poetry in Our Time*. Santa Barbara, Calif.: Talisman House, 2002. A collection of challenging readings of Bronk's generation of poets that clearly centers on the importance of Bronk's presence and his revolutionary work with philosophical poetry. Talisman was Bronk's longtime publisher.

Gilmore, Lyman. *The Force of Desire: A Life of William Bronk*. Santa Barbara, Calif.: Talisman House, 2006. This biography, shaped with Bronk's assistance, provides helpful insight into both Bronk's intellectual development and his reclusive life.

Kimmelman, Burt. *The "Winter Mind" of William Bronk*. Madison, N.J.: Fairleigh Dickinson University Press, 1998. Useful analysis of Bronk's poetry that locates it within a broad tradition of New England nature poetry (rather than philosophical poetry) that runs from Emerson to Frost.

Weinfield, Henry. *The Music of Thought in the Poetry of George Oppen and William Bronk*. Iowa City: University of Iowa Press, 2009. Probing analysis of the tradition of metaphysical poetry in the United States and, using correspondence between Oppen and Bronk, defines the philosophical dilemmas that center Bronk's poetry.

Joseph Dewey

GWENDOLYN BROOKS

Born: Topeka, Kansas; June 7, 1917
Died: Chicago, Illinois; December 3, 2000

PRINCIPAL POETRY

A Street in Bronzeville, 1945
Annie Allen, 1949
"We Real Cool," 1959
The Bean Eaters, 1960
Selected Poems, 1963
"The Wall," 1967
In the Mecca, 1968
Riot, 1969
Family Pictures, 1970
Aloneness, 1971
Black Steel: Joe Frazier and Muhammad Ali, 1971
Aurora, 1972
Beckonings, 1975
Primer for Blacks, 1980
To Disembark, 1981
Black Love, 1982
The Near-Johannesburg Boy, 1986
Blacks, 1987
Gottschalk and the Grande Tarantelle, 1988
Winnie, 1988
Children Coming Home, 1991
In Montgomery, 2003
The Essential Gwendolyn Brooks, 2005

OTHER LITERARY FORMS

In addition to the poetry on which her literary reputation rests, Gwendolyn Brooks published a novel, *Maud Martha* (1953); a book of autobiographical prose, *Report from Part One* (1972); and volumes of children's verse. An episodic novel, *Maud Martha* makes some use of autobiographical materials and shares many of the major concerns of Brooks's poetry, particularly concerning the attempts of the person to maintain integrity in the face of crushing environmental pressures. *Report from Part One* recounts the personal, political, and aesthetic influences that culminated in Brooks's movement to a black nationalist stance in the late 1960's. She also wrote introductions to, and edited anthologies of, the works of younger black writers. These introductions frequently provide insight into her own work. Several recordings of Brooks reading her own work are available.

ACHIEVEMENTS

Working comfortably in relation to diverse poetic traditions, Gwendolyn Brooks has been widely honored. Early in her career, she received numerous mainstream literary awards, including the Pulitzer Prize in poetry in 1950 for *Annie Allen*. She became poet laureate of Illinois in 1969 and has received more than fifty honorary doctorates. Equally significant, numerous writers associated with the Black Arts movement recognized her as an inspirational figure linking the older and younger generations of black poets. Brooks's ability to appeal both to poetic establishments and to a sizable popular audience, especially among young blacks, stems from her pluralistic voice, which echoes a wide range of precursors while remaining unmistakably black. Her exploration of the United States in general and Chicago in particular links her with Walt Whitman and Carl Sandburg. Her exploration of the interior landscape of humanity in general and women in particular places her in the tradition of Emily Dickinson and Edna St. Vincent Millay. At once the technical heir of Langston Hughes in her use of the rhythms of black street life and of Robert Frost in her exploration of traditional forms such as the sonnet, Brooks nevertheless maintains her integrity of vision and voice.

This integrity assumes special significance in the context of African American writing of the 1950's and 1960's. A period of "universalism" in black literature, the 1950's brought prominence to such poets as Brooks, LeRoi Jones (Amiri Baraka), and Robert Hayden. During this period of intellectual and aesthetic integration, Brooks never abandoned her social and racial heritage to strive for the transcendent (and deracinated) universalism associated by some African American critics with T. S. Eliot. Responding to William Carlos Williams's call in *Paterson* (1946-1958) to "make a start out of particulars and make them general," Brooks demonstrated unambiguously that an African American writer need not be limited in relevance by concentrating on the black experience.

The 1960's, conversely, encouraged separatism and militancy in African American writing. Even while accepting the Black Arts movement's call for a poetry designed to speak directly to the political condition of the black community, Brooks continued to insist on precision of form and language. Although Jones changed his name to Amiri Baraka and radically altered his poetic voice, Brooks accommodated her new insights to her previously established style. An exemplar of integrity and flexibility, she both challenges and learns from younger black poets such as Haki R. Madhubuti (Don L. Lee), Sonia Sanchez, Carolyn Rodgers, and Etheridge Knight. Like Hughes, she addresses the black community without condescension or pretense. Like Frost, she wrote technically stunning "universal" poetry combining clear surfaces and elusive depths.

Brooks, a recipient of more than fifty honorary doctorates, was also appointed to the Presidential Commission on the National Agenda for the 1980's; she was the first black woman elected to the National Institute of Arts and Letters. She was named consultant in poetry (poet laureate) to the Library of Congress for 1985-1986. Her honors include the Shelley Memorial Award (1976) and the Frost Medal (1989), both awarded by the Poetry Society of America; the Langston Hughes Award (1979); the Aiken Taylor Award in Modern American Poetry from *Sewanee Review* (1992); and the Medal for Distinguished Contribution to American Letters from the National Book Foundation (1994). She also received the Academy of American Poets Fellowship in 1999.

BIOGRAPHY

Gwendolyn Elizabeth Brooks's poetry bears the strong impress of Chicago, particularly of the predominantly black South Side where she lived most of her life. Although she was born in Topeka, Kansas, Brooks was taken to Chicago before she was a year old. In many ways, she devoted her career to the physical, spiritual, and, later, political exploration of her native city.

Brooks's life and writings are frequently separated into two phases, with her experience at the 1967 Black Writers' Conference at Fisk University in Nashville serving as a symbolic transition. Before the conference, Brooks was known primarily as the first black Pulitzer

Prize winner in poetry. Although not politically unaware, she held to a somewhat cautious attitude. The vitality she encountered at the conference crystallized her sense of the insufficiency of universalist attitudes and generated close personal and artistic friendships with younger black poets such as Madhubuti, Walter Bradford, and Knight. Severing her ties with the mainstream publishing firm of Harper and Row, which had published her first five books, Brooks transferred her work and prestige to the black-owned and operated Broadside Press of Detroit, Third World Press of Chicago, and Black Position Press, also of Chicago. Her commitment to black publishing houses remained unwavering despite distribution problems that rendered her later work largely invisible to the American reading public.

Educated in the Chicago school system and at Wilson Junior College, Brooks learned her craft under Inez Cunningham Stark (Boulton), a white woman who taught poetry at the South Side Community Art Center in the late 1930's and 1940's. Brooks's mother, who had been a teacher in Topeka, had encouraged her literary interests from an early age. Her father, a janitor, provided her with ineffaceable images of the spiritual strength and dignity of "common" people. Brooks married Henry Blakely in 1939, and her family concerns continued to play a central role in shaping her career. The eleven-year hiatus between the publication of *Annie Allen* and *The Bean Eaters* resulted at least in part from her concentration on rearing her two children, born in 1940 and 1951. Her numerous poems on family relationships reflect both the rewards and the tensions of her own experiences. Her children grown, Brooks concentrated on teaching, supervising poetry workshops, and speaking publicly. These activities brought her into contact with a wide range of younger black poets, preparing her for her experience at Fisk. As poet laureate of Illinois, she encouraged the development of younger poets through personal contact and formal competitions.

The division between the two phases of Brooks's life should not be overstated. She evinced a strong interest in the Civil Rights movement during the 1950's and early 1960's; her concern with family continued in the 1980's. Above all, Brooks lived with and wrote of and for the Chicagoans whose failures and triumphs she saw as deeply personal, universally resonant, and specifically black. She died in Chicago on December 3, 2000, at the age of eighty-three.

ANALYSIS

The image of Gwendolyn Brooks as a readily accessible poet is at once accurate and deceptive. Capable of capturing the experiences and rhythms of black street life, she frequently presents translucent surfaces that give way suddenly to reveal ambiguous depths. Equally capable of manipulating traditional poetic forms such as the sonnet, rhyme royal, and heroic couplet, she employs them to mirror the uncertainties of characters or personas who embrace conventional attitudes to defend themselves against internal and external chaos. Whatever form she chooses, Brooks consistently focuses on the struggle of people to find and express love, usually associated with the family, in the midst of a hostile environment. In constructing their defenses and seeking love, these people typically experience a disfiguring pain. Brooks devotes much of her energy to defining and responding to the elusive forces, variously psychological and social, which inflict this pain. Increasingly in her later poetry, Brooks traces the pain to political sources and expands her concept of the family to encompass all black people. Even while speaking of the social situation of blacks in a voice crafted primarily for blacks, however, Brooks maintains the complex awareness of the multiple perspectives relevant to any given experience. Her ultimate concern is to encourage every individual, black or white, to "Conduct your blooming in the noise and whip of the whirlwind" ("The Second Sermon on the Warpland").

A deep concern with the everyday circumstances of black people living within the whirlwind characterizes many of Brooks's most popular poems. From the early "Of De Witt Williams on His Way to Lincoln Cemetery" and "A Song in the Front Yard" through the later "The Life of Lincoln West" and "Sammy Chester Leaves 'Godspell' and Visits UPWARD BOUND on a Lake Forest Lawn, Bringing West Afrika," she focuses on characters whose experiences merge the idiosyncratic and the typical. She frequently draws on black musical forms to underscore the communal resonance of a character's outwardly undistinguished life. By ty-

Gwendolyn Brooks (©Jill Krementz)

ing the refrain of "Swing Low Sweet Chariot" to the repeated phrase "Plain black boy," Brooks transforms De Witt Williams into an Everyman figure. Brooks describes his personal search for love in the pool rooms and dance halls, but stresses the representative quality of his experience by starting and ending the poem with the musical allusion.

"WE REAL COOL"

"We Real Cool," perhaps Brooks's single best-known poem, subjects a similarly representative experience to an intricate technical and thematic scrutiny, at once loving and critical. The poem is only twenty-four words long, including eight repetitions of the word "we." It is suggestive that the subtitle of "We Real Cool" specifies the presence of only seven pool players at the "Golden Shovel." The eighth "we" suggests that poet and reader share, on some level, the desperation of the group-voice that Brooks transmits. The final sentence, "We/ die soon," restates the carpe diem motif in the vernacular of Chicago's South Side.

On one level, "We Real Cool" appears simply to catalog the experiences of a group of dropouts content to "sing sin" in all available forms. A surprising ambiguity enters into the poem, however, revolving around the question of how to accent the word "we" that ends every line except the last one, providing the beat for the poem's jazz rhythm. Brooks said that she intended that the "we" not be accented. Read in this way, the poem takes on a slightly distant and ironic tone, emphasizing the artificiality of the group identity that involves the characters in activities offering early death as the only release from pain. Conversely, the poem can be read with a strong accent on each "we," affirming the group identity. Although the experience still ends with early death, the pool players metamorphose into defiant heroes determined to resist the alienating environment. Their confrontation with experience is felt, if not articulated, as existentially pure. Pool players, poet, and reader cannot be sure which stress is valid.

Brooks crafts the poem, however, to hint at an underlying coherence in the defiance. The intricate internal rhyme scheme echoes the sound of nearly every word. Not only do the first seven lines end with "we," but also the penultimate words of each line in each stanza rhyme (cool/school, late/straight, sin/gin, June/soon). In addition, the alliterated consonant of the last line of each stanza is repeated in the first line of the next stanza (Left/lurk, Strike/sin, gin/June) and the first words of each line in the middle two stanzas are connected through consonance (Lurk/strike, Sing/thin). The one exception to this suggestive texture of sound is the word "Die," which introduces both a new vowel and a new consonant into the final line, breaking the rhythm and subjecting the performance to ironic revaluation. Ultimately, the power of the poem derives from the tension between the celebratory and the ironic perspectives on the lives of the plain black boys struggling for a sense of connection.

"THE MOTHER"

A similar struggle informs many of Brooks's poems in more traditional forms, including "The Mother," a powerful exploration of the impact of an abortion on the woman who has chosen to have it. Brooks states

that the mother "decides that *she*, rather than her world, will kill her children." Within the poem itself, however, the motivations remain unclear. Although the poem's position in Brooks's first book, *A Street in Bronzeville*, suggests that the persona is black, the poem neither supports nor denies a racial identification. Along with the standard English syntax and diction, this suggests that "The Mother," like poems such as "The Egg Boiler," "Callie Ford," and "A Light and Diplomatic Bird," was designed to speak directly of an emotional, rather than a social, experience, and to be as accessible to whites as to blacks. Re-creating the anguished perspective of a persona unsure whether she is victim or victimizer, Brooks directs her readers' attention to the complex emotions of her potential Everywoman.

"The Mother" centers on the persona's alternating desire to take and to evade responsibility for the abortion. Resorting to ambiguous grammatical structures, the persona repeatedly qualifies her acceptance with "if" clauses ("If I sinned," "If I stole your births"). She refers to the lives of the children as matters of fate ("Your luck") and backs away from admitting that a death has taken place by claiming that the children "were never made." Her use of the second person pronoun to refer to herself in the first stanza reveals her desire to distance herself from her present pain. This attempt, however, fails. The opening line undercuts the evasion with the reality of memory: "Abortions will not let you forget." At the start of the second stanza, the pressure of memory forces the persona to shift to the more honest first-person pronoun. A sequence of spondees referring to the children ("damp small pulps," "dim killed children," "dim dears") interrupts the lightly stressed anapestic-iambic meter that dominates the first stanza. The concrete images of "scurrying off ghosts" and "devouring" children with loving gazes gain power when contrasted with the dimness of the mother's life and perceptions. Similarly, the first stanza's end-stopped couplets, reflecting the persona's simplistic attempt to recapture an irrevocably lost mother-child relationship through an act of imagination, give way to the intricate enjambment and complex rhyme scheme of the second stanza, which highlight the mother's inability to find rest.

The rhyme scheme—and Brooks can rival both

Robert Frost and William Butler Yeats in her ability to employ various types of rhyme for thematic impact—underscores her struggle to come to terms with her action. The rhymes in the first stanza insist on her self-doubt, contrasting images of tenderness and physical substance with those of brutality and insubstantiality (forget/get, hair/air, beat/sweet). The internal rhyme of "never," repeated four times, and "remember," "workers," and "singers," further stresses the element of loss. In the second stanza, Brooks provides no rhymes for the end words "children" in line 11 and "deliberate" in line 21. This device draws attention to the persona's failure to answer the crucial questions of whether her children did in fact exist and of whether her own actions were in fact deliberate (and perhaps criminal). The last seven lines of the stanza end with hard "d" sounds as the persona struggles to forge her conflicting thoughts into a unified perspective. If Brooks offers coherence, though, it is emotional rather than intellectual. Fittingly, the "d" rhymes and off-rhymes focus on physical and emotional pain (dead/instead/made/afraid/said/died/cried). Brooks provides no easy answer to the anguished question: "How is the truth to be told?" The persona's concluding cry of "I loved you/ All" rings with desperation. It is futile but it is not a lie. To call "The Mother" an antiabortion poem distorts its impact. Clearly portraying the devastating effects of the persona's action, it by no means condemns her or lacks sympathy. Like many of Brooks's characters, the mother is a person whose desire to love far outstrips her ability to cope with her circumstances and serves primarily to heighten her sensitivity to pain.

Perhaps the most significant change in Brooks's poetry involves her analysis of the origins of this pervasive pain. Rather than attributing the suffering to some unavoidable psychological condition, Brooks's later poetry indicts social institutions for their role in its perpetuation. The poems in her first two volumes frequently portray characters incapable of articulating the origins of their pain. Although the absence of any father in "The Mother" suggests sociological forces leading to the abortion, such analysis amounts to little more than speculation. The only certainty is that the mother, the persona of the sonnet sequence "The Children of the Poor," and the speaker in the brilliant sonnet "My Dreams, My Works Must Wait Till After Hell" share the fear that their pain will render them insensitive to love. The final poem of *Annie Allen*, "Men of Careful Turns," intimates that the defenders of a society that refuses to admit its full humanity bear responsibility for reducing the powerless to "grotesque toys." Despite this implicit accusation, however, Brooks perceives no "magic" capable of remedying the situation. She concludes the volume on a note of irresolution typical of her early period: "We are lost, must/ Wizard a track through our own screaming weed." The track, at this stage, remains spiritual rather than political.

POLITICS

Although the early volumes include occasional poems concerning articulate political participants such as "Negro Hero," Brooks's later work frequently centers on specific black political spokespeople such as Malcolm X, Paul Robeson, John Killens, and Don L. Lee. As of the early 1960's, a growing anger informs poems as diverse as the ironic "The Chicago *Defender* Sends a Man to Little Rock," the near-baroque "The Lovers of the Poor," the imagistically intricate "Riders to the Blood-Red Wrath," and the satiric "Riot." This anger originates in Brooks's perception that the social structures of white society value material possessions and abstract ideas of prestige more highly than individual human beings. The anger culminates in Brooks's brilliant narrative poem "In the Mecca," concerning the death of a young girl in a Chicago housing project, and in her three "Sermons on the Warpland."

"SERMONS ON THE WARPLAND"

The "Sermons on the Warpland" poems mark Brooks's departure from the traditions of Euro-American poetry and thought represented by T. S. Eliot's *The Waste Land* (1922). The sequence typifies her post-1967 poetry, in which she abandons traditional stanzaic forms, applying her technical expertise to a relatively colloquial free verse. This technical shift parallels her rejection of the philosophical premises of Euro-American culture. Brooks refuses to accept the inevitability of cultural decay, arguing that the "waste" of Eliot's vision exists primarily because of people's "warped" perceptions. Seeing white society as the embodiment of these distortions, Brooks embraces her blackness as a potential counterbalancing force. The first "Sermon on the Warpland" opens with Ron Karenga's black nationalist credo: "The fact that we are black is our ultimate reality." Clearly, in Brooks's view, blackness is not simply a physical fact; it is primarily a metaphor for the possibility of love. As her poem "Two Dedications" indicates, Brooks sees the Euro-American tradition represented by the Chicago Picasso as inhumanly cold, mingling guilt and innocence, meaningfulness and meaninglessness, almost randomly. This contrasts sharply with her inspirational image of the Wall of Heroes on the South Side. To Brooks, true art assumes meaning from the people who interact with it. The wall helps to redefine black reality, rendering the "dispossessions beakless." Rather than contemplating the site of destruction, the politically aware black art that Brooks embraces should inspire the black community to face its pain with renewed determination to remove its sources. The final "Sermon on the Warpland" concludes with the image of a black phoenix rising from the ashes of the Chicago riot. No longer content to accept the unresolved suffering of "The Mother," Brooks forges a black nationalist politics and poetics of love.

"THE BLACKSTONE RANGERS"

Although her political vision influences every aspect of her work, Brooks maintains a strong sense of enduring individual pain and is aware that nationalism offers no simple panacea. "The Blackstone Rangers," a poem concerning one of the most powerful Chicago street gangs, rejects as simplistic the argument, occasionally advanced by writers associated with the Black Arts movement, that no important distinction exists between the personal and the political experience. Specifically, Brooks doubts the corollary that politically desirable activity will inevitably increase the person's ability to love. Dividing "The Blackstone Rangers" into three segments—"As Seen by Disciplines," "The Leaders," and "Gang Girls: A Rangerette"—Brooks stresses the tension between perspectives. After rejecting the sociological-penal perspective of part one, she remains suspended between the uncomprehending affirmation of the Rangers as a kind of government-in-exile in part two, and the recognition of the individual person's continuing pain in part three.

Brooks undercuts the description of the Rangers as "sores in the city/ that do not want to heal" ("As Seen by Disciplines") through the use of off-rhyme and a jazz rhythm reminiscent of "We Real Cool." The disciplines, both academic and corrective, fail to perceive any coherence in the Rangers' experience. Correct in their assumption that the Rangers do not want to "heal" themselves, the disciplines fail to perceive the gang's strong desire to "heal" the sick society. Brooks suggests an essential coherence in the Rangers' experience through the sound texture of part one. Several of the sound patterns echoing through the brief stanza point to a shared response to pain (there/thirty/ready, raw/sore/corner). Similarly, the accent cluster on "Black, raw, ready" draws attention to the pain and potential power of the Rangers. The descriptive voice of the disciplines, however, provides only relatively weak end rhymes (are/corner, ready/city), testifying to the inability of the distanced, presumably white, observers to comprehend the experiences they describe. The shifting, distinctively black, jazz rhythm further emphasizes the distance between the voices of observers and participants. Significantly, the voice of the disciplines finds no rhyme at all for its denial of the Rangers' desire to "heal."

This denial contrasts sharply with the tempered affirmation of the voice in part two, which emphasizes the leaders' desire to "cancel, cure and curry." Again, internal rhymes and sound echoes suffuse the section. In the first stanza, the voice generates thematically significant rhymes, connecting Ranger leader "*Bop*" (whose name draws attention to the jazz rhythm that is even more intricate, though less obvious, in this section than in part one) and the militant black leader "*Rap*" Brown, both nationalists whose "country is a Nation on no *map*." "Bop" and "Rap," of course, do not rhyme perfectly, attesting to Brooks's awareness of the gang leader's limitations. Her image of the leaders as "Bungled trophies" further reinforces her ambivalence. The only full rhyme in the final two stanzas of the section is the repeated "night." The leaders, canceling the racist association of darkness with evil, "translate" the image of blackness into a "monstrous pearl or grace." The section affirms the Blackstone Rangers' struggle; it does not pretend to comprehend fully the emotional texture of their lives.

Certain that the leaders possess the power to cancel

the disfiguring images of the disciplines, Brooks remains unsure of their ability to create an alternate environment where love can blossom. Mary Ann, the "Gang Girl" of part three, shares much of the individual pain of the characters in Brooks's early poetry despite her involvement with the Rangers. "A rose in a whiskey glass," she continues to live with the knowledge that her "laboring lover" risks the same sudden death as the pool players of "We Real Cool." Forced to suppress a part of her awareness—she knows not to ask where her lover got the diamond he gives her—she remains emotionally removed even while making love. In place of a fully realized love, she accepts "the props and niceties of non-loneliness." The final line of the poem emphasizes the ambiguity of both Mary Ann's situation and Brooks's perspective. Recommending acceptance of "the rhymes of Leaning," the line responds to the previous stanza's question concerning whether love will have a "gleaning." The full rhyme paradoxically suggests acceptance of off-rhyme, of love consummated leaning against an alley wall, without expectation of safety or resolution. Given the political tension created by the juxtaposition of the disciplines and the leaders, the "Gang Girl" can hope to find no sanctuary beyond the reach of the whirlwind. Her desperate love, the more moving for its precariousness, provides the only near-adequate response to the pain that Brooks saw as the primary fact of life.

OTHER MAJOR WORKS

LONG FICTION: *Maud Martha*, 1953.

NONFICTION: *The World of Gwendolyn Brooks*, 1971; *Report from Part One*, 1972; *Young Poet's Primer*, 1980; *Report from Part Two*, 1996.

CHILDREN'S LITERATURE: *Bronzeville Boys and Girls*, 1956; *The Tiger Who Wore White Gloves*, 1974; *Very Young Poets*, 1983.

EDITED TEXT: *Jump Bad: A New Chicago Anthology*, 1971.

BIBLIOGRAPHY

Bloom, Harold, ed. *Gwendolyn Brooks*. Philadelphia: Chelsea House, 2000. From the series Modern Critical Views. Includes an introduction by Bloom and provides a solid introduction to Brooks.

Bolden, B. J. *Urban Rage in Bronzeville: Social Commentary in the Poetry of Gwendolyn Brooks, 1945-1960*. Chicago: Third World Press, 1999. A critical analysis focused on the impact of Brooks's early poetry. Bolden examines *A Street in Bronzeville, Annie Allen*, and *The Bean Eaters* in clear historical, racial, political, cultural, and aesthetic terms.

Bryant, Jacqueline Imani, ed. *Gwendolyn Brooks and Working Writers*. Chicago: Third World Press, 2007. Contains seventeen essays by writers, educators, and friends of Brooks describing encounters with the poet and how she influenced them.

"Gwendolyn's Words: A Gift to Us." *Essence* 31, no. 11 (March, 2001): A18. Begins with an account of Brooks's early life and documents the sequence of her compositions. Also covers her professional relationship with Haki R. Madhubuti, who helped publish her works.

Kent, George E. *A Life of Gwendolyn Brooks*. Lexington: University Press of Kentucky, 1990. This biography, completed in 1982 just before Kent's death, is based on interviews with Brooks and her friends and family. Integrates discussions of the poetry with a chronicle of her life. Especially valuable is an extensive recounting of the events and speeches at the 1967 Fisk conference, which changed the direction of her poetry. D. L. Melhem's afterword provides an update to 1988.

Melhem, D. L. *Gwendolyn Brooks: Poetry and the Heroic Voice*. Lexington: University Press of Kentucky, 1987. Beginning with a biographical chapter, Melhem employs a generally laudatory tone as he subsequently looks closely at the earlier poetry collections. He surveys the later works within a single chapter and also examines *Maud Martha* and *Bronzeville Boys and Girls*. Melhem's treatment gives attention to both structures and themes. The bibliography of her works is organized by publisher, to show her commitment to small black-run presses after the late 1960's.

Mickle, Mildred, ed. *Gwendolyn Brooks*. Pasadena, Calif.: Salem Press, 2009. Part of the Critical Insights series, this collection of critical essays examines aspects of Brooks's work such as her relation to the Harlem Renaissance and her legacy.

Mootry, Maria K., and Gary Smith, eds. *A Life Distilled: Gwendolyn Brooks, Her Poetry and Fiction.* Urbana: University of Illinois Press, 1987. Looks at Brooks's sense of place, her aesthetic, and the militancy that emerged in her "second period." The middle section comprises essays on individual collections, while the book's final two essays examine *Maud Martha.* The selected bibliography lists Brooks's works and surveys critical sources in great detail, including book reviews and dissertations.

Washington, Mary Helen. "An Appreciation: A Writer Who Defined Black Power for Herself." *Los Angeles Times*, December 8, 2000, p. E1. Discusses the young Brooks who attended the 1967 Fisk University Writers' Conference, encountered young black militants led by Amiri Baraka, and was converted. She branded her earlier writing "white writing" and resolved to change.

Wright, Stephen Caldwell, ed. *On Gwendolyn Brooks: Reliant Contemplation.* Ann Arbor: University of Michigan Press, 1996. This resource judiciously selects and assembles the most important writings to date about the works of Brooks in the form of reviews and essays. Three-part organization helpfully separates the reviews from the essays and the later essays from the rest.

Craig Werner

STERLING A. BROWN

Born: Washington, D.C.; May 1, 1901
Died: Takoma Park, Maryland; January 13, 1989

PRINCIPAL POETRY

Southern Road, 1932
The Last Ride of Wild Bill, and Eleven Narrative Poems, 1975
The Collected Poems of Sterling A. Brown, 1980

OTHER LITERARY FORMS

Sterling A. Brown produced several studies of African American literature: *Outline for the Study of the Po-* etry of American Negroes (1931), *The Negro in American Fiction* (1937), and *Negro Poetry and Drama* (1937). With Arthur P. Davis and Ulysses Lee, he edited *The Negro Caravan* (1941). Brown also published numerous scholarly pieces in leading journals on subjects relating to African American culture and literature.

ACHIEVEMENTS

Sterling A. Brown is considered an important transitional figure between the Harlem Renaissance era and the period immediately following the Depression. Brown's fame is based not only on his poetry but also on his achievements as a critic, folklorist, scholar, and university teacher. As an acknowledged authority on African American culture, Brown served on many committees and boards and participated in numerous scholarly and research activities. Among these were the Carnegie-Myrdal Study, the American Folklore Society, the Institute of Jazz Studies, the editorial board of *The Crisis*, the Federal Writers' Project, and the Committee on Negro Studies of the American Council of Learned Societies.

Brown's poems and critical essays have been anthologized widely, and he was a memorable reader of his own poetry, especially on such recordings as *The Anthology of Negro Poets* (Folkways) and *A Hand's on the Gate.* He cowrote an article with Rayford Logan on the American Negro for *Encyclopaedia Britannica.* Brown was a Guggenheim Fellow (1937-1938) and a Julius Rosenwald Fellow (1942). He was an eminent faculty member at Howard University in Washington, D.C., from 1929 to 1969. *The Collected Poems of Sterling A. Brown* was selected for the National Poetry Series in 1979. Brown won the Lenore Marshall Poetry Prize in 1981, the Langston Hughes Award in 1982, and the Frost Medal, awarded by the Poetry Society of America, in 1987.

BIOGRAPHY

Born into an educated, middle-class African American family, Sterling Allen Brown was the last of six children and the only son of Adelaide Allen Brown and the Reverend Sterling Nelson Brown. His father had taught in the School of Religion at Howard University since 1892, and the year Brown was born, his father also became the pastor of Lincoln Temple Congregational Church. The person who encouraged Brown's literary career and admiration for the cultural heritage of African Americans, however, was his mother, who had been born and reared in Tennessee and graduated from Fisk University. Brown also grew up listening to tales of his father's childhood in Tennessee, as well as to accounts of his father's friendships with noted leaders such as Frederick Douglass, Blanche K. Bruce, and Booker T. Washington.

Brown attended public schools in Washington, D.C., and graduated from the well-known Dunbar High School, noted for its distinguished teachers and alumni; among the latter were many of the nation's outstanding black professionals. Brown's teachers at Dunbar included literary artists such as Angelina Weld Grimké and Jessie Redmon Fauset. Moreover, Brown grew up on the campus of Howard University, where there were many outstanding African American scholars, such as historian Kelly Miller and critic and philosopher Alain Locke.

Brown received his A.B. in 1922 from Williams College (Phi Beta Kappa) and his M.A. in 1923 from Harvard University. Although he pursued further graduate study in English at Harvard, he never worked toward a doctorate degree; however, he eventually received honorary doctorates from Howard University, the University of Massachusetts, Northwestern, Williams College, Boston University, Brown, Lewis and Clark College, Lincoln University (Pennsylvania), and the University of Pennsylvania. In September, 1927, he was married to Daisy Turnbull, who shared with him an enthusiasm for people, a sense of humor, and a rejection of pretentious behavior; she was also one of her husband's sharpest critics. She inspired Brown's poems "Long Track Blues" and "Against That Day." Daisy Turnbull Brown died in 1979. The Browns had one adopted child, John L. Dennis.

In 1927, "When de Saints Go Ma'ching Home" won first prize in an *Opportunity* writing contest. From 1926 to 1929, several of the poems that Brown later published in *Southern Road* were printed in *Crisis*, *Opportunity*, *Contempo*, and *Ebony and Topaz*. His early work is often identified with the outpouring of black writers during the New Negro movement, for he shared with those artists (Claude McKay, Countée Cullen, Jean Toomer, and Langston Hughes) a deep concern for a franker self-revelation and a respect for the folk traditions of his people; however, Brown's writings did not reflect the alien-and-exile theme so popular with the writers of the Renaissance.

Brown's teaching career took him to Virginia Seminary and College, Lincoln University (Missouri), and Fisk University. He began teaching at Howard in 1929 and remained there until his retirement in 1969. He was also a visiting professor at Atlanta University, New York University, Vassar College, the University of Minnesota, the New School, and the University of Illinois (Chicago Circle). Several years after coming to Howard, Brown became an editor with the Works Progress Administration's Federal Writers Project. Along with a small editorial staff, he coordinated the Federal Writers Project studies by and about blacks. Beginning in 1932, Brown supervised an extensive collection of narratives by former slaves and initiated special projects such as *The Negro in Virginia* (1940), which became the model for other studies. His most enduring contribution to the project was an essay, "The

Sterling A. Brown (©Scurlock Studios)

Negro in Washington," which was published in the guidebook *Washington: City and Capital* (1937).

Brown's first fifteen years at Howard were most productive. During this period (1929-1945), he contributed poetry as well as reviews and essays on the American theater, folk expressions, oral history, social customs, music, and athletics to *The New Republic*, *Journal of Negro Education*, *Phylon*, *Crisis*, *Opportunity*, and other journals. His most outstanding essay, "Negro Characters as Seen by White Authors," which appeared in *Journal of Negro Education* in 1933, brought attention to the widespread misrepresentation of black characters and life in American literature. Only after Brown's retirement from Howard in 1969 did he begin reading his poems regularly there. This long neglect has been attributed to certain conservative faculty members' reluctance to appreciate a fellow professor whose interests were in blues and jazz. Brown was widely known as a raconteur. Throughout his career as a writer, he challenged fellow African American writers to choose their subject matter without regard to external pressures and to avoid the error of "timidity." He was a mentor who influenced the black poetry movement of the 1960's and 1970's, and poets such as Margaret Walker, Gwendolyn Brooks, Langston Hughes, and Arna Bontemps, along with critics such as Addison Gayle and Houston Baker, learned from him.

In the five years before his retirement, Brown began to exhibit stress caused by what he perceived to be years of critical and professional neglect as well as unfulfilled goals. Inclined toward periods of deep depression, he was occasionally hospitalized in his later years. He died in Takoma Park, Maryland, on January 13, 1989.

ANALYSIS

The poetry of Sterling A. Brown is imbued with the folk spirit of African American culture. For Brown, there was no wide abyss between his poetry and the spirit inherent in slave poetry; indeed, his works evidence a continuity of racial spirit from the slave experience to the African American present and reflect his deep understanding of the multitudinous aspects of the African American personality and soul.

The setting for Brown's poetry is primarily the South, through which he traveled to listen to the folk-

tales, songs, wisdom, sorrows, and frustrations of his people, and where the blues and ballads were nurtured. Brown respected traditional folk forms and employed them in the construction of his own poems; thus he may be called "the poet of the soul of his people."

SOUTHERN ROAD

Brown's first published collection of poems, *Southern Road*, was critically acclaimed by his peers and colleagues James Weldon Johnson and Alain Locke, because of its rendering of the living speech of African Americans, its use of the raw material of folk poetry, and its poetic portrayal of African American folk life and thought. Later critics such as Arthur P. Davis, Jean Wagner, and Houston Baker have continued to praise his poetry for its creative and vital use of folk motifs. Some of the characters in Brown's poetry, such as Ma Rainey, Big Boy Davis, and Mrs. Bibby, are based on real people. Other characters, such as Maumee Ruth, Sporting Beasley, and Sam Smiley seem real because of Brown's dramatic and narrative talent. He is also highly skilled in the use of poetic techniques such as the refrain, alliteration, and onomatopoeia, and he employs several stanzaic forms with facility. Brown's extraordinary gift for re-creating the nuances of folk speech and idiom adds vitality and authenticity to his verse.

Brown is successful in drawing on rich folk expressions to vitalize the speech of his characters through the cadences of southern speech. Though his poems cannot simply be called dialect poetry, Brown does imitate southern African American speech, using variant spellings and apostrophes to mark dropped consonants. He uses grunts and onomatopoeic sounds to give a natural rhythm to the speech of his characters. These techniques are readily seen in a poem that dramatizes the poignant story of a "po los boy" on a chain gang. This poem follows the traditional folk form of the work song to convey the convict's personal tragedy.

Brown's work may be classed as protest poetry influenced by poets such as Carl Sandburg and Robert Frost; he is able to draw on the entire canon of English and American poetry as well as African American folk material. Thus he is fluent in the use of the sonnet form, stanzaic forms, free-verse forms, and ballad and blues forms.

In *Southern Road*, several themes express the essence of the southern African American's folk spirit and culture. Recurring themes and subjects in Brown's poetry include endurance, tragedy, and survival. The theme of endurance is best illustrated in one of his most anthologized poems, "Strong Men," which tells the story of the unjust treatment of black men and women from the slave ship, to the tenant farm, and finally to the black ghetto. The refrain of "Strong Men" uses rhythmic beats, relentlessly repeating an affirmation of the black people's ability and determination to keep pressing onward, toward freedom and justice. The central image comes from a line of a Carl Sandburg poem, "The strong men keep coming on." In "Strong Men," Brown praises the indomitable spirit of African Americans in the face of racist exploitation. With its assertive tone, the rhythm of this poem suggests a martial song.

Some of the endurance poems express a stoic, fatalistic acceptance of the tragic fate of African Americans, as can be seen in "Old Man Buzzard," "Memphis Blues," and "Riverbank Blues." Another important aspect of the endurance theme as portrayed by Brown is the poetic characters' courage when they are confronted with tragedy and injustice. In the poem "Strange Legacies," the speaker gives thanks to the legendary Jack Johnson and John Henry for their demonstration of courage.

"THE LAST RIDE OF WILD BILL"

Brown's poems reflect his understanding of the often tragic destinies of African Americans in the United States. No poet before Brown had created such a comprehensive poetic dramatization of the lives of black men and women in America. Brown depicts black men and women as alone and powerless, struggling nevertheless to confront an environment that is hostile and unjust. In this tragic environment, African American struggles against the schemes of racist whites are seen in "The Last Ride of Wild Bill," published in 1975 as the title poem of a collection. A black man falls victim to the hysteria of a lynch mob in "Frankie and Johnnie," a poem that takes up a familiar folktale and twists it to reflect a personal tragedy that occurs as a result of an interracial relationship. Brown emphasizes that in this story the only tragic victim is the black man. The retarded white girl, Frankie, reports her sexual experience with the black man, Johnnie, to her father and suc-

ceeds in getting her black lover killed; she laughs uproariously during the lynching. "Southern Cop" narrates the mindless killing of a black man who is the victim of the panic of a rookie police officer.

However, Brown's poems show black people as victims not only of whites but also of the whole environment that surrounds them, including natural forces of flood and fire as well as social evils such as poverty and ignorance. Rural blacks' vulnerability to natural disasters is revealed in "Old King Cotton," "New St. Louis Blues," and "Foreclosure." In these poems, if a tornado does not come, the Mississippi River rises and takes the peasant's arable land and his few animals, and even traitorously kills his children by night. These poems portray despairing people who are capable only of futile questions in the face of an implacable and pitiless nature. The central character of "Low Down" is sunk in poverty and loneliness. His wife has left and his son is in prison; he is convinced that bad luck is his fate and that in the workings of life someone has loaded the dice against him. In "Johnny Thomas," the title character is the victim of poverty, abuse by his parents and society, and ignorance. (He attempts to enroll in a one-room school, but the teacher throws him out.) Johnny ends up on a chain gang, where he is killed. The poem that most strongly expresses African American despair for the entire race is "Southern Road," a convict song marked by a rhythmic, staccato beat and by a blues line punctuated by the convict's groaning over his accursed fate:

> My ole man died—hunh—
> Cussin' me;
> Old lady rocks, bebby,
> huh misery.

SLIM GREER POEMS

The African American's ability to survive in a hostile world by mustering humor, religious faith, and the expectation of a utopian afterlife is portrayed in poems depicting the comical adventures of Slim Greer and in one of Brown's popular poems, "Sister Lou." The series of Slim Greer poems, "Slim Greer," "Slim Lands a Job," "Slim in Atlanta," and "Slim in Hell," reveal Brown's knowledge of the life of the ordinary black people and his ability to laugh at the weaknesses and foolishness of blacks and whites alike. With their rich exaggerations, these poems fall into the tall tale tradition of folk stories. They show Slim in Arkansas passing for white although he is quite dark; or Slim in Atlanta, laughing in a "telefoam booth" because of a law that keeps blacks from laughing in the open. In "Slim Lands a Job," the poet mocks the ridiculous demands that southern employers make on their black employees. Slim applies for a job in a restaurant. The owner is complaining about the laziness of his black employees when a black waiter enters the room carrying a tray on his head, trays in each hand, silver in his mouth, and soup plates in his vest, while simultaneously pulling a red wagon filled with other paraphernalia. When the owner points to this waiter as one who is lazy, Slim makes a quick exit. In "Slim in Hell," Slim discovers that Hell and the South are very much alike; when he reports this discovery to Saint Peter, the saint reprimands him, asking where he thought Hell was if not the South.

"SISTER LOU"

In "Sister Lou," one of his well-known poems, Brown depicts the simple religious faith that keeps some blacks going. After recounting all the sorrows in Sister Lou's life, the poem pictures Heaven as a place where Sister Lou will have a chance to allow others to carry her packages, to speak personally to God without fear, to rest, and most of all to take her time. In "Cabaret," however, Brown shows the everyday reality that belies the promises God made to his people: The black folk huddle, mute and forlorn, in Mississippi, unable to understand why the Good Lord treats them this way. Moreover, in poems such as "Maumee Ruth," religion is seen as an opium that feeds people's illusions. Maumee Ruth lies on her deathbed, ignorant of the depraved life led by her son and daughter in the city, and needing the religious lies preached to her to attain a peaceful death.

"REMEMBERING NAT TURNER"

Brown's poems embrace themes of suffering, oppression, and tragedy, yet always celebrate the vision and beauty of African American people and culture. One such deeply moving piece is "Remembering Nat Turner," a poem in which the speaker visits the scene of Turner's slave rebellion, only to hear an elderly white woman's garbled recollections of the event; moreover, the marker intended to call attention to Turner's heroic

exploits, a rotting signpost, has been used by black tenants for kindling. A stoic fatalism can be seen in the poem "Memphis Blues," which nevertheless praises the ability of African Americans to survive in a hostile environment because of their courage and willingness to start over when all seems lost: "Guess we'll give it one more try." In the words of Brown, "The strong men keep a-comin' on/ Gittin' stronger."

OTHER MAJOR WORKS

NONFICTION: *Outline for the Study of the Poetry of American Negroes*, 1931; *The Negro in American Fiction*, 1937; *Negro Poetry and Drama*, 1937; *A Son's Return: Selected Essays of Sterling A. Brown*, 1996 (Mark A. Sanders, editor).

EDITED TEXT: *The Negro Caravan*, 1941 (with Arthur P. Davis and Ulysses Lee).

BIBLIOGRAPHY

Davis, Arthur P. "Sterling Brown." In *From the Dark Tower: Afro-American Writers, 1900-1960*. Washington, D.C.: Howard University Press, 1982. A comprehensive study by the dean of African American critics, who knew Brown personally and taught with him at Howard University on African American writers during the 1950's. The essays on individual writers are supplemented by ample introductory material, and there is also an extensive bibliography, listed by author.

Ekate, Genevieve. "Sterling Brown: A Living Legend." *New Directions: The Howard University Magazine* 1 (Winter, 1974): 5-11. A tribute to the life and works of Brown in a magazine published by the university where he taught for forty years. This article analyzes Brown's literary influence on younger poets and assesses his importance in the African American literary canon.

Sanders, Mark A. *Afro-Modernist Aesthetics and the Poetry of Sterling A. Brown*. Athens: University of Georgia Press, 1999. Criticism and interpretation of Brown and his poetry in the context of twentieth century African American literature and intellectual life.

Thelwell, Ekwueme Michael. "The Professor and the Activists: A Memoir of Sterling Brown." *Massachusetts Review* 40, no. 4 (Winter, 1999/2000): 617-

638. A fond memoir of Brown written by one of his students at Howard University. Offers a glimpse into Brown's personality, political bent, and place as a black intellectual during the tumultuous 1960's.

Tidwell, John Edgar, and Steven C. Tracy, eds. *After Winter: The Art and Life of Sterling Brown*. New York: Oxford University Press, 2009. A collection of critical essays on Brown's works, as well as interviews with those who knew him. Also contains a bibliography and discography.

Wagner, Jean. "Sterling Brown." In *Black Poets of the United States, from Paul Laurence Dunbar to Langston Hughes*. Urbana: University of Illinois Press, 1973. A comprehensive and insightful study of the poetry of Brown, covering the subjects, themes, and nuances of his poetry. Wagner's writing on Brown is warm and appreciative.

Betty Taylor-Thompson

WILLIAM CULLEN BRYANT

Born: Cummington, Massachusetts; November 3, 1794
Died: New York, New York; June 12, 1878

PRINCIPAL POETRY

The Embargo: Or, Sketches of the Times, a Satire, 1808
Poems, 1821, 1832, 1834, 1836, 1839, 1854, 1871, 1875
The Fountain, and Other Poems, 1842
The White-Footed Deer, and Other Poems, 1844
Thirty Poems, 1864
Hymns, 1864, 1869
The Poetical Works of William Cullen Bryant, 1876
The Flood of Years, 1878

OTHER LITERARY FORMS

William Cullen Bryant wrote a substantial body of prose: tales, editorials, reviews, letters, appreciations, sketches or impressions, and critical essays. In 1850, he published *Letters of a Traveller: Or, Notes of Things Seen in Europe and America*; in 1859, *Letters of a Traveller, Second Series*; and in 1869, *Letters from the East*. He reviewed the careers of a number of his contemporaries in such pieces as *A Discourse on the Life and Genius of James Fenimore Cooper* (1852) and *A Discourse on the Life and Genius of Washington Irving* (1860). In 1851, he published his *Reminiscences of the "Evening Post,"* and in 1873, a collection of *Orations and Addresses*. His *Lectures on Poetry*, delivered to the Athenaeum Society in 1826, was published in 1884.

ACHIEVEMENTS

William Cullen Bryant's central achievement as a man of letters was his contribution to the developing sense of a national identity. Although Bryant's verse is often indistinguishable from the eighteenth and nineteenth century English verse of his models, he begins to draw lines of contrast, first, by his choice of subject matter—prairies, violets, gentians, Indian legends—and, second, by developing a characteristic poetic voice that can be seen in retrospect to be the early stage of the development of a nationally distinctive poetry.

Bryant's participation in the formative stages of American poetry was a natural corollary to the second of his two major achievements, his career as a journalist. As the editor and part-owner of the New York *Evening Post* for almost fifty years, he championed liberal social and political causes that were as much a part of the newly emerging national identity as was his poetry. His vigorous support of freedom of the press, of abolition, of the Republican Party, and of John Frémont and Abraham Lincoln, are among his most notable achievements as a journalist.

Although minor in comparison with his two major achievements, Bryant's lectures on poetic theory to the Athenaeum Society in 1826 shed light on his own poetry and on some of the cultural assumptions of his period. Bryant's emphasis on "moral uplift and spiritual refinement" as the aim of poetry is balanced by his interest in native speech and natural imagery as resources to be tapped by the poet.

BIOGRAPHY

William Cullen Bryant was born on November 3, 1794, in Cummington, Massachusetts, to Peter Bryant and Sarah Snell Bryant. The poet enjoyed a close family life and, from an early age, benefited from the positive influences of both parents, as well as from those of his maternal grandfather, Ebenezer Snell. The latter's Calvinist influence, though muted, is evident in the language of the poetry and in the recurrent image of an angry God threatening retribution for humankind's sins. His mother's gentler religious influence bore directly on his precocity as a reader in general, and of the Bible in particular, at the age of four. Bryant was later to remember those conducting the religious services of his very early childhood experiences as "often poets in their extemporaneous prayers."

A counter, and as time passed more prevailing, influence was that of his liberal physician father, Peter Bryant, who encouraged the poet in his early experiments with satires, lampoons, and pastorals. Under that encouraging tutelage, Bryant published his first poem

of substance, "The Embargo," in 1808, at the age of thirteen; three years later, he set about translating the third book of the *Aeneid*. In 1817, Peter Bryant took copies of several of his son's poems to his friend Willard Phillips, one of the editors of the *North American Review*. "Thanatopsis" and one other poem were published immediately in the journal's September issue. "Inscription for the Entrance to a Wood" and "To a Waterfowl" appeared subsequently.

Meanwhile, Bryant had been preparing himself for a legal career and was admitted to the bar in 1815. He began practicing law in 1816 in Great Barrington, Massachusetts. In 1825, he assumed editorship of the *New York Review*, and in 1829, he began his fifty-year career as a major journalist when he became part-owner and editor-in-chief of the New York *Evening Post*. From that position he was to champion freedom of speech, abolition, the right of workmen to strike,

William Cullen Bryant (NARA)

Frémont, the Republican Party, and Lincoln and the Union cause. When he died in 1878, the *Evening Post* continued his policies under the leadership of his son-in-law, Parke Godwin.

Although Bryant was to continue writing poetry throughout his life, most of it, and particularly those poems on which his reputation rests, was written by the early 1830's. By the middle of the century, though he was still an active and vigorous journalist, he had become something of an institution to writers such as Nathaniel Hawthorne, Herman Melville, and Oliver Wendell Holmes. Ralph Waldo Emerson included Bryant among the imagined faculty of his ideal college, because, as he noted in his journal, "Bryant has learned where to hang his titles, namely by tying his mind to autumn woods, winter mornings, rain, brooks, mountains, evening winds, and wood-birds. . . . [He is] American."

Bryant married Frances Fairchild in 1821. They had two daughters, Fanny and Julia, who inherited the sizable estate left at his death on June 12, 1878. His death resulted from a fall and head injury on May 29.

ANALYSIS

William Cullen Bryant wrote his poetry over a fifty-year span, but the apex of his career came in the early 1830's, very close to an exact midpoint between William Wordsworth's 1800 preface to the second edition of *Lyrical Ballads* and Walt Whitman's *Leaves of Grass* (1855). In retrospect, Bryant's poetry, especially his blank verse, can be seen in terms of a development moving from Wordsworth's theories and examples to the American model of Whitman's free verse, celebrating the self and the newly emerging national identity. At its best, Bryant's verse reflects the evolutionary dynamics of a national poetry in the making; at its worst, it is stale repetition of eighteenth century nature poetry, cast in static imitation of Wordsworthian models.

Bryant's affirmative resolution of his brooding preoccupation with the mutability of all things is another characteristic that places him in the early mainstream of the emerging national literature. He will continue to be read for his place in literary history, for the fuller understanding of the development of that national literature of which he contributes, even if his verse is wholly uncongenial to the contemporary reader. His celebration of the American landscape and his affirmation of a progressive spirit became overtly central themes for Ralph Waldo Emerson, Henry David Thoreau, and Whitman. Bryant's best poetry prefigures the American Renaissance in both content and form, theme and style, and thus he continues to be read, and to be readable, as one of America's literary pioneers.

"THANATOPSIS"

"Thanatopsis," one of Bryant's earliest successes and his most enduring one, survives as a poem rather than as an artifact because its rhythmic and syntactic fluidity has kept it readable. Blank verse has always offered the poet writing in English the best medium, short of free verse, for such fluidity, and that fact, along with the survival of the Romantic ideal of a natural or colloquial language, goes a long way toward explaining the poem's survival. Because, however, it is obvious that not all of Bryant's blank verse has been so successful, "Thanatopsis" invites a more detailed examination. The basis of its rhythmic character lies primarily in the relationship between the blank verse structure and the sentence structure. Because few of the lines are end-

stopped, the syntactic rhythm is stronger than the theoretical rhythm of blank verse—that is, of five-stress, iambic lines. An examination of the great variety of sentence length relative to line length and of the accentual stress pattern of both will provide some illustrative detail for this aspect of the poem's character.

There are three thematic sections in the poem, the second beginning at line 31, with "Yet not to thine . . . ," the third at line 73, with "So live. . . ." The opening independent clause of section 1, ending with a semicolon in line 3, has all the rhetorical quality of a sentence. It and the opening sentence of section 2 are two-and-a-half lines long. The third section has only one sentence, running through the final nine lines of the poem. Two other very long sentences are those beginning at line 8, running over eight lines, and at line 66, running over six. The two shortest sentences are at lines 29 and 60, respectively. The first of these, beginning with "The oak/ Shall send his roots abroad," has twelve syllables, two more than the blank verse line. The latter has only nine syllables, one short of the prescribed ten. Even this shortest sentence, however, occupies parts of two lines, thus contributing to rather than diminishing the dominance of the syntactic over the verse structure. That dominance prevails in large part simply because of the variety of sentence lengths, which constitute a variety of rhetorical subunits within the thematic and blank verse structures of the poem. The relationship between these syntactical subunits and the blank verse can be best illustrated by simple scansion of representative passages.

The poem begins with a two-and-a-half line independent clause: "To him who in the love of Nature holds/ Communion with her visible forms, she speaks/ A various language. . . ." If, for the sake of illustration, one ignores the sentence-sense of this phrase, the first two lines scan perfectly as iambic pentameter. The artificiality of the resulting illustration is so apparent, however, as to prompt a quick second scansion of the clause as a whole, which shifts the emphasis from line units to grammatical units—to, in this case, an introductory prepositional phrase, a relative clause, and a main clause. In that second scansion, "who," as the first word of the relative clause, is stressed, immediately throwing off the iambic regularity of the first reading. "In" loses its stress, becoming the first syllable of an anapest, "in the love." A second anapest occurs in line 2 in "visible forms." The most dramatic alteration of the blank verse line comes at the end of the grammatical unit in line 3, where the rhythm shifts momentarily from rising to falling, to the dactyl of "various," and the trochee of "language."

The opening lines of section 2, lines 31 through 33, maintain a greater iambic regularity than does the first clause, although at the end of the sentence, "couch," the first word of line 33, is stressed and is followed by the anapest "more magnificent."

In the closing nine-line sentence of the poem, the syntactic counterpoint to the blank verse rhythm is of a more subtle kind. The opening anapests of line 74, "The innumerable," *if* one sounds the schwa in the middle of the word, is followed immediately by the initial stress of "caravan." The rhythm of the prepositional phrase "in the silent halls," of line 76, prevails over the artificiality of a strict iambic reading, which calls for a stress on "in." Anapests occur in each of the final four lines. Line 78 has an initial stress on "Scourged," and the final line has the interesting juxtaposition of stresses in "About him," that is probably best described as a spondee.

The language of "Thanatopsis," particularly the dominance of syntactical over blank verse rhythm, is very close to what might be called the vernacular mode. Except for its diction, the "still voice" of the poem approximates, almost as closely as does Whitman's free verse, the voice of American colloquial speech. A dramatic illustration of that characteristic can be made by reading "Thanatopsis" side by side with almost any poem of Henry Wadsworth Longfellow's. Adjustments must be made from the late twentieth century perspective to accommodate Bryant's diction and imagery to that sense of his achievement, but in "Thanatopsis" those adjustments can be made rather easily. Except for the second-person pronouns, "thee," "thou," and "thine," there is very little diction that dates the poem.

IMAGERY

If Bryant's rhythm and diction point forward in time to the emerging American voice, his imagery and his overt moral didacticism provide the ballast that holds him most securely to his own time. The general and abstract plane of much of his imagery clearly reflects eighteenth century influence. In some instances, it clogs the otherwise fluid syntax, effectively cutting off any prospects of vitality for the modern sensibility. One of his better poems, "A Forest Hymn," suffers in this way because of the density of images such as "stilly twilight," "mossy boughs," "venerable columns," "verdant roof," and "winding aisles."

Although the imagery of "Thanatopsis" is typical in this respect—that is, its imagery is more general and abstract than particular and concrete—it does not impede the syntactic flow of the poem. This is due, in part, to the fact that the subject of the poem, the meditation on death, calls for and sustains general imagery as much as any subject can. The "innumerable caravan" of the dead and the "silent halls of death" have no concrete, experiential counterparts. The "gay" and "the solemn brood of care," on the other hand, do, and they contribute to that eighteenth century ballast that counteracts Bryant's forward motion. Those countermelodies of the static and the dynamic, of the past and of the present progressive, are nowhere more evident than in the closing lines of the first section of the poem, which juxtapose the stock images of the "insensible rock" and the "sluggish clod" with the concrete imagery of one of the most memorable lines in American poetry: "The oak/ Shall send his roots abroad and pierce thy mould."

The blank verse and the theme of "Thanatopsis" together make the general imagery less obtrusive than it is in many of Bryant's poems. The same can be said of his overt moral didacticism, which is better sustained in this blank verse meditation on death than it is in poems such as "The Yellow Violet," "To the Fringed Gentian," and "To a Waterfowl," where the fragile lyricism is overburdened for twentieth century sensibility by the didactic uses to which he puts the flowers and the birds.

"A FOREST HYMN" AND "THE PRAIRIES"

Other blank verse poems that hold up well in much the same way as does "Thanatopsis" are "A Forest Hymn" and "The Prairies," although the eighteenth century stock imagery somewhat impedes the syntactic and rhythmic flow of the former. "The Prairies," on the other hand, is remarkable for the fluid sweep of its opening thirty-four lines of impressionistic description, motivated by Bryant's first visit to Illinois in 1832. The marvelously vibrant sense of life in these lines provides an excellent example of the major counterpoint in Bryant's poetry to the stoic resignation evinced in the earlier meditation on death. The terms of that early poem are broader than those of what might be called a mortality theme; the counterpoint in Bryant is really between the two larger themes of mutability and plenitude. His prevailing preoccupation is not so much with mortality as with change, and that somber theme is countered by his affirmative sense of a natural plenitude that guarantees a continuing replenishment of all that passes.

OTHER MAJOR WORKS

NONFICTION: *Letters of a Traveller: Or, Notes of Things Seen in Europe and America*, 1850; *Reminiscences of the "Evening Post,"* 1851; *A Discourse on the Life and Genius of James Fenimore Cooper*, 1852; *Letters of a Traveller, Second Series*, 1859; *A Discourse on the Life and Genius of Washington Irving*, 1860; *Letters from the East*, 1869; *Orations and Addresses*, 1873; *Lectures on Poetry*, 1884; *The Letters of William Cullen Bryant*, 1975-1992 (6 volumes; William Cullen Bryant II and Thomas G. Voss, editors); *Power for Sanity: Selected Editorials of William Cullen Bryant, 1829-1861*, 1994.

TRANSLATIONS: *The Iliad of Homer*, 1870; *The Odyssey of Homer*, 1871, 1872.

EDITED TEXT: *A Library of Poetry and Song*, 1871.

BIBLIOGRAPHY

Brown, Charles H. *William Cullen Bryant*. New York: Charles Scribner's Sons, 1971. A well-written, comprehensive, and reliable account of Bryant's life. The study of Bryant's long career at the *New York Evening Post* is excellent. Little literary analysis.

Donovan, Alan B. "William Cullen Bryant: Father of American Song." *New England Quarterly* 41 (December, 1968): 505-520. Identifies the importance of Calvinism and neoclassicism in shaping Bryant's Romantic verses. Finds in Bryant's work "the first native articulation of the art of poetry."

Foshay, Ella M., and Barbara Novak. *Intimate Friends: Thomas Cole, Asher B. Durand, and William Cullen Bryant*. New York: New York Historical Society, 2000. An examination of the friendship among Bryant and the two painters.

Justice, James H. "The Fireside Poets: Hearthside Values and the Language of Care." In *Nineteenth-Century American Poetry*, edited by A. Robert Lee. New York: Barnes & Noble, 1985. Asserting that the Fireside poets established poetry as an American treasure, Justice presents Bryant as one of the firmest to show how personal values could be merged with public service. His conversion from older verse styles to newer, Romantic ones is the focus of the discussion of his work. Includes notes and an index.

Krapf, Norbert. *Under Open Sky: Poets on William Cullen Bryant*. New York: Fordham University Press, 1986. This resource, which includes both prose and poetry by twenty contemporary poets, pays tribute to Bryant, the United States' first nature poet. The writings give both a broad and deep appraisal of Bryant's poetic legacy.

McLean, Albert F. *William Cullen Bryant*. Rev. ed. Boston: Twayne, 1989. The first four chapters survey Bryant's life, examine his poems of nature, analyze "Thanatopsis" in detail, and classify several poems of "progress." The last three chapters evaluate Bryant's prose and translations, explicate his poetic theory and style, and review his reputation. Includes chronology, notes, a select bibliography, and an index.

Muller, Gilbert H. *William Cullen Bryant: Author of America*. Albany: State University of New York Press, 2008. A biography of Bryant that looks at him as an important American literary voice.

Nevins, Allan. *The "Evening Post": A Century of Journalism*. New York: Russell and Russell, 1922. Includes a long account of Bryant's accomplishments as an editor, praising his business judgment, his cultural influence, and his liberal stance on social issues.

Peckham, Harry Houston. *Gotham Yankee: A Biography of William Cullen Bryant*. 1950. Reprint. Folcroft, Pa.: Folcroft Library Editions, 1970. Correcting misrepresentations of Bryant, Peckham describes him as a poet with an interesting personality and an interesting career as a journalist and poet. In eleven chapters, Bryant's life is narrated from its beginnings, when he was a delicate child, through his legal work of drudgery, to his last years of eloquence. Contains illustrations, notes, a bibliography, a chronology, and an index.

Phair, Judith Turner. *A Bibliography of William Cullen Bryant and His Critics: 1808-1972.* Troy, N.Y.: Whitston, 1975. An extremely useful annotated bibliography of critical commentary on Bryant.

Ringe, Donald A. *The Pictorial Mode: Space and Time in the Art of Bryant, Irving, and Cooper.* Lexington: University Press of Kentucky, 1971. Bryant is given priority among writers who shared a pictorial aesthetic. Representation of space in Bryant's poetry is analyzed as a view of expansive nature, with precision of detail in the play of light and shadow. Time is examined as a force of contrast and continuity. Includes notes and an index.

Lloyd N. Dendinger

CHARLES BUKOWSKI

Born: Andernach, Germany; August 16, 1920
Died: San Pedro, California; March 9, 1994

PRINCIPAL POETRY

Flower, Fist, and Bestial Wail, 1960
Longshot Poems for Broke Players, 1962
Poems and Drawings, 1962
Run with the Hunted, 1962
It Catches My Heart in Its Hand, 1963
Cold Dogs in the Courtyard, 1965
Crucifix in a Deathhand, 1965
The Genius of the Crowd, 1966
The Curtains Are Waving, 1967
At Terror Street and Agony Way, 1968
Poems Written Before Jumping out of an Eighth Story Window, 1968
A Bukowski Sampler, 1969
The Days Run Away Like Wild Horses over the Hills, 1969

Fire Station, 1970
Mockingbird Wish Me Luck, 1972
Me and Your Sometimes Love Poems, 1973 (with Linda King)
While the Music Played, 1973
Burning in Water, Drowning in Flame, 1974
Africa, Paris, Greece, 1975
Scarlet, 1976
Love Is a Dog from Hell, 1977
Maybe Tomorrow, 1977
Legs, Hips and Behind, 1978
We'll Take Them, 1978
Play the Piano Drunk Like a Percussion Instrument Until the Fingers Begin to Bleed a Bit, 1979
Dangling in the Tournefortia, 1981
The Last Generation, 1982
War All the Time: Poems, 1981-1984, 1984
The Roominghouse Madrigals: Early Selected Poems, 1946-1966, 1988
Last Night of the Earth Poems, 1992
Bone Palace Ballet: New Poems, 1997
What Matters Most Is How Well You Walk Through the Fire, 1999
Open All Night: New Poems, 2000
The Night Torn Mad with Footsteps, 2001
The Flash of Lightning Behind the Mountain: New Poems, 2003
Sifting Through the Madness for the Word, the Line, the Way: New Poems, 2003
Slouching Toward Nirvana: New Poems, 2005 (John Martin, editor)
Come on In! New Poems, 2006
The People Look Like Flowers at Last: New Poems, 2007
The Pleasures of the Damned: Poems, 1951-1993, 2007 (Martin, editor)

OTHER LITERARY FORMS

In addition to poetry, Charles Bukowski (byew-KOW-skee) published stories and novels and first achieved recognition with *Notes of a Dirty Old Man* (1969). This volume brought him to the attention of many who were previously unfamiliar with his work. In conjunction with his first novel, *Post Office* (1971), and a volume titled *Erections, Ejaculations, Exhibi-*

tions, and General Tales of Ordinary Madness (1972), about half of which was reissued in *Life and Death in the Charity Ward* (1973), *Notes of a Dirty Old Man* established his reputation as a no-holds-barred commentator, full of rage yet capable of surrealistic farce. In addition to subsequent novels, which include *Factotum* (1975), *Women* (1978), *Ham on Rye* (1982), and *Hollywood* (1989), there is *South of No North: Stories of the Buried Life* (1973), which reprints both *Confessions of a Man Insane Enough to Live with Beasts* (1965) and *All the Assholes of the World and Mine* (1966); a picture narrative of his trip abroad, *Shakespeare Never Did This* (1979); a screenplay, *Barfly* (1987); and assorted illustrations. His sketches underscore his farcical tone, especially in *You Kissed Lilly* (1978), a satire of the comics in which his Thurberesque style complements his prose.

ACHIEVEMENTS

Charles Bukowski was awarded few honors during his lifetime. In 1974, he was given a National Endowment for the Arts grant, and he won a Loujon Press Award and the Silver Reel Award from the San Francisco Festival of the Arts for documentary film. Bukowski was always considered a maverick who was perceived by many academics and literary institutions to be hostile and antipoetic. His frank approach to life and writing is still too often considered simplistic or crude. Although Bukowski's literary achievements are still widely unrecognized and critically undervalued in the United States, he is already considered a classic American author in Europe. A new era of appreciation seemed to begin in the 1990's with the publication of several laudatory collections of critical analyses of his works. Few people familiar with Bukowski's work are indifferent to it. Although he neither won nor curried favor among academic or mainstream poets, he has attained an international reputation and has been widely translated. From the first, he sought to create a "living poetry of clarity," which defies the proprieties and "cages" established by academics and editors. He has been compared to Henry Miller, Jack London, Louis-Ferdinand Céline, Antonin Artaud, François Villon, and Arthur Rimbaud and had an acknowledged influence on Tom Waits, his musical heir.

Charles Bukowski (Ulf Andersen/Getty Images)

Bukowski carried the Beat manifesto to its logical conclusion without compromising his vision or pandering to the idolatrous public. By incorporating the vantage point of the underclass, he artistically wrought the unfashionable voices of the streets, the factories, the racetracks, and other less seemly social enclaves. He fused the rawness of life with a personal sensitivity; he conveyed the horrors as well as the pathos of poverty, blue-collar jobs, hangovers, and jail yards. He was never a media personality, as the Beats were. Once it became financially feasible, he began refusing all invitations for readings to guard his private self, convinced that it was readings that had killed Dylan Thomas. This reticence, with his exclusive reliance on small publishers, made his international reputation all the more impressive.

Perhaps Bukowski's most significant achievement was his successful forging of a new American poetics characterized by its accessibility and its spontaneous narrative voice. Unlike T. S. Eliot's "vertical poetry," Bukowski's is a "horizontal poetry" that photographs the jagged surfaces of society and forces the reader to peer into the baser regions of human existence, to see humankind for what it is. His unique blend of powerful, physical imagery and sardonic wit allows the reader to grasp and yet transcend the essential absurdity of existence.

BIOGRAPHY

One cannot come to terms with the poetry of Henry Charles Bukowski, Jr., without acknowledging the fact that his is an extremely personal and autobiographical poetry; the terror and agony are not merely "felt-life" but life as Bukowski knew it. His survival was a thing of wonder. As Gerald Locklin notes, he "not only survived problems that would kill most men [but] survived with enough voice and talent left to write about it." He was a practicing alcoholic whose life revolved around the racetrack, women, and writing.

Born Heinrich Karl Bukowski to a German mother and an American soldier father on August 16, 1920, in Andernach, Germany, Bukowski came to the United States in 1922 with his family. They settled in Los Angeles, later the milieu for much of Bukowski's work. His father, a milkman, was a harsh and often violent man who struggled with his own powerlessness by wielding a razor strap. The resultant hostility and animosity is evident in many of the younger Bukowski's poems. Coupled with a blood disease that left his face badly pockmarked, Bukowski was predisposed to a life on the fringes of society.

At about the age of sixteen, partly to escape and partly because of a desire to become a writer, Bukowski began to haunt the public library, seeking literary models. His own self-directed reading was far more important in shaping his literary credo than the two years he spent at Los Angeles City College. He was drawn to the works of Louis-Ferdinand Céline, John Fante, Fyodor Dostoevski, Ivan Turgenev, and the early Ernest Hemingway; in later years, he was attracted by Franz Kafka and Albert Camus. Just as the creative writing class in which he had enrolled seemed fraudulent and banal, however, so too did the voices of many of the "masters."

Bukowski's career as a writer had a rather fitful start. After receiving hundreds of rejections, "Aftermath of a Lengthy Rejection Slip" was accepted by *Story* in 1944 and *Portfolio* published "Twenty Tanks from Kasseldown." These publications were followed by ten years of virtual silence during which only four pieces were published. Toward the end of this literary hiatus, two important changes occurred. He began working sporadically at the post office, where he stayed fourteen years (until 1970, when John Martin of Black Sparrow Press convinced him to quit). This job provided the first steady source of income Bukowski had known. More important, however, was the shock of landing in the charity ward in 1955, near death from a bleeding ulcer. After receiving eleven pints of blood, he emerged "900 years older," promptly disregarded the warnings to quit drinking, and began publishing poetry in various little magazines. It was his appearance in *Outsider* and his friendship with editors Jon and Gypsy Lou Webb, who dubbed him "outsider of the year" in 1962, that launched his career. With their assistance, he began to develop an important reputation among editors and readers of the little magazines, ultimately establishing a friendship with John and Barbara Martin, who published the bulk of his work.

The barrage of women in his work revealed Bukowski's penchant for womanizing; he seemed to fall from one affair to another, yet his work revealed several significant pairings. Toward the beginning of his ten-year silence, he met Jane, "the first person who brought me any love," and began a relationship that was to continue until she finally died of alcoholism. Although their relationship, as *Factotum* demonstrates, was interrupted by intervening affairs, his cross-country meandering, and his two-and-a-half-year marriage to Barbara Fry, a Texas millionairess who edited *Harlequin*, it was a durable bond that inspired countless sensitive poems. Following Jane's death, Bukowski became involved with Frances, who bore his only child, Marina. Much later, both Linda King and Linda Lee Beighle were to play central roles in his life. The works dedicated to these women constitute a tribute of sorts and demonstrate that while his personal life was often tempestuous, he had the capacity and need for love. This is important to bear in mind to avoid misreading his oeuvre by exaggerating his sexism. Bukowski published prodigiously in his last decade and died from leukemia in 1994.

ANALYSIS

Living on the periphery of society, Charles Bukowski forged a brutally honest poetic voice. The futility and senselessness of most human endeavor conjoined with the desperation and essential solitude of the individual are constants reinforcing his "slavic nihilism." The trick, he suggested, is "carrying on when everything seems so terrible there is no use to go on. . . . You face the wall and just work it out. . . . Facing it right with yourself, alone." It is this kind of courage and stoicism that informs Bukowski's canon. He was neither a poet's poet nor a people's poet, but a personal poet who used his craft to ensure his own survival.

Bukowski's "tough guy" image was less posturing than self-protective. One senses that he was an idealist soured by the ravages of time, wearied by political betrayals, and rather appalled by the vacuity of the American left and contemporary American writers who seemed to be playing it safe and producing pallid prose and senselessly arcane poetry. Interestingly, in his best poems, the tough guy persona falls away and one discovers a sensitive poet who chose to adopt a savage bravado. Clearly, he knew the reality of the seamy side of life; his poetry teems with grotesque and sordid imagery; but unlike those who would write in order to reform, Bukowski was content to capture the pathos and rawness of the streets.

Bukowski's first four chapbooks properly acclimate the reader to his dual vision—his rawness and his compassion. They also reveal the risks inherent in this kind of personal, reportorial poetry. At his best, he blended seemingly incongruous elements to plunge the reader into a surreal landscape. At his worst, he succumbed to self-pity, mired in his own mundane reality.

FLOWER, FIST, AND BESTIAL WAIL

Flower, Fist, and Bestial Wail is the most consistently crafted of the four books and includes one of his best-known poems, "The Twins," which transforms his lingering animosity toward his father into a transcendent statement of shared humanity and mortality. The poem is replete with antithetical images: "We looked

exactly alike, we could have been twins. . . . he had his bulbs on the screen ready for planting while I was laying with a whore from 3rd street." His own ambivalence is suggested by the scarecrow image he presented as he realized "I can't keep him alive no matter how much we hated each other." So, he stands, "waiting also to die." Read in conjunction with "All-Yellow Flowers," "The Twins" establishes one of the dominant motifs in Bukowski's work—the transient nature of life and the exaggerated import that human beings attach to ephemera.

These poems have the cadence of impending catastrophe. Beginning with "Ten Lions and the End of the World," Bukowski moved from the mundane to the apocalyptic without missing a beat; he forged a vantage point that is both ironic and sentimental as he pondered the cost of the pell-mell pace of modern life.

In Bukowski's world almost anything was possible. Although the potential for violence was ever present, it defied logic. His was the spirit of farce. He constantly challenged the contours of reality. He employed a farcical dialectic to conjoin the bizarre and the mundane; he used brutal undercutting, as in "Love Is a Piece of Paper Torn to Bits," in which a ship out of control and a wife being "serviced" by another are divested of significance while a worrisome cat is promoted to center stage. By focusing on the cat and the "dishes with flowers and vines painted on them," he effectively understated his angst. Similarly, in "I Cannot Stand Tears," a guard kills a wounded goose because "the bird was crying and I cannot stand tears."

Also evident in this first volume is Bukowski's justification for callous machismo as a defense against "the lie of love"; he established his argument by infusing his poems with countless oxymorons that rearranged the signposts of reality. In "Soiree," a bottle becomes a "dwarf waiting to scratch out my prayers," and in "His Wife, the Painter," a bus becomes "insanity sprung from a waving line"; he spoke of the sunlight as a lie and markets smelling of "shoes and naked boys clothed." "Soiree" also announces the impossibility of sustaining a relationship; "Did I Ever Tell You" captures the tragicomic element of love. The inescapable conclusion from this panoply is that love is futile, duplicitous, or, at best, based on mutual concessions. This explains the frequent crassness in Bukowski's work, which was already evident in "No Charge."

LONGSHOT POEMS FOR BROKE PLAYERS

Longshot Poems for Broke Players contains several poems that do justice to the existentialism and craftsmanship that Bukowski demonstrated in his first volume. "The State of World Affairs from a Third Floor Window," for example, melds an essentially voyeuristic point of view with reflections on a nuclear-infested world. Its tone is mellow and its counterpoint suggests the possibility of survival. Survival, it seems, is a matter of perspective, a point forcefully echoed in "The Tragedy of the Leaves," which embodies Bukowski's belief that what was needed was "a good comedian, ancient style, a jester with jokes upon absurd pain; pain as absurd because it exists." It concludes with an empathetic identification with his landlady "because the world had failed us both."

The surrealism of "What a Man I Was," which lampoons the legendary status of various Western heroes, is accelerated and refined in "The Best Way to Get Famous Is to Run Away," which revolves around the proverbial desire to live underground, away from the masses and the absurdity of explaining "why." Inherent in this piece, as well as in "Conversations in a Cheap Room" and "Poems for Personnel Managers," is the unattainability of resonance, the inability to comprehend the suffering of others: "Age was a crime . . . Pity picked up the marbles and . . . Hatred picked up the cash." A blend of the sensitive and ironic, an easy movement through cliché and culture dignifies these pieces. The result is a litany of sorts dedicated to those who have fallen through the cracks of the dream, unveiling a world of fraudulent promises that routinely casts aside those who do not conform to the dictates of propriety.

RUN WITH THE HUNTED AND IT CATCHES MY HEART IN ITS HAND

Run with the Hunted, the most uneven of Bukowski's early works, is more freewheeling than *Poems and Drawings*; it displays flashes of insight in "Old Man, Dead in a Room" and reaches innovative heights in "Vegas." Bukowski interwove the abstract and the concrete to capture the impossibility of communication and the essential insanity of social and artistic conven-

tion. The majority of the poems, however, seem self-indulgent and pointlessly crass.

Having gained recognition from the early chapbooks, Bukowski assumed a surer direction. *It Catches My Heart in Its Hand* culls some of the best from the early chapbooks and adds many new pieces. In this work, Bukowski mocked his own former self-pity and transforms it into a literary device with which to document the passage of time, as in "Old Poet" and "The Race." The danger of sanctifying art receives a lighter handling in "The Talkers," which is both a critique of art for art's sake and a renunciation of those who would hide behind abstraction and pretense.

CRUCIFIX IN A DEATHHAND AND THE GENIUS OF THE CROWD

Artistic distance is even more evident in *Crucifix in a Deathhand*, which centers around reawakened memories, senses deadened by the workaday world, and actual confrontations with death. In "Sunflower" and "Fuzz," for example, Bukowski muted his personal voice to universalize his own anguish; he often seemed, as in "Grass," to be observing himself. The workaday world, the province of "little men with luck and a headstart" emerges as deadening in "Machinegun Towers & Timeclocks" and "Something for the Touts, the Nuns, the Grocery Clerks and You. . . ." Bukowski was equally contemptuous of the bovine mentality of the masses and the group-think of the counterculture. In "This," he elevated himself above any prescriptions and became his own measuring rod. His is the stance of the loner, seeking pleasures where he finds them and deferring to no one. Survival, he suggested, demands egotism; otherwise, one can only await the fiery cleansing of the bomb contemplated in "A Report Upon the Consumption of Myself."

Bukowski's disdain for all that is average becomes more overt in a single-poem chapbook, *The Genius of the Crowd*, a jeremiad cautioning the poet to avoid the profane influence of culture. More boldly than any previous poem, it unmasks Bukowski's contempt for the masses and asserts that "There is enough treachery, hatred, violence, absurdity in the average human being to supply any given army on any given day." This is reinforced by the suggestion that most preaching is duplicitous, a game of mirrors.

COLD DOGS IN THE COURTYARD

A very different impression is gleaned from *Cold Dogs in the Courtyard*, over which Bukowski was given editorial control. In a prefatory note, he explained that he chose those poems that he felt had been unduly neglected. What emerges is a collection keynoted by an almost tender melancholia. "Imbecile Night," for example, establishes a delicate balance with which he endured the dreary cadence of darkness. Informing these poems is a sense of awe as he notes the consonance of nature's marvels and human invention, especially apparent in "It's Nothing to Laugh About." Compounding this is the poignant juxtaposition of the substantial and the ephemeral, as in "Existence," a poem built around the post office and the exaggerated importance attached to "dead letters." Like the roof in "2 Outside as Bones Break in My Kitchen," the letters maintain but fail to nurture the human spirit.

In "Layovers," the memories of lost love and the dreams of renewal serve as a reprieve from Bukowski's encounters with death. Serving a similar function are encounters with the unexpected, as in "Experience," and anarchistic protests such as the one depicted in "What Seems to Be the Trouble, Gentlemen?" These poems work, in part, because they lack the self-congratulatory tone of *The Genius of the Crowd* and the self-indulgence of *The Curtains Are Waving*, which reveals the limits of Bukowski's style; in an attempt to come to terms with his angst, he is left decrying his fate.

AT TERROR STREET AND AGONY WAY

By the time *At Terror Street and Agony Way* appeared, Bukowski had apparently regained artistic control; the volume substitutes self-mockery for self-pity. Although he continued to probe the plight of those caught under the technocratic juggernaut, he did so more emblematically and with greater levity. In "Red and Gold Paint," he conceives of luck and art as miracles against the cunning caprices of bosses, wars, and the weather. It is only playing against the odds, he repeatedly suggests, which ensures survival. Those who relinquish the good fight or never begin, he implied in "Reunion," may ingratiate themselves, but they never really live.

This volume is more thematically unified by the primacy of terror and agony in Bukowski's perspective.

The lost innocence of "As I Lay Dying," the gratuitousness of "Beerbottle," and the resultant agony of blinding dreams in "K. O." quietly undergird the wanton destruction of "Sunday Before Noon" and the defeated dreams of "7th Race." Similarly, "I Wanted to Overthrow the Government" records Bukowski's suspicion of revolutionary schemes: "The weakness was not Government but Man, one at a time . . . men were never as strong as their ideas and . . . ideas were governments turned into men."

POEMS WRITTEN BEFORE JUMPING OUT OF AN EIGHT STORY WINDOW AND A BUKOWSKI SAMPLER

Bukowski's next volume, *Poems Written Before Jumping out of an Eight Story Window*, constitutes a reversal. Absent are the literary allusions, the calm and urbanity of *At Terror Street and Agony Way*. The old shrillness is back as Bukowski donned the "beast" persona and vented his spleen, abandoning all finesse. Rapine, murder, and gothic elements dominate; an alcoholic fog blurs his vision. Even the best piece, "The Hairy Hairy Fist, and Love Will Die," despite its relentless "beat" and its examination of the individual turned back on himself, deafened by silence, is reduced in magnitude.

The publication of *A Bukowski Sampler* in 1969 signaled a change. In a little less than eighty pages, Doug Blazek assembled some of the best of Bukowski's work. His selection, a fairly representative one allowing the neophyte a full taste of Bukowski, also includes an editor's introduction, a letter from Bukowski, and several tributes from admirers of his work. Published about six months after *Notes of a Dirty Old Man*, the volume was directed at the growing Bukowski audience and the burgeoning counterculture.

THE DAYS RUN AWAY LIKE WILD HORSES OVER THE HILLS

While *The Days Run Away Like Wild Horses over the Hills* again culls poems from the early chapbooks, the majority of the pieces are new and fresh. Since the book was dedicated to Jane, it is not surprising to find death as the leitmotiv. What is surprising is the almost sensual tone. In several poems to Jane, one can feel both the depth of Bukowski's love and the anguish which her death occasioned. While there are the obligatory accounts of womanizing, these pale before his elegies to Jane and his references to Frances and Marina. His attitude is encapsulated in "Birth," where the male dominion is muted by "small female things and jewels."

Allusions are multiplied without pretension; in "Ants Crawl My Drunken Arms," he criticized the banality of popular culture that prefers Willie Mays to Bach and the killing realities that essentially devoured Arthur Rimbaud, Ezra Pound, and Hart Crane. In "The Sharks" and "The Great One," the artist emerges as victim, and in "The Seminar" and "On a Grant" the pretense and incestuousness of the literary establishment are mocked through both the form and the content of the poems.

MOCKINGBIRD WISH ME LUCK

In *Mockingbird Wish Me Luck*, his next collection, Bukowski probed the culturally sanctioned disparities and skewed priorities which produce "shipping clerks who have read the Harvard Classics" and allow the powerful "a 15 percent take on the dream." "Hogs in the Sky" suggests that survival is a miracle, and yet, no more than a proper rehearsal for death "as old age arrives on schedule." The paraplegic who continues to play the longshots in "The World's Greatest Loser" is merely an extreme illustration of the fact that "nobody had any luck." Hence, the aspiring writer becomes a random assassin in "The Garbageman" and an ace crapshooter in "Moyamensing Prison."

Much of the humor in these poems is self-deprecatory, as in "The Last Days of the Suicide Kid," but subtler ironies emerge as well: the cost of success in "Making It" and the very real risk of becoming a noted writer in "The Poet's Muse." Bukowski recognized that often the skid row bums have more brains, more wit, and sometimes more satisfaction than those who have "won." Again it is a question of perspective—something which is a rare commodity in America, he notes in "Earthquake."

The second part of this volume is teeming with primordial images and energies. Monkey feet, lions, and mockingbirds stalk and taunt the poet and reader while the mass media relentlessly promote diversions and distractions. The gullibility of the masses, not a new theme, is used to establish Bukowski's own superiority

and contempt for platitudes. Recording his experiences with the draft board in "WW2," he compared himself to the draftees, concluding, "I was not as young as they." Not as young, perhaps, because he, like Robinson Jeffers, whom he eulogizes in "He Wrote in Lonely Blood," has solitary instincts and an understanding of what is essential. However, in both "The Hunt" and "The Shoelace," he realized that it is the little things which tip the scale and "sometimes create unemployed drunks . . . trying to grab for grunion."

The final section of *Mockingbird Wish Me Luck* is unified by the risks of love. Love, a tenuous miracle, endures for Bukowski only with Marina, who is the subject of several poems. "The Shower" suggests that others, like Linda King, will eventually pass out of his life despite the depth of their mutual feelings. At the other extreme are the large number of women who are sought because they are, by definition, "one-week stands." The only alternative to the ebb and flow is represented by the "old fashioned whore" and the "American matador" who opt out of conscriptive relationships.

BURNING IN WATER, DROWNING IN FLAME

These conversational poems are often riddled by the banter and banality which characterize the bulk of daily interactions, yet Bukowski insisted on the need for style—"a fresh way to approach a dull or dangerous thing." Herein lies the key to Bukowski's poetic credo—he did not seek new themes, but, rather, reworked the old from a new angle of vision. This approach is especially germane to *Burning in Water, Drowning in Flame*, which reprints many poems that had gone out of print and redirected his probing of such phenomena as love's impermanence. *Burning in Water, Drowning in Flame* constitutes a fitting conclusion to the third stage of Bukowski's career. Including sections of poems from *It Catches My Heart in Its Hand*, *Crucifix in a Deathhand*, and *At Terror Street and Agony Way* (to which *The Curtains Are Waving* has been added), it was a testimony to his growing reputation, and, having been published by one of the more prestigious small presses, accomplished the aim of *A Bukowski Sampler* with considerable finesse.

In addition to making selections from earlier volumes, this one includes a section of new poems. These are not gentle poems. Beginning with "Now," which compares writing poetry with lancing boils, Bukowski moved to "Zoo," which questions whether, in fact, humans have evolved significantly. "The Way" represents a brutal culmination, resembling the cascading cadence of Allen Ginsberg's "Howl" (1956, 1996) while managing not to fall away or to lose its sardonic tone.

The reportorial style which informs these poems is wryly explained in "Deathbed Blues" and panned in "My Friend, Andre," and while it is not always effective, at its best it gives testimony to the moral dignity which is attainable despite the depravity which threatens to consume the human spirit. "Death of an Idiot," which calls to mind "Conversations with a Lady Sipping a Straight Shot" in *The Days Run Away Like Wild Horses over the Hills*, displays compassion and achieves its impact by understatement.

LOVE IS A DOG FROM HELL

Bukowski's later poetry is more persistently autobiographical and more finely honed than his earlier work. Many of the poems, especially in *Love Is a Dog from Hell*, have fictional analogues in *Women*. A tendency already apparent in "Hell Hath No Fury . . ." in *Burning in Water, Drowning in Flame*, becomes more evident here; the poems often seem merely to have been transplanted into (or from) the novel. Similarly, several of the poems in *Dangling in the Tournefortia* correspond to *Shakespeare Never Did This*, and others clearly reveal the influence of Bukowski's move to San Pedro—a move which has not tempered his perspective.

Love Is a Dog from Hell, like the chapbook *Scarlet* which it incorporates, has loves and lusts as its primary focus. The proper context for viewing these poems is suggested by Bukowski's comment that "love is ridiculous because it can't last and sex is ridiculous because it doesn't last long enough." It was the tragicomedy which impelled him. Refusing to defer to feminist sensibilities, he related one sexual adventure after another, capturing both the eternal search and the predictable defeats which await everyone in "Another Bed."

Women are portrayed in a variety of stances; sometimes merely objects, they are at other times capable of turning the male into an object, as the black widow spider in "The Escape" and the teeth mother in "A Killer" are inclined to do. The women range from aspiring artists and reformers to whores, and the latter have the edge "because they lie about nothing." While some may take offense at the sexism in these pieces, it seems to cut both ways; the men are no less demeaned than the women. This is still the world of the streets where proprieties and pretense fall away. In poems such as "One for Old Snaggle-tooth," dedicated to Frances, Bukowski's sensitivity is economically and precisely conveyed.

The second section is concerned with the tragedies and inhumanities which transform artists into madmen or panderers. "What They Want" reads like a top ten list of artistic casualties. The artist emerges as vulnerable and damned in "There Once Was a Woman Who Put Her Head in an Oven," which calls to mind poet Sylvia Plath. However, in "The Crunch," Bukowski suggested that the artist is able to utilize the isolation and failure that drive others over the edge. Both survival and creativity seem to demand solitude, as long as it is not irreversible.

PLAY THE PIANO DRUNK LIKE A PERCUSSION INSTRUMENT UNTIL THE FINGERS BEGIN TO BLEED A BIT

Primarily a reissue of several chapbooks, *Play the Piano Drunk Like a Percussion Instrument Until the Fingers Begin to Bleed a Bit* lacks the thematic unity of the preceding volume, but it does demonstrate Bukowski's iconoclasm and his ability to revive old themes. The title deadpans the conception of the typewriter as a musical instrument, a theme first introduced in "Chopin Bukowski" in *Love Is a Dog from Hell*.

Beginning with "Tough Company," which turns poems into gunslingers waiting to receive their due, Bukowski unleashed his acerbic wit against ersatz holiday gaiety, feigned idealism, parental protocol, the notion of a limited nuclear war, and the pretense of civilization, which is compared to fool's gold in "Through the Streets of Anywhere." While there is a sense of absurdity and subterfuge rampaging through these poems, there is also a sense of durability and substance. Again the losers at the racetrack bars, in the bowels of the slaughterhouses, and in the sterile rooming houses are pummeled but maintain their dignity, accepting their exclusion and their inability to affect their fates:

"We are finally tricked and slapped to death like lovers' vows, bargained out of any gain." They await the arrival of the urban renewal cranes in "2347 Duane," and while they occasionally master the bravado of Bogart, as in "Maybe Tomorrow," more often they simply await death, as in "The Proud Thin Dying." If one is careful, "Horse and Fist" implies, one may yet survive despite the open-endedness of the game. In the meantime, it is best to "play the piano drunk like a percussion instrument until the fingers begin to bleed a bit."

DANGLING IN THE TOURNEFORTIA

There is an interesting movement in *Dangling in the Tournefortia*. Several of the early poems are retrospective, establishing a counterpoint against which to view his status—something which is overt in poems such as "Guava Tree." It seems that he was suspicious of his newly won success, recognizing that he "can fail in many more ways now," as he said in "Fear and Madness," knowing that there are more "suckerfish" who will insist upon intruding and fretting about the state of his soul. However, "Notes Upon a Hot Streak" revealed the pleasure he took in the "lovable comedy" which "they are letting me win for this moment."

While success did not temper his perspective, it did temper his rage; even his references to his father's brutality were softened, and while death continued to loom, it no longer threatened to overwhelm him or his poetry. The more balanced tone is reinforced by his use of the tournefortia, a tropical tree with delicate flowers and a fleshy fruit, as a metaphor for the interplay of love and lust, being and nothingness. Again the tempestuous love affairs are paraded, sometimes callously but often with a quick parry, as in "The Descent of the Species" and "Snap Snap." In "The Lady in Red," he explores the compensatory function served by heroes such as Dillinger during the Depression; in "Fight On" and "Blue Collar Solitude," the needed respite offered by a good street brawl and/or several drinks; and in "Nothing," seeing a supervisor besotted somehow eases the pain and agony of the job.

THE LAST GENERATION

As one of the most prolific and well-known underground poets, Bukowski pinned his success on the authenticity of his voice. Even a casual encounter with his work reveals the lack of pretense and the refusal to kowtow to the critics. He refused to be beaten; as he suggested in *The Last Generation*, a single-poem broadside, it may be harder to be a genius with the proliferation of publishers and writers, but it is worth the attempt. There are too many unsung characters of the "unholy parade" and too many poems which demand to be written.

Bukowski's bawdiness no less than his free-form style constituted a manifesto of sorts. American poetry has long been cautious and unduly arcane, thereby excluding a large part of the potential poetry audience and a wide range of subjects and sentiments. Booze, hard loving, and horse racing, while not generally seen as poetic subjects, dominate Bukowski's oeuvre. His crassness, which weakened some of his pieces, was in his best work complemented by a sensitive understanding of the fringes of society. Beneath the veneer, one senses a man who was unaccustomed to and rather afraid of love; a man who simultaneously disdained and applauded the masses because of his own ambivalent self-concept.

COLLECTIONS OF THE 1990'S

In the 1990's Bukowski softened a bit and reflectively examined his feelings about aging and death. His last book of poems published in his lifetime was *Last Night of the Earth Poems*, his longest poetry collection. Like all his poetry, the poems here are rich in sarcasm and filled with antiauthoritarian diatribes, madness, satire, and death. However, while death has always been a facet of Bukowski's poetry, here it is not the death that stalked Bukowski through forty years of poetry, resulting from alcohol abuse or depravity. Rather, it is the end of a long-lived life. Bukowski reveals that he is and has been involved in the great seasonal cycles of life: birth, death, and rebirth; pain, sorrow, and love. The subtle sensitivity of the volume is also present in its obvious love poems, many seemingly addressed to Linda Lee Beighle.

Bone Palace Ballet is divided into five sections that outline his life, from recollections that romanticize his drunken youth as a time when there was a "feeling of/ joy and gamble in/ the air" ("Beeting on the Muse") to the final section presenting poems that take stock of his life and square-off with death. *Open All Night*, like the collection of his poems titled *What Matters Most Is How Well You Walk Through the Fire*, is an expansive volume full of the grizzled mutterings that readers have come to expect from Bukowski: Former lovers, binge drinking, disillusioned souls, and the racetrack are well represented. Like other works of the 1990's, however, *Open All Night* reveals a more wistful Bukowski, an aging writer who was fearlessly confronting his mortality. Writing was never about praise or fame, he says, but "for myself/ to save what is left of/ myself." Bukowski is finally able to admit: "I've had a good run./ I can toss it in without regret."

OTHER MAJOR WORKS

LONG FICTION: *Post Office*, 1971; *Factotum*, 1975; *Women*, 1978; *Ham on Rye*, 1982; *You Get So Alone at Times That It Just Makes Sense*, 1986; *Hollywood*, 1989; *Pulp*, 1994.

SHORT FICTION: *Notes of a Dirty Old Man*, 1969; *Erections, Ejaculations, Exhibitions, and General Tales of Ordinary Madness*, 1972; *Life and Death in the Charity Ward*, 1973; *South of No North: Stories of the Buried Life*, 1973; *Bring Me Your Love*, 1983; *Hot Water Music*, 1983; *The Most Beautiful Woman in Town, and Other Stories*, 1983; *There's No Business*, 1984; *The Day It Snowed in L.A.*, 1986.

SCREENPLAY: *Barfly*, 1987.

NONFICTION: *Shakespeare Never Did This*, 1979 (photographs by Michael Montfort); *The Bukowski/ Purdy Letters: A Decade of Dialogue, 1964-1974*, 1983; *Screams from the Balcony: Selected Letters, 1960-1970*, 1993; *Reach for the Sun: Selected Letters, 1978-1994*, 1999 (Seamus Cooney, editor); *Beerspit Night and Cursing: The Correspondence of Charles Bukowski and Sheri Martinelli, 1960-1967*, 2001 (Steven Moore, editor).

MISCELLANEOUS: *You Kissed Lilly*, 1978; *Septuagenarian Stew: Stories and Poems*, 1990; *Run with the Hunted: A Charles Bukowski Reader*, 1993; *Betting on the Muse: Poems and Stories*, 1996; *Charles Bukowski: Portions from a Wine-Stained Notebook—Uncollected Stories and Essays, 1944-1990*, 2008 (David Stephen Calonne, editor).

BIBLIOGRAPHY

Cain, Jimmie. "Bukowski's Imagist Roots." *West Georgia College Review* 19 (May, 1987): 10-17. Cain draws a parallel between Bukowski's poetry and the work of William Carlos Williams, America's premier Imagist poet. Cain claims that Bukowski's rough-and-tumble poetry shows palpable Imagist influences. For advanced students.

Cherkovski, Neeli. *Bukowski: A Life*. South Royalton, Vt.: Steerforth, 1997. This volume is "a slightly different version" of Cherkovski's *Hank: The Life of Charles Bukowski*, published in 1991. Its strength resides in the writer's close access to the subject during their early friendship and material from interviews with Bukowski. It purports to include the "wilder stories" which Bukowski regretted were previously omitted. The bibliography has been updated.

Harrison, Russell. *Against the American Dream: Essays on Charles Bukowski*. Santa Rosa, Calif.: Black Sparrow Press, 1994. An excellent study that examines Bukowski's critique of the work ethic in his poetry and prose.

McDonough, Tom. "Down and (Far) Out." *American Film* 13 (November, 1987): 26-30. McDonough discusses how Bukowski's real-life alcoholism was portrayed in the 1987 biographical film *Barfly*. In the film, the drunken Bukowski was played by actor Mickey Rourke, while Faye Dunaway played his drinking companion. Gives an interesting popular insight into Bukowski's life.

Sounes, Howard. *Charles Bukowski: Locked in the Arms of a Crazy Life*. New York: Grove, 1999. Sounes indicates at the beginning of this book how Bukowski strived markedly to "improve upon" his life and make it even "more picaresque" than it was. Successfully conjures up the voice of this outrageous character and offers clear-eyed insight into his extraordinary life.

Wakoski, Diane. "Charles Bukowski." In *Contemporary Poets*, edited by James Vinson and D. L. Kirkpatrick. 4th ed. New York: St. Martin's Press, 1985. Wakoski traces Bukowski's rising popularity but laments the fact that though "Americans . . . honor truth," and Bukowski's poems are distinguished by their unself-pitying truthfulness, he has not received much serious criticism. Includes a list of his publications up to 1984.

Weizmann, Daniel, ed. *Drinking with Bukowski: Rec-*

ollections of the Poet Laureate of Skid Row. New York: Thunder's Mouth Press, 2000. Essays by friends of Bukowski such as Wanda Coleman, Raymond Carver, Karen Finley, Paul Trachtenberg, Fred Voss, and Sean Penn.

C. Lynn Munro
Updated by Sarah Hilbert

WITTER BYNNER

Born: Brooklyn, New York; August 10, 1881
Died: Santa Fe, New Mexico; June 1, 1968

PRINCIPAL POETRY

An Ode to Harvard, and Other Poems, 1907
The New World, 1915
Spectra: A Book of Poetic Experiments, 1916
Grenstone Poems, 1917
The Beloved Stranger, 1919
A Canticle of Pan, 1920
Pins for Wings, 1920
Caravan, 1925
Indian Earth, 1929
Eden Tree, 1931
Against the Cold, 1933
Guest Book, 1935
Selected Poems, 1936
Take Away the Darkness, 1947
Book of Lyrics, 1955
New Poems, 1960
Light Verse and Satires, 1978
Selected Poems, 1978

OTHER LITERARY FORMS

Witter Bynner (bih-NUR) was a man of letters, and he wrote several plays, numerous reviews, and a considerable amount of miscellaneous prose, along with some widely acclaimed literary translations. His plays include *Tiger* (pb. 1913), *The Little King* (pb. 1914), and *Cake* (pb. 1926). Most important among his prose productions are *The Persistence of Poetry* (1929) and *Journey with Genius: Recollections and Reflections*

Concerning the D. H. Lawrences (1951). Bynner's translations include, from Greek, Euripides' *Iphigenia in Tauris* (1915); from French, *A Book of Love* (1923), by Charles Vildrac; and from Chinese, *The Jade Mountain: A Chinese Anthology* (with Kiang Kang-hu), which appeared in 1929, and *The Way of Life According to Laotzu: An American Version* (1944).

ACHIEVEMENTS

Although many of Witter Bynner's literary contemporaries left the United States to seek inspiration in Europe, Bynner himself, after visiting Europe, decided to remain in the country of his birth. During his long life, he developed a passion for Chinese culture and for Mexico, but he remained a conspicuous part of the American community of letters from early in the century until his last days in Santa Fe, New Mexico. In 1910, Bynner was a charter member of the Poetry Society of America. In 1954, the Poetry Society of America awarded Bynner the Gold Medal of the Alexander Droutzkoy Memorial Award, and in 1962, he was elected to the National Institute of Arts and Letters. He served as chancellor for the Academy of American Poets from 1946 to 1966.

BIOGRAPHY

Harold Witter Bynner was born in Brooklyn, New York, on August 10, 1881. His early childhood was spent in New York; Norwich, Connecticut; and, after his father died in 1891, Brookline, Massachusetts, where Bynner completed high school. From 1898 to 1902, he attended Harvard University, where fellow student Wallace Stevens recruited him for the staff of the Harvard *Advocate*. Upon graduation from Harvard, Bynner secured a semieditorial position with *McClure's* magazine, where he remained for four years, during which time he associated with a number of professional writers, including O. Henry, and resolved to pursue a writing career. Eventually, Bynner left New York and *McClure's* and moved to New Hampshire to write. He also began giving lectures on literature and supporting the movement for women's suffrage.

Bynner began publishing volumes of his poetry in 1907 with *An Ode to Harvard, and Other Poems*. He also experimented with drama and engaged in some translation during this early period. Being both annoyed and amused by the pretensions of trendy literary movements in this period, Bynner and his friend Arthur Davison Ficke created a bogus movement based on ludicrous aesthetic principles. This supposed movement, Spectrism, was a satirical takeoff on the 1912 London movement called Imagism, and to Bynner's delight, it actually duped a number of writers and critics who should have known better but who could not resist associating themselves with the latest fad. In the course of developing this hoax, Bynner adopted the nom de plume of Emanuel Morgan, a name he often employed even after the hoax had been recognized for what it was.

After some publications that were part of his Spectric joke, Bynner's next publication was a volume titled *Grenstone Poems*. In the year of this book's publication, Bynner and Ficke visited Asia, and Bynner's subsequent enthusiasm for Chinese culture became a shaping force on the rest of his life. In 1918, he met Kiang Kang-hu, a Chinese scholar, and the two eventually agreed to collaborate on the English translation of some Chinese poetry. This translation project was to be the most ambitious literary effort of Bynner's career. Drawing upon Kiang Kang-hu's expertise in Chinese language and literature, Bynner applied his own fluency of phrasing and felicity of diction to the Chinese texts. The complete translation of the three hundred poems would appear as *The Jade Mountain* in 1929.

In 1922, Bynner moved to Santa Fe, where he was visited by D. H. Lawrence and his wife, Frieda. He journeyed with them on an expedition to Mexico described decades later in *Journey with Genius*. He continued writing poetry and plays and, in 1929, published the essay "The Persistence of Poetry." Living in Santa Fe, still a small and rather sleepy community with a significant population of artists, Bynner combined his literary endeavors with his concerns for issues that were not to become fashionable until after his death (racial justice and environmentalism). He spent most of the rest of his life in Santa Fe, with frequent visits to Mexico, where he bought a house in Jalisco in 1940. In 1926, Bynner had met Robert Hunt, who moved to Santa Fe in 1930, becoming Bynner's assistant and companion for more than thirty years.

Bynner continued to write and publish poetry throughout the 1930's. In 1937, he received a substantial inheritance upon the death of his mother. In 1943, working without the assistance of his old friend Kiang Kang-hu, Bynner began a "translation"—actually a version based upon other translations—of a work he was to publish in 1944 as *The Way of Life According to Laotzu*. Another volume of poetry, *Take Away the Darkness*, appeared in 1947. In 1950, Bynner and Hunt spent several months in North Africa and Europe. In 1952, the two men again visited Europe, returning to New Mexico in the late autumn.

Despite his age, Bynner was still composing poetry, although at a diminished pace. By the mid-1950's, Bynner's health had begun to deteriorate seriously, and he had become nearly blind. Hunt, who was considerably younger, assumed responsibility for his care. Bynner produced another volume of poetry, *New Poems*, in 1960, as he approached the age of eighty. It was the last collection published while he was alive. In 1962, Bynner was elected to the National Institute of Arts and Letters. Less than two years later, his companion and caretaker Hunt died of a sudden heart attack. Bynner himself suffered a major stroke early in the next year. He remained under constant medical care in Santa Fe until his death on June 1, 1968.

ANALYSIS

Witter Bynner's poetry has not enjoyed popularity in the years since his death, probably because he wrote mainly for himself and was consequently his own best audience. This fact sets him apart from the more famous poets of the twentieth century, and any assessment of his work as a whole must take this fact into consideration. Readers tend to find him facile to the point of glibness, and his wit sometimes seems misplaced. It is also easy, perhaps excessively so, to dismiss his quasi-mystical philosophical convictions. However, when a general assessment of the poetry of the first half of the twentieth century is made, Bynner emerges as an honest if garrulous voice and a poet whose response to the modernist predicament is quite possibly as creditable as anyone else's.

"AN ODE TO HARVARD"

Bynner's first significant published poem was "An Ode to Harvard." In this poem, written at the beginning of his long career, Bynner assumes an imposing poetic voice which speaks in hieratic tones that implicitly warn against the analysis of vision. The incantatory rhymes reinforce the Wordsworthian tone, and the whole passage resounds with an honest sincerity rarely, if ever, paralleled in Bynner's subsequent poetry. However, the very uniqueness of this poem requires the reader of Bynner to examine it carefully. When Bynner sent William Butler Yeats a copy of his poem, the great Irish poet responded, "you have the control of a powerful, eloquent, vehement language and thought that rushes on impetuous to its sentient end." It is not clear what Yeats meant by "to its sentient end," but Bynner evidently soon changed his mind about continuing to write in this fashion, and he adopted the witty, facile, sometimes even gossipy style that pervaded his work for the next half-century. However, the assertion in this passage of the oneness of life, the shared destiny of living things, remains one of Bynner's essential poetic premises throughout his long life.

POETIC FORMS AND THE UNITY OF LIFE

In "The Dead Loon" (*Grenstone Poems*), Bynner reflects upon the random killing of a wild bird by "a clever fool," an event that brings him a nightmarish vision of his own death. He concludes, "That dead loon is farther on the way than we are," but states it "is with me now and with the evening star."

As in the Harvard ode, Bynner concludes with a vision of the unity of life, here illuminated by "the evening star," Venus, the divine power of love. The poetry of Bynner increasingly foregrounds wit and the picturesque, and the playful and the clever become dominant concerns, perhaps too often, but it is only fair to point out that Bynner remains a poet of compassion who is concerned with justice in all things, except perhaps when it comes to other literary people. His poetry ranges in form from free verse to formal, structured patterns; his primary characteristic is finesse. In another poem from *Grenstone Poems*, this finesse is evident in the characteristic lines:

> She has a thousand presences,
> As surely seen and heard
> As birds that hide behind a leaf
> Or leaves that hide a bird.

This musical quatrain makes no pretense of profundity, but its pleasing structure is momentarily enigmatic, and the birds and leaves of the final two lines form a chiasmus, which is one of Bynner's favorite poetic devices. Such a chiasmus ends his poem "D. H. Lawrence," which concludes, "Whether you are a man wishing to be an animal/ Or an animal wishing to be a man." Here the structure emphasizes the paradoxicality of life and the relativity of perspective, and surely it suggests the importance for Bynner of synthesizing colloquial language, poetic form, and the most natural modes of human thought.

"EPITHALAMIUM AND ELEGY"

One of the most direct personal statements in Bynner's poetry is made in his "Epithalamium and Elegy" (1926), which begins, "My single constancy is love of life." In this poem, he celebrates life and declares that he will be content to depart from it in time. Bynner found this theme in Chinese poetry as well, as may be seen in in a passage he translated from Laozi (Laotzu) nearly twenty years later: "It is said, 'there's a way where there's a will';/ But let life ripen and then fall./ Will is not the way at all:/ Deny the way of life and you are dead."

The poet's passion for life is often suggested by his meditations upon death, which he frequently describes in terms of physical disintegration. In "Epithalamium and Elegy," he had asked, "Can I be tragical, in having had/ My love of life by life herself subdued?" However, the prospect of disintegration was implicit even in the closing lines of the Harvard ode, and Bynner faces it directly in such poems as "Idols" (1929) and "Correspondent" (1935), which begins "Words, words and words! What else, when men are dead,/ Their small lives ended and their sayings said,/ Is left of them?"

Bynner ultimately decides to defy ordinary disintegration, commanding in "Testament" (1947) that his body be burned. The lines suggest a passion for remaining whole, while later Bynner acknowledges the impossibility of doing so.

OTHER MAJOR WORKS

PLAYS: *Tiger*, pb. 1913; *The Little King*, pb. 1914; *Snickerty Nick*, pb. 1919 (with Julia Elsworth Ford); *Cake*, pb. 1926.

NONFICTION: *The Persistence of Poetry*, 1929; *Journey with Genius: Recollections and Reflections Concerning the D. H. Lawrences*, 1951.

TRANSLATIONS: *Iphigenia in Tauris*, 1915, 1956 (of Euripides); *A Book of Love*, 1923 (of Charles Vildrac); *The Jade Mountain: A Chinese Anthology*, 1929, 1939 (with Kiang Kang-hu); *The Way of Life According to Laotzu: An American Version*, 1944.

EDITED TEXT: *The Sonnets of Frederick Goddard*, 1931.

MISCELLANEOUS: *The Selected Witter Bynner: Poems, Plays, Translations, Prose, and Letters*, 1995 (James Kraft, editor).

BIBLIOGRAPHY

Kraft, James. *Who Is Witter Bynner? A Biography*. Albuquerque: University of New Mexico Press, 1995. A treatment of Bynner's colorful life supplemented by selections from his poems and letters, along with a number of photographs.

_____, ed. *The Selected Witter Bynner: Poems, Plays, Translations, Prose, and Letters*. Albuquerque: University of New Mexico Press, 1995. A characteristic selection of Bynner's writings, introduced by the editor and including a chronology, a bibliography, and a useful index.

_____. *The Works of Witter Bynner: Selected Poems, Light Verse and Satires, the Chinese Translations, Prose Pieces, Selected Letters*. New York: Farrar, Straus and Giroux, 1978. The main source of primary materials and an essential work for Bynner studies.

Lindsay, Robert O. *Witter Bynner: A Bibliography*. Albuquerque: University of New Mexico Press, 1967. This detailed descriptive bibliography of Bynner's publications is valuable, although the list of secondary sources is out of date.

Wilbur, Richard. "The Poetry of Witter Bynner." *American Poetry Review* 6, no. 6 (November/December, 1977): 3-8. A perceptive commentary on some specific poems and Bynner's poetry in general, written by a distinguished poet.

Robert W. Haynes

C

HAYDEN CARRUTH

Born: Waterbury, Connecticut; August 3, 1921
Died: Munnsville, New York; September 29, 2008

PRINCIPAL POETRY

The Crow and the Heart, 1959
Journey to a Known Place, 1961
The Norfolk Poems, 1962
Nothing for Tigers, 1965
The Clay Hill Anthology, 1970
For You, 1970
From Snow and Rock, from Chaos, 1973
Dark World, 1974
The Bloomingdale Papers, 1975
Brothers, I Loved You All, 1978
The Sleeping Beauty, 1982, 1990
If You Call This Cry a Song, 1983
Asphalt Georgics, 1985
The Oldest Killed Lake in North America, 1985
The Selected Poetry of Hayden Carruth, 1985
*Tell Me Again How the White Heron Rises and
    Flies Across the Nacreous River at Twilight
    Toward the Distant Islands*, 1989
Collected Shorter Poems, 1946-1991, 1992
Collected Longer Poems, 1993
Scrambled Eggs and Whiskey: Poems, 1991-1995,
    1996
A Summer with Tu Fu: A Sequence of Poems,
    1996
Doctor Jazz, 2001
*Toward the Distant Islands: New and Selected
    Poems*, 2006 (Sam Hamill, editor)

OTHER LITERARY FORMS

Hayden Carruth (kar-REWTH) edited *The Voice
That Is Great Within Us: American Poetry of the Twentieth Century* (1970), a highly regarded and widely
taught anthology of modern American poetry, and *The*
Bird-Poem Book (1970). *Working Papers: Selected Essays and Reviews* (1982) and *Effluences from the Sacred Caves: More Selected Essays and Reviews* (1983)
collect essays and reviews, mainly of modern and contemporary poetry. *Sitting In: Selected Writings on Jazz,
Blues, and Related Topics* (1986) collects Carruth's
music criticism.

ACHIEVEMENTS

Versatile, independent, and prolific, Hayden Carruth had a long and distinguished career as poet, editor,
critic, and teacher. He was poetry editor of *Poetry*
(1949-1950) and *Harper's* (1977-1982) and the recipient of Guggenheim Fellowships (1965, 1979) and a
senior fellowship from the National Endowment for
the Arts (1988). He received honorary degrees from
New England College (1987) and Syracuse University
(1993). His many honors include the Bess Hokin Prize
(1964) and the Levinson Prize (1958) from *Poetry*
magazine, the Vermont Governor's Award for Excellence in the Arts (1973), the Shelley Memorial Award
(1979), the Lenore Marshall Poetry Prize (1979), the
Whiting Writers Award in poetry (1986), the Ruth
Lilly Poetry Prize (1990), the National Book Critics
Circle Award in poetry (1992) for *Collected Shorter
Poems, 1946-1991*, the Lannan Literary Award for Poetry (1995), the National Book Award in Poetry (1996)
for *Scrambled Eggs and Whiskey*, and the Arthur Rense
Poetry Prize (2008). *The Selected Poetry of Hayden
Carruth* was a finalist for the Pulitzer Prize in poetry in
1987.

BIOGRAPHY

Born in Waterbury, Connecticut, in 1921, Hayden
Carruth spent most of his life in New England. He was
graduated from the University of North Carolina and
earned his master's degree from the University of Chicago in 1948. Carruth's military experience during
World War II was important to his work. Perhaps even
more important, by his own account, were his struggles
with mental illness. The long and painful recovery from
being institutionalized in 1953 led to his living in relative isolation and considerable poverty in northern Vermont for much of his working life. Married four times
(the fourth time to Joe-Anne McLaughlin in 1989),

Carruth had two children, Martha, who died of cancer in her forties, and David Barrow II, the latter present in many poems as "Bo."

Carruth earned his living as a freelance reviewer and editor before taking a teaching position at Syracuse University in 1979. He accepted a one-year professorship at Bucknell University from 1985 to 1986 and returned to Syracuse University until 1991, when he was made a professor emeritus. He then turned his energy to owning and operating Crow's Mark Press in Johnson, Vermont. Carruth died on September 29, 2008, in Munnsville, New York, after suffering a series of strokes.

ANALYSIS

The work of this lifelong New Englander reflects a sustained engagement with his region and its literary traditions, but Hayden Carruth's interests and sources ranged widely through space and time. Sometimes regarded as a poetic conservative because of his interest in fixed forms, Carruth is better seen as an experimental traditionalist whose exhaustive knowledge and mastery of formal verse allowed him to use a wide variety of poetic resources. His poems range from brief lyrics to Frostian blank-verse monologues and character studies to extended sonnet sequences, notably *The Sleeping Beauty*, a book-length exploration of the spirit of romance in the late twentieth century. Carruth's reviews and essays demonstrate his tough-mindedness and fairness as well as his insistence on careful judgment and sharp distinctions. A self-described "New England anarchist," independent and widely read, he was a significant voice for intelligence, humanity, and craft in American letters.

Carruth's great themes are old ones: madness and music, isolation and community, despair at the human capacity for destruction, and hope in the beauty and terror of love and of art, "the joy and agony of improvisation," as he puts it in *Brothers, I Loved You All*. Carruth lived a life at once set apart—he began the teaching career typical of his fellow poets only in his late fifties—and finely attuned to his place and his age. Few poets are more deeply knowledgeable about literary traditions and about the range of work being done in their own time than Carruth was, as his work as poet,

anthologist, and critic reveals. His achievement was to fuse his learning, his keen eye and ear, his remarkable poetic craft, and his thoroughgoing integrity and self-awareness into a body of writing distinguished in both form and substance.

Virtually every one of Carruth's poems shows his interest in the formal qualities of verse; unlike many of his contemporaries, he did not leap from formal to free verse in midcareer but continued to experiment with a variety of stanzaic and rhythmical patterns. Although his writing always drew deeply from the natural world, his best early poems deal with the sober human experiences of war and madness, and their austere formal patterns create a sense of barely achieved emotional control.

"ON A CERTAIN ENGAGEMENT SOUTH OF SEOUL"

"On a Certain Engagement South of Seoul," from *The Crow and the Heart*, recalls the alienation and disorientation of Carruth's combat experience in crisp terza rima:

> We were unreal,
> Strange bodies and alien minds; we could not cry
>
> For even our eyes seemed to be made of steel;
> Nor could we look at one another, for each
> Was a sign of fear.

The poem ends with the speaker still turning over the experience, struggling for some kind of clarity or understanding: Does it "make us brothers" or merely "bring our hatred back?" The horror and sorrow of the war create a kinship among those who suffered them, but it is a strange bond that does not bring joy.

"ADOLF EICHMANN"

"Adolf Eichmann" (from *The Norfolk Poems*) uses terza rima to very different effect, in a grim meditation that modulates into a horrifying curse on the Nazi executioner: "I say let the dung/ Be heaped on that man until it chokes his voice." The curse continues, wishing a plague of leprosy on Eichmann in a manner reminiscent of the imprecatory psalms. The curse's culmination, however, is a sentence of emotional rather than physical punishment:

But let his ears never, never be shut,
And let young voices read to him, name by name,
From the rolls of all those people whom he has shut

Into the horrible beds.

Few poems so direct, aimed at such easy targets, avoid lapsing into sentimentality or cliché. Throughout his career, however, Carruth took the risk of addressing the most pressing and difficult topics. (He repeatedly criticized his fellow poets for avoiding the subject of nuclear holocaust.) Here the heavy, exact rhymes on "dung" and "shut" give the poem the awful resonance of a huge bell.

MENTAL ILLNESS

Carruth's struggles with mental illness are a recurrent theme in all of his work. During his hospital stay in 1953 and 1954, he wrote the long sequence *The Bloomingdale Papers*, which was lost for some twenty years and was published in full only in 1975 (although parts appear in *The Crow and the Heart*, and the sequence "The Asylum," in fifteen-line near-sonnets, was printed in *For You*). The sequence incorporates many forms, including passages of prose, sonnets, lists, and psalms. The asylum poems confront psychological terror and trace the search for stability and coherence with remarkable acuity, honesty, and courage, refusing the temptations of easy self-dramatization or confessionalism: "Prison grows warm and *is* the real asylum." Carruth pictures himself and the other asylum inmates sitting in a deep winter stillness to face "all the terrors of our inward journeys,/ The grave indecencies, the loathsome birds." This terrifying inward journey requires a "strange bravery" of one who calls himself "unbrave." The poems humanize his suffering, without romanticizing it.

Among the poems written against the fear of madness and the correlative fear of a meaningless universe, "Contra Mortem" (from *For You*) was Carruth's personal favorite. Written in the fifteen-line stanzas he used repeatedly, it is a moving meditation on the endurance of being in the face of nothingness. In its hard-won refusal to allow despair the last word, it strikes a characteristic note: "Some are moralists and some have faith/ but some who live in the free exchange of hearts/ as the gift of being are lovers against death."

FROM SNOW AND ROCK, FROM CHAOS

With *From Snow and Rock, from Chaos*, Carruth found a confidence and a characteristic voice that remained through all the widely various work he published since. Overtones of the poets he chose for his masters—William Butler Yeats, Ezra Pound, and Robert Frost, among many others—can still be heard, along with the voices of his New England neighbors, which he often captured with uncanny accuracy. However, through and above them all, Carruth's gruff, blustery presence remains constant, acute without being merely "sensitive," open to his own faults and failings without overdramatizing them, refusing easy consolations and hero worship as well:

> this was the world foreknown
> though I had thought somehow
> probably in the delusion
> of that idiot thoreau
> that necessity could be saved
> by the facts we actually have

"FREEDOM AND DISCIPLINE"

Carruth's long-standing interest in music, particularly jazz, informs his poetics in essential ways. (His instrument is the clarinet.) In "Freedom and Discipline" (from *Nothing for Tigers*), which describes concerts by Sergei Rachmaninoff and Coleman Hawkins, he ponders "why I went to verse-making . . . this grubbing art," and concludes, "Freedom and discipline concur/ only in ecstasy." He has written sympathetic and insightful jazz criticism, paying special attention to the capacity of music to capture the streams of human feeling.

BROTHERS, I LOVED YOU ALL

Music is also central to *Brothers, I Loved You All*, arguably Carruth's best single volume, and the most fully represented in *The Selected Poetry of Hayden Carruth*. There are many fine lyrics, and several long, Frostian dramatic monologues, but the centerpiece is the long poem "Paragraphs," another sequence in fifteen-line near-sonnets. "Paragraphs" draws on Carruth's deep investment in New England culture and expresses grief at the decline of that culture under industrial urbanization, the "superadded trailers, this prefab, damned fashion/ out of Monterey or Bronxville, God knows where." The poem incorporates reports of war atrocities, memories of jazz musicians (the "brothers" of the title), celebrations of natural energy, a marvelous Puerto Rican folktale of a transparent bird that flies until it dies, quotations from the anarchist Mikhail Bakunin, and much more. Amid the ravages and human destructiveness that the poem traces, Carruth isolates a few sustaining factors: his own old poems, "their inside truth that was/ (is, is!) crucial," the human effort "to wrench lucidity out of nowhere," and especially the treasured presence of the old jazzmen he regards as his superiors, and the joy and beauty of their improvising together:

>   not singular, not the rarity
> we think, but real and a glory
> our human shining, shekinah . . .   Ah,
>   holy spirit, ninefold
> I druther've bin a-settin there, supernumerary
> cockroach i'th' corner, a listenin, a-listenin,,,,,,,
>   than be the Prazedint ov the Wuurld.

Carruth's master, Pound, used to blend high intellection and dialectical misspellings like this, and the influence is plain here, though Carruth's subject matter is very much his own. Two key parts of the modernist project were to bring past and present together so that history and modernity might coexist in the poem and to create a poetic language that would include both sophisticated abstractions and the most common, rude speech. A good case can be made for Carruth as one of the most successful inheritors of that project. Considered as a whole, in fact, his work bears up well against that of the modernist masters. He is certainly more accessible than Pound, less squeamish than T. S. Eliot, and more in touch with American life than Wallace Stevens; moreover, his language is more capacious and capable of dealing in abstractions than that of William Carlos Williams. Carruth would not have made such presumptuous claims for himself, but his work was consistently of a magnitude befitting such comparisons.

THE SLEEPING BEAUTY

The Sleeping Beauty is Carruth's book-length tribute to his third wife, Rose Marie Dorn. A reworking of the Briar Rose myth, it is also an ambitious exploration of the spirit of romance, of the multiple dangers and at-

tractions of the romantic tradition. The poem blends a series of the sleeping princess's dreams—in which she is visited by Homer, Hesiod, Henry Hudson, the fictional character Heathcliff, and Adolf Hitler, among others—with the poet's memories and reflections, conversations with a gruff Vermont ghost named Amos, and hauntingly repeated glimpses of a sculpture of a woman's face buried in a stream. The face is an emblem of the mysterious, sleeping, ideal beloved, the one whom "the prince who is human, driven, and filled with love" must pursue, and of whom he must prove himself worthy. Consistently reviewed as one of the most successful long poems of the 1980's, it deserves to be better known.

IF YOU CALL THIS CRY A SONG

If You Call This Cry a Song gathers poems written between about 1964 and 1979. As the time span would suggest, it is a varied collection, with poems in many styles and modes. Difficult to summarize briefly either thematically or formally because of its diversity, the book is filled with unpredictable treasures, including an exuberant dialect version of the myth of Hermes, "A Little Old Funky Homeric Blues for Herm."

ASPHALT GEORGICS

As early as *The Norfolk Poems*, Carruth showed his fascination with popular culture and the language of ordinary people. His most memorable and sustained treatment of that subject matter comes with *Asphalt Georgics*, thirteen poems in rhyming quatrains in the common speech of upstate New York and filled with the Kmarts and suburban clutter of their lives.

> What a mishmash—the suburbs! You
>   know it. So I pray for
> Crawford, the street, the smokebush, the
>   works. I pray for no more
>
> Reagan. Well, you got to keep your
>   wig on, you can't give in
> to the dead. So what if it don't
>   mean much. It means something.

The poems are wry and stoic at once, whimsical and grim, elegiac and defiant, an engaging blend of grumpy accommodation and high spirits. They balance common speech against the rigid stanza form with a deftness reminiscent of Frost. However, these poems do not imitate or resemble Frost's; they are far less idealized and selective in their presentation of New England, much closer to the slang and materiality of the true American colloquial.

TELL ME AGAIN HOW THE WHITE HERON RISES . . .

The title of Carruth's 1989 collection, *Tell Me Again How the White Heron Rises and Flies Across the Nacreous River at Twilight Toward the Distant Islands*, suggests its main formal experiment. The lengthy titles—others include "Sometimes When Lovers Lie Quietly Together, Unexpectedly One of Them Will Feel the Other's Pulse," "The Necessary Impresario, Mr. Septic Tanck," and "Ovid, Old Buddy, I Would Discourse with You a While"—are at once elevated and farcical, ambitious and self-deprecating, whimsical and somber. Like the poems themselves, they are emblematic of a man who has won through to a deep and difficult sanity, to a knowledge of self, craft, and world that is occasionally cranky, often idiosyncratic, but always marked by a hard-edged lucidity and a rich and integral compassion. Filled with sharply realized details, carefully worked patterns of sound, and honed and balanced abstractions, the poems integrate Carruth's lifelong concerns for the music of music and of poetry, for the mysteries of love and language, and for the ways human beings find to destroy and to sustain one another.

The volume closes with "Mother," an agonized and agonizing elegy, and with a vision of his mother on her deathbed, "Penitent for the crime committed against you, victim of your own innocence,/ (Existence is the crime against the existing),/ Drifting, drifting in the uncaused universe that has no right to be." To recognize that neither humankind nor the universe has any "right" to be and yet to persist, to make such painful eloquence from that recognition: This is the achievement of Carruth.

SCRAMBLED EGGS AND WHISKEY

Carruth earned the National Book Award for *Scrambled Eggs and Whiskey*, which contains meditations on such themes as politics, history, aging, nostalgia, guilt, and love. The volume carries a voice of dejection while also expressing a kind of gratitude for the

people and things that have made his later life remarkably satisfying. In "Flying to St. Louis," he uses the phrase "alone and desperate" twice, and goes on to say "I've blamed my mother and father" for the "pain, the desperation" for sixty-five years. He mentions that "he drinks wine and swallows more pills" in "Wife Poem" and that he will "finish the wine, take/ the sleeping pills" in "Five-thirty A.M." While a tone of defeat and melancholy finds a significant place in this collection, this mood makes the moments of deep satisfaction that much more vivid. The book is dedicated to Joe-Anne McLaughlin, his fourth wife, and in "Wife Poem," he writes that she

> dropped
> down from the moon, not like some
> sylphy Cynthia at Delphi, after all she's
> not seventeen, but with the sexual grace
> and personal implacability
> of a goddess of our time.

The central focus of the book thus seems to be Carruth's recognition that he has been blessed with a gift, an offering from the cosmos.

His experience in a mental hospital in the 1950's always informs his works to some degree, and here, in "Franconia," he notes that despite the experience, he had the good fortune to find a person whose presence and support have made him "as happy, as gratified, as I've ever been,/ old friend, in all these seventy-two years." In "Resorts," he continues in amazement to say "My dear, we are in love. It's a fact, certifiable." Although in "Birthday Cake," he admits that as an old man, he's "too old to write love songs now," that impulse is at the core of the collection.

DOCTOR JAZZ

In *Doctor Jazz*—published as Carruth entered his eighth decade—the poet lauds the unexpected power of "petty endurance." The collection celebrates his devotion to jazz, as the title references: In one piece, he lovingly describes the trumpeter Dizzy Gillespie's cheeks in midblow—"monstrous fruit about to burst,/ Blood and flesh all over the bandstand." Other sections, such as "Afterlife," "Basho," and "Faxes," have Carruth conversing with a range of personas, in lines of varying lengths. "While Reading Basho," with its combination of classic haiku form with contemporary idiom, displays some of Carruth's jauntiness: "Basho, you made/ a living writing haiku?/ Wow! Way to go, man." The emotional center is a fifteen-page-long poem in memory of the poet's daughter Martha, who died of cancer in her forties. It is a furious work that details her hospital stays, ranging from the day of her birth to a final period when she looked like "a young crone."

TOWARD THE DISTANT ISLANDS

Carruth's final book of poetry *Toward the Distant Islands*, edited by Sam Hamill, is intended as a portable edition. It includes a representative sampling of the shorter poems from earlier books as well as thirteen previously uncollected poems from 2001 to 2005. Many of his most delightful character sketches and Frostian dramatic monologues, such as "John Dryden," "Marshall Washer," and "Regarding Chainsaws," are included. In addition, several poems celebrate Carruth's marriage to McLaughlin and his consequent regeneration. New poems such as "Adoration Is Not Irrelevant" and "Navel" join "Birthday Cake" and "Testament" from *Scrambled Eggs and Whiskey*. Addressed to his wife, "Testament" includes a striking example of a skillful re-energizing of a well-worn image. In the hourglass that is the speaker's life, the upper chamber was filled with "the stuff of ego," but that has gone away, leaving nothing but love accumulating below.

Consistent with the rest of his career, many poems collected in his final book are devoted to nature. His love of the natural world is apparent in "Essay on Stone" and "Naming for Love," in which he dwells lovingly on the names and characteristics of stone and rock. "Once More" and "Springtime, 1998" are meditations on seasonal change, and "August First" asserts that the sounds of nature form a discourse that includes the poet himself. Descriptions are concrete and specific: Tobey Woods and the hermit thrush or the loon on Forrester's Pond. Beneath the specificity is the mystery of the natural world. The loon's laugh represents to the speaker "... timeless/ woe," which "... seemed/ the real and only sanity to me."

As "The Loon on Forrester's Pond" suggests, Carruth always felt that the appropriate mood of a poet was sorrow. From "The Buddhist Painter Prepares to Paint" (from *The Crow and the Heart*) to "Dearest M——"

published forty-two years later, he frequently asserted that a genuine sorrow was a requirement of producing art. "Reflexive" explains that sorrow brings out the essence of human beings and shapes them. The poet, in "The Poet," is animated by pain, "... attracting/ every new injury." Certainly among the most wrenching of his poems are those about his daughter who died of cancer. One treatment of this subject, "The Little Girl Who Learned the Saving Way," is a remarkably formed ballad with a refrain in the second line of each quatrain. Meditation on her death is more bitterly expressed in "Dearest M——" in which the speaker doubts if the world has any meaning at all and then asserts that "... Mother Cosmos/ is the greatest terrorist. . . ." This poem looks forward to later poems in its frustrated inability to express all that the poet feels: "The immensity of what should be said/ defeats me. Language/ like a dismasted hulk at sea is overwhelmed/ and founders."

If Carruth was ultimately defeated by tragedy and old age, he went down fighting. His last poems include several antiwar poems. In one of his fifteen-line sonnets, "Fanfare for the Common Man, No. 2," as well as in "Complaint and Petition," he accuses the president of the United States of depravity and of tyrannizing over his own country as well as others. His political heritage is decidedly leftist, and in "A Few Dilapidated Arias," he traces it to the 1960's, when liberation was the shibboleth, and even earlier to Nicola Sacco, Bartolomeo Vanzetti, and Emma Goldman, to what he calls a heritage of revolutionary thought. In the same poem, he reasserts a lifelong credo that includes agnosticism and a love of the earth: a preference for nature worship to "... your pile of stones, your/ nasty old cathedral. . . ." In "Small Fundamental Essay," dated 1997, he rejects war, abortion, and Christ in favor of "... the miracle of the possible/ faith in the peaceful knowledge of what is true."

Aware, sometimes comically and sometimes sadly, of his advancing age, his last poems note that he was losing competence, becoming "semi-hemi-demi invalidated" and could no longer walk in his beloved woods. "February Morning" pictures an old man on a snowy day napping over a book by Robert Frost. Still inspired by nature and words from his past, he nevertheless does not shape a song but climbs the stairs to bed.

OTHER MAJOR WORKS

LONG FICTION: *Appendix A*, 1963.

NONFICTION: *Working Papers: Selected Essays and Reviews*, 1982; *Effluences from the Sacred Caves: More Selected Essays and Reviews*, 1983; *Sitting In: Selected Writings on Jazz, Blues, and Related Topics*, 1986; *Suicides and Jazzers*, 1992; *Selected Essays and Reviews*, 1996; *Reluctantly: Autobiographical Essays*, 1998; *Beside the Shadblow Tree: A Memoir of James Laughlin*, 1999; *Letters to Jane*, 2004.

EDITED TEXTS: *The Bird-Poem Book*, 1970; *The Voice That Is Great Within Us: American Poetry of the Twentieth Century*, 1970.

BIBLIOGRAPHY

Booth, Philip. "On *Brothers, I Loved You All*." Review of *Brothers, I Loved You All. American Poetry Review* 8 (May/June, 1979): 13-16. Fellow poet Booth praises Carruth's immediacy and vitality, the "tensile strength" of his use of abstractions, and his willingness to risk direct statement. Not compelled by the Frostian poems in *Brothers, I Loved You All*, Booth is cogently appreciative of the rest of the book.

Carruth, Hayden. "Hayden Carruth: An Interview." Interview by Anthony Robbins. *American Poetry Review* 22, no. 5 (September/October, 1993): 47-49. Robbins gives a brief biography of Carruth and summarizes an interview covering many subjects including Marxist ideology, E. L. Doctorow's influence on *The Sleeping Beauty*, and the development of poetic philosophy.

Feder, Lillian. "Poetry from the Asylum: Hayden Carruth's *The Bloomingdale Papers*." *Literature and Medicine* 4 (1985): 112-127. Feder gives a brief account of the writing and publication history of *The Bloomingdale Papers* and a rather stiff but useful analysis of its depiction of the poet's struggle to remake himself. She also notes connections with later works, including *Brothers, I Loved You All* and *The Sleeping Beauty*, and calls particular attention to the ongoing search for self-realization through love.

Grimes, William. "Hayden Carruth, Poet and Critic, Dies at Eighty-seven." *The New York Times*, October 1, 2008, p. C12. This obituary gives a short overview of the poet's life and career, including assessments by critics and fellow poets.

Henry, Brian. "Freedom and Discipline: Hayden Carruth's Blues." *Georgia Review* 58, no. 2 (Summer, 2004): 261-275. Henry analyzes Carruth's use of the blues in thematics as well as in technical innovations.

Schudel, Matt. "Hayden Carruth, Eighty-seven: Poems Reflected Struggles of Life." *The Washington Post*, October 1, 2008, p. B5. This lengthy obituary takes an in-depth look at the life and work of Carruth, noting his personal struggles with mental illness and the recognition he received late in life.

Seneca Review 20 (1990). *In the Act: Essays on the Poetry of Hayden Carruth*. This special issue of *Seneca Review*, edited by David Weiss, features twelve essays on Carruth's work by Wendell Berry, David Rivard, Maxine Kumin, Sam Hamill, David Budbill, and others, as well as an interview with Carruth and new poems. The essays range from personal reminiscences to formal literary criticism, and they discuss Carruth's work from his earliest poems to *Tell Me Again How the White Heron Rises and Flies Across the Nacreous River at Twilight Toward the Distant Islands*. An extensive and valuable resource.

Solotaroff, Ted. "One of Us: The Poetry of Hayden Carruth." *American Poetry Review* 39, no. 1 (January/February, 2010): 31-33. Solotaroff provides an in-depth description and assessment of Carruth's career as a poet, placing him in the context of the literary and social developments of his time.

Jeff Gundy; Sarah Hilbert
Updated by William Howard

RAYMOND CARVER

Born: Clatskanie, Oregon; May 25, 1938
Died: Port Angeles, Washington; August 2, 1988

PRINCIPAL POETRY

Near Klamath, 1968
Winter Insomnia, 1970
At Night the Salmon Move, 1976

Two Poems, 1982

If It Please You, 1984

This Water, 1985

Where Water Comes Together with Other Water, 1985

Ultramarine, 1986

A New Path to the Waterfall, 1989

All of Us: The Collected Poems, 1996

OTHER LITERARY FORMS

Raymond Carver is perhaps best known as a writer of short fiction. In addition, he wrote a screenplay and edited a collection of short stories.

ACHIEVEMENTS

Raymond Carver has been credited with rescuing both poetry and the short story from the elitists and obscurantists and giving them back to the people. His honors include the National Endowment for the Arts Discovery Award for Poetry in 1970, the Joseph Henry Jackson Award for fiction in 1971, a Wallace Stegner Creative Writing Fellowship from Stanford University in 1972-1973, a National Book Award nomination in fiction in 1977, a Guggenheim Fellowship in 1977-1978, a National Endowment for the Arts Award in fiction in 1979, the Carlos Fuentes Fiction Award in 1983, the Mildred and Harold Strauss Living Award in 1983, a National Book Critics Circle Award nomination in fiction in 1984, a finalist for the Pulitzer Prize in fiction in 1984 and 1989, *Poetry* magazine's Levinson Prize in 1985, and a Washington State Book Award in 1987. Carver was elected to the American Academy of Arts and Letters in 1988 and in that same year was awarded a doctorate of letters from the University of Hartford.

BIOGRAPHY

Raymond Clevie Carver, Jr., was born in Clatskanie, Oregon, and grew up in Yakima, Washington, where his father worked as a saw filer in a lumber mill. Like most young men growing up in that heavily forested, sparsely populated region, Carver enjoyed hunting and fishing; however, he seems to have inherited unusual intelligence, sensitivity, and ambition. His life is a story of his struggle to achieve self-actualization in spite of an impoverished background. His parents were poor and uneducated, and he himself was extremely ignorant about literature. In his teens, he enrolled in a correspondence course in creative writing, but he never finished it. His early reading was typically the westerns of Zane Grey, the fantasies of Edgar Rice Burroughs, and magazines celebrating rugged outdoor adventure.

At the age of nineteen, Carver married his teenage sweetheart, who gave birth to their first child less than six months later. Another child was born the following year, and from then on, Carver was torn between the desire to become a writer and the need to support his family. "Nothing—and, brother, I mean nothing—that ever happened to me on this earth," he said, "could come anywhere close, could possibly be as important to me, could make as much difference, as the fact that I had two children."

In 1958, Carver and his family moved to Paradise, California, where he enrolled at Chico State College (now Chico State University). One of the major turning points in his life was a course in creative writing taught by the inspiring writer and teacher John Gardner. Carver began publishing poems and short stories in college literary magazines. He continued to do so when he transferred to Humboldt State College (now University) in Arcata, California, and finally his work began to be accepted by respected literary quarterlies.

Carver was tortured by the fact that he had to support himself and his family by working at a series of mindless and often physically exhausting dead-end jobs. Among other things, he worked as a mill hand, a farm laborer, a delivery boy, a service station attendant, a stock clerk, and a janitor. His poems and stories are haunted by guilt. He felt guilty because he was not providing his family with a decent standard of living and because he did not want to be burdened with a family at all. He drank because he felt guilty, and then he felt guilty for drinking. Many American writers have been heavy drinkers, including Ernest Hemingway, William Faulkner, and Sinclair Lewis, but few have admitted it so frankly or used it so freely as subject matter for his or her work.

In 1967, Carver obtained his first white-collar job, as an editor of textbooks for Science Research Associates in Palo Alto, California. By this time he had become a heavy drinker, and only a few years later, he was fired. Still, he had continued to write stories and poetry, and in 1970, he received a National Endowment for the Arts Discovery Award for Poetry. Other monetary awards helped him to devote more time to writing. In 1971, his poems and stories began to appear in magazines such as *Esquire*, *Harper's Bazaar*, and *Playgirl*.

Part-time teaching assignments helped Carver survive to produce more stories and poetry. In 1971, he began teaching creative writing at the University of California, Santa Cruz; in 1972, he began teaching at Stanford University. In 1975, he had to drop out of an assignment at the University of California, Santa Barbara, because of his alcoholism; in the late 1970's, however, Carver was teaching writing again, even though he said he felt uncomfortable doing it.

Carver taught at Goddard College in the late 1970's and then at the University of Texas, El Paso, and at the University of Vermont. He was appointed professor of English at Syracuse University in 1980. In 1983, he

Raymond Carver (©Marion Ettlinger/ Courtesy, Atlantic Monthly Press)

was at last able to give up teaching and devote his full time and attention to writing, after receiving a Strauss Living Award, which guaranteed him an annual stipend for five years.

Carver was separated from his wife in the late 1970's and began living with Tess Gallagher, a poet and college teacher like himself who had also been born in the Pacific Northwest. Gallagher helped him to cope with his drinking problem and provided him with understanding and emotional support. She was with Carver until the time of his death from lung cancer in 1988; they were married in Reno, Nevada, less than two months before he died. Years of worry, chronic insecurity, and hard living had cut short the career of one of America's most promising writers at the age of fifty.

ANALYSIS

Raymond Carver certainly had his faults, but he also had many strengths that were responsible for making him better loved than most other writers of his generation and ultimately more famous. He was humble, modest, honest, sincere, and dedicated. He was not ashamed to acknowledge his lower-class background or the fact that he had done a considerable amount of work that required him to get his hands dirty. He did not pretend to know all—or even any—of the answers. The reader senses that Carver was someone like himself or herself, struggling to make sense out of a life that actually did not make much sense at all.

Carver's writing was always personal and autobiographical. He did not seem to know how to write any other way. This quality made him seem primitive and a mere literary curiosity to certain sophisticated critics but also endeared him to ordinary readers, many of whom felt betrayed by the trickery and emotional emptiness of much modern literature. Carver said, "My poems are of course not literally true" but acknowledged that, as in most of his short stories, "there is an autobiographical element."

Carver never got on a pulpit or a soapbox. He never blamed anyone but himself for his troubles. His writings are remarkably devoid of allusions to religion and politics, the Scylla and Charybdis of most modern writers. This was probably another thing that annoyed his critics: They wanted him to take a position—preferably one aligned with their own. A writer can toil in obscurity forever without a glance from such people, but if he begins receiving recognition, then they immediately want to bring him into their camp. Thus critics have complained that in Carver's poems there are no resolutions, no epiphanies—as if resolutions and epiphanies were something that came in boxes of twelve at the supermarket. One of Carver's writing mottos was "No cheap tricks." He steered by this motto all his life, and it always guided him in the direction of unadorned self-revelation. The photographs that appear on the backs of many of his published volumes show a big, awkward, shy-looking man with questioning eyes that are hard to look at and hard to look away from. He was the sort of plain-spoken American that Americans have always admired, not unlike Abraham Lincoln, Mark Twain, Will Rogers, and Jimmy Stewart. In an age when every television personality seems to have all the answers to life's biggest questions, it is refreshing to come upon a writer such as Carver who has no easy answers to offer. Carver will be remembered not for his depth of thought but for his depth of feeling. He saw life as a mystery, but a wonderful and fascinating mystery.

FIRES

When Carver published *Fires: Essays, Poems, Stories* in 1983, he said that he had collected in the book everything he had previously written that he considered worth keeping. In addition to two very illuminating essays about his life and his writing values, the book contains fifty of his poems dating back to 1968. Most of the themes that would appear in his later poems are evident in these early works. "Near Klamath," for example, is one of many expressions of his love for nature and particularly for fishing. Many of Carver's poems about nature remind the reader of Hemingway's passionate love for physical action in the outdoors. Hemingway was one of Carver's early literary models; they have a similar simple, straightforward style of writing and have a similar reticence to express sentimental feelings.

With Carver, one senses that his love of nature was connected with a yearning for escape from the responsibilities that plagued him—the menial jobs, the coin-operated laundries, the crying children, the endless bills, the junk cars, the squatter's life in cheap apartments and borrowed dwellings—and kept him from his writing, the only thing that gave his life meaning. In one of his better-known poems, "Winter Insomnia," he writes:

> The mind would like to get out of here
> onto the snow. It would like to run
> with a pack of shaggy animals, all teeth.

"Drinking While Driving" is one of the many pieces Carver wrote about drinking during his lifetime. "Bankruptcy" tells with wry humor how he became bankrupt for the first time at the age of twenty-eight. A similar story is told in a later poem titled "Miracle," published in *A New Path to the Waterfall*; the wry humor is still there (as it remained for the rest of his life), but his wife's reaction to this second bankruptcy was far more violent. "Deschutes River" is an interesting poem because it brings together his love for the outdoors and his personal guilt and anxiety: The poem ends with the lines "Far away—/ another man is raising my children,/ bedding my wife bedding my wife."

Some of the poems collected in *Fires* show the bad habits a naïve beginner can pick up from other writers who substitute stylistic legerdemain, erudition, wit, and exoticism for genuine feeling. "Rhodes," "The Mosque in Jaffa," and "Spring, 480 B.C." are among the poems in which Carver deals with foreign sights and sounds, evidently trying to evoke refined sentiments. Poems with this foreign flavor continue to appear in his subsequent volumes and are among the least appealing of his works. Many of them have a certain artificial or chapbook quality, as if written by a professor on sabbatical. It was inevitable that Carver's growing fame as well as his exposure to academia would tempt him to seem more cultivated than he actually was; he was most likable and most effective, however, as a simple lad from the Pacific Northwest who had barely managed to obtain a bachelor's degree.

ULTRAMARINE

The poems collected in *Ultramarine*, published in 1986, represent Carver at his best. These poems are longer, more confident. The words march across the pages almost with the brave assurance of John Milton's iambic pentameter in *Paradise Lost* (1667, 1674). Carver, however, always shunned rhyme and meter. Stylistically, he belongs to that vast modern school of poets who have abandoned all poetic conventions and try to write like someone talking to a close friend. Though his poems have rhythm, rhyme and meter would seem as grossly out of place in a poem by Carver as he himself would look in an Elizabethan costume with lace ruffles.

The question arises, why then did he continue to arrange his words in lines to look like poems? Why did he not abandon this last vestige of conventional poetry and write his thoughts as plain prose? There are several possible answers. Probably the most important one is that the appearance of a poem gives the author more freedom. Prose poems such as those written by Charles Baudelaire have never gained wide popularity. A reader faced with a prose paragraph expects a reasoned utterance, a logical progression of ideas from the first to the last sentence. The poetic format allows Carver the freedom to use exclamations, interjections, incomplete sentences, neologisms, allusions, abrupt changes of subject, or whatever else he wishes. Here are the first four lines of "In the Lobby of the Hotel del Mayo":

> The girl in the lobby reading a leather-bound book.
> The man in the lobby using a broom.
> The boy in the lobby watering plants.
> The desk clerk looking at his nails.

These fragments would seem surrealistic in a straight prose paragraph; such prose might remind one of the experimental writing of Gertrude Stein. An arrangement in lines like those of a traditional poem, however, prepares the reader to approach the words in a different way.

One of the most interesting poems in *Ultramarine* consists entirely of short fragments describing an old car that Carver once owned—or that once owned Carver.

> The car with a cracked windshield.
> The car that threw a rod.
> The car without brakes.
> The car with a faulty U-joint.
> The car with a hole in its radiator.
> The car I picked peaches for.

The poem continues in this vein for forty-four more lines and ends with the words "My car." By the time the reader finishes the poem, he or she has formed a re-

markably complete picture not only of the car, but also of Carver's life and state of mind over the long period during which he was chained to this horrible automobile. It is characteristic of Carver to take his imagery from the external world rather than search for it in his own memory. There seems to be a Japanese influence here, perhaps by way of his favorite poet, William Carlos Williams. Like many of the poems in *Ultramarine*, "The Car" deals with themes of alcoholism, debt, meaningless work, domestic unhappiness, and the longing for escape. As always, there is also a note of unconquerable humor even in this Job-like litany of despair.

There is, however, a slightly different note, a slightly different perspective. In most of these poems, Carver is now talking about the past. Life has improved for him. He has achieved recognition. He is earning some money and not having to do it with a mop or a broom. He has quit drinking. Perhaps most significantly, *Ultramarine* is dedicated to Gallagher, a fellow writer and evidently a real soul mate, someone who would be with him for the rest of his life.

"NyQuil" is one of the poems in which Carver remembers his nightmare with alcohol. NyQuil is a well-known cold medicine, but Carver was doggedly drinking it as a substitute for liquor. An acquaintance, he says, was similarly trying to break his addiction to Scotch whiskey by drinking mouthwash by the case. This externalization or projection of feelings is a common characteristic of Carver's writing—both in his poems and in his short stories. The image of a man drinking NyQuil by the tumblerful gives the reader a vivid conception of the depth of Carver's addiction to alcohol.

"Jean's TV" is another poem in which an external object serves as an extended metaphor. A former girlfriend and drinking companion named Jean calls to ask when he plans to return the black-and-white television set she had left with him when she moved out. He hems and haws until the reader finally understands: He must have sold it a long time ago to buy liquor. Carver has confessed in interviews that he was capable of doing almost anything in his drinking days; he was also apparently unusually susceptible to feelings of remorse.

In "The Possible," he talks about another former

drinking companion, this one a fellow college teacher, and makes the following interesting statement about his many years of teaching: "I was a stranger,/ and an impostor, even to myself." "Where They'd Lived" is among the poems that deal with his unhappy marriage. Like most of the poems collected in this volume, these two pieces seem to be looking back at a receding past.

One new theme appears quite prominently among the poems collected in *Ultramarine*, the book that established Carver's reputation as a poet. It is the theme of unexpected death. "Egress" tells of a man who "fell dead/ one night after dinner, after talking over some business deal." "Powder-Monkey" is the story of a coworker who is killed in a head-on collision with a logging truck. In "An Account," a friend dies of a heart attack while watching the television serial *Hill Street Blues* (1981-1987). In each of these poems, Carver seems stunned. "What does this mean?" he seems to be asking the reader. "How can this happen?"

Somehow the black shadow of death makes Carver's message to the world suddenly stand out bright and clear. Life itself is beautiful in any aspect. The human tragedy and the human comedy are two sides of the same coin. Drinking, toiling, fighting, and lying to the landlords and the bill collectors are all a part of life, and consequently they all contain their own weird beauty. Clearly, Carver was experiencing strong premonitions of his own approaching death.

A NEW PATH TO THE WATERFALL

Carver finished *A New Path to the Waterfall* shortly before he died of lung cancer. The title of the book is taken from one of the poems in the volume, "Looking for Work." The speaker dreams that he is out fishing: "Suddenly, I find a new path/ to the waterfall." His wife wakes him up, however, and tells him that he must go out and find a job. The themes of unhappy marriage, responsibilities, shortage of cash, and a desire to escape to nature are still here, even though Carver's troubles were at this point only ghosts of the past. One of the most harrowing poems in the book is "Miracle," in which he matter-of-factly and in excruciating detail describes the aftermath of his second bankruptcy proceeding. On the way home on the airplane, his wife turns in her seat and begins hitting him in the face with clenched fists.

> All the while his head is pummeled,
> buffeted back and forth, her fists falling
> against his ear, his lips, his jaw, he protects
> his whiskey.

The shadow of death is the subject that dominates this last collection of Carver's poetry. What he sensed intuitively in *Ultramarine* has become an unblinking reality. Early in his career, he had chosen to write short stories and short poems because his struggle to support a family left him no time to contemplate larger projects; ironically, now that he had leisure and a certain amount of financial security, death was pressing him even harder than the bosses and bill collectors of old. In September, 1987, Carver, a heavy cigarette smoker for many years, was diagnosed with lung cancer. Two-thirds of his left lung was removed, but the cancer recurred as a brain tumor in March of the following year. He underwent seven weeks of full-brain radiation; however, by early June, the doctors found tumors in his lungs again. He knew he had only a short time left to live.

Some of Carver's last poems are not only his most moving but also his most successful in terms of realizing his artistic aims. "Poems" reveals how he understood his creative process. His poems "came to him," and he wrote them down as if he had heard them whispered in his ear. Frequently they came to him in the form of dreams, as was the case with "Looking for Work." He was never satisfied with the original versions of his poems, however, and he polished them painstakingly for a long time before letting them out of his hands. At their best, these poems seem to have no need for rhyme or meter or any of the other paraphernalia of conventional poetry. His method might be described as functionalism: The thought finds its own form, so that thought and form seem molded to each other. "Through the Boughs" comes close to perfection in this style of poetic composition.

> Down below the window, on the deck, some ragged-
> looking
> birds gather at the feeder. . . .
> The sky stays dark all day, the wind is from the west and
> won't stop blowing. . . . Give me your hand for a time.
> Hold on

to mine. That's right, yes. Squeeze hard. Time was we thought we had time on our side. *Time was, time was,* those ragged birds cry.

These last poems by Carver are almost the royal road to understanding what many modern poets have been trying to do. They have abandoned rhyme and meter. They have abandoned what used to be called poetic diction. They write in a conversational style. They attempt to allow the poetic message to dictate the poem's own unique form. No one has expressed the essential notion behind modern poetry better than the great American thinker Ralph Waldo Emerson, who said in his essay "The Poet" that "For it is not metres, but a metre-making argument that makes a poem—a thought so passionate and alive that like the spirit of a plant or an animal it has an architecture of its own, and adorns nature with a new thing."

Ironically, the circumstances that originally kept Carver from writing became the principal material of much of his poetry and fiction. His recognition of this fact may partially explain the wry humor found in many of his most doleful poems. Drinking bouts, hangovers, guilt, divorce, and debt were recurring themes of his stories and poems. He recognized that even his own terminal illness was a powerful subject for his poetry. With characteristic naïveté and improvidence, Carver had chosen precisely the two literary forms that are hardest to sell and pay the least money when they do sell—poetry and short stories. These choices automatically condemned him to long years of poverty, with all the problems that accompanied it. (Gardner had not warned Carver and his classmates of this reality when he advised them to forget about the "slicks" and concentrate on the "little" magazines, "where the best fiction in the country was being published, and all of the poetry.") Even had he lived longer, Carver would have had a hard time making a living as a writer: He was dependent on the various disguised forms of charity that are the creative writer's lot in the age of television.

"Proposal," "Cherish," "Gravy," "No Need," and "After-Glow" all confront the imminence of death. "What the Doctor Said," in which Carver relates how a doctor informed him that he had at least thirty-two

malignant nodules on one lung and was doomed, still is tinged with that ineradicable Carver humor, his most endearing quality. Though he has no resolutions or epiphanies to offer the reader, his invincible spirit, his truthfulness and dedication, and his admirable humanity are resolution and epiphany in themselves.

Carver had started as a country yokel in a rocky region whose literary roots did not run deep; he had made the painful climb from ignorance to enlightenment, from inarticulate frustration to masterful eloquence, from anonymity to fame. Many of his poems and stories are confessions of his sins, but readers have forgiven him because they recognize in him their own faults as well as some of their virtues. He had more than mere talent with words: He had the extra quality of soul that only great writers possess. He saw literature not as a stylish game but as the most important job a person can do. When he died on the morning of August 2, 1988, his works were being read in twenty different languages, and he has a better chance of being remembered for the next few centuries than do most of his contemporaries. His career was a striking illustration of what Emerson meant when he said in "The Poet," "Thou must pass for a fool and a churl for a long season. This is the screen and sheath in which Pan has protected his well-beloved flower. . . . and though thou shouldst walk the world over, thou shalt not be able to find a condition inopportune or ignoble."

OTHER MAJOR WORKS

SHORT FICTION: *Put Yourself in My Shoes*, 1974; *Will You Please Be Quiet, Please?*, 1976; *Furious Seasons, and Other Stories*, 1977; *What We Talk About When We Talk About Love*, 1981; *Cathedral*, 1983; *Elephant, and Other Stories*, 1988; *Where I'm Calling From*, 1988; *Short Cuts: Selected Stories*, 1993.

SCREENPLAY: *Dostoevsky*, 1985.

EDITED TEXT: *American Short Story Masterpieces*, 1987 (with Tom Jenks).

MISCELLANEOUS: *Fires: Essays, Poems, Stories*, 1983; *No Heroics, Please: Uncollected Writings*, 1991 (revised and expanded as *Call If You Need Me: The Uncollected Fiction and Prose*, 2000).

BIBLIOGRAPHY

Adelman, Bob, and Tess Gallagher. *Carver Country: The World of Raymond Carver*. Introduction by Gallagher. New York: Charles Scribner's Sons, 1990. Produced in the spirit of a photographic essay, this book contains excellent photographs of Carver, his relatives, people who served as inspirations for characters in his stories, and places that were important in his life and work. The photographs are accompanied by excerpts from Carver's stories and poems.

Carver, Maryann Burk. *What It Used to Be Like: A Portrait of My Marriage to Raymond Carver*. New York: St. Martin's Press, 2006. Maryann Burk Carver recounts her tumultuous twenty-five-year marriage to Raymond Carver.

Carver, Raymond. Interviews. *Conversations with Raymond Carver*. Edited by Marshall Bruce Gentry and William L. Stull. Jackson: University Press of Mississippi, 1990. A wide-ranging collection of interviews covering Carver's career from the early 1980's until just before his death.

Gallagher, Tess. Introduction to *A New Path to the Waterfall*, by Raymond Carver. New York: Atlantic Monthly Press, 1989. The collection in which this essay appears, a collection of Carver's last poems, includes some moving reflections on his life and values as he faced the fact that he was dying of cancer. The writer of the informative and moving introduction is the person who knew him best, the poet Gallagher, who lived with him for many years and was with him at the time of his death.

Halpert, Sam, ed. *Raymond Carver: An Oral Biography*. Iowa City: University of Iowa Press, 1995. An expanded edition of a collection of conversations originally published in 1991 as *When We Talk About Raymond Carver*. Includes contributions from Carver's first wife, his daughter, an early writing instructor, and some of his lifetime friends.

Kleppe, Sandra Lee, and Robert Miltner, eds. *New Paths to Raymond Carver: Critical Essays on His Life, Fiction, and Poetry*. Columbia: University of South Carolina Press, 2008. This collection has a number of essays on his poetry as well as Tess Gallagher's introduction to the Japanese edition of *Ultramarine*.

Kuzma, Greg. "*Ultramarine*: Poems That Almost Stop the Heart." *Michigan Quarterly Review* 27 (Spring, 1988): 355-363. In her introduction to *A New Path to the Waterfall*, Tess Gallagher calls Kuzma's review of *Ultramarine* "the most astute essay on [Carver's] poetry."

Saltzman, Arthur M. *Understanding Raymond Carver*. Columbia: University of South Carolina Press, 1988. A short overview of Carver's life and work with the emphasis on Carver's short stories and one chapter devoted to his poetry. Contains a valuable bibliography of works by and about Carver.

Sklenicka, Carol. *Raymond Carver: A Writer's Life*. New York: Scribner, 2009. Biography of Carver that looks at his life and works. Contains analyses of *Ultramarine* and *A New Path to the Waterfall*.

Stull, William L., and Maureen P. Carroll, eds. *Remembering Ray: A Composite Biography of Raymond Carver*. Santa Barbara, Calif.: Capra Press, 1993. Though not a formal biography, this collection of essays covers Carver's working-class origins, his troubled first marriage, his battle with alcoholism, his teaching style, and his ultimate happiness until his death from cancer.

Bill Delaney

TURNER CASSITY

Born: Jackson, Mississippi; January 12, 1929
Died: Atlanta, Georgia; July 26, 2009

PRINCIPAL POETRY

Watchboy, What of the Night?, 1966
"The Airship Boys in Africa," 1970
Silver Out of Shanghai, 1973
Steeplejacks in Babel, 1973
Yellow for Peril, Black for Beautiful: Poems and a Play, 1975
The Defense of the Sugar Islands: A Recruiting Poster, 1979
Keys to Mayerling, 1983
The Airship Boys in Africa: A Dramatic Narrative in Twelve Parts, 1984

*The Book of Alna: A Narrative of the Mormon
    Wars*, 1985
Hurricane Lamp, 1986
Lessons, 1987 (with R. L. Barth)
Between the Chains, 1991
The Destructive Element: New and Selected Poems,
    1998
No Second Eden, 2002
Devils and Islands, 2007

OTHER LITERARY FORMS

While primarily a poet, Turner Cassity also wrote several uncollected short stories, a poetic drama (*Men of the Great Man*, contained in *Yellow for Peril, Black for Beautiful*), and an essay on the cataloging of periodicals, "Gutenberg as Card Shark," published in *The Academic Library: Essays in Honor of Guy R. Lyle* (1974).

ACHIEVEMENTS

Perhaps because of its traditional form, Turner Cassity's poetry has received less attention than it deserves. Cassity won the Blumenthal-Leviton-Blonder Prize for poetry in 1966, the Levinson Prize from the Poetry Foundation in 1971, the Michael Braude Award from the American Academy of Arts and Letters in 1993, and a Georgia Author of the Year Award for *Devils and Islands* from the Georgia Writers Association in 2007. He also was the recipient of a National Endowment for the Arts grant in 1980 and an Ingram Merrill Foundation Award in 1991. In 2008, the West Chester Poetry Conference included a "Tribute to Turner Cassity" in its program.

Although Cassity had a large group of supporters, he had little influence on the course of contemporary writing, except perhaps as a precursor of the New Formalist school. Further attention to Cassity's work should continue to reveal both the significance of his refusal to write a less traditional, more accessible type of poetry, and the importance of his unique and challenging view, a view that rewards even as it frustrates the reader's expectations of what contemporary poetry should be.

BIOGRAPHY

Turner Cassity was born Allen Turner Cassity in Jackson, Mississippi. His father, who died when Cas-

sity was four, was in the sawmill business; his mother was a violinist and his grandmother a pianist in silent-film theaters. The family moved to Forrest, Mississippi, in 1933 and later back to Jackson, where Cassity attended Bailey Junior High School and was graduated from Central High School. Cassity was graduated from Millsaps College with a B.A. in 1951 and from Stanford University with an M.A. in English in 1952. At Stanford, he studied poetry with Yvor Winters in a program that he likens to "the strict technical training a musician would get at a good conservatory."

Cassity was drafted in 1952 during the Korean War and spent the two years of his duty in Puerto Rico, an experience that provides the basis for his sequence *The Defense of the Sugar Islands*. He received an M.S. in library science from Columbia University in 1956 and served as an assistant librarian at the Jackson Municipal Library for 1957-1958 and for part of 1961. From 1959 to 1961, Cassity was an assistant librarian for the Transvaal Provincial Library in Pretoria, South Africa. Observations from his stay in Pretoria and Johannesburg frequently appear in his poems. In 1962, Cassity accepted a job at the Emory University Library in Atlanta, where he remained until his retirement in 1991.

Cassity's travels took him to the desert and the tropics, and he spent much time in California. He referred to his poems as "tropical pastorals," but this description conceals the sense of amusement and horror with which many of his speakers perceive the past. Cassity also described himself as "a burgher" in temperament and conviction, and this label is also somewhat misleading, for his poems seldom reveal a complacent attitude; his scrutiny of colonialism, while not obviously polemical, often reveals the flaws inherent in the underlying psychology of the colonist more than do more tendentious poems. Cassity died in Atlanta, Georgia, on July 26, 2009.

ANALYSIS

Detractors, and occasionally even champions, of Turner Cassity's verse argue that while technically polished, the poems are often unrewardingly distant or difficult, and that although the poet's formal talent was considerable, his range was somewhat limited. A closer reading of Cassity's work as a whole, however, reveals the complexity to be a necessary outgrowth of the poet's vision—not merely cleverness for its own sake—and the limited scope to be a false modesty. The wealth of allusion never makes the writing pedantic or pretentious; instead it reflects the poet's refusal to adopt a single, narrow perspective as his guide.

Cassity wrote terse, elliptical poems in unfashionably strict metrical form. For Cassity, the discipline of writing in meter and rhyme was prerequisite to his creative process: "without it, nothing comes into my head." However, while traditional, his verse avoids monotony and is typically supple and lively. His poems often include exotic settings or historical figures, juxtaposing them to the tawdriness of the familiar modern world. The combination of this irony with the restrained meter and diction yields a body of poetry that is formal and wittily aloof; the polish and urbanity, however, do not conceal the poet's ongoing search for a deliverance from decay and loss. Ultimately, the poet returns to his medium, language, and to his craftsmanship to find this deliverance, and in this sense Cassity was truly modern—in contrast to many contemporary poets, who, though severing ties with traditional form, fail to understand the relationship of past to present and their role in defining that relationship.

Clearly, Cassity was to some extent an heir of earlier modern poets writing in traditional modes, especially of Winters, with whom Cassity studied; many critics have also noted similarities between Cassity's work and that of W. H. Auden, Wallace Stevens, and Robert Frost. Equally evident, though, is the deft, colloquial irony of French post-Symbolists such as Jules Laforgue, and the formal control, epigrammatic wit, and social concern of eighteenth century poetry, particularly that of Alexander Pope. Still, the density of Cassity's allusions and the complexity of his contrasts—past and present, great and trivial, historical and personal—distinguish his writing from that of the traditional poet.

The growing acceptance of Cassity's terse, restrained style has led to a greater appreciation of his poetry; still, his work has yet to receive a full, comprehensive critical account. Perhaps only when the historicity of what is now called contemporary poetry becomes clear will it be possible to understand the unique merit of Cassity's contribution. In the meantime, his poetry may gradually become for the general reader less of a curiosity and more of a hallmark of a complex and significant response to the modern age.

"Seven Destinations of Mayerling"

The fact that Cassity frequently juxtaposes the noteworthy with the mundane may in part account for his being labeled a satirist. Such a strategy, however, is a means more of evaluating the past than of ridiculing the present, a means of understanding change and loss. The poem "Seven Destinations of Mayerling," for example, relocates the castle of a German baron's suicide/murder to seven sites: Arizona (across from the London Bridge, which was actually relocated there), Orlando (another Disney World), Dallas (the Budapest Hymnbook Depository), Nashville (an attraction at the Grand Ol' Opry), Milwaukee (a beer hall), Tokyo (a brothel), and Montana (a hunting lodge). Cassity's purpose here, in spite of his witty and acerbic parodies, is not to lament the banality of modern culture, for the castle, like Europe itself, is no holy relic to be venerated. Rather, by juxtaposing the contrasting and even conflicting worlds, the poet simultaneously depicts the difficulty of living outside time and change, and the capacity of the imagination, wit, poetic language, and form to create an amusement, which itself becomes the sought-after haven, the refuge.

"Gutenberg as Card Shark"

A key to Cassity's attitude toward the past may be found in his essay "Gutenberg as Card Shark," an essay primarily about the cataloging of periodicals. Cassity criticizes the tendency of librarians to efface the traces of a periodical's original state (such as deleting the advertisements from magazines); he finds these indexes of the ephemeral nature of the publication often more revealing of the time than the verbal text itself, and points out that an emphasis on the more academic nature of the publication simplifies and hence falsifies the text's reality. Behind this priority lies the preference for the genuine though ephemeral artifact (which may in fact be genuine because it is ephemeral) over the self-consciously didactic and hence derivative and unreal artwork. The article concludes: "The Gutenberg Bible was no doubt a towering achievement, but if we could retrieve entire the cultural environment of those printed playing cards which preceded it, who would not trade Scripture away?"

WATCHBOY, WHAT OF THE NIGHT?

Cassity's first collection, *Watchboy, What of the Night?*, like most of his works, is divided into several sections. The first section, "Rudiments of Tropics," consists primarily of scenes and recollections from such places as Indochina and Haiti. These poems reflect on change, chance, and loss, as in "La Petite Tonkinoise," a monologue by a Vietnamese prostitute who is an object of exploitation but also the force that controls the colonizer: "Yet I and wheel, meek where your glance is hurled,/ Combined, were Fortune, Empress of the World." The second section, "Oom-Pah for Oom Paul," extends the analysis of imperialism to South Africa. In "Johannesburg Requiem," the blacks lament a social, linguistic, and economic structure that is not theirs but which they must serve.

The section "In the Laagers of Burgherdom" celebrates with deft irony the comforts of kitsch: Café musicians complain of having to play the same tunes repeatedly (though they do have steady employment), heaven is depicted as a Hollywood production number, lovers are compared to the Katzenjammer Kids, and elderly ladies find "Grace at the Atlanta Fox" (an art deco film theater in the style of a Turkish mosque).

"THE AIRSHIP BOYS IN AFRICA"

The forty-page poem "The Airship Boys in Africa," published in *Poetry* in 1970, is dedicated "To the Crabbes: George and Buster" (a reference to the eccentric early nineteenth century poet who described simple village life in eighteenth century couplets and to the swimmer/actor hero of Tarzan films). Here again Cassity relies on an urbane mixture of kitsch and culture, in this instance to convey the failure that results when one culture attempts to impose itself on another for mere gain; the story depicts the doomed flight of a German Zeppelin in World War I to secure territory in Africa. Interweaving past with present, reality with mirage, the poet presents a wry but frightening vision. The heroism of the German crew, like their airship, is finally deflated, their mission pointless. The first chapter describes a Namibian who, talking and thinking in clicks, watches the airship crash; the poem then, in the in medias res fashion of epics, reverts to the beginning of the story and follows the crew on their mission. The final chapter describes the survivors searching for the last remaining German stronghold, one of them falling back and clicking his tongue against his teeth. This unexpected union of conqueror with conquered is repeated in the epitaph, a conclusion with nightmarish overtones of the Flying Dutchman legend:

> Full throttle low above the high savannah;
> Game running into, out of pointed shadow.
> Herr, between drummed earth and silent heaven,
> We pursue a shade which is ourselves.

Cassity's preoccupation with kitsch, as represented here and in other works, signifies neither an amused cynicism nor a predilection for form over content but an awareness of the liberating power of coming to terms with one's own culture. While admiring its technical virtuosity, Donald Davie has criticized "The Airship Boys in Africa" for what he calls a tendency toward campiness, in which the poet seeks "to always astonish, outsmart, upstage any conceivable reader." Though characterized by cleverness and wit, Cassity's poems do not lack a seriousness or a sincerity, nor are they marred by what Davie calls a lack of shapeliness; rather, they assume a shape that, while unexpected or startling, is in fact the only shape that can convey the poet's meaning. The reference to Buster Crabbe, for example, reminds the reader of the naïve and ethnocentric assumptions of the Hollywood film about civilization and savagery, progress and technology. However, whereas the naïveté of the Hollywood production obscures one's awareness of reality, so can culture—the failed Parsifal myth, the Germanic heroic code—stifle with its insistence on the reenactment of the past.

In a later poem in *Hurricane Lamp*, "Advice to King Lear," the poet describes a San Antonio theater with seats on one side of a river and a stage on the other side. During a production of *King Lear*, as the weather on the stage grows more and more threatening (thanks to the arbitrary aid of wind machines) and as Lear's situation becomes increasingly tragic, a boat passes between the stage and the audience, and the speaker admonishes the protagonist, "Get on the boat, Old Man, and go to summer." The very tackiness of the theatrical setup allows the audience to free itself from its dependence on illusion and from its slavery to the single prescribed ending. In "The Airship Boys in Africa," the poet's exposing of the tawdriness of the Teutonic myth undermines the repressive nature not only of fascism but also of the unquestioning allegiance to myth and culture.

SILVER OUT OF SHANGHAI

Even more than "The Airship Boys in Africa," Cassity's narrative poem *Silver Out of Shanghai: A Scenario for Josef von Sternberg, Featuring Wicked Nobles, a Depraved Religious, Wayfoong, Princess Ida, the China Clipper, and Resurrection Lily, with a Supporting Cast of Old Hands, Merchant Seamen, Sikhs, Imperial Marines, and Persons in Blue*, as its full title indicates, builds a poetic world out of the soundstage exoticism of such films as *Shanghai Express* (1932). Ostensibly, the story describes the attempt of a wealthy British merchant, Sir V. M. Grayburn, to smuggle silver out of Shanghai without causing a drop in silver prices; he hires a South African engineer to suggest that the ship carries gold instead, but his rivals have the ship sunk, and a last-minute salvage effort by the engineer saves the day, or at least the silver. While overtly mocking the heroics of the adventure genre, with its exaggerated characterizations, its moral chiaroscuro, and its contrived resolution, *Silver Out of Shanghai* also attacks the attempt of the colonialist to create, through manipulation, a world without change. As a character remarks to Grayburn,

> "Oh, V., you've missed the point. It's *temporary*.
> Daddy thought the Boxer Wars would end it;
> Then the Straits.
> . . . .
>   The rest of us
> Know better, Take that Afrikaaner boy
> He knows a country has to be reconquered
> Day by day.

STEEPLEJACKS IN BABEL

While the narrative of *Silver Out of Shanghai*, if not its purpose, is clear, the form of *Steeplejacks in Babel* is much more perplexing, primarily because of the elliptical nature of the diction and the allusions. Here, as elsewhere, the poet dissects the fascist and colonialist mentalities, but in several poems, he treats more sympathetically the colonialist as displaced person, particularly in "Two Hymns" ("The Afrikaaner in the Argentine" and "Confederates in Brazil"). Technically, the

poems of *Steeplejacks in Babel* are among Cassity's tersest and densest; as Richard Johnson has observed, the poet has removed "all but the essentials." The strictures of brevity, along with the formal discipline exacted by the rhymed couplets of iambic pentameter, create a poetry whose knowledge comes from its form and not the reverse. The first and last poems, "What the Sirens Sang" and "Cartography Is an Inexact Science," underscore this characteristic truth.

THE DEFENSE OF THE SUGAR ISLANDS

The Defense of the Sugar Islands marks a significant change in Cassity's writing; these poems, based on his experience as a soldier in Puerto Rico during the Korean War, are first-person accounts of events and memories (though in a sense these poems are no more or less autobiographical than any other of his poems, and one need not know the poet's life to understand the poems). From musing on his past, the speaker comes to realize and rejoice in his own fragility: "Those airs, without their scouring sand, seem more,/ Not less, sand's vessel set to measure time." In "A Walk with a Zombie" (another reference to a kitschy Hollywood film), the speaker contrasts himself as rememberer with a mummified Pharaoh: "If in my eyes the light is less,/ Yours, Pharaoh, have not looked on loss/ As mine have looked"; through memory and imagination, he can ". . . sustain/ One blood unmummied: living wound/ Of armless mills that mock the wind,/ Of crystal words I cannot say,/ Of bladed cane I cannot see."

HURRICANE LAMP

Hurricane Lamp returns to the less obviously reflective style of the earlier works, but it, too, is a progression forward, although a subtle one. The disciplined meters and richly textured allusions again contrast with the wit and ironic distance of the speaker. Here, however, the speaker begins to adopt a more colloquial diction and a less reserved stance, particularly in such poems as "Berolina Demodee" and "A Dialogue with the Bride of Godzilla."

"MAINSTREAMING" AND "SOLDIERS OF ORANGE"

In the mid-1980's, Cassity began to move away from the terse formality of his short lyrics in a series of medium-length poems (about one hundred lines long), conversational poems that are more relaxed in meter and tone than longer narratives but equally rich in juxtaposition of past and present. "Mainstreaming" and "Soldiers of Orange" are, with *The Defense of the Sugar Islands*, among Cassity's few directly autobiographical poems: "Mainstreaming" recounts the experience of soldiers assigned to work with a unit of mentally defective draftees; "Soldiers of Orange" blends memories of a meeting with a former girlfriend and her daughter, including an encounter with Dutch colonial soldiers, with present-day observations of a drive through a Louisiana that has been colonized by Vietnamese refugees.

THE DESTRUCTIVE ELEMENT

The Destructive Element contains little in the way of a new mode or vein of work for Cassity, whose style remains constant and therefore recognizable and distinctive. Clearly, he had found something that worked and continued to do it. The poems run the gamut from clear, witty, and brief epigrams to complex, allusion-laden meditative poems. The poet's distinctive mix of philosophical speculation, irony, nose-thumbing at current pieties, and complex wordplay is a constant throughout this book. However, while he remains firmly placed in the New Formalist movement, several of his poems here are also frankly humorous and deliberately ornamental, displaying a cultivated idiosyncrasy.

Cassity was, at heart, a satirist, and while his work displays hard-bitten formalism and moral seriousness, the best satirists care deeply about their subjects, and humor is their weapon of choice for assailing human shortcoming. His passion comes clear with his use of emphatic tone and acute wit, evident in "Sitting Behind Ben-Hur."

> I've a tan. I look at backs a lot. I deeply understand teamwork.
> I live in filth. Was I fastidious
> When I was free? Here sharks will have us;
> It's not as though elsewhere there are not jackals.
> Bear up. Hand and heart grow calloused.

While the persona's rationalizations of the situation are amusing, it captures his awful resignation to fate and, by extension, people's immense capacity for endurance, even as it begs the question, at what cost?

Cassity's poetry in this volume is also frequently fun, using linguistic delight—witness "Vegetarian Mary

and the Venus Flytrap" and "Never Use a Stock Ticker Without a Geiger Counter"—and playful scenarios.

> My young grandfather, for the me of four,
> Blew smoke rings. I, these long years more,
> Without much gift, can, nonetheless
> Redeem my breath from utter shapelessness.

His life of travels acted as a springboard for many of the poems in *The Destructive Element*. His years in Africa, military service in the Caribbean, and frequent jaunts across the globe form what he calls his "colonial pastorals." He analyzes how history and place intersect, and in turn produces poems that serve as a moralistic consideration on the conflict between beauty and practicality, and the many ironies that result from this conflict. He examines a place in its natural state in order to uncover the ironic contrast after it has been changed by technology and use—that is, once it has been colonized.

NO SECOND EDEN

The primary theme of the forty-four poems in *No Second Eden* is self-delusion. Using irony to support laser-like views of people's abilities to deceive themselves, the personae of these poems startle and amuse readers in Cassity's distinctive style. The book is dedicated to his mother, who passed away in 1999 at the age of ninety-six, and it bears an epigram on self-knowledge by Ivy Compton-Burnett, one of the poet's favorite writers.

Cassity derived poetic subjects from his reading, the arts, and the news headlines. Nothing was too large or too small to catch his attention when it related to the topic of pride, the major force behind self-deception. In this collection, to illustrate the topic, Cassity writes on the tenuousness of success in "J. P. Morgan," and on odd forms of beauty as in "Sensitivity Training: The Safecracker."

The poems of *No Second Eden* are metrical, and Cassity's trademark rhymed couplet is well in evidence, functioning additionally to advance the book's title theme of no second chances or new opportunities for redemption. In "WTC," on the collapse of the World Trade Center Towers in 2001, and "A Diamond Is Forever," Cassity tackles world politics, while in "Hanging On," he writes of suicide, and in " Smile

Please," the speaker is a photographer who takes pictures at lynchings. The point of the poem is to show how the photographer is dehumanized by his awareness of the inhumanity his job requires him to experience. The trajectory of time is depicted as relentless and unforgiving, providing a "little mockery, a fit rebuke" to the everyday in "Adam with a Garden Hose," whose Eden is merely a cactus garden that bears nothing more than the gardener's futile effort to be God-like.

DEVILS AND ISLANDS

A majority of the thirty-nine poems in *Devils and Islands* complement "Inward Turned, Outward Bound," the new poems in *The Destructive Element*. The dominant themes are fashion, photography, music, flight, politics, fiction, and Christianity, and Cassity uses three forms consistently: the couplet, the quatrain, and the blank verse lyric. These forms showcase his wit, ability with wordplay, and his wry sense of humor. For example, "The Last Elevator Operator, Mr. Otis Regrets" plays off two allusions, the first to the Otis elevator and the second to the Cole Porter show tune from 1934, "Miss Otis Regrets," which tells the story of a wealthy lady who kills her lover after he abandons her. The famous refrain to this song, invoked here to suggest the elevator man is obsolete, is "Miss Otis regrets she's unable to lunch today" (because she had been hanged the day before for murder). The last elevator operator ponders how people could possibly think his job was "dull" when he had the chance to wear a uniform reminiscent of the cadets in the French military academy, Saint-Cyr, and to observe people worthy of the novels and stories of Thomas Mann, whose unfinished comic novel, *Bekenntnisse des Hochstaplers Felix Krull: Der Memoiren erster Teil* (1954; *Confessions of Felix Krull, Confidence Man: The Early Years*, 1955), is directly mentioned. The elevator serves as a kind of island for a lost, more elegant past, which has given way to the devil of self-service and advanced technologies that rendered the operator unnecessary.

The title of the book is taken from "Robinson Crusoe to Capt. Dreyfus," which begins "All islands are the Devil's in a sense." The poem develops the metaphor of spatial exile as spiritual isolation, comparing Daniel Defoe's 1719 character, Robinson Crusoe, with Alfred Dreyfus, the Alsatian captain in the French army who

was falsely accused of treason and exiled to Devil's Island in the 1890's. In a variety of ways, the poet visits the theme of isolation as it is mapped across diverging experiences and ideologies. Two poems, in particular, are representative of the major contribution *Devils and Islands* makes in Cassity's oeuvre: "Production Values" and "Afterward."

In the lyric poem "Production Values," the idea of progress is tested against time. After posing the question "What is it we accept as real?" in the first line, the speaker moves deftly through comparisons of screen images from early films to those on computer screens, Hitler to Oedipus, Shakespearean boy actors who dressed as girls to actors in minstrel shows, ending with a comparison of humans to clones. The forty-one-line poem closes with these lines:

> But Jekyll knows that Hyde is there,
> And Hyde knows it is not makeup
> By which in him we see ourselves.

These lines refer to Robert Louis Stevenson's 1886 novel, *The Strange Case of Dr. Jekyll and Mr. Hyde*, in which the same man is tortured by dueling good and evil personalities. Given that societies often measure their worth by what they produce, "Production Values" takes aim, through its binary pairings of unusual subjects, at things that are produced by people and how they are valued, frequently without context or reflection on their ethical implications.

"Afterward" is a couplet poem of twelve stanzas about the resurrection of Jesus Christ and his appearance a few days later to his disciples at Emmaus. The poem begins with a close reading of the biblical passages, highlighting the rolling away of the stone, and quickly shifts to the theme of doubt. Taking for granted that the Resurrection is both an act of faith and a logical paradox, the speaker places himself in the position of Thomas, who had to put his hand into Jesus's side to believe it was really him during the dinner at Emmaus. Because Jesus died to absolve people of their sins, he beat the devil, and doubt leaves the doubter isolated on a spiritual island. The speaker takes stock of the "evidence" in these lines: ". . . To distrust the hand/ Thrust in the side is to demand/ Proof of so high a standard, sense/ Plus Second Sight could not convince./ 'The evidence of things not seen'/ Is what leap of faith has been,/ But notice 'evidence' is still/ How we describe it . . ." The easy flow of these lines and the familiarity of the story makes this poem's summary of what Jesus did before the Ascension startlingly clear and hopeful: "Eats; promises and is seen no more."

BIBLIOGRAPHY

Ash, John. "A Brash Yankee and a Southern Dandy." Review of *Hurricane Lamp*. *The New York Times Book Review*, April 20, 1986, p. 19. Appreciates this work's juxtaposition of the ordinary and the exotic. Remarks that Cassity's insistence on formality makes for rigid and monotonous reading, but his poetry is never self-indulgent or maudlin. Comments that Cassity, at his best, combines "elegance with an attractive pungency."

Barth, R. L., Susan Barth, and Charles Gullans. *A Bibliography of the Published Works of Turner Cassity, 1952-1987*. Florence, Ky.: Author, 1988. Useful compendium of Cassity's titles.

Flint, R. W. "Exiles from Olympus." *Parnassus: Poetry in Review* 5 (Spring/Summer, 1977): 97-107. Reviews Cassity's works, in particular *Yellow for Peril, Black for Beautiful*, and *Steeplejacks in Babel*. Sympathetic to Cassity in that Flint values his taciturnity and declares him a poet to watch. Quotes from *Watchboy, What of the Night?* and compares his work to Nadine Gordimer's uncompromising style.

Gioia, Dana. "Poetry and the Fine Presses." *Hudson Review* 35 (Autumn, 1982): 438-498. Gives extravagant praise to Cassity by calling him the "most brilliantly eccentric poet in America." Although Gioia clearly enjoys Cassity's poetry, he regrets how "few of his poems really show all he is capable of." Notes that *The Defense of the Sugar Islands* was a real breakthrough for Cassity, that his full range of talents came into being in these poems, which have as much emotional and intellectual force as technical virtuosity.

Steele, Timothy. "Curving to Foreign Harbors: Turner Cassity's *Defense of the Sugar Islands*." Review of *The Defense of the Sugar Islands*. *Southern Review* 17 (Winter, 1981): 205-213. Outlines the structure of the retrospective poem. Steele argues for the work's

success on balance but acknowledges some reservations, notably the "frequent density of Cassity's syntax" and the fact that important details are withheld.

Tillinghast, Richard. "Poems That Get Their Hands Dirty." *The New York Times Book Review*, December 18, 1991, p. 7. Compares Cassity's *Between the Chains* to Adrienne Rich's *An Atlas of the Difficult World: Poems, 1988-1991* (1991) and Philip Levine's *What Work Is* (1991).

Tuma, Keith. "Turner Cassity." In *American Poets Since World War II, Second Series*, edited by R. S. Gwynn. Vol. 102 in *Dictionary of Literary Biography*. Detroit: Gale Research, 1991. Provides a basic biography of Cassity and an analysis of his works.

Steven L. Hale; Philip K. Jason; Sarah Hilbert
Updated by Beverly Schneller

LORNA DEE CERVANTES

Born: San Francisco, California; August 6, 1954

PRINCIPAL POETRY

Emplumada, 1981
From the Cables of Genocide: Poems on Love and Hunger, 1991
Drive: The First Quartet, 2006

OTHER LITERARY FORMS

Nearly all the literary work of Lorna Dee Cervantes (sur-VAHN-tehz) is poetry. She was the founder and editor of Mango Publications, which published the literary review *Mango*, and she also founded and has edited the literary magazine *Red Dirt*.

ACHIEVEMENTS

Lorna Dee Cervantes's first collection of poems, *Emplumada*, won the American Book Award from the Before Columbus Foundation in 1982. Her second collection, *From the Cables of Genocide*, won the Paterson Poetry Prize and the Latino Literature Award and was nominated for a National Book Award in 1992. In 1995, she received the Lila Wallace-*Reader's Digest*

Writers' Award. *Drive* was nominated for a Pulitzer Prize in poetry and won the Balcones Poetry Prize (2006). Cervantes has also been named Outstanding Chicana Scholar by the National Association of Chicano Scholars.

BIOGRAPHY

Lorna Dee Cervantes was born in 1954 in San Francisco and moved to San Jose (the setting for several of her best-known poems) after her parents' divorce in 1959. Her ethnic identification is not only Mexican American but also Native American, and she draws on this dual heritage in her poetry. She began writing poetry at an early age and first came to notice reading "Refugee Ship" at a drama festival in Mexico City in 1974. Her poems began to appear in Chicano journals such as *Revista Chicano-Riquena* and *Latin American Literary Review*, and in 1981, the University of Pittsburgh Press published her first volume of poetry, *Emplumada*, to widespread praise.

Cervantes gained her B.A. from San Jose State University in 1984, studied for four years as a graduate student in the history of consciousness program at the University of California, Santa Cruz, and has taught creative writing at the University of Colorado at Boulder. In addition to her academic position, Cervantes has done a good deal of editorial work, encouraging other Chicano writers, and has read her poetry at numerous national and international literary festivals.

ANALYSIS

Lorna Dee Cervantes is one of the major Latina poetic voices writing in English, and at least half a dozen of her poems have been reprinted widely. Although she has written on a variety of topics, including a number of love poems, she is best known for those poems that define the situation for Mexican Americans at the end of the twentieth century, poems that are feminist and political. More than any other poet, Cervantes describes what it is like to live in two cultural worlds—or between them—and the tensions and difficulties such a limbo creates for a woman.

EMPLUMADA

Many of Cervantes's best-known poems were printed in her first collection, published in 1981. *Em-*

plumada immediately established Cervantes as a major voice in contemporary American poetry, and its best poems raised the themes and issues with which many women were struggling. Although her language is simple and direct, Cervantes uses a number of Spanish words and phrases (and includes a two-page "glossary" at the end of the book that translates them into English). What is most striking in the collection is its colorful imagery; the poems are filled with visuals of birds and flowers. For example, the collection's title, *Emplumada*, comes from the combination of two Spanish words: *emplumado*, meaning "feathered or in plumage, as in after molting," and *plumada*, a "pen flourish." The title thus implies both change and growth and the flourish of a pen. The two emerge in this collection in a woman defining her new self through her poetry. As she writes at the end of "Visions of Mexico While at a Writing Symposium in Port Townsend, Washington,"

> as pain sends seabirds south from the cold
> I come north
> to gather my feathers
> for quills.

Poet Lynette Seator has written that *Emplumada* contains "poetry that affirms Mexican-American identity as well as the identity of the poet as woman coming-of-age." Although this collection also contains love poems ("Café Solo," "The Body Braille"), the best poems ("Lots: I," "Lots: II," "Poema para los Californios Muertos") have larger feminist, ethnic, and historical subjects.

"REFUGEE SHIP"

"Refugee Ship" (from *Emplumada*) is the poem that first gained notice for Cervantes. It is a remarkable work for such a young poet, for its brief fourteen lines capture the feelings of many earlier immigrants caught between two cultures. The first stanza establishes her Latina identity and her link to her *abuelita* (grandmother). In the five lines of the second stanza, she describes her estrangement from her native culture in language and in name:

> Mama raised me without language.
> I'm orphaned from my Spanish name.
> The words are foreign, stumbling
> on my tongue. . . .

Even her physical appearance, she concludes in this stanza, looks alien: "I see in the mirror/ my reflection: bronzed skin, black/ hair." The four lines of the third and final stanza give the image of the title that so perfectly describes her situation and dilemma:

> I feel I am a captive
> aboard the refugee ship.
> The ship that will never dock.
> *El barco que nunca atraca.*

The third and fourth lines, which repeat the same phrase first in English and then Spanish, emphasize her estrangement, her sense not only of dislocation but also of being caught between two places, two lives, and never able to land or reside in either. "Refugee Ship" captures that feeling of estrangement for generations of immigrants to the United States, who were torn between two cultures and completely at home in neither.

"Oaxaca, 1974"

Closely linked to "Refugee Ship" is "Oaxaca, 1974," which was included in *Emplumada* under that title, but appeared originally and in some anthologies as "Heritage." In the poem, the narrator looks for her Mexican heritage "all day in the streets of Oaxaca," but the children laugh at her, calling to her "in words of another language." Although she has a "brown body," she searches "for the dye that will color my thoughts," or make "this bland pochaseed" ("an assimilated Mexican American," as Cervantes translates the phrase in the glossary) more Latino in her thinking. She did not ask to be brought up "tonta" (stupid), she concludes, but "Es la culpa de los antepasados" (It is her ancestors' fault):

> Blame it on the old ones.
> They give me a name
> that fights me.

If the name is Lorna, it is obviously English in derivation and says nothing of her Mexican American heritage. The poem was first titled "Heritage," and although Cervantes dropped the poem's original first word, "Heritage," when it became "Oaxaca, 1974," the idea embodied in that word still runs beneath the poem's lines and images. The poem, like "Refugee Ship," is an evocative description of the immigrant living uncomfortably between two cultures.

"Freeway 280"

Two other poems in this first collection, "Freeway 280" and "Beneath the Shadow of the Freeway," complement each other and have been reprinted in several anthologies. Deborah L. Madsen wrote, "Cervantes's poetry reveals an acute sense of the importance of geographical and cultural place," and that is nowhere more true than in these two related poems. "Freeway 280" has the theme of human versus nature: In spite of the "raised scar" of the freeway, the narrator tells readers, life thrives. Once, she wanted to leave on the same freeway, but now she has returned.

> Maybe it's here
> en los campos extraños de esta ciudad ["in the strange
> fields of this city"]
> where I'll find it, that part of me
> mown under
> like a corpse
> or a loose seed.

The opposition between humans and nature has become the means of the narrator's finding her own identity in a hometown destroyed by urban development, but where "wild mustard remembers, old gardens/ come back stronger than they were."

"Beneath the Shadow of the Freeway"

"Beneath the Shadow of the Freeway" is a longer and more complex poem (and probably Cervantes's best-known single poem) that starts in the same San Jose setting. In spite of its title and all its natural imagery, however, "Beneath the Shadow of the Freeway" is really a celebration of the power of women. In language that lifts her thoughts to a mythic level, Cervantes creates a powerful statement of Latina strength, and a reminder about those—particularly men—who so often take it away.

The poem is broken into six numbered parts; all except the first contain verse stanzas themselves. In the first section, the narrator describes the house she lives in with her mother and her grandmother, who "watered geraniums/ [as] the shadow of the freeway lengthened." "We were a woman family," the narrator declares in the next stanza, and introduces her main theme. Her mother warns her about men, but the narrator models herself more on her grandmother, who "believes in myths and birds" and "trusts only what she builds/ with her own hands." A drunken intruder (perhaps the mother's former husband) tries to break into the house in the fifth section but is scared away. In the final stanza, the mother warns the narrator, "Baby, don't count on nobody," but the narrator confesses to the reader that "Every night I sleep with a gentle man/ to the hymn of the mockingbirds," plants geraniums, ties her hair up like her grandmother, "and trust[s] only what I have built with my own hands." The poem is thus a celebration of three generations of women and contains the promise that women can be independent and still find love.

"POEM FOR THE YOUNG WHITE MAN . . ."

"Poem for the Young White Man Who Asked Me How I, an Intelligent, Well-Read Person Could Believe in the War Between Races" may be Cervantes's most blatantly political poem in *Emplumada*, but it mirrors ideas and images found throughout the collection. "I believe in revolution," she tells the Anglo man who has questioned her, "because everywhere the crosses are burning" and "there are snipers in the schools." They are not aimed at her interrogator, she says, but "I'm marked by the color of my skin."

> Racism is not intellectual.
> I can not reason these scars away.
>
> Outside my door
> there is a real enemy
> who hates me.

"I am a poet," the persona declares, "who yearns to dance on rooftops." Her "tower of words," however, cannot silence "the sounds of blasting and muffled outrage." This contradiction is continued in the poem's last lines:

> Every day I am deluged with reminders
> that this is not
> my land
> and this is my land.
>
> I do not believe in the war between races
>
> but in this country
> there is war.

As in "Refugee Ship" and "Oaxaca, 1974," the narrator is torn between two lands—but here within her own country.

FROM THE CABLES OF GENOCIDE

Cervantes's second collection of poems, *From the Cables of Genocide*, failed to match the quality and power of *Emplumada*. The poems in the book's four sections—"From the Cables of Genocide," "On Love and Hunger," "The Captive Verses," and "On the Fear of Going Down"—tend to be longer and written in a more complex style. Cervantes also makes less use of Spanish. At least four of the poems are written "after Neruda," several others "after García Lorca," and there are more classical allusions here than in *Emplumada*. Although the distinctively sharp Cervantes language and intense imagery grace the poems in this collection, fewer of them have been reprinted.

Many of the poems in *From the Cables of Genocide* record the pain and loss suffered at the ending of love, and "My Dinner with Your Memory" may be representative of this recurrent subject and situation. The imagery of a feast (bread, butter, cheese, plum brandy) works counter to the sense of pain here: "when the moon slivers my heart/ into poverty's portions." The concluding lines are ambiguous at best but certainly convey the poem's sense of loss:

> Who would hunger at the brink of this
> feast? Who would go, uninvited,
> but you and your ghost of a dog?

Other poems in the collection, such as "On Love and Hunger" and "Macho," continue this theme. There are fewer poems here that deal with ethnic or multicultural issues ("Flatirons" and "Pleiades from the Cables of Genocide" are two strong exceptions) and more that deal with the personal plight of a woman ("On Finding the Slide of John in the Garden"). Some of the best poems in the second collection—like "Shooting the Wren"—are reminiscent of poems in the first, such as "Uncle's First Rabbit."

DRIVE

Fifteen years elapsed between the publication of *From the Cables of Genocide* and Cervantes's third volume of poetry, *Drive: The First Quartet*. In spite of its subtitle, the volume actually contains five separate collections, each set off by a heavy black page and introduced by a painting or photograph. In the author's note that concludes the volume, Cervantes writes that she has always been influenced by painters and describes the paintings by her friend Dylan Morgan that introduce four of the sections. The fifth is introduced by a black-and-white photograph of Robert F. Kennedy.

The first collection, *How Far's the Water?*, contains the most political poems, dealing with topics such as genocide and injustice. The first poem in the collection is "For My Ancestors Adobed in the Walls of the Santa Barbara Mission"; others include "Coffee," "Bananas," and "Portrait of a Little Boy Feeding a Stray in Sarajevo." The second collection, *BIRD AVE*, shifts to more personal subjects: Cervantes growing up in the barrio in the 1960's and early 1970's ("On the Poet Coming of Age") and young people at a Summer Youth Leadership Institute in 1999 ("Collages"). The third collection, *PLAY*, contains three sections of spontaneous poetry workshop exercises on a wide variety of subjects that generate what Cervantes calls seven-minute poems ("Manzanita," "Thelonious Monk," "Ghosts"). The fourth collection, *Letter to David: An Elegiac Mass in the Form of a Train*, is dedicated to Robert F. Kennedy's son, David A. Kennedy, who drank himself to death on April 25, 1984. As Cervantes explains in her prefatory "Note to David" that follows photos of both the young man and his father, the poet remembers vividly the day his father was assassinated. Each of the fourteen poems in this collection is a numbered station, as in the Roman Catholic stations of the Cross, and most are preceded by a parenthetical date. For example, "Fourteenth Station" begins "*(June 5, 1968)*" and links the elder Kennedy with the poet's mother. The fifth collection, *Hard Drive*, consists of three parts: "Striking Ash," "On Line," and "Con una poca de gracia." This collection contains mostly love poems but it also includes two photographs of the poet, one accompanying the poem "Portrait of the Poet at Thirty-three." *Drive* reveals an amazing range of poetic subjects and voices, and many of the poems demonstrate Cervantes's belief in the key relationship between language and power.

"COFFEE" AND "BANANAS"

"Coffee" centers on the massacre of forty-five men, women, and children by paramilitary units in Acteal in Chiapas, Mexico, in 1997. In six sections of the ten-page poem, Cervantes denounces the slaughter—section 3 is a simple recital of the names of the victims—and the imperialism represented by U.S. corporations in Central America. The theme of the poem is best captured in the repeated cry, "No more genocide in my name." "Bananas" uses the fruit to illuminate the international sociopolitical network of plenty and poverty running from Boulder, Colorado, to the Baltic country of Estonia. In both poems, the stark language and images are at the same time personal and political.

BIBLIOGRAPHY

Candelaria, Cordelia. *Chicano Poetry: A Critical Introduction*. Westport, Conn.: Greenwood Press, 1986. In an early evaluation of Cervantes's poetry, Candelaria writes that *Emplumada* reveals a "fresh, forceful, and multifaceted" talent and places her work in the third and final phase of Chicano poetry, after protest poetry and the development of a "Chicano poetics."

Harris-Fonseca, Amanda Nolocea. "Lorna Dee Cervantes." In *Latino and Latina Writers*, edited by Alan West-Duran et al. Vol. 1. New York: Scribner's, 2004. Harris-Fonseca provides a detailed discussion of Cervantes's first two collections of poetry and the differences between them, with analyses of several key poems.

"Lorna Dee Cervantes." In *After Aztlán: Latino Poets of the Nineties*, edited by Ray González. Boston: David R. Godine, 1993. Contains a section providing a basic biography of the poet and analysis of her works, and also places her among other Latino poets.

"Lorna Dee Cervantes." In *The Bloomsbury Guide to Women's Literature*, edited by Claire Buck. New York: Prentice Hall, 1992. This entry provides basic information on Cervantes's life and works, while placing her in the feminist context.

McKenna, Teresa. "'An Utterance More Pure Than Word': Gender and the Corrido Tradition in Two Contemporary Chicano Poems." In *Feminist Measures: Soundings in Poetry and Theory*, edited by Lynn Keller and Cristanne Miller. Ann Arbor: University of Michigan Press, 1994. Detailed analyses of Juan Gomez-Quiñones's "The Ballad of Billy Rivera" and Cervantes's "Visions of Mexico While at a Writing Symposium in Port Townsend, Washington." Also touches on several other key poems in *Emplumada*.

Madsen, Deborah L. *Understanding Contemporary Chicana Poetry*. Columbia: University of South Carolina Press, 2000. An overview of Cervantes's poetry in the final chapter of this study finds that she uses angry language, passionate expression of emotions, and complex, interwoven imagery to portray the Mexican American woman's life from a feminist perspective.

Rodriguez y Gibson, Eliza. "'Tat Your Black Holes into Paradise': Lorna Dee Cervantes and a Poetics of Loss." *MELUS* 33 (Spring, 2008): 139-155. This critical analysis of "To We Who Were Saved by the Stars" and "Pleiades from the Cables of Genocide," both in *From the Cables of Genocide*, shows how Cervantes provides a way to understand losses, both historical and cultural, and shows how women deal with these losses.

Savin, Ada. "Bilingualism and Dialogism: Another Reading of Lorna Dee Cervantes' Poetry." In *An Other Tongue: Nation and Ethnicity in the Linguistic Borderlands*, edited by Alfred Arteaga. Durham, N.C.: Duke University Press, 1994. Using the linguistic theory of Mikhail Bakhtin, Savin finds that Cervantes's "poetic discourse is fragmented, divided, lying somewhere in the interspace between two cultures," but that *Emplumada* eloquently expresses the Chicano quest for self-definition.

Seator, Lynette. "*Emplumada*: Chicana Rites-of-Passage." *MELUS* 11 (Summer, 1984): 23-38. Reads Cervantes's first collection as poems that not only affirm Mexican American identity but also present a woman in the process of coming of age. Contains detailed analyses of many of the best poems in the collection, including "Lots: I," "Lots: II," "Caribou Girl," "For Edward Long," and "For Virginia Chavez."

Wallace, Patricia. "Divided Loyalties: Literal and Literary in the Poetry of Lorna Dee Cervantes, Cathy Song, and Rita Dove." *MELUS* 18 (Fall, 1993): 3-19. Wallace argues that these three poets use language creatively to overcome barriers. He sees Cervantes's poems as "often acts of assertion against restrictive social and linguistic structures."

David Peck
Updated by Peck

FRED CHAPPELL

Born: Canton, North Carolina; May 28, 1936

PRINCIPAL POETRY

The World Between the Eyes, 1971
River, 1975
The Man Twice Married to Fire, 1977
Bloodfire, 1978
Awakening to Music, 1979
Wind Mountain, 1979
Earthsleep, 1980
Driftlake: A Lieder Cycle, 1981
Midquest, 1981 (includes *River*, *Bloodfire*, *Wind Mountain*, and *Earthsleep*)
Castle Tzingal, 1984
Source, 1985
First and Last Words, 1989
C: Poems, 1993
Spring Garden: New and Collected Poems, 1995
Family Gathering, 2000
Backsass, 2004
Shadow Box, 2009

OTHER LITERARY FORMS

Fred Chappell (CHAH-pehl) first became known through his fiction. His third novel, *Dagon* (1968), received a great deal of attention, including winning the prestigious Prix du Meilleur Livres Étranger from the French Academy. He has also published collections of short stories. His tetralogy of novels—*I Am One of You Forever* (1985), *Brighten the Corner Where You Are* (1989), *Farewell, I'm Bound to Leave You* (1996), and *Look Back All the Green Valley* (1999)—which focuses on the family of Jess Kirkman, a semi-autobiographical character, in many ways mirrors the four volumes of *Midquest*, his long poem. He also has published collections of essays on poetry and has written about poetry as a *News and Observer* book columnist.

ACHIEVEMENTS

Fred Chappell's writing, particularly his poetry, is erudite and witty, yet the poems are accessible to the average reader because of his talent, humor, ability to express the profound in the colloquial, close observance of the physical as well as the spiritual world, and mastery of forms and themes. Chappell has received numerous awards for his writing and teaching. In 1968, he won the Academy Award in Literature from the American Academy of Arts and Letters, and in 1985, he and John Ashbery shared Yale University's Bollingen Prize for Poetry. In 1986, he received the O. Max Gardner Award, the highest honor the University of North Carolina can bestow on a faculty member. He won the T. S. Eliot Award for Creative Writing from the Ingersoll Foundation in 1993, the Aiken Taylor Award in Modern American Poetry from *Sewanee Review* in 1996, and the Leila Lenore Heasley Prize from Lyon College in 1999. He was named poet laureate of North Carolina in 1997.

BIOGRAPHY

Fred Davis Chappell was born in Canton, North Carolina, in the heart of the Appalachians. His parents, James Taylor "J. T." Chappell and Anne Davis Chappell, were teachers as well as farmers, and the poet grew up reading constantly and writing poetry. In 1954, he entered Duke University, where he spent his first two years drinking beer, writing, and reading on his own, until he was suspended at the start of his junior year. He returned home to the mountains where he worked in a furniture and supply store and married Susan Nicholls, who plays a central role in many of his poems. In 1959, he resumed study at Duke, where he would later receive his B.A. and M.A. in English.

While at Duke, he became friends with many fine writers, including Reynolds Price and James Applewhite, who would have a major impact on his future. He wrote an eleven-hundred page compendium to the writings of Samuel Johnson for his master's thesis. By the time he received his M.A. in 1964, he had already published his first novel, and upon graduation, he was offered a job teaching English at the University of North Carolina at Greensboro, where he would remain until his retirement in 2004. Soon after his arrival at the university, Randall Jarrell, one of the major writers in the program, died, and as a result, Chappell quickly became central to the writing program. Chappell has lived in North Carolina all his life, except for one year (1967-1968), which he, his wife, and his son Heath spent in Florence, Italy, on a Rockefeller Foundation grant.

ANALYSIS

Fred Chappell's poetry is multifaceted and varied, difficult to summarize because of the tremendous variety of styles, themes, forms, and approaches that he uses. He moves easily between the erudite and the vernacular, the profound and the comic, the individual and the collective conscience. He is at home in a multiplicity of styles, topics, and forms. In the preface to his poetic tetralogy *Midquest*, he described it as a reactionary work because he wishes to restore to his work "qualities sometimes lacking in the larger body of contemporary poetry: detachment, social scope, humor, portrayal of character and background, discursiveness, [and a] wide range of subject matter." His poetry is informed by these qualities, particularly the precise portrayal and creation of charac-

Fred Chappell (AP/Wide World Photos)

ter and background, so that the reader enters the poet's world and finds a home there. His poetry also displays the all-encompassing quality of his learning—ranging from the theories of modern physics to the writings of ancient Greeks—and a familiarity with music of all periods and the art of the ages.

MIDQUEST

Perhaps Chappell's best-known poem is *Midquest*, a long narrative poem often described by critics as a modern epic. Its four sections—*River*, *Bloodfire*, *Wind Mountain*, and *Earthsleep*—were first published as separate volumes. The titles of the four sections relate to the four elements—water, fire, air, and earth—recognized by ancient philosophers. However, these connections only begin to delineate the complexities of the poem.

Each section of *Midquest* begins with the main character, Ole Fred, waking on the morning of his thirty-fifth birthday, May 28, 1976. This immediately forms a connection with Dante's *La divina commedia* (c. 1320; *The Divine Comedy*, 1802), which begins with that author lost in a dark forest at the midpoint of his life, in other words, the biblical midpoint of thirty-five. The Dantean resonances play out in other ways throughout the poem, perhaps most enjoyably in the form of the mountain storyteller Virgil Campbell, who, like Dante's Vergil, acts as Ole Fred's guide.

Each section consists of eleven individual poems and begins and ends with Ole Fred in bed with his beloved Susan. Although each section covers the character's thirty-fifth birthday, the sections move from the present back to Ole Fred's boyhood in the mountains of North Carolina and even further back to before his birth, through stories told to him by his parents, his grandparents, Campbell, and other members of the mountain community. Ole Fred also recalls moments from his years in higher education.

The poems move from the point of view of Ole Fred to those of his close family and friends, including his wife, Susan. Some are in mountain dialect, and some are stream of consciousness. Some are epistolaries; others are dream sequences, dialogues, or tall tales. Chappell employs a wide variety of poetic forms, ranging from the oldest of traditions in English—the Old English verse structure that counts stresses, contains

the breaks known as caesuras, and uses alliteration instead of rhyme—to the open style of free verse. Other traditional forms used include blank verse, rhymed couplets, heroic couplets, terza rima, chant royal, and rhymed tetrameter.

Because of Chappell's use of mountain vernacular, humor, tall tales, and other regionalisms, sometimes his immense learning and curiosity about the world are overlooked. In *Midquest*, he not only draws on classics of literature, such as works by Dante and William Shakespeare, but also displays a wide knowledge of science, art, music, the Bible, contemporary events (the Vietnam War in particular), and classical and political philosophy. However, the poems are never too obscure, and many are funny or wise, or both.

In the second section, *Bloodfire*, Chappell's honesty, humor, wisdom, and erudition are all evident in the poem "Rimbaud Fire Letter to Jim Applewhite." The poet begins with a time in Ole Fred's youth in Haywood County when he came under the spell of Rimbaud and learned how to "derange every last one" of his senses. He reminds his friend of their freshman year in college, the places they went, his discovery of jazz, and finally his being suspended from school and going home, where he married and watched the mountains until "the mountains touched" his mind and brought him back. He concludes this set of memories with the realization that one thing he had not mentioned was ". . . what it cost our women to prop/ Our psyches up . . ." and that it would be better to "grow old and sage" rather than wind up "brilliant, young, and dead."

CASTLE TZINGAL

The collection *Castle Tzingal* contains twenty-three poems in nine different voices. An allegorical drama, it takes place in an unnamed country during the Middle Ages. Its dark and dramatic storyline, which includes political intrigue, jealousy, moral corruption, murder, and revenge, makes it a good choice for readers who revel in drama.

FIRST AND LAST WORDS

The form *First Words and Last Words* takes is illustrated by its title. The first part of the book consists of nine poems that Chappell calls prologues to various works of art, music, or literature. The first poem, "An Old Mountain Woman Reading the Book of Job," is a profoundly moving description of a lonely widow seeking solace from the Bible. Other poems refer to works by classical writers such as Aeschylus and Livy and by the mystic Leo Tolstoy. Others deal with twentieth century works such as Allen Tate's *The Fathers* (1938) and the music of Aaron Copeland. In "The Gift to Be Simple: A Prologue to Aaron Copeland's *Appalachian Spring*," the poet rewrites the Shaker tune that Copeland incorporates in his piece, pointing out how order and music bring people "round right."

The last part of the book consists of epilogues to Albert Einstein, Kenneth Grahame's *The Wind in the Willows* (1908), Johann Wolfgang von Goethe, the U.S. Constitution, Lucretius, *Beowulf* (c. 1000), and the Gospels. The middle part of the book, "Entr'acte," contains a variety of poems exploring how literature and daily life interact, including "My Hand Placed on a Rubens Drawing." Chappell's use of the imagery of hands in this poem, as in the first poem in the book, is both vividly descriptive and symbolically powerful.

SPRING GARDEN

Following a book of one hundred epigrams, appropriately entitled *C*, the Roman numeral for one hundred, Chappell put together a collection of previously published and new poems. The title, *Spring Garden*, has multiple meanings, including being part of the address of the University of North Carolina at Greensboro where Chappell taught. Among the older poems are just two from *Midquest*, along with many epigrams from *C*.

FAMILY GATHERING AND BACKSASS

Family Gathering skewers the members of a hypothetical Appalachian family who have gathered for a special occasion. The descriptions are vivid and idiosyncratic, but the family members are familiar and recognizable, including the uncle with wanderlust and the wife who makes him pay, the drunken relative, and the unforgiven and the unforgiving relatives, all very human types. Perhaps the most brilliant picture is of Elizabeth, who opens and closes the collection, a child who lives in her own world, viewing her relatives with disdain such as only an eight-year-old can show. Similarly, *Backsass* is a collection of humorous and satiric verse, beginning with a poem from Fred's answering machine. Typical of the work is "The Critic," in which the poet writes, "your novel makes no sense/ your soufflé

has already fallen// your poetry let's not go there/ your kids are strong arguments for abortion rights."

SHADOW BOX

In *Shadow Box*, Chappell experiments with the poem-within-a-poem, creating the literary equivalent of a shadow box with what might be termed a nested or embedded poem. He does this by creating an italicized poem within the body of the complete poem, which can be read on its own, yet forms an intricate part of the whole. Generally the italicized poem does not start until several lines in and ends before the complete poem does. In "Pearl," the inner poem begins in the third line:

> She held *the sorrow that had grown* unspoken
> Till it was *perfect as a sphere*, a token
> Of her secret, *with a light that shone* within
> And stood, *in an undropped tear*, a sign.

OTHER MAJOR WORKS

LONG FICTION: *It Is Time, Lord*, 1963; *The Inkling*, 1965; *Dagon*, 1968; *The Gaudy Place*, 1973; *I Am One of You Forever*, 1985; *Brighten the Corner Where You Are*, 1989; *Farewell, I'm Bound to Leave You*, 1996; *Look Back All the Green Valley*, 1999.

SHORT FICTION: *Moments of Light*, 1980; *More Shapes Than One*, 1991; *The Lodger*, 1993; *Ancestors and Others: New and Selected Stories*, 2009.

NONFICTION: *Plow Naked: Selected Writings on Poetry*, 1993; *A Way of Happening: Observations of Contemporary Poetry*, 1998.

EDITED TEXT: *Locales: Poems from the Fellowship of Southern Writers*, 2003.

MISCELLANEOUS: *The Fred Chappell Reader*, 1987.

BIBLIOGRAPHY

Bizzaro, Patrick, ed. *Dream Garden: The Poetic Vision of Fred Chappell*. Baton Rouge: Louisiana State University Press, 1997. Excellent collection of essays on Chappell's poetry through *Spring Garden*, including a foreword by George Garrett and a poem by R. H. W. Dillard, plus essays by Dabney Stuart, Kelly Cherry, Henry Taylor, and others.

Chappell, Fred. "Fred Chappell." Interview. In *The Writer's Mind: Interviews with American Authors*, edited by Irv Broughton. Vol. 3. Fayetteville: University of Arkansas Press 1990. The poet discusses his life, works, and inspirations.

_____. Interview by Shelby Stephenson. In *Appalachia and Beyond: Conversations with Writers from the Mountain South*, edited by John Lang. Knoxville: University of Tennessee Press, 2006. In this 1984 interview, Chappell discusses the mountain South and its influence on his works.

Kibler, James Everett, Jr. "A Fred Chappell Bibliography, 1963-1983." *Mississippi Quarterly* 37 (Winter, 1983-1984): 63-88. Detailed record of Chappell's primary works.

Lang, John. "Breathing a New Universe: The Poetry of Fred Chappell." *Kentucky Poetry Review* 26 (Fall, 1990): 61-65. Brief overview of Chappell's poetry for an issue of the *Kentucky Poetry Review* featuring the poet.

_____. *Six Poets from the Mountain South*. Baton Rouge: Louisiana State University Press, 2010. Chappell is one of six Appalachian poets examined in this work.

_____. *Understanding Fred Chappell*. Columbia: University of South Carolina Press, 2001. In-depth discussion of all the works of Chappell. Includes a very complete bibliography through 2000.

Mary LeDonne Cassidy

MARILYN CHIN

Born: Hong Kong; January 14, 1955

PRINCIPAL POETRY

Dwarf Bamboo, 1987
The Phoenix Gone, the Terrace Empty, 1994
Rhapsody in Plain Yellow, 2002

OTHER LITERARY FORMS

Besides writing poetry, Marilyn Chin (chihn) has translated poetry, written short fiction, and published literary interviews. She translated Gozo Yoshimasu's *Devil's Wind: A Thousand Steps or More* (1980) and, with Pen Wenlan and Eugene Eoyang, *Selected Poems of Ai Qing* (1982). Her short stories "Moon" and "Parable of the Cake" were anthologized in *Charlie Chan Is Dead Two: At Home in the World*, edited by Jessica Hagedorn (2004), and included in *Revenge of the Mooncake Vixen: A Manifesto in Forty-one Tales*, her short-story collection published in 2009.

ACHIEVEMENTS

Marilyn Chin, a Chinese American poet, has garnered numerous awards, including a Mary Roberts Rinehart Award (1983), a Virginia Center for the Creative Arts Fellowship (1983), a Wallace Stegner Fellowship from Stanford University (1984-1985), two National Endowment for the Arts grants (1985, 1991), a MacDowell Colony Fellowship (1987), a Josephine Miles Award from PEN (1994), three Pushcart Prizes (1994, 1995, 1997), a Senior Fulbright Fellowship to Taiwan (1999-2000), the Paterson Book Prize for *Rhapsody in Plain Yellow* (2003), a Radcliffe Institute Fellowship from Harvard (2003-2004), and a Glenna Luschei *Prairie Schooner* Award (2008).

Chin is passionately devoted to her craft, keenly aware of her bicultural position as a Chinese American, alert to the sociopolitical events of her times, and always sensitive—even indignant—about the issues of women in their relationships, their families, and their societies. Coming into print in the 1980's, Chin's poetic work belongs with the second decade of a contemporary renaissance of Asian American poetry. During the 1970's, in the wake of the Black Arts movement, poets such as Lawson Fusao Inada, Hagedorn, and Nellie Wong had broken a generation-long silence during which Asian American poetry had waned to a whisper. Like her immediate predecessors, Chin is engaged and caustic about the shortcomings and inequities of American life, society, and policy. However, she possesses a more highly attuned awareness of Asian events, and her study of classic Chinese texts has endowed her with a width of allusiveness and a profundity of feeling for things Chinese that are rarely equaled in her contemporaries.

BIOGRAPHY

Marilyn Mei-Ling Chin was born in Hong Kong but grew up in Portland, Oregon, and San Francisco, the daughter of George Chin and Rose (Yuet Kuen Wong) Chin. Her father was a Chinese restaurateur who abandoned his family for a blond woman. Chin earned a B.A. in Chinese literature from the University of Massachusetts, Amherst, in 1977. She became a translator for the international writing program at the University of Iowa, working with the Chinese poet Ai Qing, and received an M.F.A. in poetry from the University of Iowa in 1981. She joined the faculty of the master of fine arts program at San Diego State University in 1988. She has traveled extensively in Asia and held visiting teaching positions in Taiwan and the People's Republic of China.

Chin's issues of familial discord—the abandonment by her father, her mother's grief, and her own need to connect with her ancestry—have had a profound impact on her poetry. In an interview with Bill Moyers, Chin recalled her family's dissolution as "the fragmentation that I write about over and over again, hoping to resolve this pain; . . . I was raised by a matriarchy."

ANALYSIS

Marilyn Chin has said that, in addition to issues of family and feminism, her thematic interests include those of "bicultural identity, . . . assimilation, . . . political and global questions." Chin has been quick to add that the poet's "most formidable challenge is that presented by the art itself. . . . A poet may spend days contemplating on the next sentence, or the next image." Characteristically, Chin's imagery is brilliant, and her turns of thought and feeling are complexly personal and sociopolitical, often taking an ironic or dialectical twist. Her allusiveness is immensely adroit and plays richly with classic Chinese poets such as Li Bo, Tao Qian, or Bo Juyi, as well as Western moderns such as Robert Frost, William Carlos Williams, Charles Baudelaire, and Constantine P. Cavafy.

Her books of poetry show Chin to be a magisterial weaver of words and crafter of images. Witty, earthy, and wise, she expertly and sensitively works with Asian and Western traditions of expression, personalizing intensely complex issues of immigration and assimilation as they affect family relations, female identity, and political consciousness.

DWARF BAMBOO

Chin's preoccupation with the poetic craft is abundantly evident in *Dwarf Bamboo*, which is much more than a capable first book. The whole is the product of a subtle, gifted intelligence, a redoubtable maker of images; it forms an intensely persuasive portrayal of a woman's sensibility grappling with the perplexity and the experience of being American, Asian, and female.

One of the most striking qualities of Chin's poetry is her use of imagery—tinglingly sensuous, precise, yet often expansively allusive within both Western and Asian cultural contexts. One poem, for instance, begins: "Red peonies in a slender vase/ blood of a hundred strangers/ Wateroat, cut wateroat/ tubes in my nose and throat." The first line is precisely visual, suggestive of a painting, be it a French Impressionist still life or a scroll painting of the Ming or Qing dynasties. The clipped second line is allusively resonant of Chinese poetry, beginning with its lack of article and continuing with the "hundred" strangers, a typical Chinese locution (whereas, perhaps, the Western equivalent might be "dozens" of strangers). The literal object, the reader realizes with a pleasurable aftershock of recognition, is a blood transfusion being given to a hospital patient. Phrasings such as this point out the qualities of Chin's image-making at its best—subtle, original, sharp, and producing resonances both Asian and Western in an American context.

Chin's images are often borne on a sweeping cadence that lends grandeur to a familiar subject. Writing of the Chinese poet Ai Qing, a victim of the Cultural Revolution, Chin says: "wherever you are, don't forget me, please—/ on heaven's station[e]ry, with earth's chalk/ write, do write." The two-part cadence of the second line reinforces its images that defamiliarize and elevate a personal letter to cosmic proportions and prepare for the briefer but even more insistent two-part cadence of the last line, which must physically take the reader's breath away.

The structuring theme of Chin's book itself is Asian and American, organic and cross-cultural. The book's title posits the organic plant image and metaphor that derives from the Tang Dynasty populist poet Bo Juyi. Elaborating the metaphor, the book's first part is titled "The Parent Node" and consists of poems set in the

Asian motherlands of China and Japan. These poems also evoke ancestors, familial ones such as grandfather and uncle and literary ones such as Matsuo Bashō, and there are poems that provide poignant, emotionally charged snapshots of life during several phases of modern Chinese history.

The second section, "American Soil," shifts its scenes to the North American continent; there is a road trip from Boston to Long Beach, California, a glimpse of the Chinese American ghost town of Locke in the Sacramento Valley, and a vignette from the bigoted and eccentric Louisiana countryside. The title of one poem announces "We Are Americans Now, We Live in the Tundra," and it provides an ironic critique of America as the promised land of immigrant dreams, which is turning out to be an antispiritual and hugely industrial wasteland, a "tundra/ Of the logical, a sea of cities, a wood of cars." (The poem does not spare the immigrants' blighted country of origin either: "China, a giant begonia—// Pink, fragrant, bitten/ By verdigris and insects.") Another poem pictures the dilapidation of "Where We Live Now" in America: "A white house, a wheelless car/ In the backyard rusted// Mother drags a pail of diapers to the line." In many of these poems, one senses a young person's point of view.

"Late Spring," the book's third section, presents a more mature persona as its speaker. The poems crisscross national boundaries, resting momentarily in Hong Kong, Nagasaki, Oregon, and Oakland; they explore love, sensuality, relationships, and art; they ponder feminine and Asian American identity: *This wetsuit protects me/ Wherever I go.*"

"American Rain" is the ironic title of the fourth and final section of the book, which concludes with a mood of skepticism, if not pessimism. The long poem "American Rain" is a surrealistic and nightmarish indictment of the Vietnam War, a vortex of imagery whirling between beautiful blooms and the marl of the dead, between Ben Hai in Vietnam and Seaside in Oregon, between life-giving rain and death-dealing bombs. Ultimately, the book closes on a pessimistic phrase ("another thwarted Spring") in a poem dominated by inkwash-like bleakness ("a black tree on a white canvas/ and a black, black crow"), for though the speaker may strive "towards the Golden Crane Pavil-

ion," she is also aware of "the shape of Mara," the Buddhist symbol of death and destruction.

Dwarf Bamboo is an organically unified volume of poems that starts with the metaphor of Chinese bamboo nodes, progresses to a transplantation on American soil, continues to maturity in spring, and undergoes an ambiguous season, whether of battering or of nurturing under American rain.

THE PHOENIX GONE, THE TERRACE EMPTY

The title of *The Phoenix Gone, the Terrace Empty* derives from a poem by the Tang Dynasty poet Li Bo titled "Climbing Phoenix Terrace at Chin-ling." Li Bo's eight-line lyric remarkably touches on the themes of loss ("the terrace empty"), fleeting time ("the river flows on"), death ("ancient mounds"), separation ("the two-forked stream"), and exile ("I do not see Ch'ang-an"). These are the themes that dominate Chin's second book.

The book is organized into six sections. Not surprisingly, the first section is titled "Exile's Letter," and it contains grouped poems lamenting the loss of Chinese culture. For instance, "The Barbarians Are Coming" presents a woman defending a portion of the Great Wall from its invaders' penetration—in imagery both militaristic and suggestively sexual. "Barbarian Suite" laments how Western modes of life, thought, and speech have supplanted Chinese modes in the speaker. "How I Got That Name" is a bitter narrative raising issues of stereotyping and identity. It tells how the author's father ("a tomcat in Hong Kong trash") became so enchanted by Marilyn Monroe, the stereotypical Western blond, that he changed his daughter's Chinese name to Marilyn "after some tragic white woman/ swollen with gin and Nembutal." It also rails against the stereotype of the model minority pinned on Asian Americans by the majority to use against other minorities.

The book's second section, "The Tao and the Art of Leavetaking," is full of a sense of someone or something missing, eventually of death. The poem "Sad Guitar," for instance, projects images of incompleteness—an immigrant (missing a homeland) is blindly (missing a sense) strumming a guitar with only three fingers (missing two), and touching through his music fire, wood, and water (three of the five Chinese elements). This section's title poem is a complex and elegiac meditation on absence that stems from the experience of deep personal loss, perhaps that of a mother or a lover. It attempts to come to terms with antitheses such as utilitarianism and aestheticism, being and nothingness, plenitude and emptiness. Several positive thoughts are suggested, for example, "all fruits lead to God"—whether a peach be a utilitarian fruit to be eaten or an aesthetic object of a still life, its roots are in creation/creativity—and again "Emptiness is but one mind./ One mind is of no mind," suggesting that one must empty the mind of the distractions of "speakable" and "nameable" material things and rational thought before the nonrationalist and nonmaterialistic Dao (Tao in Chin's work) can enter in, the Dao which is even "above" Plato's "form." However, the poem ends despairingly in images of blocked or crippled creativity ("last night the verses halted") and of thwarted desire, aridity, and perhaps impotence ("the rice paper lay idle./ The black ink dry in the receptacle."

The next section, "The Phoenix Gone, the Terrace Empty," is replete with a sense of loss. The lengthy title poem is permeated with images of exile, death, and melancholy. Its speaker narrates a journey, which begins in an arduous Chinese landscape and ends in the West in regret and isolation. The speaker also travels through time to the Asian past of her immigrant parents and working-class grandparents, as well as to the afterlife of her ancestors, before returning to her American present. Throughout, images of nostalgia, conflict, and death dominate. Finally, taking stock of herself, the speaker's American assimilation incurs only the disappointment of her ancestors, "child, child/ they cried,/ 'Ten thousand years of history and you have come to this.'" Nevertheless, the traditions of Asia fit ill in America: "Shall I walk/ into the new world/ in last year's pinafore?" This inability causes "deep regret," even hints of violence: a moon "shaped . . ./ like a woman's severed ear" appears when her mother meets her Caucasian boyfriend. To her, the image of Uroborus, the snake biting its own tail, does not represent renewal but self destructiveness, a snake "eating herself into extinction." To seek sustenance from the past is to court a "dead prince" whose love only inflicts pain: "you kiss me tenderly/ where arch meets toe meets ankle,/ where dried blood warbles" in an image of footbinding. At the end of the poem, the phoenix, a symbol of renewal (and of woman), has flown, and the speaker finds herself in the present, gazing into a pond, seeing "not lotus, not lily"—neither tranquillity nor purity —but the "yellow crowfoot" creeping over her aging face.

In tune with the book's theme of loss, its fourth section, "Homage to Diana Toy," gathers into several poignant lyrics Chin's thoughts about a patient dying of anorexia in a psychiatric hospital, and its fifth section, "Love Poesy," contains several visceral poems centering on disappointment and betrayal in love relationships: For instance, one poem ends on this wry allusion to the Tang Dynasty poet Du Fu (Tu Fu in Chin's book): "My roommate's in the bathroom [expletive] my boyfriend,/ and all I have is Tu Fu."

The final section of Chin's book is "Beijing Spring," poems occasioned by the brutal crushing of the pro-Democracy movement in Tiananmen Square in 1989. They demonstrate the depth and breadth of Chin's political conscience. Anger and sorrow fill these pages, together with a mood of disillusion delicately captured in the poem "New China," whose tone and imagery hauntingly echo the "Poems on Returning to Dwell in the Country" by the fourth century poet Tao Qian.

RHAPSODY IN PLAIN YELLOW

The finely honed poems in *Rhapsody in Plain Yellow*, a title derived from William Carlos Williams's use of the color yellow, continue to develop Chin's themes of ethnicity, feminism, and death. The italicized poem "Blues on Yellow" keynotes the work. In this poem, Chin alludes to the Chinese American experience through images of gold and railroads. (The Chinese call America the Gold Mountain, and many Chinese immigrants worked extensively on railroad construction in the American West.) She also introduces the topic of interethnic relationships through the story of the canary (yellow) and her husband the crow (black), an interethnicity already suggested in the poem's title since the blues are associated with blacks. Ominously this relationship ends in death—a foreshadowing of the dominating death motif in this book. This prefatory poem concludes that death is even welcome, as it offers a temporary escape before the individual is reborn into a painful worldly existence in the Buddhist cycle of reincarnation.

As the prefatory "Blues on Yellow" also suggests, many poems in *Rhapsody in Plain Yellow* treat with being Asian in the United States, seen often as a perilous, racist land. Thus the subtle but pointed color imagery of "Millenium, Six Songs" forms a grim, accusing picture:

> Black swollen fruit dangling on a limb
> Red forgotten flesh sprayed across the prairie
> Parched brown vines creeping over the wall
> Yellow winged pollen, invisible enemies.

The first image suggests African Americans being lynched; the second line, American Indians being slaughtered on the plains; the third, Mexicans scaling walls built to keep illegal immigrants out; and the fourth, Asian Americans being regarded as the yellow peril.

Feminist issues are as prominent as ethnic ones in this book. In particular, several poems reflect on the unhappy life of Chin's mother. In "Chinese Quatrains (The Woman in Tomb 44)," Chin writes, "My father escorts my mother/ From girlhood to unhappiness"; and in "Altar (#3)," proclaims her mother's death her "finest hour." Another feminist concern that Chin discusses is the invidiousness between women of varying lifestyles. In the allegorical "The True Story of Mortar and Pestle," two sisters hurt, pound, and grind each other because one (Sister Mortar) pursues the masculine values of career success, while the other (Sister Pestle), the traditional feminine values of homemaking.

Death is the book's persistent leitmotif. The volume's beginning foregrounds the death of Chin's mother. The book's closing poem, its title poem, mourns the death of Chin's French lover Charles in an airplane crash: It is also a searing declaration of their interethnic, bicultural union. The poet-speaker's consuming love for Charles is caught in fiercely passionate images: "Say: I shall kiss the rondure of your soul's/ living marl. Say: he is beautiful . . ." ("Say," is repeated throughout the poem and also written at its beginning in Chinese—a character that suggests a mouth exhaling.) Allusions to many other tragic loves are woven into Chin's keening, from the Tang Dynasty rebel An Lu Shan who shared a mistress

with the emperor, to the poet John Keats who contracted tuberculosis and could not marry his fiancé. Chin's poem fiercely expresses a devastating sorrow and ends with a haiku-like image of profound desolation: "Hills and canyons, robbed by sun, leave us nothing."

OTHER MAJOR WORKS

SHORT FICTION: "Moon," 1993; *Revenge of the Mooncake Vixen: A Manifesto in Forty-one Tales*, 2009.

TRANSLATIONS: *Devil's Wind: A Thousand Steps or More*, 1980 (of Gozo Yoshimasu); *Selected Poems of Ai Qing*, 1982 (with Pen Wenlan and Eugene Eoyang).

EDITED TEXTS: *Writing from the World*, 1985; *Dissident Song: A Contemporary Asian American Anthology*, 1991.

BIBLIOGRAPHY

Chin, Marilyn. "Marilyn Chin." Interview by Bill Moyers. In *The Language of Life: A Festival of Poets*, edited by Moyers, Hames Haba, and Dave Grubin. 1995. Reprint. New York: Broadway Books, 2001. Chin discusses her poetry and its personal, social, and political motivations, and provides insight into several poems. She sees herself as a conduit for "historical voices, ancient voices, contemporary feminist voices."

Cucinella, Catherine. *Poetics of the Body: Edna St. Vincent Millay, Elizabeth Bishop, Marilyn Chin, and Marilyn Hacker*. New York: Palgrave Macmillan, 2010. Examines how these four women poets treat the body in their works.

Gery, John. "'Mocking My Own Ripeness': Authenticity, Heritage, and Self-Erasure." *LIT* 12 (2001): 25-45. Gery considers Chin within a minority discourse framework and compares her to Mitsuye Yamada and Trinh T. Minh-ha; he notes that Chin's articulation of emptiness is compensated by her reconfiguration of what remains and her reconstruction of race, gender, and tradition, and he provides close readings of several poems from *The Phoenix Gone, the Terrace Empty*.

McCormick, Adrienne. "'Being Without': Marilyn Chin's Poems as Feminist Acts of Theorizing." *Hitting Critical Mass* 6, no. 2 (2000): 37-58. Mc-

Cormick argues that Asian American feminist literary theory is less abstract than white feminist theory and uses Chin's "I" poems in *The Phoenix Gone, the Terrace Empty* to illustrate. She focuses especially on "How I Got That Name," "A Portrait of the Self as Nation, 1990-1991," and the book's title poem.

Slowick, Mary. "Beyond Lot's Wife: The Immigration Poems of Marilyn Chin, Garrett Hongo, Li-Young Lee, and David Mura." *MELUS* 25, no. 3 (Fall/Winter, 2000): 221-242. Slowick argues that the central aim of these four poets, as Asian Americans and children of immigrants, is to break the silence surrounding immigrants and challenge the typical American "first person, meditative poetry of self-examination."

Svoboda, Terese. "Try Bondage." *Kenyon Review* 17, no. 2 (Spring, 1995): 186-191. Svoboda claims that Chin is searching for a complex type of freedom, in which the oppressed and oppressor coexist. Tiananmen Square is a symbol for such a freedom. She also discusses the inevitable pain of assimilation in Chin's poetry.

Uba, George. "Versions of Identity in Post-Activist Asian American Poetry." In *Reading the Literatures of Asian America*, edited by Shirley Lim and Amy Ling. Philadelphia: Temple University Press, 1992. Uba compares Chin with David Mura and John Yau, pointing out the importance of identity and ideology for her.

Zheng, Da. Review of *The Phoenix Gone, the Terrace Empty*. *Amerasia Journal* 24, no. 2 (Summer, 1998): 186-191. The reviewer notes the variety of themes in Chin's poetry and argues that her poetry is a "special form of protest" reacting to all types of social injustice. He also points out some of the Chinese literary allusions in her poem.

Zhou, Xiaojing. "Marilyn Chin's Poetry of 'Self as Nation': Tansforming the 'Lyric I,' Reinventing Cultural Inheritance." In *Asian American Literature in the International Context*, edited by Rocío G. Davis and Sämi Ludwig. Münster, Germany: LIT Verlag, 2002. Zhou distinguishes between the highly subjective "lyric I" of western poets and Chin's "I," which is more aware of the need to be representative of her culture. Zhou's argument is persuasive, his-

torically grounded, theoretically sophisticated, and thoroughly at home in Chinese culture—an indispensable essay.

C. L. Chua; Teresa Ishigaki
Updated by Chua

JOHN CIARDI

Born: Boston, Massachusetts; June 24, 1916
Died: Edison, New Jersey; March 30, 1986

PRINCIPAL POETRY

Homeward to America, 1940
Other Skies, 1947
Live Another Day, 1949
From Time to Time, 1951
As If: Poems New and Selected, 1955
I Marry You: A Sheaf of Love Poems, 1958
Thirty-nine Poems, 1959
In the Stoneworks, 1961
In Fact, 1962
Person to Person, 1964
This Strangest Everything, 1966
Lives of X, 1971
The Little That Is All, 1974
Limericks: Too Gross, 1978 (with Isaac Asimov)
A Grossery of Limericks, 1981 (with Asimov)
Selected Poems, 1984
The Birds of Pompeii, 1985
Echoes: Poems Left Behind, 1989
The Collected Poems of John Ciardi, 1997 (Edward Cifelli, editor)

OTHER LITERARY FORMS

The career of John Ciardi (CHAHR-dee) as a poet both generated and nourished his other remarkably varied and prolific literary activities, particularly his influential work as a teacher, critic, and author of two popular textbooks, *How Does a Poem Mean?* (1959) and *Poetry: A Closer Look* (1963). Ciardi served as an often controversial poetry editor of the *Saturday Review* (originally the *Saturday Review of Literature*) from

1956 to 1977. There he was responsible for selecting the verse that would be published in the magazine, as well as writing highly subjective columns covering a broad range of aesthetic subjects. Several volumes of his selected essays appeared, including *Dialogue with an Audience* (1963), *Manner of Speaking* (1972), and *Ciardi Himself: Fifteen Essays in the Reading, Writing, and Teaching of Poetry* (1989). The titles themselves suggest Ciardi's awareness of the vital role of the reader (or "audience") with whom the artist must communicate and his delight in the power and versatility of words. *The Selected Letters of John Ciardi* was published in 1991.

Ciardi's work as a translator of Dante's *La divina commedia* (c. 1320; *The Divine Comedy*, 1802) was closely related to his recognition as a poet, for he chose to present all three sections of the classic work in his characteristically forceful, idiomatic American verse, professing to offer not another scholarly translation but one that based its appeal on its ability to be understood by the average reader. Ciardi worked more than twenty years on Dante's poem. The first section, *The Inferno*, appeared in 1954, *The Purgatorio* in 1961, and *The Paradiso* in 1970. A one-volume edition, with a new introduction by Ciardi, was published in 1977. Although critical opinion of his translation has varied, Ciardi himself evaluated his effort as one that "has not been a scholar's but a poet's work."

On innumerable other occasions, Ciardi commented on his own poetry (he was an especially good self-analyst) and on art in general. Essays of this sort appeared not only in his *Saturday Review* columns but also in various periodicals and prefaces to his poetry collections.

Other facets of Ciardi's talent and personality are revealed in his numerous volumes of poetry for children, mostly nonsense verse in the grand tradition of Edward Lear and Lewis Carroll. The first

of these collections, *The Reason for the Pelican*, appeared in 1959, and another volume, *Fast and Slow: Poems for Advanced Children and Beginning Parents*, was published in 1975. Ciardi also published *A Browser's Dictionary, and Native's Guide to the Unknown American Language* (1980, 1983, 1988).

Not content with the printed word, Ciardi recorded many of his poems for children, as well as his more serious work (including the Dante translations) and several discussions of poetry in general and how it can be understood. In the early 1980's, he presented a series of programs on National Public Radio entitled *A Word in Your Ear*, in which he both instructed and entertained his listeners with nontechnical etymological lore.

ACHIEVEMENTS

Whether John Ciardi ranks among the finest of contemporary poets remains to be seen; he himself defined a "modern poet" as one who has yet to stand the test of continued critical acclaim. Because he has never been identified with a "movement" and was never the spokesperson for a conspicuous cause, his popular reputation has been solely based on his poetry, essays, and personal efforts to effect a mutually meaningful dialogue with a middlebrow audience. His first poetry

John Ciardi (©Bettmann/CORBIS)

award was the Hopwood Award in poetry (1938) from the University of Michigan. He received the Levinson Prize from *Poetry* magazine in 1946, the Prix de Rome from the American Academy of Arts and Letters in 1956, the International Platform Association's Carl Sandburg Award in 1980, and the National Teachers Award for Excellence in Poetry for Children in 1982. In 1986, he received the Theodore Roethke Memorial Poetry Prize for *The Birds of Pompeii*. In his honor, the University of Rhode Island, Providence, established the John Ciardi Poetry Prize.

BIOGRAPHY

Born in 1916 in the Italian neighborhood of South Boston, John Anthony Ciardi was the fourth child and only son of Italian immigrants Concetta DeBenedictis and Carminantonio Ciardi. When he was only three years old, his father died in an automobile accident. In 1921, his mother moved the family to the Boston suburb of Medford, where Ciardi attended public school. After finishing high school in 1933, he worked a year to earn money before entering the pre-law program at Bates College in Maine, where his academic career was not very successful. In 1935, he transferred to Tufts College in Boston, where he abandoned his pre-law studies for literature and took his B.A. degree magna cum laude in 1938. In that same year, he entered University of Michigan graduate school on a tuition scholarship.

Ciardi's main interest in the Michigan program was its Hopwood Awards in poetry, and he was determined to compete for both the money and the prestige. He won first prize, a stipend of $1,200, and saw his first book of poetry, *Homeward to America*, published in 1940; his career as a poet was launched. His master of arts degree was granted in 1939, and in 1940, he began his teaching career, a vocation he pursued, with only the interruption of service in World War II, until 1961. His first position was in Missouri as instructor in English at the University of Kansas City.

In 1942, Ciardi enlisted in the United States Army Air Force and was discharged in 1945 as a technical sergeant after duty as an aerial gunner on a B-29 bomber in the air offensive against Japan. In both 1943 and 1944, while still in the service, he received presti-

gious prizes for his verse from *Poetry* magazine. After discharge from the Air Force, he returned briefly to his teaching post in Kansas City in 1946, that year marrying Myra Judith Hostetter, an instructor in journalism. He also received another prize from *Poetry* and in the fall joined the faculty of Harvard University as an instructor.

In 1947, Ciardi's second volume of poetry was published, and he joined the staff of the Bread Loaf Writers' Conference, an affiliation he continued until 1972. In 1948, he became an assistant professor at Harvard, a position he held with distinction until 1953, once being voted "the most popular professor at Harvard." The depth and strength of his vocational commitment is evident in his 1949 statement that "I make my living by writing and by teaching others to write." During this period, he was an editor at Twayne, and another collection of his poetry, *Live Another Day*, appeared. In 1950, he edited his anthology *Mid-century American Poets*, and in 1951, he lectured in Salzburg, Austria. In 1952, he was elected a fellow of the American Academy of Arts and Sciences.

That same year, the first of his three children, a daughter, was born; in 1953 and 1954, two sons were born. In 1953, Ciardi left Harvard for Rutgers University, where he remained until his resignation as a tenured professor in 1961, no longer determined to pursue the academic life of "planned poverty." In 1956, he spent much of the year in Rome on a fellowship in literature at the American Academy of Arts and Letters, also beginning in that year his long association (lasting until 1977) as poetry editor of the *Saturday Review*. In 1958, he served as president of the College English Association and the following year published his initial juvenile poetry book. In 1960, Ciardi received the first of many honorary degrees, and in 1961, he began appearing on educational television.

Working on his Dante translations, on his almost annual publications of verse collections, and at the *Saturday Review* (he reported reading approximately one thousand poems a week in his position as poetry editor), Ciardi produced an enormous literary output. From 1973 to 1974, he was a visiting professor at the University of Florida, and for a number of years was a literary "circuit rider," filling year-round lecture engagements throughout the United States. Ciardi remained active in various literary activities into the 1980's; he died in Edison, New Jersey, in 1986.

ANALYSIS

Ideally, John Ciardi's poems should be read as a whole, not as individual works, for their total effect is much greater than the sum of their various parts. Ciardi's engaging "personality" constitutes an integral informing intelligence, a presence that becomes more complex and developed as the experience of his poetry grows. His work is comparatively accessible—indeed his "first law" for all poetry is that it be easily understood by the general reader.

In an important prefatory essay to the 1949 volume *Live Another Day*, Ciardi set down thirteen prescriptive principles of his poetic creed. These fundamental rules served him as a guideline for his own poetry and as a standard for the evaluation and judgment of the works of others. An understanding of these critical precepts is important to the analysis of Ciardi's poetry.

Ciardi's first and most important rule is that the reader should be able to understand a given poem. Ciardi had little use for certain poets (T. S. Eliot and Ezra Pound among them) whom he called "baroque," inbred mannerists writing to other writers rather than generating their work from the raw material of nature "outward to the lives of men." Moreover, Ciardi believed that a poem should be affirmative and specific "about the lives of people." He recalled the origins of the genre by reminding readers that poetry should be read aloud, that its effect is to the ear not the eye. Ciardi asserted that poetry can be about any subject and may utilize any diction (no word is "not fit"), thus echoing William Wordsworth's democratic principles set forth in his preface to *Lyrical Ballads* (2d ed., 1800). Ciardi also believed that "personality" must emerge from the work, otherwise it "is dead." Pursuing more technical prosodic elements, his premises include the opinion that to succeed, a poem "must create its own form," and that ambiguities must be recognized and understood in each of their separate possibilities.

One can recognize that much of Ciardi's poetic credo is derivative, especially from the modern New Critical approach. In reference to his translations of Dante, Ciardi confessed unabashedly that he was "a thief of other men's scholarship" but argued logically and persuasively that such work has "no better purpose" than to serve other people's needs. In his own poetic principles, however, he went beyond any limited doctrinaire critical tenets and stressed the totality of a specific work, each line being "a conceived unit" of the whole. His final points were technical: He saw rhyme in the poem as "part of the total voice-punctuation" and metrics as being more successful when the conventional iambic pentameter line is less strictly observed.

Critics have declared that no two of Ciardi's poems are alike. Although that observation may be something of an overstatement, certainly both his subjects and his forms, his diction and his tone, all demonstrate both poetic inventiveness and a remarkably broad range of personal interests. Indeed, in their subjectivity lies the primary theme of this most autobiographical poet: himself and his search for orientation and stability in a protean and often hostile and uncertain world. Readers, however, soon notice certain recurring themes: the pervasive influence of his first-generation Italian background, the shattering personal loss of his father, and the anxieties and contradictions, as well as the joys, of everyday contemporary urban life. The universal problem of discovering "a self" amid its distractions lies at the heart of Ciardi's work.

In his preference for the short, usually lyric poem, Ciardi consistently used closed forms and tightly structured traditional stanzas, whether or not he employed rhyme; more often than not the reader is aware of a beginning, middle, and end. Following his own dictum advocating "common speech," Ciardi's lively vernacular diction is honestly direct, sometimes irreverent, and even crude, often employing colloquialisms. Often faulted for being repetitious and belaboring the obvious as well as for lacking a direct emotional charge in his choice of diction, Ciardi nevertheless refused to assume a philosophical stance alien to his nature, nor did he depart from his own particular "sense of the form." Perhaps his anecdotal subjects were often not equal to his masterful technical skills, but when one considers the number of poets of whom the reverse is true, Ciardi's remarkable poetic achievement comes into focus.

HOMEWARD TO AMERICA

In Ciardi's first book, *Homeward to America*, the volume that launched his career by winning the Hopwood Prize at the University of Michigan, he exhibited many of the characteristics that mark all his work—the search for and development of a self presented with wit and irony. Drawing obvious analogies between his parents' migration to the United States—their search for a "home"—and his own experience, he concludes (in "Letter to Mother") that despite their courageous and dramatic precedent, he must find his way alone. Although the weaker poems in the collection are little more than externalizations of emotions dimly felt by the young poet, in his maturity this same protesting voice rings true.

OTHER SKIES

A tone of protest is a distinctive characteristic of Ciardi's verse, especially in his early work, yet the iconoclast is no nihilist. Affirmation of life underlies even his most violent social criticism. Beginning in 1947, Ciardi began publishing strongly worded, often cynical poems. The volume *Other Skies* reflects Ciardi's war years; the forty-two poems reveal the intellectual growth forged by his military experience. Indicative of his new personal confidence and his mastery of the ironic tone is the tightly rhymed "Elegy Just in Case" that begins "Here lie Ciardi's pearly bones," in which he speculates about what would become of his decaying corpse rotting in the jungle. The bantering observations belie the grisly truth of war and its victims, yet the poem is no less effective for its flippant tone. More somberly intense is his "Poem for My Twenty-ninth Birthday," in which he identifies himself with "the soaring madness of our time," a crewman of a bomber whose mission is "to save or kill us all" by destroying the lives of unseen and unknown enemy victims. Also in this important collection is "On a Photo of Sgt. Ciardi a Year Later," one of his most widely read poems. Here he considers himself in an earlier snapshot. He appears as an illusory costumed figure, and he concludes that the reality of a subject invariably eludes the camera's eye: "The shadow under the shadow is never caught."

LIVE ANOTHER DAY

In succeeding collections the flippancy diminishes; perhaps the newly married poet underwent a humanizing transformation, an affirmation of his growing responsibilities. In *Live Another Day*, *From Time to Time*, and *As If*, he continues to recall and chronicle earlier experiences, the raw material of his emerging consciousness of self. In *Live Another Day*, he includes both his prefatory credo as a poet and a profile of his hypothetical reader. In these transitional volumes, the poet begins his attempt to reconcile his own introspective incursions with the interests of the public with whom he feels increasingly compelled to create a "dialogue."

AS IF AND I MARRY YOU

In *As If*, Ciardi includes several poems inspired by his wife, Judith, later reprinted in *I Marry You*. At the time of this collection, Ciardi was deeply involved in his translations of Dante, an involvement that forced him to reexamine his Italian roots. Much of this personal exploration is evident in powerful poems about his father. In a sharply drawn poem typical of another less elegiac strain ("Thoughts on Looking into a Thicket"), the poet offers one of his most succinct statements of his thematic stance: "I believe the world to praise it."

I Marry You, despite its popularity, is a private collection, a tribute by the poet to his happy and inspirational marriage and family life. Some critics see it as self-conscious sentimentality, but perhaps this opinion is a judgment on modern attitudes toward such intimate revelations rather than on the emotions themselves or the quality of their presentation. Not all the poems in this collection, however, are conjugal, for what some consider to be Ciardi's finest poem, "Snowy Heron," is included. Here the poet follows his earlier admonition to praise and extends the idea of espousal to include the world of nature; "I praise without a name," he proclaims, the power of the heron's flight. He feels that by whatever name one calls this spirit, the crucial act is to express glorification, adding emphasis by both beginning and ending the second six-line stanza with the imperative "but praise."

THIRTY-NINE POEMS

With the publication of *I Marry You*, Ciardi approached the height of his poetic powers. In his next collection, *Thirty-nine Poems*, which appeared in 1959, he strives to illustrate his belief that intensely personal truths about one man might well illumine the life of another. "Bridal Photo, 1906" was inspired by a picture of his parents in a frozen moment; it ends with a prayer and a benediction by their son. In his explanatory notes for this poem, Ciardi says that from this communion of a man with a piece of paper, he found himself "knowing more and more truly about myself, and about all of us."

THE 1960'S

Four collections by Ciardi appeared during the 1960's: *In the Stoneworks*, *In Fact*, *Person to Person*, and *This Strangest Everything*. The first two works are generally seen as competent, but merely covering Ciardi's familiar and recognized poetic territory. His third volume of the decade is more successful. The title poem of *Person to Person* reaffirms his ceaseless efforts to make connections with his readers despite the difficulty of any genuine personal communication ("I can reach no one"). Another commendable poem in this group is "Autobiography of a Comedian," in which "Lucky John" Ciardi honestly profiles himself; being a comic, he confesses, is the only alternative to death. Materialistic rewards, however, do not satisfy the humanist instincts and yearnings of the soul: The comedian admits, "I'm still winning what I have no real use for." Protesting the absurdity that "even scholars take me seriously," he asks plaintively and in desperation (apparently extending himself to be a spokesperson for Everyman), "How do we make sense of ourselves?"

"TENZONE"

A well-known poem from *Person to Person* is "Tenzone," an ironic debate between the poet's soul and his body. In the guise of "soul," the effaced poet (again obviously Ciardi) describes himself complacently and realistically as "the well-known poet, critic, editor, and middle-high aesthete of the circuit" for whom "some weep" because he wastes his talents, while others find the very thought of his abilities laughable. "Soul" denounces him as a "greedy pig," dead to art, a confidence man concerned only with money and whiskey. In response, "body" accuses "soul" of having a father-fixation, of being a failed poet who knows it after discovering that a "poem is belly and bone." In "Nothing Is Really Hard but to Be Real" the poet taunts his readers by declaring that the aphoristic title is

"fraudulent," only hollow "gnomic garbage." What is important is to find the truth of "our own sound" that reveals "what a man is." This argument, as well as his rhetorical gambit, is familiar Ciardi material, the theme and style not only of much of his poetry but also of his essays and lectures.

THIS STRANGEST EVERYTHING

Less successful than *Person to Person*, his best and most significant volume of the 1960's, is *This Strangest Everything*. Here there are no excellent poems, nor, for that matter, any embarrassments; Ciardi seems content to cover old ground, to write not for critical acclaim but to fulfill the expectations of his growing audience of devoted readers.

THE 1970'S

In *Lives of X*, the first of Ciardi's two collections of the 1970's, the poet offers fifteen longer narratives in blank verse, one critic seeing it as "the closest thing to a formal autobiography [Ciardi] has yet attempted." Here he traces his rich and varied life from birth onward, recalling and expanding on events described in earlier poems and offering new details from memory, especially on his desperate search for a name and an identity, as well as his struggle with the Roman Catholic Church. The other collection of this decade, *The Little That Is All*, has been called "vintage Ciardi" and is a random yet ultimately affirmative collection that expresses his concerns with objects and events in the life of a typical twentieth century man. Ranging from power mowers and blue movies to hiring a lawyer to fix his son's fourth "pot bust," the volume reflects both Ciardi's wit and his hard-won wisdom and above all his ultimately triumphant coming to terms with life. His terse yet perceptive self-assessment of the chaos of suburban existence (in "Memo: Preliminary Draft of a Prayer to God the Father") is: "I do not complain: I describe."

OTHER MAJOR WORKS

NONFICTION: *How Does a Poem Mean?*, 1959, 1975; *Dialogue with an Audience*, 1963; *Poetry: A Closer Look*, 1963; *Manner of Speaking*, 1972; *For Instance*, 1979; *A Browser's Dictionary, and Native's Guide to the Unknown American Language*, 1980, 1983, 1988 (3 volumes); *Good Words to You*, 1987; *Ciardi Himself: Fifteen Essays in the Reading, Writing, and Teaching of Poetry*, 1989; *The Selected Letters of John Ciardi*, 1991 (Edward Cifelli, editor).

TRANSLATION: *The Divine Comedy*, 1977 (*The Inferno*, 1954, *The Purgatorio*, 1961, and *The Paradiso*, 1970; of Dante's *La divina commedia*).

CHILDREN'S LITERATURE: *The Reason for the Pelican*, 1959; *Scrappy the Pup*, 1960; *I Met a Man*, 1961; *The Man Who Sang the Sillies*, 1961; *The Wish-Tree*, 1962; *You Read to Me, I'll Read to You*, 1962; *John J. Plenty and Fidler Den*, 1963; *You Know Who*, 1964; *The King Who Saved Himself from Being Saved*, 1965; *An Alphabestiary*, 1966; *Someone Could Win a Polar Bear*, 1970; *Fast and Slow: Poems for Advanced Children and Beginning Parents*, 1975; *Doodle Soup*, 1985.

EDITED TEXT: *Mid-century American Poets*, 1950.

BIBLIOGRAPHY

Ciardi, John. *The Selected Letters of John Ciardi*. Edited by Edward M. Cifelli. Fayetteville: University of Arkansas Press, 1991. Collection of correspondence with various literati including Isaac Asimov, Theodore Roethke, Muriel Rukeyser, and John Frederick Nims. Includes an index.

Cifelli, Edward M. *John Ciardi: A Biography*. Fayetteville: University of Arkansas Press, 1997. Cifelli, an expert on Ciardi's work, chronicles the rise and fall of the poet's fortune from his high profile in the 1940's and 1950's to his relative obscurity when the Beats and the confessional poets arrived.

Clemente, Vince, ed. *John Ciardi: Measure of the Man*. Fayetteville: University of Arkansas Press, 1987. This collection of essays is essential for any student of Ciardi. Authors as varied as Isaac Asimov and Maxine Kumin comment on Ciardi's multifaceted life and writing career. Covers Ciardi's work as a poet, a science-fiction writer, and an author for children.

Krickel, Edward Francis. *John Ciardi*. Boston: Twayne, 1980. A valuable introduction to the work of Ciardi. It contains a brief biography and an analytic overview of the body of his work. Supplemented by a thorough primary and secondary bibliography and an index.

Nims, John Frederick. "John Ciardi: The Many Lives of Poetry." In *John Ciardi: The Measure of the Man*, edited by Vince Clemente. Fayetteville: University of Arkansas Press, 1987. Nims addresses Ciardi as a poet and reveals his poetic bias when he praises Ciardi as a man of the world who gave up his career to write. Ciardi's experience informed his poetry, which was rich and varied.

Williams, Miller. "John Ciardi: 'Nothing Is Really Hard but to Be Real.'" In *The Achievement of John Ciardi*, edited by Miller Williams. Glenview, Ill.: Scott, Foresman, 1969. Williams edited a selection of Ciardi's poems published from the mid-1940's to the mid-1960's. Williams's essay on Ciardi is one of the best available. Suitable for all students.

Maryhelen Cleverly Harmon

SANDRA CISNEROS

Born: Chicago, Illinois; December 20, 1954

PRINCIPAL POETRY
Bad Boys, 1980
The Rodrigo Poems, 1985
My Wicked, Wicked Ways, 1987
Loose Woman, 1994

OTHER LITERARY FORMS

Sandra Cisneros (sihs-NEHR-ohs) is known largely for her fiction. Her first published novel, *The House on Mango Street* (1984), is canonical reading for middle school, high school, and college students in the United States. She received a $100,000 advance for her collection of short stories, *Woman Hollering Creek, and Other Stories*, published in 1991. Cisneros published a bilingual picture book for children, *Hairs = Pelitos*, based on a vignette from *The House on Mango Street*, in 1994. Her most ambitious work, the novel *Caramelo: Or, Puro Cuento*, was published in 2002. *Vintage Cisneros* (2004) includes selections of poetry and fiction from her other works.

ACHIEVEMENTS

A graduate of the prestigious University of Iowa Writers' Workshop, Sandra Cisneros received two grants from the National Endowment for the Arts, one for fiction (1982) and one for poetry (1987), and a Mac-Arthur Fellowship in 1995. She won the American Book Award from the Before Columbus Foundation (1985) for *The House on Mango Street*; the PEN Center West Award for Best Fiction (1992), the Quality Paperback Book Club New Voices Award (1992), the Anisfield-Wolf Book Award (1993), and the Lannan Literary Award (1991) for *Woman Hollering Creeek, and Other Stories*; the Mountains and Plains Booksellers' Regional Book Award for *Loose Woman* (1995); and the Premio Napoli Award in 2005 for *Caramelo*. She was given the Chicano Short Story Award from the University of Arizona in 1986 and the Texas Medal of the Arts in 2003. She was awarded honorary doctorates from the State University of New York at Purchase in 1993 and from Loyola University in 2002.

Cisneros is one of the most popular and well-known Chicana writers and has used her recognition to improve the lives of people in her community. In 1995, she established the Macondo Foundation, an association that supports poets and writers working for social change. In 2000, she founded the Alfredo Cisneros del Moral Foundation, which provides financial support for writers connected to the state of Texas. Her work has been translated into more than a dozen languages.

BIOGRAPHY

Sandra Cisneros was born December 20, 1954, in Chicago, to a Mexican father and a Mexican American mother. The only daughter in a family of seven children, she grew up speaking both English and Spanish. Her family frequently traveled to Mexico for extended visits with her paternal grandparents. Although her grandparents were wealthy, Cisneros's immediate family was very poor, living in small, rundown apartments in poverty-stricken neighborhoods of Chicago. She received her early education in Roman Catholic schools, but her talents and intelligence were not reflected in the grades on her early report cards.

In 1966, when Cisneros was twelve, her family purchased a house. Though the house was small and unimpressive, Cisneros had her own room, affording her privacy to read. Cisneros's mother, a voracious reader herself, exempted her from domestic responsibilities

Sandra Cisneros (©Rubén Guzmán)

so that she would have time to read. One of Cisnero's favorite childhood books was *The Little House* (1942), by Virginia Lee Burton.

In high school, Cisneros began writing and decided to major in English in college. She attended Loyola University in Chicago, where her father expected her to find a husband. As a junior, in 1974, she enrolled in her first writing workshop. In 1976, she began work at the University of Iowa Writers' Workshop. Though she received an M.F.A. in creative writing in 1978, she was not happy during her time at the Iowa workshop. As a Mexican American woman with a working-class background, she felt very much out of place. Ironically, she was able to discover her own voice there, prompted by the assigned reading of Gaston Bachelard's *The Poetics of Space* (1958). The symbol of the house, as reflected in this book and discussed in a class, eventually led to her writing *The House on Mango Street*.

After graduating from the Iowa workshop, Cisneros

returned to Chicago, where she worked as a counselor at the Latino Youth Alternative High School and wrote poetry in her spare time. Her work appeared in buses and subways as part of the Chicago Transit Authority's project, which was sponsored by the Poetry Society of America, bringing her to the attention of the poet Gary Soto, who enabled her to published a chapbook of poetry, *Bad Boys*, in 1980.

In 1980, Cisneros began working as a college recruiter for Loyola University in order to have more time for writing. A grant from the National Endowment for the Arts in 1982 allowed her to work full-time on *The House on Mango Street*, which was published in 1984. Also in 1984, Cisneros moved to San Antonio, Texas, where she worked as an arts administrator at the Guadalupe Arts Center. In 1987, she accepted her first teaching position at California State University at Chico and published *My Wicked, Wicked Ways*, a collection of poetry. A second grant from the National Endowment for the Arts in 1987 and a large advance for *Woman Hollering Creek, and Other Stories* allowed her to leave teaching and return to San Antonio and full-time writing. She published a collection of poetry, *Loose Woman*, in 1994, and a novel, *Caramelo*, in 2002, thereby earning the approval of her father.

ANALYSIS

Although Sandra Cisneros has described her poetry as more autobiographical than her fiction, many of her poems reflect the same communal voice found in her fiction. In addition, her poetry retains a strong sense of narrative despite its lyricism. Cisneros often uses Spanish words and phrases and has commented that she does this when unable to find an acceptable translation. This infusion of Spanish complements the first-person narratives relating the Mexican American experience for which Cisneros is known. Also common to her poetry is the use of repetition and sound effects such as rhyme and assonance.

MY WICKED, WICKED WAYS

The title poem of *My Wicked, Wicked Ways*, an observation of an old family photograph, sets the tone for Cisneros's first full-length collection of poetry. The photograph is of the speaker's parents, during a happier time: "Here is my mother./ She is not crying." The speaker's father is apparently attractive, and the only conflict between her parents at this time is her father's choice of shoes. The poet moves to the future, referencing another woman who will create a disruption in the marriage, then back to the photo, which also includes a baby, then again to the future: "This is me she is carrying./ I am a baby./ She does not know/ I will turn out bad."

"Six Brothers" continues the theme of disappointing one's parents. The poem, a retelling of a fairy tale by the Brothers Grimm, contrasts the worthiness of the speaker of the poem with her brothers: "Brothers, it is so hard to keep up with you./ I've got the bad blood in me I think,/ the mad uncle, the bit of the bullet." This theme is emphasized in the poem's conclusion: "My six brothers, graceful, strong./ Except for you, little one-winged, finding it as difficult as me/ to keep the good name clean."

This collection began as Cisneros's master thesis. Its first section of poems, which includes all but one of the poems printed in the chapbook *Bad Boys*, works in much the same manner as the vignettes in *The House on Mango Street* in that it presents a portrait of a poor Catholic Mexican American neighborhood. The neighborhood is a mix of violence, illness, and laughter. "South Sangamon" begins, "We wake up/ and it's him/ banging and banging// His drunk cussing,/ her name all over the hallway." The poem provides the man's previous behavior: "That day he punched her belly/ the whole neighborhood watching," and then ends, on a presumably quiet note: "she laughing,/ her cigarette lit,/ just then/ the big rock comes in." "Abuelito Who" tells the story of a sick child, Abuelito, who "can't come out to play/ sleeps in his little room all night and day/ who used to laugh like the letter k/ is sick." "Good Hotdogs" is one of Cisneros's more joyful poems: "Dash those hotdogs/ Into buns and splash on/ All that good stuff." This poem is purely a happy memory. It ends: "We'd eat/ you humming/ And me swinging my legs."

LOOSE WOMAN

The childlike personas of *The House on Mango Street* and *My Wicked, Wicked Ways* are absent from *Loose Woman*, Cisneros's second full-length volume of poetry, even though fairy tale and nursery rhyme references abound. This volume projects a voice that has chosen isolation, despite its occasional loneliness, for the sake of art. The title poem references a Grimm's fairy tale: "Diamonds and pearls/ tumble from my tongue./ Or toads and serpents./ Depending on the mood I'm in." Although placed at the end of the book, this poem sets the tone for the entire work: "By all accounts I am/ a danger to society./ I'm Pancha Villa./ I break laws,/ upset the natural order,/ anguish the Pope and make fathers cry." In this volume, the violence has turned inward. "The Pumpkin Eater" turns on irony, with the speaker saying: "I'm not/ the she who slings words bigger than rocks,/ sharper than Houdini knives," and continuing, "I keep inside a pumpkin shell/ There I do very well." In the poem, "After Everything," the speaker is more direct, noting, ". . . when I'm through/ hurling words as big as stones,/ slashing the air with my tongue," she is alone, having reached the point "After everything/ that's breakable is broken."

Despite, or because of, the inner violence projected by these poems, solitude and poetry provide solace. In "I Let Him Take Me," the poet imagines a poem as a lover, and finds that unlike a human lover, the poem ". . . never disappointed,/ hurt, abandoned." This volume is filled with love poems; however, the speaker of these poems is, most often, happy when the lover has gone. "A Man in My Bed Like Cracker Crumbs" refers to the moment after the lover has left: ". . . now I can sit down/ to my typewriter and cup// Coffee's good// House clean/ I'm alone again./ Amen." Despite the poet's happiness at remaining single, relatives express concern. "Old Maids" presents criticism directed at Cisneros about her unmarried state: *What happened in your childhood?/ What left you all mean teens?/ Who hurt you, honey?*" However, she responds, for herself and her unmarried cousins, ". . . we've studied/ marriages too long—," noting that these were "lessons that served us well."

OTHER MAJOR WORKS

LONG FICTION: *The House on Mango Street*, 1984; *Caramelo: Or, Puro Cuento*, 2002.

SHORT FICTION: *Woman Hollering Creek, and Other Stories*, 1991.

CHILDREN'S LITERATURE: *Hairs = Pelitos*, 1994.

MISCELLANEOUS: *Vintage Cisneros*, 2004.

BIBLIOGRAPHY

Cisneros, Sandra. "Sandra Cisneros." http//www.sandra cisneros.com. The author's official Web site features a biography, descriptions and reviews of her works, articles about her, interviews, and news and features.

Estill, Adriana. "Building the Chicana Body in Sandra Cisneros." *Rocky Mountain Review of Language and Literature* 56, no. 2 (Fall, 2002): 25-43. A detailed analysis of *My Wicked, Wicked Ways* that attempts to remedy the lack of critical attention Cisneros's poetry has received in comparison to her prose fiction.

Madsen, Deborah L. "Sandra Cisneros." *Understanding Contemporary Chicana Literature*. Columbia: University of South Carolina Press, 2000. A general analytical overview of Cisneros's poetry and fiction in chronological order of publication.

Mirriam-Goldberg, Caryn. *Sandra Cisneros: Latina Writer and Activist*. Berkeley Heights, N.J.: Enslow, 1998. A full-length biography. Includes bibliography, chronology, index, and photographs.

Rebolledo, Tey Diana. "The Chicana Bandera: Sandra Cisneros in the Public Press—Constructing a Cultural Icon (1996-1999)." In *The Chronicles of Panchita Villa and Other Guerrilleras: Essays on Chicana/Latina Literature and Criticism*. Austin: University of Texas Press, 2005. Explores Cisneros's reputation as a cultural icon as evidenced in the public press, both American and international. Details the controversy over the color of her home in an historic San Antonio district.

Rivera, Carmen Haydée. *Border Crossings and Beyond: The Life and Works of Sandra Cisneros*. Santa Barbara, Calif.: Praeger, 2009. Part of the Women Writers of Color series, this biography of Cisneros looks at her life and work and its relation to her ethnicity.

Tokarczyk, Michelle M. "The Voice of the Voiceless: Sandra Cisneros." In *Class Definitions: On the Lives and Writings of Maxine Hong Kingston, Sandra Cisneros, and Dorothy Allison*. Selinsgrove, Pa.: Susquehanna University Press, 2008. Grounds the work of Cisneros in feminist theory, compares the Mexican influence on her work with the Irish influence on the work of James Joyce, and argues that

Cisneros serves as the voice of the voiceless members of her Latino, and especially Latina, communities. Specifically addresses *My Wicked, Wicked Ways* and *Loose Woman*.

Nettie Farris

AMY CLAMPITT

Born: New Providence, Iowa; June 15, 1920
Died: Lenox, Massachusetts; September 10, 1994

PRINCIPAL POETRY

Multitudes, Multitudes, 1974
The Isthmus, 1981
The Summer Solstice, 1982
The Kingfisher, 1983
A Homage to John Keats, 1984
What the Light Was Like, 1985
Archaic Figure, 1987
Manhattan: An Elegy and Other Poems, 1990
Westward, 1990
A Silence Opens, 1994
The Collected Poems of Amy Clampitt, 1997

OTHER LITERARY FORMS

Although Amy Clampitt is known primarily for her collections of poems, her first serious literary efforts took the form of fiction. Clampitt wrote two full-length novels in the 1950's, although they remain unpublished. She did, however, produce some noteworthy critical work late in her career. Clampitt provided the introduction and selected the poems for Ecco Press's *The Essential Donne*, published in 1988. *Predecessors, Et Cetera: Essays*, published by the University of Michigan Press in 1991, includes several of her essays on the aesthetics of writing and on seminal literary figures she found influential on her own work. Clampitt begins the book by posing the most fundamental of questions, "What do you need to know to be a writer?" She then uses this question as a springboard for a candid and remarkably lucid discussion of the ideas of literary figures as diverse as nineteenth century novelist

Henry James and twentieth century eschatologist Hal Lindsey. In this way the essays of *Predecessors, Et Cetera* reflect the intellectual eclecticism that informs her most memorable poems.

ACHIEVEMENTS

Amy Clampitt graduated with honors from Grinnell College in Iowa in 1941, where she was also elected to Phi Beta Kappa. Her poetry began to gain significant attention relatively late in her life, but during roughly the last decade of her life, she received a number of important awards. In 1982, she received a John Simon Guggenheim Fellowship and, in 1984, an Academy Award in Literature from the American Academy and Institute of Arts and Letters. Clampitt won an Academy of American Poets Fellowship in 1985 and a three-year Lila Wallace-*Reader's Digest* Writers' Award in 1991. She became a member of the American Academy of Arts and Letters in 1987 and served as chancellor for the Academy of American Poets from 1990 to 1994. She was also writer-in-residence at the College of William and Mary in 1984-1985, at Amherst College in 1986-1987, and at Smith College in 1992-1993.

She was named visiting Hurst Professor at Washington University in 1988. Clampitt's first major collection, *The Kingfisher*, was nominated for the National Book Critics Circle Award in 1983 and was widely received by a number of major critics as one of the most important volumes of American poetry to appear in the 1980's.

BIOGRAPHY

In a rare interview with Judson Brown for *Daily Hampshire Gazette* in 1987, then sixty-seven-year-old poet Amy Clampitt remarked, "I'm very much put off by this whole thing of making human interest stories about someone who published late." Clampitt was addressing one of the most remarkable facts about her life as a poet: that her work remained relatively unnoticed until she was in her sixties. However, although she published "late," her work is generally viewed as some of the most accomplished lyric poetry to come out of the United States in the late twentieth century.

Helen Vendler remarked of Clampitt's landmark 1983 collection *The Kingfisher*,

A century from now, . . . it will still offer beautiful objects of delectation, but it will have taken on as well the documentary value of what, in the twentieth century, made up the stuff of culture.

Although she was held in similar esteem as a "culture maker" by a host of other reviewers, who championed *The Kingfisher* and its highly anticipated 1985 follow up *What the Light Was Like* as monumental achievements, Clampitt shunned the limelight that her late-found fame afforded her. Thus, the facts of her life, especially of those sixty years before she burst on the literary scene, remain scant and sporadic. It is generally known, however, that Clampitt was born in 1920 in the farming town of New Providence, Iowa.

Even though poems like "Imago" document that she was raised very much a pragmatic, hardworking daughter of the Iowa prairie ("the shirker propped/ above her book in a farmhouse parlor"), her parents did strongly encourage her to pursue her gift for language, which she demonstrated even as a girl, writing poems as early as age nine. Clampitt was schooled at Grinnell College, where she earned election to Phi Beta Kappa and received a bachelor of arts degree with a concentration in English, graduating with honors in 1941. On graduation, she was awarded a fellowship for graduate study at Columbia University, but she left before completing her first year because she found graduate study largely unfulfilling.

Clampitt found greater satisfaction in the world of work, taking a job at Oxford University Press as promotional director for college textbooks, a position she kept until 1951, when a trip to Europe beckoned. In 1952, Clampitt returned to New York to take a position as reference librarian for the National Audubon Society. She remained there, first as a researcher and later in an editorial capacity, until 1977. Turning her efforts more toward her poetry during this period, Clampitt was eventually able to publish enough in distinguished magazines and reviews in the 1970's to secure a job in 1977 as a poetry editor with E. P. Dutton. She remained there until 1982, when she left to pursue her own writing full-time.

Throughout the 1980's and until her death from ovarian cancer in 1994, Clampitt supported herself entirely from the proceeds from her books, fellowships, and personal appearances. *The Kingfisher* alone sold in excess of ten thousand copies, an almost unprecedented feat in poetry.

ANALYSIS

Often compared to the work of decidedly Metaphysical poets like John Donne, Wallace Stevens, and Marianne Moore, Amy Clampitt's poetry is, in comparison to that of most of her contemporaries, metaphorically dense, richly allusive, and structurally complex. Although she shares with many late twentieth century poets a penchant for the short lyric, her predispositions differ markedly from those of poets such as Adrienne Rich, Robert Lowell, and Sylvia Plath. Whereas these writers use poetry primarily as a vehicle for intimate self-examination, Clampitt's work celebrates the textures and intricacies of the external rather than the internal. Her poetry, time and again, looks to the natural world as the wellspring of imagination and uniformly basks in its glory. The sometimes terse, sometimes playful, always challenging idiom in which she works reflects the complexity of a world of which she is both observer and taxonomist, subject and object.

MULTITUDES, MULTITUDES AND THE ISTHMUS

Some have dismissed Clampitt's early collections *Multitudes, Multitudes* and *The Isthmus* as "a mere foreshadowing" of her later work, but writing the entry on Clampitt for *Dictionary of Literary Biography*, Robert Hosmer observed that both books contain a number of exciting poems worthy of consideration, particularly for their mythological resonance and visionary force. Poems such as "A Christmas Cactus" and "The Eve of All Souls" take on what Hosmer calls a "liturgical" assertiveness as they seek to fuse both Christian and personal mythologies into a unifying logos. Although at a mere fifteen poems *The Isthmus* is a much briefer project, it signals an important turning point in Clampitt's work. *The Isthmus* largely turns its attention from myth and allusion to natural imagery and the delights of the physical world, particularly of the place where land meets sea. Poems such as "The Lighthouse" achieve a balance between immediacy and abstraction that anticipates Clampitt's later, better-known efforts:

A dripping sleeve of incandescence
sweeps the cove, unrolls the corridor . . .
like a sleepwalking familiar—
lightening mollified, a newly
calibrated force of nature.

"THE KINGFISHER"

Critic Paul Olson observed of Clampitt's first major volume, *The Kingfisher*, that it is "a book of tough stuff, full of dirt and doctrine." Indeed his description aptly characterizes the collection's title poem, which struggles to find the meeting point between the "doctrine" of abstraction and the "dirt" of physical immediacy. Echoing Wallace Stevens's classic "Sunday Morning" in both theme and structure, "The Kingfisher" seeks to reconcile the paradox inherent in the fact that careful observation of the physical world yields both experience and distance from that experience. In effect, closeness in itself creates its own chasm between subject and object.

Clampitt chooses the Bronx Zoo's aviary as primary locus for the poem. For urbanites, the zoo's lavish variety of birds promises a refuge from the "dazzled pub crawl" of their artificial workaday environs, from a world from which "the poetry is gone." As naturally beautiful and free as the aviary's stunning variety of kingfishers, thrushes, and bellbirds are, however, the fact remains that each bird is nonetheless caged and just as confined by its environs as its observers are. This fact leads the speaker to conclude that even the birds are therefore abstractions, their sight and songs eroding, through the prism of human perception, into "a burnished, breathing wreck that didn't hurt at all."

Curiously, the poet does not see this relegation of natural beauty, this "kingfisher's burnished plunge" into abstraction, as an entirely negative thing. Instead, echoing Stevens, Clampitt asserts that the transformative nature of the imagination, that process through which it makes experience tacit to the perceiver, is precisely what makes nature real. She confidently characterizes the imagination as "an arrow/ through landscapes of untended memory: ardor/ illuminating with its terrifying currency" the process of perception.

"IMAGO"

One of the few poems that refers directly to the poet's girlhood on the Iowa prairie, "Imago" is unique among Clampitt's works in its copious use of autobiographical elements. Where most of her contemporaries would no doubt choose the first person for so obviously autobiographical a poem, even here Clampitt opts for the third person "she." Nonetheless, the reader clearly sees this poem's attempts to infuse childhood memory with mythmaking fancy. Of her Iowa childhood, Clampitt writes:

> Sometimes, she remembers, a chipped flint
> would turn up in a furrow,
>
> . . . .
>
> a nomad's artifact fished from the broth,
> half sea half land—hard evidence
> of an unfathomed state of mind.

Resonant with the land and sea imagery so prominent in her early poem "The Isthmus," "Imago" suggests likewise that the place where earth and water intersect is a flashpoint for understanding the connection between external truth and internal myth.

Clampitt conjures from sparse instants of childhood recollection the stuff of a resoundingly textured poem, one that the possible detractors she addresses may argue "has no form," but one that in her own aesthetic "trundle[s] . . . dismantled sensibility everywhere."

In a sense, it is "dismantled sensibility" that epitomizes Clampitt's poetry, particularly poems like "Imago." Weary of narrative, they seek a more sublime architecture—one that borrows heavily from both archetypal symbolism and Christian iconography. Here one sees in the same eclectic, wildly associative stanzas Jungian archetypal imagery ("the predatory stare out of the burrow") and an almost liturgical celebration of what is simultaneously both Christian and pagan ("a luna moth, the emblem/ of the born-again, . . . a totem-garden of lascivious pheromones").

"A HERMIT THRUSH"

One of the quintessential themes in Clampitt's poetry is her reminder, as friend and reviewer Mary Jo Salter puts it, that "even our memories have their physical home, and could lose it." In "A Hermit Thrush," one of the more vibrant poems from 1987's *Archaic Figure*, Clampitt meditates on both the tentativeness and tangibility with which memory informs imagination. Choosing as her setting a picnic that is for the speaker both a getaway from and a sojourn into her private myth of the world, Clampitt uses this scenario from which to announce some of her most memorable metaphysical messages. The poem formidably opens, "Nothing's certain," proceeds to assert, of our relationship with our memories, that "to/ hold on in any case means taking less and less for granted," and ends, as she does in so many of her poems, in a veiled but nonetheless omnipresent sense of triumph over the indirect but tacit with which our world makes itself known to us:

. . .   —there's

hardly a vocabulary left to wonder, uncertain
as we are of so much in this existence, this
botched, cumbersome, much-mended,
not unsatisfactory thing.

OTHER MAJOR WORKS

PLAY: *Mad with Joy*, pr. 1993 (staged reading).

NONFICTION: *Predecessors, Et Cetera: Essays*, 1991; *Love, Amy: The Selected Letters of Amy Clampitt*, 2005 (Willard Spiegelman, editor).

EDITED TEXT: *The Essential Donne*, 1988.

BIBLIOGRAPHY

Boschman, Robert. *In the Way of Nature: Ecology and Westward Expansion in the Poetry of Anne Bradstreet, Elizabeth Bishop, and Amy Clampitt*. Jefferson, N.C.: McFarland, 2009. Looks at the themes of travel, geography, cartography, and wilderness in the poetry of Clampitt as well as in that of Anne Bradstreet and Elizabeth Bishop.

Clampitt, Amy. "Amy Clampitt: An Interview." Interview by Laura Fairchild. *American Poetry Review* 16 (July/August, 1987): 17-20. In one of her few widely circulated interviews, Clampitt candidly discusses her poetry's emphasis on sound, as well as the impact classic poets Gerard Manley Hopkins and Emily Dickinson have had on her work.

Morrisroe, Patricia. "The Prime of Amy Clampitt." *New York* 17 (October 15, 1984): 44-48. Part interview and part critical analysis, Morrisroe's article emphasizes the differences between Clampitt's poetry and that of her most widely read contemporaries, "confessional" poets, such as Sylvia Plath.

Salter, Mary Jo. Introduction to *The Collected Poems of Amy Clampitt*, by Amy Clampitt. New York: Knopf, 1997. One of the most illuminating and personal sketches of Clampitt available, Salter's introduction to Clampitt's posthumously published collected poems bristles with surprising and heretofore undocumented information and anecdotes about the poet.

Spiegelman, Willard. "What to Make of an Augmented Thing." *Kenyon Review* 21, no. 1 (1999): 172-182. A thorough stylistic critique of Clampitt's work through an analysis of her *Collected Poems*.

Stein, Jean C., and Daniel G. Maroski, eds. *Contemporary Literary Criticism*. Vol. 32. Detroit: Gale Research, 1985. Focuses on the critical reception for Clampitt's seminal collection *The Kingfisher*. Points out that several critics—including Helen Vendler, Paul Olson, Peter Stitt, and Richard Howard—viewed Clampitt as "the most important new poet on the American scene" in the last quarter of the twentieth century.

Vendler, Helen. "On the Thread of Language." *New York Review of Books* 30 (March 3, 1983): 19-22. Probably the most celebrated (and quoted) review of Clampitt's work to appear in her lifetime, Vendler's ebullient review of *The Kingfisher* notes that its progression over her previous work is "dumbfounding" and that the collection as a whole serves as a remarkable "triumph over the resistance of language, the reason why poetry lasts."

Weisman, Karen A. "Starving Before the Actual: Amy Clampitt's *Voyages: A Homage to John Keats*." *Criticism* 36, no. 1 (1994): 119-138. A close reading of one of Clampitt's collections.

White, Edmund. "Poetry as Alchemy." *Nation* 236 (April 16, 1983): 485-486. White concentrates on what he views as a profound and poignant contradiction in Clampitt's work: that her poems simultaneously both suggest and shy away from narrative. As he observes of Clampitt's work, "one senses [in it] not awkwardness but rather a strange fusion of an ambition to narrate and a talent for suppressing the tale."

Gregory D. Horn

LUCILLE CLIFTON

Born: Depew, New York; June 27, 1936
Died: Baltimore, Maryland; February 13, 2010

PRINCIPAL POETRY

Good Times, 1969
Good News About the Earth, 1972
An Ordinary Woman, 1974
Two-Headed Woman, 1980
Good Woman: Poems and a Memoir, 1969-1980,
    1987
Next: New Poems, 1987
Ten Oxherding Pictures, 1988
Quilting: Poems, 1987-1990, 1991
The Book of Light, 1993
The Terrible Stories, 1996
Blessing the Boats: New and Selected Poems, 1988-
    2000, 2000
Mercy, 2004
Voices, 2008

OTHER LITERARY FORMS

In addition to her poetry, Lucille Clifton wrote prose, often for children but also for adults. *Generations: A Memoir* (1976), is included as a part of *Good Woman*. She began publishing books for children in 1970 with *Some of the Days of Everett Anderson*, short poems in a picture-book format that spawned a series about the life of a young black boy. *The Times They Used to Be* (1974) is written as a narrative poem. She wrote other picture books in prose: *The Boy Who Didn't Believe in Spring* (1973), *All Us Come Cross the Water* (1973), *My Brother Fine with Me* (1975), *Three Wishes* (1976), and *Amifika* (1977), as well as a short novel, *The Lucky Stone* (1979). In response to questions her own six children had, Clifton wrote *The Black BC's* (1970), an alphabet book that blends poetry with prose. A departure from her usual perspective, *Sonora Beautiful* (1981) features a white girl as the protagonist.

ACHIEVEMENTS

In 2007, Lucille Clifton became the first African American to be awarded the Ruth Lilly Poetry Prize

from the Poetry Foundation in recognition of her lifetime achievement. In 1988, she became the only poet ever to have two books, *Next* and *Good Woman*, nominated for the Pulitzer Prize in the same year. Clifton won the National Book Award for *Blessing the Boats* in 2000; previously, she was a National Book Award finalist for *The Terrible Stories*. She also won the Coretta Scott King Award for *Everett Anderson's Goodbye* in 1984. Other honors include an Emmy Award from the American Academy of Television Arts and Sciences, the Charity Randall Citation (1991), the Shelley Memorial Award (1992), a grant from the Eric Mathieu King Fund (1996), the Shestack Prize from *American Poetry Review* (1988), the Lannan Literary Award for Poetry (1996), the Lila Wallace-*Reader's Digest* Writers' Award (1998), the Anisfield-Wolf Book Award for lifetime achievement (2001), the Langston Hughes Award (2003), the Frost Medal from the Poetry Society of America (2010), and three fellowships from the National Endowment for the Arts (1969, 1970, 1972). She held honorary degrees from the University of Maryland and Towson State University. Clifton was elected to the American Academy of Arts and Sciences and served as chancellor of the Academy of American Poets (1999-2005). In 1991, Clifton became a distinguished professor of humanities at St. Mary's College in Columbia, Maryland. She retired in 2007.

BIOGRAPHY

Lucille Clifton was born Thelma Lucille Sayles, daughter of Samuel L. Sayles and Thelma Moore Sayles, in Depew, New York, and grew up with two half sisters and a brother. Her father worked for the New York steel mills. Her mother was a launderer, homemaker, and aspiring poet but once had to burn all her poems because her husband told her, "Ain't no wife of mine going to be no poetry writer."

Ironically, both parents encouraged Clifton to be anything she wanted to be. She was named for her great-grandmother, who, according to her father, was the first black woman to be legally hanged in the state of Virginia. The first in her family to finish high school or consider attending college, Clifton entered college at Howard University at the age of sixteen, having earned a full scholarship. After majoring in drama and attending for two years, Clifton lost her scholarship. She told her father,

> I don't need that stuff. I'm going to write poems. I can do what I want to do! I'm from Dahomey women!

After transferring to Fredonia State Teachers College in 1955, Clifton worked as an actor and began her writing career. While at Fredonia, she met novelist Ishmael Reed at a writers' group, and he showed some of her poems to Langston Hughes, who was the first to publish Clifton's writing.

In 1958, she married Fred James Clifton. They had four daughters, Sidney, Fredrica, Gillian, and Alexia, and two sons, Channing and Graham. In 1969, poet Robert Hayden entered her poems into competition for the Young Men's-Young Women's Hebrew Association Poetry Center Discovery Award. Clifton won the award and with it the publication of her first volume of poems, *Good Times*, which was chosen as one of the ten best books of the year by *The New York Times*. Prior to 1971, when she became poet-in-residence at the historically black Coppin State College in Baltimore, Maryland, Clifton had worked in state and federal government positions. She remained at Coppin until 1974. From 1979 through 1982, she was poet laureate of the state of Maryland. From 1982 to 1983, she was a visiting writer at Columbia University School of the Arts and at George Washington University. Subsequently, she taught literature and creative writing at the University of California, Santa Cruz, and later at St. Mary's College. In addition to appearing in more than one hundred anthologies of poetry, her poems have come to popular attention through her numerous television appearances.

ANALYSIS

Distinguished by her minimalist style, Lucille Clifton is sometimes compared with poets Gwendolyn Brooks and Emily Dickinson. Clifton is usually considered one of the prominent black aesthetic poets, along with Sonia Sanchez and Amiri Baraka, who were consciously breaking with Eurocentric conventions in their work. The characteristics of Clifton's craft—her concise, often untitled free verse, use of vernacular speech, repetition, puns and allusions, lowercase letters, sparse punctuation, and focused use of common

words—became her trademark style, which is clearly unfettered by others' expectations. Without worrying about convention, about boundaries—created either physically or emotionally—Clifton shares her perceptions of life by writing about the feelings humans share. Her rationale for writing poetry was to assert the importance of being human. In an interview with Michael Glaser, Clifton stated that

> writing is a way of continuing to hope. When things sometimes feel as if they're not going to get any better, writing offers a way of trying to connect with something beyond that obvious feeling . . . a way of remembering I am not alone"

She further stated that she sees writing as a way to bear witness, to hold back the darkness by acknowledging the pain of the past and then choosing a more joyful future.

Lucille Clifton (AP/Wide World Photos)

GOOD TIMES

Clifton's early work was frequently inspired by her family, especially her children, and was often a celebration of African American ancestry, heritage, and culture. In the title poem of *Good Times*, Clifton reminds all children, "oh children think about the/ good times." She juxtaposes society's perceptions and her own in the opening poem of the collection—"in the inner city/ or/ like we call it/ home"—to honor the place where she lives. Believing in the humanity of all people, she calls on each person, regardless of ancestry, to take control of his or her life. Of Robert, in the poem by the same name, she states he "married a master/ who whipped his mind/ until he died," suggesting through the image that the union was one of mutual consent. Her impatience with humans of all kinds who do not strive to improve their lot is a theme begun with this collection and continued throughout her life. Another theme that arises here is optimism, as in "Flowers": "Oh/ here we are/ flourishing for the field/ and the name of the place/ is Love."

GOOD WOMAN

One theme of the poems in *Good Woman* involves Clifton's ethnic pride, as is reflected in "After Kent State": "white ways are/ the way of death/ come into the/ black/ and live." This volume also contains a section called "Heroes," which directly extends this first theme, and ends the book with a section called "Some Jesus."

> I have learned
> some few things
> like when a man
> walk manly
> he don't stumble
> even in the lion's den.

Although the gender in this poem is male, Clifton would not limit the message to men. Overall, her early work heralds African Americans for their resistance to oppression and their survival of racism.

AN ORDINARY WOMAN

An Ordinary Woman includes poems divided into two sections, beginning with "Sisters," a celebration of family and relationships. "The Lesson of the Falling Leaves" includes the following lines:

> the leaves believe
> such letting go is love
> such love is faith
> such faith is grace
> such grace is god
> i agree with the leaves.

It is a testimony to hope, a theme that runs throughout her work. Consistently juxtaposing past with present, Clifton provides wisdom to guide the future, as in the example of "Jackie Robinson":

> ran against walls
> without breaking.
> in night games
> was not foul
> but, brave as a hit
> over whitestone fences,
> entered the conquering dark.

TWO-HEADED WOMAN

Two-Headed Woman, which invokes the African American folk belief in a "Two-Headed Woman," with its overtones of a voodoo conjurer, begins with a section entitled "Homage to Mine," moves onto "Two-Headed Woman," and concludes with "The Light That Came to Lucille Clifton." While Clifton's works often have allusions to Christianity, as in the "Some Jesus" series in *Good News About the Earth*, she refers to other faiths as well, including the Hindu goddess Kali, from "An Ordinary Woman," providing evidence of her openness to multiple ways of knowing. As a "Two-Headed Woman," in the opening poem of that section, Clifton says she has "one face turned outward/ one face/ swiveling slowly in." Spirituality and mysticism pervade this collection, as the final poem attests, with its reference to the "shimmering voices" of her ancestors, whom the poet has heard singing in the "populated air."

QUILTING

In five parts, each of the first four named for traditional quilt patterns, "Log Cabin," "Catalpa Flower," "Eight-Pointed Star," and "Tree of Life," *Quilting* seems pieced together, like a quilt. It ends with a single poem, "Blessing the Boats," in "prayer," as if the spiritual life serves as the connecting threads. Clifton honors those whose roles in history have brought about change, as in

"February 11, 1990," dedicated to "Nelson Mandela and Winnie," and "Memo," which is dedicated "to Fannie Lou Hamer." The poem's "questions and answers" ends with "the surest failure/ is the unattempted walk."

THE TERRIBLE STORIES

In *The Terrible Stories*, Clifton chronicles the terrible stories of her own life, which include her struggle with breast cancer, and the terrible stories of her people, which include slavery and the prejudice that has survived time. The last section in the book, "From the Book of David," concludes with a question from the poem "What Manner of Man." Referring to the biblical David, the poet asks how this David will be remembered "if he stands in the tents of history/ bloody skull in one hand, harp in the other?" Clifton's ability to look at history—ancient, contemporary, or personal—and find redemption in it gives humanity a way to face and survive its failures; this perspective shows her consistent faith in grace.

BLESSING THE BOATS

Blessing the Boats includes new poems as well as selected poems from *Next*, sometimes called a collection of sorrow songs, as loss is the overriding theme. Once more, "New Poems," the opening section of the anthology, records and comments on contemporary events of the twentieth century, such as school shootings, referred to in "The Times," and the bombing of black churches, referred to in "Alabama 9/15/63." It also addresses private occurrences, such as the traumas that gave rise to such poems as "Dialysis" and "Donor."

VOICES

In *Voices*, which is divided into the three sections "hearing," "being heard," and "ten oxherding pictures," Clifton continues with the themes and motifs of her earlier volumes. The first section is "a collection of persona" and personification, according to reviewer Cameron Conaway, for characters, animals, historical figures, and abstract ideas (as in the poem "sorrows") are given life and voice. Most poignant are the interior monologues of three characters seen only on cardboard boxes: Aunt Jemima, Uncle Ben, and the Cream of Wheat man. Each longs to know about home and family, common themes in Clifton's work, but it is the Cream of Wheat man who relates their collective wanderings and whose longing is the most poignant: "we

return to our shelves/ our boxes ben and jemima and me/ we pose and smile I simmer what/ is my name." Clifton's thematic concern for recapturing lost names is also emphasized in the monologues "mataoka" and "witko," as the poems respectively have subtitles that reveal more about the names of the Native Americans: "(actual name of Pocahontas)" and "aka crazy horse." In the monologues, Clifton subtly forces readers to look beyond what they think they know to acknowledge the depths of the lives of those who have been denied voice.

The issue of loss extends not only to names but also to the land. Such loss is examined in the second section with the poem "in 1844 explorers John Fremont and Kit Carson discovered Lake Tahoe," in which Clifton characteristically uses repetition of words and structure to emphasize time and another group of Native Americans—the Washoe—whose history has also been overshadowed: "in 1841 Washoe children// in 1842 Washoe warriors began to dream// in 1843 Washoe elders began to speak// in 1844 Fremont and Carson." The final line of the poem speaks volumes of the loss through its terseness.

Clifton's interest in the realm of the spiritual is also evident in *Voices*. In the first section, animals—a horse and a raccoon—express prayers, and in a "dog's god," the deity of the canine not only blesses the dog with "four magnificent legs" but also "two-legs to feed him." In the second section, Clifton moves to the personal—she is most often the speaker—and acknowledges that "the gods/ are men"; in the poem "dad," her father thinks that such ". . . gods might/ understand/ a man like me."

The third section, "ten oxherding pictures," contains a group of poems previously issued in 1988 as a limited-edition chapbook. Clifton acknowledges that these poems are based on "an allegorical series composed as a training guide for Chinese Buddhist monks," yet she wrote her poems having only a knowledge of the titles of the pictures. Nonetheless, her poems coincide with the pictures: Both are guides to enlightenment as one journeys in search of self. In the eighth poem of the series, Clifton concludes "man is not ox/ i am not ox/ no thing is ox/ all things are ox": Alone, nothing is the self; together, all is the self. This revelation is the converse of an idea expressed earlier in the collection in "mirror," where people are "... not understanding/ what we are or what we/ had hoped to be." However, through the meditation on the ten pictures, *Voices* ends with Clifton's characteristic theme of hope—that its readers come to understand what and who they are and what they hope to be through "hearing" and "being heard."

OTHER MAJOR WORKS

NONFICTION: *Generations: A Memoir*, 1976.

CHILDREN'S LITERATURE: *The Black BC's*, 1970; *Some of the Days of Everett Anderson*, 1970; Everett Anderson's Christmas Coming, 1971; *All Us Come Cross the Water*, 1973; *The Boy Who Didn't Believe in Spring*, 1973; *Everett Anderson's Year*, 1974; *The Times They Used to Be*, 1974; *My Brother Fine with Me*, 1975; *Everett Anderson's Friend*, 1976; *Three Wishes*, 1976; *Amifika*, 1977; *Everett Anderson's 1-2-3*, 1977; *Everett Anderson's Nine Month Long*, 1978; *The Lucky Stone*, 1979; *Sonora Beautiful*, 1981; *Everett Anderson's Goodbye*, 1983; *One of the Problems of Everett Anderson*, 2001.

BIBLIOGRAPHY

Anaporte-Easton, Jean. "Healing Our Wounds: The Direction of Difference in the Poetry of Lucille Clifton and Judith Johnson." *Mid-American Review* 14, no. 2 (1994). This essay suggests that Clifton's voice is distinctive because of her use of physical imagery, particularly of the body, in order to write a work that seeks to unite it with both mind and spirit.

Bennett, Bruce. "Preservation Poets." Review of *Quilting*. *The New York Times Book Review*, March 1, 1992, pp. 22-23. Poet and critic Bennett discusses Clifton's *Quilting*, noting that the first four sections are named after traditional quilting designs, yet the final section, "prayer," consists of a single poem. He believes readers familiar with Clifton's work will witness recurrent themes section by section: importance of history on the present and future, celebration of women, and life as a personal journey of spiritual growth and discovery.

Clifton, Lucille. "A Conversation with Lucille Clifton." Interview by Alexs Pate. *Black Renaissance* 8, no. 2/3 (Summer, 2008): 12-19. Author and professor Pate interviews Clifton as part of a series of conversations with authors who represent excellence in African American literature sponsored by the Givens Foundation for African American Literature and the University of Minnesota. Clifton discusses many African Americans she has known and says poetry is "mind and soul and heart, a balancing act."

_____. "Lucille Clifton." Interview by Shirley Marie Jordan. In *Broken Silences: Interviews with Black and White Women Writers*, edited by Jordan. New Brunswick, N.J.: Rutgers University Press. 1993. Jordan and Clifton explore the differences in perception between black and white women and how that affects their approaches to writing. Focuses on *Sonora Beautiful*, one of the few works by a female African American writer told from the perspective of a white protagonist.

Evans, Mari, ed. *Black Women Writers (1950-1980): A Critical Evaluation*. Garden City, N.Y.: Anchor Press/Doubleday, 1984. Devotes three substantial essays to Clifton and her work, including "Lucille Clifton," written by Clifton herself. The other two selections are Audrey T. McCluskey's "Tell the Good News: A View of the Works of Lucille Clifton" and Haki Madhubti's "Lucille Clifton: Warm Water, Greased Legs, and Dangerous Poetry."

Holladay, Hilary. *Wild Blessings: The Poetry of Lucille Clifton*. Baton Rouge: Louisiana State University Press, 2004. A study of Clifton's work, including an interview with the poet.

Koontz, Tom, and Dolores Anindon D'Angelo. "The Poetry of Lucille Clifton." In *Masterplots II: African American Literature*, edited by Tyrone Williams. Rev. ed. Pasadena, Calif.: Salem Press, 2009. Provides an in-depth analysis of Clifton's poetry that looks at her life and how it influenced the themes of her poetry and children's literature.

Lupton, Mary Jane. *Lucille Clifton: Her Life and Letters*. Westport, Conn.: Praeger, 2006. This full-length biography of the poet explores Clifton's life and work and offers insight and analysis.

White, Mark Bernard. "Sharing the Living Light: Rhetorical, Poetic, and Social Identity in Lucille Clifton." *CLA Journal* 40, no. 3 (1997): 288-305. An evaluation of Clifton's presentation of her self-identity, especially focusing on the poems "An Ordinary Woman" and "Two-Headed Woman."

Woo, Elaine. "Lucille Clifton, 1936-2010: Poet Weathered Tragedies, Celebrated Survival in Work." *Los Angeles Times*, February 21, 2010, p. A36. This obituary provides a short biography and notes her accomplishments and expression of optimism in her poems, despite her many hardships.

Alexa L. Sandmann
Updated by Paula C. Barnes

ANDREI CODRESCU

Born: Sibiu, Romania; December 20, 1946
Also known as: Andrei Perlmutter; Andrei Steiu

PRINCIPAL POETRY

License to Carry a Gun, 1970
The History of the Growth of Heaven, 1971
Comrade Past and Mister Present, 1991
Belligerence, 1993
Alien Candor: Selected Poems, 1970-1995, 1996
Poezii Alese/Selected Poetry, 2000
It Was Today: New Poems by Andrei Codrescu, 2003
Jealous Witness: New Poems, 2008
The Forgiven Submarine, 2009 (with Ruxandra Cesereanu)

OTHER LITERARY FORMS

Andrei Codrescu (kah-DREHS-kew) has written novels, including *Messiah* (1999), *Casanova in Bohemia* (2002), and *Wakefield* (2004), and a collection of shorter pieces, *A Bar in Brooklyn: Novellas and Stories, 1970-1978* (1999). He wrote the screenplay for *Road Scholar: Coast to Coast Late in the Century* (1993), which won several awards, including a Peabody Award. He has published collections of essays, including *Zombifications: Essays from National Public Radio* (1994), *Hail Babylon! Looking for the American City at the End of the Millennium* (1998), *New Or-* *leans, Mon Amour: Twenty Years of Writing from the City* (2006), and *The Posthuman Dada Guide: Tzara and Lenin Play Chess* (2009), and several memoir/travelogues, including *The Hole in the Flag: A Romanian Exile's Story of Return and Revolution* (1991) and *Ay Cuba! A Socio-Erotic Journey* (1999).

He founded and has served as editor for and contributor to the online journal *Exquisite Corpse: A Journal of Letters and Life*. He has also been a commentator on National Public Radio and a columnist for *Gambit Weekly*, a prize-winning alternative newspaper in New Orleans. He has translated the work of Lucian Blaga, a modern Romanian poet, and edited anthologies of material from *Exquisite Corpse*. He has also issued a number of audio tapes and compact discs.

ACHIEVEMENTS

Andrei Codrescu has received numerous awards and honors, including five National Endowment for the Arts Fellowships, the Big Table Poetry Award (1970), the A. D. Emmart Humanities Award (1982), Pushcart Prizes (1983, 2005), the General Electric Foundation Poetry Award (1985), the Towson State University Literature Prize (1987), the American Civil Liberties Union Freedom of Speech Award (1995), the Mayor's Arts Award, New Orleans (1996), the Literature Prize of the Romanian Cultural Foundation, Bucharest (1996), the Lowell Thomas Gold Award for Excellence in Travel Journalism (2001), the Ovidius Prize for literature (2006), and the Romania Radio Cultural Award (2008). He was awarded honorary doctorates from Shenandoah College and the Massachussetts College of Art.

BIOGRAPHY

Born Andrei Perlmutter in 1946 in communist-controlled Transylvania, Andrei Codrescu first published under the name Andrei Steiu, chosen to conceal his Jewishness in that anti-Semitic milieu. To escape from a regime he found oppressive, he emigrated to the United States in 1966, living at first in Detroit, where he associated with the Detroit Artists Workshop, founded by John Sinclair, a well-known poet and social activist. At about this time, he began publishing poetry in Romania, using the name Codrescu. After a year, Codrescu moved to New York, linking up with the New York Beat poets, and began to publish in English. After publishing his first poetry book, *License to Carry a Gun*, he moved to San Francisco; seven years later, he moved to Baltimore and ultimately settled in New Orleans. He became a United States citizen in 1981. From 1984 to 2009, he was the MacCurdy Distinguished Professor at Louisiana State University. He has two children, Lucian and Tristan, from his first marriage to Alice Henderson. He later married Laura Cole.

ANALYSIS

Andrei Codrescu's work can be seen as combining two elements: Surrealism and the expressions of a flâneur, the gentleman stroller described by Charles Baudelaire, who comments on the urban scene of which he is a part. These converge to form a goal of intensified awareness of oneself and the environment. Codrescu is both detached and involved. His rejection of convention avoids the rage of the alienated and is paradoxically both softened and made more penetrating by humor.

JEALOUS WITNESS

In *Jealous Witness*, Codrescu's fascination with the urban milieu plays a central role. In the aftermath of Hurricane Katrina in 2005, he focused on New Orleans. In "Cleaning Ladies," he expresses his fear that an urban treasure is irremediably gone:

> they were cleansing storms
> katrina and rita
> they were cleaning women
> hired by the housing boom broom
> real estate real estate
> you kept rising like the water
> but the poor kept staying on
> in the days before the storms
> then came katrina and rita
> to finish what you began
> cleansing storms oh cleaning ladies
> making realtor dreams come true
> oh look over that rising sea
> I'll take the lobster and the vino
> see the shining shining city
> it's the new new orleans rising
> coin-operated by casinos

He alludes to the underclass, including artists, once protected and even nourished by the city's special social architecture but threatened by mercantile interests and then literally swept away by the storms, but he deftly avoids anger by the playfulness of "housing boom broom" and the personification of the storms as members of that underclass. With anger controlled, the bitter sarcasm of a shining city that has become a gambling arcade slices away crass unconcern for what has been lost.

This Surrealist flâneur has made the astonishing transition from marginalized outsider, foreigner and Jew, to academic insider and uncrowned laureate. That transition has not blunted his commitment to art as manifested both in his support of freshness and experimentation in poetry through *Exquisite Corpse* and in his rejoicing in beauty. In "The Incoming Sneeze or the Old Man's Nose," he writes:

> for you there is always beauty
> you can recognize by a whiff like a perfume in a crowd
> that's what your crooked nose is for

The reference to his Jewishness is as unmistakable as is the romantic tone, and so, presumably, is the reference, conscious or not, to Edmond Rostand's *Cyrano de Bergerac* (pr. 1897; English translation, 1898).

THE FORGIVEN SUBMARINE

In *The Forgiven Submarine*, Codrescu describes his exhilarating collaborative exploration of the unconscious with his coauthor, Ruxandra Cesereanu:

> the two divers were a shook-up pianist
> and a nearsighted drunk amerikan beatnik
> banding together for dives to great depths
> a pianist with hair from neverland and an amerikan
> with transylvanian moustaches sensitized by the
>   imminence of nothingness
> his head and armpits shaved one earring in his ear new
>   age aimlessness
> gold chains jingling on his ankles setting the ocean
>   foaming
> and setting minds to work chewing the cud
> ahoy there forgiven submarine
> we are diving your way out of submerged and
>   unadorned time

The deliberately unsettling Surrealism is softened with slang and self-mockery, and the ambition of "setting minds to work" made more palatable, as it were, by the homespun metaphor of "chewing the cud."

OTHER MAJOR WORKS

LONG FICTION: *The Repentance of Lorraine*, 1976; *The Blood Countess*, 1995; *Messiah*, 1999; *Casanova in Bohemia*, 2002; *Wakefield*, 2004.

SHORT FICTION: *A Bar in Brooklyn: Novellas and Stories, 1970-1978*, 1999.

SCREENPLAY: *Road Scholar: Coast to Coast Late in the Century*, 1993.

NONFICTION: *A Craving for Swan*, 1986; *Raised by Puppets Only to Be Killed by Research*, 1987; *The Disappearance of the Outside: A Manifesto for Escape*, 1990; *The Hole in the Flag: A Romanian Exile's Story of Return and Revolution*, 1991; *The Muse Is Always Half-Dressed in New Orleans*, 1993; *Road Scholar: Coast to Coast Late in the Century*, 1993; *Zombifications: Essays from National Public Radio*, 1994; *The Dog With the Chip in His Neck: Essays from NPR and Elsewhere*, 1996; *Hail Babylon! Looking for the American City at the End of the Millennium*, 1998; *Ay Cuba! A Socio-Erotic Journey*, 1999; *The Devil Never Sleeps, and Other Essays*, 2000; *An Involuntary Genius in America's Shoes (and What Happened Afterwards)*, 2001; *New Orleans, Mon Amour: Twenty Years of Writing from the City*, 2006; *The Posthuman Dada Guide: Tzara and Lenin Play Chess*, 2009.

TRANSLATION: *At the Court of Yearning*, 1989 (of Lucian Blaga).

EDITED TEXTS: *The Stiffest of the Corpse: An Exquisite Corpse Reader, 1983-1988*, 1988; *Thus Spake the Corpse: An Exquisite Corpse Reader, 1988-1998*, 1999.

BIBLIOGRAPHY

Codrescu, Andrei. "Andrei Codrescu Brings His Unique Take on America to Idaho." Interview by Anna Webb. *McClatchy-Tribune Business News*, February 13, 2007, p. 1. Codrescu discusses everything from leaving Romania, to being with the Beat poets, to Hurricane Katrina and the city of New Orleans in Louisiana. He says the United States is "momentarily occupied by zombies," but its "future is sound."

_____. "An Interview with Andrei Codrescu." Interview by Richard Collins. *Xavier Review* 20, no. 2 (2000): 13-18. The author talks about his writings and his life.

Collins, Richard. "Andrei Codrescu's Mioritic Space." *MELUS* 23, no. 3 (1998): 83-101. Miorita, a ewe in a Romanian folk poem, warns the shepherd that he is about to be betrayed and murdered. The shepherd asks the ewe not to tell his mother that he was murdered but rather that he married the daughter of a king. So Miorita wanders, telling the tale of a wedding that never occurred. Lucian Blaga, the poet whose works Codrescu translated, defined a Mioritic space as a geography of the Romanian imagination.

Marin, Naomi. "The Rhetoric of Andrei Codrescu: A Reading in Exilic Fragmentation." In *Realms of Exile: Nomadism, Diasporas, and Eastern European Voices*, edited by Domnica Radulescu. Lanham, Md.: Lexington Books, 2002. Discussion of how Codrescu's status as an exile from his native land affects his writing.

Olson, Kirby. *Andrei Codrescu and the Myth of America*. Jefferson, N.C.: McFarland, 2005. Examines his poetry and essays and how they relate to Surrealism.

Ratner, Rochelle. Review of *It Was Today*. *Library Journal* 128, no. 13 (August, 2003): 88. Sees his poems falling into two types, everyday poems and those reflecting his experiences as an exile.

Alvin G. Burstein

HENRI COLE

Born: Fukuoka, Japan; 1956

PRINCIPAL POETRY

The Marble Queen, 1986
The Zoo Wheel of Knowledge, 1989
The Look of Things, 1995
The Visible Man, 1998
Middle Earth, 2003
Blackbird and Wolf, 2007
Pierce the Skin: Selected Poems, 1982-2007, 2010

OTHER LITERARY FORMS

Though he is primarily known as a poet, Henri Cole has written several brief statements about his writing practice and his life, frequently in response to prompts from literary societies and little magazines. Perceptive and concise as aphorisms ("A lyric poem is a MRI of what it is to be human. . . . Like a delicate instrument, it records all the little agitations of seeing and being"), these carefully fashioned pronouncements share many of the qualities of his poems and complement his work in interesting ways.

ACHIEVEMENTS

Henri Cole has won a number of the most prestigious awards available to American poets. In 2008, he received the Lenore Marshall Poetry Prize from the Academy of American Poets, granted to the previous year's most outstanding book of poetry, for *Blackbird and Wolf*. This collection also received the Ambassador Book Award from the English Speaking Union, a Lambda Literary Award, and the Massachusetts Book Award in poetry. *Middle Earth* was a finalist for the Pulitzer Prize in poetry and received the Kingsley Tufts Award and the Massachusetts Book Award in 2004. Also in 2004, he received an Academy Award in Literature from the American Academy of Arts and Letters. Cole has also won fellowships from the National Endowment for the Arts, the Guggenheim Foundation, and from the Ingram Merrill Foundation. He is also the recipient of the Berlin Prize of the American Academy in Berlin, the Rome Prize in Literature from the American Academy of Arts and Letters, the Amy Lowell Traveling Scholarship, and a fellowship from the Camargo Foundation in Cassis, France.

BIOGRAPHY

Henri Cole was born in 1956 into an American military family residing in Fukuoka, Japan. He was raised in Virginia, growing up in a home where three languages (English, French, and Armenian) were routinely spoken, only one of which he understood. He ascribes his sensitivity to tone to his dependence on vocal inflection in understanding meaning.

In the sonnet sequence "Apollo," he portrays his father ". . . making our house/ a theater of hysteria and de-spair"; in a short autobiographical essay, he describes the violence of that house, where he learned to read the signs as he heard "the household escalate toward danger—the voices of my parents growing hysterical, lamps being thrown across rooms." He reports that he was beaten from his early childhood. Many of his poems dramatize the complexity of his response to his upbringing and his parents, who are treated with gratitude, ambivalence, and satire through his collections.

Cole also notes that his household was Roman Catholic and he was both succored and mystified by his devotion and by his feelings that God remained silent to his pleas. This spiritual yearning is a continuing component of Cole's mature poetry. "My only dialogue" during that period, he writes, "was with God, whom I besieged with my prayers." He describes the solitary nature of his early years as a kind of existential state necessary for his development as a writer.

At the College of William and Mary, where he would receive a bachelor of arts in 1978, Cole began writing poetry during his junior year. He describes his apprentice work as unoriginal, wholly autobiographical, and filled with unarticulated homosexual yearning and uncertainty. One important early poetic master, however, was James Merrill, whose refined surfaces, wit, and self-exploration Cole admires, and who remained a major influence, particularly through Cole's first two books.

Cole received a master's degree from the University of Wisconsin at Milwaukee in 1980. After receiving an M.F.A. from Columbia University in 1982, he became executive director of the Academy of American Poets, a position he held until 1988. He has since held teaching positions at Smith College and Brandeis, Columbia, Harvard (where he was Briggs-Copeland Lecturer in Poetry), and Yale universities. He currently teaches at Ohio State University in Columbus.

ANALYSIS

Early in his career, Henri Cole was acknowledged as a poet of notable formal complexity and range. He has since come to disown certain of the ornamental elements of his early work: "My first poems were written with a descriptive flourish. You might say the gold bars of language hid the animal pacing in them." This criticism carries an echo of Rainer Maria Rilke's panther, with the tensed energy of the animal pacing in contained circles. However, Cole's early lines remain muscular and articulate, qualities that deepened in later books. In the poems of *The Look of Things* and particularly *The Visible Man*, the language carries a great visceral impact. The often-tormented physicality of the image and the line has remained in the later books, though the poems of *Middle Earth* and *Blackbird and Wolf* have moved toward a simplified style that is no less masterful and controlled than the earlier collections.

Though the formal characteristics of his poems have changed, Cole has remained principally a poet of the self. In rejecting the poetry of aesthetic description, Cole reminds his readers that "a poem is not just a response to the external world. It should also present the reader with a mind in action, a self in dialogue with itself." The poems enact the process of the creation of consciousness or being. Much of this exploration is played out through two of the great human metaphors of self-building: the identification and rejection children direct toward their parents and the vulnerability, ecstasy, and loss of the sexual encounter.

Though each motif carries elements of autobiography, in Cole's work, the narrative is not primary but rather is the forge of identity and the passion—often presented with Christian undertones—of a self in the process of realization. This development is not always a triumphant epiphany of self-awareness; to the contrary, it can be conditional, transitory, a moment driven as much by disgust as delectation. The repulsion and the ecstasy are both partially grounded (as are, more generally, Cole's spiritual and erotic aspirations) in his Catholic upbringing, a fact to which he points while explaining why "self-love and self-hate co-exist in my poems, as they did in life."

Many of the poems throughout the collections are in one of two forms: the self-portrait, presented with a conscious note of artifice in which the speaker becomes the object that is being created; and the ars poetica, in which the writer investigates the way he deploys language to shape and present the moment consciousness is created. The poem, after all, is an object fashioned in the same manner, and in the same moment, as the emo-

tions and conception of the self. Cole both brings a particular drama to these familiar poetic types and links the form with the feeling. He argues that "to write only a poem of language or a poem of emotion is not enough. The two must wrestle vigorously with one another, like squirrels for a nut."

THE VISIBLE MAN

Perhaps more than any other of his books, *The Visible Man* contains a contrast between linguistic pleasure and the traumatic and elegiac core of the poems. "Chiffon Morning," for example, is a harrowing depiction of Cole's relationship with his mother and of her decline into depression. "I am lying in bed with my mother,/ where my father seldom lay. Little poem,/ help me to say all I need to say, better." The poem's beautiful and decorative language—"Hair dyed, combed; nails polished; necklace-like scar/ ear-to-ear. . . ."—acts as a palliative to the severity of the scenes but is also a veil held over the suffering the woman both shares with and keeps from her son. Through the six poems of the sequence, however, the nakedness and complications of their emotional connection are gradually uncovered.

The masterful "Self-Portrait as Four Styles of Pompeian Wall Painting," written in four sonnets that correspond to the changing periods of Pompeian fresco, is a layered exploration of identity in conversation with an external work of art. The poem plays out in the manner of a cinematic montage, as the self-characterization develops in relation to the advancing stylistic periods. The first poem announces, ". . . I am as others have made me,/ imitating monumental Greek statuary/ despite my own feminized way of being," but this description is reevaluated and altered not only in relation to later styles, but also through the historical resonance of Pompeii's destruction (". . . I do not see/ the gold sky at sunset but blackbirds hurled/ like lava stones"), as well as the subjects of specific paintings ("On a faded panel of Pompeian red,/ there's an erotic x-ray of my soul:/ a pale boy-girl figure. . . ."). The result is a poem that exposes its layers in a manner reminiscent of the excavation and discovery of the city it takes as inspiration.

MIDDLE EARTH

Middle Earth begins the shift to the simplified, resonant voicings of Cole's later work. Its title may suggest the shift as his life's contradictions turn to move along the continuum toward the opposite pole. It was written, he notes, "between youth and maturity, between free verse and formalism, between plain speech and the beautiful Merrillesque style I loved when I was young, between love and hate, sorrow and joy." The development of the book's style suggested itself while Cole was living in Kyoto, where much of the collection was composed. The austere balance and quiet articulation of these lines were influenced by his surroundings and an ideal of beauty that prizes the direct over the wrought.

In "Self-Portrait in a Gold Kimono," the first named poem in the collection, Cole writes, "I cling like a cicada to the latticework of memory." The poem is written in the affectless tone of a child describing how "Growing, I am growing now," and the way in which "the essence of self emerges/ shuttling between parents," but is overlaid with the examination and elaboration of the artist, creating images and similes: "Father is holding me and blowing in my ear,/ like a glassblower on a flame."

A prefatory poem announced the project of the collection "as a man alone fills a void with words,/ not to be consoling or to point to what is good,/ but to say something true that has body,/ because it is proof of his existence." The conditions in the penultimate line, the attempt to voice a truth with body, are essential to the impulse of the poems. Once again, Cole's work strives to be not merely an act of memory for its own sake, but a search for meaning which may inhabit the self it is creating.

BIBLIOGRAPHY

Cole, Henri. "Henri Cole." Interview by Christopher Hennessy. In *Outside the Lines: Talking with Contemporary Gay Poets*, edited by Hennessy. Ann Arbor: University of Michigan Press, 2005. In this perceptive and lively interview, Hennessy and Cole talk about the poet's life, writing practices, and artistic development. A very useful presentation of many of the thematic and formal preoccupations of Cole's oeuvre. Bibliography.

Hammer, Langdon. "Apollo and Dionysus." *American Scholar* 77, no. 4 (Autumn, 2008): 64-65. A short article centered on one of Cole's aphoristic statements from an interview in which he describes his desire to be "Apollonian in body and Dionysian in spirit." Hammer discusses ways in which this is a reversal from typical expectations and provides an interesting approach to reading Cole.

McLane, Maureen N. "Is This a Table? No, This Is a Poem." Review of *Middle Earth*. *The New York Times*, April 27, 2003, p. 8. A particularly compelling review of "Middle Earth," which discusses the poet's progression from his earlier books and draws out many of the significant themes and passages of the collection.

Vendler, Helen. "A Dissonant Triad." Review of *The Zoo Wheel of Knowledge*. *Parnassus: Poetry in Review* 16, no. 2 (1991): 391-404. A review of *The Zoo Wheel of Knowledge* by the noted poetry critic and onetime colleague of Cole's, which praises the collection for its satirical sharpness and its avoidance of "ringing declarations," while calling for more astringency in its sweeter, Merrillesque moments.

Todd Samuelson

MICHAEL COLLIER

Born: Phoenix, Arizona; May 25, 1953

PRINCIPAL POETRY

The Clasp, and Other Poems, 1986
The Folded Heart, 1989
The Neighbor, 1995
The Ledge, 2000
Dark Wild Realm, 2006

OTHER LITERARY FORMS

Michael Collier has edited a number of anthologies, including *The Wesleyan Tradition: Four Decades of American Poetry* (1993), *The New Bread Loaf Anthology of Contemporary American Poetry* (1999; coedited with Stanley Plumly), and *The New American Poets: A Bread Loaf Anthology* (2000). He also published a collection of essays, *Make Us Wave Back: Essays on Poetry and Influence* (2007).

ACHIEVEMENTS

Michael Collier was awarded two National Endowment for the Arts Fellowships (1984 and 1994) as well as a Guggenheim Fellowship. On the strength of his first volume of poetry, Collier received the Alice Day Di Castagnola Award from the Poetry Society of America. His landmark collection, *The Ledge*, was nominated for the National Book Critics Circle Award in 2000. He served as poet laureate of the state of Maryland from 2001 to 2004. In 2009, he won the Academy Award in Literature from the American Academy of Arts and Letters.

BIOGRAPHY

Michael Collier grew up during the boom years of post-World War II prosperity in a comfortable upper-middle-class Catholic family, the son of a homemaker and a military pilot who became a salesman. Collier attended a parochial school in Arizona and a Jesuit high school. After graduating from Connecticut College in 1976, where he had studied with poet William Meredith, Collier received his master's degree from the University of Arizona in 1979.

During his education, Collier held a number of odd jobs, including house painting and plumbing, that contributed both to his compassion for ordinary people and to his fascination with technology, specifically the intricate systems of everyday machines. For two years following graduation, he lived in London and traveled to "exotic" lands. He experienced strikingly different cultures, visiting Africa, Japan, and even Siberia.

After returning to the United States, Collier moved to the East Coast in the early 1980's to serve as the director of poetry programs for the Folger Shakespeare Library in Washington, D.C., before joining the English Department of the University of Maryland, College Park, in 1984. He became that institution's director of creative writing. He began publishing poetry in the mid-1980's and met with immediate critical praise for a distinctive verse style recognized for its maturity, exquisite music, and graceful subtleties. While at Maryland, he accepted a number of visiting professorships at universities, including Johns Hopkins and Yale. In 1992, he joined the faculty of the creative writing program at Warren Wilson College in North Carolina.

In 1992, Collier began his association with the prestigious Bread Loaf Writers' Conference and was named its sixth director in 1995, a post previously held by, among others, Robert Frost and John Ciardi. As editor of three critically lauded anthologies of contemporary American poetry, Collier has established himself as an important critical voice. He became the editorial consultant for poetry for publisher Houghton Mifflin Harcourt. He married Kathleen Branch, a librarian, in 1981, and together they had two sons.

ANALYSIS

To read Michael Collier is to confront a series of contradictions. Although he was part of the generation that came of age during a decade of intense social and political activism, a generation caught up in the agenda of civil rights, women's rights, and the peace movement, Collier's poetry speaks of a fascination with the domestic landscape of his own childhood. His vision recalls Edwin Arlington Robinson's compassionate portraits of the misfits and eccentrics of Tilbury Town.

Although he has worked as an activist on issues ranging from local education reform to environmentalism, Collier writes verse that seldom touches such hot-button contemporary questions but is rather focused on the unsuspected dramas that occur next door and down the street. More interesting, despite his academic background, Collier writes verse that is accessible, gently musical, and inviting. Reassuringly immediate, such verse exploits the natural inflections and collisions of sound that occur in colloquial English. Collier finds such unadorned language sufficiently musical to sustain the rich tones of verse. More notable, his verse forsakes the expected academic posturings of ironic distancing and cynicism; Collier's vision is at once compassionate and humane, exhibiting a depth of emotion for his characters, who exist along the margins of the ordinary.

Collier is clearly fascinated by things, by gizmos and machines, by the sheer mechanical complex of the contemporary world: "I'm a consumer," he has said. "I like things. I'm fascinated by the mechanical world." Collier is ultimately, however, tuned to the subtler interior worlds of those who come in contact with such machines—their vulnerabilities and eccentricities amid the overwhelmingly technical culture of the modern world.

THE CLASP, AND OTHER POEMS

The opening poem of *The Clasp, and Other Poems*, "Ancestors," sets Collier's agenda: He admits that he descends from village dentists, and the poem captures those long-ago, often difficult surgical excavations into the "fleshy rose/ pulsing in the root like the heart's/ faintest hint." By comparing the rotted tooth to the heart, Collier offers the image of the clumsy dentist's painful surgeries as fitting metaphor for the work of the poet, necessarily rooting out the painful experiences of the heart, explorations that may seem barbaric but are essentially therapeutic. Despite being barely in his thirties at the time of this collection's writing, Collier clearly felt the gravitational pull of time, the uneasy responsibility of memory, and the heavy intrusion of recollection.

These poems exist simultaneously in two tenses, crossed by the shadows and dreams where the forgotten and the neglected persist: "I don't believe that what we lose/ is lost forever." Collier draws on those occasions when the difficult past unexpectedly resurfaces: rummaging among old photographs, conducting otherwise innocuous conversations, being suspended delicately between sleep and wakefulness, ministering to an ailing loved one.

In the poignant "Eyepiece," Collier struggles to glimpse the moon through a neighbor's telescope, only to find his view unexpectedly blocked when the scope snaps shut. Such denial of a fuller view unexpectedly compels him to remember his college roommate's suicide and to concede how, eventually, everyone will similarly, suddenly, inexplicably disappear. Despite the heavy pressure of the past, the persistence of memory is revealed without sentimentality or melodramatic anxiety. Musically, the poems are executed with languid sounds, with rich, long vowels and rolling consonants in a meticulous orchestration of stresses and syllables that effect a quiet, hushed reading appropriate to verse that exists on the border between past and present.

THE FOLDED HEART

Collier's second collection, *The Folded Heart*, reinforces the premise of his first: There is no larger perspective than that of the personal past. As the title suggests, here is the gift of Collier's heart, investigations into his past that are neatly, precisely fashioned (folded) within the lines of polished verse. Gathered here are recollections drawn from Collier's childhood and adolescence, narratives of his family and his Arizona neighbors, episodes that are cast in verse not to indulge nostalgia or inflate ego but rather to explore the dimensions of each experience.

Few poems are written in the present tense, although "Tonight" is a beautiful exception, in which the poet considers the view outside his office window. The mood of the rest of this collection is consistently retrospective and somber. Careful detailing makes vivid a past that Collier, distanced in time from the events, finds nevertheless pressing and immediate. The sound of the poems is appropriately gentle, a weave of soft and rolling sounds that quietly create rhythms through the light beat of syllables, one stanza frequently flowing uninterrupted into the next without the harsh intrusion of punctuation.

As though following William Carlos Williams's dictum "no ideas but in things," Collier is able to fashion a symbolic landscape without heavy-handedness. For instance, in "Lagoon," he recounts a boyhood episode when he accessed a closed golf course to steal lost balls and was chased by a guard dog, whose pursuit was ultimately curtailed by the course fence. What does the dog symbolize? Under Collier's manipulation, the dog becomes a multilayered symbol that suggests more than it means: It may represent lost youth, the thwarted hand of authority, the uselessness of rules for a boy, the shattering intrusion of the dangers of the adult world, or, perhaps, the sheer thrill of disobedience. Thus, Collier ranges over his adolescence—recollections of performing in a third-grade theater production, purchasing a pigeon from a crafty neighbor, playing air guitar, skimming a dead bat out of a neighbor's pool, waiting anxiously at the age of five for an operation to remove his appendix, eagerly anticipating his father's return from sales trips—and reclaims them, revealing how pedestrian experience, under the appropriately sensitive observation, can be coaxed into the symbolic.

In the closing poem, "The Cave," Collier audaciously refashions the living room, where his family would watch home movies of his sister's competitive diving performance, into Plato's allegorical cave. The suburban tableau thus becomes a potent symbol suggesting the timeless struggle to wish into existence the unreachable perfect.

THE NEIGHBOR

As the title *The Neighbor* suggests, Collier moves outward in his third collection, out of the confines of his own experience to re-create empathetically the shattered interior lives of those who live about him. With compassion, Collier selects those whose quiet lives belie their emotional pain: a neighbor determined to hoist, unaided, his boat onto its hitch, a door-to-door tree trimmer saddled with a hanging goiter, an Indian neighbor versed in spirituality but unable to manipulate his power mower, a boyhood friend so unsettled by the prospects of spending the night that his mother must rescue him, a neighborhood priest in a dunking booth at a parish festival, a classroom of children ducking under desks during a safety drill, the schoolyard terrorism casually visited on a helpless fat boy.

These are characters trapped in their own lives, haunted by a higher sense, an awareness of some sort of spirituality, sensitive innocents mired in the brutal realities of a world that will not affirm a higher plane. They are victims of forces they cannot even identify. Without heavy authorial intrusion to manipulate the reader's response to these characters, Collier relies on telling details to reveal the characters' interior devastations.

In "The Magician," for instance, Collier creates the portrait of suburban ennui by focusing on a neighbor who, when he walks his dogs, does simple (if mesmerizing) magic tricks for a swarm of enthralled neighborhood children until, the walk finished, he returns to his decidedly unmagical suburban home, unchains his dogs, and quietly empties his pockets of "the tiny vehicles of magic."

Other poems are far darker. In "The Rancher," a father, a sheep rancher, meets for the first time a boy who comes to his house to pick up his daughter for a date. The father's curious fascination with the sex life of his daughter (after her dates, he "lifts her dress or puts/ his hand in her Levis") reveals a disquieting, even perverted psychology. Before the two depart, the father

shows the young man his collection of frozen castrated sheep testes and intones darkly, "She'll do to you/ what I did to sheep to get these." Then, as he shuts the freezer door, the father whispers to the stunned young man that he would be glad to listen to details about what sex with his daughter is like. His, the reader understands with shattering immediacy, is a heart without love that has long ago reduced people to meat.

In "2212 West Flower Street," Collier writes of how, after a neighbor had killed his wife and committed suicide, the shocked neighborhood struggled to restore the dead man's humanity. This is precisely Collier's achievement: the humane gesture of making even his most aberrant characters accessible and human. The poet never intrudes on the revelation of these characters; quietly, carefully, he acts as a witness to their suffering. Collier's compassionate interest in such characters emerges in lines that are elegant and subtly rhythmic, giving music and dignity to such haunted souls.

THE LEDGE

If *The Neighbor* explores the residents of a physical geography, a matrix of homes and streets, backyards and bedrooms, *The Ledge* signals that in his midforties, Collier is prepared to explore that most daunting of artistic terrain, the interior of the heart. In this effort, Collier is drawn to reassuring extremes (lost and found, youth and maturity, known and unknown, sacred and profane, familiar and exotic, clear and shadowy) and to those epiphanic moments when such absolutes are revealed to be inoperative, those moments when the familiar becomes suddenly strange, the near-at-hand becomes irretrievably lost, and the everyday becomes mysterious, even unknowable.

Here, surfaces deceive and conceal. In "Safe," a man squirrels away mementos from his emotional savagings in a quarried-out book. Bosco, a neighborhood dog in "A Real-Life Drama," stands in the street with a mangled rabbit bleeding beneath his paws, a pet "taken over by the dark corner of his nature." In another, Halloween guests wearing masks reveal interior psychologies as they stand mesmerized by a raccoon casually terrorizing their outdoor picnic spread. A boy at swimming lessons, who has only to pass alone through a locker room, is overwhelmed by the experience and sends up a terrified scream, "frightened/ of the ordinary world." Bored in a hotel, Collier struggles to watch the "erotic chaos" of the scrambled signal of an adult pay-per-view channel, the familiar sexual routine becoming suddenly mesmerizing, tantalizing. The calm of a country club is shattered, literally, when a man accidentally walks through a closed sliding-glass door.

In "My Crucifixion," Collier recalls, when in the charge of a babysitter, reenacting the crucifixion with his sisters and finding himself oddly aroused as they gleefully "hammer" his hands and feet. A man swimming in a pool appears to be some sort of grotesque, finned, aquatic monstrosity. Again and again, the familiar becomes disquietingly strange—a moment of bleacher camaraderie, the familiar stadium wave, reveals uncertain anxieties over the hopelessness of such forced cheering. In the haunting "The Dolphin," Collier compares tracking the fin lines of a coursing dolphin to understanding the intricate turns of a ten-year marriage.

Familiarity cannot sustain understanding. It is the sort of world revealed by the deep dive in "Fathom and League," in which the poet is stunned by the intricate, roiling underworld of volcanoes beneath the placid calm of the ocean surface. Amid such uncertainties, Collier offers as strategy the position of a "brave sparrow" perched on the thinnest of ledges, poised, ever vigilant, amid the inexplicable terrors of the apparently ordinary: neighborhood cats, starlings, owls, blue jays. As Collier ironically reveals the mysterious in the familiar, his style is appropriately unadorned and direct. He delivers his epiphanic moments in a colloquial narrative voice, without emotional exclamations, allowing the disconcerting revelations themselves to unsettle the reader.

In the closing poem, "Pax Geologica," Collier dreams of the ocean's bottom scattered with the detritus of his own home. This detritus is a mingling of the exotic and the familiar that is a fitting emblem for his poetic achievement.

DARK WILD REALM

Dark Wild Realm takes the reader on a journey into the beautiful mystery of death without losing an appreciation for the details of everyday life. Collier's poems frequently involve quotidian occurrences. They are narrative, colloquial, and intimate. Collier is interested in what the dead leave behind as much as in the process of death itself. He tries to make sense of death, whether of the death of a bird, an insect, or an old friend.

In "Bird Crashing into Window," Collier compares a friend dying of cancer to a collapsed bird, "not all dead." This poem reflects Collier's desire to make writing more than just keeping a diary and more than just trying to characterize an emotional state. It brings readers into the room and into the lives of these two men.

In "Confessional," readers see the strong influence on Collier of his Catholic upbringing, the trappings of this religion (beeswax, smoke, sin, and snake), and the practice of prayer that allows the spirit world "through the veil" to communicate with him. Nature itself appears to contain for Collier the essence of the departed, the historical memory of ancestors with whom he, as a poet, feels duty-bound to communicate while professing to feeling uneasy with the role. Poetry does not make a god of him: It brings him too uncomfortably close to his own mortality.

In "Mortician's Son," however, Collier sees death as "human and absurd"; in "Elegy to a Long-Dead Friend," death is forgivable and essential; and in "Summer Anniversary," the voice of a dead lover appears in a dream. In "A Line from Robert Desnos Used to Commemorate George 'Sonny' Took-the-Shield, Fort Belknap, Montana," Collier is challenged by the land, trees, insects, and birds to pick up memories of the departed and transform them into the substance of poetry: the poet as shaman or Native American medicine man who plucks memories "roosting in the air" and transubstantiates them into the golden egg of poetry.

In "Shelley's Guitar," Collier conjures the elements of earth and fire to produce new life from dead matter, proving, like the poet Percy Bysshe Shelley's heart—which refused to be consumed—that the human spirit through poetry is indestructible. In "Common Flicker," Collier's preoccupation with birds' feathers, beaks, claws, and wings, a recurrent theme in his work, is once more explored. The subjects that Collier chooses are apt to be familiar; this backyard view of nature is distilled to its delicate yet profound essence.

OTHER MAJOR WORKS

NONFICTION: *Make Us Wave Back: Essays on Poetry and Influence*, 2007.

EDITED TEXTS: *The Wesleyan Tradition: Four Decades of American Poetry*, 1993; *The New Bread Loaf Anthology of Contemporary American Poetry*, 1999 (with Stanley Plumly); *The New American Poets: A Bread Loaf Anthology*, 2000; *A William Maxwell Portrait: Memories and Appreciations*, 2004 (with Charles Baxter and Edward Hirsch).

BIBLIOGRAPHY

Henry, Brian. Review of *The Ledge. The New York Times Book Review*, April 30, 2000. This short, vituperative review uses most of its words to point to places where the reviewer finds fault with the book's sentimentality and lack of insight. The reviewer begins to discuss "The Brave Sparrow" ("the book's best poem") but this brief review is closed before any insight can be gathered. There is one helpful point made in this review: a suggestion of where the "emotional intensity" of this book exists.

Longenbach, James. "Poetry in Review." *Yale Review* 83 (October, 1995): 144-147. Places Collier within a school of contemporary academic poets.

Muske-Davis, Carol. "Out of the Cradle Violently Rocking: The New Young Poets—Review." *Kenyon Review* (Summer/Fall, 2001). This discussion of three poetry anthologies published in 2000 gives an apt review of the aesthetic of Collier's *The New American Poets*.

Reel, Monte. "Everyday Life, Uncommon Passion: Poet Laureate Offers New View." *The Washington Post*, March 25, 2001, p. C5. Discusses Collier's intention to become an ambassador for poetry throughout the state of Maryland.

Virginia Quarterly Review. Review of *The Folded Heart*. (Spring, 1990). This favorable review of Collier's second book can help readers find clues into his symbolism as well as insights about the success of his narrative style.

Joseph Dewey

BILLY COLLINS

Born: New York, New York; March 22, 1941

PRINCIPAL POETRY

Pokerface, 1977
Video Poems, 1980
The Apple That Astonished Paris, 1988
Questions About Angels, 1991
The Art of Drowning, 1995
Picnic, Lightning, 1998
Taking Off Emily Dickinson's Clothes, 2000
Sailing Alone Around the Room: New and Selected Poems, 2001
Nine Horses, 2002
The Trouble with Poetry, and Other Poems, 2005
She Was Just Seventeen, 2006
Ballistics, 2008

OTHER LITERARY FORMS

Billy Collins has confined himself primarily to poetry in his printed work. Besides composing his own poetic works, he has edited a number of poetry anthologies, including *Poetry 180: A Turning Back to Poetry* (2003), *180 More: Extraordinary Poems for Every Day* (2005), *The Best American Poetry, 2006* (2006; with David Lehman), and *Bright Wings: An Illustrated Anthology of Poems About Birds* (2009). However, he has been quick to embrace other means of communicating his work. *The Best Cigarette* (1993) and *Billy Collins Live* (2005) are compact disc readings. Collins has also published online in *Cortland Review*, an electronic literary magazine. In 2002, one of his essays was included in *The Eye of the Poet: Six Views of the Art and Craft of Poetry*.

ACHIEVEMENTS

Billy Collins has been called arguably "the most popular poet in America," not only for his accessible and often humorous work in print, but also for his appearances on National Public Radio (NPR). Several of his collections have broken sales records for poetry, and he has read and talked about his work with engaging charm on NPR's *Fresh Air* in 1997 and several times on NPR's *Prairie Home Companion*, including in 2009. However, Collins is critically acclaimed as well as popular. He has received poetry fellowships from the New York Foundation for the Arts, the National Endowment for the Arts, and the Guggenheim Foundation. He has received the Bess Hokin Award (1990), the Oscar Blumenthal Award, the Frederick Bock Prize (1992), the Levinson Prize (1995), and the J. Howard and Barbara M. J. Wood Prize (1999), all from *Poetry* magazine. He has been named Literary Lion by the New York Public Library, and the Poetry Foundation made him the 2004 inaugural recipient of the Mark Twain Award for humorous poetry. His *Questions About Angels* won the National Poetry Series competition for 1990. Collins served as poet laureate consultant in poetry to the Library of Congress from 2001 to 2003 and as the New York State poet laureate from 2004 to 2006. His work has appeared in *The New Yorker*, *Paris Review*, and *American Scholar*.

BIOGRAPHY

William "Billy" Collins was born on March 22, 1941, in New York City, the son of William Collins, an electrician, and Katherine Collins, a nurse. He attended

Billy Collins (Courtesy, Random House)

parochial schools and received a B.A. from College of the Holy Cross in 1963 and a Ph.D. from the University of California, Riverside, in 1971. His primary area of study was the Romantic poets. His career has been mainly academic; in 1971, he began teaching at Lehman College of the City University of New York, where he became distinguished professor of English. He has also served as writer-in-residence at Sarah Lawrence College. He married and settled in Westchester County with his wife, Diane, an architect. He jokes that he is in competition with her, planning for his poems to outlast the buildings she designs.

Despite the domestic setting of much of his poetry, Collins's writing reveals little of his private life. In 1999, however, his career received considerable publicity when the University of Pittsburgh Press refused to allow Random House to reprint some of Collins's earlier poems, ostensibly because the university press still found them profitable. The conflict was covered in *The New York Times* and the online magazine *Salon*, leading Collins to say that he would like to forget about the mechanics of publishing and "get back to writing poems." As writing, originally a sidelight to his academic career, has become increasingly important to Collins, he has developed a lively schedule of readings and workshops, several of the latter in Ireland.

ANALYSIS

Poet Stephen Dunn, in a review of *Picnic, Lightning*, wrote, "We seem always to know where we are in a Billy Collins poem, but not necessarily where he is going." Collins has expressed his distaste for poetry that seems to have been written in code, accessible only to the cognoscenti. Such poems, he implies in the poem "Introduction to Poetry," create readers who believe that the only way to approach a poem is to "tie the poem to a chair with rope/ and torture a confession out of it," while the writer longs for readers who can "waterski/ across the surface of a poem/ waving at the author's name on the shore." That suggests why his subjects tend to be drawn from the ordinary, the events of everyone's life—driving, shoveling snow, eating dinner or breakfast. Collins's humor and accessibility go a long way in accounting for his enormous popularity as a contemporary poet. However, the easy entrée into a Collins poem belies its surprising, often profound, ending. One unusual influence provides insight into why Collins's poems take such unexpected turns. "My own poetry would have not developed in the direction it did were it not for the spell that was cast over me as a boy by Warner Bros. cartoons. These animations offered me a flexible, malleable world that defied Isaac Newton, a world of such plasticity that anything imaginable was possible." Collins often uses humor to lead the reader into a more serious and unexpected place by the poem's conclusion. "If you can create a humorous reaction in someone right away, you've drawn a circle around you and the reader so you're inside this humor, and then you can go off in other directions so the poem is not as funny at the end as it is in the beginning."

A reviewer of *Questions About Angels* said that Collins's technique produces poems that evoke no emotional response from the reader, but many readers would disagree. John Taylor, reviewing *Picnic, Lightning* for *Poetry* magazine, argued that melancholy lies just below the surface in Collins's work; indeed, his humor often seems simply a means, an invitation to serious reflection. These qualities of accessibility, humor, and regard for the everyday are present in all Collins's work from the earliest to the latest. Certainly *The Art of Drowning* and *Picnic, Lightning* seem to mark a movement into poems of greater reflection, a reduction in the number of poems of pure playfulness that marked earlier volumes, a movement that is confirmed in *The Trouble with Poetry, and Other Poems* and *Ballistics*. The witty, joking tone of *The Apple That Astonished Paris* gives way in these last volumes to a kind of relaxed meditation.

THE APPLE THAT ASTONISHED PARIS

In *The Apple That Astonished Paris*, the poems establish a list of typical Collins subjects and his approaches to them: History is represented here, along with travel, writing, books, and some examples of playful imagination. In "Flames," for example, Collins imagines Smokey the Bear, discouraged and angry at the perennial failure of his campaign against forest fires: "He is sick of dispensing/ warnings to the careless,/ the half-wit camper,/ the dumbbell hiker." Looking oddly threatening, Smokey sets out with gasoline

and matches. The poem concludes, "He is going to show them/ how a professional does it."

Collins often uses an abstract title that he subsequently explores in a variety of concrete images. In "Books," for example, the abstract title leads, in the first stanza, to a picture of an academic library at night, empty of patrons but humming with the voices of its authors resting on their dark shelves. The second stanza pictures a man in the act of reading; he is "a man in two worlds"—the physical world in which he lives as well as the book's world of imagination. The third stanza recalls the narrator's mother, reading to him in a voice that offered him the same duality. The mother's voice was both her own and at the same time the vehicle of the frightening events of the story. The narrator finally imagines "all of us reading ourselves away from ourselves." The words become like "a trail of crumbs," the trail that the reader follows into the forest of the book.

"Death" is constructed similarly. From its abstract title, Collins moves swiftly to imagining how the news of a death in the family traveled in the past and then describes the telephone as the modern means of delivering bad news. Telephones are everywhere; the reader can almost hear one ringing—"ready to summon you, ready to fall from your hand."

Many of the poems in the volume are shorter than those in Collins's later work, but they foreshadow many of his later themes and subjects—visits to Tuscany and Ireland; the imaginative creation of a town called "Schoolsville," peopled by all the students the speaker has ever taught; a miniature world history, an organization that Collins uses often, in "Personal History," where the speaker courts his love from the Middle Ages through the Industrial Revolution only to end up in this postmodern age, driving with her to the movie theater in a Volkswagen.

QUESTIONS ABOUT ANGELS

Questions About Angels seems to move to a level beyond that of *The Apple That Astonished Paris* while still using themes and subjects familiar to Collins's readers. The writer's voice also continues in its range of irony, meditation, and amusement. In this volume, however, the humor often leads to a more sharply serious conclusion. "Forgetfulness," for example, seems at first to be a humorous consideration of what happens to one's memory in middle age:

The name of the author is the first to go
followed obediently by the title, the plot,
the heartbreaking conclusion, the entire novel
which suddenly becomes one you have never read,
  never even heard of.

Collins goes on to catalog other things one might forget—the names of the Muses, the order of the planets, the address of a relative. They are so completely lost that it is as if they have retired to a remote fishing village "where there are no phones." The list and its attendant images are funny, but the poem concludes on a suddenly melancholy note: "No wonder the moon in the window seems to have drifted/ out of a love poem that you used to know by heart."

"First Reader" offers a similar experience, beginning comically with a picture of Dick and Jane, characters from the popular series of elementary school readers in the 1940's and 1950's. Collins calls them "the boy and girl who begin fiction," for that is how they functioned for children learning to read. Collins quotes a line of frequent dialogue from those school texts. "Look!" Dick and Jane constantly command each other, "pointing at the dog, the bicycle, or at their father." At the end, Collins puns on the word "look"; even as children, with our growing literacy "we were forgetting how to look, learning how to read."

The title poem of this volume exemplifies a quality Collins admires in poems—the ending that leads the reader in a direction that was not forecast by the opening. Collins has said that too often writers overplan their poems, leaving no room for imagination to begin work during the process of composition. "Questions About Angels" opens with the old question from medieval theology: "How many angels can dance on the head of a pin?" Collins labels that the only question that is ever asked about angels and offers other possibilities, questions about how angels spend their time, what their clothes are made of, particulars about their flight. Then the poem returns to the pinhead and suggests that the answer is that only one angel can dance there, an angel who Collins pictures as a jazz singer in a nightclub, one of Collins's favorite subjects, where she is dancing forever.

THE ART OF DROWNING

The Art of Drowning introduces a slight shift in Collins's style—a movement to longer poems and a narrowing of subject matter. Several poems here rise from Collins's interest in jazz, notably "Sunday Morning with the Sensational Nightingales" and "Exploring the Coast of Birdland." In "Nightclub," Collins playfully works changes on the common musical idea that "You are so beautiful and I am a fool/ to be in love with you." No one, he says, ever sings "you are a fool to be in love with me." The poem concludes with the narrator performing a fantasy bebop solo that asserts "We are all so foolish// so damn foolish/ we have become beautiful without even knowing it."

This volume also firmly establishes Collins's sense of the beauty of the mundane, his nearly sacramental reverence for the ordinary delights of a good meal ("Osso Buco") or the sight of a student writing an exam ("Monday Morning," with its allusions to Wallace Stevens's poem "Sunday Morning"). These events make him "feel like the secretary to the morning," in "Tuesday, June 4, 1991," whose task is to chronicle the weather, his coffee, the arrival of the house painters, and the antics of the new kitten, and in doing so, he seems to drench them in an almost holy light.

PICNIC, LIGHTNING

Picnic, Lightning continues with tones and subjects of *The Art of Drowning*. Again, Collins writes about the beauties of the day ("Shoveling Snow with Buddha," "Morning," "In the Room of a Thousand Miles") and jazz ("I Chop Some Parsley While Listening to Art Blakey's Version of 'Three Blind Mice'"). What seems new in this volume is the number of poems that make specific reference to other literary works. As a literature teacher, Collins naturally refers to others' writings in all his collections, but in *Picnic, Lightning* the reader finds Samuel Taylor Coleridge's "The Nightingale" in Collins's "Moon," W. H. Auden's "Musée des Beaux Arts" in "Musée des Beaux Arts Revisited," and a whole array of writers in "Marginalia," to name a few examples. "Paradelle for Susan" makes another literary reference as Collins creates a new verse form, a loopy combination of villanelle, pantoum, and sestina, to form a gentle spoof of a type of poem often produced in workshops (a subject he satirized more directly in the previous volume). "Paradelle" is accompanied by a mock-serious footnote outlining the form's complex requirements. Overall, *Picnic, Lightning* feels very much like a second part of *The Art of Drowning*.

SAILING ALONE AROUND THE ROOM

Included in *Sailing Alone Around the Room* are twenty new poems as well as selections from four previous volumes: *The Apple That Astonished Paris*, *Questions About Angels*, *The Art of Drowning*, and *Picnic, Lightning*. In this collection, Collins continues his colloquial style, which avoids the difficulty of early twentieth century poetry and eludes affiliation with any contemporary school. Although much poetry in the late twentieth and early twenty-first centuries consists of semantic ambiguity and an unclear sense of speaker or place, the poetry of Collins clearly situates the reader. "The Lesson" begins "In the morning when I found History/ snoring heavily on the couch," and the opening to "The Iron Bridge" is even more explicit: "I am standing on a disused iron bridge/ that was erected in 1902."

Such concrete orientation is an intentional feature of Collins's aesthetic. It unites poet and reader by providing a stable jumping-off point. In "The Iron Bridge," the poem's explicit setting is a vehicle used to move back in time to the ". . . workmen in shirts and caps/ rivet[ing] this iron bridge together" to "my mother . . . so tiny" in 1902 in her mother's kitchen. The poem then returns to the present with the image of a cormorant diving beneath the water under the bridge, then crescendos by pulling the past through the present and into the future by connecting the bird with ". . . my tiny mother,/ who disappeared last year,/ flying somewhere with your strange wings// kicking deeper down into a lake/ with no end or name. . . ." The solid platform that opens the poem is really a departure point for metaphysical exploration. Referencing author Henry Miller, Collins explains that the destination in his poetry is not a place but a new way of seeing things. This illuminates Collins's description of his poetry as travel literature. "The Death of the Hat," "The Butterfly Effect," and "Madmen" are other examples that provide a new way of seeing.

THE TROUBLE WITH POETRY, AND OTHER POEMS

Collins continues to be viewed by some as a jester who avoids serious contemplation in *The Trouble with Poetry, and Other Poems*. According to critic Anis Shivani, Collins maintains a trend he began in *Nine Horses*, abandoning the ideal reader for the average reader, whose literacy is inferior, and thereby losing the celestial music his poetry might otherwise have had. Others notice a gentle sadness in this volume. In a National Public Radio interview regarding *The Trouble with Poetry, and Other Poems*, Collins explained that poetry's great subject is death. However, he goes on to say that this leads him to another great subject: gratitude for life. Poems such as "House" and "Theme" are examples of Collins's ability to simultaneously express these themes. Alongside the dead one's inevitable mortality, there is joy in the simple beauties of life. In "Flock," Collins whimsically extends both of these themes by suggesting that death for some can actually be the gift, or the price, of beauty for others. He manages this observation without seeming dire by hiding the idea among a flock of sheep. Similarly in "Care and Feeding," Collins disguises concern over turning seventy by imagining spending this birthday as his own pet dog. It is just this sort of caprice that readers seem to find either superficial or deft and profound.

Poet Louis McKee calls this volume rich and mischievous. "The Lanyard" is illustrative. It begins, characteristically for Collins, with the mundane act of chancing upon the word "lanyard" in the dictionary. There is mischief as this seemingly random introduction of the idea, and then the image, of the red and white plastic lanyard leads the reader, unexpectedly, to the fatuous comparison of this useless summer-camp product with all that a mother pours into her child over a lifetime.

> Here are thousands of meals, she said,
> and here is clothing and a good education.
> And here is your lanyard, I replied.

However, the poem is rich because it does not stop at the apparent insight that "you can never repay your mother." Collins pushes on to question how it is that children, no matter their age, so often actually believe their negligible offerings are "enough to make us even."

BALLISTICS

Called by one critic American poetry's feel-good hit of the year, *Ballistics* builds on Collins's well-established reputation as the author of lighthearted, easily accessible, often comic poetry. Poems in this vein, such as "Hippos on Holiday" and "Bathtub Families," confirm the poet's claim that he writes as a hedonist in search of linguistic pleasure. Most of the poems contain Collins's characteristic colloquial language, subtle alliteration, and gentle cadences. Collins's continued awareness of his reader is also evident in this volume. In the opening poem, "August in Paris," the speaker bemoans the elusiveness of the reader: "But every time I turn around/ you have fled through a crease in the air." Also evident here is Collins's particular brand of irony, which leans much more toward delight than cynicism. The poem "Despair" does not despair but rather rejects the bleakness of much other poetry and urges celebration instead. Just as his other volumes contain parodies of other poets' famous works (consider "Lines Composed Over Three Thousand Miles from Tintern Abbey" from *Picnic, Lightning*, a play on William Wordsworth's well-known poem "Lines Composed a Few Miles Above Tintern Abbey"), here Collins takes a jab at Stevens's "The Idea of Order at Key West" with his "The Idea of Natural History at Key West." However, more serious if not less whimsical creations are also a part of this work. In "The First Night," Collins contemplates the darkness and silence of the first night of death. In "No Things," he explores the relative merits of questioning the meaning of life versus simply enjoying it.

One thing that is perhaps new in *Ballistics* is a concision characteristic of much Eastern poetry. Just two years before the publication of this collection, Collins released a book of haiku. Its title, *She Was Just Seventeen*, puns on the seventeen syllables that compose this poetic form. Collins, in discussing *Ballistics*, has described his poems as extended haiku. Specifically, "China" and "Liu Yung" demonstrate the restraint, economy of language, and deeply evoked image that are characteristic of such poetry. "Divorce," a poem of only four lines, is a stunning example:

Once, two spoons in bed,
now tined forks

across a granite table
and the knives they have hired.

This poem retains Collins's famous sense of humor while at the same time evoking the searing pain of a marriage ended.

OTHER MAJOR WORKS

NONFICTION: "Poetry, Pleasure, and the Hedonist Reader," 2002.

CHILDREN'S LITERATURE: *Daddy's Little Boy*, 2004.

EDITED TEXTS: *Poetry 180: A Turning Back to Poetry*, 2003; *180 More: Extraordinary Poems for Every Day*, 2005; *The Best American Poetry, 2006*, 2006 (with David Lehman); *Bright Wings: An Illustrated Anthology of Poems About Birds*, 2009.

BIBLIOGRAPHY

Allen, Dick. Review of *The Apple That Astonished Paris. Hudson Review* 42, no. 2 (Summer, 1989): 321. Allen praises Collins for his accessibility, noting his "friendly lines" and calling the volume an "irrepressible delight."

Alleva, Richard. "A Major Minor Poet: Billy Collins Isn't Just Funny." *Commonweal* 129, no. 1 (January 11, 2002): 21-22. Alleva calls Collins a "celebrant of the beauty and comedy that are everywhere around us in everyday life."

Collins, Billy. "Billy Collins: The Art of Poetry LXXXIII." Interview by George Plimpton. *Paris Review* 43, no. 159 (Fall, 2001): 183-216. Collins describes how he writes poetry and what inspires him.

_____. "Inspired by a Bunny Wabbit." *The Wall Street Journal*, June 28, 2008, p. W1. Collins demonstrates, in this tribute to Warner Bros. cartoons, how creativity in one medium can affect creativity in another. The plasticity of these cartoon figures, "like Ovid on speed," became a precursor to his own concept of travel poetry.

Kirsch, Adam. "Over Easy." Review of *Sailing Alone Around the Room. The New Republic* 225, no. 18

(October 29, 2001): 38-41. Claims that Collins's "true poetic gift" is "a genuine, if often debased, wit."

Laird, Nick. "Not So Mean Streets." Review of *Taking Off Emily Dickinson's Clothes*. *Times Literary Supplement* 8 (September, 2000): 29. Laird notes that the collection, which contains selections from four earlier volumes, is Collins's first publication outside the United States. He praises Collins's writing in a "Whitmanesque tradition of celebrating America and its language."

Merrin, Jeredith. "Art Over Easy." *Southern Review* 38, no. 1 (Winter, 2002): 202-214. A critical essay that judges Collins's work to be "disappointingly monotonous and slight."

Parini, Jay, ed. *The Oxford Encyclopedia of American Literature*. New York: Oxford University Press, 2004. Essay on Collins provides biographical information and literary analysis.

Shivani, Anis. "American Poetry in an Age of Constriction." *Cambridge Quarterly* 35, no. 3 (2006): 205-230. This article places Collins in context, comparing him with four contemporary poets. Shivani is generally critical of modern American poetry, claiming that it finds no meaningful correspondence to the larger world and therefore lacks power. He commends Collins for avoiding the characteristic complaining tone but considers him guilty of writing poetry on a small scale. Section 6 of this article deals specifically with Collins's poetry.

Taylor, John. Review of *Picnic, Lightning*. *Poetry* 175, no. 4 (February, 2000): 273. Taylor provides a serious discussion of this book and of *The Art of Drowning*. He describes the qualities that create Collins's "soft metaphysical touch" and the consolations that his poems offer.

Weber, Bruce. "On Literary Bridge, Poet Hits a Roadblock." *The New York Times*, December 19, 1999, p. 1. Weber gives an account of the contest between Random House and University of Pittsburgh Press over the reprint rights to Collins's poems. The article also contains some biographical information and an account of Collins's readings.

Ann D. Garbett
Updated by Susan T. Larson

CID CORMAN

Born: Boston, Massachusetts; June 29, 1924
Died: Kyoto, Japan; March 12, 2004

PRINCIPAL POETRY
Subluna, 1945
A Thanksgiving Eclogue from Theocritus, 1954
The Precisions, 1955
The Responses, 1956
The Marches, 1957
Stances and Distances, 1957
A Table in Provenance, 1958
The Descent from Daimonji, 1959
For Sure, 1959
Sun Rock Man, 1962
In Good Time, 1964
In No Time, 1964
Nonce, 1965
For Granted, 1966
For You, 1966
Words for Each Other, 1967
And Without End, 1968
No More, 1969
Plight, 1969
Livingdying, 1970
Out and Out, 1972
0/1, 1974
Once and for All: Poems for William Bronk, 1975
Aegis: Selected Poems, 1970-1980, 1983
And the Word, 1987
Of, 1990
How/Now, 1995
Nothing Doing, 1999
The Despairs, 2001
Just for Now, 2001
For Crying Out Loud, 2002

OTHER LITERARY FORMS

Cid Corman's oeuvre is immense. In addition to his many volumes of poetry, he published a large number of translations from French, German, Italian, and Japanese. These not only have appeared as separate volumes, including the work of such diverse writers as

Matsuo Bashō, Shimpei Kusano, René Char, Francis Ponge, and Philippe Jaccottet, but also lie scattered throughout his books and magazine publications. These latter include a virtual pantheon of major writers, among them Eugenio Montale, Mario Luzi, René Daumal, and Paul Celan, as well as many little-known European and Asian writers.

Corman was equally prolific as an essayist and commentator on contemporary letters. Some of his essays have been collected in *Word for Word: Essays on the Art of Language* (1977-1978) and *Where Were We Now: Essays and Postscriptum* (1991). Corman also maintained an enormous literary and cultural correspondence with other writers and intellectuals.

Achievements

Among poets of his generation, no figure stood more at the center of both poetic activity and influence than Cid Corman. As poet, translator, and one of contemporary letters' most important editors, Corman was generator, clearinghouse, arbitrator, and gadfly, presiding over one of the most fertile and creative periods of American poetry. Through his own poetry and through his editorship of *Origin* magazine, Corman was a central reference point in the poetic battleground of the postwar years. *Origin*, which published William Carlos Williams, Louis Zukofsky, Charles Olson, Robert Creeley, Denise Levertov, and Robert Duncan, performed for its time what T. S. Eliot's *Criterion*, *The Dial*, and *The Literary Review* performed for theirs as major forums for modern writing.

Both Corman's poetry and his translations, still in need of major critical attention, have been of great importance to younger writers. The essential lines of Corman's poetic style were established in his earliest books, and its simplicity of structure and depth of realization marked a maturity of stance that younger poets, in the ongoing literary ferment, have turned to as a kind of spiritual and intellectual benchmark. This early maturity, based on Corman's desire for a poetry that would not engage in the more self-indulgent (hence more popular) styles of writing of its time, claimed for poetry a philosophical sense of anonymity, a nonaggressive quality that seemed, given Corman's unique position, to be an eye in the center of the literary storm. This quality, evident in all Corman's work, gives his voice a peculiarly important place among his contemporaries, for its tact and quiet come not out of diffidence but out of a difficult assuredness not often found in American literary life. Corman won the Lenore Marshall Poetry Prize in 1975 for *O/1* and the Lannan Literary Award for Poetry in 1989.

Biography

The two major poles of Cid Corman's life were the United States and Japan, specifically Boston and Kyoto. Close study of his work shows how it embodies both the tensions of urban American life, social and literary, and the qualities of philosophical serenity and complex identification with nature associated with Asia. Corman was born Sidney Corman in Boston and attended the Boston Latin School and then Tufts University, where he graduated (Phi Beta Kappa) in 1945. He did graduate work at the University of Michigan, where he won a Hopwood Award in Poetry. Back in Boston, Corman ran what was to be the first of his "editorial" contributions to modern poetry, a weekly radio program on WMEX that presented the best of contemporary poets in the Boston area. In 1951, he began *Origin* magazine. A Fulbright to Paris and a year as an English instructor in Matera, Italy (the source for much of the material of Corman's early volumes of poetry), were the initial phases of Corman's voyaging away from the United States to discover and resolve the contradictions of literary self-exile. Such exile was, and is, Corman's major theme. After returning to the United States, Corman made the first of his trips to Kyoto, spent two years in San Francisco, and then returned to Kyoto.

In Kyoto, Corman's work and influence flourished. There he not only wrote an enormous amount of poetry but also published in a simple and elegant format *Origin* magazine, sending it back to the United States for argument, discussion, and protest, as well as distribution. For Corman, the activity in Kyoto, along with the influence of the city's famous Zen teachers, made the Japanese city one of the necessary places of pilgrimage of American poetry. To contemporary poets who visited or lived in Kyoto, such as Gary Snyder, Philip Whalen, and Clayton Eshleman, Corman's activities and, indeed, his physical presence in the coffee shop that he and his Japanese wife, Shizumi, ran, meant serious engagement and encounter with some of the strongest literary currents of the 1960's and 1970's.

Since that time, Corman continued to be active as a poet, translator, editor, essayist, and maker of fine books. His final projects, including several large volumes of poetry, influenced by Asian masters, are outlined in an interview with Gregory Dunne. Corman died in Kyoto, Japan, on March 12, 2004.

ANALYSIS

In one of his earliest books, *Sun Rock Man*, Cid Corman writes: "Already I feel breathless/ as if I have come too far,/ to find peace, to have found it." The thread linking more than thirty years of Corman's poetry, translation, and editorship is the quest back toward some deep original peace, some attempt to find a permanent home in exile. Corman's work is one long and moving dialectic, informed by his sense of having "come too far" and yet of being unable to return. The shifts, both technical and in terms of subject matter, that one discovers in his poems are like signposts pointing both forward and backward at once; they remind the reader that every act of creation has been one of destruction as well, that self-exile for Corman means also new territory.

In Corman's career, this new territory meant, geographically, first Europe, then Japan. One sees, in particular, the Japanese influence in the details of Corman's verse: his affinity for natural objects and the short, almost Asian, tightness of his forms. However, far more important has been the psychological and literary territory Corman traversed. Psychically, this terrain embraces the open spaces of poetic activity, of "making it new" as chartered by such forebears as William Carlos Williams, Ezra Pound, and Louis Zukofsky. Like the poetry of these predecessors, Corman's work is a departure from the traditional verse conventions of its time; it is marked, as well, by a willingness to bear the immediate deflections of incident, encounter, or thought much as Williams's poetry submitted to the "local" or Zukofsky's to the dictates of the musical phrase. Corman's work can be said to seek its timelessness in its very moment. Thus his poems are spontaneous registers of isolation, of immersion in somewhat

alien landscapes where both the native or local language and its cultural iconography are essentially mute; yet it is also immersion in that deeper awareness of world and people caught in the inarticulateness of their situations. In Corman, much is characterized as silent, as unknowable. Rather than raiding the inarticulate, Corman's work attempts to come to terms with it, to construct a language that seems to represent a shared act of humanity and world.

EARLY POEMS

Corman's earliest published poems, such as those in *Sun Rock Man*, attempt to render precisely these occasions of inarticulateness. In them, Corman employs an imagist or objectivist technique, which rigorously favors the recording eye over the conceptualizing mind. The poet is an agency or a recording instrument, and the abject poverty and hopelessness of Matera, an impoverished Italian hill town, is witnessed "objectively." Authorial control is maintained, as it were, only by the details to be selected. Poems such as "the dignities" or "Luna Park" operate under the force of Williams's "no ideas but in things," realized with an eye and ear for detail and tone that are compelling and satisfying; they seem to present an almost pure externality that speaks so eloquently and powerfully that comment is superfluous.

In the end, however, one feels that such poems may rely too heavily on their being a form of exotica, particularly when their occasion is almost solely the function of the poet's arrival on the scene. Indeed, the less formally accomplished poems of *Sun Rock Man* suggest a troubled and yet more fruitful ambivalence, for they sound the note that in Corman's career has its most significant distinction: a deepening capacity to express simultaneously the subjective and the objective terms of situations. As he says of his stay in Matera, "Nothing displaces us/ like our own intelligence."

MATURE POEMS

This displacement, suggesting a leave-taking that is both poetic and physical, is the major theme of all Corman's mature work. The exile is not simply one of banishment to strange lands but to a kind of Rilkean soul-work of facing out on the "speechlessness" of the world. Thus, in nearly all the poems after *Sun Rock Man*, the visual imagistic technique, while not abandoned, is forsworn in favor of rendering the physicality of voicing itself, in an attempt to say without inflation or rhetoric the meaning for the poet of such speechlessness.

Corman's poems often begin within an action, as though the poet finds himself surprised by circumstance into utterance. The prepositions or relational conjunctions, the statements containing continuous verb forms ("finding," "remembering," and so on) found at the head of many of Corman's poems are devices for signaling the organic connection between the active and changing content of the poet's situation and the arising of the poem. Rather than the "picture-making" or mimesis of the earlier poems (or of the more imagistically inclined poet), these poems are specifically linguistic occasions, not meant to hold the mirror up to nature but to sound it.

Thus, in one poem about a bell in *And Without End*, it is, as he puts it, "as if the/ air needed clearing,/ as if the sweet sound/ were a vanishing." The poem may be said to seek, like the sound of the bell, to have both its distinctness and its completeness, completeness in the sense that though sound is invisible and adds nothing visual to the picture, it permeates and thus colors everything within hearing. Such soundings have a tactful and nonjudgmental quality about them; there is, as in many other of Corman's poems, a Buddhistic or Zenlike sense of aesthetic appreciation that is, as the poem continues "so clear/ it hardly matters to say more than 'See if you can hear it'/ and 'it' is a bell."

Corman's poems have a way of establishing an equanimity or resting place for memory. They involve an uncovering effect, moving from an unspecified dramatic statement to a highly qualified core of meaning. This meaning often resides less in a particular line or statement than in the cumulative effect of passage through the poem. In a poem entitled "Back" (*O/1*), for example, a device similar to the "bell" sound of the poem discussed above uses repetition and variants of tone or phrase to advance and specify meaning. Generalized "man" becomes "me" "given to go on"; a "call/ summoning/ all plays on" until the "event" is so "taken to/ heart" that "heart at/ height flings out." The intelligence of the poem resolves itself not only ideationally but also virtually at the level of the syllable (something

Corman has learned well from Zukofsky and Olson), where each moment of development is anticipated musically. In Corman, the minims of speech are deployed much like the quavers of traditional song, functioning as both accent and resistance to the plain meanings of words.

Such fine-tuning informs all Corman's work. The poems seem to draw attention to little more than their own process of realization, as though the form of thought that the poet engenders—though given as language—takes on the characteristics of a visual construct, something cleanly and sparingly drawn. Critics have referred to the haiku-like qualities of Corman's verse, but it is perhaps more accurate to note its peculiar transformation of imagistic technique into the realm of thought, as though the processes of the mind could be delineated as carefully as the leaf on a plum branch.

This confrontation with silence—since silence cannot respond, only evoke—becomes in Corman a form of self-realization, an embodying of poetic utterance that has its root in both estrangement and participation. The poet is at all costs trying to make a home in this homelessness, and the tension of his poetry is the attempt to give this silence its due:

> Don't make me laugh
> or I'll cry: that's the cry,
> Here me, my silence,
> in silence.

The key to such poetry is that both its solipsistic and playful qualities are embedded in the ironies of ambiguity and tone. There is something deeply comic and even lighthearted in Corman's address to a language-less world—comic in the very basic sense that seriousness and any heavy-handed desire to mean are always operative under the meaning-canceling sign of death. As Corman notes in one poem:

> in time go
> words also, however true
> Man's life is a conjuring
> finally nothing once more.

This air of "finally nothing" pervades much of Corman's later work, giving the sense of exile both ease and humor, transfiguring the past and its pains into a newer richness and balance. Here the self fully recognizes itself as a transparency, an agency that works on and gives voice to its interferences. Poetic tension comes out of the drama, and new knowledge is gained in reconciliation with the modalities of the past. Thus, Corman writes:

> To bear back the lost
> is at all events
> much like entering
> the enemy's lines
> to plead for one's dead
> for burial.

Corman's poems seek out what the phenomenologists would call the "preobjective world"; that is, the world existing before overlaps of human concept and understanding. At the same time, they suggest that the self, about which it is easy to be glib, is no more easily grasped than that exterior world. The strength of the poetry derives from Corman's urge to pare down to that world, to reduce, to silence language to all but its essential qualities, to make it, as he says in "Morion," a poem about a gem that resembles a Hans Arp sculpture: "Nothing extra,/ all edge./ solid heart. What one/ offers another."

Such poetry has the feel of a natural object; its spareness resists the desire to appropriate it, calling instead for tact and subtlety in response. Unlike much contemporary poetry, Corman's poems refuse to trade on present anxieties, refuse to be converted into a form of moral coinage—there is barely a word in these poems about the "big issues." Nevertheless, they insinuate themselves into one's moral consciousness by going to ground, by addressing the self at its most affective point, the economy of its own organization:

> Doorways
> reveal my
> shadow and
> make me ask
> myself once
> more if this
> mask I wear
> of words keeps
> my body
> clear of breath.

This grounding acts like an Archimedean lever on ordinary notions of identity and thus gives an astonishing capaciousness to the small forms that Corman so skillfully uses. One would almost want to claim for this poetry a ripple effect, or claim—and here its comparison to haiku is warranted—that it introduces an irruption into the quotidian while at the same time preserving the flavor of the quotidian intact. Such poetry does not easily lend itself to paraphrase or exegesis, nor are its larger incursions into consciousness as immediate as certain more fashionable confessional modes of writing.

This delayed effect, and the fact that Corman's work is both large in bulk (he was one of the most prolific poets of his time) and scattered throughout many volumes and little-known magazines, accounts for the lack of a larger critical effort directed at his work. Another reason may be that his work, seen only fitfully, is regarded as only another part of the vast output of American lyricism.

However, Corman, rightly perceived, was not a lyric poet at all, but, like Ezra Pound, a poet of the epic. It can be said of modern poetry that the lyric has overshadowed the epic, that given the alienated or fragmented sense of self that constitutes contemporary life, the narrative drive required for the epic form can no longer be sustained. One can also read much contemporary poetry as a counter-epic, celebrating, instead of a hero's overcoming obstacles, the hero's sense of loss, discovering, like Eliot, the fragments to shore against the ruins. By contrast, Corman's poetry would intimate a third way, where the epic has merely gone interior, where the story's arc travels across and engages the adventures of consciousness. Surely Corman's poems might be letters home from such a voyage, reminders in their cumulative reconciliations of sight and sound, of place and identity, that self and world are indeed home for each other.

OTHER MAJOR WORKS

NONFICTION: *William Bronk: An Essay*, 1976; *Word for Word: Essays on the Art of Language, Volume 1*, 1977; *At Their Word: Essays on the Art of Language, Volume 2*, 1978; *Where Were We Now: Essays and Postscriptum*, 1991; *Where to Begin: Selected Letters of Cid Corman and Mike Doyle, 1967-1970*, 2000.

TRANSLATIONS: *Back Roads to Far Towns*, 1967 (of Matsuo Bashō); *Things*, 1971 (of Francis Ponge); *Leaves of Hypnos*, 1973 (of René Char); *Breathings*, 1974 (of Philippe Jaccottet); *One Man's Moon*, 1984, 2003 (of Bashō).

BIBLIOGRAPHY

Carlson, Michael. "Cid Corman: Poet Who Was Behind the Literary Magazine *Origin*." *The Guardian*, April 15, 2004, p. 27. This obituary remembers him primarily for his editorial role, but it also discusses his influence in the poetry world and his poetry.

Corman, Cid. "Interview with Cid Corman." Interview by Gregory Dunne. *American Poetry Review* 29, no. 4 (July/August, 2000): 23-28. Provides useful insights into Corman's long career, affinities with other poets, his use of the syllabic line, and his many years living in Japan.

Evans, George. "A Selection from the Correspondence: Charles Olson and Cid Corman, 1950." *Origin* 5, no. 1 (1983): 78-106. Evans presents the first 14 of 175 letters between Corman and Charles Olson. In 1950, Corman was attempting to launch a new poetry magazine. He wrote to Olson to persuade him to take on the position of contributing editor. Interesting to all students of the Objectivist movement.

Heller, Michael. *Conviction's Net of Branches: Essays on the Objectivist Poets and Poetry.* Carbondale: Southern Illinois University Press, 1985. Corman was a major figure in the Objectivist poetry movement. These essays shed light on the nature and convictions of the Objectivists. This study is suitable for advanced undergraduate and graduate poetry students.

Hinten, Marvin D. "Corman's 'The Tortoise.'" *Explicator* 54 (Fall, 1995): 43-44. One of the few academic readings of any of Corman's poems, this one elucidates without overkill, paying attention to the functional use of syllabic lines and enjambment.

Olson, Charles. *Letters for "Origin," 1950-1956.* Edited by Albert Glover. New York: Paragon House, 1989. Corman founded *Origin* magazine as a forum for Objectivist poets, and he hired Charles Olson to be its contributing editor. Their letters discuss the struggles of the periodical and of the Objectivist poetic movement. Suitable for serious Corman students.

Olson, Charles, and Cid Corman. *Charles Olson and Cid Corman: Complete Correspondence, 1950-1964.* Edited by George Evans. 2 vols. Orono: National Poetry Foundation, University of Maine, 1987. Evans presents the 175 extant letters between the founder of *Origin* magazine and its contributing editor. They reveal that Olson was initially skeptical of Corman's aims, fearing that Corman was starting a magazine with too broad a scope to serve the needs of the Objectivist poets.

Pater Faranda, Lisa. "'Between Your House and Mine': The Letters of Lorine Niedecker to Cid Corman, 1960-1970." *Dissertation Abstracts International* 44 (February, 1984): 2474A. Pater Faranda annotates the correspondence between Lorine Niedecker and fellow poet Corman, who was Niedecker's editor in the last years of her life. Their correspondence has a dramatic shape to it because it begins before her marriage and ends just before her death.

Michael Heller
Updated by Philip K. Jason

ALFRED CORN

Born: Bainbridge, Georgia; August 14, 1943

PRINCIPAL POETRY

All Roads at Once, 1976
A Call in the Midst of the Crowd, 1978
The Various Light, 1980
The New Life, 1983
Notes from a Child of Paradise, 1984
An Xmas Murder, 1987
The West Door, 1988
Autobiographies, 1992
Present, 1997
Stake: Selected Poems, 1972-1992, 1999
Contradictions, 2002

OTHER LITERARY FORMS

In addition to collections of poetry, Alfred Corn published *The Metamorphoses of Metaphor: Essays in*

Poetry and Fiction (1987), which argued the influence of Dante and the French Symbolist movement on a wide variety of writers, most notably Wallace Stevens and Marcel Proust; his best-selling handbook *The Poem's Heartbeat: A Manual of Prosody* (1997) critiqued the nature of poetic rhythms. *Atlas: Selected Essays, 1989-2007* (2008) brought together two decades of Corn's critical essays on music, art, theater, and literature. Corn also published *Part of His Story* (1997), a novel in which a gay writer, after the death of his longtime companion from acquired immuno-deficiency syndrome (AIDS), moves to London and becomes involved in the underground movement for Irish independence. Corn, whose renewed faith in Christianity informs his poetry, edited a collection of non-scholarly reflections on the continuing relevance of the New Testament, *Incarnation: Contemporary Writers on the New Testament* (1990).

ACHIEVEMENTS

As one of the New Formalists, post-World War II university poets who returned to the traditional conventions of rhythm and rhyme, Alfred Corn suffused his experiences, most notably his coming into his sexual identity, with his meditative sensibility to create verse that is both autobiographical and profoundly visionary. Early on, his poems attracted both critical praise and distinguished awards; he was recognized with the George Dillon Prize (1975), the Oscar Blumenthal Prize (1977), and the Levinson Prize (1982), each awarded by the influential journal *Poetry*. In 1982, Corn was given the Gustav Davidson Prize from New York's Poetry Society of America, the country's oldest foundation dedicated to promoting poetry. He received an Academy Award in Literature from the American Academy of Arts and Letters in 1983 and an Academy of American Poets Fellowship in 1987. Corn traveled to France on a Fulbright Scholarship and has received numerous fellowships and grants, most notably from the Guggenheim Foundation, the National Endowment for the Arts, and the Rockefeller Study and Conference Center (Bellagio, Italy). A longtime faculty member of the graduate writing program at Columbia, Corn has held appointments with several prestigious writing programs at educational institutions including Yale

University, the University of Cincinnati, Ohio State University, and the University of California, Los Angeles. In 2004, he accepted the one-year Amy Clampitt Residency in Lenox, Massachusetts, an award given annually to an accomplished poet to provide time and resources for developing new projects in the poetic arts.

BIOGRAPHY

Although known as one of the most eloquent poets of the contemporary urban experience, most notably for his evocations of Manhattan street life, Alfred De Witt Corn III grew up in rural Georgia. He was born August 14, 1943, in Bainbridge, near the Florida border. Before Corn was four, his father was drafted into the U.S. Army and subsequently stationed in the Philippines, and his mother died from blood poisoning from a burst appendix. Corn and his two older sisters were raised by friends and then relatives until his father's discharge in 1946. The family moved to Valdosta, where Corn distinguished himself in school. A devout Methodist intent on pursuing the ministry, Corn began writing poems and stories while still in high school. He accepted a scholarship to study French at Atlanta's Emory University, graduating in 1965 with highest honors. During a junior year semester abroad, Corn met and would later (1967) marry Ann Jones, despite his growing certainty of his own homosexuality (they would divorce amicably in 1971). He pursued his postgraduate study of French literature and language at Columbia University, in part because he yearned to experience New York, so central to the poetic sensibilities of two poets he greatly admired, Walt Whitman and Hart Crane.

In 1967, Corn accepted a Fulbright Scholarship and traveled for a year in France. He completed his master's degree in 1970 and, after working briefly as a freelance writer and editor, began what would become a long and distinguished teaching career, at first as a visiting lecturer at Yale (1977-1979) then on the creative writing faculty at Connecticut College before returning to Columbia in 1983. He began publishing poetry during the early 1970's, poems infused with a Whitmanesque sense of the transcendent individual, of the poet as representative self engaged in the restless investigation of the immediate, certain that the sensual world manifested a profound spiritual reality. Forsaking the fad- dish embrace of free verse with its unstructured lines, Corn worked carefully sculpted lines of traditional rhythm and rhyme. His verse immediately attracted critical attention.

By the mid-1980's, Corn's poetry had become more reflective, even metaphysical. After having spent a decade in which he was indifferent to religion, Corn underwent a powerful conversion experience (listen- ing to J. S. Bach while walking through a cemetery) and joined the American Episcopalian denomination. Deeply moved by the pressing realities of AIDS, Corn, who was openly homosexual, began to explore the im- plications of mortality and the workings of time and memory in his poetry. Indeed, his work from the late 1990's and early twenty-first century offers a sobering counterpoint to the visionary transcendence of his ear- lier work.

ANALYSIS

In the classic tradition of Dante and the American tradition of Whitman, Alfred Corn—a born-again Chris- tian, homosexual, and a southerner in cosmopolitan New York—uses the rich materials of his own experi- ence not to put forward introspective confessions but rather to create a representative self that journeys to- ward spiritual transformation across decades of poetic exploration. Corn explores the experiences of love, family, divorce, sexuality, and ultimately death. In me- tered verse that draws on a wide variety of tightly con- structed poetic forms and elevates the sheer music of language, Corn distills from the accumulated experi- ences of his representative self meditative responses to cosmic questions such as the function of the soul, the logic of time, the value of regret, the nature of love, and the necessity of art. Such a contemplative protocol gives Corn's poetry (much like that of Crane and Stevens, both acknowledged influences) a cerebral coolness; however, his verse never loses its anchorage in the immediate. Indeed, Corn's poetic eye is restless, curious about the horizontal plane; his re-creations of the contemporary cityscape and of the rural landscape of the Deep South shimmer, giving his poetry its ground- ing in place that in turn accommodates a luminous tra- jectory into the visionary.

"POEM IN FOUR PARTS ON NEW YORK CITY"

"Poem in Four Parts on New York City," the center- piece work of Corn's second collection, *A Call in the Midst of the Crowd*, is a lyrical re-creation of a bustling New York City that, in the tradition of Whitman's ag- gressiveness romanticism, renders the urban landscape as a visionary world edged with spiritual energies. Di- vided into four sections keyed to the seasons, the poem uses the city's energy to explore the nature of time itself against the work's specific narrative, the story of a young man, an artist, struggling with a difficult rela- tionship and hoping to find in reunion with his lover the harmony promised by love. To endow that relationship with a broader sensibility of place and time, Corn, amid luminous textured passages that describe the city's moods, weaves prose passages about the history of New York City taken from tourist guidebooks, news- papers, vintage encyclopedias, letters from New York City writers (among them Henry James, Edgar Allan Poe, and Crane), and even archival records of building permits in a structural strategy that deliberately evokes William Carlos Williams's urban epic *Paterson* (1946- 1958).

NOTES FROM A CHILD OF PARADISE

With vaunting ambition, Corn audaciously draws on the model of Dante's *La divina commedia* (c. 1320; *The Divine Comedy*, 1802) to structure his own account of the pivotal years in the late 1960's when, married and on a Fulbright in Europe, he accepted his own ho- mosexuality. The book-length narrative poem *Notes from a Child of Paradise*, which like Dante's spiritual epic has one hundred cantos in three sections, one of thirty-four and two of thirty-three stanzas, tells of the courtship of Alfred and Ann and their troubled mar- riage amid rising concerns over Alfred's sexual iden- tity, all set against the context of the tumultuous 1960's. Corn never exploits the various tensions of the de- cade—the struggle for civil rights, student activism, the peace movement—but rather keeps the focus on Al- fred's growth as poet as he abandons his hopelessly expanding dissertation, tinkers with fiction writing, and ultimately finds his voice in poetry (in imitation of Dante's movement from the Inferno, to Purgatory, and ultimately to Paradise). To underscore the poem as Alfred's exploration into his identity, Corn juxtaposes fragments from the historic journey narrative of Meriwether Lewis and William Clark (Alfred and Ann return to the states and drive cross-country to Oregon). In the closing canto, Alfred understands the profound implications of his identity, and Ann becomes a Beatrice-like muse, which underscores the ascendant sense of a character spiritually transformed by exploration. Each section manifests Corn's commitment to traditional poetic forms, with exquisitely chiseled stanzas and textured, lyrical, delicate, and subtle language.

AN XMAS MURDER

With the confidence of a poet at midcareer, Corn experimented in *The West Door* with extending the range of his poetic voice beyond the relatively narrow parameter of the gay poet-self (the volume, for example, contains Corn's translations of the works of other poets, most notably Pablo Neruda and Rainer Maria Rilke). As a way to signal this interest, in 1987, Corn first published *An Xmas Murder*, which he would later incorporate into *The West Door*. In the poem, an extended blank-verse monologue that recalls numerous works by Robert Frost (most notably "Home Burial" and "The Witch of Coos"), a rural Vermont doctor engages in conversation with the poet and a companion who has recently moved to the area. The doctor tells the story of how, years earlier, a local farmer, hardworking but a loner, had been beaten to death on Christmas morning and dumped into a partially frozen river by a mob from the town. A day earlier, the farmer had gotten into a confrontation with a farmhand who was too drunk to work. The doctor himself was a witness to the killing and agreed to testify against the farmhand in court (despite pressure from townfolks who felt the miserly farmer had gotten what he had deserved). The doctor relates how his own life was destroyed after his homosexuality was made public. In part a reaction to the widespread homophobia in the wake of the AIDS pandemic, the poem signals not merely an extension of Corn's formal work but also the increasingly darker tone of his later work—the doctor tells the story to warn the couple (presumably a gay couple) not to assume their Christian neighbors are what they seem (hence "Xmas" rather than "Christmas" in the title). By appropriating the rural cadences and colloquial accents of the doctor, Corn creates a character whose anxieties and loneliness come through in powerful indirection.

"1992"

"1992," the seventy-five-page poem that is the centerpiece work of *Autobiographies*, Corn's most ambitious collection, synthesizes much of the poet's career-long investigations. It shifts between lyrical sections that explore Corn's own experiences (each section is headed by a year from the past) and sections in which he creates the voices of a wide range of Americans—men and women, rich and poor, black and white, gay and straight—all characters that give the poet's ruminations a rich feel of global solidarity. Corn sustains a daring sense of exploration (the 500th anniversary of Christopher Columbus's discovery of the New World functions as motif) in which he confronts difficult questions about the nature of memory, the impact of sickness, the fragile construct of home, the tangled dynamic of regret, and ultimately the tenuousness of life itself. It is a sobering read but one that resists concession to pessimism (more than a decade of confronting the heroic struggles of AIDS patients had convinced Corn that surrender was cowardly). In the closing prose section, Corn updates the lives of the characters and leaves each update in midsentence, suggesting the compelling urgency to endure. Indeed, his autobiographical sections tell of the stability he has found in a lifetime partner. Ultimately, however, the faith Corn offers is most elaborately expressed in the poetic lines themselves, stable, formal, technically sound, and charged with Corn's sense of the abiding music of language.

OTHER MAJOR WORKS

LONG FICTION: *Part of His Story*, 1997.

NONFICTION: *The Metamorphoses of Metaphor: Essays in Poetry and Fiction*, 1987; *The Pith Helmet*, 1992 (aphorisms); *The Poem's Heartbeat: A Manual of Prosody*, 1997; *Aaron Rose Photographs*, 2001; *Atlas: Selected Essays, 1989-2007*, 2008.

EDITED TEXT: *Incarnation: Contemporary Writers on the New Testament*, 1990.

BIBLIOGRAPHY

Abowitz, Richard. "The Traveler: On the Poetry of Alfred Corn." *Kenyon Review* 15, no. 4 (1993): 204-

217. Perceptive analysis of Corn's verse that includes analysis of his formal achievement. Develops Corn's theme of exploration/travel.

Barber, David. "*Contradictions*: Poems." Review of *Contradictions*. *The New York Times Book Review*, January 26, 2003, p. 24. The reviewer finds the poems well structured and expressive, tinged with melancholy.

Barron, Jonathan N., and Bruce Meyer, eds. *New Formalist Poets*. Vol. 282 in *Dictionary of Literary Biography*. Detroit: Gale, 2003. Contains a biographical essay on Corn that examines his life and writings.

Corn, Alfred. "Alfred Corn." Interview by Christopher Hennessy. In *Outside the Lines: Talking with Contemporary Gay Poets*, edited by Hennessy. Ann Arbor: University of Michigan Press, 2005. In this insightful interview, Corn looks at his personal history and how it influences his poetry.

_____. "Alfred Corn's Web Blog." http:// alfredcorn webblog.blogspot.com. Corn's blog. Regular updates illuminate his theories on poetry, art, academics, and his relationship with readers.

Disch, Thomas. "Alfred Corn's *Present*: A Review." *Boston Review* (December, 1997-January, 1998). A broad-reaching review that uses *Present* as an occasion to consider Corn's development of voices and his interest in art and music.

Martin, Robert K. *The Homosexual Tradition in American Poetry*. Rev. ed. Iowa City: University of Iowa Press, 1998. Originally published in 1979, this groundbreaking examination of gay poetry creates a necessary context for approaching Corn. It places Corn among the visionary gay poets Whitman and Crane.

Vincent, John Emil. *Queer Lyrics: Difficulty and Closure in American Poetry*. New York: Palgrave Macmillan, 2002. Important examination of Corn's generation of gay poets that links their themes and their formal techniques with earlier generations. Includes discussion of the impact of AIDS.

Joseph Dewey

GREGORY CORSO

Born: New York, New York; March 26, 1930
Died: Robbinsdale, Minnesota; January 17, 2001

PRINCIPAL POETRY

The Vestal Lady on Brattle, and Other Poems, 1955
Gasoline, 1958
The Happy Birthday of Death, 1960
Minutes to Go, with Others, 1960
Long Live Man, 1962
Selected Poems, 1962
The Mutation of the Spirit, 1964
There Is Yet Time to Run Back Through Life and Expiate All That's Been Sadly Done, 1965
Ten Times a Poem, 1967
Elegiac Feelings American, 1970
Earth Egg, 1974
Herald of the Autochthonic Spirit, 1981
Mindfield: New and Selected Poems, 1989

OTHER LITERARY FORMS

Although Gregory Corso published mainly poetry, he also wrote a short play, *In This Hung-up Age*, produced at Harvard University in 1955; a novel, *The American Express* (1961); and two film scripts: *Happy Death*, with Jay Socin, produced in New York in 1965, and *That Little Black Door on the Left*, included in a group of screenplays entitled *Pardon Me, Sir, But Is My Eye Hurting Your Elbow?* (1968). He also wrote, with Anselm Hollo and Tom Raworth, a series of parodies, *The Minicab War*, published in London by the Matrix Press in 1961.

ACHIEVEMENTS

Perhaps Gregory Corso's greatest contribution to the Beat movement specifically and American poetry generally lies in his role as a literary paradigm for the "New Bohemianism" that appeared in the United States after World War II and through the 1950's. Although Corso never went beyond elementary school, he gained a reputation as one of the most talented of the Beat poets, a "poet's poet," a sort of *enfant terrible* of the Beats. He received teaching appointments on the basis of his reputation as a major figure in the Beat movement. He was awarded the Longview Foundation Award in 1959 for his poem "Marriage," the Poetry Foundation Award, and the Jean Stein Award in Poetry from the American Academy of Arts and Letters in 1986.

BIOGRAPHY

More than any of his contemporaries, Gregory Nunzio Corso lived the true Beat life. Brought up in the slums of New York City, with practically no formal education, Corso was, in the words of the poet-critic Kenneth Rexroth, "a genuine *naif*. A real wildman, with all the charm of a hoodlum . . . a wholesome Antonin Artaud."

He was born in New York City to poor Italian immigrant parents, Fortunato Samuel and Michelina (Colloni) Corso. His mother died when he was a child, and about this loss Corso wrote: "I do not know how to accept love when love is given me. I needed that love when I was motherless young and never had it." His unhappy childhood was marked by his being sent to an orphanage at eleven and to the Children's Observation Ward at Bellevue Hospital when he was thirteen. At that time, Corso later wrote, "I was alone in the world—no mother and my father was at war . . . to exist I stole minor things and to sleep I slept on the rooftops and in the subway." In summarizing his thirteenth year, however, Corso insists that although he went "through a strange hell that year" of 1943, it is "such hells that give birth to the poet."

After three years on the streets of New York, having lived with five different foster parents, Corso was arrested with two friends while attempting to rob a store. Instead of being sent to a boys' reformatory, Corso was sentenced to three years at Clinton Prison, where he began to write poetry. According to Corso, prison "proved to be one of the greatest things that ever happened to me." He even dedicated his second book of poems, *Gasoline*, to "the angels of Clinton Prison" who forced him to give up the often "silly consciousness of youth" to confront the world of men.

After his release from prison in 1950, Corso took on a number of short-term jobs, including manual labor from 1950 to 1951, reporting for the *Los Angeles Ex-*

aminer from 1951 to 1952, and sailing on Norwegian vessels as a merchant seaman from 1952 to 1953. He also spent some time in Mexico and in Cambridge, Massachusetts, where he was encouraged in his writing of poetry by an editor of the *Cambridge Review* and where, with the support of several Harvard students, he published his first book of poetry, *The Vestal Lady on Brattle, and Other Poems*, in 1955.

Between that time and his departure for Europe in 1959, Corso attracted widespread attention with a series of poetry readings he gave in the East and Midwest. Following the 1955 publication of *The Vestal Lady on Brattle, and Other Poems* and his meeting with Jack Kerouac, Allen Ginsberg, and Gary Snyder a year later, his poetry began to appear often in such publications as *Esquire*, *Partisan Review*, *Contact*, and the *Evergreen Review*. In 1958, Lawrence Ferlinghetti first published Corso's famous poem "Bomb" as a broadside at his City Lights Bookshop in San Francisco, as well as the book *Gasoline* in the same year. After an extended tour of England, France, Germany, Italy, and Greece, Corso returned to the United States in 1961. During the following three years, he was hired to teach poetry for a term at New York State University at Buffalo. In November, 1963, he married Sally November.

For Corso, the 1960's were marked by a divorce and more travel in Europe. After the publication of *The Happy Birthday of Death* in 1960, which included such celebrated poems as "Bomb," "Power," "Army," and the award-winning "Marriage," the work that he did in the following decade was very uneven, frequently bordering on flippancy and sentimentality, such as some of the poems in *Long Live Man* and *The Mutation of the Spirit. Elegiac Feelings American* and *Herald of the Autochthonic Spirit* were published a decade apart, appearing in 1970 and 1981, respectively. The increased intervals between offerings indicate a shift in Corso's attitude toward the relationship between the poet and his poems. During the salad days of the Beat movement, Corso had taken his cue from his contemporaries (notably Kerouac) by rejecting any mode of writing except pure spontaneity, but his later poems are much more carefully revised and tightly crafted works. This can be seen in the newer poems that appear in *Mindfield*.

Corso traveled widely over the course of his lifetime, in Mexico and Eastern Europe as well as Western Europe, and in addition to teaching at the State University of New York at Buffalo, he taught in Boulder, Colorado. He was married three times and had five children. In his later years, he became somewhat reclusive, taking part in the occasional tribute or event. He made an appearance at the funeral of Ginsberg in 1996 to say good-bye to his old friend. Ill health forced Corso to move from New York City to Minneapolis, where he lived with a daughter. He died in Robbinsdale, Minnesota, on January 17, 2001, at the age of seventy.

ANALYSIS

Two strains pervade the poetry of Gregory Corso: the Dionysian force of emotion and spontaneity, and a preoccupation with death. From Corso's early poems to his later work, one finds the recurring persona of the clown as an embodiment of the Dionysian force, as

Gregory Corso (Time & Life Pictures/Getty Images)

opposed to the Apollonian powers of order, clarity, and moderation. The clown's comedy, which has its root in the very fact of being "a poet in such a world as the world is today," ranges from the mischievous laughter of the child to the darker, often somber irony of the poet-in-the-world. This exuberance is bound up with the rebelliousness and political activism of the 1960's, as is evident in one of Corso's early and most widely anthologized poems, "Bomb." In this poem—typographically shaped like a bomb in its original 1958 publication by City Lights—Corso confronted the unalterable reality of the nuclear age and his inability "to hate what is necessary to love."

A large part of Corso's Dionysian spirit is romantic—and Corso is certainly in the tradition of Romantic poets John Keats and Percy Bysshe Shelley. He sees the child as a pure, spontaneous Dionysian being: always naturally perceptive, always instinctively aware of sham, pretense, and deception. Such perception runs throughout American literature, from the character of Pearl in Nathaniel Hawthorne's *The Scarlet Letter* (1850) to the child who "went forth" in Walt Whitman to Huckleberry Finn in Mark Twain's novel of 1884 to Holden Caulfield in J. D. Salinger's *The Catcher in the Rye* (1951). Similarly, in Corso's poetry, the child (particularly the self of the poet's recollection) stands for pure Dionysian perception without the intervening deceptions of rules and conventions.

The other strain in Corso's poetry is a passionate concern with the mystery of death, a theme that is more pervasive in his work than any other, with the exception of the pure experience of childhood. Indeed, the intermingling of these two motifs essentially characterizes the Dionysian spirit of Corso—as well as the art of the Beat generation in general. In a poem dedicated to one of his heroes, entitled "I Met This Guy Who Died" (*Mindfield*), Corso writes about a drunken outing with his friend Jack Kerouac. Taken home to see Corso's newborn child, Kerouac moans: "Oh Gregory, You brought up something to die." "How I love to probe life," Corso once wrote in an autobiographical essay. "That's what poetry is to me, a wondrous prober. . . . It's not the metre, or measure of a line, a breath; not 'law' music, but the assembly of great eye-sounds placed into an inspired measured idea."

GASOLINE

In an early collection, *Gasoline*, Corso solidifies his poetic identity in a directly autobiographical poem, "In the Fleeting Hand of Time." Here the poet casts his lot not with the Apollonian academics, who "lay forth sheepskin plans," but with life in the "all too real mafia streets." In another poem from this early collection, entitled "Birthplace Revisited," the poet captures what Allen Ginsberg referred to as "the inside sound of language alone" by virtually overturning the expected or commonplace. This brief poem opens with a mysterious figure wandering the lonely, dark street, seeking out the place where he was born. The figure resembles a character from a detective story—"with raincoat, cigarette in mouth, hat over eye, hand on gat"—but when he reaches the top of the first flight of stairs, "Dirty Ears aims a knife at me . . . I pump him full of lost watches." This is not exactly the kind of image one would expect to find in the language of the standard-bearers of Corso's time, such as Allen Tate or John Crowe Ransom. In fact, in an act of Dionysian rebellion, Corso, in a poem entitled "I Am Twenty-five," bluntly proclaims "I HATE OLD POETMEN!"—especially those "who speak their youth in whispers." The poet-clown, in true Dionysian fashion, would like to gain the confidence of the "Old Poetman," insinuating himself into the sanctity of his home, and then "rip out their apology tongues/ and steal their poems."

THE HAPPY BIRTHDAY OF DEATH

The Happy Birthday of Death presents the best example of Corso as Dionysian clown. In the lengthy ten-part poem entitled simply "Clown," Corso presents this persona more explicitly than he does in any other place when he asserts, "I myself am my own happy fool." The fool or the clown is the personification of the "pure poetry" of Arthur Rimbaud or Walt Whitman, rejecting the academic Apollonian style of the formalists. "I am an always clown," writes Corso, "and need not make grammatic Death's diameter."

Several of the poems of *The Happy Birthday of Death*, notably the award-winning "Marriage," offer critiques of respected institutions of bourgeois society. This poem, perhaps Corso's most popular, is structured around the central questions: "Should I get married? Should I be good?" In a surrealistic feast of language-play, Corso contrasts the social ritual of marriage ("absurd rice and clanky cans and shoes," Niagara Falls honeymoons, cornball relatives) with the irrational and spontaneous phrases he inserts throughout the poem, such as "Flash Gordon soap," "Pie Glue," "Radio Belly! Cat Shovel!" and "Christmas Teeth." In opposition to the conformist regimentation of suburban life, the speaker contrives unconventional schemes, such as sneaking onto a neighbor's property late at night and "hanging pictures of Rimbaud on the lawnmower" or covering "his golf clubs with 1920 Norwegian books."

LONG LIVE MAN

In his later work *Long Live Man*, Corso continued his Dionysian assault on established literary conventions. The poem "After Reading 'In the Clearing,'" for example, finds the speaker admitting that he likes the "Old Poetman" Robert Frost better now that he knows he is "no Saturday Evening Post philosopher." Nevertheless, Frost is "old, old" like Rome, and, says the poet, "You undoubtedly think unwell of us/ but we are your natural children." What Corso intends is not to suggest that youth should respect age, but rather, as William Wordsworth wrote in "Ode: Intimations of Immortality from Recollections of Early Childhood," that "the child is father to the man." As Corso points out in his urban poem "A City Child's Day," the "Grownups do not go where children go/ At break of day their worlds split apart."

Two short poems in the earlier *Long Live Man*, viewed together, seem to foreshadow the approach Corso later used to criticize the institution of marriage and, still later, in *Elegiac Feelings American* and *Herald of the Autochthonic Spirit*, Corso maintains his Dionysian critique of Apollonian standards. The first poem is entitled "Suburban Mad Song"; the second, "The Love of Two Seasons." The first asks how the wife will look at the husband after "the horns are still," when the celebration is ended "and marriage drops its quiet shoe." In other words, when the Dionysian passions of the first experiences become the frozen form, the institution of marriage, the once-happy couple "freeze right in their chairs/ troubled by the table." The only solution for such stasis, Corso seems to be saying in the other short poem, "The Love of Two Seasons," is "the aerial laughter [of] mischief."

ELEGIAC FEELINGS AMERICAN

In "The American Way," a long poem from *Elegiac Feelings American*, Corso worries that the prophetic force of Christ is becoming frozen by American civil religion. "They are frankensteining Christ," the poet says despairingly; "they are putting the fear of Christ in America" and "bringing their Christ to the stadiums." Christ, for Corso, is the pure force of reality, while religious institutions are merely perversions even as love between two people is a pure and sacred force, while marriage is profane. "If America falls," writes Corso, "it will be the blame of its educators preachers communicators alike."

HERALD OF THE AUTOCHTHONIC SPIRIT

Herald of the Autochthonic Spirit suggests not only that the poet has not withered with age but also that he has mastered an ironic voice while maintaining his comic, childlike energy. In a simple poem, "When a Boy," he remarks, first of all, how he "monitored the stairs/ alter'd the mass" in church, as opposed to the pleasure of summer camp, when he "kissed the moon in a barrel of rain." Similarly, in the poem "Youthful Religious Experience," he tells how he found a dead cat when he was six years old and compassionately prayed for it, placing a cross on the animal. When he told this to the Sunday school teacher, she pulled his ears and told him to remove the cross. The old, Corso maintains, can never comprehend the eternally young.

In another poem from this collection, "What the Child Sees," Corso depicts the child as "innocently contemptuous of the sight" of old age's foolishness. "There's rust on the old truths," Corso contends in "For Homer," and "New lies don't smell as nice as new shoes." What the poet, like the child, perceives as pleasurable is the immediate, sensual experience, such as the smell of new shoes, not the abstractions of dried-up old lies. The sadness at the root of this pleasure, however, is a sadness that appears in much of Corso's poetry, evoked by the perennial reality of death.

MINDFIELD

The 1989 collection *Mindfield* is a compilation of Corso's favorite poems throughout his career, along with new poems. Here, one can trace the maturation of the poet across three decades. Particularly revealing are the seven poems written after the appearance of *Herald*

of the Autochthonic Spirit in 1981 but previously unpublished. These poems illustrate the growth of Corso as a poet who, at the half century point in his life, had broadened the range and scope of his poetry while maintaining some of the themes that have dominated his work from the early 1950's.

In the poem "Window," written in 1982, Corso confronts the painful reality of his own mortality. The horror of death, however, becomes merely an evil invention of the older generation that, asserts the man-child Corso, is notoriously "unreliable." Writes Corso:

> . . . your parents your priest your guru are people
> and it is they who tell you that you must die
> to believe them is to die . . .

As a romantic, Corso draws his lessons from nature. Proclaiming his "contempt for death" and asserting that "the spirit knows better than the body," Corso offers the reader lines of poetry as moving as many of Wordsworth's in his assertion of immortality:

> As the fish is animalized water
> so are we humanized spirit
> fish come and go   humans also
> the death of the fish
> is not the death of the water
> likewise the death of yr body
> is not the death of life
> So when I say I shall never know my death, I mean it . . .

To Corso, death is merely another limit or restraint that he challenges throughout his poetry. When he writes, at one point, "Death I unsalute you," Corso illustrates his resistance to all limits that restrict what he sees as the limitless strength of the human spirit.

In the longest of the previously unpublished poems, "Field Report," Corso confronts the inevitable approach of old age with words that are gentle and not fearful. That poem, like most of his other later works, seems to give support to the words of Corso's contemporary and friend, Allen Ginsberg, who writes in his introduction to *Mindfield* ("On Corso's Virtues") words that, while written about a single poem ("The Whole Mess . . . Almost" from *Herald of the Autochthonic Spirit*), could be said about most of Corso's later poetry: The poem is "a masterpiece of Experience, the grand poetic abstractions Truth, Love, God, Faith Hope Charity, Beauty, money, Death, & Humor are animated in a single poem with brilliant & intimate familiarity."

In others of his previously unpublished poems from the 1980's, particularly "Hi" and "Fire Report—No Alarm," Corso grapples with such large metaphysical issues as God, mortality, immortality, and the identity of Jesus. Without God, Corso concludes ironically, the Reverend Jerry Falwell (leader of the conservative Moral Majority and the Christian Right) might well be putting onions on hamburgers. Such pithy, concrete insights are what give humor and vividness to Corso's later poetry.

OTHER MAJOR WORKS

LONG FICTION: *The American Express*, 1961; *The Minicab War*, 1961 (with Anselm Hollo and Tom Raworth).

PLAYS: *In This Hung-up Age*, pr. 1955; *Standing on a Streetcorner*, pb. 1962; *That Little Black Door on the Left*, pb. 1967.

SCREENPLAYS: *Happy Death*, 1965 (with Jay Socin); *That Little Black Door on the Left*, 1968.

MISCELLANEOUS: *Writing from Unmuzzled Ox Magazine*, 1981.

BIBLIOGRAPHY

Cook, Bruce. "An Urchin Shelley." In *The Beat Generation*. New York: Charles Scribner's Sons, 1971. Cook discusses the lives and works of key figures of the Beat generation. Corso, in a 1974 interview, charged Cook with lying about him in an interview that he conducted.

Corso, Gregory. *An Accidental Autobiography: The Selected Letters of Gregory Corso*. Edited by Bill Morgan. New York: New Directions, 2003. A collection that concentrates on Corso's critical years of 1962 to 1967.

Gifford, Barry, and Lawrence Lee. *Jack's Book: An Oral Biography of Jack Kerouac*. New York: St. Martin's Press, 1978. An extensive biography of Jack Kerouac and his relationships with others of the Beat generation, including Corso. Under the influence of Kerouac, Corso put words together in an extremely abstract, apparently accidental manner. According to Corso, Kerouac was a "strong, beautiful man."

Hamilton, Ian. *Against Oblivion: Some Lives of the Twentieth-Century Poets*. London: Viking, 2002. Contains a chapter on Corso, examining his life and works.

Knight, Arthur, and Kit Knight, eds. *The Beat Vision: A Primary Sourcebook*. New York: Paragon House, 1987. This fascinating collection includes an interview with Corso as well as a letter from Corso to Gary Snyder. The book includes vintage photographs, critical discussion of the Beat poets' place in American literature, and the impact of their controversial ideas in shaping and defining American society.

Masheck, Joseph, ed. *Beat Art*. New York: Columbia University Press, 1977. Some of Corso's drawings were included in an exhibition of work by writers associated with the Beats, and although the catalog is not illustrated, the comments on the drawings are interesting and instructive. Corso's drawings, which are also featured in *Mindfield*, are significant but often overlooked artifacts of the Beat generation.

Miles, Barry. *The Beat Hotel: Ginsberg, Burroughs, and Corso in Paris, 1958-1963*. New York: Grove Press, 2000. A narrative account of Beat poets in Paris, where some of their most important work was done. Based on firsthand accounts from diaries, letters, and interviews.

Olson, Kirby. *Gregory Corso: Doubting Thomist*. Carbondale: Southern Illinois University Press, 2002. Olson examines Corso's poetry from a philosophical point, painting him as ranging from a static Catholic Thomist viewpoint to that of a progressive surrealist.

Selerie, Gavin. *Gregory Corso*. New York: Binnacle Press, 1982. Selerie includes an interview with Corso that is particularly provocative because of Corso's comments on his books—such as *Gasoline*, *The Happy Birthday of Death*, and *Elegiac Feelings American*—as well as friends such as Jack Kerouac, Allen Ginsberg, and William S. Burroughs. Corso also provides information on his youthful crimes and time spent in prison.

Skau, Michael. *A Clown in a Grave: Complexities and Tensions in the Works of Gregory Corso*. Carbondale: Southern Illinois University Press, 2000. An examination that covers the complete works of Corso and his complex imagination, his humor, and his poetic techniques in dealing with the United States, the Beat generation, and death. Includes a bibliography of Corso's work.

Stephenson, Gregory. *Exiled Angel: A Study of the Work of Gregory Corso*. London: Hearing Eye, 1989. A full-length study of Corso's poetry, offering individual chapters on principal collections of poetry.

Donald E. Winters, Jr.

HENRI COULETTE

Born: Los Angeles, California; November 11, 1927
Died: South Pasadena, California; March 26, 1988

PRINCIPAL POETRY

The War of the Secret Agents, and Other Poems, 1966
The Family Goldschmitt, 1971
And Come to Closure, 1990 (included in *The Collected Poems of Henri Coulette*)
The Collected Poems of Henri Coulette, 1990

OTHER LITERARY FORMS

Henri Coulette (kew-LEHT) edited or coedited several volumes, including *Midland: Twenty-five Years of Fiction and Poetry from Writing Workshops of the State University of Iowa* (1961; with Paul Engle), *The Unstrung Lyre: Interviews with Fourteen Poets* (1965), and *Character and Crisis: A Contemporary Reader* (1966; with Philip Levine).

ACHIEVEMENTS

Henri Coulette's collections of poetry have received considerable critical if not popular recognition. Throughout his career, he wrote in traditional meters and beautifully crafted lyrics; in addition, he had a deft touch with the satiric epigram. The lyrics are very unusual because they are not mere description but investigations of the imagination that stretch the boundaries of reality. For Coulette, the imagination is supreme; it creates and refines the world of appearance.

BIOGRAPHY

Born in Los Angeles, Henri Anthony Coulette attended local schools, including the institution with which he continued to be associated for most of his life, California State University at Los Angeles. He taught high school English for a while. At the University of Iowa, he attended the Writers' Workshop and obtained an M.F.A. and a Ph.D. His first collection of poetry, *The War of the Secret Agents, and Other Poems* was published in 1966. It was named the Lamont Poetry Selection by the Academy of American Poets and was well received by critics. He continued to teach at California State University at Los Angeles and produced his next collection, *The Family Goldschmitt*, in 1971. A number of his subsequent poems appeared in journals such as *Iowa Review* and *The New Yorker*.

Coulette died in 1988, but a manuscript he left was turned into a collection, *And Come to Closure*, which was published in 1990 as part of *The Collected Poems of Henri Coulette*.

ANALYSIS

Henri Coulette also had a way of transforming contemporary events into poetry. *The Family Goldschmitt* touches on the assassinations of the Kennedys and Martin Luther King, Jr., as well as linking the mythical family in that volume to the concentration camps.

Coulette created an alternative to the long poem by turning his sequence in *The War of the Secret Agents, and Other Poems* into a unified whole. The tale of the secret agents is taken from Jean Overton Fuller's *Double Webs* (1958). Coulette is less interested in the individual poem than in the relationship of poem to poem. His last collection, *And Come to Closure*, is perhaps his finest work, with a broad range of beautifully crafted poems.

THE WAR OF THE SECRET AGENTS, AND OTHER POEMS

Coulette's first book, *The War of the Secret Agents, and Other Poems*, is not a random assortment of poems but a whole in which each poem connects with the others. It is divided into five sections. The first section, "The Junk Shop," portrays a world of objects that take on life when observed by the designing mind. In the first poem, "Intaglio," a picture comes alive as the speaker assigns "roles" to the persons in the picture: the bitch, the actress, and the acrobat. The figures in the picture are his "family." The speaker knows them "as an author knows a book"; it is a literary and not a personal relationship. The poem ends as the speaker is momentarily startled by the playing and calling of children outside, and he turns to "dust the frame and set the picture straight." The real world had faded as the created world of the picture became his true reality.

In "The Junk Shop," objects created by wrights, milliners, and smiths lie in disorder and disarray, but their "pride" still "abides." The end of the poem extends the role and nature of objects; they "contain us" and are "the subjects of our thought." This poem is central to the section, since it defines objects as things with power to provoke the imagination. They can tease people out of thought and lead them to important insights about the world and themselves.

"Life with Mother," another poem on the imagination, is quite different. Mother says, "everything's left to the imagination," and that enables her to become Queen Elizabeth and Alexander Hamilton. She is certain that she is being watched "by agents of the Kremlin" and is an agent herself. Actually, however, she is a "poor Irish daughter of the man/ who invented the Nabisco fig newton." The boy, presumably her son, is not charmed but appalled by her wild imagination; however, he cannot speak. The poem ends with his imagined reply to his mother's delusions: "There are ashes on all your sidewalks, Mother/ Where are ashes in my mouth." The image of ashes succeeds in puncturing her imagined world, but his negative and disloyal revelation harms him.

The last poem in this section is "The Wandering Scholar." The scholar is having a difficult time; he is pushed into the rain and on the road by his own restlessness. He proceeds to curse himself as "the libertine of verse/ Whose meters lurch where they should tread." He prays to "St Golias," a guide who can take him through the rain "into the grove no change can mar," and begs to be brought "where the Muses are." The poem is a rather conventional lyric evoking a historical situation and connecting the poet to an earlier counterpart.

The second section of the book is a group of translations of Latin poems. The first of these, three brief poems by Heredia, tell the story of Mark Antony and Cleopatra. Initially seen as heroic and imaged as "Hawk" and "Eagle," they are quickly reduced to "two parakeets upon a single perch." In the second poem Cleopatra is defeated by Antony, and their defeat is anticipated and suggested in the third.

Coulette's translation of Catullus's famous poem on love is very fine; it is racy and contemporary without violating the spirit of the Latin original. The last poem in the sequence is an amusing translation of a poem by Philippe Jaccottet; Coulette's witty style is very fitting here.

The third section, "Hermit," consists of two poems. The first of these, "Evening in the Park," is reminiscent of the poems in the first section. Sitting in his room, the speaker looks out on an empty park. He counts "tin cans and comic books" and awaits the night. The poetic description of night is immediately brought closer to earth and described by the factual "rush of stars." It then becomes more active as a "rush of thought," bringing images that take the speaker by surprise. The images bring back the day, which was filled with anger and danger. He sits thinking about the hermit of the park: "Does he name the trees?" "Does he conjure numbers?" In the last stanza, the speaker returns to observation of the park; the cans are now "jewelled with the stars," and the comic book whispers. However, "to keep my mind/ Familiar and American," he must leave, rejecting the call of the imagination, which can transform the familiar into something rich and strange, and settling for ordinary life.

"The War of the Secret Agents" has seventeen sections that tell the story of an amateurish yet heroic group of agents in World War II. In "Proem," they are described as being "out of a teen-age novel"; they came "ready to die for England" and quickly revealed their situation. The Nazi Gestapo leader in Paris, Keiffer, learns of them through the betrayal of Gilbert, one of the members of the group. Keiffer describes those he will soon arrest as his flock of sheep. He makes a deal with the leader of the secret agents, Prosper: "No harm will come to his men,/ none at all, if he cooperates." The exigencies of war, however, make his promise meaningless; in the end, fifteen hundred are sent to death, although a few survive. Keiffer is, perhaps, the most interesting character in the poem. He has an aesthetic sense and a personal style.

What happens after the death of the agents is the most intriguing aspect of the story. In the second poem of the sequence, Jane Alabaster (perhaps Jean Overton Fuller, author of *Double Webs*, 1958) writes a letter to T. S. Eliot, her editor at Faber and Faber, about her discovery that Gilbert is the traitor who sacrificed the others. Gilbert and the few who survived will give their version of the events. In the seventh poem, Cinema speaks about how he saw Prosper on the train that brought them to Germany. He speaks of how he traveled the Metro each day as a different person and how his own identity has been lost in his code name. He cannot explain the dead; they are gone and cannot speak. Phono was with Prosper when he was marched out to death. He recalls his bravado: *Show these bastards how to die.* Somewhat uncharacteristically, Prosper replied, "You show them." Phono waited for death, but it never came.

A letter from Prosper to his wife is found in poem 15; lamenting his difficulties with his agents, "Lumbering Phono, mad Cinema," Prosper says, "I must play the greybeard for these children." The poem shows Prosper to be quite human, not at all the foolish idealist of the earlier poem.

Poem 16 is the climax of the series. Jane Alabaster confronts Gilbert and his betrayal; Gilbert at first tries to deny it but finally is forced to admit that he is the one. However, his action was not treason; he was under orders from London. There was "an underground beneath the underground," and the agents were sacrificed to protect it.

The last section in the book, "Moby Jane," is satiric. It contains a poem to a computer that writes poetry, a very amusing piece called "The Academic Poet," and the title poem. In the latter, Moby Jane speaks of Herman Melville as "a terrible man" who indulged in "useless scribblings" on an unknown whale. The real "beast" was the manuscript. Moby and Jane reject "signing the necessary papers," since that would be playing Melville's game. In Coulette, even the whales have a voice and a place.

THE FAMILY GOLDSCHMITT

A less important collection than *The War of the Secret Agents, and Other Poems, The Family Goldschmitt* begins with Coulette's imaginative identification with that family when his German landlady insists that his name is Goldschmitt. He then expands the identification by noting, "There is gas escaping somewhere." Is he on a train to Deutschland? In response, he writes a letter "to the world, no! to the people/ I love, no! to my family, yes!/ The Family Goldschmitt." Members of this mythical family are portrayed near the end of the book, and their comments mark section divisions. Coulette has a wonderful ability to transform the ordinary world into something exotic and threatening.

The section "1968" is filled with social poems on that troubled year. "On the Balcony" is on the death of Martin Luther King, Jr. The speaker is King himself, contemplating "the face in that window," presumably his killer. His friends "look up at me, lingering"; the evening is "hushed and ready." Everything seems primed for some momentous event. "It will come to me, and does,/ And I am made public." This very effective poem conveys the anticipation and completion of King's assassination without melodrama. Death is seen as a transformation from the state of a private man to another plane; King now has only a "public" existence.

The short poems on the Kennedys are, perhaps, less successful. Coulette portrays the events as sensations: "Bang!Bang!Bang!/ And always in the head." The public's response is to watch television and "drive with our lights on." These poems are effective reframings of the memorable events, but not much more.

There are other political poems in this section, a satiric poem on Richard M. Nixon and one on Ernesto "Che" Guevara. Guevara's death is caused not by the Central Intelligence Agency but by the "damned Indians." His end is described as a mistake, "like being lost/ On a family picnic." Coulette then renders the facts of the death: "a body in a sink, uniforms heavy/ With braid, a group portrait." The poem ends with an image of coldness and distance: "The earth,/ it is said, is a blue star." This image suggests inappropriate feelings about the death of one so significant.

The most interesting poem in the third section, "Walking Backwards," is the title poem. As the poem opens, the speaker is walking backward beyond people and tall buildings. Failing to make a connection with the people he passes, he makes "small talk" and shows the boredom in his face. He leaves them and "the squares/ Of which I am an angle." The last stanza comments on his departure from society: He has left behind the "great truths," the voices of orthodoxy, "at the end of their chains, barking." It is a marvelous metaphor of Coulette's opposition to and spurning of conventionality and conformity.

A short section called "Simples, Nostrums" contains a comical poem on Coulette's "first novel" and three poems on family memories. "The Invisible Father" is the best of the three. Coulette addresses his father as a "wound,/ Or at best an absence." The father is described as the sun "behind us" and as "fathering our shadows toward" the mother. Finally, he "has become the music" that he practiced, and his location is "elsewhere in that strange house." The poem ends with his coming to life as the speaker hears a passage the father had practiced "suddenly in context." In this affectionate and moving poem, the father's absence is evoked and his presence restored with a new understanding.

AND COME TO CLOSURE

Coulette's last volume, *And Come to Closure*, was published two years after his death in *The Collected Poems of Henri Coulette*; it is by far his finest collection. It begins with a brilliant translation of Horace's *Odes*, "IV" (23 B.C.E., *The Odes of Horace*, 1963), and quickly moves on to a section called "Coming to Terms"; the title poem takes the speaker back to childhood, when all is possible and "everything is in our grasp." When childhood passes, however, one is an adult, "which is to say *metaphysical*, which is to say *bored*." He asks whether the "explosion" in the desert exists, and how. Is it "invisible even to itself," or does it remain in the "desert of the mind?" Should one welcome it, "as wise men an oasis, as children mirage?" The only refuge from aging and the inevitable boredom it brings is coming to terms with the limitations of the world and the necessity for imagination, Coulette's persistent theme.

The last poem in the section is the amusing "At the Writers Conference," in which the speaker is asked, "*Why do you write*?" He answers with a few words: "love," "feeling," and "thought." The answer is greed-

ily accepted, but the questioners are really after something else; "they want to publish, for they perish soon." The speaker wonders what it is like to live "bereft of a title page,/ Vanity without signature and spine." The question cannot be answered, for the secret to publication cannot be given. He exits "to their sweet applause"—actually a mockery, since he cannot satisfy their vanity or provide the key to fame.

In a short section called "The Blue Hammer," there is one fine poem, the third section of "The Desire and Pursuit of the Part." The poem begins by announcing separation: "The whole is not/ Implicit in the part." The speaker is filled with fear at the "crab/ in my gut," the "spider/ In my head." When he gets up in the cold, however, he sees before him his cats, Jerome and Miss Coots. The last stanza celebrates this simple joy: "It is enough,/ Or all I have just now." Such quiet experiences may be only a "part," but they are sufficient. This settling for ordinary pleasures is a welcome development in Coulette's work.

The fifth section contains epigrams, one of which goes beyond the narrowness of the form. The sixteenth portrays a perfect moment: "A one-eyed cat Hathaway on my lap,/ A fire in the fireplace, and Schubert's 5th" on the radio. Listening, the speaker concludes, "This is, I think,/ As close as I may come to happiness." This is a gem of a poem in which the details create a compelling world; the poet is no longer reaching beyond material things but accepting them and their joy.

The sixth section, "An Unofficial Joy," contains a number of wonderful poems. Coulette's elegy "Night Thoughts," on his friend David Kubal, is beautiful. It is not at all somber but celebrates Kubal's life with vignettes; Kubal roams the street with his dog, "pillar to post, and terribly alive." A favorite Coulette word, "elsewhere," perfectly catches Kubal's desire for escape to "some secret inner place." Having died, he is now "elsewhere," and his dead body is compared to "a windblown rose" that is "ushered to repose." The poem ends with an imaginative identification of the poet with a brother. The poem is both a joyful reminiscence and the mourning of what is gone.

"Postscript" is a brilliant villanelle in which the speaker contemplates a failed relationship. Nearly every stanza speaks of decay or undoing. The thorn outsmarts "the cunning of the rose"; there are allusions to the serpent in the garden, the "interiors none may map or chart." The last stanza sums up: "We had too little craft and too much art./ We thought two noes would make a perfect yes." Coulette handles the complicated scheme of the villanelle with great skill and ease; the repeated line, "Who was it said, Come let us kiss and part?" communicates the speaker's regret and lack of consolation in the shattering of the relationship.

"Petition" is a perfect short poem in which the speaker prays for his cat: "Lord of the Tenth Life,/ Welcome my Jerome." The second and last stanza speaks of what Jerome loves, "bird and mouse," a "man's lap," "and in winter light,/ Paws tucked in, a nap." The invention of a cat god and the portrayal of this "fierce, gold tabby" are memorable, apt exemplars of Coulette's brilliant imagination and warm affection for what is.

Other major works

EDITED TEXTS: *Midland: Twenty-five Years of Fiction and Poetry from Writing Workshops of the State University of Iowa*, 1961 (with Paul Engle); *The Unstrung Lyre: Interviews with Fourteen Poets*, 1965; *Character and Crisis: A Contemporary Reader*, 1966 (with Philip Levine).

Bibliography

Anthony, Mary. "Some Translations by Henri Coulette." *Western Humanities Review* 21 (Winter, 1967): 67-71. Anthony rates Coulette's translations of Catullus, Heredia, and Jaccottet very highly. She states that Coulette is not a literalist but a creative translator who preserves the poetry. Coulette's "rightness" in the poems, she says, is remarkable.

Clements, Robert J. "The Muses Are Heard." *Saturday Review* 49 (May 21, 1966): 30-31. In this brief review of *The War of the Secret Agents, and Other Poems*, Clements dismisses Coulette as a "Californian" poet. He does acknowledge that the poems are "contemporary" but sees little value in the book.

Coulette, Henri. Interview by Michael S. Harper. *Iowa Review* 13 (Spring, 1982): 62-84. In this intriguing interview, Coulette reveals some of his influences and sources. Some of his poems are shown to be directly based on his life. *The Family Goldschmitt*, for example, came out of Coulette's trip to Europe in 1967. The father in the poems is Coulette's own musician father.

Donoghue, Denis. "The Long Poem." Review of "The War of the Secret Agents." *The New York Review of Books* 6 (April 14, 1966): 18-21. A brief and neutral review of Coulette's long poem. Explaining that he does not know the book Coulette used as a source for the poem, Donoghue admits to some puzzlement.

Fitts, Dudley. "Quartet in Varying Keys." Review of *The War of the Secret Agents, and Other Poems*. *The New York Times Book Review*, April 17, 1966, 46-47. A very positive review. Praises Coulette's "technical adroitness" in many of the short poems in the collection. Fitts calls Coulette "a poet to watch."

Glaser, Elton. "Alias, Alas." Review of *The Collected Poems of Henri Coulette. Parnassas: Poetry in Review* 26, no. 1 (2001): 217-230. A favorable review of Coulette's book that expresses disappointment that his work is not better known.

Santos, Terry. "Remembering Henri Coulette." *Kenyon Review* 14, no. 1 (Winter, 1992): 137. A brief biographical profile of the poet.

James Sullivan

Malcolm Cowley

Born: Near Belsano, Pennsylvania; August 24, 1898
Died: New Milford, Connecticut; March 27, 1989

Principal poetry

Blue Juniata, 1929
The Dry Season, 1941
Blue Juniata: Collected Poems, 1968
Blue Juniata, a Life: Collected and New Poems,
　1985

Other literary forms

Although Malcolm Cowley (KOW-lee) began his literary career as a poet and remained a practicing poet, critic of poetry, and adviser to scores of American poets for most of his more than sixty-year career, his literary reputation derives chiefly from his prose works, which include literary criticism and literary and cultural history as well as numerous essays and book reviews written for newspapers, magazines, and literary journals. Many of Cowley's critical essays are considered to be seminal studies of major American poets and novelists, such as Hart Crane, Ernest Hemingway, and William Faulkner. In addition, Cowley's major works of literary and cultural history, including *Exile's Return* (1934, 1951), *The Literary Situation* (1954), *A Second Flowering: Works and Days of the Lost Generation* (1973), *And I Worked at the Writer's Trade* (1978), and *The Dream of the Golden Mountains: Remembering the 1930's* (1980), have served as primary sources of information about the intellectual, social, political, and historical events and issues that shaped the aesthetic practices and the social and political beliefs of modern American writers. Cowley's published books range from pioneering translations of important novels and essays by French writers of the 1920's and 1930's, such as Paul Valéry and André Gide, to editions of the works of several of America's classic nineteenth century writers, such as Walt Whitman and Nathaniel Hawthorne. His publications also include a volume analyzing the intellectual history of modern Western civilization, *Books That Changed Our Minds* (1939; with Bernard Smith), and a historical study of the African slave trade, *Black Cargoes: A History of the Atlantic Slave Trade, 1518-1865* (1962; with Daniel Pratt Mannix).

Cowley edited anthologies of several of his contemporaries, editions that significantly contributed to expanding their audience and to establishing their literary reputations. The most notable of these are *The Portable Hemingway* (1944), *The Portable Faulkner* (1946), *The Stories of F. Scott Fitzgerald* (1951), and *Three Novels of F. Scott Fitzgerald* (1953; with Edmund Wilson).

Cowley's literary journalism has been partially collected in two volumes, *Think Back on Us: A Contemporary Chronicle of the 1930's* (1967) and *A Many-Windowed House: Collected Essays on American Writers and American Writing* (1970). The only portion of Cowley's literary correspondence (most of which is housed in Chicago's Newberry Library) that has been published is a volume of letters, with explanatory narration, between Cowley and William Faulkner regarding their eighteen-year friendship, *The Faulkner-Cowley File: Letters and Memories, 1944-1962* (1966).

ACHIEVEMENTS

Malcolm Cowley was formally honored by the American cultural and educational community relatively late in his career. His fellow writers honored him early and continuously, however, by both public recognition and private expression. Because a significant portion of his work is concerned with the writer in the modern world, Cowley was an acknowledged leader and spokesperson for the American literary community for fifty years. Consequently, many of Cowley's honors were bestowed for his service to the profession of letters as much as for his individual achievements as a poet and writer.

In 1921, Cowley was granted an American Field

Malcolm Cowley (Library of Congress)

Service Fellowship permitting him to spend two years in France studying at the University of Montpellier, an experience that was crucial in exposing him to the revolutionary ideas and practices of modern artists in France. In 1927, he received the Levinson Prize for poetry. In 1939, *Poetry* magazine awarded him the Harriet Monroe Memorial Prize. In 1946, he received a grant from the National Institute of Arts and Letters, and in 1967, the newly created National Endowment for the Arts gave Cowley a ten-thousand-dollar award in recognition of his service to American letters. The Modern Language Association of America awarded Cowley its Hubbel Medal in 1978 for services to American literature. In 1980, *And I Worked at the Writer's Trade* earned for Cowley the National Book Award in the paperback autobiography category.

Cowley was elected to the National Institute of Arts and Letters in the early 1950's, and the institute membership shortly thereafter honored him by twice electing him president, from 1956 to 1959 and from 1962 to 1965. Cowley was also elected to the senior body of the National Institute, the American Academy of Arts and Letters, and he served as chancellor of that body from 1967 to 1977. These tenures were periods in which Cowley helped to supervise the creation and granting of a number of prizes and monetary awards to scores of writers both for individual works of literature and for contributions to literature over entire careers. For more than forty years, Cowley also served as an adviser, director, and vice president of Yaddo, the private foundation that provides subsidized residence for writers and artists in Saratoga Springs, New York.

Cowley served as a distinguished visiting professor at the University of Washington in Seattle in 1950; at Stanford University in 1956, 1959, 1960-1961, and 1965; at the University of Michigan in 1957; as Regents Professor at the University of California, Berkeley, in 1962; at Cornell University in 1964; at the University of Minnesota in 1971; and at the University of Warwick in England in 1973. He was awarded honorary doctorates of literature by Franklin and Marshall College, 1961; Colby College, 1962; the University of Warwick, England, 1975; the University of New Haven, 1976; and Monmouth College, 1978.

Though Cowley began publishing in the 1920's, his work remained uncollected until relatively late in his career. However, his influence on other critics, academic scholars, poets, and novelists has been substantial. His essays written while serving as literary editor of *The New Republic* from 1929 until 1944 made Cowley one of the most widely read voices of literary and cultural analysis during the years of the Great Depression and World War II. In the postwar period, academic scholars considered his writing to be a critical guide to American literature and literary history in the entire first half of the twentieth century. When Robert Spiller, Willard Thorp, and Henry Seidel Canby began work on the now standard reference work *The Literary History of the United States* (1948-1953), they asked Cowley to write the sections concerning the social history of modern American authors and the influence of American literature on foreign nations.

As adviser to one of America's foremost publishing companies, the Viking Press, for more than thirty years, Cowley played a role in developing Viking's literary publications, including such ventures as the Viking Portable Library, the paperback Compass editions, the Viking Critical Editions, and the first significant publication in America of many new writers, among them authors such as Jack Kerouac, Ken Kesey, and Tillie Olson, and a number of poets, such as Donald Hall, Philip Booth, and A. D. Hope. In the late 1940's, Cowley served on the committees that inaugurated the National Book Awards and the Bollingen Prize for Poetry, and in the early 1950's, he helped advise the Rockefeller Foundation on the funding of literary magazines.

Cowley's critical acumen concerning his own generation of writers was matched by his ability to recognize and sponsor other talented writers. He first published John Cheever and discussed his fiction with him for more than forty years. He promoted Nelson Algren from his first reading of his work in 1942 until Algren's death in 1981. In addition, a number of academic critics, such as John W. Aldridge, Michael Millgate, Larzer Ziff, and Philip Young, have attested to the influence Cowley had on their careers.

One of only a handful of American poets who have become successful literary journalists, historians, and critics, and whose prose work belongs to the canon of

American literature, Cowley gained a reputation as one of the most perceptive of modern literary analysts. He has been described as one of the most lucid English prose stylists of the twentieth century. Because of his belief in the cultural value and importance of poetry (indeed of all literature), he saw the use of language, particularly by artists and journalists, as an expression of the moral character of society, and his analysis of modern writers and their history became the distinctive achievement of his career.

BIOGRAPHY

Malcolm Cowley was born on August 24, 1898, in the small farming village of Belsano in the Allegheny hills east of Pittsburgh. His father, William Cowley, was a homeopathic physician who maintained his office in a building in an older section of Pittsburgh. The family rented an apartment in the same building, so Cowley grew up in an urban business neighborhood with few children for companionship. The Cowley summer house in Belsano had been left to William Cowley by the poet's grandmother, and it was there that Cowley's mother, Josephine (Hutmacher) Cowley, took her only child to spend the summers while her husband worked in Pittsburgh. The farm community of Belsano and Cowley's experiences there during the long summers had a profound impact on his life and poetry. He was never comfortable in urban environments. Cowley's childhood was, like that of many writers, one of periodic solitude and long hours spent alone reading and imagining. Though he received most of his early schooling in Pittsburgh, Cowley was most comfortable in the farming community of Belsano.

He entered Harvard College in 1915 on a scholarship from the Harvard Club of Pittsburgh. There he made several important literary friendships, some of them with older poets such as S. Foster Damon, Conrad Aiken, and E. E. Cummings. These friends, themselves innovators in the modern poetry movement, introduced Cowley to the work of the nineteenth century French Symbolists and to older New England poets such as Edwin Arlington Robinson and Amy Lowell, who was then a proponent of Imagism.

In the spring of 1917, Cowley volunteered for the American Field Service in France, and he served, like other Harvard writers such as Cummings, John Dos Passos, and Robert Hillyer, as part of the earliest group of Americans to see the battlefronts of World War I. Cowley drove a munitions truck for the French army for six months, then returned to New York, where he lived for several months in Greenwich Village waiting to return to college. While living a life of poverty and writing some poetry and book reviews to survive, he met and later married an older artist, Marguerite Frances "Peggy" Baird, who was a confirmed bohemian painter divorced from her first husband, the New York poet Orrick Johns. Peggy Baird introduced Cowley to many older Greenwich Village artists, as well as to Clarence Britten, then literary editor of *The Dial*, who gave Cowley books for review and indirectly initiated his career in literary journalism.

Cowley returned to Harvard in September, 1919, and graduated in the winter of 1920 after another absence spent in Army ROTC training. He had been elected president of *The Harvard Advocate* in the spring of 1918 and spent his last two college terms working to keep alive what little literary life there was at Harvard during the war years.

After college, Cowley returned to Greenwich Village, where he and Peggy lived a bohemian life again in a cheap tenement while Cowley worked as a copywriter for *Sweet's Architectural Catalogue*. He continued to do some freelance book reviewing and wrote poems and essays for magazines.

In July, 1921, Cowley went to France for two years. There he studied at the University of Montpellier and lived for short periods in Claude Monet's village of Giverney outside Paris. In Paris, his New York friend Matthew Josephson introduced him to the French Dadaist and Surrealist writers and painters, and Cowley met most of the American expatriate writers who had gone to Europe after World War I to escape the conservative, sometimes reactionary political, aesthetic, and social ideas dominating American culture in the postwar years. In France, Cowley also worked as an editor and writer for two of the most famous "little magazines" of the expatriates in those years, *Broom* and *Secession*. Although most of the American expatriates absorbed a good deal of the social, political, and aesthetic ideas of the modern European avant-garde art movement, Cowley rebelled against such ideas and began to defend the traditional aesthetic values of Western artistic realism and mimesis. His experiences in France resulted in his understanding of the aesthetic brilliance of the modern artistic revolution, but he became sharply critical of many of the modernist doctrines and practices.

When Cowley returned to New York in August, 1923, he embarked on a career that he hoped would emulate the ideal of a professional man of letters. In the latter half of the 1920's, Cowley wrote poems, essays, and book reviews for a number of the most prominent literary journals and newspapers of the time, and translated books of French literature, some of which became best sellers. Cowley was also the friend of a number of writers living near New York in the 1920's, such as Hart Crane, Allen Tate, Robert Penn Warren, and Katherine Anne Porter.

When Edmund Wilson retired as literary editor of *The New Republic* in the summer of 1929, he chose Cowley to succeed him. For sixteen years thereafter, Cowley served in a job he loved and exhausted himself in attempting to connect the world of literature and books with the world of politics, public affairs, and social history. His own poetry and prose of the time provide cultural historians with one of the best records of the tumultuous intellectual and political fervor of the Depression and World War II years.

After being forced to resign by Congressman Martin Dies in the spring of 1942 from his position as aide to Archibald MacLeish at the Roosevelt administration's Office of Facts and Figures, for allegedly being a "communist threat" to the United States because of his left-wing political sympathies during the Depression, Cowley retired from any active political involvement and moved to Sherman, Connecticut, where he had already remodeled an old barn. Thereafter he worked as a freelance writer, editor, part-time college teacher, and adviser to the Viking Press, writing and editing the books that consolidated his reputation as one of the finest American literary critics and historians of the twentieth century.

In 1932, Cowley, who had divorced his first wife, married Muriel Maurer, with whom he lived for more than fifty years. His son, Robert, became a magazine and book editor in New York. Malcolm Cowley died in New Milford, Connecticut, in March of 1989, by that time revered as an American literary institution.

ANALYSIS

To appreciate Malcolm Cowley's poetry, it is necessary to see it in relation to the major cultural movement of his time, usually described by historians as artistic or cultural modernism, or simply modernism. Modernism represented a radical break with the centuries-long traditions of Western humanistic, realistic art. The humanistic tradition was characterized by a belief that art has a moral and social function in the larger process of human civilization.

The theories and practice of modern artists developed in reaction to both the humanistic tradition of Western civilization and the profound changes in Western society that resulted from the rising prestige of science and technology, the Industrial Revolution, and the organized use of scientific knowledge and technology by modern financial capitalism. Characteristic ideas of modern art included a repudiation of any criteria except the aesthetic as a basis for judging art, and the contention that the artistic imagination is an essentially irrational, as opposed to rational, process that governs scientific investigation and ordinary human communication.

The complex and revolutionary impulse of modern art, its antinaturalist aesthetic, its repudiation of the traditions of Western art, the social alienation and rebellion of artists, and their profound hostility to modern society constituted an epochal change in art history. The sometimes confused and alienated psychology that they represented, together with the explosion of experimental forms that it produced, were manifested while Cowley was beginning his literary career. His critical study of that historical epoch and its influence on modern American writers was the subject of his most famous book, *Exile's Return*. It was also the subject of his first published book of poetry, *Blue Juniata*.

When Cowley published *Blue Juniata* in 1929, the book was described by Allen Tate as an important historical record of the entire literary generation of the 1920's. *Blue Juniata* was published at the urging of Hart Crane, who wanted it organized to reflect the "emotional record" of its author in accord with the values of modern poetics. Instead, Cowley structured the book historically in five sections, each containing poems describing periods and places that Cowley experienced with his contemporaries. The sections include poems about his years of adolescence and World War I, the years of expatriate artists in France and Europe after the war, the migration to New York and the frenzied life of the Jazz Age, and a section of miscellaneous poems reflecting the poet's sense of upheaval in the decade of the 1920's. The book mirrors Cowley's private reaction to his time and the time itself.

If the aesthetic of modern art was antinatural, the title section of *Blue Juniata* is filled with poems celebrating nature. The title is taken from a river in west-central Pennsylvania, the rural environment that Cowley loved but to which, like the childhood homes of Thomas Wolfe, Hemingway, Fitzgerald, and others of his generation, he could not "go home again."

Cowley's poems reflect the modernist poetry movement in other ways. In the second section of the book, called "Adolescence," he reprints poems written during his bohemian days after the war. Poems such as "Kelly's Barroom" imitate the style of the French Symbolist poet Jules Laforgue and his theme of youthful disillusionment. Laforgue had been recommended to younger American poets such as Cowley by Ezra Pound and T. S. Eliot, whose "The Love Song of J. Alfred Prufrock" was also derivative of Laforgue.

The third section of *Blue Juniata* consists of poems written in Europe, where many of Cowley's American friends had been influenced by the French Dadaist artists and by the international avant-garde centered in Paris and led by James Joyce, Marcel Proust, Pablo Picasso, and other European artists. Cowley's poems of those years include English versions of some of the great modernist poems, such as Guillaume Apollinaire's "Marizibill," and an ironic poem undercutting a classical theme that he entitled "Mediterranean Beach." Such poems as "Valuta" satirize the exploitation by artists of postwar Europe's economic situation, while "Sunrise over the Heiterwand" hints at the political confusion of Pound and Eliot. Another poem of Cowley's Paris years, "Château de Soupir: 1917," is a satire on Marcel Proust's monumental novel *À la recherche du temps perdu* (1913-1927; *Remembrance of Things Past*, 1922-1931). A poem entitled "Two Swans" is a commentary on the outlaw sensibility of Charles Baudelaire and later Symbolists, who maintained that poetic beauty was to be found in the bizarre and criminal underworld.

Many of the poems of the fourth section of *Blue Juniata* ("The City of Anger, Poems: 1924-1928") are portraits of literary friends. In "The Narrow House," Cowley describes Kenneth Burke as a pastoral recluse of vast ambition and hopes who has husbanded his land in rebellion against the industrial age. Another remarkable poem, "The Flower in the Sea," portrays Hart Crane's obsession with the Symbolist idea of the "Poète Maudit" and his fascination with the sea. It is a portrait whose prophecy Crane fulfilled several years later, when he committed suicide by jumping overboard in the Gulf of Mexico. One poem, "Buy 300 Steel," satirizes Cowley's friend Matthew Josephson, who was forced to work at a job he hated as a stockbroker in the Roaring Twenties. Harold Loeb, an heir to a small portion of the Guggenheim copper fortune and the man who financed the avant-garde art magazine *Broom*, is described in Cowley's poem "Tumbling Mustard" as representing the frenzied energy of the artists of the 1920's. Allen Tate, with his taste for classical poetry and poetic styles, is addressed by Cowley in his sonnet "Towers of Song."

SOCIAL AND POLITICAL THEMES

Even in his poems about New York, Cowley reveals a social consciousness that distinguished him from his peers. Two poems of the late 1920's, "The Lady from Harlem: In Memory of Florence Mills" and "For St. Bartholomew's Eve (August 23, 1927)," are overtly political, reacting to the injustices felt by liberal artists at famous trials in New York, as well as in 1927 Boston, where the anarchist immigrants Nicola Sacco and Bartolomeo Vanzetti were tried and executed. Many of Cowley's pastoral poems in *Blue Juniata* also imply a social theme. In several short narrative and descriptive poems, such as "Laurel Mountain," "Seven O'Clock," "Hickory Cove," "The Farm Died," and "Empty Barn, Dead Farm," Cowley's tone is elegiac, lamenting the declining farm communities of nineteenth century America displaced by the growing urban industialization of the twentieth century. Two other poems, "The Hill Above the Mine" and "Mine No. 6," are stark descriptions of the ruin brought to Cowley's boyhood Pennsylvania by the greed of the mining industry. All those poems reflect Cowley's deep emotional attachment to the American landscape.

Though Cowley gave a more complete and analytical history of his literary generation in *Exile's Return*, *Blue Juniata* contains many of the themes and ideas that he later developed in that book. Indeed, the final poems of his collection, "The Urn," is a concise statement, in formal stanzas, of the central experience of the entire "lost generation," their experience of exile, uprootedness, and aching memory for a country of childhood that could never be regained in the modern world.

As a critical analyst of the Depression-era literature of social commitment and a historian of modern American literature, Cowley's major prose works are descriptive, analytical, and narrative. His deepest response to the literary and political culture of the Great Depression is revealed, however, in a slim volume of poems, his second collection, published in 1941.

THE DRY SEASON

The Dry Season contains seventeen poems, most of them written between 1935 and 1941. A few poems in the collection go back to the late 1920's but had been omitted from *Blue Juniata*. These poems, such as "Tar Babies," which was originally published in the avant-garde magazine *transition* in 1928, satirize the decadent, often sexually aberrant behavior of the artistic culture of the 1920's. "The Eater of Darkness," a poem dedicated to Cowley's friend and early Dadaist enthusiast Robert Coates, describes the bizarre literary world of New York by presenting the Jazz Age in terms of Lewis Carroll's *Alice's Adventures in Wonderland* (1865). The chaotic, sometimes destructive, rebel society of modern American art had been the theme of Coates's novel *Yesterday's Burden's* (1933), which Cowley cited in *Exile's Return* as evidence of the turn by American artists in the early 1930's from modernist art and social rebellion to social involvement.

The poetry of *The Dry Season* reveals the emotional history of Cowley's own social involvement. For example, two poems, "The Mother" and "The Firstborn," are autobiographical, written after the death of his mother. Both poems reveal a sense of guilt on the part of a son who felt unable to help his parents while they suffered, like millions of Americans, from deprivation. On a visit to Pittsburgh shortly before his mother's death, Cowley had been stunned to find that his father, a doctor unable to collect payment from most of his patients, had become a partial invalid and that his mother sometimes did not have enough to eat. The plight of his family reinforced his conviction that radical measures were needed to change the American economic structure. He also felt that writers and artists could find hope, a renewed sense of relevance, and a large audience if their art mirrored the human issues of their age.

His poems "The Last International" and "Tomorrow Morning" reflect the hopes and humanist faith that comprised Cowley's passionate response to the turmoil of the time. The imagery of "The Last International" alludes to Homer, Vergil, and Dante and their visions of Hell. In Cowley's poem, however, the dead rise up to revolutionize contemporary life.

An important aspect of "Tomorrow Morning" is its intuitive recognition that radical politics and solidarity with the politically and economically disadvantaged required affiliation with political fringe groups that would taint artistic integrity and would probably tragically fail to change historical conditions anyway. Given the evils of fascism, and the economic chaos against which Cowley believed a coalition was necessary, the poem implies that artists have no choice but to work with all factions opposed to the reactionary forces and ideas of the time.

What Cowley was unprepared for was the enormity of human evil that fascism revealed and that Soviet Communism initially masked from the often naïve writers of the 1930's. He was also surprised and hurt by the sometimes savage bitterness engendered among artists by the failed political hopes of the age. After observing the bitter factionalism of intellectuals in the late 1930's and suffering with his friends from vicious attacks by apologists for both fascism and Communism, Cowley became disillusioned by his entire political experience. Poems such as "The End of the World," "Seven," "The Lost People," and "The Dry Season" metaphorically imply that the poet's heart, mind, and spirit are despondent, like stream beds in a drought, and he yearns for some answers in an age when all myths, all beliefs, and all values seem destroyed by humanity's terrible capacity for evil. Like W. H. Auden in his poem "New Year Letter" (1941), Cowley felt the political confusion of the late 1930's as a deep void, the collapse of humanistic hopes and ideals.

The Dry Season also contains a few poems written in the late 1930's that reveal Cowley's renewed love for the American landscape, pointing the way toward solace for his political disillusionment. "This Morning Robins," "Eight Melons," and "The Long Voyage" are pastoral lyrics celebrating spring and the late summer harvest when the abundance of nature provides people with sustenance to last through the "dry winter" of nature and the human heart: "Now the dark waters at the bow/ fold back, like earth against the plow;/ foam brightens like the dogwood now/ at home, in my own country." Cowley returned to the country in the 1940's, the country of American farmers and craftspeople, of small-town friendliness and the world of nature. He spent the remainder of his active literary career there defending the values in which he deeply believed.

When Cowley's collected poems were published in 1968, Kenneth Rexroth wrote in a review of the year's poetry that Cowley was an important American poet, somewhat overlooked because of his more famous peers and the brilliance of his prose.

BLUE JUNIATA

The 1968 collection *Blue Juniata* stands as a summary of Cowley's entire literary career. The book contains most of the poems from his two previous collections, with several changes of titles, some rearrangement of order, and minor revisions of content. Several previously uncollected poems are also included, while new poems from the 1950's and 1960's are collected in two final sections called "The Unsaved World" and "Another Country."

The book's structure is both thematic and historical, and it reveals the remarkable consistency of its author. The new work in the volume again reveals a writer with a strong satiric style and an acute sense of history. Poems such as "Ode in a Time of Crisis" and "The Enemy Within" are witty, ironic commentaries on the political paranoia and undemocratic practices of the McCarthy era in the early 1950's. With allusive irony, Cowley compares McCarthy's political tactics to another great scandal of American history, the Salem witchcraft trials.

Several of Cowley's finest poems of his late years are further meditations on his favorite theme, the relationship between humans and nature. Poems such as "Natural History," a sequence in five parts; "The Living Water," a poem with echoes of the nature poetry of Henry David Thoreau and Ralph Waldo Emerson; and "Here with the Long Grass Rippling," perhaps Cowley's finest long poem (with clear allusions to Walt Whitman's "Song of Myself"), indicate again his almost religious feeling for the American landscape. "Here with the Long Grass Rippling" in particular embodies a recurring theme of the American poetic tradition, a nondoctrinaire, noncreedal, yet mystical faith in the spiritual made manifest in the world of nature.

LEGACY

While modern artists often sought frantically, sometimes tragically, to revive a sense of myth, ritual, and religious emotion in the secular, materialistic culture of modernity, seeking impossible modes of escape from nature by means of art, Cowley's vision of the sacred value of the smallest insect or flower, and the interconnectedness of the natural environment with the culture of the world, reiterated his lifelong literary theme. Literature at its best is a mirror of human history and a moral criticism of contemporary society. The profound meditation of "Here with the Long Grass Rippling" also helps to explain Cowley's great analyses of the illustrious members of his own literary generation and his sensitive response to writers such as Faulkner, Hemingway, and Thomas Wolfe, and their affinities with nineteenth century America. Having himself been shaped by the revolutionary culture of modern art, Cowley journeyed backward to find his own beliefs best expressed by the radically democratic values of America's classic writers.

Cowley's collected poetry and prose thus describe the literary odyssey of modern American writers, many of whom were his closest friends. Those writers created a new aesthetic and a new ethic that were fundamentally shaped by their experience of modern art and politics. They also modified that art by their own "long voyages" back to rediscover their moral heritage in the art of Hawthorne, Whitman, and Thoreau. Cowley's "lost generation" began as Symbolists in technique and temperament, but in the end they remained faithful to the great humanistic tradition of their nineteenth century forebears, who were, after all, as Cowley was one of the earliest to notice, America's first truly modern writers.

OTHER MAJOR WORKS

NONFICTION: *Exile's Return*, 1934 (revised as *Exile's Return: A Literary Odyssey of the 1920's*, 1951); *The Literary Situation*, 1954; *Writers at Work: The "Paris Review" Interviews*, 1958; *Black Cargoes: A History of the Atlantic Slave Trade, 1518-1865*, 1962 (with Daniel Pratt Mannix); *The Faulkner-Cowley File: Letters and Memories, 1944-1962*, 1966; *Think Back on Us: A Contemporary Chronicle of the 1930's*, 1967; *A Many-Windowed House: Collected Essays on American Writers and American Writing*, 1970; *A Second Flowering: Works and Days of the Lost Generation*, 1973; *And I Worked the Writer's Trade*, 1978; *The Dream of the Golden Mountains: Remembering the 1930's*, 1980 (memoir); *The View from Eighty*, 1980 (memoir); *The Flower and the Leaf: A Contemporary Record of American Writing Since 1941*, 1985; *The Selected Correspondence of Kenneth Burke and Malcolm Cowley, 1915-1981*, 1988; *New England Writers and Writing*, 1996 (Donald W. Faulkner, editor).

TRANSLATIONS: *On Board the Morning Star*, 1925 (of Pierre MacOrlan's novel *À Bord de l'Étoile Matutine*); *Joan of Arc*, 1926 (of Joseph Delteil's biography *La Passion de Jeanne d'Arc*); *Variety*, 1927 (of volume 1 of Paul Valéry's essay collection *Variété*); *Catherine-Paris*, 1928 (of Marthe Bibesco's novel); *The Count's Ball*, 1929 (of Raymond Radiguet's novel *Le Bal du comte d'Orgel*); *The Green Parrot*, 1929 (of Bibesco's novel *Le Perroquet vert*); *Imaginary Interviews*, 1944 (of André Gide's essay collection *Interviews imaginaires*); *Leonardo, Poe, Mallarmé*, 1972 (with James R. Lawler; volume 8 of *The Collected Works of Paul Valéry*).

EDITED TEXTS: *After the Genteel Tradition: American Writers Since 1910*, 1936, 1964; *Books That Changed Our Minds*, 1939 (with Bernard Smith); *The Portable Hemingway*, 1944; *The Portable Faulkner*, 1946; *The Complete Poetry and Prose of Walt Whitman*, 1948; *The Portable Hawthorne*, 1948; *Tender Is the Night*, 1951 (by F. Scott Fitzgerald); *The Stories of F. Scott Fitzgerald*, 1951; *Three Novels of F. Scott Fitzgerald*, 1953 (with Edmund Wilson); *Great Tales of the Deep South*, 1955; *Leaves of Grass, the First (1855) Edition*, 1959 (by Walt Whitman); *Fitzgerald and the Jazz Age*, 1966 (with Robert Crowley); *The Lessons of the Masters: An Anthology of the Novel from Cervantes to Hemingway*, 1971 (with Howard E. Hugo).

MISCELLANEOUS: *The Portable Malcolm Cowley*, 1990.

BIBLIOGRAPHY

Aldridge, John W. *In Search of Heresy: American Literature in an Age of Conformity*. New York: McGraw-Hill, 1956. These ten essays derive chiefly from the Christian Gauss lectures delivered by Aldridge at Princeton University in 1954. They lament boldly the tendency toward orthodoxy, and consequently mediocrity, in the literary sphere. One chapter, "The Question of Malcolm Cowley," appraises the role of Cowley in the shaping of the literature. The criticism is perceptive and stimulating.

Bak, Hans. *Malcolm Cowley: The Formative Years*. Athens: University of Georgia Press, 1993. Bak focuses on Cowley's formative years and draws on personal interviews conducted shortly before Cowley's death as well as published and unpublished writings to trace the unfolding of his thinking and influence.

Burke, Kenneth, and Malcolm Cowley. *The Selected Correspondence of Kenneth Burke and Malcolm Cowley, 1915-1981*. Edited by Jay Paul. New York: Viking Press, 1988. This collection is a must for those who want to understand the development of Cowley's thought and critical opinions. Provides a lively narrative and a historical dialogue between two lifelong friends. The editing is masterful. The literary theories and social criticism of both Cowley and Burke are vividly accounted for. The early letters are particularly interesting.

Cowley, Malcolm. "A Conversation with Malcolm Cowley." Interview by Diane U. Eisenberg. *Southern Review* 15 (Spring, 1979): 288-299. This verbatim recording of an interview of Cowley by the compiler of *Malcolm Cowley: A Checklist of His Writings, 1916-1973* presents Cowley's impressions of the craft of writing and his recollections of his literary associates.

_____. *Exile's Return: A Literary Odyssey of the Nineteen Twenties.* New York: Viking Press, 1951. This autobiography presents Cowley's own account of his role in the expatriate movement of the 1920's. Defines and explains the "lost generation" and is an energetic, witty, sometimes touching account of the ideas that dominated the period. Provides engaging portraits of Cowley's fellow writers: John Dos Passos, Ernest Hemingway, T. S. Eliot, F. Scott Fitzgerald, and others.

_____. "Last of the 'Lost Generation.'" Interview by Peter Gambaccini. *Yankee*, March 3, 1983, 92-93, 123-130. Cowley is interviewed at his home in Sherman, Connecticut. The chatty dialogue provides a sketchy biography, especially the growth of Cowley's reputation as a critic, and provides vivid reminiscences of Hart Crane, Robert Frost, William Faulkner, and Ernest Hemingway.

Dolan, Marc. *Modern Lives: A Cultural Re-reading of "The Lost Generation."* West Lafayette, Ind.: Purdue University Press, 1996. A study of the lost generation that locates autobiographical works by Cowley, Ernest Hemingway, and F. Scott Fitzgerald in the context of their contemporaries and within an understanding of modernism.

Kempf, James Michael. *The Early Career of Malcolm Cowley: A Humanist Among the Moderns.* Baton Rouge: Louisiana State University Press, 1985. This study in six chapters, limited to Cowley's formative years at Harvard, in Greenwich Village, and in Paris, is an effort to correct earlier misrepresentations of the critic's influence and opinions. Provides a substantial basis for an evaluation of Cowley's whole career. The best chapters detail Cowley's postwar years in France.

Simpson, Lewis P. "Malcolm Cowley and the American Writer." *Sewanee Review* 84 (Spring, 1976): 220-247. Reprinted in Simpson, *The Brazen Face of History.* Baton Rouge: Louisiana State University Press, 1980. One of the very best essays on Cowley, this article is a very readable substantial examination of Cowley's writings, particularly *Exile's Return* and *A Second Flowering.* Provides a perceptive

and searching commentary on the "poetics of exile" and on the "pragmatics of the writer's life," noting that Cowley's most graphic images are those of loneliness and showing how the basic motif of alienation runs through all his work.

Travis, Trysh. "The Man of Letters and the Literary Business: Re-viewing Malcolm Cowley." *Journal of Modern Literature* 25, no. 2 (Winter, 2001/2002): 1. Discusses the life and works of Cowley, paying particular attention to his later years and his relationship with Viking.

James M. Kempf

LOUIS COXE

Born: Manchester, New Hampshire; April 15, 1918
Died: Augusta, Maine; May 25, 1993

PRINCIPAL POETRY

The Sea Faring, and Other Poems, 1947
The Second Man, and Other Poems, 1955
The Wilderness, and Other Poems, 1958
The Middle Passage, 1960
The Last Hero, and Other Poems, 1965
Nikal Seyn and Decoration Day: A Poem and a Play, 1966
Passage: Selected Poems, 1943-1978, 1979
The North Well: New Poems, 1985

OTHER LITERARY FORMS

Louis Coxe, a career academic, published extensively in academic journals on a wide variety of literary subjects as well as on his own philosophy of poetry; a number of these essays were gathered in *Enabling Acts: Selected Essays in Criticism* (1976). As a student at Princeton University in the late 1930's, Coxe first read the poetry of Edwin Arlington Robinson and was impressed enough to make him the topic of his senior thesis. His interpretive biography of Robinson, published in 1962, remains one of the most astute (and eloquent) analyses of Robinson's achievement. Coxe's widest recognition came from his coauthorship (along with Robert

Chapman) of *Billy Budd*, a 1951 Broadway production of Herman Melville's *Billy Budd, Foretopman* (1924). The adaptation was widely hailed for its lyrical grace and its vivid theatricality (it was later made into a successful film). Coxe wrote other lesser plays, most of them about historic events, for regional repertory companies.

ACHIEVEMENTS

In an era in which poets used verse to interrogate their own emotional lives or to conduct elaborate theoretical investigations and experiments into language and form, Louis Coxe produced a substantial body of poetry that harked back to an earlier era. His poetry employed the rigors of traditional rhythm and rhyme to explore the implications of moral dilemmas by positioning the poet or a vividly drawn historical character in a situation in which the narrator must confront questions of good and evil in a frighteningly empty cosmic universe. Whether writing about his experiences in the U.S. Navy during World War II or the New England countryside that he loved, Coxe found little comfort in nature and grew to despair of humanity's best attempts at nobility. For decades, Coxe was largely in the minority—he published in small if prestigious journals, periodically gathering his poems in slender volumes. Not surprisingly, Coxe's conservative poetry was routinely dismissed as old-fashioned and overly wrought; however, in 1977, when Coxe was named a fellow by the Academy of American Poets, a younger generation of readers came to appreciate his density of theme and subtlety of craft. His subsequent volume of selected poems, *Passage*, reached his widest audience.

BIOGRAPHY

Given Louis Osborne Coxe's disdain for poets who demanded that their verse reveal biography, it is not surprising that he was reticent, even after he had achieved a measure of critical recognition, to indulge in personal revelation—therefore biographical details are sketchy. Coxe was born in Manchester, a bustling urban center in southern New Hampshire. A bright student with a love of classic poetry, specifically that of Geoffrey Chaucer and John Donne, Coxe attended a private Episcopalian all-boys preparatory school, St. Paul's, in nearby Concord. He attended Princeton University, graduating in 1940 with a degree in English. He was particularly drawn to the deep pessimism and unsettling anxieties in the poetry of both Robinson and Robert Frost. He was also impressed by their mastery of conventional forms, their precise and deft handling of prosody, and the apparent simplicity of their verses in an era of burgeoning experimental poetry that worked to reject such conventions. After his graduation, he taught briefly at two preparatory schools, the Lawrenceville (New Jersey) School and the Brooks School in North Andover, Massachusetts.

From 1942 to 1947, Coxe served in the U.S. Navy, seeing action in the South Pacific theater, and all the while writing verse about what he witnessed, appalled by the amorality and the violence of war. He published those verses after his discharge and subsequently accepted a teaching appointment at Harvard (1948-1949). There he and Chapman, who had also served in the Navy, began to work on a verse drama based on Melville's allegory of good and evil set in the open ocean, *Billy Budd, Foretopman*. Initially titled *Uniform of Flesh: A Play in Three Acts* (pb. 1947), the draft went through significant revisions, losing its verse form but maintaining its lyrical feel and its unsettling symbolic ambience. It was premiered Off-Broadway as *Billy Budd* to lavish critical praise in 1951 and moved to Broadway in 1952, finding an unexpectedly large audience who saw in the play's shadowy moral dilemma a profound echo of the unsettling ambiguities of the early days of the nuclear age and the Cold War.

In 1949, Coxe had begun teaching at the University of Minnesota, where he continued to write and publish his verse. In 1956, he accepted an endowed chair in American literature at Bowdoin College in Maine, in part to return to the New England landscape that had inspired him as a child. He stayed at Bowdoin, save for a year he spent as a Fulbright lecturer teaching in Dublin (1959) and another in southern France (1971), until his retirement in 1983. Over the years, he published steadily, both poetry and critical essays. In his last years, Coxe struggled against the onset of Alzheimer's disease; his last collection, an elegiac and wistful collection of poems called *The North Well*, was published in 1985. He died eight years later of cardiac arrest at the age of seventy-five in a veterans' hospital in Augusta, Maine.

ANALYSIS

With a sensibility distinctly out of step with his postwar contemporaries, one that draws more directly from the defining lights of Louis Coxe's college years a generation earlier—most notably, Robinson and Frost—Coxe regarded poetry as an opportunity to confront a chaotic universe in which any creator-God was irrelevant and to demand from that universe some evidence of functioning absolutes. Coxe interrogated the hard realities of greed, power, lust, and, supremely, violence. The best of Coxe's characters—whether carefully realized personages drawn from history or the poet himself speaking in voiceover—come to understand that given the reality of the savage universe, heroism comes from maintaining a private morality and asserting that actions matter and that chaos cannot be the last word. Coxe's careful attention to form, consistent metrics, and patterned sounds reflects that conservative search to affirm order. His poems disdain poetic ornamentation and lyrical excess, idiosyncratic prosody, and loose structuring; instead they are always direct and tightly designed.

THE SEA FARING, AND OTHER POEMS

For Coxe, American postwar poetry was either precious and effeminate or chest-thumping xenophobic patriotic gushing. Poetry summoned into existence by a world war conceived and executed on such a global scale demanded a cosmic sensibility, a gravitas, an aggressively masculine response, and a keen and defiant intellectual questioning. Coxe drew on his years of service in the South Pacific assigned to a patrol boat, a small, lightweight battle cruiser designed to challenge destroyers through its quick maneuverability. Such a deployment placed Coxe squarely in the midst of conflict—his poems record not merely the mundane life on board but also those horrific moments of maximum engagement when inevitably questions arise concerning how mayhem becomes a necessary element of any sailor's spiritual development.

Unlike Coxe's later signature verse, the long narrative, the poems in this collection are lyrical and meditative. In the volume's defining achievement, the lengthy title poem, Coxe re-creates life on board ship through vignettes that record the anxieties, the discipline, the backbreaking routine, and the sense of impending doom.

The poem closes with the poet consigning himself to existence on a perilous and uncertain ocean, Coxe's metaphor for the existential universe that tests the fortitude of those who must, like sailors in battle, stand ultimately alone, willing to engage those formidable terrors. His poems struggle to affirm hope in the form of letters from home, conversations in the mess hall, the abiding awe over the ocean itself, and dreams of returning home. Each assertion, however, is fragile. Other poems, most prominently his sonnets to Nathaniel Hawthorne and Melville, reflect his sobering sensibility of a death-haunted universe that savages those few with the intellectual courage to confront its meaninglessness.

THE MIDDLE PASSAGE

Coxe's most accomplished and ambitious historical narrative set in blank verse, *The Middle Passage*, recounts the voyage of a Massachusetts whaler, *Happy Delivery*, in the late 1840's. Unbeknown to its crew or even its captain, the whaler has been hired as a slave ship—it is bound for the African coast, where it will pick up more than five hundred captured African men, women, and children and transport them to Cuba to work on plantations. Despite being longer than two thousand lines, the poem maintains its integrity by tracing a single powerful action: the moral corruption of the ship's nineteen-year-old physician, Canot. In ways that recall the seafaring moral dramas of both Melville and Joseph Conrad, Coxe uses a narrative frame, a retired slaver who sailed on the *Happy Delivery*, speaking some forty years later after he happens to cross paths with the dying Canot at a dockside bar in Baltimore. Canot wants to get home to Salem to die, and the narrator, still a captain, offers him passage. Days later, after Canot has been buried, he is telling Canot's story to nameless shadows in a tavern.

A happy-go-lucky sort, new to the sea, Canot is surprisingly agreeable when he is told of the ship's true mission—he is intrigued by the possibility of larger profits. As the ship nears Africa and the captain becomes less available (he is a heavy drinker), Canot assumes command. He relishes the authority. At Sierra Leone, Canot meets the amiable French slave trader DaSouza, who offers Canot, as a perk of his new command, a slave girl for his mistress. Canot accepts, seduced by his lust (he realizes the following morning that the lecherous DaSouza had watched the two of them from a window). The voyage to Cuba, the infamous Middle Passage, was to be a brisk fourteen days. The slaves are manacled side by side below deck in conditions that rapidly deteriorate. With the captain still incapacitated, Canot relishes the thrill of command, feeling that the gods of chance are on his side and that this voyage will make him wealthy.

The ship is battered for ten long days by a catastrophic storm, and more than half of the slaves drown. Desperate and seeing his profits dwindling, Canot spirals out of control. Coxe uses a fast-spreading virus (pinkeye) that renders many of the crew temporarily blind as a metaphor for Canot's loss of moral vision. Canot first strangles the captain (the captain had come out of his drunken bender and had threatened to have Canot hanged for mutiny). Then, in perhaps his most ghastly act, Canot allows his mistress to starve to death out of fear that she knows enough English to testify about the ship's conditions. When he is faced with a crew unwilling to follow his commands, Canot coolly shoots the boatswain at point-blank range. Only ninety Africans survive the voyage, but Canot, his moral fall complete, simply anticipates his next slave run.

It is the frame that allows Coxe to raise questions about the consequences of Canot's actions: Forty years later, despite his grievous actions, despite his lack of repentance, will Canot be buried in consecrated ground? It is the narrator who arranges with the church to have Canot given a Christian burial. This is Coxe's way of exposing the hypocrisy of the culture that both condemned slavery and richly profited from it.

Some critics found the cadenced rhythms of the blank-verse form distracting and mechanical, but the narrative of a young man lost within an engulfing evil and surrendering to lust, violence, and greed registered much like the grand-scale poetry of another era, poems that, like Coxe's, with plain diction, consistent meter, stately grace, and lyrical dignity, explored rather than defined the nature of the moral universe.

OTHER MAJOR WORKS

PLAYS: *Uniform of Flesh: A Play in Three Acts*, pb. 1947; *Billy Budd*, pb. 1951 (with Robert Chapman); *The General*, pr. 1954; *The Witchfinders*, pb. 1955.

NONFICTION: *Edwin Arlington Robinson*, 1962; *Enabling Acts: Selected Essays in Criticism*, 1976.

EDITED TEXT: *Chaucer*, 1963.

BIBLIOGRAPHY

Coxe, Louis. *Edwin Arlington Robinson: The Life of Poetry*. New York: Pegasus, 1969. More than any of Coxe's critical works, this introduction to Robinson, the poet most responsible for shaping Coxe's assumptions about the craft of poetry, reads like a defense of Coxe's own versification. Underscores Robinson's occasions of heroic resistance to a universe that appears chaotic.

Howe, Marvin. "Louis O. Coxe, Seventy-five: His Poems Reflected New England Roots." *The New York Times*, May 28, 1993, p. A21. This obituary contains a brief biography and notes that Coxe's poetry was written in the tradition of Robinson.

McGovern, Robert. "Louis Coxe: Misplaced Poet." *Hollins Critic* 17, no. 2 (April, 1980): 1-15. Important reading of Coxe that defines the integrity of his vision and his poetic craft. Focuses on Coxe's longer historical narratives and sees parallels to epics of moral corruption by both Melville and Conrad.

Shain, Charles E., and Samuella Shain, eds. *The Maine Reader*. 1990. Reprint. Boston: David R. Godine, 1997. This anthology of works portraying Maine includes some poetry by Coxe as well as a short biography.

Shaw, Robert B. *Blank Verse: A Guide to Its History and Use*. Athens: Ohio University Press, 2007. Although it does not specifically deal with Coxe, this is an accessible guide to the form Coxe most often employed. Provides helpful context to understanding the achievement of blank verse and investigates modern and contemporary examples.

Steele, Timothy. *Missing Measures: Modern Poetry and the Revolt Against Meter*. Fayetteville: University of Arkansas Press, 1990. Defines the modernists' rebellion against rhythm and rhyme and argues that the revolution was wrongheaded. Outlines vividly the contentious artistic climate in which Coxe's poetry must be read.

Joseph Dewey

HART CRANE

Born: Garrettsville, Ohio; July 21, 1899
Died: Gulf of Mexico; April 27, 1932

PRINCIPAL POETRY

White Buildings, 1926
The Bridge, 1930
The Collected Poems of Hart Crane, 1933 (Waldo
    Frank, editor)

OTHER LITERARY FORMS

Hart Crane's principal literary production was poetry. Other writings include reviews, several essays on
literature, and two essays on poetry: "General Aims
and Theories" and "Modern Poetry." His letters have
been published, including those between Crane and the
critic Yvor Winters and Crane's letters to his family
and friends.

ACHIEVEMENTS

Hart Crane is acknowledged to be a fine lyric poet
whose language is daring, opulent, and sometimes
magnificent. Although complaints about the difficulty
and obscurity of his poetry persist, the poems are not
pure glittering surface. When Harriet Monroe, editor of
Poetry, challenged metaphors of his such as the "calyx
of death's bounty" in "At Melville's Tomb," Crane
demonstrated the sense within the figure. In 1930,
Crane received the Levinson Prize from *Poetry* magazine.

Crane is significant, moreover, in being a particularly modern poet. He wrote that poets had to be able to
deal with the machine as naturally and casually as earlier poets had treated sheep and trees and cathedrals.
His aim was to portray the effects of modern life on
people's sensibilities. In his poetry, Crane caught the
frenzied rhythms and idioms of the jazz age.

Crane's stature also rests on his having created a
sustained long poem, *The Bridge*. Early critics looking
for a classical epic deplored the poem's seeming lack
of narrative structure. Some critics also objected to
Crane's joining the party of Walt Whitman at a time
when Whitman and optimism were in disfavor. Later

critics, however, have seen *The Bridge* as one of the
great poems in modern American literature. They find
in it a more Romantic structure, the structure of the
poet's consciousness or the structure of human consciousness.

BIOGRAPHY

Hart Crane was born Harold Hart Crane to Grace
Hart, a Chicago beauty, and C. A. (Clarence Authur)
Crane, a self-made businessman who became a successful candy manufacturer. An only child, Crane felt
that he was made the battleground of his parents' conflicts. When Crane was fifteen years old, a family trip
to his grandmother's Caribbean plantation, the Isle of
Pines, erupted in quarreling. Crane subsequently made
two suicide attempts.

When he was seventeen, Crane went to New York
to become a poet, not to prepare to enter college as his
father thought. In the next several years, Crane alter-
nated between living in Cleveland and New York,
working at low-paying jobs, primarily in advertising,

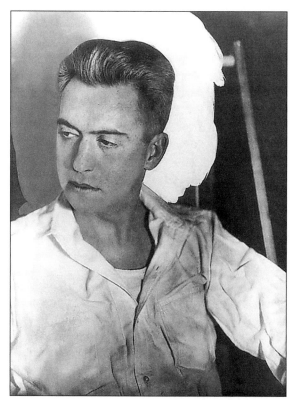

Hart Crane (Library of Congress)

jobs that drained his energy for writing poetry. Crane received little financial support from his father, who wanted Crane to commit himself to a business career. In 1917, siding with his mother in a family argument, Harold Crane began using the name Hart Crane.

In this period, Crane's poems were being published in "little" magazines. To stimulate his creativity, Crane often relied on drink and music, a habit that led him to later problems with alcohol. (His poem "The Wine Menagerie" pays tribute to the connection he found between intoxication and poetic vision.) Crane's homosexuality, which involved him in brawls and run-ins with the police, also provided him the experience of love.

"For the Marriage of Faustus and Helen" was published in 1923, a breakthrough for Crane, who previously had written only short lyrics. Poor and often unemployed, he applied in 1925 for a grant from Otto Kahn, a financier and patron of the arts. Crane received money to help support him while he worked on *The Bridge*, a poem that was to be a synthesis of the American identity. The next summer, Crane wrote a major part of his masterwork at his grandmother's plantation on the Isle of Pines, Cuba. In 1926, a collection of his poetry, *White Buildings*, was published.

Crane's stormy family life continued. In 1928, in California, after helping to nurse his sick grandmother, Crane had a final quarrel with his mother, Grace, and they never saw each other again. Shortly thereafter, Crane received a legacy from his grandmother Hart's estate, and he traveled to London and Paris. There he met Harry and Caresse Crosby, who offered to publish *The Bridge* in a special edition. In 1930 in Paris and then in New York, *The Bridge* was published.

That winter, Crane was reconciled with his father. A few months later in 1931, Crane received a fellowship from the Guggenheim Foundation. He spent a year in Mexico preparing to write a poetic drama on the conquest of Mexico. The year was marked by drinking sprees and trouble with the police for brawling and homosexuality. After traveling back briefly to Ohio for his father's funeral, Crane returned to Mexico.

At the end of his stay in Mexico, Crane had a close relationship with Peggy Cowley, who was being divorced from Malcolm Cowley. The two had plans to be married, but Crane had fits of despondency, fears about

his difficulty with writing, and anxieties about the quality of his latest poem, "The Broken Tower." After a suicide attempt that Crane feared would attract police attention, he and Peggy Cowley set sail for New York on the *Orizaba*. A stop at Havana during which Crane and Cowley lost track of each other was followed by a night on board ship during which Crane went on a violent drinking spree and was robbed and beaten. The next day at noon, Crane jumped overboard from the deck of the *Orizaba* and was never found.

ANALYSIS

Hart Crane's characteristic mode of poetry is visionary transformation. His language is that of transformation aimed at a reality beyond the surface of consciousness. Crane called the technique that subtly converts one image into another the "logic of metaphor." Like that of the French Symbolist poets—Charles Baudelaire, Arthur Rimbaud, Jules Laforgue, and Paul Verlaine—Crane's language is often vivid and obscure, a "jeweled" style that juxtaposes apparently alien entities. It is a poetry of indirection, not naming but suggesting objects or using them for an evocation of mood, for their magic suggestiveness. Sometimes choosing words for their music or texture, Crane employs the technique of synaesthesia, the correspondence between different sense modalities. Symbolists such as Crane, intuiting a correspondence between the material world and spiritual realities, aim to elicit a response beyond the level of ordinary consciousness.

Influenced by T. S. Eliot (but wanting to counteract the pessimism of the early Eliot), Crane used ironic mythological, religious, and literary echoes interspersed with snatches of banal conversation and lines from popular songs and slang. His method of achieving various perspectives almost simultaneously by the juxtaposition of such unlikely elements has been called cubist. The tension between his cubist and Symbolist methods and his Whitmanian sentiments accounts for the unique quality of Crane's style.

Crane's poetry uses visionary transformations in an attempt to encompass the modern experience. In *The Bridge*, historical figures such as Christopher Columbus, legendary characters such as Rip Van Winkle, and mythic figures such as Maquokeeta (the consort of Pocahontas) are made part of the poet's consciousness, associated with personal memories of his childhood and with scenes of modern urban soullessness. The modern scene is transmuted by the elements, which provide a standard of value and a range of alternatives. In "For the Marriage of Faustus and Helen," the classic figure of Helen of Troy is brought together with the Renaissance figure of Dr. Faustus, and the two figures with their complex contexts bring a new perspective to the streetcar, the nightclub, and the aerial battle they visit in Crane's poem. Crane learned from the Symbolists that an image can become symbolic within a private context, calling up a dense network of meanings, emotions, and associations. Such images, unlike traditional symbols, draw on the cumulative force of the poet's personal associations—his personal "language"—rather than on the common cultural heritage. Crane's poetry fuses such personal symbols with traditional symbols from the sweep of Western culture.

"FOR THE MARRIAGE OF FAUSTUS AND HELEN"

"For the Marriage of Faustus and Helen," a poem of almost 140 lines, is Crane's first long poem. It is a marriage song for Faustus, the poet in search of spiritual fulfillment, and Helen, a figure of ideal beauty. The poem begins, however, in the tawdry modern world with the mind fettered by artificial distinctions and smothered with the trivial: stock quotations, baseball scores, and office memos. "Smutty wings" in the first stanza becomes "sparrow wings" in the second as evening brings freedom from the strictures of the office.

The poet enters his experience by getting lost, forgetting his streetcar fare and forgetting to get a transfer. Between green and pink advertisements, he sees Helen's eyes across the aisle from him, half laughing. The poet wants to touch her hands as a sign of love. Helen offers him words, inspiring his poetry. The poet's promise of love makes Helen ecstatic, and like a Romantic poet, the modern poet dedicates his vision to her praise.

The setting of the next section is a rooftop nightclub with dancers cavorting to jazz played by black musicians. The scene of wild revelry is Dionysian. The abandon of the dancers is contrasted with the passivity of relatives, sitting home in rocking chairs. The poet invites the reader to experience a fortunate fall "downstairs" into sensual abandon. ("National Winter Garden" in *The Bridge* presents a much more somber and sordid version of the Fall.) Here the scene is a fallen world where people titter at death. The flapper who is the incarnation of Helen in the fallen realm should not be frowned on, however; even though it is "guilty song," sensual love, that she inspires, she is young and still retains some of the innocence of the ideal Helen.

The scene changes again in the third section, with the poet addressing a fighter pilot as an emissary of death (a problem that Crane would explore again in *The Bridge*). Crane treats war and the desecration of the heavens as the ultimate problem for the poet who would love the world and see beauty in it. It is not only eternity and abstract beauty that the poet praises but also the years, and beauty in and out of time, to which the bleeding hands of the poet pray. More advanced than business or religion, the imagination of the poet reaches beyond despair.

THE BRIDGE

The Bridge, a poem of more than twelve hundred lines, is Crane's masterwork, comparable to T. S. Eliot's *The Waste Land* (1922) and William Carlos Williams's *Paterson* (1946-1958). Although it is not a classical epic because it is not a narrative, the poem's seriousness and magnitude are reflected in its theme: The poet tries to find in himself and in the United States the possibility of the redemption of love and vision. Crane wanted the poem to be not an expression of narrow nationalism but a synthesis of the spiritual reality of the United States.

The central symbol of the poem is the Brooklyn Bridge, a product of contemporary technology that seemed in its beauty to embody humanity's aspirations for transcendence. In the poem, the bridge is seen as a musical instrument, a harp; as the whitest flower, the anemone; as a ship, a woman, a world. In a letter to Otto Kahn, his patron, Crane said that the bridge symbolizes "consciousness spanning time and space." It is a figure of power in repose, a quality that Crane ascribes in the poem to God. The bridge also symbolizes all that joins and unifies, as the bridge unites the material and the spiritual in its existence.

"TO BROOKLYN BRIDGE"

"To Brooklyn Bridge," the proem, is an invocation to the bridge, in which the central opposition of the poem is sketched out—the life-giving spirituality of the bridge versus the deadening influence of the materialistic, commercial city. The freedom of the soaring seagull in the sky is contrasted with the destructive compulsion of the "bedlamite" who jumps from the bridge, amid the jeering onlookers. The poet asks the bridge to "lend a myth to God," to be the means of belief and transcendence in the city that seems to have no ideals and nothing in which to believe.

"AVE MARIA"

In the next section, "Ave Maria," Crane goes back to the beginnings of America and to an age of faith, to Columbus after his discovery. Journeying back to Spain, Columbus meditates that he will tell the queen and her court that he is bringing back "Cathay." He will announce his discovery of a new reality, something that the poet accomplishes in his journey into history and myth. (In this section the sea acts as a bridge between the two continents.) Columbus's dedication has its counterweight, however, in Fernando, Isabella's husband, who anticipates a "delirium of jewels." Even in the discovery of America, the motive for its exploitation was present.

"POWHATAN'S DAUGHTER"

The next section of the poem, "Powhatan's Daughter," includes five sections. The first part, "The Harbor Dawn," is set in the present, with the sounds of fog horns, trucks passing, and stevedores yelling—back by the Brooklyn Bridge but enshrouded in fog. The blurring of sights and sounds by fog and water is in preparation for a blurring of time and space for a visionary journey with the poet. In the sanctuary of his room by the bridge or in his dream, the poet has an experience of love, in which his beloved is portrayed in mythic terms. Her eyes drink the dawn, and there is a forest in her hair. The mythic past lives in the present or at least in the love of the poet.

"VAN WINKLE"

The next section, "Van Winkle," shifts abruptly with the mention of macadam roads that leap across the country and seem to take the poet back to his childhood as well as to figures in American history that he learned about in school: Francisco Pizarro, Hernán Cortés, Priscilla Alden, Captain John Smith, and Rip Van Winkle. Van Winkle, who was legendary rather than historical, was a man out of time, displaced, because he refused to grow up. Here Van Winkle forgets the office hours and the pay and so ends up sweeping a tenement. He can get only menial work in a commercial society that demands a dedication to materialistic values. Van Winkle has a different, uncommercial vision. He looks at Broadway and sees a springtime daisy chain. Instead of the lifeless city, he sees a beautiful natural world.

Lines about Van Winkle are interspersed with memories of the poet's own childhood. The memories pick up equivalents for recurring symbols of the poem—the eagle for space and the snake for time. The poet remembers stoning garter snakes that "flashed back" at him. Instead of eagles, his space figures were paper airplanes, launched into the air.

Mythic journeys often involve the search for the father or the mother as a part of the search for identity. Crane introduces a possible need for that search in recounting two memories of disjunction from his parents: a glimpse of his father whipping him with a lilac switch and a more subtle denial by his mother, who once "almost" brought him a smile from church and then withheld it. Together with the smile, the mother seems to be withholding her approval and love. The final image of the section is of Van Winkle, ready for a streetcar ride, warned that it is getting late. It is time for the journey to continue.

"THE RIVER"

"The River" begins with a jumble of sounds, fragments of conversations—perhaps on the streetcar— mention of commercial products such as Tintex and Japalac, and slogans from advertising, with fragments slapped against one another, making no sense. A misplaced faith links "SCIENCE—COMMERCE and the HOLY GHOST." Unlike the sermons in stones that William Shakespeare's world could find, the slogans and jingles are meaningless.

From the streetcar, the scene switches to a magnificent train, the Twentieth Century Limited, roaring cross-country. The poem focuses on the hoboes who ride the rails and who, like Van Winkle, refuse to grow up. The men who did grow up, however, killed the last bear in the Dakotas and strung telegraph wires across the mountain streams. Those who want progress and a world of "whistles, wire, and steam" have a different time-sense from that of the wanderers. Although people like the poet's father would call the hoboes useless clods, the wanderers sense some truth and know the body of the land as alive and beautiful. In that knowledge, they are like the poet who knows the land "bare"—intimately—and loves it. The eagle of space and the serpent of time appear, adorning the body of the beloved land, but the old gods need to be propitiated because the iron of modern civilization (and especially of the railroad) has split and broken the land and the mythic faith.

The train seems now to follow the river or to become the river. Everyone becomes part of the river, which is timeless because eternal; lost in the river, each one becomes his father's father. The poet and the poem are not only traveling across the country but are journeying back into time as well. Affirming again the possibility of love, the river whose one will is to flow is united with the gulf in passion.

"THE DANCE"

In "The Dance," the poet returns to the time of Native American greatness, the time of Pocahontas. The poet imagines himself a Native American, initiated into the worldview of the brave, at home in nature, speeding over streams in his canoe. He salutes Maquokeeta, the medicine man and priest. He commands Maquokeeta to dance humankind back to the tribal morning, to a time of harmony between humankind and nature when he had power even over rainbows, sky bridges. Maquokeeta is named the snake that lives before and beyond, the serpent Time itself. The time that he creates in his dance is the time of mythic wholeness. Pocahontas, the earth, is his eternal bride, and in the dance he possesses her; time and space are made one. The poet has become one with Maquokeeta by calling him up and participating imaginatively in the dance.

"INDIANA"

The next section, "Indiana," a transitional one, is a letdown of poetic energy and drama. The verse is more prosaic and the rhymes seem strained. The explicit function of the piece is to have the national spirit passed from the Native American to the white settlers in a con-

tinuation of American history. It also chronicles the parting of a mother from a son, who is now to be independent (an important struggle in Crane's own life). The mother's pleas and clinging continue to the end of the section and almost beyond, binding the son by his pledge. Unwilling to let go, she begs for remembrance, naming the young man "stranger," "son," and finally "my friend." The relationship of friend, however, seems more request than fact, and nothing is related from the son's point of view.

"CUTTY SARK"

Once the poet has succeeded in getting away, in the "Cutty Sark" section, his verse returns to the energy and style of "The River" and earlier sections. The narrator is again the poet, introducing a tall, eerie sailor he has met in a South Street bar. Like the hoboes and perhaps like the poet, the sailor is an outcast. (In various ways he resembles Herman Melville's Captain Ahab and Samuel Taylor Coleridge's Ancient Mariner.) Like the hoboes in "The River," this sailor has a different sense of time from that of the commercial city. Instead of being tuned to the cycles of nature, the sailor's time-sense has been disturbed by the expanse of Arctic white, eternity itself. The sailor, who says he cannot live on land any more, is almost run down by a truck as he tries to cross the street, a sign of the break between the inarticulate, prophetic sailor and the cynical city.

The poet starts walking across the Brooklyn Bridge to get home, and his thoughts are still filled with memories of the clipper ships, related to the bridge in shape by being called parabolas. Just as Fernando's greed was part of Columbus's discovery of America, part of the motive for the sailing ships was "sweet opium" and the tea the imperial British sought. The poet's experience and the American experience are still a mixture of the ideal and the sordid.

"CAPE HATTERAS"

"Cape Hatteras" is a substantial section of almost 250 lines. It begins with a primitive setting, with a dinosaur sinking into the ground and coastal mountains rising out of the land. In contrast to the impersonal geological processes, the poet, who has been wandering through time and space, tells the reader that he has returned home to eat an apple and to read Walt Whitman. From Marseille and Bombay, he is going home to the

United States, to the body of Pocahontas and the sweetness of the land under the "derricks, chimneys," and "tunnels." He is returning to try to get a perspective on the exotic experiences he has had.

Next, the poet contemplates the infinity of space that is not subjugated by time and the actions of humanity, even though modern humanity can know space by "an engine in a cloud." The poet invokes Whitman and asks if infinity was the same when Whitman walked on the beach in communion with the sea. The poet's answer is that Whitman's vision lives even in the stock-market society of the present and in the free paths into the future. Opposed to Whitman's vision, however, is the fallen world of the machine, a demoniac world of unleashed power. The din and the violence of slapping belts and frogs's eyes that suddenly appear, vulnerable in the midst of such uncontrolled machinery, make the world a nightmare, an apocalyptic vision. The dance of the machines is a devilish parody of the heavenly, creative dance of the poet as the Native American priest, and America as Pocahontas.

The poet presents the scene of Wilbur and Orville Wright at Kitty Hawk with their silver biplane, praising their daring but deploring the use of the invention for war. A demoniac image that is parallel to the later image of the bridge as an anemone is the grenade as a flower with "screaming petals." Such terrible power is rationalized with theories as destructive as hail to the fertile earth. Imaginative vision cannot control the machines that have splintered space, even as the iron railroad split the land. The poet reminds the pilot that at the great speed of the airplane, the pilot has no time to consider what doom he is causing: He is intoxicated with space. The pilot's real mission is to join the edges of infinity, to bring them together in a loving union, to conjugate them. The poet follows his warning with a scene of the fighter pilot's destruction. Hit by a shell, the plane spirals down in a dance of death, and all that bravery becomes "mashed and shapeless debris."

If the fighter pilot represents a false relationship with space and infinity, Whitman is a figure with the right relationship, one whose vision of the earth and its renewal makes possible a new brotherhood. Whitman makes himself a living bridge between the sky and humanity through song. Whitman is also chief mourner of the men lost in wars, from the Civil War to Crane's time.

The next part of "Cape Hatteras" reads like a Romantic poet's declaration of his awakening to the beauty and inspiration of nature in its rhapsodic description of flowers and of heights that the poet has climbed. The declaration is followed by an apostrophe to Whitman as the awakener of the poet. Whitman is named his poetic master, the bread of angels in a eucharistic sense, and the one who began work on the bridge, the myth or imaginative construction that the poet is here creating. In Whitman, the poet seems to have claimed his poetic father: He says that Whitman's vision has passed into his hands.

"THREE SONGS"

In the next section, "Three Songs," the poet tries to work through his relationship with the feminine. In the first song, "Southern Cross," he says that he yearns for a relationship that would be heavenly, ideal, and also real. (He pictures night and the constellation of the Southern Cross.) What he has found, however, is not woman, nameless and ideal, but Eve and Magdalene, fallen women, and a Venus who is subhuman and ape-like. All the women lead to one grave, to death. The poet seems to feel disgust at the physical being of woman. He next pictures woman as a ship. Like the Ancient Mariner in Coleridge's poem, he is revolted by the generative (physical-sexual) nature of the sea. In Crane's poem, however, it is the feminine ship that is pictured as promiscuous, defiled by the masculine sea. The feminine also has qualities of a sea monster that can sting man. The Southern Cross, the poet's idealization of the feminine, drops below the horizon at dawn, and what is left is woman's innumerable spawn, evidence of her indiscriminate sexuality.

The next song, "National Winter Garden," may seem to be a continuation of the poet's disgust with women, but it is different in being given an actual, rather than an archetypal, setting. The scene is a striptease in a burlesque show. The stripper's dance is a vulgar parody of sexuality and another parody of the creative, ecstatic dance of the Indian priest-poet and Pocahontas. The burlesque queen awakens sexual appetite, but she is only pretending to have youth and beauty. Her pearls and snake ring are also fake, and the poet, who is waiting for someone else, runs away from the final "spasm." Here, however, the poet can make a reconciliation with Magdalene, with feminine sexuality, admitting its finality. Both men and women are physical and sexual; their natures are inescapable. If a woman is an agent of death, she is also an agent of birth. If each man dies alone in sexual union with her, he is also somehow born back into life, into his own sexual nature.

A third song for woman is "Virginia." The woman, Mary, is young, childlike, and possibly innocent. The poet seems to be using echoes of a popular song. Mary is working on Saturday at an office tower. She is described in chivalric terms; the poet is serenading her, and she is at least temporarily inaccessible. Flowers are blooming and bells are ringing, even if they are "popcorn bells." Like Rapunzel in the fairy tale, Mary is asked to let down her golden hair. All seems light and graceful (even though in the fairy tale the prince pays for his courtship with Rapunzel with a period of wandering in the forest, blinded). At the end of the song, the poet calls the girl "Cathedral Mary," sanctifying her, perhaps ironically.

"QUAKER HILL"

In "Quaker Hill," the tone changes from the light, playful tone of the previous song. The section begins with a diatribe against weekenders descending on the countryside. Self-absorbed, they are out of tune with nature. They also have a distorted relation with time, being eager to buy as an expensive antique a cheap old deal table whose finish is being eaten by woodlice. The poet says that time will make strange neighbors.

Meditating on time as a destroyer, the poet asks where his kinsmen, his spiritual fathers are. To find his heritage, he has to look past the "scalped Yankees" to the mythic world of the Native Americans and accept his "sundered parentage." The poet says that men must come down from the hawk's viewpoint to that of the worm and take on their tongues not the Eucharist but the dust of mortality.

This humiliation is associated with the artist's abject position in modern society. Emily Dickinson and Isadora Duncan are introduced as examples of artists scorned in their day, and the only consolation the poet offers is that pain teaches patience. He asserts that patience will keep the artist from despair, implying that

time will vindicate him. The section closes with a motif that is parallel to the fall of the fighter pilot to shapeless debris. Like the plane spiraling down, a leaf breaks off from a tree and descends in a whirling motion, but the leaf is part of a natural cycle, and the poet has put his faith in time and nature.

"THE TUNNEL"

The scene shifts back to the city in the next section, "The Tunnel." The natural world is left behind, and the poet is in the center of the gawdy theater district. References to hell, death, and "tabloid crime-sheets" make the area a wasteland. The subway, the fastest way home, is a descent into hell. The traveler cannot look himself in the eye without being startled and afraid. The sound of the subway is a monotone, but fragments of conversation are lewdly suggestive. The subway riders are the walking dead, living on like hair and fingernails on a corpse, yet "swinging" goes on persistently "somehow anyhow." The sounds of the subway make a phonograph of hell that plays within the poet's brain. This labyrinth of sound even rewinds itself; from this hell there is no exit. Love is a "burnt match." In "For the Marriage of Faustus and Helen," the flapper, the modern embodiment of beauty, was like a skater in the skies. Here the discarded match is skating in the pool of a urinal.

Suddenly the poet sees a disembodied head swinging from a subway strap. The apparition, figure of the artist scorned and destroyed by his society, is Edgar Allan Poe. Poe's eyes are seen below the dandruff and the toothpaste ads. In this banal setting, death reaches out through Poe to the poet. At this point, the subway comes to a dead stop. A sight of escape is momentary, and then the train descends for the final dive under the river.

As the train lurches forward again, the poet sees a "wop washerwoman." In the midst of the inferno, there is a positive figure of a woman. Although she is not a discoverer like Columbus, her work has dignity: She cleans the city at night. A maternal figure, she brings home to her children her eyes and hands, Crane's symbols of vision and love. A victim like Poe and the poet, the cleaning woman is bandaged. Other birth imagery here is demonic: A day being born is immediately slaughtered. The poet's greatest agony is that in this nightmare, he failed to preserve a song.

In his great agony, the poet feels the train start to ascend. Both the poet and the train are, like Lazarus, resurrected. They are returning to the natural world above ground. His vocation renewed, the poet can affirm the everlasting word. Once above ground again, the poet is at the river bank, ready to turn to the bridge.

"ATLANTIS"

With the poet resurrected, "Atlantis"—the final section of the poem—is a song of deliverance. It is an ecstatic paean to the bridge, seen as music, light, love, joy, and inspiration. More dynamic than the music of the spheres, the music of the bridge creates a divinity. It is a myth that kills death: It gives death its utter wound, just by its light, its lack of shadow. By the myth of the bridge, the cities are endowed with ripe fields. They have become natural, organic, and fruitful. The bridge is the city's "glittering pledge" forever. It is the answerer of all questions. In the poet's vision and in the poem, it is unutterably beautiful.

"Atlantis" acts as a synthesis, subsuming earlier motifs such as stars, seagulls, cities, the river, the flower, grass, history and myth, and circles and spirals. The question "Is it Cathay?" links the end of *The Bridge* with Columbus's discovery of America in the beginning, not in a mood of anxiety but in wonder at an America transfigured. The final two lines bring together time and space—the serpent and the eagle—with the music and radiance and energy of the bridge transcendent.

OTHER MAJOR WORKS

NONFICTION: *The Letters of Hart Crane*, 1952 (Brom Weber, editor).

MISCELLANEOUS: *The Complete Poems and Selected Letters and Prose of Hart Crane*, 1966 (Weber, editor); *O My Land, My Friends: The Selected Letters of Hart Crane*, 1997 (Langdon Hammer and BromWeber, editors); *Complete Poems and Selected Letters*, 2006.

BIBLIOGRAPHY

Berthoff, Warner. *Hart Crane: A Re-Introduction*. Minneapolis: University of Minnesota Press, 1989. This is a solid, concise, generally accurate discussion of Crane's life and work that corrects misrepresentations of earlier books.

Bloom, Harold, ed. *Hart Crane: Comprehensive Research and Study Guide*. Philadelphia: Chelsea House, 2003. Contains a biography of Crane and extensive analysis of works including "Voyages," "Repose of Rivers," "To Brooklyn Bridge," "The Tunnel," and "The Broken Tower."

Crane, Hart. *O My Land, My Friends: The Selected Letters of Hart Crane*. Edited by Langdon Hammer and Brom Weber. New York: Four Walls Eight Windows, 1997. This expanded and revised edition *The Letters of Hart Crane* (1952) includes separate introductions to the periods of Crane's life and an analytical index. One-third of the letters are new, and all are uncensored.

Fisher, Clive. *Hart Crane*. New Haven, Conn.: Yale University Press, 2002. A biography of the poet that uses extant documents to exhaustively examine his personal life, including his homosexuality, to link his turbulent existence with his poetic talent. Looks at the suicidal tendencies of the poet's mother and re-creates the scene of his death.

Gabriel, Daniel. *Hart Crane and the Modernist Epic: Canon and Genre Formation in Crane, Pound, Eliot, and Williams*. New York: Palgrave Macmillan, 2007. Examines the importance of Crane in modernism and in creating a new version of the epic.

Hammer, Langdon. *Hart Crane and Allen Tate: Janus-Faced Modernism*. Princeton, N.J.: Princeton University Press, 1993. Called a "brilliant study" by the reviewer for the *Times Literary Supplement*, this book focuses on the friendship between Crane and Tate, analyzing modern American poetry's progress toward professionalism and institutionalization. Includes an index.

Mariani, Paul L. *The Broken Tower: A Life of Hart Crane*. New York: W. W. Norton, 1999. Examines the life of Crane, who held a pivotal role in the development of American literature's avant-garde. Quotations from Crane's letters and poems are included throughout the narrative.

Reed, Brian M. *Hart Crane: After His Lights*. Tuscaloosa: University of Alabama Press, 2006. An examination of the poet that looks at how to interpret his works, as well as the lyric and epic form.

Tapper, Gordon A. *The Machine That Sings: Modernism, Hart Crane, and the Culture of the Body*. New York: Routledge, 2006. An analysis of Crane's work that focuses on his preoccupation with the body. Examines "The Wine Merchant," "Voyages," and "Possessions," as well as three section of *The Bridge*— "National Winter Garden," "The Dance," and "Cape Hatteras."

Kate Begnal

STEPHEN CRANE

Born: Newark, New Jersey; November 1, 1871
Died: Badenweiler, Germany; June 5, 1900

PRINCIPAL POETRY

The Black Riders, and Other Lines, 1895
A Souvenir and a Medley, 1896
War Is Kind, 1899

OTHER LITERARY FORMS

Stephen Crane is best known as a novelist and short-story writer, and deservedly so. His first novel, *Maggie: A Girl of the Streets* (1893) was an early and almost pure example of naturalistic fiction. About the time of his twenty-fourth birthday, *The Red Badge of Courage: An Episode of the American Civil War* (1895) made him famous. Of his other novels— *George's Mother* (1896), *The Third Violet* (1897), *Active Service* (1899), and *The O'Ruddy: A Romance* (1903; with Robert Barr)—only *The Monster* (1899), a novella, may lay claim to greatness. Of the scores of tales, sketches, and journalistic pieces that verge on fiction, the best are "The Reluctant Voyagers" (1893), "The Open Boat," "The Bride Comes to Yellow Sky," "Death and the Child," and "The Blue Hotel" (all in 1898). Of Crane's dramatic efforts, there is *The Ghost* (pr. 1899, with Henry James), performed in a room at Crane's home in England. According to one contemporary review, the play was a mixture of "farce, comedy, opera, and burlesque." His only other play is a slight closet drama called *The Blood of the Martyr* (pb. 1940).

ACHIEVEMENTS

As one of the first impressionistic writers—Joseph Conrad called him "The Impressionist"—Stephen Crane was among the first to express in writing a new way of looking at the world. Impressionism grew out of scientific discoveries that showed how human physiology, particularly that of the eyes, determines the way everything in the universe, everything outside the individual body and mind, is seen. People do not see the world as it is, yet the mind and eye collaborate to interpret what is for Crane, at least, a chaotic universe as fundamentally unified, coherent, and explainable. The delusion is compounded when human beings get together, for then they tend to create even grander fabrications, such as religion and history. Although Crane is also seen as one of the first American naturalistic writers, a Symbolist, an Imagist, and even a nihilist, the achievements that justify these labels all derive from his impressionistic view of the world.

Crane's major achievement, both as a fiction writer and a poet, is that he so unflinchingly fought his way through established assumptions about the way life is. He is the logical end of a long line of American Puritans and transcendentalists who believed in the individual pursuit of truth. The great and perhaps fitting irony of such logic is that Crane repudiated the truths in which his predecessors believed. In his fiction, he uses the old genres, but his impressionistic style denies their validity; in his poetry he attacks tradition directly, in part through what he says and in part by how he says it. Rejecting everything conventional about poetry in his day—rhyme, rhythm, conventional images, "safe" metaphors that never shocked Victorian sensibilities—Crane ends by denying things much more important: nationalism, patriotism, the greatness of individual and collective man, the existence of supernatural powers that care and protect and guide. In his best fiction and occasionally in his poetry, Crane faces squarely the horror of a meaningless universe, although he was unable to build a new and positive vision on the rubble of the old.

BIOGRAPHY

Born in a Methodist parsonage in Newark, New Jersey, Stephen Crane was the fourteenth and last child of a minister whose family had been in America for more than two centuries. On his mother's side, almost every man was a minister; one became a bishop. By the time his father died in 1880, Crane had lived in several places in New York and New Jersey and had been thoroughly indoctrinated in the faith he was soon to reject. Also around that time, he wrote his first poem, "I'd Rather Have—." His first short story, "Uncle Jake and the Bell Handle," was written in 1885, and the same year he enrolled in Pennington Seminary, where he stayed until 1887. Between 1888 and 1891, he intermittently attended Claverack College, the Hudson River Institute, Lafayette College, and Syracuse University. He was never graduated from any of these schools, preferring baseball to study. In 1892, the New York *Tribune* published many of his New York City sketches and more than a dozen Sullivan County tales. Having apparently forgotten Helen Trent, his first love, he fell in love with Lily Brandon Munroe. That year, too, the

mechanics union took exception to his article on their annual fete, which resulted in Crane's brother, Townley, being fired from the *Tribune*.

In 1893, Crane published at his own expense an early version of *Maggie*. William Dean Howells introduced him to Emily Dickinson's poetry, and in the next year he met Hamlin Garland. Also in 1894, the Philadelphia *Press* published an abridged version of *The Red Badge of Courage*.

The year 1895 is notable for three things: During the first half of the year, he traveled in the West, where he met Willa Cather, and in Mexico for the Bachellor Syndicate; *The Black Riders, and Other Lines* was published in May, and *The Red Badge of Courage* appeared in October. By December, he was famous, having just turned twenty-four. In 1896, he published *The Little Regiment, and Other Episodes of the American Civil War* and fell in love with Cora Stewart (Howorth), whom he never married but with whom he lived for the rest of his life.

In January, 1897, on the way to report the insurgency in Cuba, he was shipwrecked off the Florida coast. Four months later, he was in Greece reporting on the Greco-Turkish War. Moving back to England, he became friendly with Joseph Conrad, Henry James, Harold Frederic, H. G. Wells, and others. During that year, he wrote most of his great short stories: "The Open Boat," "The Bride Comes to Yellow Sky," and "The Blue Hotel."

Never very healthy, Crane began to weaken in 1898 as a result of malaria, which he had contracted in Cuba while reporting on the Spanish-American War. By 1899, Crane was back in England and living well above his means. Although he published *War Is Kind, Active Service,* and *The Monster, and Other Stories,* he continued to fall more deeply in debt. By 1900, he was hopelessly debt-ridden and fatally ill. Exhausted from overwork, intestinal tuberculosis, malaria, and a will to experience life almost unmatched in literary history, Crane died, not yet twenty-nine years old. He left behind works that fill ten sizable volumes.

Stephen Crane (Library of Congress)

ANALYSIS

Stephen Crane's poetry, like his life and fiction, consists almost entirely of "enormous repudiations."

Filled with vivid animism, startling metaphors, strident naturalism, and bitter nihilism, the poetry repudiates the God of Crane's father, the natural order seen as benevolent by the Romantics and transcendentalists, the brotherhood of humankind in any areas except sin and blind conformity, the rightness and glory of war, the possibility of justice, the grandeur of love, even humanity's ability to perceive a modicum of truth clearly. Repudiation is fundamental to his poetry. He rejects rhyme, among other things, and in doing so he anticipates Ezra Pound, Carl Sandburg, and Wallace Stevens, whose poetry came to fruition only in the twentieth century. Crane often went further than these poets by eschewing the rhythms that had defined lyric and narrative verse for more than two thousand years.

Crane never referred to his work as "poetry"; he almost invariably referred to his "lines." Once, however, he alluded to the didactic, nearly therapeutic, nature of his poems by calling them "pills." Unlike the fiction, which is often hauntingly and ironically lyrical, the poetry consciously strives for what Crane called a "tongue of wood." This tongue produced a sound that jarred against the ears of his contemporaries, and for the most part, as Crane himself observed, "in truth it was lamentable." Although Crane managed to avoid writing in the rhymed and metered style that filled the poetry libraries of his day, the cost to the quality of his lines was great. For example, few poets with Crane's credentials could write the following without knowing just how lamentable it was: "Now let me crunch you/ With the full weight of affrighted love."

Although he was seldom this guilty of what Pound later called "emotional slither," Crane nevertheless failed, most of the time, to re-create and liberate in his poetry the intensity of his thought and emotion. Love, for example, is sometimes a biological trap and sometimes a vehicle for defying the Protestant ethic that damned those caught in love's sensuality. As a trap, love can even descend to a pathological fetishism, producing some of Crane's most "lamentable" lines: "I weep and gnash/ And I love the little shoe/ The little, little shoe." On the other hand, as a way of throwing down a gauntlet before accepted Protestant belief, it can produce some of Crane's most beautiful lines. "Should the wide world roll away" depicts a love so enthralling and encompassing that the speaker denies any need for the other props that support humankind. The poem flies in the face of convention by adding sex to Huck Finn's decision to "go to Hell" rather than betray Jim: "Neither God nor man nor place to stand/ Would be to me essential/ If thou and thy white arms were there/ And the fall to doom a long way."

GOD AND THE CHURCH

Not always so summarily dismissed, God appears in a score or more of the poems as himself, nature, or some other metaphor. It could even be said that God manifests three different faces: as God the Father, he is malevolent and capricious; as God the Son, he is kindly and pitying; as the Holy Ghost, he is indifferent. "A man said to the universe," Crane's most anthologized poem, depicts a God who responds to humankind's insistent cry for recognition ("Sir, I exist!") by both acknowledging the "fact" and refusing to be bound by any "sense of obligation" as a result of it. God is similarly indifferent in "God fashioned the ship of the world carefully." Only here the indifference is more clearly deistic: Once the world was made, God went bowling.

A kindly God appears in the second stanza of "The livid lightnings flashed in the clouds" as "whispers in the heart" and as "melodies,/ Distant, sighing, like faintest breath." A pitying God appears obliquely as Christ in a Spanish-American War poem called "The Battle Hymn." He is a sacrifice not only of God (the "Father of the Never-Ending Circles") but also to God from the jingoistic war spirit of American patriots during that "splendid little war." In "There was One I met upon the road," where humankind is presented to God as a mass of sin, God's response is to look "With kinder eyes" and say, "poor soul." Conversely, if the poem is read ironically—that is, if God is taken as the creator of sin—then the God of this poem is not pitying but, rather, cruel and malevolent.

Most often, God is malevolent and unyielding, hateful and unworthy of worship. In many poems, man looks at him with "grim hatred," as a capricious dealer of death, a denier of man's suffering, a bully, and a firm upholder of the Darwinian belief in the survival of the fittest. In "To the Maiden" and "The Ocean said to me once," God is nature, but still basically malevolent, instructing the seeker in the latter poem to tell a nearby woman that her lover has been "laid/ In a cool hall" with a "wealth of golden sand." In the next stanza, she is also to be told that her lover's hand will be heaped with corpses "Until he stands like a child/ With surplus of toys."

Since Crane also heaps bitter abuse on the Church, it sometimes remains unclear as to whether the God that Crane depicts as malevolent is Crane's God or whether it is God as seen by the Church. In a number of poems, the Church is viewed as the betrayer of the New Testament God of compassion. Everywhere, "figures robed in black" are revealed as hypocritical and evil: "You say you are holy," "With eye and with gesture," "There was a great cathedral," "Walking in the sky," "Two or three angels," "A row of thick pillars," "If you would seek a friend among men," and a host of others bitterly accuse the Church of irrelevance. As Crane sees it, the Church not only fails to help man live on this planet, this "space-lost bulb," as he calls it in "The Blue Hotel," but also actively makes life more difficult.

THE MYTH OF BROTHERHOOD

Another of humankind's beliefs pilloried by Crane is brotherhood. The "subtle battle brotherhood" that fails to keep Henry Fleming from running away in *The Red Badge of Courage* becomes a banal and damnable conformity in the poetry. "'Think as I think,' said a man" is a short piece in which the speaker chooses instead to "be a toad." Patriotism is a collective "falsity," a "godly vice" that "makes us slaves." The rather good poem "When a people reach the top of a hill" is one long irony against "the blue battalions" of collective action. Responding to a question about mob courage, Crane once wrote in a letter: "The mob? The mob has no courage. That is the chatter of clubs and writers." In his poetry, as elsewhere, Crane shared the nineteenth century's fear of the mob. The only brotherhood that exists in Crane's poetry is a brotherhood of sin, as shown in "I stood upon a high place."

Although the most obviously insane use of the mob occurs in war, and although Crane made his reputation on war fiction, war as a theme does not loom very large in his poetry. "I suppose I ought to be thankful to 'The Red Badge,'" Crane wrote, "But I am much fonder of my little book of poems, 'The Black Riders.'" *The Black Riders, and Other Lines*, Crane thought, was "about life in general," while *The Red Badge of Courage* is a "mere episode in life." Aside from a few poems that allude to the Spanish-American War, war is more generalized, as in the poem beginning "There exists the eternal face of conflict."

INJUSTICE

The theme of injustice ranges among the poems from the yellow journalism of American newspapers in Crane's day to the cosmic injustice of God to humankind. In all cases, Crane is bitterly insistent that justice simply does not exist. One particular injustice, however, overshadows all others: the injustice of wealth. Wealth as wealth is not questioned, but rather what it seems to do to people who have it and to those who do not. Charity, for example, is "a lie." It is given by "bigoted men of a moment" as food that "turns into a yoke." The recipients are expected "to vanish/ Grateful because of full mouths." However, the poem warns the charitable that their turn will come: "—Wait—/ Await your turn." Only once in the ten volumes of his collected works does Crane complain about his poverty, and even then he does so in self-mockery, choosing a Chaucerian "complaint to his purse." The wealthy are "fat asses," "too well-dressed to protest against infamy." Successful people are "complacent, smiling," and "stand heavily on the dead."

The major theme of Crane's poetry, as Milne Holton's *Cylinder of Vision* (1972) has shown about the fiction, is humanity's utter inability to perceive the truth and its amazing willingness to believe that it does indeed see it. For Crane, the world is chaotic, and all humankind's beliefs about God and nations, about religions and history, are almost entirely delusory. He never resolves, for example, the conflict between the malevolent and the pitying God, choosing instead to let it stand in several two-stanza poems in which one stanza describes God the beast and the other the God of compassion. "When a people reach the top of a hill" is read by Daniel Hoffman as praise of the American nation and the triumph of humanity over fate, but it may also be read ironically as an exposure of utter delusion. Everywhere in the poetry, there are "gardens lying at impossible distances." In one poem, "A man saw a ball of gold in the sky," Crane uses his characteristic cosmic point of view to allow the man to climb into the sky only to find the gold ball made of clay. When he returns, the man finds the ball again made of gold: "By the heavens, it was a ball of gold." Misperception can involve delusion, as in "I saw a man pursuing the horizon," and monumental egotism, as in "I looked here," which takes William Shakespeare's "My mistress' eyes are nothing like the sun" another step by saying that her real beauty is irrelevant since he perceives her as beautiful. In another poem, Crane says it more directly. In the thirteen lines of "If you would seek a friend among men," the speaker notes seven times that all one needs to know about people is that they are "crying their wares." As with most of Crane's poetry, this theme can be traced to the Bible: All is vanity.

Ultimately, Crane's poetry is a protest against the conditions of life and against the lies humans tell themselves to make life tolerable. That protest sustained his brief poetic career, although in time, he did become less angry with God for not existing or at least for not paying attention. Crane is modern in the sense that, like most modern poets, he rejected both the theism and the humanism of the nineteenth century, but he lived too early to benefit from the experiments of others who were also soon to reject them.

OTHER MAJOR WORKS

LONG FICTION: *Maggie: A Girl of the Streets*, 1893; *The Red Badge of Courage: An Episode of the American Civil War*, 1895; *George's Mother*, 1896; *The Third Violet*, 1897; *The Monster*, 1898 (serial), 1899 (novella; pb. in *The Monster, and Other Stories*); *Active Service*, 1899; *The O'Ruddy: A Romance*, 1903 (with Robert Barr).

SHORT FICTION: *The Little Regiment, and Other Episodes of the American Civil War*, 1896; *The Open Boat, and Other Tales of Adventure*, 1898; *The Monster, and Other Stories*, 1899; *Whilomville Stories*, 1900; *Wounds in the Rain: War Stories*, 1900; *Last Words*, 1902.

PLAYS: *The Ghost*, pr. 1899 (with Henry James; fragment); *The Blood of the Martyr*, pb. 1940 (wr. 1898?).

NONFICTION: *The Great Battles of the World*, 1901; *The War Dispatches of Stephen Crane*, 1964.

MISCELLANEOUS: *The University of Virginia Edi-tion of the Works of Stephen Crane*, 1969-1975 (10 volumes).

BIBLIOGRAPHY

Benfey, Christopher E. G. *The Double Life of Stephen Crane*. New York: Knopf, 1992. A narrative of Crane's life and literary work that argues that the writer attempted to live the life his works portrayed. Includes bibliography and index.

Berryman, John. *Stephen Crane*. Rev. ed. New York: Cooper Square, 2001. Berryman, himself a major American poet, eloquently explains the patterns of family conflict that appear in Crane's works. Includes notes and index.

Bloom, Harold, ed. *Stephen Crane*. New York: Bloom's Literary Criticism, 2009. A collection of literary criticism on Crane's major works. Also examines his life and chief influences on his writing.

Davis, Linda H. *Badge of Courage: The Life of Stephen Crane*. Boston: Houghton Mifflin, 1998. This biography of Crane depicts him as a perpetual adolescent who was very much an enigma.

Knapp, Bettina L. *Stephen Crane*. New York: Frederick Ungar, 1987. A succinct introduction to Crane's life and career, with a separate chapter on his biography, several chapters on his fiction, and an extensive discussion of two poetry collections, *The Black Riders, and Other Lines*, and *War Is Kind*. Includes a detailed chronology, a bibliography of primary and secondary sources, and an index.

Monteiro, George, ed. *Stephen Crane: The Contemporary Reviews*. New York: Cambridge University Press, 2009. A collection of reviews of Crane's works, including his poetry collections, when they were published.

Sorrentino, Paul. *Student Companion to Stephen Crane*. Westport, Conn.: Greenwood Press, 2006. Volume contains a chapter focusing on Crane's poetry.

_____, ed. *Stephen Crane Remembered*. Tuscaloosa: University of Alabama, 2006. Sorrentino brings together nearly one hundred documents from acquaintances of the novelist and poet for a somewhat more revealing look at Crane than has heretofore been available.

Wertheim, Stanley. *A Stephen Crane Encyclopedia.*

Westport, Conn.: Greenwood Press, 1997. A very thorough volume of Crane information. Includes bibliographical references and an index.

Wertheim, Stanley, and Paul Sorrentino. *The Crane Log: A Documentary Life of Stephen Crane, 1871-1900*. New York: G. K. Hall, 1994. Stanley and Sorrentino, editors of *The Correspondence of Stephen Crane* (1988), have attempted to counter many of the falsehoods that have bedeviled analyses of Crane's life and work by providing a documentary record of the author's life. Opening with biographical notes on persons mentioned in the text and lavishly sourced, *The Crane Log* is divided into seven chapters, beginning with the notation in Crane's father's diary of the birth of his fourteenth child, Stephen, and ending with a newspaper report of Crane's funeral, written by Wallace Stevens.

Chester L. Wolford

ROBERT CREELEY

Born: Arlington, Massachusetts; May 21, 1926
Died: Odessa, Texas; March 30, 2005

PRINCIPAL POETRY

For Love: Poems, 1950-1960, 1962
Words, 1967
Pieces, 1969
A Day Book, 1972 (includes poetry and prose)
Robert Creeley: An Inventory, 1945-1970, 1973
Hello, 1976 (expanded 1978; as *Hello: A Journal, February 29-May 3, 1976*)
Selected Poems, 1976
Later, 1979
The Collected Poems of Robert Creeley, 1945-1975, 1982
Mirrors, 1983
Memory Gardens, 1986
Window: Paintings, 1988 (paintings by Martha Visser't Hooft)
Selected Poems, 1991
Life and Death, 1993 (expanded 1998)

Echoes, 1994
So There: Poems, 1976-1983, 1998
For Friends, 2000
Drawn and Quartered, 2001 (with Archie Rand, artist)
Just in Time: Poems, 1984-1994, 2001
If I Were Writing This, 2003
The Collected Poems of Robert Creeley, 1975-2005, 2006
Selected Poems, 1945-2005, 2008 (Benjamin Friedlander, editor)

OTHER LITERARY FORMS

Robert Creeley worked in a number of literary genres, including the short story (a collection, *The Gold Diggers*, was published in 1954 and revised in 1965) and the novel (*The Island*, 1963). *A Day Book* includes both prose and poetry. Creeley's nonfiction includes *A Quick Graph* (1970), *Presences* (1976), *Collected Essays* (1983), and *The Collected Prose* (1984). His ten-volume correspondence with Charles Olson was published in 1980-1996 as *Charles Olson and Robert Creeley: The Complete Correspondence*. His *Day Book of a Virtual Poet* appeared in 1998.

ACHIEVEMENTS

Robert Creeley is one of the most celebrated American postwar poets. Early identified as a member of the Black Mountain, or Projectivist, school, he established his individuality with a series of striking works and transcended early factionalism to find a place in most anthologies of the period for a poetry that has no peer. He brought the modernist vision and achievements of William Carlos Williams and Ezra Pound through the changes that profoundly altered the world after 1945 to give them fresh life in his distinctive wry diction and approach to poetic conventions. *For Love*, his first collection to receive wide distribution, had by 1978 sold more than forty-seven thousand copies; it was nominated for a National Book Award in 1962, the year of its publication.

Creeley won a range of additional awards during his long career: the Levinson Prize in 1960 and a Leviton-Blumenthal Prize in 1964 for groups of poetry published in *Poetry*, a Guggenheim Fellowship in poetry from 1964 to 1965 and in 1971, a Rockefeller Foundation grant in 1966, and a Union League Civic and Arts Poetry Prize in 1967. He won many honors in the 1980's, including the Shelley Memorial Award (1981), a Frost Medal (1987), a National Endowment for the Arts grant, a Leone d'Oro Premio Speziale in Venice, a Fulbright Award, and a Walt Whitman citation of merit. He was named poet laureate of New York State (1989-1991) and won the America Award for Poetry (1995), the Lila Wallace-*Reader's Digest* Writers' Award (1996), the Bollingen Prize and a Chancellor Norton Medal (both 1999), a Lifetime Achievement Award from the Before Columbus Foundation (2000), and the Lannan Lifetime Achievement Award (2001). He became a member of the American Academy of Arts and Letters in 1987 and served as chancellor for the Academy of American Poets from 1999 to 2002.

BIOGRAPHY

Robert White Creeley was born in Arlington, Massachusetts, in 1926 (a year that was to prove an *annus mirabilis* for American poetry, for others born that year include Allen Ginsberg, Frank O'Hara, Paul Blackburn, and Lew Welch). Creeley lost his father, Oscar, a doctor, at the age of four, and thereafter lived with his mother and sister in the nearby town of West Acton. At fourteen, he won a scholarship to the Holderness School in Plymouth, New Hampshire. He entered Harvard University in 1943. When he turned eighteen, being unfit for military service because of a childhood accident that had cost him an eye, he joined the U.S. Ambulance Corps and was sent to Burma. After World War II ended, he returned to Harvard, but he eventually left without taking a degree.

In 1946, Creeley was married to his first wife, Ann McKinnon. About this time, he struck up the close friendship with Cid Corman that was to lead to the launching of Corman's groundbreaking journal *Origin*. This journal published much of Creeley's early work and also the work of Charles Olson, an older poet with whom Creeley corresponded daily for two years. At that time, Olson was rector of Black Mountain College in North Carolina, and Creeley became editor (in absentia) of the *Black Mountain Review*, another key vehicle of what came to be called projective verse (after

Olson's essay of that name), Black Mountain poetry, or, more generally, the new American poetry. Creeley had been living in the south of France and then in Mallorca, Spain, but on the dissolution of his marriage in 1955, he came to teach at Black Mountain College. That same year, he was awarded his bachelor's degree at Black Mountain.

In 1956, however, Black Mountain College dissolved, and Creeley made his way to San Francisco, where he met the Beat writers Jack Kerouac, Allen Ginsberg, Kenneth Rexroth, and Gary Snyder. He then moved to Albuquerque, New Mexico. In 1960, he earned an M.A. from the University of New Mexico, where he was then teaching. During this period, he met Bobbie Louise Hawkins, who became his wife.

During the 1950's, Creeley had published seven volumes of verse, as well as a book of short stories, *The Gold Diggers*. A substantial selection of his poems was included in Donald Allen's 1960 Grove Press anthology, *The New American Poetry, 1945-1960*, a landmark collection that helped make the reputation of

Robert Creeley (©Bruce Jackson/Courtesy, New Directions)

Creeley and of a number of his peers and associates. In 1962, Scribner's issued *For Love*, essentially a collection of the poems that had appeared in the seven earlier books; the following year, his novel *The Island* was published, also by Scribner's.

After teaching at the University of British Columbia in 1962-1963, Creeley returned to New Mexico. In 1966, he took a job teaching at the State University of New York at Buffalo, and in 1978, he was appointed to an endowed chair there, so that he became the Gray Professor of Poetry and Letters. Although he taught for short stints at other universities, Buffalo remained his residence, and he continued his affiliation with the State University of New York until his death in 2005. In 1991, he served as the director of the poetics program at San Francisco State College for one year, and throughout the 1990's and into the twenty-first century, he participated in numerous poetry readings and writers' conferences.

In 1976, his second marriage ended; shortly thereafter, he was married once more, to Penelope Highton. Creeley and Highton would have two children; Creeley also had several children from his previous marriages. Creeley died of complications of lung disease at a hospital in Odessa, Texas, on March 30, 2005.

ANALYSIS

Robert Creeley focused on the difficult turning points of relationships, on the role language has to play in such moments, given that expectations are governed by one's vocabulary and that one thinks as one's language allows. Although his work is far from therapeutic, it has found an audience that to some extent had been readied by the increasing experience of psychotherapy among Americans of the late twentieth century and a growing awareness of the individual as instance of a system. However, this is to view the work's appeal from the base of the pyramid, as it were; its great strength is its vertical appeal, that it has something in it for readers who know little of modern poetry but also yields much when subjected to critical scrutiny. In his writing, Creeley took up where Samuel Beckett left off: Creeley addressed his readers from a world in which the worst has already happened, yet one in which there is still life and the need to act.

Creeley's greatest strength was to write a poetry of immediacy while "saving the appearances" by preserving traditional forms. Although he departed from these formal conventions for a period, he was to return to them. In any case, it was his ability to combine the radical content and approach of his early work with the use of conventional form that won for him fame and a wide readership. Colleagues such as Charles Olson, Robert Duncan, and Edward Dorn did more, arguably, to align their vision with its mode of expression; yet it may be that Creeley, in giving voice to his vision within the more recognizable confines of traditional verse, rendered a clearer picture of the gulf that separated the second half of the twentieth century from the first. He appears to be saying, "This is how the quatrain or the couplet must be used, given our new content." In this way, Creeley became one of the new sensibility's foremost translators into forms apprehensible to those still imbued with the old. No doubt part of his success derived from the fact that both sensibilities existed—and sometimes battled each other—within him; in several passages, he alluded to the nineteenth century expectations with which he was reared.

What was the essence of this other, radically new sensibility? It was an awareness of the atomic bomb, the Nazi death camps, a Europe that had been left "like a broken anthill" (as Ezra Pound said) with twenty million dead, gigantic catastrophe brought about by long-range human design, unimaginable chaos created by careful planning. This was a world in which lamp shades were made out of human skin, in which human beings were persuaded to surrender in the service of abstract causes. Readers today have heard of these horrors so often and for so long that perhaps only a poem or an anecdote can break through the scar tissue that shields their feelings and revive something of the shock and despair so widely, and so deeply, felt when Creeley began his writing career. Creeley taught by the anecdote, and perhaps the two that follow will give some sense of that time, and of the approach this poet and others took toward the grim events of the 1940's: to face them down and survive, to attempt to lead their generation out of the shadows toward some possible faith in life on which action might be based.

Asked about his empty socket, and whether he had

ever thought of wearing a glass eye, Creeley said that he had used one at one time. One evening in barracks in India, however, he had taken out the glass eye for the night and set it on the bedside table. As he reclined on his bed, he watched an Indian janitor sweeping the floor, coming closer and closer to the bedside table, and then bumping against it, so that the glass eye fell to the floor, where it broke. Because of wartime conditions, it would, he knew, take at least four months to get a replacement shipped to India. By that time, he might have been moved on to the theater of war, and in any case, his socket would have shrunk so that the new eye would not fit. Therefore, he took to wearing an eyepatch over the empty socket. In the early 1950's, when Creeley was living in a village in France, there were around him so many who had been maimed in the war—who were minus an arm or a leg, fingers or toes—that he saw no point in covering up his own loss. Protecting others from the shock of his empty socket and pretending to himself that the facts were otherwise struck him as equally futile in a world so substantially damaged.

The second illustrative incident took place during Creeley's time in Burma. His ambulance team had been assured by the local military unit that a certain village had been taken by the U.S. Army and that the enemy had been driven out. However, when Creeley and his crew arrived at the village, the first thing they spotted was a Japanese tank driving down the main street. Fortunately, they were able to back into the forest without being spotted. As the poet himself remarked of this incident, if they had taken the official word for it and not trusted the evidence of their senses, they would have been dead.

Although Creeley's poetry and prose of the 1950's contain little in the way of content that refers explicitly to wartime conditions or to the great horrors alluded to above, they are nevertheless permeated with the kind of wry awareness these two anecdotes suggest. For Creeley, as for other American poets of his generation, linear logic is less to the point than immediate perception, a plan is probably inferior to a hunch, and now always packs the possibility of transcending history. Still, any such attitude toward experience must allow for self-contradiction and ambivalence: What was a sensible line of conduct a moment ago can suddenly become not so.

"THE IMMORAL PROPOSITION"

Creeley developed a very sure way of presenting such knowledge in his poetry—for example, in "The Immoral Proposition":

> If you never do anything for anyone else
> you are spared the tragedy of human relation-
>
> ships. If quietly and like another time
> there is the passage of an unexpected thing:
>
> to look at it is more
> than it was. God knows
>
> nothing is competent nothing is
> all there is. The unsure
>
> egoist is not
> good for himself.

To turn this poem into a prose precis—"If you never do anything for anyone else, you are spared the tragedy of human relationships. If quietly and like another time there is the passage of an unexpected thing: to look at it is more than it was. God knows nothing is competent, nothing is all there is. The unsure egoist is not good for himself"—is no doubt to obtain part of the information being transmitted. What is lost in this alteration, however, reveals the essence of Creeley's poetry. In the first place, much happens around the line breaks. A Creeley line, being a breath line—speech-based, that is, with the line being the cluster of speech between two pauses—is always end-stopped: to hear the poet read aloud from his own work, a thing he made a frequent practice of doing, is to be assured of this fact. That brief but telling pause makes all the difference in the world between the last two lines. One reading thus yielded is "The unsure egoist is not"—period; another is "The unsure egoist is not [all there is]" or "is not [competent]." To add these to the first probable reading, "is not good for himself," enriches the mix. When one realizes that one has the alternative of hearing the final line as a kind of postscript, "[and therefore] good for himself," either ironic or not, one begins to appreciate the full complexity of both the poem and the general type of situation the poem addresses. Creeley made himself master of the pivotal word or phrase that, set at the end of a line, could be read both ahead and back—as with "egoist is not"—to embody more fully the kind of charged situation to which the poet found himself drawn. "To look at it is more/ than it was. God knows" is another cluster that stands on its own, as well as leading on to become part of a further statement. Remarkable also is the line break between lines 2 and 3, isolating the fourth syllable of "relationships" so that it takes on a peculiar autonomy and tangibility, as if to become those well-known "ships that pass in the night."

"The Immoral Proposition" is free verse, but it does not look much like the kind of poem that rubric brings to mind; it is too even, too balanced, too symmetrical. In fact, lines 1 and 2 consist of thirteen syllables each, while there is only a syllable's difference between lines 3 and 4, lines 5 and 6, and lines 9 and 10. Although they lack end rhyme, then, these have close similarity in length and thus have the feel of true couplets. Creeley showed great adroitness with his management of line length, as he did with his line breaks; the poem "The Warning" is a shining example of this:

> For love—I would
> split, open your head and put
> a candle in
> behind the eyes.
>
> Love is dead in us
> if we forget
> the virtues of an amulet
> and quick surprise.

Lines 1, 3, and 4 of the first stanza are four syllables long; line 2—the line that speaks of splitting something open to insert something extra—has seven syllables, or three extra. In this poem one finds end rhyme also, though in no regular pattern, and to some extent dependent on the reader's ear for half rhyme.

"BALLAD OF THE DESPAIRING HUSBAND"

Perhaps Creeley's most hilarious use of rhyme is in a poem called "Ballad of the Despairing Husband," where the measure used, that of the old song "Little Brown Jug," is played with and against to good effect:

> My wife and I lived all alone,
> contention was our only bone.
> I fought with her, she fought with me,
> and things went on right merrily.

As this and the following two quatrains disclose, Creeley was an accomplished humorist, with a sure grasp of the use of exaggeration for comic effect. Humor is not often as open in Creeley's work as it is here, but it occurs frequently enough that the practiced reader has learned to listen for the comic twist in any Creeley piece.

AESTHETIC VERSUS ACTUAL

In Creeley's work one finds a wide range of tones, with the sentimental occurring about as often as the comic. Sentimentality breaks in toward the end of "Ballad of the Despairing Husband," when the poet abandons the quatrains in iambic tetrameter in favor of longer, looser lines. Despite some playful phrases—"Oh lovely lady, eating with or without a spoon" (rhymes with "afternoon"); "Oh most loveliest of ladies"—the speaker has in effect stepped outside the frame of the poem to implore a woman who is no longer an amusing caricature but a real person.

This tension between the aesthetic and the otherwise actual sometimes is a strength in Creeley's work, but there are occasions, as here, where the reader might well judge Creeley's decision to step outside the poem to have been mistaken. The poem had been a deliberately two-dimensional rendering of important affairs of the heart, telling its portion of the truth most winningly. It ought not to have been interrupted with this other implied truth—that poems are limited, while the heart overflows. However, this is a risk run by the poet who draws extensively on personal experience for his material—especially personal experience of love.

At times, Creeley appears to judge it honest and human to break the aesthetic frame and speak in his own person. He is right in one sense; as Marianne Moore wrote of poetry, "There are things important beyond all this fiddle." Still, "this fiddle" is precisely what poetry is, and it is one thing to replace one set of conventions with another, but an entirely different enterprise to assume—perhaps unwittingly—that conventions can ever be dropped. Creeley's least satisfactory prose work, *A Day Book*, suffers greatly because this distinction is overlooked. In all fairness, it must be acknowledged that there are readers who prize such works and passages above Creeley's others and are thrilled to find the poet reduced to such vulnerability. However, these readers would probably not think very much of such raw confession emanating, word for word, from a less notable personage. They confuse gossip with art.

WORDS

By the mid-1960's, Creeley's reputation was secure. Two hugely popular poetry conferences, one at the University of British Columbia in Canada and the other at the University of California, Berkeley, had brought Creeley and his colleagues together with an audience of younger poets, professors, and counterculture enthusiasts, guaranteeing dissemination of their works and words. Creeley was being invited to read and speak in many distinguished venues in North America, Europe, and Asia; he had won Guggenheim and Rockefeller grants; his books were selling far beyond the usual for poetry. In 1967, *Words*, his first collection since *For Love*, appeared, earning for him further critical acclaim. Here the focus is less on domestic crises—at least explicitly—and more on the crisis in language. For a lyric poet who is attempting to close the gap between self and the person who utters the poem, to reduce authorial irony, and to abolish the fiction of the dramatic monologue, the contemporary disturbance in language, the growing unease concerning the gap between the word and the thing, must be a constant concern. In "The Pattern" in *Words*, Creeley writes:

> As soon as
> I speak, I
> speaks. It
> wants to
> be free but
> impassive lies
> in the direction
> of its
> words.

Such is the difficulty that these stanzas verge on nonsense verse, not least because the line breaks enforce many alternate readings beyond what syntax states. One thing is clear, though: The poet (and perhaps the poem itself) speaks of being trapped in an identity for which the habits of a vocabulary and the rules of a language, with their host of associations, are not flexible enough to allow entry or exit. This quandary becomes increasingly the burden of Creeley's writing in the late 1960's and the 1970's.

PIECES AND A DAY BOOK

In the late 1960's the twin courses of Creeley's poetry and prose began to be combined, first in *Pieces* and next in *A Day Book*. The latter consists of entries for thirty days during the course of a year, together with poems written more or less during the same period. *Pieces* consists of much briefer notebook jottings, many too short to be classified unequivocally as either poetry or prose. Among these are both prose passages and distinct poems, including "The Finger," one of the clearest embodiments of Creeley's thought. This poem speaks of the act of attention as paramount, certainly taking precedence over any plan, and it exemplifies its conclusions throughout, shifting from instance to instance as the poet recalls these.

Elsewhere in *Pieces* are many short registrations of event and thought, "quick takes," mental snapshots, the germs from which more conventional poems might have been built, had Creeley seen the point of such superstructure. At this time, however, he decided to avoid such conventions. The process of these pieces is as important as the product.

RANGE OF PROSE WORK

Creeley's innovative drive produced, in 1976, the work *Presences*, a series of prose texts written according to his preconceived system—permutations of 1, 2, 3, in a variety of sequences, a page to a number (for example, 2 = 2 pages). Within these restrictions, and rather obliquely addressing himself to the work of the sculptor Marisol, Creeley wrote an astonishing range of prose styles, from fairly conventional narrative to "cut-ups"—or pieces that read like cut-up material. The overall effect is to foreground the language—the means and the material of the writer's craft—even while delivering many of the familiar aspects of fiction and autobiography. Later, in 1984, when Calder & Boyars published Creeley's *The Collected Prose*, which included *The Island*, *The Gold Diggers*, and *Presences*, he included a newly written work, *Mabel*. Here too he writes according to permutations of 1, 2, 3. The range of style and tone is less than in *Presences*, and for much of the book, the narrative means are quite straightforward; yet the conception is innovative—to write an autobiography by focusing on the women in his life, a life not so much fictionalized in this work as at times exaggerated and seen in the light of gender.

SO THERE

As his prose creations continued to be innovative, Creeley's poetry in later years tended to settle for the same verse conventions as at the outset, but without the torque whereby the statement plays against the line breaks. The lines in the later work tend to be more pedestrian, and the poems more a recording of something noted than a drama of assertion and denial. The medium, poetry, is more taken for granted, without the challenging and questioning of *Words* and *Pieces*. Creeley's world, too, changed profoundly during the course of his career.

In bringing together the works of three volumes of poetry from the late 1970's and early 1980's (*Hello: A Journal, February 29-May 3, 1976*; *Later*; *Mirrors*), *So There* calls attention to important changes in the poet's life: the end of one marriage, the beginning of another, the birth of a son, and the transition from middle age to life as, in Creeley's words, "a young old man." Readers can also discern changes in his poetry: a movement away from proto-language-writing and a movement toward the preoccupations that came to characterize his later work, themes centered on the past, bleak reflections on the future and death, and affirmations of the present, despite losses past and still to come: "But now—/ but now the wonder of life is/ that it is at all."

Creeley called forth the American language as he heard it in its varied forms, from the cheerful repetitions of pop music ("Hello"), to the poignance of familiar phrases—be happy, be good—when sounded as a final good-bye to his friend, Max Fienstein ("Oh Max"). "Later" returns to locations from the poet's boyhood, while "Hello" captures the reader's interest for its unusual groupings of poems: The poems are organized by date and place yet offer few details of place. Instead, they tend to focus on the self in new and unfamiliar places—alone, apart, and occasionally confused. His experiences in travel bring to his mind a number of his present circumstances: decrepit houses in Singapore prompt him to muse on his own body's impermanence; the whir of a hotel air conditioner reminds him of the American Southwest. As he notes, "Same clock ticks/ in these different places."

LIFE AND DEATH

Creeley's poetry in the late 1990's showed a growing difference when compared with his earlier work. In *Life and Death*, for example, short, abstract poems find a place in the volume, as in collections past, but here they are balanced by longer sequences: "Histoire de Florida," "The Dogs of Auckland," "There," "Inside My Head," and the title poem itself. Critics have noted that here his poems, dealing with old age and the closure of life itself, take up the problems of poetic closure and resistance to closure—a theme so central to Creeley's poetics—in ways that appear more flexible and wise than the attitude of his earlier work. He seems no longer absolutely committed to a poetics of indeterminacy but attempts to reconcile the open-ended process of writing with the recognition that consciousness eventually comes to an end. Although death "will separate/ finally/ dancer from dance" and end what was a continuing process, it also is a form of absolute openness: It means the dissolution of boundaries and embodiment altogether.

It is apt, then, that the themes of this book center on this binary of life and death, and the chasms and similarities between them: old age, the death of friends, the persistence of love and memory even when the known object disappears from the world. The long poem that opens the volume, "Histoire of Florida," uses a colorful palette in describing a Floridian landscape to render an image of old age as a sunny promontory from which to look back:

> Waking, think of sun through
> compacted tree branches,
> the dense
> persistent light.
>
> Think of heaven,
> home,
> a heart of gold,
> old song of friend's
>
> dear love and all
> the faint world it
> reaches to,
> it wants.

OTHER MAJOR WORKS

LONG FICTION: *The Island*, 1963.

SHORT FICTION: *The Gold Diggers*, 1954 (expanded 1965, as *The Gold Diggers, and Other Stories*); *Mabel: A Story and Other Prose*, 1976.

NONFICTION: *A Quick Graph*, 1970; *Presences*, 1976; *Charles Olson and Robert Creeley: The Complete Correspondence*, 1980-1996 (10 volumes); *Collected Essays*, 1983; *Day Book of a Virtual Poet*, 1998.

EDITED TEXTS: *Mayan Letters*, 1953 (by Charles Olson); *Selected Writings of Charles Olson*, 1966; *Selected Poems*, 1993 (by Olson); *The Best American Poetry, 2002*, 2002; *George Oppen: Selected Poems*, 2003.

MISCELLANEOUS: *The Collected Prose*, 1984 (novel, stories, radio play); *On Earth: Last Poems and an Essay*, 2006.

BIBLIOGRAPHY

Altieri, Charles. "Robert Creeley's Poetics of Conjecture: The Pains and Pleasures of Staging a Self at War with Its Own Lyric Desires." In *Self and Sensibility in Contemporary American Poetry*. New York: Cambridge University Press, 1984. Brilliant discussion of a key element in Creeley's work: the struggle between representation and the activity of representing. The imperatives of this struggle, says Altieri, connect Creeley's poetry to the romantic attempt to create a language, a rhetoric, that can express "the opposition between thinking and thought."

_____. "The Struggle with Absence: Robert Creeley and W. S. Merwin." In *Enlarging the Temple*. Lewisburg, Pa.: Bucknell University Press, 1979. Altieri provides a useful discussion of Creeley's aesthetics of presence, an epistemological inquiry into the dialectics of presence and absence in his writings. Creeley "is trying to resolve the dualisms of man and nature, subject and object, and embody their harmonious inter-relationships. . . . But [his] solution tends to be solipsistic."

Bernstein, Charles. "Hearing 'Here': Robert Creeley's Poetics of Duration." In *Content's Dream: Essays, 1975-1984*. Los Angeles: Sun & Moon Press, 1986. This essay features an approach, incorporating, without specific attribution, many phrases and sentences from Creeley's writing into Bernstein's arguments. Focuses on how language intervenes in any investigation—even or especially the investigation of the self conducted by Creeley. Qualifies Creeley's "heroic stance" in interesting ways.

Clark, Tom. *Robert Creeley and the Genius of the American Common Place: Together with the Poet's Own Autobiography*. New York: New Directions, 1993. A biography from the author's conversations with Creeley. Includes Creeley's "Autobiography," a talk he gave at New College of California in 1991, and photographs of Creeley and family and friends.

Faas, Ekbert, with Maria Trombacco. *Robert Creeley: A Biography*. Hanover, N.H.: University Press of New England, 2001. Examines the first fifty years in the life of the poet. Faas juxtaposes different perspectives and makes Creeley's "voice" present in the narrative.

Ford, Arthur. *Robert Creeley*. Boston: Twayne, 1978. A journeyman's account of the work up to 1976, with biographical linkages that give this book much of its utility. Strong on the notion of development from *For Love* through *Words* to *Pieces*. Attention is also given to the prose works.

Foster, Edward Halsey. *Understanding the Black Mountain Poets*. Columbia: University of South Carolina Press, 1995. This discussion of the Black Mountain poets contains valuable information on Creeley as well as on Charles Olson and Robert Duncan.

Pekar, Harvey, et al. *The Beats: A Graphic History*. Art by Ed Piskor et al. New York: Hill and Wang, 2009. Comic legend Harvey Pekar provides a history of the Beat poets in this graphic book. Contains an entry on and references to Creeley.

Rifkin, Libbie. *Career Moves: Olson, Creeley, Zukofsky, Berrigan, and the American Avant-Garde*. Madison: University of Wisconsin Press, 2000. A collective group portrait covering a significant amount of twentieth century literary and intellectual history. Rifkin investigates the career choices of writers and the development of the literary canon.

Von Hallberg, Robert. "Robert Creeley and John Ashbery: Systems." In *American Poetry and Culture, 1945-1980*. Cambridge, Mass.: Harvard University Press, 1985. Von Hallberg's piece is exceptionally interesting, illuminating Creeley's oeuvre from a striking perspective: that of the systemization of American thought and culture.

David Bromige
Updated by Sarah Hilbert

VICTOR HERNÁNDEZ CRUZ

Born: Aguas Buenas, Puerto Rico; February 6, 1949

PRINCIPAL POETRY

Papo Got His Gun! and Other Poems, 1966
Snaps, 1969
Mainland, 1973
Tropicalization, 1976
By Lingual Wholes, 1982
Rhythm, Content, and Flavor, 1989
Red Beans, 1991
Panoramas, 1997
Maraca: New and Selected Poems, 1965-2000,
    2001
The Mountain in the Sea: Poems, 2006

OTHER LITERARY FORMS

Victor Hernández Cruz (krews) wrote about poetry in an early pamphlet, *Doing Poetry* (1970). In *Stuff: A Collection of Poems, Visions, and Imaginative Happenings from Young Writers in Schools—Opened and Closed* (1970), coedited with Herbert Kohl, he offers a gathering of young writers' poems that outline his fundamental commitment to poetry and poetic expression, as well as his dedication to teaching. With Leroy Quintana and Virgil Suarez, Cruz edited *Paper Dance: Fifty-five Latino Poets* (1995). This was the first anthology of Latino poets from diverse origins: Cuba, Colombia, Dominican Republic, Ecuador, Guatemala, Puerto Rico, and Mexico.

In addition to short fiction, Cruz has written the unpublished novels "Rhythm Section/Part One" and "Time Zones," both of which explore the migration and musical themes of his poetry. Excerpts from the former appear in Maria Theresa Babin's *Borinquen: An An-*

thology of Puerto Rican Literature (1974). In four of his major poetry collections, Cruz has included prose works that offer insights into his life and aesthetics. He has also published articles in various journals, including *The New York Review of Books*, *Ramparts*, *Evergreen Review*, and *The Village Voice*.

ACHIEVEMENTS

In New York, Victor Hernández Cruz edited *Umbra* magazine from 1967 to 1969 and was cofounder of the East Harlem Gut Theater. In 1970, he was invited to be a guest lecturer at the University of California, Berkeley, and then served in the Ethnic Studies Department of San Francisco State College (now University) from 1971 to 1972. He worked with the San Francisco Art Commission (1976) and the Mission Neighborhood Center (1981). With novelist Ishmael Reed, he formed the Before Columbus Foundation.

Cruz served as a visiting professor at the University of California, San Diego (1993), and at the University of Michigan, Ann Arbor (1994). In 1974, he was given the Creative Arts Public Service Award, and in April, 1981, *Life* magazine featured Cruz in its celebration of twelve North American poets. He also earned a National Endowment for the Arts creative writing award (1989) and a John Simon Guggenheim Memorial Foundation Fellowship (1991). Cultural critic Bill Moyers interviewed Cruz for an eight-part Public Broadcasting Service series, *The Language of Life*, which aired June 23 to July 28, 1995. This program was subsequently released as a book and as an audiocassette. *Maraca* was shortlisted for the Griffin Poetry Prize in 2002. Cruz became a chancellor of the Academy of American Poets in 2008.

Cruz's legendary ability to give dynamic poetry readings has twice made him World Heavyweight Poetry Champion in Taos, New Mexico. He has also participated in discussions and readings sponsored by La Fundación Federico García Lorca and at the Universidad de Alcalá.

BIOGRAPHY

Victor Hernández Cruz was born in Aguas Buenas, Puerto Rico, a small town about twenty miles from San Juan. The streets were unpaved, but he absorbed the native song and poetry as well as the poetic declamations of his grandfather and uncle. His family migrated to New York in 1954 and settled in the tenements of the lower East Side of Manhattan. He attended Benjamin Franklin High School and began to write verse. At the age of sixteen, he composed his first collection of poetry, *Papo Got His Gun! and Other Poems*. Cruz and his friends duplicated and distributed five hundred copies to local bookstores.

In 1967, the *Evergreen Review* helped launch Cruz's career when the journal featured several of these poems. Thus, while still in high school, he became a published poet. In 1969, he released his second collection of poems, *Snaps*, and gained national attention. In the 1960's, his neighborhood had become a center of intellectual and social ferment as part of the Civil Rights movement. Beat poetry, protest poetry, and feminist poetry mixed with political activism and music to form the social milieu. Ishmael Reed, Allen Ginsberg, and LeRoi Jones (Amiri Baraka) were major influences, and Cruz was intrigued by the developing Nuyorican (New York/Puerto Rican) poetry movement, which often claims him.

In 1969, Cruz moved to Berkeley, California, to become poet-in-residence at the University of California. In 1973, he published a third collection of poems, *Mainland*, which chronicles his migrations from New York to California and back again. In *Tropicalization*, Cruz expands his Caribbean and Spanish sensibility. His next work, *By Lingual Wholes*, includes some poems printed in both Spanish and English, for in San Francisco he found many Latino artists who helped him develop from North American poet into a poet for both English- and Spanish-speaking peoples.

After the publication of *Rhythm, Content, and Flavor*, Cruz moved back to Aguas Buenas, where he was born. He came into close contact with the local oral traditions and was deeply affected by them. In 1991, he recorded these sensations in *Red Beans*, and next he began working on a book of poems in Spanish. *Panoramas* provides a sensuous blend of Puerto Rico's Taino, Spanish, and African legacies in fantastic imagery that illuminates the Caribbean culture for the world. In 2001, Cruz published *Maraca*, a collection of new and selected poems spanning the years 1965 to 2000. Al-

though he continues to travel, performing his poems from Madrid to San Francisco, he is the only well-known Puerto Rican poet writing in English who chose to return to live on the island of his birth.

ANALYSIS

Victor Hernández Cruz was the first of the Puerto Rican poets writing in the English language to reach a broad American audience. However, rather than label him an English-language poet, it is more accurate to view him as a bilingual or a multilingual writer. Cruz enjoys his native language, with its Arabian and African words and its unique rhythms and patterns. His poetry incorporates many strains: his family's vital oral tradition, traditional Spanish, New York-Puerto Rican slang, and black English. He discovered various "Englishes" and was intrigued by fellow writers, such as Polish author Joseph Conrad, who wrote in English as a second language.

SNAPS

After the early success of *Papo Got His Gun! and Other Poems*, a chapbook that had gained notice in *Evergreen Review*, Random House published *Snaps*. This collection's hip, barrio voice, its jazzy rhythms, and its snapshot technique of realistically portraying street life brought Cruz immediate recognition. Random House honored his irreverence for grammar and formalities of style and thus helped launch the young poet's ongoing fascination with the relationship of sound and sense, of language and life.

The poems capture the true essence of urban ghetto life. Clacking subways, dance clubs, smoking, girl-watching, and knife fights form the gritty realities of street life. The rapid staccato of half-learned English enriches the poems. Cruz's language here is the sublanguage used to present Spanish Harlem's subculture. His speaker in these primarily narrative poems uses street slang as well as surrealistic humor to create a vivid picture of the danger and energy of the culturally diverse lower East Side. There is constant movement: on subways, uptown, downtown, inside, outside, walking, and driving. In "Megalopolis," the speaker presents snapshots from the window of a car moving through the urban sprawl of the East Coast:

let those lights & trees & rocks
talk/ going by / go by   just sit
back/ we / we go into towns/   sailing the
east coast / westside drive   far-off
buildings look like castles / the kind
dracula flies out of / new england of houses

The poem goes on to end with quick vignettes of a poet inciting riot, urban bombs, "laurence welk-reader's digest ladies" with bouffant hairdos secured with hair spray, billboards "singing lies," and "the night of the buildings/ . . . singing magic words/ of our ancestors." This ending points to another aspect of Cruz's poetry: traveling through time as well as space.

MAINLAND

Mainland records Cruz's poetic migration across the United States. The motion/mobility theme of *Snaps* here moves from intracity travel to interstate and, finally, to international migrations. The collection begins in New York, traverses the Midwest to California and the Southwest, and ends with a visit to Puerto Rico, followed by the return to New York.

These poems show the power of the memory of the Caribbean—its music and dance, its food, language, people, and culture—all working to recenter the poet once he returns to the realities of New York urban life. "The Man Who Came to the Last Floor," which ends the collection, employs surrealistic humor. A Puerto Rican immigrant with a bag of tropical seeds arrives in New York and rents a sixth floor apartment. Singing and dancing in his apartment, he accidentally flings the seeds of tropical fruits from his window.

A policeman was walking down the avenue
and all of a sudden took off his hat
A mango seed landed nicely into his
curly hair

The policeman does not notice the seed, which then grows into a flourishing five-foot tree that bears a mango. With this surreal image, Cruz presents the subtle, almost subversive, "tropicalization" accomplished by immigrants as they plant seeds to revitalize the northern urban landscape.

TROPICALIZATION

In an increasingly lyrical vein, Cruz collects in *Tropicalization* the images and rhythms of the Carib-

bean in poetry and prose poems. This collection presents a renewed vision of the United States, tropicalized, surrealistically transformed by the beat of its Hispanic population. Here Cruz uses more experimental structures to capture the spiritual side of barrio life, and he also enlarges upon the blending of Spanish and English ("Spanglish," or code-switching), always a characteristic of his work. He handles English as an amalgam capable of easily incorporating new words and innovative syntaxes.

In "Side 24," he cheerfully juxtaposes English and Spanish, cement and tropical oranges (*chinas*):

Walk el cement
Where las chinas roll
Illuminating my path
Through old streets

As part of the "ethnic" avant-garde, Cruz does not regard his Puerto Rican home with anger or despair, as Abraham Rodriguez does, nor does he look back with sadness, as does Judith Ortiz Cofer. He cheerfully delights in his ethnic identity, which he sees as tropicalizing the North, as bringing oranges and salsa to the cement and the chill of the United States.

BY LINGUAL WHOLES

Continuing his themes of contrasting and merging the sounds of two cultures and languages, Cruz again includes both poetry and prose in *By Lingual Wholes*. This collection is slower paced and more pensive than the earlier works; again, music, dance, and Spanglish coalesce in a dynamic and positive expression of multiculturalism. Cruz removes barriers of culture and language, illustrating the wholeness possible in living in and creating from two cultures and languages.

The title suggests the wordplay that will follow as Cruz proves himself a master of pun, whimsy, paradox, and concrete poetry. In addition, these poems explore a deeper heritage of Puerto Rican folklore and myth, as well as a whole range of historical events and characters. Never didactic, Cruz invites readers to participate in genial handshakes across cultures.

In the sixth poem of the collection, "Listening to the Music of Arsenio Rodriguez Is Moving Closer to Knowledge," Cruz plays tribute to the blind African-Cuban musician and composer. In New York, the Caribbean community enjoyed this music under the label "salsa." The speaker raves about salsa's power and gaily ridicules researchers who attempt to study it and "understand" it. They totally miss the dance music's intrinsic warmth and tropical passion, which is to be experienced and absorbed, not analyzed and understood.

RHYTHM, CONTENT, AND FLAVOR

In his collection *Rhythm, Content, and Flavor*, Cruz selects poems from his earlier works and adds a new work, "Islandis: The Age of Seashells." Here he continues to interweave images of the urban and natural worlds, and he reaffirms his Puerto Rican culture as the source of music and knowledge. Like lost Atlantis, with its tropical breezes and its kinship with the ocean, Puerto Rico creates a music reminiscent of the medieval "music of the spheres." As he also notes elsewhere, poetry for Cruz is "la salsa de Dios"; God is the origin of all poetry and music, and poetry is the music of God.

RED BEANS

Red Beans contains poems, prose essays, and a manifesto on poetry. The "red" of the title is the color of beans, shirts, earth, the Red Sea, "Red pepper/ In a stew," all representing the vitality and urgency Cruz finds in the "red beings," his Puerto Rican ancestors. He also draws on his earliest memories of hearing English in "Snaps of Immigration": "At first English was nothing/ but sound/ Like trumpets doing yakity yak." Later, the sound of poetic language is celebrated in "An Essay on Williams Carlos Williams":

> I love the quality of the
> spoken thought
> As it happens immediately
> uttered into the air
> Not held inside and rolled
> around for some properly
> schemed moment

Cruz continues to emphasize the naturalness, the oral spontaneity of true poetry. "Corsica" adds a focus on the joyful interplay of cultures and languages which had always been a theme in Cruz's poetry. He announces that Puerto Rico and Corsica are "holding hands" underneath the "geologic plates," that both islands see the same moon. Never narrowly ethnic, Cruz celebrates the creative merger of culture and language.

He ends this volume showing his receptivity to other cultures:

> I wait with a gourd full
> of inspiration
> For a chip to fall from
> The festival fireworks
> To favor me
> And set me on fire.

PANORAMAS

The poems and essays of *Panoramas* present a civilized and gracious tone as they transport readers to the magic world of the Caribbean, which celebrates its blend of Taino, African, and Spanish legacies. The poems and essays also illuminate Latin American/Caribbean culture in the United States and beyond. Rather than conflict, Cruz suggests a harmonious merger and a creative synthesis of disparate ideas and people.

OTHER MAJOR WORKS

NONFICTION: *Doing Poetry*, 1970.

EDITED TEXTS: *Stuff: A Collection of Poems, Visions, and Imaginative Happenings from Young Writers in Schools—Opened and Closed*, 1970 (with Herbert Kohl); *Paper Dance: Fifty-five Latino Poets*, 1995 (with Virgil Suarez and Leroy V. Quintana).

BIBLIOGRAPHY

Aparicio, Frances R. "'Salsa,' 'Maracas,' and 'Baile': Latin Popular Music in the Poetry of Victor Hernández Cruz." *MELUS* 16 (Spring, 1989/1990): 43-58. Explores and delineates the sound, beat, and rhythm of popular Latin American music in Cruz's poetry; also shows how this music tropicalizes American culture and gives a sense of cohesion and identity to immigrants. Aparicio notes that, when read aloud, the work sounds like jazz poetry.

Cruz, Victor Hernández. "Victor Hernández Cruz." Interview by Bill Moyers. In *The Language of Life: A Festival of Poets*, edited by Moyers. New York: Doubleday, 1995. In an interview with the poet, Moyers examines the blend of cultures that have influenced Cruz's poetry; also outlines the poet's rural roots and his absorption of bolero and salsa musical rhythms.

Kanellos, Nicolás. *Victor Hernández Cruz and la Salsa de Dios*. Milwaukee: University of Wisconsin Press, 1979. Focuses on the essentially Puerto Rican side of Cruz's poetry with special emphasis on the African-Caribbean strains of salsa, whose origins Cruz locates in Africa and the pre-Columbian West Indies.

Torrens, James. "U.S. Latino Writers: The Searchers." *America* 167 (July 18-25, 1992). Takes a sociological and psychological approach, noting that Cruz writes of numbing poverty and of the immigrant's struggle for dignity. Also explores the immigrant writer's need to belong to a group.

Waisman, Sergio Gabriel. "The Body as Migration." *Bilingual Review* 19 (May 1, 1944): 188-192. Explores Cruz's understanding of the three influences in Puerto Rican culture: indigenous (Taino), Spanish (including that of Arabs, gypsies/Roma, and Jews), and African (especially that of the Yorubas). Also examines his use of wordplay, metaphor, and synaesthesia. The primary focus here is on *Red Beans*.

Marie J. K. Brenner

COUNTÉE CULLEN

Born: New York, New York; or Louisville, Kentucky; or Baltimore, Maryland; May 30, 1903
Died: New York, New York; January 9, 1946

PRINCIPAL POETRY

Color, 1925
The Ballad of the Brown Girl: An Old Ballad Retold, 1927
Copper Sun, 1927
The Black Christ, and Other Poems, 1929
The Medea, and Some Poems, 1935
On These I Stand: An Anthology of the Best Poems of Countée Cullen, 1947

OTHER LITERARY FORMS

Countée Cullen (KUH-lehn) wrote nearly as much prose as he did poetry. While serving from 1926 through most of 1928 as literary editor of *Opportunity*, a magazine vehicle for the National Urban League, Cullen wrote several articles, including book reviews, and a series of topical essays for a column called "The Dark Tower" about figures and events involved in the Harlem Renaissance. He also wrote many stories for children, most of which are collected in *My Lives and How I Lost Them* (1942), the "autobiography" of Cullen's own pet, Christopher Cat, who had allegedly reached his ninth life. Earlier, in 1932, the poet had tried his hand at a novel, publishing it as *One Way to Heaven* (1932). In addition to articles, reviews, stories, and a novel, the poet translated or collaborated in the writing of four plays, one of them being a musical. In 1935, Cullen translated Euripides' *Medea* for the volume by the same name; in 1942, Virgil Thomson set to music the seven verse choruses from Cullen's translation. With Owen Dodson, Cullen wrote the one-act play *The Third Fourth of July*, which appeared posthumously in 1946. The musical was produced at the Martin Beck Theater on Broadway, where it ran for 113 performances; this production also introduced Pearl Bailey as the character Butterfly.

ACHIEVEMENTS

Countée Cullen's literary accomplishments were many. While he was a student at DeWitt Clinton High School, New York City, he published his first poems and made numerous and regular contributions to the high school literary magazine. From DeWitt, whose other distinguished graduates include Lionel Trilling and James Baldwin, Cullen went to New York University. There he distinguished himself by becoming a member of Phi Beta Kappa and in the same year, 1925, by publishing *Color*, his first collection of poems. In June, 1926, the poet took his second degree, an M.A. in English literature from Harvard University. In December, 1926, *Color* was awarded the first Harmon Gold Award for literature, which carried with it a cash award of five hundred dollars. Just before publication in 1927 of his second book, *Copper Sun*, Cullen received a Guggenheim Fellowship for a year's study and writing in France. While in France, he worked on improving his French conversation by engaging a private tutor and his knowledge of French literature by enrolling in courses at the Sorbonne. Out of this experience came

The Black Christ, and Other Poems. In 1944, the poet was offered the chair of creative literature at Nashville's Fisk University, but he refused in order to continue his teaching at the Frederick Douglass Junior High in New York City.

BIOGRAPHY

Countée Cullen was born Countée LeRoy Porter, although scholars remain uncertain as to the place of his birth. He was raised by Elizabeth Porter, who is thought to be his grandmother and who brought him to Harlem. When Porter died in 1918, Cullen was adopted by the Reverend and Mrs. Frederick A. Cullen; the Reverend Cullen was minister of the Salem Methodist Episcopal Church of Harlem. The years spent with the Cullens in the Methodist parsonage made a lasting impression on the young poet; although he experienced periods of intense self-questioning, Cullen appears never to have discarded his belief in Christianity.

During his undergraduate years at New York University, the young poet became heavily involved with figures of the Harlem Renaissance; among these Harlem literati were Zora Neale Hurston, Langston Hughes, Carl Van Vechten (a white writer who treated black themes), and Wallace Thurman. After the appearance of *Color* in 1925 and the receipt of his Harvard M.A. in June, 1926, Cullen assumed the position of literary editor of *Opportunity*. At the end of October, 1926, he wrote one of the most important of his "Dark Tower" essays about the appearance of that great treasure of the Harlem Renaissance, the short-lived but first black literary and art quarterly *Fire* (issued only once). He contributed one of his best poems, "From the Dark Tower," to *Fire*. About the solitary issue, Cullen wrote that it held great significance for black American culture, because it represented "a brave and beautiful attempt to meet our need for an all-literary and artistic medium of expression."

On April 10, 1928, Cullen married Nina Yolande Du Bois, daughter of one of the most powerful figures of twentieth century black American culture, W. E. B. Du Bois; the two were married at Salem Methodist Episcopal Church. This union proved to be of short duration, however; while Cullen was in Paris on his Guggenheim Fellowship, his wife was granted a decree of divorce. The marriage had not lasted two years. Much of Cullen's poetry deals with disappointment in love, and one senses that the poet was himself often disappointed in such matters.

In 1940, however, after Cullen had taught for several years at the Frederick Douglass Junior High School of New York, he married a second time; on this occasion he chose Ida Mae Roberson, whom he had known for ten years. Ida Mae represented to the poet the ideal woman; she was intelligent, loyal, and empathetic, if not as beautiful and well-connected as his former wife.

When Cullen died of uremic poisoning on January 9, 1946, only forty-two years old, the New York newspapers devoted several columns to detailing his career and praising him for his distinguished literary accomplishments. However, nearly thirty years after Cullen's death, Houston A. Baker deplored (in *A Many-Colored Coat of Dreams: The Poetry of Countée Cullen*, 1974)

Countée Cullen (Library of Congress)

the fact that no collection of his poetry had been published since the posthumous *On These I Stand*, nor had any of his previously published volumes been reprinted. Indeed, many volumes of this important Harlem Renaissance poet can be read only in rare-book rooms of university libraries.

ANALYSIS

In his scholarly book of 1937, *Negro Poetry and Drama*, Sterling A. Brown, whose poems and essays continue to exert formidable influence on black American culture, remarked that Countée Cullen's poetry is "the most polished lyricism of modern Negro poetry." About his own poetry and poetry in general, Cullen himself observed, "Good poetry is a lofty thought beautifully expressed. Poetry should not be too intellectual. It should deal more, I think, with the emotions." In this definition of "good poetry," Cullen reflects his declared, constant aspiration to transcend his color and to strike a universal chord. However, the perceptive poet, novelist, essayist and critic James Weldon Johnson asserted that the best of Cullen's poetry "is motivated by race. He is always seeking to free himself and his art from these bonds."

The tension prevalent in Cullen's poems, then, is between the objective of transcendence—to reach the universal, to enter the "mainstream"—and his ineluctable return to the predicament his race faces in a white world. This tension causes him, on one hand, to demonstrate a paramount example of T. S. Eliot's "tradition and the individual talent" and, on the other, to embody the black aesthetic (as articulated during the Harlem Renaissance). In his best poems, he achieves both. Transcending the bonds of race and country, he produces poetry that looks to the literature and ideas of the past while it identifies its creator as an original artist; yet, at the same time, he celebrates his African heritage, dramatizes black heroism, and reveals the reality of being black in a hostile world.

"YET DO I MARVEL"

"Yet Do I Marvel," perhaps Cullen's most famous single poem, displays the poet during one of his most intensely lyrical, personal moments; however, this poem also illustrates his reverence for tradition. The sonnet, essentially Shakespearean in rhyme scheme, is actually Petrarchan in its internal form. The Petrarchan form is even suggested in the rhyme scheme; the first two quatrains rhyme *abab*, *cdcd* in perfect accord with the Shakespearean scheme. The next six lines, however, break the expected pattern of yet another quatrain in the same scheme; instead of *efef* followed by a couplet *gg*, the poem adopts the scheme *eeffgg*. While retaining the concluding couplet (*gg*), the other two (*eeff*) combine with the final couplet, suggesting the Petrarchan structure of the sestet. The poem is essentially divided, then, into the octave, wherein the problem is stated, and the sestet, in which some sort of resolution is attempted.

Analysis of the poem's content shows that Cullen chose the internal form of the Petrarchan sonnet but retained a measure of the Shakespearean form for dramatic effect. By means of antiphrastic statements or ironic declaratives in the first eight lines of the poem, the poem's speaker expresses doubt about God's goodness and benevolent intent, especially in his creation of certain limited beings. The poem begins with the assertion that "I doubt not God is good, well-meaning, kind" and then proceeds to reveal that the speaker actually believes just the opposite to be true; that is, he actually says, "I do doubt God is good." For God has created the "little buried mole" to continue blind and "flesh that mirrors Him" to "some day die." Then the persona cites two illustrations of cruel, irremediable predicaments from classical mythology, those of Tantalus and Sisyphus. These mythological figures are traditional examples: Tantalus, the man who suffers eternal denial of that which he seeks, and Sisyphus, the man who suffers the eternal drudgery of being forced to toil endlessly again and again only to lose his objective each time he thinks he has won it.

The illustration of the mole and the man who must die rehearses the existential pathos of modern human beings estranged from God and thrust into a hostile universe. What appeared to be naïve affirmations of God's goodness become penetrating questions that reveal Cullen himself in a moment of intense doubt. This attitude of contention with God closely resembles that expressed by Gerard Manley Hopkins in his sonnet "Thou Art Indeed Just, Lord." The probing questions, combined with the apparent resolve to believe, are indeed close; one might suggest that Cullen has adapted Hopkins's struggle for certainty to the black predicament, the real subject of Cullen's poem. The predicaments of Tantalus and Sisyphus (anticipating Albert Camus's later essay) comment on a personal problem, one close to home for Cullen himself. The notion of men struggling eternally toward a goal, thinking they have achieved it but having it torn from them, articulates the plight of black artists in the United States. In keeping with the form of the Petrarchan sonnet, the ninth line constitutes the *volta* or turn toward some sort of resolution. From ironic questioning, the persona moves to direct statement, even to a degree of affirmation. "Inscrutable His ways are," the speaker declares, to a mere human being who is too preoccupied with the vicissitudes of his mundane existence to grasp "What awful brain compels His awful hand," this last line echoing William Blake's "The Tyger." The apparent resolution becomes clouded by the poem's striking final couplet: "Yet do I marvel at this curious thing:/ To make a poet black, and bid him sing!"

The doubt remains; nothing is finally resolved. The plight of the black poet becomes identical with that of Tantalus and Sisyphus. Like these figures from classical mythology, the black poet is, in the contemporary, nonmythological world, forced to struggle endlessly toward a goal he will never, as the poem suggests, be allowed to reach. Cullen has effectively combined the Petrarchan and the Shakespearean sonnet forms; the sestet's first four lines function as an apparent resolution of the problem advanced by the octave. The concluding couplet, however, recalling the Shakespearean device of concentrating the entire poem's comment within the final two lines, restates the problem of the octave by maintaining that, in the case of a black poet, God has created the supreme irony. In "Yet Do I Marvel," Cullen has succeeded in making an intensely personal statement; as Johnson suggested, this poem "is motivated by race." Nevertheless, not only race is at work here. Rather than selecting a more modern form, perhaps free verse, the poet employs the sonnet tradition in a surprising and effective way, and he also shows his regard for tradition by citing mythological figures and by summoning up Blake.

REGARD FOR TRADITION

Cullen displays his regard for tradition in many other poems. "The Medusa," for example, by its very title celebrates once again the classical tradition; in this piece, another sonnet, the poet suggests that the face of a woman who rejected him has the malign power of the Medusa. In an epitaph, a favorite form of Cullen, he celebrates the poetry of John Keats, whose "singing lips that cold death kissed/ Have seared his own with flame." Keats was Cullen's avowed favorite poet, and Cullen celebrates him in yet a second poem, "To John Keats, Poet at Spring Time." As suggested by Cullen's definition of poetry, it was Keats's concern for beauty which attracted him: "in spite of all men say/ Of Beauty, you have felt her most."

"HERITAGE"

Beauty and classical mythology were not the only elements of tradition that Cullen revered. Indeed, he forcefully celebrated his own African heritage, exemplifying the first of the tenets of the black aesthetic. "Heritage" represents his most concentrated effort to reclaim his African roots. This 128-line lyric opens as the persona longs for the song of "wild barbaric birds/ Goading massive jungle herds" from which, through no fault of his own, he has been removed for three centuries. He then articulates Johnson's observation that this poet is ever "seeking to free himself and his art" from the bonds of this heritage. The poem's speaker remarks that, although he crams his thumbs against his ears and keeps them there, "great drums" always throb "through the air." This duplicity of mind and action force upon him a sense of "distress, and joy allied." Despite this distress, he continues to conjure up in his mind's eye "cats/ Crouching in the river reeds," "silver snakes," and "the savage measures of/ Jungle boys and girls in love." The rain has a particularly dramatic effect on him; "While its primal measures drip," a distant, resonant voice beckons him to "'strip!/ Off this new exuberance./ Come and dance the Lover's Dance!'" Out of this experience of recollection and reclaiming his past comes the urge to "fashion dark gods" and, finally, even to dare "to give You [the one God]/ Dark despairing features."

THE BLACK CHRIST

The intense need expressed here, to see God as literally black, predicts the long narrative poem of 1929, *The Black Christ*. This poem, perhaps more than any other of Cullen's poems, represents his attempt to portray black heroism, the second tenet of the black aesthetic. Briefly the poem tells the tale of Jim, a young black man who comes to believe it is inevitable that he will suffer death at the hands of an angry lynch mob. Miraculously, after the inevitable lynching has indeed occurred, the young man appears to his younger brother and mother, much as Jesus of Nazareth, according to the Gospels, appeared before his disciples. Christ has essentially transformed himself into black Jim. Although the poem contains such faults as a main character who speaks in dialect at one point and waxes eloquent at another, and one speech by Jim who, pursued by the mob, speaks so long that he cannot possibly escape (one may argue that he was doomed from the start), it has moments of artistic brilliance.

Jim "was handsome in a way/ Night is after a long, hot day." He could never bend his spirit to the white man's demands: "my blood's too hot to knuckle." Like Richard Wright's Bigger Thomas, Jim was a man of action whose deeds "let loose/ The pent-up torrent of abuse," which clamored in his younger brother "for release." Toward the middle of the poem, Jim's brother, the narrator, describes Jim, after the older brother has become tipsy with drink, as "Spring's gayest cavalier"; this occurs "in the dim/ Half-light" of the evening. At the end, "Spring's gayest cavalier" has become the black Christ, Spring's radiant sacrifice, suggesting that "Half-light" reveals only selective truths, those one may be inclined to believe are true because of one's human limitations, whereas God's total light reveals absolute truth unfettered. Following this suggestion, the image "Spring's gayest cavalier" becomes even more fecund. The word "cavalier" calls up another poem by Hopkins, "The Windhover," which is dedicated to Christ. In this poem, the speaker addresses Christ with the exclamation, "O my chevalier!" Both "cavalier" and "chevalier" have their origins in the same Latin word, *caballarius*. Since Cullen knew both French and Latin and since Hopkins's poems had been published in 1918, it is reasonable to suggest a more than coinciden-

tal connection. At any rate, "Spring's gayest cavalier" embodies an example of effective foreshadowing.

Just before the mob seizes Jim, the narrator maintains that "The air about him shaped a crown/ Of light, or so it seemed to me," similar to the nimbus so often appearing in medieval paintings of Christ, the holy family, the disciples, and the saints. The narrator describes the seizure itself in an epic simile of nine lines. When Jim has been lynched, the younger brother exclaims, "My Lycidas was dead. There swung/ In all his glory, lusty, young,/ My Jonathan, my Patrocles." Here Cullen brings together the works of John Milton, the Bible, and Homer into one image that appears to syncretize them all. Clearly, the poet is attempting to construct in Jim a hero of cosmic proportions while at the same time managing to unify, if only for a moment, four grand traditions: the English, the biblical, the classical, and, of course, the African American.

"HARLEM WINE"

While *The Black Christ* dramatizes black heroism, it also suggests what it means to be black in a hostile, white world. Not all the black experience, however, is tainted with such unspeakable horror. In "Harlem Wine," Cullen reveals how blacks overcome their pain and rebellious inclinations through the medium of music. The blues, a totally black cultural phenomenon, "hurtle flesh and bone past fear/ Down alleyways of dreams." Indeed, the wine of Harlem can its "joy compute/ with blithe, ecstatic hips." The ballad stanza of this poem's three quatrains rocks with rhythm, repeating Cullen's immensely successful performance in another long narrative poem, *The Ballad of the Brown Girl*.

"FROM THE DARK TOWER"

Although not as notable a rhythmic performance as "Harlem Wine" or *The Ballad of the Brown Girl*, "From the Dark Tower" is, nevertheless, a remarkable poem. It contains a profound expression of the black experience. Important to a reading of the poem is the fact that the Dark Tower was an actual place located on New York's 136th Street in the heart of Harlem; poets and artists of the Harlem Renaissance often gathered there to discuss their writings and their art. Perhaps this poem grew out of one of those gatherings. The poem is more identifiably a Petrarchan or Italian sonnet than "Yet Do I Marvel"; as prescribed by the form, the octave is arranged into two quatrains, each rhyming *abbaabba*, while the sestet rhymes *ccddee*. The rhyme scheme of the sestet closely resembles that in "Yet Do I Marvel."

The octave of "From the Dark Tower" states the poem's problem in an unconventional, perhaps surprising manner by means of a series of threats. The first threat introduces the conceit of planting, to which the poem returns in its last pair of couplets. The poet begins, "We shall not always plant while others reap/ The golden increment of bursting fruit." The planting conceit suggests almost immediately the image of slaves working the fields of a Southern plantation. Conjuring up this memory of the antebellum South but then asserting by use of the future tense ("We *shall* not") that nothing has changed—that is, that the white world has relegated modern African Americans to their former status as slaves, not even as good as second-class citizens—Cullen strikes a minor chord of deep, poignant bitterness felt by many blacks during his lifetime. However, what these blacks produce with their planting is richly fertile, a "bursting fruit"; the problem is that "others reap" this "golden increment." The poet's threat promises that this tide of gross, unjust rapine will soon turn against its perpetrators.

The next few lines compound this initial threat with others. These same oppressed people will not forever bow "abject and mute" to such treatment by a people who have shown by their oppression that they are the inferiors of their victims. "Not everlastingly" will these victims "beguile" this evil race "with mellow flute"; the reader can readily picture scenes of supposedly contented, dancing "darkies" and ostensibly happy minstrel men. "We were not made eternally to weep" declares the poet in the last line of the octave. This line constitutes the *volta* or turning point in the poem. All the bitterness and resentment implied in the preceding lines is exposed here. An oppressed people simply will not shed tears forever; sorrow and self-pity inevitably turn to anger and rebellion.

The first four lines of the sestet state cases in defense of the octave's propositions that these oppressed people, now identified by the comparisons made in these lines as the black race, are "no less lovely being dark." The poet returns subtly to his planting conceit by citing the case of flowers that "cannot bloom at all/ In light,

but crumple, piteous, and fall." From the infinite heavens to finite flowers of Earth Cullen takes his reader, grasping universal and particular significance for his people and thereby restoring and bolstering their pride and sense of worth.

Then follow the piercing, deep-felt last lines: "So, in the dark we hide the heart that bleeds,/ And wait, and tend our agonizing seeds." As with "Yet Do I Marvel," Cullen has effectively combined the structures of the Petrarchan and Shakespearean sonnets by concluding his poem with this trenchant, succinct couplet. The planting conceit, however, has altered dramatically. What has been "golden increment" for white oppressors will yet surely prove the "bursting fruit" of "agonizing seeds." The poem represents, then, a sort of revolutionary predeclaration of independence. This "document" first states the offenses sustained by the downtrodden, next asserts their worth and significance as human beings, and finally argues that the black people will "wait" until an appropriate time to reveal their agony through rebellion. Cullen has here predicted the anger of James Baldwin's *The Fire Next Time* (1963) and the rhetoric of the Black Armageddon, a later literary movement led by such poets as Amiri Baraka, Sonia Sanchez, and Nikki Giovanni.

Whereas these figures of the Black Armageddon movement almost invariably selected unconventional forms in which to express their rebellion, Cullen demonstrated his respect for tradition in voicing his parallel feelings. Although Cullen's work ably displays his knowledge of the traditions of the Western world, from Homer to Keats (and even Edna St. Vincent Millay), it equally enunciates his empathy with black Americans in its celebration of the black aesthetic. At the same time that his poetry incorporates classicism and English Romanticism, it affirms his black heritage and the black American experience.

OTHER MAJOR WORKS

LONG FICTION: *One Way to Heaven*, 1932.

PLAYS: *Medea*, pr., pb. 1935 (translation of Euripides); *One Way to Heaven*, pb. 1936 (adaptation of his novel); *St. Louis Woman*, pr. 1946 (adaptation of Arna Bontemps's novel *God Sends Sunday*); *The Third Fourth of July*, pr., pb. 1946 (one act; with Owen Dodson).

CHILDREN'S LITERATURE: *The Lost Zoo (A Rhyme for the Young, but Not Too Young)*, 1940; *My Lives and How I Lost Them*, 1942.

EDITED TEXT: *Caroling Dusk*, 1927.

MISCELLANEOUS: *My Soul's High Song: The Collected Writings of Countee Cullen, Voice of the Harlem Renaissance*, 1991 (Gerald Early, editor).

BIBLIOGRAPHY

Baker, Houston A., Jr. *A Many-Colored Coat of Dreams: The Poetry of Countée Cullen*. Detroit: Broadside Press, 1974. This brief and somewhat difficult volume examines Cullen's poetry in the context of a black American literature that is published and criticized largely by a white literary establishment. Presents a new view of Cullen's poetry by holding it up to the light of black literary standards.

Ferguson, Blanche E. *Countée Cullen and the Negro Renaissance*. New York: Dodd, Mead, 1966. The only book-length study of Cullen for many years, this volume is a highly fictionalized biography. In a pleasant and simple style, Ferguson walks readers through major events in Cullen's life. Includes eight photographs, a brief bibliography, and an index.

Hutchinson, George, ed. *The Cambridge Companion to the Harlem Renaissance*. New York: Cambridge University Press, 2007. This work on the Harlem Renaissance contains a chapter comparing Cullen and Langston Hughes.

Onyeberechi, Sydney. *Critical Essays: Achebe, Baldwin, Cullen, Ngugi, and Tutuola*. Hyattsville, Md.: Rising Star, 1999. A collection of Onyeberechi's criticism and interpretation of the work of several African American authors. Includes bibliographic references.

Perry, Margaret. *A Bio-Bibliography of Countée Cullen*. Westport, Conn.: Greenwood Press, 1971. After a brief biographical sketch, Perry offers a valuable bibliography of Cullen's works and a sensitive reading of the poetry.

Pettis, Joyce. *African American Poets: Lives, Works, and Sources*. Westport, Conn.: Greenwood Press, 2002. This work on African American poets contains an entry describing the life and works of Cullen.

Schwarz, A. B. Christa. *Gay Voices of the Harlem Renaissance*. Bloomington: Indiana University Press, 2003. Schwarz examines the work of four leading writers from the Harlem Renaissance—Cullen, Langston Hughes, Claude McKay, and Richard Bruce Nugent— and their sexually nonconformist or gay literary voices.

Shucard, Alan R. *Countée Cullen*. Boston: Twayne, 1984. A basic biography detailing the life and works of Cullen.

Tuttleton, James W. "Countée Cullen at 'The Heights.'" In *The Harlem Renaissance: Revaluations*, edited by Amritjit Singh, William S. Shiver, and Stanley Brodwin. New York: Garland, 1989. Examines Cullen's years at New York University and analyzes his senior honors thesis on Edna St. Vincent Millay. Tuttleton argues that this period was very important to Cullen's emergence as a poet.

Washington, Shirley Porter. *Countée Cullen's Secret Revealed by Miracle Book: A Biography of His Childhood in New Orleans*. Bloomington, Ind.: AuthorHouse, 2008. This work by Cullen's niece asserts that Cullen was born James S. Carter, Jr., in New Orleans to James S. Carter, Sr., the first licensed African American dentist in Louisiana, and to Gussie Yeager Carter.

John C. Shields

E. E. CUMMINGS

Born: Cambridge, Massachusetts; October 14, 1894

Died: North Conway, New Hampshire; September 3, 1962

Also known as: e. e. cummings

PRINCIPAL POETRY

Tulips and Chimneys, 1923

&, 1925

XLI Poems, 1925

Is 5, 1926

W: Seventy New Poems, 1931

No Thanks, 1935

1/20 Poems, 1936

Collected Poems, 1938

Fifty Poems, 1940

1 × 1, 1944

Xiape, 1950

Poems, 1923-1954, 1954

Ninety-five Poems, 1958

One Hundred Selected Poems, 1959

Selected Poems, 1960

Seventy-three Poems, 1963

E. E. Cummings: A Selection of Poems, 1965

Complete Poems, 1913-1962, 1968

*Etcetera: The Unpublished Poems of E. E.
Cummings*, 1983, 2000; George James Firmage
and Richard S. Kennedy, editors)

OTHER LITERARY FORMS

In addition to poetry, E. E. Cummings also published two long prose narratives, *The Enormous Room* (1922) and *Eimi* (1933); a translation from the French of *The Red Front*, by Louis Aragon (1933); a long play, *Him* (pb. 1927); two short plays, *Anthropos: The Future of Art* (pb. 1944) and *Santa Claus: A Morality* (pb. 1946); *Tom: A Ballet* (pb. 1935); a collection of his own drawings in charcoal, ink, oil, pastels, and watercolor, *CIOPW* (1931); his autobiographical Harvard lectures, *i: six nonlectures* (1953); and a collection of his wife's photographs with captions by Cummings, *Adventures in Value* (1962).

Of these, *The Enormous Room* and *Eimi* are of particular interest because of their contributions to Cummings's critical reputation and to his development as an artist. The former is the poet's account of his three-month confinement in a French concentration camp in 1917. It was hailed on its appearance as a significant firsthand account of the war and has become one of the classic records of World War I. It is also significant in that it is Cummings's first book, and, although prose, it reflects the same kinds of linguistic experimentation and innovation apparent in his poetry. Also reflecting his stylistic innovations is *Eimi*, Cummings's account of a trip to Russia, which has a topical vitality similar to the war experiences. The major themes of the critical response to Cummings's poetry, which developed in the 1920's, were implicit in the responses to *The Enormous Room*. Those themes, explicit by

1933, also helped to shape the criticism of *Eimi*.

Similar to the two prose narratives, *Him*, a long, expressionistic drama, is also representative of Cummings's development and of his critical reputation. Experimental and distinctive, the drama was produced in 1928 by the Provincetown Players. In the program notes, Cummings cautioned the audience against trying to understand the play. Instead, he advised the audience to "let it try to understand you." As with the poetry and the prose, there were outraged cries claiming that the play was unintelligible, although there was also an affirmation of the lyrical originality and intensity of the play. The recognition of Cummings's lyrical talents was gradually to replace the often angry rejections of his work because of its eccentricity.

Stylistically distinctive and important in any full assessment of his achievement is the collection of Cummings's presentations as the annual Charles Eliot Norton Lecturer in Poetry at Harvard, *i: six nonlectures*. Of immediate interest, however, is the autobiographical content of the lectures. The first lecture is titled "i & my parents" and contains poetic and affectionate sketches of his mother and father; the second is titled "i & their son." The final four, less pointedly autobiographical in the usual sense of the word, are an exploration of the relationship between the poet's values and his sense of personal identity, between what he believes and what he is.

ACHIEVEMENTS

E. E. Cummings is not usually included in the first rank of modernist poets, which always begins with T. S. Eliot, William Butler Yeats, and Ezra Pound and is, more often than not, rounded out with Wallace Stevens and William Carlos Williams. Two aspects of his career, however, give his achievement a great deal of significance. First, he was on the cutting edge of the modernist, experimental movement in verse. Pound, at the center of that movement, was dedicated to restoring value and integrity to the word by breaking the mold of the past, and in that cause, he evangelically admonished the poets of his generation to "make it new." Although a disciple of no one, Cummings led the assault on conventional verse, pushing experimentation to extremes and beyond with his peculiarly distinctive typography and his unconventional syntax, grammar, and punctuation. Although he paid the price of such experimentation, which brought charges of superficiality and unintelligibility, he served the modernist movement well by helping to educate an audience for the innovations in verse and prose of the second and third decades of the twentieth century.

Second, Cummings was not only a leading experimenter in an age of experimentation but also an intense lyric poet and an effective satirist. As a lyricist, he celebrated those experiences, values, and attitudes that lyric poets of all times have celebrated, and high on his list was love—sexual, romantic, and ideal or transcendental. His love poetry often reminds readers of Renaissance poets because of its subject matter, diction, and imagery. He is often bawdy, often sentimental, sometimes concrete, sometimes abstract, but almost always intense. Many of his lyrics express a childlike joy before nature and the natural state; he also celebrated personal relationships, particularly in his well-known tributes to his father and mother.

As a satirist, Cummings's principal target is man en

E. E. Cummings (Library of Congress)

masse. This thrust is the opposite of the celebration of individuality, a principal subject of his lyricism. In poems with a military setting, he satirically attacks not the military but the submergence of the individual into the mass that the military often brings about. He attacks the same submergence in poems that seem to be attacking modern advertising or salespeople. Neither, however, is the real object of his scorn; it is not modern advertising but the mass mind of the mass market that it engenders that he lashes out at in several of his most effective satiric pieces.

Cummings celebrates love, spontaneity, individuality, and a childlike wonder before nature. He attacks conformity, the mass mind, progress, and hypocrisy. His greatest achievement is that in an age of experimentation in verse, and in an age defensive and self-conscious about feeling, he fashioned a personal, highly idiosyncratic style that at its best provided him with effective vehicles for some of the finest lyric and satiric poetry of the modernist period.

Among the honors and awards he received were the *Dial* Award in 1925, Guggenheim Fellowships in 1933 and 1951, the Levinson Prize from *Poetry* magazine in 1939, the Shelley Memorial Award in 1945, the Academy of American Poets Fellowship in 1950, and a special citation by National Book Awards in 1955 for *Poems, 1923-1954*. He was awarded the Boston Arts Festival Award in 1957 and the Bollingen Prize for Poetry in 1958.

BIOGRAPHY

Edward Estlin Cummings was born in Cambridge, Massachusetts, on October 14, 1894, the first of two children born to Edward Cummings and Rebecca Haswell Clarke. His father was a Harvard graduate and lecturer, an ordained Unitarian minister, and pastor of the South Congregational Church from 1909 to 1925. Cummings received his degree magna cum laude from Harvard in 1915 and a Harvard M.A. the following year. A landmark in his career came in 1952 when he returned to Harvard to deliver the Charles Eliot Norton Lectures. Subsequently published as *i: six nonlectures*, all of which are highly personal and autobiographical, the first is of particular interest because of its affectionate, idealized portraits of his parents.

Cummings went to France in 1917 to join Norton Harje's Ambulance Corps. A combination of unfortunate and nearly ludicrous events led to his incarceration by the French authorities on suspicion of disloyalty. He and a friend were confined in a concentration camp at La Ferté Mace from late September through December, 1917. That experience is the subject matter of Cummings's first book, *The Enormous Room*, which has come to be regarded as a classic account of personal experience in World War I. Although prose, it launched the poet's career and, because of its style, set the tone and, implicitly, some of the basic themes that were to characterize the responses to his poetry for the next two decades. Before 1922, Cummings had published poems in the *Harvard Monthly*, in *The Dial*, and six poems in *Eight Harvard Poets*, but it was *The Enormous Room* that began his critical reputation. His first book of poems, *Tulips and Chimneys*, was published in 1923.

In 1923, Cummings moved to Patchin Place in New York City and lived there, spending the summers at his family's place in New Hampshire, until his death in 1962. Cummings traveled to Russia in 1931 and converted that experience into the second of his two major prose works, *Eimi*. In 1932, he married Marion Morehouse, a model, actress, and photographer. It was his third marriage and it survived. She died in 1969. The three decades Cummings spent with Marion and the nearly four decades at Patchin Place deserve emphasis in a biographical sketch because they provide a perspective that brings some balance to the poet's reputation as a bohemian enfant terrible. Although he never lost the cutting edge of his capacity to shock, he lived a relatively settled life devoted to painting and writing poetry.

ANALYSIS

Since E. E. Cummings rarely used titles, all those poems without titles will be identified by reference to the Index of First Lines in *Complete Poems, 1913-1962*. An analysis of Cummings's poetry turns, for the most part, on judgments about his innovative, highly idiosyncratic versification. Some of Cummings's critics have thought his techniques to be not only cheap and shallow tricks but also ultimately nonpoetic. There was, from the early stages of his career, general agree-

ment about his potential as a lyric and satiric poet. As that career developed through his middle and late periods, negative criticism of his verse diminished as affirmation grew. Although there always will be dissenting voices, the consensus for some time has been that his innovative verse techniques and his lyric and satiric talents were successfully blended in the best of his work.

"R-P-O-P-H-E-S-S-A-G-R"

Cummings wrote both free verse and conventional verse, particularly in the form of quatrains and sonnets. He also imposed on conventional verse the combination of typographical eccentricities and grammatical and syntactical permutations that constitute his distinctive hallmark. There is a considerable range between his most extreme free-verse poems, where the hallmark is superimposed, and his most conventional sonnets, where the hallmark is barely discernible. An example of the extreme is his "grasshopper" poem, "r-p-o-p-h-e-s-s-a-g-r," which is at the same time a masterpiece and a failure. The poem is a masterful blending of form and content, an achievement that might be described as pure technique becoming pure form. It fails as a poem, however, to move the reader or to matter very much except as a witty display of pyrotechnics. Its achievement, nevertheless, is a considerable one, and it serves as a useful model of one kind of poem for which Cummings is best known.

The poem "r-p-o-p-h-e-s-s-a-g-r" is structurally a free-verse poem in which Cummings employs many of his distinctive typographical devices. The word "grasshopper" occurs four times in the poem, its letters jumbled beyond recognition the first three times. The grasshopper's leap, capturing the essence of grasshoppers, brings its name into proper arrangement. Cummings also uses parentheses to break up words and to signal recombinations of letters and syllables resulting in conventional spelling, syntax, and meaning. At the literal and figurative center of the poem is the word "leaps," which links the first two versions of the word "grasshopper" to the final two, culminating in the resolution of the proper arrangement of letters. Cummings's diagonal typography for the word "leaps" is intended to render spatially, in the visual terms of a painter, the conceptual meaning of the word.

VISUAL EFFECTS

A poem of even less substance than "r-p-o-p-h-e-s-s-a-g-r," and therefore illustratively useful in the same way, is the "leaf-falling" poem "1(a." The four words of the poem, "a," "leaf," "falls," and "loneliness," are arranged along a vertical line with two or three letters or characters on each horizontal line, except for the final five of "iness." Thus, the poem begins with "1(a," with the rest of the poem directly below, two or three letters at a time, spaced out to suggest two triplets, set off by an opening, an intervening, and a closing single line. The use of the two parentheses, setting off "a leaf falls," actually helps in the reading of the poem. To the extent that the slender column of letters on the relatively vast whiteness of the page visually complements the theme of the poem, human loneliness engendered by the cyclical dying of the natural world in the fall of the year, Cummings has again succeeded in an effective union of form and content.

Other examples of this kind of verse are poems depicting a black, ragtime piano player ("ta"), a sunset ("stinging"), and a thunderstorm ("n(o)w/the"). The arrangement on the page of the portrait of the piano player is very much like that of "loneliness," as is the second half of the poem depicting a sunset by the sea. Cummings attempts in the thunderstorm poem to create visual effects to complement the conceptual meaning of the words "lightning" and "thunder." In one line, he states that the world "iS Slapped:with;liGhtninG"; thunder in the poems appears as "THuNdeR." These five poems represent some of Cummings's more effective uses of several of his most representative devices, particularly eccentric typography and spatial arrangement intended to create special visual effects. Often successful, these same devices at times fail completely, merely producing involved semantic puzzles hardly worth the effort necessary to solve them. More important, however, is the fact that the same features of versification exemplified by these poems of relatively little substance are to be found in his very best lyric and satiric poetry, the best of which stands between the highly eccentric versification of "r-p-o-p-h-e-s-s-a-g-r" and his relatively conventional uses of the sonnet form.

SONNETS

Cummings wrote many sonnets. A convenient sampling of his uses of the form is to be found in *Is 5*, which begins with five sonnets and closes with five. The first five are portraits or sketches of prostitutes and are among the few Cummings poems with titles—in this example, the respective names of each of the women. The subject matter of the final five sonnets of the collection, in sharp contrast to the portraits, is romantic love, and this set is more conventional than the portraits of the prostitutes. Cummings's best lyric poetry tends to be his more conventional verse: A comparative reading of the second and the tenth sonnets of *Is 5* will illustrate Cummings's mastery of conventional lyric forms.

Three observations can be made about the second sonnet of *Is 5*, the portrait of Mame ("Mame") and the tenth ("if I have made,my lady,intricate"). First, the former is a portrait of a prostitute, while the latter is addressed to "my lady." Second, Mame speaks in a Brooklyn dialect, such as "duh woild," "some noive," and "dat baby." What little quoted speech there is in "if I have made,my lady,intricate" is not dialect and would not be obtrusive in a Renaissance sonnet. Third, Mame's sonnet is relatively loose structurally, while my lady's is one of Cummings's most conventional. The loose structure of the former results largely from the dramatic presentation, particularly as it calls for the use of fragmented speech in dialect. Both sonnets are conventional syntactically, grammatically, and typographically. Formally and thematically, "if I have made,my lady,intricate" stands in dramatic contrast to "r-p-o-p-h-e-s-s-a-g-r." The sonnet is one of Cummings's better lyric poems, the best of which make use of the formal eccentricities of "r-p-o-p-h-e-s-s-a-g-r" in the poet's successful blending of traditional subject matter with his personally distinctive, modern verse forms.

LYRIC POETRY

Cummings's principal lyric subject matter is his celebration of romantic, sexual, and transcendental love and of the beauty, physical and spiritual, of lovers. A good example of a successful blend of his distinctive versification with a traditional lyric subject is "(ponder,darling,these busted statues." Formally, the poem might be thought of as standing near the middle of the range defined by the extremes of "r-p-o-p-h-e-s-s-a-g-r" and "if I have made,my lady,intricate." As such, it represents well the characteristics of Cummings's poetry. The blend of versification with a traditional subject is effective because of the appropriateness of the fragmented verse to the imagery of broken statuary and architectural ruins and of both to the poem's carpe diem theme.

The most obvious aspect of Cummings's distinctive verse is typographical, his sparse and erratic use of capitals and of parentheses. These particular details function in this poem of lyric substance to further understanding. Two sets of parentheses clearly delineate the three sections of the poem, the first and last being enclosed by them. The capitalization gives emphasis to the "Greediest Paws" of time and to the all-important "Horizontal" business. In addition to the typography, two examples of Cummings's manipulation of syntax also contribute to understanding his style: verse paragraphs 3 and 6. As with the typography, the unconventional syntax contributes to the unmistakable distinctiveness of Cummings's verse without in any way impeding the reader's comprehension and hence appreciation of the poem.

The poem "(ponder,darling,these busted statues" is the modern poet's address to the perennially coy mistress. As in Andrew Marvell's poem "To His Coy Mistress" (1650), the woman is asked to consider the mutability of all things and urged, since time passes irrevocably, to get on with meaningful "horizontal" business. Marvell's plea turns on his images of the grave and the desert of eternity. Cummings, the quintessential modern, stands with the woman among the architectural ruins of a past that must be not so much denied as ignored, or, at least, turned away from. Although it is a lesser poem than T. S. Eliot's *The Waste Land* (1922), it shares with that landmark of the modernist period the fragmented artifacts of the past. More important, Cummings, like Eliot, is addressing the fundamental question of their time: What does one do in the midst of such ruins? Cummings's answer, "make love," is direct, obvious, and highly ironic; it is not simply flippant and clever. The poet's urgent request to get on with the important horizontal business is one of the most traditional lyric responses to the overt awareness of mortality, one of humankind's principal talismans down through the centuries against the certainty of death.

The poems "somewhere i have never travelled,gladly beyond" and "you shall above all things be glad and young" provide good examples of Cummings's celebration of transcendental love. It should be noted that the categories, physical or sexual love and transcendental love, are not mutually exclusive. That is, nothing in "(ponder,darling,these busted statues" precludes the possibility that the lovers see something in each other deeper and more enduring than sex. However, it would be foolish to deny the sexual suggestiveness of the imagery of "somewhere i have never travelled,gladly beyond."

The poem "since feeling is first" is an explicit celebration of feeling, the wellspring of all lyricism. Examples of his affirmation of spontaneity, of nature, and of the natural and the childlike selves can be found in "when god lets my body be," "i thank You God for most this amazing," "in Just-," and "O sweet spontaneous." Cummings's intense tribute to his father, "my father moved through dooms of love," and his slight but moving poem for his mother, "if there are any heavens my mother will(all by herself)have," extend the range of lyric subject matter to include filial affection. The poem "anyone lived in a pretty how town" is Cummings's allegorical "everyman" which has a poignancy similar to that of Thornton Wilder's *Our Town* (1938).

These poems provide examples of Cummings's principal lyric subject matter. They also constitute a group useful for studying the formal variety found in some of his best poetry. Two of them, the poem on his father and "anyone lived in a pretty how town," are fairly conventional quatrains given a twist by Cummings's characteristic grammatical distortion: The parts of speech exchange roles. For example, the father moves "through griefs of joy" and sings "desire into begin." Everyman of "anyone lived in a pretty how town" "sang his didn't" and "danced his did." In general, the key to this special vocabulary, here and in other poems, is that the present, immediate, concrete, and spontaneous are being affirmed, while their opposites are being rejected. "Is" is superior to "was." The "dooms of feel" are to be celebrated; the "pomp of must and shall" scorned. In addition to these examples of Cummings's quatrains, this group also contains another of his fairly conventional sonnets, "i thank You God for most this amazing," and several free-verse poems, including "in Just-," and "O sweet spontaneous." As a group, they illustrate and support the generalization stated earlier that Cummings makes the most effective use of his distinctive devices in his more substantive lyric poetry.

Satiric poetry

Because satirists use lyricism to intensify their satirical thrusts, there is often no hard line between satiric and lyric poetry. The distinction for Cummings in particular is more a matter of emphasis than a clear-cut distinction. Because so much of his poetry is primarily satirical, however, it is profitable to consider several appropriate examples. It is also instructive to note that, as with his best lyric poetry, his best satiric pieces are those characterized by an effective blending of his distinctive devices with the resources of traditional verse. An excellent example of such blending and of the use of lyric intensity for satiric purposes is "i sing of Olaf glad and big."

The poem looks and even sounds like free verse. It is, however, an intricately constructed set of interlocking quatrains and couplets in four-stress lines. The loosening of what sounds like very regular verse is effected by the spacing on the page and by the counterpoint of sentence or sense structure against the verse structure. That tension between verse and sense is intensified by the characteristic use of parentheses and syntactical inversions. As in "(ponder,darling,these busted statues," the parentheses are used conventionally for humorous asides, as when readers are told that colonel left the scene "hurriedly to shave," and for emphasis, as in the passages on Olaf's knees and Christ's mercy. The syntactical inversions effectively provide emphasis and hardly impede understanding. The hyphenating of the word "object-or" catches the genius of Cummings's style at its best. The poem is about a conscientious objector who becomes an "object" in the hands of his fellow soldiers.

The satire is directed not at the military or against war, but at the lockstep, group mentality that, although fostered particularly by the military, may be found in the highly organized structures of all institutions: corporate, religious, academic. For Cummings, affirmation of the bravery of the individual places heavy emphasis on "individual," and it is the group, crowd, or gang that is being indicted. The irony of the closing lines strongly suggests that the military is but the protective arm of the nation or culture locked into value

systems symbolized by abstractions such as the nation's "blueeyed pride." Olaf, blond and blue-eyed, fits the abstraction, and hence his culpability is compounded. He was "blonder," however (that is, nearer the ideal of bravery and of manhood), than most and willing to pay lip service to the ideal, while others lose themselves in the false security of the crowd.

Two other satires set in the context of war but directed at more fundamental targets are "my sweet old etcetera" and "plato told." The first satirizes, in a light vein, attitudes very close to those of the soldiers of "i sing of Olaf glad and big." Aunts, sister, mother, and father all think war is glorious, while the soldier, who describes them, lies in the muddy trenches, thereby refuting the grandiose notions of those safe and comfortable at home. The satire "plato told" comes closest to being an indictment of war, but its focus is really on the obtuseness of "him," on his failure to understand what everyone has been telling him, which is that war is hell. All three of these "war" poems satirize a failure to see reality.

"Poem: Or, Beauty Hurts Mr. Vinal," one of Cummings's few titled poems, is a harsh but clever indictment of modern advertising and, implicitly, of the culture from which it derives. Cummings piles up actual lines from advertisements for garters, gum, shirt collars, drawers, Kodaks, and laxatives juxtaposed with fragments of lines from "America the Beautiful" and fragmented allusions to Robert Browning in the sixth verse paragraph. The poem makes fun of the glibness and excessive claims of advertising but then takes a turn toward the end to focus on Cummings's primary satiric target: men and women, "gelded" or "spaded," who have allowed themselves to be manipulated into anonymous units of the "market." Cummings makes the same point in one of his harshest sonnets, "a salesman is an it that stinks Excuse." Almost savage in tone, the poem once again links various seemingly incongruous activities in terms of the marketplace: the selling of "hate condoms education . . . democracy." The focus of Cummings's attack shifts from its ostensible targets—the military, advertising, and a salesman—to processes that rob people of their individuality and freedom of choice.

Cummings's innovative genius as a versifier, excessive in many of the lesser poems, is modified and restrained in his poems of substance, effecting in many of them happy unions of form and content. He is, as a result, a modernist poet of consequence.

OTHER MAJOR WORKS

PLAYS: *Him*, pb. 1927; *Tom: A Ballet*, pb. 1935; *Anthropos: The Future of Art*, pb. 1944; *Santa Claus: A Morality*, pb. 1946.

NONFICTION: *The Enormous Room*, 1922; *CIOPW*, 1931 (drawings); *Eimi*, 1933; *i: six nonlectures*, 1953; *Adventures in Value*, 1962 (photographs by Marion Morehouse).

TRANSLATION: *The Red Front*, 1933 (a selection of poems by Louis Aragon).

BIBLIOGRAPHY

Ahearn, Barry, ed. *Pound/Cummings: The Correspondence of Ezra Pound and E. E. Cummings*. Ann Arbor: University of Michigan Press, 1996. These interchanges cast light on both the poets and their times. Includes bibliographic references.

Bloom, Harold, ed. *E. E. Cummings*. Philadelphia: Chelsea House, 2003. A collection of essays on various aspects of the work and life of the poet Cummings.

Cowley, Malcolm. *A Second Flowering: Works and Days of the Lost Generation*. New York: Viking, 1973. Contains a chapter on Cummings that focuses on his life in the 1920's and 1930's. Discusses his philosophy and evaluates his poetry.

Dumas, Bethany K. *E. E. Cummings: A Remembrance of Miracles*. London: Vision Press, 1974. Contains a chapter on Cummings's life and several chapters analyzing his poetry, prose, and dramatic works. Includes a bibliography and indexes.

Flajšar, Jiří, and Zénó Vernyik, eds. *Words into Pictures: E. E. Cummings' Art Across Borders*. Newcastle, England: Cambridge Scholars, 2007. Contains essays examining Cummings's poetry and drama, particularly with respect to the limits of the linguistic, political, visual, and spatial vision of the poet.

Kennedy, Richard S. *Dreams in the Mirror: A Biography of E. E. Cummings*. New York: Liveright, 1980. A detailed, scholarly study of Cummings's life that discusses his poems and his philosophical views. Includes a chronological list of Cummings's works, a bibliographical essay on secondary works, an index, and illustrations.

_____. *E. E. Cummings Revisited*. New York: Twayne, 1994. Primarily an analysis of Cummings's major writings, it also provides a condensed version of his life interspersed with the analysis. Includes a chronology of the poet's life, a bibliography of works by and about him, an index, and numerous illustrations.

Kidder, Rushworth M. *E. E. Cummings: An Introduction to the Poetry*. New York: Columbia University Press, 1979. Kidder focuses on enduring values in Cummings's poetry. His commentaries are fresh and insightful, often correcting existing misconceptions. Includes a bibliography and indexes.

Lane, Gary. *I Am: A Study of E. E. Cummings' Poems*. Lawrence: University Press of Kansas, 1976. A good reference for new readers. Reprints selected poems, appending detailed discussions designed to make the obscure and complicated devices transparent. The critical apparatus features complete notes, an index, and a bibliographical note.

Sawyer-Lauçanno, Christopher. *E.E. Cummings: A Biography*. Naperville, Ill.: Sourcebooks, 2004. Massive in scope and in number of pages, this biography and literary study of Cummings is readable, comprehensive, and highly recommended.

Lloyd N. Dendinger

J. V. CUNNINGHAM

Born: Cumberland, Maryland; August 23, 1911
Died: Waltham, Massachusetts; March 30, 1985

PRINCIPAL POETRY
The Helmsman, 1942
The Judge Is Fury, 1947
Doctor Drink, 1950
Trivial, Vulgar, and Exalted: Epigrams, 1957
The Exclusions of a Rhyme: Poems and Epigrams, 1960

*To What Strangers, What Welcome: A Sequence of
    Short Poems*, 1964
Some Salt: Poems and Epigrams . . ., 1967
Selected Poems, 1971
*The Collected Poems and Epigrams of J. V.
    Cunningham*, 1971
The Poems of J. V. Cunningham, 1997

OTHER LITERARY FORMS

J. V. Cunningham wrote scholarly and critical essays on Statius, Geoffrey Chaucer, William Shakespeare, and Wallace Stevens, as well as on a number of other poets and aspects of poetry. He edited a literary anthology, *The Renaissance in England* (1966), and wrote commentaries on his own poetry under the titles *The Quest of the Opal: A Commentary on "The Helmsman"* (1950) and *The Journal of John Cardan: Together with "The Quest of the Opal" and "The Problem of Form"* (1964). The volume into which his prose was collected is extremely valuable in the study of his poetry, not only for his penetrating essays on style and form but also for his scholarly discussions of literary modes and periods, which cast light on his own poetic practice.

ACHIEVEMENTS

During the early 1930's, when J. V. Cunningham was composing the first of the poems that he later considered worth printing, T. S. Eliot and Ezra Pound were exerting a powerful influence on modern poetry. In many respects a literary maverick, Cunningham objected particularly to the growing disregard of poetic meter and to Archibald MacLeish's dictum that "A poem should not mean/ But be." While pursuing degrees at Stanford University and beginning his career as an English instructor, Cunningham wrote uncompromisingly metrical poems that always meant something. Although he taught in several leading universities, he achieved prominence as scholar and poet only on his appointment as chair of the English department at the young Brandeis University in Waltham, Massachusetts, in 1953; thereafter, he gained many honors: Guggenheim Fellowships in 1959 and 1967, a National Institute of Arts and Letters Award in 1965, and designation as only the second University Professor at Bran-

deis in 1966. He was awarded an Academy of American Poets Fellowship in 1976.

His highly disciplined, concise, and intellectual poetry won acknowledgment from literary scholars such as Yvor Winters and Denis Donoghue, as well as from the makers of many poetry anthologies. In addition, Cunningham's teaching influenced a younger generation of poets, particularly Alan Shapiro.

BIOGRAPHY

Although he was born in Cumberland, Maryland, in 1911, James Vincent Cunningham's earliest recollections were of Billings, Montana, where the family settled when he was about four years old. After growing up in Montana and in Denver, Colorado, and briefly attending St. Mary's College in Kansas, he earned his A.B. and Ph.D. at Stanford University, where he also taught English.

From 1945, when he achieved his doctorate, until 1953, he taught at the Universities of Hawaii, Chicago, and Virginia, publishing two books of poetry and a book on Shakespearean tragedy during this period. Recognition followed at Brandeis University, where Cunningham taught from 1953 until his retirement in 1982.

Married and divorced twice earlier, Cunningham was married to Jessie MacGregor Campbell in 1950. Following his appointment to Brandeis, the Cunninghams settled in Sudbury, Massachusetts, between Waltham and Worcester, where she taught English at Clark University. He died on March 30, 1985, at the age of seventy-three.

ANALYSIS

J. V. Cunningham's small but distinguished corpus of poetry (he preferred to call it verse) challenges many modern assumptions. In an age dominated by freer forms, he devoted himself to meter, fixed stanzas, and—more often than not—rhyme. His poems are taut, plain, and philosophical, with the feeling tightly controlled. The proportion of general statement to sensory detail is high, as is that of abstract words to concrete and imagistic language. Although he eschewed the self as the focus of lyric, he had a highly proprietary attitude toward his poems, insisting that they belonged essentially to him rather than to his readers. He appeared quite content to reach a relatively select readership capable of appreciating the subtlety and precision of his work. In both theory and practice, he went his own way, often in contradistinction to, sometimes in defiance of, the norms of twentieth century lyric.

THE COLLECTED POEMS AND EPIGRAMS OF J. V. CUNNINGHAM

As a scholar trained in the Greek and Latin classics and in English Renaissance poetry, he brought the predilections of his favorite literary periods to his own verse. His classicism emerges in a number of ways. Cunningham's favorite form, the epigram, was perfected in Latin by Martial in the first century C.E. and in English by Ben Jonson early in the seventeenth century. More than half the poems in *The Collected Poems and Epigrams of J. V. Cunningham* are termed epigrams, while a number of others have epigrammatic qualities. Although he called only one of his poems an ode, a number of others fall within the tradition of the Horatian ode. He frequently imitates—or rather seeks English equivalents for—Latin stanzas and meters. It is no accident that his favorite stanzas, like those of Horace in his odes, are quatrains, sometimes with the contours and movement of the Roman poet's Alcaic meter, and couplets, which were Martial's and Jonson's preferred way of rendering the terse and witty statements of epigram.

Another aspect of his classicism is his fondness for Latin titles such as "Agnosco Veteris Vestigia Flammae" (I recognize the traces of an old flame), "Timor Dei" (the fear of God), and "Lector Aere Perennior." The last of these illustrates his penchant for allusion, as it appropriates a famous Horatian phrase about poetry being a monument more lasting than bronze and applies it to the *lector*, the reader of the poetry. Wittily manipulating a Latin commonplace about the fame of poets, some basic concepts of medieval Scholasticism, and Pythagoras's theory of the transmigration of souls, Cunningham argues that the poet's immortality inheres not in the poet, who, except as a name, is forgotten, but in the reader—in each successive reader for whom the poem comes to life again. Adapting phrases from Horace is one of his favorite ploys. Horace wrote *odi profanum vulgus* ("I hate the common crowd"); Cun-

ningham, "I like the trivial, vulgar, and exalted." He also appropriates the old but relatively rare Latinate word *haecceity*, meaning "thisness," to express his own theory that the preoccupation with any particular "this" is evil.

Often, he takes advantage of Latin roots to extend meaning. One of his lines in "All Choice Is Error"— "Radical change, the root of human woe!"— reminds the reader that "radical" means root. His poem "Passion" requires for its full effect an awareness that *patior* (whose past participle, *passus*, provides the basis of the English word) means "suffer," that *patior* is a passive verb (he calls passion "love's passive form"), and that the medieval derivation *passio* was used not only in theological discourse, referring to Christ's suffering, but also in philosophical discourse, to indicate that which is passive or acted on. Sometimes his employment of etymology is very sly, as in his phrase "mere conservative," where, clued by his awareness that "conservative" is an honorific to Cunningham, the reader benefits from knowing that *merus* means "pure," a fact now obscured by the English adjective's having changed from meaning "nothing less than" to "nothing more than."

Classical poets also manipulated syntax for emphasis in ways that are not always available to English poets, but Cunningham plays the sentence against the line variously, using enjambments in such poems as "Think" and "Monday Morning" to throw into striking relief words that might otherwise be obscured. He is fond of classical syntactical figures such as chiasmus. "So he may discover/ As Scholar truth, sincerity as lover" exhibits this reversal of word order in otherwise parallel phrases. It might be noted that Cunningham shares with many free-verse poets a liking for visually arresting enjambments and displacements; he differs primarily in adjusting them to the formal demands of meter.

What might be called Jonsonian neoclassicism favors poets such as Horace and Martial, who treat of their subjects in a cool and somewhat impersonal tone, carefully regulating—though not abjuring—feeling and striving for the general import of their subjects. Readers of Jonson's lyrics will recall his poem "On My First Son," which illustrates these traits well, though dealing with a heartrending experience, the death of a young son. Jonson generates not only a quiet but unmistakable sense of grief and resentment but also a corrective admonition against the moral dangers of selfishness and presumption in lamenting such a common occurrence too much. Cunningham's "Consolatio Nova" (new consolation), on the death of his publisher and champion, Alan Swallow, exhibits many of the same virtues. It generalizes, and no feeling overflows, but the careful reader sees that the loss is a specific and deeply felt one. A similarly quiet tone and controlled feeling mark "Obsequies for a Poetess."

A scholar himself, Jonson would have appreciated "To a Friend, on Her Examination for the Doctorate in English" and, except for the feminine pronoun and the latter-day degree, would have recognized in the title a perfectly appropriate theme for a poem, for in both classical and neoclassical Renaissance poetry, friendship rivaled love as a theme. "The Aged Lover Discourses in the Flat Style" is also Jonsonian from its title onward, Cunningham even adapting to his own sparer person some of Jonson's physical description in "My Picture Left in Scotland." The modern poet's fine "To My Wife," though more paradoxical than Jonson was as a rule, illustrates well the classical restraint in dealing with love. It is a poem of four quatrains in cross-rhymed tetrameter, the first two presenting images of landscape and the seasons, the last two modulating to quiet statement dominated by abstractions: terror, delight, regret, anger, love, time, grace.

Two more reputed classical virtues are simplicity and brevity. At first glance, Cunningham's poems do not seem unfailingly simple, for although the language itself is not notably difficult, the thought is often complex and usually highly compressed. Cunningham displays no urge to embellish or amplify, however, and his assessment of his own style as plain or "flat" is accurate. Brevity can test the reader's comprehension, and brevity is the very essence of Cunningham's poetic. Of the 175 original poems and epigrams in his collected verse, the longest is thirty-six lines, and many are much shorter. It is a small book for a man who wrote poetry for more than forty years. The classical model here is perhaps Vergil, traditionally thought to be happy with a daily output of an acceptable line or two. For Cunning-

ham, the perfection of a lyric outshines any number of diamonds in the rough.

THE FOLLY OF PARTICULARITY

Although Cunningham's classically inspired challenge to modern poetry was thoroughgoing and persistent, he did modify it over his career. He disapproved vigorously of poetry that merely recounts experience or indulges in emotion, and his early poems in particular concentrate on interpreting experience and subduing emotion. An early poem, "All Choice Is Error," sets forth a conviction that because choice signifies not merely the preference of one thing for another but also the rejection of all other possibilities, choice must be seen as evil, even if it is necessary evil. Choices restrict life, and the habit of favoring particularities in verse—a habit of twentieth century poets, in Cunningham's view—is an especially lamentable habit. This poem develops the theme with reference to lovers' traditional fondness for carving their initials on such surfaces as tree trunks provide. Since there can be few people who have not reflected on the folly of thus publicizing a choice that all too soon may look silly or embarrassing, it is a clever motif to illustrate his point about the folly of particularity. The poem celebrates time and the elements, which smooth the lovers' initials. What remains is recognizable as love, but the specificity of the lovers is happily lost.

"Haecceity" carries this theme further. It is a more philosophical poem, based on the argument that the actualization of any possibility is the denial of all other possibilities. Cunningham knows that people must make choices and that morally it may be better to choose one thing over another, but at the same time, choice is inherently evil because of the exclusions it necessitates. A consequence of this conviction that to restrict any general possibility to one manifestation constitutes evil is that any particular poem setting forth this idea is evil, a paradox that Cunningham does not hesitate to admit.

Because humans have a fundamental urge to carry out choices, to achieve particularity, and because all choices are equally denials of the remaining possibilities, on what basis is choice to be made? Cunningham, struck by the arbitrary and even despairing nature of many human choices, reasoned that carefully considered judgments would assure the best, or least damaging, decisions. He came to doubt reason's capacity to best emotion, however, particularly since the latter is more likely to enlist the assistance of religion. (Cunningham was reared a Roman Catholic and gave up all religious beliefs in his maturity, but he realized that his early religious training continued to influence his imagination, and references to Catholic doctrine appear in some of his mature poems.) In his commentary *The Quest of the Opal*, Cunningham discusses the poems he wrote in his attempts to escape the consequences of his theory of the evil of particularity. Although his intellectual search bore little fruit, some interesting poems, including "Summer Idyll," "Autumn," and "The Wandering Scholar," resulted.

"THE HELMSMAN"

Meanwhile, Cunningham was discovering a more satisfying way of dealing with experience in "The Helmsman." He had been much interested in Horace's ode 1.9, in which the poet describes Mount Soracte under its cap of snow and then modulates to his frequent theme of carpe diem, or "seize the day," embodied in a celebration of young love. Cunningham hoped to imitate the way Horace's images delicately implied the theme rather than merely exemplifying it. "The Helmsman," a poem about "the voyage of the soul . . ./ Through age to wisdom," imitated Horace procedurally as well as formally. It builds on memories and disappointments along the way, asserting the need to strike out on one's own, ever alert lest he slip and drown like Vergil's Palinurus in the fifth book of the *Aeneid* (c. 29-19 B.C.E.; English translation, 1553). Wisdom "comes like the ripening gleam of wheat" to this voyager, "flashing like snakes underneath the haze." In the second half of the poem, the imagery imitates that of another Horatian ode, 1.7, in which Teucer, an ancient king of Troy, prepares festively for a dangerous voyage with his cohorts. Security is only an illusion: The wheat may not ripen, the voyage may come to naught. The voyager must acknowledge the possibility of defeat but not flag in his pursuit.

AUTOBIOGRAPHICAL THEMES

By his own admission, Cunningham's poetry was becoming more autobiographical, although hardly in the manner of, for example, Robert Lowell. The closing poem of the second group in *The Collected Poems and Epigrams of J. V. Cunningham* draws on recollections of the landscape of his childhood. "Montana Pastoral" is a good example of Cunningham's ability to revive old modes by unexpected departures from convention. Over the centuries, poets have rung many changes on pastoral, turning Theocritus's and Vergil's shepherds into other rural types, into pastors in the ecclesiastical sense (John Milton's "Lycidas") or even into denizens of Lewis Carroll's *Alice's Adventures in Wonderland* (1865), as William Empson has suggested in *Some Versions of Pastoral* (1935). Cunningham's speaker can find no evidence of the supposed pastoral virtues in the wild and bleak Montana landscape. More precisely, the poem is an antipastoral, gaining its effect by holding out in its title the perennially attractive promise of the simpler, more wholesome life but then detailing briskly and briefly the harshness of the land.

INNOVATIONS

Cunningham found other ways of being new. He experimented with meters, including syllabic ones freer than most free verse in all but line lengths. "Think," for example, uses a seven-syllable line with three variously placed stresses per line, while "Monday Morning" uses a nine-syllable line with four stresses per line. In his essay "How Shall a Poem Be Written?" Cunningham cites precedents for such types of syllabic lines, although chiefly ten-syllable ones, in Thomas Wyatt, John Donne, and Sir Philip Sidney. In the eighth poem of his *To What Strangers, What Welcome* sequence, he tries blank-verse tetrameter, extremely rare in English poetry.

TO WHAT STRANGERS, WHAT WELCOME

It is tempting to read this sequence autobiographically. The earlier of the fifteen short poems take a traveler westward in the United States. Along the white lines of highways and barbed-wire fences, past tumbleweed and locoweed, the speaker wends his way. He stops in Las Vegas, takes in gaming and shows unenthusiastically, and finally passes through desert to the land of redwood trees and the Pacific surf. In the eleventh poem, the speaker turns back toward the East and, after more desert, prairie, and "stonewalled road," is found at the end relaxing in New England. The poems also allude to a love affair, although rather obscurely.

While the nominal subject of the sequence is a transcontinental automobile trip, it may perhaps be read also as a telescopic account of Cunningham's career. Born in Maryland, he went west to Montana and Colorado with his family, received most of his higher education at Stanford University (not far from the redwoods and closer yet to the surf), and, after teaching mostly at points intermediate, gravitated to New England, specifically to Brandeis University in Massachusetts, where he received the swift academic preferment that had been denied him everywhere else and where he remained for the duration of his working life. The title of the sequence—an ironic twist on the western "welcome, stranger"—becomes more ironic if one reads into it a kind of career résumé, since by far the heartiest welcome Cunningham ever received was in that urban, New England university under Jewish auspices. It must be noted, however, that the sequence does not end triumphantly but in a series of questions about identity, as if "what welcome?" remains a query without an answer.

There is much more description and concrete detail than in Cunningham's earlier poetry. He seems more inclined to imply, rather than state, his theme. The "I" of the sequence is more like the first person in the work of his autobiographical or confessional contemporaries in verse, more often found in the midst of specific, yet offhand, experiences: "I drive Westward," "I write here," "I go moseying about." It is impossible to find, difficult to imagine, Cunningham "moseying" in his earlier poetry. The footloose sequence raises a series of questions about love, fulfillment, identity. While it does not appear to answer any of them, the tone is that of a modern man responding dryly and sarcastically to Walt Whitman, the ingenuous traveler of the open road, who reveled not only in the redwoods but also in their destruction by men determined to rival them in grandeur. Cunningham's road, with its boundaries of interminable white lines and barbed wire, speaks of a land whose greatness remains but whose lack of hospitality looms, and man no longer seems commensurate with it, save in degree of unfriendliness.

To What Strangers, What Welcome confirms what careful readers of Cunningham's verse had surely already recognized: that he was very much a man of his own time, a man whose poetic theory was in no danger of turning into a pale imitation of a Roman of the Empire or an Englishman of the age of Elizabeth I. Not only in subject matter but also in form, he seemed to be edging closer to the prevailing poetry of his time. His verse in the sequence is measured but flexible and untrammeled.

Despite his sometimes intransigent defiance of the poets in Whitman's train, Cunningham objected to vers libre far less than to the assumption, unfortunately still common among its advocates, the meter is passé and that free forms constitute the only defensible mode of poetry in the later twentieth century. Despite the strictness of so much of his practice, he conceded that much modern verse is also metrical, for it departs from, often returns to, and inevitably is measured against, meter as a norm. His attitude in this respect does not differ greatly from that of another strict metrist, Robert Frost, who also loved classical poetry, found the limitations of traditional forms an irresistible challenge, and even suspected free-verse poets of unacknowledged but nevertheless recurrent iambic tendencies.

EPIGRAMS

The epigrams, which are found at the end of his collection of original poetry, are more regular. They represent poems both early and late in his career and are the best exemplars of his fondness for wit, brevity, and a cool and often satirical tone. That they are also twentieth century poems is evident from the titles that some of them bear: "With a Detective Story," "History of Ideas," "For a College Yearbook," "New York: 5 March 1957," "Towards Tucson." In short, they are full of subjects, concepts, and attitudes unimaginable to Martial, Ben Jonson, or Walter Savage Landor. There are some for which Latin equivalents might have been composed two thousand years ago, but only because they are about universal types and habits.

The epigrams are about love, drink, music, grief, wisdom, illusion, calculus, Freudianism, and many other things. They vary considerably in tone: reflective, cynical, sardonic, risqué, indecent, smug, earnest. They contain lapses in taste and judgment, but virtually all of them display an alert intelligence. Writing in an age not very interested in the epigram, Cunningham proves its durability and his right to be considered with the masters of this ancient form. A free-verse epigram would be a contradiction in terms; thus, to deny the legitimacy of Cunningham's art is to deny the possibility of the contemporary epigram.

POETRY IN TRANSLATION

The Collected Poems and Epigrams of J. V. Cunningham concludes with twenty-one translations of classical, medieval, and Renaissance Latin poems. Like the epigrams, these poems were written over many years. The most rollicking is his translation of "The Confession of Bishop Golias," attributed to the Archpoet of Cologne, a twelfth century figure. The finest, however, are of classical Latin poetry.

One might suppose that by the twentieth century, no one would be able to find a new way to render Catullus's famous couplet "Odi et amo," but Cunningham succeeded in finding a new equivalent for its final word, *excrucior*. This poem is about the lover who does not know why he both hates and loves his girl but feels it and is "tormented" or "tortured," as translators usually have it. Cunningham concludes with "I feel it and am torn." His choice, simpler and yet more graphic, is certainly justified, for the cross (*crux*, from which *excrucior* derives) tore the flesh of the crucified as the conflicting emotions tear Catullus's lover's psyche.

Cunningham also translated the Mount Soracte ode of Horace, whose procedure he found so instructive. Somewhat more formal and literal than other modern versions, his translation avoids the casual, even flippant, effect of those who bend over backward to avoid sounding archaic and bookish and, as a result, answers to the dignity of Horace's theme:

> Tomorrow may no man divine.
> This day that Fortune gives set down
> As profit, nor while young still
> Scorn the rewards of sweet dancing love,
>
> So long as from your flowering days
> Crabbed age delays.

Why Cunningham did not choose to translate more of Horace for publication is a nagging question; surely few writers have been as well qualified to do this poet justice.

In one of his most valuable critical essays, Cunning-

ham discusses his translation of Statius's poem on sleep. By reviving a comparison first made in the late nineteenth century by the great Latin scholar J. W. Mackail between the Latin poem and William Wordsworth's sonnet "To Sleep," Cunningham establishes six points of contrast between the poetry of Horace, Vergil, Statius, and many modern poets, on one hand, and William Wordsworth, along with many medieval and Tudor lyric poets, on the other. The first has to do with the relative complexity of the meter that was used by the earlier group, the second with the playing off of syntax against meter, which the medieval-Tudor group seldom did. The earlier group determined the length of the poem relatively freely, while the later group worked with a fixed idea of length. The earlier group did not match thought units to formal divisions, whereas the later group did. The paraphrasable meaning of the early group is implicit, of the later group explicit. Conceptually, the earlier group's poems exhibit continuity and degree, while the later group's are more likely to show discontinuity, identity, and contradiction. The reader must consult the essay "Classical and Medieval: Statius on Sleep" for clarification and exemplification of these differences.

What is important to see is that the group referred to above as the earlier includes not only Roman poets of antiquity but also many modern poets. According to Cunningham, the tendency of the English lyric over the centuries has been from the medieval-Tudor practice to that best exemplified by Horace, Vergil, and Statius. Far from carrying on warfare with these modern poets, whom Cunningham does not name but who surely include T. S. Eliot, Wallace Stevens, and presumably even William Carlos Williams, together with their followers in contemporary poetry, Cunningham in effect finds these moderns to be classical in a number of important ways. In his own translation of Statius's poem, he employs the now unfashionable form of blank verse, but he has clearly attempted to achieve the six qualities that he has designated as at once classical and modern. The translation ends:

> If this long night some lover
> In his girl's arms should willingly repel thee,
> Thence come, sweet Sleep! Nor with all thy power

Pour through my eyes—so may they ask, the many,
More happy—: touch me with thy wand's last tip,
Enough, or lightly pass with hovering step.

He has not declared a truce with modern poetry, and his diction will not impress many readers as typically modern, but in at least some respects, his verse and that of his contemporaries attain peaceful coexistence.

OTHER MAJOR WORKS

NONFICTION: *The Quest of the Opal: A Commentary on "The Helmsman,"* 1950; *Woe or Wonder: The Emotional Effect of Shakespearean Tragedy,* 1951; *Tradition and Poetic Structure: Essays in Literary History and Criticism,* 1960; *The Journal of John Cardan: Together with "The Quest of the Opal" and "The Problem of Form,"* 1964; *The Collected Essays of J. V. Cunningham,* 1976.

EDITED TEXTS: *The Problem of Style,* 1966; *The Renaissance in England,* 1966; *In Shakespeare's Day,* 1970.

BIBLIOGRAPHY

Cunningham, J. V. Interview by Timothy Steele. *Iowa Review* 15 (Fall, 1985): 1-24. In this delightful and revealing look at Cunningham's life and ideas about poetry, the poet describes writing poetry as a "professional task," not a mystical act. He defends the practice of meter and abhors its decline in recent poetry.

Kerrigan, William. "J. V. Cunningham's Meditation on Method." *Sewanee Review* 109, no. 1 (Winter, 2001): 65. Praises Cunningham as the greatest writer of English epigrams since Ben Jonson.

Pinsky, Robert. "Two Examples of Poetic Discursiveness." *Chicago Review* 27 (Fall, 1975): 133-141. Pinsky sees Cunningham's "discursiveness" as a positive quality. It is "concise and accurate" and without the usual poetic devices of imagery and irony. He claims that this leads to poetry that has the power and authority found in Ben Jonson's poetry.

Rathmann, Andrew. Review of *The Poems of J. V. Cunningham.* *Chicago Review* 43, no. 3 (Summer, 1997): 107-103. Rathmann gives a critical analysis of Cunningham's work and laments the fact that Cunningham is not more widely known despite the admiration of many contemporary poet-critics.

Shapiro, Alan. "'Far Lamps at Night': The Poetry of J. V. Cunningham," and "The Early Seventies and J. V. Cunningham." In *In Praise of the Impure: Poetry and the Ethical Imagination: Essays, 1980-1991.* Evanston, Ill.: TriQuarterly Books, 1993. Shapiro, a former student of Cunningham at Brandeis University, believes that Cunningham deserves to be more "highly esteemed." He analyzes a few poems and shows that Cunningham did not blindly follow traditions but set his poetry against them to create a fruitful intertextuality.

Stall, Lindon. "The Trivial, Vulgar, and Exalted: The Poems of J. V. Cunningham." *Southern Review* 9 (Spring, 1973): 1044-1048. Stall claims that Cunningham's "intelligibility" is responsible for his lack of fame. Stall states that Cunningham has restored the epigram to seriousness and brought that ancient form a new power.

Stein, Robert A. "The Collected Poems and Epigrams of J. V. Cunningham." *Western Humanities Review* 27 (Fall, 1973): 23-25. An evenhanded review of Cunningham's poems. Stein states flatly that Cunningham has written some great poems. He also sees some liabilities, especially Cunningham's use of too many clever paradoxes.

Robert P. Ellis

D

PHILIP DACEY

Born: St. Louis, Missouri; May 9, 1939

PRINCIPAL POETRY

The Beast with Two Backs, 1969
Fist, Sweet Giraffe, the Lion, Snake, and Owl, 1970
Four Nudes, 1971
How I Escaped from the Labyrinth, and Other Poems, 1977
The Boy Under the Bed, 1979
The Condom Poems, 1979
Gerard Manley Hopkins Meets Walt Whitman in Heaven, and Other Poems, 1982
Fives, 1984
The Man with Red Suspenders, 1986
The Condom Poems II, 1989
Night Shift at the Crucifix Factory, 1991
What's Empty Weighs the Most: Twenty-four Sonnets, 1997
The Deathbed Playboy, 1999
The Adventures of Alixa Doom, and Other Love Poems, 2003
The Mystery of Max Schmitt: Poems on the Life and Work of Thomas Eakins, 2004
Mr. Five-by-five, 2005
Three Shades of Green: Poems of Fatherhood, 2006
The New York Postcard Sonnets: A Midwesterner Moves to Manhattan, 2007
Vertebrae Rosaries: Fifty Sonnets, 2009

OTHER LITERARY FORMS

Philip Dacey has coedited two anthologies, the influential *Strong Measures: Contemporary American Poetry in Traditional Forms* (1986) with David Jauss and *I Love You All Day, It Is That Simple* (1970) with Gerald M. Knoll. In his first years at Southwest State University, from 1971 to 1976, he edited the literary journal *Crazy Horse*, in 1974 contributing an interview

with Robert Wilbur that would influence his own writing. In addition to expressing his fascination with Walt Whitman in his own poetry, Dacey explored the poet's life and character in a play in the first issue of *Mickle Street Review*, published in 1979 by the Walt Whitman House Association.

ACHIEVEMENTS

Philip Dacey's major career awards include a Woodrow Wilson Fellowship (1961), the New York YM-YWHA Poetry Center Discovery Award (1974), two National Endowment for the Arts Fellowships (1975 and 1980), two Minnesota State Arts Board Fellowships (1975 and 1983), a Bush Foundation Fellowship (1977), the Loft-McKnight Fellowship (1984), and a Fulbright lectureship in Yugoslavia (1988).

Dacey began winning awards for his poetry early in his career. Honors include the Yankee Poetry Prize in 1968, the Poet and Critic Prize in 1969, and the Borestone Mountain Poetry Award in 1974. He took first prize in the G. M. Hopkins Memorial Sonnet Competition in 1977 and first prizes in poetry awarded by the literary magazines *Prairie Schooner* and *Kansas Quarterly* in 1977 and 1980, respectively. Dacey won Pushcart Prizes in 1977 and 1982. He also received the Edwin Ford Piper Award from the University of Iowa Press in 1990, the Carolyn Kizer Poetry Prize from *Poetry Northwest* in 1991, and the Flyway Literary Award for Poetry from Iowa State University in 1997. He won the Peace Corps Writers Poetry Award in 2000 for *The Deathbed Playboy*, the International Merit Award from *Atlanta Review* in 2003 for "From the Front," and the $1000 Turning Point Prize from WordTech Communications, Cincinnati, in 2004 for *The Mystery of Max Schmitt*.

Dacey's poem "The Birthday" was set to music by David Sampson and performed at Carnegie-Mellon Institute in 1982. His long poem "The Musician" was set to music by Elizabeth Alexander for the American Master Chorale and received its debut performance in 1994 with the Wisconsin Chamber Orchestra at the First Congregational Church of Madison. The Southwest Minnesota Orchestra and Chorus in 2003 performed his poem "Ear Abounding," arranged by Robert Whitcomb.

Dacey played an important role in the New Formalism movement in American poetry. His interview with Wilbur, the poet considered central to the revival of formalism in American poetry, and the anthology *Strong Measures* helped solidify the movement.

BIOGRAPHY

Philip Dacey spent his early years in Missouri and graduated from St. Louis University in 1961. He served in the U.S. Peace Corps, teaching high school in eastern Nigeria from 1963 to 1965. He married Florence Chard in 1963. The marriage, which ended in 1986, produced two sons and one daughter. After his Peace Corps experience, Dacey served as an instructor at Miles College in Birmingham, Alabama, in 1966, and earned his M.A. in 1967 from Stanford University. He then returned to St. Louis to serve as an instructor in English at the University of Missouri until 1968. In 1970, he joined the faculty of the department of English at Southwest State University in Marshall, Minnesota, and served jointly as professor of English and coordinator of creative writing through 1990. One of his most significant publications while at Southwest State University was an interview with poet Wilbur, published in the fall, 1974, issue of *Crazy Horse*. Wilbur's ideas about traditional poetics would heavily influence Dacey's eventual turn toward poetic formalism.

Dacey served as distinguished poet-in-residence at Wichita State University in 1985 and was awarded residencies by the Corporation of Yaddo and the Ragdale Foundation, also in the 1980's. In 2003, he served as Eddice B. Barber Visiting Writer at Minnesota State University at Mankato.

Long active in arts organizations, Dacey was founder and director of the Minnesota Writers' Festival in 1978, and founder and director in 1986 and 1989 of the Marshall Festivals. He served as member of the arts review board for the Minnesota School and Resource Center for the Arts in 1988. In December, 2004, he and his partner, Alixa Doom, moved from Minnesota to New York's Upper West Side.

Dacey has given numerous readings from his own works, not only in the United States but also in Ireland, Yugoslavia, and Mexico. In 1992, he founded the performance trio Strong Measures with his sons, Emmett and Austin, combining poetry and music.

ANALYSIS

Although Philip Dacey initially nursed the ambition of becoming a novelist, he early realized that his talent was better adapted to a considerably shorter form. His poetry is often marked by a witty approach to those most personal of matters, love and sex. Even so, some of the sensibility of the novelist can be detected in his preoccupation with historical figures, who become major characters in his poems. Many of his quasi-biographical yet imaginative poems have focused on Gerard Manley Hopkins and Walt Whitman. He has also turned his eye toward painter Thomas Eakins.

In his poetry, Dacey has consistently pursued an interest in poetic form. This focus may have helped him overcome difficulties he has faced in establishing his personal voice as a poet. Many of his works have suffered from an incomplete command of tone, especially noticeable when he takes a more humorous approach to his subjects.

His greatest accomplishments have tended to fall within two distinct areas. His early, somewhat haphazard pursuit of a poetry of sexuality and love has matured through the years into a more reflective approach to personal matters, as represented by such works as "North Broadway & Grand." His imaginative poems, taking the point of view of such characters as Whitman and Hopkins, often seem to spring from the same font of inspiration as these more overtly personal poems.

Distinct from these are Dacey's works of a more purely imaginative nature, in which accidents of phraseology or the incongruities of contemporary life have inspired poems of a nearly absurdist nature. The accidents and incongruities serve as the building blocks of a fabricated, artificial reality, as in the poems "The Shopping List," "Four Men in a Car," and "Serenade." These works immediately and unabashedly reveal themselves to the reader as artifice and display Dacey's talent for witty and entertaining verse.

"THE SLEEP"

Dacey's 1977 Pushcart Prize-winning poem "The Sleep," a delicately balanced poem about the sexual act, approaches its subject through evocation rather than description: "The limbs begin to believe in their gravity./ The dark age of faith begins, a god below/

Draws down the body, he wants it/ And we are flattered." In the last of its three sections, the poem compares the point of sexual climax with a kind of departure. "Already we are forgetting/ Where we were/ And left from." Despite being a poem about so intense an experience, the language of the poem has a flattened and perhaps even melancholy feel to it. This may suit the poem's secondary subject, for it is also a poem offered in memory of poet Anne Sexton.

THE MAN WITH RED SUSPENDERS

The reflective and highly personal poem "North Broadway & Grand" acts as a preface to *The Man with Red Suspenders*. Also a memorial, it is addressed to Dacey's brother Owen, who was "the Dancing Policeman of St. Louis," and to the memory of their late sister Joan. The poet immediately connects the strands of their separate lives in the opening lines: "O, when she died/ he was the traffic cop/ again." The poet describes Owen as being present, at least symbolically, at Joan's death:

> only this time he was there
> at the crossroads
>
> to lead her home,
> his sister, through
> the deepening dark,
> no light but that
>
> of his presence

The poem ends with what seems to be an official statement of Owen's abilities as traffic cop: He could direct moving traffic at the city's worst intersection, where even traffic-guidance machines had failed before him. The poet ascribes Owen's unusual success to a purely human element.

> Put Dacey in. And the human
> touch eased
> the knot, jam, block,
> and everyone got home
> safe, everyone.

"North Broadway & Grand" is a poem of reassurance, offering a vision of a loved one's death eased by the "human touch."

Numerous poems in *The Man with Red Suspenders*

owe more to imagination than to experience, and often seem to play more on shallow expectation than worldly wisdom. "The Hitchhiker" speaks from the point of view of a figure apparently intent on being sheerly contrary: "If you are light,/ I am dark./ If you are clean/ I have grease/ on my knapsack." The short lines emphasize the brittle tension created by the intrusion of an unwanted presence in a private car. At the end of the poem, the discomfort prevails, for the hitchhiker switches places with the driver.

In "Dialing a Wrong Number," Dacey creates a second-person figure, possibly a male, who has found himself talking with the wrong person on the telephone, despite having taken precautions against this: "You know you have dialed/ the right number./ You were careful." The person who answers is both the wrong person and the right one: "She says she gets nothing these days/ but wrong numbers/ and has come to need them." The unintended connection becomes, by the end of the poem, yet another hoped-for connection that may never happen again.

"The Shopping List" takes a more decisive step toward imaginary circumstances. The first-person speaker of the poem is immersed in a dreamlike experience, in which he cannot make the items on his shopping list correspond to the items he takes off the shelf. The reader comes to presume the speaker is male because of what he finds when he turns: "I U-turn into the next/ aisle and find women on display,/ parts and whole,/ frozen or fresh." When he makes this turn, not only the store but his shopping list, too, changes. "Now every item/ refers to women./ My mother is on the list/ and my sister." In plain, unadorned language, the poem moves the reader through a dreamlike shopping experience toward a vision of an empty soul full of yearning, lost among other lost souls: ". . . the store opens/ onto a vast plain./ People walk there,/ as if forever,/ shopping for nothing."

Other poems in the collection, such as "Someone," "He Restricts Himself to Reading One Poem a Day," and "Waiting for the Mail," take a similar approach in conjuring up an image or idea with some element of strangeness about it, and developing that image or idea in the manner of a narrative. All share a flatness of imagery and plainness of style, as if nonpoetic diction might lend a sense of reality to these episodes of unreality.

Perhaps appropriately, the sense of unreality is most pronounced in the title poem, "The Man with Red Suspenders," which is presented as a kind of improvisation on a theme suggested by a moment in a writing class. A teacher's comment, that "you can't write a story about a man with red suspenders," inspires the subsequent series of playful comments. It begins, "I am the man with red suspenders,/ alive in this poem./ For years I wandered from short story to short story,/ seeking admittance." The poem self-consciously embraces an artificial situation and remains at the level of simple artifice through to its end: "I am as pleased as Punch/ to be here."

THE DEATHBED PLAYBOY

The title poem, "The Deathbed Playboy," is a long narrative poem detailing the interaction between a son and father at the latter's deathbed. The father has requested a copy of *Playboy* magazine. The son supplies the copy and watches his father examining it, but he wonders if he had misheard his father. Regardless of whether or not his father had actually asked for the magazine, the son comes to the conclusion that bringing it was an appropriately life-giving and affirmative act at that near-death moment.

Although the writing has a relaxed, unconstrained feel, the poem is written in iambic pentameter, with end-rhymes arranged in a quatrain pattern. The overall poem is not broken into quatrains, however, but into larger sections with varied numbers of lines. The end-rhymes, often being slant rhymes, are unobtrusive.

A second notable long poem in iambic pentameter, with slant-rhymed couplets, appears in this collection: "Harry Stafford: Whitman at Timber Creek" presents a narrative of a young man caring for an older one. In this case, the first-person narrator, Harry Stafford, is looking after "a famous poet, taken ill." In caring for and observing Whitman, who to a great degree oversees his own recovery through highly idiosyncratic rest and recreation, Harry plants within himself the seeds for what he will become when he, too, is older. Harry remembers Whitman's remarks to him and reflects that "my kind/ ways to him must somehow someday come round/ home to me, because everything came round."

The maturity conveyed by this poem, and by "The Deathbed Playboy," stands in contrast to Dacey's earlier tendency to embrace the flip and coy, in both language and subject, in his poems.

The poem "North Broadway & Grand," from *The Man with Red Suspenders*, reappears in *The Deathbed Playboy* as the second part of "Difficult Corners." The new first section, "Introduction to 'North Broadway & Grand,'" is a more pointedly narrative work, giving the background on "the traffic cop who dances as he works." It offers contrasts to the earlier work in its tone, imagery, and language.

The Deathbed Playboy contains several of the poems of artifice typical of Dacey's work. Perhaps the most adroit is "Recorded Message," an improvisation on the theme of an answering-machine message reached by a caller at an unresponsive business. "Four Men in a Car" is a playful depiction of the situation stated in the title, colored by nursery-rhyme allusions. Other poems of this sort include "The Neighbors," which imagines Saddam Hussein and George H. Bush as the poet's suburban neighbors, and "Trousers," which presents a list of imaginative thoughts relating the idea of generosity to the article of clothing.

"FROM THE FRONT"

In 2003, Dacey's "From the Front" was honored by the *Atlanta Review*. In this poem of nine three-line stanzas, the poet employs his use of flattened image and mundane events to focus on an antiwar message. The poem begins, "'War is the ultimate story,'/ the frontline correspondent/ says on the radio.// I'm having my breakfast,/ pouring the un-ultimate milk/ over my un-ultimate cornflakes." The poet's breakfast is marked by a gesture of affection between him and the woman he loves, after which she ". . . smiles/ a smile from the story of peace,/ of two people learning// not to go to war/ against each other." That "story of peace" proves central to the poem, for it has a chapter of "blank pages" that ". . . says so much/ about the art of story-telling,/ ultimately."

In avoiding cleverness and substituting the mundane for artifice, "From the Front" is effective in its consideration of "story," and what "story" must be for the popular media. The title, "From the Front," suggests that the quiet domestic scene is the real story.

THE MYSTERY OF MAX SCHMITT

Although Dacey has continued to work in free verse during the first decade of the twenty-first century, he has given special emphasis to the sonnet, beginning with *The Mystery of Max Schmitt*. To some degree, Dacey's growing focus on this traditional form is natural, in that some of his earlier work, especially his coedited anthology *Strong Measures*, has contributed to the growing receptivity among readers of American poetry to the use of meter and rhyme and has influenced younger poets who identify with New Formalism.

Dacey employs the sonnet form in *The Mystery of Max Schmitt* to give various characters their voice: The painter Eakins talks about painting; a prostitute speaks about being a nude model; and Whitman discusses Eakins's nude models. Dacey's efforts meet with mixed results, although the characters' voices tend to mute the awkwardness of the form itself.

THE NEW YORK POSTCARD SONNETS

The poet continues to explore the sonnet form in *The New York Postcard Sonnets* and *Vertebrae Rosaries*. While Dacey's poems on Eakins show their greatest strength when at their most free and relaxed, these collections rely entirely on structured verse. Dacey's tendency to title his sonnets in such informal terms as "found sonnet" or "postcard sonnet" may reflect his own attitude toward them, for as poems, they tend toward light entertainment and minor observation. Given that *The New York Postcard Sonnets* followed the poet's own move to New York and that postcards are the traditional traveler's means of minor, wish-you-were-here correspondence, Dacey may have intended the book to be light in its tone and minor in its material. The poems in this volume are numbered, with their first lines serving as titles.

Dacey's fourteen-line poems are sonnets in a loose sense. When using the sonnet form, three quatrains with a couplet at the end, Dacey typically employs a slant-rhyme scheme of *abab cdcd efef* for the quatrains, with the ending couplet slant rhymed *gg*. Dacey on occasion uses other structures, for example, a six-line ending stanza with an *abbacc* slant-rhyme scheme. In some poems, the slant rhymes are fairly consistent, as in "The Public Library's Main Reading Room":

Like subway riders: close and distant at once.
Brass lamps spread hominess in Bly's "favorite
room in the world." (From Robert, rare good sense.)
Changing times: each laptop has its outlet.

The slant rhymes are all on consonant endings, with "once" paired with "sense" and "favorite" with "outlet." In other cases, as in "My Sunday at the Met. Surrealist Max Ernst," the slant rhymes are based more freely on tonal resemblances, as in the matching of "Ernst" with "monster," and "parade" with "Dada." As is typical of poems using slant rhyme, traditional rhymes sometimes do surface, contributing to the musical sense of the lines.

Surprisingly for a university professor with decades of experience, Dacey sometimes ends the sonnets on homily-like lines, as occurs in "With Juilliard a fifteen-minute walk away." After noting that he is at Juilliard so often that he "should be paying rent," the middle quatrain continues with simple observations: "Maybe I miss my students. Or it's just plain fun/ to watch so many Asian females first bow/ and sit as if they were delicate porcelain,/ then turn into terrors and rip the keys off the piano." After a few more observations, he offers the closing couplet: "And no student's here because of Daddy's dough./ You can't buy Beethoven; hours of practice show."

VERTEBRAE ROSARIES

In *Vertebrae Rosaries*, the predominant tone again is light and humorous. The opening sonnet, "Serenade," which offers metrical entertainment of the Ogden Nash variety, is based on an Associated Press release about non-English speakers choosing the words "cellar door" as having a beautiful sound. Like some earlier poems, it is about an interesting but minor oddity of phrase. Light verse is not the whole focus of *Vertebrae Rosaries*, however: This book benefits from its variety of subject matter, with some sonnets and sonnet-groupings taking on subjects of more weight. In "Prayer," for example, the poet offers a prayer that he avoid his old mistakes in pursuing his current love, while "Postcards from Vietnam" and "The Vietnam Veterans Memorial (D.C.)" are somber in tone. Others, such as "George Ballanchine: Centro Sonnet," reflect Dacey's continued interest in writing from the point of view of famous individuals from the past.

OTHER MAJOR WORKS

EDITED TEXTS: *I Love You All Day, It Is That Simple*, 1970 (with Gerald M. Knoll); *Strong Measures: Contemporary American Poetry in Traditional Forms*, 1986 (with David Jauss).

BIBLIOGRAPHY

Caplan, David. "In That Thicket of Bitter Roots." *Virginia Quarterly Review* 80, no. 4 (Fall, 2004): 115-134. An essay on the renewed interest in metrical verse being displayed by American poets, including Dacey.

Folsom, Ed. "Philip Dacey on Whitman: An Interview and Four New Poems." *Walt Whitman Quarterly Review* 19, no. 2 (Summer, 2001): 40-51. An exploration of Dacey's continuing fascination with Walt Whitman.

Hedin, Robert, ed. *Where One Voice Ends Another Begins: One Hundred Fifty Years of Minnesota Poetry*. St. Paul: Minnesota Historical Society, 2007. This anthology gives a place of prominence to Dacey, who exerted considerable influence in Minnesota poetry during the last third of the twentieth century.

McPhillips, Robert. *The New Formalism: A Critical Introduction*. Rev. ed. Cincinnati: WordTech Communications, 2005. An overview of and introduction to the movement Dacey helped create.

Stitt, Peter. "The Necessary Poem." *Ohio Review* 19, no. 2 (Spring/Summer, 1978): 101-112. Stitt's examination of Dacey's poetry is valuable for its discussion of tonal consistency. While appreciative of the poet's strengths, he takes an uncompromising look at Dacey's failures of voice.

Stuart, Dabney. "Sex and Violence." *Tar River Poetry* 26, no. 2 (Spring, 1987): 46-53. Stuart explores Dacey's concern with sexuality as a topic, especially in reference to the poems of *The Man with Red Suspenders*.

Wallace, Ronald. "An Air a Wound Sings." *Chowder Review* 9 (1977): 93-94. Wallace's examination of Dacey's earlier work, couched in entirely positive terms, is useful for its assessment of Dacey's affirmative and celebratory approach.

Wilbur, Richard. Interview by Philip Dacey. In *Conversations with Richard Wilbur*, edited by William Butts. Jackson: University Press of Mississippi, 1990. The *Crazy Horse* interview of Wilbur, conducted in 1974 and included in this collection, proved to be influential in Dacey's own career.

Mark Rich
Updated by Rich

ROBERT DANA

Born: Allston, Massachusetts; June 2, 1929

PRINCIPAL POETRY

My Glass Brother, and Other Poems, 1957
The Dark Flag of Waking, 1964
Some Versions of Silence, 1967
The Power of the Visible, 1971
In a Fugitive Season: A Sequence of Poems, 1979
Starting Out for the Difficult World, 1987
What I Think I Know: New and Selected Poems, 1991
Yes, Everything: New Poems, 1994
Hello, Stranger: Beach Poems, 1996
Summer, 2000
The Morning of the Red Admirals, 2004
The Other, 2008

OTHER LITERARY FORMS

Robert Dana is the editor of *Against the Grain: Interviews with Maverick American Publishers* (1986) and *A Community of Writers: Paul Engle and the Iowa Writers' Workshop* (1999). Transcripts of interviews he conducted with notable literary figures have been published in academic journals, including *American Poetry Review* and *Midwest Quarterly*. He has contributed essays and literary criticism discussing poetry and poets to such periodicals as *The New York Times*, *Kenyon Review*, *North American Review*, and *Georgia Review*.

ACHIEVEMENTS

Robert Dana's body of work was recognized with the Rainer Maria Rilke Prize (1984), New York University's Delmore Schwartz Memorial Award (1989), and the Carl Sandburg Medal for poetry (1994). In 1980, he was chosen to participate in the White House Salute to Poetry and American Poets. Dana's landmark volume, *Starting Out for the Difficult World*, was short-listed for the 1988 Pulitzer Prize. He won a 1996 Pushcart Prize for his poem, "Take It or Leave It," published in *Kenyon Review*. Dana received the Danforth Teacher Study Grant in 1959 and 1960, and a Ford-Associated Colleges of the Midwest grant in 1966 and 1967. He was awarded fellowships for poetry in 1962 and 1963 from the Mary Roberts Rinehart Foundation and grants from the National Endowment for the Arts in 1985 and 1993. He served as the poet laureate of Iowa from 2004 until 2009.

BIOGRAPHY

Robert Patrick Dana's Depression-era childhood in the Boston area was, by any measure, complicated—a trauma, he has said, "from which I never recovered." Born on June 2, 1929, at Allston, Massachusetts, to Margaret (Devine) Dana, he never met his biological father, Samuel, an Italian milliner who was already married with five children when he entered into a lengthy affair with Dana's Irish Catholic mother. When Dana was seven, his mother, only forty, died of pneumonia. Dana, abandoned by his father, was separated from his older half sister, Mary Virginia Clancy (who later became a nun), and the siblings were sent to live with relatives and foster parents. The troubled Dana ran away several times. His guardians expected him to work, performing such undesirable tasks as chopping tobacco. Dana often sought solitude by exploring nearby woods, collecting butterflies, and fishing.

Although an indifferent student, he recalled being entranced by the works of Edgar Allan Poe, "the right music for a morbid boy with a miserable past and a dark future." From 1946 to 1948, Dana served in the U.S. Navy as a radio operator in Guam. To relax, he wrote poetry and stories mimicking Poe's style and unsuccessfully tried to form a swing orchestra. He returned to Massachusetts, briefly attending Holyoke Community College before selling his raincoat and watch to buy a one-way bus ticket west to Des Moines, Iowa, to attend Drake University, a private school, which he selected

largely because a friend had received a postcard advertising it.

Dana thrived at the school. His faculty adviser, the poet Edward Mayo, introduced him to the works of Robert Frost, T. S. Eliot, Ezra Pound, and W. H. Auden, none of whom Dana had read before. He concentrated on his schoolwork to improve his writing skills. Dana also reported on sports events for the *Des Moines Register* to supplement G.I. Bill funds that paid his tuition. He considered a career as a journalist or musician. After completing his bachelor of arts degree in 1951, Dana taught high school for a year in northwestern Iowa. He married Mary Kowalke on his birthday, June 2, 1951; they had one son, Richard, and two daughters, Lori and Arden.

In 1952, Dana enrolled in the prestigious Writers' Workshop at the University of Iowa, where he took poetry workshops with Paul Engle, Pulitzer Prize winners John Berryman and Karl Shapiro (who was *Poetry* editor at that time), and future Pulitzer Prize winner Robert Lowell. While he was a graduate student, Dana resided in Cedar Rapids, where his wife taught high school, twenty-five miles northwest of campus, often hitchhiking to Iowa City for his poetry workshops. Dana earned a master of arts degree in June, 1954, writing his thesis, "My Glass Brother, and Other Fragments (Poems)," which was the basis for his first book, *My Glass Brother, and Other Poems*, published in 1957.

For more than forty years, Dana taught English as distinguished poet-in-residence at Cornell College in Mount Vernon, Iowa, thirty miles north of Iowa City. Dana started as an English and journalism instructor in 1954. He began publishing poetry in small presses in 1955, although he would not release his first major collection for more than a decade, and also served as editor for Hillside Press from 1957 through 1967. Dana was promoted to assistant professor in 1958 then associate professor in 1962, receiving the rank of full professor six years later. His second book of poems, *The Dark Flag of Waking*, was published in 1964, and he completed one to three new poetry books per decade throughout his career. He arranged for *North American Review*, which had been published in Boston before it was suspended, to resume publication based at Cornell College in 1964. Dana served as that journal's editor-in-chief through

1969. In 1967, he also became editor of the campus literary magazine, *Open Field*. During the 1960's, Dana and his family briefly resided in Mexico.

Dana and his first wife divorced in 1973. That year, he became a contributing editor for *American Poetry Review*, continuing in that position through 1988. He served as his department's chair from 1974 to 1978. On September 14, 1974, Dana wed Margaret "Peg" Sellen. Beginning in the mid-1970's, Dana traveled widely, accepting appointments as visiting writer-in-residence at universities in the United States and abroad, including the University of Florida and Stockholm University. From 1980 to 1983, Dana was a contributing editor to *New Letters*. Dana expressed his admiration for small presses in 1986, when he edited *Against the Grain*, a collection of interviews he conducted with the publishers of small presses. In 1991, he agreed to become a contributing editor for *North American Review*.

Dana's poetry has been published in prominent periodicals such as *Iowa Review*, *Poetry*, *The New Yorker*, *Paris Review*, *Ploughshares*, and *Sewanee Review*, and anthologies such as *Snakebird: Thirty Years of Anhinga Poets*, edited by Rick Campbell and C. L. Knight (2004). Dana has published several poetry collections in limited editions or pamphlets, including *Blood Harvest* (1986), *Wildebeest* (1993), and *Hard Candy* (2008). He has judged writing contests for poets, including the Anhinga Prize for Poetry. Dana and his colleagues established the Des Moines National Poetry Festival in the early 1990's, and he has continued to serve as a consultant for and participant in that annual event.

In April, 1994, Cornell College sponsored a weekend honoring Dana and his work. Alumni who had studied with him provided money to establish a Robert Dana Award to recognize excellent Cornell College student writers. After retiring in 1994 and becoming a professor emeritus, Dana, who considered himself a midwesterner by choice, remained in his adopted Iowa, living in Coralville near the University of Iowa, and continued to write verse. He traveled to Great Britain, Italy, and Africa with his wife, discussing poetry at the University of Dar-es-Salaam, Kenyan colleges, and other schools. By 2001, a bronze panel featuring Dana had been embedded in the sidewalk of Iowa City's

Iowa Avenue Literary Walk; it displayed an excerpt from his poem "Summer in a Very Small Town."

In September, 2004, Governor Tom Vilsack and Lieutenant Governor Sally Pederson appointed Dana as poet laureate of Iowa. In addition to presenting poems for state occasions, Dana also traveled throughout the state for readings and workshops at colleges, schools, and libraries. Dana and his daughter created a gold-foil seal imprinted with cornstalks and lettering to designate books written by Iowa poet laureates. Dana's half-sister died in Massachusetts in December, 2004, and he returned to Boston to attend her funeral. Her death inspired his poem, "Ora Pro Nobis," printed in *Prairie Schooner* and included in his collection *The Other*. Dana observed the dedication ceremony in October, 2005, at Poet's Park in Cedar Rapids, where his poem "Lines Written Between Dream and Sleep" had been etched into a large stone. In January, 2006, Dana addressed the Iowa state legislature, reading his poem "A Short History of the Middle West."

Governor Vilsack reappointed Dana to another term as laureate in 2006, and Dana performed those duties until 2009. In May, 2008, the Coralville Public Library unveiled his poem "Library" on a bronze marker, and his poem "In Praise" was etched on the Iowa Workers' Monument in Des Moines. He recorded his poetry for podcasts distributed on the Internet. Dana often visited the Cornell College campus for poetry readings. On April 28, 2009, that school hosted "An Evening with Poet Robert Dana." Dana also participated in an October, 2009, radio broadcast reading his poetry at Iowa City's independent bookstore, Prairie Lights.

ANALYSIS

A lapsed Catholic, Robert Dana offers a profound sense of a fallen, often brutal world compelled by chance rather than governed by any design. His approach is much like that of Lowell, his teacher at the Iowa Writers' Workshop. Although deeply impressed by the sheer force of the natural world, particularly the limitless edge of the ocean and the forbidding prairie of his adopted Midwest, Dana cannot sustain comfort in the unaffected love of such natural wonders. He is too aware of the insubstantiality of the natural world, how every part of it—and ultimately every person within it—must perish. His vision, then, is ultimately sobering, even tragic, despite touches of humor and the reassurance he has found in the experience of love with his second wife, Peg.

Dana studied Chinese philosophy and has taught Asian literature. Not willing to dwell on the emotional calamities of his personal past or to anticipate the rewards of some dubious afterlife, he counsels, with Zenlike calm, the embrace of the moment. His poetry, particularly his later work, revels in the sheer delight of discovering the rich textures of the ordinary. For him, that is the poet's job: to cast the passing moment and the unobserved object into the noble shape and reassuring permanence of language. The poet's only magic, he said, "is with words . . . their sounds, their taste, their soft or their steel feel."

Although trained in formal poetics while at the Writers' Workshop, Dana came to find natural expression in open verse. Its music, so apparently improvisational, often goes unheard by the impatient ear, but his verse manages syllables, stresses, and vowel and consonant sounds to create an engrossing aural event. He once compared his verse lines to jazz: "I wanted to achieve in words what the jazz musician achieves in notes and time signatures." Dana said his style presented his reactions to his comprehensive observations through his various senses regarding what he was experiencing. He emphasized that poems enabled such moments to survive beyond their occurrence. Dana compared writing poems to a form of reporting scenes and events. Critics have referred to his work as being descriptive, and Dana has concurred that he strives to share the realism of what he sees and hears through poetic devices so his readers can interpret those images to perceive similar sights and sounds.

As Dana aged, his poetry became less morbid, although he still appropriated death as a theme. In *The Other*, Dana presents mortality as a sadness to mourn while celebrating the lives he grieves. He juxtaposes imagery, his wife breathing while she sleeps with the husk of his sister lying in her casket. Dana recognizes joys of routine activities and expresses memories of places he has lived and people he has known without becoming too nostalgic. He delights in the satirical aspects and incorporates dark humor in his poetry to balance the serious, sometimes macabre or depressing, tone. He notes that his use of sarcasm and irony is sometimes so subtle that critics fail to notice it. Aspiring to continue advancing his craft, Dana endeavors to create poetry in unique styles and structures that differ from his previous work.

SOME VERSIONS OF SILENCE

Dana's first major collection, *Some Versions of Silence*, published just two years shy of his fortieth birthday, divides into three strikingly different sections. In the first are traditional narrative poems in which Dana, like Frost or Edwin Arlington Robinson, captures the anxieties, frustrations, and surprises of quotidian experience, the recollections of a poet locked in time, bound to the real. They are moments of generous inclusion for the reader, poems about resilient fall flowers, crowded supermarkets, signs along a highway, and the trying experience of love.

With disconcerting—and deliberate—abruptness, the second section forsakes such familiarity. These poems, like Pound's experiments in strict imagism, do not have the reassuring flow, music, or rhythms of free verse. These are spare, minimalist bits, cryptic occasions for meditation, like Zen koans that cannot be adequately explained or paraphrased. "What word./ One/ without syllable,/ without edge;/ more moving/ but more/ than moving." They are abstract reflections that eschew metaphor and image and refuse commentary on the events that occasioned them.

In the closing section, Dana brings together these two impulses—the concrete and the abstract—to create quasi parables. Palpable objects are given a spiritual resonance. Under the poet's careful eye, caged birds, hawks in flight, a comb left in an empty room, autumn trees, lightning, and the descent of night can all be coaxed into suggestive symbols within slender lines that nevertheless sing. The closing poem, "The Stonecutter," tells of a craftsperson fashioning from heavy stone the subtle curves of a woman. It is a fitting image of the isolated poet finding consolation in the exertion of craft itself as a strategy for discovering the spectacular in the unpromising.

THE POWER OF THE VISIBLE

The poems in *The Power of the Visible* resist easy summary. They are Dana's most Eastern-influenced works, enigmatic, fragmentary verses with scant sense of plot, place, or character. These are cool, clean, precise, impersonal poems that speak, thematically, of the hunger for permanence amid flux, for stability amid the rush of inevitable movement. In "The Stone Garden," Dana offers a telling Zen allegory of the monumental efforts of a man to fashion a tidy garden; he then goes in to read the newspaper obituaries, a sobering reminder of the untidiness of the larger world. Love here is inaccessible, even a burden. Achingly close to a natural world that is frustratingly inscrutable, paralyzed within the vastness of time and space, many of the poems are slender presences, thin ribbons of words amid forbidding white spaces. Dana offers as solution the poem itself, the calming music of the lines. What transfixes the reader here is the language, particularly Dana's gift for unexpected coinages, striking figurative phrases, and unusual diction, that transmutes the ordinary into the delightful: "a boredom of summer storms," "the sliding/ murder of the calendar," skin that clings like "a jacket and gloves of ice," a woman's face that is "a page of snow," and pink pigs that "blister the hillside." It is the poet as conjurer and alchemist (one selection concerns a dying Merlin) who provides the reader with what the poems so desperately seek: a place apart, albeit aesthetic, amid the chaos.

IN A FUGITIVE SEASON

The poems in Dana's third major volume, *In a Fugitive Season*, mark the beginning of his reclamation of what he termed "the hard details of reality." These poems recall Dana's earlier sense of forbidding vastness but are vivid and concrete. The vastness is both natural (images include mountains, prairies, night skies, snowstorms, and the sun) and temporal (in a cycle of European poems, he visits Stonehenge and ruins of ancient civilizations). The contemporary world is a palpable presence, although harshly disappointing—Dana writes powerfully of the 1968 assassination of Senator Robert Kennedy, the anxieties of nuclear apocalypse, the political evil of the 1970's Watergate scandal. Love, specifically the heated connection of passion, is vividly recreated. Although such a world cannot offer meaning or logic, Dana refuses despair. As he counsels his cynical students:

> . . . this planet
> does its crazy slow turn under us
>
> And miles away
> even my midwestern burg
>
> twinkles
> through the blue drizzle.

Dana departs from his earlier solutions (withdrawal and meditation) and offers radically new strategies—engagement and observation, allowing the open eye to be stunned by the sheer sensual impact of the world, recalling the humane Imagism of William Carlos Williams, an influence Dana readily acknowledged. The poet, then, is to remind readers tempted to abandon wonder and to expect disappointment that the world around can shatter with its color, shade, and line. It is too much to expect meaning but enough to delight in the play of surfaces. The world is much like Dana's preferred syntactic strategy: fragments that come together to create a sense of wholeness.

> I see that I am what I always was
>
> that ordinary man on his front steps
> bewildered under the bright mess of the heavens
> by the fierce indecipherable language of its stars

STARTING OUT FOR THE DIFFICULT WORLD

The title *Starting Out for the Difficult World* might appear ironic, given that at its publication Dana was nearing the age of sixty. The poetic argument here is decidedly different from that of earlier work, though, and represents a significant starting point for Dana. At long last ready to share in the intimacy of the reader-writer relationship, he violates the keen loneliness that had long haunted his poetry by bonding with the reader. Unlike previous collections, this one deploys direct address, manipulating a recognizable, consistent "I"—an orphan, brother, friend, husband, teacher—in a real place, a New Englander transplanted to the prairie. Dana reveals a generous eye and an aching heart as well as a deep fascination for the everyday—subzero mornings, a diving hawk, homemade bread, lightning storms, summer heat, gulls feeding on a beach, and even cockroaches.

These poems, reassuringly concrete and accessibly written with the easy flow of conversational intimacy, boldly attest to a self that may not be significant but is nevertheless valuable. In the moving "At the Vietnam War Memorial, Washington, D.C.," Dana writes of locating a single name on the memorial wall, and determining to rescue that name's individuality from such a forbidding catalog, he recalls a photograph taken shortly before the soldier's death. In a brutal world that oppresses with the implied inconsequentiality of the individual, Dana demands that "we shout our names, cut/ them, like these [names], into air/ deeper than any natural shadow." Within a flow of time that no one can ease, against the shapeless fears of the impending intrusion of mortality, Dana offers the generous notion that here and now must be enough, that love is worth the risk of its failure, and that every day the open eye can find consolation in the simplest objects.

YES, EVERYTHING

As if to confirm Dana's affirmation of the self in the real world, the poems collected in *Yes, Everything* are about places—familiar and exotic, contemporary and ancient, domestic and foreign—that are very real: "This is short-grass/ prairie," he says in "Tanzania," "not a simile/ or a metaphor." Dana takes the reader to the Irish countryside; a campsite in Yellowstone National Park; a beach along the Indian Ocean; the Serengeti Plain in suffocating heat; a Helsinki railroad terminal, where he watches a couple furiously kiss; and a rain-spattered Paris sidewalk. Importantly, he includes the less exotic: a parking lot at a Florida Winn Dixie supermarket; a deserted Iowa golf course; and in perhaps the collection's most affective moment, the slender "Genesis," Dana recalls being with his wife, quite naked and shivering "amid the stunned animals," in a field just outside their Iowa home, a place that, despite being literally in their backyard, Dana compares to Eden. Not simply lexical postcards, these poems speak to the relationship between the responding self and an unfamiliar world.

Dana's position as traveler/visitor/tourist and the experience of otherness implicit in travel allow him the opportunity to explore what has always fascinated him: the implications of loneliness and the cosmic self, rootless and homeless. In the volume's penultimate poem—whose title, "Here and Now," handily summarizes his larger philosophy—Dana unpacks a new hibachi and ponders the distant pain of his Massachusetts childhood ("I remember the gilded/ and pinched and downcast/ faces of Boston women") but affirms only the "pliers/ and screwdriver . . . I believe/ in this. Here. And now." The metaphor of travel thus allows Dana to suggest that the eye has every reason to be compelled by every glance it takes, that every place, even the familiar, has the capacity to stun.

Stylistically, the poems are opulently detailed and reassuringly concrete. Most of them are direct narratives with locales that are lovingly, sensually detailed, vivid with colors colliding in unexpected harmonies. Appropriately, the music here comes subtly in modulations of syllables and shifts in stresses that allow lines to fold gently into one another. It is a tonal effect best appreciated in reading the poems aloud. Particularly effective is "Rapture," a loving ode to a stretch of Carolina beach at night that captures the heaving surf in a complex medley of long vowels, rolling "-ing" words, and soft consonants.

SUMMER

It is not altogether surprising that a poet so compelled by the urgency of now, so convinced that the material world has meaning beyond its obvious surfaces, would produce—at an age when most people are consumed by regrets, fears, or sentimental nostalgia—a volume of verse eloquently tuned to the power of the moment. Like its title, *Summer*, the poems are vibrant and urgent. The lines themselves flow, seldom stopped by end punctuation. "Why can't we," he asks in "Lines Written Between Dream and Sleep," "learn to sip the light/ as sweet bees do?" In "Awake," the poet recounts the quiet drama of a house stirring to life, each object speaking its own language of resurrection. These are not narratives but rather observations: a cold morning at his bird feeder, the first hard storm of winter, a twelve-tone wind chime, a clutch of robin's eggs, late morning coffee, a neighborhood sugared by an early morning snow, trees afire in autumn, a sleeping cat, a deep-dish pizza. They are moments snatched from the approach of mortality (in "Thyme," as he ponders a friend's cardiac scare, he is drying a bumper crop of thyme/time). Such is the treasure each is given every morning.

Dana's readers are cautioned not to be like his neighbors who "look at the sea and see only the sea." The volume closes with Dana strolling alone in a heavy beach fog, where he finds in the cloaking mist his voice suddenly stilled and useless. Dana does not panic. Rather he whistles: a sweet Chopin adagio and then "Stardust" and "On the Sunny Side of the Street," the irrepressible affirmation of, respectively, beauty, love, and hope in a forbidding environment that will not permit him either to look back from where he has come or see ahead to where he is going.

THE MORNING OF THE RED ADMIRALS

Reminiscent of the butterflies named in this collection's title, the theme of metamorphosis resonates in *The Morning of the Red Admirals*. In three sections, Dana explores his role and growth as a poet as his poems undergo a transition, evolving from a compositional style to an improvisational presentation. He provides definitions of regional and archaic words he uses as figurative devices in these poems. The title poem, "The Morning of the Red Admirals," introduces the butterfly metaphor for change that unites this collection. Dana admires butterflies he observes flying and interacting with him, flowers, and objects in his yard. He perceives his encounters with the butterflies as transitory so that they can gain sustenance and energy to prepare for flight beyond his world.

In this collection's first group, "Walking the Yellow Dog," Dana presents eighteen poems in which he describes people, animals, and places. Some, such as the middle-aged woman and her retriever in this section's title poem, are strangers in a newspaper photograph who represent how Dana imagines many people live. Others, as in ".com," are familiar, including his dying neighbor and his wife; his death, although expected, awakens Dana's awareness of his suburban community's routines, both human and nature, and the quiet absence of such traditions as women giving food to the bereaved, a silence that unnerves him. He balances violence and the potential of apocalypse with images of domestic peace and innocence in "Mercy, Perhaps" and "This Time," revealing how themes of fear, disruption, and resilience are all relevant to contrasting images of destruction and security.

The second section, "In Panama," consists of Dana's prose exposition describing his inspiration to write "The Morning of the Red Admirals." His observation of butterflies triggers memories of his boyhood enthusiasm to learn about those insects. The butterflies' visit is a catalyst provoking Dana to assess the value of his poetry and question whether he has sufficient passion for his writing, equivalent to the zeal he had as a child for butterfly collecting. He frets that his style has become stagnant, stating that he desires to improvise and create poems that cannot immediately be attributed to him. Dana refers to a scientific article discussing the varied, nonrepetitive wing movements that red admiral butterflies perform to fly. He considers the butterflies' constantly changing wing motions to be the essence of improvisation, guiding him to achieve an unexpected, dynamic voice for his poems.

The third part, "Ten Thousand Wingbeats, Five Hundred Heartbeats," consists of twelve poems that show Dana's transition to an improvisational style. Some critics suggest that Dana placed words and lines in patterns—fragments of thought and sentence structures that ignore formal grammar rules—on pages to mimic fluctuations of butterfly flight. Dana's improvisational poems incorporate autobiographical elements as his thoughts wander. Dana acknowledges how aging alters him and time has escaped in "Stepping Lightly." He helplessly watches his dying cat's physical decline, foreshadowing his own weakening body. In "Chimes," Dana hints of timelessness while hearing heavenly music when he and another cat peacefully watch rainfall modify the night landscape as summer wanes. He is content knowing that he fully embraces life and its unexpected epiphanies.

OTHER MAJOR WORKS

EDITED TEXTS: *Against the Grain: Interviews with Maverick American Publishers*, 1986; *A Community of Writers: Paul Engle and the Iowa Writers' Workshop*, 1999.

BIBLIOGRAPHY

Brunner, Edward. "From Deep Space: The Poetry of Robert Dana." *Iowa Review* 22, no. 3 (1992): 115-134. Indispensable overview of Dana's verse that traces its evolution from early Formalist verse and minimalist experiments. Particularly focused on Dana's strategy for violating the poet's profound isolation by offering art itself as mediating terrain. Close readings of several key Dana poems.

Dana, Robert. "'Better to Go in Rags': An Interview with Robert Dana." Interview by Sara Pennington. *Chattahoochee Review* 27, no. 2 (Winter, 2007): 12-20. Dana responds to critical reaction to *The Morning of the Red Admirals*. He explains why he risks writing poems that deviate stylistically from his previous works. "Better to go in rags" is a line from "Spindrift," a poem in *The Morning of the Red Admirals*, in which Dana criticizes the commercialization of poetry.

_____. "An Interview with Robert Dana." Interview by Lowell Jaeger. *Poets and Writers* (July/August, 1991): 13-21. Revealing discussion centering on Dana's sense of language and his place in twentieth century poetics. Contains candid biographical information.

_____. "Unleashing the Comic Muse: An Interview with Robert Dana." Interview by Guy Lebeda. *Weber Studies: Voices and Viewpoints of the Contemporary West* 22, no. 3 (2006): 2-13. Dana discusses his disappointment that critics often do not recognize or simply ignore humorous and satiric elements of his poetry, including poems in *The Morning of the Red Admirals*. Comments regarding educational and publishing experiences that shaped his style and explains duties associated with being named Iowa poet laureate.

Holinger, Richard. "Transcendental Bouquet." Review of *Yes, Everything*. *Iowa Review* 25, no. 3 (1995): 168-171. Explores Dana's Buddhist sense of the connectedness of everything and the beauty in the mundane. Places him within the transcendentalist school of Ralph Waldo Emerson and Henry David Thoreau.

Low, Denise. "A Morning Free of Measure." Review of *The Morning of the Red Admirals*. *Kansas City Star*, August 8, 2004, p. 6. Former Kansas poet laureate Low praises Dana's use of language, specifically classical and Old English vocabulary, and a butterfly metaphor to represent changes in his ap-proach to writing poems. Examines the effectiveness of Dana's shift in style and structure in this collection's second and third parts.

Joseph Dewey
Updated by Elizabeth D. Schafer

PETER DAVISON

Born: New York, New York; June 27, 1928
Died: Boston, Massachusetts; December 29, 2004

PRINCIPAL POETRY

The Breaking of the Day, and Other Poems, 1964
The City and the Island, 1966
Pretending to Be Asleep, 1970
Walking the Boundaries, 1974
A Voice in the Mountain, 1977
Barn Fever, and Other Poems, 1981
Praying Wrong: New and Selected Poems, 1957-1984, 1984
The Great Ledge, 1989
The Poems of Peter Davison, 1957-1995, 1995
Breathing Room: New Poems, 2000

OTHER LITERARY FORMS

In addition to his life as a poet, Peter Davison carved out a distinguished career as an editor, including his many years as poetry editor of *The Atlantic Monthly* and as a consulting editor at Houghton Mifflin. *Hello, Darkness: The Collected Poems of L. E. Sissman* (1978), a posthumous collection edited by Davison, won the National Book Critics Circle Award in poetry in 1978.

Davison also wrote two autobiographical works: *Half Remembered: A Personal History* (1973), which recounts the story of his life from birth until his early forties, and *The Fading Smile: Poets in Boston, from Robert Frost to Robert Lowell to Sylvia Plath, 1955-1960* (1994), which offers his personal perspective on a significant midcentury poetry renaissance. *One of the Dangerous Trades: Essays on the Work and Workings of Poetry* (1991) is a collection of essays on poetry and poets.

ACHIEVEMENTS

Peter Davison's poetic career was launched auspiciously after he won the Yale Series of Younger Poets competition in 1964. From the very beginning, his work gave evidence that he is heir to what might be termed the New England tradition of self-examination, a process marked by a penchant for using the outer world as a metaphor for one's inner life. In this regard, he learned much from his early mentor, the American poet Robert Frost.

Davison also discovered his literary vocation during the 1950's and 1960's, when confessional poetry, a lyric mode of personal outpouring, was the vogue. His preference for formal regularities, however, distinguishes his work from that of other poets of the time, such as Sylvia Plath and Anne Sexton, because he has a tendency to use the artifice of the poem not to indulge in guilt and self-effacement and to risk drowning himself in his own feelings but to give shape to his emotions so that they can be clarified.

In the final analysis, Davison succeeded in charting a conservative course, punctuated by flirtations with topical subjects and free verse. He won the Academy Award in Literature of the National Institute of Arts and Letters in 1972, the James Michener Award of the Academy of American Poets in 1981, the New England Book Award for Literary Excellence from the New England Booksellers Association in 1995, and the Massachusetts Book Award in poetry in 2001.

BIOGRAPHY

Born in New York City to Edward and Natalie (Weiner) Davison, Peter Hubert Davison spent his formative years in Boulder, Colorado. His father, a poet and English expatriate, taught at the University of Colorado. Here his family hosted some of the most important poets and novelists of the day because of his father's management of a significant national writing conference each summer. Thus, Peter Davison grew up in a privileged intellectual environment.

After he graduated from Harvard University in 1949 with a bachelor's degree in history and literature, Davison spent a year as a Fulbright scholar at Saint John's College of Cambridge University in England. In 1951, he was drafted into the military, and he served for

two years in the psychological warfare division of the U.S. Army. Following his discharge in 1953, Davison worked in New York City for two years as an editor at Harcourt, Brace and Company before moving to Boston in 1955 to join the staff of Harvard University Press and, in 1956, Atlantic Monthly Press.

Shortly after his move to New England, he also began to consider the possibility of writing poetry. Davison was influenced in this decision by a number of factors. He was inspired by the example of the young poet Sylvia Plath, with whom he had a brief love affair, and by his acting success in verse plays produced by the Poets' Theatre in Cambridge. He also credits years of serious psychoanalysis with helping him not only come to grips with his own identity but also find himself as a writer.

By the end of the 1950's, the course of his subsequent life was set. His was a life in letters, divided between poetry and publishing. Davison directed the Atlantic Monthly Press until 1979, when he became its senior editor. He left that position in 1985 to become a consulting editor at Houghton Mifflin, where he remained until 1998.

It is, however, his personal and not his professional life that most informed his verse, especially his responses to family connections and places of residence. He married for the first time in 1959; that union produced two children, Edward Angus and Lesley Truslow Davison. His first wife, Jane Auchincloss Truslow, was a writer. After her death in 1981, Davison married architect Joan Edelman Goody in 1984, and from then on he divided each year between his country home in West Gloucester, Massachusetts, about a mile from the ocean, and his city home in Boston. Davison died of pancreatic cancer at his city home on December 29, 2004.

ANALYSIS

From the time he took up the pen, Peter Davison characterized the act of writing poetry as an exercise in self-discovery. This assertion is validated by his very first volume, *The Breaking of the Day, and Other Poems*, which set the stage for all his later work by establishing the poet's two principal approaches to charting the parameters of self-identity: the individual's relationship to other people (parents, lovers, friends, and mentors) and the individual's relationship to nature. However, for Davison, who understood with often somber irony that what he sought was essentially unknowable, poetry was both a means and an end.

THE BREAKING OF THE DAY, AND OTHER POEMS

The centerpiece of Davison's first volume, *The Breaking of the Day, and Other Poems*, is probably the poem titled "Not Forgotten," a five-part elegy for the poet's mother, who died of cancer in 1959. This poem, one of many that Davison wrote in response to his sometimes ambivalent relationship to his parents, was the earliest of his poems to attract considerable critical attention. It chronicles the poet's experience of loss, from a state of mute numbness to a faltering acceptance of his mother's death because of his abiding sense of her "hovering/ In a hundred places."

Similarly, the title poem of the volume, the seven-part "The Breaking of the Day," focuses on the parent-child relationship. In this case, the poet assumes the role of Jacob, a biblical patriarch of the book of Genesis, wrestling with his own personal angel until the crack of dawn. The struggle described in the poem is symbolic of Davison's own coming to grips with the double displacement that he felt because of his upbringing: the betrayal he felt because of his mother's suppression of her own heritage (only at the age of thirteen did he learn that he was half Jewish) and the inhibition he felt about his own writing goals because of his father's failure to live up to his early promise as a poet. In the end, there is no sign from God, his father's incarnation in the poem; there is only the continuing quest for identity, a journey that the poet pursues from book to book for the next forty years. Davison learns only that he must "Put God in words," or find his own poetic voice.

PRETENDING TO BE ASLEEP

Perhaps as an outgrowth of his own experience with psychoanalysis, Davison devoted his third volume, *Pretending to Be Asleep* (1970), to the complexities of the psyche and his hope, as he explored his poetic vocation, to find some balance between ego and id, between a conscious response to external experience and the mysterious prompting of imaginative insight. "How

are we to see what must be seen," the poet asks in a poem titled "The Losing Struggle," "before shaping our language to the sound of it?"

Achieving this equilibrium between awareness and what Davison calls "unawareness" is difficult at best. At times, as in "Old Photograph," another poem about summoning up memories of his dead mother, Davison registers a failure of the imagination: "How can I keep in touch/ When there is nothing to touch?" However, in other pieces, such as the fourteenth and final section of the title poem, "Pretending to Be Asleep," Davison marvels at finding poems on his desk ready for him to revise. "When did this happen?" he asks, amazed by the unconscious activity of his brain. However, once the id has done its work, the ego takes over. "I know my job," he avows. "Possession they say is nine points in the poem."

WALKING THE BOUNDARIES

With his fourth volume, *Walking the Boundaries*, Davison's focus shifts from the desire to explore the boundaries of self as delineated by the relationships that one has with others, from the formative connections to one's parents and mentors to the adult interactions with friends and lovers. Instead, perhaps prompted by his purchase of a twelve-acre farm in West Gloucester in the late 1960's, Davison turns to nature as a metaphor of the self.

The most resonant example of this new mode might be the four-part series titled "Walking the Boundaries." The first section "West, by the Road" speaks of autumn, a season when "Roots hunch and contract, their blood runs thin." The section "South, by the Wall" celebrates spring, when we will "breed till our brains burst/ with the bluebell music of flickers and grackles"; and "East, by the Cliff" registers a time when the "sleeping marsh" endures a "season of waiting for light." It is clear by the fourth section, "The Woodcock," that the seasons of the year have provided metaphors for the seasons of life.

"Body at least is bound within a landscape," the poet asserts, "an earth that holds us fastened to the seasons." This condition creates "boundaries we cannot cross" except through the exercise of song. Like the woodcock that creates "music that clambers skyward through the dark," the poet can strive beyond the limits imposed by prevailing conditions through the exercise of his creative imagination.

A VOICE IN THE MOUNTAIN

The next volume, *A Voice in the Mountain*, continues Davison's poetic use of nature and its rhythms as keys to unlocking the mysteries of the human experience. The poem "Cross Cut," for example, reveals that even though its "gangrened upper branches" seemed to indicate that it was "dying from the top," the stump of a recently hewn pear tree shows signs of life at the core. Even though the "cross-cut" tree had lived to twice the poet's age, there is a lesson for Davison to learn about his own persistent fertility.

In "Haskell's Mill," Davison imaginatively recreates a now-lost, late seventeenth century grist mill that once used the tidal currents to turn a giant wheel to grind corn, and he conjures up the figure of the original miller, who "held the balance between sea and land,/ the sun and moon, the water and the stone." Contrasted to the uneasy present, when "nothing is produced and little earned," the mill represents a "primal world" and a way of life characterized by a harmony of human effort and natural force.

BARN FEVER, AND OTHER POEMS

Although he continued to write of his relationship to others, especially his parents, his wife, and other poets, Davison's most heralded pieces in *Barn Fever, and Other Poems* are the poems that use natural fact to illuminate personal experience. The seven-part "Wordless Winter," for example, compares the emotional paralysis he is experiencing as he bears witness to the death of his first wife, Jane, to the phenomenon of a winter drought in New England. "Snow has forgotten itself," the poet writes, just as his own heart is seized by a frozen aridity.

Nature is a subject that requires close observation and specificity of description. It is a challenge that Davison faces with aplomb. In the title poem, "Barn Fever," for example, the poet describes his own barn, whose lower half of "Cape Ann stone" is two hundred years old. Inheriting such a barn that others have allowed slowly to decay, the poet puzzles over ways to "heal" it even though it has ceased to have any practical purpose because his farm is no longer devoted to agriculture. As an "emblem of the past," a remnant of lives

lived closer to the land than most people's, the barn in this poem is a companion structure to the old mill in "Haskell's Mill." Both poems resonate with the nostalgia inherent in the country verses of Davison's early poetic mentor, Frost.

BREATHING ROOM

Davison always experimented with form. Most of the poems in *Breathing Room*, for instance, are formatted in eight stanzas, seven tercets or triplets of lines followed by a concluding quatrain. As he explains in the preface to the book, Davison used this structure to create what he tentatively calls "audiographs," poems meant to be read aloud, to conform to the patterns of breathing.

In subject matter, these poems echo the concerns of earlier volumes; they attempt to define the self through one's engagement with other people and the natural world. As with his earlier work, the poems of relationships are generally not as satisfactory as the poems in which he plays the role of naturalist. In this book, he writes in "A Ballad" of the "immortal mismarriage" of poets Sylvia Plath and Ted Hughes, and he revisits in "My Father's Hundredth Birthday" his poet-parent's impressive declamatory talents. These people-centered poems contain no revelations for the committed reader of Davison's work.

Despite his insistence in "Getting over Robert Frost" that the most important lesson that he learned from the older poet was the "trick of not trusting a line// unless it flickered with/ my own odor," Davison's best poems remain those that can be labeled essentially Frost-inspired. They sing of regret in a rural setting.

The poem "Seaside Summer Quarry" offers a case in point. "Rapt" in the sights and sounds around him, the poet laments the futility of trying to fix upon the page the "stolen abstractions" inspired by how a "water lily shivers and/ shrugs its shadow over/ a green platter of leaf" or how "gold strands of sunlight thread/ through the hemlocks."

OTHER MAJOR WORKS

NONFICTION: *Half Remembered: A Personal History*, 1973, 1991; *One of the Dangerous Trades: Essays on the Work and Workings of Poetry*, 1991; *The Fading Smile: Poets in Boston, from Robert Frost to Robert Lowell to Sylvia Plath, 1955-1960*, 1994.

EDITED TEXTS: *Hello, Darkness: The Collected Poems of L. E. Sissman*, 1978; *The World of Farley Mowat: A Selection from His Works*, 1980; *The Book Encompassed: Studies in Twentieth-Century Bibliography*, 1992; *Night Music*, 1999.

BIBLIOGRAPHY

Contemporary Literary Criticism 28 (1984): 99-104. A significant sampling of book reviews from the beginning of Davison's career as a poet up to the publication of *Barn Fever, and Other Poems*.

Davison, Peter. *Half Remembered: A Personal History*. Rev. ed. Ashland, Oreg.: Story Line Press, 1991. The poet's autobiography provides many insights into his life and writing.

Hewitt, Geof. "Peter Davison." In *Contemporary Poets*. New York: St. James Press, 1996. A summary of the poet's life and work with commentary by Davison and some critical analysis.

Ratner, Rochelle. Review of *Breathing Room: New Poems*. *Library Journal* 125 (August, 2000): 109. A brief review of the collection *Breathing Room*. Ratner traces Davison's argument that poetry should be composed in keeping with the capacities of the human breath to an earlier contention by American poet and essayist Charles Olson in 1950. The reviewer favors Davison's nature-inspired poems because they are more precise in detail and more demanding.

Rotella, Guy. *Three Contemporary Poets of New England: William Meredith, Philip Booth, and Peter Davison*. Boston: Twayne, 1983. This is the most comprehensive treatment of the first half of Davison's poetic career. The author attempts to grapple with the themes and techniques of the poet's first six books in an effort to define Davison's place in the New England literary tradition. In this regard, Rotella contends that at the heart of Davison's creative achievement is his nature poetry.

Young, Vernon. "Raptures of Distress." *Parnassus* 3 (1975): 75-89. A laudatory piece on Davison's relationship to other poets who write of the somber realities of life's mutability.

S. Thomas Mack

CARL DENNIS

Born: St. Louis, Missouri; September 17, 1939

PRINCIPAL POETRY
House of My Own, 1974
Climbing Down, 1976
Signs and Wonders, 1979
The Near World, 1985
The Outskirts of Troy, 1988
Meetings with Time, 1992
Ranking the Wishes, 1997
Practical Gods, 2001
New and Selected Poems, 1974-2004, 2004
Unknown Friends, 2007

OTHER LITERARY FORMS

Although Carl Dennis is one of the most prolific and successful American poets of the late twentieth and early twenty-first centuries, he came relatively late to poetry. His first collection did not appear until he was in his mid-thirties. Before then and after, Dennis, a career academic, published literary criticism in prestigious academic journals. As Dennis's national reputation as a poet grew, so did interest in his critical writings. He drew on nearly a quarter century of his publications to fashion *Poetry as Persuasion* (2001). The volume, dealing with writers such as Walt Whitman, Emily Dickinson, and William Butler Yeats, argued for the importance of voice in a poem, how a poet must define a specific voice to establish an effective intimacy with a reader. The book also offered practical advice for working poets on using irony, point of view, symbols, and rhythm and rhyme in free verse to achieve a resonant and stable voice in a poem.

ACHIEVEMENTS

In a body of poetry marked by a subtly musical, almost conversational voice, Carl Dennis, profoundly influenced by a spiritual perception of the material universe, draws on everyday experiences to distill from them quiet and understated insights that create an intimacy with the reader. In the first few decades of his career, he published regularly, and his verse drew critical praise but did not enjoy a wider success. He was a poet's poet. He received the Theodore Roethke Prize from *Poetry Northwest* (1980) and the Bess Hokin Prize (1995) and the J. Howard and Barbara M. J. Wood Prize (1997), both from *Poetry* magazine. He was awarded a variety of fellowships, most notably from the Guggenheim Foundation (1984), the National Endowment for the Arts (1988), and the Rockefeller Study Center in Bellagio, Italy (1988). However, his stature as a poet grew, beginning in 2000, when he was selected for the prestigious $100,000 Ruth Lilly Poetry Prize, presented annually to a poet for lifetime achievement. Then, in 2002, his *Practical Gods* was the surprise choice for the Pulitzer Prize in poetry.

BIOGRAPHY

Carl Dennis was born in St. Louis to a mother who was a nurse and a father who started a hugely successful chemical company specializing in elastomers and adhesives. Dennis's parents encouraged their three sons to learn a musical instrument. Dennis's older brother Robert would become an avant-garde choral composer known primarily for his musical contributions to the 1969 experimental musical *Oh! Calcutta!* However, rather than pursue music, before he turned six, Dennis began writing, some poetry but mostly fairy tales in which the fabulous, even magical elements provided him escape from the constraints of suburban life.

Restless, curious, and certain only of his love of literature, Dennis found the college experience disappointing. He was searching, he would later say, for the Platonic ideal of gifted students and wise teachers engaged in lively discussion of literature in order to gain life lessons from centuries of great writings. Dennis first attended Oberlin College, then the University of Chicago, before completing his undergraduate degree at the University of Minnesota in 1961. In 1966, he completed his Ph.D. at the University of California, Berkeley, and immediately accepted a teaching position in nineteenth century American literature at the State University of New York at Buffalo. He would remain in Buffalo for his entire career, enjoying a variety of academic promotions until he retired in 2001 to become the university's artist-in-residence.

Early in his career, Dennis pursued academic writing, publishing numerous articles on, among other subjects, Yeats, Nathaniel Hawthorne, Jones Very, and William Shakespeare. By his late twenties, however, he found literary criticism growing less engaging. He turned to poetry, as he would later explain, not to publish his verse but rather because writing verse gave him joy. The initial response to his poetry was encouraging. At a time when academic poetry was given to erudite obscurities and self-indulgent ornamentation, editors and critics were attracted by Dennis's understated lyrical voice, which offered insights drawn from everyday experiences. Dennis's early work was often compared to the subtle minimalism of short-story writer Raymond Carver. Dennis's reputation continued to grow as he worked steadily, publishing numerous volumes of verse. As his verse evolved, Dennis began to investigate the spiritual dimension of life, drawing on a variety of religious systems and myth structures to forge a particularly contemporary spiritual sensibility that invested the material universe with the potent influence of gods, angels, demons, and saints without insisting on any single theology. Even as his reputation grew, Dennis remained grounded in the classroom, where he loved engaging his students in the lively art of explicating texts, of listening to the voice of the poet, and of testing readings of classic texts. After his receipt of the Pulitzer and the publication of his collected poetry in 2004 and a new volume of verse in 2007, Dennis enjoyed increased recognition.

ANALYSIS

What strikes a first-time reader of Carl Dennis's verse is the accessibility of his free-verse poetic line, the familiarity of the everyday images and experiences he selects for treatment, and the comforting wisdom such images and experiences afford the reader. Inspired by Whitman's notion of the reader of poetry as a friend of the poet and the poem itself as an occasion for intimacy between writer and reader, who are otherwise strangers, Dennis created a sense of intimacy in his poetry. This feeling of intimacy—in an era when much academic poetry delighted in formal experimentation, obscure topics, pretentious allusions, and elaborate linguistic ornamentation—gives Dennis's poetry its warmth, even when the insights are troubling. The poetry reads as if it is being spoken, not written, and conveys a feeling of reassurance, even camaraderie. Often compared to Billy Collins in his choice of subject matter and poetic line, Dennis, like Collins, provokes harsher assessments from more academic readers who find in such light poetry the threat of bathos and regard its wisdom as little more than clichés. However, Dennis's verse, as indicated by his receipt of a Pulitzer, continues to speak to a wide audience attracted to his wry insights, his careful eye for observation and detail, and his colloquial verse line (itself actually carefully measured and sculpted with a subtle play of vowels and consonants, rhythms and pauses).

SIGNS AND WONDERS

Signs and Wonders, Dennis's third collection, published as part of the Contemporary Poets series of Princeton University Press, earned widespread national attention for Dennis. It reflects the sense and sensibility of his early work, before it would become more specifically spiritual. These are poems of precise and careful observation, describing the oppressive feel of muggy nights, the weighty business of sorting through a collection of old photographs, a gathering of bird-watchers, and the poet digging through a heavy snow in Buffalo, New York. These meditations on such everyday occasions, like the fairy tales young Dennis so loved, contain clear and straightforward insights into the foibles and quiet heroics of being alive and testify how the world speaks to the alert and the sensitive. The insights are commonplace enough to be anyone's, and the verse line is unadorned, direct, as if someone is talking. This sense of conversation is underscored by Dennis's frequent use of the word "you" and his use of rhetorical questions, both strategies that pull the reader into the dynamic of the poem. However, Dennis's voice is that of someone sensitive to the implications of experience. Several poems make pointed reference to Whitman, whose passionate, soulful call to intimacy with the reader is strongly reflected in Dennis's collection. The perceptions verge on cliché—difficult moments are best endured with dignity; vanity distracts the spirit; the slenderest moments of grace and beauty should be embraced; time passes with puzzling logic leaving only the bittersweet burden of memory; and friendship is life's splendid reward. They are not diffi-

cult truths and are not burdened by elaborate philosophical reasoning but rather are expressed with quietly underplayed humor and ironic understatement. Dennis's signature informality and accessibility help these poems convey insights into loneliness, pain, and longing.

PRACTICAL GODS

Practical Gods, Dennis's Pulitzer Prize-winning collection, published when Dennis was sixty-three, reflects the profoundly spiritual direction Dennis's verse began to take in the mid-1980's. That spirituality, which draws from Dennis's longtime interest in American Transcendentalism, is not driven by any theology nor is its argument drawn from any institutional religion. Dennis's earlier work has a decidedly secular feel and reflects his fascination with the subtleties of the horizontal plane of experience; therefore, these poems speak without apology or irony of the soul, how the material world cannot stand for a moment to be simply what it is. The traumatic experiences of loss, regret, and longing are far deeper here than in his earlier work, as the poet passes into late middle age. In the heartbreaking "St. Francis and the Nun," one of Dennis's most frequently anthologized poems, the message of the Catholic saint, known for his easy communication with birds and animals, extolling them to relish the joy of life, is juxtaposed with a young nun dying too soon, craving only some kind of explanation as to why her brief life contains such terrible suffering. In the collection's closing poem, the poignant "The God Who Loves You," the poet ponders how gods—not specifically the Christian God but any deity—can bear to watch individuals who, had they made other choices, would have led much different lives. The gods must endure the pain of unmet expectations and frustrations of which mortals remain completely unaware. The poem expresses a most wrenching twist on the conventional notion of prayer.

In the poems of *Practical Gods*, the poet's vocabulary freely draws on religious notions: Dennis investigates the implications of eternity, the tension between damnation and salvation, the logic of suffering, the practical worth of the concept of sin, and the dimensions of agape. Using allusions from religious literature—largely the Bible and classical mythology—the verse demands confidence in transcendence, that experience, emotions, and reality participate in something higher, something radiant beyond the measure of the senses. Dennis never resorts to simplistic New Age bromides (his gods, after all, are practical); rather he offers, poem to poem, a cool kind of stoicism that accepts the complications of existence and dares nevertheless to affirm its cosmic implications against the stubborn evidence of humanity's inconsequentiality in a harrowing post-Enlightenment universe.

OTHER MAJOR WORK

NONFICTION: *Poetry as Persuasion*, 2001.

BIBLIOGRAPHY

Altieri, Charles. "Sensibility, Rhetoric, and Will: Some Tensions in Contemporary Poetry." *Contemporary Literature* 23, no. 4 (1982): 451-479. A groundbreaking early reading of Dennis by a fellow poet, who sees in Dennis's early poetry a nascent romanticism (like that of John Ashbery and Robert Pinsky) that celebrates something higher in human nature.

De Nicola, Deborah. *Orpheus and Contemporary Poems on Greek Myth*. Lebanon, N.H.: University Press of New England, 1999. Investigates a critical aspect of Dennis's poetry within the context of other contemporary poets who juxtapose mythic elements with modern experiences.

Dennis, Carl. *Poetry as Persuasion*. Athens: University of Georgia Press, 2001. Collects a lifetime of readings of poets most influential on Dennis's own poetry. Investigates the relationship between reader and writer, which is central to Dennis's own poetry.

Ford, Marcia, and Andrea Jaeger. *Finding Hope: Cultivating God's Gift of a Hopeful Spirit*. Woodstock, Vt.: SkyLight Paths Press, 2006. Uses Dennis's late poetry as examples of contemporary poets who tap traditional spirituality as a strategy of hope in difficult moments of crisis. Insists too stridently on Dennis as a Christian poet.

Grossberg, Benjamin S. Review of *Unknown Friends*. *Antioch Review* 66, no. 1 (Winter, 2008): 189-191. This review of Dennis's collection on the distance between friends and the connections between strangers notes that at his best, Dennis "transmutes casual language into convincing lyricism."

Ryan, Michael. *A Difficult Grace: On Poets, Poetry, and Writing*. Athens: University of Georgia Press, 2000. Accessible and illuminating reading of Dennis's generation of poets. Particularly strong on how poets create voice and shape the dynamic of reader participation.

Joseph Dewey

TOI DERRICOTTE

Born: Detroit, Michigan; April 12, 1941

PRINCIPAL POETRY

The Empress of the Death House, 1978
Natural Birth, 1983
Captivity, 1989
Tender, 1997

OTHER LITERARY FORMS

A 1997 memoir, *The Black Notebooks: An Interior Journey*, is the most popular nonfiction work of Toi Derricotte. The book, expanded from twenty years of diaries, reveals how it feels to look white and be black in the United States. The work met appropriate controversy during a time when the nation, at the behest of then-president Bill Clinton, was trying to generate a dialogue on racial abuses past and present. Derricotte also cowrote with Madeline Tiger Bass *Creative Writing: A Manual for Teachers* (1985), published by the New Jersey State Council on the Arts. The Library of Congress's *The Poet and the Poem from the Library of Congress: Toi Derricotte* is an archival recording produced in October, 1998, by the Library of Congress's Magnetic Recording Laboratory in Washington, D.C. It is one of four video or audio presentations that profile Derricotte's life and work.

ACHIEVEMENTS

Toi Derricotte has forced the American poetry establishment to rethink its assumptions about African

Americans and women. Her work evolved through the 1970's, during the rise in black feminist awareness and what some scholars call the second Renaissance in black writing, or the Black Arts movement. She first won recognition from the New School for Social Research with its 1973 Pen and Brush Award for an untitled poetry manuscript. She went on to win recognition and fellowships from the Academy of American Poets in both 1974 and 1978. The National Endowment for the Arts bestowed awards in 1985 and 1990. She won the nomination for the 1998 Pushcart Prize, a Folger Shakespeare Library Poetry Book Award, a Lucille Medwick Memorial Award from the Poetry Society of America, and a United Black Artists' Distinguished Pioneering of the Arts Award.

BIOGRAPHY

Born April 12, 1941, into a Detroit family separated from most of the city's African American community by class and lighter skin, Toinette Derricotte (then Webster) wrote as a way to find solace in an existence filled with alienation. Her parents, Benjamin Sweeney Webster, a mortician, and Antonia Banquet Webster Cyrus, a systems analyst, divorced when she was a teenager. The young girl quickly learned to hide her thoughts on the page.

Writing was a first passion, but after high school, the shy teen studied psychology at Wayne State University with visions of a doctorate. Plans changed in December, 1961, when she gave birth to son Anthony, and in July, 1962, Derricotte married artist Clarence Reese. The union lasted two years. In 1967, she married banker Bruce Derricotte. They separated in 1991.

Parenthood's realities led Derricotte to major in special education. She started teaching in 1964 with the Manpower Program. She finished a bachelor's degree in 1965. In 1966, Derricotte became a teacher for mentally and emotionally retarded students at Detroit's Farand School. In 1969, Derricotte left her hometown to teach remedial reading at Jefferson School in Teaneck, New Jersey. The job lasted a year.

She taught for money, but always wrote. In 1973, Derricotte began a four-year stint on the *New York Quarterly* staff. The following year she started a fifteen-year residency with the New Jersey State Council on the Arts Poet-in-the-Schools program. Those years set the direction of her life as author, mentor, and teacher.

The Empress of the Death House, her first collection, was published in 1978. The next year she founded a retreat to foster the development of African American poets in a culturally sensitive atmosphere. That involvement ended in 1982 but was reborn in 1996, when she collaborated with Cornelius Eady to create Cave Canem, a summer workshop in upstate New York.

In 1983, *Natural Birth* was published. Derricotte graduated from New York University with a master's degree in creative writing the next year. The 1985 publication of *Creative Writing: A Manual for Teachers*, coauthored with Madeline Bass, followed.

In 1988, twenty-one years after she left home for New Jersey, Derricotte moved to Norfolk, Virginia, to teach at Old Dominion. The next year, *Captivity* was published. In 1990, she spent a year as Commonwealth professor in the English department of George Mason University in Fairfax, Virginia. In 1991, she moved to the University of Pittsburgh.

Throughout her writing career, Derricotte has immersed herself in classes, readings, and contributions to a various magazines and journals, such as *Pequod*, *Iowa Review*, *Ironwood*, *Northwest Review*, *Poetry Northwest*, *American Poetry Review*, *Bread Loaf Quarterly*, *Massachusetts Review*, *Ploughshares*, and *Feminist Studies*. Many of her poems and essays appear in anthologies, as well.

During 1992 and 1993, she served on faculties of summer workshops at Squaw Valley, the University of South Florida, and the College of Charleston. The decade ended with the publication of *Tender* (1997), the 1997 memoir *The Black Notebooks*, and, in 2000, a reissue of *Natural Birth*.

ANALYSIS

Toi Derricotte's candor has been compared with the simple clarity of Emily Dickinson and honest communication of Walt Whitman—but only by those unfamiliar with African American poetry. Derricotte's blunt eloquence is typical of poets in the period from the mid-1960's to the mid-1970's, known as the Black Arts movement, which some scholars have considered to be the counterpart of the Black Power movement. Derricotte's style and themes are more similar to those of Nikki Giovanni or Mari Evans than to those of nineteenth century white Americans.

Derricotte is unique in her confessional treatment of racial identity. "My skin causes certain problems continuously, problems that open the issue of racism over and over like a wound," she once wrote. That statement hangs over her photograph on the African American Literature Book Club Web site as tribute to the talent she displays in the ability to turn poignant racial episodes into instruments that sometimes strike readers' consciences with jackhammer force and, at others, soothe their souls.

"I'm not an Emily Dickinson scholar, but I have loved her for many, many years, for many reasons," she wrote in *Titanic Operas: A Poet's Corner of Responses to Dickinson's Legacy* (edited by Martha Nell Smith and Laura Elyn Lauth): "One of the reasons is because of her great courage to look at things—the most terrifying, the most beautiful—without flinching."

"Her poems begin in ordinary experiences," Jon Woodson writes of Derricotte in *Contemporary Women Poets*, "but she dissects the routine definitions supplied by society as a way towards making discoveries about what unsuspected resources the self actually contains." That aptly describes what a reader will find in any of the author's poems.

The prizewinning writer treats womanhood and race as media through which she bares her torments and forces readers to look more closely than ever before at often evaded aspects of the human experience. She writes about being an African American woman in the late twentieth century, but the work is likely to resonate with readers in any culture and time who understand that life holds more questions than answers.

THE EMPRESS OF THE DEATH HOUSE
Derricotte's early works focused on death and birth. The theme is heavy in her first book, *The Empress of the Death House*, where "The Grandmother Poems" discuss her childhood experiences in her grandparents' Detroit funeral home. Her mother's stepfather owned the business. Although her grandmother was sickly,

she used two thousand dollars of her own money to send Derricotte's father to mortuary school, so that he might join a more stable line of work.

The Empress of the Death House grapples with the plight of women who survive abuse in an effort to sort out her feelings about her grandmother and mother. The understanding was a step on the path to self-awareness and helped her to understand her personal reactions to motherhood. In *American Book Review*, reviewer Joe Weixlmann, who wrote about *Natural Birth*, said *The Empress of the Death House* opens readers' eyes to the "indifference or contempt" with which the world treats African American women.

NATURAL BIRTH
Natural Birth, in both its 1983 and 2000 editions, is an extension of Derricotte's investigation into the lives of African American women. The collection candidly probes the birth process as an experience that hurts too much and humiliates. This poem is a "tour de force, at once a book-length experimental poem, an exploration of the extremes of human experience, and an examination of the social construction of identity," Woodson wrote of the 1983 Crossing Press version. Of the 2000 edition, Eileen Robinson wrote in *Black Issues Book Review*:

> *Natural Birth* is a triumph of one woman's spirit that will appeal to readers who are looking for depth, emotion, originality and truth. . . . Derricotte has completed a moving testament to teenage mothers, and mothers everywhere, who survive the miracle of birth. It is also a special gift to their children who grow stronger for understanding the very human fears and pains of the women who brought them here.

Natural Birth takes writings about death, birth, and transcendence to another level. Derricotte reaches for the truth that most unwed mothers might like to tell. She reaches inside the experience of childbirth for the thoughts that most mothers might want to share.

In *Contemporary Authors*, Derricotte is quoted as saying that her Catholic school education taught that confession made a person "whole" or "back into a state of grace." She concludes,

> As a black woman, I have been consistently confused about my 'sins,' unsure of which faults were in me and

which faults were the results of others' projections. . . . truthtelling in my art is also a way to separate my 'self' from what I have been taught to believe about my 'self,' the degrading stereotypes about black women.

CAPTIVITY

Captivity shifted the focus from gender to race, sliding from portraits of general poverty to intricate sketches of urban students. The book places the American slave experience at the root of many issues in today's black experience. The dehumanization and commercialization of African Americans' slave ancestors has been cited as a root cause of black poverty, fractured family structures, violence, and continued oppression. *Village Voice* reviewer Robyn Selman called the book "a personal exploration yielding truths that apply to all of us."

TENDER

Derricotte's fourth book of poetry, *Tender*, does a similar favor. The uncharacteristically short title poem appears to talk about meat and begins "The tenderest meat/ comes from the houses/ where you hear the least// squealing." It does not take much reflection to see the metaphor about pain-filled lives. In the collection's preface, Derricotte urges readers to use the poem as a hub in exploring, as she calls the book's structure, "a seven-spoked wheel." The poet continues to wrestle with the meanings of death, birth, and transcendence. She writes, "Violence is central to our lives, a constant and unavoidable reality."

Derricotte's enduring legacy might be that, as she herself observed of Emily Dickinson, she does not flinch, whether the subject is political or sexual, and that courage is especially well demonstrated in *Tender*. For example, in "Clitoris," she discusses oral sex and her emotional response to it graphically and with lush imagery.

Like many in her generation, Derricotte never let go of the optimism of the 1960's about a positive evolution in American attitudes and treatment of women and blacks. At the same time, she does not hesitate to display bitter disappointment at where the country is along the road. For example, in "After a Reading at a Black College," also from *Tender*, she looks forward with both hope and skepticism:

Maybe one day we will have
written about this color thing
until we've solved it. Tonight
when I read my poems about
looking white, the audience strains
forward with their whole colored
bodies. . . .

. . . . .

. . . though frightened,
I don't stop the spirit.
Hold steady, Harriet Tubman whispers,
Don't flop around.

Once again, the best part of Derricotte's work is that, no matter how scathing, it is unapologetic. "People would like inspiring books that tell them what to do, something like *Five Steps Not to Be a Racist*," she told Don Lee in a 1996 interview in *Ploughshares*, the Emerson College literary journal. "That's just not the truth. The easy solutions don't really prepare one for the hard work that needs to be done." She goes on,

I feel the need to represent what's not spoken. I discover a pocket in myself that hasn't been articulated, then I have to find a form to carry that. Speaking the unspeakable is not that hard. The difficulty is in finding a way to make it perfect, to make it have light and beauty and truth inside it.

OTHER MAJOR WORKS

NONFICTION: *Creative Writing: A Manual for Teachers*, 1985 (with Madeline Bass); *The Black Notebooks: An Interior Journey*, 1997.

EDITED TEXT: *Gathering Ground: A Reader Celebrating Cave Canem's First Decade*, 2006 (with Cornelius Eady).

BIBLIOGRAPHY

Andrews, William, et al., eds. *The Oxford Companion to African American Literature*. New York: Oxford University Press, 1996. Contains a thorough, concise resume of Derricotte's life.

Derricotte, Toi. "The Night I Stopped Singing Like Billie Holiday." In *Shaping Memories: Reflections of African American Women Writers*, edited by Joanne Veal Gabbin. Jackson: University Press of Mississippi, 2009. A biographical reflection by Derricotte on her life.

Johnson, Sheila Goldburgh. "*Captivity*." In *Master-plots II: African American Literature*, edited by Tyrone Williams. Rev. ed. Pasadena, Calif.: Salem Press, 2009. An in-depth analysis of *Captivity* that examines themes and meanings as well as the critical context.

Pettis, Joyce. *African American Poets: Lives, Works, and Sources*. Westport, Conn.: Greenwood Press, 2002. A discussion of African American poets that focuses on their lives and how they affected their work. Contains a chapter on Derricotte.

Powers, William F. "The Furious Muse: Black Poets Assess the State of Their Art." *The Washington Post*, October 1, 1994, p. H1. This article reports on a Harrisburg, Virginia, gathering of thirty African American poets and about 250 writers, critics, and scholars to define qualities that set black poetry apart from the American mainstream. The feature story offers insight into Derricotte's personality.

Robinson, Caudell M. "Where Poets Explore Their Pain While Others Beware the Dog." *American Visions* 14, no. 5 (October, 1999): 30. Profiles Derricotte's thoughts on writing and efforts to promote the art among African Americans through a summer workshop in upstate New York.

Vincent F. A. Golphin

JAMES DICKEY

Born: Atlanta, Georgia; February 2, 1923
Died: Columbia, South Carolina; January 19, 1997

PRINCIPAL POETRY

Into the Stone, and Other Poems, 1960
Drowning with Others, 1962
Helmets, 1964
Two Poems of the Air, 1964
Buckdancer's Choice, 1965
Poems, 1957-1967, 1967
The Eye-Beaters, Blood, Victory, Madness, Buckhead, and Mercy, 1970
The Zodiac, 1976

The Strength of Fields, 1977
Head-Deep in Strange Sounds: Free-Flight Improvisations from the UnEnglish, 1979
Falling, May Day Sermon, and Other Poems, 1981
The Early Motion, 1981
Puella, 1982
The Central Motion: Poems, 1968-1979, 1983
The Eagle's Mile, 1990
The Whole Motion: Collected Poems, 1945-1992, 1992

OTHER LITERARY FORMS

James Dickey was a novelist as well as a poet, having published *Deliverance* (1970) and *Alnilam* (1987). *The Suspect in Poetry* (1964) and *From Babel to Byzantium* (1968) are important collections of criticism on modern and contemporary poetry. *Self-Interviews* (1970), *Sorties* (1971), *Night Hurdling: Poems, Essays, Conversations, Commencements, and Afterwords* (1983), and *The Voiced Connections of James Dickey* (1989) are collections of essays, addresses, journal notes, and interviews. *Spinning the Crystal Ball* (1967) and *Metaphor as Pure Adventure* (1968) are influential pamphlets based on addresses Dickey delivered while serving as consultant in poetry to the Library of Congress. Dickey also wrote a number of essays and book reviews for popular periodicals and newspapers, as well as screenplays and music for several films, two children's books, and four coffee-table books (in collaboration with various graphic and photographic artists).

ACHIEVEMENTS

Though James Dickey's subject matter varies widely, the primary tension underlying most of his writing involves the relationship between romantic individualism and power. In Dickey's work, this relationship is often played out through attempts to relate the self to the large rhythms of the universe, a process that Dickey depicts as a necessary, yet potentially destructive, catalyst in individuals' efforts to endow existence with consequence. This paradoxical vision often drew the ire of the critical establishment, but despite the controversy his writings generated, Dickey enjoyed an abundance of academic and popular acclaim for his work in a variety of genres. Among the awards he garnered are a fellowship from *Sewanee Review* (1954), the Union League Civic and Arts Poetry Prize (1958), the Vachel Lindsay Award (1959), the Longview Foundation Prize (1959), a Guggenheim Fellowship (1962), an award in literature from the National Institute of Arts and Letters (1966), the National Book Award in Poetry (1966) and the Melville Cane Award from the Poetry Society of America (1966) for *Buckdancer's Choice*, the French Prix Medicis (1971) for *Deliverance*, *Poetry*'s Levinson Prize (1981) for poems from *Puella*, the Corrington Award for Literary Excellence from Centenary College of Louisiana (1992-

James Dickey (Washington Star Collection, D.C. Public Library)

1993), and the Harriet Monroe Memorial Prize (1996). Dickey was named consultant in poetry (poet laureate) to the Library of Congress (1966-1968) and was elected to the National Institute of Arts and Letters and the American Academy of Arts and Sciences. In 1977, President Jimmy Carter selected him to read at the inaugural concert gala, making Dickey and Robert Frost the only poets up to that time to read at an American presidential inauguration. In 1983, he was invited to read the poem "For a Time and Place" at the second inauguration of Richard Riley, governor of South Carolina.

BIOGRAPHY

Born to lawyer Eugene Dickey and Maibelle Swift Dickey in the Atlanta suburb of Buckhead, James Lafayette Dickey was a mediocre high school student who preferred the athletic field to the classroom. After becoming an acclaimed football player at North Fulton High School, Dickey went on to play wingback at Clemson College in 1941 before joining the Army Air Corps the following year. Dickey was assigned to the 418th Night Fighter Squadron because of his exceptional night vision. He flew more than one hundred combat missions in the South Pacific, for which he was awarded several medals, including the Distinguished

Flying Cross. After World War II, Dickey enrolled at Vanderbilt University with the intention of pursuing a career as a writer. In 1949, he earned a B.A. in English magna cum laude; he stayed on at Vanderbilt to take an M.A. in English, writing a thesis titled "Symbol and Imagery in the Shorter Poems of Herman Melville." While at the university, he also joined the track team and won the Tennessee State High Hurdles Championship. He published several poems in the campus literary magazine and one in *Sewanee Review*; he also married Maxine Syerson, with whom he had two sons.

In 1951, Dickey began teaching at Rice University before being recalled by the Air Force to fight in the Korean War. Following his discharge, Dickey returned to teach at Rice briefly, before earning a fellowship from *Sewanee Review*, which he used to travel and write in Europe. In 1956, he returned to teach at the University of Florida, but after disputes with the university administration over his teaching assignment and a sexually explicit poem he read to a group of faculty wives, he left Florida to become a copywriter and executive for an advertising firm in New York. A year later, Dickey returned to Atlanta to work as senior writer and creative director for the local Coca-Cola bottler, later moving to other firms, where he engineered the Lay's potato chip and Delta Airlines accounts. During this period, Dickey continued publishing poetry in little magazines, eventually winning several awards, including a Guggenheim Fellowship, which allowed him to quit advertising and spend 1961-1962 writing in Italy.

During the 1960's, Dickey's reputation underwent a meteoric rise, as he established himself as one of the major poets of his generation and won a series of major awards. After serving as poet-in-residence at several universities—including the University of Wisconsin, where he won the National Book Award and was the subject of a feature article in *Life* magazine—Dickey accepted the chair of Carolina Professor in English at the University of South Carolina, where he continued to teach. In 1976, Maxine Dickey died, and Dickey married Deborah Dodson, with whom he had a daughter in 1981. Dickey continued to live and write at a vigorous pace, producing two novels in the last ten years of his life. From 1989 to 1994, he served as a Yale Younger Poets contest judge. He died in Columbia, South Carolina, on January 19, 1997.

ANALYSIS

In his poetry and novels, James Dickey often explored what extreme, and sometimes violent, situations reveal about the human condition. Dickey's poetry and fiction of the late 1950's to the 1970's are characterized by startlingly original images and a strong narrative thrust, through which he expressed, and assessed, the belief that volatile qualities are an inherent and necessary, yet potentially destructive, part of the human animal. In the late 1970's, Dickey turned to a reflective, language-oriented approach, less immediately accessible and more self-conscious, but he continued to explore his previous themes. Though his themes remained fairly constant, it should be noted that stylistically Dickey was a relentless experimenter, always looking to cover new ground in the terrain of poetic possibilities.

INTO THE STONE, AND OTHER POEMS AND DROWNING WITH OTHERS

The poems of Dickey's first two collections, *Into the Stone, and Other Poems* and *Drowning with Others*, are generally short, tightly structured, and highly rhythmic. Although these poems are often anecdotal, they do not so much unfold in time as focus on a specific psychological experience. In essence, these poems are short dramatic parables, describing a moment in which the first-person narrator experiences an epiphany resulting in a more unified and aware self. Through the brief situation presented, Dickey attempted to make a visceral impact on the reader that would become a continuing part of that person's consciousness, intensifying and altering the way in which the person experienced the world by restoring, in Ralph Waldo Emerson's words, "an original relationship to the universe."

These qualities are apparent in "Sleeping Out at Easter," which suggests how Dickey handled the theme of communion with nature in his early work. The narrator's description of his "resurrection" on Easter morning resonates with Christian and pagan overtones, making the dramatic situation—a man waking at daybreak after sleeping out in his backyard—assume a mythic, mystic dimension: "My animal eyes become human/ As the Word rises out of darkness."

The steady, flowing, melodic quality of the anapestic meter enhances the feeling that the experience happens without encumbrance. In each of the first five stanzas, the last line repeats the stanza's first line. The concluding line of each stanza is italicized and used as a refrain, producing the hypnotic quality of an incantation, and the sixth and final stanza consists entirely of the italicized refrains. The result is a sense of continuity and unity, as the poem's lines echo themselves as effortlessly as the narrator accepts the dawn and his newfound self. Dickey captures an organic unity of theme and technique that arrests and annihilates time through the image of first light, creating a new world around the narrator as he grasps the "root," and "source," of all life and of his most elemental self; it is a moment of pure religious transcendence, involving a sense of immortality achieved through communion with the permanent essence of nature.

The poem is more than an account of its narrator, however, for Dickey clearly intended it to initiate change in the reader as well. He directly addressed the reader through the use of second person in the fourth and sixth stanzas (the other four stanzas are presented in first person). These stanzas are completely italicized, indicating a transcendent voice that reverberates through all things. Similarly, the light that accompanies the new day spreads everywhere, touching everything simultaneously, symbolizing the renewal and coming together of all things. In the first stanza, the waking man declares, "My sight is the same as the sun's," and in the fifth, he describes his child, who, "mouth open, still sleeping,/ Hears the song in the egg of a bird./ The sun shall have told him that song." The transformation becomes complete in the poem's last three lines ("The sun shall have told you this song,/ For this is the grave of the king;/ For the king's grave turns you to light"): The reader ("you") is also included.

Aside from these two stanzas, Dickey primarily used first person in "Sleeping Out at Easter," as in most of his poems. When the narrator experiences transcendence he enters into a state of unity with nature ("My sight is the same as the sun's"), with the consciousness of the child, and with the reader. The narrator achieves this state without struggle; the tightly controlled, steady, almost monotonous metrics reflect the ease, godlike power, and control over experience that distinctly mark Dickey's first two books.

HELMETS

In *Helmets*, Dickey continued to explore the themes of his earlier poetry; nevertheless, *Helmets* is a transitional volume in the Dickey canon. Although there are still many short poems relying on radically subjective narrative images—poems that express control and metaphysical certainty—there also appear longer, more diffuse poems that suggest doubt and a reduced sense of control. Some of the poems in *Into the Stone, and Other Poems* and *Drowning with Others* draw on the everyday, but the emphasis is (with one or two exceptions such as "A Screened in Porch in the Country") on achieving a "superhuman" transcendent state, and transcendence is always gained. Though there are still plenty of poems of this kind in *Helmets*, in some of the poems—"Cherry Log Road," "The Scarred Girl," "Chenille"—the epiphanies are more modest and more fully human. Other poems—"Springer Mountain" and "Kudzu"—represent a more purely comic vein than his previous work.

"Approaching Prayer," one of Dickey's finest poems, indicates the manner in which the visionary mo-

ment and the role of violence began to evolve in Dickey's later work. It begins with the lines "A moment tries to come in/ Through the windows, when one must go/ Beyond what there is in the room." Instead of being plunged right into a religious experience as in "Sleeping Out at Easter," the reader witnesses a struggle, as the narrator wanders around uncertain of what he is doing. He must "circle" and go "looking for things" before he can "produce a word" he is not even sure of.

Like an amateur shaman, the narrator begins to dress for a ritual ceremony he has never previously performed, as he accumulates objects that encompass a range of experience and retain contradictory associations. The things he gathers before attempting prayer are all associated with death—the head of a boar he killed, his dead father's sweater and gamecock spurs—but also hold positive value: The hog's head represents the narrator's "best and stillest moment"; the spurs and sweater contain the memory of his father. The spurs and the hog's head are also associated with violence, and the narrator declares that his "best" moment involved violence.

After the narrator puts on the objects, he begins, through the dead hog's glass eyes, to discover another "best and stillest moment" by lining himself up with the stars in the night sky. A vision explodes before him, as "hunting" and being hunted become symbolic of the visionary moment: The narrator must experience the contrary roles. Hunting involves physical action requiring discipline and spontaneity; it also contains a deeply imaginative quality. In playing out their own parts, the predator and the prey each imaginatively enter the other's consciousness. The man must be able to think like the beast, and the beast must try to anticipate the man. When the narrator "draws the breath of life/ For the dead hog," he begins to experience the role of the prey. He is able to see himself through the eyes of the other, and a greater range of knowledge begins to open up before him.

When he views himself from the perspective of the hog, "stiller than trees or stones," the images of himself as hunter, prey, and praying freeze in his mind, shearing away time. As the narrator imagines himself goring a dog and feeling the hair on his (the hog's) back stand up, he also feels the hair that was on his head as a young man stand up. Through this thoroughly original moment, the past and the present, and the perspectives of predator and prey, merge.

As the narrator experiences killing and being killed at the same instant, the universe comes into balance, signaling his acceptance of life and death. This balance consists of stillness and motion—a universe in which the "moon and the stars do not move" and where "frantic," violent action takes place. The arrow the narrator uses to kill the hog is characterized as a shaft of light—symbolic of unity and revelation—that connects the hunter and the hog. This culminates in a unity of vision that allows him to maintain his "stillest" moment until something he compares to a shaft of light from an exploding star (suggestive of the arrow that connected hunter and hog) shoots through him, letting him feel his own death. At this point he has participated in the complete gamut of life and death. He has seen his death as a "beast" (through the eyes of the hog) and as an "angel": He has felt the light of the cosmos flare through him. When his death becomes a reality for him, he realizes that the full cycle of life contains death and violence for himself as well as for the "other." Prayer here does not result in discovery of a god who holds out the promise of an immortal soul, but in a vision that holds many dimensions of experience. Only through experiencing the contraries can real prayer be achieved, because only through full knowledge of those contraries can life be fully comprehended.

SPLIT-LINE TECHNIQUE

The greater length and variety of metrical structure of "Approaching Prayer" demonstrate the increased poetical confidence and flexibility Dickey attained with *Helmets*. In subsequent collections, *Buckdancer's Choice*; *Falling, May Day Sermon, and Other Poems* (first released in *Poems, 1957-1967*); *The Eye-Beaters, Blood, Victory, Madness, Buckhead, and Mercy*, and *The Zodiac*, this trend continued through Dickey's development of the split-line technique, which aims at creating a type of poetic stream of consciousness.

Dickey did not describe the mental processes he depicted through the split line as orderly or logical but in terms suggesting revelation: "fits," "jumps," "shocks," "electric leaps," "word-bursts," "lightning-stamped."

He saw "insight" as a matter of instinctual associations that intellectual reasoning disrupts. By breaking up his lines into "clusters of words," Dickey attempted to capture "the characteristics of thought when it associates rapidly, and in detail, in regard to a specific subject, an action, an event, a theme."

"MAY DAY SERMON"

"May Day Sermon to the Women of Gilmer County, Georgia, By a Woman Preacher Leaving the Baptist Church" is a good example of Dickey's use of the split line. The woman preacher who narrates the poem speaks in long, sprawling sentences that form hyperbolic and melodramatic masses of language. She tells the story of a religious zealot who, after discovering that his daughter has been sleeping with her boyfriend, drags her naked into the barn, chains her, and whips her while reciting biblical passages. Frenzied and near mad, the woman preacher tells the story through a tidal wave of images from the rural South. Much of the imagery is mixed and contradictory, suggesting the confusion in her own mind and the paradoxical qualities of the relationship between Christian values, especially as embodied in southern fundamentalism, and natural sexual drives. Dickey saw the poem as a commentary on "the malevolent power God has under certain circumstances: that is, when He is controlled and 'interpreted' by people of malevolent tendencies."

Dickey expressed this theme by reversing traditional Christian symbols. He describes the female narrator and God in terms of a snake. The "Lord" referred to in the first line gives "men all the help they need/ To drag their daughters into barns," suggesting the brutal, sadistically sexual use of God by some in the fundamentalist South. The psychosexual nature of the experience is indicated by the father's chaining the girl to the "centerpole," the opening of the barn door to show the "pole of light" that "comes comes," and the "unbending" snake. Sexual associations are also created through the narrator's use of snake imagery to describe God ("Jehovah . . . Down on His belly") and herself ("flickering from my mouth").

Sight, the imagination's ability to see the implications of events to find God, becomes the poem's central focus, as it takes on a deeply voyeuristic quality. First, the narrator asserts that the "Lord" watches the "abominations" the girl's father performs, but as the reader moves deeper into the passage it becomes increasingly clear that the vision is the narrator's. Instead of seeing the "abominations" she claims God witnesses, the narrator sees an orgiastic dance, as the animals "stomp" and the girl "prances": The narrator is imaginatively possessed by the scene, not simply relating it for the benefit of her audience.

As the girl is beaten, she fights against her father and "King James" by experiencing a vision of her lover, which is generated through her dance with the animals, giving her the power to transform the beating into a vision of God. Though a vision of the "torsoes of the prophets" begins to form, it quickly "dies out" as the naturalistic forces of "flesh and the Devil twist and turn/ Her body to love." Her God becomes a lover, "the dear heart/ Of life" located in the sexual urge. Like Christ on the cross refusing to recant, she refuses to deny the god she has just discovered, declaring "YOU CAN BEAT ME TO DEATH/ And I'll still be glad." Also like Christ, whose physical suffering on the cross resulted in a heightened state of spiritual awareness, the girl can "change all/ Things for good, by pain." The animals know "they shall be saved . . . as she screams of sin."

Rather than choking off her desires, the father's beating awakens her passion all the more intensely. Indeed, God, her lover, and her father are all conflated. The girl refers to "God-darling" as her "lover" and "angel-stud." Her cry "you're killing" after asking her God and lover to "put it in me" and to "give," like her use of the pronoun "YOU," can be seen as directed to God, the lover and the father. The beating assumes a sadistic sexual dimension for the woman preacher, whose "to hear her say again O again" is both part of her narrative to the congregation and a call for the beating and lovemaking to continue. Physical urges that, from a traditional point of view, are inspired by "flesh and the Devil" cannot be extinguished.

As God is pain and pleasure for the woman preacher, God is also death ("it is true/ That the kudzu advances, its copperheads drunk and tremendous"), birth ("young deer stand half/ In existence, munching cornshucks"), and, above all, sex. The woman preacher rants that the women of the congregation, like the girl, must every spring awaken to "this lovely other life-pain between the thighs." The girl has suffered her father's beating so that other women can "take/ The pain they were born for." This pain is not the sadistic torment the girl endures and transforms, but the pain that "rose through her body straight/ Up from the earth like a plant, like the process that raised overhead/ The limbs of the uninjured willow." In other words, the woman preacher claims that women must discover God in the natural passionate ache of love and giving birth. This urge springs from the earth and is part of the continuing process of life, leaving the world "uninjured" and intact, unlike the pain the father inflicts with a willow branch torn from a tree.

However, Dickey portrayed the father's beating as awakening the girl's—and the woman preacher's—sexual passion. Moreover, Dickey's woman preacher proceeds to present a male fantasy of women's perceptions and desires as she glorifies the phallus by demanding that the congregation "understand about men and sheaths." The images she uses to explain herself to the congregation are all of process, movement, "flowing," picturing existence as a constantly evolving cycle, in which male sexuality provides the impetus, "the very juice of resurrection." The poem concludes with the girl murdering her father by driving an icepick between his eyes, releasing all the animals on the farm, and roaring off with her lover on a motorcycle. The girl and her lover follow no actual road or track but disappear on the "road of mist," which moves through and envelops all nature, and they can be heard returning each spring as a reminder of the primacy of the forces of the flesh. This mythic vision inspires the woman preacher to urge the congregation to leave "God's farm," find their lovers, and go to "Hell"—that is, experience the natural world of physical drives that she believes the Bible condemns.

Though "Sleeping Out at Easter," "Approaching Prayer," and "May Day Sermon" differ radically in style, like many of Dickey's poems they concern people's attempts to gain a greater intimacy with the vital forces of the natural world. Though these particular poems present this endeavor as an affirmative experience, in "The Fiend," the novel *Deliverance*, and other works

Dickey portrays this process as menacingly destructive.

PUELLA

With *Puella* and *The Eagle's Mile*, Dickey continued to push the limits of his artistic achievements through even more intrepid experimentation. *Puella*, which is Latin for "young girl," consists of a series of relatively short poems written from the perspective of an adolescent emerging into womanhood. "Doorstep, Lightning, Waif-Dreaming" typifies this collection through its emphasis on moments of revelatory manifestation and its use of audibly charged language. The poem begins with the line "Who can tell who was born of what?" and proceeds to capture the mystery of creation and self-creation by describing the young woman's thoughts as she watches a thunderstorm unfold from the doorstep of her home. Through acoustically resonant language—"vital, engendering blank/ The interim spraddling crack the crowning rollback/ Whited out *ex nihilo*"—Dickey described the "shifting blasts" of thunder and lightning that culminate in the young woman's realization of the vitality within her ("I come of a root-system of fire") as she beholds her powers of self-sufficiency. In its entirety, *Puella* is a resounding celebration of natural processes, independence, and the strength and power of womanhood.

THE EAGLE'S MILE

With *The Eagle's Mile*, Dickey continued to foreground the sounds of poetic language while exploring the self's relationship to nature; however, instead of using narrative as does much of his previous work, these poems are deeply reflective meditations. "Daybreak" describes an individual's thoughts and sensations as he observes the forces of nature while standing on the beach. The narrator realizes that the auroral and tidal processes have no choice but to follow the laws that dictate their patterns, and he finds that it is impossible not to think of the human condition while making such observations. Although he feels that he has "nothing to say" to the waves, which show no signs of autonomy, he thinks that perhaps by staring into the shallows, which are "shucked of all wave-law," he can discover something about his relationship to the world. He imagines that by doing so he could see his own reflection and the reflection of the clouds and sky merging into one image, suggesting that some force, somewhere, must have conceived of and created a unified design that allows him and the world to exist.

"Daybreak" characterizes *The Eagle's Mile*, and much of Dickey's poetry, in its emphasis on the power of the psyche's imaginative capacities. Though in the past Dickey had shown that such idealism contains potential dangers, the rewards Dickey discovered reflect his belief in the human spirit's insatiable desire to extend itself beyond conventional boundaries, embracing a heightened state of emotional responsiveness and a capacity for glory.

OTHER MAJOR WORKS

LONG FICTION: *Deliverance*, 1970; *Alnilam*, 1987; *To the White Sea*, 1993.

SCREENPLAY: *Deliverance*, 1972 (adaptation of his novel).

TELEPLAY: *The Call of the Wild*, 1976 (adaptation of Jack London's novel).

NONFICTION: *The Suspect in Poetry*, 1964; *A Private Brinkmanship*, 1965 (address); *Spinning the Crystal Ball*, 1967; *From Babel to Byzantium*, 1968; *Metaphor as Pure Adventure*, 1968; *Self-Interviews*, 1970; *Sorties*, 1971; *The Enemy from Eden*, 1978; *In Pursuit of the Grey Soul*, 1978; *The Starry Place Between the Antlers: Why I Live in South Carolina*, 1981; *The Poet Turns on Himself*, 1982; *The Voiced Connections of James Dickey*, 1989; *Striking In: The Early Notebooks of James Dickey*, 1996 (Gordon Van Ness, editor); *Crux: The Letters of James Dickey*, 1999; *The One Voice of James Dickey: His Letters and Life, 1942-1969*, 2003 (Van Ness, editor); *Classes on Modern Poets and the Art of Poetry*, 2004; *The One Voice of James Dickey: His Letters and Life, 1970-1997*, 2005 (Van Ness, editor).

CHILDREN'S LITERATURE: *Tucky the Hunter*, 1978.

MISCELLANEOUS: *Night Hurdling: Poems, Essays, Conversations, Commencements, and Afterwords*, 1983; *The James Dickey Reader*, 1999.

BIBLIOGRAPHY

Bowers, Neal. *James Dickey: The Poet as Pitchman*. Columbia: University of Missouri Press, 1985. Focuses on Dickey as a public figure who was not only a successful poet but also a successful promoter of his work and of poetry in general. The study serves as a good introductory overview of Dickey as a media phenomenon.

Dickey, Christopher. *Summer of Deliverance: A Memoir of Father and Son*. New York: Simon & Schuster, 1998. A biography of Dickey written by his son. Includes bibliographical references and an index.

Dickey, James. Interviews. *The Voiced Connections of James Dickey*. Edited by Ronald Baughman. Columbia: University of South Carolina Press, 1990. This collection of interviews covers Dickey's career from the mid-1960's to the late 1980's. Baughman, who taught at the University of South Carolina with Dickey, has selected important and lively interviews. A useful chronology and a helpful index are included.

Hart, Henry. *James Dickey: The World as a Lie*. New York: Picador USA, 2000. A narrative biography detailing the rise and self-destruction of a literary reputation. Little of Dickey's prose or verse is quoted for analysis, and the book relies on Dickey's interviews and those held by the power of his personality.

Kirschten, Robert. *James Dickey and the Gentle Ecstasy of Earth: A Reading of the Poems*. Baton Rouge: Louisiana State University Press, 1988. Provides one of the best readings of Dickey's poems. Employs four hypotheses—mysticism, Neoplatonism, romanticism, and primitivism—to identify Dickey's characteristic techniques and thematic concerns.

_____, ed. *Critical Essays on James Dickey*. New York: Maxwell Macmillan International, 1994. Provides early reviews and a selection of more modern scholarship. Authors include Robert Bly, Paul Carroll, James Wright, and Wendell Berry. Bibliography and index.

Suarez, Ernest. "Emerson in Vietnam: Dickey, Bly, and the New Left." *Southern Literary Journal*, Spring, 1991, 100-112. Examines controversial elements in Dickey's poems and the adverse critical reaction to Dickey's work. His complex metaphysics collided with the politics of a historic particular, the Vietnam War, generating a New Left critical agenda that could not accommodate the philosophical underpinnings of his poetry. The result was widespread misinterpretations of Dickey's work.

_____. "The Uncollected Dickey: Pound, New Criticism, and the Narrative Image." *American Poetry* 7 (Fall, 1990): 127-145. By examining Dickey's early uncollected poems and his correspondence with Ezra Pound, Suarez documents Dickey's struggle to move out from under modernism's domination and arrive at his mature poetic aesthetic.

Thesing, William B. *Reading, Learning, Teaching James Dickey*. New York: Peter Lang, 2009. A teaching guide by a colleague of Dickey. Thesing examines Dickey's life, his novels, and most popular poems, using a range of critical approaches.

Thesing, William B., and Theda Wrede, eds. *The Way We Read James Dickey: Critical Approaches for the Twenty-first Century*. Columbia: University of South Carolina Press, 2009. A critical look at Dickey's works that takes into account the cultural and societal influences created by and affecting the poet.

Ernest Suarez

EMILY DICKINSON

Born: Amherst, Massachusetts; December 10, 1830
Died: Amherst, Massachusetts; May 15, 1886

PRINCIPAL POETRY

Poems, 1890
Poems: Second Series, 1891
Poems: Third Series, 1896
The Single Hound, 1914
Further Poems, 1929
Unpublished Poems, 1936
Bolts of Melody, 1945
The Poems of Emily Dickinson, 1955 (3 volumes; Thomas H. Johnson, editor)
The Complete Poems of Emily Dickinson, 1960 (Johnson, editor)

The Selected Poems of Emily Dickinson, 1996
The Poems of Emily Dickinson, 1999

OTHER LITERARY FORMS

In addition to her poetry, Emily Dickinson left behind voluminous correspondence. Because she was so rarely out of Amherst—and in her later life so rarely left her house—much of her contact with others took place through letters, many of which include poems. Like her poetry, the letters are witty, epigrammatic, and often enigmatic. They are available in *The Letters of Emily Dickinson* (1958, 3 volumes; Thomas H. Johnson and Theodora Ward, editors).

ACHIEVEMENTS

Reclusive throughout her life, Emily Dickinson garnered little recognition for her poetry during her lifetime, but her legacy to American literature in general and poetic form in particular is an achievement few have surmounted. As surely as William Faulkner and Ernest Hemingway, different as they were, brought

American fiction into the twentieth century, so Walt Whitman and Emily Dickinson brought about a revolution in American poetry. By the mid-nineteenth century, American lyric poetry had matured to an evenly polished state. Edgar Allan Poe, Ralph Waldo Emerson, and Herman Melville were creating poetry of both power and precision, but American poetry was still hampered by certain limiting assumptions about the nature of literary language, about the value of regular rhythm, meter, and rhyme, and about imagery as ornamental rather than organic. For the medium not to become sterile and conventionalized, poets had to expand the possibilities of the form.

Into this situation came Dickinson and Whitman, poets who—except in their commitment to writing a personalized poetry unlike anything the nineteenth century had thus far read—differ as widely as do Faulkner and Hemingway. Whitman rid himself of the limitations of regular meter entirely. Identifying with the common man, Whitman attempted to make him into a hero who could encompass the universe. He was a poet of the open road; Whitman journeyed along, accumulating experience and attempting to unite himself with the world around him. For him, life was dynamic and progressive. Dickinson, however, was the poet of exclusion, of the shut door. She accepted the limitations of rhyme and meter, and worked endless variations on one basic pattern, exploring the nuances that the framework would allow. No democrat, she constructed for herself a set of aristocratic images. No traveler, she stayed at home to examine small fragments of the world she knew. For Dickinson life was kinesthetic; she recorded the impressions of experience on her nerves and on her soul. Rather than being linear and progressive, it was circular: "My business is circumference," she wrote, and she often described the arcs and circles of experience. As carefully as Whitman defined himself by inclusion, Dickinson defined herself and her experience by exclusion, by what she was not. Whitman was a poet of explanation; Dickinson, having rejected expansion, exploited suggestion.

Different as they were, however, they are

Emily Dickinson

America's greatest lyric poets. Although Dickinson was barely understood or appreciated in her own lifetime, she now seems a central figure—at once firmly in a tradition and, at the same time, a breaker of tradition, a revolutionary who freed American poetry for modern thought and technique.

BIOGRAPHY

"Renunciation is a piercing virtue," wrote Emily Elizabeth Dickinson, and her life can be seen as a series of renunciations. Born in 1830 of a prominent Amherst family, she rarely left the town, except for time spent in Boston and trips to Washington and Philadelphia. She attended the Amherst Academy and Mount Holyoke Female Seminary. Although she was witty and popular, she set herself apart from the other girls by her refusal to be converted to the conventional Christianity of the town. Her life was marked by a circle of close friends and of family: a stern and humorless father, a mother who suffered a long period of illness and whom Emily took care of; her sister Lavinia, who likewise never married and remained in the family home; and her brother Austin, who married Sue Gilbert Dickinson and whose forceful personality, like that of his wife, affected the family while Emily Dickinson lived, and whose affair with Mabel Todd, the editor of the poems, precipitated family squabbles that affected their publication.

Additionally, there was a series of men—for it almost seems that Dickinson took what she called her "preceptors" one at a time—who formed a sort of emotional resource for her. The first of these was Samuel Bowles, the editor of the neighboring Springfield, Massachusetts, *Republican*, which published some of her poetry. Charles Wadsworth was the minister of a Philadelphia church; a preacher famous for his eloquence, he preached one Sunday when Dickinson was in Philadelphia, and afterward they corresponded for several years. In 1862, however, he and his family moved from Philadelphia to the West Coast. Dickinson immediately sent four of her poems to Thomas Wentworth Higginson, at *The Atlantic Monthly*, for his advice, and they began a long friendship; although Higginson was never convinced that Dickinson was a finished poet, he was a continuing mentor. Finally, late in life, Dickinson

met Judge Otis Lord, and for a time it seemed as if they were to be married; this was her one explicitly romantic friendship, but the marriage never took place. There were also less intense friendships with women, particularly Mabel Todd, who, despite her important role in Dickinson's life, never actually met her, and with the writer Helen Hunt Jackson, one of the few to accept Dickinson's poetry as it was written.

The nature of the relationships with the "preceptors" and their effect on the poetry is a matter of much controversy. It is complicated by three famous and emotional "Master" letters that Dickinson wrote between 1858 and 1862 (the dates are partly conjectural). Who the master was, is uncertain. For Johnson, Dickinson's editor, the great influence was Wadsworth, and although their relationship was always geographically distant, it was he who was the great love, his moving to California the emotional crisis that occasioned the great flood-years of poetry—366 poems in 1862 alone, according to Johnson. For Richard B. Sewall, author of the standard biography, Bowles was the master.

Whatever the case, it is true that after 1862, Dickinson rarely left her house, except for a necessary visit to Boston where she was treated for eye trouble. She wore white dresses and with more and more frequency refused to see visitors, usually remaining upstairs, listening to the conversations and entering, if at all, by calling down the stairs or by sending in poems or other tokens of her participation. She became known as the "Myth of Amherst," and from this image is drawn the popular notion of the eccentric old maid that persists in the imagination of many of her readers today. However, it is clear that whatever the limits of her actual experience, Dickinson lived life on the emotional level with great intensity. Her poetry is dense with vividly rendered emotions and observations, and she transformed the paucity of her outward life into the richness of her inner life.

Richard Wilbur has suggested that Dickinson suffered three great deprivations in her life: of a lover, of publication and fame, and of a God in whom she could believe. Although she often questioned a world in which such deprivations were necessary, she more frequently compensated, as Wilbur believes, by calling her "privation good, rendering it positive by renunciation." That she lived in a world of distances, solitude, and renunciation, her biography makes clear; that she turned that absence into beauty is the testimony of her poetry.

ANALYSIS

During her lifetime, only seven of Emily Dickinson's poems were published, most of them edited to make them more conventional. After Dickinson's death, her sister Lavinia discovered about nine hundred poems, more than half of the nearly 1,775 poems that came to form the Dickinson canon. She took these to a family friend, Mabel Todd, who, with Dickinson's friend Thomas Wentworth Higginson, published 115 of the poems in 1890. Together they published a second group of 166 in 1891, and Todd alone edited a third series in 1896. Unfortunately, Todd and Colonel Higginson continued the practice of revision that had begun with the first seven published poems, smoothing the rhymes and meter, revising the diction, and generally regularizing the poetry.

In 1914, Emily Dickinson's niece, Martha Dickinson Bianchi, published the first of several volumes of the poetry she was to edit. Although she was more scrupulous about preserving Dickinson's language and intent, several editorial problems persisted, and the body of Dickinson's poetry remained fragmented and often altered. In 1950, the Dickinson literary estate was given to Harvard University, and Thomas H. Johnson began his work of editing, arranging, and presenting the text. In 1955, he produced the variorum edition, 1,775 poems arranged in an attempt at chronological order, given such evidence as handwriting changes and incorporation of the poems in letters, and including all variations of the poems. In 1960, he chose one form of each poem as the final version and published the resulting collection as *The Complete Poems of Emily Dickinson*. Johnson's text and numbering system are accepted as the standard. His job was thorough, diligent, and imaginative. This is not to say, however, that his decisions about dates or choices among variants must be taken as final. Many scholars have other opinions, and since Dickinson herself apparently did not make final choices, there is no reason to accept every decision Johnson made.

Dickinson's poetry is at times sentimental, the extended metaphors occasionally too cute, the riddling tone sometimes too coy. Like any poet, that is, she has limitations; and because her poetry is so consistent throughout her life, those limitations may be more obvious than in a poet who changes more noticeably. They do not, however, diminish her stature. If she found her place in American literature only decades after her death, it is a place she will not forfeit. Her importance is, of course, partly historical: With Whitman she changed the shape and direction of American poetry, creating and fulfilling poetic potentials that make her a poet beyond her century. Her importance, however, is much greater than that. The intensity with which she converted emotional loss and intellectual questioning into art, the wit and energy of her work, mark the body of her poetry as among the finest America has yet produced.

THEMES AND FORM

One of Emily Dickinson's poems (#1129) begins, "Tell all the Truth but tell it slant," and the oblique and often enigmatic rendering of Truth is the dominant theme of Dickinson's poetry. Its motifs often recur: love, death, poetry, beauty, nature, immortality, and the self. Such abstractions do not, however, indicate the broad and rich changes that Dickinson obliquely rings on the truths she tells. Dickinson's truth is, in the broadest sense, a religious truth.

Formally, her poetry plays endless variations on the Protestant hymn meters that she knew from her youthful experiences in church. Her reading in contemporary poetry was limited, and the form she knew best was the iambic of hymns: common meter (with its alternating tetrameter and trimeter lines), long meter (four lines of tetrameter), and short meter (four of trimeter) became the framework of her poetry. That static form, however, could not contain the energy of her work, and the rhythms and rhymes are varied, upset, and broken to accommodate the feeling of her lines. The predictable patterns of hymns were not for Dickinson, who delighted in off-rhyme, consonance, and, less frequently, eye-rhyme.

"I LIKE TO SEE IT LAP THE MILES"

Dickinson was a religious poet more than formally, but her thematic sense of religion lies not in her assurance, but in her continual questioning of God, in her attempt to define his nature and that of his world. Although she was always a poet of definition, straightforward definition was too direct for her: "The Riddle we can guess/ We speedily despise," she wrote. Her works often begin, "It was not" or "It was like," with the poem being an oblique attempt to define the "it." "I like to see it lap the Miles" (#585) is a typical Dickinson riddle poem. Like many, it begins with "it," a pronoun without an antecedent, so that the reader must join in the process of discovery and definition. The riddle is based on an extended metaphor; the answer to the riddle, a train, is compared to a horse; but in the poem both tenor (train) and vehicle (horse) are unstated. Meanwhile, what begins with an almost cloying tone, the train as an animal lapping and licking, moves through subtle gradations of attitude until the train stops at the end "docile and omnipotent." This juxtaposition of incongruous adjectives, like the coupling of unlikely adjective and noun, is another of Dickinson's favorite devices; just as the movement of the poem has been from the animal's (and train's) tame friendliness to its assertive power, so these adjectives crystallize the paradox.

"IT SIFTS FROM LEADEN SIEVES"

"It sifts from Leaden Sieves" (#311), another riddle poem, also begins with an undefined "it," and again the movement of the poem and its description of the powerfully effacing strength of the snow, which is the subject of the poem and the answer to the riddle, is from apparently innocent beauty through detailed strength to a quietly understated dread. The emotional movement in the famous riddle poem "A Route of Evanescence" (#1463) is less striking, since the poet maintains the same awed appreciation of the hummingbird from beginning to end; but the source of that awe likewise moves from the bird's ephemeral beauty to its power.

"IT WAS NOT DEATH, FOR I STOOD UP"

Riddling becomes less straightforward, but no less central, in such a representative Dickinson poem as "It was not Death, for I stood up" (#510), in which many of her themes and techniques appear. The first third of the poem, two stanzas of the six, suggest what the "it" is not: death, night, frost, or fire. Each is presented in a couplet, but even in those pairs of lines, Dickinson manages to disconcert her reader. It is not death, for the

persona is standing upright, the difference between life and death reduced to one of posture. Nor is it night, for the bells are chiming noon—but Dickinson's image for that fact is also unnatural. The bells are mouths, their clappers tongues, which are "Put out"; personification here does not have the effect of making the bells more human, but of making them grotesque, breaking down as it does the barriers between such normally discrete worlds as the mechanical and the human, a distinction that Dickinson often dissolves. Moreover, the notion of the bells sticking out their tongues suggests their contemptuous attitude toward humankind. In stanza 2, it is not frost because hot winds are crawling on the persona's flesh. The hackneyed phrase is reversed, so it is not coolness, but heat that makes flesh crawl, and not the flesh itself that crawls, but the winds on it; nor is it fire, for the persona's marble feet "Could keep a Chancel, cool." Again, the persona is dehumanized, now grotesquely marble. While accomplishing this, Dickinson has also begun her inclusion of sense data, pervasive in the first part of the poem, so that the confrontation is not only intellectual and emotional but physical as well.

The second third of the poem changes the proportions. Although the experience is not actually any of the four things she has mentioned above, it is like them all; but now death, the first, is given seven lines, night three, frost only two, and fire is squeezed out altogether. It is like death because she has, after all, seen figures arranged like her own; now her life is "shaven,/ And fitted to a frame." It is like night when everything that "ticked"—again mechanical imagery for a natural phenomenon—has stopped, and like frosts, which in early autumn morns "Repeal the Beating Ground." Her vocabulary startles once more: The ground beats with life, but the frost can void it; "repeal" suggests the law, but nature's laws are here completely nullified.

Finally, in the last stanza, the metaphor shifts completely, and the experience is compared to something new: drowning at sea. It is "stopless" but "cool"; the agony that so often marks Dickinson's poetry may be appropriate to the persona, but nothing around her, neither people nor nature, seems to note it. Most important, there is neither chance nor means of rescue; there is no report of land. Any of these conditions would justify despair, but for the poet, this climatic experience is so chaotic that even despair is not justified, for there is no word of land to despair of reaching.

Thus, one sees many of Dickinson's typical devices at work: the tightly patterned form, based on an undefined subject, the riddle-like puzzle of defining that subject, the shifting of mood from apparent observation to horror, the grotesque images couched in emotionally distant language. All this delineates that experience, that confrontation—with God, with nature, with the self, with one's own mind—which is the center of Dickinson's best poetry. Whether her work looks inward or outward, the subject matter is a confrontation leading to awareness, and part of the terror is that for Dickinson there is never any mediating middle ground; she confronts herself in relation to an abyss beyond. There is no society, no community to make that experience palatable in any but the most grotesque sense of the word, the awful tasting of uncontrollable fear.

"I KNOW THAT HE EXISTS"

Dickinson often questions the nature of the universe; she senses that God is present only in one's awareness of his absence. She shares Robert Frost's notion that God has tricked humankind, but while for Frost, God's trick is in the nature of creation, for Dickinson it is equally in God's refusal to answer people's riddles about that creation. She writes of the "eclipse" of God, and for Dickinson, it is God himself who has caused the obscurity. The customary movement in her explicitly religious poetry is from apparent affirmation to resounding doubt. Poem #338 begins with the line "I know that He exists." While Dickinson rarely uses periods even at the end of her poems, here the first line ends with one: a short and complete affirmation of God's existence, but an affirmation that remains unqualified for only that one line. God is not omnipresent, but exists "Somewhere—in Silence"; Dickinson then offers a justification for God's absence: His life is so fine that he has hidden it from humans who are unworthy. The second stanza offers two more justifications: He is playing with people, and one will be that much happier at the blissful surprise one has earned. However, the play, in typical Dickinson fashion, is a "fond Ambush," and both the juxtaposition of incongruous words and the reader's understanding that only villains engage in ambush indicate how quickly and how brutally the tone of the poem is changing.

The last half begins with "But," and indeed 256 of Dickinson's poems, nearly 15 percent, have a coordinate conjunction as the first word of the middle line: a hinge that links the deceptive movement of the first half with the oblique realization that takes place in the second. The lines of poem 338 then become heavily alliterative, slowing the reader with closely linked, plosive *p*'s before she begins the final question: "Should the glee—glaze—/ In Death's—stiff—stare." The quasi subjunctive, another consistent poetic stance in Dickinson, cannot mask the fact that there is no open possibility here, for death must come, the glee will glaze. Then the fun—it is God's fun of which she writes—will look too expensive, the jest will "Have crawled too far!" Although the last sentence is in the form of a question, the poem closes with an end mark stronger than the opening period, an exclamation point that leaves no doubt as to the tone the poem takes.

RELIGIOUS POEMS

This same movement appears in Dickinson's other overtly religious poems. Poem #501 ("This World is not Conclusion") likewise begins with a clear statement followed by a period and then moves rapidly toward doubt. Here God is a "Species" who "stands beyond." Humans are shown as baffled by the riddle of the universe, grasping at any "twig of Evidence." Man asks "a Vane, the way," indicating the inconstancy of that on which humans rely and punning on "in vain." Whatever answer man receives is only a narcotic, which "cannot still the Tooth/ That nibbles at the soul." Again, in "It's easy to invent a Life" (#724), God seems to be playing with humans, and although the poem begins with humanity's birth as God's invention, it ends with death as God's simply "leaving out a Man." In poem #1601, "Of God we ask one favor," the favor requested is that God forgive humankind, but it is clear that humans do not know for what they ask forgiveness and, as in Frost's "Forgive, O Lord," it is clear that the greater crime is not humanity's but God's. In "I never lost as much but twice" (#49), an early but accomplished work, God is "Burglar! Banker—Father!" robbing the poet, making her poor.

One large group of Dickinson's poems, of which

these are only a sample, suggests her sense of religious deprivation. Her transformation of the meter and rhythm of hymns into her own songs combines with the overt questioning of the ultimate meaning of her existence to make her work religious. As much, however, as Dickinson pretends to justify the ways of her "eclipsed" God to humanity, that justification never lasts. If God is Father, he is also Burglar. If God in his omnipotence finds it easy to invent a life, in his caprice he finds it just as easy to leave one out.

"I TASTE A LIQUOR NEVER BREWED"

Dickinson just as persistently questions nature, which was for her an equivocal manifestation of God's power and whims. Although there are occasional poems in which her experience of nature is exuberant (for example, "I taste a liquor never brewed," #214), in most of her work the experience is one of terror. A synecdochist rather than a symbolist, she describes and confronts a part of nature, that scene representing the whole. For her nineteenth century opposite, Whitman, the world was one of possibilities, of romantic venturing forth to project oneself onto the world and form an organic relationship with it. For Dickinson, the human and the natural give way to the inorganic; nature is, if like a clock, not so in its perfect design and workings, but in its likeliness to wind down and stop.

"I STARTED EARLY—TOOK MY DOG"

"I started Early—Took my Dog" (#520) is characteristic in its treatment of nature, although uncharacteristic in the romantic venturing forth of the persona. For the first third of the poem, she seems to be in control: She starts early, takes her pet, and visits the sea. The sea is treated with conventional and rather pretty metaphor; it is a house with a basement full of mermaids. Even here, however, is a suggestion that something is amiss: The frigates extend "Hempen Hands"; the ropes that moor the ships are characteristically personified, but the substitution of "hempen" for the similar sounding and expected "helpin'" (the missing *g* itself a delusive familiarity) suggests that the hands will entwine, not aid, the poet. As so often in Dickinson, the natural world seems to be staring at her, as if she is the chief actor in an unfolding drama, and suddenly, with the coordinate conjunction "but," the action begins. The sea is personified as a man who would attack her. She flees.

He pursues, reaching higher and higher on her clothes, until finally she achieves the solid ground, and the sea, like a docile and omnipotent train, unconcerned but "Mighty," bows and withdraws, his power there for another day.

"I DREADED THAT FIRST ROBIN, SO"

Whenever Dickinson looks at nature, the moment becomes a confrontation. Although she is superficially within the Puritan tradition of observing nature and reading its message, Dickinson differs not only in the chilling message that she reads, but also because nature refuses to remain passive; it is not simply an open book to be read—for books remain themselves—but also active and aggressive; personification suggests its assertive malevolence. In #348 ("I dreaded that first Robin, so"), the initial part of the poem describes the poet's fear: Spring is horrible; it shouts, mangles, and pierces. What Dickinson finally manages is merely a peace with spring; she makes herself "Queen of Calvary," and in deference to that, nature salutes her and leaves her alone.

"A NARROW FELLOW IN THE GRASS"

The same accommodation with nature occurs in #986, "A narrow Fellow in the Grass," where the subject, a snake that she encounters, is first made to seem familiar and harmless. Then the poet suggests that she has made her peace with "Several of Nature's People," and she feels for them "a transport/ Of cordiality," although one expects a more ecstatic noun than cordiality after a sense of transport. Dickinson concludes with a potent description of her true feelings about the snake, "Zero at the Bone," a phrase that well reflects her emotion during most confrontations, internal or external.

"APPARENTLY WITH NO SURPRISE"

One of Dickinson's finest poems, #1624 ("Apparently with no surprise"), a poem from late in her career, unites her attitudes toward nature and God. Even as Frost does in "Design," Dickinson examines one destructive scene in nature and uses it to represent a larger pattern; with Frost, too, she sees two possibilities for both microcosm and macrocosm: accident or dark design. The first two lines of her short poem describe the "happy Flower." The personified flower is unsurprised by its sudden death: "The Frost beheads it at its play—/ In accidental power—/ The blonde Assassin passes on—." In common with many American writers, she reverses the conventional association of white with purity; here the killer, the frost, is blonde. Although she suggests that the power may be accidental, in itself not a consoling thought, the two lines framing that assertion severely modify it, for beheading is rarely accidental; nor do assassins attain their power by chance.

Whichever the case, accident or design, there is finally little significant difference, for nothing in the world pays attention to what has happened. "The Sun proceeds unmoved," an unusual pun, since unmoved has the triple meaning of unconcerned, stationary, and without a prime mover; it measures off the time for a God who does approve.

SELF AND SOUL

Thus, when Dickinson turns her vision outward, she looks at essential reality translated, often appallingly, into human terms. The alternative vision for Dickinson is inward, at her own self, and despite the claims of her imperial language, what she sees there is just as chaotic and chilling as what she sees without. "The Soul selects her own Society," she writes in #303, and she makes that society a "divine Majority." "I'm Nobody," another Dickinson poem (#288) begins; but in her poetry, the explicit movement is from no one to someone, from the self as beggar to the self as monarch: empress or queen. Out of the deprivation of her small society, out of the renunciation of present pleasures, she makes a majority that fills her world with aristocratic presence. However, for all that affirmation, the poems that look directly inward suggest something more; her assurance is ambiguously modified, her boasting bravado is dissipated.

MADNESS AND REASON

Occasionally, Dickinson's poetry justifies her internal confusion in conventional terms. Poem #435, "Much Madness is divinest Sense," makes the familiar assertion that, although the common majority have enough power to label nonconformists as insane and dangerous, often what appears as madness is sense, "divinest Sense—/ To a discerning Eye." Usually, however, her poetry of the mind is more unsettling, her understanding more personal. "I Felt a Funeral, in my Brain" (#280) and "'Twas like a Maelstrom, with a notch" (#414), employing the drowning imagery of "It

was not Death," are the most piercing of Dickinson's poems about the death of reason, the chaotic confrontation with the instability within. They also indicate the central ambiguity that these poems present, for the metaphor that Dickinson favors for the death of reason is literal, physical death: the tenor, insanity; the vehicle, death. However, one is never quite sure whether it might not be the other way around: the central subject death; the metaphoric vehicle, the death of reason. Through this uncertainty, these poems achieve a double-edged vitality, a shifting of idea and vehicle, foreground and background.

The awareness of one's tenuous grasp on his own reason seems clearest in "I felt a Funeral, in my Brain," for there the funeral is explicitly "in," although not necessarily "of," the speaker's brain. The metaphor is developed through a series of comparisons with the funeral rites, each introduced by "and," each arriving with increasing haste. At first the monotony of the mourners' tread almost causes sense to break through, but instead the mind reacts by going numb. Eventually the funeral metaphor gives way to that of a shipwreck—on the surface, an illogical shift, but given the movement of the poem, a continuation of the sense of confusion and abandonment. The last stanza returns to the dominant metaphor, presenting a rapid series of events, the first of which is "a Plank in Reason" breaking, plunging the persona—and the reader—back into the funeral imagery of a coffin dropping into a grave. The poem concludes with "And Finished knowing—then," an ambiguous finish suggesting both the end of her life and of her reasoning, thus fusing the two halves of the metaphor. These two readings of the last line do not exhaust its possibilities, for there is another way to read it: The speaker finished with "knowing" not as a gerund object, but as the participial modifier, so that even at the moment of her death, she dies knowing. Since for Dickinson, awareness is the most chilling of experiences, it is an appropriately horrible alternative: not the end of knowing, but the end while knowing.

DEATH

Death is not merely metaphorical for Dickinson; it is the greatest subject of her work. Perhaps her finest lyrics are on this topic, which she surveyed with a style at once laconic and acute, a tone of quiet terror conveyed through understatement and indirection. Her power arises from the tension between her formal and tonal control and the emotional intensity of what she writes. She approaches death from two perspectives, adopts two stances: the persona as the grieving onlooker, attempting to continue with life; her own faith tested by the experience of watching another die; and the persona as the dying person.

In such poems as "How many times these low feet staggered" (#187), where the dead person has "soldered mouth," and "There's been a Death, in the Opposite House" (#389), where the windows of the house open like "a Pod," the description of death is mechanical, as if a machine has simply stopped. The reaction of the onlookers is first bewilderment, then the undertaking of necessary duties, and finally an awful silence in which they are alone with their realization of what has occurred.

"The last Night that She lived"

Poem #1100, "The last Night that She lived," best illustrates all these attitudes. It oscillates between the quietly dying person—whose death is gentle, on a common night, who "mentioned—and forgot," who "struggled scarce—/ Consented"—and those, equally quiet but less capable of giving consent, who watch the death occur. First there is the conventional idea that they who watch see life differently: Death becomes a great light that italicizes events. However, as the poem continues with the onlookers' random comings and goings and their feelings of guilt over continuing to live, there is little sense that their awareness is complete.

After the death, Dickinson provides one stanza, neatly summarizing the final understanding: "And We—We placed the Hair," the repeated pronoun, the little gasp for breath and hint of self-dramatization, fills part of the time with what must be done. Then there is nothing left to do or to be said: "And then an awful leisure was/ Belief to regulate." The strange linking of "awful" with "leisure," the disruption of syntax at the line break, and the notion that the best belief can do is regulate leisure, all suggest in two lines the confusion and disruption for those who remain alive.

"Because I could not stop for Death"

By consensus the greatest of all Dickinson's poems, "Because I could not stop for Death" (#712), explores death from the second perspective, as do such poems as "I Heard a Fly buzz—when I died" (#465) and "I died for Beauty" (#449), in which one who has died for beauty and one who has died for truth agree, with John Keats, that truth and beauty are the same—the poet adding the ironic commentary that their equality lies in the fact that the names of both are being covered up by moss.

"Because I could not stop for Death" unites love and death, for death comes to the persona in the form of a gentleman caller. Her reaction is neither haste to meet him, nor displeasure at his arrival. She has time to put away her "labor and . . . leisure"; he is civil. The only hint in the first two stanzas of what is really occurring is the presence of Immortality, and yet that presence, although not unnoticed, is as yet unfelt by the persona. The third stanza brings the customary metaphor of life as a journey and the convention of one's life passing before his eyes as he dies: from youth, through maturity, to sunset. Here, however, two of the images work against the surface calm: The children out for recess do not play, but strive; the grain is said to be gazing. "Grazing" might be the expected word, although even that would be somewhat out of place, but "gazing" both creates unfulfilled aural expectations and gives the sense of the persona as only one actor in a drama that many are watching.

Again, as is common in Dickinson, the poem is hinged by a coordinate conjunction in the exact middle. This time the conjunction is "Or," as the speaker realizes not that she is passing the sun, but that "He passed us." The metaphoric journey through life continues; it is now night, but the emotions have changed from the calm of control to fright. The speaker's "Zero at the Bone" is literal, for her clothing, frilly and light, while appropriate for a wedding, is not so for the funeral that is occurring. The final stop—for, like the first two stanzas, the last two are motionless—is before the grave, "a House that seemed/ A Swelling of the Ground." The swelling ground also suggests pregnancy, but this earth bears death, not life. The last stanza comments that even though the persona has been dead for centuries, all that time seems shorter than the one moment of realization of where her journey must ultimately end. Death, Dickinson's essential metaphor and subject, is seen in terms of a moment of confrontation. Absence thus becomes the major presence, confusion the major ordering principle.

OTHER MAJOR WORKS

NONFICTION: *Letters*, 1894 (2 volumes); *The Letters of Emily Dickinson*, 1958 (3 volumes; Thomas H. Johnson and Theodora Ward, editors); *Open Me Carefully: Emily Dickinson's Intimate Letters to Susan Huntington Dickinson*, 1998.

BIBLIOGRAPHY

Barnstone, Aliki. *Changing Rapture: Emily Dickinson's Poetic Development*. Hanover, N.H.: University Press of New England, 2006. A study of Dickinson's poetry that challenges the notion that she wrote at the same level and in the same style throughout her career. This work chronicles her progression as a writer and breaks her poetry into four distinct stages that exemplify her growth and changing style from youth through old age.

Bloom, Harold, ed. *Emily Dickinson*. New York: Bloom's Literary Criticism, 2008. Essays on Dickinson examine her life, her poetry, and the culture in which she lived.

Borus, Audrey. *A Student's Guide to Emily Dickinson*. Berkeley Heights, N.J.: Enslow, 2005. This handbook helps students understand the poetry of Dickinson. Topics include poems about death, nature, time and eternity, and literary devices. Includes a chronology.

Bouson, J. Brooks, ed. *Emily Dickinson*. Pasadena, Calif.: Salem Press, 2010. A variety of new and classic essays on Dickinson's life and work.

Eberwein, Jane Donahue. *An Emily Dickinson Encyclopedia*. Westport, Conn.: Greenwood Press, 1998. Edited by a founding board member of the Emily Dickinson International Society as well as a professor of English. Covers a wide range of topics, from people important in Dickinson's life to her stylistic traits.

Grabher, Gudrun, Roland Hagenbüchle, and Cristanne Miller, ed. *The Emily Dickinson Handbook*. Amherst: University of Massachusetts Press, 1998. A collection of essays covering Dickinson's poetry, poetics, and life. Useful reference with extensive bibliography.

Habegger, Alfred. *My Wars Are Laid Away in Books: The Life of Emily Dickinson*. New York: Random House, 2001. A biography of Dickinson that makes extensive use of source documents to examine her development as a person and as a poet.

Keane, Patrick J. *Emily Dickinson's Approving God: Divine Design and the Problem of Suffering*. Columbia: University of Missouri Press, 2008. By focusing on Dickinson's poem, "Apparently with no surprise," Keane examines Dickinson's religious beliefs and her doubt.

Kirk, Connie Ann. *Emily Dickinson: A Biography*. Westport, Conn.: Greenwood Press, 2004. In addition to providing a complete biography of Dickinson, Kirk looks at problems with editing Dickinson's manuscripts and issues of publication.

Martin, Wendy, ed. *The Cambridge Companion to Emily Dickinson*. New York: Cambridge University Press, 2002. Contains eleven new essays of Dickinson scholars that cover the poet's biography, poetic themes and strategies, and the historical and cultural context in which she was writing.

Howard Faulkner

DIANE DI PRIMA

Born: Brooklyn, New York; August 6, 1934

PRINCIPAL POETRY

This Kind of Bird Flies Backward, 1958
Dinners and Nightmares, 1961, 1974 (stories, poetry, prose)
The New Handbook of Heaven, 1963
Earthsong: Poems, 1957-1959, 1968
Hotel Albert: Poems, 1968
Revolutionary Letters, Etc., 1971, 2007
Freddie Poems, 1974
Selected Poems, 1956-1975, 1975
Loba, Parts I-VIII, 1978
Pieces of a Song: Selected Poems, 1990

Loba, 1998
Ones I Used to Laugh With: A Haibun Journal,
   2003
TimeBomb, 2006

OTHER LITERARY FORMS

Although Diane di Prima (dee PREE-muh) is best known for her poetry, she has published more than twenty volumes of poetry and prose and has written and produced a substantial number of plays. She is the author of two prose memoirs, the highly erotic novel-memoir *Memoirs of a Beatnik* (1969, 1988), which contributed significantly to making her the most widely known woman poet of the Beat generation, and *Recollections of My Life as a Woman: The New York Years, a Memoir* (2001), a remembrance of her growing feminist consciousness in the 1950's and 1960's. Di Prima has also translated poems from Latin and written several treatises on Paracelsus, the sixteenth century alchemist and physician. She has expressed her opinions on poetics, politics, feminism, and the Beat generation in numerous interviews.

ACHIEVEMENTS

Diane di Prima has received grants from the National Endowment for the Arts (1973 and 1979) and an honorary degree from St. Lawrence University (1999). She was a finalist for poet laureate of San Francisco in 2002 and 2005 before becoming the city's fifth laureate in 2009, and she was a finalist for poet laureate of California in 2003. She has garnered such honors as the Secret Six Medal of Valor (1987), the National Poetry Association lifetime service award (1993), the Aniello Lauri Award for creative writing (1994), the Fred Cody Award for lifetime achievement (2006), and the Reginald Lockett Lifetime Achievement Award (2008). As a female member of the Beat generation, she has had to labor under the stereotype of "Beat chick," characterized by Jack Kerouac as girls "who say nothing and wear black." The last decades of the twentieth century brought a gradual revision of this stereotype and greater recognition for her work. Although her poems have received little academic or critical attention, they have attracted a growing number of devoted readers.

George F. Butterick has argued that di Prima's greatest contribution to the poetry of her generation lies in her work as an organizer and editor/publisher, beginning with her collaboration on *The Floating Bear*, a monthly publication she published together with her occasional lover LeRoi Jones (who later changed his name to Amiri Baraka) in 1961 and for which she served as editor until 1969. Also in the 1960's, she founded Poets Press, which published some thirty books of poetry and prose of such well-known figures as Herbert Huncke and Timothy Leary, as well as the anti-Vietnam War anthology *War Poems* (1968), edited by di Prima herself.

Even though di Prima has often been described as a minor constellation next to stars of the Beat generation such as Kerouac, Allen Ginsberg, William S. Bur-

Diane di Prima (©Allen Ginsberg/CORBIS)

roughs, and Gregory Corso, her mature work since the 1970's deserves critical attention. She is an important catalyst and chronicler of the bohemian counterculture of her generation. For more than half a century, despite sweeping changes that have transformed society, di Prima has remained true to many of the central tenets of radical thought as established by the Beats: rejection of government propaganda, exploration of mental and physical sensations, spirituality, spontaneity, and hope for a world free of constraints.

Biography

Diane di Prima was born in Brooklyn, New York, to first-generation Italian immigrants Francis di Prima and Emma Mallozzi di Prima. In interviews and in autobiographical writings, she emphasizes the strict, conservative upbringing to which a young girl of Italian ancestry was subjected during the 1930's, the years of the Great Depression. She credits her anarchist grandfather, Domenico Mallozzi, with sowing the seeds for her subsequent rebellion against this confinement by taking her to anarchist rallies and reading the works of Dante to her. She began writing when she was seven years old and, by the age of fourteen, had already decided to become a poet. She enrolled at Swarthmore College in 1951, intending to major in theoretical physics. In 1953, she abandoned her academic career and moved to New York's lower East Side, beginning her bohemian life as a poet and activist, and like her male counterparts, she freely experimented with sex and drugs. During this time, she met Ezra Pound, who—because of his public support for Italian dictator Benito Mussolini—had been institutionalized at St. Elizabeths Hospital, a mental institution in Washington, D.C., where she visited him several times. Pound found encouraging words for her fledgling attempts at poetry, and the two corresponded for some time.

A decisive factor in di Prima's career was her introduction in 1957 to the founding members of the Beat generation, a group with whom she remained closely connected for the next decade. Indeed, di Prima is considered the most important female writer of the Beat generation and features prominently in every anthology of that group. In 1958, Totem Press (founded by Jones) published her first collection of poetry, *This*

Kind of Bird Flies Backward, the first of many works of poetry, prose, and drama.

During her years in Manhattan, di Prima published and edited several poetry magazines and newsletters and helped found the New York Poets Theatre in 1961. She married for the first time in 1962, to actor-director Alan Marlowe; they divorced in 1969. She married poet Grant Fisher in 1972, but they divorced in 1975. The two marriages resulted in five children (Jeanne, Dominique, Alexander, Tara, and Rudra), whom she raised, and her life as a single mother was strongly reflected in her poetry. In 1965, she moved to upstate New York and participated in Timothy Leary's psychedelic community at Millbrook. At other times, she traversed the continent in a Volkswagen bus, in the style of the male Beat writers and the Merry Pranksters, reading her poetry in churches, prisons, and schools.

In 1969, di Prima moved to the West Coast, a more hospitable place for female writers, and became involved with the Diggers, a radical community action and guerrilla theater group that supplied free food, medical care, housing, and musical concerts for street people. The move to the West Coast signaled the beginning of di Prima's gradual move away from the radical social-political emphasis of the Beat writers and toward a more contemplative life, including the study of Zen Buddhism, alchemy, and Sanskrit.

In the 1970's, di Prima became an instructor at the Jack Kerouac School of Disembodied Poetics at Naropa Institute in Boulder, Colorado; in the same decade, as part of the Poetry in the Schools programs, she held workshops and residencies in Wyoming, Arizona, Montana, Minnesota, and elsewhere. During the 1980's, she taught courses in the hermetic and esoteric traditions in poetry at the New College of California in San Francisco, and she has since taught at the California College of Arts and Crafts, the San Francisco Art Institute, the California Institute of Integral Studies, and Napa State Hospital. She was the cofounder of the San Francisco Institute of Magical and Healing Arts, where she also taught from 1983 to 1991. In 1971, she started work on *Loba*, a long, visionary serial poem; parts 1-8 were published in 1978 and an expanded and revised version was published in 1998.

The deaths of many of the best-known male writers

of the Beat generation led to a renewed interest in the women associated with this movement, resulting in a substantial number of autobiographies and memoirs, including di Prima's *Recollections of My Life as a Woman*, which candidly chronicles her involvement with the Beat movement in the 1950's and 1960's, as well as her growing self-confidence and autonomy as a woman poet determined to shed the label of "Beat chick."

A<small>NALYSIS</small>

Diane di Prima's poetry falls into two clearly distinguished chronological and thematic categories. Her works from 1957 to 1975 are suffused with the idiom of the Beat generation, the language of the hipster and personal rebellion. Di Prima considers her association with the poets of the Beat generation and the San Francisco Renaissance as seminal for her work, as she explained in an interview:

> Don't forget, however great your visioning and your inspiration, you need the techniques of the craft and there's nowhere, really to get them . . . they are passed on person to person and back then the male naturally passed them to the male. I think maybe I was one of the first women to break through that in having deep conversations with Charles Olson and Frank O'Hara.

Further evidence of this mentoring process can be seen in the fact that Jones, through his Totem Press, published di Prima's first collection, *This Kind of Bird Flies Backward*, and Lawrence Ferlinghetti wrote a brief "non-introduction by way of an introduction" for it. The volume is full of Beat terminology, such as "hip," "cool," and "crazy." Although she saw herself, as did most of the female Beat writers, inhibited by the "eternal, tiresome rule of Cool," she also acknowledges that Ginsberg taught her to have confidence in her own spontaneity and emphasized the importance of technical writing skills. The best view of this phase of di Prima's work can be found in her collection *Selected Poems, 1956-1975*, which extracts her favorite poems from *This Kind of Bird Flies Backward* to *Freddie Poems*.

The second part of her work covers the period after she moved to Northern California in 1970. It is charac-

terized by a less strident tone, a gradual decline in use of the Beat vocabulary, and a growing concern with spiritual and ecological matters, particularly her increasing involvement in Buddhism and her role as a woman and mother. Much of this changing perspective can be found in her collection *Pieces of a Song*. Many commentators consider the long serial poem *Loba* the most typical work of di Prima's mature creative period.

D<small>INNERS AND</small> N<small>IGHTMARES</small>

Di Prima's second poetry collection, *Dinners and Nightmares*, is dedicated to her "pads & the people who shared them with me." The first part consists of descriptions of meals she has shared with a variety of people in the bohemian milieu of New York, and there is good reason to believe that most of these sketches are in fact based on real people and events. The second part is a collection of poetic "nightmares," dark contrasts to the more pleasant dinners of the first section. The nightmares deal with the squalid living conditions on the lower East Side, with thwarted or hopeless love affairs, or with standing in unemployment lines:

> Then I was standing in line unemployment green
>   institution green room
> green people slow shuffle. Then to the man ahead said
>   clerk-behind-desk,
> folding papers bored and sticking on seals
>   Here are your twenty reasons for living sir.

Some of the "nightmares" are expressed in imagistic one-liners: "It hurts to be murdered" or "Get your cut throat off my knife."

The collection concludes with a section called "More or Less Love Poems," terse vignettes of love in the hipster pads, where "coolness" thinly disguises anguish and fear of loneliness:

> Yeah that was
> once in a lifetime
> baby
>
> you gotta be clean and
> with new shoes
> to love like I love you.
>
> I think it won't happen again.

Or even more pithily:

You are not quite
the air I breathe
thank God.

so go.

It is possible to see rebellion and defiance in these lines, as well as an obstinate insistence on living life on her own terms, but while there is little self-pity (that would not have been "cool"), it is impossible to overlook her feelings of anguish and isolation.

EARTHSONG

The collection *Earthsong* was edited by Marlowe, di Prima's then-husband, and published by Poets Press. In the introduction, Marlowe writes, "these poems contain the hard line of the fifties, and the smell of New York winters, cold and grey, as well as Miles Davis' jazz and the search for new forms." Di Prima reveals her extensive classical reading in a lighthearted Beat parody of Elizabethan poet/dramatist Christopher Marlowe's pastoral "The Passionate Shepherd to His Love" (1599), which she turns into "The Passionate Hipster to His Chick." The collection also includes probably her best-known and most frequently anthologized poem. Untitled in *Earthsong*, the poem appears in *Selected Poems, 1956-1975* as "The Practice of Magical Evocation" and is a strident response to Gary Snyder's chauvinist poem "Praise for Sick Women" (from *Riprap*, 1959). In that poem, Snyder characterizes women as fertile and only confused by discipline. Di Prima's response is an unashamed acceptance of her femininity ("I am a woman and my poems/ are woman's: easy to say/ this"). She converts "fertile" into "ductile," emphasizing a woman's adaptability and strength in the face of male demands and expectations ("bring forth male children only"). Her final question, "what applause?" is rhetorical, indicating that women can expect no reward or even acknowledgment for their efforts. In *Recollections of My Life as a Woman*, di Prima sets the record straight when she writes:

Disappointment or loss marked the men of that world. And silence; one simply didn't talk about it. Disappointment and silence marked the women too. But there the silence lay deeper. No tales were told about them. They did not turn from one career to another, "take up the law," but buried the work of their hearts in the basement, burned their poems and stories, lost the thread of their dreams.

LOBA

Di Prima began working on *Loba* in 1971, and part 1 of this long serial poem first appeared in the Capra Chapbooks series in 1973. Expanded over the next two decades, book 1 (parts 1-8) was published in 1978, and in 1998, Penguin published a full, though probably not final, version. The poem is characteristic of di Prima's post-Beat poetry: It is an attempt to emulate the mythical wanderings of the *Cantos* (1925-1972) of her first mentor, Pound. The title is a reference to the figure of the she-wolf (*loba* in Spanish), the symbol of fierce maternal love in many cultures and particularly in Native American lore. *Loba* is a long journey of exploration of the feminine consciousness, beginning in primeval myths and archetypes.

Book 1 concentrates on matters of the flesh, while book 2 focuses on the soul. Di Prima has indicated that a yet-to-be-written book 3 would concern itself with the spirit. The work exhibits the poet's vast literary background, with allusions to Iseult, Persephone, and Lilith, all contained in a loosely joined series of philosophical, humorous, and lyrical poems. In one section, di Prima invokes Ginsberg's "Howl" (1956) when she writes: "who walked across America behind gaunt violent yogis/ & died o-d'ing in methadone jail/ scarfing the evidence."

Loba is a difficult poem and should not be read with the intent of finding and recognizing all the references to literary characters and myths. The she-wolf is di Prima's fundamental female hero, whose mythical wanderings allow the poet to touch on all her favorite subjects—politics, religion, erotic love, and ecology—and to display her great versatility in manipulating a wide variety of poetic forms and themes.

Di Prima's poetry has been criticized as uneven and sometimes obscure. There can be no doubt, however, that most of her poems, particularly of the early period, are accessible to the average reader and live up to the definition of poetry and the role of the poet she expressed in a 1978 interview:

The poet is the last person who is still speaking the truth when no one else dares to. . . . Pound once said, "Artists are the antennae of the race." . . . And we see very dramatically in our time how . . . the work of Allen [Ginsberg] and Kerouac in the 1950's and so on has informed the 1970's.

REVOLUTIONARY LETTERS

Originally published in 1971 and reissued several times before the 2007 edition produced by Last Gasp, *Revolutionary Letters* is one of the few significant literary efforts to emerge from the end of the hippie era. The new edition features re-edited earlier poems and is supplemented with later work.

Dedicated to her anarchist grandfather, *Revolutionary Letters* is di Prima's blank-verse chronicle of the cultural upheaval that began in the late 1940's and early 1950's with the Beats and metamorphosed into the counterculture of the 1960's before running out of steam in subsequent decades. Despite the apparent failure or suspension of the revolution, di Prima continues to be the standard-bearer, an army of one. She still proudly holds aloft the black, tie-dyed flag of utopian anarchy, the symbol for an idealized world in which individuals of all persuasions peacefully coexist without the necessity of government intervention or control, free to enjoy all the possibilities of mental, physical, and spiritual life to the fullest.

The earlier poems in the volume—some of them like haiku or epigrams in their brevity and impact—are upbeat and hopeful, in keeping with the ebullient, volatile nature of the late 1960's, when they were written. Drawing from a wealth of sources (alchemy, astrology, the history of the labor movement, Asian religions, and the female experience), di Prima keenly observes the flaws of society that detract from the ultimate freedom she espouses. She attacks obsolete traditions (such as the notion of feminine inferiority), beliefs (such as the public perception that the media always tell the unvarnished truth), and condemns meek compliance and the machinations of bureaucracy. She cajoles, warns, exhorts, and advises. In one early "letter," she confidently notes that it is not whether the revolution she envisions will happen, but simply a matter of when. In others, she reminds readers to wear shoes so they will not hurt their feet when they run away and to fill the bathtub with water in the event of government-manufactured crises.

At the time of their writing, di Prima's letters were strong, powerful statements from a pioneering female spokesperson for radical change. With the passage of the years, however, their relevance to current events has been lost, and they now seem like antique moments preserved in amber.

Later letters, in which the poet seems to realize that the revolution has failed—or is at least on hiatus—are angrier in tone, less forgiving. "Revolutionary Letter #40," for example, paints a bleak picture of a devastated United States: burning oilfields, ruined cities, abandoned vehicles, and downed power lines. "Revolutionary Letter #51" maintains that those who submit to a system become slaves. "Revolutionary Letter: Memorial Day 2003" is essentially a listing of those di Prima contends gave their lives for some form of freedom, from Paracelsus to Ferdinando Nicola Sacco and Bartolomeo Vanzetti, from John Brown to Leo Trotsky, and from Socrates to Malcolm X. More contemporary letters dealing with di Prima's concept of utopia are less grounded in reality. Her idealized, anarchistic postrevolutionary world—where men, women and children love and live off nature's bounty without restrictions—is a wonderful concept, but in light of the human species' penchant for contention, seems impossible to attain.

"NOTES TOWARD A POEM OF REVOLUTION"

"Notes Toward a Poem of Revolution" was published in a limited edition by di Prima's Eidolon Editions, as *Towers Down: Notes Toward a Poem of Revolution* (2002), and contained "Towers Down" by Clive Matson. Both poems also appeared in the antiwar anthology, *An Eye for an Eye Makes the Whole World Blind: Poets on 9/11* (2002). Matson's poem is a reaction to the traumatic terrorist attacks of September 11, 2001. Di Prima's poem, which was reprinted in the 2007 edition of *Revolutionary Letters*, is a series of fourteen short pieces—similar in tone and style to the more strident poems in that collection.

As might be expected, given the poet's lifelong anarchistic stance, di Prima, while sympathetic toward the victims of the tragedy, strongly condemns the behavior of the United States that resulted in the attacks. By aggressively seizing the role of the world's police officer and in broadening the gap between the haves and have-nots, she seems to be saying, the United States has made such atrocities inevitable. Although such suicidal acts as flying loaded passenger planes into populated buildings are inexcusable on a human scale, they are nonetheless understandable as gestures of frustration at the inability to change the way of the world through the normal channels of negotiation and compromise; collateral damage in the continuing war for the hearts and minds of the globe's citizens is part of modern reality. Poignantly, in a few brief lines, di Prima sums up the contemporary situation by comparing it to a child's game: ". . . nobody/ can hog the marbles & expect/ the others to play."

OTHER MAJOR WORKS

LONG FICTION: *Memoirs of a Beatnik*, 1969, 1988; *The Calculus of Variation*, 1972.

PLAYS: *Paideuma*, pr. 1960; *The Discontent of a Russian Prince*, pr. 1961; *Murder Cake*, pr. 1963; *Like*, pr. 1964; *Poet's Vaudeville*, pr. 1964 (libretto); *Monuments*, pr. 1968; *The Discovery of America*, pr. 1972; *Whale Honey*, pr. 1975; *ZipCode: The Collected Plays of Diane di Prima*, 1992.

NONFICTION: "Light / and Keats," 1978; "Paracelsus: An Appreciation," 1979; *Recollections of My Life as a Woman: The New York Years, a Memoir*, 2001.

EDITED TEXT: *War Poems*, 1968.

BIBLIOGRAPHY

Charters, Ann. *The Portable Sixties Reader*. New York: Penguin Classics, 2003. An anthology featuring a collection of more than one hundred pieces: essays, poetry, and fiction from some of America's outstanding writers of the decade, including works by di Prima. Provides perspective on the times.

Di Prima, Diane. "Diane di Prima." http://dianediprima .com. Official Web site of di Prima lists her works, readings, reviews, and workshops. Also provides links to other informational sites.

_____. "Diane di Prima." Interview by David Meltzer and Marina Lazzara. In *San Francisco Beat: Talking with the Poets*, edited by Meltzer. San Francisco: City Lights, 2001. In 1999, di Prima discusses her development as a poet, including an early commitment to poetry; her meetings with Beat poets such as Allen Ginsberg and Robert Duncan; her connection to Millbrook and Timothy Leary; her years in the San Francisco area and her involvement with the Diggers; and her discovery of Buddhism.

_____. "Pieces of a Song: Diane di Prima." Interview by Tony Moffeit. In *Breaking the Rule of Cool: Interviewing and Reading Women Beat Writers*, edited by Nancy McCampbell Grace and Ronna Johnson. Jackson: University Press of Mississippi, 2004. Di Prima discusses the influences on her writing, as well as the community of the Beat movement.

Johnson, Ronna, and Nancy McCampbell Grace, eds. *Girls Who Wore Black: Women Writing the Beat Generation*. New Brunswick, N.J.: Rutgers University Press, 2002. Contains an essay on di Prima, as well as an overview on women in the Beat generation.

Knight, Brenda, ed. *Women of the Beat Generation: The Writers, Artists, and Muses at the Heart of a Revolution*. 1996. Reprint. San Francisco: Conari Press, 2000. A well-illustrated anthology containing essays, poems, and short autobiographical pieces from the long neglected women—including Denise Levertov, Joanna McClure, Carolyn Cassady, and di Prima—who associated with and worked alongside the men of the Beat generation. Includes a short biography of di Prima and a number of her poems.

Peabody, Richard, ed. *A Different Beat: Writing by Women of the Beat Generation*. London: Serpent's Tail, 1997. This anthology of writings by the women of the Beat generation places di Prima in context. Firsthand accounts of these women's experiences are provided by Jan Kerouac, Joyce Johnson, Hettie Jones, di Prima, and others, who attest to the decidedly sexist times. An introduction provides an overview of the social and cultural background.

Pekar, Harvey, et al. *The Beats: A Graphic History*. Art by Ed Piskor et al. New York: Hill and Wang, 2009. Comic legend Harvey Pekar provides a history of the Beat poets in this graphic book. Contains an entry on and references to di Prima.

Waldman, Anne, ed. *The Beat Book: Writings from the*

Beat Generation. Rev. ed. Boston: Shambahla, 2007. This anthology contains an overview of the Beat generation and a short biography of di Prima, along with a selection of her poems.

Franz G. Blaha
Updated by Jack Ewing

OWEN DODSON

Born: Brooklyn, New York; November 28, 1914
Died: New York, New York; June 21, 1983

PRINCIPAL POETRY

Powerful Long Ladder, 1946
Cages, 1953
The Confession Stone, 1968 (revised and enlarged
    as *The Confession Stone: Song Cycles*, 1970)
The Harlem Book of the Dead, 1978 (with James
    Van Der Zee and Camille Billops)

OTHER LITERARY FORMS

Owen Dodson's contribution to the theater is significant, from his first involvement at Bates College in 1933 to his work on a production of his own play, *Till Victory Is Won* (first produced in 1965), by the Carnegie Hall Opera Ebony four months before his death in 1983. He published or produced eight plays between 1935 and 1965. Dodson wrote two autobiographical novels, *Boy at the Window* (1951), reprinted as *When Trees Were Green* (1967), and *Come Home Early, Child* (1977). In addition, he wrote short fiction, published in various anthologies, as well as a screenplay and radioplays.

ACHIEVEMENTS

Although poetry was Owen Dodson's first love, his need for drama led him to writing plays, but they were poetic drama. Throughout his time at Yale, he attempted to devote himself totally to drama, but continued to write poetry. The impact of his first collection of poetry, *Powerful Long Ladder*, was such that his peers and seniors assimilated him into the canon of standard African American poetry; his poems appeared in principal black poetry anthologies of the 1950's, although he had stopped writing poetry.

While at Yale, Dodson was awarded a stipend of $3,200 from the Rockefeller General Board for his expressed interest in "forming a Negro Theater where Negroes may have plays presented." With this end in mind, Dodson wrote numerous plays. In 1943, following his service in the U.S. Navy, he received a Rosenwald Fellowship to write plays for an African American theater, but failed to fulfill his obligation. In 1952, after finishing *Boy at the Window*, Dodson, with the help of poet W. H. Auden, secured a Guggenheim Fellowship "for creative activity in the field of fiction," in the amount of $3,500.

BIOGRAPHY

Owen Vincent Dodson was the ninth and last child born to Sarah Goode Dodson and Nathaniel Dodson on November 28, 1914, in Brooklyn, New York. Dodson's father, a journalist, member of the American Press Association, and editor of the Negro News Service, exerted enormous influence on his son through his literary associations. Dodson's mother died when he was eleven, and his father died the following year, so Dodson was raised by Lillian Dodson, his oldest sibling. She moved the family near Thomas Jefferson High School, which Dodson attended from 1928 to 1932.

In high school, Dodson achieved excellence in poetry reading and won various prizes in elocution. He wrote poems mostly dealing with the deaths of members of his family. Befriended by the well-known Folger family, owners of Standard Oil, Dodson and his brother Kenneth helped matriarch Mary Wells with family dinners and babysitting, and, in return, were allowed to accompany her to musical programs, motion pictures, lectures, and plays—all encouraging Dodson's love of theater. He graduated from high school with a B average, with As in elocution, and received a scholarship for Bates College in Lewiston, Maine.

As a freshman at Bates, while studying John Keats's poetry, Dodson boasted to his professor that he could write a sonnet as good as one of Keats. His professor commanded him to each week submit a sonnet he had written until either he could surpass Keats or he graduated. At Bates, Dodson refined his poetry, primarily sonnets, publishing some of them in small publications. However, despite his passion for poetry, he continued playwriting, receiving an invitation to enroll in Yale School of Drama. During his three years at Yale, he achieved a reputation for notable productions of his own plays. In 1939, with his M.F.A. in hand, Dodson accepted a teaching position at Spelman College in Atlanta, Georgia, where he mingled with the black intelligentsia and experienced racism in the South. In 1940, his beloved brother Kenneth died.

In 1941, Dodson became a visiting professor of drama at the newly established department of communication of the Hampton Institute in Virginia. Within six months, however, Dodson, fearful of German domination of the United States, enlisted in the U.S. Navy. While in the Navy, he produced a weekly program honoring black servicemen and featuring morale-boosting

Owen Dodson (New York Public Library)

plays. He continued to write poetry largely because of his realization that a great many individuals had suffered. His poetry was published in *The Negro Caravan* (1941; Sterling A. Brown, Arthur P. Davis, and Ulysses Lee, editors), an anthology of black literature, in which he was described as an "aware" black poet.

In 1946, Dodson published his first volume of poetry, *Powerful Long Ladder*. The following year, he accepted the position of professor of drama at Howard University, in Washington D.C., where he remained for twenty-five years, writing and producing his plays. He retired from Howard in 1967, suffering from ill health. His second volume of verse, *The Confession Stone*, was published in 1968. He died of heart failure in 1983.

ANALYSIS

As Owen Dodson was unable or unwilling to confine himself to any specific genre, his poems are also far-ranging in subject, style, and form. Reflecting his classical, humanistic education, his poetry frequently alludes to mythological or classical figures. Just as his drama is poetic, his poetry is dramatic and intense. Although highly skilled in the writing of sonnets, he also wrote free verse. Unlike most of the African American poets of his day, who attempted to lay bare the black experience in the United States, Dodson, instead, speaks emotionally, expressing pain and sorrow for those who have no voice.

POWERFUL LONG LADDER

Powerful Long Ladder is permeated with sorrow throughout—sorrow for those individuals suffering from the domination and brutality of racism, from conditions of war, and from grief over the deaths of loved ones. Some of Dodson's verse written while he was in the U.S. Navy focuses on his awareness of the suffering of others. "Black Mother Praying" (1943), written in free verse, is one of his most famous poems. Dodson relates an African American woman's anguished pleading for God's help in response to the brutal treatment of African Americans during the summer, 1943, race riots, sparked by competition between blacks and whites for higher-wage jobs in war industries. Another poem dating from his service period, "Jonathan's Song, A Negro Saw a Jewish Pageant, 'We Will Never Die,'" was engendered by Dodson's visit to a Jewish celebration of life. Dodson and a Jewish friend attended a candlelight ceremony commemorating Jews who had died as a result of racial hatred; Dodson's recognition of the suffering of the Jews produced a passionate emotional poem mingling the suffering of the two races. In 1940, during the Battle of Britain, Dodson composed "Iphigenia," whose reference to mythological Agamemnon's daughter, who was sacrificed in order for the Argive fleet to fulfill its mission, comments on the sacrifice of the innocent English people being slaughtered to satisfy the world's corrupt people. Dodson uses a tone of great sorrow as he internalizes the world's pain.

In "Poems For My Brother, Kenneth," in the first poetry selection, Dodson presents various perspectives of his brother. Kenneth appears regularly in Dodson's dreams, giving him directions, and then disappears back into his grave; in every thought, Dodson is overcome with memories of Kenneth. Dodson questions the relevance of World War II to him in view of Kenneth's death. Much as his mother's death years earlier had eroded Dodson's faith in God, Kenneth's death has now destroyed any hope of life after death for Dodson. He perceives Kenneth's body in the ground as "awaiting nothing." Dodson proclaims, "There will be no resurrection."

Dodson's concern for the dignity of black people in a white world of almost universal disrespect for them compelled him to compose poems in memory of African Americans whose accomplishments and personal virtues were exceptional. Poems in *Powerful Long Ladder* include a tribute to Samuel Chapman Armstrong, founder of Hampton Institute, and to "Miss Packard and Miss Giles," founders of Spelman College, and a eulogy for fellow poet, Countée Cullen. The book also contains three choruses from his verse drama *Divine Comedy* (pr. 1938); *Some Day We're Gonna Tear Them Pillars Down*, a drama that cries out for freedom; and "Sorrow Is the Only Faithful One," a personal poem that sets forth sorrow as his enduring lone companion.

THE CONFESSION STONE

The Confession Stone, begun in 1960 and finished after he had retired from Howard University, spans the

three days from Good Friday to Easter morning. The poems are grouped into cycles involving Jesus' entire family: poems or letters from Joseph to Mary; entries from "Journals of Magdalene"; Joseph's letters to Martha, sister of Lazarus; Joseph's letters to Pontius Pilate, Judas, and God; and a single response from God. The title of the work refers to a rock whereon individuals kneel and wrestle with pain and misery, and the characters in the collection appear to be on the hard stone of confession. Dodson's purpose in writing the poems, as is the purpose of most of his poetry, is to reach some reconciliation or terms with God. In the poem, Dodson appeals to God for some sign of recognition and promises not to speak of Calvary. God's cryptic response insists that Dodson has not been deserted.

The cycle of poems originated with Dodson's appearance on stage in 1941 as Judas in Lenore J. Coffee and William Joyce Cowen's *Family Portrait* (first produced in 1939) in which the Holy Family is portrayed as human beings. Dodson began the cycles with a sorrowful Mary mourning for her son—poems that composer Robert Fleming set to music and arranged for contralto Maureen Forrester to perform at Carnegie Hall. The cycle of songs continues to be sung at Easter Services.

THE HARLEM BOOK OF THE DEAD

Other Dodson poems were published in *The Harlem Book of the Dead*, a book of photographs taken by noted photographer of rituals, James Van Der Zee, who recorded funerals in the 1920's, 1930's, and 1940's for the benefit of relatives and posterity. The book was a collaborative effort between Van Der Zee, who also was the subject of an interview; Camille Billops, who furnished a text; Owen Dodson, whose poems accompanied, largely in juxtaposition, the photographs; and Toni Morrison, who provided an introduction. For one photograph of a woman arrayed in funeral attire, Dodson juxtaposed his "Allegory of Seafaring Black Mothers," in which he mythically speaks of mothers telling fortunes, milking goats, and scrubbing the ship's deck while sailing on the sea. Beneath the photograph of another deceased woman, Dodson deals with images of death's decay, but announces a resurrection so glorious and vivid that it startles the angels.

OTHER MAJOR WORKS

LONG FICTION: *Boy at the Window*, 1951 (also known as *When Trees Were Green*, 1967); *Come Home Early, Child*, 1977.

SHORT FICTION: "The Summer Fire," 1956.

PLAYS: *Deep in Your Heart*, pr. 1935; *The Poet's Caprice*, pb. 1935 (appeared in the December, 1935, issue of *Garnet*); *Including Laughter*, pr. 1936; *Divine Comedy*, pr. 1938 (music by Morris Mamorsky); *The Garden of Time*, pr. 1939 (music by Shirley Graham); *The Ballad of Dorrie Miller*, pr., pb. 1943 (also known as *The Ballad of Dorie Miller*, 2002); *Everybody Join Hands*, pr., pb. 1943; *Freedom the Banner*, pr. 1943; *New World A-Coming*, pr. 1943; *The Third Fourth of July*, pb. 1946 (with Countée Cullen); *Bayou Legend*, pr. 1948; *Till Victory Is Won*, pr. 1965 (with Mark Fax; opera); *The Shining Town*, pb. 1991 (wr. 1937).

SCREENPLAY: *They Seek a City*, 1945.

RADIO PLAYS: *Old Ironsides*, 1942; *Robert Smalls*, 1942; *The Midwest Mobilizes*, 1943; *Dorrie Miller*, 1944; *New World A-Coming*, 1945; *St. Louis Woman*, c. 1945 (adaptation of Cullen and Arna Bontemps's play); *The Dream Awake*, 1969.

NONFICTION: "Twice a Year," 1946-1947; "College Troopers Abroad," 1950; "Playwrights in Dark Glasses," 1968; "Who Has Seen the Wind? Playwrights and the Black Experience," 1977; "Who Has Seen the Wind? Part II," 1980.

BIBLIOGRAPHY

Grant, Nathan L. "The Unpublished Poetry of Owen Dodson." *Callaloo* 20, no. 3 (Summer, 1997): 619-626. Contains selections of Dodson's unpublished poetry, scavenged from handwritten or typewritten papers and found in various folders. Some are early versions of later published poems or represent mere ideas, abandoned as failures. Some portions are illegible or missing.

Hatch, James V. *Sorrow Is the Only Faithful One: The Life of Owen Dodson*. Urbana, Ill.: University of Chicago Press, 1993. Sympathetic, well-detailed biography of Dodson written by his friend, who interviewed Dodson extensively and gained access to limitless information.

"Owen Vincent Dodson." In *Contemporary Black Biography*, edited by Ashyia Henderson. Vol. 38. Farmington Hill, Mich.: Gale Group, 2003. Informative article on Dodson, his background, deaths of family members, education, literary accomplishments, homosexuality, struggles with segregation, alcoholism, and illness.

Shuman, R. Baird. "Poetry of Owen Dodson." In *Masterplots II: African American Literature*, edited by Tyrone Williams. Rev. ed. Pasadena, Calif.: Salem Press, 2009. Provides in-depth analysis of Dodson's poetry, including themes and meanings and the critical context.

Weixlmann, Joe. "A Review of Owen Dodson's *Jazz in Praise of the Lord*." *Black American Literature Forum* 14, no. 2 (Summer, 1980): 53-54. Discussion of Dodson's taped performance of his own selected poems with regard to tone and range of emotion in stirring renditions of poems concerning segregation.

Mary Hurd

EDWARD DORN

Born: Villa Grove, Illinois; April 2, 1929
Died: Denver, Colorado; December 10, 1999

PRINCIPAL POETRY

The Newly Fallen, 1961
From Gloucester Out, 1964
Hands Up!, 1964
Geography, 1965
Idaho Out, 1965
The North Atlantic Turbine, 1967
Gunslinger I, 1968
The Cosmology of Finding Your Spot, 1969
Gunslinger I and II, 1969
Gunslinger II, 1969
The Midwest Is That Space Between the Buffalo Statler and the Lawrence Eldridge, 1969
Twenty-four Love Songs, 1969
Songs, Set Two: A Short Count, 1970
The Cycle, 1971

A Poem Called Alexander Hamilton, 1971

Spectrum Breakdown: A Microbook, 1971

Gunslinger Book III, 1972

The Hamadryas Baboon at the Lincoln Park Zoo, 1972

Recollections of Gran Apachería, 1974

Semi-Hard, 1974 (with George Kinball)

The Collected Poems: 1956-1974, 1975

Manchester Square, 1975 (with Jennifer Dunbar)

Slinger, 1975 (includes *Gunslinger* books I-IV and *The Cycle*)

Hello, La Jolla, 1978

Selected Poems, 1978 (Donald Allen, editor)

Yellow Lola, 1981

Captain Jack's Chaps: Or, Houston, 1983

Abhorrences, 1984

High West Rendezvous, 1997

Way More West: New and Selected Poems, 2007

OTHER LITERARY FORMS

Edward Dorn wrote one novel, *The Rites of Passage: A Brief History* (1965, revised as *By the Sound* in 1971) and one book of short stories, *Some Business Recently Transacted in the White World* (1971). In addition, he published numerous books of essays and translations.

ACHIEVEMENTS

Edward Dorn's writing has been compared by critics to that of Walt Whitman for its joy in American themes, to that of Ernest Hemingway for its idiomatic speech, to that of Ezra Pound for its humor and erudition, and to that of Thomas Wolfe for its panoramic view. More accurate, however, are the criticisms claiming that his work defies paraphrasing and that his philosophy is likely to be different from that of his reader, who will emerge with a less inhibited and consequently more benevolent and tolerant view of the world. Dorn was called a "master of contemporary language," and *Gunslinger* has been called a "masterpiece of contemporary poetry."

Dorn taught at Idaho State University, at the University of Kansas, at Northeastern Illinois State University, at Kent State University, at the University of Essex (Colchester), at the University of California,

Riverside and San Diego, and at Muir College. At the time of his death, he was an associate professor of English at the University of Colorado in Boulder and a director of the writing program. He was twice a Fulbright Lecturer in American literature at Essex; he received National Endowment for the Arts grants in 1966 and 1968, a fellowship from the University of New Mexico in 1969, and the American Book Award from the Before Columbus Foundation in 1980. He was poet-in-residence at the University of Alaska and at the University of Michigan, Ann Arbor.

Dorn read at the Folger Library; the Cambridge Poetry Festival; the University of Durham, England; King's College (the University of London); and Westfield College. He gave the Olson lectures at the State University of New York in 1981.

BIOGRAPHY

Edward Merton Dorn attended a one-room schoolhouse for most of his first eight grades. The poet he read most frequently was James Whitcomb Riley, whose writing appeared in the local newspapers because he was from the neighboring state of Indiana. Dorn attended the University of Illinois, Urbana, and Black Mountain College, where he graduated in 1955. At Black Mountain College, in a liberal, creative environment, Dorn was associated with the rector Charles Olson, the poets Robert Creeley, Robert Duncan, Joel Oppenheimer, John Weiners, and Paul Blackburn, as well as the painter Franz Kline, the composer John Cage, and many other stimulating people. He held such disparate jobs as those of a logger in Washington State and a reference librarian at New Mexico State University in Santa Fe. During the mid-1960's, he was the editor of *Wild Dog* magazine.

In 1969, he married Jennifer Dunbar, and they had a son, Kidd, and a daughter, Maya. For the last two decades of his life, he led the University of Colorado's creative writing program. In his later years, Dorn was much concerned, in his writing and teaching, with the culture and geography of the West, writing numerous essays on the subject that were eventually collected in *Way West: Stories, Essays, and Verse Accounts, 1963-1993* (1993). He died of pancreatic cancer on December 10, 1999, in Denver, Colorado.

Analysis

Typically called a Black Mountain poet, Edward Dorn commented that there is no Black Mountain "school" with a single style or ideology, but that instead Black Mountain College meant a "school" in the true sense of the word, a climate in which to acquire and satisfy a thirst for the "dazzle of learning" and an appreciation of its value.

Referring to the poetry of the much-revered Charles Olson, Dorn claimed that he was not sure what "breath-determined projective verse" was; he simply wrote in "clots" of words, and when a line began to lose its energy, he began a new one. This intuitional line division leads to free verse, which utilizes some end-rhyme and, more often, internal rhyme. Dorn's long narrative poems (*Idaho Out* and *Gunslinger*) have the structure of an odyssey punctuated by stops and encounters.

Dominant themes

Dorn's major themes can be pinpointed by naming certain representative figures in his work. The eccentric entrepreneur and film mogul Howard Hughes represents all that is wrong with today's world, from isolation to selfishness to unbounded competitiveness. Daniel Drew, the robber baron, is the prototype of earlier American acquisitiveness. Dick Tracy, the comic-strip detective, is a pop figure familiar to all. Parsifal is not only the ideal knight, symbolic of the unrecoverable past in the mistaken view of most Americans, but also a part of the mythology ever-present in Dorn's poetry. Composer John Philip Sousa, associated with a period of history that seems in retrospect more pleasing than the present, elicits both a love for music and an almost sentimental reminiscence about an Illinois childhood. There remains the geranium, the lovely scarlet bloom that flourishes in the West and represents in Dorn's poetry the feminine Indian principle, and the trees—the box elder of his youth and the piñon of his adult years.

The West

Heeding the advice of Olson, his mentor at Black Mountain College, to "dig one thing or place" until he knew more about it than anyone else, Dorn chose the American West. That vast area became the locus and the vehicle for Dorn's major concerns: displaced persons and minorities, greedy entrepreneurs, ecology, the role of the poet, and, most important, survival. Be-

lieving that the United States government created its own first subdivisions with the passage of the Homestead Act, he noted that after a century of "planned greed," what remains are cowboys who live in ranch houses and pull plastic boats behind their highly horse-powered wagons. If a cowboy actually owns a horse, he does not ride it. Although Dorn generally loved this new world, he sometimes found it so evil that he thought it should not even have been discovered. Major villains are the "real-estate agents," who have converted "SPACE" to space by subdividing it, while the victims are the immigrants who came in "long black flea coats," Indians who now "play indian and scoff wieners and Seven Up," and the land itself.

"Sousa"

Although most ordinary citizens are relatively impotent in the face of money, acquisition, and imperialism, Dorn believed that the poet has the potential to alter perception and thought, to be, in Olson's phrase, "of the company of the gods." Art aids in humankind's survival. In the poem "Sousa," Dorn suggested that Sousa's music is an antidote to the crash course on which the world has embarked, and even a means of figuratively irrigating the wasteland. In a Dylan Thomas-like phrase, he recalled "the only May Day of [his] mind," the octagonal bandstand, the girls' billowing summer dresses, and ladybugs—all associated with Sunday afternoon occasions. Pleading with "John" (Philip Sousa) to pick up his "phone," Dorn deplores the fact that the nation, which has lifted the "chalice of explosion," can no longer be amused by Sousa's martial music. Noting that Sousa's marches are benevolent—the kind in which no one is injured—the poet concludes the poem with a brief prayer that the friends he has loved and left will have "cut wood to warm them."

"The Rick of Green Wood"

Wood is significant in Dorn's work, not only because it can literally warm bodies, but also because it is one of the natural objects to be lost in the despoliation of the West, and because Dorn himself worked as a logger. The box elder tree, associated with his youth in Illinois, and the piñon tree of the West and his adult life, appear frequently in the poems. "The Rick of Green Wood," which appears at the beginning of both

The Collected Poems, 1956-1974 and *Selected Poems*, serves to introduce not only the theme of wood and the comfort it will offer his family but also the poet himself: "My name is Dorn," he tells the woodcutter as the two converse in the November air. The friendly atmosphere is chilled by the warning that "the world is getting colder"—colder because of a lack of communication between its people and because of a depletion of its resources. Like Robert Frost's invitation to see the newborn calf and clear the pasture spring, and Emily Dickinson's "Letter to the World," Dorn's "The Rick of Green Wood" invites the reader to participate in the poet's world and to read on to learn more about the woodyard and the West beyond it.

ENGLAND

As Frost, Pound, and T. S. Eliot did before him, Dorn observed his homeland from England for a time; in all fairness, he admitted that the United States is "no more culpable" than England, and he finally decided that what happens in Minnesota was really more his business than what happens in England. Dorn took himself back home, but not before advising two jaded English poets who think that everything has already been said that they should make something up, "get laid" and describe that experience, or see what hope they can offer the world.

In the West once more, Dorn parodied the "Home on the Range," where Sacagawea wears a baseball cap and eats a Clark bar, and cowboys are good old boys who ride in trucks with gun racks. Concerned as always with the fate of men living in the United States and on the North American continent, Dorn offered suggestions: Ignore the rigid patterns of society; the person who is different may be the one worth listening to.

LITERARY INFLUENCES

In his introduction to *The Lost America of Love: Re-reading Robert Creeley, Edward Dorn, and Robert Duncan* (1981), Sherman Paul declares that his book concerns, much more than he had expected, the relationship of these poets to their "beloved predecessor," Walt Whitman. Dorn had affinities with the Transcendentalists, with Henry David Thoreau (in spite of the fact that he refers to Thoreau as a "god damn sniveler") and his conception of the "different drummer," his attitude toward civil disobedience, and his love for land

and nature; and with Ralph Waldo Emerson, who claimed to be "an endless seeker—with no past at my back." Dorn was closest, however, to Whitman. His poem "Wait by the Door Awhile, Death, There Are Others" recalls by its title and subject Whitman's "When Lilacs Last in the Dooryard Bloom'd" and contains several Whitmanesque references to his body, which Dorn said is younger than he is. Inviting himself to enter himself, Dorn confessed that he does so with great pleasure. One can almost smell Whitman's divine armpits. Some of Dorn's many "songs" could have been subtitled "Song of Myself"; in a burst of enthusiasm like that of the Transcendentalists, who thought humans divine, Dorn announces that many of his gods have been men and women.

Other literary influences are numerous. Dorn's world was frequently like that of Lewis Carroll, where nothing is what it appears to be. "The New Union Dead in Alabama" recalls Allen Tate's "Ode to the Confederate Dead," but with a bitter difference: These men have died as a result of national hypocrisy, a gelding mentality, and a gelding culture. In "Home Again," the "green hand that rocks the cradle" is reminiscent of both Whitman and Dylan Thomas. The quotations and allusions in *The North Atlantic Turbine*, published in London, are reminiscent of Eliot. This is not to say that Dorn was not original. The opposite, rather, is true. He combined old radio characters with Parsifal and Beowulf as adeptly and nimbly as Eliot did in *The Waste Land* (1922).

"WORLD BOX-SCORE CUP"

In spite of, or perhaps because of, all his literary kinships, Dorn was his own man. As Paul comments, "You don't mess with Dorn; he knows the score, and what is more . . . he has figured it out for himself." The score is, of course, lopsided, a fact satirically expressed in the poem "World Box-Score Cup," whose commentator, Stern Bill, broadcasts, from Yanqui-Go-Home Stadium, a game between the Haves (best fed, mostly English speaking) and the Havenots of the world. America, who can hardly be expected to be impartial, is the referee, and Al Capp is the captain of the Haves. Because the Havenots have no shirts, numbers are painted on their backs in whitewash; permanent paint is considered unnecessary, for obvious reasons. Players from the undeveloped squad have to be carried onto the field, an act distasteful to the developed players because of the smell of their nearly dead opponents. Stern Bill, who constantly uses the jargon of sportscasting, declares that this contest is one of the few places for people from both sides of the aluminum curtain to get together to work off their conflicting ideologies.

Stern Bill explains that the carcasses of undeveloped players will no longer be used in dog food because of the complaints of animal lovers that the meat was neither hygienic nor nutritional. At halftime, he interviews Harry Carry (who has a Japanese accent) and John Malcom Fuggeridge, whose strangely dressed companion proves to be Truman Capote (also known as Trustworthy Kaput, a southern degenerate). The last interviewees are Elizabeth Taylor's four dogs, who are accorded more dignity than are members of the Havenot team. As Dorn said, democracy has to be "cracked on the head" frequently to keep it in good condition. In this twentieth century "Modest Proposal," he is cracking at his caustic best. He once stated that one function of the poet is to stay "as removed as possible from permanent associations with power." Here he strikes out at the tendency of the United States to believe in its own invincibility and to interfere in other nations' affairs, at the same time condemning selfish greed in all nations—and all of this in sports jargon.

Dorn's satire was pointed, and he was not above using a few gimmicks. As the cover of *Hands Up!* is opened, two hands reach out to the reader, but as the book is closed, the hands suggest a nose-thumbing. In *Hello, La Jolla*, Dorn apologized for the amount of "calculated" white space and invites the readers to fill it in. As he "roadtests" the language, he uses outrageous puns ("a mews," "pater"-"potter," "tiers of my country," "End-o-China," "Would you Bolivia it?," and "Vee-et," explained as the past tense of "eat"); archaic spelling ("sunne," "starre," "goe"); inversions (an Indian sings in his "daughter" tongue; a vacuum adores Nature; men go to the unemployment agency); and, in an age that has found such exact rhymes unfashionable, places "Trinity" with "infinity," "cuff" with "enough," and "cancer" with "dancer."

GUNSLINGER

His major opus, *Gunslinger*, years in the making, appeared one slim volume at a time but is available in a one-volume edition. Robert Duncan has called it an American *Canterbury Tales*, and indeed a crew of sophisticated Muppet-pilgrims could say, "To Taos we finally came." George Gugelberger has dubbed the work a space (-d out) epic, but under any name it entertains. The characters, who come out of Western motion pictures, comic books, and science fiction, include the Slinger himself, a "semidios" who drifts along the "selvedge of time" and who is a prototype of the Western strong man. A crack shot, he is headed toward Las Vegas in quest of Howard Hughes, who possesses the power once reserved for the gods. Robart (Rob-art), the foil for Gunslinger, is named for Howard Robard Hughes and is an evil, lawless, greedy entrepreneur.

"I" is the initiate, the likable dude who dies in *Gunslinger II* but is preserved for "past reference" when he is embalmed with five gallons of acid and finally revived as Parmenides' secretary. Gunslinger explains "I's" function as that of setting up the "bleechers" (*sic*) or booking the hall when the soul plays a date in another town. Lil, who is the Great Goddess, the female principle, and the prostitute with a heart of gold; Cool Everything, an acid freak; the Stoned Horse, Lévi-Strauss; and a "heliocentric" poet complete the list of pilgrims. The horse (horsepower) rides *inside* the stage and is, of course, a Pegasus. The travelers meet a Ph.D. named Doctor Flamboyant, who confesses that he had to "take his degree" because the subject of his dissertation—last winter's icicles—could not be found.

Gunslinger, who observes that all the world is a cinema with Holy Writ as the script, visits a town called Truth or Consequence, whose residents ordered the truth and got the consequences. As the travelers get "inside the outskirts," the horse is horrified to learn that the green plots of the village contain the kind of grass that has to be mowed. When some local horses escape, their owner fires ten rounds so fast that the bullets stick together, his gun falls apart, and he becomes an Old Rugged Statue. The Stoned Horse, who sells the statue for twenty thousand pounds by starting a rumor that it is an Andy Warhol disguise, comments, "There's less to that village than meets the eye."

The townspeople crowd suspiciously around "I" because he looks strange. When they observe, "He hasn't got a *Pot* . . . ," "I" is saved by the magical appearance of a pot in his right hand. Slinger thanks the assembly for the "Kiwanis and Lions welcome," and Lil annotates (*sic*), "So this is Universe City," the name suggesting not only "university" but also the fact that people are much alike wherever one goes.

When the travelers "decoach" in Old Town and Cool Everything announces, "We're Here!" Slinger comments, "Sounds like an adverb disguised as a place." Amid puns on "head" and "para-dice," Cool Everything tells Lil his name, and she notes that if he does not stay away from tobacco, he might do just that. After a neat bit of internal rhyme: "'I is dead,' the poet said," Lil complains, "That aint grammatical, poet."

GUNSLINGER BOOK III

Gunslinger Book III introduces J. Edgar Whoever and the date February 31, along with the news that the horse had promised his mother not to join the Sierra Club. Slinger observes that everyone in this state (New Mexico) is fat because the citizens all think that "torque" is a relationship between tongue and fork. Their code is "Sllab," which must be spelled backwards to determine its true seriousness, and the first information it reveals is that Chester A. Arthur was America's first president, no matter what anyone says. The Slinger's quest is unsuccessful because his intended destination, Las Vegas, proves to be a "decoy" controlled by Big Money. The book ends at the Four Corners power plant, with "power" retaining a dual sense.

The speech of *Gunslinger* is that of hipsters, scientists, the media, bureaucracy, computers, comic books, Western slang, metaphysics, and pop culture. Dorn claimed he handled language like a material, keeping it in "instant repair." In *Gunslinger*, he proved to be a virtuoso at juggling words, mining their ambiguous meanings, placing them in surprising positions, and finally using them "to make things cohere."

Why did Dorn choose the West as his Yoknapatawpha? The most obvious answer is that this is the area in which Americans were the last pioneers; the West is also the locale of America's principal myth—the same myth of the Wild West so effectively debunked by Stephen Crane and now treated more lovingly by Dorn. His poem "Vaquero" describes the last, delicate cowboy, his wrists embossed, his eyes as blue as the top of the sky, a wistful study in color by sometime painter Dorn. Another reason for his choice of the West is the admiration he held for the courtesy, humility, and hospitality of the Indians and Spanish-speaking people who live there; he also was attracted to the casual atmosphere of the West, a place as figuratively remote as possible from Wall Street, Detroit, and Pittsburgh.

THE POET'S ROLE

A summary of Dorn's concerns would have to include the tension between humanity and landscape brought on by greed. Although people occasionally appreciate the beauties of land forms, as in *Gunslinger* ("Don't move . . . the sun rests deliberately on the rim of the sierra"), they have imposed a sameness on places by selling fast-food franchises, by constructing lookalike houses, by upsetting nature's balance, by allowing the careless rape of the land, by adopting a universal American dialect as standard, and by recognizing certain pop elements as part of national, not regional, culture. Space and place were at one time important, but thanks to people's avarice, they have lost much of their beauty as well as their identity.

To Dorn, a possible solution to this problem lies in the fact that language is a means of imposing order and discovering the natural order that humans have disarrayed. The person who can best utilize language is, of course, the poet, who is equipped to communicate because of his facility with words. He can look objectively at what other people do with language as a means of justifying commerce and even war, at the same time demonstrating through his poetry what a marvelous weapon language can be—directly in the area of criticism, and indirectly by exuberant wordplay.

What, in Dorn's view, is the role of the poet? He wondered aloud about the familiar; he demonstrated the pleasure to be recovered from doubt; he rose above differences; he arbitrated because of his dexterity with words. He is, in short, a shaper.

OTHER MAJOR WORKS

LONG FICTION: *The Rites of Passage: A Brief History*, 1965 (revised as *By the Sound*, 1971, 1991).

SHORT FICTION: *Some Business Recently Transacted in the White World*, 1971.

NONFICTION: *What I See in the Maximus Poems*, 1960; *Prose I*, 1964 (with Michael Rumaker and Warren Tallman); *The Shoshoneans*, 1966 (with photographs by Leroy Lucas); *Book of Daniel Drew*, 1969; *Views and Interviews*, 1978, 1980 (Donald Allen, editor); *Ed Dorn Live: Lectures, Interviews, and Outtakes*, 2007.

TRANSLATIONS: *Our Word: Guerrilla Poems from Latin America*, 1968 (with Gordon Brotherston; of José Emilio Pacheco's poetry); *Tree Between Two Walls*, 1969 (with Brotherston; of Pacheco's poetry); *Selected Poems*, 1976 (with Brotherston; of César Vallejo's poetry); *The Sun Unwound: Original Texts from Occupied America*, 1999 (with Brotherston).

MISCELLANEOUS: *Way West: Stories, Essays, and Verse Accounts, 1963-1993*, 1993.

BIBLIOGRAPHY

Clark, Tom. *Edward Dorn: A World of Difference.* Berkeley, Calif.: North Atlantic Books, 2002. A sympathetic biography by Dorn's close friend, a fellow poet. Relies heavily on letters from family and friends and on Dorn's work, both published and unpublished. Contains an epilogue—drawn from letters, journals, and poems—that describes Dorn's losing fight with cancer.

Costello, James Thomas. "Edward Dorn: The Range of Poetry." *Dissertation Abstracts International* 44 (July, 1983): 167A. This ambitious work examines Dorn's poetry in relation to his contemporaries and the influence in his work of the American West, politics, the Plains Indians, and even theoretical physics. Many major ideas in modern American writing are identified and explored. The range of works cited spans *The Newly Fallen* to *Yellow Lola*.

Dorn, Edward. "An Interview with Edward Dorn." Interview by Tandy Sturgeon. *Contemporary Literature* 27 (Spring, 1986): 1-17. In this compelling interview, Dorn discusses the difficulty of characterizing and judging the effects of political poetry. Dorn also explains his scorn for the flaccid academic tradition in writing and expresses his desire to invigorate the genre. This extensive and well-conducted interview offers an extraordinary glimpse into Dorn's mind and art.

_____. "An Interview with Edward Dorn." Interview by John Wright. *Chicago Review* 39, no. 1 (1993). A forty-four-page interview in which Dorn discusses his past and his work as a poet, teacher, and scholar.

Elmborg, James K. *A Pageant of Its Time: Edward Dorn's "Slinger" and the Sixties.* New York: Peter Lang, 1998. This critical study explores the poet's depiction of life in the 1960's. The author argues that *Gunslinger* is best read as a reaction to the state of the nation in the 1960's. Bibliography and index.

Foster, Thomas. "Kick(ing) the Perpendiculars Outa Right Anglos: Edward Dorn's Multiculturalism." *Contemporary Literature* 38, no. 1 (Spring, 1997): 78-105. Examines the book-length poem *Gunslinger*.

Paul, Sherman. *The Lost America of Love: Rereading Robert Creeley, Edward Dorn, and Robert Duncan.* Baton Rouge: Louisiana State University Press, 1981. A personal and intimate reflection on the power of these poets as experienced by the author. Paul explores Dorn's creative relationship to Walt Whitman, the effects of the Great Depression and World War II on Dorn's work, and the bedfellows of poetry and politics as they relate to Dorn's poetry.

Richey, Joseph, ed. *Ed Dorn Live: Lectures, Interviews, and Outtakes.* Ann Arbor: University of Michigan Press, 2007. This collection of interviews and lectures, along with an introduction and a bibliography, is a good source of information on Dorn's views.

Von Hallberg, Robert. "This Marvellous Accidentalism." In *American Poetry and Culture, 1945-1980.* Cambridge, Mass.: Harvard University Press, 1985. This excellent chapter on Dorn details the effects of his education, life experiences, and politics on his poetry. Dorn and his correspondence are frequently quoted, thereby giving authority to Von Hallberg's assertions. An accessible account of the many influences at play in Dorn's poetry.

Wesling, Donald, ed. *Internal Resistances: The Poetry of Edward Dorn.* Berkeley: University of California Press, 1985. Wesling asserts that this collection of essays is the first book to address—as its sole concern—Dorn's poetic achievements. All phases of Dorn's poetry are represented in these lucid observations that illustrate Dorn as a self-reflexive, historical, ironic and, finally, post-postmodern poet. Dorn's opus, *Slinger*, is especially well studied in this book.

Sue L. Kimball

MARK DOTY

Born: Maryville, Tennessee; August 10, 1953

PRINCIPAL POETRY

Turtle, Swan, 1987
Bethlehem in Broad Daylight, 1991
My Alexandria, 1993
Atlantis, 1995
An Island Sheaf, 1998
Sweet Machine, 1998
"Turtle, Swan" and "Bethlehem in Broad Daylight": Two Volumes of Poetry, 2000
Source, 2001
School of the Arts, 2005
Fire to Fire: New and Selected Poems, 2008
The Veiled Suite: The Collected Poems, 2009

OTHER LITERARY FORMS

Mark Doty (DOH-tee) has written three memoirs; *Heaven's Coast: A Memoir* (1996) is a moving personal account of the illness and death from acquired immunodeficiency syndrome (AIDS) of Doty's partner Wally Roberts; *Firebird: A Memoir* (1999) concerns Doty's often difficult early life and his discovery of his calling as a poet; *Dog Years* (2007) recounts his symbiotic relationship with two canine companions. *Still Life with Oysters and Lemon* (2001) is an extended essay on how people use art to see and understand the world around them.

ACHIEVEMENTS

Mark Doty has received numerous awards for his work. He won the Theodore Roethke Prize from *Poetry Northwest* (1986), the Los Angeles Times Book Prize for poetry (1993), and the Whiting Writers' Award

(1994). *My Alexandria* earned him the T. S. Eliot Prize for Poetry (1995), making him the first American recipient, and was selected for the National Poetry Series. He won the Bingham Poetry Prize (1996), the Ambassador Book Award (1996), and the Lambda Literary Award (1995) for *Atlantis*. Doty has also received the Witter Bynner Prize for Poetry (1997) from the American Academy of Arts and Letters, two additional Lambda Literary Awards (2001 and 2008), the Thom Gunn Award (2002), and the National Book Award (2008) for *Fire to Fire*. He has been honored with fellowships from the Guggenheim Foundation and Ingram Merrill Foundation and the Lila Wallace-*Reader's Digest* Writers' Award (1999). *Heaven's Coast* received the PEN/Martha Albrand Award for a first book of nonfiction.

BIOGRAPHY

As a child, Mark Doty often moved with his family (his father was a civilian employee of the Army Corps of Engineers). During his high school years in Tucson, Arizona, encouraged by poet Richard Shelton, Doty began to consider poetry seriously. He has said that he believes such mentoring is crucial to a beginning poet's development. Certainly Shelton and his household introduced Doty to an artistic world that was otherwise unavailable to him.

Doty received a B.A. from Drake University, in Des Moines, Iowa, where he also taught for a year. During this time, uncertain how to deal with his sexual orientation, he was married for a short time. He also began to publish poetry, although he later repudiated his earliest volumes as being both immature and untrue to his still-closeted identity. (He now considers his earliest book to be *Turtle, Swan*.) After he was divorced, he moved to Manhattan, where he fell in love with Wally Roberts, a window dresser for a department store. The two remained together for the rest of Roberts's life. During this time, Doty worked part time on an M.F.A. in creative writing from Goddard College in Montpelier, Vermont, where he and Roberts later lived for a time and renovated an old house. Doty later taught at Goddard.

Turtle, Swan was published by Godine in 1987. Early reviews praised its quiet tone in presenting the

Mark Doty (©Miriam Berkley)

gay experience in terms of the general human experience, which includes suffering. In 1989, Roberts was diagnosed with AIDS; the same year, the couple discovered Provincetown, Massachusetts. Moved by the beauty of the place and reassured by the support of its gay community, they decided to settle there—the paternal side of Doty's family can trace its New World ancestry to the pilgrims' landing on Cape Cod in 1620. When Roberts died in 1994, the experience was wrenching for Doty, who for a time was completely unable to write or even read. He found a release from grief in writing *Heaven's Coast*, the memoir in which he describes the experience of Roberts's illness.

In the latter half of the 1990's, Doty taught writing at various schools, including the Iowa Writers' Workshop at the University of Iowa, the Columbia School of the Arts, and the University of Utah. When he began to teach one semester each year at the University of Houston, he and his partner, writer Paul Lisicky, started dividing

their time between Texas and their two-hundred-year-old house in Provincetown. In 2009, Doty joined the faculty at Rutgers University in New Jersey.

ANALYSIS

Central to Mark Doty's work is his position as a gay poet; it informs all his poetic vision. Although he draws his subjects from a wide range of human experience, he views those subjects—as any writer must—through his own eyes. In Doty's case, those are eyes that have observed much beauty but also the painful experience of growing up gay in the 1950's and 1960's, the hatred expressed in American homophobia, and the grief of losing a lover to the ravages of AIDS. When a reviewer asked him about a "gay aesthetic," Doty noted that although gay people exist in as much variety as all human beings, a "sense of disjunction between surface and substance" is probably an essential part of gay life. A common theme in Doty's work examines the mutability of all things human; everything is ultimately fated to die, the poet says, but people must love anyway.

The relationship between surfaces and what lies beneath them is a recurrent motif in Doty's work both as he examines human experience and as he examines the external world. To discuss that relationship, he often uses the language of painting, a subject of abiding interest, as *Still Life with Oysters and Lemon* demonstrates. His diction draws frequently on the vocabulary of surface textures and colors.

A typical Doty poem is long, containing many short lines and short free-verse stanzas, although he sometimes uses rhyme. His poems often incorporate a narrative element, but Doty's real goal usually lies in the meditation that accompanies the narrative, not in the event itself. In their engagement with Doty's work, readers may feel they are accompanying the poet as he himself navigates the initial experience and struggles to understand its implications.

Doty has said that he is searching for ways to make his poetry political without relying on the language of the polemic or the harangue. He sees the possibility of making such poetry out of the materials of his own life, for he says that even when people tend their own gardens, they find that they have taken stances regarding social or political issues.

MY ALEXANDRIA

The poems of *My Alexandria* demonstrate this balance between the private and the political very powerfully as they address the AIDS epidemic and Roberts's illness. In "Fog," Doty records the events that surrounded his and Roberts's being tested for the HIV virus. The poem's central metaphor is blood, like the color at the heart of the peony buds in the front garden or the blood Doty lost by a nick from the garden shears. As they wait the three weeks for the results, Doty sees blood everywhere, feels it welling up like a wine fountain. They pass time by consulting the Ouija board, and as they do, they find that all the spirits seem eager to speak "to someone who isn't dead yet." One of the spirits seems to say that "M. has immunity" (Doty was immune) and, enigmatically, that "W. has." Another spirit identifies God as being in the garden, and the speaker, Doty, concurs, perhaps because the garden is a place of so much dying as well as growth.

When they meet the public health care worker, they get the news. She gives Roberts "the word that begins with *P*"—positive, though Doty suggests that "planchette" (the marker for the Ouija board) or "peony" or any other word would be preferable. At last he asks what one of the Ouija spirits asked: "Kiss me,/ in front of the screen, please,/ the dead are watching." He goes on: "They haven't had enough yet./ Every new bloom is falling apart." The fog of the title is the word the spirits use when "they can't speak clearly." Now, Doty says, it is the word he too must use for what he cannot say.

The long poem "The Wings" uses an angel as its central metaphor. The poem begins at a country auction, where a boy lies on the grass, waiting for his parents, and falls asleep while reading. The boy's parents waken him, and he leaves the magic world of dream and fiction to go back into "the world of things." As he slings his parents' purchase—a pair of snowshoes— across his back, he looks suddenly like "an angel/ to carry home the narrative of our storied,/ scattering things."

In the poem's next section, Doty recalls some of the things he and Roberts collected through the years. Once they picked apples in an abandoned orchard, where the grasses were still flattened from where deer had been lying. Once they found a rabbit cage containing a pair of homemade painted pine rabbits—a find any collector would treasure. That day calls up memories of the German film *Der Himmel über Berlin* (1987; *Wings of Desire*, 1988), in which angels are willing to give up their immortality for the sake of human experience. Doty agrees with the angels—who would not trade being an angel for such experiences? As he recalls the vivid scenes of that autumn day, he concludes "Don't let anybody tell you/ death's the price exacted/ for the ability to love. . . ."

The next section takes place at an exhibition of the AIDS quilt—the huge memorial quilt made up of hundreds of blocks dedicated to people who died of AIDS. Doty notes that many of the blocks are made of clothing of the dead; he concludes that these intimate blocks remind the viewer of "one essential, missing body." He goes on: "An empty pair of pants/ is mortality's severest evidence."

The poem's location moves into the autumn garden, a place in which errors can be corrected, plants can be lifted and reset in better places. The speaker says he is making an angel here, evidently using plantings to make an angelic shape. The image calls to his mind a dream in which he rescued a bird that loved him. When he took it from the closet and gave it water, "it began to beat the lush green music/ of its wings, and wrapped the brilliant risk/ of leaves all around my face."

Later, in Doty's class, his students puzzle over why the writer they are studying is so interested in mortality, and Doty says he longs to explain to them the image of the angel he has made, how it represents what is unthinkable between him and Roberts. It leans over his desk, over the bed where Roberts sleeps, just as the angels in the film watched their human charges. Doty names the angel *unharmed*. Its message seems to be that attachment to mortal beings is as futile as it is necessary to one's life as a human being: "You die by dying/ into what matters, which will kill you,/ but first it'll be enough."

ATLANTIS

The poems of Doty's next collection, *Atlantis*, form a testimony to the suffering AIDS causes both in those who have the disease and in the people who must watch them in their battle. The first poem of the collection,

"Description," defends Doty's attention to the appearance of things: "What is description, after all,/ but encoded desire?"

The effects of AIDS are described in "Grosse Fuge." The title refers to the fugue, a form in classical music involving a series of variations on a motif. The poem uses this form as it recalls the autumn Robert Shore ("Bobby" in the poem) spent with Doty during Shore's last months before his AIDS-related death. The poem circles repeatedly through Bobby's incoherent but evocative pronouncements. At the same time, the speaker is studying the fugue form to appreciate Ludwig van Beethoven's "Grosse Fuge," the patterns and autumnal tone of which seem to match Shore's decline. The form, like the disease and even this poem, seems without resolution: "What can I do but echo/ myself, vary and repeat?"

"Atlantis," the collection's long central poem, deals directly with Roberts's last days and with those of others who died of AIDS. The poem's six sections are linked by references to dreams. In the first, Doty recounts a dream in which his dog races into the road and is hit by a car. In the second, Roberts relates a dream in which he sees a light at the end of a tunnel but says that he is not yet ready to join the beings streaming toward it. The third describes the dreams of others who have AIDS. The last three sections name other sorts of dreams. Section 4 introduces the dream city of Atlantis, apparently rising from the tidal marsh with an implied promise of life. The plumber's daughter in section 5 intends to cling to life for the sick loon she has found, just as Roberts stubbornly grasps this world, a commitment dramatized by his stroking the new dog that has joined the household in the last section, a sign of his doomed determination to live.

SOURCE

Source seems to signal the poet's gradual emergence from an extended exploration of the topics of mortality and loss. In part because of his determination to move on with his life after the death of Roberts in 1993 and in part because of his relationship with Lisicky, his partner since 1995, the book is marked by a greater emphasis on being alive in the moment.

In "Principalities of June," Doty argues that living in Provincetown on the tip of Cape Cod offers daily evidence, especially in early summer, of the theory that all matter is fractured light. According to the poet, the "broken planes" of the white houses reflected in the harbor and refracted by the cloudbank serve as "phrase-books of day" or useful guides to some new language. In this case, it may very well be the language of renewal and regeneration, "articulated most of all" in the roses, "which mount and swell" on the arbor next to the house the poet shares with Lisicky. Doty asserts that roses are "built to contain/ sunlight . . ." and that in so doing, they contain the moment, which is paradoxically both fragmentary and complete.

Doty revisits, in *School of the Arts*, his abiding preoccupation with the intersection of people's inner and outer lives, especially how the poet or any artist must finally step outside himself and view experience from the perspective of the reader or audience.

Exploiting those skills that the poet has developed in navigating the genre of nonfiction, especially the memoir, "Heaven for Paul" translates personal narrative into a lesson of universal import. Doty recounts how he and his partner, Lisicky, faced the possibility of their own deaths while passengers on a plane forced to make an emergency landing. After the initial shock, ". . . crying a little/ and holding each others' hands . . . ," they each settled into a separate stance: Lisicky found tranquility and ". . . imagined himself turning toward/ what came next, an un-seeable *ahead*," while Doty could not envision a heaven but "only the unimaginable shape of not-myself—." In essence, each man represents one of the two basic human hypotheses concerning the nature of death: On the one hand, there is the hope of "transcendence," and on the other, the dread of "dissolution."

Only in framing the recollected experience as art can Doty step outside himself and gain a larger perspective. In so doing, for example, he comes to wonder why it would matter to him, ". . . on the verge of this life," that a female passenger would disapprove of two men holding hands. Later, at the end of the poem, when he confronts a second crisis—the threat of tornadoes approaching the airport after the plane's "wobbling" but safe descent—Doty has reached a state of philosophical composure, able to comment on God's possible intention regarding such life-threatening moments: "... either to torment us/ or to make us laugh, or both. ..."

FIRE TO FIRE

Besides containing a substantial sampling of poems from seven previous collections, *Fire to Fire* features twenty-three new pieces, which were published as a separate volume in England under the title *Theories and Apparitions* (2008). In particular, the eleven poems that grapple with a "theory," or lyric speculation about a certain topic, follow the poet's characteristic formula in that they are both confessional—rooted in some autobiographical experience—and universal.

In "Theory of Marriage (The Hug)," Doty revisits the canine companions that he first introduced to readers in his memoir *Dog Years*: a black retriever named Arden and a golden retriever named Beau. In their interaction with Doty and his partner, Lisicky, the dogs display contrasting behavior. Beau generally would "... offer his rump/ for scratching ..." while facing away from the one performing that act and "... looking out/ toward whatever might come along to enjoy"; on the other hand, "Arden would turn his head toward the one/ he loved ..." and "butt the top of his skull" against that person.

Thus, each dog offers a contrasting perspective on the nature of marriage. Beau regards his relationship to his human caretakers as a secure foundation from which to explore other possibilities—his stance can be interpreted as a canine variation on what some might call an "open marriage"; in contrast, Arden demonstrates the act of "... vanishing// into the beloved ..." and thus achieving a complete and exclusive union.

Very often the personal experience that serves for Doty as a trigger for poetic composition involves the contemplation of or engagement with art. In the case of "Theory of Incompletion," the poet recounts how while painting "doorways and bookcases" in his apartment, he suddenly became enraptured by a radio broadcast of a performance of George Frideric Handel's opera *Semele* (1744). According to Greek myth, Semele seeks to unite with Jupiter, the king of the gods, in his divine form, and because she is mortal, she is consumed in the act of their union. Just as Semele was dissolved by her desire, the poet surrenders to the moment and is suspended in time.

The speaker theorizes "... either it's the latex fumes or the music itself," but the end result is the same; he is enveloped in "... the rapture/ of denied closure. ..." He sits, leaning back on the rungs of his stepladder, immersed totally in the music, the "gorgeous rising tiers of it/ ceasing briefly then cascading again." This is the very nature of ecstasy, which is simultaneously "self-enfolding, self-devouring."

OTHER MAJOR WORKS

NONFICTION: *Heaven's Coast: A Memoir*, 1996; *Firebird: A Memoir*, 1999; *Still Life with Oysters and Lemon*, 2001; *Dog Years*, 2007.

EDITED TEXT: *Open House: Writers Redefine Home*, 2003.

BIBLIOGRAPHY

Baker, David. *Heresy and the Ideal: On Contemporary Poetry*. Fayetteville: University of Arkansas Press, 2000. In a chapter on how poets think, Baker argues that Doty is generally a detached observer of life because his need to instruct often undercuts the impulse to feel.

Bing, Jonathan. "Mark Doty: The Idea of Order on Cape Cod." *Publishers Weekly* 243 (April 15, 1996): 44-46. Doty discusses his working methods in reference to his prose work as well as to his poems.

Doty, Mark. Interview by Michael Glover. *New Statesman* 126 (May 30, 1997): 44-45. The interview contains some biographical detail about how Doty came to poetry. The poet also comments on the effect of Roberts's death on his writing.

_____. "Mark Doty." http://www.markdoty.org. Doty's home page contains a brief biography, a list of his books, information on readings and projects, and links to reviews, interviews, and selected poems and essays.

_____. "Mark Doty." Interview by Christopher Hennessy. In *Outside the Lines: Talking with Contemporary Gay Poets*, edited by Hennessy. Ann Arbor: University of Michigan Press, 2005. Doty discusses poetic composition, how he converts personal experience into art.

Glover, Michael. Review of *Atlantis. New Statesman* 125 (July 26, 1996): 47. Glover calls Doty the best

American poet since the death of Robert Lowell and gives some attention to his imagery and diction.

Landau, Deborah. "'How to Live. What to Do.': The Poetics and Politics of AIDS." *American Literature* 68 (March, 1996): 193-226. Discusses the work of four poets as literary responses to the AIDS epidemic; examines Doty's work in detail.

Logan, William. *The Undiscovered Country: Poetry in the Age of Tin.* New York: Columbia University Press, 2005. In an essay devoted to Doty's work, this controversial critic examines the poet's use of language and his characteristic stylistic devices.

Wonderlich, Mark. "About Mark Doty." *Ploughshares* 25 (Spring, 1999): 183-189. The profile contains some biographical information as well as brief discussions of *My Alexandria*, *Atlantis*, and *Sweet Machine*.

Ann D. Garbett
Updated by S. Thomas Mack

RITA DOVE

Born: Akron, Ohio; August 28, 1952

PRINCIPAL POETRY

The Yellow House on the Corner, 1980
Museum, 1983
Thomas and Beulah, 1986
Grace Notes, 1989
Selected Poems, 1993
Mother Love, 1995
On the Bus with Rosa Parks, 1999
American Smooth, 2004
Sonata Mulattica: A Life in Five Movements and a Short Play, 2009

OTHER LITERARY FORMS

Rita Dove has published *Fifth Sunday* (1985), a collection of short stories; *Through the Ivory Gate* (1992), a novel; and *The Poet's World* (1995), a collection of essays. *The Darker Face of the Earth*, a verse drama, appeared in 1994.

ACHIEVEMENTS

Rita Dove's literary honors include grants and fellowships from the National Endowment for the Arts, the Academy of American Poets, the Guggenheim Foundation, and the General Electric Foundation. She spent 1988-1989 as a Senior Mellon Fellow at the National Humanities Center in North Carolina. She served as poet laureate consultant in poetry to the Library of Congress from 1993 to 1995 and poet laureate of the Commonwealth of Virginia from 2004 to 2006. She also was a special bicentennial consultant (poet laureate) to the Library of Congress along with poets W. S. Merwin and Louise Glück in 1999-2000. She became a chancellor of the Academy of American Poets in 2006.

In 1987, her collection *Thomas and Beulah* made her the first black woman since Gwendolyn Brooks to win the Pulitzer Prize. She has also been awarded the Peter I. B. Lavan Younger Poets Award (1986), several Ohioana Book Awards for Poetry (1990, 1994, 2000), the Charles Frankel Prize/National Humanities Medal (1996), the Heinz Award in the Arts and Humanities (1996), the Sara Lee Frontrunner Award (1997), Levinson Prize from *Poetry* magazine (1998), the John Frederick Nims Translation Award (1999; together with Fred Viebahn), the Duke Ellington Lifetime Achievement Award (2001), the Emily Couric Leadership Award (2003), the Common Wealth Award of Distinguished Service (2006; with others), the Lifetime Achievement Award from the Library of Virginia (2008), and the Fulbright Lifetime Achievement Medal and the Premio Capri (both in 2009).

BIOGRAPHY

Born in 1952 in Akron, Ohio, Rita Francis Dove is the daughter of Ray Dove and Elvira (Hord) Dove. She received a B.A. in 1973 from Miami University (Ohio) and then studied modern European literature at the University of Tübingen, Germany, on a Fulbright Fellowship. She returned to the United States to earn an M.F.A. at the highly regarded Iowa Writers' Workshop at the University of Iowa in 1977. She held a number of teaching posts and traveled widely in Europe and the Middle East, later becoming a professor of English at the University of Virginia. During the summer of 1998, the Boston Symphony Orchestra performed her song cycle of a woman's life, *Seven for Luck*, with music by John Williams. From January, 2000, to January, 2002, she wrote a weekly column, "Poet's Choice," for *The Washington Post*. Dove married Fred Viebahn, a writer, in 1979; they had a daughter, Aviva Chantal Tamu Dove-Viebahn in 1983.

ANALYSIS

In a period when much American poetry is condemned as being merely an exercise in solipsistic navel gazing, and when African American poetry more specifically seems to have lapsed into hibernation after the vigorous activity of the Black Arts movement, Rita Dove steps forth with a body of work that resoundingly answers such criticism. Hers is a poetry characterized by discipline and technical proficiency, surprising breadth of reference, a willingness to approach emotionally charged subjects with aesthetic objectivity, and a refusal to define herself only in terms of blackness. She combines a novelist's eye for action and gesture with the lyric poet's exalted sense of language. Dove's distinguishing feature is her ability to turn a cold gaze on the larger world with which she has to interact as a social being—and as an African American woman. That gaze is filtered through an aesthetic sensibility that regards poetry as a redemptive force, a transformational power.

The startling scope of Dove's learning opens for her poetry a correspondingly vast range of topics and concerns, but the most persistent, and the one that most distinguishes her work from that of poets in the 1970's and 1980's, is history. She is constantly laboring to bring into focus the individual struggle in the ebb and flow of the historical tide. A second major concern is cultural collision, the responses of an outsider to a foreign culture, and she pursues this theme in a number of travel poems. Dove also plumbs the circumstances of her life as a way of confronting the puzzle of her own identity—as an African American, as a woman, as a daughter, as a parent—but she manages self-dramatization without self-aggrandizement.

Dove has been lauded for her technical acumen. Although much modern poetry is best characterized by a certain casualness and laxity, she has created poetry in which no verse is "free." Each poem gives the impression of having been chiseled, honed, and polished. Her poems evolve into highly individual structures, rather than traditional forms, although it is possible to find an occasional sonnet neatly revised and partially hidden. More often she stresses rhythm and sound and uses interior rhyme, slant rhyme, and feminine rhyme to furnish her stanzas with a subtle organizing principle, what she calls the "sound cage" of a poem. Her idiom is predominantly colloquial, but she can adopt the stiffened, formal diction of the eighteenth and nineteenth centuries when evoking personas from those periods. In her mastery of the craft, Dove reveals an attitude toward poetry itself—a deeply felt love and respect—that also influences the approach a reader must take to it. Her work makes demands on the reader because of that love.

Dove's first two volumes, *The Yellow House on the Corner* and *Museum*, provide a balance between the personal or individual and the social or cultural. Each is divided into sections that allow the author to address concerns that she wishes for now to remain separate. It

Rita Dove (Fred Viebahn/Courtesy, Pantheon Books)

has also been noted that the titles of these two books signal a shift in Dove's emphasis from the homely and familiar, "the yellow house," to the more sophisticated and arcane "museum." This generalization should not, however, obscure the fact that the poet's interests in these books overlap considerably. *Museum* is the more consciously organized, with its sections pointedly titled and each dealing with a central topic—history and myth, art and artifact, autobiography and the personal past, life in the modern world.

Dove's next volume, *Thomas and Beulah*, represents her coming of age critically, a step into the position of a leading African American poet. It allows her to extend her continual dissertation on the single person striving in the midst of historical flux; at the same time, she can pursue her abiding interest in her own family romance, the question of heritage. Following *Thomas and Beulah*, and still availing itself of a variety of themes, *Grace Notes* is by far the most intensely autobiographical of her works, becoming a study in limitation and poignant regret. How, she seems to ask here, does one grant to daily life that ornament or variation that magically transforms it? *On the Bus with Rosa Parks* examines the panoply of human endeavor, exploring the intersection of individual fates with the grand arc of history.

THE YELLOW HOUSE ON THE CORNER

Poems in *The Yellow House on the Corner* often depict the collision of wish with reality, of heart's desire with the dictates of the world. This collision is made tolerable by the working of the imagination, and the result is, for Dove, "magic," or the existence of an unexplainable occurrence. It is imagination and the art it produces that allow the speaker in "This Life" to see that "the possibilities/ are golden dresses in a nutshell." "Possibilities" have the power to transform this life into something distinct and charmed. Even the woman driven mad with grief over the loss of her son (or husband?) in "The Bird Frau" becomes a testament to possibility in her desire to "let everything go wild!" She becomes a bird-woman as a way of reuniting with her lost airman, who died in the war over France. Although her condition may be perceived as pathetic, Dove refuses to indulge sentimentality, instead seeing her madness as a form of undying hope.

The refusal to indulge sentimentality is a mark of Dove's critical intelligence. It allows her to interpose an objectifying distance between herself and the subject. She knows the absolute value of perspective, so that while she can exult in the freedom that imagination makes possible, she recognizes that such liberty has its costs and dangers too. Two poems in particular reveal this desire and her wariness: "Geometry" and "Sightseeing." In the former, Dove parallels the study of points, lines, and planes in space with the work of the poet: "I prove a theorem and the house expands:/ the windows jerk free to hover near the ceiling,/ the ceiling floats away with a sigh." Barriers and boundaries disappear in the imagination's manipulation of them, but that manipulation has its methodology or aesthetic: "I *prove* a theorem. . . ."

In "Sightseeing," the speaker, a traveler in Europe after World War II, comes upon what would seem to be a poem waiting to happen. The inner courtyard of a village church has been left just as it was found by the villagers after an Allied bombing raid. It is filled with the shattered cherubim and seraphim that had previously decorated the inner terrace of the building: "What a consort of broken dolls!" Nevertheless, the speaker repudiates any temptation to view the sight as the villagers must—"A terrible sign. . . ." Instead she coolly ponders the rubble with the detached air of a detective: "Let's look/ at the facts." She "reads" the scene and the observers' attention to it as a cautionary lesson. The "children of angels" become "childish monsters." Since she distinguishes herself from the devout villagers, she can also see herself and her companion in the least flattering light: "two drunks" coming all the way across the town "to look at a bunch of smashed statues."

This ability to debunk and subvert expectations is a matter of artistic survival for Dove and a function of her calm intelligence. As an African American poet, she is aware of the tradition of letters into which she steps. Two other poems imply that this tradition can be problematic. In "Upon Meeting Don L. Lee, in a Dream" Dove encounters Lee (now known as Haki R. Madhubuti), a leading figure in the Black Arts movement, which attempted to generate a populist, specifically black aesthetic. The figure that emerges from Dove's poem, however, is unable to change except to self-destruct: "I can see caviar/ Imbedded like buckshot between his teeth." Her dream-portrait of Lee deflates not only his masculinity but his status as cultural icon as well. In "Nigger Song: An Odyssey," Dove seems to hark back further for a literary forebear and finds one in Brooks, the first black woman to win the Pulitzer Prize. Although by 1967 Brooks would have come to embrace the black nationalism that Lee embodied, Dove's poem echoes the Brooks of an earlier time, the composer of "We Real Cool." In her evocation of "the nigger night," Dove captures the same vibrant energy that Brooks both celebrates and laments with the realization that the energy of urban African American youth is allowed no purposeful outlet and will turn on itself. She writes: "Nothing can catch us./ Laughter spills like gin from glasses."

Some of the most compelling poems in Dove's first book are in a group of vignettes and portraits from the era of American slavery. These poems not only reveal her historical awareness but also allow her to engage the issue of race from a distance. Dove wants her poetry to produce anger, perhaps, but not to be produced only by anger. One example of this aesthetic distance from emotion might be "The Abduction," a brief foray in the voice of Solomon Northrup. Northrup is a free black lured to Washington, D.C., by "new friends" with the promise of good work, and then kidnapped and sold into bondage. Dove dwells on the duplicity of these men and Northrup's susceptibility to them, yet no pronouncements are made. The poem ends with the end of freedom, but that ending has been foreshadowed by the tightly controlled structure of the poem itself, with each stanza shortening as the scope of the victim's world constricts to this one-line conclusion: "I woke and found myself alone, in darkness and in chains." The indignation and disgust that such an episode could call forth are left entirely to the reader.

MUSEUM

Dove's next volume, *Museum*, is itself, as the title suggests, a collection of historical and aesthetic artifacts. The shaping impulse of the book seems to be retrospective, a looking back to people and things that have been somehow suspended in time by legend, by historical circumstance, by all-too-human emotional wish. Dove intends to delve beneath the publicly

known side of these stories—to excavate, in a sense, and uncover something forgotten but vital. The book is filled with both historical and mythical figures, all sharing the single trait of muted voice. Thus, "Nestor's Bathtub" begins: "As usual, legend got it all/ wrong." The private torment of a would-be martyr is made public in "Catherine of Alexandria." In "The Hill Has Something to Say," the poet speculates on the buried history of Europe, the cryptic messages that a culture sends across time. In one sense, the hill is a metaphor for this book, a repository of signs and images that speak only to that special archaeologist, the reader.

In the section titled "In the Bulrush," Dove finds worthy subjects in unlikely places and draws them from hiding. "Banneker" is another example of her flair for evoking the antebellum world of slavery, where even the free man is wrongly regarded because of his race. In the scientist Benjamin Banneker, she finds sensitivity, eloquence, and intelligence, all transformed by prejudice into mere eccentricity. Banneker was the first black man to devise an almanac and served on Thomas Jefferson's commission to lay out the city of Washington, D.C., but the same qualities that lifted him to prominence made him suspect in the eyes of white society. Dove redeems this crabbed conception of the man in an alliterative final passage that focuses attention on his vision:

> Lowering his eyes to fields
> sweet with the rot of spring, he could see
> a government's domed city
> rising from the morass and spreading
> in a spiral of lights . . .

A third section of the book is devoted entirely to poems about the poet's father, and they represent her efforts to understand him. It is a very personal grouping, made to seem all the more so by the preceding sections in which there is little or nothing directly personal at all.

In the final section, "Primer for the Nuclear Age," Dove includes what is one of her most impressive performances. Although she has not shown herself to be a poet of rage, she is certainly not inured to the social and political injustice she observes. Her work is a way of channeling and controlling such anger; as she says in "Primer for the Nuclear Age," "if you've/ got a heart at all, someday/ it will kill you." "Parsley," the final poem of *Museum*, summons up the rank insanity of Rafael Trujillo, dictator of the Dominican Republic, who, on October 2, 1957, ordered twenty thousand black Haitians killed because they could not pronounce the letter *r* in *perejil*, Spanish for parsley. The poem is divided into two sections; the first is a villanelle spoken by the Haitians; the second describes General Trujillo on the day of his decision. The second section echoes many of the lines from the Haitians' speech, drawing murderer and victim together, suggesting a disturbing complicity among all parties in this episode of unfettered power. Even though Dove certainly wants to draw attention to this event, the real subject here is the lyric poet's realm—that point at which language intersects with history and actually determines its course.

THOMAS AND BEULAH

Thomas and Beulah garnered the Pulitzer Prize, but it is more important for the stage it represents in Dove's poetic development. Her first two books reveal a lyric poet generally working within the bounds of her medium. The lyric poem denies time, process, change. It becomes a frozen moment, an emotion reenacted in the reading. In *Thomas and Beulah*, she pushes at the limitations of the form by stringing together, "as beads on a necklace," a whole series of these lyric moments. As the poems begin to reflect on one another, the effect is a dramatic unfolding in which the passing of time is represented, even though the sequence never establishes a conventional plot. To accomplish this end, Dove creates a two-sided book: Thomas's side ("Mandolin," twenty-one poems) followed by Beulah's ("Canary in Bloom," twenty-one poems).

The narrative moves from Thomas's riverboat life and the crucial death of his friend Lem to his arrival in Akron and marriage, through the birth of children, jobs, illness, and death. Beulah's part of the book then begins, moving through her parents' stormy relationship, her courtship with Thomas, marriage, pregnancy, work, and death. These two lives transpire against the historical backdrop of the great migration, the Depression, World War II, and the March on Washington; however, these events are practically the only common elements in the two sides of the story. Thomas and Beulah seem to live separate lives. Their communication with each other is implicit in the survival of the marriage itself. Throughout, Dove handles the story through exacting use of imagery and character.

Thomas emerges as a haunted man, dogged by the death of his friend Lem, which occurs in the opening poem, "The Event." Thomas drunkenly challenges Lem to swim from the deck of the riverboat to an island in the Mississippi. Lem drowns in the attempt to reach what is probably a mirage, and Thomas is left with "a stinking circle of rags/ the half-shell mandolin." In "Courtship," he begins to woo Beulah, but the poem implies that the basis of their relationship will be the misinterpreted gesture and that Thomas's guilt has left him with a void. He casually takes a yellow silk scarf from around his neck and wraps it around her shoulders; "a gnat flies/ in his eye and she thinks/ he's crying." Thomas's gift, rather than a spontaneous transfer of warmth, is a sign of his security in his relative affluence. The show of vulnerability and emotional warmth is accidental. The lyric poet in Dove allows her to compress this range of possibility in the isolated gesture or image. Beulah's life is conveyed as a more interior affair, a process of attaining the wisdom to understand her world rather than to resist it openly. In "The Great Palace of Versailles," Beulah's reading becomes her secret escape from the nastiness of the whites for whom she works in Charlotte's Dress Shoppe. As she lies dying in the final poem, "The Oriental Ballerina," the contemplation of the tiny figurine seems a similar invitation to fantasy, but her sensibilities have always been attuned to seeing the world as it is, as it has to be, and the poem ends in a brief flurry of realistic details and an air of acceptance; there is "no cross, just the paper kiss/ of a kleenex above the stink of camphor,/ the walls exploding with shabby tutus. . . ."

GRACE NOTES

Grace Notes marks Dove's return to the purely lyric mode, but an autobiographical impulse dominates the work to an unprecedented degree. More than in any of her previous collections, the poet can be seen as actor in her own closet drama, whether as a young child learning a rather brutal lesson in the southern black school of survival ("Crab-Boil") or as a mother groping for a way to reveal feminine mysteries to her own little girl ("After Reading *Mickey in the Night Kitchen* for the Third

Time Before Bed"). The willingness to become more self-referential carries with it the danger of obscurity, the inside joke that stays inside. Dove, however, seems to open herself to a kind of scrutiny and challenge that offer no hiding place, and that assay extends to her own poetic practice. In "Dedication," a poem in the manner of Czesław Miłosz, Dove seems to question the veracity of her own technical expertise: "What are music or books if not ways/ to trap us in rumors? The freedom of fine cages!"

In the wickedly ironic "Ars Poetica," she places herself on the literary chain of being with what might pass for self-deprecation. Her ambition is to make a small poem, like a ghost town, a minute speck on the "larger map of wills." "Then you can pencil me in as a hawk:/ a traveling x-marks-the-spot." However, this hawk is not a songbird to be taken lightly. The very next poem in the book unleashes the bird of prey in Dove (a pun she surely intends); in the aptly titled "Arrow," she exposes the sexism and racism of an "eminent scholar" in all of its condescending glory. This focus on the autobiographical element is not to imply that the range of subjects in *Grace Notes* is not still wide-ranging and surprising. Echoes of her earlier books sound clearly; so does the wit that makes them always engaging: "Here's a riddle for Our Age: when the sky's the limit,/ how can you tell you've gone too far?"

MOTHER LOVE

In *Mother Love*, Dove survives her overused source material, the myth of Demeter and Persephone, by transforming it into something deeply personal. She allows herself to be inhabited by the myth, and Dove's Demeter consciousness reveals that every time a daughter walks out the door, the abduction by Hades begins again. Dove's persona adopts Persephone's stance in "Persephone in Hell"; here, Dove recalls, at twenty, enjoying the risks of visiting Paris. She felt her mother's worry but asserts, "I was doing what she didn't need to know," testing her ripeness against the world's (man's) treachery. Dove employs loose sonnet shapes in these poems, giving herself license in order to provide authentic contemporary voices. At once dramatic, narrative, and highly lyrical, these poems more than fulfill the expectations of those who anointed her at the outset of her career.

ON THE BUS WITH ROSA PARKS

On the Bus with Rosa Parks is a more miscellaneous collection, but with several cohesive groupings. The "Cameos" sequence provides sharply etched vignettes of working-class life, a recurrent subject in Dove's writings. The closing sequence, from which the entire collection takes its name, explores the interface of public and private lives in contemporary African American history. As ever, Dove is a superb storyteller whose film-like poems are energized by precise imagery and tonal perfection.

AMERICAN SMOOTH

The title, *American Smooth*, refers to the name Dove herself gave to a ballroom dance in which the partners separate and become free to improvise and express themselves individually. In the title poem, two partners achieve such perfect harmony in their dancing that for a few seconds they forget technical points like keeping their frame and instead feel as if they are flying. Dance imagery shows up in several other poems in this collection, which displays Dove's cosmopolitanism. In "Rhumba," each short line takes place during one measure of this three-step dance, and there is an unspoken dialogue between the two partners. In "Fox Trot Fridays," a couple escapes from the grinds of their daily existence by going dancing for one night each week and, for a short time, perhaps just the length of one song, find happiness. Another couple finds passion when they dance together in "Bolero." The only African American woman at a country club dance wears a red dress, makes a grand entrance, and waltzes in "Brown." "The Castle Walk" refers to a ballroom dance created by Vernon and Irene Castle, who taught ballroom dancing to the social elite of New York during the early twentieth century. In this poem, based on an actual event before World War I, they engage an African American band to play at a society dance. The band puts forth their best effort, although they know that their audience is incapable of truly appreciating their ragtime-style music. Men dance the cake-walk at a picnic in "Samba Summer" for the benefit of the women and children in attendance. Using different points of view, including the title character's, Dove describes one of the most famous dancing performances in history in "The Seven Veils of Salome."

Dove delves into African American history with seven poems that salute the 369th Infantry Regiment of the U.S. Army. During World War I, this African American unit spent 191 days in the trenches. "The Passage" describes their voyage across the Atlantic from Newport News, Virginia, to France. The well-educated narrator suffers from sea sickness, worries about German submarines and stormy weather, and thinks he sees a whale from the ship one day. In "Alfonzo Prepares to Go over the Top," a soldier prepares to leave the relative safety of his trench and take part in a bayonet charge during the Battle of Belleau Wood. The regiment marches in a 1919 victory parade on Fifth Avenue in New York in "The Return of Lieutenant James Reese Europe." Decades later in "Ripont," an African American family attends a memorial service at a battlefield where the regiment once fought.

Another event in African American history forms the subject of "Hattie McDaniel Arrives in Coconut Grove." The accomplishments of McDaniel create a sense of ambivalence in many blacks: She was the first African American actor to win an Academy Award, but she did so playing Mammy, a stereotypical role as a black servant, in *Gone with the Wind* (1939).

OTHER MAJOR WORKS

LONG FICTION: *Through the Ivory Gate*, 1992.

SHORT FICTION: *Fifth Sunday*, 1985.

PLAY: *The Darker Face of the Earth*, pb. 1994, 2000 (verse drama).

NONFICTION: *The Poet's World*, 1995.

EDITED TEXTS: *The Best American Poetry, 2000*, 2000; *Conversations with Rita Dove*, 2003 (Earl G. Ingersoll, editor).

BIBLIOGRAPHY

Bloom, Harold, ed. *African American Poets: Robert Hayden Through Rita Dove*. Philadelphia: Chelsea House, 2003. Contains a short biography on Dove and the essay "Rita Dove's Shakespeares," by Peter Erickson.

Dove, Rita. Interviews. *Conversations with Rita Dove*. Edited by Earl G. Ingersoll. Jackson: University Press of Mississippi, 2003. Part of the Literary Conversations series, this work gathers numerous interviews with Dove, many of them looking at the process of writing.

McDowell, Robert. "The Assembling Vision of Rita Dove." *Callaloo* 9 (Winter, 1986): 61-70. This article provides an excellent overview of Dove's accomplishments in her first three books and places her in the larger context of American poetry. McDowell argues that Dove's distinction is her role as "an assembler," someone who pulls together the facts of this life and presents them in challenging ways.

Newson, Adele S. Review of *On the Bus with Rosa Parks*. *World Literature Today* 74, no. 1 (Winter, 2000): 165-166. Newson examines the collection section by section, suggesting that the book forms an overall story bonded by related imagery and linked through digressions. In it, readers hear "the voice of a community's history and human response."

Pereira, Malin. *Rita Dove's Cosmopolitanism*. Urbana: University of Illinois Press, 2003. A critical analysis of Dove's poetry, literary criticism, drama, and fiction. Pereira states that Dove is most responsible for initiating a new era in African American poetry.

Righelato, Pat. *Understanding Rita Dove*. Columbia: University of South Carolina Press, 2006. Provides literary analysis of Dove's work through *American Smooth*.

Shoptaw, John. Review of *Thomas and Beulah*. *Black American Literature Forum* 21 (Fall, 1987): 335-341. This review isolates specific verbal tactics that Dove employs. It also addresses the problem of narrative and the difficult task Dove set for herself in telling the story as she did.

Steffen, Theresa. *Crossing Color: Transcultural Space and Place in Rita Dove's Poetry, Fiction, and Drama*. New York: Oxford University Press, 2001. Examines both Dove's linguistic devices and the cultural contexts of her work.

Vendler, Helen. *The Given and the Made: Strategies of Poetic Redefinition*. Cambridge, Mass.: Harvard University Press, 1995. One of the foremost literary critics of poetry discusses Dove's poetry in this collection of lectures.

Walters, Jennifer. "Nikki Giovanni and Rita Dove:

Poets Redefining." *Journal of Negro History* 85 (Summer, 2000): 210-217. Discusses Giovanni and Dove as African American women who found their voices through writing.

Nelson Hathcock; Philip K. Jason
Updated by Thomas R. Feller

NORMAN DUBIE

Born: Barre, Vermont; April 10, 1945

PRINCIPAL POETRY

The Horsehair Sofa, 1969
Alehouse Sonnets, 1971
In the Dead of the Night, 1975
Popham of the New Song, and Other Poems, 1975
The Prayers of the North American Martyrs, 1975
The Illustrations, 1977
Odalisque in White: Two Poems, 1978
A Thousand Little Things, and Other Poems, 1978
The City of the Olesha Fruit, 1979
The Everlastings, 1980
The Window in the Field, 1981
Selected and New Poems, 1983
The Springhouse, 1986
Groom Falconer: Poems by Norman Dubie, 1989
The Clouds of Magellan, 1991
Radio Sky, 1991
The Mercy Seat: Collected and New Poems, 1967-2001, 2001
Ordinary Mornings of a Coliseum, 2004
Insomniac Liar of Topo, 2007

OTHER LITERARY FORMS

Norman Dubie (DUH-bee-ay) has contributed several critical pieces to such journals as *American Poetry Review*, *Poetry*, and *Iowa Review*, but he is known primarily for his poetry.

ACHIEVEMENTS

Norman Dubie is one of America's most important and innovative contemporary poets. Since the publica-

tion of his first volume of verse when he was twenty-three years old, Dubie has, on the average, published one book every two years, accumulating an impressive body of work. At a time when American poetry has been both praised and criticized for its preoccupation with intimate personal experience, Dubie has sought to see the world through the eyes of historical figures from many different times and places—painters, fellow writers, individuals of all sorts—whose distinctive perspectives he adopts for the duration of a poem.

In 1976, Dubie won the Bess Hokin Prize from *Poetry* and the Modern Poetry Association for "The Negress, Her Monologue of Dark Crepe." He has also received creative writing fellowships from the National Endowment for the Arts and the Guggenheim Foundation. In honor of Dubie's literary achievements, the University of Iowa, where he received his M.F.A. degree, houses the Norman Dubie Collection in its library. In 2002, Dubie won the PEN Center USA Literary Award for *The Mercy Seat*.

BIOGRAPHY

Norman Evans Dubie, Jr., was born on April 10, 1945, in Barre, Vermont. His father, Norman Evans Dubie, Sr., was a clergyman, and his mother, Doris Dubie, was a registered nurse. Dubie was educated in Vermont and received his undergraduate degree at Goddard College in Plainfield, graduating in 1969. In 1968, while a student at Goddard, Dubie married Francesca Stafford, and the couple had one child, Hannah, Dubie's only child.

Leaving Vermont after his graduation, Dubie studied creative writing in the M.F.A. program of the Iowa Writers' Workshop at the University of Iowa. He received his degree in 1971 and began lecturing in the workshop afterward. From 1971 though 1972, Dubie was the poetry editor of *Iowa Review*; from 1973 through 1974, he edited *Now*. During this period, his first marriage ended in divorce.

When Dubie left the University of Iowa, he became an assistant professor of English at Ohio University in Athens. He retained this position from 1974 through 1975; during this period, Dubie published three volumes of poetry: *The Prayers of the North American*

Martyrs, *Popham of the New Song, and Other Poems*, and *In the Dead of the Night*. Following the publication of these collections, Dubie left Ohio University and accepted a position at Arizona State University.

Dubie was writer-in-residence at Arizona State from 1975 until 1976. He was a lecturer there from 1976 until 1983 and was then promoted to the rank of full professor of English. In 1976, he became the director of Arizona State's graduate writing program.

In 1975, Dubie was remarried, to Pamela Stewart, a poet and a teacher. Five years later, this marriage also ended in divorce. In 1981, Dubie remarried again, this time to Jeannine Savard, also a poet.

Dubie frequently contributes to many magazines, including *Paris Review*, *The New Yorker*, *American Poetry Review*, *Antaeus*, *Antioch Review*, *Field*, and *Poetry*.

ANALYSIS

In his introduction to Norman Dubie's *The Illustrations*, poet Richard Howard says that Dubie's poetry centers on "the experience which has the root of *peril* in

Norman Dubie (©Chris Pickler)

it, the ripple of danger which enlivens the seemingly lovely surfaces, the 'ordinary' existence." That perilous quality is evident in nearly all Dubie's work; it is the very thing that guarantees its success. Still, "the ripple of danger" creates a difficult poetry too, embracing experience in exciting, innovative ways. The ordinary becomes extraordinary. As Howard puts it, "Dubie identifies that experience, by reciting it, with his own life to a hallucinatory degree: We are not to know what is given and what is taken, what is 'real' and what 'made up.'"

The juxtaposition of "real" and "fiction" is particularly engaging in much of Dubie's early work. In *Alehouse Sonnets* and *The Illustrations*, Dubie wrote historically based poems in the form of dramatic monologues. Perhaps it is this for which Dubie is best known; not only do these monologues create a space in which the poet can move outside himself and the time in which he lives, but also they allow him the intellectual advantage of innovation as well as imagistic and allusive complexity. The result is an engaging, demanding verse. Readers must work to understand; they must either clarify the obscurity or be resigned to the "hallucinatory"; readers must not relent in the attempt to discover the value of such complexity. These are imperatives; readers have no choice.

Still, one reader will find Dubie's work elegant and beautiful; the next will find it distant and foreign, purposely ignoring accessibility. Both appraisals may be justified. Dubie's demands on his poetry and on his readers, however, set him apart from nearly all other contemporary poets. His is an original, fanciful voice, and often the distinction he makes between reality and fancy is fuzzy. This creates a sometimes lethargic, somnambulant effect, quite like walking along some foggy, hazed-over street under white lights, dreamy, disembodied, and more than a little disenchanted. The reader is much like the character in "Hazlitt Down from the Lecture Table" (*Alehouse Sonnets*) who " . . . just/ sat out the stupor in a corner."

This seems to be Dubie's exact intention, though. Dubie's imagination draws him—and readers—away from the mundane, real world and intensifies that "stupor" by displacing him to a paradoxical, mundane, exotic world. The lives of Dubie's characters, their triumphs and their failures, are no more special than are those of his readers—and no worse. The difficulty, then, is the importance readers may attribute to the allusive figures or to the thick, ambiguous imagery. One assumes that the allusion means something essential or that knowledge of the allusion will clarify the poem. Readers may puzzle for an interminable time, trying to unravel an obscure image. Each of these, however, is a failed reading; such scrutiny may aid comprehension, but it will not guarantee tidy answers. The man who "sat out the stupor" knows and accepts this.

The importance of Dubie's contribution to the poetics of his time is evident. More than most of his contemporaries, Dubie has risked much to offer an unusual, resonant voice. Granted, his poems are difficult, evasive at times, incomprehensible at other times, yet his imagination addresses very real issues. That Dubie expects his readers to work is really no fault inherent in his poetry; already, too many other poets write easy, disposable verse. Dubie's poetry is not disposable. It will not let its readers let it loose.

ALEHOUSE SONNETS

While some of Dubie's critics find his work incomprehensible, still others accuse him of being too impersonal. This is especially so in Dubie's early writing. *Alehouse Sonnets*, for example, is characterized by a detached, unidentified persona. All one knows of the persona is his affinity to William Hazlitt, the nineteenth century English critic, whom he addresses throughout the book. One can imagine, after reading *Alehouse Sonnets*, a companionship made between men of two different centuries and, most likely, two different lifestyles. Time and place cannot erase humankind's disappointments, however, for the characters in the poems share those experiences universally. To juxtapose the contraries of time and place, Dubie approaches his subjects and his characters with calculated distance. The poet hovers over the characters, sometimes coming in, intruding, but usually standing not far off, aloof and watchful.

To fault this as being impersonal is also a misreading of Dubie's work. As Lorrie Goldensohn has written of Dubie, "What mostly gets left out is the explicitly autobiographical self. The self, that darling of contemporary poetry, here has little to do; it appears to be just an-

other dreamer, usually present as a disembodied voice rummaging around . . . interchangeable with others." Contemporary poetry is excessively burdened with poems of "self," and Dubie's poems offer a refreshing break from that tendency. The fanciful mind discovers commonality of experience, how the persona's life, Hazlitt's, the poet's, and the reader's are much the same. The verse does not need to be autobiographical, because Dubie is writing everyone's biography. The poem cannot be personal; as Dubie wrote in "Address to the Populous Winter Youths," "Nearness exasperates."

IN THE DEAD OF THE NIGHT AND THE ILLUSTRATIONS

In the several collections that immediately followed *Alehouse Sonnets*, Dubie continued to experiment with deliberate distancing. Rather than addressing only one allusive figure—Hazlitt, for example—Dubie would address numerous historical personages or speak through them. *In the Dead of the Night* and *The Illustrations* are most notably characterized by a profusion of allusions to artists. A quick listing of Dubie's titles present many: "The Suicide of Hedda Gabler," "Charles Baudelaire," "Seurat," "El Greco," "Sun and Moon Flowers: Paul Klee, 1879-1940," "The Czar's Last Christmas Letter: A Barn in the Urals," and "Horace." In particular, *The Illustrations* handles these monologues with mastery.

Quite literally, one can approach the poems of this volume as "illustrations." Dubie, himself, is the illustrator, the artist whose own perceptiveness becomes the voices of his characters. The illustrations are of any number of stories, and readers involve themselves in as many ways as their experiences will allow. For,

> In a world that
>
> Belongs to a system of things
> Which presents a dark humus with everything
>
> Living

In this excerpt from "These Untitled Little Verses . . ." in *The Illustrations*, readers discover, as Dubie knows, vital connections.

SELECTED AND NEW POEMS

As his career has progressed, however, Dubie has discovered the limitations of his dramatic monologues. *Selected and New Poems*, while including a generous selection from earlier volumes, introduced a noticeable change in Dubie's manner. The emotional excessiveness of his earlier work was toned down, and many of the new poems eschewed the dramatic monologue for a more personal voice. David Wojahn, reviewing this book in *Western Humanities Review*, remarked that while the new poems "do not match the ambition of some of the earlier poems . . . they are often better crafted and more genuine." That Dubie's style changed is indicative of his desire to move ahead. It also puts Dubie into a certain degree of peril: His writing is turning inward, becoming personal and—if more lyrical—more conventional.

THE SPRINGHOUSE

The Springhouse is a promising extension of the new material found in *Selected and New Poems*. What makes *The Springhouse* remarkable is Dubie's ability to move away from the style and subjects that brought him acclaim while still reveling in his mastery of rich verbal textures. The result is a collection of thirty highly intimate lyrics—poems of youth, religious belief, and love. The new note of intimacy in *The Springhouse* is unmistakable: Readers who found themselves fighting through the earlier dramatic monologues will find the poems of *The Springhouse* similarly dramatic but infinitely more delicate and accessible.

Consider, for example, "Hummingbirds," which suggests that the world is hostile to its fragile creatures:

> They have made a new statement
> About our world—a clerk in Memphis
> Has confessed to laying out feeders
> Filled with sulphuric acid. She says
>
> God asked for these deaths . . . like God
> They are insignificant, and have visited us
>
> Who are wretched.

The "new statement" is that human beings are wretched because they find hummingbirds and God insignificant; they are poorer because of it. This is hardly the Dubie of the earlier collections, the one who distanced himself from his subjects and his readers, who disdained closeness. Similarly, "Old Night and Sleep," dedicated to Dubie's grandfather, moves readers:

> A cold rain falls through empty nests, a cold rain
> Falls over the canvas
> Of some big beast with four stomachs
> Who eats beneath a white tree
> In which only a dozen dry pods are left . . .
>
> Some new sense of days being counted.

The poem is a lamentation, an emptiness of soul accounted for visually in sensuous imagery. Things are drizzly, vague, empty; loss of a loved one makes one feel this way, makes one aware of one's own temporal existence.

THE MERCY SEAT

With *The Mercy Seat*, Dubie rejoined the literary world after a ten-year publishing hiatus. The book is divided into two sections; the first chronicles his poems from 1967 to 1991, while the second half presents new poetry. Like past works, his language continues to be spare and often sorrowful but nonetheless rich and vigorous in its forms. Here Dubie continues his exploration of dramatic monologues with the recasting of the world's great tales, bringing forth lesser historic events and making them moments of redemptive, imaginative beauty. However, his foot is also placed firmly in the current era: By dedicating the book to the Dalai Lama, modern political realities and the true stakes of the world anchor his complexly balanced poems.

ORDINARY MORNINGS OF A COLISEUM AND INSOMNIAC LIAR OF TOPO

Dubie's wide reach continues in *Ordinary Mornings of a Coliseum*, a collection that includes the poems "Nightmare with Heat Lightning," a story truly visual and filled with detailed description, and "Death by Compass," on the poet Arthur Rimbaud. Dubie's *Insomniac Liar of Topo* is filled with a randomness that seems to struggle for an all-encompassing language of feelings. It is a continuation of his neo-Surrealist vision that includes poems on the war and violence in Iraq and on the search through the world's religions for a "god" to follow.

BIBLIOGRAPHY

Anderson, Jon. "On Norman Dubie's Poems." *Iowa Review* 3 (Fall, 1973): 65-67. This article offers a reading of Dubie's work on two levels: the empathetic, which results from the poet's attempt at communication, and the aesthetic, which is the reader's personal judgment. Anderson's interpretation utilizes both sensibilities, although the latter is clearly favored in his examination of *Alehouse Sonnets*, "The Dugouts," and "Northwind Escarpment," among others.

Clark, Kevin. "Synchronous Isolations: 'Elegies for the Ocher Deer on the Walls at Lascaux' by Norman Dubie." *American Poetry* 5, no. 2 (Winter, 1988): 12-32. Clark draws upon the concepts of Carl Jung, Albert Einstein, and Søren Kierkegaard to illuminate Dubie's vision and technique in this important long poem. This is an exemplary study, its methodology applicable to much of Dubie's work.

Dubie, Norman. "Return from Silence." Interview by Mary Gannon. *Poets and Writers* 32, no. 6 (November/December, 2004): 32-42. Dubie discusses, among other topics, his return to publishing, his mentors, his book *Ordinary Mornings of a Coliseum*, and how practicing Tibetan Buddhism has influenced his writing.

Leavitt, Michele. "Dubie's 'Amen.'" *Explicator* 56, no. 1 (Fall, 1997): 55-56. A close reading reveals Dubie's technique of multiple juxtapositions that create provocative but incomplete analogies. The poem insists that by evading responsibility for brutality, human beings inevitably come to share it.

Raab, Lawrence. "Illustrations and Illuminations: On Norman Dubie." *American Poetry Review* 7 (July/August, 1978): 17-21. Raab examines the amalgamation of time periods and subjects in Dubie's poetry—from Greek mythology to Victorian England and Ovid to Nicholas I—and explores Dubie's methods of arguing and instructing his characters. Perhaps Raab's most valuable and insightful observation of Dubie's work is that his poetry is about the "little things" that, when seen clearly, appear large.

St. John, David. "A Generous Salvation: The Poetry of Norman Dubie." *American Poetry Review* 13 (September/October, 1984): 17-21. St. John uses the collection of Dubie's poems *Selected and New Poems* as a jumping-off point for an examination of the poet's major themes, including a fascination with the living and dead, with personal and historical realities, and with the principle of "release." St. John assists readers by publishing the full text of the poems discussed.

Slattery, William. "My Dubious Calculus." *Antioch Review* 52, no. 1 (Winter, 1994): 132-140. At once sarcastic and cautiously admiring, Slattery questions the value of perceived ambiguities and opacities in Dubie's style. Slattery discusses the structure of each volume in Dubie's "trilogy" (*Springhouse*, *Groom Falconer*, and *Radio Sky*), commenting on the lack of neat resolutions and the way in which Dubie's images suggest unforgettable stories about people in desperate situations.

Wojahn, David. "Recent Poetry." *Western Humanities Review* 38 (August, 1984): 269-273. Wojahn explores the transition of Dubie's style as it becomes more subdued and lyrical in his work *Selected and New Poems*. Because this process was then incomplete, the value of Wojahn's article lies in its careful and evocative examination of Dubie's early style with its dramatic monologues, extreme situations, and idiosyncratic syntax.

Young, David. "Out Beyond Rhetoric." *Contemporary Poetry and Poetics* 30 (Spring, 1984): 83-102. The career and work of Dubie are carefully and thoroughly examined in this ambitious assessment of the poet's life, themes, and expression of his ideas, which can range from the difficult to the nearly incomprehensible. This important and insightful examination is worthy reading for scholars and enthusiasts alike.

Mark Sanders; Philip K. Jason
Updated by Sarah Hilbert

ALAN DUGAN

Born: Brooklyn, New York; February 12, 1923
Died: Hyannis, Massachusetts; September 3, 2003

PRINCIPAL POETRY

General Prothalamion in Populous Times, 1961
Poems, 1961
Poems Two, 1963
Poems Three, 1967
Collected Poems, 1969
Poems Four, 1974
Sequence, 1976
New and Collected Poems, 1961-1983, 1983
    (includes *Poems Five*)
Ten Years of Poems: From Alan Dugan's Workshop
    at Castle Hill Center for the Arts, Truro,
    Massachusetts, 1987
Poems Six, 1989
More Poems: From Alan Dugan's Workshop at
    Castle Hill Center for the Arts, Truro,
    Massachusetts, 1994
Poems Seven: New and Complete Poetry, 2001

OTHER LITERARY FORMS

The literary accomplishments of Alan Dugan (DEW-guhn) centered on the medium of poetry.

ACHIEVEMENTS

Alan Dugan had been publishing poems in literary magazines for a number of years—winning an award from *Poetry* as early as 1947—before his first book of poetry was published in 1961. That book, *Poems*, enjoyed one of the greatest critical successes of any first volume of poems in the twentieth century. Dudley Fitts awarded it the Yale Series of Younger Poets Award; it also won the National Book Award and the Pulitzer Prize (1962). Poet Philip Booth called it "the most original first book that has appeared . . . in a sad long time."

Dugan published subsequent volumes of poetry, similar in style and range to his first volume. Dugan received the Rome Fellowship from the American Academy of Arts and Letters (1962), a Guggenheim Fellowship (1963-1964), and the Rockefeller Foundation Fellowship (1966-1967). He won the Levinson Prize from *Poetry* magazine in 1967 and the Shelley Memorial Award in 1982. *Poems Seven* earned the National Book Award in Poetry from the National Book Foundation in 2001 and the Massachusetts Book Award in poetry in 2002. Dugan received the Lannan Literary Award for Poetry in 2002.

BIOGRAPHY

Born in Brooklyn, Alan Dugan spent most of his life in New York City. His stint in the Army Air Corps during World War II was of importance to him, and a number of his first published poems were portraits of servicemen. He attended Queens College and Olivet College, and received his B.A. degree from Mexico City College. He married Judith Shahn, the daughter of the painter Ben Shahn. After the war, he held a number of jobs in New York City, working in advertising and publishing and as a maker of models for a medical supply house. These jobs made him dissatisfied with the world of office work, which he satirized in his poetry.

The success of his first book of poems in 1961 led to his winning a series of awards and fellowships that gave him more time for his poetry. He was a member of the faculty at Sarah Lawrence College from 1967 through 1971, and he helped found the Fine Arts Work Center in Provincetown, Massachusetts, in 1968. In 1985, he received an Academy Award in Literature from the American Academy and Institute of Arts and Letters. Dugan gave many poetry readings, and after adjusting to his high voice and the purposely undramatic, cold presentation, audiences found that his style of reading fit the poems.

ANALYSIS

Alan Dugan brought a completely developed style to his first remarkable volume, *Poems*. That style was colloquial, spare, and tough, fitting the bleak vision of much of his poetry. Dugan has been characterized as a poet lacking in charm, and truly, he made no attempt to be charming, only intense and truthful. His mocking, ironic style fit the narrowness of his outlook, and both the achievement and the weakness of his poetry rest on it. Whether Dugan wrote of war, love, or work (his key subjects), he confronted them with a similar ironic stance. His poetry is against sentimentality, even against transcendence, a kind of antipoetry.

Dugan's language makes it evident that he belonged to the colloquial tradition of American poetry. In a manner somewhat reminiscent of William Carlos Williams, Dugan reversed the expectations of the reader of love or nature poetry, turning sentiment into irony. Like Williams, and like contemporary poets such as James Wright and Philip Levine, Dugan set his poetry in the city and expressed sympathy for, and identification with, the urban working class. Although Dugan's poems seldom rhyme, they often employ traditional meters and stanza as well as free verse. The emphasis on form—even, on a few occasions, the resort to pattern poems—often creates an interesting tension with his dominant plain style.

"HOW WE HEARD THE NAME"

"How We Heard the Name," the poem that Dudley Fitts, the judge of the Yale Series of Younger Poets, selected for its "strangeness" despite "the greyness of diction and versification," is typical of Dugan's work. In part, this poem depends for its meaning on a classical allusion, a surprisingly common technique in this tough-talking urban poet. At the center of the poem is the battle of Granicus, one of Alexander the Great's most famous victories, but Dugan has singled out a seemingly trivial historical oddity: Alexander wrote that he won the battle "with no help from the Lacedaemonians."

In Dugan's poem, the river brings down the debris and dead of the battle until it also brings down a soldier on a log. The speaker of the poem inquires about the source of this grim pollution, and the soldier sardonically tells him of the famous victory won by the Greeks "except/ the Lacedaemonians and/ myself." He explains that this is merely a joke "between me and a man/ named Alexander, whom/ all of you ba-bas/ will hear of as a god." The antiheroic stance, the directness of the language, the casualness of the mention of Alexander, and the comedy of "ba-bas" to characterize those who believe a mere man can be a god, make up a microcosm of Dugan's tone and style. This is a voice that has come to joke about Caesar, not to praise him, yet reserves its greatest contempt for the sheeplike followers of great

Alan Dugan (Gillian Drake/Courtesy, Provincetown Arts Press)

leaders. No apologies are made for running away from the battle, and the reader is left with the feeling that it was the action of an intelligent man who, like the Lacedaemonians, knew when not to fight.

WAR POETRY

Dugan often spoke sarcastically of war, whether it was one of Alexander's, the American Civil War, the two World Wars, or the Vietnam War—all of which make appearances in his poetry. In a "Fabrication of Ancestors," Dugan sums up his attitude toward all wars when he praises his ancestor, "shot in the ass," who did not help to win the war for the North but wore on his body a constant "proof/ of the war's obscenity." In the curious "Adultery," Dugan contrasts the insignificance of private immoralities with greater public evils—the world of "McNamara and his band" and "Johnson and his Napalm Boys," who wipe out the lives of entire cities in Vietnam. Dugan does not plan to be among "the ba-bas."

"LOVE SONG: I AND THOU"

Love is another dominant subject of Dugan's work, and he approached it in much the same tone of fierceness and irony that informs his poems about war. In these poems he turns to the war between the sexes, its battles and betrayals. "Love Song: I and Thou" is one of Dugan's most skillful poems and is deservedly one of his most frequently anthologized. In a complicated brew, it mixes the techniques of allegory and allusion with Dugan's terse colloquial style. It illustrates the basic paradox of much of his verse: the dominant conversational, flat tone that all the reviewers have emphasized, merging with elaborate poetic devices—devices that only a few commentators have mentioned. The overriding figure is the comparison between a man's life and a house, a badly built house, in this case. The opening line of the poem declares how badly it is built: "Nothing is plumb, level, or square." It is a house with a corresponding life in considerable disarray, a house for which, on one level, the speaker insists on taking responsibility ("I planned it"), yet whose chaos, on some other level, must be blamed on a higher power ("God damned it"). The description of the house becomes a description of the ancient quarrel concerning the roles of free will and determinism in a person's life.

Also running throughout "Love Song: I and Thou" is a comparison-contrast between the speaker and Christ: "By Christ/ I am no carpenter." This reference concludes in the final lines about crucifixion in a passage that suddenly introduces the love song promised by the title. The title's "I and Thou" is a reference to the modern Jewish philosopher Martin Buber; "I-Thou" is the language he used to describe a true and vital love relationship between equals, as opposed to "I-It." The ending of Dugan's poem, however, creates a highly ambiguous feeling. In what sounds like tender talk, "I need . . . a help, a love, a you, a wife," the speaker is asking for someone to nail his right hand to the cross. He cannot finish his crucifixion by himself; he needs a helpmate, a nailer. One critic finds the language very touching, but there seems to be a bitter joke at the heart of this complex poem.

"LETTER TO DONALD FALL"

Although Dugan sometimes praised the world of sexuality ("the red world of love"), his enthusiasms were almost always tempered by irony. In a "Letter to Donald Fall," he makes a list of "my other blessings after friendship/ unencumbered by communion." They include

> a money making job, time off it, a wife
> I still love sometimes unapproachably
> hammering on picture frames, my own city . . .
> and my new false teeth. . . .

The words "sometimes unapproachably," which manage to go both forward and backward, suggest Dugan's attitude toward love. Even more typical is the comic introduction of his false teeth, which become a parallel to the approaching spring. The teeth seem to him to be "like Grails" and they talk to him, saying, "We are the resurrection/ and the life." Amidst some amusing images of spring coming to the city, Dugan comes as close as he can to satisfaction when he addresses his friend with the symbolic name in the final line of the poem: "Fall, it is not so bad at Dugan's Edge."

"COOLED HEELS LAMENT AGAINST FRIVOLITY, THE MASK OF DESPAIR"

The Muse, too, is tough in the poem with the amusing title, "Cooled Heels Lament Against Frivolity, the Mask of Despair"; she is a kind of distant boss, keeping the poet waiting in her office, as she swaps stories with the "star-salesmen of the soul." He seems to speak to her with slim hope of any positive response:

> Dugan's deathward darling; you
> in your unseeable beauty, oh
> fictitious, legal person, need
> be only formally concerned. . . .

If the fanciful Muse seems cold and indifferent, it is because there is not much to look forward to in one's encounters with the real world of bosses and work.

"ON A SEVEN-DAY DIARY"

That world of work is often portrayed in Dugan's poetry as a necessary but painful evil. "No man should work, but be" is the dream that cannot be fulfilled because "poverty is worse than work." "On a Seven-Day Diary" comically sums up Dugan's attitude with the insistent refrain, "Then I got up and went to work." It is repeated five times for the five weekdays, but "Then it's Saturday, Saturday, Saturday!" The speaker excitedly proclaims that "Love must be the reason for the week!" as he lists the pleasures of the weekend. However, he drinks so much on Saturday night that most of Sunday is lost, and—as one might expect from Dugan—the poem ends with "Then I got up and went to work."

"ON ZERO"

War, love, and work make a similarly dour pattern in Dugan's poetry—the grayness of Monday always returns. This was a poet whose longest published poem is entitled "On Zero," and whose attitude toward change might be summed up in the closing lines of "General Prothalamion in Populous Times": "the fall/ from summer's marching innocence/ to the last winter of general war." Reading a collection of Dugan's poems can be harrowing. His is a world where freedom is something to be feared, where to meet the morning is to confront "the daily accident," and where "sometimes you can't even lose"; yet Dugan often brings enough skill and humor to his work to overcome the darkness of the vision. What has been said of other writers who have been called cynical or misanthropic can be said of his work as well: The very energy of his language and the vitality of his wit belie his pessimism.

POEMS SIX

In a 1989 interview, Dugan himself complained about the slightness of the poems he wrote in the 1970's. In the same year, he published *Poems Six*, which attempts to get back to the more ambitious mode of his earlier volumes. Even for those accustomed to the bitterness of Dugan's work, however, the poems in this volume seem still bleaker in vision. The language of nausea and excrement often dominates Dugan's responses to the world's and his own difficulties.

In the opening poems of this volume, Dugan often confronted political subjects more directly than he had in the past. "Take on Armageddon" is addressed to Ronald Reagan. After talking about the final battle, the poem ends in a description of a world where there will be "no more insects, and no more you and your rotten God." In "Love and Money," Dugan describes a moment in Johnstown, Pennsylvania, when a steelworkers' strike and a convention of baton twirlers are taking place at the same time. The strikers "didn't touch the girls or the mills/ because they weren't theirs," but the speaker declares the mills do belong to the strikers since they built them and ran them. Their inability to recognize this, however, leads to the conclusion that "There is no left-wing politics in America left/ There is the International Baton Twirlers Association."

In *Poems Six*, Dugan continues to concentrate on his subjects of work, war, and love, and on occasions—as he did in his earlier volumes—to mix his tough-guy talk with allusions to classical literature and mythology. He tells his audience that as a child he used his statuette of Erato, Muse of lyric poetry, as an exercising dumbbell. He would "grab her by the neck and ankles when I got her alone/ and pump her up and down." Now the statue remains behind in silent rooms in Brooklyn as the traffic outside is leaving "for New York and the Wild West."

Possibly the most successful poem in *Poems Six* is the final one: "Night Scene Before Combat." The trucks moving in convoy outside his window in the middle of the night become a complicated symbol for the speaker, containing poetry, war, and death: "Did you know/ that metaphor means Truck/ in modern Greek? Truck. Carryall." He feels a battle within himself between staying with the woman he addresses and joining the convoy that rumbles by outside. The trucks, however, prevail, and the speaker turns to the woman "for one last time in sleep, love,/ before I put my uniform back on,/ check my piece, and say So long."

POEMS SEVEN

The year 2001 saw publication of the collection *Poems Seven*, a grand compendium of four hundred pages and covering Dugan's entire forty-year career. Along with early war poems, the collection includes three dozen new, previously uncollected, poems. *Poems Seven* earned the National Book Award in Poetry from the National Book Foundation.

BIBLIOGRAPHY

Atlas, James. "Autobiography of the Present." *Poetry* 125 (February, 1975): 300-301. This review emphasizes Dugan's acute observations about commonplace moments in daily life. Atlas criticizes the later poems of Dugan for adopting a hectoring and polemical tone.

Boyers, Robert. "On Alan Dugan." In *Contemporary Poetry in America*, edited by Robert Boyers. New York: Schocken Books, 1974. A clear and thorough overview of Dugan's poetry. Despite his limitation in range, Dugan is praised as a moralist in difficult times. Boyers believes that the best poems make "a temporary truce with the miserableness of the world."

Dugan, Alan. Interview by J. C. Ellefson and Belle Waring. *American Poetry Review* 19 (May/June, 1990): 43-51. In this wide-ranging interview, Dugan talks about his childhood, his parents, his early jobs (including writing for the *New York Enquirer*, later to become *National Enquirer*), and his attitude toward poetry. He expresses admiration for the poetry of Charles Bukowski and Philip Levine, contemporary urban American poets with whom he felt a kinship.

Howard, Richard. *Alone with America: Essays on the Art of Poetry in the United States Since 1950*. Rev. ed. New York: Atheneum, 1980. In this complex and difficult-to-read book, Howard finds something like paranoia at the center of Dugan's work. He believes that the poetry displays an "honest and desperate resentment and hatred," a hatred sometimes directed at language itself.

Martin, Douglas. "Alan Dugan, Eighty, Barbed Poet of Daily Life's Profundities." *The New York Times*, September 5, 2003, p. C11. Obituary of Dugan that looks at his life and his poetry.

Scharf, Michael. Review of *Poems Seven*. *Publishers Weekly* 248, no. 43 (October 22, 2001): 71. A review of the collection that garnered for Dugan his second National Book Award.

Stepanchev, Stephen. *American Poetry Since 1945*. New York: Harper & Row, 1965. Stepanchev states that nothing was sacred to Dugan. He praises him highly for the colloquial directness and honesty of his work and discovers a kind of irony in the way his simple style confronted difficult and complicated subjects.

Michael Paul Novak

PAUL LAURENCE DUNBAR

Born: Dayton, Ohio; June 27, 1872
Died: Dayton, Ohio; February 9, 1906

PRINCIPAL POETRY
Oak and Ivy, 1893
Majors and Minors, 1895
Lyrics of Lowly Life, 1896
Lyrics of the Hearthside, 1899
Lyrics of Love and Laughter, 1903
Lyrics of Sunshine and Shadow, 1905
Complete Poems, 1913

OTHER LITERARY FORMS

Though Paul Laurence Dunbar is best known for his poetry, he was a fiction writer as well. His achievements in fiction include four volumes of short stories and four novels. Criticism of Dunbar's short fiction suggests that the stories contained in *Folks from Dixie* (1898) represent his best accomplishment in this literary form. His novels *The Uncalled* (1898) and *The Sport of the Gods* (1902) acquired more critical acclaim than his other two novels, *The Love of Landry* (1900) and *The Fanatics* (1901).

In addition to his work in these more traditional literary forms, Dunbar wrote an assortment of lyrics and libretti for a variety of theatrical productions. He also wrote essays for newspapers and attempted to establish a periodical of his own.

ACHIEVEMENTS

Paul Laurence Dunbar's literary career was brilliant, extending roughly across two decades. He can be credited with several first-time accomplishments: He was the first to use dialect poetry as a medium for the true interpretation of African American character and psychology, and he was the first African American writer to earn national prominence. In range of style and form, Dunbar is one of the most versatile of African American writers.

BIOGRAPHY

Paul Laurence Dunbar was born to former slaves Joshua Dunbar and Matilda J. Murphy Dunbar on June

27, 1872. He spent his early childhood in Dayton, Ohio, where he attended Central High School. Dunbar began to write at age sixteen and gained early patronage for his work, and he was introduced to the Western Association of Writers in 1892.

The next few years of his life found him in the presence of great black leaders. He met Frederick Douglass, Mary Church Terrell, and Ida B. Wells at the World's Columbian Exposition in Chicago in 1893. He met W. E. B. Du Bois in 1896 and Booker T. Washington in 1897. These encounters influenced Dunbar's literary tone and perspective significantly. He blended the creative perspective of Washington with the social philosophy of Du Bois in order to present a valid scenario of African Americans after the Civil War.

Major James B. Pond, a Dunbar enthusiast, sponsored a trip to England for the writer that extended from February to August of 1897. Upon his return to the United States, Dunbar married Alice Moore and decided to earn his living as a writer. Between 1898 and 1903, Dunbar wrote essays for newspapers and periodicals, primarily addressing the issues of racial equality and social justice in the United States. He attempted to establish his own journalistic voice through a periodical that he named the *Dayton Tattler* in 1890. This effort failed.

During the latter years of his life, Dunbar wrote lyrics, including those for the school song for Tuskegee Institute. Dunbar died in Dayton, Ohio, on February 9, 1906.

ANALYSIS

The body of poetry produced by Paul Laurence Dunbar illustrates some of the best qualities found in lyrical verse. It is obvious that the poet concentrated on a creation of mood and that he was an innovator who experimented with form, meter, and rhyme. Equally apparent is the fact that Dunbar's creative style was influenced by the great British poetic innovators of the seventeenth and nineteenth centuries. Dunbar's commitment to speak to his people through his verse is reflected in his

dialect poetry. Writing in all the major lyrical forms—idyll, hymn, sonnet, song, ballad, ode, and elegy—Dunbar established himself as one of the most versatile poets in American literature.

The more than four hundred poems written by Dunbar are varied in style and effect. It is clear, however, that his dominant aim was to create an empathetic poetic mood resulting from combinations of elements such as meter, rhyme, diction, sentence structure, characterization, repetition, imagery, and symbolism. His most memorable poems display the influence of such masters as William Wordsworth; Robert Herrick; Alfred, Lord Tennyson; John Donne; Robert Browning; and John Keats.

Such an array of influences would ordinarily render one's genius suspect. There are common threads, however, that organically characterize the poetic expressions of Dunbar. The undergirding strain in his poetry

Paul Laurence Dunbar (Library of Congress)

is his allegiance to lyrical qualities. He carries mood through sound patterns, creates images that carry philosophical import, shapes dramatic events in the pattern of movement in his syntactic forms, and develops a rhythmic pattern that is quite effective in recitation. These lyrical qualities predominate in the best of Dunbar's poetry. Indeed, one might easily classify Dunbar's poetry in typical Romantic lyrical categories: The bulk of his poems can be classified as love lyrics, reflective lyrics, melancholic lyrics, or nature lyrics. Sometimes these moods overlap in a single poem. Consequently, an analysis of the features in Dunbar's poetry is necessarily complex, placing his lyrical qualities in the poetic traditions that shape them.

LYRICS OF THE HEARTHSIDE

Dunbar's lyricism is substantially displayed in his love poetry in *Lyrics of the Hearthside*. In "A Bridal Measure," the poet's persona beckons maidens to the bridal throne. His invitation is spirited and triumphant yet controlled, reminiscent of the tradition in love poetry established by Ben Jonson. The tone, however, more closely approximates the carpe diem attitude of Herrick.

> Come, essay a sprightly measure,
> Tuned to some light song of pleasure.
> Maidens, let your brows be crowned
> As we foot this merry round.

The rhyming couplets carry the mood and punctuate the invitation. The urgency of the moment is extended further in the direct address: "Phyllis, Phyllis, why be waiting?/ In the woods the birds are mating." The poem continues in this tone, while adopting a pastoral simplicity.

> When the year, itself renewing,
> All the world with flowers is strewing,
>   Then through Youth's Arcadian land,
>   Love and song go hand in hand.

The accentuation in the syntactic flow of these lines underlines the poet's intentions. Though the meter is irregular, with some iambs and some anapests, the force of the poet's exhortation remains apparent.

Dunbar frequently personifies abstractions. In "Love and Grief," Dunbar espouses a morbid yet redemptive view of love. While the reflective scenario presented in this poem recalls Tennyson's meditations on death and loss, the poetic event echoes Wordsworth's faith in the indestructibility of joy. Utilizing the heroic couplet, Dunbar makes an opening pronouncement:

> Out of my heart, one treach'rous winter's day,
> I locked young Love and threw the key away.
> Grief, wandering widely, found the key,
> And hastened with it, straightway, back to me.

The drama of grief-stricken love is thus established. The poet carefully clarifies his position through an emphatic personification of Grief's behavior: "He unlocked the door/ and bade Love enter with him there and stay." Being a lyric poet of redemptive sensibility, Dunbar cannot conclude the poem on this note. The "table must turn," as it does for Wordsworth in such situations. Love then becomes bold and asks of Grief: "What right hast thou/ To part or parcel of this heart?" To justify the redemptive quality he presents, Dunbar attributes the human frailty of pride to Love, a failing that invites Grief. In so doing, the poet's philosophical intuitiveness emerges with a measure of moral decorum. Through the movement in the syntactic patterns, the intensity of the drama is heightened as the poem moves to resolution. Dunbar utilizes a variety of metrical patterns, the most significant of which is the spondee. This poetic foot of two accented syllables allows the poet to proclaim emphatically: "And Love, pride purged, was chastened all his life." Thus, the principal emotion in the poem is redeemed.

The brief, compact lyrical verse, as found in Browning, is among Dunbar's typical forms. "Love's Humility" is an example:

> As some rapt gazer on the lowly earth,
>   Looks up to radiant planets, ranging far,
> So I, whose soul doth know thy wondrous worth
>   Look longing up to thee as to a star.

This skillfully concentrated simile elevates love to celestial heights. The descriptive detail enhances the power of the feeling the poet captures and empowers the lyrical qualities of the poem with greater pathos.

LYRICS OF LOVE AND LAUGHTER

Dunbar's *Lyrics of Love and Laughter* is not the best of his collections, but it contains some remarkable dialect verse. "A Plea" provides an example of this aspect of his reputation. Speaking of the unsettling feelings experienced by one overcome with love, Dunbar exhorts a lover's love object to "treat him nice."

> I ain't don a t'ing to shame,
> Lovahs all ac's jes de same:
> Don't you know we ain't to blame?
>   Treat me nice!

Rendering a common experience in the African American idiom, Dunbar typifies the emotionally enraptured lover as one who has no control over his behavior:

> Whut a pusson gwine to do,
> W'en he come a-cou'tin' you
> All a-trimblin' thoo and thoo?
>   Please be nice.

The diction in this poem is not pure dialect. Only those portions that describe the emotions and behavior of the lover are stated in dialect, highlighting the primary emotions and enhancing the pathetic mood, which is apparently Dunbar's principal intent. Typical of Dunbar's love lyrics, "A Plea" is rooted in the experience of a particular culture yet remains universal in its themes. Through his use of diction, meter, and stanzaic form, Dunbar captures fundamental human emotions and renders them with intensity and lyrical compassion.

LYRICS OF LOWLY LIFE

Reflective lyrics form a large segment of Dunbar's poetry. Some of his best poems of this type are found in *Lyrics of Lowly Life*, including the long stanzaic poem "Ere Sleep Comes Down to Soothe the Weary Eyes." This poem uses one sensory impression as a focal point for the lyrical evolution in the style of Keats. The sleep motif provides an avenue through which the persona's imagination enters the realm of reflection.

Through sleep's dream the persona is able to "make the waking world a world of lies—/ of lies palpable, uncouth, forlorn." In this state of subconscious reflection, past pains are revisited as they "come thronging through the chambers of the brain." As the poem progresses, it becomes apparent that the repetitive echo of "ere sleep comes down to soothe the weary eyes" has some significance. This refrain begins and ends each stanza of the poem except the last. In addition to serving as a mood-setting device, this expression provides the channel of thought for the literary journey, which is compared with the "spirit's journeying." Dunbar's audience is thus constantly reminded of the source of his revelations.

Dunbar reveals his poetic thesis in the last stanza. He uses images from the subconscious state of life, sleep, to make a point about death. Prior to making this point, Dunbar takes the reader to the realm of reflective introspection: "So, trembling with the shock of sad surprise,/ The soul doth view its awful self alone." There is an introspective confrontation of the soul with itself, and it resolves:

> When sleep comes down to seal the weary eyes,
> . . . .
> Ah, then, no more we heed
> the sad world's cries,
> Or seek to probe th' eternal mystery,
> Or fret our souls at long-withheld replies.

The escape from pain and misery is death; there is no intermediary state that will eradicate that fact of life. Dunbar presents this notion with sympathy and sincerity. His metaphorical extensions, particularly those relative to the soul, are filled with compassion. The soul is torn with the world's deceit; it cries with "pangs of vague inexplicable pain." The spirit, an embodiment of the soul, forges ahead to seek truth as far as fancy will lead. Questioning begins then, and the inner sense confronts the inner being until truth emerges. Dunbar's presentation of the resolution is tender and gentle.

Dunbar wrote reflective lyrics in the vernacular as well. "Accountability" espouses the philosophy of divine intention. In this poem, the beliefs and attitudes of the persona are revealed in familiar language.

> Folks ain't got no right to
>   censuah othah
>   folks about dey habits;
> . . . .
> We is all constructed diff'ent,
>   d'ain't no two of
>   us de same;

. . . . . .

> But we all fits into places dat
> no othah ones
> could fill.

Each stanza in this poem presents a thesis and develops that point. The illustrations from the natural world support a creationist viewpoint. The persona obviously accepts the notion that everything has a purpose. The Creator gave the animals their members shaped as they are for a reason and so, "Him dat giv' de squr'ls de bush-tails made de bobtails fu' de rabbits." The variations in nature are by design: "Him dat built de gread big mountains hollered out de little valleys"; "Him dat made de streets an' driveways wasn't shamed to make de alley." The poet establishes these notions in three quatrains, concluding in the fourth quatrain: "When you come to think about it, how it's all planned out it's splendid./ Nuthin's done er evah happens, dout hit's somefin' dat's intended." The persona's position that divine intention rules the world is thereby sealed.

Introspection is a feature of Dunbar's reflective lyrics. In "The Lesson," the persona engages in character revelation, interacts with the audience toward establishment of appropriate resolution, and participates in the action of the poem. These qualities are reminiscent of Browning's dramatic monologues. As the principal speaker sits by a window in his cottage, reflecting, he reports:

> And I thought of myself so sad and lone,
> And my life's cold winter that knew no spring;
> Of my mind so weary and sick and wild,
>   Of my heart too sad to sing.

The inner conflict facing the persona is revealed in these lines and the perspective of self-examination is established. The persona must confront his sadness and move toward resolution. The movement toward resolution presents the dramatic occasion in the poem: "A thought stole into my saddened heart,/ And I said, 'I can cheer some other soul/ By a carol's simple art.'" Reflective introspection typically leads to improved character, a fundamental tenet in the Victorian viewpoint. Sustained by his new conviction and outlook, the persona "sang a lay for a brother's ear/ In a strain to soothe his bleeding heart."

The lyrical quality of "The Lesson" is strengthened by the movement in the poet's syntactic patterns. Feelings of initial despair and resulting joy and hope are conveyed through the poet's syntax. The sequential conjoining of ideas as if in a rushing stream of thought is particularly effective. The latter sections of the poem are noteworthy in this regard. This pattern gives the action more force, thereby intensifying the feeling. Dunbar presents an emphatic idea—"and he smiled . . ."—and juxtaposes it to an exception—"Though mine was a feeble art." He presents a responsive result—"But at his smile I smiled in turn"—connected to a culminating effect—"And into my soul there came a ray." With this pronouncement, the drama comes full circle from inner conflict through conversion to changed philosophical outlook. Dunbar captures each moment with appropriate vigor.

"YESTERDAY AND TO-MORROW"

The subjects of love and death are treated in Dunbar's lyrics of melancholy, the third major mood found in the poet's lyrical verse. "Yesterday and To-morrow," in *Lyrics of Sunshine and Shadow*, is an example of Dunbar's lyric of melancholy. The mood of this poem is in the tradition of the British Romantic poets, particularly that of Wordsworth. Dunbar treats the melancholy feelings in this poem with tenderness and simplicity. The persona expresses disappointment with the untimeliness of life's events and the uncertainties of love. This scenario intimates a bleak future.

"Yesterday and To-morrow" is developed in three compact quatrains. Each quatrain envelops a primary emotion. The first stanza unfolds yesterday's contentment in love. The lover remembers the tender and blessed emotion of closeness with his lover: "And its gentle yieldingness/ From my soul I blessed it." The second stanza is reminiscent of the metaphysical questionings and imagery of Donne: "Must our gold forever know/ Flames for the refining?" The lovers' emotions are compared with precious metal undergoing the fire of refinement: Their feelings of sadness are released in this cynical question.

In the third quatrain, Dunbar feeds the sad heart with more cynicism. Returning to the feelings of disappointment and uncertainty, the persona concludes:

"Life was all a lyric song/ Set to tricksy meter." The persona escapes in cynicism, but the poem still ends on a hopeless note.

"COMMUNION"

"Communion," from *Lyrics of the Hearthside*, is another of Dunbar's melancholy lyrics and focuses on the theme of love and death. The situation in the poem again evokes a cynical attitude, again reminiscent of Donne. The poem presents a struggle between life's memories and death. Life's memories are primarily of the existence of the love relationship, and death symbolizes its demise. This circumstance unfolds in a dramatic narrative in the style of Browning.

The first two stanzas of the poem introduce the situation, and the mood begins to evolve in stanza 3. The poet uses images from nature to create the somber mood. The "breeze of Death," for example, sweeps his lover's soul "Out into the unsounded deeps." On one hand, the Romantic theme of dominance of nature and humanity's helplessness in the face of it creeps through; on the other hand, faith in love as the superior experience resounds. The conflict between conquering Death, symbolized in nature, and Love creates tension in the poem. Consequently, though the breeze of Death has swept his bride away, the persona announces that "Wind nor sea may keep me from/ Soft communing with my bride." As these quatrains of iambic pentameter unfold, the poem becomes somewhat elegiac in tone.

The persona solemnly enters into reflective reminiscence in the fifth stanza and proclaims: "I shall rest my head on thee/ As I did long days of yore." Continuing in stanza 6, he announces: "I shall take thy hand in mine,/ And live o'er the olden days." Leading up to the grief-stricken pledge of eternal love, the melancholic feeling is intensified. The mourner details his impression as follows:

> Tho' the grave-door shut between,
> Still their love lights o'er me steal.
>
> I can see thee thro' my tears,
> As thro' rain we see the sun.

The comfort that comes from such memories brings a ray of light; the lover concludes:

> I shall see thee still and be
> Thy true lover evermore,
> And thy face shall be to me
> Dear and helpful as before.

The drama cannot end unless the persona interacts with his audience. The audience is therefore included in the philosophical conclusion: "Death may vaunt and Death may boast,/ But we laugh his pow'r to scorn." Dunbar illustrates an ability to overcome the causes of melancholy in his lyrics of this mood. He works with contrasting feelings, cynicism, and determinism to achieve this goal. His melancholic mood is therefore less gloomy than one might expect.

"IN SUMMER"

Because Dunbar was greatly influenced by the British Romantic writers, it is not surprising that he also wrote nature lyrics. "In Summer," from *Lyrics of the Hearthside*, and "The Old Apple-Tree," from *Lyrics of Lowly Life*, are representative of his nature lyrics. "In Summer" captures a mood of merriment that is stimulated by nature. The common man is used as a model of one who possesses the capacity to experience this natural joy. Summer is a bright, sunny time; it is also a time for ease, as presented in the second stanza. Introducing the character of the farm boy in stanza 3, Dunbar presents a model embodiment of the ease and merriment of summer. Amid the blades of green grass and as the breezes cool his brow, the farm boy sings as he plows. He sings "to the dewy morn" and "to the joys of life." This behavior leads to some moralizing, to which the last three stanzas of the poem are devoted. The poet's point is made through a contrast:

> O ye who toil in the town.
> And ye who moil in the mart,
> Hear the artless song, and your faith made strong
> Shall renew your joy of heart.

Dunbar admonishes the reader to examine the behavior of the farm boy. Elevation of the simple, rustic life is prevalent in the writings of early British Romantic poets and postbellum African American writers alike. The admonition to reflect on the rustic life, for example, is the same advice Wordsworth gives in "The Old Cumberland Beggar." Both groups of writers agree that there are lessons to be learned through an examination of the virtues of the rustic life. In this vein, Dunbar advises: "Oh, poor were the worth of the world/ If never a song were heard." He goes further by advising all to "taunt old Care with a merry air."

"The Old Apple-Tree"

The emphasis on the rustic life is also pervasive in "The Old Apple-Tree." The primary lyrical quality of the poem is that the poetic message evolves from the poet's memory and imagination. Image creation is the medium through which Dunbar works here: His predominant image, dancing in flames of ruddy light, is an orchard "wrapped in autumn's purple haze."

Dunbar proceeds to create a nature scene that provides a setting for the immortalization of the apple tree. Memory takes the persona to the scene, but imagination re-creates events and feelings. The speaker in the poem admits that it probably appears ugly "When you look the tree all over/ Unadorned by memory's glow." The tree has become old and crooked, and it bears inferior fruit. Thus, without the nostalgic recall, the tree does not appear special at all.

Utilizing the imaginative frame, the speaker designs features of the simple rustic life, features that are typically British Romantic and peculiarly Wordsworthian. The "quiet, sweet seclusion" realized as one hides under the shelter of the tree and the idle dreaming in which one engages dangling in a swing from the tree are primary among these thoughts. Most memorable to the speaker is the solitary contentment he and his sweetheart found as they courted beneath the old apple tree.

> Now my gray old wife is Hallie,
>   An I'm grayer still than she,
> But I'll not forget our courtin'
>   'Neath the old apple-tree.

The poet's ultimate purpose, to immortalize the apple tree, is fulfilled in the last stanza. The old apple tree will never lose its place in nature or its significance, for the speaker asks:

> But when death does come a-callin',
>   This my last request shall be,—
> That they'll bury me an' Hallie
>   'Neath the old apple-tree.

The union of humanity and nature at the culmination of physical life approaches a notion expressed in Wordsworth's poetry. This tree has symbolized the ultimate in goodness and universal harmony; it symbolizes the peace, contentment, and joy in the speaker's life. Here Dunbar's indebtedness to the Romantic traditions that inform his entire oeuvre is most profoundly felt.

Other major works

LONG FICTION: *The Uncalled*, 1898; *The Love of Landry*, 1900; *The Fanatics*, 1901; *The Sport of the Gods*, 1901 (serial), 1902 (book).

SHORT FICTION: *Folks from Dixie*, 1898; *The Strength of Gideon, and Other Stories*, 1900; *In Old Plantation Days*, 1903; *The Heart of Happy Hollow*, 1904; *The Best Stories of Paul Laurence Dunbar*, 1938; *The Complete Stories of Paul Laurence Dunbar*, 2006 (Gene Andrew Jarrett and Thomas Lewis Morgan, editors).

MISCELLANEOUS: *In His Own Voice: The Dramatic and Other Uncollected Works of Paul Laurence Dunbar*, 2002 (Herbert Woodward Martin and Ronald Primeau, editors).

Bibliography

Alexander, Eleanor. *"Lyrics of Sunshine and Shadow": The Tragic Courtship and Marriage of Paul Laurence Dunbar and Alice Ruth Moore*. Albany: State University of New York Press, 2001. Traces the tempestuous romance of the noted African American literary couple. Draws on love letters, diaries, journals, and autobiographies to tell the story of Dunbar and Moore's affair, their elopement, Dunbar's abuse of Moore, their marriage, and the violence that ended their marriage. An examination of a celebrated couple in the context of their times, fame, and cultural ideology.

Bennett, Paula Bernat. "Rewriting Dunbar: Realism, Black Women Poets, and the Genteel." In *African-American Poets: 1700's-1940's*, edited by Harold Bloom. New York: Chelsea House, 2009. Bennett examines Dunbar from a modern feminist perspective.

Best, Felton O. *Crossing the Color Line: A Biography of Paul Laurence Dunbar*. Dubuque, Iowa: Kendall/Hunt, 1996. Discusses Dunbar's life and works, including racial issues.

Harrell, Willie J., Jr. *We Wear the Mask: Paul Laurence Dunbar and the Politics of Representative Reality*. Kent, Ohio: Kent State University Press, 2010. This collection of essays contains several on Dunbar's poetry, covering topics such as the tradition of masking as expressed in his poetry, his use of dialect, and his portrayal of soldiers.

Hudson, Gossie Harold. *A Biography of Paul Laurence Dunbar*. Baltimore: Gateway Press, 1999. A detailed biography of Dunbar with bibliographical references.

Leonard, Keith D. *Fettered Genius: The African American Bardic Poet from Slavery to Civil Rights*. Charlottesville: University of Virginia Press, 2006. Contains a chapter on Dunbar, "Writ on Glory's Scroll: Paul Laurence Dunbar's Moral Heroism," and chapters on the African American bardic tradition that provided context for understanding Dunbar.

Martin, Jay, ed. *A Singer in the Dawn: Reinterpretations of Paul Laurence Dunbar*. New York: Dodd, Mead, 1975. Contains biographical "reminiscences" and essays about Dunbar's poetry and fiction.

Primeau, Ronald, et al. *Being a Collection of Essays on Paul Laurence Dunbar by Members of the Society for the Study of Midwestern Literature*. East Lansing, Mich.: Midwestern Press, 2006. This collection of essays, presented at a conference about Dunbar and his work, contains several surveys of his poetry.

Reef, Catherine. *Paul Laurence Dunbar: Portrait of a Poet*. Berkeley Heights, N.J.: Enslow, 2000. A basic biography of Dunbar that focuses on his poetry.

Patricia A. R. Williams

ROBERT DUNCAN

Born: Oakland, California; January 7, 1919
Died: San Francisco, California; February 3, 1988
Also known as: Robert Edward Duncan; Robert Edward Symmes

PRINCIPAL POETRY

Early Poems, 1939
Heavenly City, Earthly City, 1947
Medieval Scenes, 1950 (reprinted as *Medieval Scenes 1950 and 1959*)
Poems, 1948-1949, 1950
Fragments of a Disordered Devotion, 1952
Caesar's Gate: Poems, 1948-1950, 1956
Letters: Poems, MCMLIII-MCMLVI, 1958
Selected Poems, 1959
The Opening of the Field, 1960
Roots and Branches, 1964
Writing, Writing: A Composition Book for Madison 1953, Stein Imitations, 1964
A Book of Resemblances: Poems, 1950-1953, 1966
Passages 22-27 of the War, 1966
Six Prose Pieces, 1966
The Years as Catches: First Poems, 1939-1946, 1966
Epilogos, 1967
Bending the Bow, 1968
Names of People, 1968
Achilles' Song, 1969
Derivations: Selected Poems, 1950-1956, 1969
The First Decade: Selected Poems, 1940-1950, 1969
Play Time: Pseudo Stein, 1969
Poetic Disturbances, 1970
Tribunals: Passages 31-35, 1970
Ground Work, 1971
Poems from the Margins of Thom Gunn's "Moly," 1972
A Seventeenth Century Suite in Homage to the Metaphysical Genius in English Poetry, 1590-1690, 1973
Dante, 1974
An Ode to Arcadia, 1974 (with Jack Spicer)

The Venice Poem, 1975
Veil, Turbine, Cord, and Bird, 1979
The Five Songs, 1981
Ground Work: Before the War, 1984
A Paris Visit, 1985
Ground Work II: In the Dark, 1987

OTHER LITERARY FORMS

Besides the poetic oeuvre, Robert Duncan produced a limited but essential corpus of essays concerning both his own work and life, and the work of those other writers important to him. Although *The Truth and Life of Myth: An Essay in Essential Autobiography* (1968) was published separately, it also opens the volume of his collected essays, *Fictive Certainties* (1985), and constitutes a major touchstone for an understanding of Duncan's work. "Towards an Open Universe" and "Man's Fulfillment in Order and Strife," also gathered in the same collection, are essential statements on poetics and politics. "The H. D. Book," first conceived as a study of the poetry of H. D. (Hilda Doolittle), became an encyclopedic investigation of mythopoesis and modernism, eighteen sections of which appeared in magazines during the late 1960's and 1970's. Other titles include *The Sweetness and Greatness of Dante's "Divine Comedy"* (1965) and *As Testimony: The Poem and The Scene* (1964). Duncan is also the author of two plays, *Faust Foutu: An Entertainment in Four Parts* (pb. 1959) and *Medea at Kolchis: The Maidenhead* (pb. 1965). Duncan was a spell-binding reader of his own work as well as a truly phenomenal raconteur: A multitude of tapes preserved either in private hands or in university archives bear witness to this, and future transcriptions of his talks and interviews will provide major additions to, and commentaries on, the oeuvre as it now stands.

ACHIEVEMENTS

Because of his erudition, his sense of poetic tradition, his mastery of a variety of poetic forms, and, most important, his profoundly metaphysical voice, Robert Duncan is a major contemporary poet. "Each age requires a new confession," Ralph Waldo Emerson declared, and Duncan presents his era with a voice it cannot afford to ignore. He was recognized with a Union League Civic and Arts Poetry Prize (1957), the Levinson Prize (1964) from *Poetry* magazine, and the Shelley Memorial Award (1984). *Ground Work: Before the War* was nominated for the National Book Critics Circle Award and won a National Book Award.

Although Duncan called himself a derivative poet, revealing his penetrating readings of Dante, Walt Whitman, Ralph Waldo Emerson, William Shakespeare, William Blake, and others, at the same time he generated contemporary visions, Emersonian prospects of discovery and renewal. An impressive collection of more than thirty volumes of poetry, drama, and prose constitutes Duncan's literary achievement. His serious notion of the role of the poet is evident in his many statements about his work, including the prefaces to such works as *The Truth and Life of Myth* and "The H. D. Book." Duncan wrote in a wide range of voices, including a bardic, visionary persona of high seriousness and metaphysical concerns, but he never lost his wit and joy in language-play. Not only was he a masterful lyricist, capable of penetrating epiphanies such as "Roots and Branches," but also he excelled in longer closed forms such as the serial poem ("Apprehensions," "The Continent") and the symphonic form of *The Venice Poem*. Finally, Duncan did some of his finest work in the form that is America's most distinctive contribution to world poetry in the twentieth century: the long, open-ended poem that can accommodate an encyclopedia if need be. Duncan's ongoing open poems, "The Structure of Rime" and "Passages," are in the tradition of Ezra Pound's *Cantos* (1925-1972), William Carlos Williams's *Paterson* (1946-1958), Louis Zukofsky's *"A"* (1927-1978), and Charles Olson's *The Maximus Poems* (1953-1983).

BIOGRAPHY

Robert Duncan was born Edward Howard Duncan in Oakland, California, on January 7, 1919, to Edward Howard and Marguerite Wesley Duncan. His mother died shortly after his birth, and his father was forced to put him up for adoption. His foster parents, "orthodox Theosophists," chose him on the basis of his astrological configuration. Duncan grew up as Robert Edward Symmes and published some two dozen poems under that name before resuming his original surname in 1942.

The hermetic lore imparted by his family and the fables and nursery rhymes of his childhood constitute a major influence on his work.

He attended the University of California, Berkeley, from 1936 to 1938, publishing his first poems in the school's literary magazine, *The Occident*, and joining a circle of friends that included Mary and Lilli Fabilli, Virginia Admiral, and Pauline Kael. For several years he lived in the East, associating with the circle of Anaïs Nin in New York City and with a group of poets in Woodstock that included Sanders Russell and Jack Johnson. Receiving a psychiatric discharge from the army in 1941, he continued publishing poems and, with Virginia Admiral, edited *Ritual* (later *Experimental Review*). In 1944, he published his courageous essay, "The Homosexual in Society," in *Politics*.

Returning to Berkeley in 1946, he studied medieval and Renaissance culture and worked with Kenneth Rexroth, Jack Spicer, and Robin Blaser. In 1951, he began his continuing relationship with painter Jess Collins. Duncan directly addresses the significance of his sexuality to his art: "Perhaps the sexual irregularity underlay and led to the poetic; neither as homosexual nor as poet could one take over the accepted paradigms and conventions of the Protestant ethic."

In 1952, he began publishing in *Origin* and then in the *Black Mountain Review*. In the mid-1950's, he taught briefly at Black Mountain College, further developing his relationship with Olson, whose important essay, "Projective Verse," had been published in 1950. Duncan remains the strongest link between the Black Mountain poets and the San Francisco Renaissance, although the name of such "schools" must be highly elastic to include such diverse poets as Olson, Robert Creeley, Edward Dorn, Allen Ginsberg, Lawrence Ferlinghetti, and Duncan.

The 1960's saw the publication of three major collections, the intense involvement with the poetry of H. D., and the writing of "The H. D. Book," as well as Duncan's strong commitment to antiwar politics, as evidenced in the "Passages" series of poems. By the early 1970's, his reputation had grown beyond the borders of the United States, and he often toured, giving poetry readings and publishing his works in Europe and elsewhere. In 1968, frustrated by his publishers' inability

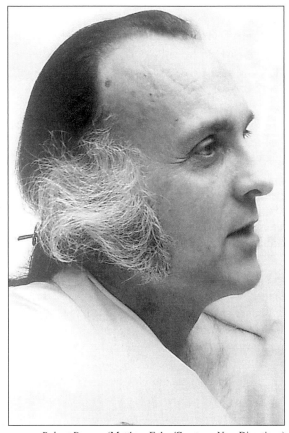

Robert Duncan (Matthew Foley/Courtesy, New Directions)

or unwillingness to print his work according to his own specifications, Duncan announced that he would let fifteen years elapse before publishing another major collection, although small, often private printings of work in progress would continue to appear throughout the 1970's and early 1980's. In 1984, New Directions published *Ground Work: Before the War*, typeset under the poet's direct supervision. *Ground Work II: In the Dark* followed in 1987, only a few months before the poet's death in February, 1988.

ANALYSIS

Of the many metaphors that Robert Duncan applied to his poetry—and very few poets have been so perceptive and articulate about their own practice—those dealing with limits, boundaries, and margins are numerous and permit a coherent if partial survey of his complex work. Such references are frequent in his poetry and are rooted in his life and his way of seeing. Living in San Francisco, at the edge of the North American continent, Duncan was acutely sensitive to the centrifugal pressures of his culture. Having been an adopted child, his identity and very name were under question during his early years. As a gay man, he felt distanced from "the accepted paradigms and conventions of the Protestant ethic." As a Theosophist, his way of thinking had been influenced by similarly unconventional assumptions. His very vision blurs distinctions and identities: He was cross-eyed, a way of seeing that he eloquently explored in such poems as "A Poem Slow Beginning" and "Crosses of Harmony and Disharmony," and that he relates to Alfred North Whitehead's "presentational immediacy."

Duncan referred to himself as "the artist of the margin," and the term is basic to an understanding of his vision and poetics. Although the concept can be traced to a number of eclectic and overlapping influences, William James's *Principles of Psychology* (1890), with its theme of the fluidity of consciousness, provides an instructive point of departure. For James, with his great interest in the "penumbra" of experience, "life is at the transitions." As he says in "A World of Pure Experience," "Our fields of experience have no more definite boundaries than have our fields of view. Both are fringed forever by a *more* that continuously develops and that continuously supersedes them as life proceeds." For Duncan as for James, life is at the edge, at the point of relationship, surprise, novelty—at the transgression of boundaries. Conceiving the universe as a constant rhythm between order and disorder, both writers (with Whitehead and John Dewey) maintained that order develops. Rejecting the extreme poles of a world of mere flux without any stability and a static world without crisis, such a worldview embraces the moment of passage as that of most intense life. Appropriately, Duncan's major ongoing poem is entitled the "Passages Poems." Primary here too is John Keats's notion of "negative capability," an acceptance of "uncertainties, mysteries, doubts, without any irritable reaching after fact and reason." Indeed, Duncan defines Romanticism as "the intellectual adventure of not knowing."

Duncan was fully cognizant of the implications that such ideas have for his poetics, scoffing in *The Truth and Life of Myth* at the "sensory debunkers" who "would protect our boundaries, the very shape of what we are, by closing our minds to the truth." The poet's charge is to challenge the boundaries of convention, with direct impact on his poetry's form: "Back of each poet's concept of the poem is his concept of the meaning of form itself; and his concept of form in turn where it is serious at all arises from his concept of the nature of the universe." Duncan's poetry challenges the boundaries of conventional ideas and conventional forms. He speaks of his poetry as a collage, an especially appropriate form for a poetry that incessantly interrogates boundaries, edges, identities. "The great art of our time," he says in "The H. D. Book," "is the collagist's art, to bring all things into new complexes of meaning."

The theme appears early in his work, developing in the poems of the 1940's and 1950's. From the first decade, in "Heavenly City, Earthly City," the poet as a "man in the solitude of his poetic form/ finds his self-consciousness defined/ by the boundaries of a non-committal sea." He apostrophizes the Pacific Ocean as an "Insistent questioner of our shores!" "A Congregation," similarly, sounds early poetic concerns of field, order, disorder, and fragmentation. In "The Festival," the fifth poem in *Medieval Scenes*, a strong early series, Duncan uses the motif of the dream to explore the unclear distinctions between wakefulness and sleep and, by extension, between ecstasy and madness, inspiration and inflated foolishness, the unicorn and the ass.

A pervasive concern with boundaries and limits is apparent in "The Venice Poem" (1948), Duncan's first indisputably major poem. In this work, based on Igor Stravinsky's *Symphony in Three Movements*, Duncan relates Berkeley to Venice and links his own lost love and self-questioning to the frustrations of Othello and Desdemona. The awareness of limits and edges crystallizes in a description of an image's coming into being: "She hesitates upon the verge of sound./ She waits upon a sounding impossibility,/ upon the edge of poetry." The final poem collected in *The First Decade*, "The Song of the Borderguard," announces by its very title Duncan's increasing awareness of transgressed boundaries: "The borderlines of sense in the morning light/ are naked as a line of poetry in a war."

The 1950's were productive years; poems written during that period include those published in *Derivations*; *Writing, Writing*; and *Letters*. Although many of these poems are all too explicitly derivative, Duncan reprints them as testimony to his roots and his past. In his 1972 preface to *Caesar's Gate*, Duncan does not use Ezra Pound's term *periplum*, but his description of the writing conveys something of the sense of a poetry "fearfully and with many errors making its way . . . seeking to regain a map in the actual." The first poem collected in *Derivations*, "An Essay at War," opens with a description of the poem "constantly/ under reconstruction," as "a proposition in movement." The poem contrasts the foolish ad hoc "design" of war itself with the imperfect pattern or design of a poem true to a changing experience. The preface to *Letters* argues that a poet's process is one of revision and disorganization, which takes place at the threshold. "I attempt the discontinuities of poetry," he announces, opening gaps that "introduce the peril of beauty." Although cynics assume that such poetry must be inflated or impossible and traditionalists abhor his assumption of a godlike role, Duncan answers both in deft lyrics such as "An Owl Is an Only Bird of Poetry," whose sure and witty inclusiveness articulates both design and disorder. Two poems near the end of *Letters*, "Changing Trains" and "The Language of Love," specifically employ the imagery of border crossing and entering new territory, clear harbingers of Duncan's major phase.

Although the early books are significant achievements, Duncan's reputation rests primarily on three major books of poetry published in the 1960's, *The Opening of the Field*, *Roots and Branches*, and *Bending the Bow*. Each is a unified whole rather than a collection of poems, and each manifests and extends Duncan's use of the theme of boundaries and margins.

THE OPENING OF THE FIELD

The terms of *The Opening of the Field* are proposed in the title, and the book's first and last poems reveal Duncan's awareness of beginnings and endings as they affect this book and much more. "Often I Am Permitted to Return to a Meadow" establishes the basic metaphor of the book, of poetry as an entry into a field of essences, "a scene made-up by the mind,/ that is not mine, but is a made place,/ that is mine." Granted entry into this field of poetic activity, the poet participates in the grand poem through his individual poems. Within this meadow, "the shadows that are forms fall," and in an act of faith ("as if"), the poet accepts it as a "given property of the mind/ that certain bounds hold against chaos." The poems seem to delineate boundaries or fields of order against chaos, but they only seem to do so because in the larger view that Duncan has of poetry and the universe, chaos or disorder are parts of a larger order. The real boundary of this poem, then, is between a state of awareness and its absence. Delineating that boundary, or more fundamentally recognizing the difference, is the responsibility of the poet. In the "disturbance of words within words," the poet's poems are constructs, architectures, flowers that turn into "flames lit to the lady." The limits and definitions of physical reality must give way before the reality of the visionary imagination.

Duncan returns to these images—indeed he never leaves them—in the final poem of this book, "Food for Fire, Food for Thought," in which he self-consciously comments on the paradox of a last poem in an open poetics: "This is what I wanted for the last poem,/ a loosening of conventions and a return to open form." The attempt to define or limit is frustrating and necessarily progressive rather than definitive. The activity, however, is the poet's preoccupation: "We trace faces in the clouds: they drift apart,/ palaces of air—the sun dying down/ sets them on fire." Fire is the concluding image, again transformed into a flower, as an "unlikely heat/ at the edge of our belief bud[s] forth." In these two poems and those in between, Duncan explores the shifting borderlines between essence and form, childhood and adulthood, flame and flower. Even as Leonardo da Vinci did, he sees "figures that were stains upon a wall" as he operates "at the edge of our belief."

The Opening of the Field includes "A Poem Beginning with a Line by Pindar," perhaps Duncan's best-known poem. Beginning with a misreading of a line from the third Pythian Ode, the poem then proclaims his recognition of a "god-step at the margins of thought." The poem is a mosaic or collage of images playing between light and dark, Cupid-sensuality and Psyche-spirituality, East and West, past and present, and it cannot be summarized here. The fourth section begins, "O yes! Bless the footfall where/ step by step the boundary walker," echoing the footstep of the poem's opening, and informs and clarifies the poet's memories and experiences. The poet, as a boundary walker, must be attuned to the elusive image or inspiration, even to a felicitous misreading of Pindar.

Other poems directly addressing the theme of boundaries include "After Reading *Barely and Widely*," a book by Louis Zukofsky, and the series "The Structure of Rime," in the second of which the poet interrogates the nature of poetry. "What is the Structure of Rime? I asked," and he is told, "*An absolute scale of resemblance and disresemblance establishes measures that are music in the actual world.*" Such a recognition of pervasive correspondences and rhymes inspires confidence in the face of difficulties and risks inherent in such poetry. In the eighth of the series, the poet is permitted to crawl through "interstices of Earth" in realizing the possible "from a nexus in the Impossible." The entire series, continuing in subsequent books and intersecting at times with other series, addresses major questions of poetry and reality.

ROOTS AND BRANCHES

Again, *Roots and Branches* enunciates in its title the basic metaphor of the book, "the ramifications below and above the trunk of vegetative life." The title lyric, one of Duncan's best, describes his delight in a monarch butterfly whose flight traces out an imaginary tree, "unseen roots and branches of sense/ I share in thought." The poet's epiphany, inspired by the correspondence between his spirit and the beauty of the common butterfly, denies yet another boundary respected by common sense, that between physical reality and a transcendent reality. Frank in its Romantic idealism, the poem evokes an Emersonian wonder at the harmony of physical and spiritual facts for a modern audience every bit as skeptical as Ralph Waldo Emerson's neighbors.

Roots and Branches closes with a more extended sequence of poems, the memorable series "The Continent," in which Duncan directly names and accepts his role as "the artist of the margin" who "works abundancies" and who recognizes that the scope of poetry "needs vast terms" because it is "out of earthly proportion to the page." On the literal level, Duncan calls for a long poem that will, like Whitman's, be creative and have "vista." Metaphorically and more significantly, he is calling for a poetry on the edge of consciousness, an expanding awareness of "marginal" realities, an openness to unusual or unconventional apprehensions. Unlike the coastal resident's awareness of the alien or the other, "The mid-Western mind differs in essentials." Without Buddhist temples or variant ways of seeing, midwesterners "stand with feet upon the ground/ against the/ run to the mythic sea, the fabulous." This is not praise for Antaeus.

The poem continues, describing a sparrow smashed on a sidewalk. More than an allusion to William Carlos Williams's famous poem, the passage illuminates the difference between having a perspective in space and time and being "too close/ for shadow,/ the immediate!" The central image of the poem, the continent, itself examines horizons, especially those between shore and land and night and day. The closing sections link such imagery with Easter (evidently the time of the actual writing of the poem) and its denial of any clear distinction even between life and death.

Far from fragmenting our beliefs and dissociating our sensibilities, such a vision asserts the oneness of things: one time, one god, one promise flaring forth from "the margins of the page." In the apparent chaos of flux and change—"moving in rifts, churning, enjambing"—both continent and poem testify to a dynamic unity. Again, at the border, at the edge of meaning, like Christopher Columbus one finds not the abyss but new worlds.

"Apprehensions" is a poem closely related to "The Continent." The central theme is again that which "defines the borderlines of the meaning." The opening chord, "To open Night's eye that sleeps in what we know by day," announces the familiar concern with overcoming common sense and sensory limitations, and with the assertion of paradoxical oneness. Quotidian preoccupations obstruct people's perspectives and limit their perceptions. In sharp contrast, the "Sage Architect" awakens "the proportions and scales of the soul's wonder" and lets light and shadow mix. The poem is a song to apprehension—both fearful and perceiving—of excavation of boundaries, resemblances, rhymes. The central apprehension is of concordances that overcome people's limited sense of shifting time, place, and boundaries in favor of an overriding order.

BENDING THE BOW

Continuing his development, Duncan followed four years later with yet another major book, *Bending the Bow*. In his introduction, he discusses his poetry with his accustomed insight, beginning by criticizing the Vietnam War, which, "as if to hold all China or the ancient sea at bay, breaks out at a boundary we name *ours*. It is a boundary beyond our understanding." Captured by a rigid form, by a fixed image of oneself, one is unable to adapt to new conditions and insights. In contrast, the pulse of the poet in moments of vision "beats before and beyond all proper bounds." The book's title establishes the contrasts of bow and lyre, war and music, Apollo and Hermes, whose tension generates this book's field. Duncan speaks of the poem not as a stream of consciousness but as an area of composition in which "the poet works with a sense of parts fitting in relation to a design that is larger than the poem" and which he knows "will never be completed."

The title lyric develops the bow and lyre analogy, articulating the central Heraclitean themes of design, connection, and unity in diversity: "At this extremity of this/ design/ there is a connexion working in both directions, as in/ the bow and the lyre." As Duncan explains in "Towards an Open Universe," the turn and return of prose and verses of poetry are phases of a dynamic unity, like the alternation of day and night or the systole and diastole of the heart. The focus of his poetry and poetics remains on the intensity of the point of transition.

While "The Structure of Rime" continues in this volume, a new series, the "Passages Poems," is also introduced, beginning with a telling epigraph: "For the even is bounded, but the uneven is without bounds and there is no way through or out of it." The first passage, "Tribal Memories," invokes "Her-Without-Bounds," and the importance of margins, borders, and boundaries continues. Describing "Passages Poems" in his introduction, Duncan states that "they belong to a series that extends in an area larger than my work in them. I enter the poem as I entered my own life, moving between an initiation and a terminus I cannot name. This is not a field of the irrational; but a field of ratios."

Among the poem's many concerns are those ratios or correspondences, and some of the most provocative insights derive from the poetic theme of margins and transitions. "The Architecture, Passages 9" demands recesses so that "there is always something around the corner." In "Wine, Passages 12," the poet celebrates even as he is threatened by "the voice/ . . . the enormous/ sonority at the edge of the void." In "In the Place of a Passage 22," the poet prays for passage in "the vast universe/ showing only its boundaries we imagine."

Like "The Structure of Rime," "Passages Poems" is an exciting achievement. Like most long poems, it resists the sort of cursory treatment that consideration of space dictates here, and the project may well be victimized by the "magnificent failure" syndrome so characteristic of criticism of American literature. Certainly it is ambitious, as Duncan acknowledges in "Where It Appears, Passage 4": "Statistically insignificant as a locus of creation/ I have in this my own/ intense/ area of self creation." Even here, the telling conditionals of "as if I could cast a shadow/ to surround/ what is boundless" indicate Duncan's full, continuing, double-edged apprehension of his enterprise and its risks.

GROUND WORK: BEFORE THE WAR

Ground Work: Before the War, published fifteen years after *Bending the Bow*, carries on the concerns of the three major collections of the 1960's. If there had been fear of a possible waning of Duncan's powers, these were unjustified. The architectonics of this large volume are highly complex, though one can easily discern a moving back and forth between familiar modes: the large-scale "grand collage" manner of the ongoing "The Structure of Rime" and "Passages Poems," and sequences of smaller, more private and sentimental lyrics, such as the most delicately rhymed "Glimpse." Both kind of workings, however, involve Duncan's familiar subject matter: revelation, knowing, the "rimes" that the poet worries out of his sympathetic readings of the past masters ("A Seventeenth Century Suite" and "Dante Études"), as well as what George Butterick has called "protest against the violation of the natural order by systematic viciousness." The short lyrics seem a clear relief after the violent engagements with the political disasters of the time, as chronicled in the *Tribunals* section of "Passages Poems," and in what is Duncan's and, maybe, the age's best political poem: "Santa Cruz Propositions." The volume ends with "Circulations of the Song," a deeply moving love poem originating in the poet's reading of Jalāl al-Dīn Rūmī's work and celebrating the years spent with the painter Jess Collins, the "constant exchange" and the shared dance of the hearth-work: After the "Inferno" of the war poems, a kind of "Paradiso" has been achieved.

This delicate point of equilibrium, however, cannot last: It belongs to that specific book, that momentary configuration; the work, the oeuvre goes on, disrupting the gained *Paradiso*, as intimations of physical disease and death enter *Ground Work II*, the next and final volume of Duncan's late work, subtitled *In the Dark* and published just months before the poet's death. Even here, however, there is no weakening of Duncan's powers: The grand sweep of the late set of "Passages Poems" entitled "Regulators" is ample proof of the poet's unrelenting energy and vision. Duncan's long illness enters the preoccupations of the book—"my Death/ rearranged the date He has with me"—without ever being able to overcome that realm of the imagination from which the poet drew his breath and strength.

DUNCAN'S ART

It is another measure of Duncan's stature and complexity that all his work is of a piece and should be read entire. A single lyric, for example, can be read by itself, or as part of a longer series in many cases (several lyrics are parts of more than one series). It must also be seen as part of the book in which it appears, since Duncan has carefully ordered his collections, and as an integral part of Duncan's canon. Finally, as he says in his introduction to *The Years as Catches*, "Poems then are immediate presentations of the intention of the whole, the great poem of all poems, a unity." Appropriately, even the boundaries of his poems are fluid and dynamic.

In his pervasive border-crossing, Duncan brings his readers news of an other that is shut out by conventional boundaries. With his artful disclosures, his imaginative vision transcends false, self-imposed constrictions. His art ultimately dissolves the very restraints and boundaries he recognizes in the act of transgressing them, and it thus weds humans to nature and to other humans, a familiar but rarely realized ideal of art.

OTHER MAJOR WORKS

PLAYS: *Faust Foutu: An Entertainment in Four Parts*, pb. 1959; *Medea at Kolchis: The Maidenhead*, pb. 1965.

NONFICTION: *As Testimony: The Poem and the Scene*, 1964; *The Sweetness and Greatness of Dante's "Divine Comedy,"* 1965; *The Cat and the Blackbird*, 1967; *The Truth and Life of Myth: An Essay in Essential Autobiography*, 1968; *A Selection of Sixty-five Drawings from One Drawing-Book, 1952-1956*, 1970; *Fictive Certainties*, 1985; *The Last Letters*, 2000; *The Letters of Robert Duncan and Denise Levertov*, 2004 (Robert J. Bertholf and Albert Gelpi, editors).

BIBLIOGRAPHY

Bertholf, Robert J. *Robert Duncan: A Descriptive Bibliography*. Santa Rosa, Calif.: Black Sparrow Press, 1986. Contains photographs of many of Duncan's books, broadsides, illustrations, and drawings.

Bertholf, Robert J., and Ian W. Reid, eds. *Robert Duncan: Scales of the Marvelous*. New York: New Directions, 1979. Collects a variety of essays, including some by contemporary poets.

Davidson, Michael. *The San Francisco Renaissance: Poetics and Community at Mid-century*. New York: Cambridge University Press, 1989. Although only chapter 4 ("Cave of Resemblances, Cave of Rimes: Tradition and Repetition in Robert Duncan") of this study of poetics and community in the Bay Area is specifically centered on the poetics of Duncan, the book as a whole is an invaluable guide to the social, political, and literary environment in which Duncan lived and worked.

Duncan, Robert. Interview. In *Towards a New American Poetics: Essays and Interviews*, edited by Ekbert Faas. Santa Barbara, Calif.: Black Sparrow Press, 1978. One of the best of many interviews.

Ellingham, Lewis. *Poet Be Like God: Jack Spicer and the San Francisco Renaissance*. Hanover, N.H.: University Press of New England, 1998. Criticism and biographic material about Spicer and the San Francisco Renaissance group that included Robert Duncan. With bibliographic references.

Everson, William. *The Last Letters*. Berkeley, Calif.: Oyez, 2000. A collection of correspondence between Everson and Duncan.

Faas, Ekbert. *Young Robert Duncan: Portrait of the Poet as Homosexual in Society*. Santa Barbara, Calif.: Black Sparrow Press, 1983. A well-researched book about Duncan's early life, the complexity of being a foster child, the East Coast years so often neglected in Duncan studies, the early radical decision to assert his gay identity, and the effects this had on the development of Duncan as a writer.

Foster, Edward Halsey. *Understanding the Black Mountain Poets*. Columbia: University of South Carolina Press, 1995. This discussion of the Black Mountain poets contains valuable information on Duncan as well as on Charles Olson and Robert Creeley.

Johnson, Mark. *Robert Duncan*. Boston: Twayne, 1988. Provides a brief but intelligent overview of the poet's life and work.

O'Leary, Peter. *Gnostic Contagion: Robert Duncan and the Poetry of Illness*. Middletown, Conn.: Wesleyan University Press, 2002. Examines Gnosticism and illness in the poetry of Duncan. In addition to analyzing Duncan's work, O'Leary discusses his influence.

Sagetrieb 4 (Fall/Winter, 1985). This special issue includes critical essays on Duncan's work, poems dedicated to him, an excerpt from "The H. D. Book," a selection of letters from Duncan to the poet William Everson, and an interview.

Mark A. Johnson

STEPHEN DUNN

Born: Forest Hills, New York; June 24, 1939

PRINCIPAL POETRY

Five Impersonations, 1971
Looking for Holes in the Ceiling, 1974
Full of Lust and Good Usage, 1976
A Circus of Needs, 1978
Work and Love, 1981
Not Dancing, 1984
Local Time, 1986

Between Angels, 1989
Landscape at the End of the Century, 1991
New and Selected Poems: 1974-1994, 1994
Loosestrife, 1996
Riffs and Reciprocities: Prose Pairs, 1998
Different Hours, 2000
Local Visitations, 2003
The Insistence of Beauty, 2004
Everything Else in the World, 2006
What Goes On: Selected and New Poems 1995-2009, 2009

OTHER LITERARY FORMS

Stephen Dunn has written nonfiction including an autobiographical memoir, *Walking Light: Essays and Memoirs* (1993, 2001) and introductions to the works of other poets. He has also edited two collections of poetry by children.

ACHIEVEMENTS

Stephen Dunn has received numerous honors for his poetry. In 2001, he won the Pulitzer Prize in poetry for *Different Hours*. Dunn received the Theodore Roethke Prize from *Poetry Northwest* (1977), the Levinson Prize (1987) from *Poetry* magazine, the James Wright Prize from *Mid-America Review* (1993), an Academy Award in Literature from the American Academy of Arts and Letters (1995), and the J. Howard and Barbara M. J. Wood Prize (2001) from *Poetry* magazine. In 1985, *Local Time* was chosen for the National Poetry Series by Dave Smith, and in 1996, *Loosestrife* was a finalist for the National Book Critics Circle Award. He has received fellowships from the National Endowment for the Arts, the Rockefeller Foundation, the Guggenheim Foundation, and the New Jersey State Council on the Arts. In addition to his readings at many colleges and universities, Dunn has read his poetry at the Library of Congress.

BIOGRAPHY

Stephen Dunn's background offers a surprising contrast to that of many of his contemporaries, because of his time spent in professional sports. After he earned his B.A. in history from Hofstra University in 1962, he spent a year as a professional basketball player. From

1963 to 1966, he worked as a copywriter for National Biscuit Company in New York City, while also attending the New School. In 1967-1968, he was employed as assistant editor with Ziff-Davis Publishing Company.

Dunn subsequently enrolled in the creative writing program at Syracuse University, where his teachers included Philip Booth, Donald Justice, and W. D. Snodgrass. After receiving an M.A. in 1970, Dunn became assistant professor of creative writing at Southwestern State University, in Marshall, Minnesota. In 1971, his first chapbook, *Five Impersonations*, was published by Oxhead Press. He served as Syracuse University lecturer in poetry in 1973-1974, and in 1974, he started teaching at Richard Stockton College in New Jersey, where he became distinguished professor of creative writing. In addition to serving as visiting professor at several universities, he served as director of the Associated Writing Programs Poetry Series in 1980-1982 and as adjunct professor at Columbia University in 1983-1987.

ANALYSIS

A disarming directness and simplicity of line characterizes the works of Stephen Dunn, as befits a poetry that quietly celebrates middle-class American domestic life. His works evoke household matters and sexual love, against the counter-theme of the discovery of personal emptiness. Dunn, or the speaker of his poems, seems to discover this emptiness both in and outside himself.

These concerns are least apparent in Dunn's early poems, where his cleverness and humor come to the fore. In "How to Be Happy: Another Memo to Myself," which appeared in *Looking for Holes in the Ceiling*, he lets ideas lead him along loosely connected thoughts, from this beginning: "You start with your own body/ then move outward, but not too far./ Never try to please a city, for example." The prose-like lines convey the sense of a man talking himself into charting a purely sensible course in life. Near the end, advice appears that Dunn seems to follow in later works: "Remember, finally, there are few pleasures/ that aren't as local as your fingertips./ Never go to Europe for a cathedral." The poem's overall tone is of one who has insights to share, even if the insights repeatedly return to the mundane.

From early in his career, Dunn's poems show a poet well centered within his own body. "Truck Stop: Minnesota" contains the line that gave his 1976 collection its name: *Full of Lust and Good Usage*. The poem offers a revery on a waitress at the truck stop, who provokes Dunn's desire and ". . . is the America I would like to love./ Sweetheart, the truckers call her." The physicality of Dunn's desire stands in contrast to his being "lost here" in a place where his "good usage" itself seems out of place.

A litany similar to that in "How to Be Happy," which seems to keep turning inward, appears in "Introduction to the Twentieth Century," from *A Circus of Needs*: ". . . And for every death/ there was a building or a poem. For every/ lame god a rhythm and a hunch, something local/ we could possibly trust. . . ." He describes setting down history books that have chronicled the century's horrors, and concludes: "In difficult times, we came to understand,/ it's the personal and only the personal that matters." In this poem, Dunn states what seems to be a declaration of belief, which will prove of significance in his later work.

NOT DANCING

In *Not Dancing*, Dunn's poems increasingly raise doubts about life and art, uncovering the difficulties to be encountered when pursuing a purely sensible course in life. In "Essay on the Personal," which begins with lines that reiterate that ". . . the personal/ is all that matters," he describes how emphasis on artistic precision has not prepared him for what life has brought him, particularly when dealing emotionally with his parents. Now he perceives that ". . . What seemed so deep/ begins to seem naïve . . ." and laments being ". . . left with style, a particular/ way of standing and saying."

Dunn directly addresses the issue of his parents in "Legacy," a longer poem that he dedicates to his father, who gambled away his savings at the racing track. The poem recalls the quietness of the unhappy family: "Nights he'd come home drunk/ mother would cook his food/ and there'd be silence./ Thus, for years, I thought/ all arguments were silent. . . ."

DIFFERENT HOURS

Although games of chance brought disaster to his parents, they assume a place of importance in Dunn's poems in *Different Hours*, as in "Another Man." The element of poignancy and regret introduced in his works of the 1980's also becomes a common ingredient in this volume. Many of Dunn's tendencies received summation in *Different Hours*, with one poem, "Visiting the Master," echoing Dunn's early advice to himself: "Use what's lying around the house./ Make it simple and sad." "At the Restaurant" includes one of his strongest statements of a growing feeling: "And there's your chronic emptiness/ spiraling upward in search of words/ you'll dare not say// without irony./ You should have stayed at home."

LOCAL VISITATIONS

Of Dunn's many explorations of domestic life, one of the most accomplished is "The Affair" from *Local Visitations*. With an almost studied plainness of language, which helps underline the sense of the honesty of the account being presented, Dunn offers an internal portrait of one who is comfortably lodged in a marriage but who begins a love affair all the same. His portrayal of the early stage of being in two relationships is finely realized, with Dunn turning sentences in on themselves in a manner that recalls his early poems:

> He took pride that he gave his divided attention
> wholly to whomever he was with.
> His wife was his better half by more than half.
> His lover was the everything
> he allowed himself partially to have.

The ending exhibits similar finesse: "It came to a choice, and he chose everything./ He left almost everything behind." "The Affair" offers no better insight into love than the physical desires of "a man who wanted too much," and it therefore remains a description of surfaces, in common with much of his earlier work. The self-critical wit Dunn deploys, however, lifts the poem above hollow portrayal.

Also notable is "Sisyphus and the Sudden Lightness," Dunn's poem chosen to appear in the ninetieth anniversary issue of *Poetry* in 2002. In *Local Visitations*, it appears alongside other poems employing the mythical figure of Sisyphus as the focal character. "Sisyphus and the Sudden Lightness" describes this doomed character's reactions when his burden is lifted, and he feels ". . . as if he had wings, and the wind/ behind him. Even uphill the rock/ seemed to move of its

own accord." Deprived of his task, he feels a new freedom, although the freedom fails to bring the expected pleasure. The poem ends, "He dared to raise his fist to the sky./ Nothing, gloriously, happened.// Then a different terror overtook him." In his depiction of Sisyphus, Dunn again unveils the sense of an emptiness that grows to overpower other pleasures.

THE INSISTENCE OF BEAUTY

In "Winter" from *The Insistence of Beauty*, Dunn examines the sense of emptiness in yet again different terms. The poem's speaker regards the "indifference of a perfect sky" and the snow on the ground below it that he realizes he would have regarded metaphorically at another point in time: "Now they seem little more than what they are." The poet is experiencing a disenchantment and reacting to the failure of art to transform common life: "And those deer prints in the driveway,/ that cardinal on a hemlock's lower branch—/ I'm amazed they don't insist or signify."

EVERYTHING ELSE IN THE WORLD

Dunn's 2006 volume, suggestively entitled *Everything Else in the World*, contains several poems that express the poet's sense that his internal empiness is infecting the world around him. Most pronounced is "Replicas," a speculative poem whose sustained conceit is borrowed from the tale of invasion by extraterrestrials. The poem's narrator, in recognizing that ". . . aliens were working here/ with their dead-giveaway, perfectly cut Armani suits," decides to host a cocktail party to befriend them. What seems striking about these "aliens" is how well-accustomed they seem to worldly success. The narrator muses, after his dog barks in a particularly telling manner, ". . . I was sure/ I couldn't afford to trust appearances ever again." As they leave and express their pleasure in the cocktail party, the emptiness behind their appearances is revealed by conformity: "Each of them used the same words,/ like people who've been trained in sales."

In "Process," which begins with the line, "I feel nothing and nothing's in my head," even the act of writing poetry seems under threat by this failure to discover meaning. All the same, Dunn conjures up solid imagery to convey his thoughts: "The ground is hard/ and my tools seem old and nothing/ reminds me of nothing. I move/ a little surface dirt around, that's all."

In "Emptiness," Dunn offers an echo of "Meaninglessness," a poem from *Loosestrife*. This short work directly addresses how deeply the speaker feels affected. In the past, he has usually ". . . hidden it,/ not knowing until too late/ how enormous it grows in the dark." The poem then reveals his new strategy, which is to "dress it plain" and to express it "to some right person." He does so to the reader, admitting "that there's something not there/ in me, something I can't name." In the poem, that "right person" is also the woman in his life. Dunn manages to swing this simple and direct poem from a statement of personal crisis to an understated poem of love, and he ends with the recognition that he is clinging to his feeling of emptiness. The juxtaposition of inner crisis and external source of hope makes this a more effective love poem than many earlier ones.

Twin emphases on physical love and the unsuccessful search for meaning give Dunn's poems a distinct quality. Even with the reader's uncertainty as to whether Dunn himself or a poetic speaker is suffering this decades-long crisis, Dunn's stance seems clear. As in the ending of "At the Restaurant" from *Different Hours*, the feeling of emptiness moves toward judgement of one who cannot establish a core of meaning. Dunn there states, "Insufficient, the merely decent man."

Other major works

NONFICTION: *Walking Light: Essays and Memoirs*, 1993, 2001.

EDITED TEXTS: *An Alibi of Gifts, a Cat of Wind: A Handbook and Anthology of Poems by Children*, 1977; *Silence Has a Rough, Crazy Weather: Poems by Deaf Children*, 1979.

Bibliography

Campion, Peter. Review of *The Insistence of Beauty*. *Poetry* 185, no. 2 (November, 2004): 133-135. An in-depth review offering insight into Dunn's overall accomplishments.

Christophersen, Bill. "Down from the Tower: Poetry as Confabulation." *Poetry* 179, no. 4 (January, 2002): 217-225. A critical response to *Different Hours*, in a review of several current poetry collections.

Coyne, Kevin. "The Greatest Poet Never Heard." *New Jersey Monthly* 26, no. 10 (October, 2001): 43-47. A profile of Dunn that emphasizes his background, including how he became interested in poetry, with discussion of his poetry's characteristics.

Dunn, Stephen. "Stephen Dunn." http://www.stephendunnpoet.com. The official Web site for Dunn provides biographical information, lists of published works and awards, commentary on his works, and links to interviews.

_____. "Stephen Dunn." Interview by Sanford Pinsker. In *Conversations with Contemporary American Writers*, edited by Pinsker. Amsterdam: Rodopi, 1985. Dunn explores his life, his poetry, and how he became a writer.

Murray, G. E. "The Collective Unconscious." *Southern Review* 37, no. 2 (Spring, 2001): 404-420. In a review of several collections of poetry, Murray gives special emphasis to Dunn's *Different Hours*.

Tromp, Ian. Review of *Different Hours*. *Times Literary Supplement* 5142 (October 19, 2001), p. 25. A discussion of Dunn's Pulitzer Prize-winning collection.

Mark Rich

E

CORNELIUS EADY

Born: Rochester, New York; January 7, 1954

PRINCIPAL POETRY

Kartunes, 1980

Victims of the Latest Dance Craze, 1985

BOOM BOOM BOOM, 1988 (limited edition chapbook)

The Gathering of My Name, 1991

You Don't Miss Your Water, 1995

The Autobiography of a Jukebox, 1996

Brutal Imagination, 2001

Hardheaded Weather: New and Selected Poems, 2008

OTHER LITERARY FORMS

Given his willingness to experiment with bringing the rhythms of both jazz and blues to the written word and his belief in poetry as performed (that is, heard) art, Cornelius Eady (EE-dee), not surprisingly, has produced several experimental theater pieces involving original scores written by jazz cellist and longtime friend Diedre L. Murray. The first production, in 1997, was a staged recitation based on *You Don't Miss Your Water*, Eady's cycle of prose poems that recounts his father's death. In 1999, Eady provided the libretto for an experimental jazz opera based on the story of Murray's brother, a gifted man lost to a life of crime and heroin addiction. That production, *Running Man* (pr. 1999), won two Obie Awards and was shortlisted for both the New York Drama Critics Circle Award and the Pulitzer Prize. His poetry collection *Brutal Imagination* contains a dramatic sequence based on the 1994 incident in which a South Carolina woman, Susan Smith, made up a story about an African American kidnapping her children to hide the fact that she had drowned them. The sequence was adapted into an off-Broadway play that won the Oppenheimer Award from *Newsday* in 2002.

ACHIEVEMENTS

Cornelius Eady emerged within the first generation of African American poets to succeed the formidable work of the Black Arts movement of the mid-twentieth century. That literary movement, an extension of the era's Civil Rights movement, created new interest in black identity. Eady continued that exploration, using his own working-class upbringing and his position as a black poet in late twentieth century America. That compelling honesty, coupled with his experiments in the sheer music of language, has garnered Eady two nominations for the Pulitzer Prize, for *Running Man* and *The Gathering of My Name*. *Victims of the Latest Dance Craze* was named the Lamont Poetry Selection by the Academy of American Poets in 1985, and *Brutal Imagination* was a finalist for the National Book Award in Poetry. He received the O. B. Hardison, Jr., Poetry Prize in 2003. A career academic, Eady has received fellowships from the Guggenheim Foundation (1993), the National Endowment for the Arts (1985), and the Rockefeller Foundation (1993), and the Lila Wallace-*Reader's Digest* Foundation (1992-1993).

BIOGRAPHY

Born in Rochester, New York, Cornelius Eady began writing poems when he was only twelve. As chronicled in *You Don't Miss Your Water*, Eady's father posed a formidable problem for the aspiring poet. High-school educated, Eady's father, employed by the city water department, had difficulty accepting literature as a valid vocation. Consequently, Eady would struggle with feelings of estrangement until his father's death in 1993. After graduating from Empire State College and then earning his M.F.A. from Warren Wilson College, Eady held teaching appointments at Sweet Briar College, the College of William and Mary, Sarah Lawrence College, Tougaloo College, and City College of New York. While at the State University of New York at Stony Brook in the 1990's, he served as director of its famous poetry center. In 1999, Eady became distinguished writer-in-residence in the M.F.A. program at New York City's innovative New School. He later joined the faculty of Notre Dame University as associate professor in English and director of the creative writing program. In 1996, along with poet Toi

Derricotte, Eady founded the Cave Canem (literally, "Beware of the Dog"), a popular program of summer workshops for African American poets.

ANALYSIS

Cornelius Eady's poetry concerns the construction of identity, the dynamics of memory and reflection as part of the interrogation of the self, and the importance of recording that complex process. Like the blues, Eady's poetry centers on the struggle to define the isolated self within a chaotic world that harbors little possibility for redemption. Like jazz, however, Eady's poetry also responds to a world that, given its essential unpredictability, can sustain authentic ecstasy. That texture, the self sustained between sadness and exuberance, is central to Eady's work. His poetry explores the roles he has played in the construction of his own identity. Not surprisingly, over the time Eady has been writing, this interrogation of the self has become more complex. Initially, Eady explored his role as urban poet; later, he examined more complex relational roles, that of husband, lover, teacher, and, supremely, son; he

Cornelius Eady (©Miriam Berkley)

later began to confront his role as an African American, specifically the struggle to construct a viable black self amid the historical and social pressures around the turn of the millennium in the United States.

The poetic line for such an investigation into the self is appropriately individual and resists conventional expectations of structure and sound. Rhythmic but not metric, Eady's line can appear deceptively simple, direct, even conversational. However, it is freedom within a tightly manipulated form. Like improvisational jazz, which can, at first hearing, seem easy and effortless, Eady's poetry is a complex aural event. His poems consciously manipulate sounds, using unexpected syncopations and cadences, enjambment, irregular spacings and emphasis, line length, and sound repetition to create an air of improvisation that is nevertheless a carefully textured sonic weave.

KARTUNES

Kartunes is a portrait of the self as young poet, an exercise in testing the reach of the imagination and celebrating the role of a cocksure poet responding originally to the world. "I want to be fresh," he proclaims, "I want words/ to tumble off my lips/ rich enough/ to fertilize/ the ground." Giddy with imaginative possibilities, Eady improvises his narrative "I" into outlandish personas (the "cartoons" suggested by the title), many culled from pop culture: He is at turns an inept terrorist, a nerdy librarian, an unhappy woman forced into a witness protection program, a dying philanthropist anxious about the approaching afterlife, a man contemplating torching his own house, the legendary Headless Horseman selecting the appropriate pumpkin to hurtle, Popeye's nemesis Bluto groomed for a date, and even Adolf Hitler posing before a mirror and dreaming of greatness.

Given such wild fluctuations in the narrative center, the poetry is given over to irreverent exuberance. Despite often centering on alienated characters existing within a contemporary environment of absurdity and brutality, the poems resist surrendering to emotional heaviness. The poems, themselves innovative in structure and sound (witness the wordplay of the collection's title), offer as resolutions the sheer animation of the engaged imagination, the possibility of love, and the ability of the world to stun with its unchoreographed wonder. With the confident insouciance of a young man, Eady argues that nothing is nobler than "laughing/ when nothing/ is funny anymore."

VICTIMS OF THE LATEST DANCE CRAZE

The interest in defining the poet and that confident sense of play animates Eady's follow-up collection, *Victims of the Latest Dance Craze*, thematically centered on the metaphor of the dance. Here the world is in constant motion—the title poem, for example, details a pulsating urban neighborhood. Like William Carlos Williams (whose influence Eady has acknowledged), the poet responds to the seductive suasion of the world that too often goes unnoticed—to a cloud passing overhead, crows battling a strong wind, a waitress's purple nail polish, the leaden feel of November, the faint stirrings of April: "an entire world," he trumpets, "on the tip of my tongue." To respond to that world is to dance, a suggestive metaphor for the body's irresistible, spontaneous response to being alive, the electric moment of the "hands . . ./ Accidentally brush[ing] against the skirts of the world." Such animation makes problematic the life of the poet so vital in *Kartunes*.

In the closing poem, "Dance at the Amherst County Public Library," the poet describes himself as a "dancing fool who couldn't stay away from words." He concedes his jealousy over those who live so effortlessly and of his own poor efforts to capture secondhand that rich experience within his poetry, his "small graffiti dance." The poetic lines here boldly strive to match the urgent call to respond originally to the world, capturing the improvisational feel of jazz: irregular patterning of lines, multiple stops and starts, a delightful matching of sounds, and wildly unanticipated rhythms.

THE GATHERING OF MY NAME

In Eady's ambitious third major collection, *The Gathering of My Name*, the tone considerably darkens as jazz gives way to the slower pull of the blues. In the opening poem, "Gratitude," Eady audaciously proffers love to those who have not welcomed him nor his poetry and confesses his greatest weakness is his "inability/ to sustain rage." It is a familiar brashness, and, indeed, the second poem ("Grace") offers one of those unexpected moments when the world sparkles: the sight of the neighborhood reflected in the waxed hood of a black sedan.

However, quickly the poems concede to a more disturbing world that crushes dreams and sours love. For the first time, Eady addresses race. Poems introduce figures such as the tormented blues singer Leadbelly or jazz great John Coltrane in the aftermath of the 1963 bombing of a Baptist church in Birmingham, Alabama. In others, a waitress in Virginia refuses to serve a black man, a passing motorist hurls racial epithets at a black man's white wife, a car breaks down in the "wrong" neighborhood. Like the blues, these are poems of pain and bad luck, the curse of awareness, the dilemma of disappointment, and the need to define the self in a harsh world. What is the poet to do? "Get it all out," Eady demands in "The Sheets of Sounds," the remarkable closing piece that is a tour de force of metrical audacity. Here, Eady captures in language the technical virtuosity and improvisational sound of Coltrane himself: "What do I have to lose,/ Actually,/ By coming right out/ And saying/ What I mean/ To say?" Honesty then compels the poet/jazz artist to let loose the spirit in all its outrage, to push art if only for a moment into uncompromising expression, the "loud humility" of a man giving himself the right to claim, as a refrain insists with typographical variations: "This is who I am."

YOU DON'T MISS YOUR WATER

Appropriately, then, in Eady's fourth collection, *You Don't Miss Your Water*, readers feel (for the first time in his work) the nearness of the poet himself. Dropping his elaborate personas, Eady speaks forthrightly of his own life. The twenty-one prose poems are stark narratives without poetic frills and without clean chronological sequencing. The reader is given an unblinking record of a son's estrangement from a father in the face of mortality, the honest struggle to come to terms with the difficult wisdom of the blues lines, "You don't miss your water/ 'til your well runs dry." Eady refuses to sentimentalize the father (he is at turns miserly, stubborn, distant, even unfaithful) or himself (he cremates the body to save money), or even death (he records the indignities of hospital treatment and the impersonal efficiency of agencies that manage the paperwork). Titles recall traditional blues songs, and the mood is elegiac, sobering, eloquent: "This is how life, sharpened to a fine point, plunges into what we call hope."

If Eady's first three volumes speak of how the imagination takes hold of the world and shapes individual identity, here he acknowledges the depth of the inevitable experience of loss and how that experience is as well part of any construction of identity. In the volume's rich closing poem, "Paradiso," Eady decides that language itself, disparaged in his earlier work as secondhand graffiti, is the sole conjurer of the afterlife, that the "key to any heaven is language."

THE AUTOBIOGRAPHY OF A JUKEBOX

The Autobiography of a Jukebox is a kind of summary text. It is divided into four sections, each of which centers on themes drawn from earlier works: the heavy intrusion of loss; the ugly realities of racism; the glorious transcendence of art, specifically jazz, within this environment of oppression; and those small unexpected moments that trigger deep emotional responses and make such a world endurable. The volume begins where *You Don't Miss Your Water* ends: dealing with harsh loss—indeed, opening poems linger within recollections of Eady's father. With a bluesy feel, other poems follow characters who discover the wounding of love, the certainty of bad luck, and the humiliations of poverty.

In the second section, Eady confronts the angry indignation over the 1991 beating of Rodney King by Los Angeles police, the federal trial in which the white officers were acquitted, and the riots that followed. It is Eady's first lengthy examination of the social dimension of the self and specifically how black identity must be defined within an oppressive white culture. To maintain dignity and to touch grace within such an environment, Eady offers in the third section portraits of jazz artists (and pioneer rocker Chuck Berry), black musicians who forged from such oppression the stuff of their art: "What/ Hurts is beautiful, the bruise/ Of the lyric." However, it is not sufficient simply to relish such aesthetic artifacts.

In the closing section, Eady quietly affirms what his first two volumes trumpeted: the imagination's ability to be stunned by the accidental encounter with something that triggers a minor epiphany in a flawed world that still permits awe—a woman with dreadlocks crossing a street, a tray of cornbread at a posh reception, the electric flow of an urban mall, and the tangy smells of a bakery. However, hard on the death of Eady's father and the anger over the King beating, these slender moments of grace are suddenly significant in ways the earlier volumes could not suggest.

BRUTAL IMAGINATION

In *Brutal Imagination*, Eady's career-long interest in defining the self takes on new maturity as he projects himself, within two unrelated poem cycles, out of the matrix of his own experience. In the first section, Eady conjures the spirit and voice of the black kidnapper that South Carolina mother Susan Smith invented as a way to hide the fact that she had drowned her two infant sons. Eady uses that lie to investigate the white culture of anger, bigotry, and anxiety within which all black identity must be fashioned. In a biting middle section, Eady suggests the dimensions of this dilemma by giving voice to the sorry racist stereotypes fashioned by a white imagination unwilling to grant blacks the dignity and complexity of legitimate selfhood: Uncle Tom, Uncle Ben, Aunt Jemina, Buckwheat, and Stepin Fetchit. The faux-kidnapper—witty, articulate, probing, caring—dominates the cycle and, specifically, the symbiotic relationship between Smith and her invention. Eady suggests how necessary the black stereotype is for whites. In the closing poem, "Birthing," which draws on excerpts from Smith's actual confession, the conjured kidnapper extends compassion to the mother, imagining the actual killing and the desperate loneliness of Smith who was driven to do the unimaginable.

The second section contains pieces from the libretto of *Running Man*. Although offered without the haunting jazz score of the original production and without the dramatic interplay of performance, the pieces nevertheless succeed in a conjuring of a sort far different from that of Smith. A southern black family, devastated by the death of its only son, struggles to explain why such a promising young man succumbed to the very life of crime that made credible Smith's vicious lie. Within the interplay of their elegiac recollections, the poetic line tightly clipped for maximum effect, the young man himself is conjured and speaks of his own promise lost to the anger of limited social expectations within the white system and to the easy out of drug addiction and crime. He is the "running man," never sure where he was running from or to: "Where I come from/ A smart black boy/ Is like being a cat/ With a duck's bill." Chained to history—the cycle begins in an old slave cemetery—blacks, whatever their talent or aspirations, must withstand the larger predatory white culture that can leave them helpless, like "fish, scooped from a pond." It is a powerful assessment of black identity at the twentieth century's close.

HARDHEADED WEATHER

The title poem of *Hardheaded Weather* describes a drive from New York City to the narrator's home in upstate New York during stormy weather, but it really is a meditation on death and friends who have died. The narrator thinks about Walt Whitman, who worked as a nurse in an Army hospital during the American Civil War, and wonders how Whitman must have felt when he had to comfort young men who were about to die.

The first section in this collection, "Lucky House," contains twenty poems describing ordinary life. The poems are ostensibly about mundane activities such as finding a couch, buying a house, moving into the house, fixing it up, recycling, surviving a blizzard, gardening, dealing with an ill mother, watching deer, mowing the grass, and surviving cancer. Eady has said that he does not normally write traditional love poetry but that he writes with love of the subject matter. The poems in this section reveal a life-affirming attitude that poetry can be found in an ordinary life, provided that the person is capable of love.

In the second section, "The Way a Long Dress Turns a Corner," Eady meditates on the September 11, 2001, terrorist attacks in "Communion." Other poems in this section reflect on Billie Holiday, Jackie Robinson, and a deceased African American journalist named Joe Wood. The poems in the first two sections were originally written from 1997 to 2003. The third section, "From *Kartunes*," reprints some of the poems from that book.

The fourth section, "The Modern World," contains previously unpublished poems from 1981. The first three, "The Professor Tries to Inspire His Poetry Students," "Charlie Chaplin Impersonates a Poet," and "Knowledge," concern a professor of poetry. Eady has personal knowledge about what it is like to teach poetry at the college level, because that is what he does for a living. In "Living with Genius," the narrator tries to

imagine what it must have been like to have been Alice B. Toklas, the companion of Gertrude Stein. American involvement with the politics of countries in Latin America was a very hot topic in 1981. The administration of President Ronald Reagan supported the Contras against the Sandinistas in Nicaragua, for example. "U.S. Involvement in 'Latin America'" imagines a Central Intelligence Agent who attempts to interrogate a guitar. The Reagan administration also indicated a willingness to entertain the possibility of a nuclear war with the Soviet Union. In "Atomic Prayer," the narrator hopes he will have time to make some symbolic actions if New York City is bombed.

The second half of the book reprints poems from his later works. Among them is "Jack Johnson Does the Eagle Rock" from 1985. Johnson, the first African American to win the world heavyweight boxing championship, was prevented from sailing on the *Titanic* because of his race. The Eagle Rock was a popular dance at the time, and Eady imagines that Johnson must have celebrated his close brush with death.

OTHER MAJOR WORKS

PLAY: *Running Man*, pr. 1999 (libretto).

EDITED TEXTS: *Words for Breakfast*, 1998 (with Meg Kearney, Norma Fox Mazer, and Jacqueline Woodson); *Vinyl Donuts*, 2000 (with Kearney, Mazer, and Woodson); *Gathering Ground: A Reader Celebrating Cave Canem's First Decade*, 2006 (with Toi Derricotte).

MISCELLANEOUS: *Poems and Stories*, 2002.

BIBLIOGRAPHY

Carroll, Rebecca, ed. *Swing Low: Black Men Writing*. New York: Carol Southern Books, 1995. In her work on seventeen black male writers, Carroll presents a biography and interview with Eady, as well as an excerpt from his work.

Harper, Michael S., and Anthony Walton, eds. *Every Shut Eye Ain't Asleep: An Anthology of Poetry by African Americans Since 1945*. Boston: Little, Brown, 1994. Contains a selection of Eady's poetry with brief critical commentary within an anthology of Eady's generation of African American poets.

Hawkins, Shayla. "Cave Canem: A Haven for Black Poets." *Poets and Writers* 29, no. 2 (March/April, 2001): 48-53. Discusses the Cave Canem workshop and retreat founded by Eady and Toi Derricotte. Eady and Derricotte recognized the need for a "haven" for black writers.

Quashie, Kevin Everod. "Cornelius Eady." In *New Bones: Contemporary Black Writers in America*, edited by Joyce Lausch, Keith Miller, and Quashie. Saddle River, N.J.: Prentice-Hall, 2001. A helpful overview of Eady's career. The introduction assesses issues and themes of Eady's generation.

Williams, Tyrone, ed. *Masterplots II: African American Literature*. Rev. ed. Pasadena, Calif.: Salem Press, 2009. Provides in-depth examinations of two of Eady's works, *An Autobiography of a Jukebox* and *Brutal Imagination*.

Young, Kevin, ed. *Giant Steps: The New Generation of African-American Writers*. New York: Perennial, 2000. A comprehensive introduction to Eady's generation.

Joseph Dewey
Updated by Thomas R. Feller

RICHARD EBERHART

Born: Austin, Minnesota; April 5, 1904
Died: Hanover, New Hampshire; June 9, 2005

PRINCIPAL POETRY

A Bravery of Earth, 1930
Reading the Spirit, 1936
Song and Idea, 1940
A World-View, 1941
Poems, New and Selected, 1944
Burr Oaks, 1947
Brotherhood of Men, 1949
An Herb Basket, 1950
Selected Poems, 1951
Undercliff: Poems 1946-1953, 1953
Great Praises, 1957
The Oak: A Poem, 1957

Collected Poems 1930-1960, Including Fifty-one New Poems, 1960
The Quarry, 1964
Selected Poems 1930-1965, 1965
Thirty-one Sonnets, 1967
Shifts of Being, 1968
Three Poems, 1968
Fields of Grace, 1972
Two Poems, 1975
Collected Poems: 1930-1976, 1976
Poems to Poets, 1976
Hour, Gnats: New Poems, 1977
Survivors, 1979
Four Poems, 1980
New Hampshire: Nine Poems, 1980
Ways of Light, 1980
Florida Poems, 1981
The Long Reach, 1984
Collected Poems 1930-1986, 1986
Maine Poems, 1988
New and Selected Poems, 1930-1990, 1990

OTHER LITERARY FORMS

In addition to poetry, Richard Eberhart wrote *Of Poetry and Poets* (1979), a prose collection divided into three parts and an epilogue. The first section is a compilation of lectures and essays on the craft of poetry. The second is a critical section in which Eberhart discusses the work of poets such as Wallace Stevens, Theodore Roethke, W. H. Auden, and Robert Frost. Five interviews and Eberhart's National Book Award acceptance speech round out the book.

Eberhart's verse plays also deserve mention. The first, *The Apparition*, printed in *Poetry* (Chicago) in 1950 and produced the same year, is a short play in which a salesman encounters a young girl who wanders into his room; she talks with him, enjoys a few drinks, and then disappears into the hallway. The second play, *The Visionary Farms*, was begun at Yaddo, the artists' colony near Saratoga Springs, New York, when the poet worked in a studio apartment next to William Carlos Williams. The play was produced in May, 1952, at the Poets' Theatre (of which Eberhart was co-founder) in Cambridge, Massachusetts. *The Visionary Farms*, which records the collapse of a family's fortune, is a satire on hucksterism. "Hurricane" Ransom misappropriates more than a million dollars from the protagonist, Fahnstock, and leaves him on the verge of financial ruin. On another level, the play is a study of American enterprise and a protest against greed. Eberhart's verse dramas are largely considered to be experiments, and though they are interesting adjuncts of the poet's craft, they are not among his finer achievements.

ACHIEVEMENTS

Richard Eberhart filled one of the fifty chairs of the American Academy of Arts and Letters and served as honorary president of the Poetry Society of America. Among his other distinguished honors are the Shelley Memorial Award in 1952, an Academy Award in Literature from the National Institute of Arts and Letters in 1955, the Bollingen Prize for Poetry in 1962, the Pulitzer Prize in 1966 for *Selected Poems, 1930-1965* (New Directions), the Academy of American Poets Fellowship in 1969, the National Book Award in 1977 for *Collected Poems: 1930-1976*, and the Frost Medal in 1986. He served as consultant in poetry (poet laureate) to the Library of Congress (1959-1961) and as poet laureate of New Hampshire. Philosophical and timeless matters of human life are explored throughout his work in unpretentious language and with gentle wit and humor. Eberhart's poetic career spanned six decades, and the poet served as a model of inspiration to such poets as Sydnea Lea, Dion Pincus, Richard Moore, Michael Benedikt, and Leo Connellan.

BIOGRAPHY

Richard Ghormley Eberhart grew up on his family's estate, Burr Oaks, in Austin, Minnesota. His early life was almost idyllic. His father, Alpha LaRue Eberhart, the son of a Methodist minister, typified the American Dream, having worked his way up from being a farmhand at the age of fourteen to becoming a business owner at the age of twenty-one. Working for the Hormel company, where he trained as a salesperson, he accumulated a fortune; by the time his son Richard was born, he had been able to buy Burr Oaks, an eighteen-room house on forty acres of land. Here the poet, his brother Dryden (b. 1902), and his sister Elizabeth

(b. 1910) enjoyed financial security until the year following the poet's graduation from high school, when tragedy struck both his mother and his father.

In 1921, a trusted member of the Hormel enterprise was found to have embezzled more than a million dollars from the company. As a result, the poet's father lost his accumulated wealth. The more serious catastrophe, however, was the poet's mother's lung cancer, which caused excruciating pain from the fall of 1921 to her death on June 22, 1922. Eberhart, who was then eighteen, stayed out of college for a year to help take care of her. It was the most profound experience of the poet's life, and it provided an impetus for his poetry and for his exploration of the meaning of suffering, what is real and unreal, the mystery of creation, and the place of the imagination in art.

Eberhart graduated from Dartmouth College in 1926. For a while, he worked as a floorwalker in a department store and as an advertising copywriter, and then shipped out as a deckhand on a tramp steamer going around the world. He jumped ship at Port Said, Egypt, and made his way to England. In 1927, he went to St. John's College, Cambridge University, where he earned a second B.A. in 1929.

The following year, 1930-1931, he served as tutor to the son of King Prajadhipok of Siam. Upon his return to the United States, he became a graduate student at Harvard University but decided not to go on for his doctoral degree. He taught at St. Mark's School from 1933 to 1940; during this time, he was responsible for bringing W. H. Auden as a guest member of the faculty for a month.

Eberhart and his wife, Helen Elizabeth Butcher, were married on August 29, 1941. The couple would have two children: Richard Butcher Eberhart, called Dikkon, and Margaret Ghormley Eberhart, called Gretchen.

After Dikkon's birth, in 1942, the Eberharts moved to Florida, where the poet received a commission as lieutenant in the United States Naval Reserve and served as a theoretical gunnery instructor. He was later transferred to the Aerial Free Gunnery Training Unit in Dam Neck, Virginia, where he wrote "The Fury of Aerial Bombardment" in the summer of 1944.

The breakthrough in Eberhart's career came with

his appointment to the faculty of Dartmouth in 1956. He also taught each spring term at the University of Florida in Gainesville in addition to serving as poet-in-residence at Dartmouth. After Eberhart's official retirement in 1970, he continued living in Hanover, New Hampshire, until his death at the age of 101 on June 9, 2005.

ANALYSIS

In his poems, Richard Eberhart returned again and again to the theme of death: death-in-life and life-in-death. His poems are, at once, a stay against oblivion and a bid for immortality. In his essay "Poetry as a Creative Principle" (in *Of Poetry and Poets*), Eberhart claimed that poetry is "a spell against death." As long as the essence of one's life exists in one's recorded work, there is immortality.

A Bravery of Earth, Eberhart's first published work, is a long philosophical and autobiographical narrative that establishes the dichotomy between the push toward life, harmony, and order and the corresponding horrors that are a constant pull toward the grave.

"THE GROUNDHOG"

"The Groundhog," perhaps Eberhart's most anthologized and acclaimed poem, is the epitome of the duality that characterizes his verse. The poem serves as a kind of memento mori that unites all living creatures in their temporality. Focusing on a dead groundhog, it develops the paradox of life-in-death. The poem additionally expresses the poet's belief that poetry is a gift of the gods—a mystical power that is relative, never absolute.

"The Groundhog" is one of four or five poems that Eberhart claimed were given to him. In a 1982 interview printed in *Negative Capability*, he described this mystical experience. These "given poems," Eberhart stated, came from "far beyond or underneath the rational mind" and hence are unusually powerful. In such an experience, he speculated, one is "allied with world consciousness." Commenting specifically on "The Groundhog," he explained that the poem was composed in "twenty minutes of heightened awareness" after he saw a dead groundhog on a friend's farm.

The body was open and the belly was seething with maggots. So here was a small dead animal, as dead as could be, and yet he was full of life, an absolute paradox. . . . He seemed to have more life in him being eaten up by maggots than if he were running along in the fields with nature harmoniously in him.

The poem cites three encounters with a dead groundhog. The first takes place "in June, amid golden fields." Here, in "vigorous summer," the animal's form began its "senseless change." The sight of it without its senses makes the poet's own "senses waver dim/ Seeing nature ferocious in him." He pokes the animal with a stick and notes that it is alive with maggots.

In autumn, the speaker returns to the place where he saw the dead groundhog. This time, "the sap [was] gone out of the groundhog,/ But the bony sodden hulk remained." The speaker's previous reaction of love and loathing, the revulsion that was the first response of the senses, is no longer present. "In intellectual chains, . . . mured up in the wall of wisdom," he brings intellect into play. He thinks about and applies reason to the experience of seeing the dead animal. In another summer, then, he takes to the fields again, "massive and burning, full of life," and chances upon the spot where the groundhog lies. "There was only a little hair left,/ And bones bleaching in the sunlight."

After three years, the poet returns again, but this time "there is no sign of the groundhog." It is "whirling summer" once more, and as the speaker's hand covers a "withered heart," he thinks of

> China and of Greece,
> Of Alexander in his tent;
> Of Montaigne in his tower,
> Of Saint Theresa in her wild lament.

Eberhart attributed the success of "The Groundhog" to the fact that he refused to delete these final lines. At a writer's discussion group in the Harvard area, where Eberhart joined other poets and read his work aloud, he was urged to end the poem with the description of the dead creature—before the mention of China and Greece, of the soldier, the philosopher, and the saint. Eberhart pointed out that the purposeful lives of these notable people distinguish them from a dead animal, the groundhog. Perhaps it can be said that an ordinary man would never have noticed the small rotting thing lying in the field had a poet not called attention to its demise. An animal leaves only bones that in time disappear; however, the lives of great men and women endure throughout time and are recorded in their works. The final lines of Eberhart's poem celebrate human achievement, the life-in-death that is beyond decay.

"FOR A LAMB"

In juxtaposition to "The Groundhog," "For a Lamb," an earlier poem about a dead animal, anticipates and highlights the import of the later work. In a field near Cambridge, England, in 1928, the speaker sees a dead lamb among daisies. "But the guts were out for crows to eat." The speaker asks, "Where's the lamb?" and then answers, "Say he's in the wind somewhere,/ Say, there's a lamb in the daisies." Although there is the sense of death as a fusion with life, there is no person in the poem to give meaning to existence. The lamb lives only because someone, a poet with creative imagination, has marked its being in the world. When there is human significance, death-in-life is transformed into life-in-death.

Eberhart believed that poetry comes out of suffering, and it was his mother's death that brought this awareness. Before she died, he had stayed out of college a year to help take care of her. According to a 1983 essay published in *Negative Capability*, this was for Eberhart "the most profound experience of my life, one that begot my poetry, an experience of depth that was inexpressible." Fifty-five years later, in an essay entitled "The Real and the Unreal," the adult Eberhart ponders the meaning of this early suffering. From memory, he says, "as part of the mystery of creation, flow poetry and music, manifold works of the imagination." One of his poems asserts that it is "the willowy Day-Bed of past time/ that taught death in the substratum." These lines exemplify Eberhart's thoughts in "The Theory of Poetry" that the first experience of the death of a loved one teaches "the bitterness but the holy clarity of truth."

LIFE-IN-DEATH AND DEATH-IN-LIFE

The final stanza of the poem "1934," reprinted in *Collected Poems 1930-1986*, defines Eberhart's premise about poetry and "life-in-death."

And I have eased reality and fiction
Into a kind of intellectual fruition
Strength in solitude, life in death,
Compassion by suffering, love in strife,
And ever and still the weight of mystery
Arrows a way between my words and me.

As a philosophical poet, Eberhart explores life's dualities. In "How I Write Poetry," he states that "everything about poetry is relative rather than absolute." Commenting on "The Cancer Cells," a poem that brings to mind his mother's terminal illness, the poet writes that the cancer cells photographed in *Life* magazine aroused in him an awareness of the simultaneity of the lethal and the beautiful, another poignant reminder of death-in-life.

In "Meditation Two," Eberhart notes that since "the Garden of Eden/ When Eve offered man the fruit of the womb and of life," human beings have been locked in dualism, "so that from the opposites of good and evil, flesh and spirit,/ Damnation and redemption, he is never absent/ But truly is fixed in a vise of these opposites." Art is a "triumph of nature/ Before the worm takes over," and it is the poet's job to "sing the harmony of the instant of knowing/ When all things dual become a unity."

The duality of the person as human and as a kind of creator and god is evident in "New Hampshire, February." Eberhart said the poem was written in the late 1930's, before he was married. One cold winter evening, he was staying in Kensington, in a cabin heated only by a kitchen stove. Two wasps fell through the roof onto the stove. At first the insects were numb, but as they moved to the center of the stove, they became lively. The poet described how he played God and shoved the creatures toward the heat, where they would become lively and buzz their wings; he would then push them away and watch them become gelid once more. The philosophical implications of this act in relation of persons to God led to the poem that concludes,

The moral of this is plain.
But I will shirk it.
You will not like it. And
God does not live to explain.

Humans' purposeful nature sets them apart from insects and animals, from wasps, spiders, gnats, seals, terns, cats, tree swallows, owls, field mice, groundhogs, and squirrels. Creatures obey "the orders of nature/ Without knowing them," but the poet who observes their blessed ignorance comments that "it is what man does not know of God/ Composes the visible poem of the world" ("On a Squirrel Crossing the Road in Autumn, in New England").

HORRORS OF WAR

"The poetry of tragedy is never dead," Eberhart states in "Am I My Neighbor's Keeper?" "If it were not so," he says, "I would not dream/ On principles so deep they have no ending,/ Nor on the ambiguity of what things ever seem./ The truth is hid and shaped in veils of error." The question of death in war, of humankind's capacity for destruction and God's tolerance of evil, is addressed in a series of poems Eberhart wrote during World War II. "The Fury of Aerial Bombardment" seems to be the best known and most anthologized of the lot. This poem's speaker says, "You would think the fury of aerial bombardment/ Would rouse God to relent." Since the time of Cain, humans have killed other humans. "Is God by definition indifferent, beyond us all?" the poet asks. The ruthlessness and senselessness of war are exposed in a lament over the death of two young men, Van Wettering and Averill, "Names on a list, whose faces I do not recall."

In "At the End of War," "God, awful and powerful beyond the sky's acre/ . . . looks down upon fighting men" and sees their bloody folly and their wickedness. The poet asks God to "forgive them, that all they do is fight/ In blindness and fury." The poem concludes with a further prayer: "And may he learn not to fight/ And never to kill, but love."

"Brotherhood of Men," an account of the death march of Bataan, similarly bewails the horrors of war. Its speaker tells what it was like to be a prisoner of war, "caught . . . on the Rock. At Corregidor/ Caged with the enemy." Here Eberhart is unsparing in graphic detail, telling of "bones softened by black malnutrition," of ulcerous legs and "heads swelled like cabbages before the soft death-rattle." He speaks of "days unendurable," when "madness was manifest, infernal the struggle."

Urine was drunk by many, rampant was chaos,
Came wild men at each other, held off attackers,
Some slit the throats of the dead,
Drank the blood outright, howled wailing,
Slit the wrists of the living, others
with knives, or with fangs ravenous,
I saw them drinking the blood of victims.

Horrible as war is, however, the narrator finds redemption in the brotherhood of man. He has a profound conviction "that we were at our peak when in the depths." The tortured group of men who "lived close to life when cuffed by death,/ had visions of brotherhood when [they] were broken,/ learned compassion beyond the curse of passion."

LIFE'S BLESSINGS

Though Eberhart railed against the evil in human nature that leads to violence and war, he was able to transcend death and destruction to acknowledge simply that to be human is to be imperfect. The poem called "A Meditation" concludes with an exhortation to let one's awareness of evil and death purify and heighten one's enjoyment of life's blessings, "easing a little the burden of our suffering/ Before we blow like the wind away."

Eberhart stated in "Learning from Nature" that he was taught "acceptance of irrationality." He recognized "the supreme authority of the imagination" because "life longs to a perfection it never achieves." In a poem whose title is an exit, "A Way Out," Eberhart noted the mocking nature of time: "but I would mock it,/ Throw hurricane force against its devil,/ Commanding it to stop." The poet acknowledged the Buddha and Jesus Christ, for they "give mankind examples of the way to go/ The ineffable, and the active means to know." The speaker wrestles with doubt and belief. His warfare is that of rationality, he says, and he "could not abrogate [his] reason East or West." In the end, however, "We can sense/ That old death will give way to new life/ As new mornings grow, Spring comes over the land."

"Love is the mystery in which to rejoice," Eberhart states in "Sphinx," and readers must not mistake his intense interest in and focus on death as indicating somberness or a lack of joy. "The Groundhog Revisiting" is a poem that celebrates life. The occasion is the wedding of the poet's daughter. A groundhog has come along and deflowered the garden; Eberhart wants to dissuade the groundhog from such destruction, not kill it, so he pours gasoline down its hole. "It's on with marriage, down with the groundhogs," he says, as he reflects on Gretchen as a child, when she could "turn six cartwheels/ Outwitting my power to put on paper/ Pure agility and grace in action." The poet offers a kind of prayer. "Grace this company in some retrospect," he says. "We are here to celebrate love and belief,/ May time bless these believers, love give them grace."

It is because of humanity's impermanence that life is precious, and Eberhart recognizes this in "Three Kids," another poem inspired by his daughter, Gretchen. He fumbles for words to describe his feelings at seeing three frisky little goats frolicking around her in a bright meadow.

> If I lived a hundred years
> No ink of mine from a passionate hand
> Could communicate to you, dear reader,
> Essence of ecstasy, this ecstatic sight
> Of joy of life, limitless freedom,
> As the girl and the young kids leaped and played.

Eberhart's delight in such youthful exuberance is informed by his awareness of death. "Flux" serves up a litany of tragedy: "the gods of this world/ Have taken the daughter of my neighbor,/ Who died this day of encephalitis," a boy, "in his first hour on his motorbike,/ Met death in a head-on collision," and a sea farmer "was tripped in the wake of a cruiser./ He went down in the cold waters of the summer." Death is sudden and inexorable. "Life is stranger than any of us expected," the poet concludes; "there is a somber, imponderable fate" that will annihilate all.

DEATH AS PREEMINENT THEME

For Eberhart, is was necessary to acknowledge the horror of death to move beyond it. Poems that embrace the theme of death represent a sizable part of his canon.

"Orchard" pictures a family, the poet's own, sitting in an automobile among fruit trees, grieving in deep silence. They have learned of the mother's impending death. In the middle time of her life, when she is "most glorious" and most beautiful, she is "stalked/ By the stark shape of malignant disease,/ And her face was holy white like all desire." "All of life and all of death

were there" among the fruit trees in the evening, but the final line says that "the strong right of human love was there" as well.

In "Grave Piece," the speaker, presumably the poet himself, says, "Death, I try to get into you," and later repeats, "I must discover inexorable Death." He feels compelled to attempt the impossible, to make "poetry to break the marble word."

Although Eberhart believed that poetry is a gift of the gods, he recognized that it requires a certain sacrifice: "Every poet is a sacrificial spirit." The poet bears this burden gladly, "gay as a boy tossing his cap up," for even when he is called to write "of tragic things and heavy/ He lives in the senses' gaiety."

Eberhart believed that the ideal life would be lived "near the pitch that is madness." He explained that the crucial word is "near." To be mad or insane would be to fail to capitalize on one's potential, but to live near madness, without being mad, would afford heightened awareness that makes poetry. For Eberhart, poetry is the bid for immortality that ultimately defeats death. It is the only way to deal with the immutable fact of mortality.

CRITICAL COMMENTARY

Eberhart's poems seldom display a light touch; they are serious and philosophical, and critics sometimes claim that they are uneven. Two advocates offer strong counters to this claim. In *Negative Capability*'s special issue on Eberhart, Arthur Gregor asserts that "poetry is significant only if it articulates the great and timeless matters of human life, anything less than that falls short of its ancient obligation." He says that Eberhart's work reminds him "of the invisible realities" at a time when "trivia has replaced the great matters of poetry." In the same issue, Sydnea Lea says that "Dick's poems, like the man himself, are engaged with matters that matter."

Certainly an examination of Eberhart's work will show that death-in-life is a consistent and predominant theme. To celebrate life, according to Eberhart, it is necessary to probe its opposite—death. "It is not necessary to live long to sense the abysmal depths of despair," he wrote as he cataloged some of the horrors: prolonged and problematical illnesses such as his mother's cancer, the pain of wrecked bodies in war, the deep eyes of those justly accused of crime, and the awesome spectacle of mental imbalance. "It is impossible," Eberhart added "to conceive of great poetry being written without a knowledge of suffering."

Eberhart stressed the fact that he was a meliorist who adjudicated between opposite ideas. "I don't accept anyone's idea as absolute, or I try not to," he says, and when one met the poet, this aspect of his personality became immediately clear. "So what can one make of all of this?" was a typical Eberhart statement, and his poems set out to respond to that question—to determine what one is to make of the grand and knotty complexity that is life. Eberhart was a poet whose creativity is a spell against death. Words from "Hardening into Print" sum up his work: "This glimpse is of an immaculate joy/ Heart suffers for, and wishes to keep."

OTHER MAJOR WORKS

PLAYS: *The Apparition*, pr. 1950; *The Visionary Farms*, pr. 1952; *Triptych*, pr. 1955; *Collected Verse Plays*, 1962; *Devils and Angels*, pr. 1962; *The Mad Musician*, pr. 1962; *The Bride from Mantua*, pr. 1964; *Chocorua*, pb. 1981.

NONFICTION: *Poetry as a Creative Principle*, 1952; *Of Poetry and Poets*, 1979.

BIBLIOGRAPHY

Engel, Bernard F. *Richard Eberhart*. New York: Twayne, 1971. An introductory biography and critical study of selected works. Includes a bibliography of Eberhart's works.

Fox, Margalit. "Richard Eberhart, 101, Poet Who Wed Sense and Intellect." *The New York Times*, June 14, 2005, p. A21. This obituary contains a short biography of the poet and notes his many achievements.

Ginsberg, Allen. *To Eberhart from Ginsberg: A Letter About "Howl," 1956, An Explanation by Allen Ginsberg of His Publication "Howl" and Richard Eberhart's "New York Times" Article "West Coast Rhythms."* Lincoln, Mass.: Penmaen Press, 1976. Ginsberg's essay casts light on both Eberhart and the times in which both poets lived.

Hoffman, Daniel G. "Hunting a Master Image: The Poetry of Richard Eberhart." Special issue of *Hollins Critic* 1, no. 4 (October, 1964). Devoted to Eberhart's poetics.

Lea, Sydney, Jay Parini, and M. Robin Barone, eds. *Richard Eberhart: A Celebration*. Hanover, N.H.: Kenyon Hill, 1980. A collection of essays on Eberhart and his work.

Negative Capability 6 (Spring/Summer, 1986). This special issue on Eberhart contains letters to the poet; commentaries and critical articles on his work; an interview; and poems, essays, and addresses by Eberhart. It is edited by Sue Brannan Walker and Jane Mayhall.

Roache, Joel. *Richard Eberhart*. New York: Oxford University Press, 1971. This book is a biography that covers the twists and turns of Eberhart's career from 1904 to 1961. Contains a selected bibliography.

Van Dore, Wade. *Richard Eberhart: Poet of Life in Death*. Tampa, Fla.: American Studies Press, 1982. A small pamphlet that deals specifically with Eberhart's study of death.

Wright, Stuart. *Richard Eberhart: A Descriptive Bibliography, 1921-1987*. Westport, Conn.: Meckler, 1989. Bibliography that looks at the works produced by Eberhart through 1987.

Sue Walker

W. D. EHRHART

Born: Roaring Spring, Pennsylvania; September 30, 1948

PRINCIPAL POETRY

A Generation of Peace, 1975
Rootless, 1977
Empire, 1978
The Awkward Silence, 1980
The Samisdat Poems, 1980
The Outer Banks, and Other Poems, 1984
To Those Who Have Gone Home Tired, 1984
Just for Laughs, 1990
The Distance We Travel, 1993
Beautiful Wreckage: New and Selected Poems, 1999
Sleeping with the Dead, 2006

OTHER LITERARY FORMS

In addition to winning critical acclaim with his poetry, W. D. Ehrhart has distinguished himself in the fields of memoir and personal commentary. He has published four volumes on his experiences during and after the Vietnam War as well as an investigative account and oral history of how the war affected the members of his boot camp platoon. He has published hundreds of personal essays and short opinion pieces on various topics in newspapers and magazines, many of which appear in his 1991 collection *In the Shadow of Vietnam: Essays, 1977-1991*.

Ehrhart has also made his mark as an editor and critic. He has edited two anthologies of Vietnam War poetry and has coedited an additional anthology of Vietnam War poetry and an anthology of Korean War literature.

ACHIEVEMENTS

While he has never enjoyed great commercial success, W. D. Ehrhart has been widely credited with establishing the American experience in Vietnam as a subject for poetry and, as Donald Ringnalda has written, is generally considered the "poet laureate of the [Vietnam] war." He has especially been in demand as a speaker and lecturer at academic conferences and universities. He served as a visiting professor of war and social consequences at the William Joiner Center, University of Massachusetts at Boston (1990), as writer-in-residence with the National Writers' Voice Project of the Young Men's Christian Association in Detroit (1996), and as a guest-in-residence at the University of Illinois at Champaign-Urbana (1998). In 2001, he held a research fellowship with the American Studies Department, University of Wales, Swansea, United Kingdom. He has received a grant from the Mary Rinehart Foundation (1980), fellowships in prose and in poetry from the Pennsylvania Council on the Arts (1981, 1988), the President's Medal from Veterans for Peace, and a Pew Fellowship in the Arts for Poetry (1993). He was also featured in episode 5, "America Takes Charge," of the Public Broadcasting Service's series *Vietnam: A Television History* and was invited to edit a special issue of the journal *War, Literature, and the Arts* (Fall/Winter, 1997).

BIOGRAPHY

William Daniel Ehrhart was born in Roaring Spring, Pennsylvania, but spent his formative years in Perkasie, Pennsylvania, where his father was a minister. The third of four sons, Ehrhart excelled in school, but the escalating conflict in Vietnam left him feeling honor-bound to postpone college in favor of military service. Reminding his parents that they had not reared him "to let somebody else's kids fight America's wars," he secured their reluctant permission to enlist in the Marine Corps at age seventeen, immediately following his high school graduation in June, 1966.

Ehrhart served in Vietnam with an infantry battalion from 1967 to 1968 and was wounded in the battle for Hue during the Tet Offensive of 1968. Discharged in 1969 with the rank of sergeant, he went on to Swarthmore College, where he became active in the antiwar movement and wrote his first published works before his graduation in 1973.

While still at Swarthmore, Ehrhart gained national recognition as a poet in *Winning Hearts and Minds* (1972), a collection of Vietnam War poetry dedicated to the cause of ending the United States' involvement. Eight of Ehrhart's early poems appeared in this collection.

After college, Ehrhart went to sea as a merchant marine and later tried both newspaper reporting and high school teaching along with earning an M.A. in creative writing at the University of Illinois at Chicago in 1978. He married in 1981, and in 1985, he made his home in Philadelphia, Pennsylvania. He earned a Ph.D. in 2000 from the University of Wales at Swansea, United Kingdom. Although he has occasionally taken short-term teaching assignments, he bills himself as an "independent scholar and teacher," earning his living primarily through his writing and his speaking engagements.

ANALYSIS

H. Bruce Franklin, in 1995, spoke for the critical consensus in praising W. D. Ehrhart for his "concision and avoidance of the mannerisms that have made 'poetry' seem like a coterie activity." Ehrhart's "distinctive flat voice speaking in a deceptively plain style," Franklin contends, gives his poetry a "visceral power" and forms the perfect stylistic complement to the "rare fusion of personal and historical vision" for which he has been widely praised. A constant theme throughout Ehrhart's poetry is the personal and collective disillusionment his generation suffered as a result of the U.S. intervention in Vietnam. Many of his poems are unabashedly polemical, and the great majority are written in free verse, Ehrhart's intention being to reach the widest possible audience. As Vince Gotera has pointed out, however, Ehrhart's apparent simplicity and earnestness belie a self-conscious artistry that involves a carefully considered selection and arrangement of language and even occasional forays into traditional poetic techniques and forms. Although he first came to prominence with his antiwar poetry, Ehrhart has not confined himself to that theme. His later poems, on a wide range of subjects, reveal a refreshing capacity for self-ironic reflection and an unabashed appreciation for the moments of grace, love, and contentment he continues to find in his own life.

A GENERATION OF PEACE

A Generation of Peace first established Ehrhart as a truth-teller par excellence and as an insightful interpreter of how the American cultural narrative failed the United States in Vietnam. His Vietnam experiences are crystallized in a series of seemingly simple and straightforward poetic vignettes illustrating the existential character of the war. "Guerrilla War," for example, bespeaks his frustration at finding himself unable to distinguish between friend and foe. The poem concludes with the honest admission that "After a while,/ You quit trying."

"Hunting" turns on the realization that, contrary to the American mythos that brought him to this point, Ehrhart has "never hunted anything in [his] whole life/ except other men." However, "such thoughts," he affirms, are quickly eclipsed by more immediate concerns, such as "chow, and sleep,/ and how much longer till I change my socks."

One of the most widely praised and culturally resonant poems to come out of this collection is "A Relative Thing," a title that Ehrhart intended as a play on the adage, "You can pick your friends but not your relatives." The poem strikes a tone of bitter recrimination over the willful ignorance of the generation that sent its sons to fight in Vietnam and bears dramatic witness to the bru-

tal realities behind much of the sanitizing rhetoric of the era. "We have been Democracy on Zippo raids,/ burning houses to the ground," the speaker complains, and made the "instruments/ of your pigeon-breasted fantasies."

"Making the Children Behave" likewise challenges the previous generation's vision of American rectitude and stands in opposition to a pervasive tendency among veteran-authors to focus on American trauma to the exclusion of the Vietnamese point of view. The poem culminates in an ironic epiphany occasioned by the speaker's earlier sense of cultural and even racial superiority. When the people in the villages through which he passed "tell stories to their children/ of the evil/ that awaits misbehavior," he wonders, "is it me they conjure?"

ROOTLESS, EMPIRE, AND THE SAMISDAT POEMS

The chapbooks *Rootless* and *Empire*, along with *The Samisdat Poems*, contain further reflections on the war's continuing effects on Ehrhart's life and the life of the country. The poem "Letter," for example, is addressed to the North Vietnamese soldier who almost killed Ehrhart in the battle for Hue during the Tet Offensive. The backdrop to the poem is the United States' 1976 centennial celebration, for which "we've found again our inspiration," the speaker wryly observes, "by recalling where we came from/ and forgetting where we've been." The poem ends with the speaker's fervent hope that Vietnam will "remember Ho Chi Minh/ was a poet" and not let their victory "come down/ to nothing."

These collections also contain reflections on perennial human themes, such as relationships, aging, and even the consolations to be found in nature. "After the Fire" is especially representative of Ehrhart's ability to celebrate the experience of love in poignant and even explicit imagery. "Turning Thirty," in fresh language, bespeaks the confusion of finding oneself suddenly older but not necessarily wiser.

TO THOSE WHO HAVE GONE HOME TIRED

A maturing of Ehrhart's vision as a public poet, one committed to addressing a growing political and popular amnesia over Vietnam, is evident in *To Those Who Have Gone Home Tired*. A restlessness and a self-ironic sense of frustration creep into many of the poems. The title poem is a far-ranging and bitter recrimination over the rapaciousness and brutality that Ehrhart sees as continuing to characterize post-Vietnam American life. "The Invasion of Grenada" likewise bespeaks his despair at popular and political appropriations of the Vietnam experience. Rejecting monuments and commemorative gestures, the speaker declares that he only wanted "a simple recognition" of the limits of U.S. power and an "understanding/ that the world . . . is not ours." What he really wanted is "an end to monuments."

The collection also contains some of his finest and most moving poems on subjects other than war. "Gifts" and "Continuity" express Ehrhart's love for his wife, while "New Jersey Pine Barrens" and "The Outer Banks" recount idyllic retreats into the world of nature. Just under the surface, and often explicitly noted, is an anxious sense that the saving graces of love and nature are only transitory and never unalloyed for someone who has committed himself to the cause of truthtelling. From the world's standpoint, he realizes, he is too readily dismissed as a "farmer of dreams" ("The Farmer") and is even considered boorish for his persistent refusal to accommodate himself to the world as it is ("Sound Advice").

THE DISTANCE WE TRAVEL

Inspired by his own trip back to Vietnam, *The Distance We Travel* is remarkable for illustrating Ehrhart's continuing capacity for reexamination and self-ironic reflection. His frustration now is directed at a culture that has appropriated the Vietnam experience for both political manipulation and popular entertainment ("For a Coming Extinction"). As the title poem and at least two others suggest, Ehrhart's former bitterness has been mitigated by the openness and friendliness he has found among the postwar Vietnamese. The result seems to have been a modicum of peace with his past, a resolution reinforced by two of his most revealing poems about his present joys, "Making Love in the Garden" and "Star Light, Star Bright."

MOSTLY NOTHING HAPPENS

One of Ehrhart's longest poems, running to 156 lines, *Mostly Nothing Happens* first appeared in two separate journals and was later reissued as a pamphlet

in 1996. It also appears in *Beautiful Wreckage*. A frankly autobiographical and personal statement, the poem places Ehrhart's present life squarely within the ironic context of his past and explores America's still unresolved legacy of racial tension. The backdrop is Ehrhart's refusal to give up on the American dream of brotherhood. He continues to live in an integrated inner-city neighborhood in the hope that his child would not "reach the age of seventeen/ with no one in her life/ who isn't white." The realization that so many of the angry young African American men he must pass day after day have no inkling of his good intentions and even resent his presence leaves him feeling understandably anxious. This anxiety occasions a poignant reflection on the first African American friend Ehrhart ever made and how this man's gentle strength helped him get through Marine recruit training. His friend, however, later died in Vietnam—an ironic fate that Ehrhart seems to hold up as an example of how the war itself only helped to exacerbate the legacy of racial disharmony and distrust he now confronts. The result, he realizes, is a depressingly familiar feeling: "Every day I'm always on patrol."

BEAUTIFUL WRECKAGE

A retrospective as well as a collection of new poems, *Beautiful Wreckage* stands as a fine introduction to Ehrhart's poetry and themes. The title poem speaks to the issue of strictly factual accuracy versus authenticity in a larger literary sense.

The collection also contains some of his finest occasional poems reflecting on his life and on the manners and mores of contemporary American life. "Not for You" is a painfully honest statement of frustrated hopes and expectations. "Prayer for My Enemies" is an ironic statement of the hypocritical pretense that Ehrhart sees as endemic to organized religion. "Rehobeth, One Last Time" shows how our self-indulgent tendency toward serial monogamy has affected a friend's life. Other poems suggest that he has made peace with his parents and with his own past ("Visiting My Parents' Grave," "What Goes Around Comes Around"). "A Meditation on Family Geography and a Prayer for My Daughter" expresses his fervent wish that his daughter will grow up to find "a place in the world/ surrounded by people who care."

SLEEPING WITH THE DEAD

Sleeping with the Dead, a collection of eleven poems, takes a look at various ways that death occurs and how people respond when confronted with death. "What Better Way to Begin" describes an anticipatory scene on "Millennium Eve" in which a father and daughter prepare to witness an explosion of fireworks in Philadelphia, the city of "brotherly love." The choice of place in this poem is ironic because the father and daughter appear to feel a sense of doom rather than a sense of patriotism while watching "the bombs bursting in air." Through images of explosive red skies and mutilated body parts, Ehrhart connotes the lasting impressions of war violence. Ehrhart's often-repeated theme of American disillusionment is evident as the daughter—who coincidentally shares the name of Ehrhart's real-life daughter—clutches her father's hand "till the last bomb's blunt concussion/ fades away as if it never were." Even though war violence may be necessary to protect a nation, Ehrhart emphasizes how its aftermath can rob one's patriotic zeal and inevitably kill an aspect of the human spirit.

"All About Death" gives a vivid account of how powerless people are in controlling their own mortalities. Ehrhart personifies death as a malicious being who "rips your heart out through your throat/ and walks away laughing." This thirty-two-line, free-verse poem is a rant about death, and the venomous tone that the speaker uses suggests that he has witnessed an incidence of senseless death. To make the accusation that "Death feels/ sorry for nothing and no one" further underscores the disdain in the speaker's tone. The speaker ends the poem by recalling how his wife "still cries out in her sleep for her [deceased] mommy." Although the level of diction in the poem conveys an adult perspective, the choice of the word "mommy" suggests that death has the ability to make people feel as though their autonomy is stripped away when death occurs, regardless of their age.

"Gravestones at Oxwich Bay" and "The Orphan" explore the feeling of emptiness that often lingers among family members after a loved one's death. Beginning with the death of an infant daughter, "Gravestones at Oxwich Bay" memorializes the sequential passing of a family. For the mother's death to be remembered as "earth exchanged for heaven," Ehrhart emphasizes the old adage that parents are not supposed to outlive their children. Although "The Orphan" also makes a poignant statement about the agonizing feeling of emptiness that results after death, the poem employs a child/adult perspective. For this "orphan" to feel as though "home [is] long gone," Ehrhart implies that a parent's death often engenders a feeling of abandonment and that death is no easier to accept even if it occurs at an age when one is expected to be prepared.

In "Home Before Morning" and "Seminar on the Nature of Reality," Ehrhart pays homage to two people whom he describes as having displayed bravery in the face of death. "Home Before Morning" describes the unyielding work of a wife and mother who never stopped working, even when her body began to shut down. The poem is also infused with a bit a political protest as Ehrhart chastises "the posturing of presidents/ and statesmen who have never heard the sound/ of teenaged soldiers crying for their mothers." By juxtaposing the image of leaders making unconscious decisions to send young men into battle, with the idea of a dying mother sacrificing herself "to be an advocate for broken souls," Ehrhart illustrates that those who are revered are often the ones less worthy of praise. In "Seminar on the Nature of Reality," Ehrhart provides a similar account of the fearlessness with which a person confronts death. While Ehrhart may suggest a sense of powerlessness in writing, "when things are very large or very small/ they don't behave the way we think they should," he emphasizes a metaphysical mood, as well as an inevitable aspect of the human psyche—to decipher between image and reality.

"All About Love," "Manning the Walls," and "Kosovo" explore present-day threats of death and destruction. "All About Love" conveys a sense of disconnect between the people and the policies that are supposed to protect a society. Both "Manning the Walls" and "Kosovo" suggest that the threat of mass destruction is not limited to originating with foreign terrorists, and that a nation must first look at the enemies that lie within its own borders.

"Sleeping with the Dead," the last poem in the collection, explores the theme of lost love, which also can cause one to feel a sense of death. The poem begins with the speaker confessing in a somewhat sarcastic tone that he never really loved the person whom he claims "almost drove me mad/ to let go." The speaker's confession initially appears to be more of a victim's declaration of independence against the power that love had over him nineteen years ago. Although he appears regretful for succumbing to love's power, the speaker accepts responsibility for letting go of his love. Ehrhart underscores the power of love to awaken the emotional side of human nature when the speaker states that this now-lost love once made him feel like he had been "raised from the dead/ after all those dead [he] slept with/ every night."

OTHER MAJOR WORKS

NONFICTION: *Vietnam-Perkasie: A Combat Marine Memoir*, 1983; *Going Back: An Ex-Marine Returns to Vietnam*, 1987; *Passing Time: Memoir of a Vietnam Veteran Against the War*, 1989; *In the Shadow of Vietnam: Essays, 1977-1991*, 1991; *Busted: A Vietnam Veteran in Nixon's America*, 1995; *The Madness of It All: Essays on War, Literature, and American Life*, 2002.

EDITED TEXTS: *Demilitarized Zones: Veterans After Vietnam*, 1976 (with Jan Barry); *Carrying the Darkness: American Indochina, The Poetry of the Vietnam War*, 1989; *Unaccustomed Mercy: Soldier-Poets of the Vietnam War*, 1989; *Retrieving Bones: Stories and Poems of the Korean War*, 1999 (with Philip K. Jason).

MISCELLANEOUS: *Ordinary Lives: Platoon 1005 and the Vietnam War*, 1999.

BIBLIOGRAPHY

Beidler, Philip D. *Re-writing America: Vietnam Authors in Their Generation*. Athens: University of Georgia Press, 1991. Argues that Ehrhart is best understood within the cultural context of his generation and sees his work as an attempt to reinstate the values and ideals the country failed to live up to in Vietnam.

Gotera, Vince F. *Radical Visions: Poetry by Vietnam Veterans*. Athens: University of Georgia Press, 1994. Remains the best overall introduction to Ehrhart's themes and technique. Gotera establishes Ehrhart as a serious artist and acknowledges his influence as a critic and editor.

Metres, Philip. *Behind the Lines: War Resistance Poetry on the American Homefront Since 1941*. Iowa City: University of Iowa Press, 2007. Discusses antiwar poetry in general, with chapters on the Vietnam War that provide perspective on Ehrhart's writing. Ehrhart recalls audience response to his reading of "A Relative Thing."

Ringnalda, Donald. *Fighting and Writing the Vietnam War*. Jackson: University Press of Mississippi, 1994. Argues that Ehrhart is one of a number of Vietnam-veteran writers whose disregard of literary convention reflects the unconventional nature of the war itself and forms a fitting strategy for challenging residual conventional wisdom.

Rottman, Larry, and Basil T. Paquet, eds. *Winning Hearts and Minds: War Poems by Vietnam Veterans*. New York: McGraw-Hill, 1972. Ehrhart debuted in this anthology. One of his most striking Vietnam poems, "Hunting," first appeared here.

Ryan, Maureen. *The Other Side of Grief: The Home Front and the Aftermath in American Narratives of the Vietnam War*. Amherst: University of Massachusetts Press, 2008. Examines Vietnam war literature primarily from its depictions of life in the United States during and after the war. Contains some references to Ehrhart.

Smith, Lorrie. "Against a Coming Extinction: W. D. Ehrhart and the Evolving Canon of Vietnam Veterans' Poetry." *War, Literature, and the Arts* 8, no. 2 (1996): 1-30. A lucid and insightful survey of Ehrhart's career and of his influence within the field.

Tal, Kali. *Worlds of Hurt: Reading the Literatures of Trauma*. New York: Cambridge University Press, 1996. Places Ehrhart squarely within the "literature of trauma" school. Tal sees Ehrhart as bearing an intensely personal witness to his traumatic experience and as resisting any and all attempts at appropriating or generalizing upon his experience.

Edward F. Palm
Updated by Theresa E. Dozier

James A. Emanuel

Born: Alliance, Nebraska; June 15, 1921

Principal poetry

The Treehouse, and Other Poems, 1968
At Bay, 1969
Panther Man, 1970
Black Man Abroad: The Toulouse Poems, 1978
A Chisel in the Dark: Poems, Selected and New,
  1980
The Broken Bowl: New and Uncollected Poems,
  1983
A Poet's Mind, 1983
Deadly James, and Other Poems, 1987
The Quagmire Effect, 1988
Whole Grain: Collected Poems, 1958-1989,
  1990
De la rage au cœur, 1992 (bilingual with French
  translations by Jean Migrenne)
Blues in Black and White, 1992 (with Godelieve
  Simons)
Reaching for Mumia: Sixteen Haiku, 1995
Jazz from the Haiku King, 1999

Other literary forms

James A. Emanuel's first book was written in prose, not poetry. His book *Langston Hughes* (1967) was one of the first detailed studies of Hughes's work. Unsatisfied with the scant critical attention given to black authors, Emanuel worked with Theodore L. Gross and edited *Dark Symphony: Negro Literature in America* (1968), the first book of its kind in nearly thirty years. A few years later, in 1972, he collaborated on another book, *How I Write Two*, this time with MacKinlay Kantor and Lawrence Osgood. *How I Write Two* explores the writing processes of several black poets, including Emanuel, Sonia Sanchez, and Gwendolyn Brooks. He served as general editor of the Broadside Critics series from 1970 to 1975. He has written a memoir, *The Force and the Reckoning* (2001), complete with poems and photos. Many of Emanuel's literary essays and book reviews appeared in books, periodicals, and journals.

Achievements

Although James A. Emanuel has been called one of the most overlooked poets of modern times, he has garnered some recognition as a critic. Arguably, his most notable achievement is the promotion of critical attention for black writers' work. He received the John Hay Whitney Fellowship (1952, 1953) and the Saxton Memorial Fellowship (1964). In 1966, Emanuel developed the first course in African American poetry to be offered at City College of New York. He also ran for a position on the Mount Vernon, New York, school board, but was defeated. "For 'Mr. Dudley,' a Black Spy" (from *Black Man Abroad*) describes the difficult experience. He was awarded two Fulbright scholarships, a professorship at the University of Grenoble in France from 1968 to 1969 and a professorship at the University of Warsaw in Poland from 1975 to 1976. Emanuel also received a Black American Literature Forum Special Distinction Award for poetry in 1978. In 1979, the American Biographical Institute named him among its Notable Americans. Emanuel invented the jazz-and-blues haiku during the 1990's. The form combines elements of jazz, blues, and the Japanese haiku. For his invention, he received the Sidney Bechet Creative Award in 1996. In 2007, he was honored with the Dean's Award for Distinguished Achievement from Columbia University.

Biography

James Andrew Emanuel, the fifth of seven children, was born in Alliance, Nebraska, to Cora Ann Mance and Alfred A. Emanuel, a farmer and railroad worker. Early on, Emanuel's parents instilled a love of language and narrative in him. He read widely, and by junior high school, he was writing detective stories and poetry. In 1939, he graduated high school and was named the class valedictorian. He took a job in Washington, D.C., as the confidential secretary to General Benjamin O. Davis, assistant inspector general of the War Department in the United States Army, and he later joined the United States Army, where he served as a staff sergeant with the Ninety-third Infantry Division in the Pacific. After World War II, he enrolled in Howard University in Washington, D.C., where he earned a B.A. degree. In 1950, he married Mattie Etha Johnson, whom he met after moving to Chicago, where he had begun attending Northwestern University and working as a civilian chief in the preinduction section of the Army and Air Force Induction Station. The couple had one child, James, Jr., who committed suicide in 1983. The couple was divorced in 1974. After earning an M.A. in 1953, Emanuel moved to New York and enrolled in a Ph.D. program at Columbia University. He earned the degree in 1962. Emanuel became an assistant professor at the City College of New York in 1962, where he would teach until 1984.

Emanuel's early work was published in college journals, but in 1958, his work began to appear in periodicals such as *The New York Times*, *Midwest Quarterly*, and *Freedomways*. In 1967, Emanuel published a critical study of Hughes, and in 1968, he coedited an anthology of African American literature, *Dark Symphony*. His first book of poetry, a collection of previously published poems, *The Treehouse, and Other Poems*, was also published in 1968.

In October of 1968, Emanuel moved to Seyssins and taught at the University of Grenoble, where he served as a Fulbright professor of American literature for a year. While living in France, he began working on poems later printed in *Panther Man*. From 1970 to 1975, he worked as general editor of the Broadside Critics Series, which published books about black poets, including Countée Cullen, Claude McKay, and Phillis Wheatley.

Emanuel served as a visiting professor of American literature at the University of Toulouse (1971-1973, 1979-1981) and Fulbright professor of American literature at the University of Warsaw (1975-1976). After his retirement from the City University of New York, Emanuel began to travel and live in Europe. Emanuel is often excluded from major anthologies, but some of his works, correspondence, and other documents are at the Library of Congress, Manuscript Division, Washington, D.C. Additional manuscripts and documents are housed in the collection at the Jay B. Hubbell Center for American Literary Historiography at Duke University in Durham, North Carolina.

ANALYSIS

James A. Emanuel's earlier poetry was largely influenced by English poets such as John Keats and William Shakespeare, but his relationship with Hughes and his close study of Hughes's work also influenced him. Some of Emanuel's poems contain vernacular, and many of them experiment with genres of music, including blues and jazz. Critics say his poems are precise and that he is adept at creating subtle phrases. Unlike the poems of many of the African American poets writing during the 1960's, Emanuel's poems rarely contain alternate spellings or innovative forms. Instead, his poems usually have rhymed quatrains and regular lines and stanzas. They are about youth, black experiences, war, manhood, and love.

THE TREEHOUSE, AND OTHER POEMS

Most of the poems in *The Treehouse, and Other Poems* were previously published in anthologies and periodicals, such as *Phylon*, *The New York Times*, and *Negro Digest*. The poems are traditional, but some reflect blues and jazz influence. Emanuel's serious poems are often about African Americans who were killed because of racism. Emmett Till, the fourteen-year-old boy who was tortured, murdered, and thrown into the Tallahatchie River in Mississippi in 1955 for whistling at a white woman, is coupled with the fairy river boy who swims forever. "Where Will Their Names Go Down?" remembers the unnamed who were subjected to similar hate crimes. "Fisherman" was inspired by time Emanual spent with his son. Other poems are about war, heroes, and the poetic process. Scholars suggest that *The Treehouse, and Other Poems* received little critical attention because the poems do not adhere to the militant, direct style of some of the African American poetry published during that time.

PANTHER MAN

Dedicated to Emanuel's City College of New York students, *Panther Man*, angry in tone, argues against racism in the United States. In the preface, Emanuel calls the volume "a reflection of personal, racially meaningful predicaments" compelled by "my feelings about the most abysmal evil in the modern world: American racism." The tone is harsher and more militant than that of *The Treehouse, and Other Poems*. Most of the poems mark Emanuel's distancing himself from the traditional poetic forms found in his earlier collection. The title poem is based on the 1969 slaying by Chicago police officers of Black Panthers Mark Clark and Fred Hampton, while "Whitey, Baby" criticizes systemic racism. *Panther Man* also contains tributes to African Americans, particularly poet Hughes and Muslim leader Malcolm X. "For the Fourth Grade, Prospect School: How I Became a Poet" and "Black Poet on the Firing Range" are about poets and how they compose, while "Fourteen" and "Sixteen, Yeah" are about youth.

BLACK MAN ABROAD

Black Man Abroad has four sections of poems arranged thematically: "The Toulouse Poems, Parts I and II," "The Warsaw Experiment," and "Occasionals." Most of the poems are set in Toulouse or another city in Western Europe, and many of them are longer and more complex than poems in earlier collections. The poems reveal speakers tackling themes that appear across Emanuel's oeuvre: childhood innocence, manhood, and racism. This volume includes the author's first romantic love poems, poems inspired by Marie-France Passard, a travel guide and librarian he met while in Europe, including "For 'Mee'" and "Lovelook Back," as well as poems about parental love. The speakers of the poems are often concerned with how the past affects the present. In some of the poems, such as "Didn't Fall in Love," the speaker refuses to allow himself to get involved in a new relationship because of past experiences. In "Goodbye No. 1," the speaker is sad because he loses something he thought he had. "Ass on the Beach, in Spain" explores the power and lure of feminine beauty over that of men. "After the Poetry Reading, Black" describes audience members' disappointment when Emanuel reads poems that do not seem to situate him as a black poet.

WHOLE GRAIN

A number of haiku, in addition to the haiku that serve as prefaces to each part of the collection, make up the 215 poems in *Whole Grain*, a collection of Emanuel's work from 1958 to 1989. Other forms are represented as well, including sonnets ("For a Farmer" and "Sonnet for a Writer"), free verse ("Topless, Bottomless Bar, Manhattan"), and rhymed quatrains ("Experience" and "I Wish I Had a Red Balloon"). Organized by themes, the collection contains poems about love, sex, race, and youth. Many of the poems, such as "Treehouse," "Whitey, Baby," "Emmett Till," and "Fisherman," are favorites among Emanuel's readers.

JAZZ FROM THE HAIKU KING

Jazz from the Haiku King, an innovative collection of various types of jazz-and-blues haiku, indicates how jazz, an African American form of music, and haiku, a Japanese form of poetry, can be complementary means of expression. "Dizzy Gillespie (News of His Death)" and "Duke Ellington" pay tribute to musicians, while "Farmer" explores the connection between a farmer and jazz. "Sleek Lizard Rhythms" describes the rhythm of jazz music. "Jackhammer," "Ammunition," and "Impressionist" speak directly to African Americans, asking them to liberate themselves and fight against injustice.

OTHER MAJOR WORKS

NONFICTION: *Langston Hughes*, 1967; *How I Write Two*, 1972 (with MacKinlay Kantor and Lawrence Osgood); *The Force and the Reckoning*, 2001 (autobiography).

EDITED TEXT: *Dark Symphony: Negro Literature in America*, 1968 (with Theodore L. Gross).

BIBLIOGRAPHY

Bloom, Harold. *Modern Black American Poets and Dramatists*. New York: Chelsea House, 1995. Provides a biography of Emanuel and excerpts from book reviews and critical essays about his work. It also includes an excerpt from "The Task of the Negro Writer as Artist: A Symposium," an essay Emanuel wrote explaining that all writers, regardless of race or ethnicity, must create work that is beautiful, powerful, and true.

Emanuel, James A. "James A. Emanuel." http://www.james-a-emanuel.com. The official Web site for Emanual contains a brief biography, a bibliography, and interviews with the author.

Fabre, Michel. *From Harlem to Paris: Black American Writers in France, 1840-1980*. Champaign: University of Illinois Press, 1993. The chapter titled "James Emanuel: A Poet in Exile" discusses Emanuel's life in France, particularly how people, sights, and experiences in and around Paris inspired his creativity, leading him to write poems such as "Lovelook Back," "Clothesline, Rue Marie," and "For Alix, Who Is Three."

Hakutani, Yoshinobu. *Cross-Cultural Visions in African American Modernism: From Spatial Narrative to Jazz Haiku.* Columbus: Ohio State University Press, 2006. The chapter titled "James Emanuel's Jazz Haiku and African American Individualism" focuses on *Jazz from the Haiku King.* The author describes how Emanuel uses haiku to convey elements of the African American experience and explains how Emanuel's work was influenced by other writers.

Holdt, Marvin. Review of *Black Man Abroad.* *Black American Literature Forum* 13, no. 3 (Autumn, 1979): 79-85. Offers an extensive examination of the work and its message.

Watson, Douglas. "James Andrew Emanuel." In *Dictionary of Literary Biography: Afro-American Poets Since 1955*, edited by Thadious M. Davis and Trudier Harris. Vol. 41. Farmington Hills, Mich.: Gale, 1985. Provides a well-developed biography and criticism of Emanuel's work.

KaaVonia Hinton

CLAUDIA EMERSON

Born: Chatham, Virginia; January 13, 1957
Also known as: Claudia Emerson Andrews

PRINCIPAL POETRY

Pharaoh, Pharaoh, 1997 (as Claudia Emerson Andrews)
Pinion: An Elegy, 2002
Late Wife, 2005
Figure Studies, 2008

OTHER LITERARY FORMS

Claudia Emerson is known principally for her poetry.

ACHIEVEMENTS

Claudia Emerson's poetry, with its rich evocation of life in the rural South, has received favorable critical attention since the publication of her first book, *Pharaoh,*

Pharaoh. She received fellowships from the National Endowment for the Arts (1994) and the Virginia Commission for the Arts (1995). She won an award from Associated Writing Programs in 1997. That same year, *Pharaoh, Pharaoh* was nominated for a Pulitzer Prize by Louisiana State University Press, which would continue to publish her work in its Southern Messenger Poets series. In 2005, she was selected by poet laureate Ted Kooser to receive a Witter Bynner Fellowship. Her *Late Wife* earned the Pulitzer Prize in poetry for 2006. She was named poet laureate of the Commonwealth of Virginia in 2008 and received the Carole Weinstein Poetry Prize in 2007 and the Donald Justice Award for Poetry in 2009.

BIOGRAPHY

Claudia Emerson was born in Chatham, Virginia, in 1957. Although Chatham is the county seat in the largest county in Virginia in geographical area, its population was only about fourteen hundred in the 2000 census. The surrounding countryside is largely made up of farms, whose primary crop was tobacco for most of the twentieth century, and tobacco-farming culture still permeates the town. Despite its size, the town has a rich history that extends back before the American Revolution. It also has a tradition of fostering the arts, especially the literary arts, and has been home to a number of nationally known writers and editors, including the poet Ellen Bryant Voigt.

Emerson attended Chatham Hall, a girls' boarding school, and graduated from the University of Virginia with a B.A. in English in 1979. She married, and the couple lived in or near Chatham for much of the next two decades. Emerson worked as a part-time rural mail carrier, branch librarian, and clerk in a used book store until she entered the M.F.A. program at the University of North Carolina-Greensboro. She imagined at first that she might use the degree (which she earned in 1991) to become an editor, but during the program, she was encouraged to develop as a poet. The result was her first book, *Pharaoh, Pharaoh.*

After the success of *Pharaoh, Pharaoh* and as her marriage began to founder, Emerson returned to Chatham Hall as academic dean (1996-1998). Her second volume, *Pinion*, was written after her divorce. In 1998, she took a teaching position at University of Mary Washington in Fredricksburg, Virginia, where she became professor of English and Arrington Distinguished Chair in Poetry. In 2000, she married musician Kent Ippolito, whose wife had died of lung cancer. Her Pulitzer Prize-winning *Late Wife* addresses her divorce and remarriage. Her fourth volume, *Figure Studies*, uses a girls' boarding school not unlike Chatham Hall to examine gender issues, including how girls are taught to be girls.

ANALYSIS

Claudia Emerson has said that she does not consider her earlier work to be particularly autobiographical; however, her poetry draws heavily on the world in which she grew up, rural southern Virginia, for its images and some of its themes. Her poems are full of farm equipment and livestock—mules, cows, tractors, and tobacco barns—and of details of rural life, such as the annual cleaning of family cemeteries or the auctions that mark the demise of a family farm. Wildlife—from snakes to deer to nightcrawlers—is everywhere in her work, and birds, including the buzzards and hawks that claim southern skies in the summer, are always present.

In interviews, Emerson has discussed the relationship between narrative and lyric poetry, noting that while she considers her works to be lyric poems, many lyric poems have a sort of narrative substructure that operates in tension with the lyric's focus on metaphor. Still, metaphor is what interests her most, as her works attest. Because most lyric poetry depends on tension for its interest, Emerson makes frequent use of form and, as she has pointed out, the tension that poetic form can create between line and sentence. Although her individual poems appear in a wide range of journals, she has said that she always thinks of each poem as part of a potential book.

PHARAOH, PHARAOH

"Searching the Title," the first poem in *Pharaoh, Pharaoh*, is a good example of Emerson's use of metaphor in that the title search in a courthouse is more a matter of heritage than of land deeds. As the speaker examines old titles, she muses on the land's history, ranging back to when no papers indicated its owners. At last, she concludes her title search. "What I know,

I own," she says, listing the hawks and crows, the beeches and pines, and the very sky as what she knows. This poem sets the volume's theme.

In "Auction," Emerson describes the sad remnants of a dead woman's life that are being offered at a farm auction. She pictures the worn combs and a crazed mirror that distorts the faces it reflects. As the people at the auction trample the dead woman's flowers, a mole's tunnel is thrust up as if by the work of "the vagrant dead" come to claim her past. In another poem, "Going Once, Going Twice," the speaker describes her father at the farm auction held after his sister died. When some cousins discover an ancient box of tintypes, he names the people in the pictures and is stunned to realize that his memory is the means by which the dead survive.

"Plagues" also examines the hold of the past on the present. A drought is making people suffer, and an elderly aunt tells the speaker that they are being punished. The seventeen-year locusts are calling "Pharaoh, Pharaoh" like the Hebrews of the Bible, begging the pharaoh for their freedom. The speaker doubts the aunt's interpretation, but by the poem's end, she says that the locusts' incessant murmur makes all their listeners feel like prisoners for whom no freedom is possible.

PINION

Pinion, a book-length narrative poem, tells the story of a tobacco farm in the 1920's, using mostly the voices of Preacher and Sister, two siblings who remained on the family farm, and that of Rose, their much younger sister. Preacher, the older brother, keeps the farm going with his endless labor, unlike his younger brother, Nate, a fiddler, a drinker, and the black sheep of the family, who appears in some of the poems. Sister, the oldest daughter, has stayed on the farm to care for her mother, whose health has been failing since the difficult birth of her last child—a "change of life baby" named Rose—and to care for her baby sister, who grows up and leaves. Rose's return to the abandoned buildings that are all that remain of the farm, long after her siblings' deaths, becomes impetus for her "recording" the voices of Sister and Preacher, giving them the means to say what they would never have said in life. Rose's voice introduces each section of the book.

The book's title, *Pinion*, offers an entry into its most central metaphor. A pinion is a wing, and birds are everywhere in the imagery of this volume, but "pinion" can also be a verb meaning to bind or restrain, just as Sister and Preacher are bound to the farm, and just as Preacher was once pinned down when his tractor—a much prized replacement for his old mule—rolled over on him. The individual lyrics of this book are woven together by not only the metaphor of wings but also other images that will seem familiar to readers of Emerson's first volume. Cows and calves, clocks, the farm bell, and the ribs of slaughtered animals (recalling Adam's rib from Genesis) appear and reappear to create the picture of lives both cloistered and claustrophobic.

LATE WIFE

The three sections of *Late Wife* are Emerson's most autobiographical and most straightforward work. The first section describes the breakup of her first marriage, the second portrays her healing as she settles into her new life alone, and the third contains a series of sonnets to her second husband.

In the first section, Emerson uses metaphor to describe the disintegration of her twenty-year marriage. In "Natural History Exhibits," the first poem in the volume, a wife says that the black rat snake kills by wrapping itself around its victim, pressing its life from it. The poem concludes when she finds a snake in the silverware drawer of her farmhouse; it "lay coiled, brooding/ on its bed of edges—blades and tines." She lets the snake escape back into the house, where her marriage already seems to rest on its own set of blades, but then regrets not killing it.

The images of the "Divorce Epistle" poems evoke the breakup of Emerson's marriage without going into detail as to what happened. "Photograph: Farm Auction" describes a picture taken by her photographer husband in which a hayfork looks like baleen from a whale, a great creature killed for trivial products. "Surface Hunting" describes a husband's collection of arrowheads, which he has found by spending hours looking down, hours his wife has treasured for providing her with solitude. "Waxwing" records how a couple rescued a baby cedar waxwing only to have it refuse to leave them when they freed it; the wife wonders whether they have done wrong by saving it in their alien world, one in which they themselves are unable to leave their crumbled relationship. In "Possessions," a wife imagines her husband's new lover boxing up her left-behind possessions to send them on; this poem is echoed in the book's last section as a new wife (Emerson) deals with keepsakes belonging to her deceased predecessor.

The second section, "Breaking Up the House," focuses on the stages of Emerson's healing after the divorce. Like the first section, it uses roughly iambic lines, and most of its lyrics are set in two- or three-line stanzas, thus setting them apart from the sonnets of the last section. One of the most arresting poems in this section is "House Sitting," in which a wife describes her temporary stay in an empty house. She spent a summer in the house without a telephone or furniture, knowing that she would soon move on and relishing the emptiness of a "house in transition" and not having to get used to anything.

The "Late Wife" section is subtitled "Letters to Kent." In its sonnets, Emerson explores her relationship with her new husband and his late wife, who died three years earlier. The sonnet is traditionally associated with love poetry, and these are indeed love poems, but of a particular sort in which a second wife recognizes the lingering presence of her husband's first wife in their marriage. The hospital in which the first wife died is still in their landscape; a few of her possessions (including the quilt under which they now sleep) are still in the house. No hostility is involved, just an honest recognition that the late wife will always be part of their marriage. "Stringed Instrument Collection" describes her husband's collection of "mandolins,/ mandolas, guitars . . ." (in contrast to her first husband's arrowheads). Her musician husband says that wood never dies; the instruments will be passed on to other hands, who will sometimes bring out from them an echo of past owners.

BIBLIOGRAPHY

Emerson, Claudia. "Claudia Emerson." http:// claudia emerson.org. The official Web site for Emerson contains a short biography, description of her books, information on readings and classes, and links to other sites.

_____. "An Interview with Claudia Emerson." Interview by Sarah Kennedy. *Shenandoah* 56, no. 3

(Winter, 2006): 27-37. Emerson offers detailed discussion about her craft, with reference to several poems from *Pinion* and *Late Wife*.

Emerson, Claudia, and Warren Rochell. "Stories (and Poems) Live in My Head: An Interview with Claudia Emerson and Warren Rochell." Interview by Tom H. Ray. *Virginia Libraries* 54, nos. 3, 4 (July-September, October-December, 2008): 40-44. Emerson discusses her life as a teaching poet.

Gates, David. "Heroine by a Hairbreadth: Before the Pulitzer, Her Book Was a Goner—It's Back." *Newsweek*, June 12, 2006, 76. Describes the difficulty in finding works of poetry, including Emerson's *Late Wife*, unless they win a prize. Notes that readers are probably missing works worth reading, like Emerson's.

Lacy, Bridgette A. "Poet of Heartbreak and Healing." *News and Observer*, June 2, 2006, p. E1. Lacy provides background on the poet and some poetic analysis in preparation for a reading Emerson gave at a local bookstore.

Logan, William. "Shock and Awe." *New Criterion* 27 (December, 2008): 36. Logan reviews multiple works of poetry, including Emerson's *Figure Studies*. He praises Emerson's work and calls it deserving of more attention, although he also labels it as slightly prissy.

Milne, Ira Mark, ed. *Poetry for Students*. Vol. 27. Detroit: Thomson/Gale Group, 2008. Contains an analysis of Emerson's "My Grandmother's Plot in the Family Cemetery."

Ann D. Garbett

RALPH WALDO EMERSON

Born: Boston, Massachusetts; May 25, 1803
Died: Concord, Massachusetts; April 27, 1882

PRINCIPAL POETRY

Poems, 1847
May-Day and Other Pieces, 1867
Selected Poems, 1876

OTHER LITERARY FORMS

Ralph Waldo Emerson's *The Journals of Ralph Waldo Emerson* (1909-1914), written over a period of fifty-five years (1820-1875), have been edited in ten volumes by E. W. Emerson and W. E. Forbes. Ralph L. Rusk edited *The Letters of Ralph Waldo Emerson* in six volumes (1939). Emerson was a noted lecturer in his day, although many of his addresses and speeches were not collected until after his death. These appear in three posthumous volumes—*Lectures and Biographical Sketches* (1884), *Miscellanies* (1884), and *Natural History of Intellect* (1893)—which were published as part of a centenary edition (1903-1904). A volume of Emerson's *Uncollected Writings: Essays, Addresses, Poems, Reviews, and Letters* was published in 1912. A sixteen-volume edition of journals and miscellaneous papers was published between 1960 and 1982.

ACHIEVEMENTS

Although Ralph Waldo Emerson's poetry was but a small part of his overall literary output, he thought of himself as very much a poet—even in his essays and lectures. He began writing poetry early in childhood and, at the age of nine, composed some verses on the Sabbath. At Harvard, he was elected class poet and was asked to write the annual Phi Beta Kappa poem in 1834. This interest in poetry continued throughout his long career.

During his lifetime, he published two small volumes of poetry, *Poems* and *May-Day and Other Pieces*, which were later collected in one volume for the centenary edition of his works. Altogether, the centenary volume contains some 170 poems, of which perhaps only several dozen are noteworthy.

Although Emerson produced a comparatively small amount of poetry and an even smaller number of first-rate poems, he stands as a major influence on the subsequent course of American poetry. As scholar, critic, and poet, Emerson was the first to define the distinctive qualities of American verse. His broad and exalted concept of the poet—as prophet, oracle, visionary, and seer—was shaped by his Romantic idealism. "I am more of a poet than anything else," he once wrote, although as much of his poetry is found in his journals and essays as in the poems themselves. In *An Oration Delivered Before the Phi Beta Kappa Society, Cam-*

bridge (1837; better known as *The American Scholar*), he called for a distinctive American poetry, and in his essay "The Poet," he provided the theoretical framework for American poetics. Scornful of imitation, he demanded freshness and originality from his verse, even though he did not always achieve in practice what he sought in theory. Rejecting the derivative verse of the Hartford wits and the sentimental versifiers of his day, he sought an original style and flavor for an American poetry close to the native grain. The form of his poetry was, as F. I. Carpenter argues (*Emerson Handbook*, 1953), the logical result of his insistence on self-reliance, while its content was shaped by his Romantic idealism. Thus his cumulative influence on American poetry is greater than his verse alone might imply.

Expression mattered more than form in poetry, according to Emerson. If he was not the completely inspirational poet called for in his essays, that may have been more a matter of temperament than of any flaw in his sense of the kind of poetry that a democratic culture would produce. In fact, his comments often closely parallel those of Alexis de Tocqueville on the nature of poetry in America. Both men agreed that the poetry of a democratic culture would embrace the facts of ordinary experience rather than celebrate epic themes. It would be a poetry of enumeration rather than elevation, of fact rather than eloquence; indeed, the democratic poet would have to struggle for eloquence, for poetry of the commonplace can easily become flat or prosaic. Even Emerson's own best verse often seems uneven, with memorable lines interspersed with mediocre ones.

Part of the problem with Emerson's poetry arose from his methods of composition. Writing poetry was not for him a smooth, continuous act of composition, nor did he have a set formula for composition, as Edgar Allan Poe advocated in "The Philosophy of Composition." Instead, he trusted inspiration to allow the form of the poem to be determined by its subject matter. This "organic" theory of composition shapes many of Emerson's best poems, including "The Snow-Storm," "Hamatraya," "Days," and "Ode." These poems avoid a fixed metrical or stanzaic structure and allow the sense of each line to dictate its poetic form. Emerson clearly composed by the line rather than by the stanza or paragraph, in both his poetry and prose, and this self-

Ralph Waldo Emerson (Library of Congress)

contained quality often gives his work a gnomic or orphic tone.

Although some of his poems appear to be fragmentary, they are not unfinished. They lack smoothness or polish because Emerson was not a lyrical but a visionary, oracular poet. He valued poetry as a philosophy or attitude toward life rather than simply as a formal linguistic structure or an artistic form. "The poet is the sayer, the namer, and represents beauty," he observed in "The Poet." With Percy Bysshe Shelley he believed that the poet was the visionary who would make people whole and teach them to see anew. "Poets are thus liberating gods," Emerson concluded, because "they are free, and they make free." Poetry is simply the most concentrated expression of the poetic vision, which all people are capable of sharing.

Thus Emerson's poems seek to accomplish what the essays announce. His poems attempt to reestablish the primal relationship between humans and nature that he sought as a substitute for revelation. Emerson prized the poet as an innovator, a namer, and a language maker who could interpret the oracles of nature. In its derivation from nature, all language, he felt, was fossil poetry. "Always the seer is a sayer," he announced in his Harvard Divinity School address, and through the vision of the poet "we come to look at the world with new eyes."

Of the defects in Emerson's poetry, the chief is perhaps that Emerson's muse sees rather than sings. Because his lines are orphic and self-contained, they sometimes seem flat and discontinuous. Individual lines stand out in otherwise undistinguished poems. Nor do his lines always scan or flow smoothly, since Emerson was virtually tone-deaf. In "The Poet," he rejects fixed poetic form in favor of a freer, more open verse. For Emerson, democratic poetry would be composed with variable line and meter, with form subordinated to expression. The poet in a democracy is thus a "representative man," chanting the poetry of the common, the ordinary, and the low. Although Emerson pointed the way, it took Walt Whitman to master this new style of American poetry with his first edition of *Leaves of Grass* (1855), which Emerson promptly recognized and praised for its originality. Whitman thus became the poet whom Emerson had called for in *The American Scholar*; American poetry had come of age.

Biography

Born in Boston on May 25, 1803, Ralph Waldo Emerson was the second of five sons in the family of William Emerson and Ruth Emerson. His father was a noted Unitarian minister of old New England stock whose sudden death in 1811 left the family to struggle in genteel poverty. Although left without means, Emerson's mother and his aunt, Mary Moody Emerson, were energetic and resourceful women who managed to survive by taking in boarders, accepting the charity of relatives, and teaching their boys the New England values of thrift, hard work, and mutual assistance within the family. Frail as a child, Emerson attended Boston Latin School and Harvard, where he graduated without distinction in 1821. Since their mother was determined that her children would receive a decent education, each of her sons taught after graduation to help the others through school. Thus Emerson taught for several

years at his brother's private school for women before he decided to enter divinity school. His family's high thinking and plain living taught young Emerson self-reliance and a deep respect for books and learning.

With his father and step-grandfather, the Reverend Ezra Ripley of Concord, as models, Emerson returned to Harvard to prepare for the ministry. After two years of intermittent study at the Divinity School, Emerson was licensed to preach in the Unitarian Church. He was forced to postpone further studies, however, and to travel south during the winter of 1826 because of poor health. The next two years saw him preaching occasionally and serving as a substitute pastor. One such call brought him to Concord, New Hampshire, where he met his future wife, Ellen Louisa Tucker. After his ordination in March, 1829, Emerson married Tucker and accepted a call as minister of the Second Church, Boston, where his father had also served. The position and salary were good, and Emerson was prepared to settle into a respectable career as a Boston Unitarian clergyman. Unfortunately his wife was frail, and within a year and a half, she died of tuberculosis. Grief-stricken, Emerson found it difficult to continue with his duties as pastor and resigned from the pulpit six months after his wife's death. Private doubts had assailed him, and he found he could no longer administer the Lord's Supper in good conscience. His congregation would not allow him to dispense with the rite, so his resignation was reluctantly accepted.

With a small settlement from his wife's legacy, he sailed for Europe in December, 1832, to regain his health and try to find a new vocation. During his winter in Italy, he admired the art treasures in Florence and Rome. There he met the American sculptor Horatio Greenough and the English writer Walter Savage Landor. The following spring, Emerson continued his tour through Switzerland and into France. Paris charmed him with its splendid museums and gardens, and he admired the natural history exhibits at the Jardin des Plantes. Crossing to England by August, he met Samuel Taylor Coleridge in London, then traveled north to visit Thomas Carlyle in Craigenputtock and William Wordsworth at Rydal Mount. His meeting with Carlyle resulted in a lifelong friendship.

After returning to Boston in 1833, Emerson gradually settled into a new routine of study, lecturing, and writing, filling an occasional pulpit on Sundays, and assembling ideas in his journals for his essay on "Nature." Lydia Jackson, a young woman from Plymouth, New Hampshire, heard Emerson preach in Boston and became infatuated with him. The young widower returned her admiration, although he frankly confessed that he felt none of the deep affection he had cherished for his first wife. During their engagement he renamed her "Lidian" in their correspondence because he disliked the name Lydia. She accepted the change without demur. Within a year, they were married and settled in a house on the Boston Post Road near the Old Manse of Grandfather Ripley. Emerson was now thirty-two and about to begin his life's work.

The next decade marked Emerson's intellectual maturity. *Nature* was completed and published as a small volume in 1836. In its elaborate series of correspondences between humans and nature, Emerson established the foundations of his idealistic philosophy. "Why should not we also enjoy an original relation to the universe?" he asked. Humans could seek revelations firsthand from nature, rather than having them handed down through tradition. A year later, Emerson gave an address before the Harvard Phi Beta Kappa Society, an event that Oliver Wendell Holmes later called "our intellectual Declaration of Independence." In his address, which is best known as *The American Scholar*, Emerson called for a distinctively American style of letters, free from European influences. Invited in 1838 to speak before the graduating class of Harvard Divinity School, Emerson affirmed in his address that the true measure of religion resided within the individual, not in institutional or historical Christianity. If everyone had equal access to the Divine Spirit, then inner experience was all that was needed to validate religious truth. For this daring pronouncement, he was attacked by Harvard President Andrews Norton and others for espousing "the latest form of infidelity." In a sense, each of these important essays was an extension of Emerson's basic doctrine of self-reliance, applied to philosophy, culture, and religion.

His self-reliance served him equally well in personal life, even as family losses haunted him, almost as if to test his hard-won equanimity and sense of purpose.

Besides losing his first wife, Ellen, Emerson saw two of his brothers die and a third become so feeble-minded that he had to be institutionalized. Worst of all, his first-born and beloved son Waldo died in 1841 of scarlet fever at the age of six. Emerson's melioristic philosophy saw him through these losses, although in his journals he later chided himself for not feeling his son's death more deeply. Despite the hurt he felt, his New England reserve would not allow him to yield easily to grief or despair. Nor would he dwell in darkness while there was still light to be found.

During these years, Emerson found Concord a congenial home. He established a warm and stimulating circle of friends there and enjoyed the intellectual company of Nathaniel Hawthorne, Henry David Thoreau, and Bronson Alcott. As his fame as a lecturer and writer grew, he attracted a wider set of admirers, including Margaret Fuller, who often visited to share enthusiasms and transcendental conversations. Emerson even edited *The Dial* for a short time in 1842, but for the most part he remained aloof from, although sympathetic to, the transcendentalist movement that he had so largely inspired. His manner at times was even offhand. When asked for a definition of transcendentalism, he simply replied, "Idealism in 1842." When George Ripley invited him to join the Brook Farm Community in 1840, Emerson politely declined. Reform, he believed, had to begin with the individual. Thoreau later rebuked him for not taking a firmer stand on the fugitive slave issue, but Emerson was by nature apolitical and skeptical of partisan causes. His serenity was too hard-won to be sacrificed, no matter how worthy the cause.

So instead he continued to lecture and write, and his essays touched an entire generation of American writers. Thoreau, Whitman, and Emily Dickinson responded enthusiastically to the appeal of Emerson's thought, while even Hawthorne and Herman Melville, although rejecting it, still felt compelled to acknowledge his intellectual presence. Lecture tours took him repeatedly to the Midwest and to England and Scotland for a second time in 1847-1848. Harvard awarded him an honorary degree in 1866 and elected him overseer the following year. His alma mater also invited him to deliver a series of lectures on his philosophy in 1869-1870. When Emerson's home in Concord burned in

1877, friends sent him on a third visit to Europe and Egypt, accompanied by his daughter Ellen, while the house and study were rebuilt with funds from admirers. He spent his last few years in Concord quietly and died in the spring of 1882. Of his life, it can be said that perhaps more than any of his contemporaries, he embodied the qualities of the American spirit—its frankness, idealism, optimism, and self-confidence. For the American writer of his age, all things were possible. If, finally, he was as much prophet as poet, that may be because of the power of his vision as well as its lyrical intensity, a power that suffused his prose and was concentrated in his poems.

ANALYSIS

Ralph Waldo Emerson's poetic achievement is greater than the range of his individual poems might suggest. Although perhaps only a handful of his poems attain undisputed greatness, others are rich in implication despite their occasional lapses, saved by a memorable line or phrase. As a cultural critic and poetic innovator, moreover, Emerson has had an immense influence through his essays and poetry in suggesting an appropriate style and method for subsequent American poets. He tried to become the poet he called for in *The American Scholar*, and to a degree, his poems reflect those democratic precepts. Determined to find distinctively American art forms, he began with expression—not form—and evolved the forms of his poems through their expression. Inspired by the "organic aesthetic" of the American sculptor Horatio Greenough, whose studio in Rome he visited in 1833, Emerson abandoned traditional poetic structure for a loose iambic meter and a variable (though often octosyllabic) line. Instead of following a rigid external form, the poem would take its form from its particular content and expression. This was the freedom Emerson sought for a "democratic" poetry.

Emerson's best poetry is thus marked by two qualities: organic form and a vernacular style; his less successful pieces, such as "The Sphinx," are too often cryptic and diffuse. These strengths and weaknesses both derive from his attempt to unite philosophical ideas and lyricism within a symbolic form in which the image would evoke its deeper meaning. "I am born a poet," he wrote to his fiancé, Jackson, "of a low class without doubt, yet a poet. That is my vocation. My singing, to be sure, is very 'husky,' and is for the most part in prose. Still I am a poet in the sense of a perceiver and dear lover of the harmonies that are in the soul and in matter, and specially of the correspondence between these and those." Correspondence, then, is what Emerson sought in his poetry, based on his theory of language as intermediary between humans and nature.

In "The Poet," Emerson announced that "it is not metres, but metre-making argument that makes a poem." His representative American poet would be a namer and enumerator, not a rhymer or versifier. The poet would take his inspiration from the coarse vigor of American vernacular speech and in turn reinvigorate poetic language by tracing root metaphors back to their origins in ordinary experience. He would avoid stilted or artificial poetic diction in favor of ordinary speech. This meant sacrificing sound to sense, however, since Emerson's "metre-making arguments" were more often gnomic than lyrical. As a result, his poems are as spare as their native landscape. They are muted and understated rather than rhapsodic, and—with the exception of his Orientalism—tempered and homey in their subject matter, since Emerson was more of an innovator in style than in substance. Emerson's "Merlin" provides perhaps the best definition of what he sought in his poetry:

> Thy trivial harp will never please
> Or fill my craving ear;
> Its chords should ring as blows the breeze,
> Free, peremptory, clear.

Emerson's poems fall into several distinct categories, the most obvious being his nature poems; his philosophical or meditative poems, which often echo the essays; his autobiographical verse; and his occasional pieces. Sometimes these categories may overlap, but the "organic" aesthetic and colloquial tone mark them as distinctly Emersonian. Two of his most frequently anthologized pieces, "Days" and "The Snow-Storm," will serve to illustrate his poetic style.

"DAYS"

"Days" has been called the most perfect of Emerson's poems, and while there is a satisfying completeness about the poem, it resolves less than might appear at first reading. The poem deals with what was for Emerson the continuing problem of vocation or calling. How could he justify his apparent idleness in a work-oriented culture? "Days" thus contains something of a self-rebuke, cast in terms of an Oriental procession of Days, personified as daughters of Time, who pass through the poet's garden bringing various gifts, the riches of life, which the poet too hastily rejects in favor of a "few herbs and apples," emblematic of the contemplative life. The Day scorns his choice, presumably because he has squandered his time in contemplation rather than having measured his ambition against worthier goals. The Oriental imagery employed here transforms a commonplace theme into a memorable poem, although the poet never responds to the implied criticism of his life; nor does he identify the "morning wishes" that have been abandoned for the more sedate and domestic "herbs and apples," although these images do suggest meanings beyond themselves.

"THE PROBLEM"

A thematically related poem is "The Problem," in which Emerson tries to justify his reasons for leaving the ministry, which he respects and admires but cannot serve. Perhaps because he was more poet than priest, Emerson preferred the direct inspiration of the artist to the inherited truths of religion, or it may have been that, as a romantic, he found more inspiration in nature than in Scripture. The third stanza of "The Problem" contains one of the clearest articulations of Emerson's "organic" aesthetic, of form emerging from expression, in the image of the artist who "builded better than he knew." The temples of nature "art might obey, but not surpass."

"THE SNOW-STORM"

This organic theory of art reached its fullest expression in "The Snow-Storm," which still offers the best example in Emerson's poetry of form following function, and human artistry imitating that of nature. Here the poem merges with what it describes. The first stanza announces the arrival of the storm, and the second stanza evokes the "frolic architecture" of the snow and the human architectural forms that it anticipates. Nature freely creates and humans imitate through art. Wind and snow form myriad natural forms that humans can only "mimic in slow structures" of stone. As the wind-sculpted snowdrifts create beauty from the materials at hand, the poem rounds on itself in the poet's implicit admiration of nature's work.

"HAMATRAYA"

One of the most intriguing of Emerson's poems is "Hamatraya," which contains an attack on Yankee land-greed and acquisitiveness, cast as a Hindu meditation on the impermanence of all corporeal things. In "Hamatraya," the crass materialism of his countrymen evokes Emerson's serenely idealistic response. No one finally owns the land, he asserts, and to pretend so is to be deceived. The land will outlive successive masters, all of whom boast of owning it. In the enduring cycle of things, they are all finally returned to the earth they claimed to possess. Emerson uses dramatic form and the lyrical "Earth-Song" as an effective counterpoint to the blunt materialism of the first two stanzas. His theme of all things returning unto themselves finds its appropriate metaphor in the organic (and Hindu) cycle of life. Hindu cosmology and natural ecology complement each other in Emerson's critique of the pretensions of private land-ownership.

"BRAHMA"

Another of Emerson's Oriental poems, his popular "Brahma," is notable for its blend of Eastern and Western thought. Here Emerson assumes the perspective of God or Brahma in presenting his theme of the divine relativity and continuity of life. Just as Krishna, "the Red Slayer," and his victim are merged in the unity of Brahma, so all other opposites are reconciled in the ultimate unity of the universe. This paradoxical logic appealed to Emerson as a way of presenting his monistic philosophy in poetic terms. The poem owes much to Emerson's study of the *Bhagavadgītā* (c. 200 B.C.E.-200 C.E.; *The Bhagavad Gita*, 1785) and other Oriental scriptures, the first stanza of "Brahma" being in fact a close parallel to the Hindu text. The smooth regularity of Emerson's ballad stanzas also helps to offset the exotic quality of the Hindu allusions and the novelty of the poem's theme.

"URIEL"

Religious myth is also present in "Uriel," which Robert Frost called "the greatest Western poem yet." Even if Frost's praise is overstated, this is still one of

Emerson's most profound and complex poems. Again it deals with the reconciliation of opposites, this time in the proposed relativity of good and evil. Borrowing the theme of the primal revolt against God by the rebellious archangels, Emerson uses the figure of the angel Uriel as the prototype of the advanced thinker misunderstood or rejected by others. Uriel represents the artist as the rebel or prophet bearing unwelcome words, roles that Emerson no doubt identified with himself and the hostile reception given *An Address Delivered Before the Senior Class in Divinity College, Cambridge . . .* (1838; better known as *The Divinity School Address*) by the Harvard theological faculty. Uriel's words, "Line in nature is not found;/ Unit and universe are round;/ In vain produced, all rays return;/ Evil will bless, and ice will burn," speak with particular force to the modern age, in which discoveries in theoretical physics and astronomy seem to have confirmed Emerson's intuitions about the relativity of matter and energy and the nature of the physical universe.

"EACH AND ALL"

Emerson's monistic philosophy also appears in "Each and All," in which the poem suggests that beauty cannot be divorced from its context or setting without losing part of its original appeal. The peasant, sparrow, seashell, and maid must each be appreciated in the proper aesthetic context, as part of a greater unity. Beauty cannot be possessed, Emerson argues, without destroying it. The theme of "Each and All" perhaps echoes section 3 on beauty of his essay *Nature*, in which Emerson observes that "the standard of beauty is the entire circuit of natural forms—the totality of nature. . . . Nothing is quite beautiful alone; nothing but is beautiful in the whole. A single object is only so far beautiful as it suggests this universal grace." The poem "Each and All" gives a more concentrated and lyrical expression to this apprehension of aesthetic unity. The poetic images lend grace and specificity to the philosophical concept of the beauty inherent in unity.

"GIVE ALL TO LOVE"

Emerson's fondness for paradoxical logic and the union of apparent opposites appears in yet another poem, "Give All to Love," which initially appears to falter on the contradiction between yielding to love and retaining one's individuality. The first three stanzas counsel a wholehearted surrender to the impulse of love, while the fourth stanza cautions the lover to remain "free as an Arab." The final two stanzas resolve this dilemma by affirming that the lovers may cherish joys apart without compromising their love for each other, since the purest love is that which is free from jealousy or possessiveness. Emerson reconciles the demands of love and those of self-reliance by idealizing the love relationship. Some commentators have even suggested that Emerson envisions a Neoplatonic ladder or hierarchy of love, from the Physical, to the Romantic, to the Ideal or Platonic—a relationship that in fact Emerson described in another poem titled "Initial, Daemonic, and Celestial Love"—but the theme of "Give All to Love" seems to be simply to love fully without surrendering one's ego or identity. The last two lines of the poem, "When half-gods go,/ The Gods arrive," are often quoted out of context because of their aphoristic quality.

"THRENODY"

A poem that has led some readers to charge Emerson with coldheartedness or lack of feeling is "Threnody," his lament for the loss of his beloved son Waldo, who died of scarlet fever at the age of six. Waldo, the first child of his second marriage, died suddenly in January, 1842. Emerson was devastated by grief, yet he seems in the poem to berate himself for his inability to sustain his grief. In his journals, Emerson freely expressed his bitterness and grief, and he gradually transcribed these feelings into the moving pastoral elegy for his son. "Threnody," literally a deathsong or lamentation, contains a mixture of commonplace and idealized pastoral images that demonstrate Emerson's ability to work within classical conventions and to ameliorate his grief through his doctrine of compensation. Some of the most moving lines in the poem describe the speaker's recollection of the child's "daily haunts" and unused toys, although these realistic details are later muted by the pathetic fallacy of external nature joining the poet in mourning the loss of his son.

"THE RHODORA"

Emerson's muse most often turned to nature for inspiration, so it is no accident that his nature poems contain some of his best work. "The Rhodora" is an early poem in which Emerson's attention to sharp and precise details of his New England landscape stands out against his otherwise generalized and formal poetic style. The first eight lines of the poem, in which Emerson describes finding the rhodora, a northern azalea-like flower, blooming in the woods early in May of the New England spring, before other plants have put out their foliage, seem incomparably the best. Unfortunately, the second half of the poem shifts from specific nature imagery to a generalized homily on the beauty of the rhodora, cast in formal poetic diction. Here Emerson's impulse to draw moralistic lessons from nature reminds us of another famous early nineteenth century American poem, William Cullen Bryant's "To a Waterfowl." This division within "The Rhodora" illustrates some of Emerson's difficulties in breaking away from the outmoded style and conventions of eighteenth century English landscape poetry to find an appropriate vernacular style for American nature poetry. Here the subject matter is distinctly American, but the style—the poem's manner of seeing and feeling—is still partially derivative.

"THE HUMBLE BEE"

"The Humble Bee" is a more interesting poem in some respects, in that Emerson uses a form adequate to his expression—a tight octosyllabic line and rhymed couplets—to evoke through both sound and sense the meandering flight of the bumble bee. As the poem unfolds, the bee gradually becomes a figure for the poet intoxicated by nature. Some of the poem's conceits may seem quaint to modern taste, but "The Humble Bee" is innovative in its use of terse expression and symbolic form. Its style anticipates the elliptical language and abbreviated form of Dickinson's poetry.

"WOODNOTES"

"Woodnotes" is a long and somewhat prosy two-part narrative poem that appears to be extracted from Emerson's journals. Part 1 introduces the transcendental nature lover ("A Forest Seer") in terms perhaps reminiscent of Thoreau, and part 2 describes the reciprocal harmony between humans and nature, in which each is fully realized through the other. The vagueness of part 2 perhaps illustrates Emerson's difficulty in capturing transcendental rapture in specific poetic language.

"CONCORD HYMN"

"Ode" ("Inscribed to W. H. Channing") and "Concord Hymn" are both occasional poems that otherwise differ markedly in style and technique. "Concord Hymn" is a traditional patriotic poem in four ballad stanzas that Emerson composed to be sung at the placing of a stone obelisk on July 4, 1837, to commemorate the Battle of Concord, fought on April 19, 1775, on land later belonging to the Reverend Ezra Ripley. The lines of the first stanza, now so well known that they are part of American national folklore, demonstrate that Emerson could easily master traditional verse forms when he chose to do so:

> By the rude bridge that arched the flood,
> Their flag to April's breeze unfurled,
> Here once the embattled farmers stood,
> And fired the shot heard round the world.

The images of the "bridge" and the "flood" in the first stanza ripen imperceptibly into metaphor in the poem's implied theme that the Battle of Concord provided the impetus for the American Revolutionary War.

"ODE"

Emerson's "Ode" is a much more unconventional piece, written in terse, variable lines, usually of two or three stresses, and touching on the dominant social and political issues of the day—the Mexican War, the Fugitive Slave Law of 1850, the threat of secession in the South, and radical abolitionism in the North. This open form was perhaps best suited to Emerson's oracular style that aimed to leave a few memorable lines with the reader. His angry muse berates Daniel Webster for having compromised his principles by voting for the Fugitive Slave Law, and it denounces those materialistic interests, in both the North and the South, that would profit from wage or bond slavery. Emerson's lines "Things are in the saddle,/ And ride mankind" aptly express his misgivings about the drift of American affairs that seemed to be leading toward a civil war. His taut lines seem to chant their warning like a Greek chorus, foreseeing the inevitable but being helpless to intervene. By the 1850's Emerson had become an increasingly outspoken opponent of the Fugitive Slave Law, and on occasion risked his personal safety in speaking before hostile crowds.

LEGACY

Despite his commitment to a new American poetry based on common diction and ordinary speech, Emerson's poetry never quite fulfilled the promise of his call, in *The American Scholar* and "The Poet," for a new poetics. Emerson wanted to do for American poetry what Wordsworth had accomplished for English lyrical poetry, to free it from the constraints of an artificial and dead tradition of sensibility and feeling. However, he was not as consistent or as thoroughgoing a poetic innovator as the Wordsworth of the "Preface" to the second edition of *Lyrical Ballads* (1800), who both announced and carried out his proposed revision of the existing neoclassical poetic diction, nor did he apply his theory to his poetic composition as skillfully as Wordsworth did. Emerson could envision a new poetics but he could not sustain in his poetry a genuine American vernacular tradition. That had to wait for Whitman and Dickinson. Perhaps Emerson was too much the philosopher ever to realize fully the poetic innovations that he sought, but even with their flaws, his poems retain a freshness and vitality lacking in contemporaries such as Henry Wadsworth Longfellow and James Russell Lowell, who were probably more accomplished versifiers. Emerson's greatness resides in the originality of his vision of a future American poetry, free and distinct from European models. It can be found in the grace of his essays and the insights of his journals, and it appears in those select poems in which he was able to match vision and purpose, innovation and accomplishment. His "Saadi" was no less a poet for the restraint of his harp.

OTHER MAJOR WORKS

NONFICTION: *Nature*, 1836; *An Oration Delivered Before the Phi Beta Kappa Society, Cambridge*, 1837 (better known as *The American Scholar*); *An Address Delivered Before the Senior Class in Divinity College, Cambridge . . .*, 1838 (better known as *The Divinity School Address*); *Essays: First Series*, 1841; *Essays: Second Series*, 1844; *Orations, Lectures and Addresses*, 1844; *Addresses and Lectures*, 1849; *Representative Men: Seven Lectures*, 1850; *English Traits*, 1856; *The Conduct of Life*, 1860; *Representative of Life*, 1860; *Society and Solitude*, 1870; *Works and Days*, 1870; *Letters and Social Aims*, 1875; *Lectures and Biographical Sketches*, 1884; *Miscellanies*, 1884; *Natural History of Intellect*, 1893; *The Journals of Ralph Waldo Emerson*, 1909-1914 (10 volumes; E. W. Emerson and W. E. Forbes, editors); *The Letters of Ralph Waldo Emerson*, 1939 (6 volumes; Ralph L. Rusk, editor); *The Journals and Miscellaneous Notebooks*, 1960-1982 (16 volumes); *Emerson in His Journals*, 1982 (Joel Porte, editor); *Political Writings*, 2008 (Kenneth Sacks, editor).

EDITED TEXT: *Parnassus*, 1874.

MISCELLANEOUS: *Uncollected Writings: Essays, Addresses, Poems, Reviews, and Letters*, 1912.

BIBLIOGRAPHY

Bosco, Ronald A., and Joel Myerson, eds. *Ralph Waldo Emerson: A Documentary Volume*. Vol. 351 in *Dictionary of Literary Biography*. Detroit: Gale/Cengage Learning, 2010. Provides primary source documents, including reviews and assessments, concerning Emerson and his works by contemporaries and by persons writing after his death.

Buell, Lawrence. *Emerson*. Cambridge, Mass.: Belknap Press, 2003. A thorough and admiring biography that presents Emerson as an international figure.

Gougeon, Len. *Emerson and Eros: The Making of a Cultural Hero*. Albany: State University of New York Press, 2009. Argues that, for Emerson, Eros is the essential cosmic force that joins humanity and the universe, and that Emerson's writings are filled with this dynamic spirit.

Myerson, Joel, ed. *A Historical Guide to Ralph Waldo Emerson*. New York: Oxford University Press, 2000. A collection of essays that provide an extended biographical study of Emerson. Later chapters study his concept of individualism, nature and natural science, religion, antislavery, and women's rights.

Porte, Joel, and Saundra Morris, eds. *The Cambridge Companion to Ralph Waldo Emerson*. New York: Cambridge University Press, 1999. Provides a critical introduction to Emerson's work through interpretations of his writing and analysis of his influence and cultural significance. Includes a comprehensive chronology and bibliography.

Schreiner, Samuel Agnew. *The Concord Quartet: Alcott, Emerson, Hawthorne, Thoreau, and the Friendship That Freed the American Mind*. Hoboken, N.J.: John Wiley & Sons, 2006. Examines the relationship among Emerson, Henry David Thoreau, Nathaniel Hawthorne, and Bronson Alcott. Sheds light on the mind behind Emerson's poetry.

Waynem, Tiffany K. *Critical Companion to Ralph Waldo Emerson: A Literary Reference to His Life and Work*. New York: Facts On File, 2010. Contains a biography of Emerson, an alphabetical list of his works, and a chronology.

York, Maurice, and Rick Spaulding. *Ralph Waldo Emerson: The Infinitude of the Private Man—A Biography*. Chicago: Wrightwood Press, 2008. A thorough biography with a chronology and selected bibliography. Describes the reaction of Emerson to Walt Whitman and his writing of "The Poet."

Andrew J. Angyal

LOUISE ERDRICH

Born: Little Falls, Minnesota; June 7, 1954

PRINCIPAL POETRY

Jacklight, 1984
Baptism of Desire, 1989
Original Fire: Selected and New Poems, 2003

OTHER LITERARY FORMS

Like many other American Indian writers, Louise Erdrich (UR-drihk) writes in various genres: short fiction, novels, memoirs, and children's literature. She has published a series of novels exploring the lives of American Indians, usually of mixed heritage, from her own Chippewa tribe. Starting with *Love Medicine* (1984), Erdrich has created an imaginative territory that has been compared to William Faulkner's Yoknapatawpha County. In addition to this "family" of novels, Erdrich coauthored, with her husband Michael Dorris, *The Crown of Columbus* (1991).

As the mother of six children, Erdrich developed an interest in children's literature and has published books for children, including *Grandmother's Pigeon* (1996) and *The Game of Silence* (2005). Her memoir, *The Blue Jay's Dance: A Birth Year* (1995), is an account of her own pregnancy and the birth of one of her daughters.

ACHIEVEMENTS

Louise Erdrich's major achievements have been in fiction. Early in her career, she was awarded first prize in the 1982 Nelson Algren fiction competition for "The World's Greatest Fishermen." This short story became a chapter in *Love Medicine*, which won the National Book Critics Circle Award for best work of fiction in 1984, the Los Angeles Times Book Prize for fiction in 1985, and the American Book Award from the Before Columbus Foundation in 1985. *The Beet Queen* (1986) won first prize at the 1987 O. Henry Awards, as well as a National Book Critics Circle Award nomination in 1986. Erdrich received the Minnesota Book Award four times, in 1997 for *Tales of Burning Love* (1996), in 2002 for *The Last Report on the Miracles at Little No Horse* (2001), in 2006 for *The Painted Drum* (2005), and in 2009 for *The Plague of Doves* (2008). *The Antelope Wife* (1998) won the World Fantasy Award for best novel in 1999, and *The Last Report on the Miracles at Little No Horse* was nominated for a National Book Award in 2001. In 2005, Erdrich was named the associate poet laureate of North Dakota, but in 2007, she turned down an honorary doctorate from North Dakota University because she found the school's mascot, the Fighting Sioux, to be offensive. Her children's book *The Game of Silence* received the Scott O'Dell Award for Historical Fiction in 2006. In 2009, *The Plague of Doves* won the Anisfield-Wolf Book Award and was also a finalist for the Pulitzer Prize in fiction. That same year, Erdrich won the *Kenyon Review* Award for Literary Achievement.

Erdrich has been awarded a number of fellowships, from The Johns Hopkins University (1978), MacDowell Colony (1980), Yaddo Colony (1981), Dartmouth College (1981), the National Endowment for the Arts (1982), and the Guggenheim Foundation (1985-1986).

BIOGRAPHY

Karen Louise Erdrich was born in Little Falls, Minnesota, the daughter of Ralph Louis, a German American teacher with the Bureau of Indian Affairs (BIA), and Rita Joanne, her French and Chippewa mother, also a teacher in the BIA school. The first of seven children, Erdrich told author Joseph Bruchac she grew up "not thinking about [her mixed blood], everybody knowing you were a mixed-blood in town. You'd go to the [Turtle Mountain] reservation to visit sometimes and sometimes you'd go to your other family. It really was the kind of thing you just took for granted." Erdrich's parents fostered her creativity. In her interview with Bruchac, she said, "Both my mom and dad were encouraging. . . . I had that kind of childhood where I didn't feel art was something strange."

Erdrich grew up in Wahpeton, North Dakota, not far from Turtle Mountain reservation, where her grandfather Pat Tourneau had been tribal chairman. Erdrich moved away from Wahpeton to enter Dartmouth College in 1972, the first year it admitted women. At

Louise Erdrich (Ulf Andersen/Getty Images)

Dartmouth, Erdrich met her future husband and collaborator, Michael Dorris, the newly hired chair of the Native American Studies department. Between receiving her B.A. from Dartmouth and entering the Johns Hopkins University master's degree program in 1978, Erdrich worked at a series of what she called "really crazy jobs," among which were beet weeder, waitress, psychiatric aide, signaler for a construction gang, lifeguard, and poetry teacher for the North Dakota Arts Council. These jobs provided her with practical experience in the world, which she later incorporated into her writing.

Erdrich's return to Dartmouth as writer-in-residence brought her back into contact with Dorris. They began exchanging poems and stories, collaborated on "The World's Greatest Fishermen," and married in 1981. They had six children: Reynold (died in 1991), Jeffrey, Madeline, Persia, Pallas, and Aza. The Erdrich-Dorris marriage was extraordinary in many respects. They collaborated fully on writing projects, although only *The Crown of Columbus* bears both names. Erdrich told Bruchac: "Michael and I are truly collaborators in all aspects of writing and life. It's very hard to separate the writing and the family life and Michael and I as people."

Erdrich had separated from Dorris when he committed suicide in 1997. She settled in Minneapolis with three of her children and began operating Birchbark Books, a bookstore. She continued to write and publish fiction and children's books, but her next work of poetry would not be published until 2003. "Being a fiction writer," she told interviewer Laura Coltelli, is "closer to the oral tradition of sitting around and telling stories."

ANALYSIS

Louise Erdrich's interest in writing can be traced to her childhood and her heritage. She told *Writer's Digest* contributor Michael Schumacher, "People in [Native American] families make everything into a story. . . . People just sit and the stories start coming, one after another. I suppose that when you grow up constantly hearing the stories rise, break, and fall, it gets into you somehow." Her parents encouraged her writing: "My father used to give me a nickel for every story I wrote, and my mother wove strips of construction paper together and stapled them into book covers. So at an early age I felt myself to be a published author earning substantial royalties."

Although most of her characters and themes grow out of her background as a Native American woman who grew up off the reservation, Erdrich's writings not only reflect her multilayered, complex background—she is both Turtle Mountain Chippewa and European American—but also confound a variety of literary genre and cultural categories. In her fiction and poetry, she plainly regards the survival of American Indian cultures as imperative. She prescribes the literary challenge for herself and other contemporary American Indian writers in her essay "Where I Ought to Be: A Writer's Sense of Place," published in a 1985 issue of *The New York Times Book Review*: In the light of enormous loss, American Indians must tell the stories of contemporary survivors while protecting and celebrating the cores of cultures left in the wake of catastrophe.

Erdrich's themes tend to focus on abandonment and return, pleasure and denial, failure, and absurdity. She raises virtually all the issues important to an understanding of the human condition: accidents of birth and parentage, falling in love, generosity, greed, psychological damage, joy, alienation, vulnerability, differentness, parenting, aging, and dying.

JACKLIGHT

The meanings of *Jacklight* radiate outward and circle back to the title poem. Instead of being trapped by the hunters' jacklights, the animals in Erdrich's poem lure the hunters into the woods: "And now they take the first steps, not knowing/ how deep the woods are and lightless." This poem's themes are typical of Erdrich: her knowledge of the natural world's wisdom, an awareness of the contentious interaction between humans and animals, and a prophetic sense that human beings need the healing power nature offers.

Following the title poem, section 1, "Runaways," explores the theme of return, most often to the natural world. Erdrich details a "quest for one's own background" in the work. She describes mixed-blood American Indians like herself searching "to discover where we are from." In "Indian Boarding School," the children running away from their off-reservation schools speak collectively that "Home's the place we

head for in our sleep." In "Rugaroo," an alcoholic man's search is so dogged that "He blew up with gas./ And now he is the green light floating over the slough." As the title poem prophesied, there is a return to the natural world and a haunting transformation.

Section 2, "Hunters," pursues the theme of the interaction between the human world and the natural—human beings having forgotten, for the most part, links with the natural world. "The Woods" presents a first-person speaker who has made the move back to the woods and who invites her lover to join her: "now when I say *come*,/ and you enter the woods,/ hunting some creature like the woman I was,/ I surround you." An integration is made, but it is bizarre and somewhat threatening: "When you lie down in the grave of a slashed tree,/ I cover you, as I always did;/ this time you do not leave." The following poem removes the threat as the speaker directly addresses her husband: "Again I see us walking into the night trees,/ irreversible motion, but the branches are now lit within." There is more companionship here, less seduction. This poem is clearly a response to the "Jacklight" poem, taking up its challenge and discovering new powers: "Husband, by the light of our bones we are going."

"Captivity" uses the narrative of Mary Rowlandson, who was captured by the Wampanoag Indians in 1676. At first repulsed by her male captor, Rowlandson will not eat the food he offers. Later, she witnesses a tribal ritual: "He led his company in the noise/ until I could no longer bear/ the thought of how I was." The poem concludes with her entreaty to the earth "to admit me/ as he was."

Section 3, "The Butcher's Wife," is a sequence of poems that share the central character of Mary Kroger, a powerful woman. These are narrative poems dealing chiefly with non-Native American material, although Kroger is a midwesterner and aware of what the land was like before white incursions. In "Clouds," Kroger says, "Let everything be how it could have been, once:/ a land that was empty and perfect as clouds." When her husband dies, Kroger goes through a transformation: "Widowed by men, I married the dark firs." Kroger has answered the call of "Jacklight." By "marrying" the woods, she has discovered unexpected powers. "At certain times," she says, "I speak in tongues."

Erdrich concludes *Jacklight* with Indian oral narratives. In "The Strange People," for example, she uses a story about the antelope. As in "Jacklight," Erdrich narrates this poem from the point of view of the animal. Initially, the antelope doe is attracted by the hunter whose "jacklight/ fills my eyes with blue fire." Though she is killed by the hunter, she does not die. A trickster figure, she becomes "a lean gray witch/ through the bullets that enter and dissolve." He is no match for her, and she leaves in the morning to return to the woods.

"Turtle Mountain Reservation" closes the volume and is dedicated to Erdrich's Chippewa grandfather. This grandpa "hitchhikes home" and comes at last to the swamp and the woods, "his hands/ that have grown to be the twisted doubles/ of the burrows of mole and badger." He is the woods. The speaker recognizes that she too comes from "Hands of earth, of this clay." This book of poems is, indeed, a return to Erdrich's roots.

BAPTISM OF DESIRE

The Roman Catholic Church teaches that there are three forms of baptism: fire, water, and desire. Any of these will establish the necessary condition for salvation to occur. In her second book of poems, *Baptism of Desire*, Erdrich focuses on desire and forms a powerful metaphor for the union of the physical and the spiritual. Subjects from her first book of poems reappear in her second. The reader recognizes Mary Kroger, for example, and also the American Indian trickster figure Potchikoo. For the most part, however, Erdrich explores new material, primarily religious but also deeply connected to her own experience as a woman, a wife, and a mother.

The most striking poem in the volume is "Hydra," which appears to be Erdrich's statement about her coming into her own as a creative being. The critic Amy Adelstein states that "Erdrich draws on the ambivalent imagery of the serpent as seducer and an initiator into the sacred mysteries." From an American Indian perspective, the hydra or snake is Erdrich's power animal, her guide and the activator of her poetic imagination: "Snake of the long reach, the margin,/ The perfect sideways motion/ I have imitated all my life./ Snake of hard hours, you are my poetry." So compelling is this "Hydra" that it explains Erdrich's ability to write poems

during pregnancy, childbirth, and the early years of her various children. In her notes to this volume, she says that most of the poems were written during periods of sleeplessness brought on by her pregnancies.

Some readers prefer the religious poems in *Baptism of Desire* to the more domestic ones. The critic Annie Finch states that they are "lush in imagery, fascinating in their suggestiveness, refreshing, often, in their very privacy." Erdrich achieves this privacy through persona poems in some cases. "The Visit," in the voice of Mary, the mother of Jesus, takes up the subject of the Immaculate Conception and the virgin birth. Erdrich's poem begins with the stark statement, "It was not love. No flowers or ripened figs/ were in his hands." Mary was told she was to become the mother of God, but this was no romantic proposition. What about Joseph, Mary's husband-to-be? "What could he do but fit the blades/ of wood together into a cradle?"

In "Avila," Erdrich writes in the voice of Saint Teresa of Ávila's brother. The opening imagery is vivid and direct, the question shocking as he asks: "Sister, do you remember our cave of stones,/ how we entered from the white heat of afternoons,/ chewed seeds, and plotted one martyrdom/ more cruel than the last?" He refers to the disasters of the Children's Crusade to free the Holy Land from Muslim rule.

"Sacraments," a long seven-part poem, is equally compelling. Erdrich discards the definitions given by the Catechism for a more private perspective. In the poem on Holy Orders, for example, she begins: "God, I was not meant to be the isolate/ cry in this body./ I was meant to have your tongue in my mouth." The speaker longs for union with her God, but the rendering is more in the vein of the fifteenth century Hindu poet Mīrā Bāī than of traditional Christianity.

In *Baptism of Desire*, Erdrich finds a spiritual element in caring for her children. In "Sunflowers," a mother and father tend to their children at night. After soothing the children, changing diapers, and providing milk, the parents return to bed and dream of "a field of sunflowers," which, like humans, are profoundly phototropic, turning their heads to the light, "to the bronze/ face of the old god/ who floats over us and burns." The spirituality here is primitive, even pagan, and much in tune with Erdrich's heritage as American

Indian. The children are like the flowers, a connection suggested but not underlined by Erdrich. Amy Adelstein comments on this suggestiveness as a trait of Erdrich's poems. She says, "It is in a dreamlike, suggestible state that the metamorphosis of shapes and identities and the confounding of time and space occur, approximating the ritual of baptism."

"Ritual," the last poem in *Baptism of Desire*, details a mother's duties as protector of her children: "I bind the net beneath you with the tendons of my wrist." Then she returns to sleep beside her husband, their bed covered with a quilt depicting "the twelve-branched tree of life." She uses this tree as metaphor for their union, which grows and spreads as a tree does, "Until the slightest twigs scrape at the solid frost-blue/ of the floor of heaven."

ORIGINAL FIRE

Original Fire, Erdrich's third book of poetry, was published in 2003, fourteen years after her last collection. In the spirit of the controlled chaos of *Love Medicine*, with its multiple narrators and nonchronological structure, Erdrich integrates five new poems amid pieces from *Jacklight* and *Baptism of Desire*, while introducing a collection of thirteen new poems under the "Original Fire" subheading. The author continues to focus heavily on themes that existed in her previous collections, in which she critiques Western religions, revels in motherhood, and ponders creation and death.

The section "The Seven Sleepers" contains three new poems, which follow an overarching theme of contradicting spiritual beliefs. The poems here are inextricably linked—each piece builds on its predecessor, necessitating that readers ponder the whole as the sum of its parts. "The Sacraments" has seven poems coinciding with the seven sacraments of Catholicism. Likewise, "Saint Clare" contains four poems focusing on specific Catholic saintly ideals and experiences. In poems such as "Christ's Twin" and "Orozco's Christ," Erdrich focuses on the duality of the sacred and secular worlds, while juxtaposing the mortal deity of Christ and the supernatural elements of American Indian spirituality.

Erdrich continues to scrutinize the brutality and hypocrisy of "civilized" Christians in two new poems: "The Buffalo Prayer" and "Rez Litany." "The Buffalo Prayer" is a scathing indictment of the ravaging of the natural world, which destroyed native culture and livelihoods. The eradicated buffalo narrate and sarcastically supplicate to Holy Ladies of "the Buffalo Bones," "Destruction Everywhere," and "the Box Cars of Skulls." These references are meant to satirize the pretenses under which the Christian colonizers destroyed the order of the natural world. Erdrich's ire for such destructive assertions of dominance by the white culture continues in "Rez Litany," which condemns the inadequate health care systems provided to native populations, whose bureaucrats ". . . preside now in heaven/ at the gates of the Grand Casino Buffet."

The final section, "Original Fire," contains thirteen new poems illustrating Erdrich's maturation both in life and in art. She focuses on relationships between mother and child, wife and husband, and humankind and nature. "New Mother" and "Little Blue Eyeglasses" portray a mother's need to comfort and protect a child from conception through adulthood. The mother-guardian-consoler theme continues into "Wood Mountain," in which a mother and son deal with the loss of a loved one, ultimately finding understanding and solace in each other.

Erdrich matures within her poetry in "Advice to Myself," in which the narrator tells herself to leave the dishes in the sink and the crumbs in the toaster, as such chores only maintain material possessions—they are not necessities. If anything, such monotonous chores promote an ongoing routine that leads to further expectations. The realization that happiness is not contingent on such trivialities sets her free.

The final poem of the collection, "Asiniig" (the Ojibwe word for stone), is representative of both grandmother and grandfather personas, whose conversation forms the basis for another creation story. The stones are the narrators, created by "original fire" and ever present. In the six individual poems that make up "Asiniig," Erdrich explores the human desire for immortality. The stones, which have myriad uses in every culture, tell people that they exist after death, if only through the stones. The stones persist in life so that people may persist in death through nature; bodies and consciousness disappear, yet, like a phantom limb, aches persist—all that remains is memory.

OTHER MAJOR WORKS

LONG FICTION: *Love Medicine*, 1984, 1993; *The Beet Queen*, 1986; *Tracks*, 1988; *The Crown of Columbus*, 1991 (with Michael Dorris); *The Bingo Palace*, 1994; *Tales of Burning Love*, 1996; *The Antelope Wife*, 1998; *The Last Report on the Miracles at Little No Horse*, 2001; *The Master Butchers Singing Club*, 2003; *Four Souls*, 2004; *The Painted Drum*, 2005; *The Plague of Doves*, 2008; *Shadow Tag*, 2010.

SHORT FICTION: "The Red Convertible," 1981; "Scales," 1982; "The World's Greatest Fishermen," 1982; "American Horse," 1983; "Destiny," 1985; "Saint Marie," 1985; "Fleur," 1987; "Snares," 1987; "Matchimanito," 1988; *The Red Convertible: Selected and New Stories, 1978-2008*, 2009.

NONFICTION: *The Blue Jay's Dance: A Birth Year*, 1995; *Books and Islands in Ojibwe Country*, 2003.

CHILDREN'S LITERATURE: *Grandmother's Pigeon*, 1996 (illustrated by Jim LaMarche); *The Birchbark House*, 1999; *The Range Eternal*, 2002; *The Game of Silence*, 2005.

EDITED TEXT: *The Best American Short Stories 1993*, 1993.

BIBLIOGRAPHY

Bak, Hans. "Circles Blaze in Ordinary Days." In *Native American Women in Literature and Culture*, edited by Susan Castillo and Victor M. P. Da Rosa. Porto, Portugal: Fernando Pessoa University Press, 1997. Bak writes an extensive analysis of the *Jacklight* poems and sees Erdrich's first book of poetry as having a different appeal from *Baptism of Desire*. He terms that appeal its "hybrid" or "amphibious" quality in that Erdrich draws on both aspects of her heritage, the German American and the Chippewa.

Chavkin, Allan, ed. *The Chippewa Landscape of Louise Erdrich*. Tuscaloosa: University of Alabama Press, 1998. Collects original essays focusing on Erdrich's writings that are rooted in the Chippewa experience. Premier scholars of Native American literature investigate narrative structure, signs of ethnicity, the notions of luck and chance in Erdrich's narrative cosmology, and her use of comedy in exploring American Indians' tragic past.

Erdrich, Louise. Interview by Joseph Bruchac. In *Survival This Way: Interviews with American Indian Poets*, edited by Bruchac. Tucson: University of Arizona Press, 1987. Erdrich discusses her poetry and her philosophy on what makes a good story.

Gould, Janice. "American Indian Women's Poetry: Strategies of Rage and Hope." *Signs* 20 (1995): 797-817. Gould discusses the dueling emotions of rape and hope that are prominent themes in Native American authors such as Erdrich, Paula Gunn Allen, and Joy Harjo. Such poetry, capable of expressing the anguish of those who strive to identify with one or more cultures, transforms from mere words on a page to an act, a performance, a song, and a strategy that aims to legitimize the rage and hope felt by an entire nation.

Hafen, Jane P. "Sacramental Language: Ritual in the Poetry of Louise Erdrich." *Great Plains Quarterly* 16 (1996): 147-155. Hafen, a Taos Pueblo Indian, examines Erdrich's books of poetry. In them, she finds evidence of the oral culture and a blending of rituals from the Chippewa and European American religious traditions. Erdrich's poetry reveals her individual voice and personal experience while at the same time connecting to the rituals of her mixed-blood heritage.

Ludlow, Jeannie. "Working (in) the In-Between: Poetry, Criticism, Interrogation, and Interruption." *Studies in American Indian Literature* 6 (Spring, 1994): 24-42. Ludlow writes a sophisticated literary analysis of Joy Harjo's "The Woman Hanging from the Thirteenth Floor Window" and Erdrich's "Lady in the Pink Mustang" from *Jacklight*. She finds Erdrich's poem potentially more empowering.

Rader, Dean. "Sites of Unification: Teaching Erdrich's Poetry." In *Approaches to Teaching the Works of Louise Erdrich*, edited by Greg Sarris, Lonnie A. Jacobs, and James R. Giles. New York: Modern Language Association, 2004. This article addresses the focuses on desire and unity in *Jacklight* and *Baptism of Desire*. Rader asserts that from a pedagogical standpoint, the readers must identity and understand the unity that exists within an individual collection and also the unity that exists throughout Erdrich's entire body of work.

_____. "Word as Weapon: Visual Culture and Contemporary American Indian Poetry." *MELUS* 27 (2002): 147-167. Native American poets Erdrich, Sherman Alexie, and Wendy Rose are the focus of this article, which discusses lyric poems by each writer. Rader argues that such lyric poetry functions as a weapon of resistance that is meant to challenge the marginalization of Native American culture.

Sawhney, Brajesh, ed. *Studies in the Literary Achievement of Louise Erdrich, Native American Writer: Fifteen Critical Essays.* Lewiston, N.Y.: Edwin Mellen Press, 2008. Several essays discuss the themes in Erdrich's work and are applicable to her poetry.

Stookey, Lorena Laura. *Louise Erdrich: A Critical Companion.* Westport, Conn.: Greenwood Press, 1999. A good study of Erdrich's works. Includes bibliographical references and an index.

Claire Keyes; Sarah Hilbert
Updated by Lydia E. Ferguson

MARTÍN ESPADA

Born: Brooklyn, New York; August 7, 1957

PRINCIPAL POETRY

The Immigrant Iceboy's Bolero, 1982
Trumpets from the Islands of Their Eviction, 1987, 1994
Rebellion Is the Circle of a Lover's Hands = Rebelión es el giro de manos del amante, 1990
City of Coughing and Dead Radiators, 1993
Imagine the Angels of Bread, 1996
A Mayan Astronomer in Hell's Kitchen, 2000
Alabanza: New and Selected Poems, 1982-2002, 2003
The Republic of Poetry, 2006
Crucifixion in the Plaza de Armas, 2008
La Tumba de Buenaventura Roig: Selected Poems/ Poemas selectos, 2008 (bilingual edition)

OTHER LITERARY FORMS

Although Martín Espada (ehs-PAH-dah) is known primarily as a poet, he also has edited two collections, *Poetry Like Bread: Poets of the Political Imagination from Curbstone Press* (1994, 2000) and *El Coro: A Chorus of Latino and Latina Poetry* (1997); translated the poetry of Clemente Soto Vélez in *The Blood That Keeps Singing: Selected Poems of Clemente Soto Vélez* (1991; with Camilo Pérez-Bustillo); and published one collection of essays in *Zapata's Disciple: Essays* (1998). A compact disc of his poetry was released in 2004 under the title *Now the Dead Will Dance the Mambo*.

ACHIEVEMENTS

Martín Espada has garnered many honors, including a Massachusetts Artists Foundation Fellowship (1984), a National Endowment for the Arts (NEA) Fellowship (1986 and 1992), the PEN/Revson Foundation Fellowship (1989) and Paterson Poetry Prize (1991) for *Rebellion Is the Circle of a Lover's Hands*, the Lilly Teaching Fellowship (1994-1995), the PEN/Voelcker Award for Poetry (1994), and a Massachusetts Cultural Council Artist Grant (1996). *Imagine the Angels of Bread* received the American Book Award for poetry from the Before Columbus Foundation (1997) and was a finalist for the National Book Critics Circle Award. *Zapata's Disciple* won the 1999 Independent Publisher Book Award in the category of creative nonfiction/ memoir. He received the Paterson Award for Sustained Literary Achievement in 2004 for *Alabanza* and in 2006 for *The Republic of Poetry*, which was a finalist for the Pulitzer Prize.

BIOGRAPHY

Born on August 7, 1957, in Brooklyn, New York, to a Puerto Rican father and a Jewish mother, Martín Espada grew up in Brooklyn. His father, Frank Espada, became active in the Civil Rights movement during the 1950's. During the 1960's, he took his son to protest meetings and rallies in an effort to educate him as to the political and social struggle that minorities must wage against prejudice, racism, and indifference. A leader in the Puerto Rican community of New York City, he later became a noted photographer. Through his father, the young Martín Espada learned about the need to fight against injustice.

Espada began writing poetry when he was fifteen.

Martín Espada (©Miriam Berkley)

He has stated that he found writing to be even more important than sleeping. Some of the odd jobs that Espada held as a young man include a bindery worker, a groundskeeper for a minor-league baseball ballpark, a night desk clerk, and a bouncer in a bar. Each of these experiences allowed him to witness the difficulties that people of color encounter on a daily basis in the United States. The many diverse settings helped him to be what Espada calls a "spy." He made the most of being a keen observer. The "mental notes" he made eventually were turned into poems. In 1981, Espada was graduated from the University of Wisconsin at Madison with a B.A. in history. He then went on to earn his law degree from Boston's Northeastern University School of Law in 1985. After earning his law degree, Espada worked as a tenant lawyer near Boston in Chelsea, Massachusetts. He was a supervisor for a legal-aid office, Su Clinica Legal, that served a clientele of primarily Spanish-speaking residents. In 1991, his wife, Katherine,

gave birth to a son. Espada became an English professor on the faculty of the University of Massachusetts at Amherst in 1993, where he has taught courses on Latino poetry and creative writing. Taking inspiration from those who came before him, he also has continued to take public stands against injustice at every turn.

ANALYSIS

Martín Espada has committed himself to living a life that does not take the status quo as the way things have to be. As a lawyer, he fought the system to make life better for those who are less fortunate. In his poetry, Espada has continued to shed light on injustices, especially those done to the Latino immigrants who have come to the United States in search of a better life. Influenced by the activist Chilean poet Pablo Neruda, Espada is a political poet in the best sense of the term. He does not write easy slogans to make himself and his audience merely feel better. He understands the immense responsibility he has shouldered in writing poems that take on sensitive topics. Espada's poetry challenges not only the audience but also the poet. He must rise above the temptation to compose mere propaganda. Coming from a Puerto Rican heritage, Espada was made well aware by the majority population at an early age not only how corrosive prejudice can be to the minority being brutalized but also how it sours an entire country.

THE IMMIGRANT ICEBOY'S BOLERO

For his first collection, *The Immigrant Iceboy's Bolero*, Espada included photographs taken by his father. The title poem refers to his father's journey to the United States. As a boy of nine, Frank Espada had to work as an ice boy. It was his job to carry large blocks of ice up the stairs of tenement buildings. Because of this heavy lifting, his back was permanently injured. The poem is a moving account of how much pressure Espada's father experienced as he attempted to make it in a new and hostile environment.

TRUMPETS FROM THE ISLANDS OF
THEIR EVICTION

Espada included Spanish translations of his poems in his second collection, *Trumpets from the Islands of Their Eviction*. In 1994, Espada published an expanded edition, which included a select number of poems from

The Immigrant Iceboy's Bolero. The poems in his second collection deal with Puerto Rican immigrants and their struggles. In "Tiburon," Espada uses the image of a shark consuming a fisherman to reflect on the relationship between the United States and Puerto Rico. The title poem shows the constant struggle of Puerto Ricans to be heard by people in the Anglo world around them. Espada opens the poem with images that give voice to the plight of immigrants coming from Puerto Rico:

> At the bar two blocks away,
> immigrants with Spanish mouths
> hear trumpets
> from the islands of their eviction.
> The music swarms into the barrio
> of a refugee's imagination,
> along with predatory squad cars
> and bullying handcuffs.

REBELLION IS THE CIRCLE OF A LOVER'S HANDS

In *Rebellion Is the Circle of a Lover's Hands*, Espada includes a Spanish translation of each poem. He writes eloquently about how what may seem personal is really also political. Individuals who go about their everyday lives working and trying to do right by their families are given a voice by a caring poet. In the short lyric poem "Latin Night at the Pawnshop," Espada expresses his concern for an entire Latin culture through the experience of finding musical instruments relegated to a pawnshop. The poem opens with the image of an "apparition of a salsa band." Instruments such as a "golden trumpet," a "silver trombone," a "tambourine," and some "maracas" all have "price tags dangling." Espada sees these price tags as comparable to a "city morgue ticket/ on a dead man's toe." The strength of this collection can be found in how Espada can take seemingly inconsequential incidents and show them to be representative of a larger offense or crime that has been done to a culture that has vibrancy and exists under the nose of the Anglo-American world.

IMAGINE THE ANGELS OF BREAD

In his fifth poetry collection, *Imagine the Angels of Bread*, Espada celebrates what has been called "the bread of the imagination, the bread of the table, and the bread of justice." The political and the personal are brilliantly wedded in a number of autobiographical poems. The poet conjures up images of family bonds, the smells of a particular neighborhood, and the lessons learned from various menial jobs. The title poem is inhabited by many elements including compassion and rage, reality and visions. Espada states that "This is the year that squatters evict landlords" and that "this is the year/ that shawled refugees deport judges/ who stare at the floor." Even though there are so many injustices of the past, the poet believes that maybe this will be the year that all the wrongs will be put right. Espada recognizes that after all the rage is vented that there must be hope for a better future. This collection won the American Book Award for poetry in 1997.

A MAYAN ASTRONOMER IN HELL'S KITCHEN

As with his earlier collections, Espada continues in *A Mayan Astronomer in Hell's Kitchen* to speak eloquently for the downtrodden, for those who have not as of yet been able to share in the American Dream. Divided into three sections, the collection opens with a section, "A Tarantula in the Bananas," that concerns the plight of Puerto Ricans in this country. The first poem, "My Name Is Espada," delineates the value of a family name and how it has survived throughout history. The word *espada* literally means "sword" in Spanish. In the poem, the poet also relates a personal history of his name:

> Espada: sword in Puerto Rico, family name of
>   bricklayers
> who swore their trowels fell as leaves from iron trees;
> teachers who wrote poems in galloping calligraphy;
>   saintcarvers who whittled a slave's gaze and a
> conqueror's beard;
> shoemaker spitting tuberculosis, madwoman
> dangling a lantern to listen for the cough;
> gambler in a straw hat inhabited by mathematical
>   angels;
> preacher who first heard the savior's voice
> bleeding through the plaster of the jailhouse;
> dreadlocked sculptor stunned by visions of birds,
> sprouting wings from his forehead, earthen wings in
>   the fire.

No matter what struggle is at hand for a person of color, a Puerto Rican, a member of the Espada family, it is possible to find strength in heritage, in a family name.

Espada concludes the first section with a short poem "What Francisco Luis Espada Learned at Age Five, Standing on the Dock." The lesson learned by young Francisco was that "Sometimes/ there's a/ tarantula/ in the/ bananas."

The second section, "A Mayan Astronomer in Hell's Kitchen," includes some of Espada's most touching poems to date. There are two poems specifically dedicated to his wife, Katherine Espada. There is humor as well as poignancy in "I Apologize for Giving You Poison Ivy by Smacking You in the Eye with the Crayfish at the End of My Fishing Line." Out of ignorance, the poet injures Katherine. He was born in Brooklyn and ignorant about how to fish, what crayfish are, and how dangerous poison ivy can be to a person's skin. The poem is humorous and touching, and also speaks to a cultural divide. The last section, "A Library of Lions," contains the most overtly political poems of the collection. The last poem, "The River Will Not Testify," details how seventeenth century Puritans butchered Native Americans. Espada writes with conviction about human dignity.

The Republic of Poetry

As in previous collections, Espada continues to believe with all his heart that poetry is a powerful medium of expression. Poetry can inspire and alter outcomes. In *The Republic of Poetry*, the poet has included twenty-six poems that hit the target, that give voice to the voiceless. In the opening section, "The Republic of Poetry," Espada reflects on the 2004 centennial celebration in Chile of Neruda's birth. He attended this tribute to a great poet, to a poet who mattered. Dictators also recognize the power of words. They attempt to hold onto power by manipulating or silencing poets. Espada speaks of the horrors inflicted on the Chilean people and on the Chilean soul. The ray of hope was extinguished by the coup that overthrew president Salvador Allende in the early 1970's. Poets are tortured and murdered for what they represent. It is unnecessary for Espada to embellish or add fanfare to these poems. The truth can stand on its own and deliver its own beckoning call.

For the second section, "The Poet's Coat," Espada wrote five very moving elegies on poets whom he holds in high esteem. The poets are Jeff Male, Julia de Burgos, Dennis Brutus, Yusef Komunyakaa, and Robert Creeley. Espada reflects on the kindness of Male, a veteran of the Vietnam War. Burgos was a Puerto Rican voice in the wilderness. Ahead of her time, she inspired future Puerto Ricans to speak out against oppression. Espada admires the poet who is willing to speak up for justice, to be a thorn in the side of terror and complacency. The final section, "The Weather-Beaten Face," brings together poems that describe the futility of war. The poet serves as a witness to all those who are willing to submit to the brutality of war, whether in Vietnam, Iraq, or another conflict. Espada believes that poetry has political, social, and moral weight. The poet must write about human experience, start an argument in order to learn a truth, and document all that history can teach.

Crucifixion in the Plaza de Armas

In *Crucifixion in the Plaza de Armas*, Espada has written about something that is very close to his heart: Puerto Rico. His family roots can be found on the island of Puerto Rico. His ancestors are never far from the poet's mind. Espada wishes to pay tribute to the spirit of those who have fought for equality and against occupation by outside forces. The word "independence" is writ large in this collection. The smells of the island fill the nostrils. There is longing in the hearts of those who moved to the United States in order to make a living.

The rich and tragic history of Puerto Rico weaves its way throughout this collection. Since its discovery by Christopher Columbus on his second voyage to the region, the island has been at the mercy of colonizers. The native people of the island were forced to be slaves of the Spaniards. The idea of independence has been considered an act of rebellion that has needed to be stopped by any means necessary. In 1937, nineteen Puerto Ricans were killed during what has come to be known as the Ponce massacre. For Espada, this human tragedy should not be forgotten. With agonizing restraint, the poet has given voice to those who want the best for those who call Puerto Rico home, who want independence at long last to become a reality.

Other major works

nonfiction: *Zapata's Disciple: Essays*, 1998.

translation: *The Blood That Keeps Singing: Se-*

lected *Poems of Clemente Soto Vélez*, 1991 (with Camilo Pérez-Bustillo).

EDITED TEXTS: *Poetry Like Bread: Poets of the Political Imagination from Curbstone Press*, 1994, 2000; *El Coro: A Chorus of Latino and Latina Poetry*, 1997.

BIBLIOGRAPHY

Campo, Rafael. "Why Poetry Matters." Review of *Zapata's Disciple*. *The Progressive* 63 (April, 1999): 43-44. Campo reviews Espada's *Zapata's Disciple* and praises the poet for his clarity of purpose and his clarity of vision.

Espada, Martín. "Give Politics a Human Face: An Interview with Lawyer-Poet-Professor Martín Espada." Interview by Sarah Browning. *Valley Advocate*, November 18, 1993. Espada speaks to the importance of keeping poetry relevant to the everyday lives of people and states that anyone who wishes to become a writer should remember to stay involved in the world. Poetry can be political without falling into the trap of being no more than mere propaganda.

_____. "Jesús Colón's Truth-Seeking Disciple: An Interview with Martín Espada." Interview by José B. Gonzalez. *Latino Studies* 5 (2007): 123-128. An insightful examination of Espada's writing process, including a discussion of his influences, his weaving of history into his poems, the importance of being a bilingual poet, and his imperative to reveal the truth in anything that he composes.

_____. "Poetry and the Burden of History: An Interview with Martín Espada." Interview by Steven Ratiner. *The Christian Science Monitor*, March 6, 1991, pp. 16-17. Espada points out that a poet can also be a historian, as he or she can put a "human face" on history and on monumental events. While important issues must be confronted directly by the poet, Espada believes that a poem suffers if the poet is overwhelmed by anger. The correct tone is of preeminent importance to Espada.

_____. "A Poetry of Legacy: An Interview with Martín Espada." Interview by Ray Gonzalez. *Bloomsbury Review*, July/August, 1997, pp. 3-4. Espada reveals how the historical past, his father, and the birth of his own son have been influential in shaping his poetry and how he sees his role as a political poet.

_____. "The Politics of Advocacy: Three Poems." *Hopscotch: A Cultural Review* 2 (2001): 128-133. Espada delineates what it takes to make a successful poem: A poem must be more than mere words and more than mere "important" topics.

Fink, Thomas. "Visibility and History in the Poetry of Martín Espada." *Americas Review* 25 (1999): 202-221. Fink details Espada's involvement in the Puerto Rican independence movement and how his heritage affects the poetry he writes. The richness and in-your-face quality of Espada's poetry make him one of the most important poets writing in English.

Keene, John R. Review of *City of Coughing and Dead Radiators*. *MELUS* 21 (Spring, 1996): 133-135. Keene reinforces how vital a poet such as Espada is on the American literary landscape. In this collection, Keene says, Espada is able to balance weighty topics with the perfect choice of words. Keene marvels at how Espada can accomplish this without ever sounding hollow or pedantic.

Salgado, Cesar A. "About Martín Espada." *Ploughshares* 31, no. 1 (Spring, 2005): 203-206. A detailed overview of Espada as poet, professor, and activist.

Jeffry Jensen
Updated by Jensen

MARI EVANS

Born: Toledo, Ohio; July 16, 1923
Also known as: E. Reed

PRINCIPAL POETRY

I Am a Black Woman, 1970
Nightstar, 1973-1978, 1981
A Dark and Splendid Mass, 1992
Continuum: New and Selected Poems, 2007

OTHER LITERARY FORMS

Mari Evans is known not just for her poetry but also for her children's books, which include *Singing Black:*

Alternative Nursery Rhymes for Children (1976) and *Dear Corinne, Tell Somebody! Love, Annie: A Book About Secrets* (1999). She has also written a number of plays, such as *Eyes* (pr. 1979) and *River of My Song* (pr. 1977), and a volume of essays, *Clarity as Concept: A Poet's Perspective* (2006). She directed *The Black Experience* for WTTV in Indianapolis between 1968 and 1973 and edited *Black Women Writers (1950-1980): A Critical Evaluation* (1983).

ACHIEVEMENTS

Mari Evans received many honors and awards, including the John Hay Whitney Fellowship (1965-1966) and the Hazel Joan Bryant Award from the Midwest Afrikan American Theatre Alliance. A Woodrow Wilson Foundation grant in 1968 allowed her to pursue her teaching career. *I Am a Black Woman* earned the First Poetry Award from the Black Academy of Arts and Letters in 1970. She received the Indiana University Writers' Conference Award (1970) and a National Endowment for the Arts Creative Writing Fellowship (1981-1982). In 1975, Marion College (later known as Indiana Wesleyan University) granted her an honorary degree, and in 1976, Bloomington, Indiana, named her Outstanding Woman of the Year.

BIOGRAPHY

Mari Evans was born and raised in Toledo, Ohio. She lost her mother at the age of seven, and her father became her primary caretaker. An upholsterer, he had a great influence on her, especially in supporting her writing. Evans published a story in the school paper when she was in the fourth grade, and her father saved it, looking on it with pride.

At the University of Toledo, Evans studied fashion design, although she did not follow it as a career. Instead, she took a position as a writer and editor for a manufacturing plant that was mostly white. Despite the racism she faced there, she continued working, developing a discipline that would serve her well in later life. Evans then began teaching and has taught or served as writer-in-residence at Indiana University at Purdue, Purdue University, Washington University (St. Louis), Cornell University, the State University of New York at Albany, Spelman College, and the University of Mi-

ami at Coral Gables. Her photo was featured on a postage stamp in Uganda in 1997, and she was nominated for a Grammy Award for Best Album Notes in 2002 for her contribution to *The Long Road Back to Freedom: An Anthology of Black Music*.

ANALYSIS

The poetry of Mari Evans is primarily directed toward African Americans, as she celebrates and explores what it means to be black. Evans uses her poetry to focus on issues that she feels strongly about, such as the Civil Rights movement and the Vietnam War, dealing directly with the emotions involved. Some of her poems are elegies for those who have died, but as a whole, her collections express joy and hope for the future, and a theme of love functions as an undercurrent.

Her poems shows the influence of other black poets such as Langston Hughes in language, rhythm, and subject matter. Jazz elements are present, creating rhythmic patterns that ebb and flow like music. Evans demonstrates her understanding of how the poems appear to readers through her use of alternative typography as well as how the poems sound when read aloud through her use of vernacular phrasing and alliteration.

I AM A BLACK WOMAN

I Am a Black Woman, probably Evans's best-known volume of poetry, brings various subjects together into a unified whole that explores a sense of love and its romantic, familial, and political effects. The first section, "To These Add One: Love Withheld Restrained," focuses on romantic love, primarily its absence. The second section deals with the emotional impact of that absence of love. The next two sections focus on familial love, mostly concerning children, and include the often anthologized "When in Rome." The last section, "A Black Oneness, a Black Strength," focuses on the political upheaval during the Civil Rights movement, with "The Great Civil Rights Law (A.D. 1964)" and "A Good Assassination Should Be Quiet," which examines the killing of Martin Luther King, Jr.

Framing this collection is the title poem, "I Am a Black Woman." By placing this poem at the beginning of the book, she prepares the reader with her strength, and by repeating it at the end of the book, she reminds the reader what that strength has brought her through.

Evans shows that despite the tragedies and heartbreaks she has outlined in poems throughout the volume, she is a strong woman:

> I
> am a black woman
> tall as a cypress
> strong
> beyond all definition still
> defying place
> and time
> and circumstance.

In *I Am a Black Woman*, Evans uses free verse and experiments with typography, employing unusual line breaks, indentations, and capitalization to emphasize elements of her poems.

NIGHTSTAR, 1973-1978

In *Nightstar, 1973-1978*, Evans increasingly relies on typography to create meaning in her poems, and she reaches out more to the readers, using the word "we" to invite the reader to become part of the community she is trying to reach.

Many of the poems in *Nightstar, 1973-1978* use the cadences of African American vernacular English to connect the poems to the black experience and to provide authenticity to those experiences that would be glossed over through the use of standard English. This use of language provides a musical quality to the work, stretching out syllables and lines and providing alliterative notes, as in "Daufuskie: Janis": "Janis sweepin/ Sweepin d'dirt right out d'door/ Janis ain playin."

Nightstar, 1973-1978 continues Evans's mission to explore social issues through her poetry. "The Expendables" recalls the bleakness of waiting for war reports from Vietnam:

> You of course
> know what is meant
> by
>   "U.S. casualties
>   were
>   . . . . light"

In "Face on the Sunwarmed Granite" and "Remembering Willie," Evans recalls and rages against the violence toward African Americans that occurred during the Civil Rights movement, and in "The Time Is Now,"

she supports a black solidarity, saying "if ever we would rise/ We could reorder space and time define/ the circumstance claim absolutes."

The penultimate poem, "Who Can Be Born Black," is one of Evans's best known.

> Who
> can be born black
> and not
> sing
> the wonder of it
> the joy
> the
> challenge.

"Who Can Be Born Black" and the closing poem, "No One Knows the Year," end the book with a sense of joy. Despite the violence and despair of the earlier poems in the collection, Evans finishes it with the triumph she feels in her heritage and her hopes for the future.

A DARK AND SPLENDID MASS

Published eleven years after *Nightstar, 1973-1978*, *A Dark and Splendid Mass* shows the experience gained by the poet in the intervening years. The anger and need to encapsulate social issues into poetry has somewhat eased in this volume, though some poems still burst forth with the need to express social problems of the early 1990's. More of the poems revolve around love, and while still Evans retains some of the alternate typography that she used in the past, she does not rely on it as heavily as she did in her previous volume.

Love, one of the themes of *I Am a Black Woman*, returns to prominence in this volume. "Celebration" does just that—it celebrates the love of two hearts that have been forced to endure hardship but are coming together in joy:

> I will bring you a whole person
> and you will bring me a whole person
> and we will have us twice as much
> of love and everything

"Celebration" is followed by "Ode to My Sons," in which Evans writes, "I wish you joy and love and strength/ a centering of mind and will."

Not all of the volume is centered on love. "Oral History: Found Poetry" relates stories told to Evans by her father, including one about her great-grandfather being lynched and one of her uncles being run out of town in Georgia. Evans has appended a note to "Alabama Landscape," dedicating the poem to "all the Black victims of 'police action' lynchings throughout the United States, and especially for Michael Taylor." Evans goes on to explain that the death of seventeen-year-old Taylor was judged to be a suicide, although at the time of his death, he was seated in the back of a police cruiser with his hands cuffed behind his back, and the fatal shot was to his temple. "Alabama Landscape" is a journey through history of running from harm, and Evans describes those running away from such violence as "vulnerable/ still unavenged."

CONTINUUM

Continuum contains a selection of older poems and some new poems, as well as a foreword by Maya Angelou that offers context for Evans's work and the meaning it has had for the black community. The older poems are interspersed with new poems. In the preface, Evans tells the reader to "Enjoy the journey as it happens, no connivance, no imposed order, no subject segments. Just life as it is lived." *Continuum* is a personal journey of her own, underscored by the selection of "Who Can Be Born Black" as the opening poem and "I Am a Black Woman" as the second poem. Thus, the volume begins by presenting the two themes that have been the most important in Evans's life and poetry.

In some cases, it is difficult to separate the new poems from the older ones, as they journey through Evans's life and the social issues she has written about in her earlier poems. However, in *Continuum*, just as in her earlier volumes, some poems speak to a distinct period of history. "September 11, 2001" is only two stanzas long and repeats itself in language that recalls the stark horror of that day:

> Malcolm said
> Chickens
> come home
> to roost

This is not the only poem that brings forth the social issues present since Evans published *A Dark and Splendid Mass.* "The Beckley Veterans Readjustment

Center" refers to veterans returning not only from Korea and Vietnam, but also from Afghanistan and Iraq.

The closing poem, reprinted from *I Am a Black Woman*, is "If There Be Sorrow." It sums up the volume and Evans's attitude toward life:

> If there be sorrow
> let it be
> for things undone
> undreamed
> unrealized
> unattained

OTHER MAJOR WORKS

SHORT FICTION: "Third Stop in Caraway Park," 1975.

PLAYS: *River of My Song*, pr. 1977; *Boochie*, pr. 1979; *Eyes*, pr. 1979 (musical; adaptation of Zora Neale Hurston's novel *Their Eyes Were Watching God*); *Portrait of a Man*, pr. 1979.

NONFICTION: "In the Time of the Whirlwind: I'm with You," 1968; "Blackness: A Definition," 1969; "Contemporary Black Literature," 1970; "Behind the Green Door," 1977 (as E. Reed); "Decolonization as Goal: Political Writing as Device," 1979; "The Nature and Methodology of Colonization and Its Relationship to Creativity: A Systems Approach to Black Literature," 1979; "My Father's Passage," 1984; *Clarity as Concept: A Poet's Perspective*, 2006.

CHILDREN'S LITERATURE: *J. D.*, 1973; *I Look at Me!*, 1974; *Rap Stories*, 1974; *Singing Black: Alternative Nursery Rhymes for Children*, 1976; *Dear Corinne, Tell Somebody! Love, Annie: A Book About Secrets*, 1999.

EDITED TEXT: *Black Women Writers (1950-1980): A Critical Evaluation*, 1983.

BIBLIOGRAPHY

Allen, Jessica. "Mari Evans." In *Encyclopedia of African American Women Writers*, edited by Yolanda Williams Page. Westport, Conn.: Greenwood Press, 2007. Presents the life and works of Evans, discussed in the context of her being African American.

Douglas, Robert L. *Resistance, Insurgence and Identity: The Art of Mari Evans, Nelson Stevens, and the*

Black Arts Movement. Trenton, N.J.: Africa World Press, 2008. Analyzes Evans's poetry and compares it to that of Nelson Stevens.

Evans, Mari. "Acclaimed Poet Mari Evans on Being a Black Writer." Interview by Herb Boyd. *Crisis* 114, no. 2 (March/April, 2007): 34-35. Evans discusses her inspirations and motivations, as well as what it means to be a black female writer. Also addresses her critical reception and writers she admires.

Foster, Frances S. "Changing Concepts of the Black Woman." *Journal of Black Studies* 3, no. 4 (June, 1973): 433-454. Gives an overview of how black female writers are changing their views and the views of others toward black women. Uses Evans as a prime example of this changing conceptualization.

Lewis, Leon. "The Poetry of Mari Evans." In *Masterplots II: African American Literature*, edited by Tyrone Williams. Rev. ed. Pasadena, Calif.: Salem Press, 2009. Presents an analysis of the poetry of Evans, looking at what it meant to be a black woman poet as well as examining her techniques and development of a voice.

Lewis, Nghana Tamu. "In a Different Chord: Interpreting the Relations Among Black Female Sexuality, Agency, and the Blues." *African American Review* 37, no. 4 (Winter, 2003): 599-609. Examines poems from a number of different African American poets, including Evans, to explore how black women are seen and how they create themselves through the use of blues influence.

Emily Carroll Shearer

WILLIAM EVERSON
Brother Antoninus

Born: Sacramento, California; September 10, 1912
Died: Davenport, California; June 3, 1994

PRINCIPAL POETRY
These Are the Ravens, 1935
San Joaquin, 1939
The Masculine Dead, 1942

X War Elegies, 1943
The Waldport Poems, 1944
War Elegies, 1944
Poems MCMXLII, 1945
The Residual Years: Poems, 1940-1941, 1945
The Residual Years, 1948
The Privacy of Speech: Ten Poems in Sequence, 1949
A Triptych for the Living, 1951
At the Edge, 1958 (as Brother Antoninus)
The Crooked Lines of God: Poems, 1949-1954, 1959 (as Brother Antoninus)
There Will Be Harvest, 1960
The Year's Declension, 1961
The Hazards of Holiness: Poems, 1957-1960, 1962 (as Brother Antoninus)
The Poet Is Dead: A Memorial for Robinson Jeffers, 1964 (as Brother Antoninus)
The Rose of Solitude, 1964 (as Brother Antoninus)
The Blowing of the Seed, 1966
Single Source, 1966
The Achievement of Brother Antoninus: A Comprehensive Selection of His Poems with a Critical Introduction, 1967
The Vision of Felicity, 1967 (as Brother Antoninus)
A Canticle to the Waterbirds, 1968 (as Brother Antoninus)
Poems of Nineteen Forty Seven, 1968
The Residual Years: Poems 1934-1948, 1968
The Springing of the Blade, 1968
Black Hills, 1973
Tendril in the Mesh, 1973
Man-Fate, 1974
River-Root: A Syzygy for the Bicentennial of These States, 1976
The Mate-Flight of Eagles, 1977
Blackbird Sundown, 1978
The Veritable Years: Poems, 1949-1966, 1978
Eastward the Armies: Selected War Poems, 1935-1942, 1980
The Masks of Drought, 1980
In Medias Res: Canto One of an Autobiographical Epic, Dust Shall Be the Serpent's Food, 1984
Renegade Christmas, 1984
The High Embrace, 1986

Mexican Standoff, 1989
*The Engendering Flood: Book One of Dust Shall Be
    the Serpent's Food (Cantos I-IV)*, 1990
The Blood of the Poet, 1994
The Integral Years: Poems, 1966-1994, 2000

OTHER LITERARY FORMS

Never hesitant about admitting his literary indebtedness to Robinson Jeffers, since it was the poetry of Jeffers that seized him as a youth and helped him realize his own vocation as a poet, William Everson wrote numerous introductions to reprinted editions of Jeffers's work, as well as a critical study, *Robinson Jeffers: Fragments of an Older Fury* (1968). Like his older mentor, Everson was intensely interested in the West as landscape and California as region, and he explored both of these concerns, as subject matter and sources for art, in *Archetype West: The Pacific Coast as a Literary Region* (1976). The importance of regional identity, as well as what he perceived to be the artist's responsibility in portraying as honestly as possible the disparity between the inner (human) and the outer (natural) landscapes, was the central focus of many of Everson's essays and lectures, many of which are contained in *Earth Poetry: Selected Essays and Interviews of William Everson, 1950-1977* (1980) and *Birth of a Poet* (1982).

ACHIEVEMENTS

The most dramatic poet of the Western landscape since Jeffers, William Everson always provoked extreme responses from his audience—either intense admiration for his painful, self-probing, and self-revealing confessionalism, or intense dislike for the extremely visceral histrionics of his verse and his voice on the reading platform. In like manner, neither his poetry nor his life was ever lukewarm. Indeed, it is difficult to consider his art as separate from his life, since his poetry was personal from the beginning of his career; it was not until his third book of poems, *The Masculine Dead*, however, that he noticeably broke away from Jeffers and moving into the intensely confessional verse for which he became known. While Robert Lowell is usually acknowledged as the first American poet since Hart Crane to advance the art of the sequence and as the

harbinger of the modern confessional mode of poetry, Everson had actually been developing the sequence form and the confessional voice since 1939, twenty years before Lowell's *Life Studies* (1959) was published. Using his literal self as a symbol of the modern predicament, Everson, as he says in *Birth of a Poet*, "spent the greater part of my life trying to probe down through the negative factors to find the living root which makes me what I am."

Probing down into himself to discover his "living root" meant, in a national sense, discovering the American character. During World War II, having taken his stand as a pacifist and having suffered the consequent about three years of incarceration in Oregon and California camps for conscientious objectors, Everson wrote some of the most incisive and forceful antiwar poetry ever to be produced in America or abroad. This did not go unnoticed, for it led to the national publication of an edition of his selected poems, *The Residual Years*, as well as a Guggenheim Fellowship in 1949.

Although Everson's entry into the Dominican Order in 1951, at which time he became Brother Antoninus, may have hurt his public following (for one poet had dropped out of sight nominally and thus publicly, and another one began to emerge), the confessional tenor of the poet's verse was intensified with his eventual entry into the "dark night of the soul" and Jungian psychoanalysis. Gradually, Brother Antoninus received greater public recognition than William Everson had: He was nominated for the Pulitzer Prize in 1959, awarded the Commonwealth Club of California Silver Medal in 1967 for *The Rose of Solitude*, and was sponsored to give public readings of his work not only throughout the United States but also in Dublin, London, Hamburg, Berlin, Munich, Rome, and Paris. He became, in short, world-renowned as the Dionysian monk who wrote dithyrambic and explicit poetry celebrating the sexual conjunction of man and woman and God. At the height of his career, however, Brother Antoninus confused his audience as Everson once had; in 1969, he abruptly left the Dominican Order and became William Everson once again.

Everson's hand-printed, limited edition of Jeffers's *Granite and Cypress* (1975) was chosen by Joseph Blumenthal, in his exhibition "The Printed Book in

America" (1977), as one of the seventy best-made books in the history of American printing. Everson received the Shelley Memorial Award from the Poetry Society of America in 1978, a National Endowment for the Arts grant in 1981, a Body of Work Award from the PEN Center USA in 1989, the Fred Cody Award for lifetime achievement in 1991, and a Lannan Literary Fellowship in 1993.

William Everson (©Christopher Felver/CORBIS)

BIOGRAPHY

William Oliver Everson, born September 10, 1912, in Sacramento, California, was the second of three children and the first son of Lewis Everson and Francelia Everson. It is noteworthy that Everson was the first son of his family because throughout his career he has stressed (in his poetry, in some autobiographical essays, and quite specifically in his autobiography, *Prodigious Thrust*, 1996) that an Oedipal complex is a key factor in his own psychology, in his strained relationship with his father, and in his relationship with the women in his life. Everson's mother, almost twenty years younger than his father, had been Roman Catholic but was forced to leave the Church to marry the man she loved (a fact of increasing importance to the poet later in his life when he converted to Catholicism). Everson's father was a Norwegian emigrant and had been an itinerant printer, musician, and bandmaster until, with a wife and children, he settled in Selma, California, in 1914, and there established the Everson Printery in 1920. As a boy, Everson looked to his mother for support, confidence, and emotional understanding, while growing increasingly intimidated, resentful, and—he has said—even hateful of his father, a taciturn and self-professed atheist who believed Christianity and faith in an afterlife were below the dignity of enlightened minds. In short, from infancy, Everson was exposed to—and often torn between—the extreme differences of his parents' dispositions and sensibilities.

Everson's first poetic attempts were love poems he wrote to his high school sweetheart, beginning in his junior year. In his senior year, he wrote topical poems for the Selma High School yearbook, *The Magnet*. After graduation (June, 1931), he enrolled in Fresno State College the following fall but remained there only one semester, during which time he had what might be called his first "literary" poem, "The Gypsy Dance" (blatantly derived from Edgar Allan Poe's "The Bells," with its strict trochaic meter and long lines), published in *The Caravan*, the Fresno State College literary magazine. Unable to find anything in college interesting enough to keep him, he returned to his parents' home (December, 1932) and remained there, while working at a local cannery, until June, 1933, when he entered the Civilian Conservation Corps (CCC). Except for short leaves of absence, Everson remained in the CCC camp for a year, but he felt intellectually deficient and painfully isolated, so he returned to Fresno State in the fall of 1934. This time, he remained enrolled for the entire academic year, and he found something that was not only interesting but also inspiring: the poetry of Robinson Jeffers. It was after this discovery that he decided to be the first poet of the San Joaquin Valley.

In 1935, again living in his parents' home, Everson had his first collection of poems, *These Are the Ravens*, published. Although the poems in the volume were not very remarkable, at twenty-three, he had begun a life-long career that would encompass much more than the San Joaquin Valley. Everson married Edwa Poulson, the young woman to whom he had written the love po-ems in high school, in May, 1938; they settled on a small farm outside Selma, she teaching elementary school and he writing his poetry and tending the vine-yard that surrounded their home. Although he was con-tent with his domestic life, the threat of America's in-volvement in the war being waged in Europe set the tenor of much of the poetry contained in his next two published volumes, *San Joaquin* and *The Masculine Dead*. In 1940, Everson's mother died; in the same year, he was forced by the Selective Service Act to take a stand on the war, and he registered as a conscientious objector. Thus, in 1943, the poet was incarcerated in a Civilian Public Service (CPS) camp for conscientious objectors in Waldport, Oregon, where he would be in-strumental in establishing the Waldport School of Fine Arts and the United Press, both precursors of the later San Francisco Renaissance.

Everson remained incarcerated, with the exception of short leaves of absence, for almost three years, dur-ing which time his father died, and he and his wife agreed to a divorce because she had fallen in love with another man; thus he lost all his familial connections with his home back in the valley. In August, 1946, two months after being released from a CPS camp in Weaverville, California, where he had been transferred earlier that year, Everson met and fell in love with Mary Fabilli, an artist and Catholic, recently divorced her-self. They were married in the summer of 1948, a year that was also important for Everson because the first national publication of a volume of his selected poetry was issued (*The Residual Years*) and because he con-verted to Catholicism on Christmas Eve of that year. Paradoxically, the Roman Catholic Church refused to recognize the Eversons' marriage because both had been married previously and Mary had been married in a Catholic ceremony; in short, their marriage was an-nulled, they separated in May, 1949, and Everson was baptized in July. A month before his baptism, he was awarded a Guggenheim Fellowship that would enable him to write with financial support for a year; the sti-

pend lasted only ten months, however, and shortly thereafter Everson entered a Catholic Worker House in Oakland, California, where he would remain for four-teen months. In June, 1951, he entered the Dominican Order at St. Albert's College in Oakland, as a *donatus*, and there he was given the name Brother Antoninus.

From *The Crooked Lines of God* through *The Haz-ards of Holiness*, the poems of Brother Antoninus emerge as a tortuous series of twists and turns as he struggles, because of his vows of celibacy, in the em-brace of Thanatos (that is, the death-urge of the self). In 1960, however, he fell in love with Rose Tunnland, a Catholic divorcé and mother of three children; it was out of this intense love relationship and the breaking of his vows that *The Rose of Solitude* emerged. Partly out of guilt but mostly out of a difference in personali-ties, this relationship was ended in 1963, but in 1965, the poet fell in love with another woman, Susanna Rickson, again broke his vows, and this time made the painful decision to leave the Dominican Order. So, in December, 1969, Brother Antoninus concluded a po-etry reading (at the University of California, Davis) by stripping off his monk's habit and walking off the platform as William Everson once again. He married Rickson six days later, and they lived at Stinson Beach until, in 1971, Everson became poet-in-residence at the University of California, Santa Cruz. He was diag-nosed with Parkinson's disease in the 1970's, although he continued to give poetry readings. He died in Daven-port, California, in 1994.

ANALYSIS

Always a poet of extremes, from the beginning of his career, William Everson expressed both need and fear, compulsion and revulsion, toward those things in his life most important to him. Much of the tension in his poetry seems to arise from his mind knowing what his heart would like to deny—that is, all is transitory, all is mutable, and there is no permanent security in life. Indeed, the major recurrent theme throughout his canon is that of thwarted love. While this is certainly not a unique theme, nor one limited to modern conscious-ness, Everson's attempt to understand the ongoing in-ternal war that he suffers (between his heart and mind) leads him, in psychological terms, to his encounter with and ultimate victory over the personal shadow-side of consciousness, and to repeated sought-after encounters with the anima or feminine side. In fact, it is the feminine side in his own consciousness, as well as that embodied in woman, for which he expresses both the greatest need and, paradoxically, the greatest fear throughout his career.

THESE ARE THE RAVENS

In the 1930's, the world was a fearful place for young Everson, as he composed his first collection of poetry, *These Are the Ravens*; even nature, which he would consistently portray as feminine, seemed hostile and malignant. In his earliest poem, "First Winter Storm," the speaker is one who hunkers indoors, afraid of the unknown and ominous unpredictability of the elemental life force that moves outside his walls ("I felt the fear run down my back/ And grip me as I lay"). Humans, in this early volume, are rendered more or less passive in the face of nature's seemingly conscious enmity toward all life, and this human condition is indicative of the poet's own relation to the world of adulthood and experience. Everson was seventeen years old when the Great Depression began in 1929. He had no career plans when he graduated from high school in 1931; he had not prepared to go to college, so his first term there proved fruitless. He returned to his parents' home to live but realized that he had become a disappointment to his father. He worked in the Civilian Conservation Corps for a year, returned to Fresno State for a year, discovered the poetry of Jeffers, and made a lifelong decision to be a poet.

Unable to support himself while pursuing his chosen vocation, however, he had again moved in with his parents, and he would remain with them until his marriage, three months before his twenty-sixth birthday in 1938. However, because he had been unable to break away from his dependence on his parents, he grew, as he wrote in *Prodigious Thrust*, into "the full status of his ambivalence with the father-hunger and father-fear, the mother-hunger and mother-fear at war within him."

The "ambivalence" he suffered manifested itself in his inability to identify with the masculine or feminine in his own personality. The constant dark moodiness he experienced he attributed to his agnatic heritage (stem-ming, that is, from his masculine precursors), and this he eschewed because he believed it to be related to male savagery and patriarchal dominance. In "I Know It as the Sorrow," for example, Everson attempts to explain the "ache" in his blood, and his recurrent "waking as a child weeping in the dark for no reason," as a psychic condition he has inherited and for which he is not, therefore, responsible. This "sorrow," he says, lies in "the secret depths" of his soul; however, while he may not be responsible for his temperament, the "warriors" of the past which he calls up, as well as their "women/ Shivering in the cliff-wind," are integral to his own perspective of life. In short, at the a priori level, he views the masculine as dominant, savage, and strong, and the feminine as receptive, docile, and weak. Although he vehemently eschews his masculine heritage—stating, at the conclusion of "Fish-Eaters," that "I find no hunger for the sword"—what he implicitly praises in heroic terms is the very thing he denounces—that is, the assertiveness of the male libido.

"WHO SEES THROUGH THE LENS"

By consistently portraying women as weak and passive creatures, while at the same time portraying men pejoratively as the exact opposite, Everson leaves himself neither gender with which to identify; in other words, by dividing himself from both his father and his mother, from the patrilineal and matrilineal inheritances, he divides himself. He becomes, therefore, the "watcher" in "Who Sees Through the Lens" (from *San Joaquin*), a man who spends his nights staring through a telescope up at the stars, a man "fixed in the obsession of seeking, the dementia for knowing," and a man so determined to understand and explain the meaning of life that he intellectually vivisects his own being for understanding. Whereas his "cold mind needles the rock" of stars at night, during the day, he divides his mind from his body as he "fumbles the sleeping seed, pokes at the sperm." This seeker is reminiscent of Jeffers's Barclay, in *The Women at Point Sur* (1927), filled with a kind of self-loathing for the corruptibility of his flesh; thus he denies his body for the monomaniacal glorification of his intellect—until, that is, his alienation becomes too painful to bear and he then strives to submerge his consciousness in sexual ecstasy. Significantly, it is in "Who Sees Through the Lens" that Everson for the first time categorizes woman as receptacle and comforter for man's intellectual frustration—a role she will be forced to play often throughout the poet's career. After he describes the "watcher," therefore, the poet beseeches him to "give over;/ Come star-bruised and broken back to the need;/ Come seeking the merciful thighs of the lover." It is between the feminine thighs, in short, that surcease may be found for the intellectual man; indeed, she offers him a momentary, mindless oblivion that he both desires and fears.

"ABRASIVE"

Woman, like everything else in life for Everson, is not to be trusted with his heart, as she changes and thus forbids his dependency on her. He is, he says in "Abrasive" (from *San Joaquin*), "torn by the wars of perpetual change," and he finds that one side of his psyche longs "to slip yielding and drowned in an ocean of silence,/ Go down into some abstract and timeless norm of reality,/ Shadow the eyes, the uneasy heart, and be done." However, while woman can grant him the momentary oblivion of consciousness, as well as the anodyne for his "uneasy heart," another side of his nature scoffs at such a need and reminds his heart that "the sun makes a fool of you," for this symbol of the masculine principle flaunts life's transitions, "shocking with seasons" those individuals who search for stasis.

THE MASCULINE DEAD

Although Everson married Poulson in 1938 and in a sense fulfilled his emotional needs while suffering his own mental chiding for succumbing to the belief that a commitment such as marriage could last, he wrote no poems to or about his wife or his love for her; instead, he wrote such poems as "The Illusion" (from *The Masculine Dead*), wherein he denigrates those people who sit in the comfort of their homes, surrounding themselves with the security of a family, while all around them people are being destroyed by the unpredictable, as "they pitch and go down with the blood on their lips,/ With the blood on the broken curve of their throats,/ With their eyes begging." What he, in his heart, wanted desperately to believe possible (that, for example, emotional security could be sustained), he found himself unable to accept intellectually; therefore, he kept his wife at a distance, for she was part of "the illusion" that made him emotionally vulnerable.

In his life, Everson took definite steps to minimize his vulnerability. He had a vasectomy, which he explains in "The Sides of a Mind" (from *The Masculine Dead*) as his attempt to avoid guilt for the pain life would inflict on his children ("each shiver of pain they ever felt/ Would ripple in to the moment of my act,/ And I will not yield"). As he writes in *Earth Poetry*, another step he took was that of subordinating his marriage to his career:

> The mistake I made . . . in regard to being an artist . . . was when I married I sacrificed the inner viability of my marriage to my career . . . I denied the primacy of her person. By reducing her to an object and sacrificing that object even to a school of thought, I denied the reality of the situation.

When the Selective Service Act was instituted in 1940, and when the United States' involvement in World War II seemed imminent, Everson took yet another self-protective step by registering as a conscientious objector. Throughout *The Masculine Dead*, which was inspired by the moral revulsion he felt over the war being waged in Europe, Everson continued to denounce his father's world of masculine and militaristic aggression. In "The Sides of a Mind," he describes himself, a poet, sitting at a table and struggling to articulate some comprehensible explanation for the confusion and destruction in the world; suddenly a political activist bursts into his room and criticizes his physical passivity: "We have time no longer for the seeds of your doubt./ We have time only for man and man/ Facing together the brute confusion of the stubborn world." Because the poet is unable to embrace his father's ethics and values (as a young man, for instance, his father had been beaten and jailed for his efforts to establish a typographical union), he learns to embrace the old man's disappointment as a testament to his own, the son's, authenticity: "Father, whatever you hoped for," he says in the second section of the poem, "I am not what you wanted./ I sit hunched in a room."

"THE PRESENCE"

What Everson once viewed as weakness, consequently, he now views as virtue in the feminine; furthermore, in "The Presence" (from *The Residual Years*), he suggests that an individual and a nation are corrupted by such a thing as war only insofar as the feminine psychic principle is corrupt. What he views as "the presence" is primal, savage, and masculine, as it "stoops in the mind, hairy and thick," destroying "norms" and "modes of arrest" when it becomes actively motivating in the conscious mind. By this "presence," he maintains, women "will be used" if they relinquish their "precepts of will" ("Throwing their bellowing flesh on the tool/ That eases the rutting sow"). By taking the pacifistic stand against the war, therefore, Everson chose to accept for himself what he saw as the traditionally feminine response to life, as he states in "Now in These Days" (from *The Residual Years*): He will "wait in these rooms," he vows, accepting "the degradation of slavery and want" imposed on him in a camp for conscientious objectors.

"THE CHRONICLE OF DIVISION"

In January, 1943, Everson was conscripted and sent to a camp in Waldport, Oregon. He would remain incarcerated for three years, during which time he composed his longest sequential and confessional poem, "The Chronicle of Division" (from *The Residual Years*). While this poem describes poignantly and incisively the human deprivation suffered by men locked up for their beliefs, the underpinning and gradually overriding focus is on the psychological condition of men without women. Paradoxically, while it had been the feminine temperament that Everson had espoused and embraced as a necessary response to what he perceived as a war caused by masculine aggression and warmongering, it was the feminine embodied in his wife that proved to be the most devastating to him. Because there had been no "primacy" in the relationship (and he gradually came to see his vasectomy as a testament to this), and because of the indefinite length of their separation, Everson's wife fell in love with another man and (in a letter) requested a divorce.

Although the poet deals with the consequent pain and feelings of rejection he experiences, throughout the poem, he discovers something within himself that is more awesome than the loss of his marriage and home: He discovers the capacity to kill, as he suddenly realizes that he desires to strangle his wife, "Till the plunging features/ Bulge and go black,/ And all his old hurt/

Lies healed on the bed." The disconcerting irony in this is immediately apparent to him, for he is locked up because he refuses to kill and yet finds within himself the desire to murder punitively; "the presence," then, "hairy and thick," hunkers in himself. Unable to accept this shadow-side of his consciousness, he attempts to purge himself of all his past familial and regional associations, believing that he might thereby conjoin his "divisible selves,/ Ill-eased with each other."

THE "WOMAN WITHIN"

With the war ended and his release from the CPS camp guaranteed in 1946, he began immediately to direct his attention, in "The Fictive Wish" (*The Residual Years*), to an introspective search for that "woman within," that woman "of his," whom he might learn to know well enough to recognize outside himself were he confronted by her. It is not surprising that Everson describes this woman in strictly physical and sexual terms, with "her breast" the "ease of his need,/ And the thigh a solace. . . ." Two months after being released from the camp, he met and fell in love with Mary Fabilli, a Catholic woman who had been recently betrayed by her husband and was also suffering the pain of rejection. In short, because of chance similarities in their respective pasts, and because he was actively searching for the woman "of his," Everson could truthfully feel about Fabilli, as he was to write in *Prodigious Thrust*, that "I knew her before I met her."

Three months after being released from his confinement in the CPS camp, Everson wrote "The Blowing of the Seed" to Fabilli and about the cathartic and rejuvenating power of their love. It is apparent that the woman had quickly become his "other self" and the nurturer of his "huge hope"; she "broke" his loneliness, he tells her, and she freed his "isolate heart." Not only has Fabilli allowed him to come "up out of darkness," allowed his courage to burst out of a "cold region" of "ash," but also her love for him has caused a new ascendancy of his masculine ego; consequently, Everson makes a 180-degree turn in attitude, abandons his "feminine," passive demeanor, and voices a traditional drive toward male primacy, wrenching their relationship into the age-old equation of strong male and weak female. This "new" attitude, voiced with a Dionysian and dithyrambic intensity, is Everson's way of compensating for the debilitating vulnerability and ultimate rejection he suffered with the breakup of his first marriage and with the treatment and alienation he suffered because of his moral position against the war. In other words, what he denied for almost ten years (that is, male aggression, libidinal masculinity, and male primacy), he affirms in *The Blowing of the Seed*; after all, the intellectual denial of the traditionally patriarchal world had involved an immense price and overwhelming nakedness emotionally, psychologically, and spiritually. While he attempts to continue writing with masculine bravado in his next poem, "The Springing of the Blade," trying to be a Whitmanesque singer of fecundity, he finds himself "strung" in "the iron dimension," his term for the past and its ineradicable cleavages and losses. Again he finds his capacity to love thwarted by his inability to live in face of the inevitable threats of infidelity that living entails—that is, the infidelity of time to life, of the real to the ideal, of the body to the spirit, and of the heart to the mind.

THE YEAR'S DECLENSION

Although Everson and Fabilli were married, their love was thwarted by another factor as well: She was a Catholic and he was not. He felt, as he expresses in "The First Absence," increasingly fearful of her possible abandonment of him; and as she began to attend religious services more frequently than she had before their marriage, he began to accompany her. Believing, therefore, that by converting to Catholicism he could secure, as he says in "The Quarrel," the "necessary certitude to start anew," he decided to do what was necessary to be baptized a Catholic. What was necessary was not what he expected, for the Church refused to recognize their marriage because it had not granted the annulment of Fabilli's first marriage; in short, they were forced to separate. Left alone, Everson was again compelled to face his own incompleteness, was again forced to face life without the emotional security of his union with another; thus, in "In the Dream's Recess," he pleads to God: "Give me the cleansing power!/ . . . Make me clean!" He needed strength now, to face his own vulnerability, and to face the inferior shadow-side of his own personality: "The sullied presence crouches in my side,/ And all is fearful where I dare not wake or dream."

THE CROOKED LINES OF GOD

Not surprisingly, after Everson decided to become Brother Antoninus, a *donatus* in the Dominican order, he set out with a convert's zealousness to denounce, in *The Crooked Lines of God*, all that he had been and believed secularly. In "The Screed of the Flesh," for example, he eschews the fleshly life he had lived with his two wives; in fact, he goes so far in his zealotry as to fictionalize his past persona as one who "gloried self,/ Singing the glory of myself." To anyone familiar with the poet's pre-Catholic verse, it is apparent that, to the contrary, Everson spent very little time "singing the glory" of himself or of his life, for his verse is tortured by self-analysis, doubt, and distrust. Obviously he intends for his conversion to purify his life and obliterate his past errors and losses, and because woman, with her tempting "merciful thighs," has hurt him the most, he claims, in "A Penitential Psalm," that his "corruptness" is his only through inheriting his mother's (and, before her, Eve's) "iniquities": "in sin did my mother conceive me!" Delegating the responsibility for his own shadow-side to another, however, could not last; thus, after his zealousness had been worn down by six years of celibacy and three years of almost total creative barrenness, in *The Hazards of Holiness*, Brother Antoninus's central poetic subject becomes his "dark night of the soul," as well as his contention with the shadow-side of his consciousness.

THE HAZARDS OF HOLINESS

The terse, almost truncated and imageless poetic lines throughout *The Hazards of Holiness* exemplify a period in Everson's life when, as expressed in "Saints," there is "No thing. Not anything," and the poet pleads to God: "Do something!/ Kiss or kill/ But move me!" Very similar to the pantheistical god in "Circumstance," a pre-Catholic poem in *San Joaquin*, who "hears not, nor sees," in "You, God," the supreme deity in this period of the poet's life is a "God of death,/ Great God of no-life." In "Jacob and the Angel," the man of the flesh and earth, Esau, becomes emblematic of Everson, and Jacob (Antoninus) must wrestle with his dark brother for supremacy—even in the face of the fact that God has apparently abandoned the celibate monk despite all his earlier confessions and self-denials. "But I?" the poet asks in "Sleep-Tossed I Lie," where he questions the value of his barrenness, bitterly imagining lovers locked in passion in the night beyond the walls of his monastery. As a result of his torturous introspection and out of the pain he suffers for the denial of the flesh, he laments: "Long have I lain,/ Long lain, and in the longing/ Fry." Again, in "Black Christ," he cries out of his barrenness, "Kill me./ . . . I beg thy kindness." Importantly, though, in the last poem of *The Hazards of Holiness*, "In Savage Wastes," a breakthrough is achieved, and the poet shows a lessening of his desire to retreat any longer into contemplation of a distant Celestial City. Instead, he affirms that "I [shall] go forth/ And return to the ways of man," no longer willing to deny his essential humanness, "And will find my God in the thwarted love that breaks between us!" With his new attitude, then, his quest for meaning and wholeness leads Brother Antoninus out of a ten-year period of celibacy and into a relationship with Rose Tunnland, to and about whom he wrote *The Rose of Solitude*.

THE ROSE OF SOLITUDE

After learning to embrace his fleshly, Esau-like nature, the poet begins to praise woman as the means through which the polarities of his psyche may be balanced and possibly synthesized, and through which he may be permitted to move closer to God. Brother Antoninus believes that, both emotionally and physically, he has been resurrected through the love for Tunnland ("I dream the dawn of the longest night: The one resurrection"); furthermore, all the poems in *The Rose of Solitude* attest to the victory of Eros (love directed toward self-realization) over Thanatos (the instinctual desire for death, as it was expressed throughout *The Hazards of Holiness*). The poet tells his reader, in "The Kiss of the Cross," that "She brought me back./ . . . I was brought back alive." Out of his desire for a sustained equipoise between the mind and the heart, the spirit and the flesh, while at the same time questioning the rightness of breaking his vows of celibacy, he pleads: "O Christ & Lady/ Save me from my law!" Ultimately, however, Brother Antoninus becomes with Tunnland like the proverbial tree that can reach heaven only if its roots have penetrated hell, as he indicates in "Immortal Strangeness":

> When we fell—
> > on the hard floor
> > in the harsh dark,
> > on the bitter boards—,
> When we fell
> We rose.

In short, the conjunction of Christ with woman at the symbolic level, conjoined at the actual level by the act of love, reveals the *felix culpa*; furthermore, the poet has come to believe that, in spite of Catholic dogma and monastic strictures, Eros and the Christ-force are nonexclusive, and so the disparity between his human needs and the mode of his existence begins to dissolve.

The relationship with Tunnland ended in separation (she fell in love with another man, the poet said in several interviews), but in 1965, Brother Antoninus met and fell in love with Rickson, to whom he wrote and dedicated *Tendril in the Mesh*, the last poem he was to write as a monk. His love for her fuses mythologies: "Kore! Daughter of dawn! Persephone! Maiden of twilight!/ . . . In the node of your flesh you drip my flake of bestowal." Through her, furthermore, he witnesses the conjunction of Eros and Christ: "Dark God of Eros, Christ of the buried blood,/ Stone-channeled beast of ecstasy and fire. . . ." At the end of the first public reading of this poem, on December 7, 1969, the poet formally left the Dominican order.

MAN-FATE

A painful period of self-doubt followed for almost five years, chronicled in *Man-Fate*. In "The Gash," for instance, the poet says, "To covet and resist for years, and then/ To succumb, is a fearsome thing." To compensate for the vulnerability and alienation he feels, Everson sets out consciously to discover a masculine persona as powerful as that of Antoninus. While it is a slow birth back to what he calls, in "The Challenge," his "basic being," he makes a decision about the "garb" of his ethos and new identity in "The Scout." Reflecting on the fact that his monk's habit is being worn by someone else in the monastery, he says that now "I assume the regalia of the Old West:/ Beads, buckskin and bearclaws. . . ." This new persona, he believes, will be his "sentinel," as he states in "The Black Hills," just as his habit had been, standing between him and the outside world of chance and abrasion. While this may be true, the primal and stereotypically male "regalia" also noticeably prevents the integration of his anima or feminine side into his consciousness, as the reader witnesses in *The Masks of Drought*.

THE MASKS OF DROUGHT

After being hired in 1971 as poet-in-residence at the University of California, Santa Cruz, Everson began to experience a lessening of his poetic output, writing only one or two poems a year for eight years. While this "drought" was certainly one he was fighting, *The Masks of Drought* was inspired by two other droughts, the literal California drought in 1977 and 1978 and the poet's sexual impotence. Throughout the volume, the latter is not only objectified but also intensified by the former, as in "Kingfisher Flat," in which the poet, lying beside his wife at night, thinks of the creek outside their home as objectifying the blocked flow of his own sexuality: "The starved stream/ Edges its way through dead stones,/ Noiseless in the night." Like the rattlesnake, in "Rattlesnake August," who when "Fate accosts—/ Licks his lip and stabs back," Everson stabs back at his age, at his physical condition, and at nature (his symbol of the feminine and her power to cause his impotence). In "Cutting the Firebreak," the poet says he is "one" with his "mad scythe" when he cuts down weeds; furthermore, the reason he and his phallic instrument are "mad" is understood when he tells the reader, in the last two lines of the poem, that the wild flowers he cuts down are, to his mind, "All the women in my life/ Sprawled in the weeds—drunk in death." In "Chainsaw," Everson goes into the woods with his saw, "the annihilate god" (and, like the earlier scythe, another phallic symbol), intending to cut down three alders, symbols of the feminine, with "woman-smooth bark,/ . . . naked skin."

Everson is attempting to impose himself on nature, by enacting the old Western code of manhood that stressed participation insofar as it led to nature's submission, but what happens throws him into an acute awareness of his human condition and folly: the third tree bucks back, kicks the saw's chain against his leg, tears his pants, but misses his flesh entirely. Nevertheless, dazed by the near catastrophe, Everson imagines

his leg's truncation, a "pitiful stump," for "Something is finished,/ Something cleanly done," and this imagined "absence" becomes distorted, transformed into a bitter reminder of the actual loss—his sexual virility. Gradually, however, he realizes the "folly" of the impulse that sent him to the woods in the first place: that is, his need to assert his maleness on the femaleness of nature to prove his virility. He acknowledges his foolishness and begins to accept his human limitations.

Although he says, in "Spotfire," that—between the extremes of his own nature—"I have seen my heart's fate/ Shaped in the balance,/ And know what I am," the last poem he composed for *The Masks of Drought*, "Moongate," indicates that he has still not realized a "balance" between his masculine and feminine sides. After staying up late one night and reflecting on all the losses in his life, Everson says that a "sudden yearn of unrealization" then "clutches" his heart, and this causes him to feel that "a dream awaits me, back in bed,/ And I turn to take it up." Significantly, in the dream he recounts in the poem, he finds himself with Poulson, back in the time before the first traumatic loss and betrayal he suffered for loving a woman. Suddenly a fox, clearly meant to represent Everson's vocation and the pursuit of success therein, darts into the poet's focus, and he abandons Poulson for his pursuit of "the illusive one." As he runs "urgently" up river, he hears the steps of someone behind him; when he turns he sees a "strange woman" who "cannot see" what it is that Everson pursues, but nevertheless, he says, "What I see she follows." After seeing her, he returns to his chase until "dusk draws down" and he can no longer follow the fox; importantly, it is only now, when he can go no farther, that he turns to face the anima image again: "And her eyes are shining, shining." Everson stated in an interview that he intended to write a sequel to this poem, and in the next poem, he would have the "strange woman" move out in front of him while the fox falls behind. It is noteworthy that the fox in "Moongate" is male.

THE INTEGRAL YEARS

While Everson's pre-Catholic poetry was published in *The Residual Years* and the Catholic poetry he wrote as Brother Antoninus was published in *The Veritable*

Years, the poetry written since his departure from the Dominican order appeared in one volume, *The Integral Years*. Smaller collections that are included in the trilogy's third volume had already been published: *Man-Fate*, *The Masks of Drought*, *Renegade Christmas*, and *Mexican Standoff*. Also included in *The Integral Years* are poems that had been published in limited editions: *In Medias Res* and "Skald" (1984), the first two cantos of an autobiographical epic titled *Dust Shall Be the Serpent's Food*.

Suffering for many years the increasingly debilitating effects of Parkinson's disease, Everson wrote poems much more slowly than he once did. However, throughout *The Residual Years*, *The Veritable Years*, and the early movements of *The Integral Years*, the poet ceaselessly affirmed and reaffirmed—by means of his own life and poetic witness—the human capacity for successful self-renewal and self-creation. Indeed, like most great artists, Everson created more than courageous life-affirming assertions; he created powerful and enduring testaments to the inexhaustible will of the human spirit to transcend mundane, gender-specific identities and to realize the integrated, whole, androgynous self.

OTHER MAJOR WORKS

NONFICTION: *Friar Among Savages: Father Luis Cáncer*, 1958 (as Brother Antoninus); *Robinson Jeffers: Fragments of an Older Fury*, 1968; *Archetype West: The Pacific Coast as a Literary Region*, 1976; *Earth Poetry: Selected Essays and Interviews of William Everson, 1950-1977*, 1980; *Birth of a Poet*, 1982; *William Everson, on Writing the Waterbirds and Other Presentations: Collected Forewords and Afterwords, 1935-1981*, 1983; *The Excesses of God: Robinson Jeffers as a Religious Figure*, 1988; *Naked Heart: Talking on Poetry, Mysticism, and the Erotic*, 1992; *Take Hold upon the Future: Letters on Writers and Writing, 1938-1946*, 1994; *Prodigious Thrust*, 1996.

MISCELLANEOUS: *William Everson: The Light the Shadow Casts, Five Interviews with William Everson Plus Corresponding Poems*, 1996 (Clifton Ross, editor); *Dark God of Eros: A William Everson Reader*, 2003 (Albert Gelpi, editor).

BIBLIOGRAPHY

Bartlett, Lee. *William Everson*. Boise, Idaho: Boise State University Press, 1985. This brief monograph provides a useful introduction to the major phases of the poet's life, his movement from Everson to Antoninus and back to Everson. Strangely, however, Bartlett focuses more on Everson's accomplishments as a master printer than his achievements as a poet. Discussion of Everson's poems is minimal.

_____. *William Everson: The Life of Brother Antoninus*. New York: New Directions, 1988. Although informative about Everson's relationship with Kenneth Rexroth in the early 1950's, as well as about Everson's place in the San Francisco Renaissance, Bartlett's study provides only cursory readings of Everson's poems and no discussion at all of the poet's second marriage to Mary Fabilli, the relationship that served as a catalyst for Everson's conversion to Catholicism. Contains an excellent bibliography.

_____, ed. *Benchmark and Blaze: The Emergence of William Everson*. Metuchen, N.J.: Scarecrow Press, 1979. A collection of twenty-two critical appraisals of the poetry and printing of Everson, this work provides an excellent overview of the poet-printer's distinguished career and accomplishments. Presented here are appraisals by such writers as Robert Duncan, Ralph J. Mills, Jerome Mazzaro, William Stafford, Kenneth Rexroth, and Albert Gelpi.

Carpenter, David A. *The Rages of Excess: The Life and Poetry of William Everson*. Bristol, Ind.: Wyndham Hall Press, 1987. A critical biography that is also a Jungian study attempts to interpret the poet's complex psychology and life via close analysis of the poetic canon and vice versa. Noteworthy here are the close, detailed discussions of Everson's long poems, such as his "The Chronicle of Division" and *Tendril in the Mesh*. Good bibliography.

Everson, William. Interviews. *William Everson: The Light the Shadow Casts*. Edited by Clifton Ross. Berkeley, Calif.: New Earth, 1996. Five interviews with Everson with corresponding poems. Offers invaluable insight into the life and work of the poet.

Herrmann, Steven. *William Everson: The Shaman's Call—Interviews, Introduction, and Commentaries.* New York: Eloquent Books, 2009. Jungian psychotherapist Herrmann was asked by Everson to collaborate on a book in 1991. This work, which contains some interviews by Herrmann, examines shamanism in Everson's poetry.

Houston, James D., et al. *The Death of a Poet: Santa Cruz Writers, Poets, and Friends Remember William Everson.* Austin, Tex.: W. Thomas Taylor, 1994. A collection of biographical essays about Everson originally published in *Metro Santa Cruz* in 1994 following Everson's death.

David A. Carpenter

F

B. H. FAIRCHILD

Born: Houston, Texas; October 17, 1942
Also known as: Pete Fairchild

PRINCIPAL POETRY

C&W Machine Works, 1983 (chapbook)
The Arrival of the Future, 1985
Flight, 1985 (chapbook)
The System of Which the Body Is One Part, 1988
  (chapbook)
Local Knowledge, 1991, 2005
The Art of the Lathe, 1998
*Early Occult Memory Systems of the Lower
  Midwest*, 2003
Usher, 2009

OTHER LITERARY FORMS

Although he is primarily known as a poet, B. H. Fairchild first published *Such Holy Song: Music as Idea, Form and Image in the Poetry of William Blake* (1980), a scholarly study drawn from his doctoral dissertation. He has also written articles on Nathaniel Hawthorne and Anthony Hecht.

ACHIEVEMENTS

Starting with *The Arrival of the Future* in 1985, B. H. Fairchild's major poetry collections have established him as a powerful voice for blue-collar workers and denizens of imperiled small-town America, particularly in the lower Midwest. Significantly, however, he rejects stereotypes; his workers are as likely to be reading the German philosopher Martin Heidegger or listening to classical music by Franz Schubert as they are to be scanning the sports pages or tuning in to pop music. A master of the blended lyric-narrative mode, Fairchild has been recognized from the start with an array of awards ranging from the National Writers' Union Poetry Competition (1984) to the National Book

Critics Circle Award (2002). *The Art of the Lathe* won him the Capricorn Award (1996), the Beatrice Hawley Award (1997), a Silver Medal from the Commonwealth Club of California (1998), the Natalie Ornish Poetry Award (1999), the PEN Center USA West Poetry Award (1999), the Kingsley Tufts Award (1999), and the William Carlos Williams Award (1999), and it was named a finalist for the National Book Award. He also received the Arthur Rense Poetry Prize (2002), a Gold Medal from the Commonwealth Club of California for *Early Occult Memory Systems of the Lower Midwest* (2002), the Bobbitt National Prize (2004), and the Aiken Taylor Award in Modern American Poetry (2005). He was the recipient of fellowships from the National Endowment for the Arts, the Guggenheim Foundation, and the Rockefeller Foundation.

BIOGRAPHY

Born in Houston, Texas, in 1942, Bertram Harry Fairchild, Jr., grew up in small oilfield and farming towns in Texas, Oklahoma, and southwestern Kansas. In high school and occasionally while attending college at the University of Kansas, where he received his B.A. in English in 1964 and his M.A. in 1968, Fairchild worked in his father's lathe shop. The lives of his high school friends and of his fellow workers figure prominently in his poems, where they are presented in dramatic contexts. The machinery of the lathe shop takes on aesthetic dimensions in his poems, as do the minimalistic, sometimes raw landscapes of marginal towns: weary hardware stores, alternately dusty and muddy roads, and raging teenagers hurtling recklessly through summer nights and trying to defeat boredom with fast cars and beer.

Fairchild configures himself as a first-person narrator and presumed protagonist in many of his most effective poems. For example, although he most likely embellishes his memories in various ways in "The Blue Buick," the long narrative poem (nearly thirty pages) at the center of *Early Occult Memory Systems of the Lower Midwest*, it must be read as a sort of *Bildungsgedicht* (poem of the writer's coming of age) and as a *Künstlergedicht* (poem of the writer's coming to vocation) as well. The Buick belongs to a couple named Roy and Maria, whose appearance in the small town of Liberal, Kansas, introduces the speaker (perhaps equal parts Fairchild and imagined character) to the outer world of Paris, ballet, the poet John Keats, the composer Wolfgang Amadeus Mozart, the philosopher Giordano Bruno, and the country music singer Patsy Cline.

Following receipt of his master's degree, Fairchild was an instructor at the University of Nebraska-Kearney (1968-1970) and then began his studies for the Ph.D. at the University of Tulsa, where he was employed as a teaching fellow (1970-1973). After completing his doctorate, he taught for three years (1973-1976) as an assistant professor at Southwest Texas State University in San Marcos, then for seven years (1976-1983) as an associate professor at Texas Women's University in Denton. From 1983 to 2006, he taught at California State University in San Bernardino, where he settled with his wife and family.

ANALYSIS

Various commentators have observed that B. H. Fairchild's work is that of a mature poet writing during his middle years, his first full-length book having appeared when he was forty-two, and they have likened him to authors such as Robert Frost, Wallace Stevens, and Richard Hugo, whose first books also were published later in life. A considerable number of his poems look back to his boyhood or to the 1950's and early 1960's; accordingly, the major risk Fairchild takes is that of nostalgia. An affectionate regard for the past, however, need not be branded with the negative connotation of "sentimental." Memories in Fairchild's poems will strike most readers as vivid, often ironic, occasionally painful, sometimes humorous, and nearly always dramatic.

David Mason begins his essay on Fairchild's poetry by citing Thomas Hobbes to the effect that memory and imagination are one, and he maintains that Fairchild is a more "thoughtful" and complex poet than has been recognized, indeed a philosophical poet, and he advises that "these poems are imagined as much as remembered." Christopher Bakken describes Fairchild's poems as "the work of apotheosis" and asserts that he writes "a poetry of the sacred; but his theology is earthbound, material, and entirely mortal."

Reviewers and other commentators have also remarked on the tension encountered in nearly every poem between allusions to individuals (often popular performers and athletes) and brand names and to individuals (often writers, artists, and composers) and titles or quotations. For example, in the frequently admired "Beauty," the opening poem in *The Art of the Lathe*, the reader encounters a Motorola radio, the popular 1960's television show *Father Knows Best*, an Allis-Chalmers tractor, and actor Marlon Brando mingled with Plato and Aristotle, nineteenth century art critic Walter Pater, author Robert Penn Warren, poet Hart Crane, and Donatello's fifteenth century bronze *David*. The first-person speaker in the poem and his wife (presumably) are visiting the Bargello gallery in Florence, but when the subject of beauty arises, naturally enough, the speaker reflects on everything from the price of soybeans and Oklahoma football to Uncle Ross's tap dancing and the autumn light pouring through venetian blinds in Kansas. A black Corvette figures in, and so does a line from James Wright's poem "Autumn Begins in Martins Ferry, Ohio."

Although long lines typical of much narrative poetry dominate Fairchild's books, he celebrates the lyrical qualities of language through subtle use of repeated vowel sounds (assonance), as in the following passage from the title poem of *Early Occult Memory Systems of the Lower Midwest*: "Cattle stare at flat-bed haulers gunning clumps/ of black smoke and hugging damaged drill pipe/ up the gullied, mud-hollowed road. . . ." Here and elsewhere in Fairchild's poems, the occasional alliteration (damaged/drill) plays a minor role to the music provided by the vowels.

THE ARRIVAL OF THE FUTURE

Fairchild's first full-length collection, *The Arrival of the Future*, consists of forty poems. The opening poem, "Machine Shop with Wheat Field," portrays a boy sleeping amid "hunks of iron turning to rust, mud pumps,/ rat-hole diggers, drill collars, odd lengths of pipe. . . ." These ordinary objects, Fairchild implies, provide suitable images and fit language for poetry. In "Angels," Elliot Ray Niederland (Fairchild takes delight in naming the characters in his poems) drives home from college hauling a load of cows, drinking from a bottle of bourbon (Ezra Brooks), and thinking about Maria Rainer Rilke's *Duineser Elegien* (1923; *Duino Elegies*, 1931) when he has an accident on an icy road. He becomes a poet, the reader is told, but the folks back home do not understand his poems.

LOCAL KNOWLEDGE

First-person speakers figure in nearly half of the thirty-five poems that make up Fairchild's second book, which first appeared in *Quarterly Review of Literature* in 1991 and was republished by W. W. Norton in 2005 with slight revisions to the text of the poems but radical reordering. The collection testifies to Fairchild's growth and sophistication as a poet, and in the five-page afterword, he comments on his discovery of himself as a reader and writer when he was a boy in Liberal, Kansas: "words filled up the empty horizon and made for me a necessary world." Although a sometimes melancholy tone prevails in poems such as "In Czechoslovakia," "The Machinist, Teaching His Daughter to Play the Piano," "The Robinson Hotel," and "Speaking the Names," the reader encounters evidence of Fairchild's sense of humor in "City of God," where "boredom is exquisite" and grief is "migratory," where a yellow Studebaker coexists with Marcel Proust and Schubert, where the Dodgers still play in Brooklyn, and where "Imperfection is a mark of divinity. God is praised/ for his lack of talent."

THE ART OF THE LATHE

The Art of the Lathe, a sixty-four-page book containing twenty-nine poems, includes a few of Fairchild's previously published poems and testifies to his careful craftsmanship. Like Elizabeth Bishop, Fairchild refuses to publish his work until he regards it as perfected; accordingly, he has not been prolific. The frequently discussed lead poem, "Beauty," embodies his attempt, as D. Z. Phillips observes, "to give expression to a beauty he finds in the lives of the people he has known, not a beauty he imposes on them." Fairchild articulates the sometimes terrifying beauty that he discovers among these hardworking men who cannot recognize it in their lives. In his two-page introduction, poet Hecht describes "Body and Soul" as "certainly the best baseball poem I know." Poems such as "Old Men Playing Basketball" are somehow humorous and poignant at once. In the title poem, which opens with the assertion that Leonardo da Vinci conceived of the first

lathe, the first-person speaker is thinking of Mozart while one of the lathe operators sings a Patsy Cline song; this is an example of T. S. Eliot's observation about the mind of the poet "constantly amalgamating disparate experience," which Hecht cites in his introduction.

EARLY OCCULT MEMORY SYSTEMS OF THE LOWER MIDWEST

Early Occult Memory Systems of the Lower Midwest, which won the National Book Critics Circle Award for 2002, runs nearly twice the length of his earlier books and represents a considerable advance in Fairchild's capacity to sustain the long narrative poem (the autobiographical poem "The Blue Buick" accounts for about one-quarter of the book). In an analogy from that poem, Fairchild embeds an implicit definition of poetry: "As with baseball and poetry, so with lathework,/ arts of precision. . . ." With words as tools, perhaps poetry is the ultimate art of precision. Fairchild also explores the genre of the prose poem in this volume, notably in three poems purportedly written by one of his recurring characters, Roy Eldridge Garcia, and in the concluding poem, "The Memory Palace." In the intense drama of "Rave On," Fairchild captures the boredom, angst, and danger of the male adolescent almost too well. Poems such as "Weather Report" and "The Second Annual *Wizard of Oz* reunion in Liberal, Kansas" provide evidence of Fairchild's humor, often mixed with a certain poignancy, and of his continued interest in the lyrical form. In the rhyming quatrains of "Weather Report," a divorced woman coming home from a self-service laundry "knows the cycles of laundry and despair," evidence of which she discovers in her laundry basket "filled with someone else's underwear."

USHER

Usher begins with "The Gray Man," which looks back to the world of manual labor under the Kansas summer sun. Although Fairchild also mentions his hometown of Liberal (the irony is obvious) in poems such as "Working Men in Their Summer Clothes," "Bloom School," and the prose poem "The Beauty of Abandoned Towns," in *Usher*, Fairchild paints a more expansive canvas, from the title poem, which concerns Nathan Gold, a Kansas boy and student at Union Theo-

logical Seminary (New York City) in 1954, to such poems as "Hart Crane in Havana" and "Wittgenstein, Dying." The former poem centers on the suicide of the
renowned modernist poet in 1932, and the latter begins
with an epigraph by Ludwig Wittgenstein, who some
consider the most important philosopher of the twentieth century. Nathan Gold returns near the end of the
book, just three days after the terrorist attacks of September 11, 2001, with a letter to his friend Sollie, in
which he writes of the poets Charles Reznikoff and
Crane. In the next poem, Maria Rasputin, daughter of
the infamous monk who served as spiritual adviser to
Russia's last czar, tells "Pyotr" (Fairchild) of her life,
connecting herself as a "freak of history" with Frieda
Pushnik, the armless and legless woman who tells her
story early in the book. In short, the dimensions of
Fairchild's world expanded enormously in this collection.

OTHER MAJOR WORK

NONFICTION: *Such Holy Song: Music as Idea,
Form, and Image in the Poetry of William Blake*, 1980.

BIBLIOGRAPHY

Fairchild, B. H. "A Conversation with B. H. Fairchild."
Interview by Paul Mariani. *Image Journal* 47 (Fall,
2005): 64-74. Fairchild comments on his love of
jazz and art, the impact of his father and his lathe
shop, the influence of various poets and writers (including William Stafford, who also graduated from
high school in Liberal, Kansas), and the blending of
narrative (horizontal lines) and lyric (vertical lines)
in his writing.

Frank, Rebecca Morgan. "About B. H. Fairchild."
Ploughshares 34, no. 1 (Spring, 2008): 192-197.
This profile traces Fairchild's history as a poet and
describes his poetry. The issue also contains a poem
by Fairchild.

Mason, David. "Memory and Imagination in the Poetry
of B. H. Fairchild." *Sewanee Review* 115, no. 2
(Spring, 2007): 251-263. Comments on remembered events in the poems and imagined or created
details, offers a close reading of "Angels," and commends Fairchild for supplying an eloquent voice for
characters who cannot speak out.

Phillips, D. Z. "Words for the Wordless." *Midwest
Studies in Philosophy* 27 (2003): 45-58. Focuses
briefly on Fairchild's use of Wittgenstein in the poems and provides close readings of "Rave On" and
"Beauty."

Ulin, David. "Poetry of Endless, Unfulfilled Desire."
Review of *Usher*. *Los Angeles Times*, July 19, 2009,
p. E9. In this favorable review, Ulin notes how
Fairchild is speaking through a variety of characters
in this work. He describes the poet as creating "an
American mythos in which the personal and the collective blur."

Ron McFarland

KENNETH FEARING

Born: Oak Park, Illinois; July 28, 1902
Died: New York, New York; June 26, 1961
Also known as: Donald F. Bedford

PRINCIPAL POETRY

Angel Arms, 1929
Poems, 1935
Dead Reckoning: A Book of Poetry, 1938
Collected Poems, 1940
Afternoon of a Pawnbroker, and Other Poems,
    1943
Stranger at Coney Island, and Other Poems, 1948
New and Selected Poems, 1956
Complete Poems, 1994

OTHER LITERARY FORMS

Kenneth Fearing had a relatively successful career
as a writer of mystery and detective fiction, combining
an ability to fashion a complex plot that concentrated
on a character trapped within the labyrinth of a large
city or organization with a strong sense of the psychology of a relatively innocent man driven to commit murder. His novels are set in the streets of Manhattan and
reflect the desperation of the Depression and the paranoia of the Cold War. Among his most enduring works
are *The Hospital* (1939), which covers an incident from

multiple points of view, *Dagger of the Mind* (1941), which examines the motives of an artist/killer from within the mind of the protagonist, and his most powerful book, *The Big Clock* (1946), which follows a man who is a witness to a crime for which he is being framed. The exceptional narrative tension of *The Big Clock* and the depth of revelation that makes the narrator especially compelling became the essential elements of the film version directed by John Farrow in 1948 and the remake called *No Way Out* (1987), which starred Kevin Costner.

ACHIEVEMENTS

During the Depression, Kenneth Fearing was recognized as a major American writer, but although he has been almost completely ignored by scholars since the 1950's and is largely unknown even to literate Americans, his poetry has scarcely been dated by the passage of time. His concern for the failure of official versions of anything to confront reality, his deep skepticism about socially sanctioned standards of "success," his recognition that urban life could provide extraordinary energy as well as desperate loneliness, and his development of a laconic, terse voice that joined common American speech with an arch tone derived from centuries-old practices of ironic styles permitted him to produce a kind of poetry that is still engaging and relevant. He was an innovative artist whose work was admired by Ezra Pound, who published him in the magazine *Exiles* in the mid-1920's. Fearing anticipated some of the rhythmic methods and structural devices of poets such as Allen Ginsberg and Robert Creeley, while extending Carl Sandburg's feeling for the proletariat into the decades when it became apparent that Sandburg's optimism was no longer justified. In his examinations of psychic survival in a world in which absurdity was overcoming reality, Fearing was a pioneer whose initial reports are an accurate and chilling rendering of the twentieth century city as a landscape of desolation.

BIOGRAPHY

Kenneth Fearing was an approximate contemporary of Ernest Hemingway, born in 1902 in the modestly prosperous suburb of Oak Park, Illinois, where Hem-ingway spent his childhood, and dying just days before Hemingway's suicide in 1961. Unlike Hemingway, however, Fearing was almost exclusively a man of the city. His public schooling and matriculation at the University of Wisconsin were designed to prepare him for a professional life similar to that of his father, who was a successful attorney in Chicago. Even at the University of Wisconsin, however, Fearing displayed aspects of the artistic temperament that mingled with his ability to handle the routines of an advertising copywriter and editor for various newspapers and magazines. His friend the poet Carl Rakosi remembers him there with a "great shock of uncut, unkempt hair . . . a low gravelly voice like Humphrey Bogart . . . always a heavy drinker who did his writing at night [and] slept all morning, skipping classes." A man on the fringe of his time, he was the focus of "admirers basking in his bohemian boldness." After completing his bachelor's degree in 1924, he worked briefly as an apprentice journalist in Chicago before moving to New York, where he settled in the celebrated artistic quarter of Greenwich Village in lower Manhattan.

Fearing spent most of the 1920's continuing his campus unconventionality, holding dead-end jobs as a salesperson and clerk while gradually connecting with political and aesthetic movements in the city's subculture. In 1927, he began a career as a writer for a public relations firms while working as a freelance journalist. Through the 1930's, he contributed stories to pulp magazines and wrote editorials for several newspapers while writing poetry steadily. His first collection of poems, *Angel Arms*, was published in 1929, and Fearing completed two other books of poems during the Depression. During this time, he was awarded a fellowship in creative writing by the Guggenheim Foundation and had begun to attend writers' conferences and give readings, but his success as a poet—his collected poems were published by New Directions in 1940—did not deter him from a venture into fiction in 1939 with *The Hospital*, a novel whose multinarrative scheme was typical of his experimental approach to problems of structure. The almost immediate commercial success of this work enabled Fearing to turn his attention to fiction as the center of his writing life, but although he worked steadily through the 1940's and 1950's in this mode, he also produced poems continuously until the mid-1950's. However, as critic M. L. Rosenthal recalled, Fearing was already "neglected in the postwar repressive backwash well underway in the late forties."

Fearing's most successful novel, *The Big Clock*, was the source of a fine film in 1948, but after *Loneliest Girl in the World* (1951), his work was not particularly successful either critically or commercially. By the time he died of cancer in 1961, he had almost completely vanished from view as a writer. A small revival of interest in his writing began in the 1990's, but his poetry is almost entirely absent from most standard anthologies, he is ignored by the academy, and critical interest remains at a very low level.

Analysis

In the rather unlikely but not inconceivable event that the detective-protagonists of Dashiell Hammett (notably Sam Spade) and Raymond Chandler (particularly Philip Marlowe) had been impelled to express their thoughts and reactions in poetic form, the result might well have resembled the work of Kenneth Fearing. Like them, he lived close to the dark underside of society—a loner who had been around, knew what unpleasant activities even well-meaning people were capable of, and instinctively sympathized with the bottom dogs who always seemed to draw a club when they needed a spade for a flush. He shared their instinctive desire to try to make sense of a world that seemed chaotic and dangerous, where decent people struggled hopelessly and ruthless, brutal ones often thrived, and he knew that his poetry—like their efforts to set some small thing right—was unlikely to accomplish much. Nevertheless, in spite of the semicynical tone of his work, he avoided a slide into nihilism by the continued effort of the work itself. Spade and Marlowe are fictional detectives who often think like poets. Fearing was a poet with the sensibility of the hard-boiled private eye, and his language—sometimes coarse, sometimes literary, usually sardonic, laconic, or even mordant—is a reflection of the film noir world he took as his subject: a world where sunlight was notably absent, dark shadows threatened to engulf everyone, claustrophobia was nearly constant, and the night seemed endless.

Angel Arms

In the early stages of his career, Fearing resembled his midwestern compatriot Carl Sandburg, but while Sandburg's affirmative *The People, Yes* (1936) expressed a belief that the common person would be triumphant, even in his first poems, Fearing was more cautious, suggesting that the best one could hope for would be "the people . . . maybe." His first subjects were people from the working class—"nifties, yeggs, and thirsties," as he put it in the street slang of the 1930's—and his close identification with their situations enabled him to capture their conditions of existence without condescension. In *Angel Arms*, his first book, the initial poem, called "St. Agnes' Eve," is a reduction of John Keats that depicts a man, awakened by gunfire at night, who gets out of bed "to scratch his stomach and shiver on the cold floor." Other poems depict a homeless woman, Minnie Spohr, rummaging "among the buckets at midnight"; a group of friends, "Andy and Jerry and Joe," drifting through the city, directionless, who "didn't know what we wanted and there was nothing to say"; a woman of the street seen in desperate dignity, "Hilda in white/ Hilda sad./ Hilda forgiving the lover who martyr'd her"; and Blake and his office coworkers, whose limited possibilities have not prevented them from feeling the excitement of life in the high-energy zone of the city:

> They liked to feel the city, away below them, stretch
> out and breathe.
> They liked the Metropolitan's red eye, and Broadway.
> They liked to hear liners on the river baying at the sky.
> They liked it all.

"The Drinkers" and "American Rhapsody (2)"

Fearing's most effective poem in this series is "The Drinkers," a precursor of William Carlos Williams's *Pictures from Brueghel* (1962), in which men in "Gonzetti's basement on MacDougal," a Greenwich Village dive, are likened to figures in a painting by Franz Hals, *Flemish Drinkers or Burghers of Antwerp*. Fearing's description is simple, straightforward, and direct, the details evoking the ethos of alienation that is one of his central subjects: "Four men drinking gin, three of them drunk. Outside is the street that sleeps and screams."

Although he never really lost his sympathy for people down and out in an "unreal city," Fearing's focus shifted from his early portraits of what was then considered "the proletariat" to poems that were designed as satirical comments on the false promises of consumerist society—promises that were close to outright lies in the midst of the Depression. He made the logical assumption that if most people were fundamentally decent, then some outside agency must be responsible for the massive neurosis he detected—a conclusion that was consistent with the political position of many left-wing artists during the 1930's. Fearing remained totally independent during his life and had as much scorn for Communist organizations as for any other, but his poems caught the contradictions in the American economic system with devastating effect. In "American Rhapsody (2)" from *Poems*, Fearing describes a man arranging a rendezvous in which the couple might "pretend, even alone, we believe the things we say," and then turns a date into a social tableau, connecting the rot in the world around them to the couple's relationship:

> You be the mother and go out and beg for food; I'll be a merchant, the man you approach, a devoted husband, famous as a host; the merchant can be a jobless clerk who sleeps on subway platforms then lies dead in potter's field; the clerk can be a priest, human, kindly, one who enjoys a joke; the priest can be a lady in jail for prostitution and the lady can be a banker who has his troubles too.

MEANING AMID SOCIAL FAILURE

In "Portrait (2)" from the characteristically named collection *Dead Reckoning*, Fearing compiles a litany of names—officious-sounding law firms, medical authorities, and well-known products—to form a hollow facade covering "nothing," a word he repeats three times at the core of the portrait. The emptiness of useless accomplishment is carried further in the first poem from "The Agency," a section in the *Collected Poems*. In "Agent No. 174 Resigns," the "agent" is a symbol for a citizen who, like Herman Melville's Bartleby, has decided to stop cooperating with "the agency," which is a figure for the institutions of organized society. This idea is explored further in the obviously named "Portrait of a Cog" and in "Yes, the Agency Can Handle

That," in which Fearing suggests that some cosmic agency has been presented as a fix for everything, but that in reality, all the essential human needs are unmet. The poem concludes with the mordant, undermining irony that Fearing often employs: "And there is no mortal ill that cannot be cured by a little money, or lots of love, or by a friendly smile; no."

It was not much of an extension for Fearing to carry the implications of social failure into a stance that paralleled the position being developed by existentialist thinkers in Europe just before and immediately after World War II. The pyramid of duplicity that he develops in poems such as "Dear Beatrice Fairfax:"—which concludes, "It takes a neat, smart, fast, good, sweet doublecross/ To doublecross the gentleman who doublecrossed the gentleman who doublecrossed/ Your doublecrossing, doublecrossing, doublecross friend"—ultimately drains every action of meaning. Thus, he tends to generalize, as in "Beware" (*Afternoon of a Pawnbroker, and Other Poems*), "Damn near anything leads to trouble,/ Someone is always, always stepping out of line." With this increasingly bleak outlook, Fearing was on the verge of the absurdist predicament that postulates nihilism or suicide as the only possible courses in a world in which nothing has any significance. His solution, in his work, was to celebrate the exhilarating, impersonal energy of the city as an almost living entity, fascinating to experience and dangerously exciting to try to master. The early poem "They Liked It" conveys this feeling, as does "Invitation," with its defiant proclamations of intent beginning, "We will make love, when the hospitals are quiet and the blue police car stops to unload prisoners," and concluding, "We will be urged by the hunger of the live. . . . We will be aroused, we will make love, we will dream, we will travel through endless spaces, and we will smile across the room." Fearing adopted the existentialist idea that even in a meaningless universe, the attempt to create meaning is ultimately meaningful. For him, this meant that the way of saying something could be a method for making the statement valid or viable, and his work both echoed some of the innovative styles of his contemporaries and anticipated the poetics of writers in the second half of the twentieth century.

One can see the modernist dictum postulated by

Ezra Pound, "Make it new," operating in poems such as "Jack Knuckles Falters," which uses quotations from a condemned man as recorded in a tabloid in the manner of John Dos Passos; in abrupt parenthetical insertions skewing the rhythms in "Jake" in the style of E. E. Cummings, as well as in a use of expostulations and nonsense expressions in "Dirge" reminiscent of Cummings ("And wow he died as wow he lived,/ Going whop to the office and blooie home to sleep and biff got married and bam had children and oof got fired,/ Zowie did he live and zowie did he die"). A kind of surrealist imagery more typical in painting or European poetry occurs in "Nocturne," with lines such as "giant pillars, filled with spiral stairs, upholding towers of sculptured night/ Where pure ether tides unroll in corridors that have no end and rise in mist." Although this type of experimental use of language is not frequent in Fearing, it is part of a spectrum of possibility that he used to establish meaning through the creative use of language. Similarly, although Fearing rarely wrote like Dylan Thomas, the poem "Denouement" uses direct address ("Sky, be blue, and more than blue; wind, be flesh and blood; flesh and blood be deathless") and nouns as verbs in rhythms that anticipate some of Thomas's work. Established forms such as the dramatic monologue are given a contemporary flavor in "Readings, Forecasts, Personal Guidance" and "Afternoon of a Pawnbroker." In his more original work with form, Fearing used a long line in a kind of bridge between Walt Whitman and Allen Ginsberg, and he anticipated Ginsberg's use of repetition in "Howl" with poems such as "Dance of the Mirrors," which uses "You" as a basic unit for variation and return, and "If Money," which manipulates why, what, where, and who in a fairly intricate scheme. Even the tight texture and elliptic syntax of Robert Creeley is forecast by "Flophouse":

> Out of the frailest texture, somehow, and by some
>   means from
> the shabbiest odds and ends,
> If that is all there is;
> In some way, of even the shaken will,
> If, now, there is nothing else left,
> Now and here in the pulse and breath.

STRANGER AT CONEY ISLAND

The combination of Fearing's range of modernist techniques combined with the dry vernacular of the hip city-dweller on the rough edges of life evokes an era without containing the poet entirely within that era. Toward the latter part of his life, Fearing began to move beyond what Kenneth Rexroth called the belief that "Western Civilization was already dead on its feet, a walking corpse bled of all value." Without actually suggesting how it might come to pass, Fearing envisioned a transcendent passage to another mode of existence. As early as "Debris," he mused on "this life," which he called "insane but true," but offered an image of serenity and renewal: "While mist rises from the cool valleys,/ And somewhere in fresh green hills there is the singing of a bird." Or in "Requiem" (1938), he could foresee a future "day like this, with motors streaming through the fresh parks, the streets alive with casual people,/ And everywhere, on all of it, the brightness of the sun." His *Stranger at Coney Island, and Other Poems* was described by Jerome Rothenberg as a poetic sequence in which Fearing's concern for vision and magic led to "an almost continuous play on the abnormal (haunted) nature of the 'real.'" Such poems as "Lanista," "Elegy," "Museum," and "This Day" from that collection project a kind of reflective confidence that the current state of social disorder could be replaced by some new and more affirmative way of living in which people might be seen "confidently waiting for the sun that will surely rise," as in the close of "Museum."

The sardonic cynic's tone that Fearing perfected was an authentic expression of his feelings of disgust with many facets of American society, but his initial identification with what Rexroth calls "the impoverished stratum of the underworld" never subsided. An accomplished literary professional and a heartland populist as well, Fearing produced poetry that was essentially unencumbered by figures of decoration that submerge a voice in a period and drain it of authority through excessive concern with the temporarily fashionable. Fearing's voice remains an effective instrument for rendering the qualities of life in the twentieth century. As M. L. Rosenthal perceptively describes him, he was "boisterously witty, alcoholic and mordant in his dead-accurate Flaubertian hostility to cruelty and cant."

OTHER MAJOR WORKS

LONG FICTION: *The Hospital*, 1939; *Dagger of the Mind*, 1941 (also known as *Cry Killer!*); *Clark Gifford's Body*, 1942; *The Big Clock*, 1946; *John Barry*, 1947 (with Donald Friede and Henry Bedford-Jones; collectively as Donald F. Bedford); *Loneliest Girl in the World*, 1951 (also known as *The Sound of Murder*); *The Generous Heart*, 1954; *The Crozart Story*, 1960.

BIBLIOGRAPHY

Anderson, Andrew R. *Fear Ruled Them All: Kenneth Fearing's Literature of Corporate Conspiracy*. New York: Peter Lang, 2003. Although this work concentrates on Fearing's fiction, it covers the theme that dominated his work, a warning against the domination of the corporate world.

Barnard, Rita. *The Great Depression and the Culture of Abundance: Kenneth Fearing, Nathanael West, and Mass Culture in the 1930's*. New York: Cambridge University Press, 1995. Analyzes the political and social views of Fearing and Nathanael West and relates them to the history of American literature and popular culture. Includes bibliographical references and index.

Burns, Jim. *Beats, Bohemians, and Intellectuals*. Nottingham, Nottinghamshire, England: Trent Editions, 2000. Fearing is one of the figures to whom a chapter is devoted in this study of American popular culture of the 1950's. Bibliographic references and index.

Dahlberg, Edward. Introduction to *Poems*, by Kenneth Fearing. New York: Dynamo Press, 1935. Dahlberg is an eccentrically interesting critic of American literature, and his singular style is perfectly suited to examining Fearing's peculiarities. A good overview of Fearing's work to that time, a sympathetic response to the poet's goals that is still timely.

Deutsch, Babette. "Flooded with the Immediate Age." *The Nation* 149 (August 19, 1939): 201-202. An essay that contends that Fearing is an ideal spokesperson for his age. Deutsch considers his poetry in technical terms, concentrating on tone and rhythm in particular.

Dupee, F. W. "Sinister Banalities." *The New Republic* 103 (October 28, 1940): 597. An essay that examines Fearing as a satirist, claiming that the poet is a representative of the "Left" and showing how he uses some of the techniques T. S. Eliot introduced in *The Waste Land* (1922).

Jerome, Judson. "Ten Poets: Rare to Overdone." *Antioch Review* 17 (March, 1957): 135-144. A balanced evaluation that identifies some of Fearing's stylistic limitations while indicating an appreciation for his development of a poetic persona in his work.

Kalaidjian, Walter. *American Culture Between the Wars: Revisionary Modernism and Postmodern Critique*. New York: Columbia University Press, 1993. Discusses Fearing's avant-garde approach to text. Primarily a poetic study, but important to an understanding of all Fearing's writings. Bibliographic references and index.

Rosenthal, David. Review of *Collected Poems*. *Village Voice Literary Supplement* 53 (March, 1987): 4. One of the few examples of a late twentieth century response to Fearing's writing, this essay shrewdly evaluates the elements of modernism that Fearing employed.

Rosenthal, M. L. "Don Kenneth and the Racket." *The Nation* 184 (January 19, 1957): 64-65. From one of the best critics to consider Fearing's poetry, this essay is an extension of the material Rosenthal developed in his book on American poets of the Depression. Very good on Fearing's use of comic modes, his creation of an individual voice, and his dissection of the American social system.

Leon Lewis

IRVING FELDMAN

Born: Brooklyn, New York; September 22, 1928

PRINCIPAL POETRY

Works and Days, and Other Poems, 1961
The Pripet Marshes, and Other Poems, 1965
Magic Papers, 1970
Lost Originals, 1972
Leaping Clear, 1976
New and Selected Poems, 1979
Teach Me, Dear Sister, 1983
All of Us Here, 1986
The Life and Letters, 1994
Beautiful False Things, 2000
Collected Poems, 1954-2004, 2004

OTHER LITERARY FORMS

Irving Feldman is known only for his poetry.

ACHIEVEMENTS

Among the most prolific and formally daring American poets of the late twentieth century, Irving Feldman was grounded in the bleak speculative meditations typical of modernism. Despite more than five decades of productivity, Feldman has remained a minority enthusiasm, respected within the university community for incandescent poems that have brought the dark tradition of Yiddish mordant humor into poetry that captures the range of the twentieth century experience. Although intimidating and highbrow at first approach, Feldman's work, richly allusive, densely erudite, and subtly structured, has garnered significant critical recognition. His first collection, *Works and Days, and Other Poems*, received the Kovner Memorial Award for poetry presented by the Jewish Book Council of America to works that best reflect the rich tradition of the Jewish experience; *The Pripet Marshes, and Other Poems* and *Leaping Clear* were both shortlisted for the National Book Award; and *All of Us Here* was nominated for the National Book Critics Circle Award in 1986. *The Life and Letters* was a finalist for the coveted Poets' Prize. He was given an Award in Literature from the American Academy of Arts and Letters in 1973.

The recipient of numerous grants and fellowships (most notably from the Guggenheim Foundation and the Academy of American Poets in 1986), Feldman received in 1992 one of the $500,000 grants from the MacArthur Foundation, the "genius" awards that annually recognize the most creative visionaries in a variety of endeavors as a way to encourage their continued work.

BIOGRAPHY

In keeping with his early allegiance to the nonpersonal poetry of high modernism, Irving Mordecai Feldman has been reluctant to share information about his own life; readers are expected to engage the poems. Not surprising, then, little is known about Feldman's upbringing. The son of Russian Jews who had come to the United States only twenty years earlier, Feldman was born in a Jewish neighborhood in Brooklyn, New York, just before the Great Depression. As Feldman was growing up, his family maintained its religious traditions for strength and consolation. As the disturbing news about the rise of Nazism filtered back to the United States from Europe, Feldman anxiously followed the fate of European Jews.

A precocious reader with an alert and curious mind, Feldman distinguished himself in school. Because of limited financial resources, Feldman attended the nearby City College of New York. He completed his bachelor's degree in social sciences in 1950 and received an M.A. from Columbia in 1953. During his time in New York, Feldman relished the coffeehouse world of the urban bohemians, the lifestyle of bold artistic expression and defiant individual creativity amid a larger world perceived to be drab, complacent, and shallow.

From 1954 until 1956, Feldman taught at the University of Puerto Rico, Rio Pedras. There he met and married avant-garde sculptor Carmen Alvarez del Olmo. In 1957, Feldman, a Fulbright fellow, taught at the Université de Lyon in central France. He returned the following year to teach at Kenyon College, a small liberal arts school in Gambier, Ohio. In 1964, Feldman accepted a position at the State University of New York at Buffalo, becoming distinguished professor of English before retiring in 1994. Known for his contrarian spirit in vigorous classroom discussions and for his demanding expectations from those young poets he chose to mentor, Feldman became an institution at his university and in the Buffalo community. All the while, Feldman pursued his poetic endeavors and maintained a considerable network of acquaintances among his generation of poets—but stayed resolutely in the margins. Even the MacArthur grant did little to encourage Feldman to pursue celebrity. Although he occasionally gave public readings (most often at the Buffalo campus where he taught), Feldman regularly turned down requests for interviews, preferring the poems to speak for themselves. On his eightieth birthday, the university created a tribute Web site that included messages from former students and colleagues and numerous testimonials by critics and poets who lauded Feldman's moral vision and the range of his formal expertise.

ANALYSIS

In turn metaphysical, allegorical, satirical, and lyrical, at once emotional and cerebral, indignant and compassionate, Irving Feldman's verse boldly defies categorization. With a moral earnestness grounded in his generation of Jewish American writers' profound reaction to the Holocaust, the poems, despite their rich variety, share a significant imperative: to define the value of the soul in a universe appallingly uninterested in such larger implications. What good, Feldman asks, is searching for clarity in a world of crushing brutalities and casual tragedies, a world defined by random death and a Kafkaesque absurdity? Feldman conceived of the Poet, always uppercase, as a troubled (at times caustic) moral visionary, defining the unsettling position of the inquiring eye and curious mind in a dark time.

That Feldman's poetry refuses easy surrender to the inevitability of pessimism, that it celebrates the value of speculation on the difficult history of the Jews, defines the intellectual satisfaction of his poetry for those readers willing to engage its obvious erudition. Influenced by modernism and by its deep investigations into a wide variety of forms and poetic lines, Feldman's work reflects a restless experimentation with and a deft mastery of virtually every traditional poetic form from haiku to lyric, from satire to allegory. His verse expands the musical range of language while maintaining a tight structure; he crafts poetic lines that reflect his belief that the work of the poet is to sculpt language into meaningful order. Unlike the Beat poets, who came of age in the same bohemian neighborhoods of 1950's New York City, Feldman found in the traditional forms of poetry a satisfying assertion of aesthetic privilege.

THE PRIPET MARSHES, AND OTHER POEMS

Although Feldman had established his reputation with *Works and Days, and Other Poems*, that collection, with its cool cerebral interrogation of philosophical issues, did not anticipate Feldman's follow-up collection, published a scant four years later. Like novelist Philip Roth, to whom Feldman is often compared, Feldman here adopts a more intimate voice, the voice of a Jewish American who came of age during the revelations of the Holocaust, the voice of the generation of witnesses who were distant from the actual events yet very much part of their implications. The empowered poet executes tightly designed lyrical constructs while the larger world defies such logic and exposes the poet's helplessness.

The prologue celebrates the omnipotence of the poet-creator shaping entire worlds within the rich confines of the imagination, and subsequent poems investigate the artist's powers and prowess (centering on the figure of Pablo Picasso). In the title poem, among Feldman's most anthologized, he imagines a poet transporting his friends from Brooklyn to the Ukraine in mid-summer, 1941, to the Jewish settlements along the Pripyat River, then imagines them as residents of the settlements with names and personalities—and then brusquely returns them to Brooklyn just moments before the Nazis arrive to execute more than six thousand Jews on the suspicion that they are harboring Soviet partisans. It is a wrenching poem in which the poet acknowledges that the imagination is ultimately powerless before such hard realities. In the collection's signature piece, "To the Six Million," Feldman addresses those who died in the Holocaust and examines the complex feelings of those Jews who bear the guilt of surviving while so many others perished, how every moment they feel the heavy shadow of the six million deceased.

THE LOST ORIGINALS

Although given the range of Feldman's formal virtuosity and the scope of his thematic investigations, it is risky to define any one collection as representative, *The Lost Originals*, published roughly at midcareer, can serve as a measure of Feldman's confident explorations of a range of themes from deeply personal recollections of growing up in Coney Island and later visiting Europe to broad metaphysical speculations about the worth of the soul itself. In poem after poem, Feldman juxtaposes the dead or the near-dead with the strength and energy of children. The poems recognize the sobering reality of death (the centerpiece is a poignant elegy to Feldman's longtime friend, the poet Charles Olson) and yet embrace with the carefree joy of a child the pleasures of things such as morning on a balcony in Barcelona, a playground vibrant with children, and the lustrous trill of an operatic tenor. Indeed, in the elegy to Olson, Feldman concludes that the poet, alone among artists, is most likely to be able to explicate the mystery of death as something immediate and, in turn, consoling.

The most profound consolation of Feldman's poetry is always the energy of language to articulate in its order, music, and exoticism (Feldman relishes startlingly unusual vocabulary) a satisfying counterargument to the chaos and ugliness of life. Formally, the poems reflect Feldman's virtuosity. The poems use at turns irregular elliptical lines or broad heavily stressed lines, intent rhythms or subtle off-beats.

THE LIFE AND LETTERS

One of Feldman's most carefully organized collections of verse, *The Life and Letters* is sectioned into three parts. Part 1 is a series of character studies, stories of relationships, of lovers and adulterers, of parents and children, poems written in accessible colloquialism and often delivered with understated humor. In "Warm Enough," for example, Feldman teases the clichéd greeting of his apartment building's elevator operator (Warm enough for you?) into mythic implications. In "Story," a friendship is shattered when a man babysitting a child is late in returning the child to its mother and she realizes how vulnerable her love of the child has made her. The volume's most anthologized poem, "The Little Children of Hamelin," describes the children from the folktale as they follow the piper up into the mountain pass only to be abandoned, their childhoods inexplicably forfeited.

In part 2, Feldman's vision turns public: The poems are caustic critiques of contemporary American culture, satirizing of its pretense, shallowness, penchant for celebrities, obsession with television, and curious fascination with talk-radio psychiatrists.

In the third part, Feldman celebrates the solution he had tendered across three decades: the poet and the power of language. He gathers poems that address the dynamic of writing, the curious responsibilities of reading, and the implications of being a poet. "How Wonderful," for example, is a tongue-in-cheek assessment of what it means to be a "difficult" poet whose poems have generated so many well-intentioned misreadings. The volume closes, appropriately, with "Entrances," a wildly funny lyrical assault of words and phrases without thematic imperative or coherent logic—just the delightful distraction and tireless energy of sounds (read aloud, the poem dazzles).

BIBLIOGRAPHY

Fishman, Charles Ades. *Blood to Remember: American Poets on the Holocaust*. St. Louis: Time Being Books, 2007. Important survey of Feldman's generation of poets, not all Jewish American, who reacted to the event of the Holocaust and how the dimension of that reaction affected even the poetry that did not directly treat the event.

Schweizer, Harold, ed. *The Poetry of Irving Feldman: Nine Essays*. Lewisburg, Pa.: Bucknell University Press, 1992. A gathering of commissioned essays, largely by working poets, that principally investigate Feldman's prosody. The collection stresses Feldman's command of a variety of demanding formal genres and his abiding faith in language.

Slavitt, David R. "'So There Were These Two Jews . . .': The Poetry of Irving Feldman." In *Re Verse: Essays on Poetry and Poets*. Evanston, Ill.: Northwestern University Press, 2005. A broad reading of Feldman's poetry by another poet—thus the analysis is largely descriptive rather than analytical. Stresses Feldman's use of Judaism and the impact of the Holocaust.

Spiegelman, Willard. *The Didactic Muse: Scenes of Instruction in Contemporary American Poetry*. New Haven, Conn.: Princeton University Press, 1989.

An argument, made by one of Feldman's most articulate readers, that his poetry draws on the ancient tradition of verse intended not merely to delight or to excite passions but rather to instruct. Takes a particular look at Feldman's satires and other public verse.

_____. *How Poets See the World: The Art of Description in Contemporary Poetry*. New York: Oxford University Press, 2005. Reading of Feldman's lyric descriptive poetry, specifically his interest in infusing, through keen observation, the everyday world of his urban landscape with a resonance and suggestivity.

Joseph Dewey

BETH ANN FENNELLY

Born: New Jersey; May 22, 1971

PRINCIPAL POETRY

A Different Kind of Hunger, 1998 (chapbook)
Open House, 2002
Tender Hooks, 2004
The Kudzu Chronicles, 2005 (chapbook)
Unmentionables, 2008

OTHER LITERARY FORMS

Beth Ann Fennelly is known primarily for her poetry. However, she also wrote *Great with Child: Letters to a Young Mother* (2006), a series of letters to a former student who was expecting her first child. Fennelly drew on her own experience of pregnancy and childbirth for the book and noted that the process of having a child is not unlike the creation of a poem, just as difficult and just as rewarding.

ACHIEVEMENTS

Beth Ann Fennelly's chapbook *A Different Kind of Hunger* won the 1997 Texas Review Breakthrough Award. *Open House* won the 2001 *Kenyon Review* Prize in Poetry for a first book. Her status as a major American poet is evident not only in the praise of

reviewers but also by the inclusion of her poems in *The Pushcart Prize 2001: Best of the Small Presses*, *The Penguin Book of the Sonnet* (2001), *Poets of the New Century* (2001), *Contemporary American Poetry* (2005), *The Best American Poetry* (2005), and *The Best American Poetry* (2006). In 2002, Fennelly received a creative writing fellowship in poetry from the National Endowment for the Arts. On March 5, 2003, she read her poetry at the Library of Congress.

BIOGRAPHY

Beth Ann Fennelly was born in New Jersey on May 22, 1971, but grew up in Lake Forest, Illinois, a suburb of Chicago on the city's North Shore. From her earliest years, she loved words and enjoyed reading, and at first, she planned to become an actress. However, though she had always had leading roles in the plays presented in her high school, after she enrolled at the University of Notre Dame, Fennelly realized that she was not as talented in acting as she had thought. Then she took a poetry workshop, and from that time on, she had no doubt about her vocation. In 1993, Fennelly received a B.A. in English, magna cum laude.

After a year spent teaching English in a Czechoslovakian coal mining village, Fennelly entered the graduate program at the University of Arkansas in Fayetteville. In 1998, she received an M.F.A. in poetry and was awarded the Diane Middlebrook Fellowship for a year's postdoctoral work at the University of Wisconsin in Madison. Fennelly told an interviewer that she was especially proud of another personal achievement that year: She competed in the Chicago marathon.

In the summer of 1999, Fennelly held a University of Arizona Poetry Center residency, and the following summer, she held a MacDowell Colony residency. From 1999 to 2002, she was an assistant professor of English at Knox College, Galesburg, Illinois. For several years, Fennelly had been married to the fiction writer Tom Franklin. The birth of their daughter Claire in 2001 inspired her to write the poems later published in *Tender Hooks*. In 2002, Fennelly accepted a position as assistant professor of English at the University of Mississippi, and the family moved to Oxford, Mississippi. Their son Thomas was born there. In 2007, Fennelly became associate professor.

ANALYSIS

With the publication of her first chapbook, Beth Ann Fennelly was recognized as a young writer who was remarkably accomplished. She has continued to produce poems that reflect her fascination with words and with ideas. In a single poem, Fennelly may be by turns thoughtful, witty, tender, harsh, and extremely funny. Above all, however, Fennelly is an honest poet, one who presents experience in all its complexity, one who is as unwilling to voice platitudes as she is to bend her ideas to fit accepted poetic forms.

OPEN HOUSE

Fennelly organized her first book-length collection, *Open House*, as a house tour. Each of the four sections of the book is likened to a room; instead of furniture, however, each contains poems linked closely in content. All six poems in the first section, "The Room of Dead Languages," have to do with words. However, they vary greatly both in tone and in form. For example, "Mother Sends My Poem to Her Sister with Post-Its" is a series of short passages scattered on the page. The mother's thoughts are just as random as the form suggests. They have only a peripheral connection to the poem she read; instead, they show that, like most mothers with grown daughters, her primary interest is not in what her child is doing now but in their relationship. Thus, she focuses on the errors in her daughter's memories and tries to find in her poem evidence that she intends to come home. Fennelly's sensitivity to the relationship between form and content is evident in the shaped poem "The Insecurities of Great Men," which keeps expanding and then dwindling; in the prose paragraph used for "My Father's Pregnancy," a restrained, factual summary of the physical process of death; and the random, scattered comments in "Cremains" that dramatize her later surrender to grief.

Fennelly's versatility is evident throughout the collection. In "The Room of Echoes," she demonstrates her ability to slip into the minds of others. For example, she speaks as one of the daughters of the English poet John Milton in "Mary Speaks to the Early Visitor at the Laying Out," as the daughter of the French painter Paul Gauguin in "Letter from Gauguin's Daughter," and as a woman deserted by her husband of thirty years in "Yield." That same imaginative power is evident in

"The Room of Paper Walls," a section made up of a single, long poem, written in various forms and fragments, in which the author assumes the persona of a creative writing teacher, which in fact is one of her own roles in life, and argues with her other persona, the poet freed from the constraints of tradition and convention. As the poem proceeds, the teacher is defeated, and the poet speaks for herself, as indeed she does in the final section of *Open House*, "The Room of Everywhere."

TENDER HOOKS

The title of Fennelly's second collection, *Tender Hooks*, is a misunderstanding of the word "tenterhooks," as a child might hear it. Since to be on tenterhooks means to be anxious, "tenterhooks" is an appropriate title for a book about pregnancy, childbirth, and motherhood, all conditions characterized by anxiety. However, Fennelly's deliberate misspelling is also an appropriate title, as the poems in the work demonstrate the tenderness the poet feels for her child, while at the same time she experiences a sense of entrapment, for, like a fish, a mother who lets herself love her child is indeed hooked and never will be released. Fennelly recognizes this in "Bite Me," when the baby's insistence on biting her mother reminds the poet of the final hours of childbirth, when the child was, in effect, gnawing her way out of her mother's body.

Fennelly describes the physical consequences of childbirth as graphically as she does the process itself. In "Three Months After Giving Birth, the Body Loses Certain Hormones," the poet lists hair loss, tooth decay, incontinence, and flabbiness as signs that although she is young, she is progressing toward death. Thus childbirth becomes a kind of initiation for the poet: Now she has a new vision of life, its cruelty as well as its joy. This ambivalence is evident in the long poem about breastfeeding entitled "Latching On, Falling Off." Breastfeeding hurts, and yet the mother desires the hurt, for it brings her not only release from the pain of a full breast but also sexual pleasure. Once the baby is weaned, the writer can once again be a sexual object to delight her husband, but she cannot help recalling wistfully the time when she and her suckling child were the only reality in the world.

Although the baby Claire is a recurring presence in *Tender Hooks*, not all the poems in the collection are about motherhood. There are speculations about religion and comments about writing. There are also descriptions of the natural world, in which the flat, frigid Illinois where the poet grew up is contrasted with the languorous South, which she has come to love. There is also a series of poems about an earlier miscarriage, which again is viewed with ambivalence, for though the poet still grieves, she knows that Claire might not have been born if the other child had lived. In the final poems, Claire is growing older and, to a degree, is moving away from her mother. The poet tries to stop time by recording every new achievement of her daughter. However, she realizes that a written record is not enough; the only answer to her sense of loss, she concludes, is to have another baby. Obviously, in the struggle between the joys and the sorrows of motherhood, it is the joys that have won.

OTHER MAJOR WORK

NONFICTION: *Great with Child: Letters to a Young Mother*, 2006.

BIBLIOGRAPHY

Betts, Genevieve. Review of *Unmentionables*. *Midwest Quarterly* 50, no. 1 (Autumn, 2008): 108-110. Although Fennelly's primary subject remains her reactions to the people and the places in her life, the poems in this collection are more complex than those in her previous works. The reviewer notes that in the section "The Kudzu Chronicles," the poet commits herself to a new identity as a southerner.

Fennelly, Beth Ann. "My Hundred." *American Poetry Review* 37, no. 5 (September/October, 2008): 35-37. Argues that by memorizing poems and then reciting them aloud, one completes the reading process. The essay includes suggestions for the use of memorization in the classroom.

Hass, Robert. "Losing Mr. Daylater: A Note on Beth Ann Fennelly." *Kenyon Review* 23, nos. 3/4 (Summer/Fall, 2001): 28-30. A perceptive analysis of "From L'Hotel Terminus Notebooks," pointing out how the poet utilizes the character of Mr. Daylater as a symbol of those forces that are the enemies of the imagination. Once he has been eliminated, Fennelly produces some of her finest poetry, nota-

bly in the sections of the poem that deal with love and death.

Olson, Ray. Review of *Tender Hooks*. *Booklist* 100, no. 13 (March 1, 2004): 1127. The reviewer is impressed by Fennelly's poetic skills, such as her instinct as to where a line should end and her "striking epigrams." No other poet deals with motherhood and with the mother-child relationship as effectively.

Rogoff, Jay. "Pushing and Pulling." *Southern Review* 41, no. 1 (Winter, 2005): 189-210. An essay on the conflicts reflected in five new books of poetry, including *Tender Hooks* by Fennelly. Rogoff notes that the poet recognizes such obvious polarities as birth/death and pleasure/pain; however, she has not yet perfected her ability to move easily between "extravagance" and "restraint."

Seaman, Donna. Review of *Unmentionables*. *Booklist* 104, no. 15 (April 1, 2008): 19. The poems in this collection are superbly crafted, and those that deal with motherhood are as honest, as direct, and as witty as those in her previous books. Fennelly is just as effective when she writes about kudzu, about the differences between Illinois and Mississippi, or about the artist Berthe Morisot.

Virginia Quarterly Review. Review of *Open House*. 78, no. 4 (September, 2002): 137-138. Praises Fennelly as a poet who takes risks, for example, including not only herself in the cast of characters but also her "poetic alter-ego," Mr. Daylater. Also admires her for including such a wide range of ideas and references in her book.

Rosemary M. Canfield Reisman

LAWRENCE FERLINGHETTI

Born: Yonkers, New York; March 24, 1919

PRINCIPAL POETRY

Pictures of the Gone World, 1955, 1995
A Coney Island of the Mind, 1958
Starting from San Francisco, 1961

An Eye on the World: Selected Poems, 1967
The Secret Meaning of Things, 1969
Tyrannus Nix?, 1969
Back Roads to Far Places, 1971
Open Eye, Open Heart, 1973
Who Are We Now?, 1976
Landscapes of Living and Dying, 1979
Endless Life: Selected Poems, 1981
A Trip to Italy and France, 1981
*Over All the Obscene Boundaries: European Poems
     and Transitions*, 1984
*These Are My Rivers: New and Selected Poems,
     1955-1993*, 1993
A Far Rockaway of the Heart, 1997
San Francisco Poems, 1998
*How to Paint Sunlight: Lyric Poems and Others,
     1997-2000*, 2001
Americus, Book I, 2004

OTHER LITERARY FORMS

Early in his career, Lawrence Ferlinghetti (fur-lihng-GEHT-ee) was very much interested in the French Symbolist poets, and in 1958, City Lights published his first and only translation of French poetry: *Selections from "Paroles" by Jacques Prévert*. His translations of pieces by an Italian poet, Pier Paolo Pasolini, appeared in 1986 as *Roman Poems*. He has also translated poetry by Nicanor Parra in *Antipoems: New and Selected* (1985) and by Homero Aridjis in *Eyes to See Otherwise* (2002). Ferlinghetti has primarily published poetry in book form, although, in addition to having written many critical and review articles that have appeared in both magazines and newspapers, he has produced a variety of works including novels, travel writing, political writing, drawings, and plays. Ferlinghetti's work crosses genre boundaries, and some of his prose works—like the novel *Her* (1960) and the travel journal *The Mexican Night* (1970)—sound so much like his poetry that it is questionable whether one should actually call them prose. He published another novel, *Love in the Days of Rage*, in 1988 and two commentaries on poetry, *What Is Poetry?* (2000) and *Poetry as Insurgent Art* (2007), the latter consisting of thoughts on poetry written over more than fifty years.

Ferlinghetti's two plays, *Unfair Arguments with Ex-istence* and *Routines*, were published by New Directions in 1963 and 1964, respectively. His interest in the theater and oral poetry led to various filmings and recordings of his readings. The two best-known performances of Ferlinghetti, "Tyrannus Nix?" and "Assassination Raga," are preserved in both film and audio recording. *Leaves of Life: Drawing from the Model* (1983) is a collection of his drawings, as is his *Life Studies, Life Stories: Eighty Works in Paper* (2003).

ACHIEVEMENTS

In 1957, Lawrence Ferlinghetti first received national attention as a result of the "Howl" obscenity trial. At that time, Ferlinghetti was recognized not as a poet but as the publisher and distributor of Allen Ginsberg's *Howl, and Other Poems* (1956). After winning the controversial trial, Ferlinghetti received enough attention to boost his own collection of poems, *A Coney Island of the Mind*, into a best-seller position. His name became strongly associated with the new, or Beat, poetry being developed on the West Coast, and Ferlinghetti became recognized as a poet of movements and protests.

Often being antigovernment in his responses, Ferlinghetti has gone so far as refusing to accept government grants for either his own writing or the City Lights publishing house. Nevertheless, he received a National Book Award nomination in 1970 for *The Secret Meaning of Things*, the *Library Journal* Notable Book of 1979 citation for *Landscapes of Living and Dying* in 1980, and Silver Medals for poetry from the Commonwealth Club of California for *Over All the Obscene Boundaries* in 1984 and for *A Far Rockaway of the Heart* in 1997. In 1977, the city of San Francisco paid tribute to Ferlinghetti by honoring him at the Civic Art Festival—the first time a poet was so recognized. The City of Rome awarded him a poetry prize in 1993, and San Francisco not only named a street in his honor in 1994 but also named him the city's first poet laureate in 1998. The poet was presented the Fred Cody Award for lifetime achievement in 1996 and the Lifetime Achievement Award from the Before Columbus Foundation in 1999. In 2000, Ferlinghetti was a joint winner, with film critic Pauline Kael, of the National Book Critics Circle's Ivan Sandrof Award for Lifetime Achievement. Furthermore, in 2001, City Lights Bookseller and Publishers was designated an official landmark. He has continued to be recognized through a wide range of awards, including the Robert Kirsch Award for body of work from the *Los Angeles Times* (2000), the PEN Center West Literary Award for lifetime achievement (2002), the Frost Medal (2003), the Northern California Book Award in poetry (2004) for *Americus, Book I*, the Association of American Publishers Award for creative publishing (2005), and the Literarian Award from the National Book Foundation (2005) for outstanding service to the American literary community.

Ferlinghetti is noted for the many public readings he has given in support of free speech, nuclear disarmament, antiwhaling, and other causes. Often overlooked by critics, Ferlinghetti has remained an active voice speaking for the American people against many institutions and practices—government, corporate, and social alike—that limit individual freedom; he stands out as a poet and a true individual.

BIOGRAPHY

Lawrence Monsanto Ferlinghetti—born in Yonkers, New York, in 1919—was the youngest of five sons of Charles Ferlinghetti and Clemence Ferlinghetti. Several months before Lawrence's birth, his father died unexpectedly of a heart attack, and his mother suffered a breakdown as a result. She was unable to care for her son and was eventually institutionalized at the state hospital in Poughkeepsie, New York.

After these humble and tragic beginnings, it is ironic that Ferlinghetti was taken and cared for by his mother's well-to-do uncle, Ludwig Mendes-Monsanto, and his wife, Emily, in their Manhattan home. It is also ironic that American-born Ferlinghetti learned French as his first language. In fact, throughout his childhood, he actually believed himself to be French, having been taken in by his great-aunt Emily, who left her husband and returned to France, her homeland. Ferlinghetti spent the first five years of his life in Strasbourg with Mendes-Monsanto, whom he refers to as his "French mother." She was eventually persuaded to return to New York to rejoin her husband, but the reunion lasted only for a short time. Ferlinghetti—who knew himself only as Lawrence Ferling Monsanto—was placed in an orphanage for seven months. Eventually, Mendes-

Monsanto reclaimed him and took him away, after leaving her husband again. This time they remained in New York.

Mendes-Monsanto took on work as a French tutor for the daughter of the very wealthy Presley Bisland and Anna Lawrence Bisland. She and Ferlinghetti lived in a small room in the third-floor servants' area until one day she mysteriously disappeared, whereupon Ferlinghetti was adopted by the Bislands.

The Bislands' son had died in early childhood. His name—and his mother's maiden name—was Lawrence, her father having founded Sarah Lawrence College near Bronxville. Presley Bisland was also a man of letters, with a profound interest in contemporary literature, although his experiences included being one of the last men to ride the Chisholm Trail on the last of the great cattle drives. The Bislands were aristocratic, adventuresome, and cosmopolitan, but also creative in spirit. In fact, Ferlinghetti maintains that Presley Bisland's writings gave him the idea that being an author was a dignified calling.

At the age of ten, Ferlinghetti was told about his natural mother, Clemence Ferlinghetti, whom he met one

Lawrence Ferlinghetti (Time & Life Pictures/Getty Images)

traumatic Sunday afternoon. He was given the choice to go with her, although he considered her a stranger, or to stay with the Bislands. He chose to stay. Unknown to Ferlinghetti, the Bislands had arranged to send him away to school. A few weeks later, he found himself boarding with a family named Wilson in one of New York City's rougher neighborhoods. Their son Bill, being older, became a hero to the young Ferlinghetti. Lawrence joined the Boy Scouts, went to baseball and football games, and was far less lonely than he had been at the Bisland mansion.

At the age of sixteen, Lawrence began to write poetry. His stepsister, Sally Bisland, gave him a book of Charles Baudelaire in translation. Ferlinghetti remembers it as the first collection of poems he read from cover to cover. He was then sent to a private high school, Mount Hernon, near Greenfield, Massachusetts. In his senior year, Anna Bisland took him for the first of a series of visits to see his natural mother and brothers at their home in Ossining.

Ferlinghetti attended college at the University of North Carolina at Chapel Hill and was graduated in 1941, after which he joined the U.S. Navy and served in World War II. It was while he was in the Navy that he received a telegram from Central Islip State Hospital saying that Emily Mendes-Monsanto, his "French mother," had died, having listed Ferlinghetti as her only living relative. This was the first he had heard of her since she had left him with the Bislands when he was ten.

In World War II, Ferlinghetti was on one of the primary naval submarine chasers coming in for the Normandy invasion. Later, in 1945, on the first day of the U.S. occupation of Japan, his ship landed there. Eventually, he was able to visit Nagasaki, where he witnessed the aftermath of the atomic bombing of that city. The devastation he witnessed left an indelible impression.

After his discharge from the U.S. Navy, Ferlinghetti returned to New York City and lived in Greenwich Village, taking on work as a mail clerk for *Time* magazine. His interest in poetry revived, and he returned to Columbia University under the G.I. Bill, receiving his M.A. degree in 1947. That summer Presley Bisland died. Soon afterward, Ferlinghetti left for Paris, where he met many literary figures. He completed work on a

thesis and was awarded a degree from the Sorbonne. He also wrote a novel, which was rejected by Doubleday. In 1949, Ferlinghetti returned to the United States for a two-week visit with Anna Bisland. In 1951, both she and Ferlinghetti's natural mother died. In the same year, after several trips back and forth between Europe and the United States, Ferlinghetti married Selden Kirby-Smith, who was known as Kirby. They moved to San Francisco, where Ferlinghetti wrote articles for *Art Digest* and book reviews for the *San Francisco Chronicle.*

Influenced greatly by Kenneth Rexroth and Kenneth Patchen, who both lived in San Francisco, Ferlinghetti soon came to be considered a political poet. He was published in Peter Martin's magazine *City Lights,* and eventually the two men collaborated to open the City Lights Bookstore in 1953. In 1955, the same year that Ferlinghetti's first book of poetry, *Pictures of the Gone World,* was published under the City Lights imprint, Martin sold Ferlinghetti his interest in the store. At about that time, Ferlinghetti became acquainted with James Laughlin, president of the publishing house New Directions. It was through Laughlin that Ferlinghetti's second book of poems, *A Coney Island of the Mind,* became a best seller.

Ginsberg came into Ferlinghetti's life from the East, bringing a poem titled "Howl" with him. Ferlinghetti was impressed with Ginsberg and published *Howl, and Other Poems.* It was this book that caused Ferlinghetti to be arrested, the charge against him being that he printed and sold obscene writings. He was eventually cleared, and partly because of the publicity, City Lights flourished.

Although Ferlinghetti and his wife, Kirby, were divorced in the early 1970's, their marriage had been relatively stable; in 1962 a daughter, Julie, was born, and in 1963, a son, Lorenzo. During the 1960's, Ferlinghetti traveled to South and Central America, to Europe, and to the Soviet Union, giving poetry readings whenever possible. In 1974, he met Paula Lillevand; they moved in together in 1978, but they parted two years later.

Ferlinghetti first took lysergic acid diethylamide (LSD) in 1967, an experience that resulted in the poem "Mock Confessional." Throughout the 1970's and

1980's, Ferlinghetti remained actively interested in political and environmental matters, his poetry inevitably reflecting his political and social concerns. During these years, he traveled extensively in Europe and sometimes in Latin America, giving readings of his poems.

In 1977, Ferlinghetti took up drawing, an interest he had left behind some twenty years earlier, and soon he was painting as well. His expressionist-style works were displayed in a formal exhibition in the mid-1980's in the San Francisco Bay area, and another show was organized in Berlin in 1990. He continued to edit volumes of City Lights anthologies throughout the 1990's. Ferlinghetti also collaborated in a video, directed by Christopher Felver, called *The Coney Island of Lawrence Ferlinghetti*, released in 1996. In it, the poet acts in autobiographical vignettes, tours places of particular meaning to him, reads his poetry, and expounds on his artistic philosophy and political views.

Ferlinghetti has continued to play an active role in the cultural and literary life of San Francisco and has traveled frequently for poetry readings, interviews, and exhibitions of his art. A 2007 show of approximately twenty of his large canvases traveled to Woodstock, New York, under the title lit.paint. New volumes of poetry have included *How to Paint Sunlight* and the ambitious *Americus, Book I*, a poetic compendium of the historical, political, and cultural past of America through the early 1960's.

ANALYSIS

Lawrence Ferlinghetti's poetry may be looked on as a kind of travelog in which he has subjectively recorded choice experiences or montages from experience, often in a jazzlike or free-associative manner. For Ferlinghetti, "reality" itself becomes metaphorical, something he endows with mythical import, although he is not a poet given to hidden meanings. Although his poetry is largely autobiographical, an adequate analysis of his poetry is possible without thorough biographical knowledge; Ferlinghetti's poetry is not excessively self-contained.

A CONEY ISLAND OF THE MIND

Whereas Ferlinghetti's poems are for the most part historical, or autobiographical, Ferlinghetti the man is a

myth, appearing as a cult hero, one of the original Beats. Sometimes a martyr to a cause, Ferlinghetti will occasionally insert his political ideologies into a poem for no apparent reason other than that they seem to fit his role. Halfway through the sometimes absurd, sometimes delightful poem "Underwear," Ferlinghetti over-extends his metaphor by becoming politically involved:

> You have seen the three-color pictures
> with crotches encircled
> to show the areas of extra strength
> and three-way stretch
> promising full freedom of action
> Don't be deceived
> It's all based on the two-party system
> which doesn't allow much freedom of choice

The reader is often seduced, but behind Ferlinghetti's speaking voice, full of American colloquialisms, is an intellect schooled in the classics, highly knowledgeable of literature, past and present—a voice full of allusions. Rather surprisingly, Ferlinghetti makes many direct references to greater works of literature by borrowing lines to suit his own purposes. Even the title of Ferlinghetti's best-selling book *A Coney Island of the Mind* is taken from Henry Miller's *Into the Night Life* (1947). One repeatedly discovers lines and phrases such as T. S. Eliot's "Let us go then you and I" and "Hurry up please it's time" ironically enlisted for use in such poems as "Junkman's Obbligato." Ferlinghetti frequently employs fragments from literature without alerting his audience to his borrowing. In "Autobiography," he states, "I read the Want Ads daily/ looking for a stone a leaf/ an unfound door"—an oblique reference to Thomas Wolfe's opening in *Look Homeward, Angel* (1929). He makes even more esoteric references to William Butler Yeats's "horsemen" in poems such as "Reading Yeats I Do Not Think" and again in "Autobiography." In "Assassination Raga," one finds a variation on Dylan Thomas's "The force that through the green fuse drives the flower." In its stead, Ferlinghetti writes of "The force that through the red fuze/ drives the bullet"—the poem being in honor of Robert Kennedy and read in Nourse Auditorium, San Francisco, June 8, 1968, the day Kennedy was buried after having been assassinated during his presidential campaign in Los Angeles.

In his role as a subjective historian and political rebel, Ferlinghetti never orates with so much pomp as to raise himself above his audience. In his meager "Charlie Chaplin" manner—Chaplin being a persona to whom he continuously compares himself in poems such as "Constantly Risking Absurdity," "In a Time of Revolution for Instance," and "Director of Alienation"—Ferlinghetti is just as capable of making fun of himself as he is of satirizing various institutions and aspects of society.

"Dog"

Whereas some poets seek to find metaphorical reflections of themselves in nature, Ferlinghetti rarely looks there for inspiration. Furthermore, being more fond of philosophy than of drama, Ferlinghetti projects a sense of conflict mainly through his own personal quest—for his true self. His feelings of alienation and the quest for environmental constants that do not restrict one's freedom are depicted in the poem "Dog" (from *A Coney Island of the Mind*), which begins: "The dog trots freely in the street/ and sees reality/ and the things he sees/ are bigger than himself. . . ." As the poem progresses, the reader comes to understand that this is an ordinary stray dog—and also Ferlinghetti in a stray-dog suit. "And the things he sees/ are his reality/ Drunks in doorways/ Moons on trees. . . ." The dog keeps on going with a curiosity that demands diversity from experience.

Ferlinghetti goes deeper, allowing the reader also to don a dog suit, to see "Ants in holes/ Chickens in Chinatown windows/ their heads a block away." Thus the reader learns that he is roaming the streets of San Francisco. The dog trots past the carcasses that are hung up whole in Chinatown. At this point, the reader learns that he "would rather eat a tender cow/ than a tough policeman/ though either might do." The reader has already been told that the dog does not hate cops; he merely has no use for them.

Here the reader begins to wonder whether being stray is conditional on having no preferences. Is the dog a Democrat or a Republican? The reader later learns that this dog is at least "democratic." Ferlinghetti does deal with unusual specifics as the dog trots past the San Francisco Meat Market, and keeps going: "past the Romeo Ravioli Factory/ and past Coit's Tower/ and past Congressman Doyle of the Unamerican Committee. . . ." Here Ferlinghetti manages to make a political statement that is alien to a dog's perspective. This "Unamerican Committee" is obviously something that Ferlinghetti the Beat poet—not the Ferlinghetti in the dog suit—has recognized. The Ferlinghetti in the dog suit says that ultimately "Congressman Doyle is just another/ fire hydrant/ to him." Thus the reader knows how the Ferlinghetti in a dog suit might treat Congressman Doyle—symbolically or not. A few lines earlier, Ferlinghetti alludes to the poet Thomas by labeling the dog "a sad young dog" (see Thomas's *Portrait of the Artist as a Young Dog*, 1940): The dog appears to be metaphorical of all poets and artists, especially Ferlinghetti himself.

Ferlinghetti proceeds to declare that a dog's knowledge is only of the senses. His curiosity already quite obvious, the day becomes:

> a real live
> > barking
> > > democratic dog
> engaged in real
> > > free enterprise
> with something to say
> > > about ontology
> something to say
> > about reality.

In this segment, a major change can be noted: Ferlinghetti has abandoned flush left margins. Beginning with the line "barking," Ferlinghetti demonstrates a newfound freedom through his staggered, free-form typography. The poem continues, and the dog himself trots more freely, cocking his head sideways at street corners "as if he is just about to have/ his picture taken/ for Victor Records." His ear is raised, and it is suggested that he embodies a question mark as he looks askew into the "great gramophone of puzzling existence," waiting and looking, just like Ferlinghetti, for an answer to everything—and it all sounds like poetry.

A Far Rockaway of the Heart

In 1997, nearly forty years after the publication of *A Coney Island of the Mind*, Ferlinghetti published a volume whose title insists that it be taken as a companion piece to the earlier work: *A Far Rockaway of the Heart*. Its 101 poems revealed that both the poet's strengths and his weaknesses were in full force as he approached his eightieth birthday. The colloquial diction is as easy as ever, but its novelty is somewhat tarnished; the wide-ranging quotation from and reference to the words of other poets is as masterful as ever, and all the more impressive as the common literary canon has all but disappeared from the cultural landscape. A number of critics noted that Ferlinghetti's styles, themes, and techniques seemed barely to have changed over the long course of his career, yet the poet himself begins the volume acknowledging this fact:

> Everything changes and nothing changes
> Centuries end
>
> and all goes on
> as if nothing
> ever ends
> As clouds still stop in mid-flight
> like dirigibles caught in cross-winds
>
> And the fever of savage city life
> still grips the streets. . . .
>
> It's as if those forty years just vanish.

Perhaps it is presumptuous of the poet to proclaim his own timelessness. However, perhaps his ongoing social and political concerns are timeless because in forty years, little has occurred to remedy the ills he sees around him, and the world goes on as absurd—and as beautiful—as ever.

HOW TO PAINT SUNLIGHT

In the introductory note to *How to Paint Sunlight*, Ferlinghetti paraphrases American painter Edward Hopper by saying that "all I ever wanted to do was paint light on the walls of life." The thirty-four poems of this volume, subdivided into four sections, each headed by a note or an epigraph, signal varying concerns with images of light and darkness. Ferlinghetti sees the world as art and light as its paint. The poet's job is to "paint" the world with authenticity and innocence and in all its various hues. Ferlinghetti also suggests that the poet is the medium, the source of the tempera and the gesso.

The poet thus creates the world anew on a canvas of former "paintings" and is astonished by each new creation.

Ferlinghetti relies on techniques familiar from earlier work: wide-ranging allusion, an oral quality, free-form lines, and humor. The first section explores varieties of light and darkness in such California landscapes as San Francisco and Big Sur. The introductory poem, "Instructions to Painters & Poets," theorizes about the connections between creating poetry and creating paintings. Subsequent poems begin with images of bright light and end with darker meditations. "Yachts in Sun" begins with the image of bright light catching the sails of the yachts on the bay and ends with the image of the dead lying drowned in the bay beneath the hulls of the boats. The second section, "Surreal Migrations," traverses world and time in search of transcendent light, incorporating allusions to Eliot, Adolf Hitler, Wolfgang Amadeus Mozart, Marcel Proust, Walt Whitman, and the Beatles. The poem ends with images of the creation of song arising from the sounds of leaves and birds. "New York, New York," the more political and sarcastic third section, focuses on urban settings and explores images of New York and personal memories of the narrator's past.

The fourth section, "Into the Interior," combines poems set in midwestern venues and transitions to meditations on the death of Beat poet Ginsberg, including one of the few prose poems of the volume, "Allen Still." Early poems in the section treat the interior of the country (the Midwest) and transition to poems that explore the human interior. "Blind Poet," a poem meant to be performed blindfolded, alludes to the poet's interior vision and to blind bards such as Homer and John Milton. The final poems of this section turn increasingly introspective as the narrator of one poem ("Mouth") laments his inability to express himself and another ("A Tourist of Revolutions") describes the superficiality of his political activism and foreshadows his own death with a wry comment: "And when I die without a sound/ I'll surely join I'll surely join/ the permanent Underground." The final poem of the section, in keeping with the overall tenor of the entire volume, is a paean to the god of light.

AMERICUS, BOOK I

Ferlinghetti's ambitious *Americus, Book I* combines both epic and palimpsest. Its title suggests that it is only the first part of Ferlinghetti's epic of the United States. The volume traces American history from the first European encounters with the natives through the death of President John F. Kennedy in 1963. Ferlinghetti's work combines political and cultural history with the individual story of its titular bardic character, Americus.

The work alludes to a variety of events, including the European colonization of North America, the French Revolution, westward expansion, and the two world wars. Much of this history takes the form of a collage of newspaper headlines, letters, and stream-of-consciousness prose poems.

Ferlinghetti sets his work firmly in the epic tradition, particularly in the third of the book's twelve sections, where the long monologue by the epic poet Homer situates the poem in the context not only of Homeric epic and Dante's *La divina commedia* (c. 1320; *The Divine Comedy*, 1802) but also of the epic works of American poets Whitman (*Leaves of Grass*, 1855), Ezra Pound (*Cantos*, 1925-1972), William Carlos Williams (*Paterson*, 1946-1958), and Charles Olson (*The Maximus Poems*, 1953-1983). Homer defines poetry in an extended catalog of inventive aphorisms that serve as an index to the themes of Ferlinghetti's poetry. Ferlinghetti alternately presents his compendium of American history and pieces together its larger cultural and artistic history, alluding to influential writers and artists.

In addition to delineating the national history and character of the United States, *Americus* also describes the personal, semi-autobiographical journey of Americus, the central character. Americus begins his journey to America in the womb of his European mother and grows up in the East with all the hopefulness and opportunity contained in the stereotypical immigrant vision of the American Dream. He experiences the horrors, the deaths, and the disillusion of World War II and, following the war, moves west. This central singer of Ferlinghetti's epic is reminiscent of Whitman's central voice in *Leaves of Grass*.

Americus is also a palimpsest, as suggested by the use of the term in the second line of the poem. A pa-limpsest is a painting or a manuscript that has been created over a previously existing work, so that sometimes the previous work shows through the new work like a ghost. Ferlinghetti layers his work over previous works by making allusions to them, a technique accentuated by the existence of the notes section at the end of the poem. In the notes, Ferlinghetti lists the numerous sources for the various quotations and references that serve as the basis for his poem, quotations that are often elided, parodied, and reworked in much the same manner as the allusions in modernist poet Eliot's *The Waste Land* (1922) or *The Four Quartets* (1943). Ferlinghetti also uses lists and catalogs in much the same manner as Whitman, trying to express the vastness and variability of America in a cornucopia of references to people, events, and impressions that help capture the American experience.

Americus provides a compendium of poetic techniques from Ferlinghetti's work. He uses free-form verse, dialogue, an oral quality, the stream-of-consciousness prose poem, humor, puns, and satire to capture the face and the sights and sounds of America and its past. Ferlinghetti notably ends this volume with a prose poem that portrays a hopeful and celebratory view of the "splendid life of the world." This final prose poem is especially striking when contrasted with the descriptions of the horrors of war and the assassination of Kennedy that precede it. The final three pages of the poem celebrate the joys of the world in all its vitality and beauty.

OTHER MAJOR WORKS

LONG FICTION: *Her*, 1960; *Love in the Days of Rage*, 1988.

PLAYS: *Unfair Arguments with Existence*, pb. 1963; *Routines*, pb. 1964.

NONFICTION: *The Mexican Night*, 1970; *Literary San Francisco: A Pictorial History from Its Beginnings to the Present Day*, 1980 (with Nancy J. Peters); *Leaves of Life: Drawing from the Model*, 1983; *What Is Poetry?*, 2000; *Life Studies, Life Stories: Eighty Works on Paper*, 2003.

TRANSLATIONS: *Selections from "Paroles" by Jacques Prévert*, 1958; *Roman Poems*, 1988 (of Pier Paolo Pasolini).

MISCELLANEOUS: *Poetry as Insurgent Art*, 2007.

BIBLIOGRAPHY

Cherkovski, Neeli. *Ferlinghetti: A Biography*. Garden City, N.Y.: Doubleday, 1979. Reviews the wrenching dislocations of Ferlinghetti's childhood, his stint in the U.S. Navy, his studies at Columbia and in Paris, and the development of his artistic and political commitments, always emphasizing the theme of the poet's search for a self. Illustrated with photographs. Provides a primary and a secondary bibliography; indexed.

Ferlinghetti, Lawrence. "Ferlinghetti." Interview by David Meltzer and Jack Shoemaker (1969) and by Meltzer, Marina Lazzara, and James Brook (1999). In *San Francisco Beat: Talking with the Poets*, edited by Meltzer. San Francisco: City Lights, 2001. Ferlinghetti discusses politics, his bookstore, his poetry, and the Beat movement and poets. The contrast between the early interview, conducted during a very active time for San Francisco, and the later interview, thirty years later, sheds light on Ferlinghetti and other Beat poets.

Fontane, Marilyn Ann. "Ferlinghetti's 'Constantly Risking Absurdity.'" *Explicator* 59, no. 2 (Winter, 2001): 106-108. This short article argues that Ferlinghetti's "drop-line" form and stanza divisions provide the structure of a visual staircase for a poem that initially seems unstructured.

Pekar, Harvey, et al. *The Beats: A Graphic History*. Art by Ed Piskor et al. New York: Hill and Wang, 2009. Comic legend Harvey Pekar provides a history of the Beat poets in this graphic book. Contains an entry on and references to Ferlinghetti.

Silesky, Barry. *Ferlinghetti: The Artist in His Time*. New York: Warner Books, 1990. A chatty biography, written with the informality and punchiness of a popular-magazine article. Based on extensive interviews with Ferlinghetti and his associates. Silesky leaves critical appraisal of the poetry to numerous poets and critics interviewed in the book's final chapter; they include Ginsberg, Robert Creeley, Paul Carroll, Ralph Mills, Diane Wakoski, and Gary Snyder. Features a selected bibliography, an index, and photographs.

Skau, Michael. *"Constantly Risking Absurdity": Essays on the Writings of Lawrence Ferlinghetti*. Troy, N.Y.: Whitston, 1989. A brief monograph, illustrated, on Ferlinghetti's works.

Smith, Larry R. *Lawrence Ferlinghetti, Poet-at-Large*. Carbondale: Southern Illinois University Press, 1983. This well-written book has one particularly interesting feature: a multicolumned chronology that parallels events in Ferlinghetti's personal life, his writing achievements, and City Lights publishing history. After presenting a "biographic portrait," Smith argues that Ferlinghetti is best placed within a European rather than American literary tradition. Smith provides a thoughtful treatment of Ferlinghetti's poetic themes and devices and surveys the prose writings and drama as well. Contains photographs, notes, a selected bibliography, and an index.

Stephenson, Gregory. *The Daybreak Boys: Essays on the Literature of the Beat Generation*. Carbondale: Southern Illinois University Press, 1990. Contains the chapter "The 'Spiritual Optics' of Lawrence Ferlinghetti," which offers a general view of Ferlinghetti's writings.

John Alspaugh; Leslie Ellen Jones
Updated by Ann M. Cameron

EDWARD FIELD

Born: Brooklyn, New York; June 7, 1924

PRINCIPAL POETRY

Stand Up, Friend, with Me, 1963
Variety Photoplays, 1967
A Full Heart, 1977
Stars in My Eyes, 1978
New and Selected Poems from the Book of Life, 1987
Counting Myself Lucky: Selected Poems, 1963-1992, 1992
A Frieze for a Temple of Love, 1998
After the Fall: Poems Old and New, 2007

OTHER LITERARY FORMS

Edward Field's most important works, aside from his poetry, are the novels he wrote in collaboration with Neil Derrick under the collective pseudonym of Bruce Elliot. The most successful of these works was the novel *Village* (1982), a chronicle of life over many decades in Greenwich Village, New York.

Field also edited an anthology titled *A Geography of Poets* (1979), which was a notable effort to showcase the works of poets from all over the United States. In 1992, Field, collaborating with Gerald Locklin and Charles Stetler, edited *A New Geography of Poets*.

ACHIEVEMENTS

In 1962, Edward Field's first collection of poems, *Stand Up, Friend, with Me*, was named the Lamont Poetry Selection, and Field was subsequently awarded a Guggenheim Fellowship in 1963. He received the Shelley Memorial Award from the Poetry Society of America in 1975, a Lambda Literary Award in 1992 for *Counting Myself Lucky*, a Rome Fellowship from the American Academy of Arts in 1981, and the Bill Whitehead Award for Lifetime Achievement and the W. H. Auden Award in 2005.

BIOGRAPHY

Born in Brooklyn to Jewish parents five years before the beginning of the Great Depression, Edward Field remained intimately associated with New York City for most of his life. His poetry frequently alludes to a childhood in which the young Field longed for a father's love, which he believed was denied to him. Field's comment in "The Sleeper" (from *Stand Up, Friend, with Me*) is telling: "when I look back on childhood// (That four psychiatrists haven't been able to help me bear the thought of)/ There is not much to be glad for. . . ." One of six children, Edward appears to have felt neglected by his parents and to have been regarded with hostility or contempt by his peers. Trained in music from an early age, Field played cello in a musical trio made up of members of his family. In 1942, while working at a Manhattan department store, Field met First Lady Eleanor Roosevelt, an occasion he was to commemorate in 2001 in the same building (now the Mid-Manhattan Library) at a reading of his own work.

Field joined the Army Air Corps in 1942 and flew twenty-five bomber missions, during which, he reported, "five planes had been destroyed by flak under me." In March of 1943, while still undergoing his military training, he was given a Red Cross package containing, among other things, an anthology of poetry. As he later wrote, "This was a bombshell. I knew immediately that I was going to be a poet." He left the military with the rank of second lieutenant, and after returning to New York, he sought to pursue his education under the G.I. Bill. He gradually came to realize that university life was not what he had hoped for and left New York University in 1948. With one thousand dollars in savings, he sailed for France. On the ship, he met a poet named Robert Friend, whom Field later credited as having introduced him to the fundamentals of modern poetry.

Remaining in Paris until the spring of 1949, Field enjoyed associating with Friend and with other members of the artistic community. Visiting London, he met poet Stephen Spender and saw T. S. Eliot. Field, though low on funds, then went to Greece, where he found himself comfortable enough to write some of the first poems he was later to publish. By 1950, he was back in New York.

After his return to the United States, Field keenly felt the atmosphere of repression that contrasted so strongly with the environments of Paris and Greece. The social intolerance that shaped many aspects of

Cold War attitudes threatened his liberty. As a nonconformist, homosexual, and Jew, he was revolted by this
intolerance, and he sought to cope with his intense anxiety by embarking on a long series of psychological
therapies.

In 1955, Field met Frank O'Hara, whose poems and
attitude toward poetry were helpful to him. Field continued to write while working in offices and endeavor-
ing to develop skills as an actor. A major event occurred in his poetic life when, in 1963, his first book of
poems, *Stand Up, Friend, with Me*, was named the
Lamont Poetry Selection. From that time on, Field led
the life of a recognized literary figure. After the publication of his first book in 1963, he received a Guggenheim Fellowship to travel abroad.

He published his second book of poetry, *Variety
Photoplays*, in 1967. The success of *Stand Up, Friend,
with Me* had made it possible for Field to earn money by
giving readings of his poetry, and he began to enjoy a
measure of financial security. His life was complicated
at this time by the illness of his companion Derrick,
whose deteriorating eyesight made him increasingly
dependent on Field, who soon began to collaborate
with his friend in the writing of fiction. After Field published *A Full Heart*, his third book of poetry, in 1977,
he and Derrick published their first novel, *The Potency
Clinic*, in 1978, using the collective nom de plume of
Elliot.

Recognizing that the New York literary establishment was exercising a domineering influence on American poetry, Field sought to balance the situation in
1979 by publishing an anthology of American poetry
titled *A Geography of Poets*. His next project was another collaboration with Derrick (as Elliot), *Village*, a
novel about life in Greenwich Village from 1845 to
1975. This novel was a best seller.

In 1987, the Sheep Meadow Press issued *New and
Selected Poems from the Book of Life*, with poems from
previous volumes supplemented by twenty-seven new
ones. *Counting Myself Lucky* was published by the
Black Sparrow Press, which also issued *A Frieze for a
Temple of Love*, a collection of poems along with an
eighty-one-page text "The Poetry File," a mixture of
memoir, gossip, and observations on poetry. In 2007,
Field published a new collection, *After the Fall*.

ANALYSIS

Edward Field's poetry is distinguished by its casualness, a characteristic he cultivated deliberately in a
reaction to the obscurity of much modern poetry. His
verse tends to be conversational in tone, syntax, and vocabulary, and usually nothing is concealed. It is easy
for the reader to forget that Field is a trained musician
and actor, yet perhaps these forms of competence contribute to the power that sometimes emerges in his
work.

STAND UP, FRIEND, WITH ME

Field's poetic voice represents the casually personal, often responding to incongruities and offering a
city-dweller's bemusement at the persistence of nature.
In *Stand Up, Friend, with Me*, for example, he describes goats, donkeys, a porcupine, and a walrus. He
illustrates his own experience with plants in the city. In
"Tulips and Addresses," he describes how he acquired
some discarded tulip bulbs and carried them about with
him for months before he found a home. He concludes:

> Now I am living on Abingdon Square, not the Ritz
>   exactly, but a place
> And I have planted the tulips in my window box:
> Please God make them come up, so that everyone who
>   passes by
> Will know I'm there, at least long enough to catch my
>   breath,
> When they see the bright red beautiful flowers in my
>   window.

A similar note sounds in "The Garden," where, after
describing the exotic plants he has sprouted from seed
in his home, he celebrates his participation in this collection of living things: "We have formed a colony in a
strange land/ Planting our seeds and making ourselves
at home."

The dominant note is the assertion of the importance
of the unaffectedly personal, a theme announced in the
volume's prologue, where, beginning with an image of
the universe, Field zooms in on the surface of the earth,
quickly focusing on New York and then on "this house,
upstairs and through the wide open door/ Of the front
bedroom with a window on the world," concluding,
"Look, friend, at me."

VARIETY PHOTOPLAYS

Variety Photoplays includes a number of treatments of Hollywood films. According to poets Stetler and Locklin, "Field has discovered and exploited the full mythological potential of old movies." These poems have such titles as "Curse of the Cat Woman," "Frankenstein," "Bride of Frankenstein," and "The Life of Joan Crawford," and they offer colloquial résumés of Hollywood films and themes. Each is a sort of dramatic monologue, a self-contained entertainment. Field's poems in fact often present comical moments that dramatize small events, as in "Plant Poems," where he assumes the persona of a scientist:

> As the leading agronomist
> in the Kharkov Agricultural
> Institute
> I want to announce the discovery
> that plants feel as we do
>
> . . . .
>
> and when you chop up a lettuce
> it is saying Ouch.

A FULL HEART

The publication in 1977 of *A Full Heart* drew fire from reviewer M. L. Rosenthal, a literary critic and editor of William Butler Yeats. Rosenthal strongly objected to what he saw as the "indefatigably prosaic" dimension of Field's poetry, a dimension that Field himself was later to defend by explaining, "I use a local New York syntax, a kind of Jewish syntax that New Yorkers use in everyday life," and "it seems to me that poetry should be easier to read than prose." Since much of *A Full Heart* presents Field's coming to terms with his most important personal relationships, Rosenthal found this casually phrased confessional mode self-indulgent and facile.

"A Full Heart" describes Field's Polish immigrant mother and her sisters, "loving women" whose burdened and unappreciated lives included only the most modest consolations. "Gone Blind" describes the impact on Field of his companion's blindness; it concludes: "Gone blind/ he has brought me light." "Visiting Home" is a long reflection on the poet's relationship with his parents, and this meditation ends with an acceptance that, if qualified, has a tone of resolution:

"I am my father's son./ Even if I can't stand it, still/ I am."

Despite Field's normal aversion to symbolism or implication, the poem "Sharks" reads very much like an exercise in the figurative. Although Field was enjoying a reasonable prosperity as literary man, he was over fifty by this time, and perhaps this poem is an anticipation of future vulnerability:

> Especially at evening
> everyone knows the sharks come in
> when the sun makes puddles of blood on the sea
> and the shadows darken.
>
> It is then, as night comes on
> the sharks of deep water
> approach the shore
> and beware, beware, the late swimmer.

A FRIEZE FOR A TEMPLE OF LOVE

A Frieze for a Temple of Love consists of three sections: a collection of Field's verse from 1993 to 1997, a long poem titled "Silver Wings: Notes for a Screenplay," and a largely prose conclusion titled "The Poetry File." The short poems included in the first section fall generally into two groups, the first of which continues the Fieldian theme of demonstrating poetic freedom by focusing on sexuality and bodily functions and the second of which acknowledges the approach of death. Both groups include expressions of Field's abiding resentment of his parents, as he remarks in "The Spirit of '76," "My parents have faded away at last./ I survived you two sickos, just,/ but it's a relief to say thanks, and goodbye." Reflecting on mortality in the final stanza of "Death Mask," Field writes:

> Life
>   a lazy buzz
> then
>   the quick sting.
>
> A long inward breath,
>   then
> the sudden
>   exhaling.

These lines carry an echo of Emily Dickinson's "I Heard a Fly Buzz When I Died," and the metaphors, unusual in Field's poems, suggest that the poet is deliberately connecting with a tradition he has long disavowed. Other passages in the book seem to reiterate Field's independence of that tradition.

In "Living Will," Field explains to Derrick's sister his preparations for death, but he makes it clear that he has not yet surrendered, for the poem ends: "May death take me/ only as I put down/ the last word."

"Silver Wings: Notes for a Screenplay" is a narrative based on Field's military service and love affairs as recalled fifty years later, and "The Poetry File," though mostly in prose, is a valuable compilation of Field's views about his own poetry and that of his contemporaries.

AFTER THE FALL

The two-part *After the Fall* contains twenty new poems and a selection by the poet from his past work. The "Fall" of the title is the destruction of New York's Twin Towers in the terrorist attack of September 11, 2001. In the title poem of more than two hundred lines, he contemplates the attendant suffering and loss of lives. For himself and his fellow New Yorkers, the poet articulates the sorrow of the occasion in his characteristically plain language; indeed, as if to dispel repressed memory, he describes images of the disaster baldly but reluctantly:

> I don't want to think of
> those inside the planes.
> I don't want to think of those trapped on the high floors.

Plodding through the disaster area, the poet murmurs,

> I don't want any of this to happen
> but it plays over and over again.

Field likens the September 11 catastrophe to other destructive assaults in history, such as those on the Tower of Babel and the Colossus of Rhodes, and reflects that both the edifices and the civilizations that built them are fragile. This observation is in keeping with the sharp attentiveness to politics shown in his other works. Moreover, many of the other poems in *After the Fall* amplify on the political scene and express his deep distrust of the George W. Bush administration. For example, in "Letter on the Brink of War," the poet likens the 2003 invasion of Iraq to the beginnings of other historical calamities: "It's one of those points in history/ that every-

thing turns on—" he says, "They even talk of shock and awe—/ another term for blitzkrieg's *sturm and drang*,// and instead of Jews, the roundup of Muslims,/ But you have to ask, Who's next?"

Another poem, "Homeland Security," depicts with sardonic humor the repressive treatment of those who might arouse even a remote suspicion of terrorist leanings:

> My advice to anybody who looks like an Arab these
> 　days is,
> when you're in a post office or jogging around the
> 　reservoir,
> never stop and jot down any notes,
> even if it's a great idea for a poem.
> . . . .
> And when they lead you away in handcuffs
> don't bother protesting your innocence and calling for a
> 　lawyer.
> You can't have one—and you're guilty.

Field declares that such pointed criticism is "how poets should be writing in this critical time," as he puts it in "What Poetry Is For," dedicated to the Nicaraguan poet Ernesto Cardenal. It is the same conviction that gave rise to the gay rights poems in his earlier volumes, a theme he returns to in *After the Fall*.

Although many poems in *After the Fall* refer to events specific to the first decade of the twenty-first century, their significance is not limited to this era. Field avoids such limitation by showing parallels between these events and those of other times. The poems also display a natural, conversational style that belies the poetic craftsmanship that, as Field puts it, makes the language "invisible."

OTHER MAJOR WORKS

LONG FICTION: *The Potency Clinic*, 1978 (with Neil Derrick; as Bruce Elliot); *Village*, 1982 (with Derrick; as Elliot); *The Office*, 1987 (with Derrick; as Elliot); *The Villagers*, 1999 (revised version of *Village*).

NONFICTION: *The Man Who Would Marry Susan Sontag: And Other Intimate Literary Portraits of the Bohemian Era*, 2005.

CHILDREN'S LITERATURE: *Magic Words: Poems*, 1998.

EDITED TEXTS: *A Geography of Poets*, 1979; *A New Geography of Poets*, 1992 (with Gerald Locklin and Charles Stetler); *Dancing with a Tiger: Poems, 1941-1998*, 2003 (of Robert Friend).

BIBLIOGRAPHY

Crow, Kelly. "Time for Recalling the Departed and Reuniting the Long-Lost Related." *The New York Times*, June 24, 2001, p. 6. A report on a reading by Field at the Mid-Manhattan Library, a building in which, when the building housed a department store, Field worked as a junior employee in 1942. Crow describes Field's reading style ("he discarded the microphone . . . and . . . bellowed") and records Field's description of Eleanor Roosevelt, whom he had met in the same building nearly sixty years earlier.

Field, Edward. "The Poetry File." In *A Frieze for a Temple of Love*. Santa Rosa, Calif.: Black Sparrow Press, 1998. This collection of miscellaneous observations on poetry and poets provides a good perspective on Field's insights and development as a poet. Always in the entertainer mode, Field tosses in a substantial amount of gossip as well.

Goldgar, Harry. "The Poets' Selections: Two Distinguished American Poets Offer Worthwhile Volumes." *St. Petersburg Times*, July 5, 1987, p. 7D. In a review of two poetry volumes, including Field's *New and Selected Poems from the Book of Life*, Field's friend Goldgar comments with enthusiasm on the poet's "plain-speaking, gut-feeling, anti-establishment" works, praising their "accessibility" and lack of inhibition. Field had briefly been in residence at Eckerd College in St. Petersburg, Florida.

Nelson, Emmanuel S., ed. *Contemporary Gay American Poets and Playwrights: An A-to-Z Guide*. Westport, Conn.: Greenwood Press, 2003. Contains a biographical essay on Field that also analyzes his works.

Olson, Ray. Review of *After the Fall. Booklist* 104, no. 3 (October 1, 2007): 17. Olson praises Field's work, calling it enjoyable to read. Notes that there is more anger and less humor in this volume.

Stetler, Charles, and Gerald Locklin. "Edward Field, Stand-Up Poet." *Minnesota Review* 9, no. 1 (1969). This essential article by two of Field's fellow poets celebrates his role in what the authors call "a full-scale renaissance of the Oral Tradition." Stetler and Locklin are particularly enthusiastic about Field's "movie poems" and the way they have "shaped or recorded patterns of our emotional lives." Associating Field's aesthetic with the media theory of Marshall McLuhan, this article explains how Field's poetry, especially in actual performance, escapes the limitations of the printed page.

Robert W. Haynes
Updated by Thomas Rankin